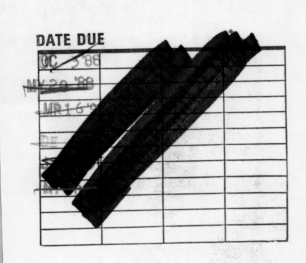

ANCIENT WRITERS

Greece and Rome

ANCIENT WRITERS

Greece and Rome

T. JAMES LUCE

EDITOR IN CHIEF

Volume I

HOMER

TO

CAESAR

CHARLES SCRIBNER'S SONS / *New York*

Library of Congress Cataloging in Publication Data
Main entry under title:

Ancient writers.

    Includes bibliographies and index.
    Contents: v. 1. Homer to Caesar—v. 2.
Lucretius to Ammianus Marcellinus.
    1. Classical literature—History and
criticism.   I. Luce, T. James (Torrey James),
1932–
PA3002.A5   1982   880'.09   82–50612
ISBN 0-684-16595-3 (set)   AACR2

1 3 5 7 9 11 13 15 17 19 Q/C 20 18 16 14 12 10 8 6 4 2

PRINTED IN THE UNITED STATES OF AMERICA.

The paper in this book meets the guidelines for permanence and durability of
the Committee on Production Guidelines for Book Longevity of the Council
on Library Resources.

EDITORIAL STAFF

LIST OF SUBJECTS

Volume I

LIST OF SUBJECTS

Volume II

INTRODUCTION

THE TWO VOLUMES of *Ancient Writers: Greece and Rome* are part of a larger series by Scribners on great literary figures of our Western heritage: *American Writers* in eight volumes, *British Writers* in eight volumes, and the forthcoming *European Writers*. For the majority of the ancients, only inference and guesswork are available in matters of basic biographical information such as birth dates: little that is reliable has come down to us about some of the greatest of them. This is particularly true for the writers of the archaic and classical periods of Greece. When the Hellenistic scholars at the great library in Alexandria began to interest themselves in these questions, they often had little more to go on than we have today. Nothing daunted, they wrote up what they found, or thought they found, in the writings themselves; frequently it seems that no other good sources existed. Embroideries and falsifications were added subsequently, to the point that many of the resultant Lives have little or no claim to truth or even to verisimilitude. Nor have many Roman writers fared better: one thinks of those mendacious creators of later imperial biographies, the Scriptores Historiae Augustae, or the lack of much sound information about early writers such as Plautus and Terence. As to the author of "On the Sublime," we do not even know his name: "Longinus" is merely a guess, and a poor one at that.

The experts invited to contribute to *Ancient Writers* were asked to write essays that would be at once sympathetic, readable, and informative—essays that a wide range of readers, from students in secondary school to advanced classical scholars, would read profitably and with pleasure. Part of the aim has been protreptic: to encourage readers to delve further into a writer by explaining his place in world literature and by making his greatness apparent. To that end the bibliographies appended to each essay include a list of English translations, editions in the original Greek or Latin, and important modern works. Translations are, with few exceptions (which are noted), those of the authors of the essays. A Chronological Table sketching the main periods of ancient history has also been included. The writers discussed in these volumes are listed chronologically in a parallel column; their lives are thus roughly correlated with the chief events of the era in which they lived. For certain writers who were intimately bound up with the major events of their day and were themselves leading historical figures, such as Demosthenes, Polybius, Cicero, and Caesar, the essays about them provide a far fuller, more reliable guide than the bare outline of the table.

We have not tried to produce articles on the model of an encyclopedia, with a standard format and even coverage, whose primary if not exclusive purpose is to transmit information. The aim here has been rather for the authors to write personal, even idiosyncratic, essays in order to show what in their eyes constitute the significant achievements of the writers of the ancient world. To be sure, information on such matters as the writer's life and works and on the background of the literary genre or genres in which he wrote is included where it is known. But coverage of these topics is subordinate. Nor have the authors always felt obliged to discuss all or even most of the works of a given writer. For some, such as Sophocles and Plautus, a review of each work has been possible; but for prolific writers like Plato, Aristotle, and Cicero, the essays would have been reduced to bare catalogs, had their surviving works been discussed seriatim. Readers will thus encounter essays of widely varying approaches in these volumes. They should know that this was our aim from the beginning.

Forty-seven essays are included. Most are concerned with individual writers; but in some, two have been paired because they wrote in the same genre and lived in the same era: Tibullus and Propertius (Latin elegy), Persius and Juvenal (satire), Lucan and Statius (epic of the Latin Silver Age), Epictetus and Marcus Aurelius (Stoic philosophy). Two essays cover a number of writers who share a common literary background: the Greek Lyric Poets (Pindar, however, is treated separately) and Hellenistic Poetry (Theocritus receives a separate essay). Note, too, that the essay on Aeschylus is prefaced by an introduction to the nature of Greek tragedy in general; even those interested in Greek and Roman comedy and the Latin tragedies of Seneca will find parts of that introduction pertinent and useful.

Little objection is likely to be raised against the writers who have been chosen for inclusion. All are major figures who either wrote significant literary works themselves or wrote about literature. Objection may well be made concerning those who have not found a place here: Why Isocrates but not Lysias? Why Josephus but not Eusebius? Such decisions were not easy, and in a few cases were somewhat arbitrary. The plan at the start was to include only writers of Greece and Rome and to fix the dividing line between *Ancient Writers* and *European Writers* by including in the former all those who were born certainly or probably before the death of the first Christian emperor of Rome, Constantine the Great, in A.D. 337. Ammianus Marcellinus, the last of our writers, just manages to qualify on this criterion; certainly he makes a fitting conclusion to the whole, since, as the admirer of the last great protagonist of pagan religion, the emperor Julian, he concludes a series of writers all of whom were pagan in their beliefs.

I want to thank the many who have contributed to these volumes for their willingness to write the essays in the first place and for the laudable results of their efforts. I have learned much from them, and am confident that their readers will too. I also want to thank the Managing Editor, Michael McGinley, and

INTRODUCTION

his staff at Scribners for their courteous help, as well as Marshall De Bruhl, Director of the Reference Book Division. Finally, I must acknowledge the debt I owe to Charles Scribner, Jr., who first asked me to undertake the task of Editor in Chief. He has a special knowledge and love of the writers of Greece and Rome. I hope these essays will give him special pleasure.

T. JAMES LUCE

CHRONOLOGICAL TABLE

ca. 2000–*ca.* 1400 B.C.	Minoan civilization flourishes in Crete	
ca. 1400–*ca.* 1200	Mycenaean civilization flourishes on the Greek mainland	
1183	Traditional date for the fall of Troy	
ca. 1200–ca. 750	**The "Dark Ages" in Greece**	
ca. 800–*ca.* 700	Rise of aristocracies in Greece	
776	Traditional date for the first Olympic Games	
753	Traditional date for the founding of Rome	
753–509	**The Regal Period in Rome**	Homer (Eighth Century?)
		Hesiod (Eighth Century)
ca. 750–ca. 500	**The Archaic Period in Greece**	
ca. 750–*ca.* 650	Major era of Greek colonization	
ca. 650–*ca.* 590	Age of lawgivers in Greece: Draco (*fl.* 620) and Solon (*fl.* 594–593) at Athens	
ca. 560–510	Pisistratus and his sons tyrants at Athens	Greek Lyric Poets
		Aeschylus (525–456)
		Pindar (*ca.* 518–*ca.* 438)
509	Tarquin the Proud, the last king in Rome, expelled	
509–31	**The Roman Republic**	
ca. 508–507	Reforms of Cleisthenes at Athens	
ca. 500–323	**Classical Greece**	
499–479	The Persian Wars: 499 Ionian Revolt	
		Sophocles (497–406)
	490 Battle of Marathon	
		Herodotus (*ca.* 484–420)
	480 Battle of Thermopylae and Salamis	Euripides (*ca.* 480–406)
	479 Battle of Plataea	
479–431	Growth of the Athenian Empire	

CHRONOLOGICAL TABLE

460–429	The Age of Pericles at Athens	
		Thucydides (*ca.* 459–399)
		Aristophanes (*ca.* 445–385)
		Isocrates (*ca.* 435–338)
431–404	The Peloponnesian War: 431–421 Archidamian War	
		Xenophon (*ca.* 428–*ca.* 355)
		Plato (428–348)
	421 Peace of Nicias	
	416 Destruction of Melos	
	415–413 Sicilian Expedition	
	413–404 Decelean War	
404–371	Spartan hegemony of Greece	
ca. 400–265	Rome's unification of Italy	
399	Death of Socrates	
387–386	"The King's Peace": Artaxerxes II, king of Persia, sets the terms of a general peace for Greece	
		Aristotle (384–322)
		Demosthenes (*ca.* 384–322)
		Theocritus (End of Fourth Century)
377	Foundation of the second Athenian Empire	
371	Battle of Leuctra: Thebes defeats Sparta	
371–362	Theban hegemony of Greece	
362	Battle of Mantinea: death of Epaminondas of Thebes	
ca. 360–336	Philip II makes Macedon into a first-ranked power in Greece	
		Menander (*ca.* 342–*ca.* 291)
338	Battle of Chaeronea: Philip II crushes Greek resistance	
336	Philip II assassinated; accession of Alexander the Great	
336–323	Conquest of the East by Alexander	
331	Foundation of Alexandria in Egypt	
323	Death of Alexander	
	Battles of the successors of Alexander for supremacy; establishment of the kingdoms of the Antigonids (Macedon), Seleucids (Syria), and Ptolemies (Egypt)	
323–146	**Hellenistic Greece**	Hellenistic Poetry
		Callimachus (*ca.* 305–*ca.* 240)
		Apollonius (*b. ca.* 295)
264–241	First Punic War: Rome vs. Carthage	
		Plautus (254–184)

CHRONOLOGICAL TABLE

218–201	Second Punic (or Hannibalic) War	
		Polybius (205?–125?)
201–146	Rome defeats the kingdoms of Macedon and Syria	
		Terence (d. 159)
146	Destruction of Carthage and Corinth	
133–31	Decline and collapse of the Roman Republic	
133–121	Tribunates of Tiberius Gracchus and Gaius Gracchus	
112–106	War with Jugurtha; Marius	
		Cicero (106–43)
		Caesar (100–44)
		Lucretius (94?–50?)
		Sallust (86–35)
		Catullus (84–54)
		Vergil (70–19)
		Horace (65–8)
82–79	Dictatorship of Sulla	
63	Catilinarian Conspiracy; consulship of Cicero	
60	Formation of the First Triumvirate: Pompey, Caesar, Crassus	
		Livy (ca. 59–ca. A.D. 17)
58–52	Caesar's conquest of Gaul	
		Tibullus (54?–18)
		Propertius (50?–15)
49	Caesar crosses the Rubicon: start of civil war with Pompey	
49–44	Dictatorship of Caesar and war with Pompeians	
48	Battle of Pharsalus: defeat and death of Pompey	
44	Assassination of Julius Caesar	
43	Formation of the Second Triumvirate: Antony, Octavian, Lepidus	Ovid (43 B.C.–A.D. 18)
42	Battle of Philippi: defeat of Brutus and Cassius	
31	Battle of Actium: Octavian defeats Antony and Cleopatra	
31 B.C.–A.D. 284	**The Roman Empire: The Principate**	
31 B.C.–A.D. 68	The Julio-Claudian Dynasty	
27	Octavian receives the title Augustus	
27 B.C.–A.D. 14	Reign of Augustus	
		Seneca the Younger (4? B.C.– A.D. 65)
A.D. 14–37	Tiberius	
		Persius (34–62)

CHRONOLOGICAL TABLE

37–41	Caligula (Gaius)	Josephus (*ca.* 37–*ca.* 100)
		Martial (*ca.* 38–*ca.* 104)
		Lucan (39–65)
		Quintilian (*ca.* 40–*ca.* 96)
		Plutarch (*ca.* 40–*ca.* 120)
41–54	Claudius	
		Statius (45?–96?)
		Epictetus (*ca.* 50–*ca.* 120)
54–68	Nero	
		Tacitus (*ca.* 55–after 117)
		Juvenal (60?–140?)
		Pliny the Younger (*ca.* 61–*ca.* 112)
		Petronius (*d.* 66)
69	Civil War: "Year of the Four Emperors"—Galba, Otho, Vitellus, Vespasian	Suetonius (*ca.* 69–after 122) Longinus (*fl.* First Century)
69–96	The Flavian Dynasty:	
	Vespasian (69–79)	
	Titus (79–81)	
	Domitian (81–96)	
96–180	The "Adoptive" Emperors (The High Empire):	
	Nerva (96–98)	
	Trajan (98–117)	
	Hadrian (117–138)	
		Lucian (*ca.* 120–after 180)
		Apuleius (*b. ca.* 120)
		Marcus Aurelius (121–180)
	Antoninus Pius (138–161)	
	Marcus Aurelius (161–180)	
180–192	Reign of Commodus	
193–235	The Severan Dynasty	
235–284	Military anarchy: start of barbarian invasions	
284–	**The Roman Empire: The Dominate**	
284–305	Diocletian	
306–337	Constantine the Great	
312	Battle of the Milvian Bridge: triumph of Christianity	
		Ammianus Marcellinus (*ca.* 330–*ca.* 395)
337–361	Constantius II	
361–363	Julian the Apostate	
378	Battle of Adrianople	
379–395	Theodosius the Great	
391	Pagan temples closed	
393	Last celebration of the Olympic Games	

LIST OF CONTRIBUTORS

Listed below are the contributors to *Ancient Writers: Greece and Rome.* An author's name is followed by his or her institutional affiliation at the time of publication, the titles of books written or edited, and the title of the essay written for the present volumes.

FREDERICK M. AHL. Professor of Classics, Cornell University. Author of *Lucan: An Introduction* and of a book on Statius' *Thebaid* (in progress). **Lucan and Statius.**

J. K. ANDERSON. Professor of Classical Archaeology, University of California at Berkeley. Author of *Greek Vases in the Otago Museum; Ancient Greek Horsemanship; Military Theory and Practice in the Age of Xenophon;* and *Xenophon.* **Xenophon.**

WILLIAM S. ANDERSON. Professor of Classics, University of California at Berkeley. Author of *The Art of the Aeneid; Ovid Metamorphoses 6–10: Text and Commentary;* and *Ovid Metamorphoses, libri xv* (Teubner Classical Text). **Persius and Juvenal.**

WILLIAM ARROWSMITH. Robert W. Woodruff Professor of Classics and Comparative Literature, Emory University. Author of Petronius' *Satyricon* (translation), and of translations of numerous plays of Euripides and Aristophanes. General Editor of *The Greek Tragedies in New Translation,* 33 vols. **Petronius.**

SAMUEL DECOSTER ATKINS. Professor Emeritus of Classics, Princeton University. Author of *Pushan in the Rigveda* and of numerous articles in scholarly journals. **Theocritus.**

HELEN H. BACON. Professor of Classics, Barnard College, Columbia University. Author, with Anthony Hecht, of *Aeschylus: Seven Against Thebes* (verse translation) and of *Barbarians in Greek Tragedy.* **Aeschylus.**

GEORGE CAWKWELL. Fellow and Praelector in Ancient History, University College, University of Oxford.

Author of *Philip of Macedon* and of articles on aspects of fifth- and fourth-century-B.C. Greek history. **Isocrates.**

EDWARD CHAMPLIN. Associate Professor of Classics, Princeton University. Author of *Fronto and Antonine Rome* and of articles on Latin literary history, prosopography, and landholding in ancient Italy. **Pliny the Younger.**

DEE LESSER CLAYMAN. Professor of Classics, Brooklyn College, The City University of New York. Author of *Callimachus' Iambi* (Mnemosyne Supplementa 59), and of numerous articles and reviews in scholarly journals. **Hellenistic Poetry at Alexandria: The Epigrammatists, Callimachus, and Apollonius of Rhodes.**

WALTER ROBERT CONNOR. Andrew Fleming West Professor of Classics, Princeton University. Editor of *Greek Orations* (book); and author of *Theopompus and Fifth Century Athens* and *The New Politicians of Fifth Century Athens.* **Thucydides.**

PETER S. DEROW. Fellow and Tutor in Ancient History, Wadham College, University of Oxford. **Polybius.**

DONALD C. EARL. Professor of Classics, University of Hull (England). Author of *The Political Thought of Sallust; Tiberius Gracchus: A Study in Politics; The Moral and Political Tradition of Rome;* and *The Age of Augustus.* **Sallust.**

DAVID JOHN FURLEY. Charles Ewing Professor of Greek Language and Literature, Princeton University. Author of *Aristotle: On the Cosmos; Two Studies in the Greek Atomists;* and an edition, with R. E. Allen, of *Presocratic Philosophy.* **Lucretius.**

JOHN ARTHUR HANSON. Professor of Classics and Comparative Literature, Princeton University. Director, American Philological Association (1972–

1975). Author of *Roman Theater-Temples* and of the Loeb Classical Library edition of Apuleius' *Metamorphoses* (in progress). Editor of *Transactions and Proceedings of the American Philological Association*, vols. 96–100, and of Monographs 25–30 of the American Philological Association. **Vergil.**

ELISABETH HENRY (B. Walker). Instructor of Classics, English, and Education, in English universities. Author of *The Annals of Tacitus: A Study in the Writing of History* and of numerous articles and reviews in scholarly journals. **Seneca the Younger.**

W. R. JOHNSON. Professor of Classics and Comparative Literature, University of Chicago. Author of *Luxuriance and Economy: Cicero and the Alien Style; Darkness Visible: A Study of Vergil's "Aeneid"*; and *The Idea of Lyric: Lyric Modes in Ancient and Modern Poetry.* **Ovid.**

C. P. JONES. Professor of Classics, University of Toronto. Author of *Philostratus: Life of Apollonius* (translation); *Plutarch and Rome*; and *The Roman World of Dio Chrysostom.* **Plutarch.**

JOHN J. KEANEY. Professor of Classics, Princeton University. Author of numerous articles on Athenian ostracism, Aristotle, Harpocration, and lexicography. **Plato.**

GEORGE ALEXANDER KENNEDY. Paddison Professor of Classics, University of North Carolina at Chapel Hill. Author of *The Art of Persuasion in Greece; Quintilian; The Art of Rhetoric in the Roman World*; and *Classical Rhetoric and Its Christian and Secular Tradition from Ancient to Modern Times.* **Quintilian.**

JAMES P. LIPOVSKY. Instructor, The Heights School (Potomac, Maryland). Author of *A Historiographical Study of Livy: Books VI–X.* **Livy.**

JOHN LOWE LOGAN. Assistant Professor of French, The Pennsylvania State University. Author of numerous articles in scholarly journals and reference books. **Longinus.**

ANTHONY ARTHUR LONG. Gladstone Professor of Greek, University of Liverpool. Joint Editor, *Classical Quarterly* (1975–1981). Author of *Language and Thought in Sophocles; Hellenistic Philosophy*; and an edition of *Problems in Stoicism.* **Epictetus and Marcus Aurelius.**

T. JAMES LUCE, JR. Kennedy Foundation Professor of Latin Language and Literature, Princeton University. Author of *Livy: The Composition of His History* and numerous articles in scholarly journals. Editor of the Arno Press reprint series in Roman history (1975). **Tacitus.**

JOHN F. MATTHEWS. Lecturer in the Middle and Late Roman Empire, and Fellow and Praelector in Ancient History, The Queen's College, University of Oxford. Author of *Western Aristocracies and the Imperial Court, A.D. 364–425; Atlas of the Roman World* (with Tim Cornell); and *The Roman Empire of Ammianus Marcellinus* (in progress). **Ammianus Marcellinus.**

GLENN W. MOST. Mellon Assistant Professor of Classics, Princeton University. Co-editor of Leibniz' *Specimen Dynamicum* and Wolf's *Prolegomena ad Homerum* (in progress); author of numerous articles on ancient poetry and philosophy and modern literary theory. **Greek Lyric Poets.**

CARROLL MOULTON. Curriculum Director, Films for the Humanities (Princeton, N.J.). Associate Editor, *Classical World* (1973–1977). Author of *Similes in the Homeric Poems; Menander: The Dyskolos* (verse translation); *Aristophanic Poetry*; and numerous articles in scholarly journals. **Aristophanes; Menander.**

GREGORY NAGY. Professor of Greek and Latin, Harvard University. Author of *Greek Dialects and the Transformation of an Indo-European Process; Greek: A Survey of Recent Work* (with F. W. Householder); and *The Best of the Achaeans: Concepts of the Hero in Archaic Greek Poetry.* **Hesiod.**

MARTHA CRAVEN NUSSBAUM. Associate Professor of Philosophy and Classics, Harvard University. Author of *Aristotle's De Motu Animalium*; and an edition (with Malcolm Schofield) of *Language and Logos* (collection of essays in honor of G. E. L. Owen) and of *The Collected Papers of G. E. L. Owen* (both in progress). **Aristotle.**

ROBERT E. A. PALMER. Professor of Classics, The University of Pennsylvania. Associate Editor of the Arno Press series Ancient Religion and Mythology (1974–1975). Author of numerous articles and reviews in scholarly journals. **Martial.**

LIONEL PEARSON. Professor Emeritus of Classics, Stanford University. Author of the Loeb Classical Library edition of *Plutarch, On the Malice of Herodotus; Demosthenes, Six Private Speeches* (commentary); *The Art of Demosthenes*; and numerous articles in scholarly journals. **Demosthenes.**

DAVID HUGH PORTER. W. H. Laird Professor of Liberal Arts and Professor of Classical Languages and of Music, Carleton College. Author of *The Harmony of the Lyre. Studies in Classical Poetry, Drama, and Music* and of numerous articles in scholarly journals. **Horace.**

LIST OF CONTRIBUTORS

BETTY NYE QUINN. Professor of Classics, Mount Holyoke College. Author of numerous articles in scholarly journals. **Caesar.**

ELIZABETH RAWSON. Fellow and Tutor in Ancient History, Corpus Christi College, University of Oxford. Author of *The Spartan Tradition in European Thought; Cicero, A Portrait;* and numerous articles in scholarly journals. **Cicero.**

CHRISTOPHER ROBINSON. Fellow and Tutor in Modern Languages, Christ Church, University of Oxford. Author of *Lucian and His Influence in Europe; French Literature in the Nineteenth Century;* and *French Literature in the Twentieth Century;* and an edition of Erasmus' translations of Lucian for *Opera Omnia Desiderii Erasmi,* vol. 1. **Lucian.**

FRANCIS HENRY SANDBACH. Professor Emeritus of Classics, Trinity College, University of Cambridge. Fellow of the British Academy. Author of *Menandri Reliquiae Selectae; Menander: A Commentary; The Comic Theatre of Greece and Rome;* and *Plutarch's Moralia* (translation with text). **Terence.**

CHARLES PAUL SEGAL. David Benedict Professor of Classics and Professor of Comparative Literature, Brown University. Author of *Tragedy and Civilization: An Interpretation of Sophocles; Poetry and Myth in Ancient Pastoral: Essays on Theocritus and Virgil;* and *Dionysiac Poetics in Euripides' Bacchae.* **Sophocles.**

SUSANNA STAMBLER. Instructor of Classics, Cornell University. **Herodotus.**

WILLIAM BEDELL STANFORD. Pro-Chancellor, Trinity College (Dublin). Author of books on classical subjects and of numerous articles in scholarly journals. **Homer.**

JOHN PATRICK SULLIVAN. Professor of Classics, University of California at Santa Barbara. Author of *Propertius: A Critical Introduction; The Jaundiced Eye* (satires and poems); *Neronian Literature: A Selection;* and *Women in Rome: A Sourcebook.* **Tibullus and Propertius.**

JAMES TATUM. Professor of Classics, Dartmouth College. Author of *Apuleius and the Golden Ass; Plautus: The Darker Comedies;* and numerous articles in scholarly journals. **Apuleius.**

G. B. TOWNEND. Professor of Latin, University of Durham (England). Author of chapters on Lucretius, Cicero's poetry, and Suetonius in *Studies in Latin Literature;* and of numerous articles in scholarly journals. **Suetonius.**

CHRISTIAN WOLFF. Professor of Classics and Strauss Professor of Music, Dartmouth College. Author of articles on Euripides and Sophocles. **Euripides.**

JOHN WRIGHT. Professor of Classics, Northwestern University. Author of *Essays on the Iliad: Selected Modern Criticism; Plautus: Curculio, Introduction and Notes;* and numerous articles in scholarly journals. **Plautus.**

ZVI YAVETZ. Lessing Professor of Ancient History, Tel Aviv University. Author of *Plebs and Princeps; Caesar in der Offentlichen Meinung;* and *Slave Wars in the Roman Republic* (in Hebrew). **Josephus.**

DAVID C. YOUNG. Professor of Classics, University of California at Santa Barbara. Author of numerous articles in scholarly journals. **Pindar.**

JAMES E. G. ZETZEL. Associate Professor of Classics, Princeton University. **Catullus.**

ANCIENT WRITERS

Greece and Rome

HOMER
(Eighth Century B.C.?)

ONE INDISPUTABLE FACT stands firmly outside the maze of controversy that surrounds the Homeric poems. Their popularity remains huge, even in the present time when so few readers can enjoy them in the original Greek. Within the last thirty-four years, one prose translation of the *Odyssey* into English has been bought by more than 2,300,000 readers and libraries, and a similar version of the *Iliad*, by more than 1,500,000. Six other new and widely read translations of the *Odyssey* and four of the *Iliad* have also appeared since 1950 in the English-speaking world alone. Among ancient books, only the Bible has a comparable record.

The present essay will try to illustrate the principal qualities that have maintained this popularity for more than two-and-a-half millennia. The method will not be that of analytical scholarship. Analytical methods, in which the stylistic and conceptual elements of a work are sorted out, examined, and, where possible, explained, are, of course, the bedrock of literary interpretation. But they generally concentrate attention on the parts rather than on the whole, on the trees rather than on the great teeming poetic forests of the *Iliad*, with its more than 100,000 words, and the *Odyssey*, with more than 80,000. It is their wholeness, their symphonic unity, their majestic architecture that makes them supreme masterpieces, together with their richness and variety of characters and events, their imagery, pathos, irony,

humor, and their all-pervading humanity. For the general reader these elements are best seen in their original contexts, not separately in lists and excerpts. Homer himself spoke of "the path of song." The succeeding pages will follow this path through his two inexhaustibly rewarding poems.

First, however, some questions about the origins of the Homeric poems must be briefly considered, although they are strictly unanswerable and for the most part unhelpful so far as enjoyment of the poetry is concerned. Yet they cannot be entirely ignored since Homeric scholarship has been obsessed by them for more than two centuries. Who composed the two poems, and when and where? There is no firm historical evidence to warrant confident replies. Each reader who has studied the possibilities has to make his own guess. The present writer provisionally accepts the widely held view that one author named Homer composed both poems in Chios or Asia Minor in the eighth century B.C.

Two other questions have greater literary relevance—how were these massive epics composed and why? As to how, Milman Parry's epoch-making demonstration that both poems contain features of oral composition has transformed Homeric criticism in the last fifty years. But again there is no firm evidence to show whether Homer himself composed orally or by writing. Generally, however, critical emphasis is now on the poems as performances—partly from memory, partly from creative improvisation—rather than as documents.

Finally, why? What were the poet's aims and intentions? Many scholars and critics since Friedrich Wolf wrote his famous *Prolegomena* in 1795 have held that Homer's aim was historical, to record famous deeds of dead heroes. But Homer makes it plain that his primary purpose was to give pleasure by the music and the substance of his "songs," as he called them, and he never dwells on any strictly historical or utilitarian purpose. His works are essentially imaginative and fictional, "admirable lies," as Aristotle affirms in his *Poetics*. They also, of course, have historical implications which historians have explored exhaustively. (Heinrich Schliemann, the German archaeologist, used them to find Troy.) Undoubtedly too, they have moralistic and educational aspects. But these are by-products of Homer's magnificent fictions. He is no chronicler or preacher or teacher. Like Shakespeare, his aim was primarily and essentially "all for your delight." The present essay will be primarily concerned with that aspect of his work, in a spirit of what one may hope is Homeric hedonism.

The opening lines of the *Iliad* define the subject and nature of the poem:

Sing, Goddess, of the wrath of Achilles son of
    Peleus,
the destructive wrath which laid innumerable woes
    upon
the Achaeans and hurled many mighty souls of
    heroes into
Hades and made their bodies a prey for dogs and
    for all
birds, while the will of Zeus was being
    accomplished.

The first word in the poem—and the first word in extant European literature—is *ménin*—"wrath"—or "anger," if one wants to use a less archaic word; anger, which medieval theologians recognized as being the most destructive of the seven deadly sins and which

Seneca described as "brief madness." That is Homer's theme—and not only the anger of Achilles but also, as soon becomes evident in the poem, anger on the part of many others, both gods and men. In other words, the *Iliad* is not primarily concerned with matters of military history. It deals essentially with human and divine passions and their effects. Certainly it contains many brilliantly vivid descriptions of battles and arms and armor. But what supremely matters here, as in almost all the greater works of classical literature, is human nature—men and women, like ourselves though on a more heroic scale, acting, feeling, and suffering. That is why the *Iliad* has universal appeal and not merely historical or antiquarian interest.

The second word in Homer's first line, "Sing," is equally significant. The words he regularly uses for "poetry" and "poet" are "song" and "singer" (*aoidé,* an uncontracted form of *odé,* "an ode," and *aoidós*). These terms emphasize the musical properties of early Greek poetry (which will be considered later). The process of composing poetry, Homer implies, consists primarily in hearing the song that the Muse sings to him and transmitting it to his audience. Elsewhere we are told that the "god-inspired singer" is a "public worker" (*dēmioergós*) like seers, doctors, and carpenters (*Odyssey* 17.382–385), and he is welcomed to people's homes because he "gives delight by singing." In other words, poets are professional entertainers whose primary aim is to give pleasure. Emphasis on pleasure and entertainment as the primary function of the poetic art, as Homer sees it, recurs in other passages. At its best, poetry, Homer implies, acts like magic: it "charms" (*thélgei*) and "casts a spell" (*kēlēthmós*). It can also have a pleasurable, therapeutic effect, being able to assuage even the bitter wrath of Achilles when he "delighted his heart" with singing and playing the lyre (*Iliad* 9.186–189)—a remarkable premonition of Aristotle's doctrine of emotional *katharsis.*

The third word, "Goddess," makes it plain that Homer is not relying on his own memory and art for the success of his poem. He needs supernatural aid from the Muse and, as indicated later in the poem, from her sisters. In modern terms this means that the impetus to compose true poetry lies beyond the control of a poet's conscious mind and will. Needless to say, memory, knowledge, and artistry play a large part in poetic composition. But what makes poetry true poetry is "inspiration," as critics from Democritus and Plato to Robert Frost have continuously affirmed.

Two other features of the exordium deserve notice. It gives a brief picture of one of the horrors of war—corpses being mangled and devoured by dogs and birds. Later in the poem Homer describes war's nobler aspects as well as its miseries—courage, endurance, comradeship, and even chivalry and courtesy at times, in contrast with its ghastly wounds and pitiful agonies. He recognizes that battle is the supreme test of manhood, but he also recognizes that its main results are pain and sorrow for men and especially for women. Consequently, the *Iliad* is a tragic poem, a somberly magnificent tragic poem, though not—thanks to Homer's artistry—a depressing poem. But the *Odyssey*, where the hero is a man of intelligence rather than passion, has a happy ending.

Finally, "the will of Zeus was being accomplished." Commentators have disagreed about what precisely this will of Zeus was. Its general meaning is plain: Homer had a pious belief that above all the chaos and complexity of the events related in his poem a steady divine purpose ruled. We should remember this when we come to consider the follies and frailties of the Olympian divinities as portrayed in several episodes of the *Iliad*. But such a belief in a divine plan does not imply optimism, as it would in an age that had faith in the ultimate benevolence of its deity. The earlier Greeks had no confidence in divine philanthropy. They bowed to the superior knowledge and power of their gods, but expected no paternal kindness from them. This, too, is the stuff of tragedy.

The main narrative of the *Iliad* begins with a question and answer: "Which of the gods caused the strife between Achilles and Agamemnon? It was Apollo." Apollo is angry, we are told, at the ill treatment of his priest, Chryses, by Agamemnon. Agamemnon had taken the daughter of Chryses as a prize in war. When her father came, dressed in priestly garments and bringing a rich ransom, to ask for her release, Agamemnon arrogantly refused, though all the rest of the Achaeans opposed him. So Chryses prayed to Apollo for vengeance.

Now Apollo comes storming down from Olympos with anger in his heart. With his terrible death-dealing arrows he shoots the deadly plague first into the dogs and mules of the camp and then into the Achaeans themselves. For nine days the funeral pyres blaze continuously.

On the tenth day the goddess Hera intervenes. (Angry because Paris, prince of Troy, did not award her the prize of supreme feminine beauty, she always sides with the Greeks.) She prompts Achilles to call a council of the Achaean leaders. There, he makes the reasonable suggestion that they should consult the prophet of the army, Calchas, as to why Apollo is angry with them. In reply, Calchas says that he will tell them, but first—and this is significant for our understanding of the character of Agamemnon—Achilles must promise to protect him if Agamemnon is angered at what he has to say. (Homer uses four different words for anger here.) Achilles promises. Calchas reveals that Apollo is angry because Agamemnon refused to release Chryseis, the priest's daughter.

Agamemnon is furious. "His dark inward parts were mightily filled with wrathful spirit: his eyes flashed like shining fire." He abuses Calchas and says that he values Chryseis more highly than his wife Clytemnestra—an ominous remark in view of what happened when he returned home after the war. But because he desires the safety of the Achaean host, he will consent to release her, provided that he is given satisfactory compensation. Achilles flares up at this. He calls Agamemnon "most possession-loving of all men" and refuses to let him take anything that has already been allocated to another leader. If, however, Zeus grants them possession of Troy, then Agamemnon can have a triple or quadruple share of the booty. (It should be remembered here that the Homeric heroes consistently believed that their personal honor was directly involved in their physical possessions. To deprive a man of his property against his will meant a loss of honor as well as a loss of wealth.)

In reply, Agamemnon first addresses Achilles courteously enough. But he soon goes on to accuse him of trying to cheat him with mere promises. He says that if the Achaeans will not give him recompense, he will take it by force from one of three heroes, Achilles himself or Ajax or Odysseus. (In this quiet way Homer introduces the next two outstanding heroes among the Achaeans after Achilles and Agamemnon.) Then Agamemnon gives orders for Chryseis to be brought back to her father, adding a gratuitous insult to Achilles by calling him "most violent of all men."

With a fierce scowl, Achilles hurls back insults in return. He complains that while he bears the chief burden of the fighting, Agamemnon gets the lion's share of the plunder. Finally, he threatens to abandon the war and return home. "Go if you want to," Agamemnon replies. "You're the most hateful to me of all the Achaean princes—always fond of strife and wars and battles." Then he threatens to take Achilles' favorite captive woman, Briseis, to replace his own. Naturally this infuriates Achilles. He draws his sword to attack Agamemnon. Athena (another divine partisan of the Achaeans, since she too was slighted by Paris) intervenes and drags Achilles back by his hair. She commands him to desist, promising that if Agamemnon fulfills his threat, Achilles will eventually receive triple compensation for his loss. Achilles reluctantly sheathes his sword—"but he certainly did not cease from his anger." He abuses Agamemnon as a drunkard, shameless as a dog and cowardly as a deer, and swears he will fight no more for him.

Before Agamemnon can reply, another hero comes forward, Nestor, the aged King of Pylos, "pleasant of speech, the clear-voiced orator of the Pylians, from whose tongue flowed utter-ance sweeter than honey." He regularly intervenes in the *Iliad* to try to restrain the fierce passions of the younger heroes. Although something of a Polonius at times in his rambling sermons and reminiscences, he stands out luminously as an embodiment of wisdom combined with eloquence. In a speech that gives relief from the high tension of the recent exchange of insults, he appeals for moderation from the two angry princes. When Nestor has finished, Agamemnon excuses his indignation on the ground that Achilles has been challenging his supreme authority. Achilles says that his personal honor is being impugned, but he concedes that he will allow Briseis to be taken from him without resistance. If, however, Agamemnon tries to confiscate any of his other possessions, then "dark blood will at once spurt out upon the spear." (Homer constantly uses a specific detail instead of an abstract phrase.)

The assembly is now dissolved. Achilles withdraws to his hut (not a tent: the Achaeans have now been nine years in or around the Troad). Agamemnon now arranges for the return of Chryseis. A ship is prepared, and Odysseus is chosen to perform the diplomatic task. We may note how the hero of the *Odyssey* first enters the action of the *Iliad*. (Most scholars believe on stylistic and other grounds that the *Iliad* is the earlier poem.) He is described here as *polúmētis*, literally "of much wise counsel" or "of many wise plans," *métis* implying both practical intelligence and its results: no other hero is so described. Throughout the *Iliad*, he acts as the serviceable and sensible man who performs tasks that need tact and sagacity, as well as distinguishing himself for courage and enterprise at times. Five other heroes are more prominent in the poem—Achilles, Hector, Agamemnon, Ajax, and Diomedes. But we are made aware from time to time that Odysseus has unique qualities of his own and that he does not quite fit into the conventional pattern of old-fashioned heroism.

Fixed epithets such as *polúmētis* are a regular feature of Homer's poetry (and of oral poetry in general). Already in this first book,

Achilles has been given his special descriptive term "swift-footed." Agamemnon in turn is introduced as "wide-ruling" and "lord of men." (These distinctive descriptions differ from other descriptions that are shared by heroes in general, like "glorious" and "god-descended.") Those applied to the three main actors in the first book give us a basic conception of their qualities: Agamemnon is the greatest king in authority and power among the Achaeans at Troy; Achilles excels in physical prowess; Odysseus is primarily concerned with planning and achieving the most beneficial course of action. In what follows, these special epithets will be italicized.

To return to the story: after Odysseus' departure, Agamemnon orders a ritual purification of the Achaean host and a sacrifice of bulls and goats "beside the barren sea." Then he sends two "nimble" heralds to fetch Briseis from Achilles' hut. Achilles, we are told, "certainly did not rejoice at seeing them." But he receives them courteously and considerately—"You are not to blame, but Agamemnon with his pernicious heart." He hands over the "fair-cheeked" Briseis without making any difficulty.

Next comes a scene that perturbed, and perhaps still may perturb, readers who believe that heroes should never cry—the "stiff-upper-lip" tradition, which first became dominant in parts of Western Europe in the nineteenth century. When Briseis is taken away, Achilles bursts into tears and goes out alone on the shore of the "gray sea." There he calls to his mother Thetis to come and grant him revenge on Agamemnon. He is still "pouring out tears." (Dryden contemptuously compared Homer's heroes to St. Swithun's Day, always raining.) Thetis, a sea-goddess, rises from the waves swiftly "like a mist," gently touches her son's hand, and asks what ails him. Achilles rather impatiently replies, "Why do you ask when you, as a goddess, know it already?" and then describes his grievance in nearly fifty lines. Thetis promises to try to persuade Zeus to satisfy her son's vengefulness. (Homer uses her speech to remind us that Achilles himself is doomed to die young,

though that will happen beyond the end of the *Iliad*.)

Attention returns to Odysseus. He sails with Chryseis to her father's home and supplicates him to pray to Apollo to remove the plague. Apollo consents. A sacrifice of animals follows, and then a feast, and then joyful festivities with dance and song and hymns in honor of the god—"and he, as he heard it, felt pleasure in his heart." Another characteristic feature of Homer's style can be seen in this incident—the typical scene. In describing events that naturally recur in the course of his narrative, such as sacrifices or feasts or the handling of a ship or arming for battle, Homer regularly repeats phrases and features. Artistically, these repeated passages have the pleasing effect of repetitions of motifs in music. At the same time, since the poet could sing these prefabricated passages from memory, they gave him opportunities for coining new phrases and for thinking ahead about his new material. This prompts the question of how much of Homer's poetry is traditional, that is, derived from previous bards and poets, and how much original. It cannot be answered with any certainty until pre-Homeric poetry is discovered. All the eloquent and sometimes illuminating books that have been written on this problem are guesswork. The present writer's guess is that when the name of a single person is attached to two superb poems, he is likely to have been a genius of outstanding originality, though, like any master-architect he would freely use materials that had been cut and shaped by others before him.

The second day of the main action is introduced with the customary formulaic line

When the early-rising, rosy-fingered dawn appeared.

(This is a third notable feature of Homer's style—the stereotyped, unchanging formula for introducing recurrent actions or events. Again, we cannot say for certain how many were composed by Homer himself and how many were inherited. It hardly matters, so far as our enjoyment of the poem is concerned.) The Greek mission to Chryses makes its way back to the Achaean encampment, the ship speeding on with "the purple wave roaring at its stem." Eleven days pass without any recorded event. Presumably they are spent in recovering from the effects of the plague. Then the scene shifts from the Troad to Olympos. Thetis successfully beseeches Zeus the cloud-gatherer to let the Trojans temporarily inflict heavy casualties on the Achaeans so that the withdrawal of Achilles may be regretted, and she returns to her undersea abode.

Now a scene of domestic bickering between the king and queen of the gods is enacted on Olympos, our first introduction to the discordant relations that prevail among them in the *Iliad*. Hera, having observed the presence of Thetis, suspects that Zeus has been plotting behind her back. She addresses him as "deception-planner" and asks who has been plotting with him—"You've never yet dared voluntarily to tell me what you've had in mind." Zeus replies quite politely: she mustn't expect to be told everything he plans, but she will certainly be the first of the gods and goddesses to hear "what is reasonable to be told." Then "large-eyed" (literally "ox-eyed": the eyes were considered the chief factor in female beauty by the ancient Greeks) Hera angrily calls her husband "Most dreadful of the children of Cronos" and continues to abuse him. He commands her to sit down and be silent if she wants to avoid physical violence. Frightened, Hera obeys. The rest of the Olympians are agitated. Her son Hephaistos, that famous craftsman, comforts white-armed Hera and offers her nectar, the wine of the gods. Hera smiles and takes it. All the Olympians drink with her. Unquenchable laughter breaks out among them as they watch lame Hephaistos bustling around with the drink. (These sudden bursts of tremendous mirth recur in Olympos.) The Olympians continue their feasting and festivity with music and song from Apollo and the Muses. Then, when "the bright light of the sun had set," each of them goes to lie down in the room that the fa-mous, *lame-in-both-limbs* Hephaistos had made for them. Zeus, too, "the lightning-maker," retires to the bed where "he formerly slept when sweet sleep came to him ... and beside him slept golden-throned Hera."

This is a brilliantly composed cadence to the passionate scenes that precede it. Artistically it is admirable. But for critics who think it necessary to consider poetry in terms of theology and ethics, serious perplexities obviously arise. What are we to make of divinities who quarrel and bicker and take sides and deride physical deformities? The question is not a new one. As early as the sixth century B.C., philosophers and moralists attacked Homer for attributing some of the worst of human failings to the gods. (Later in the poems we hear of gods telling lies, committing adultery, and wounding one another in battle.) Early defenders of Homer's reputation explained their conduct as being allegorical, representing the interactions of physical phenomena like fire, water, air, or of abstract qualities like love, strife, and so on. But few later Greeks, except the Stoics, accepted allegorizations of that kind.

In trying to explain the portraiture of the gods in the *Iliad*, one must remember that Homer is an artist, not a theologian or a moralist. Whatever we say about the mores of the Olympians, aesthetically and artistically these gods are magnificently effective and satisfying. They are not mere "gods from the machine" like those who, at the beginning and ending of Greek tragedies, arrange and control the plot, though at times Homer's gods serve that purpose. Nor are they pious ideal pictures of what a devoutly religious person would like the gods to be. For Homer they are a set of fascinating characters, larger than life, uninhibited by most of the limitations that bind human beings, but subject to human passions. They are beautiful but sometimes mean and petty. They are pleasure loving, but their pleasures are often marred by painful emotions. Sometimes they are sublime; sometimes they are ridiculous. We catch a glimpse of sublimity in the scene between Zeus and Thetis. When the father of gods

6

and men, as he is called elsewhere, consents: "Then he nodded assent with his blue-black eyebrows, and the ambrosial locks of the Lord quivered on his immortal head, and great Olympos reeled." It is said that when Pheidias made his sublime chryselephantine statue of Zeus at Olympia, he had this passage in mind.

There is another problem with Homer's gods. As we have seen, it was Athena who intervened to stop Achilles from attacking Agamemnon with his sword. Frequently, elsewhere in the poems, we find similar interventions, sometimes when the hero already seems to have made up his mind. This "double motivation," as it has been called, perhaps results from lack of knowledge about the hidden workings of the mind. Not that Homer is psychologically naive, as some scholars have suggested. But the mystery of a sudden momentous decision or a sudden change in characteristic conduct may have seemed to him to need some objective explanation, as when the impetuous Achilles decided not to attack Agamemnon. The Olympians provided that. They also provided a second dimension to the whole story, a second stream of action that sometimes flows on apart from human affairs and sometimes merges with them. Besides—and this is perhaps what attracted Homer most—they offered immensely rich potentialities for fanciful characterization and humor and even for gentle satire. To suggest that we should conclude that Homer himself—about whose personal opinions we know nothing for certain—must have been an agnostic or a crypto-monotheist (as agnostic or monotheistic critics would like to have him) is, to say the least, irrelevant to the literary appreciation of his poetry. And to point out that there are inconsistencies between the portraiture of the gods in the *Iliad* and in the *Odyssey* is equally irrelevant from a literary point of view. The *Odyssey* as Homer conceived it needed a different kind of divine will, and for him, artistic considerations were paramount.

The second book of the *Iliad* begins with Zeus's execution of his promise to Thetis. He sends a dream—or rather Dream personified—to tell Agamemnon a flat lie: if the Achaeans can be persuaded to attack at once, they will capture Troy. When Agamemnon hears this in his sleep, he calls an assembly. But he makes a curious decision that has troubled many commentators. He advises the Achaeans not to go into battle as the dream had ordered, but to abandon the expedition and go home—"Let us flee with our ships to our native land, for we shall never capture Troy with its broad streets."

Some interpreters take Agamemnon's exhortation to retreat as a subtle maneuver: he hopes to provoke so strong a reaction that the Achaeans will be all the more eager to fight. This is possible. But Homer would probably have made such an intention clear. In any case, the Achaeans readily take his advice at its face value. Two dynamic similes express their sudden mass movements toward the ships. They are like "tall waves of the sea . . . when they are raised by the east wind or by the south wind rushing out of the clouds from Father Zeus," and "like a rich field of corn when, stirred by the blasts of the southwest wind, it bows all its ears of grain." The dust rises high from their hurrying feet, and one can hear the din of their shouting in Homer's echoing onomatopoeic words, *alalētós* and *aüté*. They begin to prepare their ships for sailing away.

Hera sees the threat to her hopes of destroying Troy. She sends her ally Athena to stop the flight. Athena goes to Odysseus, equal to Zeus in intelligence, and tells him to check the rout. He persuades the leaders to stop with a well-judged short speech. He uses rougher methods with the men of low rank, striking them with his staff and abusing them and telling them that they must obey their leaders. (His remark, "Rule by the many is not a good thing: let there be one ruler, one prince to whom the child of crafty-minded Cronos has given the power," became a motto for supporters of the divine right of monarchs in the sixteenth century and after.)

The host assembles again "with clamor as when a wave of the boisterous sea thunders on a wide shore and the broad tide roars." Now

Homer produces one of those totally unexpected interventions that give a sudden new interest to his main narrative. A man of the people, such as Odysseus has just been striking with his staff, stands up in the assembly. He is described as being hideously ugly—lame-footed, bandy-legged, round-shouldered, egg-headed, thin-and-patchy-haired (all unique terms in the Homeric poems—no formulaic diction here). In shrill, harsh tones he abuses Agamemnon for his acquisitiveness and urges the host—"Base reprobates, Achaean women, not men"—to abandon Agamemnon and the war.

At once Odysseus rises, denounces the rabble-rouser Thersites, and threatens dire punishment if he repeats his foolish and ill-judged advice. Suiting his action to his words, Odysseus strikes him across the face with his staff. Thersites, weeping and with a bloody weal on his forehead, crouches down "with a wild look." Then, when the rest of the assembly praises Odysseus highly for quelling the agitator, he at once makes a long speech urging the Achaeans to stay and fight on, since according to a prophecy, Troy must fall in the tenth year, and it is now the ninth. Nestor supports him, and Agamemnon resumes command with directions to prepare for battle.

The Thersites incident is most vividly presented. Though the agitator appears for less than seventy lines, he makes an unforgettable impression. (He became a proverbial figure in the later tradition: Shakespeare re-created him memorably in his *Troilus and Cressida*.) Contemporary political thinkers may regard him as a pioneer of democracy and pacifism, but there is not the slightest trace of sympathy in Homer's description of him and his actions. On the contrary, here for once in his two poems, Homer displays open partisanship on the basis of class and politics.

After sacrifice and prayer to Zeus, heralds go out to muster the troops for battle. Four elaborate similes mark the importance of the occasion with emphasis both on sight and sound. The bronze armor of the assembling host flashes like a fire on the mountainside. The noise of their movements is like the clamorous cries of flocks of large birds in an Asian water meadow. Their numbers are like swarms of flies round pails of rich milk in the springtime, or like large flocks of goats tended by goatherds. Agamemnon stands out among the captains in stature and power like a great bull in a thronging herd.

The moment is also given special importance by an invocation to the Muses asking them to inform the poet about the leaders and their ships—"for we poets only hear reports about them and know nothing for certain, while you are goddesses and are omnipresent and omniscient." What follows next has caused an immense amount of controversy and speculation—the so-called "Catalog of the Ships." In the remaining 384 lines of the second book, Homer gives, with much topographical detail, the names of the leaders of the Achaeans and Trojans, their places of origin, and, in the case of the Achaeans, the numbers of their ships and men. It is not relevant here to discuss how much of this information is reliably historical. Our concern is with its literary value.

It is true that its lists of men and places are much longer than anything else of the same kind in the Homeric poems, and they certainly bring the narrative to a long halt. Also, as many critics have observed, it is hardly the time and place, now in the ninth year of the war, to present a roll call of this kind. On the other hand, the material is handled with high poetic skill. Many of the place-names are distinguished by the addition of pleasing epithets, as in "Thisbe with its many doves," "Arne with its many grape-clusters," "hollow, glen-filled Lacedaemon," and "grassy Haliartos." At times, too, the poet gives personal details about the persons named, as when we are told that Nireus, who brought the smallest number of ships (only three), was the most beautiful of all the Achaeans except for Achilles but was weak and had few followers. Further, the clustering place-names have a euphony and resonance that please the attentive ear—as in similar strings of names in poets like Milton and Vergil. And we know from other Greek poets that Greek audiences enjoyed hearing about remote and fabulous places.

The best explanation of this mixture of "catalog" and poetry is perhaps that Homer took over a body of material from some earlier source, improved it poetically, and placed it here to emphasize the magnitude of the forces involved in the consequences of Achilles' wrath. To object that it is untimely to introduce such a roll call at this late stage of the Trojan war is to confuse poetic time with historical time. Besides, Homer is not trying to describe the war as a whole but only the consequences of the wrath.

After the much shorter Trojan "catalog" at the end of book 2, the two armies move forward to the conflict with the Trojans making a clang, clang, clang of armor (*klangē* repeated three times in four lines of the Greek) like the clangor of bird flocks in the sky. In contrast, the Achaeans move forward in fierce silence (a touch of chauvinism, perhaps, on Homer's part). The dust rises up from the armies' feet like mist on mountaintops. But the expected clash of arms does not come. Paris—or Alexandros, as he is called here and often elsewhere—steps forward and challenges Menelaos to single combat. Menelaos gladly accepts and advances. Paris panics and retreats. Hector roundly abuses him as "superbly handsome but a deceiver of women." Paris replies courteously and in a self-deprecatory way—an endearing mannerism of his—and says he'll fight Menelaos in a formal duel, the winner to have Helen. Hector proposes this to the Achaeans. They accept. Preparations are made to swear a solemn oath that the result of the duel will be binding.

Now the scene shifts for the first time to the city of Troy. The elders of the Trojans, including King Priam, are sitting on the wall overlooking the battlefield in the plain below. Forced by old age to desist from warfare, they are still good talkers, "like cicadas in the trees of the woodland with their lily voices." (This is a surprising and beautiful synesthetic meta-

phor, but its meaning is disputed: perhaps it implies a voice that is well shaped, clear in outline, and free from ugly, jarring harmonics in contrast with, for example, the croaking of frogs.) Now Helen appears among them. Here, on her first appearance, a less sophisticated writer might have described her beauty in detail. Homer prefers to describe its effect on what might be expected to be a very unsympathetic audience. He makes the sad, war-weary old men pay her a supreme tribute: "Surely there is no blame on the Trojans and on the well-greaved Achaeans that they should suffer woes for a long while for the sake of such a woman, when she looks so astoundingly like the immortal goddesses." Then, realistically, they add, "All the same, such as she is let her depart in the ships and leave behind no further woe for us and our children."

This method of expressing the qualities of a character in terms of other characters' impressions and not by direct descriptions is strongly favored by Homer. He uses it again in the next scene. Priam asks Helen to identify the leaders of the Achaeans as they muster their forces on the plain below. He inquires in turn about Agamemnon (a very tall, beautiful, and kingly figure), Odysseus (smaller but broader, and like a sturdy ram leading a flock of sheep), and Ajax (massive in head and shoulders). Helen, in reply, first addresses Priam very respectfully and then says that she wishes she had died rather than leave her home and come to Troy, so sad is she at all the suffering she has caused. Then she identifies the three heroes.

At the end of the scene, Homer introduces a touch of pathos. Helen says she misses her twin brothers Castor and Polydeukes (Pollux) among the Achaeans. In fact they were dead, but "she did not know that the *life-giving* earth held them in Lacedaemon." (Whether Homer intended a further touch of pathos in the term "life-giving" here is uncertain.)

The narrative returns to the confronting armies. Priam arrives from Troy. In his presence, Agamemnon swears an oath that the winner of the duel between Menelaos and Paris shall keep Helen and her possessions. Solemn sacrifices and libations follow. Achaeans and Trojans pray to Zeus and the other gods that if either side breaks the agreement, "then let their brains and their children's brains be poured on the ground like the wine of this libation, and may their wives be enslaved," a prayer that eventually worked against the Trojans.

After due preparations, Paris and Menelaos begin their fight. Paris casts his *long-shadowing* spear first but fails to pierce Menelaos' shield. Menelaos in return pierces Paris' breastplate with his spear, but fails to wound him. Drawing his sword, he strikes Paris' helmet. His sword shatters in his hand, so he leaps forward and seizes Paris by the helmet and starts dragging him along. Aphrodite comes to the rescue. (She always acts as Paris' protector because he awarded her the prize for beauty.) Breaking the bindings of his helmet so that it comes away in Menelaos' hand, she surrounds Paris with a protective mist and brings him home to his perfumed bedroom. (A military scholar has noted how the Homeric gods anticipated the use of the smoke screen in warfare.)

The characterization in the episode that follows is particularly subtle and pleasing. First, Aphrodite orders Helen to go and meet Paris, now "radiant with beauty and fine garments: you'd say that he was going to a dance rather than returning from battle." Helen, recognizing the goddess, who is disguised as an old woman, by "her lovely breasts and gleaming eyes," replies angrily and tauntingly. Is Aphrodite trying to deceive her again? Does the goddess want to take her away to some other foreign city now because Menelaos has defeated Paris and wishes to take Helen ("hateful me") home? Let Aphrodite marry Paris herself or become his slave, since she finds him so attractive. "I won't go to him—I would deserve blame if I did—and I won't prepare, and share, his bed. The Trojan women will all blame me afterwards—and my heart is confused with grief."

But one cannot successfully resist a goddess. Aphrodite, in a rage, threatens woeful consequences for both the Trojans and the Achaeans and an evil doom for Helen herself if she rebels. Frightened, Helen wraps herself in her shining silver robe to slip past the Trojan women unrecognized and silently follows laughter-loving Aphrodite. She sits down in front of Paris, averting her eyes, and taunts him with his inferiority to Menelaos as a warrior. Paris, always mild in his responses, asks her not to abuse him and claims that Menelaos won the victory by the help of Athena. Then he asks Helen to let him make love to her, for he has never felt such a desire for her before, not even in the earliest days of their infatuation. After this passionate appeal, Helen silently follows Paris to bed. She still cannot resist Paris in that mood. The testimony to the power of sheer physical attraction—"sweet desire," as Homer calls it—has seldom been expressed with finer effect or with such masterly restraint. Meanwhile, on the field of combat, Agamemnon claims victory for Menelaos and demands the return of Helen and her possessions.

Homer excels in skillful contrasts. The temporary reconciliation of Paris and Helen is set against another scene of angry bickering among the divinities on "the golden floor" of Olympos. Zeus suggests that Menelaos should now take Helen and that Troy should be left in peace. Nothing would please the vindictive Hera and Athena less. After a heated dispute, Zeus agrees to let Athena go and provoke the Trojans into breaking the truce. She persuades the Trojan Pandaros to shoot an arrow at Menelaos. After a prayer to the archer-god Apollo, Pandaros obeys. "The bow twanged, the string gave a loud scream and the sharpened arrow sprang forward, eager to take flight into the melee."

Homer, who rarely intervenes personally in his poems, has an endearing way of speaking to a few of his heroes directly from time to time, especially Menelaos and Patroclos. "Nor, Menelaos," he says, "did the blessed immortal gods forget you." Athena diverts the arrow, "as when a mother keeps a fly away from her child when he lies in pleasant sleep." As a result the arrow only grazes his skin. But the dark blood flows out from the wound. Homer, always conscious of the aesthetic beauty even of cruel or painful things, adds an unusual simile to give vividness to the image of the red blood on the warrior's white flesh: "As when a woman . . . stains ivory with red dye to make a cheekpiece for horses, and then it is stored in a treasury and many horsemen pray to own it but it is kept as a delight for the king, so, Menelaos, were your shapely thighs and shins and fine ankles stained with blood." Agamemnon fears for his brother's life but is reassured. The medical doctor of the Achaeans, Machaon, son of the healer demigod Asklepios, is summoned. He treats the wound successfully.

The Trojans, encouraged by the wounding of Menelaos, now attack in force. Agamemnon goes among the Achaeans to urge them to fight bravely. When he comes to Odysseus, he taunts him as a "crafty-hearted master of evil wiles" and as a coward. Odysseus, angry for once, fiercely tells him that he's talking sheer nonsense. Agamemnon smiles at this and addresses Odysseus more civilly, saying that in fact they both think much the same way—"and if any bad thing has been said just now, let the gods nullify it all." Typical of Agamemnon to insult and cajole in turn so nonchalantly! He goes on to abuse Diomedes, thereby provoking an angry reply from Diomedes' companion Sthenelos. But Diomedes rebukes Sthenelos and says he has great respect for Agamemnon's authority.

Then, like a great wave of the sea gathering force in the main and crashing down with a deep roar on the resounding coastline, the ranks of Achaeans move remorselessly into battle, the leaders giving commands, the common soldiers obeying in silence. The Trojan forces, on the contrary, advance with loud and dissonant cries among them—like an enormous flock of bleating sheep. Athena urges the Achaeans. Ares exhorts the Trojans. They are accompanied by Terror and Fear and "ever-raging Strife."

A lively description of the clash of arms and armor follows. We hear the din of battle with its cries of pain and joy—men yelling and suffering, destroying and being destroyed, the ground streaming with blood. The voices and confusion are like one of those terrible "flash floods" that sweep down the mountainsides in Greece after a heavy rain, carrying devastation with it. The battles continue, with many interruptions, through the next four books.

Modern readers may find Homer's sustained descriptions of battles rather tedious at times. Not that they are tediously presented. In fact they are diversified with incomparable skill. It is their subject matter, not their poetic qualities, that tends to cause us to lose interest. Unless we are students of archaic warfare, Homer's ballistic and anatomical technicalities are likely to tire, just as detailed commentaries on baseball or football soon lose the attention of people who know and care little about such games. But Homer's audience of men in an era of constant warfare probably found these duels supremely interesting. They would appreciate all the finer points as fully as Elizabethan audiences must have appreciated the various maneuvers in Shakespeare's scenes of fighting.

Even a reluctant reader, however, must admire the amazing variety in Homer's hundreds of killings and woundings—so many different offensive and defensive maneuvers, so many heartfelt speeches, so many touches of pity for beauty destroyed, parents bereaved, wives widowed, children orphaned, so many vivid similes to give a background of normal life, so many synonyms for the brute fact of death—"Crimson death and mighty doom seized his eyes"; "He slept the bronze sleep"; "Dark night came down over his eyes"; "He breathed out his spirit"; "Death hid him round"; and others.

Homer does not spare us the ugliest and most painful features of war, the mutilations and indignities, the spilled blood and the entrails exposed—"the spear wounded him in the navel, and all his guts gushed out." At the same time he notices, with the perceptive eye of a painter and the sharp ear of a musician, the varied

11

sights and sounds of the battlefield. He sees the gleam and flash of arms and armor, the stains of blood on white flesh, the surging movements of the troops, the bristling spears of a regiment advancing. He hears all the crashes and thuds and splinterings and shoutings and groans and cries of heavily armored warriors fighting and falling, and he often suggests the quality of these sounds in onomatopoeic words. He feels the chill of "the cold bronze" on a warrior's warm flesh.

In fact, Homer has put much of his finest artistry into his battle scenes. And he constantly humanizes them. We are always made aware of the cost in terms of pain and grief. Besides, just when the chronicle of death and wounds might become unendurable, with superb timing he introduces episodes of a quite different kind, which take one's mind completely away from the gore and din of the battlefield.

Book 5 was given the title *The Championship of Diomedes* by some ancient editor. It is the first of a series of mass slaughterings in which prominent heroes on either side perform outstanding feats of valor and destruction. Diomedes, like a mountain torrent in full spate, slays many Trojans and, when encouraged by Athena, fights and wounds Aphrodite, who intervenes to rescue her son, Aeneas, from his attack. He wounds her in the arm "through the fragrant dress which the Graces themselves had made." Then laughter-loving Aphrodite— where is her laughter now?—flees to her mother in Olympos and is comforted by her with recollections of how other gods suffered in the past. Confused fighting follows, Hera, Apollo, Athena, and Ares joining in. On the Trojan side, Hector and Aeneas (destined to survive the sack of Troy and to become, according to Vergil, the ancestor of the Caesars of Rome) are the chief champions for the Trojans.

Homer relieves the tension of these battle scenes with two celebrated episodes. In the first, Diomedes, still on the rampage, encounters Glaukos, a leader of the Lycian allies of the Trojans. Diomedes asks him who he is. Glaukos begins his reply with an arresting reflection on

the transience of human life. Alexander Pope, whose long note ably defends the passage from "severe and groundless criticisms," translates it with fine poetic effect:

Like Leaves on Trees the Race of Man is found,
Now green in Youth, now with'ring on the Ground,
Another Race the following Spring supplies,
They fall successive, and successive rise;
So Generations in their Course decay,
So flourish these, when those are past away.

Then Glaukos proceeds to relate his ancestry in a long speech. It includes the story of Bellerophon and the Chimera, that fire-breathing monster with a lion's foreparts, a goat's body, and a serpent's tail. It also contains the earliest reference to a written message (as opposed to the usual recited ones) in European literature, the only one of its kind in the Homeric and Hesiodic poems.

Glaukos' philosophical reflection on human life gives a deep perspective to all that happens in the *Iliad*. Momentous and terrible as its events are, viewed in terms of man's long history they are like passing seasons in the cycle of the years. Death is inescapable, but life continually renews itself. Diomedes, a pragmatic young hero, makes no comment on Glaukos' aphorism. But he recognizes that Glaukos is a hereditary guest-friend of his family. Then the two warriors leap from their chariots and clasp hands affectionately. What follows this noble interchange may seem rather an anticlimax in our time. "Then," says Homer, "Zeus took away Glaukos' good sense: he exchanged his armor with Diomedes, gold for bronze, the worth of a hundred oxen for the worth of nine." Homer, like most Greeks of antiquity, did not believe that it is more blessed to give than to receive, or that getting the best of a bargain was beneath the dignity of an aristocratic hero.

The second peaceful episode set among the battles of books 5 to 8 is one of the most famous in all Greek literature. It is a supreme example of Homer's skill in pathos. Hector leaves the battlefield and returns to Troy to ask the women to supplicate Athena for her favor. He tells his mother, Hekabe, to arrange this and refuses her offer of a refreshing drink. Next, he meets Paris and Helen and has brief but revealing exchanges with them. Helen expresses deep self-reproach for bringing so much trouble on the Trojans and then with "honeyed words" asks Hector to sit and talk with her in her misery. He politely refuses, saying that he is on his way to see his wife and infant son, since he cannot be sure that he will ever return from battle again. (Helen's last words to him perhaps speak more for the poet than for her tragic self—"we on whom Zeus laid an evil fate, so that we may be renowned in song for future generations." This is a poet's answer to the problem of pain: at least it provides good material for poetry.)

These are only preliminaries to the greater drama that now takes place between Hector and Andromache. She comes to meet him, accompanied by a nurse carrying Astyanax, "tender in heart, just a baby, Hector's darling son, like a beautiful star." Hector smiles when he sees him. But Andromache is in tears at the thought of what will happen to herself and the child if Hector dies and Troy falls. Half chiding and half appealing, she begins, "Uncontrollable man, your warlike spirit will destroy you, and you have no pity for your infant son and unlucky wife. . . . I have no one else to protect me. . . . Don't go back and be killed, leaving your son an orphan and your wife a widow. . . ."

Hector answers her gravely: of course, he is deeply concerned for her; but the heroic code compels him to fight again—"I am ashamed at what the Trojan men and the *long-robed* Trojan women would say if I were to skulk like a dastard away from warfare—and my spirit does not allow me, since I have learned always to be brave and to fight in the front line of the Trojans, winning great fame for my father and for myself." Yet, he adds, "I well know in my heart and spirit that there will come a day when sacred Troy will perish, with Priam wielder-of-the-stout-spear and his people." He grieves, he

says, more for Andromache than for his mother or father or brothers because he foresees the day when the victorious Achaeans will drag her and Astyanax into slavery.

Then comes a brilliant touch. Hector is still dressed in all his bright but terrifying armor. (Two of his recurrent epithets are "with flashing helmet" and "gleaming in bronze.") He reaches out to take Astyanax in his arms. The child, frightened at the sight of his father in battle dress, and especially at the terrible nodding of the plume on the top of the helmet, screams and shrinks back into his nurse's arms. Hector and Andromache both start to laugh at this. Hector takes off his terrifying helmet, takes his baby son in his arms, kisses him, tosses him in the air, prays that he may be outstanding among the Trojans and—a surprisingly self-deprecatory wish for a Homeric hero—that he may be much better than his father in battle, "and may he give delight to the heart of his mother." Andromache takes the child to her fragrant bosom "laughing tearfully"—*dakruóen gelásasa*—a unique and marvelously effective phrase. Hector, full of pity, caresses her: "Don't be too sorrowful: no one will hurl me into Hades until destiny decrees: no man can escape his destiny. Go now to our home and work at your weaving and spinning . . . the war will be the men's concern and especially mine. . . ." Not masculine chauvinism, this, but, in modern terms, "occupational therapy": work is the best anodyne. Then Hector goes back to the fighting. Andromache, in floods of tears and often turning back to look at him, laments with her attendant women, "for they no longer thought that he would return from battle, escaping the rage and strength of the Achaeans."

No scene in Greek literature surpasses this in its depth of feeling or its embodiment of the eternal conflict between masculine and feminine principles of conduct. This, Homer says, is what war and anger can cause within the sacred bonds of marriage and parenthood. This is how two gentle and loving people will have their happiness wrecked. Criticism that it is structurally premature to introduce these fare-

13

wells so early in the poem is based on the assumption that modern critics know better than the ancient Greeks how to compose a heroic epic. Actually, the scene would gravely upset the balance of the poem if it were kept until nearer Hector's death.

On his way back to the battlefield, Hector meets Paris. He, lighthearted as ever and full of physical exuberance after his encounter with Helen, prances along like a stall-fed stallion with its mane floating free over its shoulders. He has no worries about his wife and no child to care for. He greets Hector breezily: "Sorry, comrade, if I kept you waiting." Hector answers: "Everyone knows that you're a mighty warrior, but you just don't like fighting, and I'm sad when I hear the Trojans saying ugly things about you. Let's go: perhaps Zeus will grant us to set up the mixing-bowl of freedom in our halls, when we've driven the well-greaved Achaeans from Troy." Liberty or death—how often have the Greeks all through their history proclaimed that choice!

In books 7 and 8, the battle rages on with an appearance of much confusion. Technically, it is in the interests of the plot development that this should be so. For a while, in Yeats's words, "Things fall apart," until at last Achilles returns. Tolstoy creates much the same atmosphere in his *War and Peace*. The main combatants now are Ajax, "huge of stature with a grimly smiling face and mighty strides," Diomedes, and Teucer. But the fighting is frequently interspersed with speeches, similes, and nonmilitary scenes, as when nine leading champions of the Greeks draw lots to decide who will fight Hector, when the Achaeans decide to build a defensive wall around the ships, when a truce is made to bury the dead, and when the gods continue their endless intrigues and bickerings. The eighth book ends with a much admired simile to describe the campfires of the Trojans as they bivouac for the night near the camp of the Trojans.

Matters have now reached a crisis for the Achaeans. Total victory for the Trojans seems imminent. Agamemnon calls an assembly and again advises withdrawal from the war. Diomedes says that he and Sthenelos at least will fight on. Nestor deferentially advises Agamemnon to try to appease Achilles with lavish gifts and to persuade him to join the battle again. Agamemnon consents. He does not actually apologize for his actions, but he admits that he was infatuated, a victim of *Até* and of blameworthy emotion. He proposes to offer Achilles lavish compensation, including the hand of one of his three daughters in marriage and a rich dowry. He will also swear an oath that he has not had sexual intercourse with Briseis (whom he, of course, will now return). Three delegates are chosen to visit Achilles with this offer—Odysseus, Ajax, and Achilles' old tutor, Phoenix, who first appears on the scene here. They go to Achilles' hut and find him "giving pleasure to his heart" by singing songs—"famous stories of men"—to the accompaniment of his lyre. He receives them warmly and hospitably. After a feast, with Patroclos significantly in the background, Odysseus, forestalling a gesture from Ajax to Phoenix to lead off, produces an accomplished piece of "situational rhetoric." He begins, tactfully as elsewhere, by praising Achilles' hospitality. Then he argues: the Achaeans are in terrible peril; only Achilles can save them; Hector rages unchecked; only Achilles can prevent disaster. Then he switches his argument: "Remember your father, Achilles, how he warned you against quarrelsomeness." Next he rather perfunctorily describes Agamemnon's offer: he probably knows that this is least likely to persuade Achilles to relent. He ends with a renewed appeal for compassion toward the Achaean host "who honour you as a god," and with a remark about Hector's destructive rage. Pity, filial affection, pride, rivalry with Hector, these are the motives on which Odysseus relies, more than on Agamemnon's offer.

Achilles is not persuaded. After an opening remark about how he hates people who say one thing and think another—does he mean Odysseus or Agamemnon, or does he simply mean that he admires frankness and is going to be frank himself?—Achilles says he doesn't see why he should fight just for the sake of another man's wife, especially when Agamemnon thought nothing of confiscating another man's beloved slave-woman. He threatens to sail away with his followers tomorrow. As for all those gifts and offers, he has plenty of possessions at home and plenty of marriageable women there, too. Why should he risk his life to destroy Troy? Life is more valuable than any other thing. The Achaeans had better find some other way of saving themselves and their ships. So let Odysseus and Ajax go back and report failure while Phoenix stays on.

This is a powerful piece of indignant oratory. Anger has made Achilles say some things against his own nature, such as his threat to return home and his assertion that a life without fame might be more acceptable than a glorious short life. In fact, by the end of the book he clearly has withdrawn his threat to sail home, since he tells Ajax that he will not fight until his own encampment is directly attacked by Hector.

After Achilles' reply to Odysseus, Phoenix begins the longest speech in the *Iliad*. With tears in his eyes, he first says that if Achilles returns home he feels bound to go with him, because Achilles' father, Peleus, entrusted his son to his charge to teach him to be "a speaker of words and a doer of deeds." (The emphasis on oratorical as well as practical training for a young hero is noteworthy.) Phoenix then describes how he had come as an exile to the kingdom of Peleus and had been treated there like a son. Placed in charge of the infant Achilles, he had cherished him as a baby and as a youth. To give poignancy to these memories, he adds a vivid detail: when he fed baby Achilles with sips of wine at a feast, the child used "to bubble them back" over his tutor's tunic. (Is Phoenix hinting here that Achilles, even in early infancy, was apt to reject offers?) One can imagine—but Homer does not say it—how Achilles might smile at this touch.

Immediately after this, Phoenix makes a direct appeal to Achilles to "tame his great anger." Even the gods themselves are appeasable, though their power and valor are greater than any man's. In a striking allegorical personification he says that "Supplications"—that is, prayers for appeasement—are daughters of Zeus: they are lame and wrinkled and dim-eyed in contrast with the Spirit of Destruction, *Atè*, who is strong and sound in limb and quicker to run forward: but the Supplications follow after her to heal the harm. If a man rejects their requests, *Atè* will attack him. Phoenix admits that Achilles would be justified in maintaining his wrath if no requital were offered. But now Agamemnon has promised full recompense for his injury, and two of Achilles' best friends among the Achaeans, Odysseus and Ajax, have come to plead with him.

Next, Phoenix tells a long and complicated story about a hero, Meleager, who was eventually persuaded to abandon anger and save his people from destruction. He ends with a practical point. If Achilles relents now, he will be amply rewarded, and the Achaeans will honor him "as a god." If he waits until he is compelled to fight, when the Trojans are about to win total victory—clearly, Phoenix does not believe Achilles intends to go home—then he will have less honor and no gifts.

Achilles, addressing Phoenix in affectionate terms, first asks him not to try "to confuse him with lamentations and grief," and then refuses. A brief appeal from Ajax also fails. Odysseus and Ajax return to a council of the Greek leaders and report Achilles' refusal. Bold as ever, Diomedes says that it was a waste of time trying to persuade him: they should all just go and have a meal and a good sleep and then fight in the morning. He promises to fight in the front line. "Then all the princes, admiring the speech of Diomedes *tamer-of-horses*, agreed, and poured a libation and went, each to his hut, and there they lay down and received the gift of sleep."

"But sweet sleep did not hold Agamemnon, *son of Atreus, shepherd of the hosts*, as he turned many things over in his mind . . . and his groans come thick and fast like lightning-

15

flashes." So the next book begins, book 10. In his nocturnal anxiety Agamemnon goes to Menelaos and finds him even more disturbed with fears of imminent disaster. In the darkness they go round the camp arousing other heroes and checking the sentinels. Nestor in council suggests that they should send spies into the camp of the Trojans. Diomedes volunteers to go. Several others offer to be his companion. He chooses Odysseus. They arm and set out. (This passage has the now famous reference to the "boar's tusk helmet" and also mentions Autolycos, Odysseus' rascally grandfather who will reappear in the *Odyssey* and in Shakespeare's *The Winter's Tale*.) Meanwhile, Hector and the Trojans have also decided to send a spy among the Achaeans. They choose Dolon ("Trickyman," a kind of foil to the wily Odysseus), who is caught, interrogated, and killed by the two Achaeans. They proceed to explore the camp of the Thracian allies of the Trojans, killing their chieftain with many of his men and capturing his famous horses. The two heroes return, report the success of their foray, attend to the horses, bathe first in the sea and then in hot baths, sit down together to a meal, and offer a grateful libation of wine *as-pleasing-as-honey* to Athena for her protection during their dangerous enterprise.

This is a thoroughly enjoyable book with its lively style and unusual atmosphere. But its unity with the rest of the poem has been questioned by commentators since antiquity. They assert that it was composed as a separate lay by Homer and incorporated into the *Iliad* later. This assertion can neither be proved nor disproved. Undoubtedly, there are stylistic features not found elsewhere in the *Iliad*, as distinct from the *Odyssey*, and some of them have been stigmatized as "late." It is also true that the incident does nothing to advance the plot of the whole poem. But it is skillfully integrated into the night after Achilles' refusal, and its atmosphere of anxiety, uncertainty, and darkness is very apt for that occasion. Also, it gives the wily Odysseus and the bold Diomedes an excellent opportunity to use their special talents.

The *Iliad* would be a less rich poem without it.

The next eight books of the poem are mostly concerned with fighting. Several champions on each side are given opportunities for outstanding feats of valor—among the Achaeans: Agamemnon, Idomeneus ("gray-haired though he was"), Odysseus, and especially Ajax; among the Trojans: Hector, Aeneas, and Deiphobos. Though at times modern readers may be inclined to skip over the gory details, they will do so at their peril, so effectively, and often unexpectedly, does Homer introduce memorable phrases, aphorisms, and images into the speeches and similes. For example, in a very long and perhaps designedly tedious oration by Nestor, we find the striking advice given to Achilles by his father always to be the best and outstanding above all the others, which admirably epitomizes the competitive heroic creed. Again, Hector, when refusing to be cowed by a bad omen, nobly affirms, "One omen alone is best, to fight and defend one's own homeland." And the poet's mood noticeably changes from time to time. Sometimes, as we have seen, he emphasizes the harsh cruelty of battle; sometimes he brings out its glories; sometimes he expresses marked pity for its victims when their "tender" and "lily-like" flesh is lacerated. By these devices, and by many others, with supreme artistic tact he never lets the action grow monotonous.

One famous episode in this part of the poem is the deception of Zeus by Hera. When it looks as if Zeus's temporary support of the Trojans, to please Thetis, will bring disaster on the Greeks, Hera decides to use her physical charms to make Zeus lose interest in anything but lovemaking and sleep. She proceeds to make herself look supremely beautiful and attractive. First—to quote Pope's voluptuous version, reminiscent of passages in his *Rape of the Lock*—

... she bathes and round her Body pours
Soft Oils of Fragrance, and ambrosial Show'rs....

16

Thus while she breath'd of Heav'n, with decent
 Pride
Her artful Hands the radiant Tresses ty'd;
Part on her Head in shining Ringlets roll'd
Part o'er her Shoulders wav'd like melted Gold.
Around her next a heav'nly Mantle flow'd,
That rich with Pallas' labour'd Colours glow'd;
Large Clasps of Gold the Foldings gather'd round,
A golden Zone her swelling Bosom bound.
Far-beaming Pendants tremble in her Ear,
Each Gemm illumin'd with a triple Star. . . .

Then, she goes to Aphrodite and borrows her magical girdle in which are "love and desire and intimate talk and coaxing which steals away the reason even of firm-minded men." Next, she persuades the god of sleep to be her accomplice. Thus prepared, she goes and finds Zeus watching the battle from Mount Ida. "At once, when he saw her, love overwhelmed his shrewd wits, as much as when they first mingled in lovemaking, deceiving their dear parents." Hera pretends that she is on her way to visit Father Ocean and Mother Tethys. Zeus insists that she postpone her visit and says, rather tactlessly, that never before in all his other love affairs—and he specifies seven of them—has he felt "*sweet* desire" so strongly. Hera consents. The earth sends up fresh herbage and flowers to make a thick and soft bed for them, and there they lie, modestly enveloped in a golden cloud that glitters with dewdrops. Afterward, when Sleep has overpowered the happy god, Hera slips away and organizes support for the Achaeans.

The Trojans are now in retreat again. Zeus awakes, pities them, and with a terrible scowl abuses Hera, threatening her with fearsome punishment. She goes to Olympos and advises the gods to obey Zeus. (There is an unusual simile here: Hera speeds as fast as "the mind of a man who has traveled widely and thinks with strong yearning 'Would I were there, or there' and has many such wishes." This psychological comparison is only paralleled in the *Odyssey* when ships are described as being "as swift as a wing or as thought." Here Homer is probably drawing on his own experience of the rapidity of the creative imagination.) Trouble follows among the Olympians. Eventually Apollo is sent to rally the Trojans. They attack in force and come to the defensive wall which the Achaeans have recently built. (There has been much analytical trouble over this.) Apollo breaks it down "as a child does to a sand castle near the sea, who, having made it to delight his childish heart, scatters it again with hand and foot just for pleasure, too."

This is a great crisis. Hector is now in full fury, like the War God and like a devastating forest fire in the mountains: there is foam round his mouth, blazing light in his eyes, and terror in the flashing gleam of his famous helmet. Even Ajax retreats before him. At this moment of desperation Patroclos, Achilles' dearest friend and companion, decides to intervene. He goes in floods of tears to Achilles, who unsympathetically asks him, "Why are you weeping like a baby girl running to her mother and holding on to her dress?" Patroclos describes the dire peril of the Achaeans. If Achilles himself will not help them, will he let him, Patroclos, go in his place? Achilles "with great feeling" emphasizes that his anger is unabated and he will not himself fight. But he consents to let Patroclos go against the Trojans and says he will lend him his armor. Achilles orders him to come back from the battle as soon as he has saved the ships from destruction.

At this turning point in the poem, Homer invokes the Muses to tell him how the Trojans began to succeed in their aim of setting fire to the ships. Achilles, when he sees the flames breaking out, orders Patroclos to arm at once. A full description of his arming follows—the fine greaves with silver fittings, the "starry" breastplate, the mighty shield of bronze, the horsehair-crested helmet, and the two mighty throwing-spears (but not, we are told, Achilles' huge thrusting-spear of ashwood from Mount Pelion, for only Achilles could wield that mighty weapon). Next, Achilles orders his charioteer to prepare his chariot with his two immortal horses, Xanthos and Balios ("Bay" and "Dapple"). He encourages his followers, the Myrmidons, to support Patroclos bravely and sends Patroclos away with a prayer for his success and safety. Zeus grants the first, but not the second.

A lively simile of wasps pouring furiously out of their roadside nest when provoked by silly children expresses the energy and intensity of their onslaught. Almost at once Patroclos rescues the *hollow* ships from the Trojan attack, giving the Achaeans a brief respite, as when a cloudy sky suddenly clears "and all the mountain-peaks and the sharp headlands and the wooded glens appear and the bright boundless upper air breaks through."

Though the Trojans withdraw a little, they still fight on. Gradually, Patroclos wins the upper hand. Even Hector flees. To stop the rout, Sarpedon, leader of the Lycians, leaps from his chariot and confronts Patroclos. (We know that Patroclos will kill him: Zeus, his father, has already predicted his death.) Zeus pities him and would like to save him, but Hera argues against this, offering as a consolation that when Sarpedon dies, Death and *kind* Sleep should bear away his body for honorable burial in Lycia. Reluctantly Zeus agrees. As a sign of his grief he sends a shower of raindrops like blood. Then Patroclos wounds Sarpedon fatally with one cast of his spear through the chest. He falls like a forest tree cut by woodmen with their sharp axes to be timber for a ship. (One may note in the addition "for a ship" how Homer often adds "irrelevant" touches to his similes, leading our minds for a moment into another sphere of life.) As he lies stretched out in front of his chariot grasping the blood-stained dust, Sarpedon utters deep cries like a bull caught in the jaws of a tawny lion. A tremendous battle ensues over his corpse. Eventually, Apollo rescues it, and the twin brothers, Death and Sleep, bear it away for burial far off in his native land.

The ancient Greeks believed that in life, as in a stormy sea, waves of grief and pain often come in triads of increasing force. Homer's three major death scenes fit into that pattern: first Sarpedon's, then Patroclos', then Hector's,

each being more momentous than the other—a crescendo of themes with bold variations. The best parallel in modern art is perhaps to be found in musical symphonies where a subject is introduced several times with amplifications and developments.

Hector returns to fight Patroclos and with Apollo's help kills him. "Then with weakening voice you spoke to him, horseman Patroclos." (A similar phrase was formerly used about Hector when he was gravely wounded; it will be repeated of him when he is dying at the hands of Achilles: as these are its only three occurrences, the repetitions are likely to be significant.) He predicts that he will soon be avenged by Hector's own death at the hands of Achilles. "Then his spirit left his limbs and went in flight down to Hades, bewailing his fate and the loss of his manhood and youthful vigour." Hector scornfully challenges his prophecy—"Who knows whether it may not be Achilles, son of fair-tressed Thetis, who will be killed by my spear?"

Menelaos advances to rescue Patroclos' corpse and kills an elegant young Trojan, Euphorbos. His lovely long hair, plaited and bound with bands of silver and gold, is steeped in blood as he lies like a beautiful, tall olive branch covered with white blossoms that has been shaken to the ground by a strong blast. (These static, still-life similes come as a welcome change from the many images of wild animals hunting and being hunted.) Hector approaches, drives Menelaos back, strips off Patroclos' armor and puts it on himself. Tremendous fighting follows with the corpse of Patroclos being dragged to and fro by the contestants. Achilles still remains in ignorance of his companion's death.

Two brief moments of relief are given in this sanguinary episode. The horses of Achilles, having been brought safely out of the melee by their charioteer, become like human beings for a moment and bewail the fate of Patroclos, standing "still as a gravestone on the barrow of a dead man or woman." Tears flow from their eyes, and their luxuriant manes are soiled by the earth as they droop their heads in sorrow. Zeus sees and pities them. "Poor creatures, did we give you, ageless and immortal as you are, to a mortal prince, Peleus, so that you should share the woes of men? Surely there is nothing in the world more miserable than man...." Zeus promises to protect them from the Trojans.

The second brief moment of relief from the agonies of the battlefield comes when Ajax, baffled by a darkness sent by Zeus, cries out in dismay, "Father Zeus, rescue the sons of the Achaeans from under the mist: make the air clear again, grant sight to our eyes: slay us at least in the light...." Longinus in his famous treatise On the Sublime singled out this prayer for special praise. It has many overtones—the Greek love of light and fear of darkness, a heroic desire not only to die gloriously but to be seen to die gloriously, and the whole wide range of associations that the word used here for "light," pháos, carried with it.

At last the news of Patroclos' death and spoliation is brought to Achilles. His anguish is terrible. He pours dust and ashes on his head and dress and falls prostrate on the ground. The Achaean messenger, Antilochos, son of Nestor, keeps holding his hands for fear Achilles would cut his own throat. His mother, Thetis, hears his terrible groans and hastens to him with an attendant train of thirty-three sea-nymphs, all euphoniously named, in a lovely litany that gives great solemnity to the epiphany of the sea-goddess. She comforts her son, who expresses his remorse at the effects of his anger. She persuades him not to join in the fight until she has a suit of armor made for him by Hephaistos himself. He promises, and she departs to Olympos.

But the threat to the corpse of Patroclos looms larger. Hera sends Iris, messenger of the gods (whose track through the sky is the rainbow), to command Achilles to make a brief appearance. He comes out, radiating a terrifying bright aureole kindled round him by Athena—like the hero-light of the ancient Celtic champions—raises himself above in view of the fighters and shouts a great war cry as loud as a trumpet call. Terrified by the sight and the sound, the Trojans reel back. Patroclos' corpse is rescued. For a while the battle pauses.

Thetis arrives in Olympos and persuades Hephaistos—his celestial smithy is fully described—to make armor for her son. He fashions a magnificently ornamented shield. Homer spends over 130 lines, about 900 words, on its decoration. It portrayed a city at peace: with weddings, feastings, dancing, music, a quarrel, and a quiet judgment; and a city at war: with two armies, flashing armor, war gods, an ambush, a cattle raid, battles, deities of destruction, and many corpses. Also there were scenes of ploughing and harvesting, of vintage and herding, and of further dancing (with a notable reference to Diadalos and Ariadne of Knossos in Crete). Hephaistos made a breastplate, too, "brighter than glowing fire," a helmet, "fair and finely adorned with a golden crest," and greaves of "pliant tin." It would be pointless to question the metallurgy of all this Olympian craftsmanship. What matters is the poetry, and it is all golden.

Thetis brings the armor down to Achilles. Achilles takes "the glorious gifts of the god" in his hands, delighted at their fine workmanship. But he thinks anxiously about the condition of Patroclos' body: will flies settle in its wounds and breed worms to ravage it? Thetis promises to preserve it with ambrosia and nectar. She tells Achilles to summon an assembly and announce the ending of his anger against Agamemnon. Achilles does so. In a long speech, Agamemnon blames "Zeus and Fate and the Fury that walks in darkness, and Áté, the eldest daughter of Zeus" ("her feet go softly, not treading on the ground, but down on men's heads she goes to harm them"). Even Zeus, he adds, suffered from her when Heracles was being born—a long story as he recounts it.

Achilles wants all the Achaeans to go out and fight at once. Anger against Hector is now his ruling passion. Against his demand for immediate action, Odysseus, that sensible hero—which is something of a contradiction in terms—advises that the Achaeans should first have a meal. Like Napoleon, he knows that an army marches on its stomach. Achilles impatiently refuses all delay. Odysseus resolutely presses his advice: "You are much mightier in battle, but I am far ahead of you in intelligence, because I am older and have learnt more: men soon get too much of fighting, and they can't feel grief for a dead man with their stomachs: survivors must think of eating and drinking." Achilles makes no reply.

Agamemnon arranges for his gifts to be brought to Achilles and swears an oath that he has not touched Briseis. Homer, who avoided sketching her portrait in the opening scenes of the poem, now lets us see her clearly for a moment. When, like *golden* Aphrodite, she arrives at Achilles' hut and sees the corpse of Patroclos, she throws herself down beside it with shrill cries, "tearing her breasts and tender throat and beautiful face." Calling him "Patroclos dearest favorite of mine in my misery," she remembers how he comforted her when Achilles had taken her captive and how he was "always sweetly kind" to her. The other captive women join in the lamentations—"seemingly for Patroclos, but each for her own personal sorrows."

Achilles finds no joy in Agamemnon's honorable restitution. It only prompts him to express his grief for Patroclos more fully. He still refuses to eat, but Athena gives him nectar and ambrosia to sustain his strength. Now the armor is brought out from the ships, "helmets with their bright sheen and bossy shields and breastplates with solid plates and ashwood spears," and "their gleaming light reached up to the sky, and the whole land around smiled at the lightning-flash of the bronze." (In this way Homer skillfully modulates from the mood of static grief to one of resplendent action, and from the gloom of Achilles' hut to the sensuous joy of brilliant light effects.) As Achilles dons his new armor, his eyes flash and his teeth chatter with passionate eagerness for battle and revenge. Then he grimly rebukes his two immortal chariot horses for failing to bring Patroclos safely back. One of them, Xanthos, miraculously given a voice by Hera, answers him back, blam-

ing Apollo for Patroclos' death and predicting Achilles' own ultimate doom. Achilles replies that he knows all about his own doom and drives his chariot and horses forward with a yell.

All is set now for the death of Hector. But Homer postpones the climax for nearly 800 lines, that is, for over an hour's singing or speaking time. (He makes a similar long postponement before the slaughter of the suitors in the *Odyssey*.) Book 20 begins with an order from Zeus that the gods should fight on one side or the other in the battle. Before they come to blows, Apollo urges Aeneas to contend against Achilles. (The prominence given to this Trojan prince here may be due to dynastic as well as to poetic reasons.) Their duel is inconclusive. Aeneas escapes with a miraculous leap over many ranks of men and chariots. Then Hector advances to meet Achilles. At this point a new reader may be inclined to think, "Now at last the battle royal will begin." But no: once again Homer uses his device of "retardation." Apollo saves Hector with a protective mist. Achilles drives his chariot on, red to its axles with the blood of slaughtered Trojans. He ruthlessly rejects a long and pitiable appeal for mercy from Lycaon with the words, "Patroclos died, a much better man than you, and I, too, must die when fate decrees. . . ."

Continuing the merciless slaughter, Achilles fills the river Scamander (called Xanthos by the gods) with corpses. The river god emerges and rebukes him for defiling his streams. A furious battle between the hero and the god ensues, like that of the Sumerian hero Gilgamesh with Humbaba or Beowulf with Grendel. When Achilles is almost overwhelmed, Hera sends Hephaistos to rescue him with parching fire. The water of the river seethes with the heat. Its eels and other fishes are distressed. (The imagination in this book sometimes approaches the grotesque.) The river is tamed. But now the gods begin their general fight. "They hurled themselves in with mighty clatter: the broad earth resounded and the great sky gave a trumpet call." In fact, what follows is more a war of words than of wounds—"a ridiculous harlequinade" is what Walter Leaf, the best English editor of the *Iliad*, called it. This goes too far, but undeniably some of this book is peculiar. (Geniuses often have their peculiar phases.)

At long last, in book 22, the great climax comes. "Destructive doom" compels Hector to await Achilles' onslaught outside the walls of Troy despite the pitiful entreaties and gestures of his father and mother. Then for a moment his courage wavers. Should he retreat to safety? Once again he steels his resolution with the words he used in answer to Andromache's pleas, "I fear the blame of the Trojan men and the *long-dressed* Trojan women." Yet he wonders whether he should disarm himself and go to Achilles and offer him the return of Helen and a gift of great treasures? "Foolish thought: he would slay me like a defenseless woman. Better to join battle as soon as may be and see to which of us Zeus will grant triumph."

Achilles approaches, brandishing his dreaded Pelian spear. Hector trembles at the sight and flees away like a dove from a hawk. A long pursuit takes them past familiar places in the Trojan landscape, scenes of pleasure, perhaps, in Hector's childhood. (There is a bonus here for scholars interested in topography.) Zeus pities Hector and wishes to save him. His implacable daughter Athena demands death. Zeus lets her have her way. Meanwhile, on the Trojan plain the fateful pursuit has been going on and on, as in a nightmare when pursuer and pursued seem never to succeed in coming closer. Decisively, Zeus lifts up the scales of destiny, balancing the fates of Hector and Achilles. The scales decree Hector's doom. Apollo abandons him.

Bright-eyed Athena, taking the form of a Trojan friend, persuades Hector to stand and face Achilles. Hector asks Achilles to promise that the victor will give the other's body to his kinsfolk for decent burial. Achilles refuses: "Lions do not pledge oaths with men; wolves have no concord with lambs: now you will pay in full for the sorrows of my comrades." They fight. Eventually, Achilles drives the point of his spear right through Hector's soft neck. (But the windpipe was not severed, we are told, so that he could still speak: Homer is careful about such touches of verisimilitude.) Hector, with weakening voice, begs Achilles to spare his corpse. Achilles replies: "Dog, do not supplicate me by my knees or by my parents: I only wish that my spirit and passion would move me to cut off your flesh and eat it raw, for what you have done. Nothing can keep the scavenging dogs from your head." Hector, dying, says Achilles has "an iron spirit" and predicts his death. Then "his soul fled from his limbs and went down to Hades, mourning his fate and the loss of his manhood and youth."

Brutal scenes follow. The Achaeans come and admire the spectacular size and shape of Hector's corpse. But none leave without adding to its wounds. Achilles slits Hector's ankles, ties them to his chariot, and drags him in sight of the city. "And as he was dragged through the rising dust-cloud, his blue-black hair spread out, and his head, once so graceful, lay all in the dust, for then Zeus had granted to his foemen that they should do outrageous things to him in his own homeland."

Priam and Hekabe watch all this from the walls of Troy. Their lamentations and those of all the people fill the city. It is "as if all high-sited Troy was smoldering with fire, right down from its citadel." Priam can hardly be held back from rushing out to beg his son's body from Achilles. Andromache has not yet heard the news. She is preparing a hot bath for her husband when he comes home from battle—"Poor foolish woman, she did not know that he, very far from such baths, had been overcome by Pallas Athena, at the hands of Achilles." Then Andromache hears the shrill cries and groans from the walls. With trembling limbs and wildly beating heart she rushes, like a madwoman, to learn the cause, though she already guesses it. From a tower she sees Hector being dragged remorselessly down to the Achaean ships. The expression of her grief is heartrending.

Now in the Achaean camp, Achilles and the

Myrmidons mourn again for Patroclos. They honor his corpse with a cavalcade of their chariots and then, after a lavish funeral banquet, Achilles and his followers go away on the shore of the boisterous sea. When Achilles has fallen asleep, the spirit of Patroclos appears to him in a dream and complains that he should be able to sleep while the body of his dearest friend lies unburied. Achilles promises to give him full funeral honors. He tries to embrace the ghost, but it gives a shrill screech and vanishes away under the earth like a wisp of smoke.

At dawn, Achilles sends men and mules to the woods to fetch timber for a funeral pyre and musters his Myrmidons in a funeral procession. The pyre is built, the corpse is placed on it, sacrifices are burned (including twelve Trojan youths, their throats having been kindly cut first), and finally the "iron force" of fire is applied. Achilles bids Patroclos farewell. To comfort the vengeful spirit of his friend, he promises to give Hector's corpse to the scavenger dogs. (But Aphrodite and Apollo protect and preserve it.)

The corpse, like Shelley's on the Italian coast, is slow to burn. Achilles prays to the north and west winds to come and fan the flames. Iris brings his message to the palace of the winds where they are all banqueting together. The two winds come blustering over the sea and increase the flames. Achilles tends the blazing pyre all night. In the morning the Achaeans quench the smoldering ashes, gather the bones, place them in a golden casket, and bury them under a hero's mound.

Homer, careful as ever not to harrow his audience's feelings too long with sorrowful scenes, now introduces a comparatively light-hearted episode, which at the same time gives scope for enjoyment of a favorite activity of the Greeks in antiquity, athletic sports. They consist of contests in chariot racing, boxing, wrestling, running, dueling with spears, throwing the weight, archery, and casting the javelin. This also gives him an opportunity to bring all the chief heroes of the Achaeans on to the scene again in what is the last appearance for all except Achilles. As in his battle scenes, the poet makes use of each event to illustrate character. Nestor shows his wisdom in giving advice to his son on how to win the chariot race: his son, with youthful rashness, drives dangerously and loses the race. In the wrestling the *wily* Odysseus throws the massive Ajax with a crafty trick. Then Achilles, fearing Ajax's wrath if defeated in the final throws, intervenes and gives prizes to both heroes. Next, Odysseus with the help of Athena, "like a mother," defeats in the footrace the lesser Ajax, who slips and has his face covered in cow dung—at which the Achaeans laugh merrily. When Agamemnon rises to contest the javelin throw, Achilles tactfully cancels the contest, gives him the prize, and provides another for his opponent. Some minor heroes appear for a moment, as when Epeios, later celebrated as the builder of the Wooden Horse, wins the boxing but makes a derisory throw with the discus—at which the Achaeans laugh again.

After these games the rest of the Achaeans turn to supper and sleep, but not Achilles. He lies awake, restlessly turning now on his back, now on his face, now on his side, as he yearns for Patroclos and remembers "how many things he achieved and how many the sufferings he endured with him when they thrust their way through battles and through sorrowful seas." Unable to lie still, he starts up and roams wildly along the seashore. (Notably, Achilles in the *Iliad* shows this Byronic trait of seeking solitary consolation by the sea.) At dawn he harnesses his chariot and drags Hector's corpse three times round the tomb of Patroclos.

The gods, with the exceptions of Hera, Poseidon (who is still rancorous because an earlier king of Troy cheated him), and Athena, pity Hector's corpse. Apollo persuades Zeus to arrange for its ransoming. Thetis goes to her son and tells him that he must allow this. Storm-footed Iris speeds to Priam and informs him of Zeus's decision. Soon now, a modern reader might think, Hector's body will be brought home and buried. But Homer's technique of retardation comes into action again, and nearly three hundred lines elapse before Priam reaches Achilles' hut. First Hekabe tries to dissuade him, unsuccessfully. He goes to his treasury and selects opulent gifts for Achilles—garments, rugs, ten talents of gold, tripods, cauldrons, and a specially fine goblet from Thrace: "he spared nothing, so greatly did he wish to ransom his dear son." Then he angrily drives the Trojans out of his palace and abuses his sons as liars and playboys (literally "dancers"). A wagon is prepared and loaded with the gifts. Hekabe pours a libation and asks Priam to pray to Zeus for a favorable omen. An eagle with wings as wide as the door of a rich man's lofty-roofed bedroom appears on the right hand, the side of good omen, and swoops through the town, gladdening the hearts of the Trojans.

Priam's journey to the hut of Achilles is described with equal amplitude. Zeus orders Hermes to help him. Hermes puts on his golden sandals, which carry him like the wind over land and sea, and takes his magical staff, and then, disguised as a princely youth, he meets Priam. There is darkness now over the land. A lengthy exchange of speeches follows between him and the Trojan king.

At last Priam, aided by Hermes, reaches Achilles' hut. There he finds Achilles still seated at table after a meal. "Great Priam" goes forward and dares to touch Achilles' hands, those "dreadful, man-slaying hands which had killed so many of his sons." "Think of your own father, Achilles" (Hermes has advised him to begin like that); "he is the same age as I am, advanced on the baneful path of old age. But he still has the joy of hoping that he will see his dear son returning from Troy, while I, in contrast, am utterly undone by fate...." He adds with a pathetic touch of vanity, "I have dared what no man on earth has dared before, to kiss the hand that slew my own son."

Achilles is deeply moved by the mention of his father. Taking Priam by the hand, he gently thrusts him away. Then side by side, they weep together, Priam for man-slaying Hector, Achilles for his father and for Patroclos. Then

"when glorious Achilles had full pleasure of mourning"—Homer recognizes here and elsewhere the fact that the physical expression of sorrow can give a pleasant sense of relief, just as poetry and song about sad things can give deep pleasure—he raises Priam up, "pitying his gray head and gray beard." He speaks to Priam first in admiration for his courage in daring to approach the man who killed so many of his sons—"you must have a spirit like iron." (How tactful and courteous of him to begin by praising an aged hero for his courage—or, rather, how admirable of Homer to make his heroes behave so nobly when they are not deranged by passion!)

Then, like many heroes when they are trying to subdue their natural impulses—one thinks of the great speech by Ajax before his suicide, in Sophocles' play—Achilles philosophizes for a moment about life. Zeus, he says, has casks of good fortunes and evil fortunes on each side of his throne. From these he apportions to each man his destiny: some receive a mixture of good and evil, some only evil. Achilles' own father first was greatly blessed, but his grief will be great when his only son dies. Hector's father was supremely blessed with wealth and sons, but now....

Priam, knowing that he has succeeded, asks Achilles to take the gifts and let him go back at once with Hector's body. At this point Homer presents a superb touch of characterization. For a moment Achilles' wrath flares up again, because Priam has tried to prescribe what he should do and how he should do it. An Achilles will not be hurried: he will do things in his own way. Scowling fiercely, he replies, "Don't provoke me, old man ... take care that you do not stir up my spirit in its agony, for fear that, guest and suppliant though you are, I may violate the injunctions of Zeus." Priam, terrified—as who would not be?—acquiesces. To release his fierce energy, Achilles leaps up like a lion, goes out, unyokes Priam's chariot, and takes the gifts. But he generously leaves some fine garments to serve as Hector's shroud—again a touch of admirable considerateness. He orders servants to wash and anoint the corpse out of sight of Priam so that he should not witness the painful process. When the body has been prepared, Achilles himself raises it and places it on Priam's wagon. As he does so, he groans and calls out to Patroclos' spirit not to feel resentment, promising to give him, even in Hades, a share of Priam's rich gifts.

Returning, he suggests to Priam that they should have a meal together, reminding him that even Niobe, in her grief at losing six sons and six daughters at once, took food. As they sit at table, Priam gazes in wonder at Achilles, "like a god to see," and Achilles gazes in turn at Priam with his noble features and discourse. "But when they had taken their pleasure in looking at each other," Priam asks for a bed to be made ready for him so that they both "may take pleasure in sweet sleep." (With this double reference to pleasure, Homer is telling us, it seems, that life and nature offer compensations even in the saddest times, if we will accept them.) Achilles makes sure that Priam's bed is placed where no chance visitor from the Achaean camp might see it, and at Priam's request he promises to hold the Achaean forces back for eleven days during Hector's burial rites. He then presses the old man's wrist to reassure him and goes away to sleep in his inner room, "and the fair-cheeked Briseis lay beside him." That is the last we see of Achilles in the *Iliad*. In contrast with his recent savagery, he has now appeared as a model of noble and generous behavior, except in that one fearsome moment when his anger blazed out again.

There is no parting scene after this. Homer avoids it, and we must bow to his judgment. Instead, Hermes comes to Priam and bids him leave at once for fear that the other Achaeans should discover and capture him. When Homer wishes his characters to move fast, they move fast. Within seven lines Priam is back in Troy with the body of Hector. The Trojans pour out to meet him. In turn Andromache, Hekabe, and Helen lament for Hector—Helen praising him for his gentleness toward her—"for nobody else in *broad* Troy was tender and friendly, but all shuddered at me."

Preparations are made for the funeral. Wood is gathered, the pyre is built and lit. When the corpse is consumed, Hector's brothers and companions gather his white bones from the ashes, wrap them in soft crimson robes, place them in a golden casket, lay them in a grave, and heap a mound of great stones over it. Then the mourners assemble for a sumptuous banquet in the home of Priam, that god-nurtured king. The last line of the poem is:

And so they tended the burial of Hector tamer of horses.

The wrath is over; its victims are buried; the mourners have feasted; the poem is ended. We have witnessed a triumph of humanity and a masterpiece of the poetic art.

No prose summary could do anything like justice to the somber magnificence of the last book of the *Iliad*, and much less to the 100,000 words of the whole great epic. So many touches of deep emotion and subtle sympathy have to be omitted, so many vigorous actions, lively speeches, splendid descriptions, vivid similes, and striking metaphors. Yet it is hoped that some impression of Homer's art has been conveyed in the preceding pages, especially of his mastery of climax and suspense, and of his ever-changing textures of anger and affection, tears and laughter, cruelty and kindness, hate and love, sorrow and joy, in such a way that readers may turn or return to the poem itself for full enjoyment.

The *Odyssey* is both a simpler and a more complex poem than the *Iliad*—simpler because it centers on one man and his associates, more complex because it moves backwards and forwards in time and traverses many different regions. The opening lines make its subject clear—"Tell me, Muse, of the resourceful man [*polútropon*, literally "of many turns": Homer uses it only of Odysseus] who was driven far astray when he had destroyed the sacred citadel of Troy: he saw the cities of many men and got to know their minds: he suffered many heartfelt woes in the sea as he strove for his own life and for his homecoming with his companions." The term used here for homecoming, *nóstos*, is a key word. (How the various Achaean heroes came home after their victory at Troy was apparently a favorite theme before Homer, for he refers to several other *nostoi* in the *Odyssey*.) In fact, from the point of view of plot rather than of character, the *Odyssey* might be called *The Nostos of Odysseus or How Odysseus Made His Way Home to His Wife Penelope and to His Kingdom in Ithaca, and What Happened There*.

Two other phrases in the introductory lines deserve attention. "Tell me, Muse" contrasts with "Sing, Goddess" in the first line of the *Iliad*. Perhaps it indicated that poetry had become less akin to song since the earlier poem was composed. Secondly, the tenth line reads, "Tell us, too, Goddess, about these things from some beginning or other," which apparently implies that the story of Odysseus had already been extensively told. Nothing similar is said about the story of the wrath of Achilles. We are also told in the opening lines that the companions of Odysseus all perished before reaching home, because they foolishly ate the cattle of the sun god, and that Odysseus himself has not reached home yet. He is still "in want of his homecoming and his wife," marooned on the island of the nymph Calypso, "glorious among goddesses." We are warned, too, that even when Odysseus does reach home, he will not have escaped danger, and that Poseidon will harass him mercilessly until then, though all the other gods pity him in his exile. (We soon learn the reason for Poseidon's anger—the blinding of his son, the Cyclops: but Homer's hearers may have known this already.)

The main narrative begins with a discussion among the gods in the absence of Poseidon, who is away at a feast with the Ethiopians. Zeus begins with some reflections on the theme that mortals should not blame their sufferings on the gods but on their own reckless transgressions. The bright-eyed goddess Athena seizes the opportunity to say that her heart is distressed for wise-hearted Odysseus, who "In his yearning to see the smoke rising up from his own land wants to die." (Exile was always an intolerable grief to Greeks.) She reminds Zeus how Odysseus gave him pleasure with his sacrifices at Troy—"Why, then, are you so odious towards Odysseus?" (The paronomasia is in the Greek: it suggests a connection between a verb meaning "to be angry with someone" and the name "Odysseus," and perhaps implies that he, in contrast with Achilles, was a victim—not an agent—of wrath.) Zeus, the cloud-gatherer, agrees to let Odysseus come home. Hermes is sent to summon him from Calypso's island. Athena volunteers to go to Ithaca and send Telemachos on a voyage in search of news about his absent father. (Telemachos is now a youth of about twenty, having been an infant in arms when Odysseus went to fight at Troy.)

The next four books are taken up with the doings of the godlike, prudent Telemachos, and we do not meet Odysseus again until the fifth book. Analytical scholars have argued that this is a breach of unity, so that the *Telemachy*, as they call it, must be an addition to the original poem about Odysseus. Against that, it may be argued that authors often hold back the entrance of their main character to increase expectation and suspense; that it gives depth and perspective to the crisis in Ithaca; that the style and content of these books are fully Homeric; that Homer, as we have seen in the *Iliad*, often makes wide digressions from his main theme; and most important of all for those who care more about the poetry than about the poet, these *Aventures de Télèmaque* (to borrow the title of François Fénelon's famous 1699 variation) are a brilliant piece of creative fiction.

Athena arrives at the palace in Ithaca disguised as an old friend of Odysseus. Telemachos receives her courteously and hospitably.

HOMER

In his speech of welcome, he expresses deep pessimism about his father's fate. Athena encourages him to be more hopeful and persuades him to act against the insolent suitors of Penelope who are now infesting her home. We are given a glimpse of them eating and drinking, playing a board game, dancing and listening to the songs of Phemios, the greatly popular bard of Odysseus. Telemachos presses Athena to stay on for further hospitality, but she declines, having told him that he must go on a journey to the Peloponnesos to seek news of his father. Then she departs, flying like a bird through the smoke hole in the roof. Telemachos, recognizing her godhead, gains courage and spirit and goes to meet the suitors.

The most renowned bard is now singing a divine song to the suitors about "the sorrowful homecoming (*nóston*) of the Achaeans." Wise-hearted Penelope hears it in the upper room where she usually stays during the day. She comes down and asks the bard to sing a different song, "since he knows many other enchanting themes," and not one which renews her deep sorrow for her absent husband "whose fame extends through Hellas and central Argos." To her surprise, her son, who has suddenly become adult and independent as a result of Athena's visit, rebukes her: "Why do you grudge the bard his giving pleasure in whatever way his mind turns? Audiences like songs on the newest themes." He orders her to go back to her room and look after her spinning and weaving. She, in astonishment at the change in her son, obeys.

Now the suitors make an uproar in "the *shadowy* halls." Telemachos tells them to go to their own houses. Two ringleaders reply: Antinoös, always a bully, abuses him; Eurymachos, a less arrogant type, is more civil. (There were, we are told later, a hundred and eight suitors in all—a notable proof of Penelope's attractiveness. Homer wisely characterizes only a few of them.) The suitors spend the rest of the day in dance and song. At nightfall Eurycleia, his nurse and his father's before him and now acting as housekeeper, leads Telemachos to his bedroom with a torch. (Described here with a unique epithet as "shrewd in planning," she becomes an important figure later in the plot.) In a quiet ending, like that of the first book of the *Iliad*, she carefully folds Telemachos' clothes, hangs them on a peg near his *carved* bed and goes out, closing the door with its silver hook and leather thong to pull the latch. (Domestic details of this kind, phrased in fine poetry, take the place of Iliadic descriptions of weapons.) The young prince lies awake all night in his blanket of sheep's wool thinking about the journey that Athena has ordered.

Then "when the rosy-fingered, early-rising dawn appeared"—that memorable formula which Homer uses twenty-seven times—Telemachos and his two swift dogs (dogs are pets in the *Odyssey*, not eaters of corpses as in the *Iliad*) go to an assembly of the Ithacans. There he complains bitterly about the conduct of the suitors, bursting into angry tears at the end of his speech. The populace pities him, but Antinoös abuses him and blames Penelope for the suitors' long wooing. He describes her famous delaying ruse of weaving a shroud for Odysseus' father during the day and unraveling it at night for three years until a disloyal servant betrays her. The suitors will not leave, he asserts, until Penelope marries one of them. Telemachos answers that he can't force his mother to marry against her will. Suddenly Zeus sends an omen of two eagles swooping down and attacking the assembly. A soothsayer interprets it as prophesying the return of many-deviced Odysseus (who, we are told, had promised that he would come back in the twentieth year). Further heated debate follows. The assembly breaks up.

Telemachos goes down to the seashore, like Achilles, and Athena comes in the disguise of Mentor, a guardian appointed by Odysseus, and encourages him to be worthy of his father. He returns, deep in thought, to the palace to challenge the suitors further. One of them hopes he may die on his journey. Telemachos goes out to make preparations. Eurycleia, though shocked to hear of his decision, helps

26

him. He makes her swear not to tell Penelope about it until ten or eleven days have passed. Soon "the sun sank and all the streets were cast in shadow" (another fine formula used eight times in the *Odyssey*). Athena lays a deep slumber on all the suitors and, in the shape of Mentor, leads Telemachos to his ship. They sail off. "The darkling wave sounded loud as it surged round the speeding cutwater: the ship ran on, making a path over the wave . . . all night and through the dawn she cleaved her way." (The first half of the *Odyssey* is full of vivid seascapes.)

Next day they reach Pylos where Nestor has his palace. Nestor and his son receive Telemachos and Mentor (Athena) warmly. When Nestor learns who they are and what they are seeking, he lives up to his Iliadic reputation for loquacity in a speech of almost a hundred lines, full of reminiscences, remarking, "if you were to stay with me for five or six years, I couldn't tell you all the troubles we suffered at Troy." It all amounts to no information about Odysseus. (A reference here to the murder of Agamemnon by Aigisthos implies a contrast that runs all through the *Odyssey* between Agamemnon's fate on his return home to a faithless wife and her paramour and Odysseus' happier fortune.)

After further discourse, in which Telemachos' pessimism is rebuked by Athena, and Nestor gives further lengthy information about the homecomings of other Achaeans "until the sun sank and the darkness came," Athena takes flight "like a seabird," to the astonishment of all. Telemachos is persuaded to stay the night at Pylos. Next morning, Nestor and his six sons offer an elaborately described sacrifice of a cow with gilded horns to Athena. Then Nestor's youngest daughter, Polycaste, bathes, oils, and clothes Telemachos—a normal Homeric custom that has pained some prudish critics. After a meal, a chariot is prepared for Telemachos, and he sets out with one of Nestor's sons for Sparta, making an intervening stop, briefly mentioned, at a house on the way. After another day's journey he reaches the palace of Menelaos and Helen.

This visit gives Homer an opportunity to portray something that would be likely to please an early Greek audience enormously—the domestic life of Helen after her return from Troy. It is a very skillful and charming picture. Her entrance is deliberately delayed. First the visitors are given time to dine and to admire the opulence of the palace with its "lightning-flash of bronze and gold and electrum and silver and ivory." Then Menelaos speaks to them at some length about his sufferings after he left Troy. An affectionate reference to Odysseus—Menelaos has not yet learned who his visitors are—causes Telemachos to weep. While Menelaos is wondering what to do, Helen makes a spectacular entry, "like Artemis of the golden distaff," accompanied by three attendant women bringing her folding chair, a coverlet of soft wool, and a remarkable silver workbasket fitted with wheels. (The comparison with the chaste goddess Artemis, and not Aphrodite, no doubt shows Helen's changed ethos.) In the scene that follows, she shows herself to be perceptive, considerate, regretful about her Trojan escapade, and conscious now of her husband's good looks and good sense.

She immediately notices that one of the strangers looks like great-hearted Odysseus. Menelaos agrees. Nestor's son tells them that his companion is in fact Telemachos. Fairhaired Menelaos at once expresses his grateful affection and his deep regret at Odysseus' failure to return home. All begin to weep at memories of the past. Soon Helen decides to cheer things up. She puts a powerful drug into their wine—so strong an anodyne that "even if one's mother and father were to die, or if a brother or dear son were to be slaughtered by the sword before one's eyes, one would not cry." (Homer adds some details about how Helen had been given it in Egypt, where there is abundance of beneficial and harmful drugs and everyone is highly skilled in medicine. This is typical of the many fascinating sidelights on the ancient world that Homer supplies: but here the main purpose is to give prominence to this unusual drug, whatever it was.)

To gain time for her medicine to take effect, Helen tells a story about how Odysseus came into Troy as a spy, disguised as a beggar, and how he was recognized and treated well by her. Menelaos adds reminiscences about Odysseus' stratagem of the Wooden Horse, and what it was like to be one of those inside it when Helen went round it and called out their names, "imitating the voice of the wives of all the Achaeans"—a strange incident not described elsewhere. Then Telemachos suggests that all should go to bed, and Helen carefully sees that they are provided with beautiful crimson rugs and coverlets and woolly tunics.

Next day Menelaos asks Telemachos why he came to Sparta. (Homeric etiquette prescribed that such questions should not be asked until hospitality has been given.) Telemachos tells him that he has come in search of information about his father and describes the sad state of affairs in Ithaca. Menelaos, in the first long simile in the *Odyssey* (there are much fewer than in the *Iliad*), says that the suitors will be like deer trapped by a lion when Odysseus returns. Then in a long narrative he recounts how, on his way back from Troy, he came to an island off the coast of Egypt. There he encountered a magician named Proteus, the Old Man of the Sea, who had the power to change his shape. (Hence the word "protean" in English, and the original title of the first chapter of James Joyce's *Ulysses*.) Helped by Proteus' daughter, Menelaos compelled the magician to tell him about the *nóstoi* of other Achaeans and learned that Odysseus is detained on Calypso's island. Prudent Telemachos, having heard this, courteously declines Menelaos' invitation to stay on for ten or eleven days by saying that he would gladly stay for a year, so much has he enjoyed Menelaos' stories, but that he must go back to his waiting companions at Pylos. The Spartan King, good at the battle cry, smiles with pleasure at the politeness and thoughtfulness of the young Ithacan prince and prepares to send him off with lavish gifts.

The scene changes back to Ithaca. The suitors are astonished to learn about Telemachos' departure and approve their ringleader Antinoös' suggestion that they send a ship to waylay the youth on his return and, Antinoös implies, kill him. When Penelope hears this, she is paralyzed and dumbstruck for a while with grief and dismay. Though comforted a little by Eurycleia, she goes without food and drink, worrying about her son. When at last "pleasant sleep came, and she lay back and slept and all her limbs were relaxed," Athena sends a dream to assure her that Telemachos will return safely. When wise-hearted Penelope asks the dream-shape if Odysseus is alive, however, she is refused that information and left in suspense. Meanwhile, the suitors lay their ambush for Telemachos.

There the *Telemachy* ends. In it, we have heard high praise of Odysseus from Nestor, Menelaos, Helen, Telemachos, and Mentor. We have witnessed the arrogance and malevolence of the suitors and the anxious grief of Penelope. We have learned how Odysseus yearns for his home and family and how his family yearns for him. The stage is now set for his appearance at the center of the narrative.

Book 5 begins with another council of the gods at which Athena again persuades Zeus to let Odysseus return home. This has already been decided by Zeus at the beginning of the poem, but it is not Homer's way to say something like "As you will remember, over two thousand lines ago the gods. . . ." It is much simpler and more effective to create briefly the decisive council without any harking back. Oral poetry avoids confusing its hearers by asking them to recall earlier developments in the plot: each present event demands all their attention.

At Zeus's command, Hermes binds on his winged sandals, takes his magical rod, and sets out like a bird over the waves of the violet-colored sea to Calypso's beautiful island. It is described with idyllic detail: the air is perfumed with the scent of burning cedarwood; alder trees and poplars and fragrant cypresses are there; many wild birds, a vine with richly clustering grapes, copious springs of water, and meadows filled with violets and wild celery—

"Even an immortal god would gaze at it in wonder and would feel joy in his heart." Hermes finds Calypso in her cave and tells her, after the customary hospitality, that she must let Odysseus go. She shudders at the bad news and complains that the gods are jealous when goddesses and mortals are happy together, but reluctantly consents. Meanwhile, we have been told that great-hearted Odysseus is alone on a sea-cape, lamenting and wailing and gazing with tears in his eyes over the unharvested sea—a strange introduction by modern standards to the hero of a great epic poem. There Calypso finds him as he yearns to get back to his own home and wife, for "the nymph pleased him no longer, though he slept with her nightly, he unwilling, she willing, in her hollow cave."

Calypso, glorious among goddesses, rather brusquely tells Odysseus to stop lamenting and make preparations for sailing home. He can hardly believe it and asks her to swear an oath that she does not plan to harm him. With a smile she calls him a wily rascal and swears to him by earth and heaven and the inviolable Styx. After a meal she tries to persuade him to stay, offering him immortality and claiming that she, as a goddess, is more beautiful than Penelope. Odysseus politely refuses, but they have pleasure that evening in their last lovemaking. Next day Odysseus builds a boxlike boat whose construction is elaborately and uniquely described. On the fifth day Calypso bathes, dresses herself in perfumed garments, and brings provisions for Odysseus' voyage. No words of parting are recorded, but "gladly did the glorious Odysseus spread his sails to the favorable breeze."

On the eighteenth day, high shadowy mountains appear on the horizon. But before Odysseus reaches land, Poseidon, now returned from feasting with the Ethiopians, sees him and sends a tremendous tempest. Saved from drowning by a kind sea-nymph, Odysseus struggles ashore on an unknown island. He makes a bed of leaves under an olive tree and falls fast asleep.

The scenes that follow are among the most delightful in the Homeric poems, thanks to the charming spontaneity of their protagonist, Nausicaä, the young daughter of Alcinoös, king of the Phaeacians. The story, too well known to need recounting, tells how, prompted by Athena, Nausicaä goes to the seashore to wash the royal linen, encounters Odysseus, and escorts him to her city. In age and mind she stands somewhere between Shakespeare's Rosalind and Lewis Carroll's Alice, young enough to call her father "Daddy dear" and to play ball with her girl companions, and old enough to be on the verge of marriage—and as beautiful as Artemis, the virginal goddess. Odysseus, storm-beaten and stark naked, has to use all his adroitness in situational rhetoric to win her sympathy and help. She amusingly lectures the much-enduring Odysseus on the fact that Zeus sometimes gives misfortunes even to noble and virtuous people—"so you must altogether endure your sufferings, stranger." There was a risk that the picture of a naked seaman conversing with an innocent girl could have been ludicrous for the hero, but Homer avoids it with consummate artistry, ennobling Odysseus with a powerful lion-simile and causing Athena to make him look supremely handsome during the incident, like silver gilded with gold and with "hyacinthine" hair.

Scholars have suggested that this encounter between a kind of fairy princess and a stranger prince, who later defeats all the local lads in competitive sports, is based on a type of folktale which often recurs in European literature—*la princesse lointaine* who marries the "dark horse." This may be so, but Homer firmly subordinates it to his main narrative without leaving any sense of lost romance or sentimental heart-burnings. When Nausicaä and Odysseus meet each other again in the Phaeacian palace, they say good-bye briefly and calmly—"Remember me when you reach your native land"—"I shall remember you with prayers of gratitude always, for you gave me my life, girl."

Instructed by Nausicaä to appeal to her mother, Queen Arete, who apparently is the controlling character in Phaeacia (her strange silences and questions have prompted much critical speculation), Odysseus enters the palace, after admiring its wonderful gardens and magical statues, and prostrates himself at her knees as a suppliant. (He had prudently omitted this traditional gesture with Nausicaä.) She does not reply, but King Alcinoös treats him courteously and hospitably. Eventually, the Queen shoots a sharp question at him—"Who are you, and who gave you the clothes you are wearing?" (Nausicaä had given him some of her laundry to wear.) Avoiding a direct answer, Odysseus relates how he left Calypso's island, was shipwrecked on the seacoast of Phaeacia, and met the princess there—a richly detailed account, but he doesn't tell his name. (This has caused further perturbation to critics who, often being professional examiners themselves, think that everyone should answer a question directly, precisely, and succinctly. In fact, Homer is probably employing his customary technique of delaying a major climax to an extent that modern readers find almost intolerable.) Odysseus ends his long reply by telling a white lie to protect Nausicaä from blame for not having conducted him personally to her parents. Alcinoös, having first remarked in his outspoken manner that Odysseus seems to be just the kind of man he would like his daughter to marry, promises him escort home tomorrow if he prefers not to stay. The episode ends with the much-enduring, glorious Odysseus asleep "on a carved bed in the loud-echoing portico."

Book 8 offers another welcome example of Homeric retardation. Despite Alcinoös' promise to escort him home "tomorrow," Odysseus is kept on to witness something of the easy, self-indulgent life of the Phaeacians, who love "feasting and lyre-music and dancing and changes of clothes and hot baths and beds." First, it is agreed at a council that an escort ship should be prepared for Odysseus' journey home. Then comes a banquet with music and song from the bard Demodokos, who moves Odysseus to tears with a song about an incident in his heroic past. (Does Homer's description of this bard tell us something about Homer him-

self or not? One can only guess.) Next, there is an athletic contest in which Odysseus, when rather rudely challenged by an insolent young Phaeacian, shows supreme prowess and then boasts inordinately about his prowess as an athlete. Alcinoös, always a perceptive and genial host, intervenes to soothe things down and calls on the bard to sing an amusing and slightly risqué song about how Hephaistos trapped his wife Aphrodite in adultery with Ares. Next, two sons of Alcinoös dance a pas de deux with a crimson ball. Odysseus tactfully praises them. Alcinoös responds with promises of rich guest-gifts. At a second feast, the bard sings about the Wooden Horse and the sack of Troy. Odysseus weeps at these memories of his heroic past. Alcinoös observes him and asks him why he weeps.

Now at last comes the denouement. Odysseus, after exuberant praise of the lavish banquet and the singing of the bard (Plato found his superlatives regrettably hedonistic), proclaims, "I am Odysseus son of Laërtes, of concern to all men for every kind of wiliness. My fame reaches to heaven and my dwelling place is Ithaca, fair in the evening light . . ." (eudeielos, or perhaps "finely clear" like "Delos": the problem of whether Homer's Ithaca is modern Ithaca has vexed many earnest seekers after factuality in poetry). Then at line 39 of book 9, the story of the Odyssey begins, chronologically speaking, with the statement, "The wind took me from Troy."

The first port of call on his homeward voyage was a town which he promptly sacked—as much a normal procedure for energetic Homeric heroes as for a Drake or a Raleigh—losing six companions from each of his twelve ships. Importantly for the plot, he was given some particularly potent wine there by a priest of Apollo: it served afterwards to befuddle the Cyclops' wits. Sailing southward, he reached Cape Maleia in the south of the Peloponnesos, always a danger point for seamen. A tempest sent by Zeus the cloud-gatherer drove him past it—and probably right out of the normal world into a kind of wonderland (though many scholars and yachtsmen have spent happy days in trying to locate its sites in the Mediterranean).

It would be superfluous to recount the world-famous incidents that now occur to delight our imagination and to test Odysseus' prudence, courage, and endurance. They have become proverbial among all western nations from Russia to Peru—the Lotus-Eaters, the Cyclops, the king of the Winds, the Laestrygonians, Circe, the Sirens, Scylla and Charybdis, and the Cattle of the Sun. But some subtler features are sometimes overlooked. For instance, in the supreme triumph of Odysseus' resourceful intelligence, the discomfiture of the Cyclops, the wily hero had no less than four problems to solve: how to render the cannibalistic ogre powerless to hurt him and his men further, how to prevent his fellow Cyclops from helping him, how to get the enormous stone away from the mouth of the cave, and how to get out of the cave past Polyphemos' huge, groping hands. All these he successfully solved, most famously with his "No-man" ruse—a brilliant piece of paronomasia that Homer echoes in several subsequent variations.

Secondly, in the same incident, why does Odysseus uncharacteristically behave so imprudently in staying on in the cave despite his companions' warnings, and in shouting so recklessly from his escaping ship? (Perhaps this is a relic of an older folktale in which the hero was a brash Jack-the-Giant-Killer?) And does Homer intend us to be sorry for Polyphemos in his blindness as he talks affectionately to his pet ram (with Odysseus clinging precariously underneath)?

Or again, are these fairyland figures intended to be allegorical, emblems of the trials and temptations which pilgrim man must encounter on his voyage through life—the Lotus-Eaters representing lethargic apathy (akēdía, accidia, "sloth"); the Cyclops, barbarous violence; Circe, sensual indulgence which bestializes men; the Sirens, paralyzing infatuation (cleverly they tempt Odysseus with a promise of boundless information, not with voluptuous delights); Scylla and Charybdis, an inescapable choice between two evils? Homer's intentions here, as elsewhere, are inscrutable. But many readers of the *Odyssey*, from the Stoics to James Joyce, found encouragement and inspiration in allegorical interpretations of these fantastic creatures.

Book 11 stands apart from the rest of the supernatural tales, and provides the first of a fascinating series of literary descents into Hades that extends through Aristophanes, Vergil, Dante, and Milton to modern times. The primary reason for the inclusion of such an episode may have been because such a descent was a traditional feat for beneficial heroes such as Orpheus, Heracles, and Theseus. (Homer motivates it rather weakly by making Circe say that Odysseus must consult the spirit of the prophet Tiresias.) The poet presents the Land of Spirits in amazingly varied aspects, blending traditional themes with quite unexpected incidents and setting the whole episode in an uncanny atmosphere of darkness and distress. Among the traditional figures of earlier mythology that appear are a series of beautiful heroines from several parts of Greece, three great sinners being punished for their transgressions—Tityos, Tantalos, and Sisyphos—and the Theban prophet Tiresias. (His mysterious prophecy that Odysseus would have to undergo further travels after his return to Ithaca prompted many splendid poems in the later tradition, most notably those by Dante, Tennyson, and Nikos Kazantzakis.) Here again we meet the spirits of the three chief Iliadic heroes, Agamemnon, Achilles, and Ajax. The first two lament their untimely deaths. Agamemnon warns Odysseus against treacherous wives. Achilles says he would rather work as a laborer on the farm of a poor man than lord it over the souls of the dead, but he is comforted by Odysseus' praise of his only son. Ajax, implacably angry at his defeat by Odysseus in a contest for heroic excellence, preserves a majestic silence—the model, probably, for Dido's silence toward Aeneas in Avernus in Vergil's *Aeneid*. Most poignant of all is Odysseus' unexpected meeting with the spirit of his mother, Anticleia.

When she first appears, he, with characteristic pragmatism, postpones letting her speak until he gets the necessary information about his return home from the prophet. Then mother and son converse with deep affection. In the end, Odysseus tries three times to embrace her, but she, "like a shadow or a dream," offers no substance to his grasp—another motif that Vergil, always ready to imitate his epic master, effectively borrowed.

When the poet has decided that he has offered a fully satisfying feast of infernal scenes, he again shows his ability to move his characters very fast when he wants to. Suddenly, Odysseus panics at the thought that Persephone, queen of Hades, might send some terrifying Gorgonlike visage out of the recesses of Hell to petrify him with horror. In eight lines he is, quite convincingly, back with Circe.

One must recognize that there are several reasons for having doubts about authorship in this book. But whether composed by one poet or several poets, it is all magnificently arresting and superbly surprising. Besides, it is skillfully integrated into the main narrative, as when Arete breaks in with her first words of praise for Odysseus after she has heard the account of his meeting with his mother and his description of the beautiful heroines of antiquity.

Book 12 brings us past the Sirens and Scylla and Charybdis (with a brief glimpse of the Clashing Rocks and a notable reference to the story of Jason and the Argonauts) to the final disaster for Odysseus' companions, their eating of the forbidden Cattle of the Sun and the subsequent storm that sinks Odysseus' last ship. (Before that, as their numbers steadily diminished in various catastrophes, some of the men have emerged with names and characteristics of their own.) Odysseus alone survives to reach Calypso's island. And there his long after-dinner speech comes full circle—a massive example of Homer's favorite "ring-composition."

Homer uses a memorable line to describe the effect of this great story on the listening Phaeacians: "Through the *shadowy* halls they were held by the charm of his story." This is an audience's supreme tribute to a totally captivating performance, not immediate applause but a moment of entranced silence while the spellbound listeners escape from the enchantment (*kēlēthmós*). The ancient literary critics called this poetic power *psuchagogía*, "control of hearts and minds."

King Alcinoös is so impressed by Odysseus' narrative that he arranges even greater guest-gifts for him. But Odysseus longs for the time of his departure, as a tired ploughman who has toiled all day with wine-dark oxen longs for sunset. When it comes, he bids courteous farewells to Alcinoös and to Arete, who adds special, personal gifts to his collection. Then the ship sails, speeding on over the purple waves of the boisterous open sea as fast as a four-horsed chariot or a swooping hawk, while Odysseus sleeps a deep, sweet sleep—"he who had formerly suffered so many griefs in his heart as he thrust on through wars and woeful waves, now sleeping soundly, forgetful of what he had suffered."

While the morning star, brightest of all, is still shining in the sky, the ship reaches Ithaca. Quietly, the Phaeacian crew put their noble passenger and his gifts ashore near a cave of the Nymphs (whose strange description has occasioned much speculation by both allegorists and topographers). They return to Phaeacia and to a mysterious fate caused by the still vengeful Poseidon. Meanwhile, Odysseus, who has rather improbably slept through his disembarkation, has awakened. Here, Homer contrives another of the brilliant, unpredictable twists in his story. Athena wraps the scenery in a divine mist so that Odysseus fails to recognize his own island and fears that he may have landed again on an island of savages—have the Phaeacians tricked him? He carefully counts his guest-gifts and finds they are intact. Then, still yearning for his homeland while he is actually in it, he walks sadly along the seashore. Soon Athena, disguised as a young shepherd—"altogether tender in appearance, such as the sons of princes are"—meets him. The following conversation between the goddess and the anxious, misled hero has been universally admired for its subtle intimacy. (The fact that the female character is disguised here as a man gives it the piquancy of one of Shakespeare's similar scenes, as for example when Rosalind exchanges pleasant raillery with Orlando in *As You Like It*.) The most amusing feature in Odysseus' case is that when he, the renowned deceiver, tells a protective lie about his identity, he is playfully deceived and affectionately mocked by Athena—"What a cunning, tricky, obstinate, versatile rascal you are . . . but you are courteous, too, and shrewd-minded and persevering, so I'll help you to the full." Odysseus' rueful replies to this divine banter are admirably contrived. But his joy at learning that he is in Ithaca at last is overwhelming. He kneels down and kisses the beloved ground with a prayer to the local nymphs. Then, like old friends, hero and goddess sit side by side and plan how he can kill the suitors.

If Homer had been in a hurry to finish his story, through shortage of time or through impatience in his audience, he could have ended it adequately now within a few hundred lines by bringing Odysseus directly to his palace to outwit the suitors and regain his wife and kingdom. But our poet never seems to have felt pressures of time or of audience satiation. Like the modern author of a best-selling book, he apparently could always command ample time and an insatiable public for as much expansion as he wanted. The present essayist has neither of these advantages, nor has he the incantatory charm of Homeric poetry to sustain his narrative. So he must summarize the eight books between Odysseus' arrival in Ithaca and his victory over the suitors very briefly, though some of Homer's finest characterization will be lost in the process.

Disguised by Athena as a beggar and told to go first to the outlying farm of a loyal and likeable servant, Eumaios, the illustrious swineherd (he was of noble birth), he spends three days there, talking at great length with a plethora of ingenious lies about his own identity and past history. Meanwhile Telemachos, evading

the suitors' ambush, arrives there and eventually recognizes, very movingly, his long lost father. They make further plans for destroying the suitors. Then they go separately to the town. Outside the palace Argos, the favorite dog of Odysseus, now twenty years old and sadly decrepit and neglected, recognizes Odysseus (by smell, no doubt) through his disguise, wags its tail, droops its ears in welcome . . . and dies—a favorite scene ever afterward with dog lovers. Later, inside the palace, Odysseus is roughly handled, and the suitors behave outrageously. Penelope sends for the beggar to ask him for news of her husband, but this crucial meeting is postponed for a long while. Odysseus fights the local beggar in a vigorous boxing match. Penelope, prompted and beautified by Athena— there are echoes here of the adornment of Hera in the *Iliad*—makes a striking entrance into the hall. The suitors are paralyzed with admiration: "their hearts were exchanged by her beauty, and all of them prayed to lie with her in bed." (Significantly, this is the first time Odysseus sees her after twenty years.) Taking advantage of the attention, Penelope remarks that suitors usually offer gifts to the object of their wooing. The suitors, including even the evil Antinoös, take the hint and offer fine presents. Then they turn to abuse and maltreat Odysseus again.

Book 19 brings the meeting between Odysseus and Penelope. But first comes the dramatic moment when Odysseus' old nurse, Eurycleia, while washing his feet and legs by Penelope's order, discovers the scar of a boyhood wound and recognizes her master. (The story of how he got it in a boar hunt with his grandfather Autolycos of Parnassos gives precious glimpses of Odysseus' birth and youth.) The ensuing dialogue between Odysseus and the still unsuspecting Penelope—but some scholars believe she is beginning to sense his identity—is full of irony and pathos. It needed a heart of iron, we are told, for Odysseus not to reveal himself prematurely. Finally, she announces her intention to settle the question of her marriage once and for all: whoever of the suitors can string the massive bow of Odysseus and shoot an arrow through a line of axeheads can marry her. (The motivation for this sudden decision is not made clear, but obviously it is necessary for the impending climax.)

Further retardation, achieved with customary inventive skill, delays this crucial event all through book 20, while Odysseus suffers further insults and agonies, but is comforted by a favorable omen from Zeus. One extraordinary moment intervenes. Theoclymenos, a seer brought from the Peloponnesos by Telemachos, suddenly has a vision of the suitors' imminent doom. He sees darkness descending on their heads, "a blaze of groaning," tears on their cheeks, blood on the walls and on the porch, and the courtyard full of ghosts descending to the gloom of Erebos. It is over in a minute or two when the suitors laugh it off with a joke. Stylistically, it shows Homer's ability to produce a weird, uncanny atmosphere when it suits his plot.

Now we come to the first major climax. The bow is brought in. The line of axes is arranged. (The exact nature of the shooting test is disputed.) Two suitors fail to string the bow. Odysseus asks to be allowed to try. The suitors refuse, but Telemachos insists. Odysseus handles the familiar weapon sensitively and firmly, then strings it—and the string "sings beautifully to his touch like a swallow's cry." The suitors are dismayed. Zeus thunders. Odysseus seizes an arrow, shoots it through the axes, calls for action to Telemachos, strips off his rags, leaps on the high threshold with the bow in his hand, and exultantly cries, "Now I shoot at another mark, and let Apollo aid me." It is one of the great climactic moments of all literature, as so many authors, artists, and critics have attested.

Now, with Telemachos and two faithful servants, the hero ruthlessly slaughters all his enemies in the hall—first their ringleader Antinoös (the name implies hostility), then the other named suitors, and finally the anonymous rabble. Homer uses all his Iliadic skill in varying the ways each man dies. During the massacre, tension is increased when Melanthios, a disloyal servant, manages to get some weapons to

the suitors. At a critical moment Athena makes an appearance to encourage and aid her hero. Only two are spared: Phemios, the bard who sang for the suitors only by compulsion—Homer consistently implies that bards should be treated with reverence and generosity—and Medon, the palace herald.

Now all the suitors are dead, lying in the blood and dust like a shoal of fish netted and heaped on the sand "yearning for the waves of the sea." (Here, as elsewhere, the poet shows pity for suffering animals, and perhaps, too, he implies a touch of pity even for the suitors.) Odysseus sends for Eurycleia. When she sees Odysseus, triumphant and terrible like a blood-bespattered lion among his prey, she starts to shout out in triumph. Odysseus, with remarkable restraint for a hero, tells her, "It is not a pious thing to exult over slain men: it was destiny and evildoing that caused their doom." But immediately he asks her to tell him which of his servingwomen were accomplices and paramours of the suitors. Odysseus orders them to be killed with sharp-edged swords, but Telemachos chooses to hang the twelve of them by the neck from a long rope, like birds in a snare, so that they should die "most pitifully. . . . They struggled with their feet for a little while, but not for very long." The treacherous Melanthios is punished with even greater ferocity: his nose and ears are cut off, his genitals torn away and thrown as raw meat to the dogs, and his arms and legs severed. Sheer atrocity is not confined to the *Iliad*.

Vengefulness having been fully satisfied, and the hall restored to order and fumigated with sulphur, Odysseus orders Eurycleia to bring in his loyal servants and to summon Penelope. The servants affectionately greet their master and are greeted by him individually with tears of joy. Eurycleia tells Penelope that Odysseus is home and has slain the suitors. Penelope thinks she is mad. Eurycleia presses the truth on her. Penelope joyfully embraces the old nurse, but instead of rushing to meet Odysseus—she has learned caution in her twenty years of loneliness—she asks for further assurance, wavering between belief and disbelief. Perhaps, she thinks, some god is deceiving them. (She would remember how Zeus had used various deceptions to seduce other married women.) Eventually, she goes down to the hall, anxiously wondering what she should do. Should she stand apart and question this stranger, or should she embrace and kiss her alleged husband?

What follows is one of Homer's greatest scenes, rivaling in its happier way even the tragic encounter of Priam and Achilles. (Technically the *Odyssey* is a kind of comedy, the *Iliad* a tragedy.) Homer exploits his finest artistry to win our sympathy for his long-suffering heroine and at the same time to demonstrate that she is the equal of Odysseus in intelligence as well as endurance. (Homer consistently shows less male chauvinism than almost any other author in antiquity.) Penelope decides to hold back. For a while she and Odysseus—he is now sitting calmly in the firelight—gaze at each other in silence. Telemachos cannot understand their restraint. He breaks in impatiently, "Mother, unnatural mother, how can you keep away from my father? Surely your heart is harder than stone!" She pleads amazement and uncertainty. Understandingly—and perhaps rather patronizingly—Odysseus smiles and says that it's probably because he looks so filthy with slaughter: he'll go and have a bath, then no doubt Penelope will be more willing to accept him. Meanwhile, he adds (always keeping an eye on practical affairs), arrangements must be made to prevent the kinsmen of the suitors from knowing what has happened.

After his bath, Athena beautifies him as a goldsmith gilds silver (exactly as in his encounter with Nausicaä). Then "looking like immortal gods," he returns and sits down where he was before and speaks to his wife, beginning, "You're a strange tough-hearted, unfeminine woman...." Penelope answers, "You're just as strange..." and then very cleverly sets a test for Odysseus by casually ordering Eurycleia to move their nuptial bed out of the royal bedroom for him to sleep in. Caught off his guard

and deeply moved, he exclaims, "Woman, that's a heartrending thing you've said ... how can our bed be moved when I myself fixed it to the floor?" Now comes Homer's masterstroke: Penelope, instead of exulting at her cleverness in extracting a final proof of Odysseus' identity, bursts into tears, embraces him, and appeals for his wise and loving forgiveness. Their mutual joy is complete. Athena delays the horses of the Dawn-goddess to prolong it. But a shadow falls on their rejoicing when Odysseus recalls that his trials are not quite over yet, for the prophecy of Tiresias must be fulfilled. Penelope finds comfort here in the fact that at least he has been promised a happy old age in the end. Then a maid prepares their long-disused conjugal bed; "Gladly then, as of old, they came to the place [or the custom] of their bedding."

That is line 296 of book 23. Many modern scholars have taken this to be the end of the original *Odyssey*. (A similar belief can be extracted from an ambiguous remark by Aristarchus and Aristophanes of Alexandria that it is the *télos* of the *Odyssey*.) Undeniably, there are serious anomalies in the style and content of the succeeding episodes. But is it probable that Homer would have left Odysseus' father, Laërtes, uncomforted on his lonely farm, and the problem unsolved of how to cope with the vengeful relations of the suitors? Besides, there is much of high poetic and dramatic merit in this "continuation."

Next, after Odysseus and Penelope have both "had their pleasure in delightful lovemaking," they "have pleasure" again in telling each other what happened to them during their long separation, first Penelope, then Odysseus. At last the dawn comes. Odysseus, after some words of sympathy for the sufferings they have both had to endure, arms himself and summons Telemachos and his two loyal henchmen to prepare to meet the suitors' kinsmen.

At this point, the narrative of Odysseus' actions is drastically interrupted by a strange episode. We are shown the god Hermes conducting the spirits of the dead suitors, squeaking like bats in a cave, to "the asphodil meadow" where the spirits of the dead dwell (as described in book 11). There they meet the spirits of the Iliadic heroes. Two of these, Agamemnon and Achilles, describe their own misfortunes, and in return one of the suitors describes how Odysseus won his revenge. "O fortunate resourceful Odysseus," Agamemnon exclaims. "You had a virtuous and faithful wife, while I met murder at the hands of mine, to the abiding shame of women." There the episode breaks off abruptly. It has been strongly criticized for irrelevance and for stylistic anomalies. On the other hand, it gives emphasis to the deserved destruction of the suitors, it provides a final eulogy of Penelope, and it offers another glimpse of famous heroes, always a welcome event to Greek audiences. Besides, it has distinct poetic merit, and its synopsis of how Odysseus triumphed, like the earlier synopsis of his wanderings, would please the audience, like a musical coda which briefly recalls the main motifs of a long opus.

The central narrative now resumes. Odysseus goes and finds his father working in pitiable circumstances on his farm. Strangely, he tells him a lie about his own identity before he reveals himself. (Critics have found it hard to motivate this deception, but it is dramatically very effective.) He enlists Laërtes to fight with him against the kinsmen of the suitors. Soon Laërtes has the supreme joy, for an old warrior, of regaining his martial strength and valor by the aid of Athena, and of then killing one of the enemy. Finally, the goddess, with the consent of Zeus, intervenes to impose peace on both sides—"Pallas Athena, maiden daughter of aegis-bearing Zeus, seeming like Mentor in form and voice." With those simple formulaic phrases, the poem very quietly ends.

It is with a strong sense of inadequacy that the preceding outlines of Homer's poems are concluded by the present writer, compressed, as they are, to less than a tenth of the originals and deprived of Homer's poetic diction. Some impression, however, may have been conveyed of the speed, variety, and directness of Homer's narrative; of his subtle characterization; of his masterly use of similes, metaphors, and epithets; of his irony, pathos, and compassion; and especially of the firm grip that he keeps on the development of his narratives despite so many dazzling digressions. It is this combination of superb architectonics with inexhaustible invention that makes Homer so fully worthy of Dante's title for him, *poeta sovrano*.

But something more has to be said if full justice is to be done to Homer's poetic powers. As we have seen, he described poetry as "song" and emphasized its incantatory effects on an audience. This implies that the musical elements in his diction were of great importance, as one would expect in poetry composed to be performed before an audience. These elements will now be briefly considered.

For his musical purposes, Homer could use three main qualities of vocal sounds—meter, timbre (or tone-color, the German *Klangfarbe*), and pitch variation. For meter, his dactylo-spondaic hexameters provided him with a noble marching rhythm, eminently suitable for the processional pageantry of his epics. For timbre, Homer commanded a dialect of Greek that was particularly rich in resonant vowels and sharp consonants—probably a poetic diction evolved during many generations of bardic craftsmanship and not a spoken dialect. For controlled pitch variation, ancient Greek offered a feature unique, in its fully developed form, among the languages of Europe. This was the built-in tone scale, which formed an essential element in the pronunciation of almost every word, as indicated in post-classical times by the three Greek accentual marks. (There is uncertainty about the phonetic value of the grave accent, but the evidence for the acute and circumflex is fairly clear.) This inherent pitch variation enabled ancient Greek poets to choose words for the sake of their melodic quality as well as for their rhythm and tone color. (It should be remembered that early Greek epic poetry was probably pronounced in a tone of voice intermediate between singing and talking, perhaps rather like plainsong, and not in conversational tones.)

Homer could use these three elements, rhythm (meter), timbre, and pitch variation, in two distinct ways—either to support his conceptual meaning or to provide an independent musical accompaniment to his narrative. The first use can be seen in its simplest form in onomatopoeic words like *éklangxan* and *klanggé* (compare "clangor" and "clang"); *língxe*, for the high note of a plucked bowstring (a thinner sound than "twang"); *sisd-*, for "sizzle"; and *alalétós*, for a "hullabaloo." But Homer generally preferred to employ less obvious kinds of phonetic mimesis. Many readers, for example, have found pleasure in hearing the trotting of mules in the rhythm and assonance of *Illiad* 23.116: *Pollà d'ánanta kátanta páranta te dochmiá t'élthon* (literally: "They went many ways, upwards and downwards and sideways and crossways"). Similarly, they have felt the laborious straining efforts of Sisyphos as he strives to push his boulder up the hill (*Odyssey* 11.593–600) in the phrase *lâan áno ótheske* ("he kept pushing the stone upwards") with its repeated alphas and straining omegas (and perhaps with a hint of "Ah, ah, oh, oh!"). Then, as the rock slips from his grasp, we can hear it go bumping down the hill and settling at the bottom in *aûtis épeita pédonde kulíndeto lâas anaidés* ("Then back again to the ground rolled the remorseless stone"). Again, in the first line of the song of the Sirens (*Odyssey* 12.184): *Deûr'ág'ión, polúain' Odyseû, méga kûdos Akhaión* ("Come hither, much-renowned Odysseus, great glory of the Achaeans") the dactyls are divided so as to suggest a lyrical anapaestic rhythm, and there are no heavy consonant clusters to make the texture thick and harsh as in *trikhthá te kaì tetrakhthà* ("in three pieces and in four": *Iliad* 3.363; *Odyssey* 9.71).

In examples of that kind there is a sound-for-sound equation. But Homer also offers sound-for-sight equations in which the pleasant effects (euphony) or ugly effects (cacophony) represent a visual scene. One line particularly admired for its euphony describes a flowing river (*Iliad* 18.576): *Pàr potamòn keládonta, parà rhodanòn donakéa* ("Along the sounding river, along the swaying reed-beds"). Contrast the harsh-sounding line Demosthenes is said to have repeated in order to eliminate his stammer (*Odyssey* 5.402): *Rhókhthei gàr méga kûma potì kseròn epefroio* ("For a great wave crashes down on the stark mainland"), or the phrase used to describe how a wounded warrior's "guts gushed out on the ground," *khûnto khamaì kholádes* (*Iliad* 4.526, 20.181), or the word *kekakóménos*, "uglified" (*Odyssey* 6.137), used to express Odysseus' filthy appearance after long struggles in stormy seas. Noticeably in these examples there is a predominance of cacophonous gutturals.

These mimetic effects are not the most important function of euphony in Homer. They are intermittent and sporadic. What remains to be considered now pervades the whole of each poem. This is a sustained word-music that is made out of the three main acoustic factors and sounds continuously from line to line in long or short phrases as the punctuation indicates. For this purpose a vocabulary rich in vowels is particularly valuable. Homer's dialect gave him great scope in this, allowing him to use uncontracted and extended forms like *boóosa, goóosa,* and *ekhéessa*, "shouting," "groaning," and "echoing," and even such an extraordinary form—can any other poetic diction rival it?—as *aáatos*, "inviolable." And he likes to achieve the same expansion of tone color in proper names with almost Polynesian vocalism like Nausicaä, Aiaie, and Oloöson. Sometimes he constructs whole lines in which the vowels greatly outnumber the consonants, as in *Iliad* 2.266: *Huiées huionoí te bíes Herakléeíes* ("Sons and grandsons of the mighty Herakles"). At other times he exploits sound patterns in which the consonants predominate, tickling our ears with jingles like *Zeû kúdiste mégiste* ("Zeus most glorious, most mighty") (*Iliad* 2.412 and elsewhere); *nekúon amenénà kárena*, "feeble heads of the dead" (perhaps, but the meaning was disputed even in the time of Aristophanes: *Odyssey* 10.521 and elsewhere); and the line *Khrè kseînon paréonta phileîn, ethélonta dè pémpein* ("One should be kind to the staying guest, but send him on when he wishes to go") (*Odyssey* 15.74). These are like proverbs, made memorable by rhyme and assonance. Indeed, an important function of all word-music is to make words more memorable, especially in oral literature.

The ancient Greek critics saw a further potentiality in the poetic sound effects. They believed that the music of poetry affected the emotions of those who heard it in much the same way as instrumental music did. A notable witness is Longinus, the author of the treatise *On the Sublime*. He asserts in chapter 39 that "the arrangement of words, which is a kind of harmony of the language implanted by nature in man, touches not merely the hearing but the soul itself . . . and by the combined effect of the blending and variety of its own sounds . . . introduces into the souls of those who are nearby the emotion that affects the speaker. . . ." He concludes, "But it is lunacy to dispute about things that are widely admitted, since experience is sufficient proof." (We must remember in this connection that the ancient Greeks were convinced that music had deep and strong ethical effects.)

Modern scholars are sometimes inclined to discount this effect of *psuchagogía*, "psyche-controlling," as it was termed in antiquity. They would dismiss such interpretations as fanciful and even absurd. Are they more likely to be right in a matter of this kind than native Greek speakers? But emotional responses are highly subjective and cannot easily be measured and quantified. So readers—or hearers, rather—must judge for themselves. The present writer, at least, certainly feels these emotional responses at times. To him the opening lines of the *Iliad* and the *Odyssey* suggest quite different moods by a combination of the three acoustic factors. In the *Iliad*, *Ménin áeide theá Pēlē-*

ïádeō Akhiléos ("Sing, Goddess, of the wrath of Achilles son of Peleus"), the dominant vowel is eta; the rhythm is slowed down by the spondee in the fourth foot and by the difficulty of pronouncing the patronymic of Achilles, *Pēlēïádeō*, with its internal hiatus and synizesis; and the two circumflex accents prescribe a salient rising-falling intonation at the beginning and ending of the line. In the *Odyssey*, *Ándra moi énnepe, Moûsa, polútropon hòs mála pollà* ("Tell me, Muse, about the man of many turns"), the dominant vowel is alpha; the dactyls move on unchecked to the end of the line; and the single circumflex accent is unemphatically placed. The effect of these contrasting sound patterns is, on the one hand, to create a feeling of melancholy and of strain at the opening of a tragic and pessimistic poem and, on the other, to impart a sense of buoyancy and unchecked movement to the beginning of the poem that ends in peace and harmony (though for a moment this feeling is checked at the beginning of the next line by the tongue-twisting word *plángkhthē* ("was driven astray").

The total effect of Homer's musicality combines mimetic, aesthetic, and emotive elements in a continuous, polyphonic orchestration of rhythm, tone-color, and melody that is magnificently sustained through the whole of each poem. Among English poets, only Milton, perhaps, in his *Paradise* poems offers such rich symphonic effects. Like an ever-flowing river—sometimes swift, sometimes sluggish, sometimes rough, sometimes smooth, sometimes roaring, sometimes murmuring—it carries the listener steadily onward in its currents. As we move downstream our chief concern is, indeed, to watch the vivid scenes and momentous events and arresting figures to be seen all round us—ships, cities, palaces, farmhouses, battles, banquets, deaths, marriages, gods, heroes, women, children, slaves, monsters, stars in the sky, clouds on the hills, the glorious radiance of Greek sunshine flashing on bronze and gold and marble, and so on in endless variety. These sights hold our attention so powerfully that we hardly notice the sounds and movements of the stream that bears us past them. Yet if we listen and respond to its movements, the pleasure of our journey is richly increased.

No translation can adequately transmit this "strong-wing'd music of Homer," as Tennyson called it. Even those which are genuinely poetic, like Chapman's and Pope's, substitute a different kind of music, and that, too, generally at the cost of fidelity to Homer's meaning. Less poetic and more faithful versions may enable readers to understand and enjoy the visual and intellectual elements in the poems. But the living voice of the poet himself, so miraculously recorded and preserved in those black marks on white pages, can only be heard in his own resonant Greek.

Selected Bibliography

TEXTS

Note: See also the section COMMENTARIES below.

ILIAD

The Iliad, edited by T. W. Allen and D. B. Monro. 2 vols. Oxford, 1920.
The Iliad, edited by T. W. Allen. 3 vols. Oxford, 1931.
The Iliad, edited by P. Mazon. 4 vols. Paris, 1947–1949.

ODYSSEY

The Odyssey, edited by T. W. Allen. 2 vols. Oxford, 1917.
The Odyssey, edited by V. Bérard. 3 vols. Paris, 1939–1946.
The Odyssey, edited by P. von der Mühll. Basel, 1946.

For the textual transmission in general, including that of the papyri, see J. A. Davison in A. J. B. Wace's *A Companion,* etc. (pp. 215–219), as listed below, and the earlier publications cited in it.

TRANSLATIONS SINCE 1930

The dates given are those of the first editions.

ILIAD

Chase, A., and W. G. Perry, Jr., trs. Boston, 1950.
Fitzgerald, R., tr. New York, 1974.
Graves, R., tr. *The Anger of Achilles. Homer's Iliad.* Garden City, N. Y.,1959; London, 1962.
Lattimore, R., tr. Chicago, 1951.
Rieu, E. V., tr. Harmondsworth, 1950.

ODYSSEY

Andrew, S. O., tr. London, 1934; 1948.
Cook, A., tr. New York, 1967.
Fitzgerald, R., tr. Garden City, N. Y., 1961.
Lattimore, R., tr. New York, 1967.
Rieu, E. V., tr. London, 1946.
Shaw, T. E., tr. New York, 1932.
Shewring, W., tr. New York, 1980.

For critical studies on translating Homer, see Packard and Meyers' *Bibliography,* p. 175, the works cited below by H. W. Clarke and C. Nelson, and W. Arrowsmith and R. Shattuck, eds., *The Craft and Context of Translation* (New York, 1961).

COMMENTARIES

ILIAD

Ameis, K. F., C. Hentze, and P. Cauer. 4 vols. Leipzig, 1905–1932. Reprinted Amsterdam, 1965.
Leaf, W. 2 vols. 2nd ed. London, 1900–1902.
———, and M. A. Bayfield. 2 vols. London, 1895–1898.
Leeuwen, J. van. 2 vols. Leiden, 1912–1917.
Monro, D. B. 2 vols. 4th ed. Oxford, 1894–1899.
Willcock, M. M. Books 1–12. London, 1978.

ODYSSEY

Ameis, K. F., C. Hentze, and P. Cauer. 4 vols. Leipzig, 1910–1920.
Leeuwen, J. van. 2 vols. Leiden, 1917.
Merry, W. W. 2 vols. Oxford, 1887; 1902.
———, J. Riddell, and D. B. Monro. 2 vols. 2nd ed. Oxford, 1886; 1901.
Stanford, W. B. 2 vols. 2nd rev. ed. London, 1964–1965.

HOMERIC GRAMMARS

Monro, D. B. *Grammar of the Homeric Dialect.* 2nd ed. Oxford, 1891.

Chautraine, P. *Grammaire homérique*. 2 vols. Paris, 1942–1953.

CONCORDANCES, INDEXES, AND LEXICONS

ILIAD AND *ODYSSEY*

Autenrieth, G. G. P., ed. *A Homeric Dictionary for Schools and Colleges*. Translated by R. P. Keep. Norman, Okla., 1958; London, 1960.

Bechtel, F., ed. *Lexilogus zu Homer*. Halle, 1914.

Cunliffe, R. J., ed. *Lexicon of the Homeric Dialect*. 2 vols. Glasgow, 1924–1931.

Ebeling, H. *Lexicon Homericum*. 2 vols. Leipzig, 1880–1885.

Snell, B., and H. J. Mette, eds. *Lexikon des frühgriechischen Epos*. Vol. 1. Göttingen, 1955–1978.

ILIAD

Prendergast, G. L. London, 1875. Revised by B. Marzullo. New York, 1971.

ODYSSEY

Dunbar, H. Oxford, 1885.

SELECTED LITERARY STUDIES SINCE 1930

Austin, N. *Archery at the Dark of the Moon: Poetic Problems in Homer's Odyssey*. Berkeley, 1975.

Bérard, V. *Introduction à l'Odyssée*. 3 vols. Paris, 1933.

Beye, C. R. *The Iliad, the Odyssey, and the Epic Tradition*. New York, 1966.

Bowra, C. M. *Homer*. London, 1972.

———. *Tradition and Design in the Iliad*. Oxford, 1930.

Carpenter, R. *Folk Tale, Fiction and Saga in the Homeric Epics*. Berkeley, 1956.

Clarke, H. W. *The Art of the Odyssey*. Englewood Cliffs, N. J., 1967.

———. *Homer's Readers: A Historical Introduction to the Iliad and the Odyssey*. Newark, N. J., 1981.

Dihle, A. *Homer-Probleme*. Opladen, 1970.

Eisenberger, H. *Studien zur Odyssee*. Wiesbaden, 1973.

Erbse, H. *Beiträge zum Verstandnis der Odyssee*. Berlin, 1972.

Fenik, B. *Homer: Tradition and Invention*. Leiden, 1978.

———. *Studies in the Odyssey*. Wiesbaden, 1974.

———. *Typical Battle Scenes in the Iliad. Studies in the Narrative Techniques of Homeric Battle Description*. Wiesbaden, 1968.

Finley, J. H. *Homer's Odyssey*. Cambridge, Mass., 1979.

Finley, M. I. *The World of Odysseus*. 2nd ed. London, 1977.

Gaunt, D. M. *Surge and Thunder: Critical Readings in Homer's Odyssey*. London, 1971.

Griffin, J. *Homer on Life and Death*. New York, 1980.

Hainsworth, J. B. *The Flexibility of the Homeric Formula*. Oxford, 1968.

Kakridis, J. T. *Homeric Researches*. Lund, 1949.

———. *Homer Revisited*. Lund, 1971.

Kirk, G. S. *Homer and the Oral Tradition*. Cambridge, 1976.

———. *The Songs of Homer*. Cambridge, 1962.

———, and A. Parry. *Homeric Studies. Yale Classical Studies* 20. New Haven, 1966.

Lee, D. J. N. *The Similes of "The Iliad" and "The Odyssey" Compared*. Melbourne, 1964.

Lesky, A. *A History of Greek Literature*, translated by James Willis and Cornelis de Heer. London, 1966.

———. *Homeros*. Stuttgart, 1967.

Lord, A. B. *The Singer of Tales*. Cambridge, Mass., 1960.

Mazon, P. *Introduction à l'Iliade*. Paris, 1940.

Merkelbach, R. *Untersuchungen zur Odyssee*. Munich, 1951.

Moulton, C. "Homeric Metaphor." *Classical Philology* 74: 279–293 (1979).

———. *Similes in the Homeric Poems*. Göttingen, 1977.

Mühll, P. von der. *Kritisches Hypomnema zur Ilias*. Basel, 1952.

Nagler, M. N. *Spontaneity and Tradition: A Study in the Oral Art of Homer*. Berkeley, 1974.

Nagy, G. *The Best of the Achaeans: Concepts of the Hero in Archaic Greek Poetry*. Baltimore, 1980.

Nelson, C., ed. *Homer's Odyssey: A Critical Handbook*. Belmont, Calif., 1969.

Oldsley, B., ed. "The Homeric Epic." *College Literature* 3, no. 3 (1976). Seven essays by various authors.

Page, D. *Folktales in Homer's "Odyssey."* Cambridge, Mass., 1973.

———. *The Homeric "Odyssey."* Oxford, 1955.

Parry, A., ed. *The Making of Homeric Verse: The*

Collected Papers of Milman Parry. Oxford, 1971. (See also Kirk, above.)

Redfield, J. M. *Nature and Culture in "The Iliad": The Tragedy of Hector.* Chicago, 1975.

Schadewaldt, W. *Von Homers Welt und Werk.* 4th ed. Stuttgart, 1965.

———. *Iliasstudien.* 3rd ed. Darmstadt, 1966.

Scott, W. C. *The Oral Nature of the Homeric Simile.* Leiden, 1974.

Severyns, A. *Homère.* 3 vols. Brussels, 1944–1948.

Shipp, G. P. *Studies in the Language of Homer.* 2nd ed. Cambridge, 1972.

Stanford, W. B. *The Ulysses Theme.* 2nd ed. rev. Oxford, 1968.

Steiner, G., and R. Fagles, eds. *Homer: A Collection of Critical Essays.* Englewood Cliffs, N. J., 1962.

Taylor, H., Jr., ed. *Essays on "The Odyssey."* Bloomington, 1963.

Thornton, A. *People and Themes in Homer's Odyssey.* London, 1970.

Trypanis, C. A. *The Homeric Epics.* Wartminster, 1977.

Vivante, P. *The Homeric Imagination: A Study of Homer's Poetic Perception of Reality.* Bloomington, 1970.

Wace, A. J. B., and H. Stubbings, eds. *A Companion to Homer.* London, 1962.

Wender, D. *The Last Scenes of "The Odyssey."* Leiden, 1978.

Whitman, C. H. *Homer and the Heroic Tradition.* Cambridge, Mass., 1965.

Willcock, M. *A Companion to "The Iliad."* Chicago, 1976.

Woodhouse, W. J. *The Composition of Homer's "Odyssey."* Oxford, 1930.

PUBLICATIONS ON HOMERIC EUPHONY

Allen, W. S. *Vox graeca: The Pronunciation of Classical Greek.* 2nd ed. Cambridge, 1974.

Daitz, G. *A Recital of Ancient Greek Poetry.* New York, 1978. Reviewed in *Hermathena* 127: 33–38 (1979).

Havelock, E. A. *Preface to Plato.* Oxford, 1963.

———. *Prologue to Greek Literacy.* Cincinnati, 1971.

Packard, D. W. "Sound-patterns in Homer." *Transactions of the American Philological Association* 104: 239–260 (1974).

Shewan, A. "Alliteration and Assonance in Homer." *Classical Philology* 20: 193–209 (1925).

Stanford, W. B. "Euphonic Reasons for the Choice of Homeric Formulae?" *Hermathena* 108: 14–17 (1969).

———. *The Sound of Greek.* Berkeley, 1967. With bibliography and a record.

———. "Sound, Sense and Music in Greek Poetry." To be published in a forthcoming issue of *Greece and Rome.*

———. "Varieties of Sound-effects in the Homeric Poems." *College Literature,* 3, no.3:219–227 (1976).

BIBLIOGRAPHIES

D. W. Packard and T. Meyers list 3,840 publications on Homer, with a subject index and index locorum, in *Bibliography of Homeric Scholarship: Preliminary Edition 1930–70* (Malibu, Calif., 1970), a most valuable aid to all students. For previous surveys, see the Packard and Meyers listings of F. M. Combellack, E. R. Dodds, J. B. Hainsworth, A. Lesky, H. N. Mette, and D. Mülder. Subsequent publications are discussed by K. Myrsiades in Oldsley above, and A. Heubeck in Fenik, *Homer,* etc., above. Publications from 1914 onward are listed in J. Marouzeau, ed., *Dix années de bibliographie classique* (Paris, 1927) and J. Marouzeau et al., eds., *L'année philologique* (Paris, 1928–   ).

W. B. STANFORD

HESIOD

(Eighth Century B.C.)

THE HESIODIC QUESTION

FROM THE VANTAGE point of the ancient Greeks themselves, no accounting of Hesiod is possible without an accounting of Homer as well. In the fifth century B.C., Herodotus was moved to observe (2.53.2) that the Greeks owed the systematization of their gods—we may say, of their universe—to two poets, Homer and Hesiod. The current fashion is to argue, from the internal evidence of their poetry, that both lived sometime in the latter half of the eighth century, roughly three hundred years before Herodotus composed his *Histories*—although there is considerable controversy about which of the two was earlier. For Herodotus, as for all Greeks of the classical period, however, the importance of Homer and Hesiod was not based on any known historical facts about these poets and their times. Whatever Homer and Hesiod may have meant to the eighth century, the only surviving historical fact about them centers on what their poems did indeed mean to the succeeding centuries extending into the historical period. From Herodotus and others, we know that the poems of Homer and Hesiod were the primary artistic means of encoding a value system common to all Greeks.

In this connection it is worthwhile to correct a common misconception: Homer is not simply an exponent of narrative any more than Hesiod is an exponent of purely didactic poetry. The explicitly narrative structure of epic, as is the case with myth and mythopoeic thinking in general, frames a value system that sustains and in fact educates a given society. Conversely, as we shall see, the teachings of Hesiod frame an implicit narrative about the poet and his life.

The question is, Why were these two poets universally accepted by the Greeks of classical times? Such acceptance is especially remarkable in view of the striking diversity that characterizes Greece throughout this period. Each *polis* (city) was a state unto itself, with its own traditions in government, law, religion. Moreover, the diversity that prevailed among the many city-states of Greece had already taken shape by the eighth century, the very era that scholars agree in assigning to Homer and Hesiod. How, then, could the diversification of the Greeks coincide with the consolidation of their poetic heritage? The evidence of archaeology helps provide a partial answer. In the eighth century, the emergence of distinct city-states with distinct localized traditions was simultaneous with a countertrend of intercommunication among the elite of these city-states—the trend of Panhellenism. The patterns of intercommunication were confined to a few specific social phenomena, all datable to the eighth century: organization of the Olympic Games; establishment of Apollo's sanctuary and oracle at Delphi; organized colonizations (the Greek word for which is *ktísis*); proliferation of the alphabet.

Another phenomenon that may be included is Homeric and Hesiodic poetry, featuring overall traditions that synthesize the diverse local traditions of each major city-state into a unified Panhellenic model that suits most city-states but corresponds exactly to none. Erwin Rohde cites in particular the Homeric and Hesiodic concept of the Olympian gods, which transcends the individual concepts of these same gods as they are worshiped on the level of cult in the localized traditions of the city-states. We have in this example what amounts to internal evidence corroborating the external evidence summed up in Herodotus' statement: Homeric and Hesiodic poetry systematized the city-states' diverse ideologies about the gods into a set of attributes and functions that all Hellenes could accept. (The earliest unambiguous attestation of the word *Panéllēnes* in the sense of "all Greeks" is in Hesiod, *Works and Days* 528.)

The notion that the Homeric and Hesiodic poems were a Panhellenic phenomenon going back to the eighth century leads to the tempting scenario of connecting a likewise Panhellenic phenomenon, alphabetic writing: it too, after all, is dated to the eighth century. According to this scenario, the Homeric and Hesiodic poems were enshrined for the Greeks because they were written down, thus becoming fixed texts that proliferated throughout the Hellenic world. The problem is, how exactly are we to imagine this proliferation? It is clear that literacy was a tenuous phenomenon at best throughout the archaic period of Greece, and the Panhellenic spread of the Homeric and Hesiodic poems during this period stretching from the eighth to the fifth century could hardly be attributed to some hypothetical circulation of manuscripts. To put it bluntly: it seems difficult to imagine an incipient eighth-century reading public—let alone one that could have stimulated such widespread circulation of the Homeric and Hesiodic poems.

The argument for an archaic reading public is actually rendered pointless by the historical fact that the medium of transmitting the Homeric and Hesiodic poems was consistently that of performance, not reading. One important traditional context of poetic performance was the institution of Panhellenic festivals, though there may well have been other appropriate public events as well. The competing performers at such public events were called rhapsodes (*rhapsōidoí*; see, for example, Herodotus, 5.67), one of whom has been immortalized in Plato's *Ion*. We learn that this rhapsode Ion has come from his home in Ephesus to compete with other rhapsodes by reciting Homer at the festival of Asclepius in Epidaurus (*Ion* 530a). In the dialogue as dramatized by Plato, Socrates ascertains that Ion is a specialist in Homer, to the exclusion of Hesiod and Archilochus (*Ion* 531a and 532a)—the implication being that there are other rhapsodes who specialize in these other poets. Socrates and Ion then go on to discuss the different repertoires required for the rhapsodes' recitation of Homer and Hesiod (see especially *Ion* 531a–d). In fact, Plato elsewhere presents Homer and Hesiod themselves as itinerant rhapsodes (*Republic* 600d). The examples could be multiplied, but the point is already clear: the proliferation of the Homeric and Hesiodic poems throughout Greece in the archaic period (and beyond) did not depend on the factor of writing.

Even if Homer and Hesiod were meant to be heard in performance, not read, there are those who insist that writing was an essential factor at least in the composition and transmission of their poetry. Here we must turn to the study of oral poetry, as perfected by Milman Parry and Albert Lord. The fieldwork of these scholars was based on the living poetic traditions of the South Slavic peoples, and the theories that were developed from their fieldwork were then tested on Homeric—and later on Hesiodic—poetry. The findings of Parry and Lord have on occasion been viewed with suspicion by prominent Hellenists, who fear that the analogy between the typical Yugoslav *guslar* and a Homer demeans the latter and overly exalts the former. This is to misunderstand the intellectual basis of fieldwork—and of anthropological research in general. The mechanics of living traditions, however lowly they may seem to Hellenists, can provide indispensable information for extensive typological comparison with those of other traditions, living or dead.

We learn from the experience of fieldwork that composition in oral poetry becomes a reality only in performance, and that the poet's interaction with his audience can directly affect the form and content of composition as well as of performance. Moreover, the actual workings of formulaic diction are to be ascertained directly in the dimension of performance—a dimension that is of course now extinct in the case of the Homeric and Hesiodic texts. In studying this factor of performance as reflected by the living South Slavic traditions, Parry and Lord worked out criteria of formulaic behavior that, when applied to the Homeric text, establish it too as oral poetry. For example, one reliable indication of oral poetry is the principle of economy as it operates on the level of each individual performance; each position in the verse tends to allow one way, rather than many ways, of saying any one thing. As it turns out, this principle is at work in Homeric poetry as well, which suggests that the composition of the *Iliad* and the *Odyssey* is also a matter of performance. The principle of economy, as G. P. Edwards has demonstrated, is also at work in Hesiodic poetry; moreover, both Homeric and Hesiodic poetry reveal parallel patterns of general adherence to and occasional deviation from this principle.

If, then, the Homeric and Hesiodic poems are reflexes of oral poetry, we can in theory eliminate writing as a factor in the composition of these poems, much as we have eliminated it as a factor in their performance. The absence of writing would suit, at least superficially, the findings of Parry and Lord: in the South Slavic traditions, oral poetry and literacy are incompatible. But now we have to reckon with a new problem, one raised by the study of oral poetry itself. The findings of Parry and Lord also suggest that composition and performance are aspects of the same process in oral poetry, and

that no poet's composition is ever identical even to his previous composition of the "same" poem at a previous performance, in that each performance entails a recomposition of the poet's inherited material.

The problem, then, is this: How could the Homeric and Hesiodic poems survive unchanged into the historical period without the aid of writing? One solution is to posit that the poems were dictated by their illiterate composers. But we have already noted that the hypothetical existence of fixed texts in, say, the eighth century cannot by itself account for the proliferation of Homeric and Hesiodic poetry throughout the city-states. That process, as we have also noted, must be attributed long-range to the recurrent competitive performances of the poems over the years by rhapsodes at such events as Panhellenic festivals. Thus we must resort to positing the existence of early fixed texts only if the competing rhapsodes really needed to memorize written versions in order to perform, and for this there is no evidence.

On the contrary, there is evidence that the rhapsodes preserved in their performances certain aspects of poetic diction that would not have been written down in any early phase of the textual transmission. In the postclassical era of the Alexandrian scholars, when accentual notation was for the first time becoming canonical, it was observed that rhapsodes maintained in their recitations certain idiosyncratic accent patterns that did not match current pronunciation. We now know from cognate accentual patterns in Indo-European languages other than Greek that these aspects of rhapsodic pronunciation are deeply archaic—surely the heritage of Homeric and Hesiodic diction. To repeat, there seems no way for these patterns to be preserved textually from the archaic period, and we are left with the conclusion that the rhapsodes were much more than mere memorizers of texts.

True, the rhapsodes were not oral poets in the sense that this concept is defined by Parry and Lord on the basis of their fieldwork on South Slavic traditions: by the time of Plato, rhapsodes seem to have been performers only, whereas the oral poet technically performs while he composes, composes while he performs. Looking beyond Yugoslavia, however, we find oral poetic traditions in other cultures where the factor of performance has become separated from that of composition—as revealed, for example, in the Old Provençal contrast of *trobador* (composer) and *joglar* (performer). There are also oral traditions, like those of the Somali, where composition may precede performance without any aid of writing. These and other examples are discussed in Ruth Finnegan's *Oral Poetry*, which is useful for its adjustments on the Parry-Lord theories, though it sometimes confuses oral poetry with the kind of free-associative improvisations that mark certain types of modern poetry in the West.

"Improvise" is a particularly pernicious word when applied to traditional oral poetry—including that of Homer and Hesiod. An oral poet in a traditional society does not "make things up," since his function is to re-create the inherited values of those for whom he composes/performs. As perhaps the most striking available example, I cite the Vedas of the Indic peoples—a vast body of sacred poems displaying the strictest imaginable regulation in form as well as content—and formalizing the ideology of the priestly class without change for well over two millennia. It should be added that, despite the availability of writing, the authority of the Vedas to this day abides in the spoken word, not in any written text. Moreover, the Vedas have been transmitted unchanged, as a fixed "text," for all these years by way of mnemonic techniques that had been part of the oral tradition. Given the authority of the Homeric and Hesiodic poems by the time they surface in the historical period of Greece, it is not unreasonable to suppose that their rhapsodic transmission entailed comparable mnemonic efforts—which need not have required writing at all. In theory, though, written texts of the Homeric and Hesiodic poems could have been generated at any time—in fact, many times—

during the lengthy phase of rhapsodic transmission.

In the case of Homeric and Hesiodic poetry, composition and proliferation need not have been separate factors. It is not as if a composition had to evolve into perfection before it was disseminated throughout the city-states. Rather, in view of the Panhellenic status ultimately achieved by the Homeric and Hesiodic poems, it is more likely that their composition and proliferation were combined factors. These poems, it appears, represent the culmination of compositional trends that were reaching their ultimate form, from the eighth century onward, in the context of competitive performances at Panhellenic festivals and other such events. By way of countless such performances for over two centuries, each recomposition at each successive performance could become less and less variable. Such gradual crystallization into what became set poems would have been a direct response to the exigencies of a Panhellenic audience.

Recalling the testimony of Herodotus and others to the effect that Homer and Hesiod provide a systematization of values common to all Greeks, we may go so far as to say that "Homer" and "Hesiod" are themselves the cumulative embodiment of this systematization—the ultimate poetic response to Panhellenic audiences from the eighth century onward. An inevitable consequence of such evolution from compositional trends to set poems is that the original oral poet, who composes while he performs and performs while he composes, evolves with the passage of time into a mere performer. We must not be too quick to dismiss the importance of the rhapsode, however: he must have been a master of mnemonic techniques inherited directly from oral poets. Even in such minute details as accentual patterns, as we have seen, he preserved the heritage of a genuine oral poet. The etymology of *rhapsōidós* (stitcher of songs) reveals a traditional conceit of the oral poet as overtly expressed by the poet himself in cognate Indo-European poetic traditions. There is, then, no demotion implicit in the formal distinction between *rhapsōidós* and *aoidós* (singer)—which is the word used by the Homeric and Hesiodic poems to designate the genuinely oral poet. It is simplistic and even misleading to contrast, as many have done, the "creative" *aoidós* with the "reduplicating" *rhapsōidós*. We must keep in mind that even the traditional oral poet does not really "create" in the modern sense of authorship; rather, he re-creates for his listeners the inherited values that serve as foundations for their society. Even the narrative of epic, as we have noted, is a vehicle for re-creating traditional values, with a set program that will not deviate in the direction of personal invention, away from the traditional plots known and expected by the audience. If, then, the *aoidós* is an upholder of such set poetic ways, he is not so far removed from the *rhapsōidós* as from the modern concept of "poet."

The more significant difference between *aoidós* and *rhapsōidós* lies in the nature of their respective audiences. The *rhapsōidós*, as we have seen, recites the Homeric or Hesiodic poems to Hellenes at large—to listeners from various city-states who congregate at events like Panhellenic festivals—and what he recites remains unchanged as he travels from city to city. On the other hand, the typical *aoidós* as portrayed in, say, the *Odyssey* (9.3–11) sings to a strictly local community. As the studies of Wilhelm Radloff concerning the oral poetry of the Kirghiz peoples have made clear, the oral poet in a local situation will of course adjust his composition/performance to the nature of his audience. For example, the presence of rich and distinguished members of society will prompt the Kirghiz *akyn* (poet) to introduce episodes reflecting traditions that glorify their families. Now the local audiences of Greece in the eighth century must have challenged the poet with a veritable kaleidoscope of repertoires; each city would have had its own poetic traditions, often radically different from those of other cities. We have a reference to the regional variety of poetic repertoires in the *Iliad* (20.249). Moreover, even the traditions of any

given city could change radically with successive changes in population or government.

The obvious dilemma of the oral poet is that each of the various local traditions in his repertoire will have validity only when it is performed in the appropriate locale. With the surge of intercommunication among the cities from the eighth century onward, the horizons for the poet's travels would continually expand, and thus the regional differences between one audience and the next would become increasingly pronounced. The greater the regional differences, the greater the gap between what one community and another would hold to be true. What was held to be true by the inhabitants of one place may well have been false to those of another. What is true and false will keep shifting as the poet travels from place to place, and he may even resort to using alternative traditions as a foil for the one that he is re-creating for his audience. This device is still reflected in *Homeric Hymn* 1, where the poet declares in his prayer to Dionysus that the god was not born in Drakanos or in Ikaros or in Naxos or by the banks of the Alpheios or even in Thebes (vv. 1–5), and that those who claim any of these proveniences are *pseudómenoi* (lying; v. 6); he goes on to say that the god was really born at the mountain Nyse (vv. 6–9; compare *Hymn* 26.5). The localization of this Nyse is a separate problem, and the point now is simply that various legitimate local traditions are here being discounted as lies in order to legitimize the one tradition that is acceptable to the poet's audience.

There is a parallel poetic device that inaugurates the *Theogony* of Hesiod, at verses 22–34, which we will understand only by first examining the testimony of Homeric poetry about poetry itself. In the *Odyssey*, Odysseus himself tells stories like an oral poet who has to keep adjusting his composition/performance to the exigencies of his diverse audiences, and in such contexts the resourceful hero is explicitly likened to a poet (11.368, 17.518). It is in the manner of a poet that he tells his "Cretan lies" (compare 17.514, 17.518–521). As he finishes telling one such Cretan tale to Penelope, Odysseus is described in these words:

> He assimilated many lies [pseúdea] to make them look like genuine things. . . .
>
> (Odyssey 19.203)

Earlier, Eumaeus had described other wanderers who, just as the disguised wanderer Odysseus is doing now, would come to Penelope with stories about Odysseus that are calculated to raise her hopes:

> It's no use! Wanderers in need of food
> are liars [pseúdontai], and they are unwilling to tell true things [aléthea muthésasthai]. . . .
>
> (Odyssey 14.124–125)

Odysseus himself fits this description: before telling his major tale of the Odyssey in the court of Alkinoös, he asks the king to let him eat first, since his gastér (belly) is making him forget his tales of woe until it is filled with food (7.215–221). Such a gambit would be typical of an oral poet who is making sure that he gets an appropriate preliminary reward for entertaining his audience.

The root for "forget" in this last passage is léth- (7.221: léthánei), the functional opposite of mné- (remember, have in mind), a root that can also mean "have the mnemonic powers of a poet" in the diction of archaic poetry. Mnémosúné, mother of the Muses (Theogony 54, 135, 915), is the very incarnation of such powers. The conventional designation of poetic powers by mné- has been documented by Marcel Detienne, who also shows that the word a-léth-és (true) is thus originally a double-negative expression of truth by way of poetry. The wanderers who are described in the passage above as being unwilling to tell the truth are cast in the mold of an oral poet who compromises poetic truth for the sake of his own survival. Similarly in the court of Alkinoös, Odysseus as poet is implicitly threatening to withhold the truth of poetry by explicitly blaming his gastér.

With these passages in mind, we come finally to Theogony 22–34, retelling Hesiod's encounter with the Muses. These goddesses, as daughters of Mnémosúné, not only confer the mnemonic powers of poetry on the poet of the Theogony but also offer to endow his poetry with truth, as they themselves announce to him:

> Shepherds living in the fields, base objects of reproach, mere bellies [gastéres]!
> We know how to say many lies [pseúdea] that look like genuine things,
> but we can also, whenever we are willing, proclaim true things [aléthea gér úsasthai].
>
> (Theogony 26–28)

"Truth," which itinerant, would-be oral poets are "unwilling" to tell because of their need for survival (oud' ethélousin at Odyssey 14.124–125), is "willingly" conferred by the Muses (eút' ethélomen). We see here what can be taken as a manifesto of Panhellenic poetry, in that the poet Hesiod is to be freed from being a mere "belly"—one who owes his survival to his local audience with its local traditions: all such local traditions are "lies" in face of the "true things" that the Muses impart specially to Hesiod. The conceit inherent in the Panhellenic poetry of Hesiod is that this overarching tradition is capable of achieving something that is beyond the reach of individual local traditions. As in the Homeric Hymn 1 to Dionysus, the mutually incompatible traditions of various locales are rejected as lies, in favor of one single tradition that can be acceptable to all. In the case of Hymn 1, this goal seems to be achieved by assigning the remotest imaginable traditional place of birth to the god (Nyse is pictured as "near the streams of Aiguptos," v. 9). In the case of the Theogony, we see this sort of process in a global dimension: the many local theogonies of the various city-states are to be superseded by one grand Olympian scheme.

As we have noted already, the Olympus of Hesiodic and Homeric poetry is a Panhellenic construct that elevates the gods beyond their localized attributes. It is a historical fact about

Greece in the archaic period that whatever can be classified as religious practice or ideology was confined to the local level, and a survey of the attested evidence, as gleaned from sources like Pausanias or epichoric inscriptions, reveals clearly that each city had a very distinct pattern of cults. A given god as worshiped in one city could be radically different from a god bearing the same name as he was worshiped in another city.

Under these circumstances, the evolution of most major gods from most major cities into the integrated family at Olympus amounts to a synthesis that is not just artistic but also political in nature, comparable with the evolution of the Panhellenic games known as the Olympics, another crucial phenomenon originating in the eighth century. As in any political process, the evolution of the Panhellenic poems would afford some victories and many concessions on the part of each region: some one salient local feature of a god may become accepted by all audiences, while countless other features that happen to contradict the traditions of other cities will remain unspoken. For example, Cythera and Cyprus may well be recognized as places that the newborn Aphrodite first visited (the narrative specifies that she did so in that order; see *Theogony* 192–193), but very little else about their local lore will ever come to the surface in Hesiodic and Homeric poetry.

The oral poet as represented by the poetry itself is one who can sing both epics and theogonies, as we learn in this description of the poetic repertory of Phemios:

> ... the deeds of men and gods, upon which the poets confer glory [*kléos*]. ...
>
> (*Odyssey* 1.338)

So also in this description of a generic poet:

> But when a poet,
> attendant [*therápōn*] of the Muses, sings the glories [*kléos*] of earlier men
> and the blessed gods who hold Olympus. ...
>
> (*Theogony* 99–101)

In view of the diversity that existed among the cities, an oral poet would have needed for his repertoire a staggering variety of traditions for composing epics and theogonies, which could in the end be rejected as "lies" by the poets of the ultimate epic and ultimate theogony, Homer and Hesiod. Panhellenic poetry can still tell us how an actual epic was being composed by Phemios in the *Odyssey* (1.326–327), or how Hermes composed a theogony for Apollo in the *Hymn to Hermes* (425–433). Yet such Panhellenic poetry, ascribed to the ultimate poets, is itself no longer oral poetry in the strict sense: it is being performed by rhapsodes. (In the case of the Homeric poems, the compositions have even become too long for any single performance.) Moreover, oral poetry has not survived. The emergence of artistic marvels like the uniquely "truthful" and Panhellenic *Theogony* of Hesiod from among countless "deceitful" and local theogonies of oral poets entails not only the crystallization of the one but also the extinction of the many.

HESIOD, POET OF THE THEOGONY

It would be simplistic to assume that the "truth" of the Muses about the genesis of all the gods the Greeks have in common would ever be conferred upon just any poet. Hesiod's *Theogony* in fact presents its composer as the ultimate poet. The very name *Hēsíodos* at *Theogony* 22 means something like "he who emits the Voice." The root $*i_\cap eh_1$ of *Hēsí-* recurs in the expression *óssan hieîsai* (emitting a [beautiful/ immortal/lovely] voice), describing the Muses themselves at *Theogony* 10, 43, 65, 67, while the root $*huod-_{2\cap}$ of *-odos* recurs as $*hud-_{2\cap}$ in *audé* (voice), designating the power of poetry conferred by the Muses upon the poet at *Theogony* 31. In this way *Hēsíodos* embodies the poetic function of the very Muses who give him his powers.

Also, the generic poet's epithet, "*therápōn* [attendant] of the Muses" (*Theogony* 100), literally identifies Hesiod with these divinities and implicitly entails not only his ritual death but also his subsequent worship as cult hero (compare Nagy, *Achaeans*, p. 297; the poetic word *therápōn*, conventionally translated as "attendant," is apparently borrowed from an Anatolian word, attested as Hittite *tarpan-alli*, "ritual substitute"). We may compare the generic warrior's epithet, "attendant of Ares" (*Iliad* 2.110, 6.67, for instance), which identifies the hero with the god of war at the moment of his death (Nagy, *Achaeans*, pp. 292–295). Although the Homeric poems offer little direct testimony about the cults of dead warriors, they reveal extensive indirect references to the ideology of hero cults. The actual evidence for the existence of hero cults in the eighth century and thereafter comes from archaeology, and there is reason to believe that the historically attested cults of the Homeric heroes are no mere reflex of Homeric poetry; rather, both the cults and the poetry represent interacting aspects of a broader phenomenon. By the same token, it appears that an ideology reflecting the cult of the poet Hesiod is built into the poetry of Hesiod.

This statement would of course be an absurdity were it not for the fact that the very identity of Hesiod within his poetry is consistently determined by the traditions that are the foundation of this poetry. As we are about to see time and again, the persona of Hesiod as reflected by his poetry is purely generic, not historical. This is not to say that Hesiod is a fiction: his personality, as it functions within his poetry, is just as traditional as the poetry itself, and he is no more a fiction than any other aspect of Hesiodic poetry. A word more suitable than fiction is myth—provided we understand genuine mythopoeic thinking to be a traditional expression of a given social group's concept of truth.

Of course, Hesiodic poetry refers to itself not as the gradual evolution of poetic traditions into compositions on a Panhellenic scale but, rather, as the one-time creation of one ultimate poet

whose self-identification with the Muses, for him both a bane and a blessing, makes him a cult hero. Besides the poet's name and the epithet "*therápōn* of the Muses," the most striking sign of Hesiod's stance as hero is dramatized in the scene describing his first encounter with the Muses. The goddesses are antagonistic to the poet's local origins, but aid him anyway by transforming his repertoire from localized "lies" into the "truth" that all Hellenes can accept; they give Hesiod a *skêptron* (staff, scepter) as an emblem of his transformation from shepherd to poet (*Theogony* 30).

This narrative is typical of traditional Greek myths that motivate the cult of a poet as hero. In the *Life of Archilochus* tradition, for example, the diffusion of which can be historically connected with the actual cult of Archilochus as hero on his native island of Paros from the archaic period onward, we find another story about the poet and the Muses. On a moonlit night, young Archilochus is driving a cow toward the city from a countryside region of Paros known as the *Leimônes* (Meadows) when he comes upon some seemingly rustic women, whom he proceeds to antagonize with mockery. The disguised Muses respond playfully to his taunts and ask him to trade away his cow. Agreeing to do so if the price is right, Archilochus straightway falls into a swoon. When he awakens, the rustic women are gone, and so too is the cow; but in its place Archilochus finds a lyre that he takes home as an emblem of his transformation from cowherd to poet (Mnesiepes Inscription E$_1$, II, 23–38).

The similarities between Archilochus and Hesiod extend further. As a clue, we note that the epithet "*therápōn* of the Muses" is applied to Archilochus precisely in the context of the story retelling the poet's death (Delphic Oracle 4, Parke and Wormell ed.). Then again, just as Archilochus was worshiped as cult hero in his native Paros, so was Hesiod in Askra—until his homeland was obliterated by the neighboring city of Thespiai, and the reputed remains of the poet were transferred by the refugees from

Askra to a new cult precinct at Orkhomenos, a rival of Thespiai (Aristotle, *Constitution of the Orkhomenians*, frag. 565, Rose ed.; Plutarch ap. Proclus commentary). According to another tradition, contradicting the one emanating from Orkhomenos (Plutarch, *Banquet of the Seven Sages* 19.162c), Hesiod was buried and venerated as hero in the cult precinct of Zeus Nemeios at Oineon in Ozolian Lokris (*Certamen*, p. 234, Allen ed.; compare Thucydides, 3.96). In the myth that serves to validate this tradition, the murdered poet's corpse is said to have been originally cast into the sea, only to be carried ashore on the third day by dolphins (*Certamen*, p. 234.233, Allen ed.)—a narrative scheme that is particularly appropriate to a cult hero in whose honor a festival is founded (as in the case of Melikertes and the Isthmian Games).

In short, the lore about Hesiod fits a general pattern that is characteristic of a local cult hero, and the parallelism of Hesiod and Archilochus in this regard becomes even more noteworthy. The local cult of Archilochus at Paros, as we have seen, is the actual source of the myth about the poet's transformation from cowherd into poet. In the case of Hesiod's transformation from shepherd into poet, however, the myth is built into the *Theogony* itself. Since the hero cult of Hesiod is just as much a historical fact as the cult of Archilochus, and since both these cults are deeply archaic in nature, it is possible that the Hesiodic cult is ultimately a locus of diffusion for the Hesiodic poems, just as the Archilochean cult seems to be for the Archilochean vita.

Moreover, the Archilochean vita tradition may well have been the actual context for the preservation of Archilochean poetry itself, with a narrative superstructure about the poet's life serving as a frame for "quoting" the poet's poems (compare the "quoting" of Aesop's fables in the *Life of Aesop* tradition). This arrangement is in fact suggested by the format of the Mnesiepes Inscription, the Parian document that proclaims the hero cult of Archilochus and then proceeds to tell the story of his life (starting with the incident of the cow and the lyre). Granted, this document is late (third century B.C.) and may reflect literary mannerisms characteristic of the Hellenistic era. It is also true that the genre of the poet's vita in general tends to degenerate—from traditional narratives that are parallel to the poems into what can only be called fictions that are arbitrarily derived from the poems. Still, the program of the Mnesiepes Inscription is to document and motivate cult practices in a sacred precinct that is actually named after Archilochus (the *Arkhilókheion*), and in such an ancestral religious context invention seems out of the question.

The relevance of this information about Archilochus to Hesiod becomes clear when we consider the name of the man to whom Apollo is said to have given the command to institute the hero cult of Archilochus: *Mnēsiépēs*, meaning "he who remembers the word(s)." It seems as if the foundation of the poet's cult goes hand in hand with remembering the poet's words. Given the historical fact that the poems of Archilochus, like those of Homer and Hesiod, were recited at public competitions by rhapsodes (Athenaeus, 14.620c), we may envision a pattern of evolution parallel to that of the Homeric and Hesiodic poems. In other words, the oral poetic traditions of Paros could eventually have become crystallized into a fixed collection of poems retrojected as creations of the ultimate poet Archilochus and disseminated by way of rhapsodic transmission in the context of the poet's hero cult. We may directly compare the *Homērídai* (sons of Homer) and *Kreōphuleîoi* (sons of Kreophulos), organizations of reciters whose very names imply that their "founding fathers" were cult heroes.

In this connection a brief word is in order about a Panhellenic tendency inherent in all archaic Greek poetry—not just the Homeric and Hesiodic. It is a historical fact that each major poetic genre in the archaic period tends to appropriate the surface structure of a single dialect to the exclusion of all others. For example, the elegiac poetry of even the Doric areas is characterized by Ionic diction, as we see in the poems of Theognis (Megara) and Tyrtaeus (Sparta); conversely, the diction of choral lyric will be a synthetic form of Doric even for Ionic poets like Simonides and Bacchylides.

Before we consider any further the evolution of the local Boeotian poetic traditions of Hesiod into the Ionic hexameters of the Panhellenic *Theogony*, it is instructive to ask this related question: Why should the local Doric traditions of a city like Megara evolve into the Ionic elegiacs of a Theognis? The answer is given by the poetry itself: the goal of this poetry, the poet says, is to be heard by all Hellenes everywhere (Theognis, 22–23, 237–254). It seems as if such a goal can be reached only with the evolution of the local poetry into a form that is performable at Panhellenic events. In the case of the elegiac, that form would be Ionic. And such evolution entails, again, the eventual crystallization of oral poetic traditions into the kind of fixed poems that are the repertoire of rhapsodes. Who, then, is the poet? As we shall observe in the next section, Theognis too—like Archilochus and other masters of lyric—may be considered an idealized creation of the poetry in which he has an integral function—and which he is credited with creating.

There is an important difference, however, between the poems of a Hesiod on the one hand and of a Theognis or an Archilochus on the other. The difference is one of degree: these three figures, among others, seemingly have in common an intent to address all Hellenes, but Hesiod has far more authority than all the other poets. A Theognis or an Archilochus speaks from the perspective of his own city, though the localized aspects of the city are shaded over and the Panhellenic aspects are highlighted. In the case of Hesiod, however, the perspective is meant to be that of all cities. This transcendence is of course facilitated by the historical fact that the figure of Hesiod has no native city to claim him, since Askra was destroyed by Thespiai. Because Askra is no more, its traditions need not infringe on those of other cities.

By allowing Hesiod to speak as a native of Askra, the Panhellenic tradition is in effect making him a native of all Greek cities, as we shall see in our survey of the *Works and Days*. The *Theogony* too expresses this transcendence, in two interrelated ways: the form in which the Muses are invoked and the nature of the gift that they confer on Hesiod.

We begin with the second. Whereas the mark of Archilochus' transformation from cowherd to poet in his nighttime encounter with the Muses is a lyre, Hesiod's transformation from shepherd to poet in his likewise nighttime encounter (*Theogony* 10) is marked by their gift of a *skêptron* (staff, scepter; v. 30). There has been much fruitless debate over such questions as whether this gift implies that Hesiod had not learned how to play the lyre, and not enough attention has been paid to the implications of the word *skêptron* as it is actually used in archaic poetry. The *skêptron* is a staff held by kings (*Iliad* 1.279, 2.86), by Chryses as priest of Apollo (1.15, 1.28), by Teiresias as prophet (*Odyssey* 11.90), by *kērūkes* (heralds; *Iliad* 7.277), or generally by one who stands up to speak in the *agorē* (assembly; *Iliad* 3.218, 23.568).

Perhaps the most revealing example of such an *agorē* is in the *Iliad* (18.497), where it is presented as the context of an archetypal *neîkos* (quarrel) visualized on that timeless microcosm of a frozen motion picture, the Shield of Achilles. While the two nameless litigants are seen formally quarreling with one another, partisans of each side shout their preferences (*Iliad* 18.502), and each of the seated *gérontes* (elders) at the assembly waits for his turn to stand up with *skêptron* in hand and speak in favor of one side or the other (18.505–506). As each elder speaks, taking the staff from the attending heralds, he is described as rendering *díkē* (judgment/justice; 18.506); moreover, a prize awaits the one who "speaks *díkē* in the most straight manner" (18.508).

Such an elder is the equivalent of the generic *basileús* (king) as described in the *Theogony* (80–93). Moreover, the king's function of speaking *díkē* at the assembly is in fact a gift of the Muses, as the *Theogony* itself tells us. The just king is imbued, from childhood on, by the Muses (*Theogony* 81–84), and he decides what is *thémis* (divine law; v. 85) by way of "straight *díkē* [plural]" (v. 86)—in the context of the assembly (vv. 86, 89, 92).

In sum, the *skêptron* given to Hesiod by the Muses indicates that the poet will speak with the authority of a king—an authority that emanates from Zeus himself (*Theogony* 96; *Iliad* 1.238–239, 9.97–99). The point is, just as Zeus has authority over all other gods, so also the poet who formalizes this authority by telling how it all happened thereby implicitly has authority over all other poets.

Next we turn to the invocation of the Muses in the *Theogony*. At first blush, Hesiod hardly fits the image of a poet whose authority transcends that of all other poets. He is situated in Askra (*Works and Days* 640), a remote Boeotian settlement at the foot of Mount Helikon, which in turn is described as the local cult place of the Muses (*Theogony* 1–7). Such a localization, as well as the poet's self-identification as Hesiod, has conventionally been interpreted as a primitive assertion of individualism in contrast with Homer's elevated anonymity.

This is to misunderstand the inherited conventions of the *Theogony*. As we can see from the theogony performed by Hermes himself to the accompaniment of his lyre in *Hymn to Hermes* 425–433, the traditional format of such a composition is that of a prelude (the classical Greek word for which is *prooímion*). The internal evidence for this format has been extensively studied by Hermann Koller (the key word in the *Hymn to Hermes* is *amboládēn* [playing a prelude] at v. 426), and it will suffice here to note that the *Homeric Hymns*, including the *Hymn to Hermes*, are also preludes (thus Thucydides at 3.104.4 refers to the Homeric *Hymn to Apollo* as a *prooímion*). The conventional closure of the *Hymns*, *metabḗsomai állon es húmnon* (as at *Hymn to Aphrodite* 293), literally means "I will move on to the rest

of my song" (not " . . . to another hymn," as most translators render it). The rest of a performance introduced by a prelude may be technically any poetic/musical form, but the one form that is specified by the *Homeric Hymns* themselves is the deeds of heroes (31.19, 32.19)—which would be some form of epic or catalogue poetry.

Still, the fact is that the *Iliad* and the *Odyssey* have survived without any fixed preludes, although the availability of such preludes is documented by Crates of Pergamon (*Vita Homeri Romana*, p. 32, Wilamowitz ed.). The prelude is the prime context—practically the only context—for the archaic poet to identify himself, speak in his own persona, and describe the circumstances of his performance (compare Theognis, 22; Alcman, frag. 39, Page ed.; even in choral lyric it is the prelude in which the first person is more appropriate to the poet than to the chorus). Thus the notorious contrasting of Hesiodic self-identification with Homeric anonymity is invalid—if indeed the self-identification of Hesiod is happening within a prelude. Moreover, the self-identification of Homer is attested in another genuine prelude, the Homeric *Hymn to Apollo* (166–176).

The proposition that the *Theogony* is, from a purely formal point of view, a complex prelude that invokes all the gods can be tested by adducing the larger *Homeric Hymns* as simplex preludes, each of which invokes one god. Admittedly these *Hymns* are unwieldy as functional preludes precisely because of their sheer size, and there may well be an element of *ars gratia artis* in their evolution. Since preludes traditionally appear in a variety of metrical forms, the fact that the *Homeric Hymns* were composed in hexameter suggests that they were closely affected by the specific form of the epic poetry that they preceded; moreover, if the epic compositions were to evolve into monumental size, then so could the preludes that introduced the epic performances. Despite the monumental size of the larger *Hymns*, however, the point remains that they maintain the traditional program of a functional prelude, one that is worthy of Panhellenic performance. This program can be divided into five stages:

    1. the invocation proper; naming of the god

    2. application of the god's epithets, conveying either explicitly or implicitly his efficacy on the local level of cult

    3. a description of the god's ascent to Olympus, whereby he achieves Panhellenic recognition

    4. a prayer to the god that he be pleased with the recognition that has been accorded him so far in the performance

    5. transition to the rest of the performance.

These five stages may or may not be explicit in any given *Hymn*. For instance, in the shorter *Hymn to Hermes* (18.5–9) the admission of Hermes as an Olympian god (stage 3) is suggested by way of mentioning the delay of his admission during the confinement of Maia in her cave; in the longer *Hymn to Hermes* (4.5–9), by contrast, the closely corresponding mention of this delay is followed by a lengthy narrative that elaborates on the god's subsequent admission. This narrative in the longer *Hymn* takes us all the way to verse 578, where we finally reach stage 4; by contrast, stage 4 in the shorter *Hymn to Hermes* is reached by verse 10.

Such an example of extreme length and brevity in two *Homeric Hymns* to the same god, achieved by expansion and compression, respectively (the mechanics of both phenomena are a sure sign of oral poetry), can be compared with the length of the *Theogony* and the brevity of *Homeric Hymn* 25. Technically, both *Hymn* 25 and the *Theogony* are hymns to the Muses, and the first six hexameters of the seven-hexameter prelude have direct formal analogues in the longer:

Hymn 25.1	*Theogony* 1
Hymn 25.2–5	*Theogony* 94–97
Hymn 25.6	*Theogony* 963

Whereas the short hymn is a simplex prelude that motivates the genesis of the Muses, the long hymn is a complex prelude that first mo-

tivates the genesis of the Muses, who are then invoked to motivate the genesis of all the gods, which is the theogony proper. But from verse 964 onward, the *Theogony* is no longer formally a theogony, in that the subject matter shifts from the *theôn génos* (genesis of gods, as at *Theogony* 44, 105; compare 115) to the genesis of demigods born of gods who mated with mortals (compare *Theogony* 965–968); the latter theme, which amounts to catalogue poetry about heroes and heroines, is actually expressed as *génos andrôn . . . hemithéōn* (genesis of men who were demigods) at *Homeric Hymn* 31.18–19—a theme to which *Hymn* 31 announces itself as a formal prelude.

To repeat, verses 1–963 of the *Theogony* are from the standpoint of form a hymn to the Muses, serving as a prelude to the catalogue of heroes and heroines that survives at verses 965–1020 of the *Theogony*—and that interconnects with Hesiod fragment 1. The significant modification in this hymn to the Muses is that it becomes primarily a monumental hymn to Zeus and all the Olympian gods; thus at stage 4, where the poet may be expected to pray that the Muses be pleased with what has been composed so far, he in fact prays to win the pleasure of all the Olympians generated in his *Theogony*.

Thus verses 1–963 of the *Theogony* are not a single, but rather a composite, hymn in comparison with most *Homeric Hymns*. The hymn proper is at verses 36–103, culminating at 104 in a separate stage 4 in which the poet prays exclusively to the Muses; then, starting at verse 105, the expected stage 5 of transition (to whatever composition might follow the prelude) is implicitly postponed and replaced by a reapplied hymn to the Muses running all the way to verse 962, followed at last by a reapplied but cumulative stage 4 at verse 963. We may compare *Hymn to Apollo* 165–166, a stage 4 appropriate to Apollo as he is worshiped in the Panionian context of his birthplace Delos: the poet first prays to Apollo and then greets the Deliades, a chorus of female singers/dancers who seem to be a local manifestation of the Muses, with a formula that elsewhere conveys a stage 4 prayer. Then, at verses 177-178, the expected stage 5 of transition is explicitly postponed and followed at verses 179-544 by a reapplied hymn to Apollo as he is worshiped in the Panhellenic context of his abode at Delphi; there is a reapplied stage 4 at verse 545, where the poet again prays to Apollo, followed at last by the stage 5 of transition at verse 546.

In the case of the *Theogony*, verses 105-962 amount to an expanded variant of the compressed hymn at verses 36-103, just as verses 179-544 in the *Hymn to Apollo* amount to an expanded variant of the compressed hymn at verses 1-165. There is an important formal difference, however, between the compressed version at verses 36-103 of the *Theogony* and the expanded version of verses 105-962: whereas both are simultaneously a prelude and a theogony—just like the composition performed by Hermes in *Hymn to Hermes* 425-433—the compressed version is more of a prelude and the expanded version is more of a theogony.

The expanded version is the *Theogony* proper, told by Hesiod in his own persona and "retelling" what the Muses had told him. The compressed version, on the other hand, is told only indirectly: in this case the theogony related by the Muses to Hesiod is merely paraphrased, as it were, in the context of describing what the goddesses sang as they went up to Mount Olympus.

Verses 1-21 of the *Theogony* present yet another indirect version (thus there are altogether three versions of theogony in the *Theogony*). Here too the theogony related by the Muses is paraphrased, this first time in the context of describing what the goddesses sang as they came down from Mount Helikon. In this version the Muses are invoked as Helikonian (*Theogony* 1-2), not Olympian as everywhere else in the *Theogony*. Moreover, the thematic order of the Muses' theogony, which they sing and dance (*Theogony* 3-4) as they come down from the summit of Mount Helikon, is the inverse of what they sing and dance (*Theogony* 70) as they go up to the summit of Mount Olympus (which is stage 3 in the program of a Panhellenic hymn).

In the first theogony, at *Theogony* 11-20, the Muses are described as starting their narrative with Olympian Zeus (v. 11) and moving their way "down" from the other Olympian gods—Hera, Athena, Apollo, Artemis, Poseidon (vv. 11-15)—all the way to the previous divine generations (vv. 16-19) and then to the primordial forces, Earth, Okeanos, Night (v. 20). These same Muses, after they encounter Hesiod at the foot of Mount Helikon, are described in the second theogony (*Theogony* 36-52) as starting their narrative with Earth/Sky (v. 45) and moving their way "up" to the Olympian gods, culminating with Zeus himself (v. 47; the word *deúteron* [next] here denotes merely the order of this theogony, and therefore does not slight the importance of Zeus). It is important that this narrative direction of the Muses' second theogony, which determines the direction of Hesiod's third and definitive theogony at verses 105-962, corresponds to stage 3 in the program of a Panhellenic hymn, the ascent to Olympus of the divinity who is being praised.

We see here a transformation of the Muses from local goddesses on Mount Helikon into Panhellenic goddesses on Mount Olympus. As they start their way down the slopes of Helikon, they are described as *énthen apornúmenai* (starting from there) at *Theogony* 9—corresponding to *énthen apornúmenos* (same meaning) at *Hymn to Apollo* 29, where the verse goes on to proclaim the transformation of Apollo from lord of his native Delos into lord of all mankind. In their local setting the singing and dancing Helikonian Muses resemble the Deliades of the *Hymn to Apollo*. Like the Muses (for example, *Hymn to Apollo* 189-190), the Deliades are Apollo's attendants (v. 157), and the poet seems to be praying to them and Apollo together at stage 4 of his hymn (vv. 177-178). Further, the Deliades too seem to sing and dance (compare Thucydides, 3.104.5 and Euripides, *Herakles* 687–690); it is as if the performances of the Helikonian Muses and the Deliades were envisioned as lyric rather than hexameter poetry.

Moreover, the relationship of Hesiod to the Helikonian Muses parallels the relationship of Homer to the Deliades (the *Hymn to Apollo* unmistakably claims Homer as its composer). The self-dramatized encounter of Homer with the Deliades leads to the poet's promise that he will spread their *kléos* (glory) by mentioning them in his poetry as he travels throughout the cities of mankind (*Hymn to Apollo* 174–175; compare v. 156, where this glory is already presented as a fait accompli); in other words, the Deliades will have a place in Panhellenic poetry. Similarly, the encounter of Hesiod with the Helikonian Muses leads to the poet's glorifying them with the *Theogony*, which is technically a Panhellenic hymn to the Muses; in this way the local goddesses of Helikon are assimilated into the Panhellenic goddesses of Olympus.

We may also compare Hermes' miniature theogony as paraphrased in the *Hymn to Hermes* 425–433; this theogony is technically a hymn to the mother of the Muses, Mnēmosúnē (v. 429), who is described as the deity presiding over and defined by the characteristics of Hermes (for the diction, compare Callimachus, *Hymn to Apollo* 43). In the same way the Helikonian Muses preside over and are defined by the characteristics of Hesiod—characteristics that they themselves had conferred upon him.

And here we finally see why it is essential for the *Theogony* that Hesiod should have his local origins at the foot of Mount Helikon. As an expression of the Helikonian Muses, he possesses characteristics that are beyond the immediate sphere of the Olympian Muses. As we have seen, the goddesses confer upon him a staff (*Theogony* 30), an emblem of authority that is the province of kings and that emanates from Zeus himself. Also, as his very name Hēsíodos proclaims, the Muses of Helikon endow the poet with *audé* (*Theogony* 31), a special voice that enables him not only to sing a theogony (vv.

33–34) but also to tell the future as well as the past (v. 32). Whereas the generic protégé of the Olympian Muses and Apollo is an *aoidós* (poet) who composes the equivalent of Homeric epos and hymns (compare *Homeric Hymn* 25.2–3 and *Theogony* 94–103), Hesiod as protégé of the Helikonian Muses has the powers not only of a poet but also of what the Greeks would call a *kêrux* (herald) and a *mántis* (seer).

As some recent studies have demonstrated in detail, the Indo-European heritage of Greek poetry entailed an original overlap of what eventually evolved into the separate functions of poet-herald-seer. This overlap still survives, not only in the characterization of Hesiod as protégé of the Helikonian Muses but also in the paradigm of Hermes as protégé of Mnēmosúnē.

By virtue of singing a theogony, Hermes is said to be *kraínōn* or "authorizing" the gods (*Hymn to Hermes* 427). The verb *kraínō*, as Emile Benveniste shows, denotes sovereign authority as exercised by kings and as emanating from Zeus himself. It conveys the notion that kings authorize the accomplishment of something and confirm that it will be accomplished (as at *Odyssey* 8.390). A typological survey of ritual theogonic traditions native to diverse cultures throughout the world reveals that a basic function of a theogony is to confirm the authority that regulates any given social group. By singing a theogony and thus "authorizing" the gods, Hermes is in effect confirming their authority.

Hermes later enters into an agreement with Apollo whereby the two gods divide their functions between themselves, and in the process Hermes gives Apollo his lyre along with the powers that go with it (*Hymn to Hermes* 434–512), while Apollo gives Hermes a *rhábdos* (staff) described as *epi-kraínousa* or "authorizing" the ordinances that Apollo has learned from Zeus himself (vv. 531–532). While granting this much authorization to Hermes, Apollo specifically excludes the sphere of divination that is appropriate to the oracle at Delphi (vv. 533–549); but Apollo does include the sphere of divination that is appropriate to the Bee Maidens of Mount Parnassos (vv. 550–566). These Bee Maidens also *kraínousin* or "authorize" (v. 559): when they are fed honey, they are in ecstasy and tell *alēthéē* (truth; vv. 560–561), but they *pseúdontai* (lie) when deprived of this food (vv. 562–563). Such ecstatic divination is achieved with fermented honey—a pattern typical of an early stage when *aoidós* (poet) and *mántis* (seer) were one. When the Bee Maidens are in ecstasy, they *kraínousin* by telling of future things that will really come to pass.

The division of attributes between Apollo and Hermes dramatizes the evolutionary separation of poetic functions that are pictured as still integral at the time when Hermes sang the theogony. But then Hermes cedes the lyre to Apollo and confines himself to the primitive shepherd's pipe (*Hymn to Hermes* 511–512) so that Apollo can take over the sphere of the poet. Apollo also takes over the sphere of the seer on a highly evolved Panhellenic level (his oracle at Delphi), leaving to Hermes the more primitive sphere of the seer as a local exponent of the sort of "truth" that is induced by fermented honey. But the "newer" god's dramatized affinity with the more primitive aspects of poetry and his actual inauguration of Apollo's poetic art by way of singing a theogony indicate that Hermes—not Apollo—is in fact the older god, and that his "authorizing" staff and his "authorizing" Bee Maidens are vestiges of an older and broader poetic realm. From a historical point of view, Apollo and his Olympian Muses are the newer gods: they represent a streamlining of this older realm into the newer and narrower one of Panhellenic poetry.

Similarly, Hesiod's relationship with the Helikonian Muses represents an older and broader poetic realm that the poet then streamlines into the newer and narrower one of a Panhellenic theogony by way of synthesizing the Helikonian with the Olympian Muses. The *skêptron* (staff) and the prophetic voice that Hesiod receives from the Helikonian Muses, speakers of both falsehood and truth, are analogous to the Hermetic *rhábdos* (staff) and Bee Maidens, likewise speakers of both falsehood and truth. It seems as if the Muses of Olympus inherit the genre of theogony from the Muses of Helikon, just as Apollo gets the lyre from Hermes, composer of the first theogony. For a Panhellenic theogony to happen, the Muses have to come down from Helikon and go up to Olympus, through the intermediacy of Hesiod.

Just as Hermes is the archetypal *kêrux* (herald) and *mántis* (seer), so Hesiod embodies these two functions along with that of the *aoidós* (poet) by way of the Helikonian Muses. (These local Muses, as Pausanias, 9.29.2–3 reports, are Melétē [practice], Mnémē [memory], and Aoidḗ [song]; these names correspond to the processes involved in the composition and performance of oral poetry.) The figure of Hesiod requires these local Muses in order to compose a theogony, but he also requires the Olympian Muses in order to compose Panhellenic poetry. His own implicit reward for assimilating the Helikonian Muses into the Olympian is that his local gifts, a staff and a voice that are both appropriate to a local theogony, become in a Panhellenic context the emblems that establish his ultimate authority as poet, emanating from the ultimate authority of Zeus as king.

HESIOD, POET OF THE WORKS AND DAYS

Hesiod's ultimate authority as poet, emanating from the ultimate authority of Zeus as king, is put to the test in the *Works and Days*. In the prelude to the poem (vv. 1–10), which is formally the equivalent of a hymn to Zeus, the supreme god is implored to "straighten the divine laws [*thémis*] with your judgment [*díkē*]" (v. 9) while the poet proceeds to say *etétuma* (genuine things) to his brother Perses (v. 10). Thus the actions of Zeus and the words of Hesiod are drawn into an explicitly parallel relationship.

The actions of Zeus are a model for the ideal king as visualized in the *Theogony*: imbued by the Muses (vv. 80–84), he "sorts out the divine laws with straight judgments" (vv. 85–86). Thanks to his straight judgments, the king is also able to bring to an end even a great *neíkos* (quarrel; v. 87). We are reminded of the *neíkos* pictured on the Shield of Achilles (*Iliad* 18.497), adjudicated by elders who pronounce *díkē* with *skêptron* in hand (vv. 505–508). Curiously, the idealized king in the *Theogony* is not represented as holding a *skêptron*; instead, this symbol of the authority that emanates from Zeus is conferred by the Muses upon Hesiod (*Theogony* 30). It is as if the Muse-imbued king were cast in a mold that could fit the poet.

This is not to say that Hesiod is a king; rather, as we shall see, the *Works and Days* elaborates an authority that replaces and transcends that of kings. The impetus for the entire poem is in fact a *neíkos* between Hesiod and Perses (v. 35), but this quarrel will not be stopped by any ideal king; the poet wishes that he and his brother would settle it themselves (v. 35), "with straight judgments, which are the best, being from Zeus" (v. 36). The original cause of the quarrel between the two brothers is this: after they had divided up their inheritance from their father (v. 37), Perses forcibly took some of Hesiod's fair share (v. 38), thereby enhancing the prestige of greedy kings "who wish to pronounce this judgment" (vv. 38–39). These kings, characterized by Hesiod as "gift-devouring" (vv. 39, 221, 264), are anything but ideal, and the poet threatens that they will be punished for their "crooked judgments" (vv. 250, 264).

As we shall see, what ultimately settles the quarrel of Hesiod and Perses is not any king, but the *Works and Days* itself, elaborating on the concept of *díkē* in the sense of "justice." So far, the translation offered for *díkē* has been "judgment," which is how we must interpret the word in the immediate contexts of *Works and Days* 39, 249, and 269. In each of these instances, an accompanying demonstrative (*ténde*; see also *táde* [these things] at v. 268) forces a translation such as "this judgment," referring short-range to the unjust pronouncement that the greedy kings wish to make. Such contexts even help us understand the etymology of *díkē*: the ideal king "sorts out" (verb *diakrínō*, at *Theogony* 85) what is *thémis* (divine law) and what is not (v. 85) by way of *díkē* (v. 86), which is an indication (as in Latin *indic-āre*, where -*dic*- is cognate with Greek *díkē*), hence "judgment." Long-range, however, any ad hoc "judgment" can be turned into "justice" by Zeus, who is the authority behind all human judgments. Thus, when Hesiod implores Zeus to "straighten the divine laws with *díkē*" (*Works and Days* 9), the supreme god's "judgment" is the same as "justice." This action of Zeus, to repeat, is coefficient with the words of Hesiod to Perses (v. 10), in the context of a quarrel that the two of them must "sort out" for themselves (verb *diakrínō* again, this time in the middle voice; v. 35).

The figure of Hesiod resorts to words in reacting to the violent seizure of his property by Perses. First he tells Perses the story of Prometheus and Pandora (*Works and Days* 42–105), motivating the prime theme of man's inherent need to work the land for a living. Then he tells Perses the myth of the five generations of mankind (vv. 106–201), which shows in detail how mankind becomes elevated by *díkē* (justice) and debased by its opposite, *húbris* (outrage). The fifth and present generation, which is the Age of Iron, is a time when *díkē* and *húbris* are engaged in an ongoing struggle. As happens elsewhere in myths about the ages of mankind, the present encompassed by the final age merges with the future and becomes a prophecy: in a deeply pessimistic tone, Hesiod predicts that *díkē* will finally lose to *húbris* (*Works and Days* 190–194). Next, Hesiod tells the fable of the hawk and the nightingale (vv. 202–212), addressing it to kings who are *phronéontes*, or "aware" (v. 202). Again the tone is pessimistic, at least in the immediate context: the hawk seizes the nightingale, described as an *aoidós* ("singer," that is, poet; v. 208), simply because he is more powerful (vv. 206, 207, 210), and he boasts of having the ultimate power of either releasing or devouring his victim (v. 209).

At this point Hesiod turns to Perses and, applying all that he has just told him, concludes by urging his brother to espouse *díkē* and reject *húbris* (*Works and Days* 213). He warns that the fulfillment of *díkē* is an eventual process, and that *díkē* will in the end triumph over *húbris* (vv. 217–218). Personified as a goddess, Díkē will punish greedy men who "sort out divine laws [verb, *krínō*; noun, *thémis*] with crooked judgments [*díkē*]" (vv. 220–223), and "who drive her out, making her not straight" (v. 224; compare *Iliad* 16.387–388). Then follows the paradigm of the two cities: the city of *díkē* becomes fertile and rich (vv. 225–237; compare *Odyssey* 19.109–114), while the city of *húbris* becomes sterile and poor (vv. 238–247).

Having defined justice as an eventual process (*Works and Days* 217–218), Hesiod invites the greedy kings to reconsider "this judgment [*díkē*]" that they had wanted to pronounce in response to the forcible taking of Hesiod's property by Perses (v. 39). We now see that kings who make "this judgment" (v. 269) are thereby making the goddess Díkē "not straight" (v. 224), and that the goddess will eventually punish such men through the power of her father, Zeus (vv. 220–224, 256–269). The eventuality of justice is also clearly defined in the poetry of Solon: men who forcibly take the property of others (frag. 4.13) are thereby guilty of *húbris* (v. 8) in violating the foundations of Díkē (v. 14), who will come to exact just punishment "with the passage of time" (v. 16).

The *Works and Days* dramatizes the actual passage of time required for the workings of Díkē. At the beginning of the poem, we find the goddess implicitly violated through the forcible taking of Hesiod's property by Perses and through the crooked judgment pronounced in the unjust brother's favor by the greedy kings. At verse 39 "this judgment" is still implicitly crooked as the poet begins to teach about Díkē, and the initial teachings are still pessimistic about the outcome of the struggle between *húbris* and *díkē*, as also about the power of the hawk/king over the nightingale/poet. By the time we reach verses 249 and 269, however, "this judgment" is seen in the light of the vengeance that Díkē herself will take on those who violated her. Perses is now urged to espouse *díkē* in the sense of "justice" (v. 275), since

those without it will devour each other like wild beasts (vv. 275–278).

The moral of the fable about the hawk and the nightingale hereby becomes explicit: the hawk/king who threatens to devour the nightingale/poet as proof of his power is utterly disqualified as an exponent of justice. Moreover, since only those kings who are *phronéontes* (aware) will understand the fable (v. 202; compare the idealized kings at *Theogony* 88, who are *ekhéphrones* [aware]), the greedy kings are implicitly disqualified even from understanding the moral, in view of their general ignorance (see *Works and Days* 40–41). And if the kings cannot be exponents of justice, they are utterly without authority and their raison d'être is annihilated. In fact, after verse 263, the kings are never heard of again in the *Works and Days*.

As for Perses, he is being taught that, in the end, it is the man of justice who gets rich (vv. 280–281), while the man who forcibly takes the property of others (vv. 320–324) will have wealth "only for a short while" (vv. 325–326). By the time we reach verse 396 of the *Works and Days*, Perses has been reduced to utter penury and now comes to beg from Hesiod. But the poet refuses to give him anything, teaching him instead to work the land for a living (vv. 396–397). While the authority of justice as emanating from Zeus and as represented by Hesiod is taking hold, even the sense of indignation originally felt by the poet against his brother begins to recede; already by verse 286, he is expressing his good intentions toward Perses. Toward the latter half of the poem, the figure of Perses recedes in favor of a generalized second person singular: it is as if Perses were now tacitly ready to accept the teachings of his righteous brother.

In the end, then, *díkē* (justice) is totally vindicated in the *Works and Days*, and its eventual triumph is dramatized in the time that elapses in the course of the poem. Moreover, the function of the king as the authority who tells what is and what is not *thémis* (divine law) by way of his *díkē* (judgment) is taken over by the poem.

The vantage point is Panhellenic, in that all the cities of the Hellenes are reduced to two extreme types, the city of *díkē* (vv. 225–237) and the city of *húbris* (vv. 238–247). Even the consistently plural use of *basileîs* (kings) in the *Works and Days* suggests a Panhellenic perspective: from the Homeric tradition we see that each city is ruled by a single king.

With the elimination of kings, the *Works and Days* can address itself to any city of, say, the eighth century or thereafter—whether its government is an oligarchy, a democracy, or even a tyranny. And what the poem in effect communicates is the universal foundation of the law codes native to each Greek city-state.

Even in a democracy like Athens, the laws of Solon, as his own poetry proclaims, are founded on the authority of Zeus as king (frag. 31). Just as Zeus is the one who "straightens what is crooked and withers the overweening" (*Works and Days* 7), as he is implored by Hesiod to "straighten the divine laws with *díkē*" (v. 9), so also Solon's Eunomíē (good government by way of good laws) is a goddess who "shackles those without *díkē*" (frag. 4.33), "blackens *húbris*" (4.34), "withers the sprouting outgrowths of derangement" (4.35), and "straightens crooked judgments [*díkē*]" (4.36). In the *Theogony* we find that Zeus himself fathered Eunomíē, as well as Díkē (v. 902); moreover, their mother is Thémis, the incarnation of divine law and order (v. 901), and it is significant that Zeus married her after defeating Typhoeus and swallowing Metis, the last two remaining threats to cosmic order.

Assuming the stance of a lawgiver, Solon says in his poetry that he "wrote down" his laws after having adjusted "a *díkē* that is straight" for the noble and the base alike (frag. 36.18–20). But besides this written law code, we must also keep in mind the poetic traditions attributed to Solon; and in these traditions the figure of Solon functions not only as a lawgiver, as we see here, but also as a personal exponent of *díkē* by virtue of his life as dramatized through his poetry. In one poem, for example, Solon prays to the Muses that they give him

wealth and fame (frag. 13.1–4), and that they should allow him to help his friends and hurt his enemies (13.5–6). He yearns to own possessions but renounces any thought of forcibly taking any from others, which would be "without *díkē*" (13.7–8); sooner or later, *díkē* would have revenge (13.8). More specifically, deeds of *húbris* will surely be punished by Zeus, who appears like a violent wind (13.16–25; compare again *Iliad* 16.384–392).

In the poetic traditions of Megara, as represented by the oligarchical Theognis, we find a remarkable parallel: here too the poet prays to Zeus that he may help his friends and hurt his enemies (vv. 337–338). If Theognis could only exact retribution, by the time he dies, from those who had wronged him, then he would have the fame of a god among men (vv. 339–340). We may note the similarity between this aspiration and what happens to Lycurgus of Sparta: this lawgiver is declared to be like a god by Apollo's oracle at Delphi (Herodotus, 1.65.3) and is made a cult hero after death (1.66.1). Theognis goes on to say how he has been personally wronged: his possessions were forcibly taken from him (Theognis, 346–347). So too with Hesiod: Perses had forcibly taken some of his possessions (*Works and Days* 37, in conjunction with 320).

Like Hesiod, moreover, Theognis initially admits pessimism about any success at retribution (v. 345), and in his apparent helplessness he expresses the ghastly urge to drink the blood of those who had wronged him (v. 349). The cryptic mention here of a *daímōn* (spirit) who would supervise such a vengeance (vv. 349–350) reminds us of the countless invisible *phúlakes* (guardians) of Díkē who stand ready to punish wrongdoers in *Works and Days* 249–255 and who are identical to the *daímones* of stylized cult heroes at verses 122–126 (see J. P. Vernant, *Mythe et pensée*, pp. 21–22). The guardians of Díkē are described as coefficients of Díkē, who is likewise pictured as standing ready to punish wrongdoers (*Works and Days* 256–262); similarly in the poetry of Solon, it is Díkē who in due time punishes wrongdoers (frag. 4.14–16). Theognis, however, has conjured up the starker alternative of a bloodthirsty revenant, who may even turn out to be the poet's own self after death.

Although the particulars may vary, Theognis, like Hesiod and Solon, is presented through his poetry as a personal exponent of *díkē* by virtue of his life as dramatized through his poetry. But, unlike Solon's poetry, which can refer to the *díkē* of a written law code as well (frag. 36.18–20), the poetry of Theognis can refer only to the *díkē* that emerges from his teachings, addressed to his young *hetaîros* (comrade) Kyrnos and to various minor characters. Still, this *díkē* has the force of a law code handed down by a lawgiver, as Theognis himself proclaims: "I must pronounce this *díkē*, Kyrnos, along a straight line and norm, and give equal portion to both sides, with the help of seers, portents, and burning sacrifice, so that I may not incur shameful reproach for veering" (vv. 543–546). Like Solon, who protects "both sides" and allows "neither side" to win (frag. 5.5/6), Theognis presents himself as giving an equal share to "both sides" (v. 544), elsewhere advising Kyrnos to walk "the middle road" (vv. 219–220, 331–332) and to give to "neither side" that which belongs to the other (v. 332).

The fact that Theognis pronounces "this *díkē*" (v. 544) in a setting of sacrifice and ritual correctness (v. 545) is significant in view of Hesiod's instructions in the latter part of the *Works and Days*, where moral and ritual correctness are consistently made parallel. At verses 333–335, Hesiod's concluding injunction to shun "deeds without *díkē*" is followed up by this further advice:

> To the best of your ability, sacrifice to the immortal gods in a holy and pure manner, burning sumptuous thigh-portions; and at other times propitiate them with libations and burnt offerings, both when you go to bed and when the holy light comes back, so that they may have a gracious heart and disposition, and so you may buy another man's holding, rather than have him buy yours.
>
> (336–341)

As the *Works and Days* proceeds, the advice becomes more and more meticulous: for example, one must not cut one's nails at a "feast of the gods" (vv. 742–743). Or again, a man must not urinate while standing up and facing the sun (v. 727), nor on a road (v. 729), nor into rivers or springs (vv. 757–758). We may compare the parallel advice in the Indic *Law Code of Manu* 4.45–50: "Let him not void urine on a road . . . nor while he walks or stands, nor on reaching the bank of a river. . . . Let him never void faeces or urine . . . while looking towards a Brahman, the sun, water, or cows."

The legal traditions of the Indic peoples are clearly cognate with those of the Greeks, and in this connection it is especially interesting to observe the use of *memnēménos* (being mindful) at *Works and Days* 728, in the specific context of the injunctions now being considered, as well as elsewhere (*Works and Days* 298, 422, 616, 623, 641, 711). The root *men-/ *menh-/ *mneh- of *me-mnē-ménos* recurs in the Indic name Mánu-, meaning "the mindful one": this ancestor of the human race gets his name (which is cognate with English *man*) by virtue of being "mindful" at a sacrifice. Manu is the prototypical sacrificer, whose sheer virtuosity in what Sylvain Lévi has called "the delicate art of sacrifice" confers upon him an incontestable authority in matters of ritual. Since ritual correctness is the foundation of Indic law, the entire Indic corpus of legal/moral aphorisms is named after him.

There is a parallel thematic pattern in the *Precepts of Cheiron*, a poem attributed to Hesiod (scholia to Pindar, *Pythian* 6.22) in which Cheiron the Centaur instructs the boy Achilles. The one fragment that we have (frag. 283) contains the initial words spoken by the centaur, in which he tells Achilles that the very first thing the young hero must do when he arrives home is to sacrifice to the gods. In a fragment from the Epic Cycle (*Titanomachy*, frag. 6, p. 111, Allen ed.), Cheiron is described as the one who "led the race of mortals to justice [*dikaiosúnē*] by showing them oaths, festive sacrifices, and the configurations of Olympus." There are also parallel formal patterns shared by the *Precepts* and by the *Works and Days* (336–337, 687–688), as well as by Theognis (99–100, 1145 in conjunction with 1147–1148).

The interaction between Cheiron and Achilles in the *Precepts of Cheiron* is so strikingly similar to the one between Hesiod and Perses and the one between Theognis and Kyrnos that F. G. Welcker was led to propose, in the preface to his 1826 edition of Theognis, that Perses and Kyrnos are generic figures whose dramatized familiarity with Hesiod and Theognis makes it possible for these poets to offer well-intended advice to their audiences, who really consist of strangers. Such Near Eastern typological parallels as *Ahiqar and Nadan* and the *Proverbs of Solomon* add to the probability that these figures are indeed generic. Nevertheless, at least in the case of Perses, Martin West and other scholars resist accepting this probability, primarily because the historicity of even Hesiod is thereby endangered, "and no one supposes Hesiod himself to be an assumed character."

Throughout this presentation it has been generally argued that the persona of the poet in any given archaic Greek poem is but a function of the traditions inherited by that poem; accordingly, West's specific argument requires no ad hoc rebuttal here. Suffice it for now to observe that there are analogues to the complementary characterizations of Hesiod and Perses even in Homeric poetry. One example is the challenge issued by Odysseus to the suitor Eurymakhos at *Odyssey* 18.366–375: the resourceful king, disguised as beggar-poet, is challenging the idle usurper of his possessions to a hypothetical contest (the word for which is *éris* [strife], at 18.366; compare *Works and Days* 11–26, esp. v. 26) in "working the land" (the word for which is *érgon*, again at 18.366, and also at 18.369; compare *Works and Days* 20, for example).

Or again, there are analogues to the complementary characterizations of Theognis and Kyrnos in the *Works and Days*. For example, Hesiod pointedly teaches that one should not make one's *hetaîros* (comrade) equal to one's own brother (v. 707). This negative injunction then becomes an excuse for displaying the poetic traditions available for teaching a *hetaîros* instead of a brother, since Hesiod goes on to say in the next verse: "but if you should do so [make your *hetaîros* equal to your own brother], then...."

What follows in the next several verses is a veritable string of aphorisms that deal precisely with the topic of behavior toward one's *hetaîros* (vv. 707–722), and there are numerous striking analogues to the aphorisms explicitly or implicitly offered by Theognis to his *hetaîros* Kyrnos (for instance, *Works and Days* 710–711, 717–718, 720 and Theognis 155–158, 945, 1089–1090, respectively). Conversely, Theognis pointedly defines a true friend as a man who puts up with a difficult *hetaîros* as if he were his brother (vv. 97–100). By implication, one simply has to put up with a difficult brother. Theognis is uncertain whether his being a friend to Kyrnos is actually reciprocated: he challenges the fickle youth either to be a genuine friend (v. 89) or to declare that he is an enemy, overtly starting a *neîkos* (quarrel) between them (vv. 89–90). We may compare the *neîkos* between Hesiod and Perses, which is indeed overt (*Works and Days* 35) but at least is settled in the course of the poem. By contrast, no overt *neîkos* ever develops between Theognis and Kyrnos, and neither is Theognis ever assured that Kyrnos is a genuine friend.

In reckoning with different samples of archaic Greek poetry, we must of course avoid the assumption that parallel passages are a matter of text referring to text; rather, it is simply that any given composition may refer to traditions other than the ones that primarily shaped it, and such different traditions may be attested elsewhere. Still, it is almost as if Theognis here were alluding to a Perses, or as if Hesiod were actually giving advice on how to treat a fickle Kyrnos.

Hesiod and Perses are not the only key characters in the *Works and Days*. Their father's very essence retells some of the key themes that shape the composition. He came from Kyme in Asia Minor (v. 636), sailing the seas in an effort to maintain his meager subsistence (vv. 633–634), until he settled on the mainland at Askra, a place that is harsh in the winter, unpleasant in the summer—in short, never agreeable (vv. 639–640).

This description of Hesiod's Askra, generally accepted as empirical truth by scholars from Strabo onward, seems exaggerated at best: the region is in fact fertile, relatively protected from winds, replete with beautiful scenery, and actually mild in the winter as well as the summer (P. W. Wallace, "Hesiod and the Valley of the Muses," p. 8). Why, then, does Hesiod present a deliberately negative picture of his native Askra? The answer emerges when we reconsider the city of Kyme, which, in sharp contrast with Askra, is the place that Hesiod's father left, "fleeing from poverty, not from wealth" (*Works and Days* 637–638). We see here a pointed contrast with a theme characteristic of *ktísis* (foundation) poetry, a genre that concerned itself with the great colonizations launched toward distant lands from cities of the mainland and its periphery (for a collection of fragments and commentary, see the 1947 dissertation of Benno Schmid).

One of the thematic conventions of foundation poetry is that the great new cities that sprang up in Asia Minor and elsewhere in the era of colonizations were founded by intrepid adventurers fleeing from the poverty that overwhelmed them in the old cities. A worthy example is Kolophon, one of whose founders was "the man in rags," Rhákios, who got his name "because of his poverty and shabby clothes" (scholia to Apollonius of Rhodes, 1.308). So also in the poetic traditions of Megara, which celebrated the city's role as starting point for the foundation of many great cities in the era of colonizations (see K. Hanell, *Megarische Studien*, pp. 95–97), Theognis urges that one must travel over land and sea in search of relief from baneful poverty (vv. 179–180). In sum, when

Hesiod's father traveled all the way to Askra from Kyme, thereby fleeing poverty, he was in effect reversing the conventional pattern of colonization as narrated in foundation poetry.

To repeat, we have here a pointed negative reference as well: Hesiod's father fled from poverty and did not flee from wealth. The theme of wealth conjures up a distinctive feature of foundation poetry, where the colonizers advance from rags to riches, eventually making their new cities fabulously wealthy. Again a worthy example is the city of Kolophon, which in time grew excessively rich (Athenaeus, 12.526a, quoting Xenophanes of Kolophon frag. 3). From Theognis, 1103–1104 we learn that the mark of this excess was *húbris* (outrage), which led to Kolophon's utter destruction. This fate, as the poet warns, is now looming over Megara as well. Further, we see that the *húbris* afflicting Megara is manifested specifically as greed for the possessions of others, and that it brings about the ultimate debasement of the city's nobility (Theognis, 833–836).

Such warnings about debasement and even destruction by *húbris* recall the Hesiodic scheme of the two cities: while the city of *díkē* becomes fertile and rich (*Works and Days* 225–236), so that no one needs to sail the seas for a living (vv. 236–237), the city of *húbris* becomes sterile and poor (vv. 238–247), and its people are afflicted either by wars (v. 246) or by the storms that Zeus sends against them as they sail the seas (v. 247). From the standpoint of foundation poetry, as we have seen in the instance of Kolophon, the same city can begin at one extreme and end at the other. As he leaves Kyme, Hesiod's father flees the poverty of a city implicitly ruined by *húbris* (*Works and Days* 637–638), and he is in effect fleeing from the debris of what had been the golden age of colonization (for a Homeric reference to foundation poetry, specifically to narrative conventions that picture colonization in a golden age setting, see *Odyssey* 9.116–141).

Settling down in Askra, Hesiod's father has found a setting marked by a stylized harshness that conjures up the iron age. Whereas *díkē* and *húbris* characterize the golden and the silver ages, respectively (*Works and Days* 124, 134), both characterize the iron age simultaneously. So too with Askra: it is neither a city of *díkē* nor a city of *húbris*. Still, the place is full of characteristics that pull in one direction or the other. For example, the name Askrḗ itself means "sterile oak" (Hesychius, s.v.). While barrenness marks the city of outrage (*Works and Days* 242–244), a fertile acorn-bearing oak is a prime image in the city of *díkē* (vv. 232–233: note here the phonetic similarity of *drûs/ákrē* [top of the oak] with Askrḗ). The local lore as reported by Pausanias (9.29.1) has it that Askra was founded by Oíoklos (he who is famous for his sheep; compare *Works and Days* 234 and *Theogony* 26), son of a personified Askra who mated with Poseidon, and by Otos and Ephialtes, who were also the first to sacrifice on Helikon to the Muses. These two brothers, however, are elsewhere clearly exponents of *húbris* (*Odyssey* 11.305–320, especially 317 in conjunction with *Works and Days* 132, preliminary to the destruction of the Silver Generation because of their outrage, v. 134).

As we have seen earlier, the struggle of *díkē* against *húbris* in the iron age of mankind appears at first to be a lost cause, but the corresponding struggle, in Askra, of Hesiod as exponent of *díkē* against Perses as exponent of *húbris* turns into a universal triumph for justice and for the authority of Zeus. In this light we may consider the meaning of the name Pérsēs. Since this character, unlike Hesiod, is confined to the *Works and Days*, the meaning may have something to do with the central themes inherited by this composition. Now the form Pérsēs is a residual variant, through a split in declensional patterns, of Perseús, and we may compare such other formal pairs as Kíssēs (*Iliad* 11.223) and classical Kisseús. Moreover, the form Perseús is related to the compound formant *persi-* of the verb *pérthō* (destroy), and it is not without interest that the direct objects of *pérthō* are confined in Homeric diction to *pólis* (city), its synonyms *ptolíethron* and *ástu*, or the

name of a *pólis*. Since Perses is primarily an exponent of *húbris* in the *Works and Days*, we may recall the traditional theme expressed by Theognis: *húbris* destroys the city (vv. 1103–1104, for example).

Of course *húbris* destroys cities only figuratively: more precisely, it is Zeus who destroys cities because of their *húbris*—which is actually what he does to the archetypal city of *húbris* at *Works and Days* 238–247. In this sense the name Pérsēs formalizes the negative side of what Zeus does to those marked by *húbris*. Thus it may be significant that Perses is addressed as *díon génos* (descendant of Zeus) by his brother Hesiod at *Works and Days* 299—and that this title is elsewhere applied only to the children of Zeus (for instance, Artemis at *Iliad* 9.538). Moreover, from the fifth century onward, the name of the father of Hesiod and Perses is attested as *Díos* (see, for example, Ephorus of Kyme, F. Jacoby, *Fragmente der griechischen Historiker*, 70 F 1). Thus the split between Hesiod and Perses as exponents of *díkē* and *húbris*, corresponding to the split between the city of *díkē* and the city of *húbris*, is genetically reconciled in a figure whose name carries the essence of Zeus, much as Hesiod and Perses become reconciled in the course of the *Works and Days* through the utter defeat of *húbris* by the *díkē* of Zeus.

Hesiod's pervasive affinities with Zeus, as with Apollo and his Olympian Muses, are paralleled by his affinities with the goddess Hekate as she is celebrated in *Theogony* 404–452. Like Zeus, this goddess is an ideal paradigm for the Panhellenic nature of Hesiodic poetry. Thanks to the sanctions of the supreme god (*Theogony* 411–415, 423–425), Hekate has title to a share in the divine functions of all the gods (vv. 421–422). Accordingly, the invocation of Hekate at a sacrifice is tantamount to a blanket invocation of all the other gods as well (vv. 416–420). Because of her relatively recent, maybe even foreign, origins, this synthetic goddess Hekate is an ideal Panhellenic figure (compare the choice of "foreign" Nyse as the genuine birthplace of Dionysus in *Homeric Hymn* 1.8–9): she can manifest even her ritual dimensions in Hesiodic poetry, unlike the historically older gods who are each worshiped in different ways by each city-state—and whose ritual dimensions are therefore consistently screened out by the Panhellenic poems of Hesiod as well as Homer.

The parallelism of Hekate with Apollo and his Muses also has a bearing on the Panhellenic authority of Hesiod. We start with the fact that Apollo and Hekate are actually cousins: their mothers, Leto and Asteríē, are sisters (*Theogony* 405–410), and the latter name is identical to the "god-given" name of Delos, Apollo's birthplace (Pindar, *Paean* 5.42 in conjunction with *Hymn* 1, frag. 33c.4, Snell and Maehler ed.). The shared grandparents of Apollo and Hekate are Phoíbē and Koîos; the first name is the feminine equivalent of Apollo's primary epithet Phoîbos (as at *Theogony* 14), while the second is cognate with the Indic *kaví* (poet/seer) (see above for a discussion of Apollo's relationship to the generic *aoidós* [singer/poet] and *mántis* [seer]). The name Hekátē is the feminine equivalent of Apollo's epithet Hékatos (as at *Hymn to Apollo* 1). Most important, the name of Hekate's father, Pérsēs (*Theogony* 409), is identical to that of Hesiod's brother.

Hekate is the only legitimate child of Pérsēs the god, and as such she is *mounogenēs* (*Theogony* 426, 448). By contrast, Perses the man is distinctly not the only child of Dios, being the brother of Hesiod, who in turn implicitly wishes he were an only child: he advises that the ideal household should indeed have a *mounogenēs* (only child) to inherit the possessions of the father (*Works and Days* 376–377). What would happen if Hekate were not an only child is suggested by the story about the birth of Eris (strife) in *Works and Days* 11–26, presented as a traditional alternative to the story reflected in *Theogony* 225.

The *Works and Days* affirms that there is not just a *moûnon . . . génos* (single birth) of Eris (v. 11), as we see in the *Theogony* (v. 225), but that there are in fact two Erides (*Works and Days* 11–12). The younger and secondary one of these Erides is negative in her stance toward mankind, but the older and primary one is positive: she instills the spirit of competition, which motivates even the idler to work the land for a living (*Works and Days* 12–24). In that Eris is the parent of Neîkos (quarreling; *Theogony* 229), the *neîkos* between Hesiod and Perses (*Works and Days* 35) is motivated by Eris. At first it seems as if it had been the maleficent and secondary Eris that had done so, but as the quarrel eventually reaches a resolution with the triumph of Hesiod's *díkē* over Perses' *húbris* in the *Works and Days*, we realize that it must have been the beneficent and primary Eris all along. The point is, just as an undivided negative Eris can split into a primary positive and secondary negative pair, so an undivided positive Hekate could by implication split into a primary negative and a secondary positive pair. Thus it is beneficial for mankind that Hekate should remain an only child: the primary child in a hypothetical split of the *mounogenēs* Hekate figure would presumably take after the father Pérsēs, whose name conveys the negative response of gods to the *húbris* of mankind. Similarly, Hesiod and Perses are a primary positive and secondary negative pair, and the secondary child Pérsēs has a name that conveys, again, the negative response of Zeus to the *húbris* of mankind. As for the father of Hesiod and Perses, his name, Dîos—to repeat—carries the essence of Zeus.

The special thematic relationship of Hesiod with the figure of Hekate raises questions about a revealing detail in the *Works and Days*. Despite all the advice given by Hesiod to Perses about sailing, the poet pointedly says that he himself has never sailed on a ship except for the one time when he traveled from Aulis to the island of Euboea (vv. 650–651). There follows a pointed reference to the tradition that the Achaean expedition to Troy was launched from Aulis (vv. 651–653). The *Iliad* acknowledges Aulis as the starting point of the Trojan expedition (2.303–304), and according to most versions it was there that Agamemnon sacrificed his daughter Iphigeneia to Artemis (for instance, *Cypria*, Proclus summary, p. 104.12–20,

Allen ed.). In the Hesiodic *Catalogue of Women* (frag. 23a.15–26), we read that the sacrificed Iphigeneia (here called Iphimede, vv. 15, 17) was thereupon made immortal by Artemis, and that as a goddess Iphigeneia became Artemis-of-the-Crossroads (vv. 25–26), otherwise known as Hekate (Hesiod, frag. 23b = Pausanias 1.43.1).

Hekate, as the *Theogony* (vv. 435–438) tells us, aids those who compete in contests, and the poet cites athletic contests in particular. When Hesiod crosses over from Aulis to Euboea, he is traveling to an occasion of contests, the Funeral Games of Amphidamas at Chalkis (*Works and Days* 654–656). Moreover, Hesiod competes in a poetic contest at the games—and wins (vv. 656–657). He goes home with a tripod as prize, and dedicates it to his native Helikonian Muses (vv. 657–658). Finishing his narrative about the prize that he won in the poetic contest, Hesiod pointedly says again that this episode marks the only time that he ever made a sea voyage (v. 660).

Hesiod's only sea voyage is ostentatiously brief, with the distance between Aulis and Euboea amounting to some 65 meters of water. There is a built-in antithesis here with the long sea voyage undertaken by the Achaeans when they sailed to Troy. Perhaps the antithesis was meant to extend further: Aulis is an original setting for the *Catalogue of Ships* tradition, transferred to a Trojan setting in the *Iliad* only because this particular epic starts the action in the final year of the war. But even the *Iliad* acknowledges Aulis as the starting point of the Achaean flotilla. Moreover, the strong Homeric emphasis on navigation as a key to the Achaeans' survival (for example, *Iliad* 16.80–82) is in sharp contrast with the strong Hesiodic emphasis on the poet's personal inexperience in navigation—especially in view of Hesiod's additional emphasis on Aulis as the starting point for not only his short sea voyage but also for the long one undertaken by the Achaeans. Perhaps, then, this passage reveals an intended differentiation of Hesiodic from Homeric poetry.

In this light it is not out of place to consider a variant verse reported by the scholia at *Works and Days* 657. In this variant we find Hesiod declaring that his adversary in the poetic contest that he won was none other than Homer himself:

> defeating god-like Homer in song, at Chalkis

instead of

> winning in song, [I say that I] got a tripod
> with handles on it

There is no proof that this variant verse is a mere interpolation (from an epigram containing the same verse, ascribed to Hesiod in *Certamen*, p. 233.213–214, Allen ed.). Also, to argue that this verse may be part of a genuine variant passage is not to say that the surviving version about the tripod is therefore not genuine. In archaic Greek poetry, reported variants may at any time reflect not some false textual alteration but, rather, a genuine traditional alternative that has been gradually ousted in the course of the poem's crystallization into a fixed text.

Furthermore, there is an attested traditional story that tells of the contest of Homer and Hesiod (*Certamen*, pp. 225–238, Allen ed.), juxtaposing the *Life of Homer* and the *Life of Hesiod* traditions. In its present form it is a late and accretive reworking that has generated much controversy about its authorship, a problem that cannot be addressed here. One thing is sure, however: the basic premise of the story—that Homer and Hesiod competed in a poetic contest—exhibits the characteristics of a traditional theme. This theme, moreover, corresponds to a basic truth about archaic Greek society: the performance of poetry, from the days of the oral poets all the way to the era of the rhapsodes, was by its nature a matter of competition.

PROSPECTS

A definitive assessment of Hesiod's poems is elusive, since we still know so little about their background. The best hope is that there will be further progress in rigorous internal analysis and in systematic comparison with other attested Greek poetic traditions, so that tomorrow's reader may better appreciate the mechanics and aesthetics of Hesiodic poetry. Even so, we shall always fall far short, unable ever to recover all that this poetry presupposes of its own audience at large.

To treat Hesiod simply as an author will only accentuate our inability, in that he represents a culmination of what must have been countless successive generations of singers interacting with their audiences throughout the Greek-speaking world. Whatever poetic devices we admire in the poems have been tested many thousands of times, we may be sure, on the most discerning audiences. Even the unmistakable signs of a Hesiodic poem's structural unity are surely the result of streamlining by the tradition itself, achieved in the continuous process of a poem's being recomposed in each new performance.

With the important added factor of Panhellenic diffusion, however, the successive recompositions of Hesiodic poetry could in time become ever less varied, more and more crystallized, as the requirements of composition became increasingly universalized. Of course the rate of such crystallization, and even the date, could have been different in each poem or even in different parts of the same poem. From this point of view, we can in principle include as Hesiodic even a composition like the *Shield of Herakles,* though it may contain references to the visual arts datable to the early sixth century. Scholars are too quick to dismiss this poem as not a genuine work on the basis of the dating alone, and it then becomes all the easier for them to underrate its artistic qualities on the ground that it is merely an imitation of Hesiod.

Critics also have noticed that the conclusion of the *Theogony* at verses 901–1020 is formally and even stylistically distinct from the previous parts of the poem. But this part is also functionally distinct from the rest, and we may note in general that different themes in oral poetry tend to exhibit different trends in formal—even linguistic—development. To put it another way: different contexts are characterized by different language. An explanation along these lines is surely preferable to a favorite scenario of many experts, in which the *Theogony* was somehow composed by a combination of one Hesiod and a plethora of pseudo-Hesiods. Worse still, some will even attribute the constitution of the poem to a dreary succession of redactors. Whatever the arguments for multiple authorship may be, there is predictably little agreement about how much or how little can be attributed to the real Hesiod. In sum, it seems preferable to treat all Hesiodic poems, including the fragments, as variable manifestations of a far more extensive phenomenon, which is Hesiodic poetry.

Another obstacle to our understanding of Hesiodic poetry, perhaps even harder to overcome, is the commonplace visualization of Hesiod as a primitive landlubber of a peasant who is struggling to express himself in a cumbersome and idiosyncratic poetic medium clumsily forged out of an epic medium that he has not fully mastered. Hesiod's self-dramatization as one who works the land for a living is thus assumed to be simply a historical fact, which can then serve as a basis for condescending speculations about an eighth-century Boeotian peasant's lowly level of thinking. It is as if the poetry of Homer and Hesiod were primitive raw material that somehow became arbitrarily universalized by the Greeks as a point of reference for their poetry and rhetoric in particular, and as the foundation of their civilization in general. Of course, if critics go on to treat such poetry as a producer rather than a product of the Greek poetic heritage, it is easy to find fault whenever we fail to understand. Over the years Hesiod especially has been condemned for many offenses against the sensibilities of modern literary critics. Perhaps the most shortsighted of the many charges leveled against him is that he is, on occasion, capable of forgetting his starting point.

There are, to be sure, those who have articulately conveyed the cohesiveness and precision of Hesiodic poetry. I single out the work of Jean-Pierre Vernant, whose findings about such key Hesiodic themes as Prometheus and the ascendancy of Zeus are so definitive that no attempt has been made here to offer a summary. There is also the work of Peter Walcot, whose repertoire of Near Eastern parallels to aspects of the *Theogony* and the *Works and Days* serves to illuminate the inner workings of Hesiodic composition. The value of these analogues is not to be underrated, and the absence of any mention of them up to this point may now be remedied by citing Martin West's commentaries, which contain an illustrative collection of references. It is worth noting, however, that such Near Eastern parallelisms may in any given instance be a matter of typology rather than of direct borrowing. Given the universality of mythopoeic thinking, even the most striking convergences in detail may turn out to be nothing more than a typological analogue: we are reminded of the Inca parallels to the Pandora myth, which seem closer to the Hesiodic version than do some of the Near Eastern parallels generally cited as Hesiod's "sources."

One of the most neglected areas in the general study of Hesiod, as also in this specific presentation, is the artistry of the poems. With our fragmentary understanding of the Hesiodic tradition, some special effects that would have delighted the intended audience will be forever lost to us, while others will emerge only in their barest outlines. It seems appropriate to bring this survey to a close with one such dimly perceived set of special effects, illustrating simultaneously the richness of the poetry and our own poverty of understanding.

In *Works and Days* 504–563, a much-admired passage about the harshness of winter, the North Wind is described as it descends upon trees along the side of a mountain, penetrating the skin of all living things in its path with its cold blast (vv. 507–518). The imagery here is pointedly sexual, as a study by Calvert Watkins of parallel imagery in other Indo-European traditions clearly shows. Then follows (vv. 519–525) the contrasting image of a sen-

suous young girl taking a bath in her warm and comfortable boudoir, safely sheltered from the piercing wind and "not yet knowing the ways of golden Aphrodite" (v. 521); meanwhile, the *anósteos* (boneless one) is gnawing at his own foot in his cold and wretched haunts (vv. 524–525). Now the word *anósteos* is paralleled as Indic *anasthá-* (boneless one), a kenning for "penis," while the Greek word for "gnaw," *tendó* (v. 525), is related to the Irish *teinm* (*laído*), "gnawing (of marrow)," a magical process leading to knowledge by divination. Thus the "boneless one," by gnawing his foot, "knows," in contrast with the inexperienced young girl.

But the allusiveness extends even further. The "boneless one" is also to be understood as an octopus (compare the syntax of *Words and Days* 524, containing *anósteos*, with that of Hesiod, frag. 204.129, containing *átrikhos* [hairless one], or snake), an animal that is conventionally pictured in Greek lore as eating its own feet when it is hungry. The hungry octopus eating its foot is described as living in cold and wretched haunts (*Works and Days* 525), and this image of poverty takes us back to an earlier image of a poor man in winter, holding his swollen foot in his emaciated hand (vv. 496–497); the Proclus commentary here cites an Ephesian law to the effect that a child could not be exposed until his father's feet were swollen with famine. Our thoughts turn to Oidípous, "he whose feet are swollen," and the story of his exposure.

In this connection we come to yet another occurrence of the word *poús* (foot) in this passage about winter: at *Works and Days* 533–535, the winter storm is described as making everyone hunch over like a *trípous* (three-footed) man (v. 533; compare v. 518). This kenning, which designates a man leaning on a walking stick, corresponds to the *aínigma* (riddle) of the Sphinx as solved by Oidípous (Sophocles, *Oedipus Rex* 393, 1525). Like the "boneless one" who "gnaws" his foot and thereby knows by divination (*Works and Days* 524), Oedipus knows by virtue of solving the riddle of the

Sphinx. The oracular tone of this passage is sustained later (at *Works and Days* 571) with another kenning, *pheréoikos* (he who carries his house, or snail), which is introduced by the expression *all' hopót' àn* (but whenever . . .) (v. 571), a frequent introductory phrase in oracles.

This much said, we are still typically far from understanding all the implications of this passage, just as we are far from understanding all that can be understood about Hesiod and his world.

Notes

The Hesiodic Question

Panhellenic authority of Homer and Hesiod as reported by Herodotus (2.53.2): also Xenophanes, frag. B 10 Diels-Kranz (on Homer) and Heraclitus, frag. B 57 Diels-Kranz (on Hesiod). Panhellenism as a trend verified by archaeology: Snodgrass, pp. 421, 435. The Olympian gods as a Panhellenic model: Rohde, pp. 94–95. Poetic performances at Panhellenic festivals: Nagy, p. 8, sec. 15, n.1. Further reports on recitations by rhapsodes of Archilochus and other poets: Athenaeus, 14.620c. Principle of economy as indication of performance of *Iliad* and *Odyssey*: Nagy, "Formula and Meter," pp. 245–246. Accent patterns in Homeric poetry that point to oral transmission by rhapsodes: Wackernagel, p. 1103. Mnemonic techniques used for transmission of the Vedas: Kiparsky, pp. 99–102. Indo-European poetic theme of "stitching songs" as a traditional conceit of oral poet: Durante, pp. 177–179. Constraints against deviation by poet from traditional story patterns: Nagy, pp. 265–275. Regional variety of poetic repertoires as reflected in *Iliad* 20.249: Nagy, pp. 272–274. Poetry of *ktísis* (foundation), its vulnerability to changes in population or government: Nagy, pp. 140–141, 273. Stance of Odysseus as oral poet: Nagy, pp. 233–237. Poet's implicit withholding of truth by way of explicit blaming of his *gastér* (belly): Svenbro, p. 54. Passages in *Odyssey* and elsewhere concerning the *gastér* of the generic poet: Svenbro, p. 54; Nagy, pp. 229–233. Composition of epic poetry by Phemius as described in *Odyssey* 1.326–327: Nagy, p. 97.

Hesiod, Poet of the Theogony

Etymology of Hēsíodos: Nagy, pp. 296–297; Peters, p. 14. Etymology of Hómēros and applicability of the name as epithet of Muses: Nagy, pp. 297–300. Archaeological evidence for hero cults in eighth century B.C.: Snodgrass, pp. 191–193, 398–399. Hero cults not simply "inspired" by Homeric poetry: Nagy, p. 115, sec. 28, n.4. Ideology of cult of Hesiod as built into Hesiodic poetry: Nagy, pp. 296–297. Connection of *Life of Archilochus* tradition with cult of Archilochus at Paros: Nagy, pp. 303–308. Remains of Hesiod buried at Oineon in Ozolian Lokris: see comments of Pfister, p. 231, n.861. Remains of Hesiod carried ashore by dolphins, parallel to: remains of Melikertes carried ashore, festival of Isthmian Games founded in his honor; see Pfister, pp. 214–215, n.788. Lore about Hesiod as typical of lore about cult heroes: Brelich, p. 322. "Quoting" of poems of Archilochus in the vita of Archilochus, compared to "quoting" of fables of Aesop in *Life of Aesop* tradition: Nagy, pp. 279–288. Vitae of poets as an unstable genre: Nagy, p. 306. Meaning of name Mnēsiépēs: Nagy, p. 304, sec. 4, n.3. *Homērídai* and *Kreóphuleîoi*: their "founding fathers" as cult heroes: Brelich, pp. 320–321; Nagy, pp. 8–9. Connections between quarrel of two litigants pictured on Shield of Achilles and quarrel of Agamemnon and Achilles: Muellner, pp. 105–106. Epic and catalogue poetry designated as *érga/érgmata*: *Homeric Hymn* 31.19/32.19. Epic poetry designated as *kléa phōtôn . . . hēmithéōn*: *Homeric Hymn* 32.18–19; catalogue poetry designated as *génos andrôn . . . hēmithéōn*: *Homeric Hymn* 31.18–19. Self-identification of "Homer" as composer of *Homeric Hymn to Apollo* (166–176): Nagy, pp. 5–6, 8–9. Variety of metrical forms in preludes: Koller, pp. 170–171. Compression and expansion as signs of oral poetry: Lord, pp. 99–123. Interconnection of

Theogony 965–1020 with Hesiod, frag. 1: Nagy, pp. 213–214, sec. 3, notes 1, 3. Heritage of overlap between *aoidós* (poet) and *kêrux* (herald): article by Mondi; heritage of overlap between *aoidós* and *mántis* (seer), as reflected in practice of ecstatic divination by way of fermented honey: article by Scheinberg.

Hesiod, Poet of the Works and Days

Pervasive theme, in *Works and Days*, of mankind's elevation by *díkē* (justice) and debasement by *húbris* (outrage): Vernant, *Mythe et pensée*, pp. 13–79. Fable of hawk and nightingale in *Works and Days* 202–212 as connected with *Works and Days* 801 and 828: West, p. 364. (Verse 828 was followed by further verses on the subject of *ornithomanteía* [divination by birds], which were athetized on dubious grounds by Apollonius of Rhodes and are now lost; if the *Works and Days* ended with the *ornithomanteía*, the relevance of the fable of the hawk and nightingale to the overall structure of the poem is further enhanced.) Noun *dóxa* (fame) at Solon, frag. 13.4 is parallel to related verb *dokéō* (seem) at Theognis, 339. Parallels between *Works and Days* and *Law Code of Manu*: West, pp. 334–335. Manu as prototypical sacrificer: Lévi, p. 121. Questions raised about historicity of Hesiod and Perses: West, pp. 33–34. Odysseus and suitor Eurymakhos in *Odyssey* 18.366–375 as analogous to Hesiod and brother Perses in *Works and Days*: Svenbro, pp. 57–58. Odysseus as beggar-poet: Nagy, pp. 228–242. Name Rhákios as "man of rags": Schmid, pp. 28–29. *Odyssey* 9.116–141 as reference to *ktísis* (foundation) poetry: Nagy, pp. 180–181. Stylized harshness of Askra as parallel to harshness of iron age: West, p. 197. Name Pérsēs as variant of Perseús: Perpillou, pp. 239–240. Name Perseús as related to compound formant *persi-* of verb *pérthō* (destroy): Perpillou, p. 231. Relationship of Greek *Koîos* and Indic *kavî-*: Chantraine, p. 553. *Works and Days* 11–26, split of Eris into two Erides, one positive and one negative: Nagy, pp. 313–314. Maleficent aspects of Hekate, as represented in ar-

chaic Greek iconography: Vermeule, p. 109. Distance between Aulis and Euboea: West, p. 320. Competition as a pervasive aspect of Greek poetic performance: Durante, pp. 197–198.

Prospects

Formal and stylistic distinctions between *Theogony* 901–1020 and the rest of the poem: commentary of West, ed., *Theogony*, p. 398. Inca parallels to Pandora myth: Sinclair, p. 13. Sexual imagery in *Works and Days* 507–518: Watkins, p. 231. Concept of *anósteos* (boneless one) as kenning for "penis": Watkins, p. 233. Irish *teinm* (*laído*), "gnawing of marrow," as magical process leading to knowledge by divination: Watkins, p. 232. Concept of *anósteos* as kenning for "octopus"; Greek lore about the octopus as eating its own feet when starving: West, p. 290. Riddle of Sphinx as solved by Oidípous: besides Sophocles, *Oedipus Rex* 393, 1525, see Asclepiades in F. Jacoby, ed., *Fragmente der griechischen Historiker* 12 F 7, and the comments by West, p. 293.

Appendix

The Language of Hesiod

The figure of Hesiod can proudly announce his local origins and still speak in a language that has evolved to match the language of Panhellenic hymns, which in turn have evolved to match the language of the epics that they inaugurate. The poet of the *Theogony* can even equate the artistry of composing a Panhellenic theogony with that of composing an epic (vv. 100–101)—and the ritual context that a local theogony would surely entail is for us all but forgotten.

In fact, the diction of Hesiodic poetry is so akin to the Homeric that its self-proclaimed Boeotian provenience would be nearly impossible to detect on the basis of language alone. What is more, the Ionic phase of evolution and eventual crystallization is actually even stronger in the Hesiodic tradition than in the Homeric.

Granted, there have been attempts to establish linguistic differences between Homer and Hesiod, the most interesting of which is the finding that the first- and second-declension accusative plural endings -$\bar{a}s$ and -ous occur in preconsonantal position far more often in Hesiodic than in Homeric diction; also, that in prevocalic position they occur less often (see G. P. Edwards, *The Language of Hesiod in Its Traditional Context*, pp. 141–165). This phenomenon has been interpreted to mean that we are somehow dealing with the native speaker(s) of a dialect in which these accusative plurals have been shortened to -$\breve{a}s$ and -$\breve{o}s$; this way the beginning of the next word with a consonant would not matter because the resulting -$\breve{a}s$ C- and -$\breve{o}s$ C- do not produce overlength, whereas -$\bar{a}s$ C- and -ous C- do. Now it is true that Homeric diction tends to avoid overlength (-$\bar{V}$C C- as distinct from -$\breve{V}$C C- or -$\breve{V}$ C-), but it does not follow that Hesiodic diction matches this tendency; rather, in line with the fact that the formulaic behavior of Hesiod generally reveals fewer constraints, and hence less archaism, than that of Homer, it could be that the higher proportion of preconsonantal -$\bar{a}s$ and -ous in Hesiod reveals simply a greater tolerance for this type of overlength than in Homer.

As it happens, accusative plurals ending in -$\breve{a}s$ and -$\breve{o}s$ are decidedly not a feature of the Boeotian dialect. As for the sporadic occurrences of first-declension -$\breve{a}s$ before vowels, it is not true that this phenomenon is limited to Hesiodic diction, as is generally claimed. There are sporadic occurrences in Homeric diction as well, including the *Hymns* (for instance, at *Iliad* 5.269, 8.378; *Odyssey* 17.232; *Hymn to Hermes* 106). It is difficult, granted, simply to rule out the possibility that this phenomenon is a reflex of Doric dialects, where first- and second-declension -$\breve{a}s$ V- and -$\breve{o}s$ V- are indeed attested. Still, it seems preferable to account for the entire problem in terms of the Ionic dialects, which represent the final and definitive phase in the evolution of both Homeric and

Hesiodic poetry. The formulaic evidence could go back to a pre-Ionic stage common to all Greek dialects, with accusative plurals ending in

$$-\breve{a}ns\ V\text{-} \qquad -\breve{a}ns\ C\text{-}$$
$$-\breve{o}ns\ V\text{-} \qquad -\breve{o}ns\ C\text{-}.$$

Then we may posit an intermediate stage common to all dialects (and still attested in some) with

$$-\breve{a}ns\ V\text{-} \qquad -\breve{a}s\ C\text{-}$$
$$-\breve{o}ns\ V\text{-} \qquad -\breve{o}s\ C\text{-}.$$

In the final Ionic stage, prevocalic -$\breve{a}ns$ and -$\breve{o}ns$ became -$\bar{a}s$ and -ous, which were extended to preconsonantal position as well:

$$-\bar{a}s\ V\text{-} \qquad -\bar{a}s\ C\text{-}$$
$$-ous\ V\text{-} \qquad -ous\ C\text{-}.$$

But the intermediate stage, by way of formulaic repositionings of words from prevocalic to preconsonantal contexts and vice versa, could have left sporadic traces of "contaminations":

$$-\breve{a}s\ V\text{-} \qquad -\bar{a}s\ C\text{-}$$
$$-\breve{o}s\ V\text{-} \qquad -ous\ C\text{-}.$$

There would be more such traces in Hesiodic than in Homeric poetry simply because the Hesiodic reflects a lengthier span of evolution in the Ionic hexameter tradition. The point remains: not only does Hesiodic poetry implicitly claim to be like Homeric poetry (as at *Theogony* 100–101) but it also shares fully in its formal heritage.

Even within Homeric poetry, the *Odyssey* is perceptibly different from the *Iliad* in featuring more instances of preconsonantal -$\bar{a}s$/-ous and fewer instances of prevocalic -$\bar{a}s$/-ous, although this gap between the *Odyssey* and the *Iliad* is not nearly as great as the one between the Hesiodic poems on the one hand and the Homeric on the other (R. C. M. Janko, *Studies in the Lan-*

guage of the *Homeric Hymns and the Dating of Early Greek Epic Poetry*). Still, these data correspond to an overall pattern, as established on the basis of several other linguistic criteria: the *Odyssey* had a lengthier span of evolution in the Ionic hexameter tradition than the *Iliad,* while the Hesiodic poems combined had an even lengthier span than the *Odyssey.*

The pervasive Ionic heritage of Hesiodic poetry extends from form to content. The one month name overtly mentioned in the *Works and Days, Lēnaión* (v. 504), happens to occur in many Ionian calendars (though not in the Athenian), and even the morphology (ending in *-ón*) is distinctly Ionic. Now each city-state had its own idiosyncratic calendar, and there were significant variations in the naming of months even among states that were closely related; it comes as no surprise, then, that the overt mentioning of month names was generally shunned in archaic Greek poetry, with its Panhellenic orientation. Thus it is all the more striking that an exclusively Ionic name should surface in the poetry of Boeotian Hesiod. At best we can justify the name *Lēnaión* as tending toward a Panhellenic audience in that it is native to most Ionian cities at least; moreover, the meaning of the name is transparent, in that it is derived from *lḗnai* (devotées of Dionysus). Even so, the name and its form are more Panionian than Panhellenic. Moreover, the description of the wind Boreas as it blows over the sea from Thrace in the verses immediately following the mention of *Lēnaión* reflects a geographically Ionian orientation parallel to what we find in the *Iliad.*

In sum, not only does Hesiodic poetry implicitly claim to be like Homeric poetry, but it also shares fully in its predominantly Ionic formal heritage.

Selected Bibliography

Note: An asterisk denotes a basic reference work.

Allen, T. W., ed. *Homeri Opera,* V. Oxford, 1912.

Benveniste, E. *Indo-European Language and Society,* translated by E. Palmer from the 1969 French version. Coral Gables, Fla., 1973.

Brelich, A. *Gli eroi greci.* Rome, 1958.

Chantraine, P. *Dictionnaire étymologique de la langue grecque,* I–IV. Paris, 1968–1980.

Cook, R. M. "The Date of the Hesiodic *Shield.*" *Classical Quarterly,* 31:204–214 (1937).

Detienne, M. *Les maîtres de vérité dans la Grèce archaïque,* 2nd ed. Paris, 1973.

Di Gregorio, L., ed. *Scholia vetera in Hesiodi Theogoniam.* Milan, 1975.

Dickie, M. W. "*Dike* as a Moral Term in Homer and Hesiod." *Classical Philology,* 73:91–101 (1978).

Duban, J. "Poets and Kings in the *Theogony* Invocation." *Quaderni Urbinati di Cultura Classica,* 33:7–21 (1980).

Durante, M. *Sulla preistoria della tradizione poetica greca,* II: *Risultanze della comparazione indoeuropea,* Incunabula Gracea 64. Rome, 1976.

*Edwards, G. P. *The Language of Hesiod in Its Traditional Context.* Oxford, 1971.

Evelyn-White, H. G., ed. and trans. *Hesiod, the Homeric Hymns and Homerica,* 2nd ed. Cambridge, Mass., 1936.

Finnegan, R. *Oral Poetry: Its Nature, Significance, and Social Context.* Cambridge, 1977.

Gagarin, M. "*Dikē* in the *Works and Days.*" *Classical Philology,* 68:81–94 (1973).

Giangrande, G. "Der stilistische Gebrauch der Dorismen in Epos." *Hermes,* 78:257–277 (1970).

Hanell, K. *Megarische Studien.* Lund, 1934.

Havelock, E. A. *Preface to Plato.* Cambridge, Mass., 1963.

Hunt, R. "Satiric Elements in Hesiod's *Works and Days.*" *Helios,* 8:29–40 (1981).

Janko, R. C. M. *Studies in the Language of the Homeric Hymns and the Dating of Early Greek Epic Poetry.* Ph.D. dissertation, Cambridge University, 1979.

Kiparsky, P. "Oral Poetry: Some Linguistic and Typological Considerations." Pp. 73–106 in B. A. Stolz and R. S. Shannon, eds. *Oral Literature and the Formula.* Ann Arbor, Mich., 1976.

Koller, H. "Das kitharodische Prooimion: Eine formgeschichtliche Untersuchung." *Philologus,* 100:159–206 (1956).

Lévi, S. *La doctrine du sacrifice dans les Brāhmanas.* Paris, 1966.

*Lord, A. B. *The Singer of Tales.* Cambridge, Mass., 1960.

*Merkelbach, R., and M. L. West, eds. *Fragmenta Hesiodea.* Oxford, 1967.

HESIOD

Miller, A. "The 'Address to the Delian Maidens' in the *Homeric Hymn to Apollo*: Epilogue or Transition?" *Transactions of the American Philological Association*, 109:173–186 (1979).

Minton, W. W. "Homer's Invocations of the Muses: Traditional Patterns." *Transactions of the American Philological Association*, 91:292–309 (1960).

*——. *Concordance to the Hesiodic Corpus.* Leiden, 1976.

Mondi, R. J. "CKHΠTOYXOI BACIΛEIC: An Argument for Divine Kingship in Early Greece." *Arethusa*, 13:203–216 (1980).

Muellner, L. *The Meaning of Homeric EYXOMAI through its Formulas.* Innsbruck, 1976.

Nagy, G. "Perkūnas and Perunŭ." Pp. 113–131 in *Antiquitates Indogermanicae: Gedenkschrift Hermann Güntert.* Innsbruck, 1974. On the creation myths implied by *Theogony* 35.

——. "Formula and Meter." Pp. 239–260 in B. A. Stolz and R. S. Shannon, eds. *Oral Literature and the Formula.* Ann Arbor, Mich., 1976.

——. *The Best of the Achaeans: Concepts of the Hero in Archaic Greek Poetry.* Baltimore, 1979.

Parry, A., ed. *The Making of Homeric Verse: The Collected Papers of Milman Parry.* Oxford, 1971.

*Paulson, J. *Index Hesiodeus.* Lund, 1890.

Perpillou, J.-L., *Les substantifs grecs en -EYC.* Paris, 1973.

Pertusi, A., ed. *Scholia vetera in Hesiodi Opera et dies.* Milan, 1955.

Peters, M. *Untersuchungen zur Vertretung der indogermanischen Laryngale im Griechischen.* Vienna, 1980. See p. 14 on *Hēsíodos.*

Pfister, F. *Die Reliquienkult im Altertum.* 2 vols. Giessen, 1909.

Pucci, P. *Hesiod and the Language of Poetry.* Baltimore, 1977.

Radloff, W. *Proben der Volksliteratur der nördlichen türkischen Stämme, V: Der Dialekt der Kara-Kirgisen.* St. Petersburg, 1885.

Rohde, E. *Psyche: The Cult of Souls and Belief in Immortality among the Greeks,* translated by W. B. Hillis from the 1920 German edition. New York, 1925.

*Rzach, A., ed. *Hesiodi carmina, editio maior.* Leipzig, 1902.

Scheinberg, S. "The Bee Maidens of the Homeric Hymn to Hermes." *Harvard Studies in Classical Philology,* 83:1–28 (1979).

Schmid, B. *Studien zu griechischen Ktisissagen.* Freiburg, 1947.

Schwartz, J. *Pseudo-Hesiodea.* Leiden, 1960.

Sinclair, T. A., ed. *Hesiod, Works and Days.* London, 1932.

Snodgrass, A. M. *The Dark Age of Greece: An Archaeological Survey of the Eleventh to the Eighth Centuries.* Edinburgh, 1971.

Solmsen, F., ed. *Hesiodi Theogonia, Opera et Dies, Scutum.* Oxford, 1970.

Stolz, B. A., and R. S. Shannon, eds. *Oral Literature and the Formula.* Ann Arbor, Mich., 1976.

Svenbro, J. *La parole et le marbre: Aux origines de la poétique grecque.* Lund, 1976.

Vermeule, E. *Aspects of Death in Early Greek Art and Poetry.* Berkeley, 1979.

Vernant, J.-P. *Les origines de la pensée grecque.* Paris, 1962.

——. *Mythe et pensée chez les Grecs.* 2 vols., 2nd ed., with new pagination. Paris, 1974.

——. *Mythe et société en Grèce ancienne.* Paris, 1974.

Wackernagel, J. *Kleine Schriften.* 2 vols. Göttingen, 1953.

Walcot, P. *Hesiod and the Near East.* Cardiff, 1966.

Wallace, P. W. "Hesiod and the Valley of the Muses." *Greek, Roman and Byzantine Studies,* 15: 5–24 (1974).

Watkins, C. "ANOCTEOC ON ΠOΔA TENΔEI." Pp. 231–235 in *Étrennes de septantaine: Mélanges Michel Lejeune.* Paris, 1978.

West, M. L., ed. and comm. *Hesiod, Theogony.* Oxford, 1966.

——, ed. and comm. *Hesiod, Works and Days.* Oxford, 1978.

GREGORY NAGY

GREEK LYRIC POETS

I

THE MODERN READER who comes to Greek lyric poetry for the first time finds a rich store of pleasures. Consider Alcman's fragment:

No longer, O honey-voiced holy sounding maidens,
Can my limbs carry me. If only, if only I were a
    kingfisher,
Which flies with the halcyons upon the wave's
    flower,
Fearless of heart, the sea-purple holy bird!
                                                    (*PMG* 26)[1]

We are moved by the pathos with which the aging poet contrasts his own debility with the youthful vigor of the girls and at the same time we are struck by the imaginative vitality with which he compensates himself for his body's weakness by fantasizing himself a legendary bird, borne gracefully just above the top of the waves into which any man (or girl) would sink struggling. We admire the poetic mastery with which Alcman, turning the foam of the imagined wave into a metaphorical flower (with connotations of land, springtime, and youth), demonstrates that, old as he is, he has lost nothing of his creativity. And we enjoy the flirta-

tious generosity with which he offers the girls' ephemeral youthfulness the opportunity to share immortality by participating, as halcyons (themselves, by legend, mourners for mortality), in his own poetic fantasy. Or consider the lines often attributed to Sappho:

Set now is the moon,
And the Pleiades; and the middle of the
Night; and the hour goes by;
And I lie down to sleep alone.
                                        (*PMG* 976)

We respond to the grammatical simplicity of the clauses, in which emotion seems to express itself without mediation, and to their straightforward coordination, whereby each clause slips past as gently but irrevocably as the hours of loneliness. We also imagine in all its distinctness the implied situation: an evening toward the end of winter (in Greece, the season when the Pleiades set in the middle of the night), against whose familiar chill (and hints of future warmth) the girl reacts with a desire for love. She waits and watches, and not finding the object of her desires on earth she seeks complicity in the most feminine of celestial bodies; abandoned finally by these too when they vanish below the horizon, she follows their motion downward and inward into her bedroom and into herself; here she first becomes fully aware of the extent of her solitude, recognizing that, when all nature has retired, she alone remains

---

[1] *PMG* is an abbreviation for *Poetae Melici Graeci,* one of the basic texts of Greek lyric poetry. See the bibliography at the end of this essay for abbreviations referring to other basic texts.

awake. The girl feels herself both a part of wider natural processes and irremediably divorced from them. In the moon and stars she has found a companionship that her loved one has denied her, but she has been disappointed in the end by them as well. We recall that the Pleiades were once girls, who turned into stars in order to escape the amorous pursuit of Orion—who, now himself a constellation, forever follows them to the horizon in vain.

Reading such passages, we feel them to be quintessentially lyrical. Clearly, we have certain expectations that we are gratified to find fulfilled by them; but what exactly do we mean when we call them "lyric poetry"?

Some of us, indeed, may be taken aback by the phrase and may wonder what other kind of poetry there is besides lyric. For a number of reasons it has become possible in modern times to identify poetry itself, in its truest or most essential form, with the lyric. The modern expansion and consequent fragmentation of the reading public has jeopardized the exemplary status of drama for theories of poetry, while until relatively recently the novel has been excluded as prosaic from the center of modern aesthetics. Within the broad field of the remaining literature, comprising many possible nondramatic and nonnovelistic genres, the lyric has acquired predominance. Again, there are evident historical reasons for this predominance: the privatization of the aesthetic experience, the intense interest in the individual's spontaneity and originality, and the withering away of many of the social institutions for which earlier poets had made their contribution to public occasions. All these factors, which help to make up the distinctive nature of the experience of literature in the past two centuries or so, have made it possible for poetry in general to be equated with the lyric in the minds of some readers. This is not to say that satires or poems for affairs of state have altogether ceased to be written; but these tend to be relegated to a secondary rank, whereas the essence of poetry is often located instead in a lyric impulse.

It is evident that identifying literature with poetry and poetry with lyric poetry does not help us very much toward understanding the specificity of the lyric. Thus there is good reason to draw here upon a more ancient tradition, with roots in antiquity but revived in the eighteenth century, that distinguishes three literary genres: epic, drama, and lyric. Modern theories that concern this triad have for the most part defined the lyric mode along one of two axes: the subjective and the formal.

Lyric poetry has often been thought to depend primarily upon the poet's subjectivity. As the necessary and sufficient reason for a lyric poem's coming into being, the poet's personality—his hopes and passions, his vicissitudes and fears—has been thought an adequate criterion for explaining the poem's nature and character. The lyric poet pours out in unpremeditated strains the most primal emotional impulses that move him; or, if he reflects upon these impulses, it is only so as to make his experience more intelligible to himself. We as readers are not thought to occupy his attention: his self-absorption is so thorough that, at the extreme, he speaks to himself, and we are unintended eavesdroppers. Such a theory can favor a simplicity of thought and expression that approximates the lyric to the ballad and folk song, but it can also justify a highly esoteric, enigmatic poetry organized around a set of private symbols to which an audience might not have easy access. What becomes highly problematic with such a definition of lyric is any rationalizing tendency in the poem that seeks to generalize individual experience so as to make it universally available, or any rhetorical strategy that deploys certain techniques to achieve determinate effects in the reader. This is the notion of the lyric that John Stuart Mill, for example, had in mind when he distinguished eloquence as *heard* from poetry as *overheard*, and wrote, "Poetry is feeling confessing itself to itself, in moments of solitude, and bodying itself forth in symbols which are the nearest possible representations of the feeling in the exact shape in which it exists in the poet's mind." This is also what James Joyce meant when he

76

had Stephen Dedalus define the lyrical form as that "wherein the artist presents his image in immediate relation to himself." And it is why we tend to think of love as a particularly appropriate subject for lyric poetry, for what other emotion moves most of us so deeply and so privately?

This subjectivist determination of lyric poetry has dominated literary theory at least since Hegel and has characterized the expectations of even relatively uninformed readers for about as long. But within the past century or so, a number of writers have attempted to define the lyric differently, this time in terms of certain formal characteristics—grammatical, linguistic, rhetorical—that permit it to be analyzed not in terms of the psychology of its author, but rather in its difference from other kinds of discourse. Poe singled out brevity as an important criterion: "I hold that a long poem does not exist. I maintain that the phrase, *a long poem*, is simply a flat contradiction in terms." More recent authors have considerably refined this descriptive terminology. Most frequently, theorists have pointed to a dissociation of complicated, clearly organized, logical structures in favor of relatively autonomous, smaller units of signification. Thus asyndeton (paucity of conjunctions) is privileged at the expense of polysyndeton (wealth of conjunctions), and, among conjunctions, copulative or temporal ones ("and, and then") at the expense of causal or final ones ("because, so that"). The phrase or word rather than the sentence or paragraph bears the weight of communication; sentences tend to be structured paratactically (by coordination) rather than hypotactically (by subordination); repetition of sounds, words, phrases, or lines plays an important role. Roman Jakobson has correlated such features with a rhetorical preference for metaphor as against metonymy. Also, attention has been drawn to the general predominance of present-tense verbs and "shifters," words that have meaning only with reference to the situation of utterance: "I, you, now, here. . . ." To be sure, upon closer inspection the objectivity claimed by such formal the-

ories of lyric is impaired by the fact that they all depend, directly or indirectly, upon a subjectivist determination of what, to begin with, is to count as lyric; that is, such theories merely lead to a formal description of certain features of a class of utterances that has already been delimited precisely in terms of the presumed subjectivity of their speakers. But these formalist theories have nevertheless provided a useful set of categories for systematizing and generalizing the expectations that many of us bring to lyric poetry and the aspects of it to which most of us respond.

Returning to the two passages with which we began, we may now see more clearly why they strike us as so lyrical: both are expressions of emotions felt deeply, privately. Both are short and grammatically simple. Both imply logical connections rather than asserting them. The reader who pursues such lyric moments finds that his expectations are often fulfilled by the Greek lyric poets—perhaps not least because they are for the most part transmitted to us in tiny fragments quoted by later authors or unearthed on Egyptian papyri. Much of Sappho's poetry, most of the erotic lyrics of Ibycus and Anacreon, and occasional fragments of Archilochus, Alcman, Mimnermus, and Alcaeus seem to fulfill most of the criteria for lyric poetry outlined above. But soon the reader begins to have doubts. Where will he find outpourings of subjectivity in Sappho's mythological wedding song for Hector and Andromache (*PLF* 44) or in Alcman's longest surviving fragment (*PMG* 1), a choral ode written to be sung and danced by a group of maidens at a religious ceremony, providing in its first half an account of a sanguinary local myth and in its second half bantering praise for the maidens' beauty and merits and references to the rituals performed concurrently? How will he revise his expectations for lyric brevity when he discovers that Stesichorus' *Geryoneis* (*SLG* S7–87) was at least 1,300 lines long and that his *Oresteia* (*PMG* 210–219) filled two books in the ancient edition of his works? Nor will he find that any of the other formal criteria modern theorists have established for the lyric escape frequent violation at the hands of the Greek lyricists. Faced with such disappointment, he may indeed prefer to neglect those poems that do not correspond to his categories. But if instead he is willing to revise those expectations so as to come to a fuller understanding of the entire corpus of the Greek lyric poets, then he may legitimately demand an explanation of what is meant by applying to their works the term "lyric poetry."

Nowadays, when we hear the phrase "lyric poetry," very few of us are likely to think at once of a lyre; yet this musical instrument provides its etymology and explains its usage. Epic poetry was recited to the accompaniment of a type of lute (the *phorminx* or *kitharis*), just as poetry in elegiac couplets was usually recited to the accompaniment of a kind of flute (the *aulos*). Lyric poetry, on the other hand, was sung: here the lyre provided the instrumental accompaniment for a melodic voice, not just a chanting one. Musicality is what distinguishes the Greek lyric from other literary genres. This is why the older and more accurate term the ancients applied to this kind of poetry is not "lyric," but "melic": for *melos* designates a tune or melody, whether of a bird (as of a nightingale in the undated, but probably fifth-century *Homeric Hymn* 19.16), a musical instrument, or the human voice. Thus Plato, after discussing tragedy and comedy in the *Republic* (3.398d), moves on to the subject of lyric poetry *(melos)*, and asserts that it is made up of words *(logos)*, a musical component (a scale or mode, *harmonia*), and rhythm or meter *(rhuthmos)*. Every ancient lyric poem was written to be sung. Many modern lyric poems have attempted to imitate this condition by such stylistic devices as the refrain, and a few modern poems have attained it by being set to music.

The fragments we discussed at the beginning, like all the rest of Greek lyric poetry, have come to us without their melodies; of the three components Plato distinguished, the words have been transmitted, their meter can be analyzed, but their musical quality has been lost

forever. And since the time of Plato, "lyric" has come to replace the earlier "melic" to describe this kind of poetry. Between these two facts, oddly enough, there may be a direct correlation. Both are consequences of the crucial mediating role played by Alexandrian literary scholars in the Hellenistic period. No autograph manuscript of an ancient Greek lyric poet has survived to us from antiquity. Indeed, as we shall see in more detail later, the very fact of the survival of a number of lyric poems beyond the lifetime of their authors and original audiences is a perplexing matter, one that raises questions we are likely never to resolve. But when, after the collapse of the traditional Greek world in the fourth century B.C., scholars at the royal court at Alexandria decided to collect and systematically organize all that remained of the literary masterpieces of that vanished age, they gathered together whatever they could find not only of the epic, tragic, and comic poets, but also of the melic. What interested them, as far as we can tell from the evidence, was exclusively the poets' words. The fact that we know nothing of the poets' music means that those scholars, those narrow funnels through which all earlier literature had to pass to reach us, either themselves knew nothing of it or else had access to it but were not interested in it or did not understand it. In fact as early as Plato a certain indifference to melic music and rhythm and an emphasis on the verbal component is evident; thus the same passage of the *Republic* mentioned above discusses at length the question of the moral suitability of what poetry conveys with its words, but entrusts not to Socrates but to one of his interlocutors a familiarity with the technical vocabulary appropriate to *harmonia* (3.398e–399c), and permits both partners in the conversation to disclaim unashamedly any expert knowledge in matters of rhythm and meter (3.400a–c). Indeed, Plato asserts several times that the dominant component is the words and that melody and rhythm must be made to follow these (3.398d, 400a, d). So, too, Aristotle in his *Poetics* identified rhythm, language, and harmony as the means of poetic imitation (1.1447a21–23); but he himself concentrated almost exclusively on language, assigning the technical details of meter to experts in that field (20.1456b34, 38) and tipping his hat twice to the sensual pleasure the musical element provides (6.1450b15–16, 26.1462a15–17) but otherwise entirely neglecting it. In this regard, as in many others, the Alexandrian editors may have inherited and institutionalized an Aristotelian prejudice; but it is no less imaginable that no musical notation had ever reached them, or that, even if it had, the enormous changes in Greek music that had intervened in the fifth and fourth centuries would have made any such notation unintelligible to them.

Thus the Hellenistic scholars performed a first selection by filtering out the *melos* from the melic poets, for whatever reason, and presenting the poetry in their editions as words in meter. But they performed a second selection as well: they selected out from all preceding lyric poetry the works of nine poets as worthy of preservation (in the form of editions) and study (in the form of commentaries). It is probably not accidental that what may well be the earliest usage of the term *lyrikos* to refer to what had earlier been called a melic poet is an epigram listing nine poets as the nine canonical lyric ones:

To Pindar the Poet and to the Remaining
Lyric Poets

Pindar, holy mouth of the Muses; and, babbling
    Siren,
    You too, *Bacchylides*; and Aeolian graces of
        Sappho;
And script of *Anacreon*; and you, *Stesichorus*, who
    drew off Homer's flow in your own labors;
And the sweet page of *Simonides*; and *Ibycus*, you
    who gathered
    The delightful flowers of Persuasion and of boys;
And sword of *Alcaeus*, which often shed the blood
    of tyrants,
    Protecting the fatherland's statutes;

And woman-singing nightingales of *Alcman*—may
    all you be gracious,
    You who established the beginning and the end
    for all lyric.

(*Anthologia Palatina* 9.184)[2]

For the anonymous author, who has been dated roughly to 100 B.C., the lyric poets are already an exclusive canon, one transmitted to him in the form of written texts: although he retains conventional traces of their original oral nature in his descriptions of Pindar, Bacchylides, and Alcman, far more significance attaches to his references to the script of Anacreon and the page of Simonides. In later Greek as well, although the term *melos* does not disappear, its usage is increasingly restricted to discussions of literary genres, where the *melos* is distinguished from epic and drama. "Lyric" on the other hand begins to be used in the first century B.C., always referring to the canon of the nine lyric poets and gradually becoming the dominant term in all other usages as well. Hence "lyric" as a designation is tied to the end of the living tradition of lyric song and to the beginning of its study in the form of written memorials rescued from a distant and now unfamiliar past. Paradoxically, "lyric" seems to denote musicality—but instead characterizes the written text.

The epigram states that these nine poets established lyric's beginning and end, and we may take this in two senses: first, in terms of chronology, for later poets, whatever their qualities, were no longer admitted to this closed elite; and second, in terms of merit, for these are the poets who demonstrated by their genius the very limits that lyric poetry could attain. The exclusiveness of this canon was never violated: thus Corinna, a Boeotian poetess whose date is controversial but who seems most likely to have written in the Hellenistic period, is occasionally praised as being worthy to be added to the list as a tenth member, but never suc-

[2]*The Greek Anthology.*

ceeds in acquiring a permanent place on it. Horace begins his *Odes* with the hope that he will be inserted into the ranks of the lyric poets (*Odes* 1.1.35–36), but nowhere claims to have attained this goal.

It has been suggested by some scholars that this group represents not those poets whom the Alexandrian philologists judged to be better than the others, but rather includes all those lyric poets whose works were available in sufficient quantities to warrant an edition. But this conclusion is most unlikely: we know the names of a number of other poets besides these nine; the very number nine, identical as it is with the traditional number of the Muses, is significant; and in other genres we know that these scholars selected the poets they considered best. In any event, these nine poets soon came to be regarded not merely as the very best, but as qualitatively different from all later ones. Thus the author of this epigram addresses to them what is, regarded generically, a hymn to the gods, invoking them by name and special attribute and closing with a prayer for their favor. He himself, of course, is writing an epigram rather than a lyric poem, since, as a mere mortal, he does not dare to compete with them on their own territory; but even so he claims to be obliged to obtain their favor if his own poetry, whatever it is, is to be at all successful. We may regard his prayer as having been only partially fulfilled: he does achieve a certain elegance in his distribution of the nine names (three in the first couplet, beginning as always with Pindar as the greatest of the lyric poets; two each in the next two couplets, in each case with half a line for the first and a line and a half for the second; a full couplet for the eighth and the beginning of another full one for the ninth). But the epithets he applies to the individual poets are either so vague as to be no less appropriate to any other one (Pindar, Bacchylides, Anacreon, Simonides) or else the most unimaginative commonplaces about the themes or nature of their poetry (Sappho, Stesichorus, Ibycus, Alcaeus, Alcman).

In the very mediocrity of this poem we may see a hint of the dark side of the reverence later generations accorded the canonical nine: as *melic* poets they had flourished in a context where occasional hopes for literary immortality had precluded neither intimate connection to real social occasions and the immediacy of their lives nor dialogue, both polemical and respectful, with other poets; as *lyric* poets, stripped of the melodies they had once sung and confined within written editions, hedged by commentaries and preserved in libraries, they came to exercise a restraining influence on the literature of later antiquity. As names, as figures for an ideal poetry, they retained an enormous influence. They continued to be read widely: Cicero's comment that even if he could live a second time he would not have leisure enough to read the lyric poets (Seneca, *Epistles* 49.5) is the exception that proves the rule; in Greek, not to know "the three of Stesichorus" (whatever they were) was a proverb for ignorance. But oddly their poetry itself seems to have rarely inspired emulation by later poets in antiquity. Theocritus wrote four poems in Greek Aeolic meters (*Idylls* 28–31), of which at least one (29) seems to have been based on Alcaeus, and a plea for patronage (*Idylls* 16) filled with reminiscences of Pindar. Callimachus wrote a recently rediscovered victory poem modeled on Pindar. Many epigrams in *The Greek Anthology* take the form of encomia or epigraphs for the archaic Greek lyric poets, yet surprisingly few display any degree of familiarity with their works. Papyri and citations bring us very few additional later lyrics, either folk songs or more sophisticated varieties. In Latin, the prestige of Horace should not blind us to the fact that his lyric poems, like those of Catullus and Statius, fall outside the mainstream of Roman literature. Horace himself frequently refers to the canonical nine Greek lyric poets, explicitly placing himself within their tradition and putting familiar tags from their better-known poems at the beginnings of several of his own; yet in spirit, themes, and social role he is far closer to the Hellenistic Greek poets. Like virtue, the greatest Greek lyric poets were praised—but neglected. Even modern lyric poetry, for all its recurrent phases of reverence for Pindar or Horace, has its roots not in archaic Greece, but in medieval Europe.

We may be tempted to regret the twin facts that the Alexandrian scholars filtered out both the music from the lyric poets and the canonical nine from all other lyric poets; but we need not reproach them too severely. It is quite true that these poets wrote only to sing and that the loss of their melodies means we can never recreate the original form of their poems in its totality. But the effect of music, perhaps more than any other art form, is closely bound up with the culture in which it is produced, and the examples of Chinese or Arabic music, even those old Provençal songs for which the melodies have survived, suggest that if by some miracle the tunes for ancient Greek lyric were rediscovered and—miracle within miracle—they could be accurately transposed into modern musical notation, they would impress most listeners as no more than exotic. We would be glad to hear them sung, but it would be naive to assume that they would have an effect on us anything like what they had on their original audience, to whom the scales and harmonies were familiar from childhood. As for the second filtering, it would have been of considerable historical interest to have extensive samples from the many other lyric poets contemporary with the nine who have survived; but we may well wonder how good their literary quality would have turned out to be. The ancient scholars did indeed choose; but we have every reason to believe they chose wisely. What is more, the fame of the canonical nine poets attracted to their names the anonymous works of other poets who wrote in the same genre or were influenced by them: for example, the fifth Olympian in the Pindaric collection is almost certainly not by him, and numerous epigrams were falsely attributed to Simonides. Famous examples in other genres include the *Rhesus* ascribed to Euripides and much of the body of work transmitted under the name of Theognis. These spurious poems give us a sense

of what we are missing. All in all, it does not seem to be that much.

Finally it must be added that there is a modern tendency to lump together with the nine poets of the lyric canon two other groups of ancient Greek poets: those who wrote more or less scurrilous invectives in iambic and trochaic meters, especially Archilochus, but also Semonides and Hipponax and others like them; and those who wrote in elegiac couplets on a great variety of themes, including military (Calinus, Tyrtaeus), erotic (Mimnermus), and gnomic or symposiastic (particularly Theognis). These poets come from the same period of Greek cultural history as do the truly lyric poets, and they can be (and are occasionally in this essay) used to cast light on the social conditions and general themes of the nine. However, the only reason to consider them fundamentally similar is that their works also correspond now and then to the modern notion of lyric poetry as short and highly personal. But as we have seen, this notion is not entirely appropriate for the Greek lyric poets themselves. No one in antiquity thought of the iambic and elegiac poets as writing within the lyric genre. In the pages that follow they are not discussed at great length.

II

Collectively, the nine lyric poets span the whole physical extent of the Greek world and the historical period from about 650 to 450 B.C. They may be divided roughly into four generations. Alcman, the earliest, was active in the second half of the seventh century and confined his literary career entirely to Sparta. A second group was born around the third quarter of the seventh century and lived well into the sixth century: Stesichorus from the western extremity of the Greek world, from southern Italy and Sicily; Sappho and Alcaeus from the eastern extremity, from the island of Lesbos off the coast of Asia Minor. Like Alcman, these poets were primarily local in interest and orientation. Only in the subsequent wave, those poets born in the first half of the sixth century and whose careers extended through its second half, do we begin to find authors voluntarily leaving their birthplace and moving throughout the Greek world: Ibycus, born in southern Italy, came to the island of Samos after he had established a reputation in Italy; Anacreon, born in Teos, an Ionian city on the coast of Asia Minor, left first, like Ibycus, for Samos and thereafter for Athens and probably Thessaly. Simonides was born slightly later, in the middle of the sixth century on the island of Ceos near the southeast tip of Attica; but his longevity allowed his literary career to extend well into the fifth century (approximately 556–468 B.C.). His travels throughout the Greek world, at least to Athens, Thessaly, and Sicily, set a precedent for his younger contemporaries, who were born toward the end of the sixth century and died around the middle of the next one: Bacchylides, also from Ceos like his uncle Simonides; and Pindar of Thebes (about 518–438 B.C.), who survived Aeschylus by twenty years.

These two centuries have come to be known as the Lyric Age of Greece. They witness the most decisive transformations in Greek society before the second half of the fourth century B.C., when at last many of the institutions established in this period collapsed. The world of the Homeric epics is, to be sure, a mixture of idealizations of the distant past, memories of the intervening Dark Ages, and elements of the contemporary mid-eighth century; but though this mixture cannot be disentangled, those epics depict a society fundamentally different from that of the classic age of the fifth and fourth centuries. Homeric society is organized around the familial household, ruled by an aristocrat and seeking an economic self-sufficiency that precludes intimate and permanent commercial ties with other households. There is a king, who in an ill-defined manner has precedence over the aristocrats but in some way depends on their assent, and there is the large mass of the common people, who are summoned to assembly but whose will is not binding. There is very lit-

tle apparatus of state, no written constitution or established laws, neither well-defined political offices nor rules for eligibility and administration; even the basic concept of the citizen is lacking. The primary means of economic exchange are barter and reciprocal gifts; coinage is unknown. What counts as Greece is only the mainland, Ithaca, Crete, Rhodes, and a few nearby islands; the rest of the world is inhabited by foreigners, legendary races, and monsters. If fifth-century society, with its well-established and generally nonroyal political systems, its colonies stretching from Italy to Africa to the Black Sea, and its complicated monetary economy, is radically different from the world of the Homeric epics, this is in large measure the achievement of the Lyric Age. Growth in population, establishment of the polis, and intensive colonization began in the middle of the eighth century, at around the time of Homer; but only in the seventh century did the foundations for the future of Greece begin to be laid in earnest.

Not that the transition was easy or smooth: on the contrary, this is a period of enormous social upheaval throughout the Greek world. The term that most exactly designates the extremes reached by this social unrest is *stasis*, violent dissension or conflict. The political figure who most fully exemplifies this period is the tyrant. A number of Greek cities underwent at least one tyranny, of greater or lesser duration, during these two centuries. Indeed, the first great period of Greek tyranny almost exactly coincides with the lifetimes of the nine lyric poets: the first recorded usage of the word is in Archilochus (West, 19.3) in the middle of the seventh century. The first known historical tyrants—Pheidon of Argos, Cypselus of Corinth, Theagenes of Megara, and Orthagoras of Sicyon—must be dated to roughly the same time. The sixth century witnessed celebrated tyrannies at Corinth (the Cypselids: Periander and Psammetichus), Sicyon (Cleistenes), Athens (failed attempts by Cylon around 632 and Damasias in 582–580; then after 560 the Peisistratids: Peisistratus, Hippias), and Samos (Polycrates). The last major tyrannical dynasty of this period, that of the Deinomenids in Sicily (Gelon, Hieron, Thrasybulus), was overthrown in 466 B.C.

It is important to stress that the Greek tyrant was not necessarily an evil despot in the sense that the word came to mean later. Instead the term in this period designates a man who suddenly and unconstitutionally seizes absolute power within a city, often by force, and retains that power in direct identification with himself and his immediate family until the dynasty he has attempted to establish is toppled. Historically the tyrants were a shortcut on the road toward democratization of the Greek city-states. They tended to come from the ranks of the traditional aristocracy and not from the wider class of citizens who had attained wealth in the economic expansion after the eighth century. The military, if not yet constitutional, importance of the newly wealthy to the city was institutionalized during the early seventh century in the abandonment of the traditional military strategy (the individual aristocratic spear-thrower, supported by the large mass of unarmed or lightly armed commoners) and the adoption of the hoplite phalanx (a tightly knit formation of heavily armed, spear-thrusting men, each of whose shields helped protect his neighbor, who were only of military usefulness when they all fought together). Nevertheless the tyrants generally came to power by claiming to represent the political and economic interests of this wider and hitherto disenfranchised class. Though not true democrats in any sense of the word, their historical effect was to contribute to the dissolution of the archaic power base of the older aristocrats and to widen access to political office. Whatever their self-understanding (we shall turn to this question shortly), they represent a force for innovation in Greek political history and step upon its stage as Greece's first true individuals: around their names cluster anecdotes of power, passion, and violence but also of sagacity and glory approximating them to the gods, and of transgressions prohibited to men—and, too, of

inevitable punishment, of humiliation and torment almost beyond human imagination. Polycrates' immense good fortune, for instance, is memorialized in the story of the valuable ring he cast into the ocean to avoid the enmity of the gods—only to have it return later in the belly of a fish offered up to him as homage by one of his subjects (Herodotus, 3.40–43). And in the end, Polycrates too was punished for exceeding the limits set to mortals: he was tricked by Oroetes, Persian governor of Sardis, into sailing to Magnesia, where he was crucified so horribly that Herodotus spares us the details (3.120–125).

With the exception of Alcman, whose city, Sparta, was unusually stable during this period and was not ruled by a tyrant until the end of the third century B.C., each of the Greek lyric poets was in some way affected by tyranny and *stasis*. This becomes all the more striking when it is recalled that, for all their visibility and importance, the early tyrants were a rather restricted phenomenon geographically: only in the cities near the Saronic Gulf were they concentrated. Hence the regularity of the connections between lyric poetry and tyranny is anything but self-evident. In the first generation after Alcman, these connections are direct and personal. Stesichorus is reported by Aristotle (*Rhetoric* 2.20.1393b8–22) to have attempted to dissuade his fellow citizens at Himera from granting their military leader, Phalaris, a bodyguard, by warning them with an animal fable that they would be paving the way for his tyranny. We know that Sappho was exiled at least briefly during the decades of *stasis* in Mytilene (*Marmor Parium* 36: *PLF* 98b).

It is in the life of Alcaeus that we can most closely follow the intimate involvement of a citizen who happened also to be a poet in the political turmoil of his time, for about half of his surviving poems are taken up with this theme. Indeed, Strabo reports (*Geography* 13.617) that these poems of Alcaeus were called "poems of *stasis*"; and Dionysius of Halicarnassus remarked that if one removed the meter from Alcaeus' political poems one would find political rhetoric (*On Imitation* 421). The events of this period were ones with which Alcaeus was deeply connected—usually as the odd man out. Around 612–609 B.C., a first tyrant on Lesbos, Melanchrus, was overthrown by Alcaeus' brothers and Pittacus; later Pittacus formed an alliance with Alcaeus against a new tyrant, Myrsilus, but Pittacus seems then to have betrayed Alcaeus and joined forces with Myrsilus. Alcaeus celebrated Myrsilus' eventual death in exuberant lines—"Now a man must get drunk, and with all his might / Drink, since Myrsilus has finally died!" (*PLF* 332)—that inspired Horace's ode on the death of Cleopatra (*Odes* 1.37). But if Alcaeus hoped that his own chance for power had now come, he was sorely disappointed. The citizens of Lesbos, whom one presumes to have grown weary of the shortsighted and selfish factionalism of Alcaeus and people like him, chose Pittacus (who was later revered throughout Greece as one of the Seven Sages) as temporary ruler in order to put down dynastic factionalism: he spent ten years doing this, then voluntarily abdicated. Alcaeus greeted Pittacus' election with contempt (*PLF* 348). At least twice during these years he was exiled, and some of his poems complain of the bitterness of the exile's lot (for example, *PLF* 130). His political poems vary between complaints against treachery and political rivals, admonitions to rescue the endangered ship of state, disconsolate flights to the bottle after a defeat, and exhortations to action like this:

The large house gleams with bronze; and the
   whole roof has been well equipped
With shining helmets, from which white horse-hair
   plumes wave downwards,
Adornments for the heads of men; and shining
   bronze greaves, a bulwark
Against the strong arrow, hang upon pegs,
   concealing them,
And corselets of new linen and hollow shields are
   piled up,
And beside them Chalcidian swords, and beside
   them many belts and tunics.
These are not to be forgotten, because we have
   taken upon ourselves this task from the
   beginning.

                     (*PLF* 357)

We might well think (as did Athenaeus, who quotes these lines, 14.627a) that musical instruments would have been more suitable decorations for the house of a poet than weapons of war; but this would be to misunderstand the relationship between politics and poetry in Alcaeus. Alcaeus was first and foremost a political animal who defined himself by his success or failure in the political arena; what role this left to his poetry we shall see subsequently.

In the generations that followed, lyric poets no longer participated so directly in the political process but became dependent on established tyrants for patronage. Ibycus may be regarded as a transitional figure: for the proverbs "more old-fashioned than Ibycus" and "more foolish than Ibycus" are explained by the ancient sources with reference to a story of his having refused the tyranny offered him by his fellow citizens in Italy and instead withdrawing to Ionia. Ibycus' refusal, historical or not, may be taken as the model for a new conception of poetry: the poet is now no longer in the first instance a citizen of his native town, engaged with his whole being in its political life, but is instead a professional, one whose skills set him apart from other people and can be sought after by those who wish to make use of them. Although this new role may remind us in some ways of the older Homeric or Hesiodic rhapsodes, it is important to stress the differences: the new poets provide lyric, not epic, poetry; they move far beyond the confines of their native regions; they adapt the contents of their songs to their audiences; and they seem entirely dependent on patronage.

Patronage is one thing the tyrants seem to have been eager to provide. Several of the Greek tyrants energetically fostered the arts (one is reminded of the Ptolemies and Attalids three centuries later): the poet Arion was summoned from Lesbos to Corinth by Periander and developed the dithyramb in that town; Ibycus left Italy for the court of Polycrates of Samos, where he was joined by Anacreon; Peisistratus beautified Athens with a large-scale building program, while his son Hipparchus reorganized the recitations of Homer at the Panathenaic festivals and brought to Athens Anacreon (after the fall of Polycrates) and Simonides. Nor was this dependence of poetry upon power restricted to the tyrant as patron: Anacreon may have stayed at the court of King Echecratidas in Thessaly, and Simonides was certainly associated with the royal Thessalian families, the Scopads and the Aleuads. With Simonides begins the long list of Greek poets patronized by the Sicilian tyrants, including Pindar (whose powerful patrons came from most other parts of the Greek world as well), Bacchylides, and Aeschylus.

Where consumers were so eager, suppliers eventually realized that they could turn a profit. Simonides was regarded by the ancients as having been the first to write poems for money, a practice that Pindar disparaged (*Isthmians* 2.1–11) but which ancient scholars accused Pindar himself of having favored to the point of avarice. Aristotle reports that Simonides once refused to write a victory ode for a winner in the mule race, on the grounds that mules were not a subject that could inspire him to poetry, but that, once the price had been raised, Simonides complied with a poem beginning, "Hail, daughters of wind-footed horses!" (*Rhetoric* 3.2.1405b23–28). We also owe to Aristotle an anecdote that epitomizes the relation between poet and patron at the end of the Lyric Age:

> There are many people who need things from those that have them. Hence what Simonides said about the wise and the wealthy to the wife of Hieron, who asked him whether it was better to be wealthy or wise. He said, "wealthy, for I see the wise spending their time sitting at the doors of the wealthy."
>
> (*Rhetoric* 2.16.1391a7–12)

It is often suggested that the lyric poets, like the tyrants, represented a new age in the development of Greek culture, an age glorifying the individual in all his unique specificity at the expense of the community and valuing the immediate present and the innovative over the past and the traditional. In particular, lyric poetry is seen as competing with Homer, and by implication or assertion repudiating him as the model for literature, and with the Homeric epic as the paradigm for behavior. Thus Bruno Snell devotes one of the longest and most interesting chapters of his influential book, *The Discovery of the Mind,* to "The Rise of the Individual in the Early Greek Lyric." Hermann Fränkel, speaking of "the sudden swing from epic to lyric," writes of the lyric poets' sense of human ephemerality:

> The current situation of the individual finds artistic expression in short lyric poems which speak a direct, open, and natural language corresponding to the new realism. In a single poem the reaction of the speaker to what is at that moment happening is given an objective existence. Epic is now an anachronism. Its solemn and ceremonial language is no longer suitable for what men have to say. There is no longer any belief in fixed characters such as epic employs. With neutrality and detachment epic tells us of men long dead; but now the fates of other men long ago do not interest the poet—life can now be understood only by living it.
>
> This is roughly the attitude of lyric poetry at the time when its founder Archilochus broke with traditional ideologies in order to put something totally new in their place.
>
> (*Early Greek Poetry and Philosophy,* p. 136)

This is an attractive notion for the modern sense of the development of literature, a notion that received its most authoritative formulation in Hegel's deduction of the necessary historical succession of objective epic, then subjective lyric, and finally synthetic drama. It seems to make exemplary sense of a fragmentarily transmitted poem addressed by Ibycus to the tyrant Polycrates (*PMG* 282a), which opens for us with a brief sketch of the fall of Troy:

And they sacked Dardanian Priam's
Great, famous, prosperous city,
Having started from Argos
By the plans of great Zeus,

For the sake of blonde Helen's beauty
Waging a many-hymned strife
In tearful war,
And woe went up to much-suffering Pergamum
Because of golden-haired Aphrodite.

But now it is my desire to hymn
Neither host-deceiving Paris
Nor slender-ankled Cassandra
And the other children of Priam

And the nameless day of the taking
Of high-gated Troy; nor shall I recount
the splendid courage
Of the heroes whom hollow

Many-pegged ships brought
For Troy as an evil, those noble heroes;
Whom lord Agamemnon
Ruled, a Pleisthenid king, leader of men,
Son of Atreus, his noble father;

And these things the skilled Muses,
the Heliconians, could embark on well in speech,
But a long-lived mortal man
Could not tell them all. . . .

Ibycus goes on to provide a summary catalog of the Greek heroes who set sail from Aulis and concludes with a reference to Zeuxippus, son of Hyllis:

But to him Troilus
Was compared, as to bronze
Thrice-refined gold,

By Trojans and Danaans
For his lovely beauty.
These men have a share in beauty forever,
And you too, Polycrates, will possess undying fame
As far as song and my own fame can give it.

It seems that the themes of the epic are simply rejected in favor of a poetry directed to the immediate situation. The "many-hymned" strife, with its piled-up, tired epithets, need not be celebrated by yet another hymn; the poet has lost the desire to sing of the two crucial moments of the Trojan cycle, the mustering of ships that began the Trojan War and the sack of Troy that ended it. Instead the poet turns to the

present, to his patron, who will be made no less famous than Homer's heroes by a poet grown suddenly conscious of his own poetry and his own fame. May we take this poem as an emblem for the new spirit of the Lyric Age?

By no means. To begin with, lyric poetry was at least as ancient in Greece as epic. Homer makes numerous references to varieties of poetry that were later composed by the Greek lyricists: songs for solo performance (a Linus-song, *Iliad* 18.567 ff., and a song while weaving, *Odyssey* 5.61–62), as well as songs for choruses (a wedding song: *Iliad* 18.491 ff.; paeans to Apollo: *Iliad* 1.472–74, 22.391–92; dirges: *Iliad* 18.50–51, 314–16, 24.720 ff., *Odyssey* 24.58 ff.). There can be no doubt that Alcman did not invent the choral lyric or the love poem, just as Archilochus was not the first to compose iambs and elegies: in each case they were drawing on centuries-old traditions. But the earlier lyricists have been lost to us forever because their poems were not written down. It is true that the productions of the lyric poets were set down in writing later than the Homeric epics. It is also true that, with few exceptions (Peisander of Cameirus, Panyassis of Halicarnassus, Choerilus of Samos, Antimachus of Colophon), epic poetry ceased to be composed after the seventh century. But the explanations for these two phenomena are quite different and must be kept carefully separated. The tardiness with which the lyric poets were committed to writing is due simply to the primacy of Homer in Greek culture and to the slowness with which writing was diffused during this period. In an age in which it was not self-evident that everything should be written down and in which the materials and skill needed for writing were not widespread, it is not surprising that the texts regarded as by far the most important were written down long before others. What is more, Homer's monumental epics, with their panHellenic and transhistorical pretensions, required memorialization and diffusion (which could best be provided by writing) in a way that lyric poetry did not: for lyric poetry, at least at the beginning of the Archaic Age, was uniquely bound up with the moment of its performance and had no aspirations beyond the immediate place and time (one thinks of the insoluble difficulties Alcman's local and topical allusions provide the modern scholar). Hence there was no compelling need to write down lyric poems. The fact that they were eventually put into writing is likely to be less a tribute to the superiority of the canonical nine over their predecessors than a symptom of the gradual proliferation of writing itself as something taken for granted. We can find a trace of the impact of writing on archaic Greek poetry in a celebrated passage of Theognis (19–26): the poet claims here that he has set a seal on his verses, so they cannot be filched or exchanged for worse ones without anybody's noticing and so everyone will say they are the verses of Theognis. About the identity of this seal there has been much scholarly dispute; but surely it is nothing else than the fact that Theognis has committed his poetry to writing, so that reference to an authorized written exemplar will be enough to establish the authenticity of elegiac distichs performed in (or without) his name. Hence writing establishes for the first time the possibility of literary property—and, we may add, the universal and permanent fame of Cyrnus, addressee of Theognis' poetry (237–254). It is surely no accident that only the later archaic Greek poets, such as Pindar and Bacchylides, frequently asserted that the fame they conferred was not bound by limitations of space and time: for it took a long time before the implications of writing were evident for poetry.

As for the decline of epic after Homer, it is explained by the oral nature of the Greek epic tradition: the oral composition of epic poetry could not long survive the advent of writing, even if writing was slowly diffused. Furthermore the evident popularity of the *Iliad* and *Odyssey* meant that bards were soon expected to provide recognizable versions of these poems rather than widely variant ones or poems about other parts of the epic cycle. On the other hand, oral composition and transmission seem not to have played the same kind of

decisive role in lyric poetry, so that this genre could flourish in an age gradually becoming accustomed to writing. Hence the belatedness of the Greek lyric poets is historical accident, not historical necessity. In other words, the evident differences between Homer and the lyric poets are not of historical succession, but of literary genre.

What is more, the attitude of the lyric poets toward Homer is much more complex and respectful than some modern scholars allow. The earlier lyric poets treated the subject matter of traditional epic in lyric meters—whereby their language was largely Homeric, and many Homeric phrases and formulas found a comfortable place in their largely dactylic rhythms. As the author of the pseudo-Plutarchan *On Music* put it, "Stesichorus and the archaic melic poets composed epic verses and put melodies around them" (chapter 3). What is most striking is that these earlier epic lyricists uniformly steered clear of the contents of the *Iliad* and *Odyssey*, and instead drew their material from other parts of the Trojan cycle or from other epic sagas—another testimony to Homer's predominance. The seventh-century lyric poets Sacadas and Xanthus are reported to have composed, respectively, a *Sack of Troy* and an *Oresteia* (*PMG* 699-700). Stesichorus' dependence on epic material was a byword in antiquity; besides the poems referred to previously in this article, he too wrote a *Sack of Troy* (*PMG* 196-205) and evidently long lyrics about the Argonauts, the Calydonian boar hunt, and Theban myths, among others. Sappho's wedding song for Hector and Andromache has already been referred to; Alcaeus wrote poems about Helen (*PLF* 42, 283), Ajax's rape of Cassandra (*PLF* 298, *SLG* S262), and Achilles' plea that Thetis intercede with Zeus (*PLF* 44). Nor do the later lyric poets abandon the extended narration of epic materials: Ibycus too wrote a *Sack of Troy* and a poem on the Calydonian boar hunt; Longinus reports (15.7) that Simonides wrote vividly about the appearance of the ghost of Achilles over his tomb when the Greeks were preparing to sail away from Troy; Pindar drew on the legend of the Argonauts for a victory ode that was over 530 lines long in the ancient editions (*Pythian* 4).

But even when the lyric poets wrote about their own experience, they often could not, or would not, free themselves from Homer's influence: for the prestige of Homer in Greek culture meant that he provided the form that made their experience intelligible to them. Alcaeus' catalog of his weapons, in the poem quoted previously, is thoroughly Homeric in the language of its references to the gleaming bronze (*Iliad* 13.801, 16.664, 18.131, 23.27), the shining helmets (*Iliad* 17.269), the waving horsehair plumes (*Iliad* 6.469, 11.41–42, 15.537), the bulwark against arrows (*Iliad* 5.316); the epic vocabulary functions in this context almost as an assurance of success in battle. Ibycus' poem to Polycrates is not only filled with epic reminiscences throughout the sections in which it deals with material from the Trojan War; even its assertion that no man could list in detail all the Greek heroes is borrowed directly from Homer (*Iliad* 2.484–492). Also, in the poem's final address to the tyrant, the "undying fame" promised him is a quotation from Homer (*Iliad* 9.413), a phrase assigned by Achilles, greatest of Homer's heroes, to himself: Polycrates, named by a poet in this heavily Homeric context, is offered a prospect of future fame that can be validated only by appeal to the very poet Ibycus might at first have seemed to reject.

Indeed the works of all the lyric poets are marked by frequent reminiscences of Homer and appeals to his authority. Alcman may have asked the Muse to sing a new song for him (*PMG* 14a); but he himself wrote of Ajax and Memnon (68), of "illustrious Ajax" (69; compare *Iliad* 23.779), of "Dysparis" (77; compare *Iliad* 3.39); he told the story of Odysseus' preparations for sailing past the Sirens (80) on the basis of a version slightly different from the *Odyssey* (12.177), and elsewhere (81) varied another line from the same poem (6.244). Sappho justified her longing for the absent Anactoria by adducing the authority of Homer's Helen, who had

also felt that the one she loved was more important than anything else in the world (*PLF* 16); in exactly the same way, Homer's heroes had often buttressed moral arguments by appeal to mythic examples. Alcaeus, somewhat varying Sappho's language, reminded her what disasters Helen's love had led to and how much more respectable a wife Thetis had been (*PLF* 42, 283). Ibycus writes about the profound effect love has upon him:

Eros, once again looking at me meltingly
From beneath dark eyelids,
Drives me with manifold bewitchments
Into the Cyprian goddess' infinite nets
Oh, I tremble as he approaches,
Just as a yoke-bearing prize-winning horse near
    old age
Goes unwillingly with its fast chariot to the race.

                                    (*PMG* 287)

Why are Eros' eyelids dark? Presumably because in Homer that adjective is reserved for the eyelids of only the most powerful gods (Zeus: *Iliad* 1.528, 17.209; Hera: *Iliad* 15.102). And the simile at the end of the text should remind us of Homer's use of the same image with exactly the same words for the haste with which Achilles moves eagerly to attack Troy (*Iliad* 22.21–23)—with this crucial difference, that in Homer the racehorse has not passed its prime and does not shy away from the race. Athenaeus (11.463a) ascribes to Anacreon an epigram rejecting strife and tearful war (the contents of the *Iliad*) as unsuitable for songs at a drinking party and suggesting instead erotic poetry—but doing so in language that, with the exception of only one word, is directly derived from Homer. The use of Homeric diction and imagery in Pindar and Bacchylides is too rich and thoroughgoing to need exemplification here.

There is thus a curious parallel between the lyric poets and the tyrants. For although the tyrants may well in the end have been a force for innovation in Greek political history, they consistently attempted to legitimate themselves by appeal not to the future (which they were in fact preparing) but to the past (which they claimed to be perpetuating or restoring): they portrayed themselves as guardians of archaic cults and traditional values, which they were restoring to a new grandeur after the decadence of the more recent past. Pheidon claimed to be the heir of Herakles and to be recovering the "heritage of Temenos," which dated back five centuries. Cleisthenes moved the remains of the legendary hero Melanippus to expel the cult of the Argive Adrastus, his ancient enemy. Peisistratus had himself declared tyrant by a tall and beautiful woman who, dressed in armor and mounted on a chariot, was proclaimed to be Athena herself and was driven through Athens. Such devices may seem clumsy: it was certainly more sophisticated (if perhaps not more effective) to sponsor the arts, both to magnify the present to the splendor epitomized by the world of Homer's heroes and to memorialize it for the future in the way that Homer had done so impressively. For this purpose the lyric poets—who themselves, for their own various reasons, had frequent recourse to the epic poetry of the past—were perfectly suited. To be sure, the lyric poets sometimes did address themselves to the immediacies of their own experience and introduce their names and personalities into their poetry; but very often they could do this only by means of the tools that Homer provided them. Their goal was on occasion, the here and now; surprisingly often, their path took them through Homer.

III

Oddly enough, the importance of the most fundamental generic distinction within ancient lyric poetry, that between monodic and choral lyric, was not recognized in antiquity: only one ancient author, Plato (*Laws* 6.764d–e), alludes to it, and only in passing. The one extensive analysis of the kinds of lyric poetry transmitted from antiquity, the *Chrestomathia* of Proclus (available only in epitome: Photius, *Bibliotheca* 319b33 ff.), does not provide much help toward understanding the nature of archaic lyric; not only is it quite late, but it also pays for the attempt at an overly schematic organization by degenerating rapidly into arbitrariness and confusion: it begins with poems to the gods and poems to men, then adds poems to both gods and men, only to append a fourth and entirely miscellaneous category; it separates men and gods too rigidly and ignores monody entirely. The Alexandrian scholars applied no uniform system of classification to the authors they edited: thus Sappho's books of poems are divided by metrical considerations, whereas Pindar's are classified in terms of the occasions for which he wrote. Hence in classifying the poems ourselves, we must have recourse to inference from the texts, indirect evidence, and reasonable hypotheses. In the following pages, therefore, we cannot claim certainty, only plausibility.

The most obvious difference between monody and choral lyric is in their modes of performance: monody was sung in solo presentation by a poet who accompanied himself on the lyre, whereas choral lyric was performed by a chorus, which simultaneously sang the words and danced to them, accompanied by the lyre and sometimes other instruments. But there are other differences as well. The language of monody tended to be close to the ordinary dialect spoken by its composer, whereas that of choral lyric was usually a highly artificial mixture of a variety of dialects, with a strong Dorian coloring. The stanzas of monody are generally shorter and metrically less complicated than those of choral lyric. There is a certain tendency for monodic poetry to be strophic (each stanza has an identical metrical structure) and for choral lyric to be triadic (the meter of a first strophe is repeated exactly in an immediately following antistrophe, after which comes an epode with a different metrical pattern; this group of three units is then repeated a number of times), but no hard and fast rule can be made. On the one hand, choral lyric was occasionally strophic: thus, at the beginning of the Lyric Age, there is no metrical reason to compel division of Alcman's maiden song into triads; while at the end of the age, a number of Pindar's victory odes are written in strophic form (*Olympian* 14; *Pythian* 6, 12; *Nemeans* 2, 4, 9; *Isthmians* 8). On the other, some poetry in triadic form is most likely to have been monodic in performance. For example, Stesichorus' lengthy lyrics are organized metrically as repeated groups of strophe, antistrophe, and epode, but it is hard to imagine a chorus singing and dancing a poem several thousand lines long; the mere fact that Ibycus' poem to Polycrates is also organized triadically does not prove that it was performed by a chorus rather than by the poet alone; Pindar's triadic Third Pythian Ode was not occasioned by any real athletic victory and seems most likely to have been a personal ode for the tyrant Hieron; and even the familiar stanzas of Sappho and Alcaeus, though always printed as groups of four lines, are metrically triadic in form (two identical shorter lines followed by one longer one).

Yet another difference is in the geographical regions where these two forms of lyric poetry were popular: monody was most popular in the eastern part of the Greek world, the Ionic and Aeolic cities in or near Asia Minor (Sappho and Alcaeus came from Lesbos, Anacreon from Teos); the poets of choral lyrics tended to come from western Greek colonies (Stesichorus, Ibycus) or central Greece (Alcman from Sparta, Pindar from Thebes, Simonides and Bacchylides from Ceos) and to receive commissions primarily from Dorian cities, including those in Sicily.

These differences are largely formal in nature: they provide a useful terminology for describing the various modes of lyric poetry but do not fully explain how the modes functioned. What role, if any, did Greek lyric poetry play in the societies in which it was produced? Can we discern any differences in social function between monody and choral lyric?

The evidence is scant but it may suffice to permit a tentative generalization. Monodic poetry was performed at informal occasions for small groups bound together by ties of friendship and common interest, and served the social function of uniting these into cohesive wholes and setting them apart from and against other groups in the same city. Choral poetry, on the other hand, tended to be sung at formal celebrations that unified the city as a coherent totality in its acknowledging of divine benefit and human achievement, and served socially to guarantee the integration of the city as a whole, in distinction to other cities. We may be tempted to characterize the difference between these two types of lyric poetry in terms of the modern contrast between private and public. These categories, however, can be used only with the greatest diffidence: for the apparent privacy of much monodic poetry is not that of the spontaneous, introspective individual, but rather that of the small group outside of which the archaic Greek individual can scarcely be conceived. Also, the public character of much choral poetry, rather than excluding the possibility of individual assertions by the poet, seems instead almost to demand such assertions as long as they are integrated into the public celebration. By its nature, therefore, monody concentrates on the personal relations between an individual poet and another member of his own group of friends, or that group as a whole, or individuals outside that group. Choral lyric emphasizes the relations between man and god, in observing cult rituals whereby a city honors its gods, in honoring extraordinary human success that can come only through the favor of the gods, and in witnessing moments of transition in the lives of individuals that can only be accomplished successfully by the grace of the gods. Hence in general monodic poetry has two primary modes: erotic for those within the same group and invective against those outside it. The two primary modes of choral poetry are hymnic for the gods and encomiastic for men. As long as these general principles are not treated too restrictively, they may be helpful in clarifying some otherwise curious persistent features of archaic Greek lyric poetry.

Because the Greek choral odes were long and complex, the fragmentary nature of what has survived makes it extremely difficult to form a clear picture of their original nature. Only Pindar has come down to us by means of medieval manuscripts, whereas Bacchylides was partially rescued from oblivion by the discovery of a papyrus edition of some of his poems in Egypt in 1896. For the rest we depend for the most part on brief citations and guesswork. We have especially little evidence for the early choral lyrics with which archaic Greek cities honored their civic divinities on regular ceremonial occasions: hymns to Zeus and other gods, paeans to Apollo, dithyrambs to Dionysus. But there are two other kinds of choral lyric for which we can fortunately get some sense of their role in the Greek community: the maiden song (partheneion) and the victory ode (epinician). Of the partheneia of Alcman we have most of one (PMG 1: the so-called Louvre-Partheneion, discovered in 1855) and parts of another (PMG 3); on the basis of these we may venture some inferences about the character of the choral odes that accompanied rites of transition in ancient Greece: the coming of age (partheneion) and marriage (hymenaios and epithalamion).

Although the interpretation of the Louvre-Partheneion is highly controversial, it was most likely sung by a chorus of ten girls under the direction of a chorus leader named Hagesichora, while they performed a ritual dedication of an object (probably a robe, possibly a plough) to a goddess of the dawn at a ceremony performed just before sunrise. The members of the chorus single out one girl, Agido, for praise for her beauty; but her own qualities pale in comparison with those of Hagesichora. It is possible but far from certain that Hagesichora and Agido were involved in a ritual footrace in conjunction with the ode, and that a rival chorus called the Pleiades were competing with the performers of this song for a victory. In any case, the ceremony most probably celebrates the coming of age as the point of transition for the maiden from the status of child to nubile woman: the group that used to number eleven girls has now been reduced to ten, because Agido has become a woman. She is, to be sure, not yet as fully one as Hagesichora, their director and instructress: consequently the chorus, who disparages its own lack of attractiveness, limits its praise for the charms to which Agido has already attained by contrasting them with the more perfect fulfillment embodied in Hagesichora. Agido is compared to the sun, whose rising she invokes: the threshold of adulthood corresponds to the dawn with which the performance of the poem coincides, just as adulthood itself, represented by the golden hair and silvery face of Hagesichora, is correlated with the risen sun and full daylight, toward which the ceremony as a whole aims. But the passage toward that goal (one in which the younger girls too are involved) is fraught with dangers, and its attainment lies in the hands of the gods. At the moment of transition, when things are no longer and not yet stable, the possibilities for failure are manifold, and the success wished for by humans can be provided only by gods. Hence the finery in which the members of the chorus have dressed themselves for the occasion is not enough to protect them: they need Hagesichora, together with Agido, to mediate with the gods and to ensure that their offering will be received with favor. But it is with the gods that fulfillment itself lies. This superiority of the gods to men is the burden of the whole first mythological part of the poem, of which only fragments survive: here the legend of the destruction of the sons of Hippocoon, Spartan heroes, is moralized as proof of the irresistible might of Destiny and Providence, oldest of gods: "for the unshod valor / Of men should not fly to heaven / Or try to marry Aphrodite" or other goddesses (15-19). The limit of human wisdom is the recognition that there is a vengeance wreaked by the gods on human presumption and that only that mortal is happy who weaves his day happily to the end without a tear (36–39): hence the light of Agido can be praised, for she has accomplished just this by successfully attaining this new stage and setting the members of the chorus an example they can only hope to be able to emulate when their time comes.

Myth and ritual here are closely bound up with one another: the former demonstrates the folly of human arrogance, the latter implores divine favor for the achievement of human desire. The maturity of Agido, who we have reason to believe belonged to a leading family of Sparta, concerns the community as a whole, for the ritual that announces her coming of age introduces her to the entire city as an eligible marriage partner and authorizes her entrance into the ranks of its adult members.

Alcman's second partheneion (*PMG* 3) juxtaposes Astymeloisa (who plays the role in this poem that Agido plays in the first) with the gathered host of the people and etymologizes her name as "she who is an object of concern to the populace" (*melēma damōi: PMG* 3.74). Alcman's maiden songs provide a poetic voice for the society as a whole to praise one of its children for having attained adulthood and to ask the favor of the gods so that others can do likewise. In the Louvre-Partheneion the bantering tone of the chorus' disparagement of itself and its praise for Agido and Hagesichora is a gentler form of the ribald jests that characterize the choral poetry sung at that other important rite of passage, the wedding, such as the hymenaeal lyrics of Sappho. This may be interpreted as apotropaic, intended to forestall possible divine displeasure.

The same apotropaic tendency is even more apparent in those choral lyrics that celebrate extraordinary human achievements. The athletic victor, for example, is praised for having attained a success that approximates him, if only briefly, to the felicity of the gods, but at the same time he is warned that he is only a man after all and will be destroyed if he forgets his nature and presumes he is a god.

Bacchylides' splendid third epinician was written to celebrate the victory of Hieron, tyrant of Syracuse, in the chariot race at the Olympic Games of 486 B.C. In rhapsodic style the poet begins by invoking the Muse to celebrate two goddesses especially revered in Sicily, Demeter and Persephone, and Hieron's victorious horses, which brought him the garland of victory and caused the multitude of spectators to exclaim at his Zeus-given political power and at the generosity with which he displays his wealth. That display is manifested by the poet's descriptions of the celebrations and hospitality with which Syracuse is filled and the golden tripods Hieron has dedicated to Apollo at Delphi. Man's obligation to honor the gods with such gifts is then illustrated with an extended account of the mythicized fate of Croesus, king of Lydia: when the Persians captured his capital, he preferred self-immolation to humiliation and, on his pyre, reproached the apparently ungrateful gods, who were neglecting his many gifts to them; but, at the last moment, the flames were quenched by a sudden downpour sent by Zeus, and Croesus and his family were whisked away by Apollo to the legendary land of the Hyperboreans. Such was the reward for Croesus' piety: but, among Greeks, none has surpassed Hieron in this regard, and only an envious man will refuse to accord the Syracusan victor the praise he deserves. The military prowess of Hieron's youth has yielded now to a riper wisdom that knows how ephemeral human happiness is and does not forget Apollo's advice to Admetus: one should live each day both as though the morrow were one's last and as though one would live fifty more years of deepest wealth, acting in any event with piety and regarding the joyous contentment of the just as the highest kind of profit.

Bacchylides concludes by contrasting the permanence of the natural elements with the irreversible temporality of human life:

Yet the gleam of excellence does not wane
Together with mortals' bodies, but instead
  The Muse nourishes it. Hieron, you have
    displayed

The finest blooms of felicity
  To mortals; for a man who has done well
Silence brings no adornment;
  Instead, with the revelation of fine things
One will praise too the grace of the honey-tongued
  Nightingale of Ceos.

(3.90–98)

Like most other Greek epinicians, Bacchylides' ode deploys alternately two strategies that at first sight contradict one another: on the one hand, it dissociates Hieron from all other men, dwelling on the victor's unique achievement and correlating him with the gods; on the other hand, it emphasizes the differences between Hieron and the gods and explores what the victor has in common with all other men. Within this poem, the former movement occupies most of the beginning and focuses attention on Hieron's political power, wealth, and athletic achievement: the gathered masses of Greeks are introduced proclaiming his difference from themselves, and the poet honors Hieron by associating him with Croesus, who (despite his historical reality) functions as a mythic paradigm for wealth and bliss that no mortal dare hope for. But the transition to Apollo's advice initiates a second movement, in which it is now discovered that Hieron, for all his triumph, shares distinctive features with all other human beings, features that set them forever apart from the gods: uncertainty about the future, mortality, aging, death. The victor, standing at the border between human and divine, partakes of both realms: he displays to men the glory to which they can attain and at the same time demonstrates that beyond this they cannot go.

We may correlate this doubleness of the poet's strategies of praise with a certain ambiguity in the social role of the victor himself. For on the one hand, the victorious athlete confers glory not only on himself and his family but also on his city as a whole. Syracuse and all Syracusans share in Hieron's triumph, and it is no accident that Bacchylides begins by naming two of the most prominent Sicilian civic divinities. Greek cities knew well how to honor the athletes who conferred such honor on them. For the rest of his life a victor received a special place of honor at public festivals; the city walls might be breached in order to mark his triumphal entry from the games, and his image was sometimes stamped on his city's coins. In Sparta the Olympian victor was accorded a place next to the king on the battlefield; at Athens he dined at public expense in the Prytaneion. But on the other hand, the victor is distinguished as unique from all his fellow citizens: after all, only he has attained this pinnacle of glory.

We may well suspect that the pride a community took in its victor was sometimes not entirely free of resentment for his special privileges. Indeed, the figure of the envier, so common in epinician poetry and introduced here too by Bacchylides (3.67–68), suggests as much. Hence the victor must both be praised as exceptional and at the same time integrated into his community as a whole. The emphasis on Hieron's differences from all other men focuses praise on his uniqueness and thereby on the unique glory that accrued to Syracuse. But also the advice of Admetus reminds Hieron and the audience that the victor is after all a man such as they and placates the potentially envious by indicating to them that they are fundamentally not different from him.

The harmony with which the chorus members, delegated representatives of the city as a whole, perform the epinician, symbolizes the unity of the city in its acknowledgment of the victor's extraordinary prowess and ordinary limitations. Hence it is the poet who provides the city with a voice in which it can proclaim its glory and its integrity; and it is not inappropriate that Bacchylides ends his poem by correlating the lasting fame his poetry can truthfully confer on human excellence with the fame that men will bestow on the poet himself. On the level of the victor, the apparent contradictoriness of the twin strategies is overcome by assigning to Hieron both the glory of success and the knowledge of his own limitations; on the level of the poet, by the integration of both into a coherent artistic unity. Poet and victor, as often in Pindar and Bacchylides, are here intimately linked; they provide the means for the city to reflect publicly on its own capacities and constraints, and each depends upon the other.

Choral lyric, then, plays an important role in the public self-consciousness of the archaic Greek city; monody, on the other hand, seems to have been linked to no civic ritual, performed at no communal occasion, and directed to the unanimous acknowledgment of no object of general concern. Instead the monodist functioned for the most part within the smaller group of those connected with one another by bonds of kinship, friendship, and political alliance. His poems were performed at private and informal banquets or drinking parties and tended to ensure the cohesiveness of the small group in its difference from others within the same city. Most of the monodic poets composed lyrics of two sorts: those stressing the relationships of friendship, trust, and love among members of the same group, and those excluding others from that group by criticizing or attacking them. The erotic and the invective are thus the two sides of the coin of archaic Greek monody: it is here that the link between the melic poets and such writers of iambs and elegies as Archilochus and Theognis is closest.

In particular, Theognis' poetry, explicitly connected with the symposium or private drinking party, is filled with warnings that the good should associate only with one another and should avoid association with the base, and it alternates praise for friendship within the symposiastic group with disparagement of other groups within the city. Anacreon is most familiar to us as the author of erotic lyrics in praise of young boys; but we also have an extended fragment of another poem of his, in choriambs and iambs, in which he viciously satirizes a parvenu named Artemon (PMG 388; compare 424). Alcaeus' exhortations to drinking and his pledges of loyalty to his comrades are balanced by the harshness of his attacks on members of rival political groups. The events he discusses,

tyranny and *stasis*, are often supremely important for the city of Mytilene as a whole, but he treats them not from the perspective of the city but rather in terms of their impact on himself and his comrades. Because this group of friends is simultaneously an informal political party, the general social function of Alcaeus' monody—to strengthen loyalties within the small group and to deepen the gulf between it and others—takes on a thoroughly political coloring. But his poems are never public pronouncements on political events from the point of view of the entire community: instead, they are defiantly self-assertive.

We may grasp the fundamental differences between choral and monodic lyrics most clearly by contrasting the choral with the monodic hymn: the choral hymn is performed for the sake of the whole city at an established ritual occasion; the monodic hymn invokes divine favor for personal purposes within the informal context of the private party. Thus Anacreon prays to Dionysus that the god will help him seduce Cleoboulus (that the poet will be able to have his way with the boy once the latter is drunk: PMG 357). Also, Alcaeus composes a hymn to the Dioscuri in their capacity as rescuers of sailors at sea, without any apparent connection to public ritual and perhaps only to ensure a safe voyage for himself or a comrade (PLF 34a). Such poems were written for an immediate occasion. The fact that they survived the moment for which they were composed and could be passed on to later centuries is quite remarkable; but already in Aristophanes' time Alcaeus and Anacreon were recognized as the masters of the drinking songs called *skolia*, which were popular at Athenian symposia in the sixth and fifth centuries B.C. (compare Athenaeus, 15.694a). It may be conjectured that this singing of songs aided in the transmission of their poems.

It is in the poetry of Sappho that Greek monody attained its most memorable fulfillment, and thus it is fitting that this brief survey of Greek lyric conclude with some remarks about her. For with the exception of Pindar, Sappho is the only Greek melic poet to have become part of world literature—a fact all the more remarkable when we recall that, until this century, the corpus of her transmitted writings included only two texts longer than four lines. Of course her reputation is not derived exclusively, or directly, from her poetry: from the authors of the Athenian Middle and New Comedy of the fourth century B.C., among whom she was a favorite subject for plays of a certain sort (thus Diphilus, in his comedy *Sappho*, made the seventh-century poet Archilochus and the sixth-century poet Hipponax her lovers: Athenaeus, 13.599d), to Lord Byron's "The isles of Greece, the isles of Greece! / Where burning Sappho loved and sung," she has become the emblem of a spontaneous and overwhelmingly sexual passion in (and often for) women that has entranced centuries of male imaginations in those to whom the transmitted poems need not have been well known (but for whom the term "lesbian" could still have quite a definite meaning). The best comment on biographical speculations of this sort, to which Sappho more than any other ancient poet was subjected, was made by Seneca:

> Didymus the grammarian wrote four thousand books: I would feel sorry for him if he had merely read so many useless things. Among those books are investigations "On the Native Country of Homer," "On the True Mother of Aeneas," "Was Anacreon More of a Drunkard or a Lecher?" "Was Sappho a Prostitute?" and other things which, if you knew them, ought to be forgotten. Go ahead now and complain that life is not long enough!
>
> (*Epistles* 88.37)

The historical truth that can be inferred from Sappho's poems may be less flamboyant than the colorful fictions with which posterity has adorned them, but it may make no less strong a claim upon our attention.

Comparison of the poems of Sappho with those of her contemporary Alcaeus reveals a surprising degree of similarity in the social function underlying their obvious differences of subject matter. Both poets disparage their rivals in the harshest of terms. Alcaeus may mock Pittacus as "Potbelly" (*PLF* 129.21) and invoke the baseness of his origin (348) and his father's drinking habits (72); but Sappho is no less severe in her contempt for Andromeda, who can be captivated by a rustic and unfashionable girl (57), for Gorgo, with whom people are quite fed up (144), or for the thoroughly tiresome Irana (91). Many of Alcaeus' poems were composed for drinking parties and advise sharing in the festivities without restraint: thus Melanippus should drink with Alcaeus precisely because of death's inevitability (38a); Bycchis and the other members of a party should forget a laboring ship (perhaps the ship of state, perhaps an aged courtesan) and instead devote themselves to drinking (73); Bycchis again should drown his sorrows in wine (335); the rain outside (338) or the rising of Sirius (347) are reasons enough for a party. So too Sappho, in another of the purely personal hymns characteristic of monody, summons Aphrodite from Crete to take part in a private celebration (2); another poem urges Dica to put festive garlands on her hair (81b). Again, both poets freely discuss family matters in their lyrics: Alcaeus tells of his brother Antimenidas' service as a mercenary soldier among the Babylonians (350); and Sappho expresses the hope that her own brother may return safe from a foreign voyage (5), mocks his love for a certain Doricha (15b, 202, 203), and mentions her mother (98a) and her daughter Cleis (98b, 132, 150).

Of course, many of Alcaeus' poems concern the struggle for political power, but none of Sappho's do. Yet this fact largely reflects the exclusion of women from the political process, typical of ancient Greek society, and should not mislead us into overlooking what the two poets have in common. Both Sappho and Alcaeus preside over small groups in competition with other groups. For both, loyalty within the group is balanced by enmity toward those outside it. And for both the worst imaginable crime is the treacherous breach of trust whereby someone from one's own group goes over to the enemy—compare Alcaeus' attack on Pittacus' faithlessness (129) with Sappho's reactions to Gongyla's leaving her for Gorgo (213), Attis' leaving her for Andromeda (131), Mica's leaving her for the women of the house of Penthilus (71), and other, for us nameless, similar cases (1, 55). For whatever reasons, the poetry of Sappho emphasizes more than that of Alcaeus the links of friendship within a group and gives those links an unmistakable homoerotic coloring. But the longing for absent members of the group (16, 94, 96), like the praise for the beauty of its present members (22, 23, 39, 95), functions no less importantly in Sappho's poetry to integrate the small group than Alcaeus' exhortations to drinking do in his: beauty and love may take the place among women that politics and strife occupy for men, but the social institutions mirrored in their poems remain surprisingly similar.

Thus in Sappho's more famous poem, the one that inspired Catullus' superb translation (51):

He seems to me to be equal to the gods,
That man, whoever sits opposite to you
And listens nearby to you speaking sweetly

And laughing seductively—this indeed
Has set my heart in my breast trembling;
For as soon as I look at you briefly, I can no longer
  say anything,

But my tongue is silent, a delicate
Fire suddenly has run down beneath my skin,
With my eyes I see nothing, my ears are rumbling,

A chilly sweat covers me, trembling
Seizes me completely, I am paler
Than grass, I seem to be just short of dying.

But all must be endured, since . . .

(31)

The extreme of self-control in the analysis of experience is combined here with the extreme of the lack of self-control in the experience analyzed. With an almost clinical dispassion, Sappho catalogs the symptoms of overwhelming passion. Seeing the girl, she may be struck dumb: but her poem is extraordinarily eloquent. The man who sits opposite the girl may seem a mere pretext for the poem: he is invoked in the beginning and perhaps functions as an implicit contrast to Sappho in his divine bliss (as opposed to her torment) or divine strength (as opposed to her weakness); but he is made unidentifiable and vague and is dropped from the explicit level of the extant poem after the first stanza. Instead, the focus shifts to the unnamed girl; but even the girl, as an autonomously existing person, may seem to disappear in the face of the violence of the symptoms her sight unleashes: Sappho sees her in the second stanza, but by the third can no longer see anything at all. For us, the emphasis may seem entirely on the poet. Sappho's body is atomized into a collection of discrete local catastrophes: the organs of perception and expression fail her, and she becomes the anonymous battlefield on which contradictory forces, fire and cold, moisture and dryness, meet in confused opposition.

In reading this poem, we may incline to forget the girl and to concentrate on Sappho's turbulent emotions; but its wit and sophistication consist in its delicately advising us to do exactly the opposite. For at the moment of blindness to which it refers, any self-consciousness on the part of the poet is excluded: she may not be able to see the girl, but she cannot be capable of perceiving herself any more clearly. And at the moment of lucidity in which the poem is composed, Sappho has enough distance from her plight to be able to analyze it in detail as entirely due to the effect of the girl. To linger on "burning Sappho" is to neglect the social function of praise that informs and legitimates the poem in favor of an emotional pathos that is in fact reconstructed only in order to serve that function. The love that Sappho expresses may indeed have been heartfelt; but the stanzas in which she alludes to her passion are surrounded by a frame in which that passion is inextricably bound to particular social institutions, and which we ignore at our risk. It is in fact the beauty of the unnamed girl that is the burden of the poem and the justification for its composition and performance: every detail Sappho provides is designed to testify, not to the poet's susceptibility, but to the girl's seductiveness. Sappho's poem bears no trace of the "egotistical sublime," of the narcissistic fascination with the private self so characteristic of some modern poetry: if we remember its social frame, we shall be fairer to her—and to the other Greek melic poets as well.

Selected Bibliography

BASIC TEXTS

PLF = Poetarum Lesbiorum Fragmenta, edited by E. Lobel and D. L. Page. Oxford, 1955.

PMG = Poetae Melici Graeci, edited by D. L. Page. Oxford, 1962.

SLG = Supplementum Lyricis Graecis. Poetarum Lyricorum Graecorum Fragmenta Quae Recens Innotuerunt, edited by D. L. Page. Oxford, 1974.

West = Iambi et Elegi Graeci ante Alexandrum Cantati, edited by M. L. West. 2 vols. Oxford, 1971–1972.

Bacchylides, edited by B. Snell and H. Maehler. 10th ed. Leipzig, 1970.

OTHER GENERAL TEXTS

Anthologia Lyrica Graeca, edited by E. Diehl. Leipzig, 1924–1952.

Elegy and Iambus, Greek Elegiac and Iambic Poets, edited by J. M. Edmonds. 2 vols. Cambridge, Mass., and London, 1931. Loeb Classical Library. Unreliable texts.

Lyra Graeca, Greek Lyric Poets from Eumelus to Timotheus excepting Pindar, edited by J. M. Edmonds. 3 vols. Cambridge, Mass., and London, 1922–1927. Loeb Classical Library. Unreliable texts.

Lyrica Graeca Selecta, edited by D. L. Page. Oxford, 1968.

Poetae Lyrici Graeci, edited by T. Bergk. 4th ed. Leipzig, 1878–1882.

TRANSLATIONS

Barnstone, W. Greek Lyric Poetry. Bloomington, Ind., 1961.

Bowra, C. M., and T. F. Higham. Oxford Book of Greek Verse in Translation. Oxford, 1938.

Lattimore, R. Greek Lyrics. 2nd ed. Chicago, 1960.

INDIVIDUAL POETS

ALCMAN

Calame, C., ed. Les choeurs de jeunes filles en Grèce archaïque. 2 vols. Rome, 1977.

Page, D. L., ed. Alcman. The Partheneion. Oxford, 1951; New York, 1979.

SAPPHO AND ALCAEUS

Lobel, E., ed. Alkaiou Melē, the Fragments of the Lyrical Poems of Alcaeus. Oxford, 1927.

————. Sapphous Melē, the Fragments of the Lyrical Poems of Sappho. Oxford, 1925.

Martin, H., Jr., ed. Alcaeus. Twayne's World Authors Series. New York, 1972.

Page, D. L., ed. Sappho and Alcaeus. An Introduction to the Study of Ancient Lesbian Poetry. Oxford, 1955.

Rösler, W., ed. Dichter und Gruppe. Eine Untersuchung zu den Bedingungen und zur historischen Funktion früher griechischer Lyrik am Beispiel Alkaios. Munich, 1980.

Voigt, E.-M., ed. Sappho et Alcaeus. Amsterdam, 1971.

ANACREON

Gentili, B., ed. Anacreon. Rome, 1958.

BACCHYLIDES

Jebb, R. C., ed. Bacchylides. The Poems and Fragments. Cambridge, 1905.

CORINNA

Page, D. L., ed. Corinna. London, 1953.

COMMENTARIES

Campbell, D. A. Greek Lyric Poetry. A Selection of Early Greek Lyric, Elegiac and Iambic Poetry. London and New York, 1967.

Gerber, D. E. Euterpe. An Anthology of Early Greek Lyric, Elegiac and Iambic Poetry. Amsterdam, 1970.

Smyth, H. W. *Greek Melic Poets.* London, 1900; New York, 1963.

INDEX

Fatouros, G. *Index verborum zur frühgriechischen Lyrik.* Heidelberg, 1966.

CRITICAL STUDIES

Andrewes, A. *The Greek Tyrants.* New York, 1963.

Bowra, C. M. *Early Greek Elegists.* Cambridge, Mass., 1938.

————. *Greek Lyric Poetry. From Alcman to Simonides.* 2nd ed. Oxford, 1961.

Burn, A. R. *The Lyric Age of Greece.* London, 1960.

Davison, J. A. *From Archilochus to Pindar. Papers on Greek Literature of the Archaic Period.* London and New York, 1968.

Färber, H. *Die Lyrik in der Kunsttheorie der Antike.* Munich, 1936.

Finley, M. I. *Early Greece. The Bronze and Archaic Ages.* New York, 1970.

Fränkel, H. *Early Greek Poetry and Philosophy: A History of Greek Epic, Lyric, and Prose to the Middle of the Fifth Century.* Translated by M. Hadas and H. Willis. New York, 1975.

Griffith, J. G. "Early Greek Lyric Poetry." In M. Platnauer, ed., *Fifty Years (Plus Twelve) of Classical Scholarship.* Oxford, 1968.

Halporn, J. W., M. Ostwald, and T. G. Rosenmeyer. *The Meters of Greek and Latin Poetry.* Rev. ed. Norman, Okla., 1980.

Harvey, A. E. "The Classification of Greek Lyric Poetry." *Classical Quarterly* 49:157–175 (1955).

Jaeger, W. *Paideia: The Ideals of Greek Culture.* Translated by G. Highet. 2nd ed. New York, 1945.

Kirkwood, G. M. *Early Greek Monody. The History of a Poetic Type.* Ithaca and London, 1974.

Pfeiffer, R. *History of Classical Scholarship. From the Beginnings to the End of the Hellenistic Age.* Oxford, 1968.

Pickard-Cambridge, A. *Dithyram, Tragedy and Comedy.* Revised by T. B. L. Webster. 2nd ed. Oxford, 1962.

Raven, D. S. *Greek Metre.* 2nd ed. London, 1968.

Snell, B. *The Discovery of the Mind. The Greek Origins of European Thought.* Translated by T. G. Rosenmeyer. New York, 1960.

————. *Poetry and Society. The Role of Poetry in Ancient Greece.* Bloomington, Ind., 1961.

Snodgrass, A. *Archaic Greece. The Age of Experiment.* Berkeley and Los Angeles, 1980.

Treu, M. *Von Homer zur Lyrik. Wandlungen des griechischen Weltbildes im Spiegel der Sprache.* 2nd ed. Munich, 1968.

Webster, T. B. L. *Greek Art and Literature 700–530 B.C.* London, 1959.

West, M. L. *Studies in Greek Elegy and Iambus.* Berlin, 1974.

Wilamowitz-Moellendorff, U. von. *Sappho und Simonides. Untersuchungen über griechische Lyriker.* Berlin, 1913.

————. *Die Textgeschichte der griechischen Lyriker.* Berlin, 1900.

GLENN W. MOST

AESCHYLUS

(525–456 B.C.)

AESCHYLUS AND EARLY TRAGEDY

ESCHYLUS WAS BORN into a society in which almost all significant public and private occasions—funerals, weddings, celebrations of military or athletic victories, prayers for deliverance from siege or plague or drought, the turning points of the agricultural year—were marked by choral performances, some improvised, some fixed by long tradition, some commissioned, composed, and rehearsed for the occasion. In the competition for the commission for the choral lament in honor of the men who fell at Marathon (the battle in which the Athenians single-handedly defeated the Persian expeditionary force in 490 B.C.), Aeschylus lost to his older contemporary, the lyric poet Simonides. Sophocles at about age fifteen won acclaim for leading the chorus celebrating the battle of Salamis, the great naval victory of the combined Greek forces over the Persians in 480 B.C. Such performances were formalized versions of long-established social patterns. Even today, in the more remote Greek villages at the news of a death, the women, as a matter of etiquette when not of personal grief, raise the wail, and at the funeral a close relative improvises a song of mourning to which the women respond in chorus.

A chorus is a group of people more or less homogeneous in age, sex, and social station witnessing, participating in, responding to an event in which they are deeply involved. Their common interest in the outcome makes them act as a unit. A tragic chorus is such a group. It was part of tragedy not as an archaic survival (in the more individualistic society of fourth-century Athens nonchoral forms of drama quickly developed), but because it represented, in only slightly conventionalized form, a social reality. Because choral behavior is alien to us, we think of the chorus as intensifying the formality and artificiality of the genre. In fact, it expresses something quite close to daily reality and, like other elements of tragedy, can be treated in a more or less stylized way.

Though the alphabet had been in use for more than two hundred years when Aeschylus was born, literature hardly existed in our sense of something experienced primarily from the written page. Until well into the fourth century B.C., verbal arts were still performing arts; the written text was not so much a work of art in its own right as a performing artist's score, usually involving music—also the work of the poet—as well as words. The lyric poet Archilochus boasts of his skill in leading the dithyramb, a choral performance in honor of Dionysus. The tragedians were composers and choreographers as well as poets. In addition, they trained their own choruses, directed their own plays, and performed in them themselves. Sophocles started a new style for tragic poets when he gave up acting in his plays.

It is not without significance that the Greek word for literary style, *lexis*, comes from the root *leg-*, which has to do with speech, whereas our word "style" derives from the Latin *stilus*, a writing implement. The shift from seeing literature as performance to seeing it as something written on a page, the separation of words from music, must have begun in Aeschylus' lifetime. It was an accomplished fact by the end of the fourth century. Aeschylus and his fellow poets of the fifth century wrote for performance and probably never conceived of their works except as performed. In performance the centrality of the chorus was inescapable. Aesthetically, dramatically, symbolically, music—audible as song and the notes of the pipe, visible as dance—was an essential element of the composition. In order to experience even partially the richness and complexity of tragedy, the modern reader must try to recapture in imagination this lost dimension of choral performance.

In fifth-century Athens, tragedies usually had only one performance, in a competition at the spring festival of Dionysus, where they could be awarded first, second, or third prize by a panel of specially appointed citizens. In order to compete the poet submitted his work to one of the city's chief elected officials and "asked for a chorus." If the work was accepted this official appointed a *choregos*, a wealthy citizen who paid the costs of production, principally hiring a piper, and equipping and training a chorus, or rather four choruses since poets competed not with one but with four plays.

A poet "received a chorus" for a tetralogy consisting of three tragedies and a comic finale called a satyr play. This was a short, rowdy play with a chorus of satyrs, which made festive fun with tragic form and traditional stories. One satyr play has survived entire, Euripides' *Cyclops*, a burlesque of the Cyclops episode in *Odyssey* 9; and sizable fragments of several others have been preserved. No tetralogy has survived, but we have one trilogy, Aeschylus' *Oresteia*, which presents in *Agamemnon*, *Libation Bearers*, and *Eumenides* the working-out of the curse on the house of Atreus through the successive homecomings of Agamemnon, of his

son Orestes, and finally of the Furies. The lost satyr play, *Proteus*, was on the related theme of the adventures of Agamemnon's brother Menelaus in Egypt, on his way home from Troy.

From surviving titles it is clear that not every tetralogy, even of Aeschylus, had such close story connections as *Oresteia*. In many cases there is no discernible relation between the four titles; for example, Aeschylus' *Phineus*, *Persians*, *Glaucus*, *Prometheus*, the last a satyr play not to be confused with *Prometheus Bound*. Even in such a sequence some kind of thematic or aesthetic unity should not be ruled out. Skillful dramatists would probably avoid the dramatic equivalent of a piece of music with movements in unrelated keys. The musical analogy is probably valid, since the representation of a tragic story through impersonation originated in the dancing, singing dithyrambic choruses.

Impersonation, the root of drama, is instinctive. It occurs spontaneously in the play of children and adults, and in one form or another is incorporated into the art and ritual of most cultures. As far as we know, drama as an art form—a story not narrated but told through impersonation, composed, rehearsed, performed primarily as entertainment—came into existence in the Western world in Attica in the mid-sixth century B.C., when to the dithyrambic choruses, probably already using mime and impersonation, were added a prologue and speeches spoken, not sung, in verse by their conductor/composer/director. Attic tradition attributed this revolutionary shift from lyric impersonation to telling a story through impersonation to a poet named Thespis. This kind of tragedy, in which a single actor and a chorus, with a leader who perhaps occasionally spoke, acted out a story in spoken and sung verse with dance and gesture, was the earliest form of drama as artistic composition.

About the dithyramb out of which tragedy was believed to have developed, we know only that it was a poem in honor of, but not necessarily about, Dionysus sung and danced by a chorus of fifty boys or men elaborately costumed but not masked. One may speculate that like the rhapsodes' performances of the Homeric poems, it was highly mimetic, and perhaps involved direct impersonation. The seeds of drama existed in the lyrical exchange between the solo voice of the poet/director of the dithyramb and the chorus. This character became an actor when he began to speak (in verse) as well as sing. Since a tragic chorus numbered twelve in Aeschylus' day, augmented to fifteen by Sophocles, the four choruses of a tetralogy would have been close in number to the dithyrambic chorus. It seems possible that the tetralogy form and the smaller chorus came into being when Thespis or one of his contemporaries recognized the dramatic possibilities of dividing the fifty-man dithyrambic chorus into four choruses of twelve. The two leftover persons could have been used as nonspeaking actors, those indispensable characters who attend on royalty, go on errands, carry bodies in and out, restrain prisoners, hand people weapons, in general perform the secondary business involved in the acting out of a story. When there is the possibility of changing the scene and the actor's identity in relation to four separate choruses, several different kinds of action can occur within the scope of one choral performance.

Dithyrambic as well as tragic competitions were a constant feature of festivals in honor of Dionysus. The principal occasion was the City Dionysia in late March, the opening of the sailing season when Athens had the opportunity to display herself both to her own citizens and to visiting representatives of the cities that made up the Delian League, the alliance of Greek maritime states of which she was the leader. Each year three tragic poets competed, having been granted a chorus the previous summer. This allowed six to eight months for rehearsal and indicates something about the care taken with the productions. To have a tetralogy selected was already in some sense to have been successful in a competition, but there was beyond that the possibility of first, second, or third prize. The names of the poet and the *choregos*,

the titles of the plays, and their rank in competition were part of the official records of the city of Athens. A victory with a tragic or a dithyrambic chorus was the occasion for lavish celebration. In Plato's *Symposium* the guests are all suffering from hangovers acquired the day before at the formal party celebrating the poet Agathon's victory with a tragic chorus.

Tragedy was a new art form, and Thespis was one of the poets presenting plays when, about 534 B.C., roughly ten years before Aeschylus was born, Pisistratus, tyrant of Athens, reorganized the spring festival of Dionysus in Athens to include performances of tragedies. By the time Aeschylus was old enough to "ask for a chorus" the Athenians had expelled the Pisistratid dynasty, established a democratic government, and instituted at the City Dionysia the system of tragic and dithyrambic competitions that existed with relatively little change during the artistic life of Aeschylus, Sophocles, and Euripides. In Athens, choral drama became an established art form with developed conventions for comedy as well as tragedy. Comedy was included in the official competitions considerably later, about 486. From Thespis' time through the late fourth century—about two hundred years—tragedy was a local phenomenon, composed and performed primarily for festivals of Dionysus in and around Athens.

In this period of about two hundred years, during which choral tragedy flourished as a living, changing art form in its original home, several thousand plays must have been composed and performed. Aside from the three great tragedians and their works, we know for this period the names of 94 tragic poets and the titles of over 200 tragedies, principally from allusions or quotations in other writers, both contemporary and later. In addition, tattered bits of ancient papyrus rolls that have survived, sometimes for millennia, in Egypt's rain-free climate, preserve titles and fragments of lost plays and disjointed scraps of information about writers and productions. Of all these plays, by late antiquity only a small selection, perhaps for the standard school curriculum, of

AESCHYLUS

Aeschylus, Sophocles, and Euripides was regularly read, seven plays each of Aeschylus and Sophocles, ten of Euripides. These, with nine more of Euripides, including the satyr play *Cyclops*, that survived by a lucky accident, plus bits and pieces of lost plays, are all that remain of tragedy. Of several thousand plays, only these thirty-three survive, and even these are only a fraction of their authors' work. Aeschylus and Sophocles each wrote over ninety plays, Euripides about 120. Their lost works exist, if at all, as fragments of the kind described above.

After their deaths the great tragic artists of the fifth century—Aeschylus, Sophocles, and Euripides—quickly became classics. Their plays and new plays modeled on them were performed not only in Athens but wherever Greek was spoken, in the cities of Greece, Asia Minor, Egypt, South Italy, and later in Latin versions in Latin-speaking cities. Of these later tragedies in Greek and Latin, in form at least modeled on fifth-century Athenian tragedy, we have only fragments except for nine by the first-century A.D. philosopher-statesman Seneca and a tenth attributed to him that is probably spurious. Though Seneca's plays have appropriated the externals of fifth-century Greek tragedy, they are a fundamentally different art form with its own laws and beauties. They have choruses but they are not "choral." The choruses are aesthetically and thematically integrated, but unlike those of their models they are not actual people for whom the action has some kind of crucial ongoing meaning. In truly choral drama the members of the chorus, because of their profound human involvement, constitute the matrix of the action. They are indispensable, as characters in the drama, to its realization, as they are not for Seneca.

Even by the late fourth century, choral tragedy—with its mythological subjects, its grand preoccupations, ethical, social, psychological, cosmic—was already an "archaic" art form, an expression of a deeply communal way of life that except on the village level was going out of existence. A new form of drama without chorus, with made-up stories about contemporary middle-class people with their slaves and hangers-on, the so-called New Comedy, the original romantic comedy, developed in Athens and quickly became popular elsewhere as the appropriate form for this "modern" world, focused on personal relationships and individual fulfillment.

Aeschylus' father, Euphorion, was a member of the old Athenian aristocracy from the Attic town of Eleusis. Aeschylus was about fifteen when the Pisistratids were expelled. His first tragedies were presented under the recently restored democracy. His first victory was in 484, six years after the battle of Marathon, in which he fought and in which his brother Cynegirus was killed. He lived through the Persian occupation of Attica and central Greece in 480–479 and probably also fought in the battle of Salamis. His earliest extant tragedy, *Persians*, presents the impact of the Persian defeats on the Persian court in Sousa. It was performed along with three other plays in 472 and won a first prize. Pericles, then about twenty-three years old, was the *choregos*.

Aeschylus witnessed and was part of the beginnings of the post-Persian War flowering in Athens of the arts, of democratic institutions, of military, above all of naval, power that we call the age of Pericles. It was a time of confidence and idealism when Athens was achieving a dominant position in the Greek world as leader of the Delian League, and the more destructive aspects of that leadership had not yet manifested themselves.

In 468 Sophocles won a victory with his first chorus, apparently over Aeschylus. From then on the two poets frequently competed with each other. Euripides was granted his first chorus in 455, the year after Aeschylus died. Aeschylus made two, possibly three, trips to Sicily, where, like his contemporaries the lyric poets Pindar, Simonides, and Bacchylides, he enjoyed the patronage of the tyrant Hieron in his court at Syracuse. Sometime after 476, when Hieron founded the city of Aetna, Aeschylus composed a play (now lost) in celebration of the event. At Hieron's request he also did a second production of *Persians*. Pindar combines the themes of these two plays, the founding of the city and the repulse of the "barbarians" (Persians and their allies in the eastern Mediterranean, Etruscans and Carthaginians in the western Mediterranean) by the Greeks in a choral ode whose immediate occasion is Hieron's victory in the chariot race at Delphi in 470 (*Pythian* 1). It seems possible that Pindar's victory ode and Aeschylus' two plays were all performed in the course of one grand celebration commemorating the achievements of Hieron's rule.

Near the end of his life (it must have been after the production of *Oresteia* in the spring of 458), when Hieron had been dead about ten years, Aeschylus returned to Sicily. He died there at Gela in 456. The people of Gela buried him with many honors, at public expense. His gravestone bore the following inscription: "Aeschylus, an Athenian, son of Euphorion, is covered by this monument. He died in wheat-bearing Gela. To his warlike spirit the hallowed ground of glorious Marathon will bear witness, and so will the long-haired Medes. They experienced it." If the tradition is correct that Aeschylus himself composed it, he chose to be remembered as a soldier rather than a poet.

A scholar of the fourth century A.D. writes of Aeschylus, "the Athenians considered him the father of tragedy, and summoned him, even when he was dead, to the festival of Dionysus. For works of Aeschylus were presented in revival by their decree, and won victories all over again" (Philostratus, *Vita Apollonii* 6.11). Philostratus is referring to the fact that though other tragic poets won victories with posthumous presentations, only Aeschylus was honored with a formal decree of the people of Athens that anyone who wished to enter the competition with a work of Aeschylus should "receive a chorus." For the Athenians he was the father of tragedy, both because of his mastery of the tragic emotions of pity and fear, and, in a more literal sense, because the forms and conventions of tragedy that he adapted or worked out are, except for some relatively minor developments that are discussed later, the conventions of tragedy as we know it.

An ancient biography, preserved in some manuscripts, records that his tomb was frequented "by those whose livelihood was tragedy," who made offerings there and performed his plays. As the father of tragedy he was accorded the status and graveside cult of a culture hero.

Fifty years after Aeschylus' death, in the spring of the year following the deaths of both Euripides and Sophocles, Aristophanes in *Frogs* showed what Aeschylus and tragedy meant to the Athenians. Perhaps Philostratus had this play in mind when he wrote that the Athenians "summoned him [Aeschylus], even when he was dead, to the festival of Dionysus." In two senses that is literally what happens in *Frogs*: first because Aristophanes brings Aeschylus into the theater as a character, competing and winning a poetry contest in Hades with Euripides; second because it is Aeschylus rather than his favorite Euripides that Dionysus chooses to bring back from Hades to help Athens regain her nerve in the disastrous times near the end of the Peloponnesian War. Dionysus' explanation of why he has come to Hades suggests what the dramatic choruses meant to the city: "I came down after a poet. What for? So that the city could be saved and stage her choruses. So, whichever of the two has the best advice for the city that's the one I plan to take with me" (1418–1421). He then asks the two poets for a judgment about the brilliant and disruptive leader of the extreme democrats, Alcibiades. Two things are notable here: It is the judgment of a poet that can "save" the city from tearing itself apart over Alcibiades; and the sign of salvation is restoration of choral performances as they were before the bad times restricted them. In contrast to Euripides, who makes a lofty and rhetorically elegant moral statement with no indication of what kind of action the city should or could take, Aeschylus gives stern, old-fashioned advice: the Athenians must face up to the fact that in encouraging Alcibiades they have, as he says—

apparently alluding to *Agamemnon* 717 ff.—reared a lion cub in the city (*Frogs* 1431). His remedy is nothing less than tragic confrontation, a coming to terms with an act that cannot be undone. Faced with their own tragedy it is the "father of tragedy" that the people of Athens will summon from Hades to help them come to terms with what they have brought on themselves. Aristophanes seems to be suggesting that the audience of a tragedy should be invited not only to witness the great figures of the past confronting irreversible disaster but also to discover in themselves the ability to confront their own terrible realities.

CONVENTIONS OF CHORAL TRAGEDY

During Aeschylus' lifetime and, if the tradition is correct, largely as a result of his shaping, tragedy evolved from one-actor choral drama to what we know as Greek tragedy. Working not only as poet but also as composer, actor, choreographer, chorus master, director, he established the scenic as well as the literary conventions that are, with relatively minor developments, the conventions of the tragedy of Sophocles and Euripides. The great differences we feel between him and his successors are not in basic form but in different treatment of form.

Information about the fifth-century stage and its dance, music, costume, and production is meager, often from later periods, and unreliable. Archaeological evidence is minimal. Evidence from contemporary visual arts is rich and vivid but not informative, since it is rarely possible to detect how realistic these representations of dramatic performances are. Much that is represented as the practice of the classic stage, the exaggerated masks and boots for instance, was devised considerably later as a suitably grand way of presenting the "classics." The texts of the plays have come down to us without music,[1] stage directions, or choreography, and with few and frequently confused indications of who is speaking or singing. There are some, not always reliable, comments and anecdotes of later ancient writers, but for the most part we must take the text as our guide to the visual as well as the auditory dimension of tragedy—to gesture, movement, dance, costume, scenery, properties, even exits and entrances, what Aristotle in the *Poetics* called "spectacle." Aristotle's playing down of this dimension, his insistence that tragedy should be able to make its effect through reading alone, is based on the sound perception that plays that rely on acting and scenic effects to move the audience are less tragic than those with inherently tragic stories. It has had the unfortunate effect of diverting attention from much that was significant, in some cases essential, in choral drama.

In a performance for which the presence of a chorus is a precondition, the two chief means of choral expression, dance and song, with all that goes with them in terms of musical and visual effects, must have a greater and more integral function than in the nonchoral forms of drama we are accustomed to. Spectacle in choral drama involves not only scenery, costume, and stage effects, but choral gesture, movement, and grouping, and that combination of the visual and the auditory that is the dance. As I hope to show more concretely in discussing individual plays, it is dramatically significant whether words are sung or spoken, what gestures are made, what properties are used by chorus and actors. One of the critic's tasks is to determine from such clues as the texts provide the special emphases that these devices contributed. The visual and musical dimensions were probably more essential to choral drama than the blazing colors that once gave complexity to the now blank surfaces of Greek sculpture and architecture. There is much that we can

---

[1]A few papyrus fragments of tragic lyrics with musical notation have been discovered, but there is no certainty about how to read the "notes."

never know about music and spectacle, but it is well not to forget their importance in choral performance and to try to imagine what they may have contributed to our texts.

What Aeschylus had to work with was a singing, dancing, miming chorus and a leader who sang and spoke as a solo voice in response both to the chorus and to a single actor. They performed on a circular or nearly circular outdoor orchestra (dancing floor) with some kind of temporary building across the back. The audience occupied the hillside that rose in a semicircle from the level of the orchestra. Chorus and actors entered from the sides into the orchestra or through doors in this stage building. There were no lights or curtain. Actors and chorus wore masks. Up to the end of the fifth century, these basic theatrical conditions were only slightly modified. The theater was given permanent form in stone, with seats for the audience, ramps leading into the orchestra on either side, *perhaps* with a slightly raised stage in front of the scene building (both the archaeological and the literary evidence are unclear). Scene painting, probably in the form of panels or a backdrop in front of the stage building, was an innovation of Sophocles (Aristotle, *Poetics* 1449a). Developments in dramatic devices were somewhat more extensive but did not alter basic form. Aeschylus, according to Aristotle (*Poetics* 1449a), added a second actor and gave first place to spoken as opposed to sung portions, and Sophocles added a third actor (an innovation adopted by Aeschylus in *Oresteia* and probably also in *Prometheus*). Three actors remained the norm. This does not limit a play to three characters, since with masks one actor can play several roles. But it limits the number of speaking characters simultaneously on stage to four, three actors and the chorus leader. Nonspeaking parts played by extras—servants, armed escorts, the jury in *Eumenides*—are a feature of most plays.

From the beginning three styles of delivery were used: speech, recitative, and song, with appropriate meters for each. Even in one-actor

tragedy there were probably spoken exchanges between actor and chorus leader as well as set speeches by the actor. Recitative can be choral or for solo voice. It is often, but not always, used for the entrance of the chorus, even more frequently for the much shorter choral exit song. In moments of excitement there is sometimes a shift from speech to recitative. The chief meter for speech is a six-foot iambic line, called iambic trimeter. Like English iambic pentameter, which was developed in emulation of Seneca's Latin version of this meter, it is capable of a wide range of effects, from something close to ordinary speech to sonorous high poetry. All the possibilities for song are exploited—full chorus, chorus broken up into two or more groups, solo song, and lyric exchange between chorus and one or more solo voices. Finally, speech and song are sometimes combined when actor or chorus leader speak in trimeters and chorus or actor sing in reply. Few translators give reliable indications of the shifts from one form of delivery to another.

There is no rhyme in Greek poetry, but in every type of Greek verse there is a varied and refined use of the melodic and rhythmic possibilities of language, most richly exploited, as might be expected, in sung passages. The music of the choral and solo lyrics of tragedy is lost, but the verbal music remains. Those who do not read Greek have to take this on faith, since it can only be communicated through live demonstration in Greek.

It is an oversimplification to say that the lyric, or sung, passages of tragedy are emotional, the spoken rational. Choral song can be speculative, narrative, expository, and some of the most intense moments of tragedy are in spoken passages. Nevertheless sung passages use poetic language and music to explore, elaborate, and intensify mood and feeling in ways not available to speech alone. Passages that combine speech and song dramatize their contrasting effects. In the first part of the Cassandra scene of *Agamemnon*, a literal-minded and confused chorus, speaking, try to make sense of Cassandra's horrific prophetic vision communicated in song; as the horror, though not the sense, of her vision begins to reach them, the chorus also shift to song. More ironically, in *Seven Against Thebes*, Eteocles, speaking "rationally," prepares for armed encounter with his brother, while the chorus of Theban women, singing "emotionally," try to dissuade him.

Many of the conventions of tragedy are determined by its choral form and the conditions of performance and must have been part of tragedy from the beginning. They are built into the genre and appear in the latest as well as the earliest plays, but not according to any rule or system prescribing which, how many, where, or how they should be used. There is great freedom and inventiveness in their application. Most of the "rules" of tragedy were formulated after the fact. Fifth-century tragedy was fluid and experimental, creating conventions rather than being bound by them. Poets innovated in any way that suited their poetic purpose.

To set the scene before the entrance of the chorus, a prologue in the form of a speech by a single actor or a dialogue between two actors is a customary but not an inevitable part of a tragedy. In the days of Thespis, who is credited with its introduction, it must have been spoken by the actor. It would perhaps be particularly needed when there was no help from a second actor or sophisticated scenery to convey the information that a modern audience usually finds in the program—time, place, identity of actors and chorus. No surviving play of Sophocles or Euripides is without such an introductory scene, but Aeschylus felt free in *Persians* and *Suppliants* to omit it and to begin with the entrance of the chorus, who deliver the necessary information in the course of their entrance song. As an ancient commentator on *Persians* observes, "The chorus functions as prologue."

On a stage without curtain or lights, getting the chorus into the orchestra at the beginning and off at the end is an inevitable part of every play. There is a traditional way of doing this, which again is observed only when it serves the artistic and dramatic needs of the situation. In slightly less than half the surviving plays the chorus enters with anapestic recitative, whose ordered rhythms suggest some kind of ordered progression into the orchestra. Many other kinds of entrances exist. In *Seven Against Thebes* the chorus of women, panicked by the prospect of the sack of the city, rush on apparently in no order at all singing in the most agitated of all lyric meters, the dochmiac, which more often occurs at a crisis of the action or in a lament following a catastrophe. Frequently the final exit of the chorus is marked by a short passage of anapestic recitative delivered by the chorus or an actor; but the chorus of *Persians* exit singing an iambic lament, and the chorus of *Agamemnon* apparently exit in silence, in fear or disdain of the last insolent words of Aegisthus and Clytemnestra.

An antiphonal lament for solo voice and chorus called a *kommos* (from the root *kop*, "beat," referring to beating the breast in mourning) is a common but not inevitable part of tragedy. The term seems to have been used loosely not only for this form of lament but for any song for chorus and solo voice. The exit song of *Persians* is a conventional *kommos*, with Xerxes crying out in grief and the chorus responding. The choppy iambic dimeters, monotonously repeated, reproduce the sound and rhythm of breast beating. A *kommos* can have two solo voices—Orestes and Electra in *Libation Bearers*, Antigone and Ismene in *Seven Against Thebes*. The *kommos* of *Libation Bearers* turns into a prayer for vengeance. There is no *kommos* in *Suppliants*, *Prometheus*, or *Eumenides*, though *Prometheus* has a sorrowful choral ode describing how earth's inhabitants grieve for Prometheus. In *Oedipus at Colonus*, which piles grief on grief until the final illumination, there are three *kommoi*, one of them not a lament but a scene of violent conflict in which Creon and his armed soldiers drag Antigone from the stage while the chorus call for help.

The antiphonal structure of *kommos* is also used for exchange of information and for occasional scenes of conflict. In the *kommos* of

Persians the chorus repeatedly ask for missing Persian princes by name. Xerxes must respond to each name by confirming that its owner is dead. In the second half of the Cassandra scene of *Agamemnon*, which is a *kommos* in the looser sense of the word, Cassandra is struggling to impart, and the chorus to grasp, the meaning of her prophetic vision. Information can be communicated antiphonally in speech as well as song. Question and answer in iambic trimeter often breaks down into symmetrical one-line, or in moments of great excitement half-line, exchange. In *Persians* the ghost of King Darius elicits the details of the Persian defeat from the queen in such a line-for-line exchange. This device, called *stichomythia* (speaking in lines) also lends itself to intense verbal conflict, for example, the final confrontation of Orestes and Clytemnestra in *Libation Bearers.*

Passages that combine speech or recitative and song, because of their antiphonal structure, are frequently used to express conflict. Eteocles' confrontations with the women of Thebes in *Seven Against Thebes*, Pelasgus' with the daughters of Danaus seeking sanctuary in *Suppliants*, Athena's with the Furies outraged at Orestes' acquittal in *Eumenides*, take this form. In *Agamemnon* the chorus of Argive elders also hurl accusations at Clytemnestra, as they mourn their dead king in traditional lyric manner, while she, the wife who should be the chief mourner singing the solo dirge, repels their charges and proclaims a victory in anapestic recitative, standing over the corpse of the husband she has murdered. The effect is richly operatic. I think of the moment in *Trovatore* where the monks chant their prayers for the soul of the condemned troubadour while he and Eleanora sing a love duet and the soldiers their military march. Members of the chorus frequently engage in short spoken exchanges including *stichomythia*, but are rarely given speeches of more than four or five lines.

"Drama" comes from the root *dra-*, to do. A drama is something done, an action, not necessarily physical, that, as Aristotle describes it (*Poetics* 1449–1450a), leads to good fortune or the reverse. Such an act is Prometheus' refusal to reveal the secret that Zeus must learn if he is not to fall from power. The essence of such action, and therefore of drama, is choice between conflicting views or forces—in this case between Zeus and Prometheus and the cosmic powers they represent. With Aeschylus' introduction of the second actor it became possible to present extended conflicts explored on several levels at once: Eteocles assigning defenders of the seven gates of Thebes in response to the messenger's description of the attacking captains, Clytemnestra inducing Agamemnon to trample the wealth of the house, Prometheus defying Zeus in the person of his emissaries. Though extended debates in paired speeches do not occur in Aeschylus' plays, his introduction of the second actor made such scenes, so characteristic of later tragedy, possible. To him we owe the means of representing directly the collisions of forces and personalities that make drama, as well as the more ideological confrontations that we find in Sophocles and Euripides.

In one-actor drama, onstage action was of necessity limited, and large-scale events and violence, often the cause or the outcome of choice, were difficult to represent. Much of the time, actor and chorus must have been responding to the account of an offstage event. The extended lyrical narrative, the convention of the messenger scene, and its extension the long narrative speech all reflect this reality. Lyrical narrative of events that are basically part of the action becomes less common as three-actor drama becomes established. But even with the greater freedom to present complex events and physical conflict that three actors afford, a preference for presenting such events in narrative speeches persisted. Perhaps the principal reason for this is the taste for great narrative of an audience reared on recitations—of Homer first of all, but also on the performances of great choral lyric narratives of which only a few not very representative examples have survived. Perhaps also the poets recognized that the account of an eyewitness—

of the murder of Laius or the self-blinding of Oedipus—is often more convincing, therefore more not less tragic, than simulated onstage violence. The presence of the chorus as a witness who might be expected to become involved is a practical obstacle to staging such events, though perhaps not as serious as is sometimes claimed. There is no hard and fast rule that the chorus can never leave the stage during the drama. Two notable instances in extant plays are *Eumenides* and Sophocles' *Ajax*. May there not have been many more among the lost plays?

Until the coming of cinema some kind of "messenger scene" was the only way that such events as the central matter of *Persians*—the defeat of Xerxes' fleet at Salamis and the disasters of the overland retreat of the land army through central and northern Greece—could be represented dramatically. But the messenger scene is not an inadequate substitute for a wide-screen spectacular. The point of the messenger scene in *Persians* is not reliving the events directly but experiencing them through the responses of the messenger, the chorus of Persian elders, and the queen. This is equally true for those two most famous messenger speeches of tragedy: in *Oedipus the King* the description of Jocasta's suicide and Oedipus' self-blinding, and in *Bacchae* of the dismembering of Pentheus by his mother and the other Theban maenads. The persistence of the messenger scene was the result of artistic choice rather than of mechanical adherence to convention. The kinds of stories that furnish the matter of tragedy tend to focus on action in the sense described above: the conflicts that culminate in choice and their irreversible consequences. By its very nature the messenger scene widens the scope of such actions to include their impact on narrator, chorus, and any other characters on the stage. This is in the spirit of tragedy, which is never just about the fate of individuals but is also about the implication of their actions for every person in the story and, by extension, for all human audiences.

TRAGIC STORY AND TRAGIC CHORUS

Homer, particularly in the *Iliad* as Aristotle pointed out, furnished the pattern for the tragic story. The *Iliad* is not the story of the Trojan War. Its action covers fifty-odd days near the end of that ten-year struggle and focuses closely on only a few of those, turning points, critical moments of choice leading up to Achilles' climactic choice to return to battle and fight Hector. Because it *enacts* a story *musically*, tragedy has an even narrower focus than epic, with the heightening of intensity that compression, direct representation, and music realize. As epic narrates, tragedy reenacts, not the whole event but the moment of critical choice that has irreversible consequences, usually for everybody on the stage, the moment that is the culmination of many past events, the turning point after which everything is permanently different. The essence of tragedy is the moment of concentrated awareness of irreversibility, of that which nothing can undo, in the light of which life, for any survivors on stage and off, including the audience, will henceforth be lived.

The magnitude of the tragic event, the reason for presenting it in choral performance, lies in its implications not just for those we think of as principals but for all participants. Spectators, even readers two millennia later, are participants. For this reason Greek tragedy does not end with the catastrophe, the quick tableau of a stage littered with bodies that we are used to from Elizabethan tragedy. The *Iliad* does not end with Achilles' victory and Hector's death, but spends two more books in contemplation of the aftermath. The last third or quarter of a tragedy is usually devoted to the unfolding by chorus and survivors of the meaning of the event. The implications of the Persian defeat must be experienced in the form of the antiphonal lament by Xerxes and the Persian elders in which every source of grief and humiliation is agonizingly recalled. Tragedy is not a simple reenactment but an act of assimilation. Not only the occurrence but its implications must be lived through on the stage and by the audience. This living-through is part of the event, its completion and validation, the means by which, for all its brevity, the tragic moment becomes a permanent possession of humanity.

The Greek word for the critical moment that is the focus of every tragedy is *kairos*. It was so important an element in the way the Greeks saw life that sometime in the fifth century it emerged objectified as a god, with a cult of his own. The god's cult statues are bald on the back of the head with a long lock of hair on the forehead. Unless you "take time by the forelock" as he flashes past, the chance of capturing him is gone for good.

Tragedy's focus on the brief critical moment guarantees a certain unity of action even in so-called episodic tragedies. *Trojan Women*, a favorite example of an episodic plot, is no exception. Every apparently discontinuous episode is part of the moment when, with the Greek ships poised for departure, the captive Trojan women are allotted as spear brides to the Greek chieftains, in reparation for the carrying off of Helen to Troy. Helen herself, Menelaus' prize, is presented as such a captive "Trojan" bride. When the aged queen Hecuba prepares the body of her grandson Astyanax for burial instead of for his wedding, the abnormality of all the "weddings" of the play is underlined. The allotment is also, fatefully, a kind of Trojan retaliation for the fate that Paris' bride brought on Troy. For the whole play from prologue on is designed to show that the Trojan "brides" whom the ships bear homeward will bring to the Greeks destruction like that which Helen brought to the Trojans. It is this moment, as fateful for Greece as for Troy, that gives the play its focus and its double terror.

The so-called unities of time and place were not rigidly observed rules but general practices that were consequences of this focus on the critical moment. The more concentrated the moment the less room there is for long lapses of time or changes of scene. Nevertheless there are many plays containing one or the other or both. It is reported that Aeschylus created five scene changes in the play composed for Hieron of Syracuse to celebrate the founding of Aetna. Because the brief tragic moment is the summation and fruition of all that has led up to it and the determinant of what is to follow, most plays encompass much more than they enact. Here too the *Iliad* sets the pattern. The culmination of the wrath of Achilles in the duel with Hector is the pivot of the whole Trojan War. And in presenting it as the turning point in the series of events that starts with the rape of Helen and reaches beyond the death of Achilles to the fall of Troy, the poem encompasses, without narrating, the whole war. What is enacted in *Oedipus the King* is Oedipus' discovery of a series of long past events and the reactions to that discovery of Oedipus, Jocasta, Kreon, and the Theban elders. Encompassed is the history of the curse in the house of Laius and its connection with the riddle of mortality. *Trojan Women* enacts the allotment of spear brides but it encompasses the whole war and its aftermath from the rape of Helen through the disastrous homecomings. It is the concentration of meanings past, present, and future in the moment enacted on the stage, not just the fate of individuals, that gives tragedy its impact.

The stories that were found suitable for tragedy were stories of a special kind of event: as just suggested, an event of a magnitude to affect and have meaning for people other than those directly involved, an event significant enough to call for the presence of a chorus. We refer to such a story as a myth.[2] Myth and chorus are the distinguishing characteristics of Greek tragedy. One seems to imply the other, and both disappear together from the more individualistic drama of the late fourth century.

Usually the myth, the story, was of an event of the legendary past thought to have some

---

[2]The Greek word *muthos* means any story. It could be used even of the made up plots of New Comedy.

basis in history, *Lear* or *Cymbeline* rather than the more documentable history of Shakespeare's chronicle plays. The involvement of gods, directly as stage presences or indirectly through such devices as fulfillment of prophecy, is a sign of the event's magnitude, its significance for a wider community. It does not make the stories unhistorical ("mythological" in our sense of fanciful or unreal) in the view of the Greeks, as readers of Aeschylus' younger contemporary Herodotus can readily see. Occasionally a more recent event was seen as having the kind of significance that calls for the presence of a chorus, as in Aeschylus' *Persians*, the only surviving example that deals with events of the Persian War, in some of which Aeschylus himself had taken part. On stage we witness the Persian response to Xerxes' defeat. But beyond this, the significance for other defeated peoples and for Greeks and other victors, though not directly shown, is reflexively implied. The full range of the action's impact is indicated by the involvement of the gods, which is as great in this play as in any dealing with the legendary past. Though there were a few tragedies with made-up stories—none by any of the three great tragedians, however—the preference was for what was thought of as a real event, usually of the remote past. A choral performance is a response to an event that affects a community's sense of itself and its relation to the gods. Almost inevitably such an event is conceived as an actual rather than an imaginary occurrence.

The action of tragedy, then, like the action of the *Iliad* and *Odyssey*, involves the gods and the cosmic order of which both mortals and gods are part. This order is the context for all tragedies, though the three tragedians differ greatly in their attitudes toward it and their ways of representing it. Some knowledge of its outlines, therefore, is important for understanding tragedy. The cosmic order is the system of Justice, *Diké*, enforced and administered by Zeus and the Furies, an order that includes, but is not confined to, the moral order on which

human society is based. If the sun departed from its course, said the philosopher Heraclitus (*ca.* 500 B.C.), the Furies would drive it back. Homer and Hesiod, in a perhaps anachronistic reading, were thought of as authorities for the fifth-century version of this system, which prescribes for everything in creation its proper place.

The gods, though immortal and infinitely more powerful than mortals, are, like mortals, part of this creation, not its creators. Zeus, mightiest and most wise of all the gods, administers and enforces the cosmic order, but he did not create it or establish its rules. Like his predecessors, Kronos and Uranos, he rules conditionally and can be overthrown if he disregards *Diké*. He is a creature not a creator, subject in the last analysis to the cosmic order like all other creatures. The gods have a different place in the scheme from that of mortals, and they are governed by different rules, but transgression of those rules can lose them their privileges and throw the universe into chaos, which may involve human beings too. And human transgressions make trouble among gods.

Such interaction of gods and mortals is implicit in every tragedy, explicit in a few, particularly *Oresteia* and *Prometheus*. In *Oresteia* the chain of human actions culminating in Orestes' acquittal by a jury of Athenian citizens precipitates a cosmic crisis in which the Furies, underworld powers outraged at the Olympian gods for their support of Orestes and Athens, threaten to destroy Athens. In *Prometheus*, Prometheus, a god, has conferred a god's prerogative, fire, on mortals. In the struggle between him and Zeus that follows, Zeus's continued rule and the existence of mankind are both in jeopardy. In spite of the poetry of mystery and power that Aeschylus bestows on him, Zeus is no Jehovah. It is important to realize that in tragedy gods and mortals and gods and gods interact, explicitly or implicitly, sometimes to reaffirm the old order, sometimes to create new relationships and perhaps new kinds of consciousness in the cosmos.

Violators of *Diké* are in the most literal sense transgressors, oversteppers (see Latin *trans-gredi*, to step across, and Greek *parabainein*, to overstep, the customary verb for violations of *Diké*). For *Diké* assigns a place and a function to each part of creation. To overstep the boundaries of this assigned place is a violation of fundamental order that threatens the whole system. It is felt as pollution requiring purification since it mingles what was designed to be kept separate.

In the human sphere, transgression, overstepping, occurs in terms of the "unwritten laws" *(agraphoi nomoi)* that are the basis of social order and civilization, everything that distinguishes human beings from animals. These laws prescribe and circumscribe human behavior in certain fundamental relationships. They enjoin reverence between host and guest, for oaths, for the rights of suppliants, for kindred, and always of course for the gods, who punish violations of these laws. Overstepping, the use of violence in any of these contexts, introduces animal behavior into the human sphere. It is a form of pollution that, unless checked, proliferates in the community, sometimes in the cosmos.

Unlike codified law, the unwritten laws are part of the cosmic system enforced by Zeus and the Furies. The Furies appear wherever *Diké* has been violated. By tracking down and punishing the transgressor they restore order and prevent pollution from spreading. They are objectifications of the fury of the victims of outrage, not primitive demons but expressions of the psychological reality that violence breeds violence. Their avenging presence is a symptom not a cause of pollution. By virtue of their function they are double in nature, as their two names indicate: they are both *Erinyes*, "Strife creatures" (the poets derived this name, possibly incorrectly, from *eris*, strife), pursuers of the transgressor, savage and implacable embodiments of anger; and *Eumenides*, "Kindly Ones," benign and gracious fosterers of order and creativity both physical and spiritual.

It is because a tragic event involves a violation of *Diké*, usually a transgression of unwritten law, that it has consequences and meaning not just for the transgressors but for all who must suffer or witness the disruption of order. It is this, in the last analysis, that gives the event its wider application, what I have called its magnitude, the reason for the presence of a chorus. The pity and fear of tragedy arise in part from its demonstration of how inevitably, and without regard for the cost in human suffering, the gods move to expel pollution and restore order. The system rights itself with a certain grand impersonality to which human victims are merely incidental. Our ideas of sin and repentance are alien to this system of retribution. Most of all with Aeschylus, but to a large degree with Sophocles and Euripides too, one should think not of sin and repentance but of pollution and purification in a quite external sense, less of the tainted soul of the transgressor and more of the community polluted and disrupted by his or her presence.

The most obvious, but not the most common, way of integrating the workings of *Diké* into a tragic story is through the onstage presence of a god, as prologue or *deus ex machina*, or of gods as actors, individually or in chorus. More frequently the gods and *Diké* are represented indirectly through oracle, dream, and prophecy, through miracle on stage or reported, or through the dramatic use of ritual. Any or all of these in every possible combination, usually reinforced by complex imagery, are used to convey the cosmic context of tragic action.

Fulfillment of prophecy in some form is part of the action of a very large number of tragedies. What happens has been foretold or foreshadowed, usually enigmatically. Foreknowledge is possible because there is a cosmic order, imperfectly grasped by mortals, more fully known to the gods. When what has been foretold comes to pass, this order is validated. When Apollo's oracle at Delphi seems to have erred, the chorus of *Oedipus the King* foresee moral chaos and declare that they can no longer perform their choral dances or worship the gods (895–910). This is only one of many tragedies that represent the disaster and pollution that follow from disregarding or misunderstanding prophecy.

In tragedy it is most often Apollo, god of purification and healing, harmony in all its senses, who transmits knowledge of the future to mortals through his oracle at Delphi or through his priests. This knowledge can lead to the affirmation of order that comes with understanding the event in the context of *Diké*. Such understanding, even when it is not after the fact, as it usually is, rarely comes without much suffering. Other common devices of foreshadowing are omens, dreams, ominous names (the most familiar example is Oedipus, which means both "swollen foot" and, more prophetically, "knowing foot"), and curses, righteous prayers for vengeance that the Furies are bound to enforce.

It is sometimes held that because so much is foreknown and foretold, Greek tragedy is a tragedy of fate in which human beings have no choices. In what sense, if at all, are mortals responsible for their actions if the gods have foreknowledge and the power and obligation to maintain the cosmic order? For the Greeks, as for us, free will is a paradox. The complexity of moral choice is represented by assigning to it multiple causes, human and divine. Clytemnestra murders her husband because she is the instrument of the curse on the house of Atreus, part of the system of retribution that seeks to rid the community of pollution, but also because he murdered their daughter, because during his prolonged absence she conceived a passion for another man, and because it is her nature to seek redress even by the most extreme means. Freudians might call her action "overdetermined."

But whatever the determining circumstances, human or divine, the person is presented as choosing freely. Circumstance limits choice, but the will is not constrained, though the judgment is often clouded with passion. Mortals, though infinitely less powerful than gods, are responsible for their actions, whether they choose with judgment in control, like Orestes' deciding in *Libation Bearers* to murder his mother in spite of her appeals to filial piety or like Eteocles' deciding in *Seven Against Thebes* against the impassioned urging of the chorus to murder his brother, they act when passion has taken away judgment; or like Oedipus in *Oedipus the King*, they act in complete and unavoidable ignorance. Orestes' case with its ultimately fortunate outcome is an exception. The human condition is inherently tragic, since most choices must be made with insufficient knowledge and with judgment clouded by passion. In this state of mental blindness and delusion (which the Greeks called *Até*) mortals "overstep" and let loose pollution and the Furies that come to restore order.

Since the disruption of order is a disruption of the relation of the community and its gods, it often creates a dilemma over ritual, which regulates these relations. How and by whom can Polynices be buried *(Antigone)*? How shall the division of the inheritance of Eteocles and Polynices be justly adjudicated *(Seven Against Thebes)*? How can the homecoming feast and sacrifice be performed *(Oresteia)*? How and by whom shall Oedipus be buried *(Oedipus at Colonus)*? Can Dionysus be worshiped in Thebes *(Bacchae)*? The action of tragedy is sometimes a search for a new ritual to fit a new state of affairs or a change in the situation that will make the celebration of an old ritual possible. The chorus—as representatives of that larger group affected by the disruption—are frequently the ones who perceive and articulate the ritual dilemma. The institution of a new rite or the reaffirmation of an old one is the sign of restored equilibrium between the community and the gods.

Even more frequent than such overall structuring is ritual in the form of onstage actions in response to particular events, most often performed by the chorus. Many choral songs are also ritual acts called forth by the circumstances, not interludes but necessary parts of the action. Formal supplication, the requesting and granting of sanctuary, is such an act. Lament in the form of *kommos*, discussed above, sometimes combined with funeral rites, is a part of most tragedies. There are prayers of every kind, for deliverance from siege, plague, and other misfortune, for victory, for vengeance, for a safe journey in this world or to the next, prayers of celebration and thanksgiving, of blessing and cursing. Aeschylus has two great necromantic scenes. In *Persians* the chorus, standing over the tomb of Darius, raise the ghost of their dead king from the grave, and in *Libation Bearers* the chorus at the tomb of Agamemnon help Orestes and Electra to nerve themselves for matricide by calling up from underground and incorporating into themselves the wrath of the slaughtered king-father. It is because ritual is a visible expression of the relation between the community and the gods that it plays so large a role in tragedy, both in individual scenes and as an element of overall structure. Many tragedies end with the establishment of a cult that is both the sign of restored harmony and a means by which the wider group on and off the stage can own for itself the meaning of the tragic event.

The action of tragedy, when it involves the fulfillment of prophecy, or the solution of a ritual dilemma, or the identification and elimination of pollution, can itself be a means of extending the scope of the event to include the larger community and its cosmic context. This structure can also be symbolic, part of a system of imagery that is still another means of widening the reference and thereby intensifying the impact of onstage action. The action of *Persians* is both a fulfillment of prophecy and a coming to terms with a ritual dilemma. As will be shown more fully below, it is also, like *Oedipus the King*, a series of revelations, uncoverings of events already past, each one represented as a progression from darkness into light. This imagery of darkness and light reinforces and is reinforced by the action, which is literally a process of enlightenment as to the meaning of Xerxes' defeat, in terms of a dream, an oracle, and a ritual dilemma.

In addition to its other uses, imagery, as just indicated, can be a means of conveying the wider context of the event. As the play unfolds, the storm that pervades *Seven Against Thebes* comes to connote the periodic outbreaks of the Fury in the house of Laius that result in parricide, incest, and fratricide. The predators—hunting dogs, lions, wolves, snakes, eagles—that haunt *Oresteia* all allude to Furies who pursue and hunt down the transgressor. The hunting imagery of Euripides' *Hippolytus* evokes both the purity and freedom of Artemis the huntress and the snares in which Aphrodite entangles her less than pure victims.

The tragic story, then, is complex and cosmic in scope. One and the same onstage action, such as the series of revelations in *Persians* or the conflict over the burial of Polynices in *Antigone*, can have many aspects. It can simultaneously fulfill prophecy, resolve a ritual dilemma, implement a system of images, and do several other things besides. The brief critical moment enacted on the stage is itself many faceted. In addition, as I have indicated, it encompasses far more than it enacts: the past of which it is the culmination, the future that it brings forth, and the cosmic scheme that governs the affairs of gods and mortals. The extraordinary impact of the tragedies comes partly from this richness, this compression of so much into the crucial moment, a fact already observed by Aristotle, who admired the intensity of tragedy, its ability to achieve its effect in a small compass (*Poetics* 1462a–1462b).

By its nature the tragic story calls forth a chorus of persons with a common interest in its outcome. Who they are is determined by the nature of the event being enacted, of which they are somehow representative by virtue of their collective involvement. They furnish the titles of a majority of the extant plays of Aeschylus, many of Euripides, only one of Sophocles. They do not, as is sometimes alleged, represent the Athenian community, since they are frequently slaves, women, foreigners, sometimes gods, whatever collectivity is the most directly concerned in the event. They are one of the means by which what would otherwise remain an individual experience is magnified and generalized. For example, *Libation Bearers* is fittingly named from its chorus of house slaves, female prisoners of war. Survivors of homes violated and destroyed by violence, they are eager accomplices of Orestes and Electra, children of the violated house of Atreus, disinherited and reduced to virtual slavery. The rage with which they urge matricide generalizes the rage of the children of Agamemnon by associating it with the rage of all victims of violence against the domestic sanctities.

There is no single prescribed way in which a chorus functions. It is difficult to find a description that fits even the small number of plays that we know, beyond saying that it is one of the actors and participates in most of the ways that actors participate. Chorus leader and individual chorus members are frequently involved in dialogue, with the limitation that members of the chorus do not make extended speeches. In *Eumenides* and in *Suppliants* of both Aeschylus and Euripides, among extant plays, they are a principal actor. Even when not directly part of the main conflict they are never just spectators, but always in some sense victims or beneficiaries of the event—mourning, celebrating, urging action, not simply as sympathizers but as interested parties. Sometimes they perform some action indispensable to the plot.

In the days when nonchoral drama was coming into existence and tragedies were being composed in which choruses were merely musical interludes, Aristotle wrote, "One ought to consider the chorus one of the actors. It should be part of the whole and participate in the action not in the manner of Euripides but in the manner of Sophocles" (*Poetics* 1456a). Aristotle does not specify what he sees as the difference in treatment of the chorus by Sophocles and Euripides, but the statement that the chorus functions as an actor and part of the story is unambiguous. It seems possible that his criticism of Euripides is not that the chorus is insufficiently integrated in the action (in the surviving plays this is not the case), but that in some cases it lacks the qualities of a group and could as well be represented by a single actor.

AESCHYLEAN TRAGEDY

So far I have spoken about tragic form and tragic story as they appear with characteristic variations in treatment, in the surviving works of the three major tragedians. In what follows I attempt to see the extant plays of Aeschylus as much as possible in their totality as choral performances of which music and visual effects were organic parts. But first a few words should be said about the general qualities that distinguish them from the plays of the other two tragedians.

Aeschylus wrote between ninety and one hundred plays. He must, therefore, have presented twenty-three to twenty-five tetralogies. If our records are correct, thirteen of these took first prize in his lifetime, including all of the extant plays, with the possible exception of *Prometheus*, about which we have no information. He had, of course, many posthumous victories. Sophocles appears to have had an even higher proportion of first prizes, perhaps as many as two-thirds of his productions. Euripides, who competed at least twenty-two times, took first prize only four times in his lifetime.

Four of Aeschylus' seven extant plays are from different tetralogies. *Persians* was the second play of a sequence of unknown subject produced in 472; *Seven Against Thebes* was the third play in an *Oidipodeia* produced in 467; *Suppliants* was probably part of a Danaid tetralogy produced between 466 and 463; and *Prometheus Bound* seems to have come first or second in a *Prometheia* of unknown date but probably close in time to *Oresteia*. The remaining three, *Agamemnon*, *Libation Bearers*, and *Eumenides*, belong to *Oresteia*, produced in 458. All our plays, then, are works of Aeschylus' mature art, belonging to the last sixteen years of his life. None is evidence for the earlier form of tragedy. The five tetralogies, twenty plays in all, must have represented a large part of Aeschylus' culminating artistic achievement.

The seven plays are in some ways profoundly different from each other, but they have a grandeur, a remoteness from daily life—wonderfully parodied in Aristophanes' *Frogs*—

that is typically Aeschylean. The prominence of song, of the high poetic tone of lyric verse, is one source of this grandeur. For all three dramatists the proportions of song to speech vary considerably from play to play in ways that seem determined more by dramatic needs than by chronology. *Agamemnon*, written two years before Aeschylus died, has the third highest proportion of song of all his plays; *Eumenides* in the same trilogy has the second lowest. Overall, however, in Aeschylus' plays, lyric passages tend to be somewhat longer and the proportion of song to speech higher than in the plays of Sophocles and Euripides. Though there is no tragedy whose range of meanings would not be restricted if the lyric passages were removed, and many tragedies contain extended lyric narratives—the sack of Troy in Euripides' *Trojan Women* (511–567), Deianeira's violent wooing in Sophocles' *Trachiniai* (497–530)—Aeschylus alone uses lyric narrative to present events that are essential to the story—the departure of Xerxes with his army and navy in *Persians*, the action of the curse in the house of Laius in *Seven Against Thebes*, the events at Aulis in *Agamemnon*, Io's deliverance in *Suppliants*. So vivid are these lyrical excursions into the past that it is difficult, when remembering the plays, not to think of them as actual scenes. This too contributes to the grandeur and solemnity of the action.

Aeschylus' characters are monumental, even when they are not literally larger than life, as they are in *Eumenides* or *Prometheus*, where most are divinities. This is in part because, though his characterizations are complex and his plots well-laid and tightly unified, his emphasis, in contrast to that in later tragedy, is not on conflict between or within individuals or on intrigue and the shocks and surprises it can generate, but on the obsessive states of mind that can lead to violation of the unwritten laws: Xerxes' restless drive for mastery in *Persians*, Clytemnestra's gloating fury in *Agamemnon*, Eteocles' fratricidal rivalry in *Seven Against Thebes*.

Whether or not there are gods on stage, the cosmic frame, the workings of *Dikē*, is always explicitly and concretely presented. Where Sophocles hints at a cosmic order based on some kind of justice obscurely governing human affairs, and Euripides equivocates about the existence of cosmic justice, Aeschylus spells it out, not without paradoxical elements that leave it still a mystery in spite of the vividness and clarity with which it is realized. Aeschylus does not minimize the violence and indifference to individual suffering in the workings of this system, but he seems not only to acknowledge it as what is but also to affirm it as what ought to be: as the basis of morality for mortals.

Characters and action appear monumental in part because of this prominence of the cosmic frame. When seen as part of a cosmic process, the obsessions and sufferings of mortals are magnified but, paradoxically, also diminished, because they are subordinate to something still more momentous. In *Seven Against Thebes* pity and fear at Polynices' and Eteocles' fratricidal hatred merges with awe at the way the Fury and Ares force equality on both brothers. Mortals are ennobled by being part of a cosmic event, but their own merely human concerns lose some of their immediacy. No tragedy of Aeschylus ends as do many tragedies of Sophocles and Euripides (*Oedipus the King* and *Trojan Women*, for example) with the focus on a single human being making a gesture of self-affirmation in the face of the irreversible disaster. *Prometheus* is no exception, for Prometheus is immortal, and for immortals nothing is irreversible. In *Agamemnon*, *Libation Bearers*, and *Seven Against Thebes*, the characters who might be expected to make such a gesture are dead. But even in *Persians*, *Suppliants*, and *Eumenides*, where such characters survive, the primary affirmation comes from a chorus, not an individual.

Style is another aspect of Aeschylean grandeur. Of all the dramatists, he most affects the grand language and stylistic devices of epic: the accumulation of epithets and gorgeous periphrases, the long narrative and descriptive speeches, and that favorite device of epic, the catalog or list of names, places, objects used as a structuring device and to add weight and solemnity as well as to convey information important to the story. A general air of solemnity, remoteness, and formality is contributed to by a vocabulary with a high proportion of words not in daily use, literary words, strange and archaic forms from earlier poets, many ponderous compounds (some apparently his own creations), and a large number of words that are either his own coinages or so rare as not to appear in any other surviving texts.

Like the events it conveys, Aeschylus' language is dense and obscure with multiple meanings. The chorus of *Persians* describe Persian preeminence in land warfare as god-given (101), then go on to describe their attempt to become masters of the sea as something learned (109), therefore not divinely ordained. They have flouted destiny by "trusting in finely twisted cables and devices that transport people" (114). This is not just bombast and mystification. It can be a periphrasis not only for the ships in which the Persians misguidedly put their confidence but also for the bridges made of boats (described earlier in the same song, 70–71), grappled to cables that Xerxes had had slung across the Hellespont and the Bosporus so that his army could cross on foot the waters that divide Asia and Europe. Xerxes went beyond the Persians' original error of trying to become seafarers like the Greeks. With his boat bridges he sacrilegiously tried to yoke (Aeschylus' word) the lands of Persia and Greece that fate had separated with the divine element, the sea. Already in the first choral song, one characteristically complicated and obscure phrase, by compressing both the earlier, lesser, transgression and Xerxes' later and more dire one, foreshadows the catastrophe.

The concreteness of the phrase from *Persians* is also characteristic. Like his contemporary Pindar, Aeschylus vividly materializes ideas and events. The effect is extraordinarily rich, a dense jumble of physical beings and objects charged with meaning. In *Frogs*, part of the poetry contest in Hades is to weigh verses in an actual scale to see which are heavier. Aeschylus' verses win over Euripides' every time.

The verses of Sophocles and Euripides are as rich in figures of speech that when pressed yield as many and as complex meanings, but their surfaces are smoother, suppler, lighter. They are less loaded down with visualized material, creatures, and things, and their vocabulary is on the whole closer to daily speech. Their complex systems of images and motifs are less obvious because they are less relentlessly materialized and highlighted with poetic language. In *Oedipus the King* allusions to seeing and not seeing, walking, running, wandering are so naturally part of what is being said and done that it takes a while to realize that they are also part of the imagery of knowledge that is associated with eyes and feet. Aeschylus' images and motifs are so concretely visible, audible, sensible that they seem present on the stage, as indeed they often are. The roar of the storm that symbolizes strife unloosed in *Seven Against Thebes* is physically present not only in the powerfully onomatopoeic descriptions of its violence that pervade the play but also, even more physically, in the storms of lamentation of the chorus. The figures of the black-robed Fury and steel-clad Ares haunt the action like additional characters, as in some sense they are, since it is they who enforce the equal division of the inheritance in the only way it can be achieved, through the deaths of the two brothers. Ares, the Fury, and the storm are also present as themes in *Oedipus the King*, but not so visibly and audibly.

Frequently in Aeschylus' plays verbal images are objectified on the stage and become literally part of the action. In *Oresteia* the net in which the Furies trap transgressors becomes associated with the actual robe in which Clytemnestra entangles Agamemnon in the bath, the same blood-spattered robe that Orestes, fresh from matricide, exhibits to the chorus as proof of his mother's guilt. The Furies themselves, mere images in the first two plays, become visible on stage only when they make their appalling entrance as the chorus of the last play of the trilogy. Through such devices action becomes symbolic as much as images become real.

Even more than other poets Aeschylus exploits that special form of concreteness that reifies language by treating the physical properties of words as embodiments of the reality they refer to. Throughout *Persians*, Persian losses are estimated over and over in a special vocabulary. Words for wealth and words for measuring, weighing, and counting proliferate as alliteration of *p* makes audible play with the fact of loss of Persians *(Persai)* and their wealth *(ploutos)*. Words as physical sound extend the association of Persia with wealth into a partial identification that implies that the diminishing of wealth is a diminishing of identity.

Punning, particularly with names as indicative or prophetic of fate and identity, is another way in which Aeschylus reifies language. The mission of devastation of the Persians is described with an infinitive of a verb that means "to sack"—*persai* (178). Xerxes plans not only to sack but to "Persian" Greece, to replace Greek freedom with Persian despotism. Because Zeus's name is inflected on the root *di-* (genitive *Dios*, dative *Dii*, accusative *Dia*) it is possible in *Seven Against Thebes* (670–671) and *Libation Bearers* (948–952) to see the *Di-* of the name *Dikê* (justice) as a true indication that she is Zeus's child.[3] *Di-* is also the root meaning "two." The doubleness of Zeus, of *Dikê*, of the situation in *Oresteia*, the fact that there are not one but two "rights" involved at every stage of the action: all are expressed in a twinning motif that pervades the trilogy. This is announced in the first lines of the chorus' entrance song not only with an image—the two sons of Atreus likened to twin eagles circling a robbed nest—but by characterizing the sons of Atreus with four occurrences in three lines of the same root *di-*: *antidikos . . . dithronou Diothen kai diskeptrou times ochuron zeugos* ("bringing counterjustice . . . the steadfast pair yoked in authority, twin-throned from Zeus and twin-sceptered": 41–43). Zeus, *Dikê*, and doubleness are conflated through the physical properties of words. This

characteristically Aeschylean trait is rarely reproducible in translation.

The visual aspect, also characterized by splendor and concreteness, is designed to reinforce the action as it does in those modern ballets which enact a story. There is a tradition that in *Seven Against Thebes* a certain Telestes performed with such effect that "by his dancing he revealed what was taking place." (Athenaeus, *Deipnosophistai* 1.22a). One can only conjecture that he mimed the sack of the city that the chorus of Theban women imagine in their second song, and the rage, madness, and grief of Laius, Oedipus, and his sons that are described in the chorus' last two songs.

Pageantry of the kind we associate with opera is widespread in Aeschylus' plays. There are chariot entrances, processions, supplementary choruses, crowds of extras, complex ceremonials. There are also many detailed, complicated actions executed on stage. Prometheus is fettered to the rock nail by nail. In *Seven Against Thebes* the play reaches its climax as Eteocles puts on his armor piece by piece, six in all. Clytemnestra's maids spread the ensnaring carpet from the door of the palace to Agamemnon's chariot, and he removes his sandals before stepping on it. Most, perhaps all, of such scenes of carefully detailed action are examples of the objectification of imagery discussed above.

As this discussion has perhaps already suggested, however dense, ornate, and obscure the language, however complex the moral issues, Aeschylus' plays are simple as well as grand: simple in their single-minded subordination of everything to one all-encompassing cosmic concern; simple also by virtue of a certain earthiness of perception and vocabulary, both violent and tender, to which the concreteness of his language often contributes. The chorus of *Seven Against Thebes* visualize the sack of a city in horrifyingly down-to-earth detail: girls dragged by the hair, screams of bloodied infants, bellowing looters egging each other on, grain from gutted storerooms scattered and trampled in the streets (321–368). In *Libation Bearers*, at the center of *Oresteia*, the Furies'

[3] The virgin goddess *Dikê*, daughter of Zeus, should not be confused with the cosmic order of *Dikê*, which antedates the Olympian gods and to which Zeus and the other gods are subject.

function of nurture, finally made explicit at the end of *Eumenides,* is presented in its most fundamental form. Immediately after the episode in which Clytemnestra has been unable totally to conceal her relief at the false report of Orestes' death, his old nurse, a house slave, reacts to the same news with tearfully loving memories of soiled diapers and broken nights with a fretful baby (734–782). Just as Aeschylus' characters, in comparison with those of Sophocles and Euripides, seem at the same time more monumental and less centrally the subjects of his plays, so the plays themselves, for all their grandeur, have a fundamental earthiness and simplicity not found in either of the other two tragedians.

PERSIANS

Persians, the second and only surviving play of the tetralogy that contained *Phineus, Glaucus,* and the satyr play *Prometheus,* was produced in 472. As far as the myths go, the missing plays could have dealt with "barbarians"[4] and Greeks in conflict. The scanty fragments neither support nor rule out this possibility. Though the earliest of the extant plays, it was composed only sixteen years before Aeschylus' death. Beyond the fact that it is a two-actor play, there is little to suggest an early stage of tragic or of Aeschylean art.

The chorus, like that of *Agamemnon,* are elders, representatives of king and nation to whom in moments of public crisis all characters first address themselves. In both plays, the chorus—advising, greeting arriving royalty with due ceremonial, receiving information, explanations, self-justifications—are an index of the nature of the upheavals in their respective communities.

---

[4]The basic meaning of *barbaros* is "someone who does not speak Greek, who says, 'ba ba.'" For Greeks, who knew barbarians principally as highly civilized Persians and Egyptians, it does not connote primitivism. The extent to which it is pejorative depends on the degree of prejudice of the speaker.

As I have already pointed out, the onstage action of *Persians,* like that of *Oedipus the King,* is a series of discoveries of events already past and a recognition of their meaning. Each stage of the transition from ignorance to knowledge, off stage and on, is marked by the imagery of darkness followed by light that reveals a devastation greater than could have been imagined. The sun rising over the bay of Salamis reveals the Greek fleet, not fleeing in disarray, but advancing in battle order upon the Persians, exhausted by a night of standing guard in the straits. The sun rising on the Persians fleeing across the frozen river Strymon melts the ice and precipitates them to their deaths. Darius, rising into the light from the darkness of the underworld, reveals still further disasters to befall the Persian forces.

Alternations of darkness and light are also part of the imagery of *Oedipus the King,* for modern Westerners perhaps the most dramatically immediate of all the ancient tragedies. It is ironic that many critics have found *Persians,* with the same basic imagery and pattern of action as Sophocles' play, technically primitive and undramatic, too static and remote to be tragic. I believe this is a misperception that arises from not recognizing the chorus' central role in redefining the status of the fallen king. It is through their words and actions that we come to recognize the drama, what has been done, the nature of the irreversible event that is Persia's and Xerxes' tragedy.

I have chosen to demonstrate rather fully the way the chorus of *Persians* functions just because it is harder to perceive in this play than in any other play of Aeschylus. I hope that the demonstration may provide the reader with a workable critical approach to the plays in which this aspect is not so fully discussed.

The discovery of the Persian disaster takes place in three stages—initial foreboding, revelation, and finally confrontation of the consequences. Each of these stages in turn is in two parts.

In the first part of the first stage the chorus are alone on stage, King Xerxes' trusted councillors assembled near the royal palace in Sousa for consultation, as they tell us in their opening song. Their enumeration of the host sent forth from Persia to cast the yoke of slavery about the Hellenes, like an epic catalog, lists by name the leaders of seventeen different contingents and also names parts of the empire that have contributed men and ships. They sing of the irresistible multitudes of men and ships and chariots, of the yoking of the Bosporus and the Hellespont with bridges of boats, of Xerxes, "a man like a god . . . glaring the black glance of a blood-dappled serpent" (80–81) in his Syrian chariot with his escort of spearmen; but their account is undercut by fear. No word has come of the vanished host. Persia is drained of men and treasure. In empty beds princesses of Persia weep and tremble.

In the second part of this stage, fear and foreboding deepen and the splendor of Persian despotism is made visible with the arrival of the queen, Xerxes' mother, widow of King Darius. The elders prostrate themselves in reverence as she enters in a chariot, with a gorgeous retinue, to consult about some ominous occurrences, particularly about a dream of the night before, and to inquire about the unknown people at the edge of the empire whom Xerxes seeks to subject to Persia. In her dream Xerxes tried to yoke to his chariot two sisters, one in Greek, one in Persian dress. The Persian was pleased and docile, but the Greek overturned and shattered the chariot. Xerxes, thrown out, rent his kingly garments, and Darius tried to comfort him. The dream and other ominous events reinforce the half-voiced fears of the previous scene that the yoking of Europe and Asia with the bridges of boats is against destiny and doomed and predicts the destruction of the symbols of kingship, chariot and robes, that precipitates the ritual dilemma of the play. The elders' veiled suggestions, in their answers to the queen's questions about the Greeks, of a force and vitality out of proportion to their numbers and material resources adds to the atmosphere of foreboding.

In the second stage the fears and prophecies of the first stage are more than confirmed, first by a messenger who brings news of the naval defeat in the bay of Salamis and the disasters of the overland retreat, then by the ghost of Darius, who explains the catastrophe in terms of Persian destiny and history and of Xerxes' blindness and folly, and who foretells disaster for the part of the army that Xerxes has left behind him in Greece. This two-stage revelation, of the immediate past by the messenger, and of the remote past and of the future by Darius, is in effect two "messenger scenes." With the song of the chorus that separates them they make up more than half the play (603 lines out of 1,077). This is the dramatic heart of the action, the irreversible tragic event that we witness through the words of messenger and ghost and the responses of chorus and queen.

The messenger's account of the battle of Salamis harps on the relatively small numbers of the Greeks and the enormous numbers of the Persians. His casualty list, naming eighteen Persian leaders, echoes without repeating verbatim the list of vanished princes of the opening choral song, and his description of Xerxes on the heights above the bay of Salamis tearing his kingly garments is a literal fulfillment of part of the queen's dream. He sees the hand of god in the victory of so few over so many and in the way the forces of nature seemed to conspire to destroy the retreating army. Departing, the queen admonishes the chorus to comfort Xerxes if he arrives before her return and to provide him with an escort to the palace to replace the one that has been lost, "so that misfortune not be added to misfortune" (531). So important is it that the king of kings not appear unattended like an ordinary person.

At the dead center of the play between the two scenes of revelation, the chorus sing a song that is itself another revelation, a kind of action. Awe and reverence for the great king are gone. It begins as a cry of rage at Xerxes mixed with almost unbearable grief and horror and goes on to visualize in the last two stanzas Persian vassals liberated, no longer paying tribute or prostrating themselves in reverence, tongues no longer under guard, the yoke shattered. In spite of the grief of the singers this passage bursts on the ear like a shout of joy, an unintended hymn to freedom, with the multiplied *l*-sounds (thirteen lambdas in twenty-two words) of Greek words for "free" *(eleutheros)* and "release" (on the root *lu-*). Fear and reverence for a king "like a god" are replaced by rage, grief, and horror at a fellow mortal. The rigidity and terror of the enslaved cities (the Athenian audience would think of the Greek cities of Asia Minor) are dissipated in a burst of energy and joy. The song prepares for the last scene where, as we shall see, Xerxes' fall from godlike status is ratified. Far from being the interlude that choral odes are often said to be, it is the pivot of the whole action.

The return of the queen underlines the changed status of the royal house. She comes on foot, without her royal chariot, her entourage reduced to one or two attendants who carry the offerings and libations that are used in the elaborate necromantic ritual with which the chorus sing Darius up from the underworld. Earliest of all stage ghosts, like his successors he is subject to a curfew, has to be informed about current events, but has more than human knowledge of past and future events. As he appears in all the insignia of Persian royalty, the elders prostrate themselves and do not find the courage to address him directly until almost the end of the scene. From the queen he learns of the present disaster. With the authority of one returned from the grave he confirms earlier intimations that the gods have collaborated with human folly. Zeus has caused the premature fulfillment of an old oracle, in response to Xerxes' defiance of destiny, his blindness in imagining that Greeks can be controlled by the same means as Persians, the sacrilege of his attempt to yoke the straits, a mortal trying to control a god. There are more disasters to come. Few of the Persians still in Greece will live to come home. They will perish on the field of Platea in requital for the sacrilegious destruction of the temples, altars, and images of the Greek gods. Zeus is their punisher. Darius returns to the darkness under the earth, and the queen de-

parts (her final exit) to fulfill Darius' last admonition to her, to procure proper clothing for Xerxes. Without the gorgeous trappings of royalty the Persian king is scarcely a king.

The two-part structure of the final stage, the confrontation and reorientation, mirrors that of the first stage, the chorus first alone singing, then with a royal personage, at the beginning of the play the queen, at the end her son. The premonitions and fears of the beginning are now confronted as realities. The song that precedes Xerxes' entrance, like the song that precedes the queen's first entrance, is an epic list, in this case an enumeration of lost wealth, Greek coastal and island cities conquered by Darius and now lost by Xerxes. The greatness of Darius' triumph in the past, which occupies most of the song, is a measure of the greatness of Xerxes' defeat in the present, referred to only in the last two lines. For the audience of Athenians and their allies, the triumph that the song celebrates must have been felt as their own rather than Darius'.

Xerxes enters on the last grief-stricken lines of the song:

But now, without question, these reversals are god sent.
　We endure,
Beaten and overwhelmed in the battering sea.
(905-906)

In tattered garments, on foot, without his royal chariot and escort, he is the literal fulfillment of the queen's dream, the reversal of the glories of the opening song and of the song just ending. This change from godlike king to mere man is visually emphasized by the chorus' failure to prostrate themselves as they had for the queen and Darius. In the following *kommos* the chorus—raging, accusing, grieving—present Xerxes with name after name of Persian princes (twenty-seven in all), and Xerxes confirms their deaths with anguished cries, in a final enumeration of losses that echoes the lists of names of the opening song and the messenger's speech. The climax of this final revelation of Xerxes as fallible mortal is visual as well as verbal and musical. The king of kings calls on the chorus to look on the remnant of his followers (like the queen on her second entrance he probably has one or two attendants), at his quiver almost emptied of arrows, at his torn garments, and finally cries, "I am stripped [literally "naked," *gumnos*] of my escort" (1036). The new escort that forms to conduct him to his palace is a ritual acknowledgment of his new, vulnerable, merely human state, the mourning chorus, on foot, beating their breasts, lacerating their cheeks, tearing their hair.

In providing this escort, so different from the one that has been lost, the Persian elders implement the queen's parting instructions and in some sense restore Xerxes to kingship, however drastically transformed. The new escort objectifies and sums up the new state of affairs, in which a semidivine king has been replaced by one who is human, fallible, vulnerable. More than the queen, more even than Darius, it is the chorus who gradually expose this new state of affairs and give it final expression in this last scene.

The principal action of *Persians* is a series of revelations of disasters, some past, some still to come, which lead to the final revelation of Xerxes' changed relation to the chorus and, by implication, to the empire. As I hope this account has suggested, several other actions are taking place simultaneously, all of them aspects of this primary action and all of them together constituting the richness of the play. The three lists of Persian names (forty-nine names, some used more than once to add up to fifty-nine in all) that structure the play in the opening scene, the messenger scene, and the final scene suggest that each stage in the revelation is a stage in the enumeration of Persian losses, a vast accounting of wealth in men and treasure left behind in Greece. This is emphasized by words of emptying and filling (Xerxes' quiver is empty, the bay of Salamis is crammed with Persian dead), by words for counting, measuring, weighing, and by the proliferation of words for wealth, reinforced as previously described, by

frequent alliteration in *p*. The diminishing of wealth comes to imply a diminishing of Persian identity, as the loss of the symbols of royalty comes to imply a diminishing of godlike royal status. Another simultaneous action is the working-out of the ritual dilemma posed by the destruction of these symbols, the finding of an appropriate escort to replace the one lost in Greece.

The action of *Persians* is also, like the action of so many tragedies, a fulfillment of prophecies, an almost literal fulfillment of the dream reported by the queen and also of the earlier prophecies about Persian destiny hinted at in the opening song of the chorus and made explicit by Darius. The action can also be described as the disruption of cosmic order by Xerxes in his blind drive for dominance beyond what fate has ordained for Persia and its restoration with the Persian defeat. Because the actions are all facets of a single action, it is difficult to describe one without alluding to the others. The structure is characteristically Aeschylean. It is a complex unity in which past events precipitated by the blind act of an individual are discovered to be a fulfillment of destiny and create a dilemma that is resolved by an appropriate ritual response. In *Persians*, as in Aeschylus' other plays, many other actions unfold simultaneously as part of this basic pattern. This multiplicity of actions all tending to one conclusion is perhaps the main reason for the play's uncanny vitality.

The sum of all these actions exposes the once godlike king to himself, to his subjects, to us, as naked, frail, and vulnerable, evoking pity and fear like any other mortal who greatly aspires and fails and is forced to blame himself. The reflex of this action is a celebration by indirection of the victory and liberation of the Greeks, an affirmation of the vitality and idealism that made it possible for so few to beat off so many, reinforced by allusions to the contrast between the hierarchical authoritarian ways of Persia and the freedom and equality of Greece. Up to a point Persian grief is the measure of Greek joy. But it is also a warning. For *Persians* is not about evil, "slavish" Persians vanquished by noble, "free" Greeks. It is about human error such as all of us are prone to, which is why it evokes not the vainglory of West triumphing over East but the pity and fear that we feel for fellow mortals.

SEVEN AGAINST THEBES

Seven Against Thebes,[5] produced in 467, was the third play of an *Oidipodeia,* a tetralogy about the house of Laius, father of Oedipus. The other plays were *Laius, Oedipus,* and the satyr play *Sphinx.* Like *Oresteia,* the tetralogy dealt with the working out through three generations of a curse originating in an old transgression. But whereas in *Oresteia* the curse is ultimately deflected and the family saved, the curse in the house of Laius ends only with the annihilation of the race. The title of the satyr play as well as the content of the surviving play make it likely that its theme was the central problem of the house of Laius, the riddle of mortality that is also the riddle of personal identity. Without the text of *Laius* we cannot be sure what the original transgression was. From the choral account in *Seven Against Thebes* we learn only that the Delphic oracle thrice warned Laius that if he died childless the city would be safe (745–749). The first two plays must have dealt with the murder of Laius by Oedipus, the son who should not have been begotten, and with Oedipus' cursing of his sons, Eteocles and Polynices, who were also his brothers, because in some way not specified in the surviving play they mistreated him after the discovery of his incest and parricide.

In *Seven Against Thebes* the sons' contest over who shall inherit their father's rule in Thebes has led to open war. Its focus is the critical moment when Polynices' attack on his native city at the head of an army of Argive allies culminates in single combat between the brothers in which each kills the other, literally fulfilling their father's curse that they shall apportion their heritage with the sword (786–790).[6]

In a final scene following a choral lament over the brothers' corpses, a herald reports that the city has determined to deny Polynices burial as a traitor while granting funeral rites and an honorable grave to Eteocles. In defiance of the city Antigone announces her intention to bury Polynices. In their exit song the chorus divide, one half following Antigone and the body of Polynices, the other following the body of Eteocles. Scholars have questioned the authenticity of this scene and suggested that it is the work of a fourth-century interpolator influenced by Sophocles' *Antigone.* It is at least conceivable that the similarities with *Antigone* are due to Aeschylus' influence on his younger contemporary, rather than the other way around. As far as language and style go, the scene could just as well be the work of Aeschylus as of a skillful interpolator. One reason for questioning it is that since Antigone's only role in the previous action has been as a solo voice in the lament, it seems tacked on. But in the final scenes of *Agamemnon* and *Prometheus* new characters (Aegisthus, Hermes) are introduced, though with somewhat more preparation. Another objection is that it makes the trilogy end with a new outbreak of conflict instead of with the resolution that, through the deaths of Oedipus' sons, frees the city from pollution. Ultimately the issue, still being debated, turns on whether the scene is an appropriate and "Aeschylean" way to end the trilogy.

The action takes place inside the besieged city before a public building, in front of which are statues of the city's gods. The onstage drama

---

[5]Though the play is referred to by this title in Aristophanes' *Frogs* 1021 (405 B.C.), in the text Aeschylus refers only to the city of Cadmus and Cadmeans, never to Thebes and Thebans.

[6]Lines 727–733, in which the chorus describe the inheritance as as much native earth as it takes to bury a man, are usually said to be a variant form of the curse. I believe that they are not part of the original curse, but a consequence of the sons' rejection of all other forms of equality. Like other ominous sayings, the curse could have been fulfilled in a benign way, e.g., the brothers could have used a sword to inscribe on the earth a plan of Theban territory and divide it equally. See following on Ares as divider.

is mainly between Eteocles and the chorus of Theban women whose panic he tries to restrain, and who in turn try to restrain his fratricidal rage. In the last (disputed) scene the drama shifts to Antigone and the herald. Like Zeus in *Prometheus* and the Hellenes in *Persians*, Polynices, the other pole of the conflict, is on stage only in the words of others.

As in *Persians* a large part of the story is conveyed in messenger scenes and choral narratives. The principal action of the play, which takes place off stage, is the allotment of their inheritance, which is also the fulfillment of their father's curse, to the sons of Oedipus, who, since they refuse to divide the kingdom equally, have equal shares forced on them in the most malign form: enough native earth to be buried in. Allotment is the subject of each of the four messenger scenes (three if the last scene is not genuine) and of the two great choral songs that frame the report of the fratricide. In the prologue a scout reports to Eteocles the Argive preparations for attack and describes the nighttime ritual in which the Argive leaders, dipping their hands in bull's blood, swear to sack Thebes or die and then draw lots to determine which of them will lead the attack on each of the seven gates. The chorus of Theban women rush in, panicked by the sights and sounds of the advancing army, and throw themselves in wild supplication on the statues of the gods. In a contest that begins with the chorus singing their fears and Eteocles speaking words of rebuke and ends in line-by-line spoken exchange, Eteocles reduces them to silence and departs to see to the defenses after ordering the women to substitute a prayer for victory for their ill-omened outcries. But the chorus cannot control their fears. After one stanza of panicky prayer their song turns into a vision of what will happen to them if the city is sacked. In the central messenger scene, which follows, the same scout gives the details of the allotment described in the prologue. He reports to Eteocles on the names, personalities, and shield devices of the seven Argive captains who are leading the attack at the seven gates, and Eteocles re-

sponds to each description more briefly with a description of the Theban captain he will allot to ward off each attacker. His final and fatal act, which sets the stage for fratricide, is to allot to himself the defense of the seventh gate, where, as he has just heard, Polynices has been assigned by lot to lead the attack. The offstage and onstage allotment takes 311 lines, almost a third of the play, 69 lines more than the central messenger scene of *Persians*.

The messenger leaves, but the action goes on as the chorus try and fail to dissuade Eteocles from defending the seventh gate. Like their first contest with their king, this contest begins with the chorus singing and Eteocles speaking, and ends with a spoken line-for-line exchange. But the roles are reversed. It is the chorus now who are urging reason and control and Eteocles who is being carried away by uncontrollable feelings. After his departure the women in a horrified prevision of the fratricide sing of the enactment of the ritual of allotment of inheritance by "a stranger . . . a bitter distributor of wealth and possessions, savage minded iron, who apportions the lots, shaking out [the one that determines] that they shall dwell in as much land as can hold them dead, with no share of the wide plains" (727–733). After describing the transgressions of Laius and Oedipus that led up to this, they return to the allotment of the inheritance by iron, now specifically linked with Oedipus' curse that they should divide their inheritance with the sword (785–789).

A messenger confirms these fears. At six gates the Argives have been defeated, their leaders slain, but at the seventh there has been an allotment of property with iron (818–819). The two brothers have murdered each other. Their bodies are carried on stage, and in the lament that follows "the bitter resolver of strife . . . whetted iron" is identified with "the bitter, evil distributor of wealth, Ares, who makes the father's curses come true" (941–946). Ares, god of war, embodiment of hatred and violence, apportions the inheritance and thus becomes the Fury's partner in implementing the curse. The last scene, whether or not it is genuine, stays within this pattern, as Antigone contests with the herald the city's refusal to grant Polynices the inheritance allotted him by the sword, enough native earth to bury him.

The ritual of lamentation that accompanies burial is as much a part of the inheritance as the grave itself. The choral lament over the bodies of the brothers (822-960), which with the addition of the solo voices of Antigone and Ismene becomes a genuine *kommos* (961-1004), is therefore part of the implementation of the allotment. Either the play ends with the consummation of this double ritual for both brothers or, if the last scene is genuine, with a new ritual dilemma. Polynices is denied his divinely sanctioned share in mourning and burial, and the dilemma is only partially resolved when it is accorded him illegally by Antigone and half the chorus.

From the prologue on, Eteocles is presented as a man attempting to control forces that he imperfectly understands and by which he is ultimately swept away. These are the forces of Ares and the Fury, for whom the recurrent image is a storm, objectified in the raging warriors (embodiments of Ares) outside the walls and inside the walls by the weeping women to whom Eteocles reacts as if they were Furies, capable of destroying the city with their ill-omened cries. Thanks to Eteocles, Thebes is proof against storming women and storming army. As the messenger who announces the defeat of the attackers says (794-797), the city rides out the storm. But Eteocles and Polynices, in the words of the chorus, are overwhelmed and swept away "down the wind of lamentation ... to the sunless, all welcoming unseen shore" (852-860). For them the storm of violence climaxes in fratricide, the storm of grief in the onstage lament over the corpses. Polynices, leading an armed attack against his native city, summons Ares to enforce his claim. Eteocles calls on the "curse and overwhelming Fury of my father" (70) to protect the city. But neither brother understands or controls the forces they have called up. Inevitably both are swept to destruction by the forces they themselves have unloosed. Simultaneously with the allotment of the inheritance and the fulfillment of the curse, this symbolic storm runs its course.

The allotment of the inheritance is also the solution of a riddle that takes many forms but is ultimately *the* riddle of the house of Laius, the riddle of mortality and personal identity. Though Polynices appears as the attacker and Eteocles the defender of the father's land and city, Oedipus has cursed *both* sons for some act of filial outrage. As the action will reveal, they are mirror images of each other, equal in rights as well as wrongs. They must therefore divide the inheritance equally. But, since each claims exclusive right to the father's land and city, equal division can be achieved only in death. By repeatedly associating land and mother (Sophocles does the same in his plays about the house of Laius), Aeschylus reveals the psychological reality underlying this all or nothing position. Beneath the rivalry over land and kingship is the violence of incestuous rivalry among three sons of one mother, Oedipus, Eteocles, and Polynices. It is the closeness of those who are "all too much of one blood" (940) that makes all compromise impossible. This imagery makes it almost certain that Aeschylus' version of the offense that caused Oedipus to curse his sons in the previous play was some attempt to curtail or preempt his rights in the common mother. A reference to this three-way rivalry, which is the clue both to the irreconcilable violence and to the identity of the brothers, ends the lament. In their common grave they will be "sharing a bed with the father" (1004). When the ritual of allotment is consummated the riddle of identity is answered. Side by side in native earth all three have equal shares of the mother they contended over.

In the first half of the prologue, when Eteocles presents his plans for dealing with the crisis of the Argive attack to a group of silent citizens, he appears as a man with the illusion rather than the reality of calm and control. Though he claims to have a firm grip on the rudder of the ship of state, he hints at a storm of lamentation that could overwhelm the city.

Sophocles in the prologue of *Oedipus the King* evokes both the tableau and the language of this scene as though to point to the parallels between Oedipus and his son, both men who appear to have grasped the situation, to have answered the riddle, but who lack real control because of not understanding their own role in the crisis, the riddle of their own identity. Under Eteocles' statesmanlike manner there are hints of uncertainty, even panic. There is both rigidity and unnatural violence in the way he reduces the chorus to silence. Though he seems unfazed by the messenger's descriptions of the frenzied attackers and their terrifying shield devices, calmly selecting defenders qualified to cope with the particular threat each attacker poses, at the report that his brother is leading the attack at the seventh gate he breaks out with imprecations and cries of grief and refuses to hear the chorus' pleas for restraint.

In this central scene the motif of the riddle becomes explicit. Eteocles confronts each attacker and each shield device described by the messenger as a riddle to which he must find the right answer. The purpose of the shield devices is magically to terrify, and so paralyze, the enemy. Eteocles must therefore find a fitting opponent for each attacker and fitting words with which to turn the threat of his shield device. As he tells off the defenders he unmasks the attackers, exposing the self-destructive impiety of their frenzied violence and turning their threats and terrifying blazons back upon themselves.[7] Against Parthenopaios, the fifth attacker who swears that he will sack Thebes even in spite of Zeus and bears on his shield a sphinx devouring a Theban, he opposes Aktor, whose tongue makes no claims but whose spear hand "sees what must be done" (554). The monster sphinx will not invade Thebes again,

but beaten back under a hail of weapons will turn on her bearer for exposing her to such punishment. In a similar manner he turns the words and blazons of each attacker into a prophecy of destruction for the attacker, not the city. But like all the other blazons, and like the riddle that Oedipus answered, the sphinx has a particular and personal application for the house of Laius that Eteocles does not deal with. Like his father he reads the riddle for the city but not for himself. There is something mechanically moralistic in the way he deals with the first six attackers that suggests the mask rather than the reality of the wise and self-controlled leader.

The theme of the mask is brought home in the description of the one truly just man among the attackers, the sixth, Amphiaraus, priest of Apollo, who carries a blank shield because he "wishes not to *seem* but to *be* best" (592). Eteocles knows that this undisguised opponent is more formidable than the previous five with their delusive and self-deluding shield devices. Eteocles, though he can unmask others and revere the power of the undisguised truth, does not know what lies beneath his own mask. This begins to be clear only after he has heard the description of the seventh attacker at the seventh gate, Polynices, yelling threats against the city and his brother, and carrying a shield on which the figure of the maiden goddess *Diké* leads an armed man into the city. In words spelled out on the shield she proclaims a message that can be read in two ways: "I shall lead this man home [*kataxo*, also means "lead down to death"], and he shall possess [*hexei*, also means "have to wife"] his father's city, and [enjoy] return to [*epistrophas*, also means "overthrow of"] his house" (647–648). In the context one must infer that he and his shield device are equally deluded and delusive. *Diké* will prevail and the second, unacknowledged, meaning will come true.

At the description of Polynices and his shield device Eteocles abandons his statesmanlike calm and proclaims, with exclamations of rage and grief, that the father's curses are coming to

---

[7]Eteocles describes the shield device of only one defender, the fourth, Hyperbios, with Zeus wielding a thunderbolt on his shield. He confronts Hippomedon, who has on his shield the monster Typhon, whom Zeus slew with the thunderbolt. It is not clear from the text whether or not the defenders Eteocles dispatches to each gate actually appear on stage. If they do each must have a similarly appropriate answering blazon on his shield.

fulfillment. He correctly reads the riddle of the blazon as it applies to his brother. If the name of *Diké* means anything, then the covert rather than the overt meaning must apply to the impious attacker of the mother city and would-be brother murderer. But immediately, without seeming to see how it may also apply to himself, he announces that he himself will defend the seventh gate. Proclaiming, "Who can more justly claim that station, ruler against ruler, brother against brother, hater against hater?" (673–675), he demands his armor. Like his brother, he contemplates brother murder under the sign of *Diké*. Beneath the calm statesman-like surface lies Polynices' twin, as he immediately demonstrates by transforming himself into just such another impious warrior. As he puts on each piece of armor—greaves, breast-plate, sword, helmet, shield, and spear—in the canonical sequence of epic arming scenes—the chorus try and fail to persuade him to assign someone else to defend the seventh gate. Against their warnings and appeals to reason he invokes the hatred of the gods for the house of Laius and the demands of honor and departs for the seventh gate, transformed from civilian ruler to armed warrior, the visual counterpart of Ares, the bitter divider of the inheritance. In a fitting climax to this drama of shields Eteocles assumes his own in the last moments of the scene. Is it conceivable that it should not have a device that would in some way answer that of his brother? I suggest that its emblem was the Fury, upholder of *Diké* and enforcer of curses, whom he himself had invoked to defend the city.

The Fury is at work. As the chorus end their song, "But now I shudder lest consummation [of curses] be wrought by the darting Fury" (790–791), a messenger enters and announces that the city is victorious at six gates and "holy Apollo, Lord of Sevens, has captured the seventh, bringing to fruition for the race of Oedipus Laius' ancient folly" (800–802). Apollo, purifier, lord of the harmonies of the seven-stringed lyre and the seven planets, has replaced the Fury whose presence is the sign of

pollution and violence. When the bodies are brought on stage the chorus confirm the messenger's view. The inheritance is equally divided, the curses and Delusion (*Até*) have triumphed, the Fury storm has swept away the two brothers and subsided (960). Their deaths bring to an end the fury of outraged parents and children in the house of Laius that the Fury embodies.

The Fury hovers in the background from the beginning of the play, breaks out in full force at the climax of the central scene, and subsides leaving the brothers dead and the city safe. If the last scene is genuine, this is a tenuous and temporary safety. In denying Polynices his god-given portion the city takes on the delusion that one brother has a greater claim than the other. This must reactivate the curse and make inevitable a future outbreak of the Fury in which the city, like the family, will find release from pollution only in annihilation. Such a bleakly prophetic ending is in keeping with the story from an epic now lost, but familiar to Aeschylus' audience, that the sons of the attacking leaders sacked Thebes to the ground in retaliation for the refusal of burial rites to their fathers. It makes the choral song about the sack of the city, like the song about Ares and the Fury, a true premonition.

SUPPLIANTS

Suppliants is the earliest example of a frequently used story pattern found with variations in plays of widely different tone and character, in Aeschylus' *Eumenides*, in Sophocles' *Oedipus at Colonus*, and in several plays of Euripides. A refugee from some kind of persecution requests sanctuary, which is granted, usually after some resistance. The pursuers then attempt to seize and carry off their victim and after a struggle, often violent, are driven off or reconciled by the granters of sanctuary. Since supplication is a request for a special kind of hospitality, hospitality is often an important theme. In *Suppliants* the refugees are the fifty daughters of Danaus, represented by the chorus. Led by their father they have fled from Egypt to Argos, their ancestral home, and sought sanctuary in a shrine on a hill outside the city to avoid forced marriage with the fifty sons of their father's brother, Aegyptus.[8]

Partly because it survives in only one error-laden manuscript, and perhaps also because it deals with a religious mystery, it is the most obscure of the extant plays.[9] Line 8, which might tell us *why* Danaus and his daughters consider marriage with the sons of Aegyptus as pollution, is hopelessly corrupt. Whether they repudiate marriage in itself or marriage with kindred or simply dislike their suitors, is not clear. Even more than *Agamemnon*, the play ends in unresolved violence and contradiction that call for a sequel. The Danaids have been granted sanctuary by the Argives and forcibly rescued from an Egyptian attempt to kidnap them. But the Egyptians are threatening war, which could lead to forced marriage, and the Danaids are calling on Zeus to save them as he saved their ancestress Io. Paradoxically Io's deliverance was itself a form of marriage in which Io, mystically united with Zeus, gave birth to a god. We know the general outlines of the rest of their story. Danaus, perhaps yielding to force, betrothed his daughters to the hated sons of Aegyptus, but ordered them to murder their husbands on their wedding night. All but one obeyed. Hypermnestra, yielding to love, spared Lynceus and they became the progenitors of a new Argive dynasty.

Probably, therefore, *Suppliants* is the first of a series of plays that traced this story through to its resolution, as *Oresteia* traced the consequences of Agamemnon's murder through to their resolution. The lost plays, *Egyptians, Danaids,* and *Amymone,* are thought to constitute the rest of the tetralogy. The satyr play *Amymone* seems to have continued the theme of suitors accepted and rejected. We know from other sources that Amymone, one of the Danaids, sent by her father to find water when they landed in Argos, was harassed by a satyr and rescued by Poseidon, who, in gratitude for favors then accorded him, showed her the spring of Lerna.[10]

A recently discovered papyrus mentions a victory of Aeschylus sometime between 466 and 463. Two of the four titles are legible, *Danaids* and *Amymone.* If *Suppliants* was in fact part of a tetralogy that included these titles, then it is later than *Persians* and *Seven Against Thebes,* and not, as the scholarly consensus once had it, an example of supposedly primitive early tragedy. No doubt the play's frustrating obscurity and the fact that it uses only two actors contributed to this view; but more important, its structure seemed clumsy and undramatic to critics used to seeing drama in terms of individuals and the chorus as an archaic and increasingly superfluous survival. For in this play not only is the chorus the principal actor, but also the actors themselves almost always, except in the scene between the Egyptian herald and the Argive king, talk with the chorus rather than each other. If the late date is correct, this fact is not a sign of undeveloped dramatic technique but a function of the fact that the chorus *is* the principal actor, the center of the drama. The same phenomenon occurs for the same reason in *Eumenides,* the latest surviving play of Aeschylus, unless *Prometheus* is later.

The play falls into two parts, the second considerably shorter than the first, but of almost identical pattern. In each section Danaus

---

[8]If the relatively late date for the play mentioned below is correct, the fifty maidens, by a convention also found in vase painting where two or three figures can represent a crowd, were represented by a chorus of twelve. Some of those who believe the play to be "primitive" and early argue for a chorus of fifty, like the dithyrambic chorus. This involves the additional complication that the text requires a like number of Egyptians to attack, Argives to rescue, and handmaidens to accompany the chorus—expensive and crowded.

[9]*Libation Bearers* also survives in only one manuscript. But there we have the rest of the trilogy to throw light on the obscurities of a faulty text.

[10]A few, very brief, fragments from the other three plays exist, and one sizable one from *Danaids*—a speech, apparently by a god, celebrating desire as a universal force.

mounts the hill on which stand sacred images of Argive gods and sights a military force approaching. The first time it is Pelasgus, king of Argos, advancing from the city with an armed escort to ascertain what strangers have just landed in his territory. The second time it is emissaries of the sons of Aegyptus, who anchor their ships in the nearby harbor and disembark seeking to recover the maidens by force. On both occasions the Danaids take refuge on the hill among the holy images and then engage in a contest with the newcomers. The first struggle is a series of wild entreaties to Pelasgus to grant them sanctuary, culminating in the threat to pollute Argos by committing suicide among the holy images if their supplication is not granted. Pelasgus leaves them praying to their ancestral gods while he and Danaus go to persuade the assembly of the people of Argos to grant the request for sanctuary. Danaus returns to report that the request has been unanimously approved with the right to dwell unmolested in Argos and with protection against all who contest it. In the second struggle the Egyptian emissary of the sons of Aegyptus and his armed followers try to drag the maidens from the sanctuary by force and are prevented only by the arrival of Pelasgus with his armed force. The Egyptians depart threatening war. The two sections are linked by a song of thanks and blessing to the people of Argos for their hospitality to Danaus and his daughters and framed by the choral entrance song and the final scene, also largely sung, in which the Danaids and their father take up their abode in Argos.

As in *Persians*, the entrance song functions as prologue. As the Danaids desperately pray for protection to Zeus of Suppliants, they make known their plight. They are refugees, escorted by their father, who have crossed the sea from Egypt and landed in Argos to ask sanctuary in the name of their kinship with the Argives through their ancestress Io. The contents of the prayer that links the two sections indicate the crucial change that takes place in the Danaids' condition and in their state of mind. By vote of the Argive people their status has been changed

from suppliant to guest. In this new situation they pray not to Zeus of Suppliants (*Hikesios*) but to Zeus of Hospitality (*Xenios*), and instead of threatening all the horrors of pollution, both that which accompanies the anger of Zeus at those who deny suppliants and that which would result from their suicide in the sanctuary, they invoke all the blessings that attend freedom from the pollution of civil violence—health and fertility for land and animals and people—and all those harmonies of the spirit that are the fruit of reverence for the unwritten laws. Their song reveals their transformation from raging victims to benevolent guests. In a comparable situation at the end of *Eumenides*, the Furies, transformed from Strife Creatures to Kindly Ones, invoke similar blessings on Athens.

The granting of sanctuary is only a temporary solution. In the next scene they are once more raging victims attacked by the Egyptians and again rescued, this time forcibly, by the Argives. But this rescue too is only temporary, for Argos is now threatened by war with Egypt. In the final scene King Pelasgus invites the chorus to choose where they wish to live in Argos, and their father returns to take charge of them. He is escorted by a company of armed Argives, assigned him by the people both as a mark of honor and for protection. As the chorus sing praises of Argos and prayers for deliverance from their pursuers, a second chorus, probably Danaus' Argive bodyguard, urges the power of Aphrodite and speculates fearfully that the reception of the fugitives may lead to war and other forms of violence.[11] The Argives have reason to be afraid. Their respect for suppliants will bring on them not only war with Egypt but the horrible pollution of the Danaids' bloody wedding night, which the next two plays are

[11] A supplementary chorus suggests a *choregos* both wealthy and generous. Many scholars think it consists of the handmaidens of the Danaids alluded to at 977–979. The concern about war seems more appropriate for Argives, and the language of both choruses suggests that the second group have granted sanctuary to the first. The finale of *Eumenides* also has a supplementary chorus.

thought to have dealt with. After calling on Zeus to deliver them as he delivered Io, the Danaids end with a prayer that "*Diké* may follow on *Diké* by means of a liberating device from god" (1071–1073).

The symmetries of this structure would be even more noticeable in performance, with Danaus twice sighting approaching strangers from the summit of the hill, the maidens twice taking refuge there among the statues, and twice descending to thank and bless the Argives. It is a structure that invites us to compare Argive and Egyptian behavior to suppliants: two groups of armed men, one, after considering all the risks, voting to receive and protect the suppliants, with force if necessary; the other laying violent hands on them and trying to drive and drag them from the sanctuary.

The play is so permeated by allusions to Io that one almost forgets she is not one of the characters. The action is a reliving of her story with a difference. In rather the same way, *Seven Against Thebes* is permeated by allusions to Oedipus, and the action relives with a difference the confrontation with the riddle of mortality and personal identity. Io, from whom both the Danaids and their would-be bridegrooms are descended, was an Argive maiden who incurred the anger of Hera, Zeus's consort, because she was desired by Zeus. Transformed into a cow and turned out into the wilderness, where she was maddened by a gadfly, she wandered over the earth and across the seas from Greece through Asia until she reached Egypt. There, miraculously released from madness and restored to human form by the touch and breath of Zeus, she gave birth to the "child of the touch" (*epaphé*), Epaphus, the divine healer, Zeus's offspring, the Egyptian bull god, and great-grandfather of the feuding brothers, Danaus and Aegyptus. The Danaids base both their appeal to Pelasgus for sanctuary and their many appeals to Zeus for release from their pursuers on their descent from Io and Epaphus. They offer knowledge of her story, elicited in line-for-line exchange with the king, as proof of their identity. The central song of the play, in which they pray to Zeus for deliverance as they wait to hear whether the people of Argos will vote to grant them sanctuary, is a lengthy retelling of her story. While their fate is being decided off stage, they revert to the origins of their situation, as the chorus of *Seven Against Thebes* revert to Laius and Oedipus while Eteocles and Polynices are engaged in single combat.

The Danaids perform Io's journey in reverse. From Egypt, her destination, they return to Argos, her starting point, traveling mainly over the sea, whereas Io traveled mainly over land. Like Io they are bestialized, reduced by persecution to maddened, subhuman creatures. In the vocabulary of the play they become a herd or troop, "shepherded" by Danaus, goaded, dragged, and driven like cattle and claimed as stolen property by their Egyptian attackers, who become whirring, stinging, black, madness-inducing gadflies. The cause of their dilemma and the manner of their release also resemble Io's. Like their ancestress, the Danaids are reluctant brides, victimized by desire. Words that can mean "grasp" as well as "touch" are used to describe both Zeus's treatment of Io and the Egyptians' treatment of the Danaids, and the actions of both are characterized by a word built on the root *rhus-*, used both in words that refer to saving or protecting and words that refer to claiming or repossessing property by seizure (150, 315, 424, 727–728). Zeus can be said first to have seized Io, then to have saved her with his miraculous and gentle touch. Similarly he is both cause of her being whirled away in a storm of madness and of her being healed with his gentle breath. In the persecutor who forced her own father to turn her out into the wilderness, Io also finds a releaser and protector. He is tormentor, lover, and father in one, the violent cause and the gentle resolution. For the Danaids these three roles are separate. Unlike Io's, their father accompanies them and shares their dangers. Their persecutors and their rescuers are separate entities, those same two groups that the structure of the play seems designed to contrast, the Egyptians grabbing the maidens and claiming right of seizure, and the Argives casting their ballots for accepting them as suppliants.

The action of voting, which temporarily releases the Danaids, is also effected with the hand. In the exchange between Danaus and his daughters about the outcome of the vote (600–624), there is a rather unexpected emphasis on the hands that cast the ballots in the voting urn, in close association with several verbs meaning "ratify," "fulfill," "hold sway," "have authority" (kuroo, krateo, kraino). Elsewhere in the play these verbs are used mainly of the authoritative actions either of Zeus, who is both father and king of gods and men, or of his earthly surrogates, Danaus and Pelasgus. The Argives' fatherly, kingly gesture of voting with the hand evokes in a general way Zeus's deliverance of Io and in particular echoes the language of line 45, where the touch that impregnated Io is associated with kraino (fulfill, accomplish, hold sway). The assembly of the Argives as a sovereign body can also be called surrogates of Zeus. Their hands ratify release from torment for the maidens and restore them to human status with the offer of hospitality, as Zeus's touch released Io from the gadfly and madness and restored her human form. The imagery of storm and breath is less consistently developed in connection with the Danaids, though occasionally it seems to be hinted at.

In their constant allusions to Io, above all in the kind of resolution they imagine for themselves, the Danaids express an affinity with Io that amounts to an identification. Their references to her mystic union with Zeus are strategically placed to emphasize its importance: in the choral entrance song (17–18 and 42–46), in Pelasgus' first exchange with the chorus (313–315), as the climax of the central song about Io (575–594), and at the end of the chorus' exit song (1062–1067). To Pelasgus they describe her union with Zeus as occurring in two stages. In Argos immediately after she is changed to a cow he unites with her in bull form (300–301). When she finally reaches Egypt he impregnates her with a touch of his hand (315). Apparently the animal intercourse produces no progeny,

but the healing union through breath and touch is hardly ever mentioned without also mentioning its outcome, the divine child. The union of god and mortal brings a blessing to all humanity, Epaphus, the healing god. But not only a god is born. For Io too there is a kind of birth, or rather rebirth, from animality back to humanity, a transformation, a healing of madness, a purification.

The most explicit of several indications that Io's first forced encounter with Zeus involves sexual awakening as well as maidenly fear and pain is the gadfly from whose stinging torment she seeks release in her maddened flight across Europe and Asia. Oistros, the Greek word for gadfly, was also used at this time to signify any intense desire. At some time within about a century of the production of Suppliants it entered the Hippocratic corpus as the scientific term for sexual excitement; Latinized as oestrus it is still so used. If the persecutor is also the awakener it is not so paradoxical that it is he who finally relieves the stings of desire. However, relief comes not from normal sexual intercourse but from the touch and breath of a lover who is in some sense also a father, and results in the birth of a god of healing. The experience belongs in the domain of religious mystery and can only occur because the persecutor/lover is himself a god.

In many ways throughout the play it is suggested that the Danaids too are seeking not only escape from the Egyptians and pollution but relief from desire, from the animal longings that their suitors' pursuit has awakened. Most obviously the "liberating device" that they pray for at the end of the play is a form of impregnation. Also, in two major speeches that frame the whole action—one immediately after the choral entrance song, the other immediately before the final scene—Danaus shows an almost obsessive fear that his daughters will engage in unmaidenly, provocative behavior among the Argives. Further, after Pelasgus has rescued them from the Egyptians, he asks the maidens to choose where and how they will live in Argos. With maidenly deference they decline to choose without their father's help, but they also allude to the presence of hand-maidens who are part of their dowry, as though they imagined themselves taking up residence as prospective brides (966–979). It is, of course, a cultural necessity that they are seeking a male figure of authority to whom to subject them-selves and that they never even consider the possibility of acting on their own. Not even in suicide will they be outside male control. In death they will transfer themselves to the juris-diction of the god of the Underworld (790–791). But they seem actively and passionately to court subjection to some male who will release them from their torment, to their father, to King Pe-lasgus, to Zeus who is both father and king.

We know that in the sequel of the myth, probably also in Aeschylus' sequel, forty-nine of Danaus' daughters chose to stay within his jurisdiction by carrying out his order to murder their husbands on their wedding night—a vio-lation of the marriage bond that must result in terrible pollution. In trying to escape the pol-lution of being treated like animals by the Egyptians they pollute the land of the Argives, who treated them like people, with their terri-ble animal violence. In some versions of the myth the maidens were ultimately purified and found husbands, in others, possibly of later date, they were punished in Hades. Both ver-sions seem to emphasize the hopelessness of turning to a mortal father as the remedy for de-sire.

Perhaps Hypermnestra's choice to defy the father out of love for the enemy bridegroom is the true analogue in the mortal sphere of the device by which Io regained her human form, the entirely human way of escaping the animal condition and being reborn as fully human. Of the sisters only she followed Io in accepting healing at the hands of her tormentor. *Sup-pliants* seems to set the stage for such a conflict between loyalty to father and loyalty to hus-band. It would be very much in the manner of Aeschylus to make the action of the trilogy hinge on this and to have the Argives respond to Hypermnestra's daring choice by creating

ritual and legal safeguards against the kind of treatment the Danaids received from the sons of Aegyptus. These, of course, are speculations without factual standing. They are offered only to provide an example of what Aeschylus might have been preparing for in giving Io almost the status of another character in *Suppliants*.

PROMETHEUS

Io is a principal character in *Prometheus Bound*. One of its most important themes, mar-riage forced and voluntary, is peculiarly hers. *Prometheus Unbound*, which was known as its sequel in antiquity, is the only other title ex-plicitly associated with it. Its date and rank in competition are not recorded. It is usually dated late on stylistic grounds. I discuss it here be-cause the figure of Io links it thematically to *Suppliants*.

Certain "un-Aeschylean" peculiarities of style and structure have caused some modern scholars to claim that the play we have is not by Aeschylus but by some later fifth-century poet strongly influenced by him. Those who believe it is by Aeschylus disagree over whether it was part of a tetralogy, and if so whether it came first or second, or whether because of some spe-cial circumstances, perhaps production outside of Athens, it simply formed a dilogy with *Pro-metheus Unbound*. Some who deny it is by Aes-chylus argue that the play stands by itself and should be classified as "monodrama" and find this an additional reason for doubting its au-thenticity.

A striking peculiarity is the complexity of the stage effects called for by the text: Prometheus nailed to a crag high in the air at the beginning of the play and engulfed with the chorus, crag and all, in a cataclysm at the end; the chorus' entrance in a winged chariot (several winged chariots?); Oceanus' flying entrance and depar-ture mounted on "a four-legged bird" (395, a griffon?); Hermes' flying entrance and depar-ture. It is peculiar also in that the staging of the prologue seems to require a third actor, who is

AESCHYLUS

never needed again. Other peculiarities include significantly less choral singing (but not less choral speaking) than in the other six plays; uncharacteristic vocabulary, sentence structure, and metrical practices; and what are perceived as awkwardnesses in dramatic treatment.

One may question whether such divergences from Aeschylus' usual practice are evidence of inauthenticity, especially since "usual" is defined by such a small and chronologically limited sample of Aeschylus' total work. The atmosphere of the play—with its wilderness setting, its cast of divinities (the only mortal is Io, who is half cow), its chorus of water nymphs—is unusual enough to account for at least some of these peculiarities. Awkwardness is a dubious criterion. What we cannot explain either because we lack information about the other plays of the tetralogy and about relevant cultural facts or because the poetic structure has not been recognized, is often seen as failure of dramatic technique. Unless new evidence is discovered, the debate seems even less likely to end than the debate about the authenticity of the end of *Seven Against Thebes*. As the following discussion will show, I do not find that the play lacks dramatic coherence. It seems to me to have the same kind of complexly integrated, many-faceted structure as the other plays of Aeschylus. I therefore strongly incline to believe it is genuine.

The action revolves around a double issue of survival. Zeus, chief god of the Olympian dynasty, is punishing Prometheus, a member of the older Titan dynasty, for having rescued humanity from annihilation with the gift of fire, which he stole from the Olympian Hephaestus. But Zeus's father, Kronos, whom Zeus overthrew and succeeded as king of the gods, has laid a curse on his rebellious son. Zeus's continuance as ruler of the Olympians depends on avoiding marriage with a goddess who is fated to bear a son who will overthrow his father. Prometheus, who has knowledge of both past and future from his mother, Gaia-Themis (the compound name means earth and ancestral

wisdom), knows the identity of this bride. She is not named in the play, but we know from other sources that she was Thetis, the sea goddess whom both Zeus and Poseidon courted.

In the play Zeus, through his messenger, Hermes, tries to force from Prometheus the secret that will deflect his father's curse, and Prometheus makes surrender of the secret conditional on his release from bondage. This contest of wills over what Prometheus has done to assure humanity's survival and will not do to ensure Zeus's sovereignty is the principal conflict of the play. The cataclysm that engulfs Prometheus in the finale is Zeus's answer to Prometheus' defiant refusal to impart the secret. The play ends in deadlock but seems to look forward to a resolution, which apparently took place in *Prometheus Unbound*. Its general outlines, which we can guess at from the text of *Prometheus Bound* and the fragments of the sequel, conform with what we know of the story from other sources. Zeus learned the secret and remained on his throne. (Thetis, according to legend, married the mortal Peleus and became the mother of Achilles.) His son Herakles, Io's descendant, killed the eagle that Zeus had sent to prey upon Prometheus' liver and liberated him, and some kind of reconciliation took place. The exact sequence of events and the cause of Prometheus' relenting are not known. The freeing of Prometheus and the establishment of Zeus's power seem to have been reciprocal actions. The process of bringing them about involves not the familiar fulfillment of a curse but the averting of a curse by abstention from the action that would trigger it.

If *Prometheus Unbound* was the third play, which seems likely, since it is hard to imagine a sequel to the freeing of Prometheus and the confirmation of Zeus's rule, then the first play must have dealt with some stage of the story still earlier than the events of *Prometheus Bound*. This is unlikely to have been either Prometheus' assistance of Zeus at the time of the power struggle between the Olympians and the Titans, or their subsequent falling out over the theft of fire and his other benefactions to

132

humanity, since Prometheus narrates these at length in *Prometheus Bound*. The play seems to presuppose more knowledge than it supplies of the wooing of Thetis by Zeus and Poseidon and the cursing of Zeus by Kronos. These are possible elements of a first play.

The present play is a study in contrasting motifs of motion and immobility, hardness and flexibility. Prometheus is motionless, bound to his rock by fetters, opposing the adamantine will of Zeus with his own rocklike and immutable will, but with a mind that roves in reminiscence and prophecy from the ancient dynastic struggles of Titans and Olympians and the defenseless condition of mortals before the gift of fire to his own deliverance by Io's descendant in the thirteenth generation. In space his pronouncements cover the whole inhabited world, both Io's Greek wanderings and her circumambulation of eastern lands, and in the west Sicily and the Pillars of Herakles where the giant Typhon and the Titan Atlas are punished for their defiance of Zeus. He is visited by a series of creatures in motion, the chorus of goddesses of springs and rivers, airborne and fluid as their element, whose mood changes with every visitor; Oceanus, god of the watery realm, on his winged mount, an accommodator counseling accommodation; Io in flight, half cow, leaping and writhing under the stings of the gadfly; and finally Hermes, winged messenger of Zeus. As the play ends the cosmos itself seems to be dissolving, as earth, sky, and sea are mingled, the mountain crumbles, and the earth opens to swallow Prometheus and the chorus.

The action is framed by Zeus's intransigent violence, communicated through his ministers. In the prologue Hephaestus, god of fire, overseen by Zeus's servants Kratos (Dominion) and Bia (Violence), using the fiery arts of the smith, fetters Prometheus limb by limb to a cliff in the Scythian wilderness. Hephaestus acts under duress, out of fear of Zeus. Kratos goads him on with vindictive, jeering malice. Bia is silent, but presumably menaces and encourages. Prometheus too is totally silent until his tormentors have departed. In the final scene Hermes arrives to demand immediate surrender of the secret and describe the far worse tortures in store for Prometheus if he refuses. The chorus, who have been counseling submission like all Prometheus' other well-wishers, suddenly turn defiant and announce that they will share his fate. However represented on stage, the thunder, lightning, whirlwind, and earthquake with which the play ends are a kind of cosmic tantrum, Zeus's violent power (*kratos*, dominion, joined with *bia*, violence) objectified.

These two scenes of the violent exercise of power frame the body of the play, which consists of two sections. In the first, Prometheus in dialogue with the chorus and briefly with their father Oceanus reveals how he has come to his present predicament. In the second, also in dialogue, Io's parallel predicament is revealed and the resolution of her torment and that of Prometheus foretold. Io, like Prometheus, is a victim of Zeus's violence, in torment and banished from the human community. But in many ways she is his mirror opposite rather than his double. Prometheus is a god, male, whose mind and will remain free though his body is immobilized as a punishment for having chosen to defy Zeus. Io is a mortal, female, whose mind and will are constrained by madness, though her body is condemned to endless motion as punishment for having been chosen as the object of Zeus's desire. Prometheus has brought fire from heaven to earth, but mortal Io has kindled the fire of passion in Zeus who inhabits the sky (590, 650). This parallelism and complementarity is reinforced by the structure of the two sections. They are of nearly equal length and each has three parts. But whereas in the first section the past is emphasized, and Prometheus' ultimate release and reconciliation with Zeus is only hinted at, in the second section, though Io's past misfortunes are also recounted, the future is foretold in some detail: both Io's ultimate release from suffering through Zeus's miraculous touch and Prometheus' release, which will be its long-range outcome.

In these two sections the constraining power exercised by Zeus through *kratos* and *bia* is contrasted with the liberating power exercised by Prometheus, the power of mind and of the quality known as *kharis*. The mind through knowledge of both past and future (*Prometheus* means "foresight") can deliver humanity from bondage to nature through understanding the uses of fire. English has no single word that covers all the meanings of *kharis*. It is a spontaneous grace or favor that evokes, or should evoke, a like response, and may be part of such personal relationships as compassionate fellow feeling and passionate love. Our word "charity" is derived from it. It also designates Aphrodite's attendants, the three graces or *kharities*.

When Titans and Olympians were struggling for power, Prometheus learned from his mother that craft, not violence, was destined to prevail in the cosmos. Since his fellow Titans refused to avail themselves of his wily devices, he offered them to Zeus, who prevailed because of them. This act of *kharis* and foresight was followed by another. For Zeus, in dividing up the spoils of victory, left out humanity and planned to destroy them. Prometheus alone of the gods opposed Zeus and saved the human race from destruction, then saved them again, for they would have perished without a share in the goods of the cosmos, by craftily stealing fire for them. In his benefactions to Zeus and to humanity, *kharis* and foresight are interwoven. Zeus's punishment of Prometheus for his *kharis* toward humanity is a poor return for the *kharis* he himself received from Prometheus.

The play's contrast between what is freely performed as *kharis* and what is extorted by *bia* is emphasized by a refrainlike recurrence of words meaning "willing" and "unwilling." It is a device comparable to the weighing and counting motif of *Persians* or the twinning motif of *Oresteia*. In every scene the opposition between Zeus's overwhelming power and violence and *kharis*, linked in some way with mental activity, is an important element. In the prologue both Kratos and Hephaestus jeer at the craft and "mortal-loving disposition" (12, 28) that have brought Prometheus to grief. In contrast Oceanus, the chorus, and Io offer *kharis* in the form of sympathy and compassion and receive it in turn when Io and Prometheus satisfy their curiosity. The Oceanids' first words after their entrance song are a request for the whole story of Prometheus' quarrel with Zeus. At the end of his account of his benefactions to Zeus and to humanity, Prometheus in turn urgently begs them to leave their chariot to hear the whole of his story and share his pain.

Oceanus comes not only to sympathize but with an offer to intercede with Zeus on Prometheus' behalf, if only Prometheus will be a little less defiant. Reminding him of Zeus's intransigence, Prometheus rejects this offer of *kharis* almost contemptuously, as something Oceanus is unable to deliver and dismisses him with a warning of the risks he runs in associating with the enemies of Zeus. Oceanus' ineffectiveness and Prometheus' intractability reinforce the apparent hopelessness of the deadlock between Zeus and Prometheus. The Oceanids respond with a mournful song in which they express the grief of earth and all her creatures for the benefactor who brought fire from heaven to earth and for his fellow Titans. Their song evokes the infancy of civilization, humanity just emerging from their animal condition, for the earthly mourners they name dwell in places remote and wild in Athenian eyes—Asia, Colchis, Scythia, Arabia, Caucasus. No cities are mentioned, and the high cultures of Persia, Greece, and Egypt are not referred to.

When the song is over, Prometheus renews his request to the chorus for their attention, which they give him while he explains his "crime" in detail, how through the gift of fire mortals, who had previously been like infants, achieved consciousness and control of their faculties (443–444). With fire Prometheus gave mortals awareness of self and the world, of the seasons and the risings and settings of the heavenly bodies, of numbers and letters, with a consequent "flowering" (7) or "welling-up" (110) of technology and the arts, culminating in medicine, divination, and the discovery of metals in the depths of the earth. At the end he hints at Zeus's subservience to fate and at the secret that can force him to free Prometheus, but when the chorus press him for more information he grows enigmatic.

The song the chorus now sing expresses their terror at the breakdown of the reciprocity of *kharis* between Prometheus and Zeus and Prometheus and mortals. Their model of *kharis* is feast and sacrifice, that shared celebration of gods and mortals in which favors are exchanged. Their prayer always to enjoy such feasting is sharpened by their terror at seeing that Zeus seems to have forgotten what he owes Prometheus, and mortals are too weak and vulnerable to come to the aid of their benefactor. They end with one more image of *kharis* and feasting when they contrast the song they now sing for Prometheus with the song they sang for his marriage with their sister, when "you *persuaded* Hesione with bride gifts and brought her as a wife to share your bed" (559–560). It is on this final note of *kharis*, the willing bride entering the bridegroom's house after her family has been suitably compensated with gifts, that Io, an unwilling bride surrendered under threat of force by an unwilling father, enters.

Io's entrance in the form of a cow, first asking in chanted anapests where she is, and almost immediately breaking into a mad song of agonized appeals to Zeus as she leaps about under the stings of the gadfly, could not have been anticipated by the audience and must have had a shocking impact. Io begs two favors from Prometheus, that he will tell her what still lies in store for her and explain to her as a "gift" why he is bound to the cliff. Having briefly satisfied the second request, Prometheus offers to grant the first as a gift with a warning that she is better off not knowing, when the chorus break in demanding their "share of pleasure" (631)—to hear from Io how her troubles started. Prometheus of course, since he knows both the past and the future, needs no such account. He instructs Io to grant this *kharis* to her father's sisters (Io, though a mor-

tal, is the daughter of Inachos, the principal river of Argos). Prometheus, who has identified himself to Io as "the giver of fire to mortals" (612), continues his role of giver in relation to her, as he shares with her not literal fire, but that which fire has been identified with, knowledge. Io, like Prometheus earlier in the play, bestows on the chorus the gift of her sorrowful story and receives in return their tribute of tears. This section ends with their brief song of grief and horror at the story of how her father, yielding to terrifying oracles, turned her out into the wilderness, where she took on cow form and began her gadfly-haunted wanderings.

In the second section of Io's scene, Prometheus describes the first part of the route she will take when she leaves him, through Scythia and the regions north of the Black Sea into Asia, a mere prologue, as he says, to her whole story. The account is interrupted by Io's cries, and the section ends in a line-for-line exchange between Io and Prometheus in which Prometheus mentions the fateful marriage by which Zeus can bring about his own downfall, and explains that Zeus can escape only if Prometheus is freed, and that the freer will be a descendant of Io's in the thirteenth generation.

This creates the opportunity for still another exercise of *kharis*. Prometheus offers Io a choice. She may either hear the rest of her wanderings or learn who will liberate Prometheus. But the chorus intervene with the request that Prometheus tell *both* stories, the one as a *kharis* for them, the other as a *kharis* for Io. Prometheus, agreeing, first narrates how Io will wander through the fabulous lands of the East and finally come to rest in Egypt. Before fulfilling the second part of the agreement, in order to demonstrate the accuracy of his knowledge of events he has neither witnessed nor been told about, he describes to Io how, at the beginning of her wanderings, she came to Dodona in the wild western part of Greece, where the oracular oak trees of Zeus's shrine saluted her as "glorious wife-to-be of Zeus" (834–835). This "annunciation" is thus made prelude to the account of Io's impregnation by Zeus's "dreadless hand, by touch alone" (849) and of all that followed—the birth of Epaphus, named from the touch, and five generations later the flight of his descendants, the Danaids, to Argos pursued by the sons of Aegyptus, of their bloody wedding night, and of the one who, enchanted by desire, spared her husband and with him founded the Argive dynasty whose scion, Herakles, would liberate Prometheus. As he finishes, Io cries out in another spasm of madness and flees the scene.

Io's departure, like her entrance, is marked by a choral song about marriage. In the previous song Prometheus furnished the chorus an example of the terrible consequences of opposing Zeus; in this one they take Io as an illustration of the dangers of unequal marriage in general, of which marriage with Olympians and above all with Zeus is the most disastrous of all, not only for mortals like Io, but for all creatures. Zeus's inescapable love is more terrible than his anger. The chorus identify with Io in their dread of the anguish of election, the fearful ordeal of the earth creature chosen to be bride and mother of god. Prometheus reminds them that to choose can be as dangerous as to be chosen. Only he can save Zeus from destroying himself by choosing a bride who will be the fulfillment of Kronos' curse.

The prophecies of the Io scene look forward to a resolution of the conflict between Zeus and Prometheus through further acts of *kharis*. Zeus will yield to the power of love and release Io from her torment. This will lead to Hypermnestra's act of *kharis*, also under the influence of love, and in the thirteenth generation, to the freeing of Prometheus by Herakles, a belated return from the mortal descendant of mortal Io for Prometheus' acts of *kharis* to humanity. Prometheus presumably will also yield and bestow on Zeus the gift of the fatal secret.

The action of the final scene of *Prometheus Bound* perhaps foreshadows this series of voluntary changes of attitude in the divine and mortal spheres that restore order and end suffering. Io leaves the stage proclaiming that she

is aflame with madness—heart, judgment, breath, and speech are all in chaos (877–886). Prometheus is engulfed defying Zeus and invoking, in words very close to Io's, the physical chaos, the confusion of earth, sky, and sea in the earthquake, thunder, and lightning of the cosmic cataclysm sent by Zeus. But there has been a shift of values. The chorus, who in this scene as earlier in the play have been counseling Prometheus to give up his intransigence and surrender the secret, suddenly become choosers and decide to share Prometheus' fate. When Hermes advises them to save themselves by getting out of the way, they repudiate the advice as base and announce, "With him I wish to suffer whatever must be. For [from him] I have *learned* to hate traitors, and there is no sickness that I more despise [than the sickness of treachery]" (1067–1070). As in the two preceding choruses, they see Prometheus as a source of knowledge. In return for his many acts of *kharis* in responding to their endless questioning, they bestow on him the only *kharis* that in their powerlessness they have to give, the willingness to share his fate. Prometheus' gifts to the chorus bear fruit not just in a mechanical exchange of favors but in understanding that leads to new attitudes and choices. As in most of Aeschylus' plays, the crucial gesture that clarifies the nature of the change that is coming about is given to the chorus.

In a manner that we have come to recognize as characteristically Aeschylean, the onstage action is emblematic of the wider action that the drama encompasses. The series of acts of *kharis* coupled with understanding culminates in the chorus' choice to share Prometheus' fate because of what they have learned. It reflects the original act of insight and *kharis* by which Prometheus saved humanity from destruction and anticipates the resolution of the conflict at the end of the trilogy. The chorus' change of heart is both symbolic and prophetic of an alternative to violence that can lead to accommodation. Without the rest of the trilogy, there is much that we cannot know about the details of this wider action. It seems to point to an order in which *bia* is complemented by *kharis*, in which Zeus will heal Io, Hypermnestra will spare her lover, Herakles will free Prometheus, Prometheus will impart the secret and be reconciled with Zeus.

Fire is the all-pervasive symbol of all the interacting forces in the play, both in the physical and the psychological realms. It represents the destructive power of *bia*, the lust and rage that precipitate mental chaos in the form of madness, and physical chaos in the form of a world cataclysm. It also represents the healing and procreative power of understanding and *kharis* that initiates the birth of consciousness and the arts of civilization by which humanity is rescued from helpless savagery; and the birth of the healing god, the child of the touch who is both the sign of Io's rescue from her bestial condition and the ancestor of the hero who will restore Prometheus to the community of gods and mortals. As in *Suppliants* this paradoxical force is summed up in the figure of Zeus, who is both destructive and creative, the enslaver and the liberator, the tormentor and the healer, the jealous preemptor of the fiery thunderbolt and himself the victim of the fire of desire. Both the idea and the complex imagery are characteristic. Aeschylean also is the way in which the interplay of *kharis* and *bia* involves many simultaneous actions. It is the first stage in averting the curse of Kronos and confirming the rule of Zeus, in validating Prometheus' foreknowledge, and in founding the Argive dynasty through which his liberation will be achieved.

ORESTEIA: *THE TETRALOGY*

Agamemnon, Libation Bearers, Eumenides are the first three plays of the tetralogy known as *Oresteia*. The lost satyr play, *Proteus*, treated an adventure of Agamemnon's brother Menelaus on his way home from Troy. For several reasons the three plays have a special place in the history of tragedy. The only surviving trilogy, they exemplify one way, though certainly not the only way, in which plays produced together were related to each other. They are also set apart by their powerful exploitation of the horrible. A crescendo of horrors—child murder and cannibalism, human sacrifice, husband murder, matricide, madness—culminates in the onstage appearance as the chorus of the last play of the Furies themselves, embodiments of gruesomeness and violence. Even today, read in translation, the trilogy's impact is appalling. In performance in Athens, in 458 B.C., it was shocking enough to give rise to the story, which may or may not be true, that children fainted and women miscarried in the theater when the Furies entered, not in conventional choral procession, but bursting in one by one in no order, no doubt with suitably ghastly masks, costumes, and dance movements. That each act of violence in the trilogy is performed in circumstances that make it morally necessary from the point of view of the person performing it, only intensifies horror by adding pity and fear.

Oresteia is special also in the way it ultimately deals with horror, not in tragic recognition and such transcendance as can come through acceptance of the human condition, but through transformation leading to release and joyful affirmation made possible by the integration of human events into a cosmic vision. Unlike the descendants of Laius, perhaps rather like Kronos' son, Zeus, in *Prometheus Bound*, the family of Atreus is not destroyed by the curse but is ultimately released from it by a combination of human and divine actions whose outcome is a new relation among cosmic powers and a freer, more creative society in Athens. For the family, if not for all its members, the fatal action turns out not to have irreversible consequences. In the resolution of the action, the earthly fate of individuals, their anguish and their joy, is less important than their inclusion in a divine process. *Oresteia* is the earliest surviving example of this basically untragic story pattern. It is easy to imagine similarly visionary conclusions to the Danaid and Prometheus trilogies. Sophocles' *Oedipus at Colonus* is such a story, and in lesser degree his

Philoctetes and perhaps also *Trachiniai,* and in the epic mode the *Aeneid,* the *Divine Comedy, Paradise Lost,* and *Paradise Regained.*

The essentially tragic story, which goes back to the *Iliad,* exposes the unbridgeable gap between the deathless gods and even the most glorious of mortals and links human greatness to recognition of human limitation and mortality. In this untragic story pattern human beings do enter into the divine, whether, as in *Oresteia,* while remaining mortal they become partners of the gods in a divine process, or, as in the plays of Sophocles, they undergo a transformation that gives them divine or semidivine status.

It is in the romantic story of the *Odyssey,* not the tragic story of the *Iliad,* that we find an analogous pattern. Like the *Odyssey,* these plays are in some sense successful quests with "happy" endings; and happy endings, as Aristotle pointed out (*Poetics* 1453a), are basically untragic. As in the *Odyssey,* the goal is homecoming, the obstacle offended divinity. Each hero (Orestes, Oedipus, Herakles, Philoctetes) ultimately, with divine help, regains either his original or a substitute patrimony and home. But the typical romance ending, of the *Odyssey* or the romantic plays of Euripides, emphasizes the earthly fate of individuals, their happiness or unhappiness (for example, the reunion of Odysseus and Penelope, the punishment of the maids and suitors, and the averting of the vendetta of the suitors' families). In the background, to be sure, lurks a structure that rewards the deserving and punishes the undeserving, but the story ends not with a vision of that structure but with the individuals. If the story pattern of *Oresteia* is romance, it is not romance in the Odyssean or Euripidean sense. Perhaps we can call it visionary romance or *commedia.*

The central onstage action of each play of *Oresteia* is a homecoming, the first two disastrous, the third triumphant, the last, one presumes, since it was a satyr play, hilarious and problematic. In *Agamemnon,* Agamemnon returns victorious from the sack of Troy to be murdered by his wife, Clytemnestra, who with her lover, Aegisthus, then usurps the throne of Argos. In *Libation Bearers,* Orestes, son of Agamemnon and Clytemnestra, who had been sent away by his mother when she was planning her husband's murder, returns from exile and murders his mother and her lover in retribution for his father's death and is forced by the pollution of mother's blood to flee his native land once more. In *Eumenides* two homecomings are achieved, the first off stage, the other on stage. Orestes, purified by Apollo and tried and acquitted by a jury of Athenians specially convened by Athena, is free at last to go home to Argos and take his rightful place as Agamemnon's heir. The pursuing Furies, until now outcasts, relegated by gods and mortals to outer darkness, appeased by Athena's offer of a new home and a cult in Athens, are installed there with rejoicing and festivity. The lost satyr play, *Proteus,* was also about homecoming. Menelaus, delayed in Egypt by contrary winds, ambushed Proteus, the elusive old man of the sea, and forced him to reveal what Menelaus must do to get home.

The fortunate homecoming should be celebrated with a sacrifice that furnishes both a thank offering to the gods on Olympus and the meat for a feast for the human celebrants. After Agamemnon enters his house Clytemnestra declares that preparations for the sacrifice at the household altar are complete (1056-1058). In the event Agamemnon himself is the sacrificial animal in a ritual that brings new pollution to the already polluted house of Atreus. In *Libation Bearers,* Orestes' slaughter of Clytemnestra is intended as a sacrifice to rid the house of pollution, but is itself attended by pollution that makes impossible the celebration of the feast of thanksgiving for Orestes' victorious homecoming. In *Eumenides* the chain of human sacrifice ends when the Furies are prevented from making Orestes the next sacrificial victim. At the end of the trilogy, when all forms of pollution have been dealt with, the aborted feast of thanksgiving is finally celebrated on stage, not by Argives for the homecoming of Orestes, but by Athenians for the induction of the Furies into their new home. If *Proteus* followed the version of the story we know from the *Odyssey* (4.351–592), it too, though in a different way, associated homecoming with a sacrificial feast. Proteus instructed Menelaus that favorable winds could be obtained by offering hecatombs to the gods, who were angered by his neglect of them.

In *Oresteia,* as in Aeschylus' *Oedipodeia,* the source of the pollution that manifests itself in recurring slaughter is an ancient transgression. Thyestes was banished for seducing the wife of his brother Atreus, father of Agamemnon and Menelaus. Atreus, in an apparent gesture of reconciliation, recalled him from exile and invited him to a feast at which he fed him the flesh of two of his own children. Thyestes' feast on the flesh of sacrificed children is the original polluted feast and sacrifice that is repeated with gruesome variations throughout the trilogy. Clytemnestra's lover Aegisthus, a brother of the murdered children, has been forced to live in exile. His usurpation of the Argive throne is still another homecoming, and his conspiracy against Agamemnon is motivated by revenge as well as passion.

Atreus' ancient transgression, like Laius' transgression in *Seven Against Thebes,* is outside the action of the trilogy but constantly referred to as the origin of the pollution that manifests itself in new violence in each generation. It is a violation of the unwritten laws that protect relations between kindred and between host and guest. It is Zeus *Xenios* (Zeus of Hospitality, from *xenos:* "stranger," "host," and "guest") who presides over the trilogy as outrage succeeds outrage in a context of feasting and hospitality. The opening lines of the choral entrance song of *Agamemnon* describe how Zeus *Xenios* sent the two sons of Atreus, Agamemnon and Menelaus, against Troy like twin Furies to punish Paris, the guest who carried off his host's wife. In *Libation Bearers* Orestes, returning home in disguise, is welcomed as a guest and a stranger *(xenos)* by Clytemnestra and Aegisthus whom he then murders. In the

trial scene of *Eumenides* Apollo states that the mother is related to the child not by the bond of blood but by the bond of *xené* to *xenos* (hostess to guest). Only the father contributes his blood to the child, the mother harbors and nurtures him as a stranger. This is the biological "fact" that makes it possible to declare Orestes guiltless of kindred blood. Clytemnestra, the unnatural mother, who withholds nurture and hospitality from her children, also offends against Zeus *Xenios.*

The resolution of the trilogy is a double gesture of hospitality by the Athenians to Orestes and to the Furies. To Orestes, the outcast, they give sanctuary and the protection of the law. To the Furies they give not only a home but legal status and a title. They will be known as *metoikoi* (sharers of the house), the title granted in the Athens of Aeschylus' time to resident foreigners, according them, with certain restrictions, the rights of native Athenians. The final scene of the trilogy is the festival and pageant that induct the Furies into their new home and status as members of the Athenian community.

In the ancient world when an animal was slaughtered for the feast, the Olympians received their share in the form of the smoke from the bones and fat burned on the altar. There was no feast that was not also a sacrifice through which the gods on Olympus shared in the festivities. The human sacrifices in *Oresteia,* which culminate in the Furies' thwarted desire to devour alive their sacrificial victim, Orestes, are part of the chain of polluted feasts that begins with Atreus' sacrifice of the children of Thyestes.

The choruses of the three plays reflect the impact of the crisis of pollution in three different areas of life and help to establish the total context of the action. The crisis of *Agamemnon* is political. A husband, who is also a king, is murdered, and the murderess' lover, a rival claimant to the throne, usurps the succession backed by his own armed followers and a dissenting faction in Argos. The chorus brood about the anger of the people at all the sufferings of a ten-years' war to regain one man's faithless wife and try to warn the returning king of dissension. They are, appropriately, aged councillors of state loyal to the absent king, concerned for the welfare of Argos and, after the murder of the king, for a legitimate successor who will not bring more pollution with him. The play ends with a confrontation of the two factions: Aegisthus and Clytemnestra, in control by virtue of their popular following and their tyrants' armed guard, and the old men, helpless but defiant, warning of pollution and of vengeance to come in the person of Orestes.

In *Libation Bearers* the crisis is domestic. The great affairs of war and state that take up so much of *Agamemnon* are absent, and the action narrows until it is entirely focused on mother and son in murderous confrontation. The chorus are female house slaves, "keepers of the house" (84), prisoners of war, victims—like Orestes and Electra—of outrage against domestic sanctities. They appear robed in black, bearing libations to assist Electra in making offerings at the tomb of Agamemnon. It is they who give her the courage to pray for the return of Orestes and the death of her own mother, and who lash Orestes and Electra into a frenzy of rage in which they become capable of planning and executing matricide. It is they who conceive the trick that guarantees that Aegisthus and Clytemnestra will face Orestes without their armed followers, and who persuade Orestes' old nurse to implement it. They are hardly distinguishable from those other black-robed keepers of Agamemnon's house, the Furies. Like them they demand vengeance and help to implement *Dikē*.

The chorus of divinities in *Eumenides* is an indication that the crisis is cosmic, having to do with clarifying for gods and mortals the fundamental importance of the Furies in the cosmos. Like Orestes, they have been outcast, dwellers in darkness who associate only with the irrevocably polluted, excluded from the feasts that sanctify the relations between mortals and Olympians. The court founded by Athena in Athens, which is the means of restoring Orestes to the human community, is also the means of inducing the Furies to become participants in these festivities by accepting a home and a cult in Athens.

As in Aeschylus' other plays, the action of the trilogy and of each of its three plays is many faceted: a homecoming involving the celebration of a feast and sacrifice that attempts to get rid of pollution but in the process creates new pollution, a recurrent ritual dilemma resolved in the last play. As will appear from the following discussion the feast and sacrifice also celebrate, or attempt to celebrate, a victory, and the sacrificial victim in each case is the object of a hunt that is carried on in the imagery and sometimes in the action of the play as persistently as the storm of *Seven Against Thebes* or the counting, weighing, and listing in *Persians*. In *Agamemnon* and *Libation Bearers* the homecoming feast-sacrifice-victory hunt also fulfills the curse that Thyestes laid on the whole race, that they should suffer the fate of his sacrificed children (*Agamemnon* 1600–1602). The action of *Eumenides* in resolving the ritual dilemma undoes the curse. Finally, as already mentioned, the trilogy is structured by a motif of twinning as *Seven Against Thebes* is structured by the number seven.

All these images and actions coalesce in the Furies whose homecoming victory feast and sacrifice is the ultimate goal of the trilogy; who deal with pollution by remorselessly hunting down transgressors; whose double nature, Kindly Ones (*Eumenides*) and Strife Creatures (*Erinyes*), is emblematic of all the dualities of the trilogy. Their hunting function is alluded to in countless images of predatory creatures—eagles, hawks, serpents, lions, wolves, the mythological predators Scylla and Amphisbaena—and in images of the victims of the hunt—the fledglings in the nest, the cowering hare, the quivering deer. Above all they are represented by the dog, who embodies both their functions, the keen-scented hunter of wild creatures and the steadfast watchdog, guardian of civilized life. The instruments of the hunt are everywhere: weapons, nets, snares, whips that lash on the pursuers, and torches that reveal the prey cowering in darkness. Victory is a successful hunt that will be celebrated by sacrificing and feasting on the captured wild creature.

ORESTEIA: AGAMEMNON

The action of *Agamemnon* takes place in front of the palace in Argos at the critical moment of Agamemnon's return from the sack of Troy. Through spoken and sung narrative it encompasses both the impact in Troy and Argos of the ten-years' war and the immediate and long-range antecedents of the play's action, the abduction of Helen, the sacrifice of Iphigeneia, and the feast of Thyestes, and anticipates the vengeance of Orestes. Its monumental length matches this monumental scope. Of extant tragedies only Sophocles' *Oedipus at Colonus* and Euripides' *Phoenissae* are longer, and it is the longest of Aeschylus' plays by more than 500 lines.

The action has three stages: preparation for murder, implementation, confrontation of the consequences. In the first stage Clytemnestra and the chorus receive the news of the fall of Troy and Agamemnon's imminent return, first flashed by beacon and then confirmed by a messenger who reports that Agamemnon has landed in Argos. As they prepare to welcome the long-absent husband and king, Clytemnestra's smoldering hatred and the chorus' loyalty and ambivalence about the war and the house of Atreus become apparent. In the second stage, which occupies the center of the play, the hopes and fears of the first stage are fulfilled. Agamemnon returns victorious but in a state of self-confidence that blinds him to his own danger as Clytemnestra welcomes him into the trap she has set for him. His captive concubine, Cassandra, follows him into the house, prophesying his death and her own, and almost immediately his death cry is heard. In the final stage, first Clytemnestra, standing over the bodies of her husband and his concubine, and then Aegisthus confront the chorus, proclaiming justice accomplished and the end of pollution and

threatening armed retaliation against resistance to their regime.

The complex system of images, themes, motifs that flesh out the action of the trilogy are all announced in the prologue and the opening chorus of *Agamemnon*. Dog, torch, feast and sacrifice, victory, and homecoming open the trilogy. A watchman, faithful guardian of the house of Agamemnon, keeping watch on the roof "like a dog" (3), as he says, broods on lurking pollution in the royal house and prays for "release from trouble" (1, 20). Saluting the beacon that flares up in predawn darkness to signal that Troy has fallen and Agamemnon is on his way home victorious, he calls out to Clytemnestra within to raise the cry *(ololugmos)* that accompanies the sacrifice and feast of thanksgiving.[12]

The chorus of Argive elders appear before the house to find out, as we learn part way through their opening song, why all the altars of the city are flaming with offerings (83–103). In this immensely long lyric narrative, hunting, the twinning motif, and feast and sacrifice are complexly linked as the chorus relive incidents connected with the departure of the Greek expedition against Troy ten years before. Like a pair of eagles shrieking their grief as they circle their robbed nest, the leaders of the expedition, Atreus' sons, Agamemnon and Menelaus, issued forth to punish Troy for the rape of Helen, sent like an avenging Fury against the Trojan robbers of the Greek nest by Zeus *Xenios*.

When the Greeks mustered with their ships at Aulis a portent, two eagles again, victimizers now not victims, feasting on a pregnant hare and her unborn young, was interpreted to mean that the two sons of Atreus would sack Troy as the two eagles feasted on the hare and her young. But there was something unholy about feasting on the unborn, which portended a "second lawless sacrifice without feasting" and "an unforgetting child-avenging wrath" (147–155). The fleet was paralyzed by unfavorable

---

[12]If the victim goes to the altar without resistance and dies without a struggle at the first blow, the *ololugmos* is raised as a sign that the sacrifice is auspicious.

winds until Artemis, outraged by the eagles' banquet, was appeased with the sacrifice of another innocent young creature, Iphigeneia, the daughter of the house, slaughtered "like a goat over the altar" (232). The eagles' feast, which is also described as a sacrifice (150), looks back, of course, to the feast of Thyestes as well as forward to the sacrifice of Iphigeneia and the "unforgetting child-avenging wrath" it provoked in Clytemnestra (155). It also points to the Greek excesses during the sack of Troy, hinted at later by Clytemnestra (337–347). The justified hunt of the opening simile is now an unholy feast. The eagle portent links the motif of hunting, the two great birds of prey of the opening simile sent forth by Zeus to hunt down the transgressors, with the motif of feast and sacrifice. Both simile and portent are characterized by two kinds of doubling: doubling as pairing, two eagles, two sons of Atreus; and doubling as opposition, victims becoming victimizers, the double meaning of the portent, mirrored in the refrain "Cry woe, woe, but let victory be for what is well" (138 and 159).

Clytemnestra explains to the incredulous chorus how the news of Troy's fall on the preceding night was flashed from mountaintop to mountaintop by a chain of beacons that originated on Mount Ida in the Troad. In the form of leaping beacon flames, the Fury torch that set Troy aflame is returning to Argos. The victory signal is also the signal for the wife and lover to prepare to exact retribution for their wrongs.

While the chorus brood in song over the grief caused by Paris when he "outraged the hospitable board by the theft of a wife" (401–402), and the grief and hidden anger in Argos for all the men who because of one man's wife will never come home, several days must be assumed to pass, long enough for Agamemnon's ships to get from Troy to Argos.[13] A messenger announces to Clytemnestra and the chorus that the king has safely landed in the nearby port. Here too the message is double. The beacon report is

true. Agamemnon is returning victorious with the spoils of Troy; but the other member of the kingly pair, Menelaus, has disappeared with his ship in a storm, and no one knows if he is alive or dead.

The chorus receive the confirmation of the fall of Troy not with a joyful victory song, but with a brooding song about justice, full of the dualities characteristic of the trilogy and focused on Helen, the cause of it all, wife of the vanished Menelaus. With dance and song she came to Troy, "love's flower" (743), treacherous destroyer, sent by Zeus *Xenios* against the Trojans, "a bridal, grief-bearing Fury" (748–749). Thoughts of the Fury bride who brings pollution and retribution to Troy, the violence under the beautiful surface that breaks through and destroys a whole city, lead to more general thoughts of how violence breeds violence from generation to generation. They do not say it directly, but they seem to fear that if the Fury bride brings retribution to Paris and Troy, Agamemnon and Argos may suffer a similar fate at the hands of Helen's sister, Clytemnestra.

Agamemnon now arrives in a chariot, escorted, presumably, as befits a victorious king and followed by a wagon loaded with booty and bearing his prize of war and concubine, the Trojan princess, priestess of Apollo, Cassandra. Throughout this scene she remains silent and almost unremarked in the wagon. The elders show their ambivalence in their welcome, in which they hint at their own disapproval of the war, at the deceptiveness of appearances, at false friends and sedition at home. Standing in the door of the palace, Clytemnestra also says nothing until Agamemnon's long official greeting to Argos, to its gods, and to the Argive elders is finished. Strangely impersonal, the queen first addresses a long description of her suffering and faithfulness in her lord's absence to the chorus. Finally she greets Agamemnon with fulsome and fawning flattery and invites him to

[13]It is not unusual for a choral song to be used in this way to mark the passage of hours, or days, required for an off-stage event such as a journey or a battle.

[14]The Greek word for the color is *porphura*, often translated "purple," but it seems to have been closer to crimson. It was obtained from a small shellfish also called *porphura* (Latin *murex*), an important source of wealth for Phoenicians and other Mediterranean peoples.

step from his chariot onto a crimson[14] carpet that her maids have spread from the house door to the chariot. In Greek eyes it was impious to offer to a mere human being an honor that should only be offered to a god. They found it shocking that Eastern despots claimed godlike status and accepted such honors. Agamemnon at first resists with conventional professions of reverence and piety; but when Clytemnestra presses him with a sly mixture of flattery and taunts he succumbs. Ordering a slave to unloose his sandals, he steps onto the carpet and enters the palace.

The sumptuous carpet—steeped in the blood-red dye of the murex fish, source and symbol of wealth and pomp for millennia in the Mediterranean—is part of the stored wealth of the house. It is because he feels awe at wasting and sullying that wealth by walking on it that Agamemnon removes his sandals. As he walks the trail of blood into his house he symbolically reenacts those earlier desecrations of the living wealth of the house, the slaughter of Thyestes' sons and of Iphigeneia. The chorus described Paris as "trampling the great altar of *Dikē*" (382–383). Agamemnon also tramples holy things. The carpet is also the net or snare in which Clytemnestra, a Fury bride like her sister Helen, entangles him and draws him to his doom. His surrender to her wiles, his acceptance of divine honors, his obliviousness to the danger in his own house, is a sign of the vainglory that blinds him to the fact that, like the Trojans, he is human and liable to suffer for his transgressions as he has made them suffer. He has consented to the murder of a daughter, desecrated the shrines of Troy, violated Apollo's virgin priestess, and now blandly issuing orders to his wife for the proper entertainment of his concubine, unsuspectingly enters his house, "stepping," as he says, "on crimson" (957).

This episode of military pomp, desecration, and entrapment is Agamemnon's only scene. He speaks in all eighty lines and then disappears for good. It is the center of the play and the pivot of the action. When Agamemnon confidently enters his own house defenseless and unprepared for violence, his doom is sealed.

Before she follows him, in a speech of horrifying double meanings and sinister joy, Clytemnestra voices her pride in the wealth of the house with its ever-renewed supply of crimson welling up from the boundless sea for the dying of garments. The return of her lord is the fruition of her slow ripening desires that she calls on Zeus the Accomplisher to fulfill (958–974).

The old men know that they should be feeling joy at their king's triumphant return and royal reception, but against the evidence of their senses their hearts are full of fear and premonitions of evil. Their bewildered song anticipates Cassandra's horrified previsions of the murders to come. When Clytemnestra returns briefly and tries to make Cassandra enter the house to take part, as she says, in the homecoming sacrifice, Cassandra still sits silent in the wagon. But when the queen contemptuously departs, Cassandra yields to the chorus' gentler request to leave the wagon and at last breaks her bitter silence with a wild burst of song. In a mantic fit, calling on Apollo with inarticulate shrieks, she sees a father feeding on butchered infants, a husband being snared in a robe and struck down by a wife in the bath, the Furies reveling and raising the cry over an unholy sacrifice. The chorus at first interrupt her song with puzzled questions and comments spoken by individual members, but as they become more involved in her horrific vision they too begin to sing. The end of her mad song is a heartbroken lament over her own imminent death, a *kommos* in which the chorus participate. When she stops singing and begins to speak, the same visions assail her, the Furies drunk on blood, the chain of unholy sacrifices ending with her own.

Even though in this second wave of possession she is more coherent and more gruesomely specific, the chorus, terrified and confused, understand only the allusions to the past, to the Fury lurking in the house as a result of the feast of Thyestes. At the climax of this second fit she casts away the symbols of her priestly office—the fillets, staff, and robe—that consecrate her to Apollo. The god of purification has no place in the realm of the Furies, the polluted house that she is about to enter. She herself is more a

Fury than a priestess of Apollo as she foretells the coming of a mother-slaying avenger of the two murders about to be committed. Furylike she can sniff out blood like a keen-scented dog (1093–1094), and on the threshold of the house she starts back at the stench of blood and death, which the wondering, pitying chorus assure her is only the smell of the domestic sacrifice. Despairingly she passes the threshold she calls the "gates of Hades" (1291), an unresisting sacrifice.

The old men's brief song brooding over her words is shattered as Agamemnon shrieks and shrieks again from within the palace that he has been struck a mortal blow. Then there is silence within. The sacrifice is accomplished. As though in confirmation of its unholy nature the principal victim does not die at the first blow but struggles and cries out. Their dithering over whether, all helpless and unarmed, they should assert their authority by breaking in and catching the perpetrators redhanded ends abruptly as the palace doors, thrown wide, reveal the queen blood-splattered, with the victims at her feet.

A contest of words follows between the chorus protesting the murder and espousing the cause of the legitimate heir and Clytemnestra defending and glorying in her deed. It escalates to near violence when Aegisthus with his armed bodyguard joins Clytemnestra and threatens to kill the old men if they resist or speak against his authority as ruler. The chorus interrupt her long triumphant speech with brief sung protests mingling horror, rage, and grief in the wildest of all lyric meters, the dochmiac, the meter of Cassandra's mad song and of the entrance song of the chorus of *Seven Against Thebes*. As the conflict intensifies, Clytemnestra shifts from speech to chanted anapests, and the jerky iambic dimeters that are usually accompanied by breast beating creep into the chorus' song as they mourn their fallen lord.

The queen exults, "Where I struck I stand over those whose end has been accomplished. This is my doing, I shall not deny it" (1379–1380). Pointing to the bloody robe in which Agamemnon lies entangled she boasts that it is the net in which she trapped him and proclaims, "I struck him twice and with two groans his limbs were loosed, and when he was down I struck another, a third blow, a votive offering to Underworld Zeus, Savior among the dead" (1383–1387). In the traditional banquet ritual, the third libation to (Olympian) Zeus the Savior marks the end of eating and the beginning of drinking. Clytemnestra has hunted down her victim and in a monstrous inversion of feast and sacrifice now offers him up to Underworld Zeus, Pluto, and substitutes his blood for the wine of the customary libation. "This is Agamemnon, my husband, and a corpse by the work of this right hand, artificer of *Dikē*" (1404–1406). She counters the chorus' horrified charges of pollution and warnings of Fury vengeance with the pollution of Iphigeneia's sacrifice, and calls her deed a sacrifice to her daughter's *Dikē* and Fury (1431–1433). She repudiates their blame of her sister Helen as the source of all the deaths and disasters of the war and its aftermath, but accepts their vision of herself and her sister as embodiments of the Fury bringing doom to the two sons of Atreus. She is only the agent. The Fury herself, "the bitter, ancient avenger of Atreus profferer of the hideous banquet," has "taken the form of the wife of this corpse" and offered the corpse as a sacrifice in repayment for slaughtered children (1500–1504). When the chorus ask who can fitly bury and mourn the king, she replies, in effect, that that is none of their business. "At *our* hands he fell and perished and *we* shall bury him, *without* any mourning from the household." Let him wait for that tribute of love until he is greeted by his daughter on the further shore of Acheron (1551–1559). Aegisthus and his bodyguard arrive as she is making the deluded claim that she has driven the Fury from the house.

Aegisthus shares her delusion. Seeing Agamemnon lying in "the woven robe of the Furies" (1580), he proclaims that at last he believes that the gods above take responsibility for avenging human wrongs. He relives in horrible detail the feast that his father Thyestes was proffered by Atreus and rejoices to see Atreus' son trapped in *Diké*'s snare (1611). Aegisthus' and Clytemnestra's reference to the chorus' protest as "barks" recalls the watchman of the prologue. Faithful guardians, watchdogs of Argos and the royal house as they are, they deny Aegisthus' authority and threaten him with the consequences of pollution. At the reminder that Orestes lives and may take vengeance, Aegisthus orders the bodyguard to draw their swords. The old men prepare to counter with their staffs. It is Clytemnestra who, in an unexpected change of mood, prevents bloodshed, pleading with Aegisthus, "dearest of men," that they have caused enough harm and sorrow (1654–1656). The play ends with her naively pathetic hope that she and Aegisthus can disregard the chorus' "barks" and happily order their life together (1672–1673).

ORESTEIA: LIBATION BEARERS

The action of *Libation Bearers* takes place in three stages that mirror the action of *Agamemnon*: preparation for murder, implementation, confrontation of the consequences. In the first stage, Orestes and Electra are reunited near the tomb of Agamemnon, where, with the help of the chorus, they establish contact with the spirit of their murdered father and work themselves into the state of mind where they can will and plan the murder of their mother and her lover. The other two stages unfold in front of the palace,[15] which Orestes enters to kill Aegisthus and before which he confronts and kills Clytemnestra. Finally, standing in the open doorway with his victims at his feet, he is assailed by visions of the Furies. The attempt to end pollution has resulted in still another polluted sacrifice.

In the prologue Orestes has returned from exile secretly, accompanied by his friend Pylades, who is at his side throughout the play,

though he speaks only once (three lines at the crisis of the action). Orestes' first gesture is to perform two indispensable rites—the dedication of one lock of hair in token of mourning and respect at the tomb of his dead father, and of a second lock of hair as a belated puberty rite to Inachos, the principal river of his native Argos. This confusion of the rituals of life and death that are normally kept separate suggests contamination. It is another instance of the doubleness that pervades the trilogy.

Orestes has been instructed by Apollo's oracle at Delphi to visit vengeance on his father's murderess and threatened with his father's Furies if he fails to comply. He finds Electra and a black-robed chorus of women house slaves bearing libations for a propitiatory ritual at the tomb of Agamemnon, ordered by Clytemnestra, who has been terrified by a dream that she gave birth to a serpent that drew blood from her breast when she attempted to suckle it. Electra confronts a more extreme form of the ritual dilemma raised at the end of *Agamemnon*. How can she propitiate her father's spirit with offerings from his murderess? Orestes watches his sister, inspired by the chorus, transform the ritual of propitiation into a prayer for vengeance and then reveals himself to her.

After a heartrending reunion, brother and sister join with the chorus in a traditional breast-beating, cheek-lacerating, hair-tearing *kommos* at the tomb of their father. But soon, incited by the chorus, they begin to dwell on their wrongs until they have lashed themselves into fury. The lament is transformed (in still another doubling of ritual) into a prayer for vengeance as they call on Agamemnon's spirit to return to the light to help destroy the enemy (456–460). When they shift from song to speech, they continue to pray in what is practically a necromantic rite, beating on the ground and calling on Agamemnon and the gods of the underworld to remember outrage and assist in vengeance. Agamemnon's furious spirit, summoned from his tomb, enters into his children to fit them for their Fury task. At the moment of their reunion Orestes referred to himself and

---

[15]Burials in antiquity are always outside the city walls. The tomb, therefore, must be at some distance from the palace.

his sister as nestlings (256) and "bereft offspring of the eagle father who perished in the twisted coils of the dread serpent" (247–249). When the ritual at the tomb is over he proclaims that he has become a serpent in fulfillment of his mother's dream (549–550), and, having concerted the murder plot with Electra and the chorus, departs to put it into effect. In his turn he has been transformed from helpless victim to raging beast of prey, the embodiment of the Fury, implementer of *Diké*.

Two contrasting scenes of domesticity occupy the center of the play and of the trilogy. These look back to the roots of the curse and forward to its resolution. In the first Orestes and Pylades, disguised as strangers from Phocis with a message for the queen that Orestes has died in exile, are welcomed into the palace by Clytemnestra. Barely able to hide her relief, she unsuspectingly offers them the hospitality of the house, dwelling on its abundance of warm baths, soft beds, and all other appropriate comforts.

In the second a domestic slave, Orestes' old nurse, on her way to notify Aegisthus of the arrival of guests, grieves over the false report of his death and garrulously recalls the labor and the joy of tending him as an infant. The foster mother's warmth and grief balance the mother's savage coldness and anticipate the critical moment in *Eumenides* when the mother is defined not in terms of blood relationship but of the indispensable nurture and tendance that she affords the child. As the nurse departs, the chorus make her an unconscious accomplice by persuading her to tell Aegisthus that Clytemnestra wishes him to come to the palace without his bodyguard.

These two scenes are the dramatic as well as the thematic and physical center of the trilogy. Clytemnestra has admitted Orestes, unrecognized, to the men's quarters where Aegisthus will join him, unsuspecting and without his armed protectors, as defenseless as Agamemnon in the central scene of the previous play. The two astonishing choral songs that frame them further emphasize their centrality. The first song progresses from a terrified review of the monstrous acts of violence of which human nature is capable under the stress of passion to a vision of the inevitability of punishment, however long delayed, for those who trample sacred things. "In time, to exact requital for longstanding blood, a child is brought back to the house by the renowned, the fathomless minded Fury" (648–651).

As these words are sung Orestes and Pylades return in disguise to knock at the door of the palace and are greeted by Clytemnestra. As the nurse leaves to deliver the entrapping message, the chorus pray in song that Orestes may guide his chariot with a steady hand and win the race so that they may raise the victory song in the house. They close with an exhortation to him not to quail when he confronts his mother but to have the heart of Perseus confronting the gorgon,[16] and remembering the wrongs of the living and the dead, look in the face of guilt and utterly destroy it (831–837). The simile implies that Orestes' act, like Perseus', is rational and morally necessary but performed in the face of an almost uncontrollable instinctive fear. Athena gave Perseus a mechanism for avoiding being turned to stone by this fear. Instead of looking at the gorgon directly he looked at her reflection in his shield. He looked, but with the assistance of "reflection."

When Aegisthus appears and walks unattended into the palace, the trap is sprung. Almost immediately his death cry is heard, and a servant calls for help. When the palace door is opened, Orestes is standing with drawn sword over the body, and Clytemnestra, rushing out

---

[16]Gorgons, one of whom was slain by Perseus with Athena's help, were primeval earth powers with faces so horrible that anyone who looked at them was immediately turned to stone. From early times they are represented with staring eyes, fangs, protruding tongues, and snaky locks. From about the mid-fifth century the gorgon was sometimes represented with the face of a beautiful woman. In comparing the Furies to gorgons (*Libation Bearers* 1048 ff., *Eumenides* 49–50) Aeschylus gives us a clue about how their masks looked. The double image is appropriate for the Furies, who are both Strife Creatures and Kindly Ones. One scholar has suggested that the transformation in the finale of *Eumenides* may have been responsible for the addition of the beautiful face to gorgon iconography.

from the women's quarters, sees her dead lover and recognizes her son. Face to face with his mother, Orestes has need of the heart of Perseus. When she shows him the breast that suckled him and calls him child, he nearly loses his nerve. It is at that moment that Pylades speaks his three fateful lines, helping Orestes to conquer his dread by reminding him of Apollo's oracle. There follows a line-for-line exchange between mother and son in which Orestes finds an answer for her every attempt to justify herself and to terrify him with threats of pollution. Orestes is in possession of his faculties, acting in the light of reason, fulfilling Apollo's command. The exchange with Clytemnestra is in effect the reflecting device that makes it possible to master fear. It is not an argument but a clarification of the meaning of Clytemnestra's action in murdering Agamemnon that frees Orestes to act. He ends by driving Clytemnestra at sword's point back into the doorway where Aegisthus' corpse lies. There he murders her, and there he stands silent, while the chorus sing a song of thanksgiving for the victory of justice and the end of pollution in the house.

The scene evokes the end of *Agamemnon* with Clytemnestra standing over her two victims. But Orestes' stricken silence and the chorus' joyful song are in meaningful contrast to the lament of the old men and the queen's triumphant gloating over her deed. If this interpretation is correct, Orestes, like Oedipus, is an explorer of darkness who by confronting ultimate terror widens the territory of consciousness.

When Orestes finally speaks it is clear that this conquest is not yet complete and the thanksgiving celebration is premature. As he holds up the evidence of his mother's guilt, "the trap for the beast . . . the net . . . the snare" (998–1000), the blood-spattered robe in which Agamemnon was entangled, he proclaims himself the anguished bearer of "the pollution of a victory no one would envy" (1017). His control begins to go. Furies, "my mother's dogs" (1054), avengers of her blood, visible only to him, multiply round him. Once more he flees his native

land, seeking purification at the shrine of Apollo. In their brief exit song the chorus recall the slaughtered children of Thyestes, and Agamemnon murdered in the bath, "and now the third [libation], the savior . . . or should I say the doom? When will upwelling delusion crest? When be lulled to rest and subside?" (1073–1076). The savior has been invoked with the blood of Clytemnestra, the third libation, but the feast is not the feast of thanksgiving for the victory of *Dike* but the Fury revel that still goes on in the house.

Like his father, Orestes has come home intending to celebrate a victory. He is also the victim turned victimizer who hunts down and snares his prey. Clytemnestra, the triumphant huntress who gloried in the third libation, is now the hunted animal who furnishes both the sacrifical meat and the wine for the libation. The action, like that of *Agamemnon*, is both a hunt and a sacrifice. It is also the fulfillment of Clytemnestra's dream. Orestes, the nestling bereft of his eagle father, becomes the serpent who sheds the blood of the woman who gave him life. In so doing he has provided another in the chain of unholy feasts that began with the banquet of Thyestes. The attempt to get rid of pollution has created new pollution. The ritual dilemma is still unresolved.

ORESTEIA: EUMENIDES

In basic structure *Eumenides* conforms to the standard formula for a suppliant play. Orestes, pursued by the Furies, now materialized as the chorus, is granted sanctuary first by Apollo, then by Athena and the Athenians. This results in a conflict between the pursuers and the granters of sanctuary that is resolved not by the victory of one side over the other but by integrating the pursuers more completely into the cosmic scheme.

In the first stage of the action, which takes place before Apollo's shrine in Delphi, the cosmic scope of the conflict is made plain. Having accepted Orestes as a suppliant and declared him purified, Apollo sends him to Athens to seek the protection of Athena from the still unappeased Furies, who claim him as their victim on the grounds that the stain of mother's blood can never be wiped out. Apollo, whose home is Olympus, and Orestes, an earth-dwelling mortal, are ranged against the Furies, children of night, who dwell in darkness under the earth.

In Athens, where Athena grants Orestes sanctuary, the dilemma is resolved in two stages. The Areopagus, a court of Athenians created for the occasion by Athena, declares that Orestes, already pronounced ritually pure by Apollo, is also legally not guilty, and he departs to take his rightful place in Argos as heir of Agamemnon. But the fearful wrath of the Furies, who are threatening to blight Athens with their curses, still remains to be dealt with. Athena does this by offering the Furies a home and a cult in Athens, where they will become guardians and enforcers of the laws of homicide that the Areopagus will henceforth administer. As they accept their new home and this new version of their old function as protectors and enforcers of *Dikē*, their anger dissipates and their benign aspect as spirits of blessing and increase, nurturers instead of punishers, comes into play. The trilogy ends with their triumphant induction into their new home.

The Pythia, Apollo's priestess in Delphi, opens the play with a prayer that strikes an appropriately cosmic note by invoking all the gods that have been associated with the oracle since its beginning in the primordial past. She enters the shrine to consult the oracle and reappears almost immediately, half dead with fear, to report that a suppliant with bloody hands and dripping sword occupies the innermost shrine and around him, asleep, is a troop of black-robed, snaky-locked, gorgon-faced Furies. As she flees in helpless terror Orestes comes out of the shrine, and Apollo himself appears to promise protection. By the power of Apollo the Furies, who never sleep, have been momentarily overpowered with sleep. But in Athens, as

Athena's suppliant, Orestes will find permanent release from trouble. Admonishing him not to let fear take possession of his mind (88), Apollo sends him on his way under the protection of Hermes.

The Furies' horrible animal cries are heard from the inner shrine as the ghost of Clytemnestra, piteously complaining that they neglect and dishonor her, taunts and goads them awake. It is not clear from the text just when they burst into visibility with the disordered rush the original audience found so appalling. By the time they are awake, on stage, and singing their song of outrage at Apollo's trick and the "beast's" escape from the nets (147), Clytemnestra's ghost has vanished. For she, as she says, is part of their dream. It is Apollo they confront. He reviles them as bloodthirsty, cannibalistic feasters, abhorred by the gods, and expels them from his shrine. The god withdraws, and they rush off as they rushed on: in pursuit of their prey. It is one of the rare instances of a choral exit in the course of a play. For a moment the stage is empty. When Orestes enters and flings himself as a suppliant on the statue of Athena, the scene has become Athens, and enough time has elapsed for Orestes to get from Delphi to Athens.

The Furies are not far behind. They make their second entrance sniffing blood like dogs on the track of a wounded fawn (246–247). As they throng around Orestes, who is clinging to Athena's statue, they announce that in repayment for mother's blood his living body shall furnish red blood as a drink offering for them to gulp down. They will fatten on this "drink which is not for drinking" and drag him down to darkness, wasted but still alive (264–268). He has been nurtured for them and he is consecrated to them (304). Hunted down like a wild animal, he will furnish both meat and wine for their sacrifice and feast. They then perform a gruesome ritual of incantation and consecration, dancing and droning a "binding song" around their victim as he clings to Athena's statue. Its purpose, explicit in one of the refrains, is to paralyze his will and make him totally theirs:

> Over the consecrated one this song,
> madness, frenzy, mind-destroying,
> the Furies' hymn that binds the mind,
> tuneless blight for mortals.
>
> (328–333, repeated 341–346)

But Orestes, purified and instructed by Apollo, is proof against this terror as he was not when he had visions of the Furies at the end of *Libation Bearers*. When he speaks again, after Athena appears in person to answer his supplication, he is in control and able to give the goddess a rational account of his case. Apollo has declared Orestes purified, the Furies claim he is unpurifiable. Athena declares that no individual, mortal or divine, should decide a case that, if not correctly handled, might provoke the Furies into envenoming the soil of Attica. The gravity of the situation calls for the convening of a special court to hear both sides and deliver a judgment. It is a sign of the indispensability of mortals that this court will be made up of Athena's own Athenians.

Up to this point the Furies have appeared as materializations of Cassandra's and Orestes' visions of them—prancing, gloating, cannibalistic revelers, bloodthirsty, baying dogs. In Apollo's words they are "creatures whom all spit upon, maiden crones, primaeval children, no god, no human creature, no wild beast consorts with. Sprung from outrage, they dwell in Tartarus beneath the earth in outrageous darkness" (68–73). Robed in black, they claim no part in the white-robed feasts that mortals share with Olympians (347–352). Strangers in every sense, polluted with blood of human victims, they are outcasts from every community. Their lot in the cosmos is comparable to that of bearers of pollution in the human community, such as Orestes before he was purified by Apollo, without ties or standing, excluded from feast and sacrifice and all other association.

When the Pythia stumbles on them, she has no idea who they are or where they come from and has never seen anything like them. Athena, by contrast, not only knows their names and ancestry, she greets them with courtesy and respect, repeatedly dwelling on what is due from the younger to the older gods and on the importance of their function. They in their turn respond courteously, abandoning their ghoulish reveling and unquestioningly accepting her as arbiter of their dispute. Their positive side, which Athena alone acknowledges and relates to, appears in the song they sing while she is absent recruiting her court of Athenians. It is a solemn and controlled assertion of their age-old function, of the blessings enjoyed by those who revere the altar of *Diké*, the disasters that befall those who trample it, and the affirmative force of dread, the guarantor of order, the cause of reverence from which come health and prosperity.

Orestes presents himself for trial with Apollo as his spokesman and supporter. Athena leads in her judges, eleven mute actors, who will hear the testimony and the arguments and deliver their judgment by dropping affirmative or negative ballots in a single voting urn. The Furies are bound by the convention that choruses do not make extended speeches. They make the charge of matricide in a line-for-line exchange with Orestes, who does not deny that he killed his mother. But Apollo denies the charge of shedding kindred blood, with the argument already referred to, that the child shares the blood only of the father, "him who mounts"; the mother receives the alien seed as nurse and stranger or hostess (*xené*) to a stranger-guest (*xenos*: 658–660).

This denial of any blood tie between mother and child, which is crucial since it is the basis of Orestes' acquittal, is often interpreted as downgrading the role of the mother. For several reasons this is unlikely. First of all, in an interesting inversion of the conventional view that man belongs to culture and woman to nature, the woman here has the cultural function of hospitality and nurture, the man the natural function of mounting. Secondly, in the context of the trilogy, the bonds of hospitality are at least as sacred as those of blood. The presiding god is Zeus *Xenios*. The ultimate outrage is not a violation of a blood tie, but Clytemnestra's murder of a husband and a king. When the Furies try to extenuate her deed by pointing out that she has not shed kindred blood, Apollo, who speaks with the authority of Zeus, asserts that the relation of husband and wife is even more sacrosanct than that between the giver and the receiver of an oath (217–218). Finally, the mother's role is highlighted in the centrally placed figure of Orestes' nurse, who gives life in the form of nurture, though she has not given birth, and of the Furies, who in relation to Athens are not only guests—foreigners without blood ties permanently made welcome in the city—but also nurturers who have never given birth but through their cherishing and protecting of the land, the people, and the laws become givers of life and joy. This "fact of life" is the true turning point of the trilogy: in terms of the action, it provides a legal basis for Orestes' acquittal and it breaks the chain of human sacrifice and prepares for the final resolution; in terms of the theme, it draws attention to nurture performed by females who are not blood relatives, which is to be the Furies' role in relation to Athens.

The defense ends with this crucial argument. In her instructions to the jury Athena names the court "Areopagus" from its meeting place on the hill *(pagos)* of Ares and declares that it will be a permanent institution for the adjudication of homicide in Athens, the vigilant safeguard against the outbreak of Ares between citizens that is the consequence of homicide not properly dealt with. Echoing the Furies' last song, she extols dread as the source of reverence, order, and justice and enjoins her citizens "not to cast all fear out of the city" (698). Then one by one the judges step forth and silently cast their ballots in the urn in time to eleven hostile couplets delivered alternately by the Furies and Apollo. Athena casts her own vote for ac-

quittal, and announces that if the votes are equal the accused goes free. In a moment of supreme suspense the urn is emptied and the votes are counted. The votes are equal.[17] Orestes is acquitted. With thanks to the gods and to Athens he departs for the long-deferred homecoming, innocent in the eyes of gods and mortals.

But more is involved than the problems of Orestes and the house of Atreus. The outraged Furies, singing a song of hate and rage in which they threaten to pollute and blight the soil of Attica with their dripping venom, are still to be dealt with. In a somewhat different way from the end of *Libation Bearers*, this scene also evokes the end of *Agamemnon*. While the chorus sing their passionate protest at the trampling down of ancient law by the young gods, Athena, first in speech and then in chanted anapests, counters their accusations, but with a gentleness and a courtesy entirely opposite to Clytemnestra's brutal exultation and prophetic of the opposite outcome of this contest. While the Furies rage and threaten, Athena offers them over and over a home and a cult in Athens and the office of upholding for all time the newly established court. When they finally realize that the court is not a repudiation but an affirmation of their function their opposition quickly gives way to acceptance, the song of cursing becomes a song of blessing, and their other face, the face of tenderness, replaces the gorgon face of fear and wrath.[18] The Strife Creatures *(Erinyes)* are also Kindly Ones, cherishers and nurturers *(Eumenides)*. As Athena salutes them as metics *(metoikoi:* resident foreigners) they exchange their black robes for red, assisted by a supplementary chorus of Athenians, who then escort them with torches

---

[17] According to another view there are twelve jurors, whose votes are equally divided. In that case, when Athena announces that the votes are equal she treats her own as supplementary.

[18] The change of mood may have been accompanied by a change of mask, which would not have been too difficult to effect while the supplementary chorus invested them in their red robes.

and song to their new home in a cave under the hill of Ares.[19]

For the house of Atreus and for Argos the release from trouble—for which the watchman prays in the opening of *Agamemnon* (1 and 20) and which Apollo promises Orestes at the opening of *Eumenides* (83)—seems to be achieved when Orestes is purified and acquitted and the Fury revel departs from the house. The stain that started with Thyestes' cannibalistic feast is finally wiped out. But the Athenians, faced with a new threat of pollution, take a step beyond this. Instead of getting rid of the Furies, they incorporate them into their legal, religious system. In so doing they activate their benign aspect and become recipients of the song of blessing, a veritable hymn to joy encompassing all levels of creation and ending with the prayer that civil strife may never pollute the earth with the blood of citizens. The Furies' presence as guardians of the court is the guarantee against uncontrolled pollution, the proliferation of violence within the household and the community that afflicted Argos. It is their terrible aspect that gives them the power to confer this ultimate boon. In Athena's words, "From these faces of fear I see great benefit for the citizens" (990–991). It is at the moment when the Athenians, with Athena's help, bring these "faces of fear" out of the darkness—where they have dwelt apart and unknown—into the light and make them part of the community that they become the faces of Kindly Ones.

The Areopagus, the first court of homicide, of which the Furies become the watchdogs, institutionalizes the process of bringing fear out of darkness into the light by providing a means for dealing with the instinctive rage and horror at bloodshed within the family and the community. The carefully outlined procedures of the court perform the function of Perseus' shield. They make it possible to look at the cause of contamination and judge it with flexibility and discrimination. They replace automatic expulsion of the perpetrator with a mechanism for bringing the act into the light of consciousness and reason, determining what actually took place, and deciding whether purification is possible.

Fear of the indiscriminate violence that can destroy families and cities in the wake of outrage is salutary and necessary, but may inhibit reason and lead to the sacrifice of the innocent. With the help of the court the paralysis of fear can be overcome, reason can be brought to bear, the innocent will not be sacrificed to save the community from self-destruction. Athena is quite explicit about her purpose in creating the court. It will be the means of preventing the Furies from envenoming Attica if they lose their case (476–479). When, through her gentle prompting, they finally understand that the court confirms rather than supersedes their age-old function of dealing with pollution and that they can therefore leave the realms of darkness and reside in Athens as the court's protectors with attendant honors, they stop threatening and begin blessing Athens and the Athenians.

When the Furies are given the status of metics they exchange their black robes not for the white robes in which mortals and Olympians hold festival, but for red robes like those the metics wore when they took part in Athenian state rituals.[20] The red robes set them apart as belonging to a different order, dwellers beneath the ground distinguished from those who dwell above ground and in the heavens, outsiders, not blood kindred, but outsiders who have been given a status and a home and who participate in some way in the feasts and sacrifices of mortals and Olympians. No longer confined to underworld darkness, they now have a place in both worlds. They have exchanged the invisibility of black for the visibility of red. They who

---

[19]The cult and the shrine existed in Aeschylus' day.

[20]A line seems to be missing from the passage. Athena urges the citizens to honor some unspecified characters in red robes. The context makes it almost certain that she is referring to the Furies.

have existed and functioned in darkness from the beginning of time are now known and recognized as indispensable and are given a cult.

In the first two plays of the trilogy the victory feast and sacrifice is attended with new pollution. In the pageant of the finale of *Eumenides* it is finally celebrated without a human victim. The acquittal of Orestes has broken the chain of human sacrifice. Instead of a cannibalistic revel apart from gods and mortals, the Furies celebrate their own homecoming and the victory of *Diké*. In a torchlight procession with animal (not human) sacrifice and libations, the Athenians escort them to their new home. The refrain of the escorting Athenians' song furnishes the very last words of the trilogy. "To our singing now raise the sacrificial cry" (1042 and 1047). Like the Furies themselves, the Fury emblems have all become benign. The hunting dogs are now watchdogs, the blood-red robe and the torch are now signs of consecration.

It is Athens' privilege to know the Furies for what they are. In Athena's words they "wield great influence among the Olympians and the powers beneath the earth, and with sovereign sway they make [all] plain in mortal affairs, on some bestowing song, on others again an aborted life of tears" (950–955). It is the Athenians who first see them in their totality, as bearers of horrible retribution, but also as the source of song that is part of joy and festivity. It is not in his native city but in Athens that the nature of Orestes' achievement—his overcoming of the "gorgon"—is recognized and translated into social forms. In Sophocles' *Oedipus at Colonus*, Athens is again presented as being able to accept without fear of contamination the stranger whom other communities view as an outcast and by this act of enlightened hospitality to establish a special relation with the Furies.

For Thucydides the Athenians were distinguished from other Greeks precisely by their ability to look at and discuss any situation, no matter how threatening and dangerous, from every angle before determining how they would act. This quality, perhaps more than any

other, justifies Pericles' claim in the funeral oration (Thucydides, *Histories* 2.41) that they are the "education of Hellas." The Athenians saw the source of their creative energy and their freedom to act as a willingness to know, an extension of consciousness. Their patron goddess Athena is "gorgon-eyed" and her emblem is the severed gorgon's head.

The Furies' necessary function is more effective when performed in the light of consciousness. When the face of fear is brought out of darkness, acknowledged as indispensable, and given a recognized place in the community, it becomes the face of blessing and causes a burst of light and energy. This, Aeschylus seems to be saying, sets Athens apart from other cities: to have known how to make the Furies benign, to have liberated themselves from the paralysis of fear by confronting and making proper use of fear. It is with this vision of human possibility that the trilogy ends.

APPENDIX: A NOTE ON SOURCES AND INFLUENCES

If there is anything new in this essay, it is chiefly in the synthesis and application of the ideas and findings of others who may, in some cases, be dismayed by the uses to which their contributions have been put. The responsibility for these is mine alone. Those to whom I am most indebted, both those whose works appear in the bibliography and those who read, criticized, and shared their thoughts, are gratefully listed here: F. Solmsen, B. C. Dietrich, E. R. Dodds, H. Lloyd-Jones, M. Gagarin for works on the functioning of *Diké*, Zeus, and the Furies, and M. Visser for illuminating verbal communications on the same; J.-P. Vernant, P. Vidal-Naquet, J.-P. Guépin, R. Girard, James Redfield, for their elucidations of the place of ritual in Greek life and the ideas about pollution and purification, nature and culture, sacrifice and violence that underlie tragic action; Froma Zeitlin for her pioneering articles on sacrificial imagery in *Oresteia* and also for generously sharing the fruits of her superb scholarship in conversation and correspondence over many years; John Herington, and more recently Brooks Otis, for their explorations of the implications of the nontragic structure of *Oresteia*, particularly John Herington's contribution of the term *commedia* to designate the form; O. Taplin for the impetus his work has given to attend to the long-neglected theatrical dimension of tragedy; Deborah Roberts for her illuminating treatment of prophecy in tragedy in her unpublished dissertation (Yale, 1979); George and Mary Dimock, Helene Foley, Barbara Stoler Miller, Sarah Spence, and the editor of this series, James Luce, all of whom read my manuscript in one or another of its stages, and made the right comments and asked the right questions.

I have used the Greek text of Denys Page (see bibliography). The translations are my own.

Selected Bibliography

TEXTS, COMMENTARIES, TRANSLATIONS

COMPLETE PLAYS

Aeschyli Septem Quae Supersunt Tragoediae, edited by D. Page. Oxford, 1972.

Aeschylus, edited and translated by H. W. Symth, with appendix of recent fragments edited and translated by H. Lloyd-Jones. 2 vols. Cambridge, Mass., 1971. Loeb Classical Library.

H. J. Rose, *A Commentary on the Surviving Plays of Aeschylus.* 2 vols. Amsterdam, 1958.

The Complete Greek Tragedies (in translation), edited by D. Grene and R. Lattimore. 4 vols. Vol. 1: Aeschylus; vol. 2: Sophocles; vols. 3 and 4: Euripides. Chicago, 1953.

The Tragedies of Aeschylus, edited by F. A. Paley. 4th ed. London, 1879. Text and commentary.

INDIVIDUAL PLAYS

Agamemnon, edited by J. D. Denniston and D. Page. Oxford, 1957. Text and commentary.

Agamemnon, edited and translated by E. Fraenkel. 3 vols. Oxford, 1950. Text and commentary.

Agamemnon, Libation Bearers, Eumenides. Translated with commentary by H. Lloyd-Jones. 3 vols. Englewood Cliffs, N. J., 1970. Greek Drama series.

Oresteia. Translated by R. Fagles. New York, 1966. Introduction, notes, glossary by W. B. Stanford.

The Oresteia of Aeschylus, edited by G. Thomson. 2 vols. New ed. Amsterdam, 1966. Text and commentary.

Persae, edited by A. Sidgwick. Oxford, 1903. Text and commentary.

The Persae of Aeschylus, edited by H. D. Broadhead. Cambridge, 1960. Text and commentary.

Persians. Translated with commentary by A. J. Podlecki. Englewood Cliffs, N. J., 1970. Greek Drama series.

Prometheus Bound, edited by A. O. Prickard. 4th ed., rev. Oxford, 1931. Text and commentary.

Prometheus Bound. Translated with commentary by J. Scully and C. J. Herington. The Greek Tragedy in New Translation, edited by W. Arrowsmith. New York, 1975.

Seven Against Thebes. Translated with commentary by C. M. Dawson. Englewood Cliffs, N. J., 1970. Greek Drama series.

Seven Against Thebes. Translated with commentary by A. Hecht and H. Bacon. The Greek Tragedy in New Translation, edited by W. Arrowsmith. New York, 1973.

Seven Against Thebes, edited by A. Sidgwick. Oxford, 1903. Text and commentary.

Seven Against Thebes, edited and translated by A. W. Verrall. London, 1887. Text and commentary.

The Suppliant Women. Translated with commentary by J. Lembke. The Greek Tragedy in New Translation, edited by W. Arrowsmith. New York, 1975.

The Supplices of Aeschylus, edited and translated by T. G. Tucker. New York, 1889. Text and commentary.

FRAGMENTS

Die Fragmente der Tragödien des Aischylos, edited by H. J. Mette. Berlin, 1959.

Tragicorum Graecorum Fragmenta, edited by A. Nauck. 2nd ed. Leipzig, 1889.

See also *Aeschylus,* edited by H. W. Smith, appendix by H. Lloyd-Jones, listed previously.

LEXICON

G. Italie, *Index Aeschyleus.* 2nd ed. Leiden, 1964.

AESCHYLUS

STUDIES OF AESCHYLUS AND HIS WORKS

Cameron, H. D. *Studies on the "Seven Against Thebes" of Aeschylus.* The Hague and Paris, 1971.

Conacher, D. J. *Aeschylus' "Prometheus Bound": a Literary Commentary.* Toronto, 1980.

Finley, J. H., Jr. *Pindar and Aeschylus.* Martin Classical Lectures, vol. 14. Cambridge, Mass., 1955.

Gagarin, M. *Aeschylean Drama.* Berkeley and Los Angeles, 1976.

Garvie, A. F. *Aeschylus' Supplices: Play and Trilogy.* Cambridge, 1969.

Griffith, M. *The Authenticity of "Prometheus Bound."* Cambridge, 1977.

Herington, C. J. "Aeschylus: The Last Phase." In *Aeschylus: A Collection of Critical Essays,* edited by M. H. McCall, Jr., pp. 148–163. Englewood Cliffs, N. J., 1972. Also in *Arion* 4:387–403 (1965).

Kuhns, R. *The House, the City, and the Judge: The Growth of Moral Awareness in the "Oresteia."* Indianapolis and New York, 1962.

Murray, G. *Aeschylus, the Creator of Tragedy.* Oxford, 1940.

Murray, R. D. *The Motif of Io in Aeschylus' "Suppliants."* Princeton, 1958.

The Oxford Classical Dictionary, edited by N. G. L. Hammond and H. H. Scullard. 2nd ed. Oxford, 1970. Brief, informative articles on Aeschylus, Thespis, tragedy, music, meter, etc.

Sansone, D. *Aeschylean Metaphors for Intellectual Activity.* Wiesbaden, 1975.

Solmsen F. *Hesiod and Aeschylus.* Ithaca, N. Y., 1949.

Stanford, W. B. *Aeschylus in His Style: A Study in Language and Personality.* Dublin, 1942. Reprint. New York, 1972.

Taplin, O. *The Stagecraft of Aeschylus.* Oxford, 1977.

Thalmann, W. G. *Dramatic Art in Aeschylus' "Seven Against Thebes."* New Haven, 1978.

Thomson, G. *Aeschylus and Athens.* 2nd ed. London, 1946. 3rd ed., 1966, has no footnotes.

Zeitlin, F. I. "The Motif of the Corrupted Sacrifice in Aeschylus' Oresteia." *Transactions and Proceedings of the American Philological Association* 96:463–508 (1965).

———. "Postcript to Sacrificial Imagery in the Oresteia (*Ag.* 1235–1237)." *Transactions and Proceedings of the American Philological Association* 97:645–653 (1966).

STUDIES OF TRAGEDY AND TRAGIC THEATER

Aristotle, *On Poetry and Style (Poetics),* translated by G. M. A. Grube. Indianapolis and New York, 1958. The Library of Liberal Arts.

Arnott, P. *An Introduction to the Greek Theatre.* London and New York, 1959.

———. *Greek Scenic Conventions in the Fifth Century* B.C. Oxford, 1962.

Bieber, M. *The History of the Greek and Roman Theatre.* 2nd ed. Princeton, 1961.

Dale, A. M. "The Chorus in Action in Greek Tragedy." In *The Collected Papers of A. M. Dale.* Cambridge, 1969. Also in *Journal of Hellenic Studies* 8:141–152 (1961).

Jones, J. *On Aristotle and Greek Tragedy.* New York, 1962. See also J. M. Redfield, *Nature and Culture,* listed below.

Kitto, H. D. F. *Greek Tragedy: A Literary Study.* 2nd ed. New York, 1954.

———. *Form and Meaning in Drama: A Study of Six Greek Plays and of "Hamlet."* 2nd ed. New York, 1968.

Lattimore, R. *The Poetry of Greek Tragedy.* Baltimore, 1958.

———. *Story Patterns in Greek Tragedy.* Ann Arbor, 1964.

Lesky, A. *Greek Tragedy,* translated by H. A. Frankfort. New York, 1965.

Otis, B. *Cosmos and Tragedy: an Essay on the Meaning of Aeschylus,* edited by E. Christian Kopff. Chapel Hill, N. C., 1981.

Pickard-Cambridge, A. *Dithyramb, Tragedy and Comedy.* 2nd ed. Revised by T. B. L. Webster. Oxford, 1962.

———. *The Dramatic Festivals of Athens.* 2nd ed. Revised by J. Gould and D. M. Lewis. Oxford, 1968.

Romilly, J. de. *Time in Greek Tragedy.* Ithaca, N. Y., 1968.

Taplin, O. *Greek Tragedy in Action.* Berkeley and Los Angeles, 1978.

Walton, J. M. *Greek Theatre Practice.* Contributions in Drama and Theatre Studies, number 3. Westport, Conn., 1980.

Webster, T. B. L. "Greek Tragedy." In *Fifty Years and (Twelve) of Classical Scholarship,* edited by M. Platnauer. 2nd ed. Oxford, 1968.

———. *The Greek Chorus.* London, 1970.

————. *Greek Theatre Production.* 2nd ed. London, 1970.

STUDIES OF MYTH, RELIGION, AND CULTURE

Alexiou, M. *The Ritual Lament in Greek Tradition.* Cambridge, 1974.

Dietrich, B. C. *Death, Fate, and the Gods: the Development of a Religious Idea in Greek Popular Belief and in Homer.* London, 1965.

Dodds, E. R. *The Greeks and the Irrational.* Sather Classical Lectures, vol. 25. Berkeley and Los Angeles, 1951.

Girard, R. *Violence and the Sacred,* translated by Patrick Gregory. Baltimore, 1977.

Guépin, J.-P. *The Tragic Paradox, Myth and Ritual in Greek Tragedy.* Amsterdam, 1968.

Guthrie, W. K. C. *The Greeks and their Gods.* Boston, 1954.

Lloyd-Jones, H. *The Justice of Zeus.* Sather Classical Lectures, vol. 41. Berkeley and Los Angeles, 1971.

Onians, R. B. *The Origins of European Thought.* 2nd ed., 1954. Reprint. New York, 1973.

Redfield, J. M. *Nature and Culture in the Iliad: the Tragedy of Hector.* Chicago and London, 1975.

Rose, H. J. *A Handbook of Greek Mythology, Including Its Extension to Rome.* New York, 1959.

Vernant, J.-P. *Myth and Society in Ancient Greece,* translated by J. Lloyd. Atlantic Highlands, N. J., 1980.

————, and P. Vidal-Naquet. *Tragedy and Myth in Ancient Greece,* translated by J. Lloyd. Atlantic Highlands, N. J., 1980.

HELEN BACON

PINDAR

(*ca.* 518–*ca.* 438 B.C.)

I

> The body of every man goes to meet mighty
>   Death,
> but there remains still alive an image of his
>   life. For it alone
> comes from the gods. It sleeps when our
>   arms and legs act;
> but when men are asleep, it often reveals
>   to them in their dreams
> the coming judgment of joys and pains.[1]

I N EXTANT WESTERN literature these are the first words to suggest that the human soul has its origin in the divine. They come from no theologian nor philosopher, but from "the poet of the ancient Olympic games," as our society knows Pindar (if it knows him at all). Recent technical scholarship views Pindar mainly as a rhetorician, the master of encomium, the author who knows best how to compose in praise of another man. Yet it is mistaken to regard Pindar as anything more or less than what the ancient Greeks regarded him, a lyric poet. They judged him the greatest lyric poet not so much for his versatility as for his poetic style. They found the impact of his poetry, as a whole, incomparable.

There were many lyric poets to contend for that top ranking, but most are little more than names to us now. Even the remains of such giants as Sappho and Simonides are so tattered as to prevent full and confident judgments about their poetic gifts. Only Pindar survived the Middle Ages, kept alive as Homer, Herodotus, and Sophocles were—that is, copied over and over by human hands and passed from scribe to scribe. The manuscript tradition of Pindar preserves forty-five complete poems, enough to read and judge him as a poet.

There was much more. The provocative passage that appears above comes from a funeral dirge, not an Olympic ode. Of that dirge we have no more than the snippet I quote, preserved for us because Plutarch quotes it. We have no more than a few fragments from all of Pindar's dirges. In the early Middle Ages, perhaps as barbarians overran Europe, the paper on which they were written disintegrated, and no one much cared. Most of Pindar's poems met the same fate. We have about a fourth of his work. Ancient sources say Pindar composed a total of seventeen books (full papyrus rolls) of poems in various genres. These included dirges, hymns to the gods, paeans (special hymns to Apollo), dithyrambs, and several other genres peculiar to the Greek lyric tradition. He wrote three books of *partheneia*, "maiden songs." Choruses of young women performed these poems, usually during a religious celebration. The other genres were performed by a chorus of youths or men, who both danced and sang. Pindar also wrote four books

---

[1]Fragment 131b Maehler = 131 Sandys (see bibliography). The meaning and translation of the last line are far from certain. Plutarch equates Pindar's word *eidolon* (image) here with the word *psyche* (soul), an association that goes back to Homer.

(the most in any genre) of epinician odes, poems performed by a chorus to celebrate a man's victory in one of the athletic festivals.

These four books of victory odes contain the forty-five complete poems that we possess. Each book takes its name from one of the four great athletic festivals: the Olympian, Pythian, Nemean, and Isthmian games. Titles such as "Olympian 1" do not date from Pindar's time, but from the Hellenistic age, when Alexandrian scholars collected Pindar's works, edited them, and arranged them into the seventeen books. In modern texts of Pindar, the few extant fragments of the thirteen lost books are ordinarily appended to the four books of epinicians. They are sadly scanty.

If our knowledge of his work is incomplete, we know even less of Pindar and his life. Apart from his approximate dates (*ca.* 518–*ca.* 438 B.C.) and native city (Thebes), we know almost nothing certain about his personal life. It is not that ancient sources are wholly lacking; rather, they are so unreliable that we cannot trust their information. There are a few very brief Pindaric biographies, written at the close of antiquity. They are full of details, such as the names of Pindar's parents, teachers, wife, and children. Yet these biographers had no more authentic sources for this information than we have. They too had only the poetry itself, and their method was to ransack it for any hint of an answer to the biographers' usual questions. Unfortunately, Pindar's poetry belongs to religious, public, and encomiastic genres, where those answers are not likely to be found. The failure of these ancient Lives shows in their disagreement on the information they contain. The fact that there are three different candidates for Pindar's father suggests that one ancient pastime was to pin the tag "his father" on a name in an ode. Most of the statements in the Lives are so fanciful that one cannot take them seriously: "When Pindar was a child asleep, bees filled his mouth with honey" (a portent of his mellifluous verse) or "Pindar once came upon the god Pan singing one of the poet's own songs."

In contrast with the pious Pindar of these Lives, the annotated editions from antiquity present Pindar as rather greedy and cantankerous. The scholiasts' Pindar must repeatedly reply to accusations made against him by sundry detractors and rival poets. But these scholars, too, had nothing but the poems to rely on. Their comments about Pindar's personal disputes seem to be based on patent misreadings of specific passages in the odes. They tell us much about the contentious world in which these scholars themselves lived, but almost nothing of Pindar. Until very recently the scholiasts' view of Pindar prevailed, and modern scholars merely redoubled their efforts to reconstruct Pindar's life from that same poor source, his text. A noted modern scholar, Wilamowitz, wrote a lengthy biography of Pindar, in which he presented detailed itineraries of his travels, described Pindar's relations with various individuals, his leanings and involvements in all the political questions of the day, and even the fluctuations of his bank account.

But most of this is outright historical fiction in the guise of scientific research. Even worse, this largely fictional biography of Pindar was incorporated as historical fact into most encyclopedias and modern studies on Pindar. The general reader would do well to discount what he reads about Pindar's personal life as the probable result of confusion, wrong assumptions, and impetuous misinterpretation. Although the poems convey almost nothing useful toward a Pindaric biography, they reveal much about Pindar. From his poetry we can learn of his professional life—that is, Pindar as poet—and his intellectual life, the subjects of this essay.

II

A reader who begins with the first few lines of Pindar's first poem may be enchanted and eager to continue. More likely, that reader will be mystified, and react as did the Gentleman's wife in one of Charles Perrault's tales. Upon learning that her husband was reading Pindar, the wife insisted that he read her a few lines. When he finished translating *Olympian* 1.1–7 for her, she accused him of inventing it all—just to mock her. No author, she roundly declared, would spout such unintelligible nonsense.

Pindar's reputation for difficulty matches that for excellence. A reader approaching him for the first time in translation will surely find him largely opaque. There is a maze of unknown proper names. Even familiar gods, heroes, and places may pass unknown, for Pindar often designates them by alternative phrases. Mythological narratives seem to jump around capriciously in time, and bear little relevance to their context. Sometimes a sentence demands minute knowledge of Greek literary convention. At other times a metaphor or simile will be so bold that it wholly eludes the untrained audience. Students sometimes complain that they have carefully read an entire ode—and understood nothing. Most difficult of all (even for the scholar) is keeping one's bearings on a train of thought that may change suddenly with kaleidoscopic variety.

Perhaps one's first draft of Pindar should be small, and not too heady. I suggest one of the shorter, less ambitious odes, *Nemean* 2. It celebrates the victory of an Athenian, Timodemos, in the athletic games at Nemea (probably dated in the 480's). This is Timodemos' first major victory, and it comes in a festival held in honor of Zeus. The argument of the first stanza turns on those circumstances. There was a group of men who habitually made their start with Zeus, the Homeridae ("Sons of Homer"), rhapsodes who gave public performances of the *Iliad*, the *Odyssey*, and other early epics. They usually prefaced their recitations with a short prelude of their own, and those preludes often began: "With Zeus let us begin our song." Pindar's analogy between the young athlete's initial Nemean victory and the rhapsodes' introductory song may seem specious or farfetched until we see better how it develops. From this start the athlete's career may be expected to unfold like the long epics that follow the preludes of the Homeridae. Pindar reinforces his suggestion that there is far more to come with a bookkeeping metaphor (the victory as a "down payment") that may elude the reader in translation.

That reader will miss even more in the second stanza, but may well grasp the general theme. Timonoös' son (the athlete Timodemos) and his success are a glory to Athens. His career is now favorably launched down the path of his forebears, who also won many crowns in the great games. With all these things so favorable (and the bookkeeping metaphor of a "balance due" now operative from stanza 1), Timodemos ought to win many more victories in the Isthmian and Pythian games.

So far the argument has developed with rather explicit comparisons and long periodic sentences. It has reached out to several topics, but the goals have remained clear. A hardy reader can scarcely be blamed for rechecking the place at stanza 3[2]: "It is likely for Orion to come not far from the P[e]leiades. Indeed Salamis can rear a fighting man. In Troy Hector listened to Ajax." Here is that seeming rupture of argument that may send Pindar's readers to despair or to another author. But when Pindar moves most quickly we must be most patient. Although he has not lost sight of his subject, his rhetorical methods abruptly change—to the implicit, allusive, and paratactic. Orion is the constellation, and the reader who misses it becomes more and more bewildered.

When the constellations parade across the sky, Orion the Hunter follows hard by the star cluster Pleiades. It is a simple analogy, again implying that more victories are sure to follow Timodemos' success. Pindar did not change his theme, but cut the thread for an audience unfamiliar with the sky. He could not foresee our numbers. Similarly, Greeks would hear an echo of Homer in the reference to Salamis. In *Iliad*

[2]Modern texts do not fully agree in the numeration of lines in Pindar (I follow Maehler's text). Most translations do not number the lines, and there is no uniformity. I therefore cite a passage merely by stanza number, assuming any reader may find it in any text—if resourceful enough. There is no alternative method.

7, before meeting Hector in single combat, Ajax boasts, "I was born and reared in Salamis; I'm no neophyte warrior." Relying on the echo, Pindar alludes to Ajax's valor (against Hector) at Troy and relates the passage to his victor: "Your valor, Timodemos, in the pancration brings you glory; and Acharnai, too, is long known for brave men." Once one sees that the Athenian suburb, Acharnai, is the victor's home, the A-B-B-A pattern becomes clear: "Salamis, Ajax" compares with "Timodemos, Acharnai." But these correspondences draw an analogy between the young athlete and the hero of the Trojan War that again may seem farfetched.

Timodemos' grueling event, the pancration, pitted one man against another in a combination of wrestling, boxing, and street fighting. No holds were barred, and there were no rounds. The athletes carried the attack to each other until one gave up or could not continue. Although athletics never became a substitute for war in Greece, Pindar sometimes presents the valor, achievements, and glory of the athlete and of the warrior as if cut from the same cloth. Here the unrestrained combative nature of the event invites and validates the analogy.

In the rest of stanza 4 and most of stanza 5, Pindar recounts the athletic victories of this prominent Acharnian clan, the Timodemidae ("Sons of Timodemos"). The reader who assumes this Timodemos to be the same man as the victor errs badly. He is, rather, an ancestor after whom the present victor is named, a common Greek practice. Pindar's victory catalog will not read like a modern sports page, where we find box scores more prosaic than prose itself. He usually records the victories by periphrastic means. The result maintains the tone of lyric poetry, but often at a cost to the modern audience, which may need geographical help just to grasp a victory catalog. Victories "beside Parnassus" are victories at the Pythian games at Delphi, which is overlooked by the famous mountain. Crowns won "in the valley of Pelops" come from the Isthmian games, administered by the citizens of nearby Corinth. The games at Nemea (not far from Isthmia) Pindar specifies by name, and victories "at home" are clearly in Athens.

The final sentence ends the poem as it began, with the subjects of Zeus and the athlete's recent victory. An audience familiar with the rhapsodes' preludes would recall more of their traditional formula, "With Zeus let us begin, and with Zeus let us end. Take up the song." The opening idea has informed the whole poem.

Nemean 2 is certainly not one of Pindar's best or most interesting odes. We must not judge him by it, no more than we would judge Rembrandt by a minor sketch. Yet even in its small scale and minor tendency, this poem illustrates the pitfalls that await a rash reader. The poem requires at least some knowledge of Greek culture, literary tradition, athletics, mythology, geography, and even genealogical practice. The unwary may go astray at almost any point: the Homeridae, the sudden reference to the constellations, the allusive Ajax parallel, or even the circumlocutions of the catalog. Nemean 2 also at least hints at some of the rewards for the patient, although in translation there is a disadvantage. One misses the poem's outstanding quality, a superb diction that depends not so much on grandiloquence (Pindar's vocabulary is usually rather simple) as on a crisp syntax chiseled into the stanza as onto a stone. However negligible compared with his great odes, Nemean 2 is an artistic success, coherent in its themes and true to its aims.

III

"But why," we instinctively ask, "would the greatest lyricist of Greece spend his energy versifying athletic summaries, composing poems about the future career of a pancratiast?" Why, in short, would Pindar write epinicians? In part the answer lies in his times. The Olympic games were founded in 776 B.C., before Homer composed his epics. They grew slowly in content, importance, and appeal. By the early sixth century the concept of Panhellenic athletics spread to Delphi, where the second great festival, the Pythian games, was founded in 582. Soon games began at Isthmia and Nemea, completing the "Big Four" of Greek sport. Other cities, large and small, held their own contests. By the latter half of the sixth century, athletics were a major feature of Greek society. A staggered sequence offered athletes almost continuous competition from spring to fall, and at least one of the "Big Four" every year. It appears that athletic recruiting was common, at least in the Italian and Sicilian Greek colonies. Athletes were highly esteemed and handsomely paid. The way that Greece heaped glory, money, and attention upon its athletes from about 550 to 450 B.C. has had no parallel in history until now.

We find it difficult to imagine a Greek culture, a century before Euripides and Socrates, as sports-mad as our own. Therefore we must be sure that the similarities do not obscure important differences. Unlike our secular sports, Greek games were attached to religious festivals. But the religious element is merely one index of the fundamental difference between Greek athletics and our own. Athletics were fully integrated into Greek culture as a whole: religion, government, and the arts. Contrary to our custom, the humanists and artists joined with the athletes in a reciprocal relationship. We cannot imagine a Picasso portrait of Jesse Owens, or Robert Frost composing an Olympic ode for Paavo Nurmi (with song and dance!). But in the latter sixth century B.C., athletic scenes became favorites of Greek vase painters. The best sculptors were hired to make likenesses of individual athletic stars, to be enshrined at Olympia in a kind of hall of fame. And the best poets began to write victory odes.

Because athletics were integrated with the rest of Greek culture, the epinician was no mere sports write-up. It was a complex lyric poem, set fully in the context of Greek life and the Greeks' search for life's meaning. Indeed a man of his times, Pindar responded to the athletic spirit even more strongly than we would expect—with his entire intellectual and spiritual being: "There is a divine presence in a test of human strength" (*Isthmian* 5, stanza 2—see section V below).

Pindar presents the athletic contest as a microcosm of the general human struggle for greatness, the struggle to pass beyond ordinary human limitations and enter upon achievements of permanence and distinction. Only because he saw athletics in this light could he compare Timodemos to the great hero of myth, Ajax. And only because he presents his athlete-patrons in this light could the epinician genre pass beyond the victory celebration to join the best of Western literature.

IV

As an occasional poem, the epinician is firmly rooted in the occasion of its first performance, a victory celebration for a specific individual. That is why Pindar's readers must deal with so many names of his contemporaries: the victor's father, uncle, clan, or coach. We do not know these people as the Greek audience did. Moreover, we can never fully appreciate a Pindaric ode as a total artistic performance. We lack the music and the choreography. We would greatly profit if we knew the dancers' gestures and the musical score. But their loss is not so crucial as it sounds. Homer made all Greek poets fully aware that a poem may survive its first performance—survive even its performers and its author. Pindar probably expected his poems to be severed from their music, and consciously composed with an eye on the distant future, when he would be read.

Poetry of the present can interest people of the future only if it brings its occasional subjects into relation with larger, enduring questions. Myth is the major means by which Pindar places his athletes' achievements in the timeless makeup of the world. There is a reciprocal process. By itself, neither the present nor the past implies a general truth. But by holding his contemporaries up against figures from mythology, Pindar affirms the permanence of the heroic past in its relevance to the present. Conversely, by referring his occasional subjects to mythological examples, Pindar validates their participation in a recognized pattern of human life.

A simple comparison between victor-patron and mythological hero is rare. We saw such an analogy, between Timodemos and Ajax, merely implied in *Nemean* 2. Similar is *Pythian* 1, stanza 8, but there the comparison is explicit and briefly developed. The victor, Hieron, king of Syracuse, wages battle "in the manner of Philoctetes." Pindar quickly summarizes Philoctetes' myth: the ailing hero, long mistreated by the Greek leaders, eventually played a crucial role in Troy's capture. The rather exact analogy seems to include, in the cases of both Hieron and Philoctetes, illness, failure to receive allies' proper respect, and eventual military success. Normally, though, Pindar's myths are much longer, and they illustrate general similarities of kind, not matters of precise detail.

Typical is *Pythian* 6, the central third of which narrates a tale of the Trojan War. The parallelism between the contemporary and heroic worlds is as pointed as in *Pythian* 1, stanza 8, but shows a variation. The heroic archetype, Nestor's son, Antilochus, finds his contemporary counterpart not in the victor-patron, Xenocrates, but in that man's son, Thrasyboulos. Before the myth Pindar praises Thrasyboulos for maintaining a well-known precept, that a son honor Zeus first, and his parents the same way. As the myth begins (stanza 4), Pindar cites an earlier ("in former times") example. When old Nestor was about to be killed on the battlefield of Troy, his son, Antilochus, hurried to his aid and "purchased his father's safety at the price of his own life." It was the absolute act of filial devotion, and was so recognized by others. "But that is ancient history" (end of stanza 5); "of present-day men" Thrasyboulos exhibits extreme filial piety. He is the Antilochus of his own day.

Pindar unmistakably compares Thrasyboulos to Antilochus, yet it would be silly to press the details. Thrasyboulos has not died for his father. He lives a full, successful life (stanza 6). Whatever act of filial piety merited him this praise, it was surely minor compared with the ancient hero's supreme sacrifice. But its specific nature is not relevant. The similarity between the two men is one of kind or quality, not of degree or detail. And the mythological example works in the poem. Both in the days of yore and now, there have been models of a son's devotion to his father. Illustrations taken from each period reciprocally validate each other, and imply that filial piety has a permanent place in the world. These models will still be good in the future.

The examples of Philoctetes and Antilochus are exceptional in one respect. The poet specifies their applicability to the contemporary world, and even the individuals, Hieron and Thrasyboulos, to whom they apply. Seldom is Pindar so explicit or helpful to his readers. Usually he introduces his myths with no announcement, no explanation. The audience must think for itself. The latter half of *Nemean* 1 tells the charming myth of the infant Herakles, who rises from his crib to throttle two serpents, which Hera sent to kill him. On learning of the prodigious feat, Teiresias the Seer prophesies Herakles' future greatness and eventual abode on Olympus. Pindar makes no explicit statement to compare the victor-patron, Chromios, with the Theban hero. But the context and what is known of Chromios' career lead most scholars to see an implicit comparison of the two, the Heraklean valor somehow reflected in the Syracusan knight. Again, we should not seek one-to-one equivalents and presume that the young Chromios strangled snakes in his first year. Pindar merely suggests that in valor, at least, Chromios is something like Herakles, and will receive his eventual reward.

Many readers are reluctant to accept such subtle suggestions when Pindar will not proclaim how his myths work. In many poems the relevance of the mythical subject to the occasional poem is not at all obvious, and some readers, both ancient and modern, fault Pindar for a lack of artistic unity that they see in such odes. Pindar's myths may seem at times merely enchanting, isolated stories, well told for their own sake. Pindar is indeed a major source for myth study. The mythical portions of an ode demand somewhat less specialized knowledge than others, and Greek myth almost magically fascinates Western man. A modern reader, therefore, may tend to focus on Pindar's myths as entities, and neglect the rest. Most Pindaric myths can give satisfaction that way, and I mention a few: the myths of Apollo and Cyrene (*Pythian* 9); Pelops and Tantalus (*Olympian* 1); the myth of the great Flood (*Olympian* 9); the Argonauts' quest for the Golden Fleece (*Pythian* 4); the Rhodian myths (*Olympian* 7); the young Herakles (*Nemean* 1); the young Achilles (*Nemean* 3); and the brief Oresteia (*Pythian* 11).

These and other stories may at first appear able to stand on their own right—especially since the transitions to and from them often seem willful or unmotivated. But that may be our fault, not Pindar's. Generally the reader who views a myth in isolation forfeits a full understanding of the myth itself (to say nothing of the ode as a whole). For the myth normally assumes a form determined by its integral function in its context—that is, in the entire poem.

In the engaging tale of *Olympian* 13, the Corinthian hero, Bellerophon, seeks a method to break Pegasus, the winged horse. Athena appears to him in his sleep, and lays beside him the Bridle Bit; he picks it up, and tames the horse on whose back he later performs his wondrous deeds. Even specialists have seen no close connection between this tale and Xenophon, the Corinthian track and field athlete for whom the poem is written. But a connection emerges if we look for one crucial similarity, as in a Homeric simile, instead of detailed, precise parallelism, as in medieval allegory.

The story centers not so much on the horse, the hero, or the hero's deeds as on the discovery of the Bit. Formerly the Bit did not exist. Bel-

lerophon invents it, with Athena's help. The emphasis on invention here clearly continues a theme prominent earlier in the poem. In stanza 3, Pindar praises Corinth for being a center of invention, and catalogs some of its "first ever" achievements (including invention of the Bit, later elaborated in myth). Because of the way Greeks kept athletic records, this general and recurrent theme has immediate relevance to the epinician occasion at hand. Xenophon, Pindar's victor-patron, has just set a new world record (stanza 4). He is the "first man ever" (a standard record formula) to win both the sprinting event and the all-around contest (*pentathlon*) at the Olympic games.[3]

No extant author before Pindar represents Bellerophon as the inventor of the Bridle Bit. It is likely that Pindar invented this version to suit this particular poem, adroitly adapting the Corinthian hero's myth to the innovative tradition in Corinthian history. He thus makes an excellent mythological study of the mysterious process of invention;[4] and he associates hero and record-breaking athlete through the background theme of the Corinthians' usual position at the forefront of new human achievements. The forefront of human achievements is, one might say, Pindar's usual theme song, whether he speaks of the heroic world or of his own.

Sometimes Pindar aims his praise even more directly at the athlete's homeland. The middle of *Pythian* 10 recounts Perseus' visit to the land of the Hyperboreans. There is a delightful description of the blissful life enjoyed by this wondrous mythical tribe that lives apart from

---

[3] For Greek athletic record keeping and its phraseology, see M. N. Tod in *Classical Quarterly*, 43 (1949), 105–112.

[4] For a sometimes surprisingly similar study of modern scientific invention, see T. Kuhn, *The Structure of Scientific Revolutions*, 2nd ed. (Chicago, 1970). For instance, "More often the new [theory] . . . emerges all at once, sometimes in the middle of the night, in the mind of a man deeply immersed in crisis. What the nature of that final stage is—how an individual invents . . . (or finds that he has invented a new way)—must here remain inscrutable and may be permanently so" (pp. 89–90). Or, "Scientists then often speak of the 'scales falling from the eyes' or of the 'lightning flash.' . . . On other occasions, the relevant illumination comes in sleep" (pp. 122–123). What we call "inscrutable" Pindar calls Athena.

other men in the Far North. Devotees of Apollo, they spend all their days in feasting, playing music, and dancing, without aging or falling ill, without hard work or war. This passage on the Hyperboreans can be read as merely a fine piece of utopian literature, and arranged beside such tales as the Isle of the Blest (which it resembles). But one understands the myth and Pindar's motivation for shaping it this way far better when it is placed squarely within its poem. The victor hails from Thessaly, the real North Country of classical Greece. Pindar's praise of a Hyperborean Utopia is, by extension and reflection, also in praise of the athlete's own land—the "Blessed Thessaly" of stanza 1.

One school of scholars claims that Pindar freely uses the heroic world to allegorize the various political struggles of his own day. But their arguments are poorly founded, and will not meet a scholarly test. For example, it is just a rash and willful assertion that the overweening Clytemnestra of *Pythian* 11 symbolizes the growing arrogance of imperial Athens. Nothing in Pindar's text remotely suggests that idea. The aspects of Pindar's world that he usually illustrates by mythological model are the general ones we have seen: filial piety, a victor's valor or signal achievement, the traits of his native land. He rarely mentions interstate strife within Greece, and I know no certain case where he allegorizes it in myth.[5]

Barbarians are another matter. In *Pythian* 1 the poet praises Hieron's martial successes against Phoenicians and Etruscans (stanzas 11–12) in a way that recalls stanzas 3–5, an account of Zeus's triumph over the monster of myth, Typhos. The analogy is rather clear: as Zeus is the suppressor of what is unruly and anti-Olym-

pian, so Hieron suppresses barbarian, anti-Hellenic forces. The mythological parallel gives an aura and importance to Hieron's achievements that no direct praise, however extreme, could match.

There remains one more magnificent exception to the rule that Pindar tends not to illustrate national "current events" with his myths. The myth of *Isthmian* 8 is downright awesome, both in subject matter and in poetic language. Briefly, the tale is this. At some point before the Trojan War, both Zeus and Poseidon took a fascination for the comely sea goddess Thetis, and wished to take her to bed: "Eros gripped them." They contended for her favor. But the wise goddess Themis summoned the gods to a summit conference. To the two love-struck deities she gave a brief command: "Stop that!"

Themis then explains that Thetis is destined to bear a "son more powerful than his father." If she lies with Zeus or any of his brothers, she will give birth to a new kind of god, with new weapons stronger than the trident and thunderbolt. He will overthrow the Olympian gods and their order, become the new ruler of the world.

To avert this catastrophe, Themis recommends that Thetis be married off safely to a mortal ("Let her see her son die in battle!"). Then the son stronger than his father will be no threat to the Olympians. Themis even offers a candidate worthy of a goddess: Peleus, "the most pious man in Iolcian land." The sobered gods in council nod their heads in assent to all she has said. The deed is quickly done, and Thetis bears not the destroyer of divine order but Achilles, the scourge of Troy. A catalog of Achilles' victims closes the myth, a reminder of how destructive this force would have been if unleashed against Olympus instead of Ilium.

It is a powerful myth. Especially haunting is the scene in which these great gods in highest council—shortly before, quite occupied with rather indulgent erotic pursuits—realize the extreme gravity of the situation, their own imminent Armageddon—and quickly, quietly nod assent. On me, at least, it has a profound effect.

In its context this myth is even more awe-

[5]When he broaches such subjects as a recent battle of Greek against Greek, he may generalize it, and emphasize the traditional concepts—valorous death and glory—but not national culpability or topical questions of any kind (see D. C. Young, *Pindar Isthmian 7* [Leiden, 1968], esp. pp. 45–46). Exceptions concern the colonial monarchs and politicians, such as Hieron and Chromios. In these cases Pindar is not dragging in his own interests and views on contemporary politics, but using all relevant material available for praising his patron. Damophilos' role in *Pythian* 4 is clearly extraordinary and still not fully understood.

some, more profound. Stanza 2 explains the poem's historical setting: "Some god has thrust aside from our heads a Stone of Tantalus, a burden on Greece *not to be borne.*" Scholars agree that this Panhellenic "Stone of Tantalus" (an old symbol for impending disaster) can only be the Persian invasion repulsed by the Greeks (and "some god") in the wars fought on Greek soil in 480–479. Greece, too, has just been saved from overthrow and essential extinction. In those notions—a return from the brink of utter disaster, the salvation of a way of life, quenching a threat to the most fundamental order—we find the parallels between Pindar's real world and his Thetis myth. As the Olympian world, the cosmos as we know it, was saved from the strange new lord whom Thetis would have borne, so Greece was saved from subjugation at the hands of barbarian invaders from the East. Pindar does not elaborate in stanza 2 on what a Persian victory would have meant. But his grave mythological analogy suggests that he knew the far-reaching, even "cosmic," implications. Had the Persians won, Greek civilization would not have been the same, nor would the course and development of western Europe.

V

We know almost nothing about the selection and training of an epinician chorus, and very little about its performance of an ode. The victorious athlete, or an associate of his, commissioned the poem and paid for it. But there survives no information about how this contract was made. Presumably some kind of interview between poet and patron would be required. But we do not know to what degree an athlete prescribed the contents of his poem. The epinician poets all appear to exercise a great deal of freedom. It seems that the ode was the athlete's, but the composition was the poet's—tailored to suit the occasion. Even in so unusual a poem as *Isthmian* 8 the athlete is far from forgotten. There the young pancratiast

victor, Cleander of Aegina, and his family receive their share of individualized praise; and they have their own relationships to the mythological parallels explained above.[6] Because the characters and circumstances of Pindar's patrons strongly affected what he wrote, it is time to look more closely at who they were. A fourth of Pindar's epinicians are for citizens of Aegina, an island-state just south of Athens. We know little about these Aeginetans as individuals except their names. They seem to care greatly about their heritage and family connections, no doubt belonging to that aristocracy for which encyclopedias tell us Pindar wrote. Often the family already boasts athletic victors. The Aeginetans seem, more than most, to cultivate the epinician. Simonides and Bacchylides also wrote for them, and they seem, more than most, to enjoy hearing myths about their traditional heroes, the "Aeacids" Telamon and Peleus, and their sons, Ajax and Achilles. The Aeginetans' interests seem implanted in their odes, which abound with tales of the Aeacids and with family history. For the specialist in Pindar, athletics, or Greek ethics, the Aeginetan odes offer much, including a mine of information. With notable exceptions (such as *Isthmian* 8) the casual reader may find them, as a whole, somewhat less immediately rewarding than some other odes, being more entwined with things and people removed from us.

Some readers' favorites are the odes for the Sicilian kings. For Hieron, king of Syracuse, Pindar wrote *Olympian* 1 and *Pythians* 1, 2, and 3. Hieron was one of the most powerful men in the Mediterranean, inheriting the crown from his brother, Gelon, essentially a usurper. Hieron continued Gelon's ambitious programs, creating a powerful, imposing city and ruling vast numbers with an iron hand. He also patronized poets, including Simonides, Aeschylus, and Pindar. The myths in Hieron's poems are varied and especially interesting, grand in conception, trenchant in effect. Some critics

[6]C. Carey in *Dionysiaca*, a Festschrift for Denys Page (Cambridge, 1978), pp. 27–33, and A. Köhnken in *Bulletin of the Institute of Classical Studies* (London), 22 (1975), 25–36.

think them disturbing, for punishment plays a role in all. Each reader must gain his or her own impression of each of these odes, but no serious student wili be unimpressed. They are among Pindar's most ambitious, carefully wrought poems. Pindar perhaps knew that the prominence of their recipient would put the poems, too, in the limelight, and bestowed on them additional time, care, and pains.

The same care seems apparent in poems for two other monarchs of Greek colonies (where, unlike Greece proper, monarchy was still in fashion). In *Olympian* 2 the central portion of the poem presents an astonishing doctrine of reincarnation, judgment after death, and a blissful, permanent afterlife for the pure and just. In most poems Pindar gives the traditional Greek views: Hades is the Receiver of All, and his realm is a grim land of no return. But here the recipient of the poem, Theron, monarch of Akragas, Sicily, may play an especially strong role in the choice of a central subject. He enjoyed a greater reputation for benevolence than did other monarchs of his day. If he himself did not entertain the ideas of this extraordinary doctrine (basically those of the mystery religions), they were especially at home in Akragas, the city of Empedocles. Pindar's other monarch-patron was Arkesilaos, king of Cyrene, the principal Greek city of Africa. For him Pindar wrote *Pythian* 4, a poem remarkable for its tale of Jason, the Argonauts, and Medea. It is by far the longest of Pindar's myths, the nearest to (but far from) an epic in conception.

Most of Pindar's patrons were probably men with standing, but not the power of these kings. One is the little-known Athenian Alkmaeonid. Another, Diagoras of Rhodes, comes from the East, but most hail from the mainland or colonial West. Only four are natives of Pindar's Thebes. A few may not have had the nobility of blood or position that scholars readily grant them. Hagesidamos and Ergoteles (*Olympians* 10 and 12) may belong to a class of professional athletes in the western colonies. But it is idle to speculate further on social origins, and not very relevant to reading the poems. The point is this: Pindar's patrons had much in common, but

their diversity, too, is important. They had diverse roles in life, diverse experiences, and diverse needs. And surely they had diverse expectations about what Pindar would say in their poems.

VI

A younger contemporary of Pindar, the philosopher Anaxagoras, was a one-book author. From him we can expect a coherence, a philosophical consistency. Yet in Anaxagoras' case it is difficult to find.[7] How much more unlikely in Pindar's! Each poem was composed as an entity, and performed as a complete work. A half-century separates the last datable poem from the earliest. That inconsistencies of thought exist from poem to poem should not surprise, nor can their existence be faulted in such a collection of poems. For all were first conceived, composed, and published as independent works to suit various occasions, the separate victory celebrations of some very different men.

Pythian 11 argues that the life of a king is a most undesirable lot.[8] *Olympian* 1 argues that the life of a king is the highest lot there is. There is no real contradiction here. *Olympian* 1 celebrates the victory of a king. *Pythian* 11 does not. Rather, its patron was clearly an ordinary citizen, without great political station. What is true in one case cannot be true in the other. Attempts to construct a coherent Pindaric philosophy misconstrue the nature of his work. Yet we must not, on that account, write him off as a thinker. We may still study Pindar's interests, his ideas, the problems he consistently identifies, and the solutions he offers. For these pertain to matters that all members of his varied group of patrons did have in common.

Pindar's special themes are not unique with him. Like almost all else Greek, their germ is in Homer, and other authors treat them. But with Pindar a few favorite subjects assume such importance and thoughtful development that they

[7]G. S. Kirk and J. E. Raven, *The Presocratic Philosophers,* 2nd ed. (Cambridge, 1960), p. 367.
[8]D. C. Young, *Three Odes,* pp. 1–26.

set him off even from Bacchylides, whose epinicians deal with themes fundamentally the same. They—along with Pindar's bold, highly compressed style—are the hallmarks of his work.

Pindar's foremost concern—his preoccupation—is with excellence, that category of things, acts, and qualities encompassed by the Greek word *arete*. Several studies on this aspect of Pindar's work are readily accessible elsewhere.[9] I limit myself here to one rather neglected portion of the question that relates directly to the epinician genre: the way that Pindar places all types of excellence on the same level and at the same value, whether they be physical, military, intellectual, political, or poetical. To our modes of thinking, he may seem indiscriminate; but he has his reasons.

> The race of the gods is one thing, that of men,
>   quite another.
> We both get our breath from Earth, our common
>   mother.
> Yet the powers of the two races are wholly
>   different, so that one of them is nothing—
> while the bronze heaven of the gods stays secure
>   forever.
> But we can become something *like* the immortal
>   gods
> through greatness—greatness of mind or greatness
>   of body—
> though we don't know from day to day, or night to
>   night, what course
> fate has drawn for us to run our race.
>   (*Nemean* 6.1–8)

Because the gods are, in Greek thought, those who can perform with perfection, human excellence is akin to the divine. But man can resemble the divine only when performing at the superlative level. This resemblance, I emphasize, comes through greatness, either mental or physical, and the parallel presentation of the two kinds indicates their equal standing. In our society those involved in one of these two spheres may tend to discount or ignore excellence in the other; but to Pindar excellence is

excellence. A great discus throw and a great lyric stanza are of the same high quality because there is a divine quality in each.

The most concise statement comes from *Olympian* 9: "Prowess of body and prowess of mind are due to a god."[10] Since what comes from the gods cannot be second-rate, physical excellence, as proved in the athletic contest, can be in no way inferior to other kinds. The contest itself is a flirting with divinity.

> In athletic games the victor wins the glory his
>   heart desires
> as crown after crown is placed on his head, when
>   he wins
> with his hands or swift feet.
> *There is a divine presence in a judgment of human*
>   *strength.*
> Only two things, along with prosperity, shepherd
>   life's sweetest prize:
> if a man has success and then gets a good name.
> *Don't expect to become Zeus.* You have everything
> if to share in those two blessings comes your way.
>   (*Isthmian* 5, stanzas 2–3, emphasis added)

This important passage points to the fundamental difficulty. The athletic contest, the performance, and the excellence displayed there may all be divine or nearly so. The athlete is not. Far from it.

The blunt sentence "Don't expect to become Zeus" concisely states a double-edged theme basic to Pindar's verse and thought: the theme of human limitations. The variations of the theme are, true to Pindar's style, many and inventive. He tells his patrons that they cannot pass beyond "the Pillars of Herakles" (Gibraltar, symbol for the western limit of the world); that they cannot get to the Hyperboreans' land; that they cannot get to heaven; that no human can be perfectly happy; that all men must die; and, as quoted above, that they cannot become gods (compare *Olympian* 5, end). Rhetorically these are all highly complimentary statements.

---

[9]H. Fraenkel, *Early Greek Poetry and Philosophy* (Oxford, 1975), pp. 427–504.

[10]*Olympian* 9, stanza 2 (end). The Greek is *agathoi kai sophoi*, one of Pindar's variations on the *erga* and *boulai* doublet (compare *Nemean* 8.8, *Pythian* 4.72, *Olympian* 11.19). Here *agathoi* connotes valor and success as well as physical prowess, and *sophoi* may suggest poetic wisdom, but body and mind are foremost.

They imply (as the passage above asserts) that the victor-patron has reached the absolute limit of human achievement, accomplished so much that there is nowhere else to go, no new height to scale. Pindarists aptly name it "the ne plus ultra" theme. Yet on the other side of this encomiastic beatification, the other edge cuts the other way. The limitations stated are still all too true. Even these victors are human—mortal and imperfect.

The final stanza of *Pythian* 8 speculates on the essence of man. "What is a person? What is no person? The dream of a shadow, that is Man."[11] This is the most quoted passage in Pindar, partly because of Greek pessimism's allure, partly because of the brilliant metaphor for man's insubstantiality. But it is usually quoted out of context, as if Pindar means "A despicable thing is Man." Perhaps he does. Perhaps he is. But Pindar's very next sentence vehemently countermands this pessimism: "What is a person? What is no person? The dream of a shadow, that is Man. But whenever the god-given gleam comes, a brilliant light plays upon humans, and there is a life that is sweet." The god-given gleam, which humans can experience, is Pindar's interest here, not his basic pessimism. For the gleam makes all our abjectness and mortality less difficult to bear.

But even the gleam does not fully resolve the philosophical problem stated earlier. I restate it. Essentially, mortal man is an insignificant nothing ("so that one of them is nothing"; "Man is the dream of a shadow"). But something divine is present in his contests. And his deeds, if they have true greatness, participate in the divine, and through them a man can become "something *like* the immortal gods." Yet man's mortal nature makes him unable to enjoy permanently the divine quality even of his own deeds; and when the divine light shines on man and makes him godlike, it is a transitory thing. What is needed is some way to keep the god-given gleam playing on the man and his deeds forever; some way to capture it and give it a permanence that impermanent mortals may enjoy. Pindar's solution, of course, is poetry, poetry of Pindar's kind, celebration in song. The man's song survives the man, and commits his deeds to the permanence of time. The poet captures the gleam itself and makes it immortal.

The "immortalizing" power of poetry, always a major force in Greek literature, becomes the leitmotif of Pindar's work. Poetry will not give a man immortality.[12] But it will give him "something like" immortality, and thus merits full cultivation. The alternative is to embrace that nothingness that is our nature, and to accept oblivion. Without poetry's preservative, one's immortal deeds (at least so far as the agent's benefit goes) are wasted. Pindar tells Hagesidamos, the victor-patron of *Olympian* 10:

> Whenever a man has wrought excellent deeds without song
> he comes to Hades' compound, providing
> little delight for all his toil. He has breathed in vain.

Because of its qualities, Pindar's favorite metaphors for poetry concern things that preserve or restore. In *Nemean* 8, he addresses the victor's father, himself a sprinter and Nemean victor.

> To bring your soul back again, Megas,
>
> that I cannot do. Empty is the outcome of vain hopes.
> But I can raise a talking memorial-stone of the Muses
> for your clan and the Chariadai, because
> of those four successful feet. I am happy
> to send up a cheer fitting the deeds. And a person can
> render even great toil painless, through the medicine of song.
> There existed, even long ago, the song of praise,
> even before the Seven strove against Thebes.
>
> (stanzas 8–9 [end])

---

[11]The translation of *ti de tis; ti d' ou tis* is more difficult than scholars admit. Mine is rather literal, and seeks to preserve some of the flexibility of the original.

[12]Pindar cautiously avoids applying the term "immortal" (*athanatos*) to his patrons. In fact, Greek poets are generally chary of using the term of those "immortalized" by fame, even war heroes. Tyrtaeus, 12.32 is exceptional.

The first metaphor compares the encomiastic poem to a permanent monument stone, but implies the superiority of song. Unlike the silent stone, it has a voice. *Pythian* 6 elaborates a related metaphor (stanzas 1–2). There Pindar compares the preservative power of song to that of a treasury safe. Again song emerges superior. The stone safe eventually gives way to the elements, depositing its treasure as rubble into the sea. But the safe of song, its contents embedded in the generations of men's minds, outlasts all physical storehouses. It can last as long as the race of man.

The other metaphor is medical. Pindar compares the restorative power of song to the curing incantations of a medicine man. Song is no absolute panacea for man's mortal condition. It cannot confer personal immortality ("To bring your soul back again, Megas, that I cannot do"). But, assuaging our toil and pain, it is the best "cure" available. It can give a man "something like" immortality by immortalizing those moments when he is something like the immortal gods.

The subjects of medicine, poetry, and immortality receive their fullest and finest development in *Pythian* 3, which celebrates Hieron's equestrian victories.[13] The poem begins with a long myth about Coronis (whose death is expressed through an image of plague) and her son, Asklepios. Asklepios, the god of medicine,

the god of medicine, and became the world's foremost doctor. He exhibited great art in his practice. Yet he tried to exceed human limitations; he tried to bring a man back from death. With his thunderbolt Zeus quickly smote both doctor and patient, "implanting their doom." The myth firmly demonstrates the impossibility of physical immortality for humans, however advanced the medical arts.

In the last third of the poem, Pindar compares the poet's and the doctor's ability to satisfy man's longing for immortality, the urge not to have "breathed in vain." The comparison is made by means of some verbal echoes not apparent in most translations. Poetry wins over medicine in the end. "We know of Nestor and Sarpedon, subjects of men's speech, from the epics which poetic craftsmen have made [compare Asklepios, the "craftsman of cures," stanza 1]. Excellence grows permanent through echoing songs. But few find it easy to do."

Although it is brief, the final understatement expresses much. For the word "few" seems to refer not merely to the agent of the deeds but even more to the poet who makes them last. It is as difficult to compose enduring poetry as to perform deeds worthy to endure. (No doubt many unknown and quite dead poets have vainly mouthed Horace's boast, "I shall not wholly die.") Pindar's final sentence recognizes that even poetry, the best medicine of all, may fail in its herculean task. Yet it also suggests that Pindar, too, if a successful poet, will share the profits of his "immortalizing" verse. Indeed, he got the better share. What is preserved of the patron is his deeds. What is preserved of the poet is his thoughts. We might even say his mind.

VII

A poet's entry into the ranks of the immortals depends not so much on his thoughts as on how he expresses them. Pindar's poetic style distinguishes him from other poets and earned him his preeminent place among lyricists. Sir Philip Sidney's phrase "the inimitable Pindar" refers to his style. Pindar's style provoked the begin-

[13]D. C. Young, *Three Odes*, pp. 27–68. Many of the victories that Pindar celebrates were won in the equestrian events, not the athletic events proper. These equestrian victors (who include all three monarchs) did not themselves participate in the contests. A jockey or charioteer competed on the track, and the stable owner need not even be present. Yet the owner received the name and glory of the victory. One expects some embarrassment from Pindar when he seeks to place these equestrian victors in his encomiastic system, founded on codes of valor and human performance. There may be some embarrassment, but certainly not much. Fortunately for the system, "horse-breaking" was an ancient and honored Homeric epithet, and horse rearing an activity of the heroes. The equestrian events were the most prestigious on the Greek agonistic program. To keep stables was astoundingly expensive in Greece. The equestrian victors tended to be men of high estate, with activities and achievements of note outside of the games. Pindar could concentrate on their other activities (often martial or political), and substitute their expense of money for the athletes' expense of physical effort. The equestrian odes differ from the athletic in details, perhaps somewhat even in conception, but not in essence.

ning of a Horatian ode (4.2), in which the master of poetry warns that anyone who tries to emulate Pindar is doomed to fall in failure, as Icarus fell on wax wings into the sea. Horace continues: "As a river rushes down from a mountain, raised beyond the wonted banks by the rains, so great Pindar seethes and dashes on from his profound mouth,[14] certain to win Apollo's laurel." It is astounding that Pindar gives this impression of ebullient individuality, of unwonted freedom. For he wrote in one of the most restrictive mediums ever devised. It is a wonder that a Greek choral poet could compose at all.

A Greek choral poem is divided into stanzas usually six to ten lines long. The precise metrical pattern (arrangement of long and short syllables) for each poem is unique. Within a stanza the lines exhibit a metrical motif, but they are of unequal length and no two lines are metrically the same. Thus every first stanza of a Pindaric ode is a complex metrical creation, a poetic original. Yet within a particular ode, all or most subsequent stanzas precisely match the first. This matching must follow one of two systems. For example, *Pythian* 6 uses the simpler system, called "monostrophic." All six stanzas follow precisely the same distinctive metrical pattern:

```
1  u _ u _       u u u _ u u _ u _ _ | u _ u _ u u _ ‖
2              u u u _ u u _ uūu _   u _ ‖
3              u u _    _  u _ u _ u u _ ‖
4          _ u u _ u _ _  u _ u _ u u _ |
5          u u u _ u u _ u _   _ūu _ ‖
6  u _ u _ _ | _ _ u _ u u _ _ ‖
7  u _ _   u _ u _   X _ u _
```

[14]The usual translation of *profundum os* is not "profound mouth," but something after the Lewis and Short version ("with inexhaustible copiousness of expression") or like C. E. Bennett's (Loeb) "deep-toned voice." Horace surely means these other things, too, and the *os* is mainly the poet's; but *profundus* is often used of the depth of water, and *os* of an outlet for water. The "deep mouth" somehow continues, through a *jeu de mots*, the metaphor (see E. C. Wickham, *Works of Horace*, 1 [3rd ed., Oxford, 1896], ad loc.). Horace's poetry, like Pindar's, is often too poetic, too much master of its native tongue to be transferred to another.

The single, recurrent metrical pattern for each stanza is exact. The variations admitted (at lines 2 and 7) are few and minor. There is no such freedom of substitution or resolution as in Homer's hexameters or the pentameters of Sophocles or Shakespeare.

In the other system ("triadic") the first two stanzas (called "strophe" and "antistrophe") are metrically the same, but the third has its own metrical structure. This three-stanza unit is repeated in toto throughout the poem. Thus the number of stanzas in a triadic ode must be a multiple of three, and stanzas 2, 4, 5, 7, 8, 10, 11, and so on match stanza 1, while stanzas 6, 9, 12, 15, and so on are metrically equal to stanza 3.

This is anything but free verse (whatever translations imply or medieval man believed about Pindar's odes). Once the pattern for a stanza was established, Pindar had a very limited word choice for each place in each line in any subsequent stanza. The idea to be expressed was required to fit a predetermined rhythm. Clearly, Pindar did not write like Truman Capote, who claims to compose his endings first. But the exigencies of metrical correspondence raise an interesting question. Did he always write his first lines first? In some poems the opening verse is so apt and distinctive that one readily accepts its primacy in composition and in determining the shape of all its metrical congeners in later stanzas. An example is the one-word first line of *Olympian* 13, *Trisolympionikan* ("Thrice Olympian victor").

At other times certain phenomena invite us to suspect otherwise—that is, that Pindar could have composed piecemeal and synthetically rather than lineally in an unswerving progression; that he sometimes composed a line in the midst of a poem before arriving at a final version of the opening stanza. In one sense it is pointless to investigate such uncertain matters. For they are inherently unknowable, and we can never pass beyond pure speculation. Yet the metrical correspondence raises the question of how often Pindar looked backward and forward as he wrote. And many things in his poetry suggest that he looked forward and backward more than we expect in archaic Greece. In Pindar's case speculation seems called for.

In *Olympian* 1 the eighth verse of the first strophe (and therefore the eighth verse of the other strophes and the eighth verse of the antistrophes, as well) begins with an extraordinary sequence of seven "short" syllables (UUUUUUU_U_U_U_). The rapid succession of so many shorts in a row gives an unmistakable impression of rapidity. In the fifth, sixth, and seventh occurrences of this verse (lines 66, 77, and 95) there appears within this series of seven shorts the base of the Greek word for "swift," *tachy*. Meter supports meaning exquisitely. It might be fortuitous that the meter and meaning coincide in this way on three separate occasions in the latter part of the poem. Perhaps Pindar did not realize the potential for special poetic effect until after he wrote the first four lines that contain the seven consecutive shorts (lines 8, 19, 37, and 48). But it seems more likely that he envisioned from the start a metrical form that would reinforce the idea of swiftness in his Pelops tale later in the poem, and that he composed the first instance of this eighth verse (or at least decided on its meter) with one or more of these posterior "fast" lines already in mind.

Such obvious coincidence of meter and meaning is not common in Pindar, nor are there but a few certain cases where meaning and sound coincide—that is, onomatopoeic writing. But one of these bears on the question of the compositional sequence. In *Pythian* 1, stanza 4, Pindar describes an erupting Mount Aetna, its flaming gases hurling chunks of hardened lava into the sea: "en or*ph*naisin *p*etras *ph*oinissa kylindomena *ph*lo*ks* es batheian *ph*erei *p*ontou *p*laka *s*yn *p*atago" ("In the pitch black night, a bright red flame rolls and spews forth rocks that drop sizzling into the expanse of the deep sea"). In the Greek, at least, the alliteration of "p" and "s" sounds perfectly suggests what the words themselves express: the hissing and crashing of the volcanic debris into the surf. It is difficult to imagine that Pindar composed these words

with less than a free metrical rein, that he found such right words to fit a meter already set by line 4 in stanza 1. But perhaps he did. Speculation must end, giving way to wonder.

Since the nineteenth century, Pindarists have disputed the question of repeated words in Pindar. Some claim it a mark of his style to repeat the same word or related phrases several times within an individual ode, and they view these repetitions as helpful signposts for the critic. Others argue that these repetitions result from mere chance, and do not justify interpretations that see one passage echoed in another. Certainly there is subjectivity in such interpretations, and some scholars take them to excess. But the necessary metrical recurrences imply a kind of backward-looking composition, anyway; and verbal echoes indeed occur in Pindar. No discussion of Pindar's style can rightly ignore them.

Near the end of *Nemean* 8, Pindar suggests that his poetry has a kind of restorative effect on his patrons (see section VI above), then closes the poem: "There existed, even long ago, the song of praise, even before the Seven strove against Thebes." This final sentence unmistakably echoes something earlier in the Ajax myth: "There existed, even long ago, smooth talk and deceit" (stanza 6). The earlier sentence referred to the wheedling rhetoric of Odysseus, who persuaded the Greeks to deprive Ajax of his honor and rightful prize, the armor of Achilles. The verbal repetition forces a comparison between the contemporary world and that of myth, between poems of praise and spiteful rhetoric. No Odyssean deceit can harm the victor Deinias or his father. Pindar's song preserves their honor and the true record of their achievements. And there is salvation for Ajax, too, at the end. Encomiastic poetry dates from *before* the Trojan War, even before Odysseus' deceitful rhetoric. Ajax did not fail to find his poet of praise, someone to restore his suffering honor. As Pindar says elsewhere, "Homer honored him throughout mankind" (*Isthmian* 4, stanza 10). Poetry has given both Ajax and Deinias their reward, and once again the past is reflected in the present, and the present in the past.[15]

In *Pythian* 5 the word *makar* ("blessed") occurs five times, applied to the victor himself (King Arkesilaos of Cyrene), to his home, to his associate and charioteer, to his ancestor (the founder of his city), and finally to the gods (who were more accustomed to the adjective). Pindar's insistence on connecting Arkesilaos with the concept of blessedness clearly gives the poem an unusual and frequent note of beatification.

To place especial value on single words naturally risks overinterpretation. And usually the more significant recurrences involve matters of thought, phrase, and image as well. The importance—even visibility—of such recurrences varies greatly from poem to poem, but in my opinion they are among Pindar's most effective means of expression. *Pythian* 3 restates the topic of "the near and the far" through theme and image, over and over and with great variation. That topic, in turn, bears significantly on what Pindar says about poetry and medicine in that same poem. The recurrence of the word "craftsman" (section VI, above) is merely one small element in a system of repetitions, reminiscences, and restatements so complex that it passes far beyond our scope of study.

Seldom do Pindar's verbal or figurative echoes survive translation. Many are too fragile to be converted. Most simply disappear at the hands of the translators, many of whom are not sensitive or painstaking, and inevitably function as the black holes of literature. But some of Pindar's effects are beyond the best translators' range. For they depend upon the flexibility of Greek word order, and cannot be turned into a "position determining" language such as English (which normally places subject before verb). Pindar sometimes postpones the subject of a long sentence until its very end (such as "Herakles" in *Olympian* 10, stanza 5). He thus builds great rhetorical (if not informational) suspense, as in a Latin sentence with its verb at the end.

A comparable rhetorical effect comes from enjambment over a stanza break. In the penultimate stanza of *Olympian* 2, Pindar swears an oath that no city in the past hundred years has engendered a man with a more beneficent heart or more generous hand —(stanza break as we wait to hear the name of the Man of the Century)—"than Theron." In *Nemean* 8 Pindar closes one stanza in mid-sentence: "To bring your soul back to life, Megas—." The first words of the new stanza finally complete the suspended sentence: "—that I cannot do."

Pindar's etymological and onomastic puns will escape the Greekless reader; so will his highly compressed similes. Compression is, no doubt, the foremost characteristic of Pindaric style. In *Pythian* 11 he compresses the subject matter of the first two plays of Aeschylus' *Oresteia* into twenty brief lines. Little is missing. *Isthmian* 7 expresses, in three stanzas, virtually all the ideas and themes contained in the extant battle poetry of Callinus and Tyrtaeus. All the key phrases are there in full.[16] Most readers will sense this compression in a longer passage, such as a myth. But what translator could reproduce the sometimes astonishingly terse mannerisms? "By ship nor by foot" (for "neither by ship nor by foot") is rather standard Pindarese. He even formulates his ideas on poetic economy: "If you say it just right, gathering the chief points of many things into brief space, people tend to fault you less" (*Pythian* 1, stanza 13).

In the beginnings of his poems, Pindar was willing to compromise this characteristic conciseness. His opening verses often elaborate an arresting, unusual conception, sometimes bordering on a conceit. *Olympians* 1, 6, 7; *Pythian* 1; *Nemeans* 2, 4, 6, 7, 8; and *Isthmians* 2, 5, and

---

[15]A. Köhnken, *Die Funktion des Mythos bei Pindar* (Berlin, 1971), pp. 19–36.

[16]D. C. Young, *Pindar Isthmian 7*, especially pp. 20–26 and appendix.

6 come first to mind. The first verses of *Olympian* 6 both exhibit and explain the idea.

> Golden may the front pillars be that we set
>   before our song
> as before a thick-walled room of a wondrous
>   mansion.
> At the very outset of a work
> its front should be made conspicuous and splendid.

The technique is common, but always effective. A brilliant, unusual beginning captures interest, and entices an audience into the composition. If the body of the work is well wrought (compare "thick-walled room"), no one objects that the initial grandeur and novelty are not sustained throughout.

Conversely, Pindar ends many poems without fanfare or special preparation, such as *Pythians* 6 and 9; *Nemeans* 4, 6, and 11; and *Isthmian* 8. Some critics fault Pindar on this account, complaining that his odes "trail off." True, Pindar has little of that romantic strain that makes a Beethoven reluctant to let go. Pindar's is not yet Horace's final touch, sometimes deft, sudden, and pianissimo. But, like Bach, when he is through, he is through. Sudden quiet, after so very much, has its effect, too.

The inventive, playful, almost eccentric mind that creates a Pindaric opening also lies behind many metaphors and single sentences. But these, Pindar's most charming and memorable turns of phrase, may seem bizarre when translated, banal when paraphrased. I risk but a few of my favorites. "Mute is the man whose speech does not include Herakles" (that is, "Everyone [who can!] praises Herakles"; *Pythian* 9). I find a touch of grim humor after a summary of Achilles' Trojan victims: "These are the men whom Achilles showed the way to Persephone's house" (that is, "killed"; *Isthmian* 8). And there is a lovable archness in the account of the Hyperboreans: "The Muse is never out of town on their ways" (that is, "In Hyperborean culture people constantly sing poetry"; *Pythian* 10). I doubt another reader would choose the same three first in such a matter of taste, but there is plenty for all.

VIII

The latter part of *Nemean* 10 tells the story of the Dioscuri, Castor and Polydeukes, who become embroiled with another set of brothers, Idas and Lynkeus. Castor is killed in the fight. Grief-stricken, Polydeukes calls on Zeus the Father and asks to die along with his brother. Zeus surprisingly responds, saying that he, Zeus, is Polydeukes' actual father ("You are my son!"), but that the fallen brother had a mortal sire. Zeus offers his own son immortality, and a life of perpetual bliss on Olympus. It is more than any man could dream.

But Zeus offers him a strange alternative, too. The god-born hero and his mortal brother may share each other's fates, half and half.[17] Polydeukes may be demoted, and Castor elevated, to a half-dead, half-immortal state, living one day with the gods on Olympus, the next with the dead in Hades. The devoted brothers may stay together only by exchanging home, lot, and life on alternate days. It is a fantastic conception, to be forced to choose between eternal bliss and dying more than a thousand deaths. Many authors would examine its implications, the horrors of repeated descents. But Pindar makes one of his quick endings: "As Zeus finished speaking, Polydeukes took no second thought. First he opened the eye, then the voice of bronze-armored Castor."

As in *Nemean* 8, the poem is ended, but not quite over. We must not become so fascinated with Polydeukes' choice that we forget Castor, for whom he made it. A mortal returned to life! Pindar underscores the wonder of it all (even the half-life of a Dioscurus) with the touch of

---

[17]The Dioscuri's lot of life and death, on alternate days, is Homeric (*Odyssey* 11.300–304); so also *Pythian* 11 (end). The earliest evidence for their separate origins, one from a god and the other from a mortal, is the lost epic *Cypria*. The earliest evidence for Polydeukes' choice is Pindar.

the master poet. We might say, "And Castor breathed again." But Pindar focuses on the fraternal relationship, and reverses the symbolic act Greeks customarily performed on their deceased relatives, namely to close the eyes of the loved one. Polydeukes opens his brother's eye instead of closing it, a typically Pindaric transformation of the commonplace. The return of the voice quickly signifies the miraculous boon. For absolute silence, not sound, regularly followed the traditional touch of the eye.

This myth and its brilliant final poetic stroke summarize much of what I have sought to convey about Pindar. He no doubt implies that his patrons at least approach the state of the model athletic heroes, Polydeukes and Castor. They can never fully become gods; but they pass beyond the ordinary human condition. The half-immortality becomes a poetic symbol. That is why Pindar seems so drawn to myths that raise the questions of mortality and immortality, and blur the line between them.

Classicists tend to regard Pindar as an outspoken political and religious conservative, with his head in the sand as the rest of Greece rushed hell-bent toward the skepticism of Euripides and an Athenian democracy that he abhorred. Pindar is indeed a political poet, but we must know what "political" means. If we mean "centered on the polis," then the judgment is right. Pindar stresses how the patron and his city interact, how the victory profits the city, and how the city molds its men. But if we mean that he injects his opinions on the political controversies of his day, arguing for one polis or faction over another, I do not see all the evidence that others see. Conservative he may be, in viewing government as mainly an aristocratic function, and hailing the "Dorian" constitution when he sees it (*Pythian* 1, stanza 8). But what else could we expect? It hardly merits censure, praise, or remark if a man sees as reasonable the political ideas that prevail in his culture and in various states. For Athens itself, Pindar has nothing but the highest praise. And even later in his century, there are extant few authors—even Athenian authors—with much to say for democracy.

If Pindar seems rather uninterested in politics, and unremarkably conservative there, it is not true in religion. His frequent delvings into questions about the gods, life and death, and the relationship of men and gods eclipse his political statements manyfold. As for his conservatism, the evidence suggests the opposite. What we call "religion" in Greek culture is not the same thing as religion in ours. There was no dogma, and Pindar felt free to recast myths and ideas about the gods. When he takes a sophisticated view of the divine, or denies the story of Tantalus' banquet (*Olympian* 1), he takes the steps of a concerned, forward-looking person of religious development. His motives may be as poetic as religious, and there were Greeks on the fringe, such as Xenophanes and some Homeric critics, more radical than he. But most Greeks were surely more conservative than Pindar, who partook of a literary tradition of religious sophistication that extends from Homer to Plato. Pindar even has more in common with Plato's religious upstart, Socrates (who claims the gods cannot be unjust or do harm), than with mumbo-jumbo religious conservatives who live in simple fear of the gods.

For us, at least, Pindar is at the forefront of new religious thought when he expresses ideas that we associate with the mystery religions. *Olympian* 2, their earliest extant source, is not the only place where Pindar speaks of reincarnation, reward and punishment after death, and eventual escape, through purity of soul and action, to a blessed existence.[18] This is no place to speculate on Pindar's own beliefs, nor on the origins of the mystery religions. But I note that the details of Pindar's versions have their antecedents in Homer and Hesiod: Elysium in *Odyssey* 4, and the Golden Age and Isles of the Blest (*Works and Days*). Pindar staffs his Isle of

---

[18]Besides *Olympian* 2 see *Threni* VII (129, 130, 131a), and frags. 133, 137 (which are, essentially, frags. 129, 130, 133 in J. Sandys' Loeb). My discussion above primarily concerns *Olympian* 2.

the Blest with Elysium's Rhadamanthys and Hesiod's Kronos; he refreshes it with the gentle ocean breezes of those epics. Pindar's islanders have the same freedom from toil and grief, the same festal life, as Hesiod's Golden Agers. And, taking their cue from Hesiod, the heroes of old have already found residence in Pindar's island paradise.

We cannot determine how important a role poets such as Pindar played in transmitting ideas like those of the mysteries to later generations. Surprisingly, it is to Pindar that Plato and later authors, such as Plutarch, turn first when they wish to authenticate the concepts of transmigration and immortality of the soul, judgment of the dead, and a place of permanent bliss for the pious. And the later mystery religions never really sought to divest their rather un-Homeric ideas of their epic-founded topography and cast of characters.

Pindar's subjects keep leading into questions of religion and philosophy. The nature of his work leads me to insist, once more, that he is a poet and expresses himself as nothing else. Sir Philip Sidney identified a crucial difference between poetry and philosophy. The philosopher's knowledge, Sidney wrote in 1595, "stands so upon the abstract and general that happy is that man who may understand him and more happy that can apply what he does understand." With this abstractness he contrasts the concreteness of the poet, who, Sidney claims, gives a "perfect picture" of what the philosopher says. The poet

> couples the general notion with the particular example. A perfect picture, I say, for he yields to the powers of the mind an image of that whereof the philosopher bestows but a wordish description which does neither strike, pierce, nor possess the sight of the soul so much as that other.
> (*Defense of Poesy*, p. 17, Soens ed.)

There seems no better way to demonstrate Sidney's point (and a side of Pindar that space compels me to ignore) than to juxtapose a sentence from *Nemean 7* with something from De-

mocritus, a philosopher and much younger contemporary of Pindar, who helped to found the atomist school.

> If a person should go beyond moderation, the most delightful things would become the least delightful.
> (Democritus, frag. B 233, D–K)

> Even honey can cloy, and the delightful pleasures of Aphrodite.
> (*Nemean 7*, stanza 8)

It is difficult to imagine how two people could express essentially the same thing in such different ways. Everything in Democritus is in the abstract; everything in Pindar is concrete. Syntactically, the philosopher's sentence is a future potential condition, the most complex and vague construction in standard Greek syntax (technically called a "future less vivid condition"). Pindar's is probably as direct and vivid as one could be in Greek. In length Pindar's version is a third shorter than the philosopher's (seventeen Greek syllables [five of which say "Aphrodisial"] to twenty-six). Preference, again, depends on taste. I leave to each reader which he or she finds more memorable.

In all of extant ancient literature, only one author's style can closely compare with Pindar's. Aeschylus' choral odes exhibit this chiseled conciseness, this bold allusiveness, and these reverberating echoes of theme and phrase—the difficulty, too—that we associate with Pindar. These two poets seem to be doing something other than what many of their recent poetic predecessors did. Indeed, the poetic differences between Pindar's and Aeschylus' choral odes, on the one side, and Solon and Theognis, on the other, are astonishing. The two elegiac poets often seem to be struggling merely to adapt rather commonplace Greek thought to a rather easy meter. In Pindar's and Aeschylus' choral odes, one finds a poetic style in which the poets more than control rhythm and language; they own them. And they have learned to play poetry almost as a musician plays an instrument. How their kind of inventive, compressed poetry arose from the lyric lays of Stesichorus we should very much like to know. But that chapter is not likely to be written unless we somehow acquire the work of Simonides.

Selected Bibliography

Note: An asterisk indicates that a book has been reprinted without change since 1960.

TEXTS AND SCHOLIA

Pindari carmina ad fidem optimorum codicum recensuit. . . , edited by Tycho Mommsen. 2 vols. in 1. Berlin, 1864. Indispensable for a detailed description of the manuscripts and their readings.

Pindari carmina, cum fragmentis, edited by C. M. Bowra. Oxford, 1935; 2nd ed., 1947.* The Oxford Classical Texts edition, but not recommended.

Pindari carmina cum fragmentis, edited by H. Maehler (after B. Snell et al.). Vol. 1: *Epinicia.* Leipzig, 1971. Vol. 2: *Fragmenta; Indices.* Leipzig, 1975. The standard text.

Scholia vetera in Pindari carmina, edited by A. B. Drachmann. 3 vols. Leipzig, 1903–1927.* The Teubner edition of the unusually rich Pindaric scholia.

TRANSLATIONS

"If a man should undertake to translate *Pindar* word for word, it would be thought that one *Mad man* had translated *another*" (Abraham Cowley, preface to his *Pindaric Odes* [London, 1656]).

Bowra, C. M. *Odes of Pindar.* Harmondsworth, 1969. Not recommended; it often renders Pindar's Greek with meaningless English, contains factual errors and misprints, and is vitiated throughout by Bowra's own unfounded biographical interpretations.

Conway, G. *Odes of Pindar.* London, 1972. Presents an often attractive translation, but the notes regularly follow Bowra's interpretations, and can misinform.

Lattimore, R. *Odes of Pindar.* 2nd ed. Chicago, 1976. Heretofore the most popular translation, often reveals insight, but the brief notes are misleading and the glossary inadequate. The first edition (1947), often reprinted until 1976, has so many misprints and simple errors that it cannot be recommended.

Nisetich, F. *Pindar's Victory Songs.* Baltimore, 1980. Since the difficulty of translating Pindar is proverbial, one admires all the more the achievement in this excellent new translation. The long introduction is helpful and up to date. For readability, accuracy, and attractiveness, the translation itself has no peer. The glossary and index are unusually complete, and make this an obvious choice.

Ruck, C., and W. Matheson. *Pindar, Selected Odes.* Ann Arbor, Mich., 1968. Contains translations of twenty-one odes. The translators' avant-garde approach sometimes accurately represents the effect of the original, but as often it leads to anachronisms and grotesqueries.

Sandys, J. *Odes of Pindar.* London, 1915.* The Loeb Library edition, often reprinted; has an accurate enough translation, but is cast in archaic prose and lacks stanza divisions.

Swanson, R. A. *Pindar's Odes.* Indianapolis and New York, 1974. Contains the best section on Greek athletic games and reprints some Pindaric imitations by English poets such as Ben Jonson, William Wordsworth, and Matthew Arnold.

LEXICAL AND BIBLIOGRAPHICAL AIDS

Gerber, D. *A Bibliography of Pindar, 1513–1966.* Cleveland, 1969.

————. "Pindar." *Classical World,* 70:132–157 (1976).

Slater, W. *Lexicon to Pindar.* Berlin, 1969.

Young, D. C. "Pindaric Criticism." Reprinted in *Pindaros und Bakchylides, Wege der Forschung* 134, edited by W. Calder III and J. Stern. Darmstadt, 1969. Pp. 1–95. This anthology reprints (in original language) ten essays by nine scholars on various Pindaric topics. Young's is a history of Pindaric interpretative scholarship from 1821 to 1962.

COMMENTARIES

All commentaries available in English are badly out of date and can seriously mislead, for they often employ the biographical methodology that most recent scholars reject. Yet no modern commentary on all four books is likely to appear soon, and the older works must serve. They should be used with caution, especially where they offer a biographical explanation of a passage.

Bury, J. B. *The Nemean Odes of Pindar*. London and New York, 1890.*

———. *The Isthmian Odes of Pindar*. London and New York, 1892.* Both of Bury's commentaries must be used with special caution because they employ an idiosyncratic theory of recurrent sounds.

Farnell, L. R. *Works of Pindar*. Vol. 2: *Critical Commentary*. London, 1930.* One of only two complete commentaries in English (see Fennell, below).

Fennell, C. *Pindar: The Olympians and Pythian Odes*. 2nd. ed. Cambridge, 1893.

———. *Pindar: The Nemean and Isthmian Odes*. 2nd ed. Cambridge, 1899. Both of Fennell's commentaries are noticeably superior to that of Farnell.

Gildersleeve, B. L. *The Olympian and Pythian Odes*. 2nd ed. New York, 1890.* A model of penetrating judgment and concise, vivid prose.

Seymour, T. *Selected Odes of Pindar*. Boston, 1882. Annotates fifteen poems.

GENERAL WORKS AND SPECIAL STUDIES

Since the 1960's Pindaric scholarship has sharply changed its direction. For most of the twentieth century, the prevailing view assumed that Pindar laced his odes with frequent references to his own private difficulties, even when irrelevant to the epinician at hand. Scholars thought many obscure passages inexplicable except as veiled allusions to his personal disputes with numerous detractors. E. Bundy opposed this biographical method in two highly technical pamphlets, *Studia Pindarica I* and *Studia Pindarica II* (Berkeley, 1962). By a comparative study of encomiastic themes, he showed that the passages were not so obscure as others thought, that they conformed to the normal literary conventions of the genre, and that they gave no grist to the biographical mill. At first Bundy's heterodox ideas met a chilly reception, but now most scholars accept his principal argument. Several subsequent works have developed his thesis with varying degrees of modification. This reversal of scholarly opinion on a fundamental question will explain why critical works on Pindar differ so greatly one from another. For complete bibliography and detailed assessments of the interpretative literature, see LEXICAL AND BIBLIOGRAPHICAL AIDS (above). I list here only those books that the general reader is most likely to come upon or to find useful.

Bowra, C. M. *Pindar*. Oxford, 1964. A long study that, unfortunately, cannot be recommended. Careless mistakes compound the graver errors and impetuous interpretations of the biographical school.

Burton, R. *Pindar's Pythian Odes*. Oxford, 1962. Contains an essay on each Pythian ode; some essays are excellent, others are out of date.

Finley, J. *Pindar and Aeschylus*. Cambridge, Mass., 1955. Occasionally gives insight into Pindar's poems and poetic vision, but it tends toward the impressionistic and is written in a baffling prose style that exults in vague phrases and opaque assertions.

Fraccaroli, G. *Le odi di Pindaro*. Verona, 1894. Contains a long, thoughtful introduction, quality Italian translation, and sensitive literary essays on each ode.

Hamilton, R. *Epinikion*. The Hague, 1974. Takes the recent study of the genre into mechanical and tabular forms. Hamilton attempts to reduce Pindar's poetry to a few basic, recurrent themes (represented by shorthand symbols), and studies their arrangement in the epinicians.

Lefkowitz, M. *The Victory Ode*. Park Ridge, N.J., 1976. Seeks to introduce the general reader to the epinician genre, but is limited to the odes for Hieron. The details of the argument require some knowledge of Greek.

Norwood, G. *Pindar*. Berkeley, 1945. A very readable book with some provocative comments and an idiosyncratic, misguided thesis of "symbolism." Norwood anticipated Bundy in questioning the biographical approach.

von Wilamowitz-Moellendorff, U. *Pindaros*. Berlin, 1922.* A large, learned, frequently conjectural book by a famous classicist in German. Long the virtual bible of the biographical school, it is now losing some of its favor and authority, but remains a prominent work, often cited.

Young, D. C. *Three Odes of Pindar: A Literary Study of Pythian 11, Pythian 3, and Olympian 7*. Leiden, 1968.

———. *Pindar Isthmian 7, Myth, and Exempla*. Leiden, 1971. Both of Young's works stress literary interpretation, but the details of the argument require some knowledge of Greek.

DAVID C. YOUNG

SOPHOCLES

(497–406 B.C.)

LIFE, DEVELOPMENT, CHRONOLOGY

ONE OF THE three surviving tragedians of classical Athens, along with Aeschylus and Euripides, and one of the great dramatists of world literature, Sophocles spanned in his long life (497–406 B.C.) the cultural flowering of Athens in the fifth century. He was born shortly before the first Persian invasion that ended with the Athenian victory at Marathon, and he is said to have led the victory-song that celebrated the Greek naval triumph at Salamis ten years later in 480. His youth coincided not only with the surge of confidence that these victories inspired in his native city, but also with the perfecting of tragedy as a literary form under Aeschylus, some twenty-eight years his senior. If the authority of Aristophanes and the later biographical tradition can be trusted, he was profoundly influenced by Aeschylus and felt great respect for the older writer.

If Aeschylus was in some sense a teacher, he was also a rival against whom Sophocles competed for the first dozen years of his dramatic activity. At his debut in the dramatic competitions of the Athenian Dionysia festival in 468 B.C. he won his first victory, defeating Aeschylus with the *Triptolemus*. From that time on, he was the most successful of the three tragedians in the annual competition, winning eighteen first prizes and many second prizes. He was never third. He is said to have left behind some 123 plays (that is, slightly more than thirty te-

tralogies, each consisting of three tragedies and a satyr play), of which seven survive. There are also substantial fragments of two satyr plays, the *Trackers (Ichneutae)* and the *Inachus*. A number of passages from lost plays are quoted by later writers or have come to light on papyrus fragments from Greco-Roman Egypt.

Sophocles' mature years coincided with the political and cultural supremacy of Athens usually known as the Periclean Age, named after the statesman who was also a close personal friend of Sophocles. This period saw Athens' domination of the eastern Aegean under its maritime empire, the development of full democracy at Athens, and the burst of intellectual and artistic activity represented in literature by Herodotus, Socrates, the Sophists, and Thucydides, and in the visual arts by red-figure vase-painting, the Parthenon (dedicated in 432 B.C.), the Erechtheum, the Hephaesteum, the Propylaea of the Acropolis, the sculptures of Phidias, and numerous other works.

Amid this intellectual ferment, Sophocles held a central position. He was a friend not only of Pericles, but also of Socrates and Herodotus; to the latter he wrote an elegiac poem of which nothing survives. It is clear from his work that he was also familiar with the bold ethical and political speculation in the advanced intellectual circles of Athens, although he does not show the same enthusiasm as Euripides for the new currents of thought. The ancient Life, appended to some manuscripts, reports that he "brought together from among the educated a group of companions dedicated to the Muses."

Euripides, about twelve years younger, entered the dramatic competitions in 455 B.C.; they remained rivals throughout their dramatic careers, but Sophocles was always the more popular. The long and grim conflict with Sparta during the Peloponnesian War (431–404 B.C.) cast its shadow over the mature years of both writers. Both died in its last years—Sophocles in 406, Euripides in 405. Yet some of the greatest works of Sophocles, and almost all of the surviving works of Euripides, were written in the midst of the war.

Sophocles' life presents the paradox that the poet capable of the profoundest sense of tragedy was celebrated for his serenity, personal happiness, good fortune, and integration of public spirit, religiosity, and political activity. The form of ancient drama does not permit much scope for personal revelation, but something in Sophocles' experience must have corresponded to the bleak lines in the *Oedipus at Colonus*: "Not to be born wins every accounting; next, when one comes into the light, to go there whence he has come as soon as possible. For when youth, bearer of light follies, is past, what suffering wanders afar without, what sickness does not lie within? Envy, civil war, strife, battle, killing ..." (1224–1235). As Edmund Wilson once wrote, "Somewhere even in the fortunate Sophocles there had been a sick and raving Philoctetes" (*The Wound and the Bow*, 1941).

To his contemporaries, however, Sophocles appeared a pleasure-loving and happy man, a bon vivant, fond of young boys, pious in the traditional ways, affable, supremely fortunate in the circumstances of his life. "Happy Sophocles, who lived a long life and died a happy man, a man of skill. He died well, having made many beautiful tragedies, enduring no suffering." These lines, a tribute by the comic poet Phrynichus shortly after the poet's death, reflect a popular contemporary view of Sophocles. Traces of this view appear also in Aristo-

phanes and Ion of Chios, a rather gossipy contemporary, some of whose anecdotes found their way into the Hellenistic biographies reflected in the ancient Life and into the miscellany of Athenaeus in the third century A.D. known as *Professors at Dinner (Deipnosophistai)*. We glimpse another side of the man at the beginning of Plato's *Republic*, where the aged Sophocles, in a discussion about love, rejoices in the fact that he is no longer subject to "that savage and raging despot, Eros." We are reminded of the poet's vivid representation of the power of sexual desire in the *Trachinian Women* and in the third stasimon of the *Antigone*, which begins, "Eros, invincible in battle ... " (780).

Sifting fact from fable in the case of so celebrated and so remote a figure is not easy, particularly given the tendency to mythicize the lives of great men even shortly after their deaths. Still the main outlines of his life are reasonably clear. He was born of a well-to-do Athenian named Sophillus, who was possibly the owner of an arms factory, in the part of Athens known as Colonus, which figures prominently in his last play, the *Oedipus at Colonus*. In 443–442 B.C., in the middle of his dramatic career, he served as *hellenotamias*, one of the state supervisors of the tribute exacted from the subject allies. The success of the *Antigone*, produced in 442, was apparently responsible for his election as general, along with Pericles, to put down the revolt of Samos in 441–440. The biographical tradition reports another generalship sometime later, during the Peloponnesian War. After the failure of the Sicilian expedition in 413, he was one of the ten commissioners charged with ordering the troubled affairs in Athens, and he seems to have been associated with the oligarchical coup after 411. Despite all his political activity, which is in strong contrast to Euripides' distance from public life, he was judged by his contemporary Ion of Chios as "neither clever nor energetic in political affairs, but like any decent Athenian."

His public service included not only politics but also religion. He held the priesthood of a minor healing divinity known as Alkon or Halon. The ancient Life reports that he founded a shrine of Heracles as a result of that hero's appearance to him in a dream. He also received the sacred snake of the healing god Asclepius in his house and composed a cult hymn in honor of Asclepius, of which three lines are preserved in an inscription on stone. For the pious entertainment of that divinity in his serpentine form, he received cultic honors at his death under the title *dexion*, the "receiver." It may seem hard to reconcile this traditional piety with the radical questioning of the ways of the gods in plays like the *Trachinian Women* or the *Oedipus Tyrannus (Oedipus Rex)*, but we should remember that religion in classical Greece was a matter more of cult observance than of orthodox belief. Greek religion was remarkably undogmatic. Sophocles' piety is clearly a complex matter, but it is not inconsistent with notions of the mystery of the divine and the difficulty of understanding what the gods are and how they manifest themselves in human life. Sophocles' active role in the state cults indicates his serious concern with religious matters. But it by no means indicates that he was committed to justify the ways of God to man in any simple way.

In addition to his dramatic and poetic works, he is said to have written *On the Chorus*, of which we know practically nothing. Aristotle attributes to him the celebrated comparison with Euripides, that he "made men as they should be, whereas Euripides made them as they are" (*Poetics* 25: 1460.b32). His critical reflection on his art also appears from a remark he is said to have made about Aeschylus: responding to gossip that Aeschylus wrote his tragedies when drunk, he said, "Even if he [Aeschylus] does all the correct things [*ta deonta*], he does them unknowingly" (Athenaeus 1.22b). The implication is that his own artistic practice is quite conscious and premeditated.

Sophocles' most important statement on his art is cited by Plutarch (without context, as he too often does) in his essay *On Advancement in Virtue* (7.79b). Sophocles here divides his work

into three periods. In the first, "he played out to the fullest the weighty majesty [*onkos*] of Aeschylus." In the second, he developed "the pungency and contrived artistry of his presentation." In the third, he "changed to that quality of his style which is most full of character and best."

The very existence of such a self-reflective comment is fascinating. Unfortunately, the application of these three stages to the extant works is a matter of some controversy, largely because the dating of the plays themselves is so uncertain. Traces of the Aeschylean "weightiness" of the first period are certainly evident in the surviving fragments of the earliest play, *Triptolemus* (468 B.C.) and to a lesser extent in the *Ajax*, which most scholars date between 460 and 450. The "pungent" or "bitter" quality and the "contrivance" of the second period may be plausibly used to describe the *Antigone*, dated with reasonable likelihood to 442–441. With the *Oedipus Tyrannus*, generally dated to the period 429–425 because it seems to refer to the great plague that broke out then in Athens, the poet is well within his third style, "most full of character and best."

To this final period belong three of the remaining four extant plays: *Philoctetes*, securely dated to 409 B.C. by the ancient Argument prefixed to the play; *Oedipus at Colonus*, written in the last years of the poet's life and performed posthumously in 401; *Electra*, of uncertain date, but generally regarded as a late play, perhaps between 425 and 410. *Trachinian Women* has been dated both very early (before 450) and very late (*ca.* 415). Style and dramaturgy seem to me to favor a date in the middle period, perhaps between *Antigone* and *Oedipus Tyrannus*, or 440–430 B.C.

GENERAL CHARACTERISTICS OF SOPHOCLEAN DRAMA

Sophocles created the form of tragic drama that has become dominant in Western literature. Instead of the explicitly theological concerns and cosmic scope of his great predecessor, Aeschylus, he focuses his plays on one or two protagonists of heroic proportions and engrossing, complicated character. While retaining Aeschylus' mood of deep religious seriousness, Sophocles deals with the question of divine justice and the problem of suffering in a more naturalistic way. He depicts the moral and emotional issues of credible, if grandiose, human beings, rather than cosmic themes. His focus remains clearly on the human rather than the divine world. The difference between the two tragedians is analogous to that between the severe style in early classical art, as on the pediments of the temple of Zeus at Olympia (*ca.* 470–460 B.C.), and the fully developed, human-centered art of the high classical period, as on the Parthenon frieze (*ca.* 440 B.C.).

At some point, perhaps late in his career, Aeschylus developed the connected trilogy, wherein all three tragedies at the Dionysiac performance are related to a single theme or the fortunes of a single house, as in the *Oresteia.* Sophocles did not follow his predecessor's lead in this direction, but concentrates an integral dramatic action into a single tragedy. Instead of tracing events over several generations, or even over thousands of years as in Aeschylus' *Prometheia,* Sophocles relies on a tightly unified structure and a complex plot that elicits intense but characteristic responses through powerful crises and abrupt reversals. The divine agents and the mythical past, though still important, are kept subordinate to the character of the chief protagonist and appear primarily in the lyrical generalizations of the choral odes or in philosophical speculations by chorus or actor rather than in the enacted events themselves.

A brief comparison of Sophocles' *Electra* and Aeschylus' *Oresteia* makes these differences clear. Aeschylus' trilogy ranges over three generations of the house of Atreus; Sophocles' single play centers on the character of Electra, a complex heroine who is tested in her commitment to justice and carefully studied in her shifting emotions as she arrives at her grim and hopeless resolution to take vengeance into her own hands. Rather than tracing the previous sufferings of this ill-starred family on the stage, as Aeschylus does, Sophocles only alludes to them in choral odes or in brief reminiscences by the chief characters. Instead of the cosmic scale of the Aeschylus version, which culminates in the on-stage confrontation of Olympian and chthonic divinities for the massive pageant of a divided world-order reconciled at the end of *Eumenides,* Sophocles creates an all-absorbing present moment, restricted to human actors and their emotional life. Past and future are not excluded, but they are glimpsed suggestively only through the strong foreground of the present.

Sophocles' tragic action, here and elsewhere, shows an individual in crisis about the central values of his or her life. Commitment to a dominant ideal brings the hero into painful, sometimes fatal, conflict with society, loved ones, the limitations of human existence itself. Forced to a choice, the hero refuses to sacrifice personal integrity to survival or avoiding pain. Most of Sophocles' heroes are torn between an aspiration to an almost godlike autonomy and a dependence on the rhythms of nature, on loved ones, on family and society. The tragic conflict often involves time, change, and process: the unbending laws of mortal existence versus the inflexibility of a great spirit that would break through to wider horizons and less conditioned possibilities.

One side of Sophoclean drama reflects the humanism of the Periclean Age and recalls the confident beauty of the human form as depicted on the Parthenon frieze. An important ancient critic, Dionysius of Halicarnassus (late first century B.C.), praises Sophocles for the "nobility and greatness of natures" in his characters. But equally important in his work are the uncertainty of human life, the mystery of the gods' ways, the force of the irrational and the fortuitous. This current might be described as a continuation of the Aeschylean religiosity, a sense that our lives move amid powers beyond our full grasp. Although Sophocles' heroes are never helpless victims of divine intervention like Euripides' Hippolytus, Heracles, or Pentheus, they too confront a world that throws them into apparently undeserved suffering, like Oedipus or Philoctetes. They too, for all their strength of will and integrity—indeed because of them—are subject to irrational violence and self-destructive emotions.

Sophoclean criticism has veered between the poles of idealizing his heroes' integrity and insisting on their asocial, dangerous, willful savagery. Because Sophocles depicts his characters with a fullness that encompasses both sides, his plays elude simplistic interpretation and require constant reevaluation. Each generation seems to shift its view of the poet in accordance with its own changing view of human nature and of the capacity of human life to achieve happiness and deal with suffering. Contemporary critics, predictably, have been more willing to accept a Sophocles who acknowledges the possible cruelty and injustice of the gods, the unknown and irrational in existence. But it must be pointed out that divine action in Sophocles is sufficiently mysterious that it can also be interpreted in a more positive, though not easily optimistic, light. Scholars will probably continue to argue both sides. We should be aware that in most cases at least two views are possible, and Sophocles may have intended us not to be able to take one side or the other easily.

Sophocles' transformations of Aeschylean tragedy also involved formal innovations. According to Aristotle (*Poetics* 4:1449.a15), he added a third actor and developed scene-painting. The ancient Life (4) adds that he reduced the number of members in the chorus from fifteen to twelve. The smaller chorus probably helped concentrate attention on the individual actors and also enabled the poet more easily to treat the chorus as an actor directly involved in the events onstage, an aspect of his dramaturgy that Aristotle contrasts favorably with Euripides' practice (*Poetics* 18:1456.a 25–26). Scene-painting, possibly helped by developments in wall-painting by masters like Polygnotus but

probably still rather simple, made the action more vivid. The third actor (which some ancient sources attribute to Aeschylus) gave opportunity for a greater variety of personal interaction and a greater depth and naturalness of characterization. The third actor also makes possible rich, three-way or four-way exchanges (the latter including the chorus, which often speaks in dialogue through the mouthpiece of its leader, the *koryphaios*). The tense meetings of Oedipus, Jocasta, and the Theban messenger in the latter part of *Oedipus Tyrannus* and then of Oedipus, the messenger, and the old herdsman in the next scene are perhaps the most powerful use of three actors on the Attic stage.

"The chorus," Aristotle says in the remark mentioned previously, "should be included as one of the actors and should be a part of the whole and share in the dramatic action, not as in Euripides, but as in Sophocles." This assessment of the Sophoclean chorus seems to fit the plays that have survived. In all of them the chorus takes its full share in the events onstage. It can even be deceived or misled, either by the protagonists (*Ajax*) or by the same delusions or lies that blind major protagonists (*Oedipus Tyrannus, Trachinian Women, Electra*). It can also act as the agent of deception and even become temporarily at odds with the protagonist, as in *Philoctetes*. It can be at odds with or hostile to the main hero, as in *Antigone* and, initially, in *Oedipus at Colonus*.

The chorus generally has a distinctive character of its own, sometimes better to set off the hero's tragic isolation, as in the contrast between the intimidated elders of Thebes and the proud, independent, and fearless heroine of *Antigone*. It does not serve merely as the mouthpiece of the poet or the spokesman for the accepted moral and religious views of the society. Its lyrical songs, punctuating the action at regular points, provide a means of viewing the action in a perspective different from that of the rapid, involved dialogue of the characters or of the chorus speaking in dialogue-meter as a character.

The relation of these choral odes to the main

action is one of the most discussed aspects of the interpretation of Sophocles. Although the odes are always in keeping with the character, age, and status given the chorus, their rich lyrical poetry and mythical parallels often evoke associative meanings and truths beyond what the chorus itself, as a character, can fully grasp. The odes are in the language of emotion rather than logic. Their expression of religious feelings and poetic intensity suggest rather than affirm. In *Antigone*, for example, the philosophical generalizations and often remote myths of the odes are in keeping with the personality of the elderly chorus that seeks to avoid confrontation with a ruler with whom they often disagree. But the unseen forces and divinities of which they sing point to elements in the action that become increasingly important for understanding the tragic shape of events: the irrational, the power of death and the family curse, gods like Eros and Dionysus.

Sophocles' unified focus on a single figure, the formal symmetry and proportion of the design, wherein each detail performs a proper and necessary function, and the achievement of a style both noble and plausible give his tragedies a feeling of inexorability in a framework of sustained elevation of language and intensity of situation. The harmony of these elements produces an effect variously defined as classical or serene, but it should not be confused with complacency or smug certainty. The serenity lies in the sureness of the form and in the confident mastery of language and dramatic effects. At the same time, these plays are among the most disturbing works of Western literature.

After "playing out to the full" (as Plutarch put it) the Aeschylean magniloquence of his first period, Sophocles developed a language that was flexible, dignified, sonorous, richly poetic but also capable of a wide range of inflections and subtlety of feeling. Ancient critics regarded him as an example of the "middle style," midway between the lofty grandeur of Aeschylus and the sharper, more epigrammatic and self-consciously rhetorical effects of Euripides. While praising his solemnity and magnif-

icence, some also note a certain unevenness (Longinus, *On Sublimity* 33.5), which results sometimes from his mixture of poetical elevation and fidelity to character. The prologue to *Trachinian Women* provides a good example. Deianeira opens the play with some rather trite moralizing, in not particularly distinguished language, on the uncertainties of human life. But at line 9, as she looks back to the circumstances of her marriage, a different tone suddenly appears:

> I had a river as a suitor, Achelous, who took three forms and asked my father for me, coming as a bull plain to see; another time, a glistening, twisting serpent; with man's body but bull-prowed another time; and then from down the bushy forest of his beard watery streams as from a river's springs poured down.
>
> (9–15)

This shift from commonplace reflection to imaginative description also serves a dramatic purpose, for it creates a balance between the personal emotions of a sensitive woman looking back on the sufferings of her life and an almost surreal world of mythical beings conveyed in appropriately elaborate language. The mixture is characteristic of this play, which hovers between domestic realism and the phantasmagoric shapes of a remote mythical world.

The language of the dialogue, though more straightforward than the lyrical speech of the choral odes, is often dense and intricate. In what is sometimes called "sunken imagery" apparent literal clarity reveals, on closer view, secondary or tertiary meanings, often forming a chain or sequence of images of thematic importance for the play. Oedipus' exchange with Creon early in the *Oedipus Tyrannus* may serve as an illustration:

Creon: Apollo now commands clearly to punish with (force of) hand the killers of this murdered man [i.e., Laius].

Oedipus: But where on the earth are they? Where will be found this track, hard to search out, of the ancient guilt?

Creon: In this land, he said. What is investigated is capable of being caught. What is neglected flees away.

(106–111)

Oedipus' two lines here use the metaphor of tracking, signaling the theme of the hunt prominent in the play. He combines this image, however, with words that connote intellectual examination. The Greek word for "hard to search out," *dystekmarton*, for example, also means "hard to draw logical inference"; the word for "guilt," *aitia*, also means "causation." The word for "what is investigated," *to zētoumenon*, is also a technical term for a philosophical problem. This combination of animal imagery ("track") and the intellectual vocabulary characteristic of the contemporary Sophistic movement itself expresses the anomalous contiguity of godlike intelligence and bestial helplessness in the tragic paradoxes of the hero's life.

"So well does Sophocles know how to measure the right moment that often from a brief half-line or a single word he can depict the whole character of one of his figures." This remark in the ancient Life (21) catches the quality of pregnant density in Sophocles' style. A line like Antigone's "It is my nature to share in love, not hate" (523) is a good example.

"Man's character is his *daimon*," his divinity or his destiny, the sixth-century thinker Heraclitus wrote in a much-quoted sentence. In Sophocles the relation between character and divinity is close and sometimes mysterious. *Daimon* means one's personal luck, or lot, or divinity in a larger sense. In a sense character too is luck, the fact that one is born with certain capacities or qualities. Sophocles often explores the interaction or clicking together of inward character and external circumstances, the luck, lot, or destiny—all possible translations of *daimon*—that give a life its particular stamp. In the *Ajax*, when the hero returns to sanity and is told that Tecmessa hid his son to save him from possible death from his father, Ajax replies, "Yes, that would be something appropriate to my *daimon*" (534). The reflection on his

daimon conveys, in briefest form, a mixture of bitterness and self-reproach at the degradation into which he has fallen, and also the recognition that his suffering is linked to the ungraspable essence of what he is, partly his own self, partly something beyond his control or full understanding.

The *Oedipus Tyrannus* is Sophocles' profoundest meditation on the relation between character and destiny. Looked at one way, Oedipus' life seems pure chance; viewed another way, it seems to be necessity or divine will. Sophocles gives no final answer. His gods are there not to say that life makes sense or nonsense, but to signify that the meaning of an individual life is both momentous and ultimately mysterious. Sophocles' heroes all live at the frontiers between humanity, bestiality, and divinity. Seeking absolutes and scorning the safe middle ground of compromise, they virtually call divinity to their lives, either by a direct rejection of the terms on which human life must be lived, like Ajax, or by a mysterious knowledge, won through the trial of suffering, that sets them at the limits of human experience, like Philoctetes or the Oedipus of *Oedipus at Colonus*.

In Sophocles, as in most Greek tragedy, character is not so much a matter of idiosyncratic personality as of exemplary traits set forth in strong, clear lines in universal human situations drawn from the storehouse of mythic narrative. His figures are neither types nor individualized portraits, but paradigms of great-souled humanity confronting harsh moral choices or irrational suffering. Sophoclean tragedy has nothing like the distinctive uniqueness of a Hamlet or Lear. Rather, it projects a vision of an idealized, though by no means perfect, heroic personality and explores what happens when such a figure is tested in his most essential values and strengths.

The gods, always remote, do not manipulate puppetlike humans, but embody or enforce the laws of existence, the inflexible realities of life. They may also symbolize the ultimate meaning of the heroic life; their presence indicates that such a life is great enough to implicate divinity. To be a hero in Sophocles is to be the bearer of a destiny that reaches beyond the limits of ordinary mortality, for good or ill. The hero's task is to understand and accept this fact: that his life is informed by a pattern, hitherto invisible, which he can now discern.

Oracles and prophecies have a major role in all of Sophocles' plays; but they are not to be interpreted as a mark of a deterministic philosophy of life. They indicate that the heroes' lives have a place in a large, if mysterious, world-order. It is always up to the individual how to interpret and act on the oracles. In the Judeo-Christian tradition, miracles are signs that resolve a crisis through a clear revelation of the divine will. In Greek tragedy, oracles and miracles are signs not of a resolution, but of a crisis in man's relation with the gods. One might consider an oracle for a tragic hero as a kind of negative halo, the mark of a troubling significance in his life that he must grasp and live out.

Characters often define themselves by their response to oracles. They show thereby how much of the otherness of the divine reality they can understand or accept. Jocasta in *Oedipus Tyrannus* runs away and kills herself when she recognizes the prophecy, whereas Oedipus searches it through. The wily and unscrupulous Odysseus of *Philoctetes* proves to have a more limited understanding of the oracles than the impressionable and inexperienced young Neoptolemus. The obscurity of the oracles in *Trachinian Women* or in the prologue of *Electra* is in keeping with the muffled, obscure quality of the divine order in those works. The prophecy that Creon receives as the turning point of the action in *Antigone* speaks only of the unavoidable retribution that he receives for the narrowness, insensitivity, and inhumanity of his way of life. The prophecy in the middle of *Ajax* (798) confirms a grim truth that we already know: that death is the only path open to a man like Ajax, in a situation such as Ajax now confronts. In all cases the oracle is not a substitute for human motivation, but a dimension of the action parallel to it. It indicates that the hero's acts have resonances in another register, exist on a wider plane of existence than that of ordinary men.

Like his predecessors, Sophocles draws his plots from the rich material of Greek myth, interpreted and reshaped by the poets from Homer on. The tragedian could always add or subtract details, sometimes boldly. Thus Sophocles probably invented the love between Haemon and Antigone, the descent of Heracles at the end of *Philoctetes*, and the call to Oedipus at the end of the *Oedipus at Colonus*.

Sometimes the poet's interpretations allow deeper, often older, mythical patterns to show through. Thus the *Oedipus Tyrannus* rests not only on a common myth of the search for lost identity, but also on an inversion of a foundling myth, like that of Moses or Cyrus or Romulus. Instead of becoming king and ruling happily ever after when the lost son discovers that his true parents are king and queen of the land, this hero loses the kingdom that he has already won and goes from the height of prosperity to the depths of misery. The *Antigone* sets the heroine's life in the mythical frame of the bride of death, like Persephone who descends to marry Hades, god of the underworld, but, unlike Persephone, Antigone will not return in the seasonal cycles of nature's dying and rebirth. *Philoctetes* and *Trachinian Women*, in different ways, use the ancient symbolism of a difficult journey or a mysterious crossing of water. In all cases, however, character and emotional reality remain uppermost.

Sophocles is a man of the theater as well as a poet. The pacing of Oedipus' discovery of the truth in *Oedipus Tyrannus* is one of the most powerful experiences of theatrical suspense in Western drama. The moment when the blind Oedipus at the end of the *Oedipus at Colonus* suddenly arises at the gods' mysterious thunder to lead the others to his place of appointed burial is an electrifying enactment of the old hero's power of inner vision, now recognized by the gods and made manifest in movement and gesture.

The shifting between appearance and reality

that underlies so much of Sophoclean tragedy also produces powerful stage effects of irony and pathos. In *Electra,* for example, the worn and wasted heroine, deceived by the lie that her brother Orestes is dead, appears on the stage in a moving scene of lamentation as she holds the urn that supposedly contains her brother's ashes, while the brother, in disguise, stands before her and finally breaks down and reveals the plot. The visual configuration—Electra's crushing grief, the empty urn, the disguised brother who withholds the truth until he can stand her suffering no longer—is itself emblematic of the harsh changes between deception and truth, death and life, in Electra's bleak world. In a few moments she passes through a whole range of emotions, from darkest despair to lyrical joy (1098–1231).

An analogous visual contrast between spontaneous feeling and preconceived plotting dominates the stage in the great scene of *Philoctetes*: the crippled hero collapses into a sudden coma from his ulcerous foot while the young and vigorous Neoptolemus is left standing above him, now in possession of the magical bow that he had orders to steal, but torn between his pity for Philoctetes and the commands of Odysseus and the army. Sophocles further exploits the contrast of strong and weak in this visual tableau and creates another paradoxical relation between appearance and reality: the mighty son of Achilles suddenly realizes the meaning of the oracle, that to the helpless cripple lying inert at his feet belongs the crown of victory at Troy (839–842). In this scene and in the urn-scene of the *Electra,* Sophocles takes his audience through an emotional crisis, often with an unexpected outcome: here, Neoptolemus' decision to reveal the plot; in *Electra,* Orestes' abandonment of his ruse and revelation of his true identity to his sister. In both cases the hero's suffering and endurance make lies yield to truth and touch in the other person a realm of authentic feeling that deception cannot overlay.

Sophocles is equally a master of the power of restraint, silence, and gestures that speak more poignantly than words. The silent exit of Deianeira in *Trachinian Women* and, on a smaller scale, of Eurydice, Creon's wife, in *Antigone,* and the impassioned yet guarded speech of Jocasta in *Oedipus Tyrannus* express these women's recognition of a terrible truth and a tragic acceptance of suffering. In several scenes of tense silence the audience must fill in for itself what the unspeaking protagonist onstage is thinking and feeling: Electra listening in silence to the long tale of her brother's alleged death at Delphi while Clytemnestra, her hated mother, stands by, struck by instinctive sorrow, yet also triumphant in the removal of the feared avenger (681–787); or Oedipus' long silence in *Oedipus at Colonus* as he listens to his son's attempted defense (1254–1354), holding back his reaction for nearly a hundred lines until he breaks out into bitter insults and his deadly father's curse (1354, 1372–1396). Although some of the intricacies of the choral odes might escape most of the audience of twenty or thirty thousand gathered in the theater of Dionysus, these sharply delineated scenes of grand, clear gestures and wrenching emotions could speak to all, as they still speak to us.

THE INDIVIDUAL PLAYS

Ajax

The *Ajax* is generally regarded as the earliest of the seven extant plays, exhibiting the weightiness of style in Sophocles' first or Aeschylean period. With *Antigone* and *Trachinian Women* it is also described as a diptych play because it falls into two somewhat uneven parts with the hero's death at line 865. Diptych, however, is perhaps somewhat misleading, as the hero dominates the play to the very end. His corpse, shown on the *ekkyklema,* a low platform wheeled out from the back of the stage, is a massive and forceful presence, the center of the conflicts of the latter half of the play. Alive or dead, Ajax is a point of controversy and clashing values.

SOPHOCLES

In subject matter and spirit, *Ajax* is the most Homeric of the seven plays. Sophocles draws heavily on the characterization of Ajax in the *Iliad*: the stalwart warrior, huge, loyal, steady, and unflinching in battle. It is part of the tragic reversal that this team-fighter is totally isolated from his own side and that the warrior of open, face-to-face combat resorts to a treacherous sneak attack at night against his fellow-generals. A post-Homeric epic poem narrated the story of the award of Achilles' arms, after his death at Troy, to Odysseus rather than Ajax. In the eleventh book of the *Odyssey* the shade of Ajax, implacable even in death, turns away in silence from Odysseus as he wanders in the underworld. Aeschylus had cast the tale of his death into tragic form in a lost trilogy, *Decision of the Arms*, *Thracian Women*, *Women of Salamis*.

Besides the literary sources, Sophocles was probably influenced by the hero-cult of Ajax in Athens. One of the ten Athenian tribes was named after the hero (whose native Salamis had long been a part of Attic territory), and interpreters have seen a reference to the cult in the gathering and supplication around the body in lines 1171–1181. For this play, as for *Trachinian Women* and *Oedipus at Colonus*, it must be recalled that heroization after death does not imply anything like sainthood or moral rectitude. The heroes (in the technical, cultic sense) are distinguished for their power and their special relation to the gods, often marked by sudden, violent, or mysterious death or disappearance. They are intensely local divinities, whose bodies, buried in the earth of their people, are a help and protection in war. Ajax in this play, Heracles in *Trachinian Women*, Oedipus in the *Oedipus at Colonus*—all share in some features of this cult: they are distinguished for extraordinary strength of body or spirit, have a mysterious and dangerous closeness to divinity, possess an unbending will and fiercely proud determination, die and find burial in circumstances attended by violence, mysterious isolation, and divine intervention or prophecy.

Ajax's harsh, uncompromising strength of will is contrasted with the more humane and reasonable adaptability to the necessities of human life embodied in Odysseus for public and political actions and in Tecmessa, the captive concubine of Ajax and mother of his young son, Eurysaces, for personal and familial relations.

The double dishonor in which Ajax finds himself is irreconcilable with his image of himself as a heroic warrior. Not only has he lost the prize of Achilles' arms, symbol of first place in battle, but in a fit of insane anger has stalked out of his tent at night to kill the leaders of the expedition, the Atreid chiefs Menelaus and Agamemnon and their associate, Odysseus. Athena has turned his murderous fury into madness: instead of the generals, he slaughters captured cattle (along with a couple of herdsmen). Some of the animals he brings to his tent to mutilate and torture, thinking they are the Atreids and Odysseus.

Sophocles brings the two chief protagonists on the stage in their contrasting roles: Odysseus, led by his patron goddess, Athena, divinity of cool intelligence and clarity of judgment and action, is acting responsibly in a self-appointed role of concern for the army in tracking down Ajax. Ajax enters, carrying his bloody sword, still insane, boasting to Athena (who keeps Odysseus invisible) of his revenge of the night before.

Odysseus' compassion for his old enemy's degradation, in contrast to Athena's remote justice (121–133), helps prepare for our next, and very different, view of Ajax: the *ekkyklema* reveals the interior of the tent where Ajax sits, sane but desperate, groaning amid the bloody mess left from the night before. From inarticulate cries that ignore his friends' attempts at consolation and help, he passes gradually to lyrical lamentation over his ignominy and then, in the firmness of dialogue meter, to the determination to die. That determination dominates the first two-thirds of the play, culminating in the final suicide-speech alone by the sea (815–865). The problem of what to do with the corpse (represented, doubtless, by a dummy on the *ek-*

kyklema) dominates the last third. First, Teucer, Ajax's half-brother, defends it, valiantly but without success, against the Atreids' narrow-minded enmity. Finally, Odysseus returns to the stage and persuades the Atreids to permit the burial, though he himself, as Ajax's erstwhile foe, is to be excluded from the ceremony.

Ajax will not bend to the adjustments necessary to live in a world characterized by mutability. His view is fixed on eternity, on absolutes. The only solution is to leave this world by self-chosen death. To the changeful world of mortal life the flexibility of Odysseus is the proper response, and Ajax will have none of that.

A series of multiple ironies involving change and stability fill out Ajax's tragic situation. The sword with which he takes leave of this world, planted in the earth with a fixity characteristic of the hero's rigid will (815–822), is the gift of his Trojan enemy Hector; though given in apparent friendship, it proves constant in hostility (662–665). Tecmessa remains steady in her love, the Atreids in their hate. And yet Ajax's body is saved from desecration by an enemy turned friend. Where the inflexible warrior-ethic of Teucer would fail, Odysseus' ability to see both sides and negotiate a compromise succeeds.

These contrasts between change and fixity carry political as well as ethical implications. Odysseus embodies the flexibility, reliance on persuasion and debate, and reasonableness necessary for the Athenian democracy. Ajax harks back to an older aristocratic ideal, praised and admired, but obsolescent in the circumstances of mid-fifth-century B.C. Athens. Sophocles' play, in the period 460–445, catches a moment of changing values in his society, the widening gap between the old nobility and landed aristocracy, who look back to the heroic ideals extolled in Homer and in the old poets, and the new, city-based leaders and sailors of the democracy.

But the play is far more than political allegory. It is also a powerful and richly poetical meditation on man's yearning for independence and autonomy, on the devotion to an absolute ideal of heroic honor and the heroic self, in a world where interdependence, reciprocity, mutual need, and the bonds of love and family are equally necessary for survival. Ajax leaves behind his woman, his child, his parents, to satisfy his uncompromising image of himself as a bearer of the heroic *areté*, the excellence of a warrior in a shame-culture, a society, not unlike that of Japan, where personal honor, reputation, and saving face are of primary importance. But he can count on Tecmessa to bring up the child and on Teucer and his men to protect his son and keep his body from shameful outrage (560–577). Even in the self-willed isolation of his death he does not escape his need for others. The ties of blood that link him to the changeful cycles of generation, age, decay also save him from the last dishonor, the exposure of his corpse to dogs and birds. His ultimate tragic paradox is that he can reach the absolutes of his timeless values only by plunging to the core of mortality, only through his death.

Athena's role in the play is difficult for a modern audience. She exhibits the remoteness characteristic of the Sophoclean gods: she has driven Ajax mad to protect the army, but her intervention only makes manifest the kind of response that a man like Ajax is inherently likely to make. The award of Achilles' arms to his rival and enemy signifies the collapse of a world that he has trusted to recognize his merit and to reward the kind of excellence that he has cultivated all his life. Temporary and homicidal insanity is a predictable result.

Sophocles could easily enough have accounted for Ajax's madness in purely naturalistic terms. Why then does he use Athena? As a principle of the inexorable realities of the world that the gods often signify, the laws built into the structure of reality, Athena exemplifies the hard fact that there is a price to pay for violence, egotistical self-centeredness, rejection of the conditions of mortal existence. This is the justice of the gods. Her presence on the stage also brings out the contrast with Odysseus: fellow-humans, even enemies, can pity; the gods do not. "Do you see, Odysseus, how great is the force of the gods?" she says at the end of the prologue. "And yet I pity him," Odysseus replies, "in his total misery, enemy though he is . . . , as I look to his situation no more than to my own. For I see that all of us who live are ghostly images or light smoke, nothing more" (118–126).

Sophocles' use of this divinity on the stage is markedly different from Aeschylean practice. Unlike an Aeschylean god, Athena does not so much raise the problem of causality, guilt, and retribution as set off the human wisdom of Odysseus, the feeling quality that enters relations between men, from the distant justice of the Olympians. The contrast between Athena's and Odysseus' response to Ajax's madness shows what it is to be human. The question of divine justice is not entirely lacking, as Calchas' prophecy shows; but human wisdom, not the Aeschylean theodicy, is Sophocles' main concern.

Antigone

Composed ten to twenty years after *Ajax*, *Antigone* too presents a sharp contrast between two polarized characters: Antigone who would bury her brother, Polyneices, in defiance of Creon's decree forbidding it, and Creon, king of Thebes, a harsh and self-willed monarch whose irreverence toward the dead in the name of civic order recalls the Atreid generals of *Ajax*. Antigone has something of Ajax's stubborn, suicidal determination; unlike Ajax she is fighting not just for personal honor, but for the sacred laws that demand that she give proper burial to her family-members. For all her fierceness of principle, in which she contrasts with her more yielding sister, Ismene, her life revolves about human ties and love, shown in her concern for the burial of her dead brother and her love for her intended husband, Haemon, Creon's son.

Antigone has long been considered one of the masterpieces of Greek drama. Interpretation, however, has suffered from two major forms of oversimplification. The first is Hegel's

well-known view of the play, in his *Philosophy of Fine Art* (1823–1827), which reduces it to a dialectical conflict between the principle of individualism, embodied in Antigone, and the demands of the state, embodied in Creon, both with equal claims to rightness. The other simplification treats the play as the tragedy of Creon, a tragedy of pride and folly punished by the gods. The Hegelian view is false to the facts of the play: Antigone is isolated, but does not represent a principle of the individual against the state. Her loyalties are to the family and to the religious usages in the proper treatment of the dead, not to individualism per se. Neither is Creon an embodiment of the state. His notion of political authority is revealed as narrow, self-centered, and autocratic. The interview with Haemon, who points out that the citizens of Thebes take a different and far more generous view of Antigone's acts, confirms his limited and tyrannical conception of his city (690–761).

As to the second view, it is true that Creon has a slightly longer speaking part than Antigone. But he is not powerful or interesting enough to be a tragic hero. A foolish man caught by his own irreverence, limited outlook, and egotism, he is justly punished by the gods. He merely gets what he deserves. He gains a measure of our sympathy at the end, but there is little that is truly tragic in his suffering. His story follows a rather familiar Aeschylean moral pattern: outrage, folly, and punishment *(hybris, atê, dikê)*; but it lacks the larger scope or complex conflicts of Aeschylean figures like Agamemnon, Clytemnestra, or Prometheus.

Morally and psychologically, Antigone is the center of the play. She is faced with a genuinely tragic conflict, the ultimate choice between death with integrity of her deepest commitments (burying her fallen brother) or life with silence and complicity in what she knows to be wrong. The French dramatist Jean Anouilh clearly recognized this core of her tragedy in his *Antigone* (1944; translated 1946), when he makes the heroine a proud young woman who refuses to compromise with the Nazi collaborators and forces the father of her fiancé to order her execution.

Antigone's tragedy deepens even after her act of defiance. The ode on Eros, god of sexual desire (789–801), immediately follows Haemon's attempt to defend Antigone to his father and intimates the strong and genuine love between the two young people. This element, which should of course not be exaggerated to the status of a romantic subplot, may well be Sophocles' innovation, though we know very little about this myth prior to Sophocles' version. Antigone laments that instead of being a happy bride on earth she will be a bride of Hades (806–811). Sophocles treats her love for Haemon with great delicacy: only once, in her first encounter with Creon, does she refer to him explicitly (572): "O dearest Haemon, how your father dishonors you." This line, however, has been controversial since the Renaissance, when it was first assigned to Antigone rather than to Ismene, as it is in the manuscripts; but such mistakes in the assignment of speaker in the manuscripts are notoriously frequent.

Not only Antigone's decision to bury her brother, but also the manner of her death, constitute a trial of her heroic nature. Her total isolation is all the more bitter because she is dying to defend the value of family ties. The chorus, often the confidant of the hero, is distant and not clearly sympathetic. This is, in fact, the only Sophoclean play extant in which the chorus is not of the same sex as the chief protagonist. At times, in her lyrical lamentation, Antigone seems on the verge of breaking down. But by her last speech, in dialogue-meter, she defends her decision with her own kind of logic and with conviction (891–928). Still, the emotional vehemence of her lyrical lament (806–882) allows a glimpse of the mood in which she will soon commit suicide in the underground chamber where Creon imprisons her. With characteristic austerity Sophocles does not fill in the details of her last moments. But we have seen enough of this deeply feeling young woman's intensity of love and passion to ask ourselves what she might have thought and felt in the ter-

rible time—Sophocles does not tell us how long—between the blocking up of the cave and her decision to take her own life rather than die slowly of starvation.

Antigone's personal tragedy unfolds against the large mythical pattern of the virgin bride of death, Kore or Persephone (previously mentioned). She compares herself also to a very different feminine model, the weeping Niobe, turned to stone in her grief for her children, a *mater dolorosa* fixed in the act of perpetual lamentation for lost loved ones (824–833). Antigone views herself in the lasting frame of myth and eternal forces of nature, but there is a bitter irony, for she will not reach marriage and childbirth. The motifs of love, marriage, and its loss culminate in the grimly inverted marriage in the messenger's account of Haemon's end:

> Leaning into his sword, he plunged it up to the middle into his side. Then, still conscious, he takes the girl into his weak embrace. Blowing out his sharp spray of blood, he sprinkles her white cheek with the bloody drops. A corpse beside a corpse he lies there, alas, getting fulfilment of marriage-rites in Hades' house.
>
> (1234–1241)

The marriage-in-death, instead of providing the union that would perpetuate the two houses in fruitful union, seals the doom of the house of Oedipus and leads directly to the utter obliteration of Creon's in the suicide of his wife Eurydice, who dies cursing Creon for the previous death of another son as well (1301–1305).

Antigone's tragic decision stands within the large frame of divinity and eternity that characterizes the heroic personality in Sophocles. She defends her choice of the unwritten laws in these terms:

> For those are not of now or of yesterday, but they live always, nor does anyone know when they came into the light. I had no intention of incurring punishment from the gods for infringing these, in fear of something a man's intelligence devised. For I knew full well that I would die. How not?

Yes, even if you had not made your decree. But if I die before my time, I count that as a profit. If one lives in the midst of many woes, as I do now, how does he not win profit by his death?

(456–464)

This great speech of defiance sets out the two poles of her life: devotion to the eternal laws of the nether world and a fascination with death. Death for her, as in a way for Ajax, holds the power and mystery of the timeless and the unknown. And yet as she contemplates the immediate reality of death in her last speech, she conveys not a martyr's eagerness to die, but a keen sense of the waste and loss of her young life (806–816, 876–882, 891–896).

Creon has little feeling for the mysterious realm of the gods, the underworld, human passions. When he speaks of death, it is an instrument of punishment or political power. When he uses the word *philos* (loved one), it is to designate a friend of the city. To his dictum, "The enemy is not a *philos*, not even when he is dead," Antigone replies, "By nature I am made to share in love [*symphilein*,] not in enmity" (522–523). The chorus' second ode (332–375), a famous praise of man's conquest of nature, sounds a note of triumphant rationalism of which Creon would certainly approve; but that confidence is increasingly qualified in subsequent odes, devoted to the irrational forces that emerge around both Antigone and Creon: the family curse, the power of love, the mysterious workings of the gods.

When the chorus hesitantly suggests that the first burial may be the work of the gods, Creon flies into a fury and insults them for senile stupidity (278–289). In his view the burial can only be the act of political dissidents. The first burial poses a problem: if Antigone buried Polyneices' body the first time, why does she return to do it again? The issue is never fully clarified, and scholars continue to discuss the question of the two burials. Creon's response, in any case, shows him totally insensitive to the dimension of the sacred, save as it subserves political ex-

pediency. He assumes that the will of the gods is exactly congruent with what he takes to be the authority of the city.

Even after the terrible threats of Teiresias, Creon behaves with a callous disregard for life. Instead of going at once to free Antigone, who might still be alive, he first performs the burial of Polyneices' body (ironically the burial that he forbade is thus performed three times). In the meantime Antigone has hanged herself (1195–1205). Creon's priorities exhibit the same legalistic mentality and the same insensitivity that marked his exposure of Polyneices' corpse in the first place: an act technically legal under Greek practices, but clearly inhumane in this case. As a result he is punished exactly where he is most vulnerable: in his personal relations, his house, the irrational and uncontrollable power of emotions, the inexorability of death—all the things, in short, that Antigone has championed.

That contrast between Antigone and Creon is not so much a Hegelian antithesis between individual and state as a contrast between two fundamentally different attitudes toward life: one founded on the primacy of emotion and personal ties, committed to absolute values, and informed by a feeling for the sacred; the other based on rational organization, authoritarian control, the subordination of feeling to power and domination. The tragedy lies in the circumstances that produce the clash rather than the complementation of the two sides. The failure of that union is symbolized by the unrealized marriage of Antigone and Haemon.

We cannot forget that Creon has in fact saved Thebes; and the first ode shows the city's relief and joy. But the secular humanism that he embodies, for all its brilliant success in the new intellectual movements of Sophocles' day, is also potentially inhumane and reductive, as Antigone's tragic sense of life and the doom of an accursed house that she brings with her show to the full. No simple formula, however, can exhaust the meaning of this play: its rich choral poetry, sharply drawn characters, and representation of the mysterious and ultimately inexplicable forces in our lives place it among the most powerful of the ancient dramas.

Trachinian Women

Whereas *Ajax* and *Antigone* are in some sense political plays—that is, about the relation of the city to what lies beyond or below it—*Trachinian Women* is unique in Sophocles' extant work for its lack of a clear civic background. Its subject is the destruction of a house, the house of Heracles and Deianeira. Exiled from Tiryns, Heracles has come to live in Trachis in northeast Greece, beneath Mount Oeta. Like the *Antigone,* but in a totally different way, the tragic element lies in the fact that male and female destroy rather than complement one another.

The first half of the play belongs to Deianeira, who has been patiently but anxiously waiting for Heracles to return from a fifteen-month absence on one of his many journeys. Heracles' return is announced first by a messenger and then by his companion, Lichas, who brings with him a beautiful young girl, Iole, unhappy and silent. Deianeira painfully learns the truth that Heracles fell in love with her, sacked her city, Oechalia, to get her, and is now bringing her back to live with him. Initially understanding, even forgiving, Deianeira decides to use what she thinks is a love charm to win back his affections. This is an unguent given her by the centaur Nessus and is actually a powerful poison. It is made from the clotted blood around the wound caused by Heracles' poisoned arrow when Nessus tried to carry off Deianeira while ferrying her across a river. She applies the unguent to a robe and sends it off to Heracles. Her son Hyllus soon brings back news of the charm's effect, the agonies of Heracles, for the unguent contains the deadly venom of the Hydra. Deianeira leaves the stage for the interior of her house, soon to commit suicide. Heracles enters, wearing the robe that eats his flesh. Roaring with pain, he calls for

Deianeira, whom he wants to kill with his own hand. When Hyllus tells him about Nessus and the poison, he recognizes an old prophecy, realizes that his end is near, and asks Hyllus to convey him to the top of Mount Oeta, where he must be burnt alive. Hyllus must then marry Iole. Under severe constraint Hyllus agrees, and the play ends with a sad procession toward the mountain and the troubled pronouncement, "There is nothing of this that is not Zeus."

This is the only preserved play of Sophocles about sexual passion. To some interpreters, therefore, it has seemed Euripidean in tone. Sophocles may, of course, have been influenced by his younger contemporary, but we should not forget the anecdotes about his active interest in sex or the ode on Eros in the *Antigone.* We know too that he wrote plays, now lost, on erotic subjects, for example, a *Phaedra* and a *Danae.* Our present selection of seven plays was largely determined by considerations of propriety, heroic grandeur, rhetorical interest, and suitability for the schools of late antiquity and Byzantium. Had we a larger range of his work, *Trachinian Women* might well look less anomalous.

The fact that the play is about the famous hero Heracles may have helped assure its preservation. The myth itself is not particularly well known. Sophocles probably drew on the sixth-century B.C. epic, *The Capture of Oechalia.* The choral lyricist Bacchylides told a brief version of the myth in a dithyramb (ode 16), which cannot be later than 450 B.C. Some scholars have argued that Sophocles' play prompted Bacchylides' ode, which would make *Trachinian Women* one of his earliest preserved works, but this hypothesis rests on no solid foundation.

Despite the apparent division in the action (Deianeira's departure for suicide at line 820, Heracles' arrival at line 971), the play is strongly unified by the anticipation of Heracles' arrival from the very first scene. The oracles about him, which recur throughout, also pull the play together: they create a mood of suspense and suggest an imminent crisis in his life.

This use of interlocking oracles to pace the action is perhaps another reason to date the play some years prior to the *Oedipus Tyrannus*, where the oracles are far more fully developed. Hyllus too, who has an important role in both halves, provides continuity. But like Lichas, who conveys the robe from the house to the altars where Heracles is celebrating his return, all he can bring to his two parents is death and separation.

At first glance, the play has a rather static look, partly because much of its action takes place through long set speeches. For this reason too it has been dated relatively early. But beneath a certain stiffness in the form, the events are powerful and stirring, with much packed into short compass. We see the middle-aged Deianeira coming to grips with the recognition that the beautiful captive girl, whom she pities, is to be installed in her own house as her husband's concubine. The excited ode on the power of Aphrodite, which pitted Heracles against the monstrous river-god, Achelous, to win Deianeira in the past, is beautifully placed to suggest the mounting sexual tension and jealousy (497–531). It helps prepare for the long speech in which Deianeira sets forth her decision to use the centaur's love charm, ignorant of its real power. Once that decision is made, the play drives quickly to its end: the report of Heracles' affliction, Deianeira's suicide, Heracles' vociferous entrance, and his thirst for revenge, then the calm of new understanding, leading to the preparations for his mysterious funeral pyre on Mount Oeta.

In its lack of a clear heroic center and in its nearly equal division between two protagonists, *Trachinian Women* seems to stand apart from the other six plays. Deianeira is by far the more sympathetic of the two main figures. Gentle, loving, forgiving, she resembles Tecmessa in *Ajax*. Yet Heracles, for all his anger, lust, and violence, is treated with respect as a great hero by every character in the play, Deianeira included. This is a case where it is not easy to adjust modern sensibilities to a fifth-century B.C. perspective. Clearly, Sophocles does not soften the harsh lines of this man of strong passions and brutal impulses. He has destroyed a Greek city to get a woman, and he does nothing to investigate Deianeira's motives or guilt. It is enough for him that she is behind the poisoned robe; that she did not know of the poison matters to him not a bit. When he learns the truth and hears the name "Nessus," he never turns back to Deianeira. His sole concern now is the prophecy and the future of his race. It is part of Deianeira's tragic isolation that the husband who has been the center of her thoughts and anxieties for so long has not a word of pity or even of sorrow for her, once the cause for revenge is past.

How then are we to account for the repeated eulogies of Heracles as "best of men"? Some have thought that Sophocles is being ironical, that he is playing the old heroic values off against more developed sensibilities, calling the old myth into question. Recalling Ajax, we should also remember how ambiguous these heroic figures are. Gentleness, compassion, consideration for others are not concomitants of heroic greatness. That is more likely to include egotism, strong passions of hate and love, determined adherence to a narrow code of values, an inflexible will.

Heracles fits the pattern. His greatness is inseparable from his faults. He is a civilizing hero. The Hydra and Nessus who kill him are monsters that he has exterminated from the earth in the course of his mighty labors, enumerated at length (1058–1061, 1090–1102). He is also the son of Zeus, as we are repeatedly told, and as such has a privileged destiny, signaled by oracles that he alone comprehends. His death too is heroic: for all his roaring and shouting, at the end he calls his "hard spirit" to enduring silence, "to accomplish as a thing of joy this deed of necessity" (1259–1263). He also possesses a knowledge, hidden from others, about his future descendants. He overrides the repugnance of Hyllus to marry Iole, who is after all the cause of both his parents' deaths, but Heracles knows that the young pair will become the founders of the Dorian race.

Sophocles mutes the issue of Heracles' divinization after death, although he himself exploits this old and familiar legend in the finale of *Philoctetes*. The prominence of the pyre in Heracles' commands at the end, however, at the very least raises that possibility (1190–1215). Heracles speaks of "dying" (1172), but also mentions obscurely "a cure for his sufferings" through the pyre (1208–1210), a possible allusion to being taken up to Olympus from the fire.

It is part of the contradictions around Heracles that this civilizing killer of beasts is killed by the monstrous figures of his past, the Hydra and the centaur, who symbolize the still untamed monstrosity in his own soul. His lustful violence toward Iole is no better than Nessus' toward Deianeira. Priding himself on his strength and his physique, he is destroyed in and through his body. He groans that he is reduced to weeping like a girl, defeated by a woman, not even a man with a sword (1062–1063, 1070–1075).

Deianeira's tragedy exactly complements Heracles: like him, she is destroyed in and through the things she has valued most highly — house, family, the bond of the marriage bed. Modeled after Penelope in the *Odyssey*, faithfully and patiently awaiting her lord's return, she unwittingly acts out the role of a Clytemnestra, who destroys her husband (also with a robe) on his return from the wars. This is not the tragedy of a single hero, then, but a double tragedy, the two parts closely interlocked.

The juxtaposition of contemporary realism and remote myth gives the play its peculiar quality of both familiarity and strangeness. Through this mixture Sophocles portrays the continued power of the elemental passions and instincts beneath the civilized, moderated surface of domestic life. All these years the gentle and faithful Deianeira has guarded in the safe interior of her domestic space the deadly poison of the Hydra and the centaur, creatures that belong to the savage realm of primordial violence. That venom is one of Greek literature's most expressive symbols for the explosive power of sex and the destructive force of lust,

violence, and deception, transmitted from the centaur to the wife, from the wild to the house. Sophocles' rich imagery and powerful poetry weave these themes deeply into the fabric of the action.

It is possible that Sophocles' close study of a complex female character owes something to Euripidean influence, particularly the *Alcestis* of 438 B.C. and the *Medea* of 431, works that have plausibly been adduced for dating *Trachinian Women* in the 430's. It is equally possible that Sophocles was writing, partly at least, under the impact of Aeschylus' *Agamemnon* (458–457 B.C.). As Aeschylus' tragedies were often reperformed throughout the fifth century, this influence is of only limited help for dating. In any case, *Trachinian Women* is a work of great poetic and dramatic power, rich characterization, and disturbing theology. That it does not fit the conventional definitions of Sophoclean tragedy may reflect more on modern critics than on the ancient poet. It is a play that deserves more careful and sympathetic attention than it has generally received.

Oedipus Tyrannus

If *Trachinian Women* is the most neglected of Sophocles' works, *Oedipus Tyrannus* (in English also *Oedipus Rex*, *Oedipus the King*) is by far the best known and has been the most influential. Aristotle praised its structure. Seneca, Corneille, Dryden, Voltaire, Gide, Cocteau, and others have imitated its brilliant plot. Freud drew upon it for one of his best-known theories, the "Oedipus complex," named from Oedipus' incestuous union with his mother and murder of his father. The play is also the most sustained instance of so-called Sophoclean irony, a use of language that implies one meaning for the speaker and another for the interlocutor or the spectator or both. The inexorable logic of Oedipus' discovery of his origins, the tense progression as he gradually pieces together his past, the combination of deep human sympathy for Oedipus and Jocasta with the theological questions posed by their suffering all make this play one of the great masterpieces of world literature.

The myth of Oedipus was well known in Sophocles' time and had been treated in art and literature in the centuries before the play. As usual, there was no single, authoritative version, but many variants. The *Iliad* (23.679) briefly mentions "funeral games for Oedipus who fell in battle," a form of the myth that precludes the self-blinding. The *Odyssey* mentions his incestuous marriage to his mother (here called Epikaste), but says nothing about self-blinding or exile: "In lovely Thebes he ruled over the Cadmeans, suffering pain, through the destructive counsels of the gods" (11.275–276). A lost post-Homeric epic called the *Oedipodeia*, of which a few lines survive, has his children born not from his mother/wife, Jocasta or Epikaste, but from a second wife, Euryganeia. As a number of aristocratic families in Greek cities traced their descent to Oedipus' line, this suppression of the incestuous origin of his sons may have been part of a deliberate purification of the myth in the early archaic period. Another lost epic of this time, the *Thebaid*, told of Oedipus' curses on his sons, that "war and battles should come between them." An important recently discovered papyrus fragment of Stesichorus, a poet of the late seventh century B.C. who wrote lyrical narratives on mythical subjects, contains a long speech by a Theban queen, almost certainly Jocasta or Epikaste, trying to avert the civil war in which Oedipus' two sons kill one another. Sophocles uses this part of the legend in *Oedipus at Colonus* and *Antigone*. It is probable that the lost portion of Stesichorus' poem also narrated the story of Oedipus.

The most important direct influence on Sophocles' play was Aeschylus' trilogy, *Laius, Oedipus, Seven Against Thebes* (with a satyr play, *Sphinx*), produced in 467 B.C., the year after Sophocles' debut in the dramatic competitions. Only the last play, the *Seven*, survives, but from this and a few fragments of the other two we get a good idea of Aeschylus' treatment. He emphasized the family curse, transmitted from Laius to Oedipus and thence to Oedipus' two sons, Polyneices and Eteocles. He also gave prominence to an oracle of Apollo, described thus in the *Seven* (745–749): "Three times in the Pythian oracles at the earth's mid-navel Apollo tells [Laius] that if he dies without issue he will save his city." Here the god's words take the form of prescriptive advice; Laius' refusal to heed it precipitates the ruin of his family and his city. In Sophocles the oracle is purely descriptive. It offers no course of action that could avert it: "It will be his portion to die at the hands of a son born from himself and Jocasta" (713–714). There is nothing about saving the city, nor is Laius explicitly told that he can avoid the prophecy by remaining childless. Rather than posing a conflict between familial or dynastic ambition and the salvation of the city, Sophocles raises the question of the power or helplessness of human life and the mysterious circumstances that make an individual life fortunate or miserable.

It is a widespread but erroneous view that *Oedipus Tyrannus* is primarily about oracles, prophecy, predestination versus free will. The play is much more concerned with knowledge: the limits and the kinds of knowledge and the problem of self-knowledge. In contrast to Prometheus, whose intelligence conquers and organizes nature for human convenience, Oedipus embodies a tragic knowlege gained through confronting the mysteries of his origins, the contradictions within the very conditions of his existence, his precarious place in the world and his uncertain identity. In Aeschylus, Oedipus kills his father at a crossroads near a shrine of the Furies in Boeotia. Sophocles placed the patricide at the crossroads leading from Thebes and Corinth to Delphi, the sanctuary of Apollo, one of whose injunctions was "Know thyself." The change of locale is symptomatic of Sophocles' shifting the meaning of the myth away from the power of the family curse to the question of self-knowledge.

Another misconception about the play has been equally tenacious, despite repeated refutations in the scholarly literature, namely, that

Oedipus is punished for a tragic flaw of anger, violence, or pride. It is true that Oedipus is not blameless in his anger against Teiresias and Creon; but irascibility—in both cases understandable—is hardly sufficient to merit the massive suffering that befalls him. The tragic point of the king's interview with Teiresias is not so much Oedipus' anger (for after all Teiresias shows himself equally irascible and equally violent), but the fact that the truth is revealed in just such a way and in just such language that Oedipus cannot "hear" it. Language, like other means of reaching knowledge, may prove a barrier rather than a vehicle to truth, concealing through ambiguity rather than revealing through logical distinction. In *Antigone* Sophocles had listed "speech and thought like the wind" among man's proud inventions to subdue the world, and theories about the origins and power of language began to develop about this time. Tragedy presents another view of language and communication, as of man's rational power of domination and control in general.

The tragic-flaw interpretation of the *Tyrannus* owes its prestige largely to the celebrated thirteenth chapter of Aristotle's *Poetics*, in which Aristotle singles out Oedipus (along with Thyestes) as the best example of tragic reversal or "peripety" *(peripeteia)*. Such a figure is "neither exceptional in excellence and justice, nor does he change to misfortune because of baseness and viciousness, but because of some error [*hamartia*], a man in great repute and good fortune, like Oedipus and Thyestes and the famous men from such families." The word here translated as "error," *hamartia*, can mean both "moral flaw" and "intellectual mistake." Passionate arguments have been made on both sides, but most recent scholars tend to accept the meaning "mistake" in a purely intellectual rather than a moral sense. The meaning "mistake" or "intellectual error" in fact suits the situation of both Oedipus and Thyestes better than "flaw."

Not the dangers of pride or anger, but the place of the irrational and absurd in human life and the instability of even the most solid-seeming happiness, the ease of self-deception, and the painful journey of self-knowledge are the central themes of the play. Oedipus moves from the height of success to the most feared degradation and misery, largely through no fault of his own. The circumstances that led to his killing of Laius at the crossroads and his marriage to his mother are entirely outside of his control. Even in killing Laius, as Sophocles tells the tale, Oedipus acted justifiably, under extreme provocation, albeit in anger. In Greek morality, he is not guilty of willful wrongdoing, but he is nonetheless indelibly and horribly polluted by a miasma, the physical stain of patricide and incest.

In his tragic reversal from kingship to pollution, Oedipus ironically fulfills his role as savior of Thebes, for he performs the order of Apollo that Creon brings back from Delphi, "Drive out the land's pollution" (97–98). In a fusion of opposites characteristic of the rift between appearance and reality in this play, he is simultaneously the expelled outcast and the savior-king. As Oedipus proved the savior of Thebes in the past, when he defeated the Sphinx by answering her riddle, so again he will exercise his great intelligence to release the city from its affliction. But now the riddle will be the secret of his own identity. The elders' pitiable supplication in the prologue both insists on the previous achievement and conveys their confidence in him, while also showing his responsibility and compassion as their king:

> Best of men, Oedipus, make the city stand upright. Show your concern. This land now calls you "savior" for your previous energy. Let us in no way remember your rule as one in which we came to stand upright and then fell down again. But in unstumbling security raise this city up.
>
> (46–51)

The metaphors of walking subtly link the solving of the previous riddle with the riddle of

Oedipus' past, where feet and walking play a crucial role.

Critics sometimes read the play as if it ended with Oedipus' return to the stage, blinded by his own hand, at line 1366. But the play goes on for nearly two hundred lines more. Here, Oedipus shows a greatness of another kind. He is not broken by suffering, like Creon at the end of *Antigone*. The irrational extinction of earned good fortune and exterior power reveals a new source of strength in his tragic knowledge of the uncertainties of life, the deceptiveness of its surface, the mystery of living out a pattern that has somehow been given him in the circumstances of birth, parents, situation, but is also of his own making. He does not commit suicide like Jocasta. "For no one else of mortals except me," he reasons, "can bear my sufferings." For all his misery, he does not lose his love and concern for his children, whom he embraces with deep affection. He has become a kind of second Teiresias, exchanging external sight for an inner vision beneath appearances. Even as he leaves the stage, he is still a heroic figure, clear and strong of purpose as he views himself as "most hated by the gods" and asks to be let go to wander as an outcast. Creon, the moderate, untragic man of good sense and temperate caution, warns, "In everything do not wish to have power; for the things in which you had power did not follow with you in life" (1522–1523). The moralizing closure by the chorus (1524–1530) would not be out of character, but may well be the addition of a later time.

The play's superb tightness of construction, density of allusion, and the raw power of the myth are responsible in large part for its stunning effect. Not a word is wasted. Even apparently chance utterances prove to have their irony. The play is full of double and triple meanings. Apollo's oracle of the present, that Thebes must "drive out the pollution" (96–98), gradually reveals its full meaning as it meshes with the god's other two oracles: the one given to Laius and Jocasta, that their son will kill his father (711–722), and the one given to Oedipus, that he "must have union with his mother, bring

forth a race unendurable among men, and be the killer of the father who begot him" (791–793). The way in which the essential pieces of information are disclosed bit by bit produces a feeling of suspense, inevitability, doom, and courage that are unrivaled in dramatic art. The long narratives of Jocasta and Oedipus in the middle of the play fill in the background, but the actual revelation takes place in two tense line-by-line exchanges (*stichomythy*) that build up to the greatest climaxes of the ancient Greek theater: the first when Jocasta exits in full knowledge of the truth, leaving Oedipus joyfully confident that he will finally uncover the secret of his birth (989–1085); the second when Oedipus learns the horror of that secret, detail by detail, in questioning the Corinthian messenger and Laius' old herdsman (1123–1135). In both scenes Sophocles exploits his perfected technique of three-way dialogue for its fullest theatrical and psychological effect.

The plot of *Oedipus Tyrannus* is not without flaws. Critics since Voltaire (in his *Lettres sur l'Oedipe*, 1719) have pointed out the illogicality in the fact that Oedipus, on becoming the king of Thebes, would not fully have investigated his predecessor's death, that Jocasta would not have spoken of the oracle given to her and to Laius or of her lost infant, that Oedipus would not have recounted what he knew of his origins or how he killed an old man near Delphi, that both together would not have discussed the wounds on his feet. It is hard to imagine that these objections did not occur to Sophocles. But it would be mistaken to read a Greek tragedy with the criteria of the realistic drama that has formed modern taste. A Sophoclean tragedy, like Greek tragedy in general, is a stylized representation of the highly symbolic form of narrative that constitutes myth. Viewed by a large crowd on a festal occasion in open air, it would carry the conviction of its rapid movement, dense plot, complex poetic language.

Oedipus' name means not only "swell-foot," but also "know-foot": he is to know the secret of his feet that points back to the hidden origins of his life and also back to his great triumph of knowledge, solving the Sphinx's riddle. The answer to that riddle is the mystery of man's multiple, changing identity as he passes from infancy to old age, from four feet to two to three. One of the deepest ironies in the play is that Oedipus who "knows the feet" of the riddle lacks the basic and primary knowledge given every man at birth, the name that relates him to father and mother in a house and roots him in city and family. Oedipus' name, however, comes not from acceptance in the security of a house and a city, but from exposure on the desolate mountain, his feet "yoked together" (719), made one instead of two, so that he would never walk on feet at all, that is, have no house, no parents, no passage through life.

In subtly reenacting the meaning of the riddle in his own present, Oedipus does a great deal of counting, measuring, sorting out difference and equality. At the beginning he seems "all but equal to the gods" (31); at the end he proves "equal to nothing" (1187). His guilt or innocence hangs on the question of number (as did success or failure in confronting the Sphinx), on whether the old herdsman will hold to the story of one killer, not many: "For one would not be equal to many," Oedipus reckons (845). And yet, in the truth that Oedipus' logic has not yet discovered, one *is* equal to many. He himself is not only one man, but several: the visible surface of his life hides beneath it a puzzling duality. He is not only "tyrant" or usurper, but also legitimate king, as Laius' son; not only husband, but also son of Jocasta; not only the agent of justice, but also outlaw; not only the savior, but also the source of the pollution. In the recurrent animal imagery of the play, he is both the human tracker who defeats the monstrous Sphinx and the hunted beast that "wanders beneath the wild forest and the caves, the bull of the rocks" (476–478).

In still another etymology, "Oedipus" means "know where" (*oida pou*). But he does not "know where" he belongs, whether in the city or the wild. "In the house or in the wild" is the first question he asks in investigating Laius' death (112); but that alternative soon passes to him as his inquiry takes him from house and palace back to Mount Cithaeron where Jocasta and Laius exposed their child and where the shepherds took up the crippled infant (718–719, 1026–1050, 1123–1135). When his search for Laius' murderer, and himself, has reached its end, he claims his affinity with those wild places of his origins: "Let me dwell in the mountains, where Cithaeron has its name as mine, the place which my mother and father still alive set up as my proper tomb, that I might die and they be my killers" (1451–1454). In tracing the path of his life back to the mountain, Oedipus learns who he is and "where" he is. He becomes not just the victorious solver of the Sphinx's riddle, confident in his success and intellectual control of the life-process that the riddle describes, but its tragic exemplar as he himself traverses, in a single action, the journey of life from maturity back to infancy and then forward to feeble old age, fulfilling Teiresias' prophecy (454–456): "Blind instead of seeing, beggar instead of rich, pointing his way with a staff, he will make his way to a foreign land."

Electra

Like *Oedipus Tyrannus*, *Electra* owes a great deal to its Aeschylean model, the *Choephoroe*, middle play of the *Oresteia*. As in the case of the *Oedipus* too, Sophocles has drastically recast his version. He inverts the order of the climactic events, so that Clytemnestra is killed first, Aegisthus second. It has been claimed that this rearrangement softens the horror of the matricide by ending with a murder that carries neither moral nor psychological conflicts. Clearly, in condensing the full range of the earlier trilogy into a single play Sophocles could not work out the moral questions of the *Oresteia*. But it is questionable whether the problem of the matricide is so negligible.

To clarify the strong heroic personality of Electra, Sophocles provides a foil, like Ismene to Antigone, in the figure of Chrysothemis. This weaker and more compromising sister shows what a less forceful and less committed person would become in corrupt Mycenae after Agamemnon's murder. Ill-dressed, poorly fed, maltreated, threatened, and isolated, Electra must hold out as the sole voice of justice and vengeance in the palace of her murdered father. She lives for one thing only, the return of her exiled brother to avenge the killing and punish the murderers.

For all three tragedians, the fulcrum of the plot is Orestes' return, in disguise, using a trumped-up story of his own death. Aeschylus and Euripides both place the recognition between brother and sister early in the play. They then act in concert to carry out the vengeance. Sophocles puts the recognition late. He thereby builds up suspense for this preliminary climax, emphasizes Electra's isolation, and shows the intense personal ties between brother and sister. The postponement of the recognition also enables him to ring the changes on Electra's emotions as she swings from hope at his arrival to despair at the news of his supposed death and then back to joy when she discovers him actually alive.

Unfortunately we cannot establish the exact chronological relation between Sophocles' *Electra* and Euripides'. The similarities between the two plays are clearly too great to be coincidental. Besides many verbal similarities, both works stress the maltreatment of Electra, the license of Clytemnestra, the hatred between mother and daughter, and the mother's moral and emotional vulnerability to her daughter. Euripides characteristically depicts the more sordid side of things. Was Euripides responding polemically to Sophocles' lofty tone, showing an alternative way of envisioning such a situation, or did Sophocles write his play as an answer to Euripides' harsher realism and degrading of the mythical past? We do not know. Euripides' play is now dated, on stylistic grounds, to around 420 B.C. For Sophocles' play there is no sure date, but it should be within a few years, either way, of Euripides'. The intricacy of the plot—in its own way as subtle as that of the *Oedipus Tyrannus*—argues for a late date. In its full treatment of the characters, ra-

pidity of reversals, and complicated intrigue that rests entirely with the human figures, the play resembles *Philoctetes* (409 B.C.); but stylistic features alone are too uncertain a basis for chronology.

Despite the sudden reversals and what might be considered a happy ending (insofar as the protagonists defeat their enemies and survive), the mood is grim and austere. The action centers on hatred and matricidal vengeance. The narrow enclosure of Electra's life is heavily emphasized. Death and darkness predominate in the imagery. The choral odes offer little relief, for they are rather unlyrical and focus narrowly on the present events or their immediate antecedents. They have little of the varied geography or wide-ranging mythical paradigms that one finds in the odes of the other plays.

The atmosphere of austerity comes largely from Sophocles' conception of Electra herself, "a figure so tightly bound," as Virginia Woolf perceptively wrote in *The Common Reader* (1925), "that she can only move an inch this way, an inch that. But each movement must tell to the utmost, or, bound as she is, . . . she will be nothing but a dummy, tightly bound." At her first appearance her long, lyrical lament just outside the palace gate contrasts with the practical energy and goal-directed curtness of Orestes and his old tutor (1–120). That contrast is maintained throughout and reaches its climax in the recognition scene. Here Orestes, carrying the urn that supposedly holds his ashes as part of his trick to gain access to the palace, is overcome by the sight of Electra's misery. For once faltering in his straight path to his goal, he decides not to go through with the plan of deceiving Electra and tells her the truth. Electra's lyrical cries of joy, however, are again stifled by the dangers around them and by the pressure to act before the plot is discovered or Aegisthus returns. And so Electra must once more close up feelings and suppress love and joy in favor of hatred and killing: "Do not fear that [my mother] will ever see my face bright with laughter," she reassures Orestes; "so deep has the ancient hatred melted into me" (1309–1310).

The sequence is repeated when she recognizes the old tutor, another friend. But he sternly admonishes her with the urgent necessity to act: "Now Clytemnestra is alone, no man inside" (1368–1369). It is part of Electra's tragedy that for all her triumph and ultimate vindication of justice she is able, in these circumstances, to fulfill her capacity for hatred rather than for love. This is the difference between her and Antigone, whom she otherwise resembles in devotion to the family and in determination.

Although Sophocles firmly subordinates the supernatural elements to human characterization, the repeated prayers to the Furies, the underworld deities, and to Apollo's oracles remind us that they are not entirely absent (32–38, 110–120, 634–659, 1376–1383, 1424–1425). Clytemnestra is initially troubled by bad dreams about Agamemnon, which she tries to appease by offerings at his tomb. These signs of what we would call a guilty conscience afford Electra her first chance to act against her mother, persuading her sister, Chrysothemis, not to lay Clytemnestra's offerings at the tomb. Later the grave-offerings become the occasion for an ironical inversion of appearance and reality characteristic of the mature Sophocles. Seeing Orestes' offerings at his father's grave, Chrysothemis joyfully reports his return to Electra. Electra, totally taken in by the false story of her brother's death, convinces Chrysothemis, but then is unsuccessful in enlisting her aid in performing the act of vengeance. Thus falsehood momentarily wins out over truth, death over life. This reversal is the crisis in which Electra, now believing herself totally alone, resolves to execute the vengeance by herself. This is Electra's moment of heroic trial. The recognition of Orestes in the next scene comes almost too late to reverse the erosion of her softer, more loving qualities. When she and Orestes finally are joined together, happiness is overshadowed by the terrible act of matricide. Orestes enters the house for the deed. The chorus shudders at the dreadful cries; but Electra, standing beside them, shouts out to him, "Strike if you have strength a second blow," and then again, "If only Aegisthus were there too" (1415–1416).

The sudden arrival of Aegisthus gives no time to pause, and Electra quickly shifts from open exultation to clever guile. She is now the one to take the active role in trickery, leading her enemy to his death. Yet at the very end, as her vengeance is almost complete, she asks Orestes not to prolong the final killing. These last words of hers (1483–1490), full of ambiguities, strike a note of weariness rather than joyful success. Without paying much heed to his sister's plea for a quick end, Orestes does in fact draw out his revenge, amid ominous warnings about the "present and future woes" of the house of Atreus (1493–1500).

It is hard to assess the tone and meaning of this difficult play. Technically it is one of Sophocles' best. As a work of theater, it is second perhaps only to the *Oedipus Tyrannus*. Sophocles builds up a crescendo of intense emotions from the news of Clytemnestra's dream to the first face-to-face confrontation between mother and daughter, and then to the alternations between hope and despair, joy and sorrow, in the reversals that culminate in the great recognition scene. Yet for all the manipulation of truth and falsehood, which is largely manipulation of Electra, nothing seems done only for effect. This is due to the strong unity of the play in its involving and complex central character and also to the symmetry of the plot, the seriousness of the themes, and the poetical force of the language.

Philoctetes *and* Oedipus at Colonus

The melodramatic plot structure of the *Electra* also characterizes the last two extant plays. In both *Philoctetes* and *Oedipus at Colonus* a character clearly marked as a villain—Odysseus and Creon, respectively—makes a sudden appearance, momentarily gains the upper hand, and then has to retreat ignominiously at the protagonist's victory, thanks to the aid of a strong and noble ally (Neoptolemus, Theseus). Neither play is quite a tragedy in the modern sense: both have a more or less happy ending, marked by a victory of sorts for the protagonist, as may be said for the *Electra* too. In this respect ancient tragedy is a rather open and fluid genre. Yet in all three plays the hero's victory has somber tones and contains genuinely tragic elements.

In both the *Philoctetes* and the *Oedipus at Colonus* this tragic element rests with a protagonist who has passed through terrible suffering. Diseased or polluted, enfeebled or outcast, this hero still retains an inward power and possesses thereby some mysterious and potent good that the society needs. Philoctetes owns the unerring bow that Heracles gave him in the past, and without it the Greek army cannot capture Troy. Oedipus brings to Athens the blessings that his body, to be buried in a tomb known only to King Theseus, will confer on the city. Yet the possession of such blessings does nothing to soften the harsh outlines of these figures. Philoctetes is devoured by an inward rancor as bitter as the outward ravages of his ulcerous wound. Oedipus, though full of love for his daughters, Antigone and Ismene, calls down murderous curses on the heads of his sons, Polyneices and Eteocles. "Help your friends and harm your enemies," not "Turn the other cheek," expresses the dominant ethic of these heroes (and much of Greek culture).

In both figures Sophocles has distilled the heroic personage that he had been developing since the *Ajax*: unbending will, fierce commitment to their personal loyalties and hatreds, a mysterious destiny from the gods that sets them apart from others but also makes them indispensable to the society that casts them out. Through these two outwardly ruined and physically maimed men—Philoctetes a diseased cripple, Oedipus a blind beggar polluted by incest and patricide—Sophocles expresses that paradoxical relation between outer and inner strength, physical helplessness and spiritual power, that he had presented most fully in the shifting between surface appearances and hidden truth in *Oedipus Tyrannus*.

In both these last plays divine intervention plays a large, though still obscure, role. In the *Philoctetes* the divinized hero, Heracles, descends from Olympus to resolve Philoctetes' tragic dilemma. In *Oedipus at Colonus* the gods themselves call the hero to his mysterious resting place.

The *Philoctetes*, securely dated to 409 B.C. by the ancient Argument appended to the play, is perhaps Sophocles' richest work in the three-way interaction of major characters—Philoctetes, Neoptolemus, and Odysseus. Though written as much as half a century after *Ajax*, it resembles that play in its concern with heroic integrity. Like Ajax, Philoctetes opts for suffering rather than yield to his enemies. Yet whereas Ajax must see his decision out to its inexorable end in death, Philoctetes is saved by a sudden yielding and concern on the part of the gods.

Sophocles drew on the story of Philoctetes in the post-Homeric epics about the sack of Troy. Both Aeschylus and Euripides before him had written a *Philoctetes*. The second-century A.D. essayist Dio of Prusa provides a brief comparison in his fifty-second oration. Both earlier plays, like Sophocles', centered on the persuasion of Philoctetes, whom the Greek army had left on Lemnos when he was bitten by the viper that guarded the goddess Chryse's shrine. The embittered hero is needed for the capture of Troy, but he obviously hates the army that has cruelly abandoned him. Aeschylus' version is obscure, but in both his and Euripides' play, Lemnos is inhabited. Sophocles has intensified his hero's isolation and misery by making it a deserted island. Euripides' play had the added tension that the Trojans simultaneously send an embassy to win Philoctetes over to their side. It seems probable that the role of Neoptolemus and the emphasis on Odysseus' unscrupulousness, along with the deserted island, are Sophoclean innovations.

Both the young Neoptolemus and the mature Philoctetes are, in a sense, alienated from their true natures: Neoptolemus in abandoning the heroic spirit of his father, Achilles, for the trickery and lies of Odysseus; Philoctetes in clinging to his deserted island and using the noble bow of Heracles, symbol of heroic achievement and comradeship, to maintain his savage and lonely life. Neoptolemus finally chooses the uncompromising cripple over the shifty but superficially successful Odysseus. He gets a lesson in commitment and firmness from the older man's reduced life. The embittered outcast learns from his young companion a fresh capacity for trust and friendship. Each has a complementary message for the other; and each helps the other back to a lost nobility of nature, one of the chief themes in the play. Neoptolemus finally reclaims his heritage as the son of the great Achilles; Philoctetes vindicates his right to possess Heracles' bow, rekindling in himself the spirit of heroic loyalty and friendship through which he won it.

In the process the two men undergo a series of complex reversals. Neoptolemus changes from manipulator to sympathizer. Philoctetes, though won over from mistrust to belief in his new friend, remains intractable even in the face of Neoptolemus' reasonable and concerned arguments and the prophecy of his cure at Troy. He would rather hold fast to his disease and his desolate island than help the men who left him to lonely suffering. In his decision there is a tragic choice that, for all its self-destructive harshness and unreasonable stubbornness, has its justice and commands our respect.

Were Philoctetes to persevere in this decision, he would follow the tragic path of Ajax and Antigone. Instead Heracles—no longer the violent and tormented figure of the *Trachinian Women*, but a divinized embodiment of heroic action and excellence *(aretē)*—comes from the gods to persuade Philoctetes (1409–1444). He does not add any new facts to the arguments and prophecies that Neoptolemus had cited in the previous scene; but he can speak of these with the authority of his own heroism, the suffering and the "eternal excellence" that stamped his own life with greatness.

This use of the "god from the machine" (*deus ex machina*), virtually unique in Sophocles, has

been variously interpreted. Psychologically, Heracles can be understood as the symbol of Philoctetes' capacity for friendship and heroic action: he reveals to Philoctetes what it means to have received the gift of the bow. Theologically, he shows not only the gods' recognition of his endurance and the justice of his cause, but also his place in a larger order. He announces the ineluctable demands of history, the broader pattern of which the individual human life is a part. To live on a deserted island as a lonely hunter is to be a beast or a savage, not a human being. Philoctetes is not allowed, either for himself or for others, to lead a life of meaningless suffering. He must leave behind his desert island and be healed of his festering wound— both symbols of the inward disease of hatred that separates him from other men—to share the toil, the social demands, and the rewards of his place in history.

And yet Sophocles does not entirely efface the discrepancy between human feelings and the divine will. He shows the gods as ultimately rewarding good, but not requiting evil. Philoctetes is forced to help the generals who inflicted on him ten years of lonely misery. Nothing is said of their punishment. The gods mysteriously intervene to save Philoctetes from prolonging that suffering, but its original cause is still left unexplained. Neoptolemus rather feebly cites "enduring fortunes from the gods" or "divine chance" (1316, 1326). Yet this unresolved obscurity remains as the dark and mysterious side of the divine power.

Produced posthumously by Sophocles' grandson in 401 B.C., *Oedipus at Colonus* (also called *Oedipus Coloneus*) shows the same mixture of reconciliation and harshness as *Philoctetes*. The old Oedipus, near the end of his life, has lost nothing of his intransigence. For all his physical weakness, he has the power of anger and bitterness that can repulse King Creon, who would take him back to Thebes, and he curses his sons in a spirit of unforgiving wrath. Yet we first see him leaning weakly on the arm of Antigone, his companion and support in exile, finding his way painfully to the grove of the Furies on the outskirts of Athens. His love and concern for his two daughters are touchingly drawn. Encountering the fearful reactions of the chorus of elders who inhabit the nearby village of Colonus, Oedipus courageously confronts the pollutions of his past. He argues passionately and convincingly for his moral innocence, on the grounds that he acted in ignorance, not intentionally. This is Sophocles' answer, at the legal and rational level, to the moral dilemmas of the earlier *Oedipus* some quarter-century before.

The theme of purification of the past, however, will dominate the play, literally in the ritual libations that Oedipus will perform to enter the Furies' grove as a suppliant, symbolically in his separation from the accursed Theban past that would pull him back, through Creon's violent abduction and Polyneices' entreaty. At the end, when the gods call him to his grave to be a cult-hero in the Attic land, that separation is complete. The goddesses who avenge the pollution of blood in familial crimes have proven to be not the terrible Erinyes, but the Eumenides, "the Kindly Ones." Symbolically reenacting his crime by entering a forbidden place of female powers, Oedipus finds there a place of rest and cleansing, not punishment.

This spirit of purification marks the play's conscious reuse of the earlier *Oedipus*. Sophocles combines the traditional story of Oedipus' crimes with a local legend of his burial at Colonus, where Sophocles himself had lived. As usual he has interpreted the myth in his own way and freely added details of his own invention, including probably the role of Theseus, the traditional idealized king of early Athens. At the time of writing, near the end of the Peloponnesian War, Athenian territory was under constant attack and invasion. The blessings of the hero's tomb at the city's frontier evoke nostalgically the inviolate beauty of the Attic landscape, particularly in the celebrated ode describing the grove (668–719), and also suggest a paradox in Athens akin to that in Oedipus: a spiritual greatness in the midst of apparent weakness.

The figure of Oedipus in this play is a plausible extension of what the Oedipus of the *Tyrannus* might be twenty or thirty years later. We should recall that the order of events in the myth follows the sequence of *Tyrannus*, *Coloneus*, *Antigone*, whereas Sophocles wrote the plays in the order *Antigone*, *Tyrannus*, *Coloneus*, with long intervals between. Antigone, whom we see at a point before the heroic sacrifice that she makes in the *Antigone*, is as devoted to family as one would expect. Her generous attempt to intervene in Polyneices' behalf is in character with the later portrayal, as is the intimation of tragic doom in her failure and in her selfless decision at the end of the play to return to Thebes to prevent the fratricidal battle. Creon's character is drawn in harder outlines: violent, irascible, overbearing, and unscrupulous, he is not at variance with the narrow-minded and tyrannical ruler of the *Antigone*, but he is considerably further along the path from the efficient, cautious, precise, and as yet untested figure of the *Tyrannus*.

The long debates between Creon and Oedipus in the middle of the *Coloneus* and between Oedipus and Polyneices near the end may seem too slow for the modern reader. Both scenes, however, are crucial for Oedipus' gradual separation from his polluted Theban past and for his entrance as a hero to the Athenian land. The former scene is enlivened by Theseus' melodramatic rescue of Oedipus' daughters from Creon's outrageous kidnapping. The latter is itself a miniature tragedy. Neither Oedipus nor Polyneices will bend. Antigone tries to effect a reconciliation, but to no effect, and Polyneices marches off to fulfill the terrible curses of Oedipus. One can glimpse here a trace of the old Aeschylean pattern of the family curse, but Sophocles once more subordinates supernatural mystery to the study of intense emotions and the psychological realities of bitter father-son conflict.

Oedipus' power of prophetic curse also marks his own mysterious proximity to the gods. Even as Polyneices leaves the stage for his doomed expedition, Oedipus recognizes the thunder and lightning of the gods' call to him. The frightened chorus summons Theseus. In an electrifying *coup de théâtre* Oedipus, now sure of his powers, gives instructions about his tomb and the blessings it will bring. Fully in command, the blind old man leads his children and the youthful king:

> My children, follow me. For I am revealed now your guide, as you were once your father's. Come, and touch me not, but let me find the holy tomb itself, where it is my portion to be hidden in this earth. This way. Yes, here, for here Hermes Guide of Souls leads me, and so does the goddess Persephone below. O light that is no light, once before you were mine; now for the last time my body grasps you. For now I walk the last road of my life, which I shall close henceforth within Hades' dark.
>
> (1542–1552)

The end itself is shrouded in mystery. We hear only of Theseus shielding his eyes and praying to the gods of earth and sky. Oedipus has vanished, inexplicably.

For all the sublime poetry of the hero's end, Sophocles does not allow us to remain in the realm of the gods. The last scene of the play belongs to the human survivors, the distraught and bereft sisters, Antigone and Ismene. Oedipus' mysterious end does not ease their pain at the loss of a father. Despite Theseus' consolation of a "grace from the gods below," Antigone would see her father's tomb and die. In her desperate grief we recognize the passionate violence of that Theban heritage to which she will return. She accedes to Theseus' prohibition about the tomb, but finally wins from him the promise to send her back to Thebes to avert her brothers' deaths there (1768–1776). For all of Oedipus' transcendent passage to the unknown beyond human life, we are shown clearly that the tragedy on earth is not over.

CONCLUSION

Looking back from Sophocles' last two works to *Ajax* or *Antigone*, written from three to four decades earlier, one sees that the poet has not significantly softened the lines of his heroes' personalities, but at least suggests, in his last plays, the possibility of a reconciliation between the harsh demands of the heroes' natures and the gods, even though this is mysterious or cannot occur on earth. Philoctetes is like an Ajax whom the gods, at the last minute, permit to escape from self-chosen and self-destructive suffering by showing him a way out of his intransigence. The old Oedipus of the *Coloneus* carries with him all the irrational suffering of his younger self, but now receives an answer to those terrible questions about the absurdity of life that the earlier play so urgently raised. For both Philoctetes and Oedipus the gods, after much time, give suffering a meaning. The pattern of lonely endurance and inner struggle receives an ultimate validation that becomes clear and visible to all.

It is hard to avoid the implication that in these last two plays, both written in his eighties, Sophocles is reflecting on the meaning of his own art: the power of tragedy itself to probe through the dark confusion of irrational suffering and elicit from the tragic myths blessings as well as curses. The poet, like the hero, enters the realm of the unknown and emerges into the light of eternal things. In presenting heroes who, by the simple force of their own being, break through the complicated intrigues and false appearances of the world around them, Sophocles may be more or less consciously looking back from the intellectualized relativism of his contemporaries to a view of myth and art as a vehicle still for absolute values. He seems to have achieved here something of what Thomas Mann (in "Freud and the Future") describes as the heightened insight of the mature artist who has "acquired the habit of regarding life as mythical and typical," namely, "a smiling knowledge of the eternal, the ever-being and authentic." The sublime finale of the *Oedipus at Colonus*, where the hidden divine voice calls the battered, ancient sufferer to the unknown place where his bones will confer blessings on Athens, allows us to think that Sophocles, at the end, may have viewed his own life and work in some such terms.

Selected Bibliography

TEXTS

Sophocle, edited by A. Dain and P. Mazon. 3 vols. Paris, 1955, 1958, 1970. Budé edition, excellent Greek text with facing French translation; useful introduction and notes.

Sophocles, edited by R. C. Jebb. Cambridge, 1897. Conservative Greek text.

Sophoclis Fabulae, edited by A. C. Pearson. Oxford, 1924. The standard Greek text in the U.S. and U. K. Sometimes arbitrary in emendations.

Sophoclis Tragoediae, edited by R. D. Dawe. 2 vols. Leipzig, 1975, 1979. New Teubner text, based on a fresh collation of the manuscripts.

TRANSLATIONS

Arrowsmith, William, ed. *The Greek Tragedy in New Translations.* So far comprises *Antigone*, translated by R. E. Braun. New York, 1973; *Oedipus the King*, translated by Stephen Berg and Diskin Clay. New York, 1978; *Women of Trachis*, translated by C. K. Williams and G. W. Dickerson. New York, 1978. New contemporary verse translations; full introductions.

Fitts, Dudley, and Robert Fitzgerald. *The Oedipus Cycle.* New York, 1949. Contains the two *Oedipus* plays and *Antigone*. More poetical than the Lattimore-Grene collection; rather freer with the original in the choral odes.

Lattimore, Richmond, and David Grene, eds. *The Complete Greek Tragedies. Sophocles*, vol. 2. Chicago, 1957. Various translators. Clear and contemporary idiom. Faithful but sometimes prosaic; uneven. Helpful introductions.

Storr, F. *Sophocles, with an English Translation.* 2 vols. London and New York, 1912, 1913. Loeb Classical Library. Facing Greek and English texts; rather stilted.

Watling, E. F. *Sophocles, The Theban Plays.* Harmondsworth, 1947. Colloquial and readable modern verse translation.

FRAGMENTS

Pearson, A. C., ed. *Fragments of Sophocles.* 3 vols. Cambridge, 1971. Radt, Stefan, ed. *Sophocles.* Vol. 4 of *Tragicorum Graecorum Fragementa.* Göttingen, 1977. Includes ancient biographical sources, criticism in antiquity, and testimonia.

LEXICON

Ellendt, Fridericus. *Lexicon Sophocleum.* 2nd ed. Berlin, 1872. Reprinted Hildesheim, 1965. In Latin.

COMMENTARIES

ALL SEVEN PLAYS

Cambell, Lewis. *Sophocles.* 2nd ed. 2 vols. Oxford, 1879–1881. Valuable introduction; Greek text.

Jebb, R. C. *Sophocles, the Plays and Fragments.* 7 vols. Cambridge, 1892–1907. Greek text; facing translation. Valuable introductions, notes, critical appendix. Indispensable.

Kamerbeek, J. C. *The Plays of Sophocles.* 6 vols. of 7. Leiden, 1953– . Useful introductions. No Greek text. Full-scale commentary, especially helpful for diction, linguistic and grammatical details, staging.

INDIVIDUAL PLAYS

AJAX

Stanford, W. B., ed. *Sophocles, Ajax.* London, 1963. Contains Greek text.

ELECTRA

Kells, J. H., ed. *Sophocles, Electra.* Cambridge, 1973. Contains Greek text.

OEDIPUS TYRANNUS

Gould, Thomas, ed. *Oedipus the King.* Englewood Cliffs, N.J., 1970. Contains English translation.

Sheppard, J. T., ed. *The Oedipus Tyrannus of Sophocles.* Cambridge, 1920. Contains Greek text, facing English translation, interpretive essay.

PHILOCTETES

Webster, T. B. L., ed. *Sophocles' "Philoctetes."* Cambrige, 1970. Contains Greek text.

CRITICISM

Adams, S. M. *Sophocles the Playwright.* Phoenix, supplement 3. Toronto, 1957.

Bowra, C. M. *Sophoclean Tragedy.* Oxford, 1944.

Burton, R. W. B. *The Chorus in Sophocles' Tragedies.* Oxford, 1980.

SOPHOCLES

Cameron, Alistair. *The Identity of Oedipus the King.* New York, 1968.

Cook, Albert. *Enactment: Greek Tragedy.* Chicago, 1971.

Ehrenberg, Victor. *Sophocles and Pericles.* Oxford, 1954.

Gellie, George H. *Sophocles, A Reading.* Melbourne, 1972.

Goheen, R. F. *The Imagery of Sophocles' "Antigone."* Princeton, 1951.

Jones, John. *On Aristotle and Greek Tragedy.* London, 1962.

Kirkwood, G. M. *A Study of Sophoclean Drama.* Cornell Studies in Classical Philology 31. Ithaca, N.Y., 1958.

Kitto, H. D. F. *Form and Meaning in Drama.* London, 1956.

———. *Greek Tragedy.* Garden City, N.Y., 1955.

———. *Sophocles: Dramatist and Philosopher.* London, 1958.

Knox, B. M. W. "The *Ajax* of Sophocles." *Harvard Studies in Classical Philology* 65: 1–37 (1961).

———. *The Heroic Temper.* Sather Classical Lectures 35. Berkeley and Los Angeles, 1964.

———. *Oedipus at Thebes.* New Haven, 1957.

Lattimore, Richmond. *The Poetry of Greek Tragedy.* Baltimore, 1958

———. *Story Patterns in Greek Tragedy.* Ann Arbor, 1965.

Letters, F. J. H. *The Life and Work of Sophocles.* London, 1953.

Long, A. A. *Language and Thought in Sophocles.* London, 1968.

Musurillo, Herbert. *The Light and the Darkness.* Leiden, 1967.

Opstelten, J. C. *Sophocles and Greek Pessimism.* Translated by J. A. Ross. Amsterdam, 1952.

Reinhardt, Karl. *Sophokles* (1947). Translated by F. and H. Harvey. Oxford, 1979.

Rosenmeyer, Thomas G. *The Masks of Tragedy.* Austin, Tex., 1963.

Segal, Charles. *Tragedy and Civilization: An Interpretation of Sophocles.* Martin Classical Lectures 26. Cambridge, Mass., 1981.

Taplin, Oliver. *Greek Tragedy in Action.* Berkeley and Los Angeles, 1978.

Vickers, Brian. *Towards Greek Tragedy.* London, 1973.

Waldock, A. J. A. *Sophocles the Dramatist.* Cambridge, 1951.

Webster, T. B. L. *An Introduction to Sophocles.* Oxford, 1936.

Whitman, Cedric H. *Sophocles: A Study of Heroic Humanism.* Cambridge, Mass., 1951.

Winnington-Ingram, R. P. *Sophocles: An Interpretation.* Cambridge, 1980.

Woodard, Thomas, ed. *Sophocles: A Collection of Critical Essays.* Englewood Cliffs, N.J., 1966.

CHARLES SEGAL

HERODOTUS

(*ca.* 484–420 B.C.)

THE FATHER OF HISTORY

EVEN THE HONORIFIC title that has been bestowed on Herodotus since antiquity points to some of the most vexing problems that arise in assessing him. Its obvious meaning (and what was meant by his ancient admirers) is that the *Histories* are the first work of history as we understand it, that Herodotus created a literary genre which wove rational analysis of cause and effect into an artful narrative of events, and that, as such, it served as a model for all other ancient historians. But there is a tendency among some critics to award Herodotus the paternity without granting him the substance, to suggest that, while he paved the way for history, he himself does not deserve to be called a historian. Rather than being the "onlie begetter" of the genre, he is demoted to being only the begetter. Serious students of history and historiography, therefore, have been inclined (with a few notable exceptions) to say less of the father than of the metaphorical son—Thucydides. There can be no doubt that, to judge from what that writer says, he had little respect for any of his forerunners as historians.

Many features of the *Histories* contribute to the denigration of Herodotus as a historian. The organization of the work is loose by modern (or even Thucydidean) standards; Herodotus takes an apparently inordinate pleasure in telling stories that seem to have little relevance to his historical subject, the Persian Wars; the gods fig-ure disproportionately in a work describing factual events; and imagination rather than careful documentation is responsible for too much of the information: How can Herodotus have known exactly what was said in Persian bedrooms? Comments on Herodotus by both ancient and modern critics reinforce the feeling that the virtue of the *Histories* lies less in historical analysis than in the pleasures of the text. Dionysius of Halicarnassus, a professed admirer of Herodotus writing in the age of Augustus, seems to damn the historian with praise that he surely did not mean to sound faint by complimenting him for choosing a topic that delighted readers; it is the charm of the work, not its historical accuracy, that he considers worthy of admiration. Plutarch, who found a great deal to object to in Herodotus, was forced to praise the style of the *Histories* for its sweetness and grace at the same time that he accused the historian of being untruthful. To cite but one modern judgment, the historian Edward Gibbon, in one of those footnotes for which *The Decline and Fall of the Roman Empire* is justly renowned, referred to Herodotus as one "who sometimes writes for children and sometimes for philosophers."

From the very first book of the *Histories*, it is not hard to see why these two classes of people should be named as appropriate readers. The stories of the beautiful, if imposing, wife of Candaules, of Arion and the dolphin, of Peisistratus' chicanery, of Astyages' cannibalistic dinner party, of the greatest of the Persian kings beginning his life as a simple farm boy and ending it as a wine sack—all these, on the one hand, easily excite the interest of even the most jaded of children. The emphasis on the role of fate, Solon's disquisition on the mutability of human fortune and his advice not to consider anyone happy until he is dead, the tragic tale of Adrastus and Atys—these, on the other hand, show an equal interest in ethical instruction.

Herodotus' unquestioned skill as a narrative artist leads also to comparison with his greatest predecessor in that form. Longinus calls him the "most Homeric," and Plutarch, in the passage referred to above, uses an allusion to the *Odyssey* (11.368) to impugn the veracity of the historian:

> He told "his story like a bard" not "knowingly" but sweetly and subtly.

Herodotus, indeed, invites comparison with Homer. Whole episodes seem to be designed with Homeric models in mind. When, just before embarking on the expedition to Greece, Xerxes is influenced by the advice of Artabanus to give up the enterprise, he has a dream in which a handsome young man addresses him:

> Are you changing your mind, Persian, and will you not lead your army against Greece even though you've ordered the Persians to muster? You do not do well to change and the one standing here will not forgive you. But just as you planned during the day, continue on that course.
>
> (7.12)

No reader could fail to be reminded of the "evil dream" that Zeus sent to Agamemnon at the beginning of book 2 of the *Iliad,* and no reader could fail to expect the result of obeying the vision to be as disastrous in the one case as in the other. Another clear example of imitation in episodic construction is Herodotus' description of the death of Leonidas at Thermopylae and of the struggle for his body (7.225), a passage de-signed to evoke the Homeric description of the struggle over the body of Patroclus.

Other features of the *Histories* seem equally Homeric. Herodotus' catalogs are reminiscent of the catalog of ships in the *Iliad* (book 2); when the historian speaks of the sailing of the twenty Athenian ships to help the Ionians in their revolt, an expedition that, in Herodotus' narrative, is one of the proximate causes of the Persian Wars, he describes it as "the beginning of evils" (5.97), a phrase that alludes to Homer's description of Paris' ships (*Iliad* 5.63) as "beginning evils." What is more, not only Herodotus in the narrative but his own characters in their speeches seem to have Homer constantly in mind. Croesus (1.45) attempts to ease the mind of Adrastus, accidental murderer of Croesus' son, with a phrase that echoes Priam's chivalrous exculpation of Helen in the *Iliad* (3.161 ff.). When Artabanus warns Mardonius of the dangers of the expedition against Greece, he imagines him "lying a prey to dogs and birds somewhere in the land of the Athenians" (7.10), a clear allusion to the opening lines of the *Iliad.* Similarly, Dionysius of Phocaea, exhorting the Ionians to energetic preparation against the Persians, says that their affairs are "on the razor's edge" (6.11), a reminiscence of a speech of Nestor's in the *Iliad* (10.169 ff.); and Pausanias, rejecting advice to crucify the Persian general (9.79), does so in words that recall Odysseus' rebuke of Eurycleia for exulting over the death of the suitors (*Odyssey* 22.411 ff.).

The preface to Herodotus' work provides the historian's views on how he is both like and unlike Homer, a demonstration of why the *Histories* are both Homeric and un-Homeric. In the very opening of the book, Herodotus announces that one of his aims is to prevent the deeds of the Greeks and the barbarians from losing glory, becoming *aklea.* This word harks back to the subject of Homeric epic, the glorious deeds of men (*klea andrōn*). And when, at the end of the preface, Herodotus declares that he will speak of great and small cities of men, he alludes as clearly to the opening of the *Od-*

yssey (1.3) as the earlier Homeric word does to the *Iliad*. To judge from these echoes, and from the Homeric quality that we have seen pervades the narrative, Herodotus is claiming the right to be read as a prose Homer, a historical writer of epic.

But if Herodotus claims this right, he affords equally clear indications of how his work differs from Homer's. In discussing the legend of Helen in Egypt, he shows that he regarded the decorum of epic as different from that of history:

> In my opinion, Homer knew this story, but since it was less suitable to epic poetry than the version he actually used, he deliberately rejected it, although he has revealed that he did in fact know it.
>
> (2.116)

The very opening words of the *Histories* display Herodotus' sense of the profound differences between his work and the epic poems, and one need only look at the first lines of the three works to see it:

> Sing, Goddess, the wrath of Achilles. . . .
> *(Iliad)*

> Tell me, Muse, of the man of many wiles. . . .
> *(Odyssey)*

> This is the demonstration of the research of Herodotus of Halicarnassus. . . .
> *(Histories)*

On the most basic level, Homer's poems are anonymous, and the invocation to the Muse (whether literally meant or merely a rhetorical gesture is irrelevant) provides the only authentication of what Homer says: he asks his divine inspirer to give knowledge of the subject, which he can learn from no other source.

Herodotus' opening is quite different. He names himself as author in the first words, and he claims sole responsibility for what he writes. Homer, in beginning the catalog of ships in the *Iliad* (book 2), had felt the need to reinvoke a divine authority to recall the specific details of the Greek force:

> for you are goddesses, are present and know all things,
> but we know only the report . . .
>
> (2.485–486)

Herodotus, by contrast, had been present at many of the places (if not the events) that he describes, and he shows no reluctance to speak in the first person of what he knows; he is also careful to distinguish the sources of his information. After he recounts the rationalized versions of early Greek-Asian hostilities in book 1, chapters 1–5, he dismisses them in order to report things "in our knowledge." When he goes to Egypt, he is careful to distinguish what he has seen from what he has heard:

> Thus far what I have said has been based on my own observation, judgment and inquiry; I am now going on to use accounts from the Egyptians, although I shall add to them things I myself have seen.
>
> (2.99)

First person statements, even second person addresses, are infrequent in Homer; in Herodotus, we are constantly made aware of an author who sifts evidence, makes judgments, and is the only person responsible, finally, for what is said.

The difference in attitude toward what is said between Homer and Herodotus is, in fact, embodied in the word that Herodotus gives his work, *historie*. Although it is usually translated as "research," its etymological connections are somewhat different. In the *Iliad*, the word *histor* occurs twice: once it is the term for an arbitrator in a lawsuit (18.401), and once the umpire at a race (23.486); in Hesiod and the *Homeric Hymns*, it refers to someone who knows, or who has a skill; in an old inscription from Thespiae, it is the word for a witness. (In this, it is interesting to note, the development of the word in Chinese for "history" is precisely similar: *shih*, the character for "historian," also denotes an arbiter, umpire, or record keeper in a contest.) The word *historie*, therefore, implies more than mere inquiry: it suggests both the witnessing of actions and the exercise of judgment about what is seen and heard. And in that connection, the starting points of the narratives of the *Iliad* and the *Histories* offer a sharp distinction. Where Homer begins by asking which *god* started the quarrel of Achilles and Agamemnon, Herodotus announces that he will dismiss speculations about mythic time:

> I am not going to decide which of the two stories is true, but I shall name the man I myself know was the first to attack the Greeks unjustly and then continue with my history.
>
> (1.5)

Intimately connected with the divergence of Herodotus' ideas about authorial responsibility and about the nature of evidence from those of Homer are their differing views on the nature of their subject and of its relationship to the present. Homer speaks of a distant past, one so remote that there is no real connection between it and the present time of either the author or the audience. When he says that a hero lifted a rock so huge that it would take five men nowadays to lift, or when Nestor compares the heroes of the Trojan War with those of his youth, there is a sense of historical time only in that both Homer and his Nestor feel that there was a decline, the reasons for which are neither stated nor sought, between "then" and "now." In the same way, Hesiod, telling the story of the ages of man in the *Works and Days*, is interested only in the fact of progressive decline, but demonstrates no real curiosity about how and why age gave way to age, and offers no indication of the precise link between the mythic time of the ages and the historical time in which he wrote. Homer, his Nestor, and Hesiod all look at the past, but they have none of the historian's desire to explain its development or to use it in order to understand the origins of the present. Mythic time, in these works, is filled with discontinuities, unconnected episodes, and plain gaps.

More important, perhaps, is the fact that Homer and Hesiod demonstrate an antihistorical insistence on the lack of progress, on the mere fact of decline. This is fundamentally opposed to Herodotus' desire not only to seek causes for present events in past actions, but also to point out the first discoverers of things, to illustrate growth and positive development, as is particularly the case with political institutions. The change from tyranny to democracy, the growth of constitutions, the development of Spartan *eunomia*—"law and order"—all these subjects are the hallmarks of a writer who is interested in charting, in a historical manner, the organic connections between past and present.

It is, finally, the sense of the authorial voice and its location in time that most distinguish Herodotus from Homer. Where the epic poet is merely the medium through which tradition, in the shape of the Muse, can convey a discontinuous past to an unspecific present, Herodotus has a far more active role. He bears the responsibility for what he reports; his active judgment is employed in the sifting and arranging of his material; and, above all, it is his task to bear witness. His purpose, as he states in the opening sentence, is to preserve the great deeds of the past from losing glory and from fading away. It is the function of the historian to remind his present audience of the immediate and disturbing significance of past glory.

THE SHAPE OF THE HISTORIES

Even though Homer at the opening of the *Odyssey* invites his Muse to begin the story at a place of her own choosing, while Herodotus deliberately selects a starting place that fits his own topic, the *Histories* at first sight seem to show less care in both the selection and the arrangement of material than the Homeric poems. A Muse, perhaps, was obliged to follow more exacting standards than a historian in the matter of constructing a work of art, but still it seems peculiar for Herodotus to claim at the start that his subject is the wars of Greece and Persia and then immediately to leap back to the history of Lydia, to give accounts of Media, Persia, Ionia, Egypt, Scythia, Libya, and Thrace before even approaching the immediate background to the Persian Wars. The arrangement of the *Histories* hardly seems to demonstrate a historian's sense of what is important.

Some features of Herodotus' narrative style would have appeared less unusual to contemporaries than to modern readers. Early Greek narrative did not proceed in a linear fashion; it was customary to begin from the point of immediate interest, then to give background, and only then to return to the starting point. Where a later writer would follow a stricter chronological or geographical framework, as in the case of Thucydides or Polybius, the archaic mode of narration encouraged backtracking and digression to such an extent that the clear line of the main narrative is at times obscured by what is contained in the back-circling rings. There are moments when Herodotus seems aware that all he says is not entirely germane to his historical subject and thus—to adapt the unfortunate schoolboy's description of Dante—stands with one foot in the archaic age and with the other reaches out toward the classical style. He defends the longest of his digressions by explaining that it is so long because its topic, Egypt, possesses more wonders than any other country (2.35); he interrupts a digression by telling us what we already know, that "my work has from the beginning sought out digressions" (4.30); he concludes an intricate excursus with "this is a digression from my main subject" (7.171). This self-consciousness indicates not embarrassment but rather a didactic interest in clarity and a firm sense of what his main subject is and is not. Herodotus has rightly been described as a man who could not cross the street without finding something interesting; his collection of *objets trouvés* should not, as J. D. Denniston has warned us, mislead readers into regarding him

as little more than "an entertaining old fellow with unlimited credulity and a knack for telling amusing, sometimes improper, stories in an Ionic brogue." Rather, as Denniston shows, Herodotus' achievement as a stylist is in many ways greater than that of any other Greek prose writer.

Although Herodotus' plan of composition does not follow the rigorous chronological schematism of Thucydides (and in coping with such a vast span of time and space it would be difficult to do so), that does not mean that there is no organization. The fact that it takes Herodotus five books to get to his announced topic, the conflict between mainland Greeks and Persians that begins in the Ionian Revolt, suggests to many readers that the *Histories,* or at least the first half of the work, are something of a grab-bag, that Herodotus has thrown in everything that he happened to know about the kingdoms of the East. Some critics, in the desire to make Herodotus conform to their notion of a proper historian, have all but ignored the first half of the work; others see the first half as a work in progress, showing the author's slow development into a historian; yet others believe that what Herodotus originally wrote was a history of the Persian Empire that was then condensed and rearranged into its present unwieldy form.

An unprejudiced view of the work as a whole shows that such hypotheses are not only unnecessary, but also misleading, and give a much less complimentary portrait of the author than he deserves. Herodotus, in the first place, is interested in giving explanations and accounts of that large portion of the world that would be unfamiliar to his audience. In order to demonstrate both why the Persian Wars happened and why it was so astonishing that the Greeks won, it was also necessary to give some sense of the magnitude of the Persian Empire and of the background to the wars on both continents—for the earlier history of their own land is not likely to have been much more familiar to the Greeks than that of Persia.

After his famous preface on the reciprocal snatching of women by Greeks and Asiatics, a passage clearly designed to poke fun at the methods of his predecessors, Herodotus takes as his starting point Croesus, the king of Lydia. Although not the first of the barbarians to attack the Greeks, he was the first to reduce some of them to tributary status and is therefore held responsible for initiating "unjust deeds." Croesus' attack on, and subsequent defeat by, Cyrus led to the subjection of the Greeks in Asia Minor to the Persian king, and when the Lydian kingdom becomes a part of Persia, Herodotus' interest naturally follows the history of the conqueror, telling how the Persian Empire had come into being and how Cyrus in particular had come to power. The basic outline of the remainder of the first half of the *Histories* follows the chronological development of the Persian Empire. It was Cyrus' successor, Cambyses, who conquered Egypt; that event is the occasion for Herodotus' most extensive digression, on Egyptian history and customs (book 2). Book 3 tells of the death of Cambyses, the constitutional crisis in Persia, and the succession of Darius (including the constitutional debate in 3.80–82), which is in turn the occasion for an extended account of the size, provinces, and wealth of the empire. In book 4 we read of the disastrous expedition of Darius to Scythia and of the conquest of Libya; again, the customs of both countries are elaborately described. Book 5 picks up the story of the aftermath of the Scythian expedition—postponed since 4.143—which leads directly to the Ionian Revolt, the uprising that provoked Darius' invasion of Greece in 490 B.C.

The second half of the *Histories* is far less digressive than the first. Having explained the rise and power of Persia and having, in digressions in books 1 and 5, explained why Athens and Sparta were the leading cities in Greece, Herodotus follows a more strictly chronological pattern. The Ionian Revolt leads to the campaign of Marathon (book 6), and the great battles of the war with Xerxes of 480–479 each receive a book: Thermopylae in book 7, Salamis in book 8, Plataea and the final sea battle of Mycale in book 9.

This picture of an orderly exposition of the reasons for the wars between Greece and Persia is, it must be admitted, achieved only by reducing the contents of the *Histories* to the barest summary; to read the work through is the surest way to shatter it. Even admirers of Herodotus must wonder what Egyptian burial customs or the amounts of radishes, onions, and garlic consumed by the pyramid builders have to do with the Ionian Revolt. How does the Scythian practice of making human skulls into drinking cups illuminate the battle of Salamis? Because the first half of the work is so discursive and so detailed, and because its connections with Herodotus' stated topic often seem fortuitous, it is easy to assume that the *Histories* reflect an intellectual growth from ethnography and geography to history, and that the great ethnographical excurses are somehow separable from each other and from the more "historical" parts of the work. These assumptions, still widely held, are based not only on the peculiar quality of the work itself but also on the fact that Herodotus' main precursor in prose was a geographer and ethnographer. The genesis of the *Histories* is thus explained by making Herodotus begin his researches as a pupil of the late sixth-century writer Hecataeus of Miletus.

Herodotus' apprenticeship, if it was that, was an irritable and at times disrespectful one. Hecataeus is mentioned several times in Herodotus' narrative, either because of his historical role in the Ionian Revolt or because of his writings—but it is precisely where he appears as genealogist or geographer that he seems to be the butt of Herodotean jokes. The amused contempt for Hecataeus' genealogical researches (2.143) and for the absurdly symmetrical maps of the world prevalent in Herodotus' day (which had been made by Hecataeus and, before him, by Anaximenes of Miletus) at 4.36 was not entirely justified. Hecataeus' geographical work, the *Tour of the Earth*, was followed extensively by Herodotus, as we know from fragments of it preserved by later authors. Even one of the most memorable phrases in Herodotus' Egyptian excursus—that describing

Egypt as "the gift of the Nile"—was a happy, if unacknowledged, borrowing from it.

The *Genealogies*, Hecataeus' other work, has a proud beginning to which Herodotus was clearly indebted: "Thus proclaims Hecataeus of Miletus: I write what I believe to be the truth; for many and ridiculous, so they seem to me, are the stories of the Greeks." This skepticism and intellectual hauteur may well have channeled Herodotus' own efforts in the direction of critical scrutiny of traditions. But the main targets of Hecataean rationalism, as far as we can tell, were legends about Heracles and the descendants of Deucalion—the territory, that is, of myth, not of history. Herodotus' introduction, then, conveys a distinction not only between himself and Homer, but between himself and Hecataeus. While the critical investigations of his predecessor were confined to the long-distant past, Herodotus' work was concerned with contemporary or near-contemporary events. Perhaps the most important difference between the two writers is that for Herodotus, geography and ethnography were not simply ends in themselves. Both subjects are subordinated to a much larger purpose, the explanation of the reasons for and the outcome of the wars of Greece and Persia. Hecataeus' writings, decisive though they were for Herodotus, must be understood as antiquarian research; they were not intended to serve as a comprehensive historical narrative.

If one views Herodotus' ethnographic digressions as isolated treatises, it is obvious that he owes a great deal to the methods of his predecessors. In the absence of information about their past and about their neighbors, the Greeks regularly used imagination to fill in the gaps; and while that impulse might be taken to indicate genuine curiosity about history or foreign customs, the neat symmetries of the results indicate that the goal of such descriptions was tidy systems, not the exposition of potentially uncooperative and discrete facts. The infinite variety and multiplicity of even those foreign customs that the Greeks did know were blurred, simplified, and distorted by ancient ethnographers on the constant and easy principle of polarity: that everything foreign was the opposite of things Greek, with the further corollary that the more remote the area, the more thoroughly it reversed Greek customs.

The appeal even to Herodotus of the polarity of Greek and other is shown by more than one passage in his work, but none is more memorable than his famous description of Egyptian customs:

> There the women go to market; the men stay at home and weave. Other people weave by pushing the weft up, the Egyptians push it down. Men carry burdens on their heads, women on their shoulders. Women urinate standing up, men sitting. They knead dough with their feet and gather mud and dung with their hands. . . . The Greeks write from left to right, the Egyptians from right to left.
>
> (2.35 ff.)

Even though Herodotus here appears to be like his predecessors in using Greek custom as the norm against which to judge others, his brisk and entertaining list does not really seem to be designed to reinforce a Greek in his high opinion of himself. Herodotus, indeed, seems to be aware of both the folly and the universality of tendentious ethnography. In speaking of the Persians, he observes that they

> honor most those who live nearest to them, give second place to those who are second nearest . . . and honor the least those who are farthest away. Thinking that they themselves are by far the best of mankind, they consider those who live farthest off to be the basest.
>
> (1.134)

But the entire argument of the *Histories* is itself a demonstration that Herodotus could not accept the validity of such beliefs. By the time of Plataea, the Persians were to regret that they had not taken the Greeks, among the farthest off from Persia, rather more seriously.

It is in the broader combinations of the ethnographic techniques of polarity and analogy, however, that Herodotus most shows his superiority over his predecessors, and the relationship of the two largest digressions, on Egypt and Scythia, is highly instructive in demonstrating the sophistication of his techniques and of his adaptation of the manner and matter of earlier ethnography to his own larger purposes. Egypt and Scythia were as isolated as possible, geographically, historically, and culturally, from each other, but Herodotus has managed, through a combination of accurate observations, inherited errors, and original historical insights, to bind the two together and to connect them, indirectly but in significant ways, to the rest of the work. His starting point is geographical: he draws Egypt and Scythia together because (as he mistakenly reports) Nature has already done so. The two great rivers of each country, as he states repeatedly (2.26, 33–34; 4.50), correspond to each other. He makes the Nile and the Danube both flow first from west to east and then north and south, respectively, so that their mouths are directly opposite each other. As if to correspond to their comparable rivers, the two peoples share an important characteristic, their detestation of foreign customs.

At this point, however, analogy ends and polarity begins. Egypt has only one river, and Scythia many—but their number almost equals that of the canals of Egypt, all of which were constructed under the orders of one king (4.47; 2.108). While the many rivers of Scythia are the only marvel that that country offers to its geographer (4.82), Egypt has more wonders than any country on earth, and more monuments that defy description (2.35). Egypt, with its 11,340 years of human kingship and an indeterminate period of divine government, is one of the oldest of nations, while the Scythians claim that theirs is the youngest (4.5), and they can trace only 1,000 years of history.

Specific customs of the two peoples are also diametrically opposed. Egypt is "full of physicians," each highly specialized (2.84), and the people are the second-healthiest in the world (2.77). The Scythians, in contrast, "cure" royal diseases by executing anyone found guilty of swearing a false oath by the royal hearth (4.68). Scythians never bathe in water, but instead "howl with joy" during their more pleasurable, if less salubrious, hashish saunas (4.75). Egyptian priests, on the other hand, bathe four times a day in cold water (2.37), and the entire nation prizes cleanliness. The Egyptians, the most skilled of all peoples in preserving the memory of the past, have also invented and passed on to the Greeks geometry (2.109), the names of the twelve gods (2.50), the methods of divination, and the methods of establishing public assemblies, processions, and litanies (2.58). They have developed many other customs adopted by the Greeks, including a law brought by Solon to Athens which is, according to Herodotus, a perfect law, and one which he hopes the Athenians will keep forever (2.177). Scythia, on the other hand, has no images, no temples (except to Ares, the god of war, 4.59), and, in general, no admirable arts. Like Archilochus' hedgehog, indeed, the Scythians have learned only one great thing, and Herodotus attributes it not to their ingenuity, but to their nomadic way of life (4.46): they have the ability to remain invincible and unapproachable.

In the contrast between the single wisdom and success of the otherwise unadmirable Scythians and the military failure of contemporary Egypt, the civilization most renowned for learning and sophistication, we may begin to see some reasons for the interconnection of the two digressions. In the sixth century B.C., Egypt was totally unable to resist the invasion of the most incompetent of the Persian kings, the lunatic Cambyses; but it was one of Egypt's earliest rulers, Sesostris, who had conquered Scythia, a victory that eluded Darius, surely one of the greatest of Persian rulers. Herodotus, indeed, makes that contrast explicit. When Darius desired to set up his own statue before that of Sesostris, the priest of Hephaestus did not permit it, saying that Darius had not equaled Sesostris' deeds, for Sesostris had subdued as many nations as Darius and had conquered the Scythians as well. Darius, it was reported, gave way to the priest (2.110). Egypt, though clearly a subject of great interest to Herodotus, was by the historian's lifetime a nation of defeated archivists and museum keepers. Scythia had won, or at least had not been conquered by the Persians; though its inhabitants might be nasty and brutish, its existence as a free nation was not short.

The elaborate web of connections and oppositions that binds the descriptions of Egypt and Scythia together has wider ramifications. In many ways, it is something like a text of the Heraclitean universe, which "by being at variance, agrees with itself; there is an adjustment of opposite tensions, like that of the bow or the lyre." Once the contrasts between the two most antithetical societies known to the Greeks are seen to bear directly on their success or failure in dealing with Greece's major enemy, the Persian Empire, it becomes clear that they also have a considerable significance for the explanation of the Greek defeat of Persia as well. In some sense, Herodotus portrays Greece as the synthesis of Egypt and Scythia, and the connections between Greece and the two opposite countries are mentioned more than once in the course of the *Histories*. Through its adaptation of Egyptian customs and learning, Greece has acquired elements of civilization that Herodotus can admire. But in her poverty, in comparison with the wealth of Lydia or Persia, Greece has maintained the hardiness of a primitive state. Its civilization has not softened it so much that it cannot fight bravely, and its victory is not, like Scythia's, a function of impassable terrain and nomadic life, but rather the result of its peculiar combination of intellectual and physical strength. The whole intricate and detailed argument that has been briefly summarized here is encapsulated in the remarks Herodotus attributes to Demaratus, the Spartan exile in the court of Xerxes:

> Greece has always had poverty as her companion, while courage she has acquired, attaining it through wisdom and firm law; by using courage

> Greece defends herself against poverty and bondage.
>
> (7.102)

Far from being mere curiosities of antiquarian learning, the digressions in Herodotus, like the allusions to divine intervention (to which we must turn next), serve the larger historical argument that organizes, connects, and controls the entire work.

HOMERIC GODS, IONIAN IDEAS

In many respects, the Homeric qualities of Herodotean narrative and the frequent allusions to the role of fate or the gods in the *Histories* tend to detract from appreciation of the merit of the work as history. Indeed, it must be admitted that neither rationalism nor a scientific concern for the workings of human causes on human effects is the immediate impression conveyed by the work. For if Herodotus believes that the gods had a decisive role in mortal affairs, then it is difficult to expect him to proceed in a historical manner, as the use of divine causation suggests the imposition of a violent discontinuity between one action and its result. It is therefore necessary, if we are to appreciate the historical achievement of Herodotus, to devote some space to examining the role of the divine in his work.

There are, to be sure, supernatural forces at work in the *Histories*, but they are not omnipresent, nor do they seem to work in any particularly irrational, hostile, or personal fashion. The individual Olympian gods, in fact, are remarkably absent. No Athena appears, as she does in the *Iliad*, to pull the hair of a Themistocles; no warrior in the Persian Wars is snatched away in a mist. Nor does Herodotus, for the most part, mention the names of the specific gods except in reporting the beliefs, thoughts, and actions of others. Instead, he uses far more generalized terms, and refers to "the god" or "the divine" in a most un-Homeric manner. When he does refer to the individual gods, indeed, he is capable of severely rational skepticism. In narrating the invasion of Xerxes in 480 B.C., he describes the valley of Tempe in Thessaly:

> The Thessalians say that Poseidon made the gorge through which the Peneios flows and the story is a reasonable one; for whoever thinks that Poseidon shakes the earth and that chasms which are the results of earthquakes are the works of this god, would say on seeing this gorge that Poseidon made it. It is the work of an earthquake, as it plainly appeared to me, this cleft in the mountains.
>
> (7.129)

That Herodotus does not believe in the necessity of equating an earthquake with the action of a god is clear from this passage; but it is equally clear that he recognizes that others do make such equations. And if he does not himself stress the role of gods in human affairs, he knows and reports extensively the beliefs of others. While the gods do not, as a rule, intervene in Herodotus' historical universe, the belief of the actors in his narrative in their intervention was of no small importance. Croesus believed in Delphi, and his belief led him into disastrous error. Amasis believed in divine envy of human success, and his belief led him (at least in Herodotus' account) to break off relations with Polycrates. The gods are a constant factor in Herodotus' *Histories*, but their importance lies less in their objective presence than in the influences exerted on men by belief in them. Herodotus is capable of offering criticism even of this role of the gods. He is impatient with the Spartans for being so scrupulous in divine observance that they missed battles, and even more remarkable is the attitude toward Delphi implicit in his discussion of the Athenian role in the Greek victory: after saying that it was the Athenians who saved Greece, he goes on to point out that they did so despite the prophecies of Apollo:

> Not even the threatening oracles that came from Delphi and threw them into terror could persuade them to abandon Greece, but, standing firm, they endured the invasion of their country.
>
> (7.139)

Far from emphasizing the role of the gods in the victory, Herodotus is here on the brink of praising the Athenians for their Olympian disregard of Delphi, for divinely ignoring the divine.

The gods do act in Herodotus. They send Polycrates' ring back to him in the belly of a fish (3.42); they send rain to quench the pyre on which Croesus was to be burned (1.87); they create a storm off Euboea that nearly equalizes the number of Greek and Persian ships (8.13). But although Herodotus can make his Solon tell Croesus that "the divine is wholly jealous and fond of baffling us" (1.32), Herodotus himself is extremely sparing in speaking of divine jealousy (*phthonos*) as a historical cause. There are slightly more than twenty uses of the word in Herodotus, and of those passages only six have to do with the envy of the gods. More striking, five of these passages are in speeches or letters, notably the advice of Solon to Croesus (quoted above), of Amasis to Polycrates (3.40), of Artabanus to Xerxes (7.10). And in the context of addressing a tyrant or monarch, it is certainly reasonable for an adviser to suggest that any mishap that may befall him is less the result of his own error or rash action than of the envious intervention of a hostile deity. It would certainly have been rash for Artabanus to suggest to Xerxes that the expedition to Greece was likely to fail because it did not deserve to succeed. The single instance in which Herodotus speaks of divine envy in his own person, moreover, while certainly lurid, is scarcely an example either of arbitrary action by the gods or of extensive manipulation of human history by them. The passage in question is at the end of book 4, where Herodotus recounts the death of Pheretima, the ruler of Cyrene. That gentle woman had nailed her enemies on crosses in a circle, cut off the breasts of their wives, and nailed them up too. Herodotus offers a moral conclusion to this edifying tale:

Nor did Pheretima weave her life to a successful end. As soon as she returned to Egypt from Libya after taking vengeance on the people of Barca, she died horribly. While she was still alive, she seethed with worms, since over-violent punishments enacted by human beings are hated by the gods.

(4.205)

Even though Herodotus here speaks of mankind becoming the object of envy or resentment (epiphthonoi) of the gods, the actions of Pheretima are such that divine intervention is scarcely irrational, or an example of their being "fond of baffling us"; one would be much more inclined, in such an instance, to speak of divine justice.

Even the most vivid and emphatic actions of the gods in Herodotus seem to concern the fate of individuals like Pheretima and to have little real connection with the main structures of historical causation. The most famous example of the role of divine envy in Herodotus—perhaps because it comes at the very beginning of the *Histories*—is the story of Solon and Croesus. This story, the truth of which has been doubted on chronological grounds, falls into several parts. When Solon came to visit Croesus, who was the richest of all men and, according to Herodotus, at the height of his power and prosperity, the king asked the Athenian sage, after showing him his treasuries and all his wealth, who was the most fortunate of men. The word that Croesus used for "fortunate," *olbios*, is ambiguous: it means either prosperous or happy. Croesus used it in the first sense, but Solon took it in the second, and he gave two examples of men he thought truly fortunate, thus angering Croesus greatly. On being questioned about his reasons, Solon gave the reply quoted above, about the jealousy of the gods and the insecurity of human existence:

For to my mind, you are very rich and king over many people; but as for that question you asked me I cannot yet answer you until I learn that you have ended your life happily. . . . Whoever has the greatest number of advantages and, keeping them to the end, dies a peaceful death, this man, O king, in my opinion, justly bears the name "happy." We must, in every matter, look to the end; for often the god gives men a glimpse of happiness and then ruins them utterly.

(1.32)

The second episode in this story follows immediately upon the visit of Solon, and its importance is marked by the manner in which Herodotus introduces it:

After Solon's departure, a great vengeance [Nemesis] from god seized Croesus, because, as I guess, he thought himself the happiest of men.

(1.34)

The tale that follows is singularly tragic. Croesus dreams that one of his two sons was to be killed by an iron weapon, and consequently he keeps the boy from all warfare and similar activities. But, under the supervision of Adrastus, a suppliant who has taken refuge with Croesus, he sends the son to take part in a hunting expedition, where he is killed by a misdirected shot by the same Adrastus.

No one could deny that this episode displays the workings of the divine in human affairs, that it displays a tragic attitude toward the meaninglessness of the vicissitudes of mortal fortune. Indeed, the passage is almost suspiciously tragic. *Nemesis*, divine vengeance, is mentioned only here in the *Histories*; the name of the instrument of fate, Adrastus, is not only the name of a tragic figure, the hero who knows his own fate but cannot avert it, but Adrasteia, "she from whom one cannot run away," is a cult title of Nemesis in Aeschylus. The whole episode is not only tragic; it is, quite literally, a tragedy.

But to say that the gods are responsible for the unpredictability of human life, and that happiness is rarely constant, is far from saying that all historical events are divinely determined. The third and climactic episode in the story of Croesus demonstrates that. After receiving the ambiguous oracle from Delphi that "if he should march against the Persians, he would destroy a great empire" (1.53), Croesus attacked Cyrus, the Persian king. The empire destroyed was not, of course, that of Cyrus, but Croesus' own. When he was taken prisoner, Cyrus put him on a pyre in order to burn him alive; Croesus, on the pyre, remembered the warning of Solon and called the Athenian's name aloud, so that Cyrus, being curious, asked the meaning of the name:

> Then Cyrus, hearing from the interpreters what Croesus had said, changed his mind and reflected that he, a mortal man, was burning alive another mortal, one who had been no less fortunate than himself; moreover, fearing retribution and thinking that nothing human is secure, he ordered that the blazing fire be extinguished as quickly as possible and that Croesus and those with him be brought down from the pyre. This they tried to do, but did not succeed.
>
> (1.86)

What Cyrus could not do, the gods did. Croesus called on Apollo for aid:

> Weeping, he called upon the god and suddenly in a clear and windless sky clouds gathered and a storm broke, with such violent rains that the pyre was extinguished.
>
> (1.87)

Here, without any doubt, the gods are taking a very active role in human affairs. But two reservations are in order. In the first place, in this part of the story, as in the tragedy of Adrastus, the gods' role is limited to the personal happiness or salvation of an individual. In the section of the story of Croesus that has the most historical importance, his attack on, and defeat by, Cyrus, Herodotus offers quite human reasons for the events. Croesus attacks Cyrus not because of Nemesis, but because of his greed for land (1.73). He is defeated not because of the gods, but because his tactics are singularly stupid; after he fights an indecisive battle, he simply disbands his army and does not expect

Cyrus to continue the war. When Cyrus does invade, Croesus is totally unprepared, and he is, therefore, defeated. In these matters, we are told nothing of direct influence by the gods; their only role is in sending the ambiguous oracles to Croesus, and that he misinterprets them is his fault, not theirs, a result of his willingness to believe what he wants, and thus to be seen as part of his character, not of divine causation.

In the second place, the miraculous salvation of Croesus is told in very curious language. The storm sweeps out of a clear sky, and suddenly all is well. One should compare this to a passage from the most famous poem of none other than Solon himself, describing the justice that comes from Zeus:

> But Zeus oversees the end of all, and suddenly, just as a spring wind scatters the clouds, a wind which stirs up the depths of the unplowed sea with its many waves, ravages in the wheat-bearing land the fair works of men, reaches the sky, the lofty seat of the gods, and makes the sky clear again, the warmth of the sun shines over the fertile land, there are no clouds in sight—such is the vengeance of Zeus. . . .
>
> (frag. 13, w. 17 ff.)

Both the scene between Solon and Croesus at the beginning of the story, and this description of Croesus' miraculous rescue (the result of calling on the name of Solon), seem redolent of the language and the attitudes of Solon's own writings. One may suspect (although it can by no means be proved) that, as in the mock-historical account of the origins of the Trojan War in the preface, so here the literary reminiscence is deliberate. At the least, these scenes work as a kind of *tour de force*, comparable to imitations of Homer in battle scenes; here we have imitations of the great poet and sage in an ethical context. In particular, Herodotus seems to be taking slightly less than seriously an attitude toward the world that, if true, would completely preclude the possibility of writing logical or analytic history.

The high-minded stance of the Athenian and

his gloomy understanding of what it means to be human are to a certain extent undermined by the far more practical reaction of another Athenian who visits Croesus. This time it is Alcmaeon, an ancestor of the man who used the great wealth of his family to abolish the Peisistratid tyranny and to establish democracy. Alcmaeon comes to Sardis to be reimbursed for a service he had rendered to Croesus and is offered as much gold as he can carry on his person. His greedy acceptance results in so ludicrous a transformation of his appearance that he "resembles anything rather than a human being." Croesus laughs and gives him more (6.125). The story works almost as a witty inversion of the Solon-Croesus encounter, and the best joke is that if Alcmaeon had shared his fellow citizens' scorn for Croesus' wealth, his descendants might not have been rich enough to bribe first the Delphic oracle and second the Lacedaemonians into helping them banish the tyrants and establish the democracy (5.62–63)—without which there would have been no Greek victory over Persia. Herodotus himself does not explicitly make these connections, but here as elsewhere he shows his respect for common-sensical action which cares not a whit for timid flutterings about divine jealousy.

No one, I think, could deny that Herodotus' *Histories* are overdetermined, that his views allow room for both divine and human causes for events. But it would be rash, on the basis of the few occurrences of divine envy and the limited number of specific interventions of gods in specific human events, to suggest that a belief in the gods prevented Herodotus from offering historical judgments. That something is fated to happen—as many things are in Herodotus— may mean as little as that they do happen. Even the fact that the god, or fate, or necessity, knows that Croesus is destined to be defeated by Cyrus does not mean that *he* knows it or acts in the light of such a destiny. More important is the fact that any divine arrangement does not prevent, or even interfere with, the chain of human causation that binds the *Histories* together. The reason the Persian Empire first comes into contact with the Greeks is that Cyrus conquered Croesus and that Croesus had previously conquered the Greeks. That important chain of events may ultimately have been the result of some divine plan—but Herodotus never even hints at it.

That the primary mode of divine intervention in human affairs is not envy, then, is clear; and a number of the incidents discussed lead to a different conception: that it is retribution or justice that is involved. Herodotus himself, in one passage, offers a different and rather more pleasant assessment of the activity of the gods. In describing the marvels that are found in various exotic provinces of the Persian Empire, Herodotus discourses on the winged serpents that guard the frankincense-bearing trees of Arabia, and before discussing the manner in which their number is kept down, he offers the following observation:

> And it would seem that the forethought of the divine, being wise, just as is to be expected, has made prolific all creatures which are timid and edible in order that they might not become extinct by being eaten up, while those creatures which are savage and dangerous, it has made very unfruitful.
>
> (3.108)

The contrasting examples that Herodotus gives for this assertion are the rapidly breeding rabbit and the lioness, who (in Herodotean zoology, at any rate) bears only one cub, and no more:

> The reason for this is as follows: when the cub begins to stir in its mother, having claws much sharper than those of other creatures, it tears the womb and as it grows, it scratches much more; by the time of the birth, almost nothing of the womb is left whole.
>
> (3.108)

The dismal and tragic existence of the winged serpents (the occasion for Herodotus' meditation on divine forethought) is equally instructive. We are told that they would overrun the earth were it not for the fact that the female kills the male at the very moment of impregnation, and that murder is avenged (the word is *tisis*) by the offspring who dispose of this archetypal Clytemnestra as they are born.

In the natural history embodied in these chapters, we have the rudiments of quite a different system of divine control of the world than that suggested by the concept of divine envy. While the same event might be interpreted from different points of view—the victim of cosmic forethought might well consider it, on a more personal scale, as malice or envy—a world that is governed by a system involving divine forethought or *tisis* is a far more orderly place than one in which any disgruntled divinity can wreak his will on a harmless human being.

Tisis (retribution) appears in a cosmic context in the writings of one of Herodotus' Ionian predecessors, the sixth-century philosopher Anaximander, in a remarkably similar manner, one which suggests that the historian was not totally out of touch with philosophical speculation. One of the very few extant quotations from Anaximander reads:

> The things that are pass away into those things from which they come to be, in accordance with necessity; for they render to each other penalty and requital (*díkē* and *tisis*) for their injustice, in accordance with the arrangement of time.
>
> (title unknown)

In this sentence, the interrelationship of "the things that are" is described through a legal metaphor. The encroachment of each thing on the territory of another is injustice, but in the end, because everything has to pay for this injustice, a balance is maintained among them. What is remarkable about this idea, it has been observed, is that it is a way of talking about the continuity and stability of natural change that does not involve the unpredictable intervention of the gods, but expresses, through the notions of *tisis* and *díkē*, a self-regulating mechanism of cosmic order. Like Herodotus, however, Anaximander did not leave the gods com-

pletely out of the picture, although the precise working out of his cosmology is not, because of the poor state of preservation of the fragments, particularly clear. We do know that he spoke of the indefinite, which he called "the divine," and that he endowed this indefinite with Homeric attributes for the gods, "immortal" and "unaging," and that he said that it was this divine indefinite that "steers all and governs all." Whatever the relationship of the two fragments is, it is clear that above the equal opposites, which continually pay one another for their injustice, there is a divine something that supervises the workings of the system.

It is the combination of the divine and the concept of requital that appears, in very similar language, in Herodotus' discussion of animal life in book 3. It is divine forethought that makes sure that weak animals survive, and it is the same aspect of the divine that makes certain that winged serpents do not overrun mankind. But it is not by intervention in the case of specific animals or at every moment; divine forethought, in its wisdom, has set up a system which regulates itself, which maintains, by law, a balance in nature.

A system of checks and balances operates in Herodotus on a far wider scale than just as it applies to rabbits, lions, and winged serpents, and it is worth looking in this light at the context of Herodotus' discussion of divine forethought. It is found in the long section of book 3 on the extreme regions of the earth. Having begun in 3.89 to describe the extent and organization of Darius' empire, he progresses in chapter 97 to its farthest regions, the Indians and Ethiopians, Arabia and the Caucasus. Having described the tribute received from these places, Herodotus concludes:

> The ends of the earth, it would seem, have by lot the most excellent blessings, in the same way that Greece has been assigned by far the most excellently mixed climate.
>
> (3.106)

A complex system of balances is in operation here. Even though the extreme regions are excessively hot or cold, the rigors of the climate are offset by the vast amounts of wonders they contain: gold, the largest horses and birds, wool-bearing trees, spices, and sheep with tails so long that they have to be carried in little carts. But even within this, the fortunate people of Arabia pay a penalty for the blessing of their frankincense in having to fight off the winged serpents, while those serpents in turn pay a penalty for their viciousness in the perpetual tragedy that their families reenact. Divine forethought is indeed wise, and Herodotus has seen the extent of its wisdom in far more detail than (as far as we can tell) Anaximander had. For Herodotus extends the concept of a divine order and balance from the warring elements to animals, and from animals to geography. The description of the ends of the earth embodies a sort of geography of *tisis* and *díkē*, a vision of the physical world reflecting the same principles of balanced distribution and retribution that is reflected in the animal kingdom.

Herodotus' familiarity with Ionian speculations about the order of the visible world, their adoption of systems that did not rest on the unpredictable and unreliable interventions of the Homeric gods, their theories about physical and geographical causes of human characteristics, is evident. It is an extremely important factor, for one thing, in understanding the shape of the *Histories,* and even their starting point. For Herodotus the great geographical polarity around which the work (and the events with which he is concerned) is shaped is the conflict of East and West, of Europe and Asia. He begins the work with Ionian Greece, the center, in any such system, of the known world, having characteristics of both sides, and located in a sort of limbo between the Greeks of the mainland and the Asiatics. From conflict between the Ionians and Croesus, the pattern stretches out, as the work progresses, in both directions: Croesus' war with Cyrus brings the Persians (farther east) into contact with Ionia, the Athenians' involvement in the Ionian Revolt brings them into conflict with Persia. What is more, his interest, as we have seen, in the balances and the significance of geography offers at least a

partial explanation for the discursive and ethnographic nature of the first half of the work; far from being evidence of his growth from mere geographer into true historian, it is a crucial element in the understanding of human history. For Herodotus, geography teaches; it shows laws and patterns in a world that is not governed by the whim of the gods but is ordered providentially. To quote from Gibbon once again: "Man vanishes, but geography remains through the boundless annals of time."

But the neat balances and antitheses proposed in Ionian speculation, although they attempted to describe the visible world, fail in their relevance to empirical reality, and in that the historian goes beyond them. One clear example is to be found in Herodotus' comment on the map of Anaximander and Hecataeus, which was apparently an elegant, but unfortunately imaginary, diagram:

> Indeed, I laugh when I see that many before now have drawn maps of the world, not one of them explaining matters sensibly: Ocean they make flowing around the world which they draw round as if shaped by a pair of compasses, with Asia and Europe of exactly the same size.
>
> (4.36)

Perhaps because of the well-known Greek aversion to experimental science, the early Ionian thinkers developed theories that were only that, and failed to take into account those concrete and specific facts which make a mockery of any broad generalization. The author of the Hippocratic treatise *Airs, Waters and Places* may offer, as a nod to reality, his observation (24) that the soft nature of people who dwell in meadowy regions may be stiffened up by the imposition of law, thus admitting that humans are not totally at the mercy of a theoretical system; Herodotus makes it his business, throughout the *Histories,* to investigate all the particular events that lead up to the creation of laws. In that sense, it may be just to describe Herodotus as being Homeric; for the epic world is not inhabited by theories or by type-characters, but by individuals, and it is their particularity, not their universality, that provides the model for historical narrative.

Herodotus' handling of a single crucial question, the cause of the defeat of the Persians in 480, may serve as a guideline for understanding how vast is the gap that, finally, separates him from both Homeric divine causation and from the systematic theories of the Ionian philosophers. If Herodotus were truly a believer in the activity of the gods in all human events, the argument we would expect him to use actually does appear in the *Histories*; but it is in a speech that he puts into the mouth of Themistocles:

> Let us refrain—now that we have had the good luck to save ourselves and our country, repelling so great a cloud of men—from pursuing the fleeing forces. For it is not we who have achieved this deed, but the gods and the heroes, who were jealous that one man be king of Asia and of Europe too, especially a man who is both wicked and impious; one who has made no distinction between temples and private property; who has burnt and cast down the images of the gods; who has flogged the sea and has thrown fetters into it.
> (8.109)

This superstitious thought—that the defeat of Persia was not the result of the cleverness or courage of the Athenians, but of the retribution of the gods for the impiety of Xerxes—is not one that we expect to find voiced by the cynical Themistocles, the man who tricked the Persians into fighting at Salamis. In fact, the context shows that this idea too is being used by Themistocles for his own ends. The speech of the Athenian general is given here in the hope of persuading the Greeks not to pursue the Persians into Asia, because, as Herodotus explains, he spoke "in the hope of establishing a claim upon the King." In other words, Themistocles invokes the presence of the gods less because he believes in it than because he expects it to convince the superstitious multitude he is addressing.

There could be no greater contrast to this than Herodotus' own analysis of the causes of the Greek victory in 7.139. Announcing that he will offer an opinion that he knows will not be liked by his readers, he asserts that the primary cause of the defeat of Persia was the Athenian decision to resist at all costs:

> Had the Athenians, dreading the coming danger, left their own country or had they not left it but remained and surrendered themselves to Xerxes, then no one would have tried to resist the King by sea. If no one had resisted by sea, then this is what would have happened by land: even if the Peloponnesians had cloaked the Isthmus with walls, still the Lacedaemonians would have been deserted by their allies—not a voluntary betrayal, but a necessary one, since their cities would have been captured one by one by the fleet of the barbarian and finally the Lacedaemonians would have stood alone and, standing alone, after a tremendous show of valor would have died nobly. ... So, if a man were to say that the Athenians were the saviors of Greece, he would not be exaggerating the facts. Whichever side they took, to that side the balance was sure to incline. By choosing that Greece remain free, they themselves roused to battle all the rest of the Greeks, as many as had not yet turned traitor, and they themselves (next to the gods) drove off the King.

The clear and logical explanation of what would have happened without Athens is a demonstration of the truth of his initial statement, that it was the Athenians who saved Greece. What is more, it comes as the climax to a series of sections in which Herodotus had traced the political development of Athens from the murder of Hipparchus in 514 B.C. to the battle of Marathon in 490. The theme of those sections is the celebration of the value of freedom. Even though, before the constitutional reforms of Cleisthenes, Athens had been inferior to her neighbors in the arts of war, once she had shaken off the tyrants, she was able to defeat the Boeotians, Chalcidians, Spartans, and Aeginetans with terrifying efficiency. Herodotus gives his explanation for this:

> It is clear, therefore, that while they were oppressed by a tyrant, they willingly played the

coward, as men do who work for a master; but when they were freed, each one was eager to achieve something for himself.

(5.78)

The resounding success of Marathon, in which 6,400 Persians, but only 192 Athenians, were killed, and the great battles of the war with Xerxes only confirm our impression of the advantages of *isegoria*, the right of free speech in the Assembly. The chain of causation of the Greek victory stretches back through the Athenian decision to resist the Persians in 480 to the military courage and success that are made possible by democratic political institutions.

This is neither a pious insistence on divine causes nor the abstract speculation of the Ionians. Although his statement about the military value of freedom in 5.78 has a clear parallel in a generalization about the weakness of Asiatic peoples in an Ionian medical text, it is here placed in a context of specific information and a great amount of detail about individuals, laws, events, and battles that amounts to a precise and careful historical argument. What is more, although Herodotus gives the gods some credit for the victory in a perfunctory parenthesis, "next to the gods" (and in 8.13 he even gives "the god" credit for equalizing the numbers of the Greek and Persian fleets), they have little place in the analysis. It is an argument about the human causes of success, not the divine causes of failure. We are not told, as in the story of Croesus, that Xerxes was afflicted by Nemesis, or that divine envy grudged the Persians a victory. And if, as Themistocles says, the gods did not want one man to rule two continents—an argument that is in close accord with Herodotus' geography of *tisis* and *díkē*—those gods are far in the background. Within the parameters of divine forethought, it is still up to humans to act rationally and intelligently: it was the Athenians, not divine forethought, who defeated the Persians. Within the system of divine balances that Herodotus recognized, it was still the glory of the great deeds of human beings whose memory he sought to preserve.

THE MAKING OF A HISTORIAN

Even if Herodotus had been totally immersed in the speculative philosophies of Ionia, the facts of his life and the age in which he lived would not lead one to expect him to be purely a theoretician. He was born at Halicarnassus (now Bodrum), in the southwestern corner of Turkey, probably in the year 484 B.C.—between the campaigns of Marathon and the great invasion of Xerxes. Halicarnassus was a city of Dorian Greeks who had intermarried extensively with the native Carian population; Herodotus was a member of such a mixed family, one of considerable importance in the city. Nor was he the first member of his family to have literary aspirations; one of his relatives (probably an uncle), Panyassis, wrote epic poems on Heracles and on the foundations of the cities of Ionia. It is scarcely surprising that in the *Histories* Herodotus shows a considerable interest in both subjects.

As an inhabitant of a city that had sent ships in Xerxes' expedition, and one whose status was directly affected by the Athenian victory and subsequent conquests in the eastern Aegean, Herodotus could not help being aware of the crucial role that the Persian Wars had played in the lives of all Greeks; though he may not have been old enough to remember the wars himself, he must have known veterans of the campaigns. Herodotus himself was not merely a bookish figure: the love of freedom that so animates his work played a significant part in his life. The brief biography in the ancient lexicon *Suda* records that he was driven into exile for intriguing against the tyrant Lygdamis and that he then returned to Halicarnassus when Lygdamis had been expelled.

Although it is probably fruitless to speculate on the circumstances that create a historian, there are certain striking parallels, even in this meager material, with the life of Thucydides. Like Herodotus, Thucydides' family was of mixed blood (in his case Thracian and Athenian); like Herodotus, Thucydides spent much of his life in exile from his native Athens. It is easy to see why Herodotus would have been drawn to the subject of the Persian Wars. Coming from an area that was, at least while he was growing up, on the frontier between Athenian and Persian influence; having been forced, by exile, to see more of the world than the average fifth-century Greek; being a member of a family that was neither Athenian nor Ionian nor Persian, but a combination of Dorian Greek and Carian, he will have acquired a certain distance from easy sympathy with any of the participants in the politics of the Aegean world. At the same time, his political activity will have given him a keen sense of the value of liberty and of the importance of the Persian Wars in determining the fate not only of Halicarnassus but of all Greece.

Whether or not the ancient biography is correct in saying that Herodotus returned to Halicarnassus after the fall of Lygdamis we cannot tell; but it seems unlikely that he spent much time there. The *Histories* give abundant evidence of the breadth of his travels. He was certainly in Egypt; he spent a considerable time in Samos, an island for which his affection is obvious, and he was well acquainted with Athens, Sparta, and Delphi. It is often said that he spent considerable time at Athens, in part because of a dubious tradition in an unreliable source that the Athenians gave him an immense sum of money (ten talents) for a reading of his work. He may well have given readings there, but it is equally likely that he did so at the Panhellenic festival at Olympia. As for his travels, so for his occupation, the only clues are to be found in his work, but these clues are even more unreliable. Some critics have concluded, from the number of references to commerce in the *Histories*, that his travels were the result of his being a merchant; but from the subjects in which he expresses interest in his work, we might just as well conclude that he was an architect, a doctor, a chef, a mortician, a botanist, or a priest. On such questions, speculation is not profitable.

On the later years of his life, we have slightly more information. We know that in 443 B.C. he was one of the settlers of Thurii, a colony founded under Athenian leadership on the site of the former city of Sybaris in southern Italy. Participation in this colony may have been of great significance for Herodotus, and Thurii was, in any case, an extraordinary venture. Pericles was probably responsible for it, and Thurii was designed not as a purely Athenian colony, but as a Panhellenic city. Peaceful coexistence within one set of walls of Athenians, Dorians, and others did not last long, despite the presence in the city of a number of men of great intellectual stature (it is pleasant to imagine Herodotus in Thurii conversing with Hippodamus of Miletus, the town planner, the orator Lysias, the philosophers Protagoras and Empedocles). Thurii played out in miniature its own version of the Peloponnesian War, beginning within ten years of the foundation of the colony. There was a war with Dorian Tarentum, a quarrel over whose colony it really was (which ended with Delphic Apollo being named as the founder of the place), and internal civil war *(stasis)* between Dorians and Ionians which had probably broken out within Herodotus' lifetime. After his death, the dispute was resolved in favor of Sparta rather than Athens, and the Thurians aided the Spartans during the Ionian War in 411 B.C.

Of the date and place of Herodotus' death we cannot be certain. A Byzantine source records a grave inscription for the historian at Thurii, and there is no reason to doubt it. Many scholars have assumed, from the detailed references to events in Athens in the early years of the Peloponnesian War (the latest is to an incident in 430), that he left Thurii in disgust with its internal *stasis* and returned to Athens. But, given that the Greeks in the West kept in touch with the mainland through regular commerce and through visits to the Panhellenic shrines of Olympia and Delphi, there is no reason to assume he left Thurii. It is perfectly reasonable to believe that he died in the West in the early 420's.

The circumstances of Herodotus' birth and early life at Halicarnassus and his mature years and death at Thurii provide a suitable frame for the making of the historian. But there is more to it than that. To progress, in the space of fifty years, from witnessing the triumphant defeat of the barbarians by the unified forces of the Greeks to seeing the Hellenic world split by the struggle between Dorian and Ionian, to see the liberating Athenians turn into a new, and possibly more oppressive, imperial power replacing the Great King, to settle in a colony whose purpose was to exemplify the unity of the Greeks, and to live through its dissolution through *stasis*—all this would be enough to make the least curious of men wonder what had happened, and Herodotus was far from being the least curious of men.

To find the origin of the *Histories* in a melancholy contemplation of decline and dissolution may seem to be at odds with the lofty and apparently optimistic tone of Herodotus' description of the Greek triumph of 480 B.C., but these two moods are by no means mutually exclusive. Various observations throughout the work seem to suggest that at least one of the reasons for Herodotus' writing was to point out to his contemporaries the difference between what they were doing and what their fathers had done. The opening sentence of the work, in fact, seems to direct the reader's attention to that possibility in two ways. In the first place, the tone is curiously negative; Herodotus defines his purpose as:

> In order that the memory of the past may not be effaced among men by time and that the great and marvellous achievements done by Greeks and by barbarians may not lack renown.

The sentence suggests that the great deeds of the Persian Wars are, at the time of writing, in danger of becoming *exitela,* effaced or faded, and *aklea,* without renown or memory.

In the second place, a contemporary reader would have found something rather odd about the definition of Herodotus' subject that emerges in the course of the work. In the opening the topic is announced as the wars of the Greeks and Persians, and the last event of his narrative, at the end of book 9, is the siege of Sestos in 479 B.C., a campaign in which the Greeks secured a Persian fortress on the European side of the Hellespont. Perhaps because it is, in fact, Herodotus who has defined the Persian Wars for us, we tend to think of that date as an appropriate stopping point; a contemporary audience is unlikely to have shared that belief. They would have remembered, for example, the battle of the Eurymedon in the early 460's, an even greater victory over Persia. They would have remembered the campaigns of the Athenian general Cimon and the great expansion of Athenian naval power at the expense of Persia in the years after Sestos. And they would have remembered that the formal end of the Persian Wars had taken place only in 448, with the Peace of Callias (although the existence of such a formal act is still disputed). To someone reading the *Histories* in the late fifth century, Herodotus' silence about what happened after 479 would have been as vivid as what he had said about the earlier campaigns.

Many reasons have been suggested for Herodotus' choice of ending, and a number of them seem plausible. For one thing, after Sestos the war had a very different character. It was waged in what Herodotus himself called the territory of the Persian (8.3); it became a war of aggression, not one of defense. As important, perhaps, is the fact that after Sestos, the Spartans withdrew from the war, and it was no longer the war of the Greeks and the Persians, but of the Athenians and their allies and the Persians. Had Herodotus continued the story to 448 B.C., he could not have ignored what went on in Greece at the same time: the growth of Athenian power, the so-called First Peloponnesian War of the middle of the century. In the narrative of the great battles of the Persian Wars of 490 and 480–479, Herodotus was able to describe and admire the unification of Greece against a common danger; had he gone on, he would have been compelled to describe the contentious divorce of the former yokefellows.

For some readers, both Herodotus' choice of subject and his choice of stopping place seem to have a very specific motivation, the praise and defense of Athens. Perhaps the most important piece of evidence in favor of such a view is Herodotus' praise of Athens as the savior of Greece at 7.139 (quoted above). His language there is emphatic, and by calling Athens "savior" and saying that she "held the scales" in the war, he ascribes to the city characteristics that are normally applied only to gods. Even more, at the beginning of the paragraph, he draws attention to what he is doing:

And here I am forced to state an opinion which most men will dislike but since, to me at least, it seems to be true, I shall not refrain.

This certainly seems to cast Herodotus in the role of defender and panegyrist of Athens, but it is not so simple. In the first place, Herodotus' view of the importance of Athens in 480 B.C. is almost certainly correct, and it would be a strange sort of criticism to make the historian into a partisan pamphleteer because he told the truth. And in the second place, the way he draws attention to his judgment is two-edged: by saying that the opinion of Athens' importance will be unpopular, he reminds his readers that the Athenian actions since that time have not entirely lived up to their greatness in the Persian Wars.

Other allusions to Athenian actions seem less than wholeheartedly complimentary. In the one clear reference to Pericles in the *Histories*, Herodotus tells the story of Agarista, the granddaughter of Cleisthenes, the Athenian legislator:

She, married to Xanthippus son of Ariphron, and being pregnant, saw a vision in her sleep: she thought that she gave birth to a lion, and a few days afterwards, she bore Xanthippus a son, Pericles.

(6.131)

To compare the great Athenian leader to a lion cub may seem, at first sight, wholly flattering; but to those who recall Herodotus' description (3.108, cited above) of the devastation that pro-

ducing a lion wreaks on its mother or remember Aeschylus' simile of the lion cub in the *Agamemnon*, it is a less than cheerful image.

Xanthippus appears again in Herodotus, in the very last episode of the *Histories* (9.116 ff.). After the Athenians had captured Sestos and before they sailed home with the cables of Xerxes' bridge over the Hellespont, they captured and punished the Persian commander of the district, one Artayctes. This man had, by tricking Xerxes, plundered the treasures of the shrine of Protesilaus. While he was in captivity, Artayctes saw the salted fish being cooked by his Athenian guard start to leap in the pan as if newly caught; recognizing this as an omen that Protesilaus, though dead and preserved, still had the power to punish a malefactor, Artayctes tried to bribe Xanthippus, the Athenian commander, to release him and his son. That the incorruptible Xanthippus refused the bribe may appear to be complimentary either to the Athenians in general or to Pericles, but the sequel does not. Xanthippus led Artayctes to the place where Xerxes' bridge had been fixed, and there had him nailed to a board and left him to hang, while his son was stoned to death before his eyes.

Parallels in the *Histories* suggest that this act is not merely a sign of proper severity. We are reminded not only of the "excessively cruel" punishment inflicted by Pheretima on her enemies in book 4, but of an even closer parallel in book 9. After the battle of Plataea, an Aeginetan had suggested to the Spartan general Pausanias that he should discourage future Persian outrages against the Greeks by beheading and crucifying their general Mardonius, an act that Herodotus describes as "most sacrilegious." Pausanias rejected the advice:

That deed suits barbarians rather than Greeks; and even in them we dislike it. I myself would not wish to please either the Aeginetans or anyone else who enjoys such acts; it is enough for me if I please the Spartans, by righteous deeds and by righteous speech.

(9.79)

Pausanias' speech and the nobility that he later shows in refusing to hold guilty the children of a Theban, Medizer, whose father had escaped are meant to show a noble, properly Greek way to behave, and the difference between what he does and what Xanthippus does is striking: what Pausanias condemns as barbarian and impious, Xanthippus carries out. This juxtaposition may be intended merely to reflect on the character of the two men, but another conclusion is possible. In the interval between the incidents, the Peloponnesian forces had decided that the war was over and had gone home, leaving the Athenians to besiege Sestos. It was the Athenians alone, and not the Greeks as a whole, who were responsible for the unpleasantly barbaric execution of Artayctes and his son.

However one wishes to interpret stories such as these, it is clear that Herodotus was well aware that the history of the Greek struggle against the Persians was the occasion for some deeds that were less than entirely honorable. That he was conscious of the actions that took place after 479 B.C., moreover, is clear not only from allusions to specific events of the succeeding fifty years but from certain passages that seem to suggest that the glory of the war with Xerxes was somewhat overshadowed by the sequel. Perhaps chief among these events is an incident that occurs at the very beginning of the Persian Wars proper, when the Persian fleet had just set sail from Delos to Eretria in 490. Immediately after their departure from the sacred island, it was struck by an earthquake, the first and last ever to affect it:

> And this was a portent, as I suppose, by which the god revealed to men the evils that were to come. For in the generations of Darius the son of Hystaspes and Xerxes the son of Darius and Artaxerxes the son of Xerxes, in these three successive generations more ills fell upon Greece than in the twenty generations before Xerxes, evils coming in part from the Persians, but in part from the wars for the supreme power fought by their own leaders.
>
> (6.98)

That Herodotus should report a significant omen is scarcely surprising, but the weight, solemnity, and emphasis that he gives it is striking. By saying that the earthquake was a portent of all the ills to affect Greece from both external and internal warfare for three generations, Herodotus seems for a moment to extend his subject and to undercut the glorious deeds of the Persian Wars that he is about to relate by this somber glance at the future.

The impressiveness of Herodotus' utterance here and the impression that it must have made on contemporary readers are the result not only of the formal use of patronymics to reintroduce the Persian kings, but of the chronological indications that he gives. Twenty generations before the accession of Darius, at Herodotus' normal equivalence of three generations to the century, is 1189 B.C., the period of the Trojan War. In this figure, then, Herodotus includes the entire span of time encompassed by his work, and at the same time refers to the previous great conflict between East and West that he had excluded from his subject in the preface of the *Histories*. As for the generations of the Persian kings, that period could conceivably include the years down to 424 B.C., when Artaxerxes died. As Herodotus himself was probably dead by then, however, we may take it to refer to the time until the sentence was itself written.

There are other passages of the *Histories* that show that Herodotus was not an admirer of war. One thinks in particular of Croesus' admission of the folly of attacking Cyrus:

> No one is so foolish as to prefer war to peace; for in peace sons bury their fathers, but in war fathers bury their sons.
>
> (1.87)

But one passage in particular seems to show Herodotus' horror at the war that developed between the Greek cities after the Persian Wars, the "war for supreme power," as he called it in 6.98. At the beginning of book 8, just before the battle of Salamis, Herodotus explains why the Athenians did not supply the commander in chief for the Greek fleet:

> From the start . . . there had been talk of turning over the command at sea to the Athenians. But when the allies opposed this, the Athenians yielded, considering the survival of Greece to be of utmost importance and recognizing that if they quarreled over the leadership, Greece would be destroyed. In this they judged correctly; for civil strife is as much worse than war waged by a unified people as war is worse than peace. Understanding this, the Athenians did not press their claim but yielded, only so long as they had great need of the others, as they showed: for when they had driven the Persian back and were contending for his territory, then, using the insolence of Pausanias as an excuse, they deprived the Lacedaemonians of their leadership.
>
> (8.3)

The phrase that Herodotus uses to describe the "civil strife" that is so much worse than war is a memorable one: *stasis emphulos,* "civil war within a race." The expression was not coined by Herodotus, but he gave it a very new meaning. Just as *stasis* by itself in Herodotus always refers to civil war within a city, so *stasis emphulos* and related expressions in earlier authors mean the same thing. The *polis* is seen as the furthest extent of common blood to be defined by *emphulos.* In 8.3, however, Herodotus means something quite different, as the choice is not between civil war in a city and war in general, but war between Greek and Greek and war between Greek and Persian. By changing the meaning of the phrase from intracity to intercity strife, Herodotus implies that all the Greek cities have the same relationship to one another as do citizens of the same town or members of the same family. All Greece, that is, should be recognized as a single unit, of which the individual cities are members.

The context of Herodotus' use of the phrase in 8.3, however, makes it all too clear that it is only in his view, not in that of the Greek cities, that they are all related. As he tells the story of the Athenians' decision not to press for the leadership in 480 B.C., it emerges that they did so not because they believed in Greek unity, but because they needed help from the other Greeks for their own survival, and that they abandoned that pose as soon as it was safe to do so. This contrasts markedly with their words at the end of book 8, when they reproach the Spartans for believing that they would betray Greece to the Persians:

> Your fear is base, knowing full well as you do that the Athenian spirit is such that there is nowhere on earth so much gold or a land so outstanding in beauty or excellence that, accepting such gifts, we would want to join with the Persians and enslave Greece. Many and great are the obstacles to this, even if we should desire it: first and most important, the burning and destruction of the images and temples of the gods, whom we are forced to avenge to the best of our capacities rather than come to terms with their destroyers; next, there is the kinship of the Greeks in race and speech, and the shrines of the gods and the sacrifices which we have in common, and the way of life which we all share. For the Athenians to betray all this would not be right.
>
> (8.144)

Despite the pious assertions of the Athenians here, it was obvious to any contemporary reader of Herodotus that they had not chosen to honor the "kinship of the Greeks"; and the events of the fifty years following the Persian Wars show that a speech that Herodotus gave to Mardonius, the Persian general, was all too accurate. After saying that the Greeks had seemed very reluctant to fight him in 490, all but the Athenians, Mardonius went on:

> But, as I have learned, the Greeks are accustomed to start wars very irrationally, on account of their arrogance and clumsiness. . . . Since they all speak the same language, they ought to use heralds and messengers and any means other than fighting to compose their differences. . . .
>
> (7.9)

Clearly Herodotus has here put a view that is his own into the mouth of a Persian general.

If one considers the notorious disunity of the Greeks in Herodotus' day, it may seem odd that he speaks of them as if they were all brothers. But perhaps we should consider the possibility that that is precisely the point that Herodotus wished to make. Indeed, considering the history of Greece before the Persian Wars, as told by Herodotus, together with the events of his lifetime, it seems likely that the forging of that unity during the Persian Wars was one of the "marvellous achievements" that he announces as his topic in the preface.

The unity of the Panhellenic experiment at Thurii quickly collapsed; the cooperation of the Greek cities in the Persian Wars took slightly longer to degenerate into internecine strife. But the participant in the former event is not likely to have been unaffected by the latter. By writing a history that showed how the forging of unity between the most narrow-minded, selfish, and touchy cities (and the *Histories* amply document those characteristics) led, for once, to a victory over the greatest empire in the world, he surely had his own time in mind. Thucydides may have obliquely sneered at his predecessor's work by calling it "a prize essay for the moment," but that description can have a more honorable meaning than its author intended. Herodotus' work was aimed at the immediate readers; his goal was no less than to resurrect in their minds the nation of Greece that had defeated the Persians and that was, through the pettiness and self-interest of their descendants, in danger of becoming "without renown" and "effaced."

Even if Herodotus succeeded in restoring the unity of Greece in the minds of his readers, he was not successful in having any effect on the Greeks themselves. The union of Greece was not to be seen again for many generations, and when it came, it was imposed from without. Herodotus' *Histories* do not express a tragic vision of human life, but they bring to mind the true tragedy of Greece as well as the triumphant moment that the historian recorded.

"Blessed is the man," said Euripides in a famous fragment (910) from an unknown play, "who has knowledge that comes from *historia*. He does not devise calamities for the citizens or commit injustice, but observes the ageless order of immortal nature, in what way it came to be and whence and how. Never can the practice of base deeds cleave to such men." There is much in the *Histories* that enables us to apply Euripides' accolade to Herodotus—the ultimately benign picture of a wise and provident divine power, the sense of wonder at man's energy and achievements, the countless rewards that await the determined seeker after the causes of things. But Euripides' understanding of *historia* pertains only to natural philosophers, to researchers who explained what was above and below the earth, who looked at the cosmos and not at cities, who studied strife among the elements and not wars among men. To the degree that Herodotus' researches led him to similarly detached and grand visions of a beautifully balanced universal order, a divinely protected equilibrium of natural and human forces, so far can he be called blessed. When men's deeds merit epic commemoration, when the historian can freely confer the appropriate glory upon them, then he too can be called fortunate. But it is the prerogative of the natural philosopher alone to isolate himself from sad decline and from abysmal repetitions of wasted spirit in an expense of shame. Herodotus' broader understanding of *historia* made such isolation impossible, and a story that he tells (9.16) may serve as a suitable epigraph for his life's work. At a banquet in Thebes before the battle of Plataea, a leading Persian sat next to the Orchomenian Thersander and spoke in distress of the many deaths that lay in store for the Persians in the battle. He went on to say that, though he knew a disaster was coming, he was powerless to avert it:

> Indeed this is the most hateful of sorrows among men, to have much knowledge and yet power over nothing.

Selected Bibliography

TEXTS AND COMMENTARIES

A Commentary on Herodotus, edited by W. W. How and J. Wells. 2 vols. Oxford, 1928.

Herodoti Historiae, edited by Carl Hude. 2 vols. Oxford, 1927. Text only.

Herodotus: The Fourth, Fifth and Sixth Books, edited by R. W. Macan. London, 1895. Text and commentary.

Herodotus: The Seventh, Eighth and Ninth Books, edited by R. W. Macan. London, 1908. Text and commentary.

TRANSLATIONS

Rawlinson, G. *Herodotus: The Persian Wars*. New York, 1947. Modern Library edition.

———. *Herodotus: History of the Greek and Persian Wars*, abridged and edited by W. G. Forrest. London, 1966. Forrest's introduction is excellent.

Selincourt, A. de. *Herodotus: The Histories*. Harmondsworth, 1954. Penguin edition.

Both the Modern Library and the Penguin editions are considered standard.

CRITICAL STUDIES

Benardete, S. *Herodotean Inquiries*. The Hague, 1969.

Burn, A. R. *Persia and the Greeks*. London, 1962.

Bury, J. B. *The Ancient Greek Historians*. New York, 1909. Reprinted 1958.

Collingwood, R. *The Idea of History*. Oxford, 1946.

Denniston, J. D. *Greek Prose Style*. Oxford, 1965.

Drews, R. *The Greek Accounts of Eastern History*. Cambridge, Mass., 1973.

Evans, J. A. S. "Father of History or Father of Lies: the Reputation of Herodotus." *Classical Journal* 64:11–17 (1964).

———. "Herodotus and the Ionian Revolt." *Historia* 25:31–37 (1976).

Fornara, C. *Herodotus. An Interpretive Essay*. Oxford, 1971.

Gomme, A. W. *The Greek Attitude to Poetry and History*. Berkeley, 1954.

Harvey, F. D. "The Political Sympathies of Herodotus." *Historia* 15:254–255 (1966).

Havelock, E. A. "War as a Way of Life in Classical Greece." In *Valeurs antiques et temps modernes*. Vanier Memorial Lectures, 1970–1971. Ottawa, 1972. Pp. 19–78.

Heidel, W. A. *Hecataeus and the Egyptian Priests in Herodotus, Book II*. American Academy of Arts and Sciences Memoirs, XVIII, 2. Boston, 1935.

Immerwahr, H. *Form and Thought in Herodotus*. Cleveland, 1966.

Jacoby, F. "Herodotus." In A. F. Pauly and G. Wissowa, eds., *Realencyklopädie*. Supplement 2, cols. 205–520. Stuttgart, 1913. Reprinted in F. Jacoby, *Griechische Historiker*. Stuttgart, 1956. In German; the basis for all modern studies of Herodotus.

Kirk, G. S., and J. E. Raven. *The Presocratic Philosophers*. Cambridge, 1957.

Lattimore, R. "The Wise Advisor in Herodotus." *Classical Philology* 34:24–35 (1939).

———. "The Composition of the *History* of Herodotus." *Classical Philology* 53:9–21 (1958).

Lloyd, G. E. R. *Polarity and Analogy*. Cambridge, 1966.

Momigliano, A. *Studies in Historiography*. London, 1969.

Myres, J. *Herodotus, Father of History*. Oxford, 1953.

Paassen, C. van. *The Classical Tradition of Geography*. Groningen, 1957.

Pearson, L. *The Early Ionian Historians*. Oxford, 1939.

Pembroke, S. "Women in Charge: the Function of Alternatives in Early Greek Tradition and the Ancient Idea of Matriarchy." *Journal of the Warburg and Courtauld Institutes* 30:1–35 (1967).

Starr, C. *The Awakening of the Greek Historical Spirit*. New York, 1968.

Waters, K. *Herodotus on Tyrants and Despots. A Study in Objectivity*. Wiesbaden, 1971.

Wells, J. *Studies in Herodotus*. Oxford, 1923.

White, M. "Herodotus' Starting-Point." *Phoenix* 23:39–48 (1969).

SUSANNA STAMBLER

EURIPIDES

(*ca.* 480–406 B.C.)

INTRODUCTION

EURIPIDES WAS BORN about 480 B.C., to a family of some means and in part nobility, with property on the island of Salamis, where he is said to have withdrawn to reflect and work on his plays. He was commissioned by the Athenians to write a funeral epigram for their soldiers lost in the disastrous Sicilian expedition of 414–412, and he composed (probably in 416) a victory ode for the notorious Alcibiades. In contrast to Aeschylus and Sophocles, no reports about Euripides' public offices or functions survive. He may have done some painting (pictorial qualities in his poetry support this). Toward the end of his life (after a last theatrical production in Athens in 408, which included the play *Orestes*), he left his native city on the invitation of Archelaus, king of Macedonia, in whose domain he died before the spring of 406.

Some sense of how the dramatist was perceived in his own time may be inferred from a series of caricatures in Aristophanes' comedies *Acharnians*, *Thesmophoriazusae*, and *Frogs* (produced between 424 and 405 B.C.), making due allowance for comic fantasy, distortion, and a tendency to cast the author's character from the more striking features of his plays. Clearly the comic poet was fascinated by him, both exploiting his notoriety and paying him the ambivalent tribute of continuous parody. Euripides comes off as—variously and not al-ways consistently—a standoffish character, on the grumpy side, bookish, intellectually fastidious, sarcastic, ingenious, resourceful, even occasionally, when really pressured, accommodating, and, in pathetic distress, sympathetic. Generally one has the impression that Euripides may have been both popular and disturbing to his audiences, mixing theatrical flair and powerful emotional effects with a detached, critical intellectuality. His productions won first prize four times in twenty-two competitions, which suggests that official approval may have been reluctant. He was controversial, and, it should be said at the outset, the interpretation and critical assessment of individual plays continue to be controversial.

The cause of this controversy stems partly from the dramatist's temperament, which seems to vary in the ways and places of its focus and appears to allow the representation, with equal conviction and skill, of conflicting sides of an issue—Euripides is renowned for his scenes of debate. This temperament is at once theatrical and critical, includes conviction and detachment, lyric expression and prosaic argument, idealized sentiment and harsh realism. Sophocles reportedly said that he himself represented human beings as they should be while Euripides represented them as they actually were; but that suggests too large a simplification. Euripides' work is multifaceted, with a wide range and variety in both sympathetic and critical modes. This accounts for the variety of

233

response it has elicited, and, more than with most authors, makes it easier—and important that one try not—to project particular preoccupations of a given time into his work. According to some of his followers, for example, we might see a Euripides in the light of an Ovid or a Seneca, of his first adapters and translators in the early sixteenth century (including Erasmus), of a Racine, a Voltaire, a Goethe or Schiller, a Robert Browning, a Henrik Ibsen, or, in the twentieth century, of a range of authors including George Bernard Shaw, Jean Anouilh, Jean Giraudoux, Robinson Jeffers, T. S. Eliot, Yannis Ritsos, and Edward Bond.

The variety, the elusive and disorienting quality in Euripides' plays, is closely related to the time in which they were written. In a period of intellectual ferment, Euripides is associated with the new thinkers and shows the effects of their ideas—natural philosphers like Anaxagoras and Diogenes of Apollonia, sophists like Protagoras, Gorgias, Prodicus, and Antiphon, and the successor of all of these, Socrates. Characters in his plays sometimes draw on ideas of these thinkers. More importantly, the rationalistic tendency of this movement and its questioning perspective are represented throughout the plays, but invariably in the course of a play's action, simple, critical rationalism is revealed as inadequate and drastically limited. One aspect of Euripidean tragedy, in fact, lies in its confrontation between hope in these new modes of understanding and despair at their inadequacy and failure.

Another condition affecting the understanding of the plays is the development of the genre of tragedy itself. More and more in the course of the latter part of the fifth century B.C., tragedy approaches the exhaustion of its traditional and conventional resources. For Euripides, this increasingly creates a tension between maintaining the established requirements of the genre— such as the use of a circumscribed body of myth or the presence of a participating chorus—and a need to revitalize, perhaps even break with, them by innovation and change. Though, unlike his younger contemporary Agathon, he resists a final break with the traditionally constituted elements of tragedy.

Finally, there are the social, economic, and political forces that inevitably affect so public an art as Attic tragedy. Since with a few exceptions (Aeschylus' *Persians*, produced in 472, is the one surviving example and may have been the last) tragic convention requires plots based on traditional myths, the presence of contemporary history in the plays is indirect, or rather is based more on larger issues than on specific details and references. (It is comic drama in this period that invents its plots freely, caricatures public figures on stage, and makes the larger and smaller issues of politics its common subject.) The myths presuppose a remote, archaic society, governed by kings or clan chiefs. But tragedies are run through with anachronisms, especially signaled by a vocabulary that belongs to the developing political and legal institutions of the democratic city-state, the *polis*.

An underlying feature of Attic tragedy is the confrontation of past and present: the past of the myths, including as models heroic human beings in their relations to divine forces; and the present of a contemporary society under pressure of change and adaptation, attempting to comprehend and control itself and the external forces affecting it. In Aeschylean drama this confrontation, it appears, tended to culminate in an affirmation of the present, justified, though not without undergoing the struggles and costs of a tragic process, by a capacity for both change and persuasive integration of the past. This movement from past to present is also a movement from the more confined and private sphere of the family and kinship group to the larger, public community of the *polis*.

Euripides (whose drama in this and certain other respects more obviously continues and complements Aeschylus than Sophocles) tends in almost the opposite direction. Living through a period during which the Athenian *polis* was increasingly in crisis, he appears to look backward, or rather inward, to private relations as the focal point of his drama. In this respect he anticipates the increasingly private orientation of later Greek literature. This movement in Euripides, however, is by no means straightforward. Concern for the private as such is a thread persisting throughout the plays but also subject to a variety of perspectives on its meaning and weight; and in all instances it is set against some aspect of the public sphere, as though it could be defined, or even be said to exist, only on the latter's terms.

The history of Attic tragedy could be traced roughly along the lines, first, of the formation of Athens' characteristic democratic institutions and of her emergence into historical prominence after playing a crucial role in defeating the Persians, in the first decades of the fifth century B.C.; then, in the middle decades, of the consolidation of an overseas empire; finally, in the latter part of the century, of the waves of crisis, internal and external, brought on by these developments and culminating in the Peloponnesian War, begun in 431 and finished in 404. Aeschylus' plays coincide with the first two of these phases, Sophocles' with the latter two; Euripides' surviving plays, excepting *Alcestis*, produced in 438, all fall within the period of the war.

We have eighteen plays out of seventy-four whose titles are known. (One other play, *Rhesus*, survives under Euripides' name but is probably a work of the fourth century.) A considerable number of fragments of lost plays and some information about them also survive; for about a dozen we can get some idea of individual scenes and, to a certain extent, plot elements. The surviving plays can be grouped along general chronological lines, roughly as follows: (1) *Alcestis* (438), *Medea* (431), *Hippolytus* (428); (2) *Heraclidae* (about 430), *Andromache* (about 424, perhaps earlier), *Hecuba* (about 424), *Suppliants* (about 424, perhaps later); (3) *Electra* (between 420 and 416), *Heracles* (between 417 and 414), *Trojan Women* (415); (4) *Iphigenia among the Taurians* (about 414), *Helen* (412), *Phoenissae* (about 411–409), *Ion* (about 411–408), *Orestes* (408), *Bacchae* and *Iphigenia in Aulis* (produced posthumously, shortly after 406). The date of *Cyclops*, the only

complete surviving example of a satyr play, is unknown. We do know that the first set of Euripides' plays to be produced was staged in 455, which means that his earliest surviving plays represent fully mature work.

MYTH AND DOMESTIC TRAGEDY

In *Alcestis*, *Medea*, and *Hippolytus*, Euripides represents mythical or legendary material from a domestic point of view. The individual relationships of the protagonists, or the failures of these relationships, are central. (Sophocles' *Women of Trachis*, which possibly was produced in the period of these plays, is another example, though treated differently, of such a perspective.) *Alcestis*, perhaps in part because it was played in place of a satyr play, alternates and mixes light and serious elements, and its plot turns out fortunately. But it is also characteristically elusive and shifting in tone. The story of the play—a bride or beloved's sacrifice of her life for her husband (who is often a king) or lover after all his own family have refused help, and (a story element of perhaps separate origin) the combat of a hero (usually husband or lover) with death (or a monster) for the beloved—belongs to popular folklore rather than heroic myth. The plot thus has an aura of innocence and allows miraculous events, like the postponed and reprieved death, that are not usually found in tragedy. But Euripides, in various ways, makes this fairytale world transparent.

The play is marked by an ironic wit, as in the opening confrontation of Apollo and Death (exceptionally, on stage in person), normally awesome powers in the tragic world, who here bicker, bully, and are meanly stubborn. The story itself is presented in such a way that its characters are seen in their relationships as more or less ordinary human beings, with some psychological realism, as though asking: What kind of people are these really, in this familiar story? What would it actually be like for a wife to go through with an offer to die for her husband? And for him to accept such an offer? How would a human relationship survive such a trial? What, when a father has refused to give up his life for his son's, would the two say to each other? Alcestis is part of both a domestic, ordinary world and a heroic one. The first is conveyed by report and by her effect on those closest to her: servants, children, and Admetus. Her heroism is celebrated by everyone and claimed by herself. Her sacrifice, she explains, was undertaken for the sake of the family; she says nothing about love for Admetus. If this seems odd to us, Athenians would normally have considered appropriate a prior claim of the indispensable social unit of the family with a male head, as well as a wife's reticence about her private affections. (In *Suppliants*, a wife chooses to kill herself at her husband's funeral explicitly for heroic glory and passionate love, but there, no domestic life is left to preserve.) Admetus, on the other hand, expresses passionate distress at the death of his wife. He promises not only not to marry again, as Alcestis asked (so as not to bring a hostile stepmother into the house), but also, on his own, to remain in mourning for the rest of his life. This public expression of feeling, revealing the affective side of a marriage relation, must have seemed very unusual to its contemporary audience (but Theseus' distraction at the death of Phaedra, in *Hippolytus*, is comparable). The choice to mourn indefinitely points to the deeper paradox of Admetus' situation: another died to allow him to live, but he comes to realize that his life, saved in this way, is not worth living, neither privately without his wife nor publicly with a reputation as the man who let his wife die for him.

The benign folktale is, so to speak, broken up by contradictions within human characters and social values. This happens subtly or shockingly, as in the contrast between the noble death of Alcestis and the harsh scene between Admetus and his father Pheres, shocking especially because their quarrel takes place literally over the body of Alcestis and because it contravenes so drastically the conventional, deeply held Greek pieties concerning honor due to parents. In a more general way the story is interwoven with a kind of dialectic of opposed values. At the start, the confrontation of Apollo and Death contrasts gracious favor with ineluctable necessity—the first precious, though, in the face of life's real conditions, potentially arbitrary and chaotic; the second, if that is all there is to life, degrading and repulsive. A social dimension is also suggested: Apollo is aristocratic, Death egalitarian and democratic (see lines 55–59). When Alcestis speaks for the family unit, but keeps silent about personal affection, the recognized social structure and private feeling are set apart. The quarrel of Admetus and Pheres underscores conflicting claims of blood ties and marital ties, two kinds of *philia*, "friendship" in the broadly understood Greek sense, encompassing necessary kinship bonds and freely chosen associations.

A third kind of friendship twice marks crucial turning points in the play's action, that of Admetus and the hero Heracles, a long-standing, formally recognized social relationship of *xenia* or guest-friendship. It causes Admetus, when Heracles appears in the midst of Alcestis' funeral preparations, to hide his desolate grief and insist that his friend be entertained as though nothing were wrong. Admetus suppresses his private feeling in favor of the formal obligation. This is doubly judged. The chorus, in the light of common sense, first call it folly (551); but then, in song, they celebrate the exemplary nobility of Admetus' *xenia*, linking it to Apollo, also a guest-friend (the fairytale element surfaces again here), and to the beautiful poetry and pastoral world associated with the god (569 ff., see also 8–9). At the last turn of the play's action, Heracles recalls both judgments. Admetus as a friend should have spoken freely and not kept his troubles hidden (1008–1010). Yet Heracles has already praised Admetus' noble kindness in his absence (840–842, 854–860) and has enacted his response by risking death to bring Alcestis back. A last twist is given this contrast of private feeling and a socially recognized code of behavior when Heracles insists that Admetus take care of a veiled woman he has brought along (in fact, Alcestis). Admetus faces a quasi-tragic dilemma, between refusing his friend a favor, contrary to friendship's code, and breaking his impassioned promise to Alcestis never to take another woman into his house (this dilemma resembles the paradox of Admetus' earlier situation, in which his life was saved by an event that makes it unlivable). But the folktale's happy ending is only momentarily stayed. The code of friendship wins out; Admetus regains Alcestis, though partly by having to deny her in a private sense. This conclusion—and it may be a further paradox that the basis of Alcestis' heroic sacrifice is now, strictly speaking, canceled—may suggest to a sophisticated sensibility a final irony overshadowing the folktale. Yet to a majority of its audience, the happy ending—the reuniting of the couple, the defeat of death (though that must be only temporary), Heracles' extraordinary act of friendship and cheerful heroism, and Admetus' education in adversity—must outweigh ironic qualification. The folktale, at times disturbingly undercut as we see through it to the bewildering complexities of ordinary life, survives. The countermovement of harsher realism does not so much destroy the story as allow reflection and detachment. Naive response is checked, and an ideal fantasy gains psychological and social depth.

Domestic life in *Alcestis* is recovered, after the disorienting threat of death. Because of the folktale perspective and because of the elegance of Euripides' dramatic construction, the play holds in balance its lighter and more serious elements. In *Medea* and *Hippolytus*, the domestic sphere is the scene of unmitigated disaster. These plays, with *Bacchae*, are Euripides' most powerful and accomplished tragedies.

Medea represents vengeance after love betrayed. Its main lines are simple and direct. Yet its effect is also disturbing: a violent story of personal emotions in fact involves and cuts into the fabric of Greek moral and social assumptions.

The play's dramatic power is due most directly to a concentration on the completely dominating figure of Medea and to the emotionally charged nature of the final phase of her revenge, the willful killing of her children. This concentration on a single figure, more common in Sophocles, is unique in Euripides' surviving plays (only *Hecuba* and *Heracles* approach it), and may be an experiment in the Sophoclean mode. Unlike the integrated singleness of a Sophoclean hero, however, Medea is represented in three general aspects, which both fade in and out of one another and are variously highlighted. First, there is the well-known Medea of epic legend, an exotic and barbaric figure, an Eastern princess, grandchild of the sun god Helios, and a sorceress, passionate and extreme in her love for the Greek hero Jason and in the measures she takes for his sake—betraying her father, killing her brother, and instigating the death of Jason's usurping uncle. This side of Medea, established by traditional myth, is recalled at the start of the play, then seems forgotten until near its end. When Medea first appears, she speaks as a contemporary Greek, or more exactly Athenian, woman. In this light, she is still a passionate and intelligent (or scheming) figure, but is vulnerable and victimized, as any Greek woman might be. Her life has been given over entirely to Jason, who is now leaving her for another woman for social and economic reasons and probably because he has grown tired of her. Medea articulates a woman's dilemma eloquently, evoking what must have been common contemporary experience (at least of a "middle" class): the arranged marriage, the dowry price, the bride's going to an alien house, inexperienced and at the mercy of what her husband might really be like, confined to that house, while the husband was free to make a life outside and find distraction there at any time, and, finally, facing the hazards of childbirth—greater, Medea asserts in famous, challenging lines, than thrice standing in the line of battle (231–251). Medea's own situation, moreover, is even worse, because she is an alien in a foreign country and has no family to return to once she is abandoned. To be sure, it could be said that she chose to follow and help Jason (he argues, to absolve himself from responsibility, that passion made her do it: 526 ff.) and to have burnt all bridges back to her family. Yet one can also see the extremity of Medea's situation as a deeper representation of the life of the Greek married woman, who is like an alien, feeling her family irrevocably lost, seen and probably feared by the male as a creature wholly absorbed in her emotional life, her "bed" as everyone, but especially the men, call it (ignoring, incidentally, her further involvement with children), and who is considered to have intelligence fit only for domestic scheming.

When Medea says that she would prefer fighting in battle three times to giving birth once, she could be seen to draw attention to what Greek society would regard as the essential social function of women, the reproduction of the community itself. More obviously, she challenges men's claim to superior status on the basis of their role as fighters, risking their lives for the community. A female and male perspective are combined in Medea. In addition to being a wife and mother, she is cast in the role of hero and heroic avenger. Here, personal and larger issues are at stake, again. Medea is betrayed both emotionally and personally and is the subject of a violation of a socially established sanction—the pact, in this case of marriage, sworn to by solemn oaths (20–23, 160–163, 169–170, 206–208, 410 ff., 439 ff., 492–495, 1391–1392; an example of such an oath, which Medea gets from Aegeus, is shown at 737 ff.). She is both avenger for herself and an agent of divine retribution for the violation of a sacred law. In the latter case she is a Fury, a divine scourge (1059, 1260, 1330, see also 1013–1014). In the former she is like a hero who will not brook dishonor to her person. Like the traditional hero, she is marked by a sense of her own worth, by a sense of obligation to forefathers (406), by a self-willed, stubborn determination, unswayed even by friendly advice (27–29, 103 f., 109–110, 119–120, 176–177, 590, 621, 1028), by being com-

pared to natural forces, a monster, a lion (28–29, 189, 1342–1343, 1358–1359), by acute sensitivity to ridicule (383, 405–406, 797, 1049–1050, 1355, 1362), by loyalty to friends, and, above all, by implacable hatred of enemies.

> Let no one [Medea says, summing up her plan of revenge] think me of no account or powerless, nor a quiet stay-at-home. Quite the contrary: consider me hard on my enemies and to my friends kindly. That sort of person has the life of greatest glory.
> (807–810)

And typically this heroic assertion ends with heroism's final goal and prize, (everlasting) glory or fame.

This combination of female- and male-defined roles in Medea is a main source of the play's disturbing effect and power. Mixing women's domestic sphere and the male heroic world suggests a dissolution of the boundaries that define the accepted order of Athenian society. At the same time, antagonisms between the two spheres as well as contradictions within them are uncovered. Both Medea and the chorus of Corinthian women (she easily wins their support) explicitly identify the women's world as confined and oppressed, and as misrepresented by a society that is publicly dominated by men (231 ff., 410–430, 1081–1089). This world, as a result, is only negatively defined as passive—at the mercy of powerful feelings, private and obscure. Even its most evident contribution, the bearing and raising of children—who are continually present in the play and everyone's persisting preoccupation—is barely acknowledged, if not, as in Jason's case, intensely resented (565–575). Further, the women's sphere brings into sharp focus the contradictions inherent in the men's. When Medea behaves according to the male heroic code, she takes on a particularly frightening aspect; while at the same time the problems in that code are drastically revealed. Questions are raised (as they are by Homer's and Sophocles' heroes): To what lengths can a hero go to maintain a sense of self? Is there a point at which the hero's deeds bring infamy instead of fame? Who really are the friends whom the hero helps and the enemies he harms? This latter question most clearly defines the tragic center of the play.

As in *Alcestis*, the meaning of friend *(philos)* covers a range of possibilities, some potentially contradictory. Jason was once Medea's friend, her lover, for whom she gave up and betrayed her "friends," her kinsmen. Now Jason and his new friends, his wife-to-be, Creusa, and her father, Creon, king of Corinth, are Medea's enemies; her revenge will encompass them all. Medea's friends are at first only the nurse and the children's tutor, then, through her persuasion, the chorus, and, because of her capacity to help, Athens' king Aegeus; one last friend will be her grandfather the sun, who furnishes her with the chariot on which she makes her escape. But her most particular "friends," her "dear ones," are her own children. Above all, she should help them, both as their mother and according to the heroic code. Yet the heroic code also requires revenge on one's enemies, and Medea understands that revenge is fully achieved only if Jason is struck where he is most vulnerable. As he deprived her of her life in the family, striking at the vulnerable point of her trust in their bond, so she would take from him any possibility of reconstituting a family, striking at his desire to perpetuate himself through children. In the execution of the complete vengeance the heroic code—the male model for self-asserting action in the public world—appears, by a relentless logic, to involve the killing of one's own children. Its self-destructive violence is quite literally brought home.

Medea embodies these larger issues, and their tragic clash is her anguished dilemma: can she bring herself to kill her own children? In an extended, famous monologue she debates the decision with herself (1021–1080). Her resolution wavers as she looks at the children and imagines her life without them, and again as she embraces them. She is caught in a double

bind. If she is resolute and fulfills the heroic imperative, she destroys herself as a woman and mother. The children might just be saved (1045), yet still be in great danger for having been used as the unwitting agents of the first part of the revenge plot, bringing the poisoned gifts to Creusa; we are, so to speak, at the razor's edge of tragic necessity. But if Medea acts to save the children, she must give up the fulfillment of her revenge on Jason, abandon the heroic mode, be a "cowardly woman" entertaining "soft words" (1051–1052), and so lose her identity as an independently recognized, self-asserting person. Her monologue ends, as she chooses the heroic course:

> Though I understand what sort of evil I am going to do, still, heart is stronger than what I have thought out, this heart that causes humankind's greatest evils.
>
> (1078–1080)

She articulates a division within herself, an internalization of the conflicting worlds and values around her; and she acquires true tragic stature because she herself knows her own division and the destruction it entails. After this, however, her human aspect recedes again. Her pleasure in anticipating the messenger's account of Creusa's and Creon's horrific deaths is chilling (1132–1135). She then pauses only briefly before going on to kill the children (1242 ff.). And when she reappears for the last time, up above the stage roof on her divine chariot, the corpses of the children at her side, she is once more the sorceress of legend, a superhuman being, cruelly taunting the wretched Jason below, implacable in vengeance, unassailable and godlike.

In the lines from Medea's monologue just quoted above, the word translated as "heart" *(thumos)* can describe passion, anger, and, in the case of epic heroes, a warrior's "fury." It is also the word for "self" when a character talks to himself or herself (a usage in epic poetry and in archaic lyric; Medea uses it this way in this speech: 1056), a self now tragically divided.

239

"What I have thought out" translates a word meaning "plans." Irrational feeling and reflective reason are contrasted. (There is a complication insofar as Medea has just used the word "plans" to refer to her vengeance-plan [1044, 1048], but this indicates only how the plan calculated by reason subserves the irrational passion of vengeance.) Notably, the heroic ethic that wins out in Medea's speech and subsequent action is identified with the irrational elements within her, while the humane choice, preserving the children, is identified with a reasoning element. It may be that in these lines Euripides alludes to the Socratic argument that, if reason apprehends a right course of action, the performance of the action follows unimpeded, and so "no one errs willingly" (see Plato, *Protagoras* 352d). To this intellectual optimism Euripides opposes a problematic irrationalism.

The complicated relation of reason to forces associated with emotion is further illustrated in the play by the theme of intelligence. Medea's old nurse early in the play calls the poets of the past "inept" and not "wise" *(sophos)* because their poetry did no more than enhance already festive occasions, yet they could discover no way of assuaging the grief that destroys families (190–203). *Sophos*, like *philos* (friend), is another term of varying meaning and valuation (the issues raised by both are a continuing concern of Euripides). Its meaning includes "wise," "intelligent," "skillful"—it can be used of craftsmen and poets—as well as "shrewd" and "clever" in a derogatory sense. Euripides' relation to the new intellectual movements of his time is often invoked by it. Here, used of poets, it suggests a kind of self-reference, as though Euripides, through the character of the nurse, indicates that the poetry of his play may be attempting to discover a "remedy" (199) to cure those harsh feelings, like Medea's, that threaten domestic life. Such a reflection on the function of poetry from within the drama appears to be an innovation, or an adaptation of a practice found in epic and choral poetry especially and in the comic drama of Aristophanes.

Euripides is a kind of *sophos*, a poet who not only draws traditional inspiration from the Muses but is also at work with new ideas and rational argument. Medea is also partly cast in the role of *sophos*, in addition to the three aspects of her characterization already indicated: the legendary sorceress, the contemporary Athenian woman, and the heroic avenger. Creon orders her expulsion from Corinth because he fears her cleverness, her being a "wise woman" *(sophé)*, cunning in mischief, who will employ her intelligence to be avenged (282–291). Medea's response is a demonstration of that very intelligence, which is in fact her weapon, taking the place of the male's physical and institutional force, in the struggle to maintain her life. Strategically she disavows her intelligence—while defending the plight of intellectuals, especially innovative ones, before a hostile public (292–315)—and appeals to feeling and the sanction of supplication (324 ff.). A further association of intellectuality and women is made by the chorus directly following Medea's decision to kill her children. The chorus relates itself to a reflective rationalism that it claims for women too and associates with a "Muse" (1081 ff.), linking intellectual activity with a wider culture as well as, once more, with Euripides' own dramatic poetry. What they have thought out, they say, is that, all things considered, it is better to go through life without any children (1090–1115). Here, rationality is put in the service of a purely private goal of emotional self-sufficiency that simply ignores the community's need to reproduce itself, a need apparently supported by the nonrational forces that move human beings to produce and foster their children (the argument resembles one found in the contemporary sophist Antiphon). This position, to be sure, is as weak as the individual effort of thinking in the face of society as a whole and the emotional forces underlying it. In fact, it oddly resembles Jason's fantasy wish that men might produce children without women (574–

575), making the male world essentially self-sufficient. Jason himself represents a kind of vulgar rationalism. In his confrontation with Medea (446–626)—a rhetorically shaped contest or *agon* especially characteristic of Euripidean dramaturgy and in certain respects similar to contemporary law court speeches and to the antithetical political speeches represented by Thucydides—he is purely utilitarian and self-interested (see particularly 548–549 and 600; contrast 485). His arguments are a calculated evasion of justice. It is Medea who argues for justice, integrity, and truthfulness. (In this way, too, she recalls the heroic stance of an Achilles.) The general contrast of arguments from the point of view of advantage or of justice was part of contemporary political rhetoric.

At one point in the play "wisdom," the practice of reason, is raised to an ideal status. In the central scene, Medea wins the promise of refuge from the Athenian king Aegeus. There the word *sophos* describes noble heroes of earliest Athenian legend, Pandion (665) and Pittheus (686). (It also describes Apollo's oracle, ironically "too wise" to be understood: 675.) The chorus follows this scene with a splendid and famous song in praise of Athens—whose people are "nourished on wisdom [*sophia*, the noun form of the adjective *sophos*] most renowned" in a clear atmosphere where "the sacred Muses give birth to harmony," where Aphrodite is crowned with flowers and "the Loves [*Erōtes*] form an escort for wisdom [*sophia*], helpers in every kind of excellence [*aretē*]" (824–845). All the elements that in the play produce destructive conflicts are here integrated and beneficent: wisdom, fame, traditional poetry, passion, heroic achievement, and excellence. The place where this (Corinthian) drama is being performed, and the fact of its performance—evidence of Athenian artistic culture—are here evoked in idealized form. However, the chorus' song continues and asks in horror how Medea could kill her children and then go to a place so blessed as Athens (846 ff.). This too is a kind of direct address to the Athenian audience, suggesting the question, how will they receive this complicated, disturbing, child-killing figure? The integration of intellect and passion in the ideal representation of Athenian life and their tragic, problematic interconnection, which according to this play underlies that life, are left in uneasy, unresolved juxtaposition. The final effect of the play, as so often in Euripides, is difficult to assess simply. Its emotional power is undeniable: horror at Medea's final vengeance, pity for her dilemma and the children's death. But these feelings are somewhat offset by Medea's final transformation into something more than human, by the grim but appropriate justice achieved. (It may be too that Jason finally wins some sympathy in his abject destruction; at least a conventional, male Greek audience must have found the fate of this former epic hero, who is represented rather like one of them in his self-concerned, middle-class pursuits, very unsettling.) One could ask, do the horror and pity allow one also to consider the reasons for our feeling them? Yes, if the feelings Medea arouses are sufficiently ambivalent to make us think.

Most of Euripides' plays include at the end reference to a future continuation of the myth from which the human drama making up the main body of the play was drawn, and a link from the world of the play to some contemporary ritual practice—an etiology or explanation of the practice. Medea says that she will institute a festival and ritual "in the place of this impious murder" when she buries her children in the temple of Hera at Corinth (1378 ff.), that is, the killing of the children will be commemorated in a regularly performed religious ceremony, a ceremony of sacrifice observed in Corinth at the time of the play's performance. The irrational, passionately motivated, individual act is given a kind of rational status insofar as it is harmlessly repeated as part of a predictable pattern. Medea had, in fact, earlier called the killing of her children "my sacrifices" (1054), suggesting an act charged with religious force (whether negative or positive) within a ritual order. It is tempting to draw an analogy between the imitative or commemorative repetition of the ritual and the dramatic performance that confronts the audience with an "impious murder"—the complex of social tensions implied by it—and at the same time contains it within the formal conventions of tragic poetry, and, insofar as the drama itself is part of a ritual occasion, a festival in honor of Dionysus, within a ritual framework as well. Characteristically, Euripides allows a glimpse of the most archaic, religious elements of tragic drama, alongside the interweaving of contemporary intellectual speculation and social issues.

Where in *Medea* tragic action is focused almost exclusively from the viewpoint of the central character, in *Hippolytus* the tragedy involves three major figures (and carries with it an incidental fourth, Phaedra's nurse). As in *Alcestis*, a popular folktale pattern underlies the drama's plot—the story, recurring in Greek and Near Eastern mythology, about the sexual proposals of a woman to a younger man, who refuses and is then falsely accused to his sponsor or father, the woman's husband, of having sexually propositioned or raped her (the story of Joseph and Potiphar's wife in Genesis). But to a far greater extent than in *Alcestis*, the folktale is the scaffolding for a complex drama, which very nearly, but by no means entirely, looks as though it might have happened without any miraculous or divine interference.

Medea's story is of human revenge, which at the end turns into something more than human with Medea's transformation into a magical and religious force. *Hippolytus* is a story of divine vengeance, which ends with an unusual, if fleeting, expression of human solidarity. It is probably a comment on contemporary social bias that human solidarity is achieved in this play between an Athenian father and son, while the conclusion of *Medea* involves the destruction of relationships between an alien wife and her husband, and a mother and her chil-

dren. To an extent found elsewhere in Euripides only in *Heracles* and *Bacchae*—and in a quite different, undestructive way in *Ion*—divine forces in *Hippolytus* appear quite exactly to define and restrict the course of human lives. The play is framed between opposed deities, Aphrodite and Artemis.

Aphrodite, goddess of sexuality throughout the animate world, states at the start what will happen, so that her divine prerogative, unregarded by the virginal Hippolytus, who is exclusively devoted to Artemis, will be vindicated. This, she says, is going to come about through Phaedra's passion for the young man (a manifestation of Aphrodite's power) and its being revealed to Theseus, who will then cause his son's death by calling on a wish granted him by the god Poseidon. What happens is, in fact, considerably more complicated. Phaedra, after attempting desperately to suppress her passion for her stepson, admits it to the nurse, succumbing in part to the latter's anxious solicitude and in part to the paradoxical need to let the cause of her virtuous silence be known. The nurse proceeds on her own—though Phaedra's passivity is very near acquiescence (508–525; but see also 1305)—to tell Hippolytus. His reaction, inadvertently overheard by Phaedra, is violent and abusive, and implies that he may reveal everything to Theseus. Phaedra, in despair and anger, the hopelessness of her passion irrevocably established and—a crucial matter for her—her reputation at stake, decides to kill herself and throw the blame on Hippolytus in a letter accusing him of attempted rape, the letter to be found after her death. She is moved to forestall the accusation she imagines Hippolytus will make and to be avenged on him for the harsh manner of his rejection (in this respect her motives resemble Aphrodite's: compare 728–731 and 6–14, 48–50). Theseus, in extreme distraction at the news of his wife's death and without any attempt to determine, or capacity to understand, his son's position, believes without question what he finds in Phaedra's letter. Hippolytus, in turn, who had sworn not to reveal Phaedra's passion, is consistent in his piety, keeps his oath, and thus is unable to defend himself. Yet even before he confronts Theseus, the latter has already called down the fatal curse, and in addition has ordered his son's banishment—a secular punishment as near for a Greek to death as could be imposed. Hippolytus, on his way into exile, reaches a lonely place by the sea where a bull, "a wild portent," appears out of the waves with a great roar (perhaps a grotesque recollection of the birth of Aphrodite) and drives the horses of his chariot out of control until they wreck it on the cliffs and he is mortally wounded. And so Aphrodite's purpose is achieved.

This involved web of motivations suggests the complexity of the forces affecting human lives, working from within and outside. The individual characters act according to their natures, and at the same time represent social roles and their contradictions. Phaedra is an aristocratic woman who takes that role—preserving the integrity of the family and an unimpeachable reputation—seriously. At the same time she is a woman—in another, also typical, perspective—who is subject to powerful erotic passion, which itself is partly an inherited trait (her mother, Pasiphaë, and her sister Ariadne have both been involved in illicit passions: 337–341) and represents a longing to escape the confinements of her enclosed life, to participate in what she imagines is a free existence in the natural world enjoyed by Hippolytus (208–231). The nurse attempts to guide her mistress' way according to a down-to-earth practicality and resourceful argumentativeness, both of which have affinities with a popular, democratic character. Theseus is a figure of conventional male authority with a history of sexual adventures, which have included Phaedra's sister and Hippolytus' mother. Like Jason, he is a heroic figure who comes home, bringing back some of the domestic consequences of his exploits, a wife from abroad and a bastard son. Hippolytus is a young man, at a point in life which his society would regard as transitional,

but which he embraces as a perfect ideal, devoted to a purity that allows him both self-absorption and a privileged communal life in a kind of club of young men with whom he shares the pleasures of hunting and conviviality (108–111; compare 1016–1018, 1092–1099, 1179–1180). His desire for sexual purity and his devotion to the virgin goddess Artemis, who embodies that ideal and presides over the hunter's domain, may, in turn, be a response to his status as bastard, and part of an inheritance from his Amazon mother, Hippolyta. Each character in the end acts under conditions that in themselves are understandable, even commendable—saving a reputation, saving a mistress' life, being broken by grief over a wife's death, preserving the demands of piety. Yet each is so constituted as to fail crucially to understand and communicate with the other; what they all share is the human limit of vision, which separates them. They also share membership in the same household. At the start of the play, they are spatially separated (suggesting their distance from one another in understanding), Phaedra confined in the palace (she is carried out in front of it because stage convention does not allow interior scenes), Hippolytus in the countryside, Theseus abroad on an errand at Delphi. The concatenation of events bringing them together as it does, and in the family space, precipitates the tragic outcome, destroying them all.

Whether one takes the rough, general view that Aphrodite has brought all this about, or whether one sees a more intricate pattern of causes, involving human character, happenstance, and social pressures, the tragic result is the same. In this light the play is exceptionally grim. From within it, the cries for escape (208 ff., 673–674, 732–751, 1290–1293), the voices of despair and bafflement, seem to outweigh even the expressions of pity. The play starts with doom hanging over a young, unknowing protagonist (56–57), then follows with a long sickbed scene (176–524) representing Phaedra's dilemma: she is afflicted with a "disease" (this traditional metaphor for private and public disorder pervades the play), whose nature is a mystery to all but herself (40, 269) and whose cure, once the sickness is identified, cannot be found, except in death. Then the contagion spreads to Hippolytus (730, 933). (Phaedra's passion for Hippolytus is also regarded as a disease because it is illicit, subverting a series of social norms—incest prohibition, a woman's marital fidelity, and a woman's sexual passivity.) Faced with the obscure affliction of her mistress, the nurse reflects:

> Every human life is full of pain,
> without relief from tribulations.
> Whatever is kindlier than this living
> darkness enfolds and hides in clouds.
> Whatever this is that glitters on earth,
> We reveal ourselves desperately in love with it,
> because of ignorance of another life
> and no demonstration of what is below earth;
> we drift along on mere stories.
>
> (189–197)

The bafflement before life-destroying sickness recalls the situation in Athens about a year before the production of the play, when a plague struck that, according to Thucydides (*Histories* 2.47.2), doctors could not deal with and no human skill or appeal to the gods through supplication and oracle could help. (The situation is also recalled in Sophocles' *Oedipus Tyrannus*, produced a few years after *Hippolytus*.) Only knowledge of what lies beyond human life would help, but human reason is, so to speak, by definition incapable of such knowledge. All that is left are "stories" (*muthoi*), unreliable because not susceptible to rational proof. As in *Medea*, Euripides suggests reflection on the drama itself, whose basis is made up precisely of such *muthoi*. The nurse's dilemma of understanding is like the dramatist's. Each will attempt to overcome it. The nurse, after the shock of learning the nature of Phaedra's affliction, determines simply to save her life at all costs; and to this end she draws freely on "sto-

ries" about the gods to bolster her arguments (452 ff.). In the absence of rational coherence, human life is reduced simply to maintaining itself, survival. Survival in turn requires adaptive skills; and the nurse's arguments on behalf of Phaedra's life reveal a further conflict, between a realistic assessment of the forces affecting life, notably Aphrodite's power, which drives the procreative forces of all life (447–450), and the moral, or social, imperatives. Phaedra is caught hopelessly between the two. In a surprisingly deliberate tone of argument, she articulates her dilemma as one between the capacity of rational understanding and the feelings or emotional dispositions attending action: "it seems to me that it is not that we do so badly because of the nature of our intelligence—many are certainly right-minded; we must see it this way: we understand and recognize what is good, but do not sustain the effort to achieve it" (377–382). The conflict of reason and nonrational forces recalls Medea's dilemma, but Phaedra, more passive and constrained, tries to fulfill the social role assigned to her. Yet this causes her to decide that the only honorable and rationally arguable course open to her is suicide. Both women enact in themselves the contradictions—the irrationality—of their worlds. Phaedra does so in the terms not of the male heroic imperative but of her ordinary, domestic life, subject to indolence (she is an aristocrat), pleasant talk, and reflectiveness, but without any scope for public action. Her reflections discover a further contradiction, within language itself, in the word that describes both the imperative by which she attempts (and fails) to live and the idea by which Hippolytus chooses (or is naturally disposed) to live—and also fails: *aidós*, meaning variously "shame," "restraint," "chastity," and "respect" (385 ff.; compare 78 ff.). Finally, she is confronted by society's double standards: she feels with particular intensity the pressure on a woman of her class to maintain a good name, by remaining chaste, and yet observes that secret adultery is common (406–421). Like Hippolytus, she refuses to compromise, and perishes because of her refusal. The tragedy is that the integrity of each does not mesh with the other; each is limited, and therefore both vulnerable and destructive, to self and others.

The chorus, witnessing these two fates, responds dispiritedly:

> Greatly does the gods' care for us, when it comes to the mind, take away pain; I had kept within me, in hope, understanding, now it fails me as I look over the chances and deeds of mortal life: things shift this way and that way, the span of men's lives is a continual wandering.
>
> (1102–1110)

Like the nurse, they fall back on accommodation and adaptability, their faith in understanding broken by the prospect of Hippolytus' unmerited punishment (1111–1125; compare 253–266, 467); and they go so far as to express outright anger at the gods (1146). Like the nurse, too, their sentiments represent a common, ordinary response, in contrast to the unbending, aristocratic ideals of Phaedra and Hippolytus. A larger set of conflicts, then, emerges: on the one hand, the uncompromising ideal, associated with an assumption of order, social and divine justice, and rational understanding; on the other hand, an adaptive position, assuming the irrationality and obscurity of life's meaning. The first can be related to an attempt to structure human society according to a set of articulated rules or laws (nomoi); the second involves acceptance of natural forces (physis) as an irreducible given. The first, in this drama, invites destruction; the second attempts to negotiate survival on whatever terms can be obtained. Finally, the first is associated with heroism, poetry, myth, and the gods; the second with a kind of realistic, everyday perspective, empirical rationalism, and the acceptance of chance as the moving force of events. The first is the stuff of tragedy, the second a recoiling from or evasion of tragedy. In their combination lies one of the distinctive characteristics of Euripidean tragedy and, one could say—aligning the first with an aristocratic and the second with a democratic viewpoint—of Athenian society.

The presence of the goddesses Aphrodite and Artemis appears to deny chance or random motivation, one foretelling the outline of the events we witness, the other closing them off, explaining to the human actors what has actually happened and pointing to something like a future reordering. At the same time, however, the goddesses themselves contradict each other (1301–1302, 1328–1332, 1416–1421) and act according to standards (notably vindictiveness) characteristic of human society and morally problematic (2148–2150, 97–98, 114–120, 1331–1332, 1416–1422). The sexual passion that Aphrodite represents and manipulates for her vengeance is also considered a random, unpredictable force, which "flits about," as the chorus sing, "like a bee" (561); and Artemis too is associated with the bee (77).

In the end the figure of Hippolytus embodies in the face of these entanglements both their larger contradictions and some sense of a redeeming order. Phaedra's fate recedes before his; she is, after all, only Aphrodite's agent and a woman (nothing more, unlike Medea), and her tragedy remains enclosed within the categories imposed on her by her society. Hippolytus, though perhaps psychologically simpler and less clearly sympathetic to us, is the final point of attention, in an extended spectacle of mental and physical suffering. His devotion to chastity is the remarkable feature of a more general piety. Within Greek social convention, it is highly unusual and marks him, like his illegitimate status, as anomalous (a sign too of tragic heroes—Medea, for example, and, above all, Oedipus). A figure who stands apart, he also represents a turning to a purely private life, which finds expression in his individual relationship to the goddess Artemis, and in an explicit withdrawal from the opportunities of politics that he would normally be expected to pursue (1010–1020). This privacy points to contradictions in his life. At his first entrance he addresses Artemis with a personal prayer whose beautiful language recalls the personal lyric of earlier Greek poetry (73–87). In this prayer the accepted belief that access to a sacred precinct requires ritual purity is internalized in what seems to be a new way. In fact, the particular space Hippolytus describes, an "untouched meadow," seems to be sacred only in his private imagining (no markers, man-made or designated, are mentioned). The virtue that would rightfully allow access to this precinct cannot, he claims, be taught (as the rules for the normally practiced, formal cleansing or purification would be); such a virtue is possessed only by nature, innately in one's inner being (79–81). Thus, internalizing his piety, Hippolytus also makes it exclusive. But the exclusive claim to natural virtue—which is also an aristocratic claim—conflicts with a larger sense of nature in the play as a whole, nature as a range of forces associated with goddesses like Aphrodite and Artemis (the play's view of her, too, is broader than Hippolytus'), morally indifferent and not subject to human rationality. A notable symptom of Hippolytus' narrow understanding of nature is his extraordinary misogyny (though in fact it has a long tradition in Greek literature). He speaks of women as a counterfeit coinage, not natural beings but deceiving fabrications (something like Hesiod's Pandora), and, like Jason, fantasizes about substituting for the natural process of procreation a sexless commercial transaction (618–624). This drastic rejection is curiously reflected in the end of the play.

As in *Medea*, near the end, the play's action is linked to a ritual, here practiced in Troezen (the setting of the play), which is to be a "compensation" for what Hippolytus has suffered (1423; compare *Medea* 1383). Artemis foretells the cult honors he will receive when unmarried girls perform the ritual cutting of their hair before marriage. He will "through the age's long cycle reap the greatest grief of their tears," and the maidens will "ever" be charged with "doing the Muses' work" in his honor (1426–1429). This is a beautiful fixing of a tragic career into a permanent poetic memorial—in fact, what Euripides' play has done, sustained by the

recurring ritual to which it alludes. But there is also the irony that Hippolytus, who had refused women and marriage, becomes the central figure of a cult that marks the transition to marriage and womanhood. (He himself, in his virginity, could be regarded as both male and female; he speaks of his "maiden soul": 1006.) Euripides again leaves us with a double view. In *Medea*, reference to a ritual of sacrifice is offered as a possible clue to the meaning of an ambivalent and violent story of revenge. In *Hippolytus*, a ritual of transition, a rite of passage, has a similar function. But Hippolytus suffers the trauma associated with such a ritual in a particularly brutal way, compounded by a sharp sense of injustice and for reasons more complicated than the fact that in the normal order of things he will have to give up the restricted life of a young man. The order that the ritual represents and the beautiful poetry with which the play is filled, associating natural forces and the gods, are set against the bleak prospect of isolated human life. In this play, after the consolation of a ritual prospect, after Artemis has gone—for the goddess would be tainted by the sight of death (1437–1439; Hippolytus' on stage death is unusual in tragedy)— there is a final moment of purely human reconciliation between Hippolytus and Theseus. Human and, it must be said, male. Hippolytus, having won a divine favor for the time after his death, freely, and with a nobility more innate than legitimately produced (1452–1453), grants a favor that only a human being could bestow, forgiveness. A condition of that forgiveness is the overwhelming pressure of human mortality, though Artemis' urging of it (1435; compare 1326 and 1405) is a benign, contributing factor.

WAR AND POLITICS: DRAMAS OF SUPPLICATION, SACRIFICE, AND REVENGE

In *Alcestis*, *Medea*, and *Hippolytus*, contradictory pressures—socially determined, moral, and religious imperatives; and aspects of the characters themselves, psychological forces—motivate the dramatic action. The characters appear as individual figures struggling with personal destinies. They stand out partly because their struggles take place within a separate, domestic sphere; at the same time, the presence of gods and the allusions to ritual give that sphere a wider, more universal import. In a number of subsequent plays the dominating pressures are public and political. In one way or another they have to do with war, as the enactment or result of life under political crisis. War is both the motivating background of these plays and a reflection and commentary on the effects of the contemporaneous Peloponnesian War. In the setting of war, politics takes its harshest form as the struggle between strong and weak, to which all else, all traditional values and means of social coherence, is subordinated. The most trenchant analysis of this process can be found in Thucydides' *History of the Peloponnesian War*. He singles out two exemplary moments in its first years: the plague at Athens, an irrational incursion against which (as we noted before) all human skill is helpless, and (perhaps partly as a result) a profound demoralization and indifference to moral and religious restraints follow (2.52–53); and the ferocious civil wars at Corcyra, an example of how the war fosters internal as well as external conflict and destruction (3.82–83), and how in these factional battles traditional values are undermined and perverted. This perversion, in turn, is reflected in a new instability of the language of values itself, a language once derived from the aristocratic code (3.82.4–5). The traditional fabric of public life comes unraveled; and dominating the process is an individualistic drive for revenge (3.82.7), itself a twisted form of the striving imposed by a heroic code to assert and defend one's honor. (The word for "revenge," *timória*, has the root meaning "looking after one's honor"; we could compare the relation of our words "vindictive" and "vindication.")

In the plays, these historical and social issues are represented through myth, especially the events and characters of the two great wars of heroic epic, the Trojan War and the expedition of the Seven against Thebes. The latter involves principally an internal conflict, stemming from a quarrel of brothers that ends in mutual fratricide. In tragedy this Theban war also focuses on conflicts arising from the development of the *polis*-community out of a social organization based on family ties. It makes up the subject of *Phoenissae* (at a time when Athens was severely affected by internal political struggle), and its aftermath is represented in *Suppliants* (in an earlier period of the war). Both plays include debates on the nature of government, on democracy and its rival regimes, that is, on the principles of the Greek city-state's coherence. (*Suppliants* appears more confident and rationally articulate on the claims of democracy.)

The Trojan War, and especially its background and aftermath, figures, in some form or other, in eight of the surviving plays (as well as the satyr play *Cyclops*). It is the universal or "world" war, involving all Greece as well as Asia. Though fought between Greek and non-Greek, it suggests the common humanity of both, their common subjection to cycles of defeat and victory, enslavement and freedom, and a common capacity for nobility or baseness, restraint or impious recklessness. Yet Euripides stresses the war's negative force: the suffering of the defeated; the moral degradation of the victors (in *Hecuba* and *Trojan Women*) and even of their victims (Hecuba in *Hecuba*); the irrational, deluded folly behind the war (*Helen*); and its destructive effects on private lives (*Andromache*, *Electra*, and *Orestes*). In the two Iphigenia plays and in the figure of Polyxena in *Hecuba*, sacrifice, though noble because voluntary, seems a wasted price paid for the waging of the war. Only certain motifs from the background of the war—the judgment of Paris, the marshaling of the Greek army, the heritage of the young Achilles—are presented, in choral songs, in an elaborated, lyric vein that suggests a kind of aesthetic detachment, a glimpse of a beautiful, separate world, though usually in strong contrast to a harsh, surrounding dramatic action (*Andromache* 274 ff., *Electra* 432 ff., *Iphigenia in Aulis* 164 ff., 573 ff., 1037 ff., 1283 ff.; contrast *Hecuba* 629 ff.).

Myth provides the material and the perspective from which elements of contemporary life are represented, both simplifying, by drawing on the familiar and typical, and elaborating poetically; both focusing emotional effects (especially in conjunction with heightened language, music, and dance) and distancing them in the special world of poetry and legend. However, an individual play's actual dynamics—the specific plot that defines its point of departure, development, and conclusion—are made out of a certain (restricted) number of component elements, chosen, modified, and combined to give the play its particular structure and movement and its underlying dramatic effect and meaning. The social and individual crises brought on by the pressures of war, for example, acquire their most precise expression through the shaping of a play's plot. The most important of these plot elements are supplication, sacrifice, revenge, recognition, and rescue. Scenes of plotting, devising, and executing a stratagem are often associated with revenge and rescue. One further technical feature of the drama might be mentioned here, the scene of confrontation and debate, or *agon*, setting one long speech against another, which is handled with particular virtuosity by Euripides. Insofar as it rarely causes dramatic movement of itself, however, it is not properly a plot element; rather it articulates oppositions, which may often be left unresolved.

These plot elements are technical and artistic resources with a tradition within the genre of tragedy as a whole, but they are also related to actual aspects of Greek life and institutions, and their implications change within the historical context of a play's production. For example, the revenge plot of Aeschylus' *Libation Bearers* takes part of its meaning from issues of juridical and political development in the middle decades of the fifth century B.C.; the revenge plots of Euripides' *Electra* and *Orestes* illustrate conditions of social disorder and change characteristic of the end of the century. Suppli-

cation, sacrifice, and revenge are most often associated in the plays with conditions determined by politics and war. Recognition and rescue tend to take place in more private circumstances.

Supplication as a formal plot element usually comes at the start of a play (there are also incidental supplications between individuals, for example, *Medea* 338 ff., *Hippolytus* 324 ff.). An initial spectacle of one or more people, sometimes (if time has allowed) holding wool-wrapped branches, at an altar, indicates a confrontation between the threatened weak and their powerful enemies. At the same time a test is implied of the efficacy of the altar—the religious sanction it represents—to protect the helpless, and of the willingness of the human community on whose land the altar stands to support that sanction, often at great political risk. During the latter part of the fifth century, suppliancy, one of the oldest of Greek socioreligious institutions, was in the process of change, taking on a more political and secular form that involved individuals seeking asylum with the *polis* as a whole. Euripides' use of the plot element of supplication variously reflects the issues raised by this process—the movement from personal to political relations and, under the pressures of the war, the tensions between religious sanction and political expediency. Of six plays including supplication, *Andromache* and *Heracles* show its failure; the later *Helen* and *Ion* suggest that its force is marginal; and *Heraclidae* and *Suppliants*, plays closer to the early years of the war, represent it as successful. In the latter two plays, the city called on to support the suppliants is Athens, traditionally reputed to assist outsiders in distress (a tradition still represented at the end of the century in Sophocles' *Oedipus at Colonus*).

Even in these two plays, however, the suppliant plot element is combined with others that affect its meaning. In *Heraclidae*, supplication is followed by a sequence of voluntary self-sacrifice and then revenge. Athens at first willingly undertakes the risks of protecting the suppliants, but then it cannot find among its citizens an individual sacrificial victim (a role that must be chosen by one of the suppliants themselves); and finally the city is divided, partly urging the successful suppliants to refrain from taking vengeance on their arch-enemy by execution (an execution contrary to the usual Greek practice regarding prisoners of war—usual at least until the early years of the Peloponnesian War), and yet, in the person of the Athenian chorus, weakly acquiescing in a cheap compromise that allows the revenge to be exacted after all (1053–1055; compare 250–258, 1022–1025). In *Suppliants*, the supplication is less on behalf of the protection of individuals than for the upholding of the common Greek religious custom of allowing the enemy dead to be buried after battle. It becomes the occasion of a full representation of, and apology for, Athenian intervention in a just cause—a representation recalling a number of the themes of the funeral oration of Pericles recounted in Thucydides. Against this political background, Euripides sets the inconsolable, private grief of the bereaved and the unexpected voluntary self-sacrifice of Evadne, wife of one of the fallen warriors. Unlike the sacrifice of Makaria in *Heraclidae*, performed in response to a religious mandate and for the sake of the suppliant group, Evadne chooses spontaneously to throw herself on her husband's funeral pyre. Though she expects to win glory for it, her action is entirely private and unrelated to the suppliant drama; in fact, it offsets and distracts from that drama's public and patriotic themes. Finally, in *Heraclidae*, there is revenge, though only forecast, not enacted (1143–1153, 1213–1223). In both plays Athens, the defender of the suppliants' sanctioned and just claims, gains tangible, political rewards (*Heraclidae* 1026–1034, *Suppliants* 1187–1195). And in both plays the issue of revenge complicates that moral balance. In *Heraclidae*, the balance is complicated because the reward comes through the agency of the original persecutor of the suppliants and because the suppliants, having achieved the aim of their supplication, will not act according to the moral dictates of their defenders (1009

ff.). In *Suppliants*, the balance is complicated because the promised revenge will involve a renewal of war by the grandchildren of the mourning mothers, and belies anguished calls for peace and rational conduct in political affairs (748–749, 949–954). Here the Euripidean ambivalence is most clearly shown by the fact that the spokesman of the suppliants' enemies makes the most eloquent defense of peace, "dearest to the Muses, hateful to the goddesses of vengeance" (479–493).

Sacrifice and revenge, the two commonest plot elements in Euripides' surviving plays, indicate the opposed and complementary sides of his drama. The first, in the form of voluntary self-sacrifice for family, husband, friend, or community, represents a test and proof of natural nobility; suggests an ideal; and solicits admiration for and hope in the selflessness of the young. (It is only the young, mostly young women, who offer themselves and are accepted as victims.) This plot element, common in popular folktales, perhaps first brought into drama by Euripides, appears in some form in nine plays, both early (*Alcestis*) and late (*Iphigenia in Aulis*), and as far as one can make out is not found in the other dramatists. Revenge plots, on the other hand, had long been common to the tragic genre. In these, as the example of *Medea* already illustrates, Euripides is harshly realistic, uncovering individual and social contradictions in their most destructive aspects.

The larger background of sacrifice plots is, of course, religious practice. It may well be that the elusive origins of Attic tragedy itself are partly bound up with sacrificial ritual. In each play, killing, with its concomitant excitement, terror, and sense of release, is a central action, though partly distanced in the drama; and each play constitutes an effort to understand or justify that action. The killings in tragedy are often described in the language of ritual sacrifice, while the ritual itself is theatrical, involving staging, dressing up, and playacting. Both the religious practice and the drama mark special occasions in which a human, political community bonds itself while isolating some part of itself—the principals of the sacrificial action, victims and executioners—on behalf of higher, divine powers, who sanction the bond.

This religious force is represented by Euripides as a somewhat remote, partly obscure imperative that requires the payment of an ancient, all-but-forgotten debt, essentially to the underearth powers of the dead (*Heraclidae* 402–409, *Hecuba* 36 ff., 110 ff., *Phoenissae* 931 ff., and in general, of course, *Alcestis*). In the two Iphigenia plays the antecedent reason for sacrifice remains unexplained or vague; an unfulfilled vow is mentioned in *Iphigenia among the Taurians* (17 ff.), but no cause is given for the vow. A main emphasis in the sacrifice actions is on the victim or subject, the person sacrificed. Though in a larger sense helpless or trapped, this person is shown taking active control over her (or his) role, knowingly or deliberately choosing it. In this way, the dramatist gives the archaic religious practice a human dimension and partly recovers it from the blind, compulsive spell of ritual. There is, however, a price for this movement toward a more purely human, individualized perspective. Even as the motivating forces for sacrifice are obscure, as they represent a pressure from the past that can be neither resisted nor quite comprehended, so the future effect, the wider, public value of the sacrifice, is hedged by doubt. Already Alcestis' sacrifice, though noble and impressive, had a double edge, at once saving Admetus' life and taking away his reason for living. In *Heraclidae*, Makaria's sacrifice seems to be a necessary condition of the Athenian army's successful defense of the suppliants' cause. Yet once she leaves the stage, nothing more is heard about her, while the report of the battle suggests that the victory was due to the last-minute appearance of troops gathered by Heracles' son Hyllus and the miraculous rejuvenation of the suppliants' leader Iolaus. Evadne's sacrifice in *Suppliants*, as remarked, is completely self-enclosed. In *Hecuba*, one of Euripides' darkest plays, the sacrifice of Polyxena is only a brief illumination, isolated and offset by her mother's gradual dehumanization through vengeance.

Sacrifice in *Heraclidae* and *Suppliants* (and also *Andromache*) follows a suppliant action, and it is in some measure a validation of the suppliants' claim for support. In *Hecuba*, sacrifice follows on an attempted, and rejected, personal supplication by Hecuba and the explicit refusal of Polyxena to make a supplication (342–345; compare 290). Polyxena gives up her life, then, not for any larger cause, but because she cannot see any prospect of a life worth living for an aristocrat who refuses contamination by any kind of slavery; she would rather be dead than alive as a prisoner of war. Her noble behavior at the execution, sympathetically reported by a Greek herald, wins the respect of the mass of the Greek army and slightly eases her mother's grief. Yet it does not affect Hecuba's decline under the pressures of disaster. Only the heroic manner of Polyxena's death allows it to bypass the gulf between the victors and the defeated and to avoid a suggestion of collaboration with the enemy. Polyxena's behavior elicits the pity of the herald who reports her death and the pity of her executioner (519, 566). She is described as she offers herself up for slaughter, tearing the clothes from her upper body and exposing her breasts, "most beautiful, like a statue's" (558–561). The soldiers, finally, cover her body with leaves, as though she were a victor at the Olympic games (573–574). Euripides has caught and frozen the scene as an ideal moment. Yet the executioner still strikes, and the play returns to what is actually before us, the survivors, Hecuba and her desperation.

In two later plays, the plot element of sacrifice is more directly involved in larger patterns within the overall dramatic action. The voluntary sacrifice of Menoikeus in *Phoenissae* is noteworthy not only because, like Evadne in *Suppliants*, he refuses to obey a father who would prevent it, but also because his father, Creon, rules the state that the sacrifice is intended to preserve. Euripides now raises the issue of private survival within the family, and its problematic relation to the public salvation of a community, an issue that the later years of the war, with both the increase of factionalism in internal politics and Athens' increasingly hazardous position before her enemies, had brought more sharply into focus. The public effect of Menoikeus' sacrifice, unlike Makaria's in *Heraclidae*, is brought to the audience's attention, at least for a moment (1090–1093). Yet Thebes's victory is due, finally, after a long chain of events, to quite different factors: military strategy (1093 ff.), an isolated instance of divine interference (1174–1180), and the alertness of the soldiers (1466–1471). Menoikeus' sacrifice in its purity of motive (even as he is a ritually pure victim: see 941–947) throws into relief Creon's complex situation, as a man with family feeling and interest (919 ff., 1206–1207, 1310 ff.), then as the surviving ruler of the city. As ruler he changes (no doubt hardened by his personal losses) into a complete spokesman of the city, commanding that his nephew Polyneices, leader of the expedition against Thebes, be denied burial, and that his brother-in-law Oedipus, whose family has been declared to be the root of Thebes's troubles (886–888, 1589–1591), must go into exile. This change in Creon is matched—in the elaborately designed fullness of this drama—by a change in Antigone. Early in the play, she appears as an innocent and sheltered girl with a romantic view of heroic warfare. At the end, she returns transformed by her family's calamities into a determined, heroic figure who refuses a marriage connection with the ruling house of Thebes in order to attempt, against the city's decrees, to bury her brother Polyneices and to accompany her old, blind father into exile. She refuses both the advantages and the imperatives of the public sphere for the sake of individual resistance on her family's behalf. Though not formally set out as a sacrificial action, the young girl's choice is a counterpart to Menoikeus' sacrifice. Like Makaria and Evadne, she claims "glory," "noble fame," as one of her motives (1659, 1742); Menoikeus speaks of avoiding "disgrace" and effecting "good" for one's native community (999, 1013, 1015–1018). Simple, selfless devotion to city is set against individual heroism

for family, and it is with the latter, the more dramatically integrated and emotionally compelling, that Euripides ends the play. It is notable that the more idealized representation of sacrifice is Menoikeus', probably Euripides' invented addition to the mythical material of his plot and an incident relatively isolated. (A comparable example is the figure of Theonoe in *Helen*, also probably a Euripidean invention, who represents an ideal of ritual purity combined with a moral and rational vision, and who seems central to the play's structure and yet is relatively marginal to the final working out of the plot.)

Iphigenia in Aulis is the last of Euripides' plays, together with *Bacchae*, to be written and survive (perhaps not quite finished and possibly somewhat altered after his death, though probably not in any important degree). It is entirely made out of the story of the best-known sacrifice in Greek myth. Agamemnon's sacrifice of his daughter, the necessary prelude to the Greek expedition against Troy, which is re-evoked at the end of the war ten years later by a chorus of Argive elders, had set in motion Aeschylus' *Oresteia* trilogy (*Agamemnon* 109–251). There Agamemnon is the king around whom divine conflicts and issues of divine justice are gathered; Iphigenia is a mute, unwilling victim, described, at the moment of the sacrifice, "as in a picture." Euripides' play, filled—as often in these later plays—with circumstantial incidents and characters, culminates in Iphigenia's decision to be a willing victim. The context of the story is secularized, and, in the usual Euripidean manner, the renowned characters—in addition to the father and daughter, Clytemnestra, Menelaus, Achilles, an infant Orestes, Odysseus—have their heroic dimensions reduced, particularized, and made simply human. As in *Phoenissae*, the sacrifice sharply raises issues of the relation of private life to public constraints and needs.

Agamemnon is a more closely observed version of Creon, weaker because caught in a greater variety of pressures: personal ambition, a contradictory desire to be free of public responsibility, the demands of his brother, the insistent presence of his wife, close affection for his daughter, and, finally and decisively, the desires of the army he is supposed to be commanding, abetted and manipulated by the personally ambitious Odysseus, working hand-in-glove with the seer Calchas (513–527).

Iphigenia combines aspects of both Menoikeus and Antigone in *Phoenissae*. With the former, she shares a ritual status and devotion to a public cause, though in each case with more complex implications. With the latter, she shares a claim to "glory" (1376, 1383, 1399; compare 1440, 1504, 1531) and a change in character, though more abrupt and surprising. A young, sheltered, and innocent girl, she is at one blow deceived in her expectation of a marriage and confronted with death. Her first response is an impassioned supplication for her life (1211 ff.). But then her father explains his dilemma. He is under irresistible pressure from the army, which is seized by a passion for war and a desire to recover a national honor feared lost through the abduction of a Greek woman (Helen) by a barbarian (Paris); and if the expedition is denied, the army threatens to turn against Agamemnon's own city of Argos (1264–1268). Now, Iphigenia sings a lament for herself, of which the poetry, especially in the account of the judgment of Paris, creates for her own fate a larger backdrop, distancing and softening it, and whose wider vision encompasses the anguish of family betrayal, the ruinous Helen, the circumstantial effects of Zeus as weather god, and, in anticipation, the sufferings of the Greeks as well as of all human beings (1279–1335). Her lament turns from self to the whole world. Finally, in a movement from resignation to action—and partially back to self—at the sudden entrance of Achilles, whose bride she was to have been and whose troops have turned against him for defending her (enacting what the army had threatened against Agamemnon), she responds to the critical turn of events by declaring herself ready, of her own free will, to be sacrificed. At this climax of the drama, a heroic choice, sustained by eloquence

and poetry, transcends the individual weaknesses, vacillations, vanities, and self-serving surrounding it. Iphigenia appears to have met the need of the Greeks to resolve their potentially self-destructive differences.

This marks an ideal achievement for sacrifice. No greater service for the community, the widest community of Greece itself, could be imagined. In this light, too, the play addresses a Greek world in the last stages of a war increasingly ruinous for all concerned. It implies an appeal to the common sense of self-preservation among Greek cities, as urged, for example, four years before in Aristophanes' *Lysistrata*; and linked to that appeal, with the increasing involvement of the Persians in the war, is a reminder of the united force, led by Athens and Sparta, that had withstood and defeated the Persian attack earlier in the century. Finally, the play evokes the grimly realistic principle that calls for the resolution, or deflection, of internal strife by a united war against a common, external enemy, of a Greece united against the "barbarians" (so *Lysistrata* 1133–1134; compare Aeschylus, *Eumenides* 864–865, 913–915). All this, represented in the terms of heroic myth, must have appealed to a contemporary audience. But the play has counter-currents too. Set against the public, political theme, there is a persistent preoccupation with personal encounters and relations, drawn in fine, sometimes even humorous, detail. There is the representation of sordid or futile behind-the-scenes political manipulation, and a sense of revulsion at the machinery of politics and the corruption of individual politicians (seen also in Sophocles' *Philoctetes*, produced in 409 B.C., especially, again, through the figure of Odysseus; it is a common Aristophanic theme, most despairingly in *Frogs*, produced in 405). There is the wavering purpose of the army itself, first willing to disband and go home (332–333, 803–819), and then consumed by war-lust, as though the larger purpose or justice of the expedition were irrelevant. Above all, there is the fact that to make such a unified effort possible, a father must sacrifice his daughter, deceiving her with the promise of marriage to the army's greatest warrior. Euripides draws attention to this point by the alignment of two rituals, one that precedes a marriage ceremony (718–721, 1111–1113) and one that precedes a battle, each a common Greek practice involving blood sacrifice and the goddess Artemis (433, 882, 1114, and by implication 718). For a moment, it seems, Euripides lets us see a translation of the meaning of the marriage ritual, a traumatic ritual of passage in which a young girl must leave the only home known to her, given away by her father (a betrayal) to a virtually alien life (a kind of death), for the sake of the orderly perpetuation of Greek society, seen publicly as a male enclave, an army. The preparatory sacrifice for marriage becomes a preparatory sacrifice for war, where war is regarded as a positive, productive effort. (We may recall Medea's juxtaposition of childbearing with fighting in battle.) More generally, however, Euripides creates an effect of unsettling discontinuity by evoking the archaic, ritual aspects of Iphigenia's sacrifice in a context that is immediate, contemporary, and essentially secular (the Aeschylean, theological dimensions of the story, in which the sacrifice of Iphigenia is in some sense necessary because of an offense against the goddess Artemis, are completely suppressed). The meaning of the sacrifice, then, in this play too, is in the end ambivalent. Iphigenia's own part in it is heroic, but her heroism is isolated, and perhaps does not quite still the suspicion that she is infected by the madness of the army. She enacts a harsh logic of redemption, but the play suggests that, at least at the level of the public life it represents, there may not be much left worth redeeming; and what is of value, the young and idealistic, become sacrificial victims or, as in the case of Achilles, may not survive the pressures of a corrupting environment.

The ambivalence of Euripides' presentation of sacrifice hinges on the disjunction of its personal aspect from its larger, public effect; or, to put it another way, it is due to seeing the sacrifice cut off from both a directly continuous source in the past and an effect in the future, cut off from a history and larger continuity. Insofar as sacrifice has a larger, more than personal meaning, it acquires that meaning from its religious basis, which is also a social basis, integrated with the familiar and validated experience of its audience. The development of the notion of self-chosen sacrifice is a sign of the weakness of that base, or its contradictory character: an institution as such is inadequate and part of its function falls to individual human initiative—an initiative cast in heroic form and yet coming mostly from the weakest members of the society, the young, the defeated, the female. But Euripides' locating of individual sacrifice within a religious frame suggests that, for all its limitations, such a frame or structure is felt to be necessary. The dramatist shares with the intellectual revolution of the sophists a critical, secularized sense of what the gods and religious practices may mean, but he resists any repudiation of them. He appears to see religion as too much part of the fabric of people's lives, especially, we may suppose, in the middle and lower urban and peasant classes, to be simply dismissed.

If sacrifice brings forward the weaker to perform in a heroic manner, so also does revenge, but with contrary implications. Instead of allowing the possibility of noble and selfless action, revenge reveals the destructive aspects of the heroic code. The heroism of sacrifice is something new, an effort to draw from the heroic code a positive force. The heroic impetus to revenge, on the other hand, is a legacy from the past, too deeply ingrained to be shaken off and yet, in a changing world, deeply problematic. In *Hecuba*, one notices the isolation of Polyxena's sacrifice; what underscores that isolation is Hecuba's subsequent revenge. The setting of the play, as in *Iphigenia in Aulis*, is a military camp, now in a kind of limbo—barbaric Thrace on the Greek mainland—between the ruins of Troy and the homeland cities of the Greeks, which many, we know, will reach, if at all, only after severest hardships, or, as in Agamemnon's case, only to their ruin. In this desolate place, power relations and political pressures are exposed in their rawest form, an effect of the conditions of war: "The war, taking away the easy management of daily life, is a violent teacher, and assimilates the temper of the majority to their immediate circumstances" (Thucydides, *Histories* 3.82.2). Hecuba failed in her personal supplication for her daughter's life, addressing the politician Odysseus, who argued the community's greater advantage in honoring heroes and discounted the claim of a personal obligation (299 ff.). She makes a further supplication to Agamemnon for passive complicity in her revenge for the murder of her son, and is accepted. There could be no more than personal supplications because there are no altars on this stage, and no community is present that might sustain their sanction. Agamemnon, in spite of a declaration that "this is common [that is, the common interest or basis of a shared unity] to all: that both in the case of the individual person and the *polis* the wicked men suffer and the good prosper" (903–904; compare 800–805), cannot or will not actively support Hecuba's appeal for justice. Private and political considerations inhibit him, his interest in Cassandra and the fact that the army regards the criminal, Polymestor, the Thracian warlord, as an ally or "friend" (855–863). Hecuba, like Medea, though in far more extreme conditions—the conditions brought about by war—has suffered an injustice that not only is personally devastating but is itself a crime against a moral imperative of social order. Not only was Polymestor exceptionally brutal, killing Polydoros (Hecuba's last surviving male child) out of his own greed for money and denying the mutilated body burial, but the murder also viciously violates a tie of guest-friendship with the royal house of Troy (7, 19, 26, 774, 793–794, 1247–1248). Like Medea, too, Hecuba has no recourse for justice in the society around her. She may win expressions of pity, and, after she has exacted her revenge, Agamemnon, in a remarkable reversal of judicial procedure, declares her victim guilty (1240–1251). But first she is left on her own, to pursue vengeance for herself, on

the heroic model. Passion, the extremity of grief, drives her on, as it once did Achilles—to whom her daughter was sacrificed. It drives her so powerfully that she refuses an offer of freedom (so far will Agamemnon go to meet her desperation): "so long as I may be avenged on the base I am willing to live out my whole life in slavery" (756–757). Failure, she implies, to fulfill the demands of the heroic code is equivalent to being a slave. Later, with Agamemnon as her example, she declares that no human being is free, such are the constraints of money, chance, the majority of one's fellow citizens, the city's laws (864–867); that is, she describes a gulf between contemporary Athenian democracy and heroic individualism. Yet, as in *Medea*, heroic behavior entails "barbaric" acts. Hecuba contrives the blinding of Polymestor and the killing of his children. Thus, like Medea, she passes into a realm beyond what is human: Polymestor foretells her metamorphosis into a bitch, an animal that may be associated with an avenging Fury (1265 ff.; compare 685–687 and *Medea* 1260, 1059).

The strength of this play is in its harsh concentration. There are weak and strong, friends and enemies, whose statuses shift surprisingly in the setting of a reduced, transient community represented by the Greek army, a community capable of acting like a political assembly (107 ff.) but not accessible to outsiders for justice. Here heroic ideals become remote or irrelevant, as in Polyxena's sacrifice, or else twisted, as in the effects of Hecuba's need for recompense. Beyond this there are no wider perspectives in the form of poetic memorials or lyric elaborations; nor are there any divine presences, in spite of the presence of two ghosts in the story—that of the unburied Polydoros, which opens the play, and that of Achilles, which motivates the sacrifice. Gods are rarely mentioned. Hecuba attempts to claim law, *nomos*, a transcending principle that functions by virtue of human consensus, as the highest power over gods and humans (800 ff.), but, within the play's action, in vain. There are indications in the play that some retribution awaits the Greek heroes, and these allow us to suppose a wider, if vague, balancing force at work, though this is nothing to Hecuba. In the end, the play may have served as a kind of warning to the Athenians, or as a call to reflect on the effects of war. The horrors revealed and committed are the work of non-Greek outsiders, the Thracian Polymestor and the Trojan Hecuba, yet Agamemnon, and by implication his army, cannot keep clear of them. After all, is what the barbarians do to one another so much worse than, or different from, what the Greeks, who perform human sacrifices, may do? At the assembly that determines Polyxena's fate (conducted like a contemporary Athenian assembly), Theseus' sons (who were the representative Athenian champions in *Heraclidae*) both speak in favor of the sacrifice, taking Odysseus' side against Agamemnon, "to crown Achilles' tomb with living blood" (123–127). As in *Iphigenia in Aulis*, the price of war, even in its aftermath, is the killing of a virgin girl, so that, in this case, honor may be assured the dead and may continue to be the incentive for the highest heroism of the warrior in an army (134–140, 303–316; the arguments are Odysseus'). Many in the audience may have approved such a sentiment, but Euripides will have made those with any penetration uncomfortable.

In *Medea*, the action of revenge brings to light internal contradictions in the heroic code, because the code is claimed by a woman and an outsider. In *Hecuba*, revenge points to a more general crisis in the public sphere, when that sphere is dominated by war. Though Medea's enemies include the ruling family of Corinth, the play gives no sense of a political community. As a result, it seems inevitable that she should take vengeance into her own hands. Where no public justice is available, private and daemonic forces take over. Something like this happens in *Hecuba*, but with different implications because the play does represent a distinct political entity, the army, which might have brought Hecuba's enemies to justice. The spectacle of Hecuba's vengeance, then, is an explicit sign of a failure in the public world. Aeschylus' *Oresteia* (taking, like a number of Euripides' plays, both the Trojan War's origins and its aftermath as a point of departure) represents the issue of revenge as a divine concern, in the large context of the justice of Zeus, and as a family affair, which threatens both the family itself and the social community. But the trilogy is arranged as a historical progression, culminating in the institution of civic legal procedures, and in this process the gods' involvement is integrated with the final structuring of the human community, of Athens. In Euripides, on the other hand, the social structures are represented as already present, but in a state of crisis. Euripides increasingly shows how war brings back, or brings to the fore, the archaic conditions that preceded and still underlie the organization of the democratic *polis*. His plays in this way dramatize tensions inherent in the *polis* and made increasingly acute in the later years of the Peloponnesian War, tensions between (roughly speaking) the more recently evolved political principles of the democracy and the older, persisting aristocratic ethos, involving primary loyalties to family and the archaic warrior code—though by this time the aristocratic ideals have increasingly taken the form of an oligarchic factionalism, frequently bypassing family ties for more volatile kinds of partisanship and reducing the warrior code to a kind of revenge-taking that is little more than political terrorism. War, then, brings back the conditions of an older time into a changed world. The typical representation of that older time and its values is the heroic mythology from which tragedy draws its stories and characters. Thus Euripides' treatment of that mythology, a mixture of acceptance, modification, undercutting, and distancing, becomes the expression of, and a response to, the confrontation of archaic and contemporary forces in his society.

The more archaic conditions enforced by war may partly account for Euripides' increased interest in poetic and theatrical archaism. His inclusion in the later plays of older stylistic elements and dramatic techniques as well as more recondite or elaborated mythological material points in two directions. On the one hand, it suggests a withdrawal into a more purely poetic realm, seemingly distant and private. On the other hand, in the process of evoking this realm, Euripides also shows its inevitable limitations, a lack of integration or connection with a communal public world. An illustration of this kind of doubleness is *Electra*, a play in which Euripides treats the revenge story that makes up the central play of Aeschylus' *Oresteia*, the *Libation Bearers* (and is treated by Sophocles in his *Electra*, whether earlier or later than Euripides we do not know). Aeschylus' play takes place in an atmosphere of intense religious pressures, set at Agamemnon's tomb and then in front of the royal palace. Euripides relocates the setting to the countryside at some distance from the scene of the original crime and its civic context. This rural setting in which the central stage building represents a cottage not a palace, a chorus of country women, the old shepherd who once saved Orestes, the poor and decent independent farmer who is Electra's nominal husband, pastoral motifs in the choral songs (445 ff., 463, 704)—all suggest a private world apart, represented with some affection and even touches of humor. But these idyllic suggestions are shattered by the main story, the revenge killings. And Orestes and Electra, the heroic avengers, are themselves in turn shattered by the horror of what they have done. Euripides makes his protagonists more distinctively human and psychologically complex, and puts them into a setting that appears to give them more personal freedom of action and expression. But the revenge action, instead of projecting out into a larger future, into a newly constituted community, recoils on itself. The movement represented by Aeschylus from heroic and familial revenge to political justice is now arrested. The archaic values of heroic revenge cannot be sustained in isolation (though Sophocles' *Electra* seems almost to claim that they can). The natural, country setting of the play represents not only idyllic and beautiful impulses but also wild and savage

ones; and without reference to civil society there is no check on that savagery. *Electra* is not directly a play of political issues, but its tragedy is defined by the fact that no political order and no divine assistance are there to transform wild revenge into acceptable justice, nor to give adequate direction and larger meaning to individual human actions. In the end, both Orestes and Electra must go into exile, he before even setting foot in his native city (1250–1251; compare 594–595), she finding that there is "no greater sorrow than to leave the confines of one's native land" (1314–1315).

To be sure, the end of *Electra* appears softened by a forecast of Orestes' eventual trial and acquittal and Electra's "proper" marriage to Orestes' noble friend Pylades, that is, by a promise of their reintegration into orderly society. But to them, and in some measure to an audience who has just witnessed the action on stage, these are remote events; they may even require us to consider where such a society might be found (Orestes' trial will be at Athens, but it is not clear whether human jurors or gods will be required to bring in a just verdict: 1258 ff.). Such final divine resolutions serve primarily to recall the events of a drama to the wider frame of mythical tradition, and sometimes to relate them to a particular contemporary ritual or religious observance (we saw examples in *Medea* and *Hippolytus*). Yet these resolutions can also have an effect of discontinuity, between the immediacy and complexity of dramatic events and the more neutral narratives of their mythical sources, between the isolated, anguished human experience of the protagonists and a bland, divine reordering. Here again the contradictoriness of Euripides' drama is evident, calling for a choice among feeling, reflection, acceptance, and rejection, or some nearly impossible combination of these. The strain of such alternatives is nowhere greater than in the later sequel to the revenge story of *Electra*, *Orestes*.

Orestes represents first its hero's remorse for vengeance taken and then a new revenge attempted. The play has a remarkable range of qualities, shifting levels of style, and virtuosic manipulation, both serious and parodistic, of the traditions of its myth, the tragic treatment of that myth and tragic technique in general. The story of Orestes' revenge combines two kinds of vengeance, one the heroically defined vengeance noticed thus far in the figures of Medea, Hecuba, and Orestes in *Electra* (to which can be added Alcmena in *Heraclidae*, Orestes in *Andromache*, Heracles in *Heracles*, Creusa in *Ion*, and, in certain respects, Phaedra in *Hippolytus* and Iphigenia in *Iphigenia among the Taurians*); the other a divine vengeance, such as Aphrodite's in *Hippolytus* and Apollo's in *Electra* and *Orestes*. In the latter case, a deity or group of deities may punish human beings or a whole human community for some offense against the gods. This punishment is a revenge (one word, *timória*, can cover both notions) in defense of divine justice, at one end of the scale (thus, principally, *Electra*, *Orestes*, and *Trojan Women*), and, at the other end, of an individual god's personal prerogatives (thus Aphrodite in *Hippolytus*, Apollo in *Andromache*, Hera in *Heracles*, and Dionysus in *Bacchae*). In these last instances, divine vengeance bears a very close resemblance to heroic vengeance, exacted for the sake of individual honor, and may entail the moral ambiguity and contradictoriness of human, heroic vengeance (thus Heracles is almost simultaneously praised for his piety toward the gods and viciously punished by the goddess Hera: *Heracles* 825–861).

In *Orestes*, Orestes is represented as having acted (as he did in *Electra*) partly because of Apollo's command, that is, because a sanctioned justice requires his father to be avenged, and partly for himself, to recover his patrimony and assert himself in the community that should be his. However, the force of Apollo's sanction, already attenuated in *Electra* (see, for example, 979–981, 1245–1246), now appears radically questionable, if not actually irrelevant. Emphasis falls instead on what Orestes has done in the name of revenge, namely, killing his mother, and on its devastating effect on himself. In addition, as the importance of the

god recedes, the possibility of a secular, civic justice emerges. The archaic story of revenge is now located at the center of an existing political community, the city of Argos, which should have made Orestes' heroic revenge unnecessary—he should have taken Clytemnestra to court. But, as though he had no such recourse, like Medea and Hecuba, he did not. Thus, as the play begins it is he who must face the justice of the city. It is as though the heroic and divinely sanctioned mode of revenge were being put on trial by the human community. But the trial is a failure. Human justice as such turns out to be utterly compromised by factional, political interests. Even Orestes' uncle, Menelaus, a relative who should be helping him, according to the code of kin-friendship, does nothing, so as not to jeopardize a political connection.

Where *Electra* shows the savagery of the archaic code and its destructive effect on those who attempt to act in accordance with it, because of its remoteness from a world of civic order, *Orestes* shows the civic order itself deeply flawed. The cause of the flaw lies in a general human fallibility, which every single figure in the play displays in some way and which political life appears to encourage by giving it larger scope. Its more specific embodiment is the spirit of vengeance, the archaic legacy, which (in spite of all that had once been claimed in such a work as the *Oresteia*) has not yet been reconciled with the order of the *polis*. The latter part of the play offers an ironic commentary on, and surprising as well as bitter confirmation of, the implications of what preceded. After Orestes' experience of public justice, which has condemned him to death, he decides—at the suggestion of his friend Pylades—spontaneously, without divine command or particular legal claim, to take justice into his own hands and punish Menelaus' betrayal by killing his wife, Helen. Helped by Pylades and Electra, he would have accomplished this except for the last-minute intervention of Apollo.

Acting on their own, according to an heroic-aristocratic code gone awry in the changed world of the democratic *polis*, the protagonists lurch toward a conclusion that would destroy the myth their story is based on. Orestes, for instance, instead of setting off on his journey of purification and acquittal and a marriage with Helen's daughter Hermione, is about to cut the girl's throat and bring himself, his friends, and his ancestral house down in flames. Apollo's appearance, which stops all this, at once saves the characters from self-destruction and reestablishes the coherence of the myth. But if we imagine ourselves satisfied with this traditional resolution, we still cannot ignore its abrupt and arbitrary manner. The effect of the play's ending is appropriate because it is the last of a series of disorienting effects, a disorientation caused by the gap which the play opens between its representation of immediate, contemporary human and political experience and of the poetically stylized, formal, and distant world of the myth—and the traditions of the tragic genre. Euripides has made an experimental play that lets us see the possibility of the collapse and transformation of traditional tragedy based on an inherited mythology and on the inherited cultural order implied by the mythology. What makes his experiment so powerful is that this undoing of a literary form is shown to run parallel to the collapse of heroic and aristocratic values, on the one hand, and to the viability of the civic community itself, on the other. It is noteworthy that just such a parallel is indicated in Aristophanes' *Frogs*, three years later, where the passing of the great tragic tradition is linked with Athens' desperate political crisis shortly before the war's end and the city's defeat at the hands of Sparta and her own oligarchic faction.

RECOGNITION

Among the later plays of Euripides, three stand somewhat apart. *Iphigenia among the Taurians*, *Helen*, and *Ion* are often referred to as "romances." Aristophanes' *Thesmophoria-*zusae is a composite parody of this new turn in Euripides' drama, including a different kind of dramatic excitement, adventure in distant places, ingenious rescue plots, mistaken identities, surprising recognitions between long separated or lost family members, and happy conclusions. Some of these features become important ingredients of the New Comedy of the fourth century B.C., whose absorbing interest in the interplay of personal feelings in the everyday life of private citizens, particularly in situations of misunderstanding and under the sudden effects of unexpected turns of chance, are also prefigured in Euripides. Here too he is experimenting, and in ways that suggest a continuing reappraisal of the genre of tragedy itself. Aristophanes (especially in *Frogs*) indicates how Euripides' general tendency to recast the mythical heroes as ordinary, fallible human beings, often in circumstances less than heroic, was felt to be a subversion of the dignity of the genre. The wider implications of this practice, namely, that such a shift of emphasis uncovered, with a new directness and emotional sting, some of the deeper contradictions of contemporary Athenian society, must have had even greater, if perhaps less obvious, effects. *Orestes* is the most striking and direct challenge to the traditionally conceived tragic genre, though notably carried out with some of the genre's most familiar and traditional material. In the romances, Euripides once more looks to the genre's transformation, but more gently and in a roundabout way. Here, for instance, his choice of mythical material is mostly new to tragedy; the settings are remote or, as in *Ion*, distant from the usual political community; suffering and pain, though part of the story, are mostly evoked as a recollection from the past; present disasters are threatened but (narrowly) averted; the tone is sometimes mixed between light and serious; and in place of final, destructive catastrophe, there is a sense of renewal and new life. This last now is not arbitrarily imposed by a sudden divine decree (as, for example, in *Electra* or *Orestes*) but is recovered at least in part by the efforts of the human actors themselves. All in all, these plays are still tragedies or, as Aristotle requires, plays representing "high and serious action" (*Poetics* 1449.b24), at least insofar as their fortunate outcomes are always a very near thing: some kind of providential assistance—the mark of inevitable human helplessness—is required in each case. However, this assistance now hovers more ambivalently between a direct necessity represented by the specific acts of a given deity, and a vaguer force, more obscure and impalpable, represented by chance. Indeed, though gods are present in each of these three plays, the human actors tend to experience their own lives as largely moved by random, unpredictable, and unexplainable forces.

Elements making up the romances also appear earlier. There are fortunate conclusions, involving some special favor from the gods, in *Alcestis*, *Andromache*, and *Orestes*. *Andromache* and *Electra* are set in a more or less remote countryside, at a distance from a central human community (the domestic settings of *Alcestis*, *Medea*, and *Hippolytus* are also comparable). The plot elements of supplication, sacrifice, and revenge are in the romances too, though altered by their contexts. Actions of rescue, found in various forms in *Alcestis*, *Andromache*, *Heraclidae*, *Suppliants*, *Electra*, *Heracles*, and *Orestes*, are also shared. The rescues in the romances, though, are preceded by scenes of recognition lyrically elaborated to give full resonance to the feelings of those whom the recognition has reunited (*Iphigenia among the Taurians* 827 ff., *Helen* 625 ff., *Ion* 1445 ff.), a distinguishing feature (lacking, for example, in the recognition scene of *Electra*).

Long part of the repertoire of tragic actions, recognition is found first among surviving tragedies in Aeschylus' *Libation Bearers*, where it marks the return of the exiled Orestes and the joining of forces in the plot for revenge. It is strikingly illustrated by Sophocles' *Oedipus Tyrannus*, taking the form of self-recognition and the coming-to-awareness of a disastrous truth that is also the fulfillment of a god's ora-

cle. In Euripides, the scenes of recognition all involve exiles. In *Iphigenia among the Taurians* and *Helen*, they are preparatory to a joining of forces in a plot of escape that will successfully bring about the exiles' release and return. In *Electra*, as in *Libation Bearers*, recognition precedes the revenge plot, but then, as we saw, a further exile follows. In *Ion* there is first a false recognition—Xuthus, the foreign husband of the Athenian princess Creusa, is persuaded by Apollo's oracle to recognize in Ion (who is in fact the god's son) a long-lost child. This triggers a plot of revenge, undertaken by Creusa, Ion's unrecognized and unknowing mother, who imagines him to be an alien intruder into the noble ruling house of Athens. But the revenge plot is discovered and Creusa, who now faces punishment herself, takes refuge as a suppliant at the altar of Apollo. This suppliant action, like the revenge that preceded it, is diverted by an event that looks like the work both of chance and of pious inspiration (see 1186–1210, 1320 ff.). Only then, finally, does the play's whole action culminate in the true recognition of mother and son; that is, it culminates at the human level: Ion's divine father remains to be discovered and confirmed, to the satisfaction of the young man's belief.

The recognition in *Helen* averts the possibility that the heroine might be lost and abandoned forever. In *Iphigenia among the Taurians* and *Ion*, the recognitions are just in time to prevent a sister (Iphigenia) from causing her brother's (Orestes') death, and a son (Ion), his mother's (Creusa's). The recognitions dramatize one of Euripides' main preoccupations in his later plays, human ignorance and human need to know. This is the realm that Plato will describe as the area of opinion, *doxa*, which means "what people think," their consensus on a matter (a notion associated with the democratic process), and also "illusion" or what is supposed from the subjective, individual viewpoint, in contrast to what is claimed to be universal truth. Euripides has an acute sense of the drama and pathos of human ignorance. It is the decisive mark of human vulnerability, and above all of the isolated person in his or her subjective being. It is, so to speak, the passive determinant of what makes us human, and it finds powerful expression in the emotions. Hence Euripides' continual interest in human passions, especially at their extremes, in revenge, madness, and erotic passion, each a form of destructive human blindness, the first two linked to each other and to the heroic code, while erotic passion is linked to the enclosed life of women. In the romances these extremes are avoided, or rather their final consequences are stayed. Recognition in *Iphigenia among the Taurians* has been preceded by Orestes' fit of madness (modeled in its representation on the heroic madness of Sophocles' Ajax) and then is tantalizingly delayed by a kind of heroic stoicism: he would not give those he imagines to be his enemies the satisfaction of knowing his identity (500 ff.). The objective ignorance of brother and sister—for how could they possibly imagine who, in their remote and unlikely circumstances, the other may be—is abetted by an ignorance fed on subjective feeling. Iphigenia has had a dream that she misinterprets (though its meaning should have been clear enough) to mean that her brother is dead. In both Orestes and Iphigenia, a feeling of despair encloses, at least for a time, a wider capacity for understanding. Similarly Creusa's attempt on Ion's life is determined by a deeply felt sense of having been wronged, but that feeling is sparked by her mistaken assumption, on insufficient evidence, that her own child is dead (345 ff., 950 ff.). Helen too assumes that the person she most longs for, Menelaus, is dead, an assumption based only on a secondhand report that she of all people, whose life, according to this play, has been entirely determined by false report, should have been careful of.

This susceptibility to delusion based on impulses of individual feeling is complemented by concerted human effort once the delusion is overcome. After recognition has brought friends together and broken their isolation, they are able to take the initiative themselves and work out their escape. This they do, in turn, by exploiting the ignorance of others. Deceiving the barbarian kings who had constrained their lives, Iphigenia and Helen take control, and where before in their ignorance they had been subject to irony, now it is they who deliberately evoke it. Plotting and executing stratagems, otherwise associated with revenge and destruction, are in *Iphigenia among the Taurians* and *Helen* part of an exciting and revitalizing adventure. *Ion* is somewhat more complicated. Xuthus, a non-Athenian outsider, is deceived like the barbarian kings. But the plot to return Ion to an Athenian home and inheritance is planned by the god Apollo himself. This plot, however, is obstructed by those on whose behalf it was conceived. Both Creusa's despairing vengeance attempt and Ion's determined need to know his true father divert it (in addition, Ion had declared that he had no wish to go to Athens). Athena herself must appear to ensure the plot's final success. Both passion and the need to know force Apollo's hand and cause his plot to be changed, not in its final purpose but in its intent, however well-meaning and temporary, to deceive.

Pleasure in successful contrivance and the play of human intelligence extricating itself from tight places is reflected in Euripides' own shaping of these plays. They are beautiful examples of clear and closely knit dramatic construction, demonstrations of the poet's intelligent skill, his *sophia*, used to make things come out all right. In this, they differ strikingly from such plays as *Heraclidae*, *Andromache*, *Heracles*, and *Orestes*, where familiar stories are wrenched from their old moorings so that new meanings can be found in them, and the plays' effects of abruptness and discontinuity represent convulsive effects of social crisis. The romances were produced in the same years of political upheaval and reversals in the war as plays like *Phoenissae* and *Orestes*. But they represent a very different kind of response. Like such plays of this period as Aristophanes' *Birds* and *Thesmophoriazusae*, they are sometimes said to be escapist plays, entertaining distractions from contemporary Athenian life.

This they are in some degree. The successful deployment of intelligence and the achievement of survival in an irrational world suggest models of what should be sought and hoped for. Contrivance also has an element of artifice, as do the paradoxes and ironies that abound in these plays. That those, for example, who most love one another are the ones who come closest to destroying one another has emotional and dramatic force, but is also a neat theatrical trick. *Helen* goes furthest in this direction, run through with an intellectualized interplay between what is "real" and what is "imagined" or represented in speech—"deed" (or "body") and "word" in the language of the play—which is here identical with contemporary intellectual discourse. So, for instance, recognition scenes are usually between two people, one of whom has been unknown to the other since infancy, and identity, therefore, has to be established by special tokens or scars or knowledge of intimate family background. In *Helen*, however, the recognition—which is nearly thwarted—takes place between two people who recognize each other's appearance perfectly well, but one of whom refuses to believe the evidence of his eyes, so powerful is the effect of unlikelihood. The play, of course, represents two Helens, a "real" one on stage, and a divine fabrication. The fabrication has a fixed place in the story of a great war in which on her account many men were killed and a city destroyed. The Helen on-stage, who had nothing at all to do with Troy, is a private person whose existence alone we can verify, while trying to accommodate our certain knowledge that the Trojan War really took place.

What Euripides is doing here is both playful and serious. *Helen*, produced just after Athens' disastrous defeat in Sicily, is a kind of distraction for a despondent community. Yet the play also insistently evokes the deadly Helen alongside the innocent one, as well as the ruinous consequences of the Trojan War. War's folly and losses are not blindly denied but represented at a certain distance so that they can be seen with a measure of detachment and critical reflection. *Iphigenia among the Taurians* appears to be even more remote from public issues, yet it too is about something of importance to the larger community. The frame of its action has to do with ritual procedure—sacrifice—and the transfer of a barbaric cult to Attica, acknowledging the violent meaning underlying it but making its performance symbolic, working psychologically in memory but not in fact (compare the cults noted earlier that were linked to Medea's sacrifice of her children and Hippolytus' death). At the same time, the play is Euripides' version of the resolution of the long story of Orestes' revenge, a resolution unachieved in *Electra* and *Orestes* but now become possible in a distant, alien setting. The legal and political solutions to Orestes' dilemma are abandoned for a kind of religious one. The lives of Iphigenia and Orestes are finally linked to and partially absorbed by cult practices that, as they are fixed in recurring seasonal cycles, recall and give focus to an ancient sense of communal feeling and continuity. There is a similar suggestion in Helen insofar as she is assimilated through the play's poetry to the figure of Persephone and to a natural cycle of death and renewal celebrated in cult practice (compare 164–178, 243 ff., 1301 ff., 1465 ff.). *Ion* again is somewhat different. Here, Athens is directly and disturbingly recalled when Ion explains why he does not want to go there: its political life is too threatening and dangerous, it is a city "full of fear" (595 ff.). Like Hippolytus, he prefers the special, unpolitical life of his youth (621 ff.). But he really has no choice. Involvement in public life for him is part of an inevitable process of growing up. The play shows the interconnections between a life that succeeds because it is private and withdrawn and one that is hazardous and potentially tragic because involved with the lives of others and the city. But disaster is averted, a conclusion coordinated with a final patriotic forecast of Ion's lineage (he will give his name to the Ionians) and, more importantly, with the play's pervasive mythology of early Athens evoking a whole range of the city's ancient ritual traditions and celebrations.

Unlike Shakespeare's romances, which in some ways they call to mind, these plays do not represent a final sense of reconciliation or resolution. Their happy endings are achieved under circumscribed conditions, notably the exclusion of direct political themes and public contexts, except partly in *Ion*. Taken together with the other later plays they are part of Euripides' unceasing preoccupation with multiple and contradictory issues. This basic feature of his work is nowhere so strikingly illustrated as in *Bacchae*—the last completed play to survive—both by contrast with the romances and within itself.

Its story is at once political and religious; combines revenge with revelation; and raises acutely, once more, the question of the relation between the *polis* and its values, and the individual person, or, more particularly, alternate communities of persons. As in *Hippolytus*, the vindication of a deity's prerogatives sets the play in motion. But here the process of divine punishment has been made both personal and political. Dionysus himself enters directly into the action and is involved with members of his own family; but his punishment also affects the whole city (39, 44–48, 1295). Pentheus, the god's main antagonist, is a cousin. Though their unequal struggle takes a personal, sometimes even uncannily intimate form, it is also a political contest. Pentheus is the city's ruler and representative (360–362, 503, 666, 961–963). His opposition to the god is at the same time an act of impiety and a defense of a traditional civic order. Thus, a conflict is drawn between the *polis*, as a Greek, male, warrior-citizen enclave with an aristocratic code, and Dionysiac religion. This conflict is complicated by the nature of Dionysus revealed in his revenge and by the associations of his religion. The religion is represented as a way of liberation for those ignored or subordinated by the aristocratic city—women (including the aristocratic women) and the mass of ordinary people, the democratic populace, as well as (we know from historical sources) any other members of the community denied citizenship rights, such as slaves or resident aliens. In addition, the religion is associated with non-Greeks as well as Greeks (the chorus is made up of female followers of the god from Lydia) and with the universal, wild, and miraculously and demonically fertile force of nature itself. In the face of such forces the blind and ineffectual resistance of Pentheus is symptomatic of a blindness and vulnerability at the heart of the city. Yet, in a further complication, Dionysus, representative of these forces, is somehow also bound to the Greek city and aristocratic values. His punishing of Pentheus is also a kind of heroic revenge, motivated by the need for honor and status, *timé* (203–204, 321, 1378), and marked by sensitivity to insult and ridicule (516, 1081, 1378), similar, in other words, to the revenge motives of Medea or Hecuba or, indeed, of Pentheus (see 247, 319–320, 854, 1310–1312). On the other hand, the god is apparently weak, associated with women, and effeminate in appearance (233 ff., 453 ff.). Like Medea and Hecuba, he is an outsider trying to live on the terms of the Greek city, and like them he has a cunning side. He is *sophos* (shrewd) in the contriving of his vengeance (480, 489, 641, 655–656, 824, 839, 1190; in a famous refrain, the chorus equates *sophia*—the word can mean both "wisdom" and "cunning" —with the achievement of revenge: 877–881 and 897–901).

These elements of contradiction, brought to light by revenge, are gathered around the god Dionysus. This is appropriate insofar as his own nature is essentially ambivalent. He is, he tells us, "most terrible" and "most gentle" (861). The play shows both sides, moving generally from the latter—the soothing benefits and intoxicating blessings that come from the god, so beautifully evoked in the choral songs and in the narratives of the messengers from Kithaeron— to the former—the punishing power that not only leads to destruction but also (and this is something Aphrodite could not do to Hippolytus) invades completely, takes possession of the individual soul (compare 75 and 1268–1270), and makes a person mad. This movement, or shift of emphasis, is part of the play's doubleness of action. The play is an etiological account of the coming of Dionysiac religion to Greece represented principally through the process of the god's revelation of himself to the city. In this way the action is like an extended recognition, and the play, like the romances, is filled with deceptions, misunderstandings, and disguises. As in the romances, too, recognition is associated with a return, a homecoming—of Dionysus to his native Thebes. But it all goes wrong. Dionysus' plan of bringing the benefits of his religion to Thebes, like Apollo's plan for Ion and Creusa, is resisted by those for whom it is intended. But in Apollo's precinct, though the god himself is aloof and remote, a benign providence sorts things out. In Thebes, Dionysus is all too close, and the exercise of his power requires its victims. In *Ion* human pity wins out (47, 618, 1276–1277). In *Bacchae* the need to inspire fear prevails (304, 861; compare 856, 971, 1310; contrast 1120). *Bacchae*'s action of revenge, with all it implies, cuts into the action of recognition. Dionysus' homecoming is only temporary, only long enough for him to leave his mark (46–49), and the play ends with the death or exile of all its human protagonists (1333 ff., 1351 ff.). The chorus, too, will go to another land. It is almost as though Thebes were an illusion that has passed away. As for individual recognitions, they come too late. Pentheus has understood nothing until the moment of his inevitable death, and then it is no use his crying out his name to a mother who in her blind madness carries out what other recognitions had so narrowly averted (1113 ff.). Agave too has her scene of recognition, which marks her recovery from Dionysiac madness (1263 ff.; compare 1383 ff.): she is brought to the awareness of having killed her own son. The madness of Dionysus, which had earlier in the play been represented as a form of liberation, is now revealed as part of a complex that includes revenge, blindness or madness, and recovery to witness the nature of one's crimes, and that is

found also in Theseus' punishment of Hippolytus, Orestes' avenging of his father, and Heracles' avenging of his family (*Heracles* 922–1000, 1109 ff.).

The tragic effect of *Bacchae* is perhaps unsurpassed. It is the kind of play Aristotle has in mind when he says that Euripides appears to be "the most tragic" of dramatic poets (*Poetics* 13.1453.a29–30), a play in which members of a family group, usually a ruling house, do or suffer terrible things in a final disaster. *Bacchae*, in addition, represents such a disaster as part of a deep instability or crisis in the whole social structure. The play, then, shows the attractions of alternatives to that structure, yet only to suggest that one probably cannot live without it. There are, moreover, those who are unable to recognize Dionysus as a potentially beneficent god, and yet the god makes it practically impossible for such a recognition to take place (471 ff.); in some, like Pentheus, he actually seems to provoke the very impiety which he then punishes. But finally *Bacchae*, too, like *Medea* and *Hippolytus* and the other plays, suggests some compensating order. Dionysus is not only the god of extreme ambivalence, he is also the god of the theater (he appears in that role a year later in Aristophanes' *Frogs*). He makes an appearance on stage, playing the part of a human being, the Lydian stranger, and at the end of the play he appears on the palace roof as "himself," the god. We need to imagine how an actor might have indicated the difference. At any rate, the theatrical nature of the task, the play with effects of illusion, is clear. Another instance of this is the final appearance on stage of Pentheus, in which he is made to play out a sinister, grotesque, and nearly comic scene of adjusting his costume or disguise as a woman and practicing the appropriate gestures and movements (925–944). Here, Dionysus plays the part, within his play, of the play's director making backstage preparations and conducting a rehearsal. The theatrical process itself, like the tradition of the tragic genre in *Orestes*, has become part of the play's subject. This is a mark of a late, self-conscious stage in the history of an art form. Yet at the same time, this scene, like so much of the play, draws on archaic ritual material. Pentheus' mimed sex-change is part of ritual practice and is combined with another role, of the hero as—here unconscious—sacrificial victim (1114 ff.). Ritual and theater are shown overlapping. The play is not only an etiological account of the coming of Dionysus' worship to a Greek city, it is also an etiology of tragic drama. The etiological link made at the ends of plays like *Medea* and *Hippolytus*, coming after the main action with an effect of distancing, is in *Bacchae* embedded in the whole play and leads directly to the immediate, dramatic experience of its audience. The compensating order, which offsets the tragic horrors, is the beautiful order of the dramatic work itself revealed in its performance. The depth of the horror, the unflinching pursuit of its conditions, the beautiful poetry and dramatic force of its representation—all together—constitute Euripides' distinctive legacy.

Selected Bibliography

TEXTS

Euripide, edited by F. Chapouthier, H. Gregoire, L. Meridier, and L. Parmentier. 6 vols. Paris, 1925–1961. Includes all the plays except *Iphigenia in Aulis*. With French translation.

Euripides. Leipzig, 1964–1979. The Teubner text, which includes: *Andromache*, edited by A. Garzya; *Hecuba*, edited by S. Daitz; *Helena*, edited by K. Alt; *Heraclidae*, edited by A. Garzya; *Ion*, edited by W. Biehl; *Orestes*, edited by W. Biehl; *Troades*, edited by W. Biehl.

Euripidis Fabulae, edited by G. Murray. 3 vols. Oxford, 1901–1913. The standard edition, which is being revised by J. Diggle.

Euripidis Fabulae II, edited by J. Diggle. Oxford, in progress.

FRAGMENTS

Austin, C. *Nova Fragmenta Euripidea*. Berlin, 1968.
Nauck, A. *Tragicorum Graecorum Fragmenta*. 2nd ed. Leipzig, 1888. *Supplement* by B. Snell. Hildesheim, 1964.
Page, D. L. *Greek Literary Papyri* 1. 2nd ed. Cambridge, Mass., 1942.

TRANSLATIONS

Arrowsmith, W. *Alcestis*. Oxford, 1973.
Bagg, R. *Bacchae*. Boston, 1978.
———. *Hippolytus*. Oxford, 1973.
Beye, C. *Alcestis*. Englewood Cliffs, N.J., 1974.
Burnett, A. P. *Ion*. Englewood Cliffs, N.J., 1970.
Cavender, K. *Iphigenia in Aulis*. Englewood Cliffs, N.J., 1973.
Fitts, D. *Alcestis*. New York, 1936.
Grene, D., and R. Lattimore, eds. *The Complete Greek Tragedies*. *Euripides*. Vols. 1–5. Chicago, 1955–1959. The standard translations.
Kirk, G. S. *Bacchae*. Englewood Cliffs, N.J., 1970.
Lattimore, R. *Iphigenia among the Taurians*. Oxford, 1973.
Merwin, W. S., and Dimock, G. *Iphigenia in Aulis*. Oxford, 1978.

COMMENTARIES ON COMPLETE PLAYS

Benedetto, V. *Orestes*. Florence, 1965.
Biehl, W. *Orestes*. Berlin, 1965.
Bond, G. W. *Heracles*. Oxford, 1982.
Collard, C. *Suppliants*. 2 vols. Groningen, 1975.
Dale, A. M. *Alcestis*. Oxford, 1954.
———. *Helen*. Oxford, 1967.
Denniston, J. D. *Electra*. Oxford, 1939.
Dodds, E. R. *Bacchae*. 2nd ed. Oxford, 1960.
England, E. B. *Iphigenia in Aulis*. London, 1891.
Garzya, A. *Hecuba*. 2nd ed. Milan, 1966.
Kannicht, R. *Helen*. 2 vols. Heidelberg, 1969.
Lee, K. H. *Trojan Women*. London, 1976.
Owen, A. S. *Ion*. Oxford, 1939.
Pearson, A. C. *Heraclidae*. Cambridge, 1907.
———. *Phoenissae*. Cambridge, 1909.
Platnauer, M. *Iphigenia among the Taurians*. Oxford, 1938.
Roux, J. *Bacchae*. 2 vols. Paris, 1970–1972.
Stevens, P. T. *Andromache*. Oxford, 1971.
Ussher, R. G. *Cyclops*. Rome, 1978.

Wilamowitz-Moellendorf, U. von. *Heracles*. 3 vols. 2nd ed. Berlin, 1895.
———. *Ion*. Berlin, 1926.

COMMENTARIES ON PLAYS SURVIVING ONLY IN FRAGMENTS

Bond, G. W. *Hypsipyle*. Oxford, 1963.
Cantarella, R. *Cretans*. Milan, 1963.
Diggle, J. *Phaethon*. Cambridge, 1970.
Handley, E., and J. Rea. *Telephus*. London, 1957. *Bulletin of the Institute for Classical Studies*, supplement 5.
Kambitsis, J. *Antiope*. Athens, 1972.
Musso, O. *Cresphontes*. Milan, 1974.

CONCORDANCES

Allen, J. T., and G. Italie. *A Concordance to Euripides*. Berkeley, Los Angeles, and Cambridge, 1954.
Collard, C. *Supplement to the Allen and Italie Concordance to Euripides*. Groningen, 1971.

CRITICAL STUDIES

Adkins, A. W. H. *Moral Values and Political Behaviour in Ancient Greece*. New York, 1972.
Arthur, M. B. "The Curse of Civilization: The Choral Odes of the *Phoenissae*." *Harvard Studies in Classical Philology* 81:163–185 (1977).
Barlow, S. A. *The Imagery of Euripides*. London, 1971.
Burkert, W. "Greek Tragedy and Sacrificial Ritual." *Greek, Roman and Byzantine Studies* 7:87–121 (1966).
Burnett, A. P. *Catastrophe Survived*. Oxford, 1971.
———. "*Medea* and the Tragedy of Revenge." *Classical Philology* 68:1–24 (1973).
Conacher, D. J. *Euripidean Drama*. Toronto, 1967.
Connor, W. R. *The New Politicians of Fifth-Century Athens*. Princeton, 1971.
Euripide. Entretiens sur l'antiquité classique. Vol. 6. Geneva, 1960.
Finley, J. H. *Three Essays on Thucydides*. Cambridge, Mass., 1967.
Foley, H. "The Masque of Dionysus." *Transactions and Proceedings of the American Philological Association* 110:107–133 (1980).
Gould, J. P. "Hiketeia." *Journal of Hellenic Studies* 93:74–103 (1973).

Gregory, J. "Euripides' *Alcestis*." *Hermes* 107:259–270 (1979).
———. "Euripides' *Heracles*." *Yale Classical Studies* 25:259–275 (1977).
Grube, G. M. *The Drama of Euripides*. London, 1961.
Hormouziades, N. *Production and Imagination in Euripides*. Athens, 1965.
Knox, B. M. W. "The *Hippolytus* of Euripides." *Yale Classical Studies* 13:3–31 (1952). Also in Segal, below.
———. "The *Medea* of Euripides." *Yale Classical Studies* 25:193–225 (1977).
———. "Second Thoughts in Greek Tragedy." *Greek, Roman and Byzantine Studies* 7:213–232 (1966).
Lattimore, R. *Story-Patterns in Greek Tragedy*. London, 1964.
Murray, G. *Euripides and His Age*. 2nd ed. London, 1946.
Pachet, P. "Le Bâtard monstrueux." *Poétique* 12:531–543 (1972). Discusses *Heracles*.
Pucci, P. *The Violence of Pity in Euripides' Medea*. Ithaca, N.Y., 1980.
Reckford, K. "Medea's First Exit." *Transactions and Proceedings of the American Philological Association* 99:329–359 (1968).
de Romilly, J. *L'Évolution du pathétique d'Eschyle à Euripide*. Paris, 1961.
———. "Le Thème du bonheur dans *Les Bacchantes*." *Revue des Études Grecque* 76:361–380 (1963).
Segal, C. "The Menace of Dionysus: Sex Roles and Reversals in Euripides' *Bacchae*." *Arethusa* 11:185–202 (1978).
———. "The Tragedy of the *Hippolytus*." *Harvard Studies in Classical Philology* 70:117–169 (1965).
———. "The Two Worlds of Euripides' *Helen*." *Transactions and Proceedings of the American Philological Association* 102:553–614 (1971).
Segal, E., ed., *Euripides: A Collection of Critical Essays*. Englewood Cliffs, N.J., 1968.
Stevens, P. T. "Euripides and the Athenians." *Journal of Hellenic Studies* 86:87–94 (1956).
Stinton, T. C. W. *Euripides and the Judgement of Paris*. London, 1965.
Strohm, H. *Euripides: Interpretationen zur dramatischen Form*. Zetemata 15. Munich, 1957.
Trenkner, S. *The Greek Novella in the Classical Period*. Cambridge, 1958.

EURIPIDES

Webster, T. B. L. *The Tragedies of Euripides*. London, 1967.

Whitman, C. *Euripides and the Full Circle of Myth*. Cambridge, Mass., 1974.

Winnington-Ingram, R. P. *Euripides and Dionysus*. Cambridge, 1948.

Wolff, C. "The Design and Myth in Euripides' *Ion*." *Harvard Studies in Classical Philology* 69:169–194 (1965).

———. "On Euripides' *Helen*." *Harvard Studies in Classical Philology* 77:61–84 (1973).

Zeitlin, F. "The Argive Festival of Hera and Euripides' *Electra*." *Transactions and Proceedings of the American Philological Association* 101:645–669 (1970).

———. "The Closet of Masks: Role Playing and Myth-Making in the *Orestes* of Euripides." *Ramus* 9:51–77 (1980).

Zuntz, G. *The Political Plays of Euripides*. Manchester, 1955.

CHRISTIAN WOLFF

THUCYDIDES

(ca. 459–ca. 399 B.C.)

LIFE AND FAMILY BACKGROUND

The visitor disembarking from a flight at the old west airport in Athens sets foot at once, albeit with an intervening pavement, on the township where Thucydides' family lived. The area retains its ancient name of Halimous, though almost all else has changed. The economy once based on farming and fishing has shifted to the service industries of the modern metropolis, and almost all traces of the village and of the nearby cult of Demeter and Persephone, for which the area enjoyed some prominence in classical times, have disappeared under the urban sprawl and seaside delectations of contemporary Athens. The village itself seems not to have been especially rich, populous, or famous, but the cult, located right on the shore at Cape Coilias, attracted the leading women of Athens to a festival of sacred rites and dances in the fall of each year. Men were excluded, but Thucydides' family was of sufficient prominence to allow us to conjecture that its women participated in, perhaps were even leaders of, this local Thesmophoria.

That his family was closely connected to the leading families of Athens is much more than a conjecture. Thucydides' father is only a name to us, but it is a most revealing one: Olorus. In all the history of Athens we know of no other citizen with such a name, but it was the name of a king of Thrace in the late sixth century B.C. When the Athenian Miltiades, the commander whose strategy later won the victory over the Persians at Marathon, was sent out by the tyrants then dominating Athens to establish a base in northern Greece, he married a daughter of this Thracian king (Herodotus, 6.39). From this union the unusual name Olorus came to Athens and to Thucydides' family. The ancient sources that assert that Thucydides was a descendant of this marriage of the semi-Hellenized Thracian princess Hegesipyle and the famous Miltiades may simply be inferring the genealogy from the name, but the inference seems secure. It accounts, as will become clear, for much of what we know about Thucydides' connections, wealth, and place of burial close by the memorials of Miltiades' children.

Thucydides' relatives, in-laws, and more remote connections include many of the leading figures in Athenian political and social life during the fifth century, among them Pericles and his most powerful rival, another Thucydides, the son of the wrestling master Melesias. Miltiades' famous son Cimon, the commander who defeated the Persians at the battle of Eurymedon in the 460's B.C., is of course among them, as is his outspoken and controversial half sister Elpinice. Less directly there are connections to Alcibiades and to the wealthiest family of Athens, that of Callias and Hipponicus. The genealogical chart (see p. 268) shows some of the relationships. The chart is in part conjectural, and many scholars would suggest slightly different lines of descent, but overall, the close-

THUCYDIDES

ness of Thucydides' connection to the economic and political elite of Athens is beyond dispute.

Such a position implies wealth, and a good deal more wealth than is likely to have been derived from the farms and fisheries of Halimous. Thucydides himself tells us that in 424 B.C. he had "the possession of the working of the gold mines" on the Thracian coast opposite the island of Thasos (4.105.1). Since it is known that Athens confiscated Thasos' continental holdings after its unsuccessful revolt from Athens in the 460's, it may be that Thucydides held a state contract for the working of the mines. Or his right to work the mines may have been an inheritance from his Thracian relatives or a dowry from an alleged but ill-attested Thracian wife. More likely it was an informal arrangement, an understanding with some of the Thracian dynasts beyond the limits of Athenian control, whereby Thucydides arranged for the mining and extraction of the metal while paying them a percentage of the profits.

Under such an agreement Thucydides would have purchased the slaves and found the managerial and technical staff (perhaps also slaves) necessary for an efficient exploitation of

GENEALOGICAL CHART

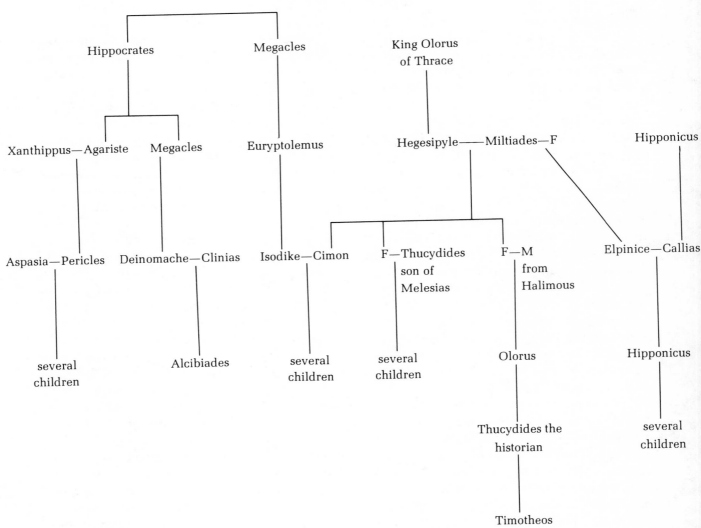

the mines. He would frequently have traveled to the area to inspect the mines and to cultivate his relations with the Thracians, though he need not have had much to do with day-to-day operations. Like his contemporary, the Athenian commander Nicias, whose wealth derived from slaves working the Attic silver mines, Thucydides would have been the arranger and negotiator, not the actual manager. But in each case substantial wealth was derived from the exploitation of mineral resources by slave labor.

If we speak of this period as the "Golden Age" of Greece, the metaphor should remind us of the economic foundation of Greece's cultural accomplishments. And we must be critical of the widespread notion that the circle of economic and political power to which Thucydides belonged was also the intellectual and cultural elite of the age. In fact, the artists and thinkers of fifth-century Athens were only rarely members of this circle.

A careful study of Athenian propertied families by Professor John Davies of Liverpool University includes a genealogical chart, almost four feet in length, that shows in much greater detail than the one above the family connections of the wealthiest and most powerful citizens. As one studies the fine print, one finds very few members of this class have any record of literary or artistic attainment. Pericles, to be sure, supervised and may have done much of the planning for the building program that included the Parthenon and other major constructions. He is said to have conversed often with the philosopher Anaxagoras, the Sophist Protagoras, and the artist Phidias. Many wealthy Athenians, moreover, gave financial support to the cultural life of their city. But the great names of the intellectual Golden Age of Athens were either immigrants or visitors like Protagoras, Gorgias, Anaxagoras, Phidias, Herodotus, and Polygnotus, or, if Athenian citizens, seem not to have been included—however well-to-do or respectable they might have been—in the charmed circle of their city's social and political elite. Neither Aeschylus,

Euripides, nor Aristophanes seems to have belonged to it. Sophocles, well known in his own day as treasurer, priest, and military commander, certainly had dealings with many of its members, but even his connection is not likely to have been an intimate one. Socrates, a stonecutter from an undistinguished family, was a curiosity when he appeared at the dinner parties given by the scions of the affluent and powerful. Some of these young men, members of the generation following Thucydides', became more engaged in the intellectual and artistic life of their city, but in his own generation Thucydides seems an exception within his social class. Men of his background were expected to know their Homer, to be able to sing and quote from memory the lyrics traditionally heard at symposia, and to possess a ready wit and the skills of improvisation. Of their training in public speaking more will be said in the next section of this essay. But it does not appear that literary accomplishments were expected of or frequently attained by his peers.

This is not to say that Thucydides turned his back on the life-style of his class. What we can tell of his early career is not atypical or unconventional. Social and political distinction was closely associated with military attainments, including, whenever possible, a generalship. Thucydides held that office in 424–423 B.C., and from that fact we can infer a good deal more about his career. To attain that office one was expected to have served with honor in earlier campaigns, to have proved oneself loyal to the democracy and reliable in battle, and to be of some maturity—at least thirty years old.

Although it follows that Thucydides was probably born before 454 B.C., nothing compels us to date his birth before 460. Indeed his reference to himself in book 5, chapter 26, has often been thought to have a defensive tone, as if he feared that someone might think he had been too young fully to comprehend the war from its outset. If we assume that he was born in the first years of the 450's, he would have grown up in the period when Pericles was the dominant political leader in Athens and would have reached prime military age when the Peloponnesian War broke out in 431 B.C. He would almost certainly have done some military service every year; his economic status would have suggested, but not required, service in the cavalry. If he did choose to serve in the cavalry, we can imagine him fighting in the engagement on the road to Eleusis in the first year of the war (2.19.2), and later attending Pericles' funeral oration for those who had died there and in the other skirmishes that had marked the first year of what would be a twenty-seven-year war.

A soldier who distinguished himself could rise to positions of intermediate command as a *lochagos* (captain) or *taxiarch* (regiment commander), especially in a time of awesome casualties caused both by the war and the great plague that devastated Attica in the years from 430 to 426. Late in the Athenian year 425–424, Thucydides stood as a candidate for the generalship from his tribe, Leontis, and was elected, probably for the first time.

At his election it could not have been foreseen how crucial the area near Thucydides' gold mines would soon become. But a brilliant Spartan commander, Brasidas, managed to move an expeditionary force through Thessaly into northern Greece and to encourage defections from the Athenian tributary allies in this region. Thucydides' familiarity with the area and his connections in the region made him an obvious choice for one of the commands in this theater, and he was soon sent to protect Athenian holdings from seizure by Brasidas. It was, if our reconstruction of his career is correct, his first significant command. And it rapidly turned to disaster. He underestimated the speed with which the enemy would move and the willingness of the citizens of the crucial city in the area, Amphipolis, to abandon their Athenian connection and accept Brasidas' offer of autonomy. By a matter of hours Thucydides arrived too late to prevent the defection of the city. No other setback in the entire war, not even Athens' ultimate defeat, had such prolonged and grievous effects on Athenian foreign policy. Even in the middle of the next century the Ath-

enian dream of recovering Amphipolis exacerbated the city's relations with Philip of Macedon and made it difficult for it to find an accommodation with this major new power to the north. Such developments, to be sure, could not be foreseen in 424, but the importance of Amphipolis was clear, and criticisms of Thucydides' generalship and even charges of incompetence and treason were inevitable if he returned to Athens. Rather than face them, Thucydides chose exile. It was twenty years until, at the end of the Peloponnesian War, he returned to his defeated city.

Exile, voluntary or enforced, was not an uncommon fate for unsuccessful military commanders in Greece. Many found it more difficult than Thucydides to withdraw with safety and comparative security. But voluntary exile shattered his political and military career, excluded him from the social circle to which he was born and from the city he had tried to serve. All the greatest Greek historians were exiles or wanderers from their native cities; no doubt some of the richness and diversity of Greek historical writing is the result of this fact. Thucydides himself makes such positive effects clear: "since because of my exile I had contact with both sides, and not least the Peloponnesians, it turned out that I had a considerable opportunity to observe at leisure something about them" (5.26.5). More important may have been an unmentioned and less readily defined effect: the severance was not just geographical, but also a cutting away from a class and its assumptions and values. Thucydides was thrown back on a project that already betokened some detachment from his milieu—his history of the war. This became his life work, still incomplete when he died, probably in the 390's B.C.

He was buried, we are told, not at Halimous, but just outside the Melite gate through the western wall of Athens, among the "Cimonian memorials." It was thus with the famous relatives on his grandmother's side that Thucydides apparently found his final resting place. Some Thucydidean scholars have concluded from this story that Thucydides had close Cimonian connections to one of the most prominent families in Athenian politics, and this has led them to emphasize his Cimonian origin and ties. From this it has become a common speculation in Thucydidean studies that he was raised in a family whose political stance was reflected by Cimon and Pericles' opponent, Thucydides the son of Melesias. This theory in turn has led to the conjecture that the historian Thucydides broke with his family, abandoned his family's stance, and became an admirer of Pericles, perhaps even an apologist for him. The links in this argument are weak, especially the assumption that the whole family, or even Cimon himself, was consistently anti-Periclean. Much more compelling is what emerges from the history itself: a proud intellectuality, a determined refusal to indulge in any simple or facile defense of the empire from which his family, class, and city had so greatly profited, and a willingness to doubt and to challenge many of the premises and commonly acknowledged truths of his time.

INTELLECTUAL BACKGROUND

Much of what we have said about Thucydides' life is inference and conjecture, and much remains unknown. Indeed, it is so frustrating not to know more about him that one is sometimes tempted to turn to the ragbag of stories gathered in the often garbled and gullible ancient biographies that are appended to the *Histories* in some manuscripts. A better effort would be to bring what can be confidently asserted about his life into relationship with our picture of the intellectual life of fifth-century Greece.

Generations of study of Thucydides' work and that of his contemporaries have made it clear that he was well aware of and deeply influenced by the intellectual developments of his time. They shaped, and now help to clarify, the one central biographical fact about him— his writing of the *Histories*. Whether Thucydides simply assimilated and reflected the in-

tellectual developments of his day, or whether he criticized and ultimately transcended them, is a challenging and controversial question whose answer is central to any interpretation of his work.

The Athens of his time was a place of remarkable intellectual and creative activity. When he was born, the Acropolis was not yet adorned by the Parthenon, Propylaea, or Erechtheum. Over the Agora no temple of Hephaestus presided. The theater of Dionysus had witnessed some of the best of Aeschylus' work, but comedy was still crude and unshaped, and the greatest dramas of Sophocles and Euripides were yet to appear. Philosophy flourished in other Greek cities, but the first great Athenian philosopher, Socrates, almost an exact contemporary of Thucydides, had not yet transformed the nature of intellectual inquiry. By the time of Thucydides' death, all had changed and the "Golden Age" of Athens had come and, just as swiftly, gone. The causes of this remarkable period of creativity are still only dimly perceived. A strong economic base was provided—first, as we have seen, by the use of slave labor to exploit the natural resources of the region and, second, but no less important, by the Athenians' integration of the Aegean into a common market untroubled by trade restrictions, Phoenician competition, piracy, or rivals to Athenian dominance. But economic explanations are not sufficient. Complex intellectual and social factors and, behind them, a deep and hard-to-chart shift in cultural values were beginning to have important effects.

During the fifth century B.C. Athens underwent a change as radical as any recorded in a comparable period in antiquity. At the beginning of the period, the city was heavily dependent upon oracle, expounder, and prophet for setting civic policy. Families long distinguished by wealth and reputation provided the principal access to these sources of authority. They supplied priests and priestesses for the various cults, traveled to Delphi and other oracular centers for guidance, expounded the oracles and the unwritten law, and provided political and military leadership. By the end of the century, these traditional sources of authority had largely been weakened or bypassed. Laws and procedures had been written down, leadership and prestige had been democratized. Oracles were still consulted, but their interpretation was not the monopoly of an elite. The citizen body as a whole resolved and sanctioned civic policy, guided by discussion in the council and assembly and by incessant public and private argument. In Athenian politics this change was most evident in the curtailment of the powers of the Areopagus council in 461 B.C., and its corollary, the insistence that before any Athenian citizen could be punished, he must be tried on a specific charge before a jury of his fellow citizens.

At the social level, the transformation in civic life opened new opportunities for classes and individuals whose role in the past had largely been to listen and to obey. At the same time it required new and sometimes distasteful strategies by aristocratic families who wished to maintain their ancestral prominence in public life. Instead of relying on such positions as priest, clan leader, or expounder, the aristocrat was now forced to devise a new formula for political success—part generosity, part public service, and part skillful argument in the assembly and self-defense in the law courts. Since the traditional education—based largely on the memorization of Homer and other poetic texts—did little to ensure the acquisition of such skills, a need arose for teachers of rhetoric and of "the political craft."

If we did not know of the existence of the Sophistic movement we would have to posit something very much like it—and might invent for it a term less charged and less misleading to English speakers than "sophistic." These itinerant teachers of political and oratorical skills—the Sophists—often taught rhetorical skills by requiring their pupils to argue both sides of an issue. It was sometimes said that the real mark of an excellent speaker was the ability to make the worse cause appear the better. Such virtuosity could only be hindered by a slavish devotion to moral absolutes. In fact, the Sophists were relativists or, more properly, situationalists; they taught that the good citizen was not the man who could apply unchanging maxims or principles to conduct, but the one who could devise the actions and words appropriate to a specific situation.

The Sophists' language shocked and provoked distrust and opposition in many quarters, although such teaching need not have posed any fundamental challenge to traditional Greek ethics. But sometimes they, or those influenced by them, articulated more radical views. Some Sophists stressed the contrast between what is natural (physis) and what is purely conventional, laws or social restraints (nomoi). Nature was identified with the drives and appetites that lead an individual or group to pursue its own interests and to seek gratification. Laws and conventions were human constructs and were sometimes represented as devices to repress the natural impulses of the stronger and to allow those who were weaker to rule. By nature, some Sophists contended, the stronger should dominate the weaker and the weaker serve the stronger.

Since Hegel, the Sophists have often been compared to the philosophes and other figures of the eighteenth-century European Enlightenment. In some respects the analogy is misleading, but it can remind us of their appeal and of the intellectual excitement they generated. They carried on in a new and seemingly more relevant way what Gregory Vlastos has called "the demolition of the supernatural," a process begun by the earlier Greek philosophers, the physiologoi. There was something fresh and daring in their willingness to challenge convention and to assert the power and irresistibility of nature. They promised security and advancement for the individual, and progress and good government for society through the elimination of antiquated and repressive structures. Yet there was no need for revolutionary activity; the Sophists could teach a man to accommodate successfully to democracy, change, and even imperialism.

Almost every aspect of the Sophistic movement is reflected in some way in Thucydides' work. The speeches in the *Histories*, for example, regularly follow the rhetorical patterns advocated by the Sophists; and Thucydides' own explanation of how he constructed the speeches is best understood as an adaptation of Sophistic ideas. After pointing out how difficult it was both for him and for his informants to keep in mind the details of specific speeches, Thucydides says that he expressed them "as it seemed to me that each of the speakers would express 'the appropriate' concerning the circumstances present at any given moment, while I kept as close as possible to the general proposition of the things actually spoken" (1.22.1). Few sentences in Thucydides' crabbed and difficult text have caused as much perplexity and debate as this one, but its explanation becomes easier when one recognizes its origin in Sophistic thought and practice. Thucydides uses the Sophistic concept of "the appropriate" and applies it to this problem of historical reconstruction. He suggests, perhaps oversimplifying, that there is one set of appropriate responses *(ta deonta)* for any rhetorical situation, given of course the general proposition the speaker is advocating. Thus while neither Thucydides nor any informant could remember the exact phraseology of a speaker, one could determine the general proposition—to make war or peace, to accept or reject an alliance, to kill or spare a conquered population—and the circumstances under which the speech was given, such as the type of audience and its disposition. From these facts one could derive the rhetorically appropriate strategy and thereby create an approximation of the original speech. Whether Thucydides always follows this formula is another question, but the influence of the Sophists helps explain his otherwise baffling statement about his method.

A similar influence can be detected in his treatment of the events of early Greek history. Here he adapts a technique based on probability that had been developed by the Sophists for use in courtroom situations. In a law case, a weak defendant might ask whether it was likely that he would have assaulted a much stronger opponent; a strong person accused of the same crime would ask whether it was likely that he would have commited it, since he would surely be suspected. Each detail of the case would be examined carefully until points were found that could be used to argue the suspect's innocence or guilt. Thucydides uses a similar technique to assess the traditional stories about early Greek history and to construct a more plausible picture of the past. In assessing the scale of the Trojan expedition, for example, he begins by arguing that it is likely that Homer, a poet, would exaggerate (1.10.3). He then uses the details of the *Iliad* to establish the number of ships sent to Troy and the average size of their crews. He thereby leads the reader to conclude that the expedition was not such a large one, considering that it was drawn from all of Greece. (Thucydides does not complete the calculation; it would yield a figure of 102,000 for the Greek army, an immense force, larger than any that engaged in the Peloponnesian War!)

Sophistic training and thought emphasized the direct conflicts of debate in the law courts and assemblies. Thucydides shares the Sophists' love of paired speeches and antitheses in thought, such as those between speech *(logos)* and deed *(ergon)*, nature and convention, power and morality. Thucydides presents this last pair in a way that reflects contemporary rhetorical thought—by using the contrast between the advantageous and the just, an important topic in oratorical training. Speakers were taught how and in what circumstances to use such arguments in their cases. In Thucydides, the arguments take on a new significance and are used to analyze the tension between power and morality that is such an important theme in the *Histories*. In the third book, for example, Cleon contends that it is just for the Athenians to put to death all the male citizens of rebellious Mytilene. His opponent, Diodotus, concedes the justice of such a punishment, but points out that the Athenians are not in a law-court situation, where considerations of the just and unjust are appropriate, but in an assembly, where the proper topic is what is advantageous or disadvantageous. He is able in this manner to outmaneuver Cleon and to argue that Athens' own self-interest dictates that the Mytileneans should be spared.

The most important affinity between Thucydides and the Sophists—one that also links him to the Hippocratics and other thinkers of this period—is a new way of looking at the past. Archaic Greeks had drawn their models and ideals in large part from their vision of earlier times; behind their own age of lead or iron lay a period remote and hard to recapture, an age of heroes, a time of rapport between men and gods, a Golden Age. The thinkers of the archaic period tended toward pessimism, emphasizing the brevity of life, the transitory nature of pleasure, and man's separation from the splendor of his past. In their view any improvement in man's lot would have to come from a reversion to earlier and happier days. Progress, if such were even possible, would actually mean regress.

The fifth-century Greeks came to reject this picture of the past. Doubts arose on two fronts. First, the earlier poets seemed to have exaggerated the cultural level and accomplishments of the past. Second, it began to appear that the direction of change had been toward improvements in man's lot. If conditions were actually improving, what must earliest man's situation have been? Without the developments made possible by the gradual accumulation of knowledge and skills, life must have been brutish and short. There could have been few defenses against cold, sickness, and wild beasts. What little protection man enjoyed must have been gained slowly and painfully over long periods of time. The Sophist Protagoras, in Plato's dialogue of that name, draws a picture of man's early existence that reflects this new view of the past. According to the story he tells, man originally lacked protection from his environment, but Prometheus stole wisdom and the arts—as well as fire—from Hephaestus and Athena, and gave them all to man.

Then by skill man swiftly articulated speech and words; he discovered shelter and clothing and shoes and beds and nourishment from the earth. Thus provided, men originally lived in scattered settlements; there were no cities. Since they were in all respects weaker, they were constantly being destroyed by the wild beasts. Their skill in handicrafts was sufficient help as far as nourishment went, but it was insufficient for war against the wild beasts. They did not have any political skill, part of which is skill in war, but they tried to form groups and to save themselves by founding cities.

(*Protagoras* 322a)

In Protagoras' story the gods eventually provide the necessary political skill, and man is enabled thereby gradually to move to higher levels of security, civilization, and material comfort.

The result of Thucydides' new method for the reconstruction of the past is a picture of early Greek history similar to the story told by Protagoras. The opening twenty-three chapters of the work, commonly called the "Archaeology," challenge the widespread notion of the epic grandeur of early Greece. The great expedition against Troy is shown to be far less splendid than the epic poets alleged and their listeners believed. Thucydides points out that the length of the Trojan War was not the mark of its grandeur but the result of persistent problems in logistics. Early Greek history is revised and scaled down as he traces the slow development of financial reserves, naval power, and united action—the requirements for large-scale accomplishments.

When Thucydides presented this new picture of the early stages of Greek civilization in the "Archaeology," it must have seemed a shocking tour de force. But in retrospect we can see how closely this portion of the work parallels other movements within the culture, and how closely it is related to the extensive reassessment of the past being conducted by Thucydides' contemporaries. The parallels, however, are not only to the Sophists, but also to the Hippocratic writers, whose new approach to medicine was one of the most important intellectual breakthroughs of Thucydides' lifetime.

In a treatise such as the Hippocratic work on *Ancient Medicine*, one detects something very similar to Protagoras' view of the past: "Our present ways of living have, I think, been discovered and elaborated during a long period of time. For many and terrible were the sufferings of men from strong and brutish living when they partook of crude foods, uncompounded and possessing great powers ..." (ch. 3, W. H. S. Jones, trans.). Through these long ages of suffering, the writer goes on, a method has emerged that promises a new and secure knowledge about sickness and health and a solution to much of man's suffering:

> ... a starting point and a road have been discovered, along which many and fine discoveries have been made over a long time and the remaining ones will be discovered if someone is talented enough and uses existing discoveries as his starting point.
>
> (*Ancient Medicine*, ch. 2)

The results of these studies were at first approximate and in need of refinement, but the early Hippocratic scientists confidently believed that their regimen could succeed with cases that formerly appeared intractable and would eventually lead to a comprehensive approach to health. Today, their claims seem naive, and their regimen, with its faith in diet, reminds us of the modern food faddists. But behind their prescriptions was a new method, free from the superstitions of earlier Greek medicine men, responsive to observation and argument, and immensely significant for the future of medicine.

Their confidence was not foreign to Thucydides. He even uses similar language at the end of the "Archaeology" in a series of observations about his method and its usefulness:

> I discovered that the past was approximately of this sort, though it was hard to trust in each indicator, one after the other.... Nevertheless, if from the aforementioned indicators someone concludes that it was approximately of the sort that I have narrated, he will not be mistaken.... For lis-

tening, perhaps, the lack of a story-telling element in these matters will appear rather unpleasant, but it will suffice as it is for all who wish not merely to have a clear view of the past but also to draw useful inferences in regard to events in the future which, human nature being what it is, will be approximately of the same sort and similar again at some point. It is composed as something to keep forever rather than as a contest piece to listen to just now.

> (1.20–22)

Thucydides affirms that he too has a method; one that, like the Hippocratics', leads not to total exactitude but to approximations that are sufficiently precise for useful inferences. It is not certain whether Thucydides always maintained this view of his method and its utility, or whether this is his final formulation of his views. But it is a bold claim with which to preface his history, polemically phrased, marking a deliberate contrast between himself and the poets and the speakers of ceremonial orations and display pieces with their nostalgic views of the past.

Many other features of Thucydides' work—his insistence on precise and unswerving observation and his careful attention to detail, for instance—link him to the Hippocratic writers. The description of the great plague in the second book of the *Histories* turns into a disquisition on the psychological and moral effects of the illness, but it begins with a careful description of the symptoms and the stages of the disease quite in keeping with the recording of individual illnesses in the Hippocratic *Epidemics*. Less obvious, but perhaps more significant, is the treatment of causation. Thucydides, like the medical writers, and in sharp contrast to the epic poets, avoids invoking any divine intervention to explain the war and its sequence. He seems to have borrowed both concepts and language from the developing medical discipline and to have achieved thereby a subtle analysis that integrates the immediate provocations to war (such as the conflicts between Athens and the Peloponnesians at Corcyra and Potidaea) with a much deeper and more general cause: the fear provoked by the growth of Athenian power. It is indeed tempting to speculate that Thucydides viewed the war as a kind of sickness affecting Greece and that he considered his own task to be similar to a Hippocratic doctor's observation of an unusual illness. This analogy does not account for all the features of the text—above all for its tendency to turn from precise observation to contemplation of the psychological and moral effects of the war—but it has the merit of emphasizing the importance of detailed observation in each type of inquiry.

When all the connections between Thucydides and Hippocratic medicine have been compiled, two features stand out as most significant. First is their common view of the past and their willingness to demythologize and deromanticize it. Its deficiencies and the sufferings of former days are brought into focus, and a new method of analysis is proposed that seems to promise improvements in the future.

These essentially *historical* attitudes appeared with surprising rapidity and prominence in many aspects of Greek culture during the fifth century B.C. They provided the basis for a new inquiry into the past and for new methods of preserving and analyzing it. At the same time, the debunking and devaluation of the past and the many forms of attack on the myth of a Golden Age were part of the radical social and cultural change affecting many aspects of Greek life at this time. The intense interest in history, as well as much of the actual historical writing, coincided with and was partially caused by the breaking down of traditional forms of authority and modes of conduct. Just as one is less likely when ill to turn today to the charms and incantations of earlier forms of healing, so the Greeks were less reliant on the patriarchal sources of authority—exegete, priest, clan leader, or elder. Instead, they based decisions on an analysis of power and its sources, on calculations and arguments derived from the study of money, trade, shipping, and the workings of human nature.

Second, besides the common view of the past

and the willingness to demythologize it, there is a strain of optimism in the Hippocratics and many of the Sophists, as there is in some portions of Thucydides' work. Progress suddenly seems possible. And to many of the thinkers of the period it appeared that the way to progress was through careful analysis of the past to obtain useful knowledge about the future. Thucydides, as we shall see, is at times critical of this idea and aware of the dark implications of the war he narrates. But he was deeply influenced by the idea of progress and of history's potential role as its agent. He knows, for example, the great claims that had been made for *logos*, a Greek word that means both speech and reason, and the argument advanced by Gorgias and others that *logos* is the most powerful of forces and hence capable of settling disputes and averting violence. Whatever the final implications of the *Histories*, one feels in the opening chapters the optimism that characterized the years before the war, and is led to contemplate the idea that advances in civilization have been a direct function of advances in Greek power and in the scale of Greek undertakings. As one reads ahead, one finds in Pericles a statesman committed to reason and to an analysis of power that points to ultimate Athenian success.

To many Athenians, even in the midst of the cultural ferment of the late fifth century, the ideas of the Sophists, the Hippocratics, and Thucydides must have seemed radical and strange. Optimism, progress, historical thinking, and new modes of argument and analysis were outlandish and sometimes thought ludicrous, frightening, or even subversive. They were the radical notions of a self-appointed and unrepresentative elite. But Thucydides consciously, boldly, addressed himself to that elite. He constructed a style that made no concessions to a popular audience. He explicitly contrasted his work with the popular forms of the day—with poetry and the encomiastic oratory heard at festivals. His text is proudly unpoetic and unmythic, unapologetically prose. It is a personal possession, not an entry in a festival contest. It is designed for a private occasion, for the individual alone in his study or gathered with a few friends who are willing to make the intense intellectual effort needed to deal with original thought expressed in a complex style. There is no place in it for romanticism or nostalgia and no trace of the Herodotean compromise wherein historical analysis is combined with a story-telling element to create for the reader a new heroic age—the resistance of Greece to barbarism.

The *Histories,* then, not only derive from the intellectual movements we have grouped together as the Greek Enlightenment, they also address precisely those segments of the population that had been most strongly affected by the Enlightenment. Everything we know about this elite suggests that they were proud of their sophistication and determined to be rigorously tough-minded. They avoided outdated subjects, old-fashioned argumentation, and sentimental clichés. They aspired to a realism about human conduct and an acceptance of the drives that shaped it. Traditional moral restraints had little force; indeed, to follow them seemed a sign of naiveté. As Democritus put it, the wise man "had no obligation to obey laws and conventions, but rather to live freely" (frag. 166). It was *physis* (nature) that led man in this direction, and in particular the drives for survival, advancement, power, and status. Self-interest had led men to devise inventions, material comfort, and methods that seemed to promise even greater advancement.

These are the ideas behind the *Histories,* the ideas that the Peloponnesian War would test with all the rigor and tough-mindedness that any Enlightenment thinker could desire.

THE LITERARY FORM OF THE HISTORIES

As in the eighteenth-century Enlightenment, a new sense of the past and of man's relationship to it characterized many of the intellectual developments of the late fifth century B.C. The new attitudes had paradoxical effects on literature and the writers of the time. They simultaneously separated many Greeks from the received picture of the past and made it urgent to develop and preserve some improved understanding of it. The new emphasis on a carefully thought-out method for reconstructing history made many of the traditional literary forms for transmitting the past appear suspect and shattered men's naive confidence in the picture they presented.

Epic poetry was especially vulnerable. It has often been noted that Greek historical writing was much influenced by the devices of epic poetry, but the relationship is not one of simple borrowing. Just as the Sophists deliberately took over the role of the poets as the teachers of Greece, so historical writing systematically displaced epic, appropriated some of its techniques, and drew to itself talent that might otherwise have carried on the poetic traditions of archaic and early classical Greece. Epic poetry was eclipsed as a form for creative expression. Similarly, tragic drama on historical subjects virtually disappeared after the middle of the fifth century. At a more general level, prose tended to displace poetry—not on the stage or in the affection of the most broadly based audiences, but in many of the works intended for a specialized or consciously intellectual audience. Philosophical works were less likely to be written in verse; pamphlets, published versions of speeches and technical treatises, and various other prose works were in circulation.

Many of these works were aimed at a relatively narrow audience and were what we might classify as subliterary. But they reflect a change of the utmost significance. A setting for literature was emerging that did not depend on ceremonial occasions, the festival, or the symposium. Literature, especially prose, acquired not just an audience but a readership—perhaps a narrow, elitist, individualistic readership, but one that could be reached without the constraints of ceremonial and collective occasions. To this readership Thucydides addressed his work, explicitly marking the contrast between his investigations and the encomiastic display pieces of the orators and the mythologized view of the past among the poets. He even chooses as his normal verb for narration *xyngrapho,* never a word for writing poetry or elevated prose, but for technical discussions, manuals, drafts, and analyses. He may himself have used this word and its cognates to refer to his work, for the title the *Histories,* while ancient, need not be Thucydidean. The work was his "treatise," grouped thereby with the new prose literature of the fifth century, ostentatiously unpretentious. It contrasted sharply with the playful but lofty poetic literature of early Greece and with the elaborate conceits and stylistic affectations of the prose of the Sophist Gorgias.

This lack of pretension contains, to be sure, an element of arrogance, perhaps even of parricide. It is an assault on the implicit pretensions of other writers. Among its casualties is a familiar figure in early Greek literature, the omniscient narrator. The voice in these early works always knows whereof it speaks, indeed it is inspired by a Muse or reports inner feelings and reactions. In this the poet is the inheritor of the long period of oral literature from which the written texts of early Greece were derived. "Oral narrative invariably employs an authoritative and reliable narrator. He is gifted, like Homer . . . , with the ability to observe an action from every side and to tell the secrets of men's hearts" (R. Scholes and R. Kellogg, *The Nature of Narrative* [New York, 1966], p. 51). But the recognition in the fifth century that progress depends on careful observation of details, refined by analysis and method into successive approximations of the truth, runs counter to the authorial pose most common in early Greek literature. In the fifth century, especially in Herodotus, we meet quite a different narrator: not the writer who knows all but the more modest recorder and analyzer, the person who does not claim to know with epic surety but who has asked questions and gathered reports, often conflicting or contradictory, and presents them

with varying amounts of analysis to the reader. He is the inquirer, the collector of stories, the reporter who conceives his job as relating what he has heard, not necessarily synthesizing all into a final truth.

Thucydides' technique is quite different from that of Herodotus, and has often caused him to be criticized as dogmatic or deceptive. In the "Archaeology" he demonstrates his method of analysis by applying it to the most intractable material, the remote past. At the end of the section he affirms, as we have seen, that his method has passed its test and can produce useful knowledge. After this point he rarely mentions variant accounts, the precise sources of his knowledge, or the methodological perplexities that stand behind his conclusions. He feels he has established his authority. Such a stance is easily condemned, especially by invoking the modern notion that the historian must constantly cite the evidence and let the reader test his inferences at every turn. But it is important not to be misled about the nature of Thucydidean narrative. Whatever its merits or weaknesses are, it is not a bland textbook history or a consensus of all the experts. Below the surface there is a constant awareness of the diversity of view and conflicts of interpretation that historical events inevitably provoke. The assurance in Thucydides' work is not that of the omniscient narrator, who knows that his audience is bound not to challenge his re-creation of an imaginary world. Rather, it is a provocation, a challenge to readers to reread, rethink, and revalue their assumptions; it is designed to encourage critical thought. But the intended object of criticism is not so much the process whereby Thucydides derived his inferences, as it is the inadequacies of the views received through the process.

This critical point of view may escape the reader who approaches the text, as we often must, without a sense of the confusions and controversies of the time when it was written. But sometimes Thucydides helps us. At the end of the "Archaeology," for example, after explaining how poorly the Athenians understand the history of the overthrow of the Pisistratid tyranny, he remarks:

> The other Greeks too make many mistakes about many other matters, not just those forgotten over time, for example, that each of the two Spartan kings has two votes, not one, and that there is a Pitanates brigade among them—which was never the case. For most people the search for truth involves no pains; they take what is available.
>
> (1.20.3)

Here Thucydides goes out of his way to challenge those who agree with Herodotus (6.57 and 9.53). Elsewhere his attack on received views is less explicit but no less significant. We know, for example, that many Greeks believed that the Peloponnesian War broke out because Pericles was unwilling to repeal an embargo Athens had imposed against her neighbors the Megareans. Thucydides never mentions this theory, but the whole construction of his first book exposes the limitations and inadequacies of such a view. The cause of the war is shown to be a much deeper process; the gradual growth of Athenian power and the consequent fear of Athens that eventually impelled Sparta to take action against it (1.23.6). By implication this is revisionist history aimed at an audience that knew the more popular version and was willing to contemplate an analysis based on a much more sophisticated concept of causation.

Even the idea that there was a single Peloponnesian War lasting from 431 to 404 B.C. seems itself to be a Thucydidean notion, and one that was by no means evident to all his contemporaries. The violence of 431 had been preceded by a long period of hostilities. Modern historians often refer to a series of battles in the 450's and early 440's as the First Peloponnesian War. But Thucydides dispatches this conflict with a quick summary in the first book and refuses to view *his* Peloponnesian War as a simple recrudescence of the old violence. He is equally insistent that the Peace of Nicias in 421

B.C. did not end the war and that the Athenian expedition to Sicily from 415 to 413 should be viewed as a part of the continuing conflict with the Peloponnesians. Thus when the Peace of Nicias does break down and the Peloponnesians resume their invasions of Attica, he treats the renewed hostilities as a new phase in a single twenty-seven-year war.

Both in his interpretation of events and in his literary form Thucydides was an innovator. Just how daring an innovator he was is hard to assess because we are ill informed, both about contemporary interpretations of the events Thucydides reported and about the range and nature of prose narrative during the period. We do know that historical writing already existed in the first half of the fifth century, as did prose genealogies and mythologies. Before the end of the century Ion of Chios had written his memoirs, and Stesimbrotus of Thasos his polemical sketches of prominent Athenian politicians. There was an abundant pamphlet literature, of which one notable example is the attack on Athenian democracy included in the works of Xenophon under the title "The Civic Arrangements [*Politeia*] of the Athenians." Recent studies have suggested that biography was already emerging as a literary form in this period and that fictitious narratives were beginning to circulate. Some of these works were ephemeral; others were eclipsed by the more polished successors of later ages, but we can now begin to see Thucydides as part of a great flourishing of prose literature in the late fifth century.

The most important implication of this observation can be missed if one approaches this literature anachronistically. We distinguish—in part because the Greeks came to distinguish—the separate literary forms of history, memoir, romance, and biography. But these distinctions were by no means always firmly drawn. If one looks, for example, at the remains of Ctesias' *Persica*, a work of the early fourth century that blended personal reminiscences, a historical account of contemporary Persia, and imaginative narratives about legendary and mythic figures, it is clear that the work fits none of the later genres. Rather it is an example of a mixture from which, by a process of gradual differentiation, many later forms developed.

Thus Thucydides was writing at a time when prose literature was growing exuberantly but had not yet been pruned, shaped, and neatly separated. Unlike Ctesias, Thucydides preferred to include in his work a relatively narrow range of material, almost entirely political and military, and he seems not to have enjoyed playing with the boundary line that separates fact from fiction. But his commitment to a precise and factual narrative of the war did not find a ready-made pattern. Even as seemingly simple a matter as finding a satisfactory chronological structure for his work posed difficult problems. No predecessor seems to have developed a pattern that would be satisfactory for a conflict as long and fought on as many fronts as the Peloponnesian War. The calendars of the various Greek states were complex, difficult to synchronize, and not readily understood outside their own area. And there was a more fundamental dilemma: a strictly chronological account would fragment the treatment of extended operations, while the presentation of a major undertaking from beginning to end would obscure the chronology and the connection with other simultaneous events. Thucydides' solution to the problem was a compromise that let the war itself shape the narrative pattern. He exploited the fact that there was a fairly clear campaigning season in the warm months of the year. Events are narrated year by year with a formula to mark the transition: "and the second year ended of the war which Thucydides wrote up" (2.70.5). Each year begins with the campaigning season in the spring and is divided into two sections: the "summer," or the normal campaigning season, and the "winter," the rest of the year. Within these units Thucydides normally narrates each major campaign continuously, returning to extended actions in subsequent seasons or years.

This chronological system seems to be Thucydides' own invention, not something borrowed from a predecessor or imposed by some rigid genre. It is a good example of the flexibility and indeterminacy in historical writing at this stage in its development and a reminder of both how much Thucydides had to work out for himself and how inadequate are some of the models of the development of historical writing that suggest a straight-line progression from early historians such as Hecataeus, through Herodotus ("the father of history"), to Thucydides and thence to the fourth-century historians. Basic problems in historical narrative were confronted anew by many of these historians, and many influences were at work on the shaping of history as a literary form.

This is particularly the case with Thucydides' relationship to Herodotus. That he knew the works of Herodotus is clear, if only from his criticism of errors that he found in Herodotus. The *Histories* never mention "the father of history" by name. Some ancient writers say that Thucydides' father, Ŏlorus, brought him to a reading by Herodotus at which the young historian-to-be burst into tears. But the story is unreliable and may be very misleading, especially if we think of an impressionable Thucydides influenced by the completed masterpiece of Herodotus. The date of the publication of Herodotus' work is by no means certain, and the stories of his public readings in Athens do not inspire confidence. His history cannot have reached its final form until the early years of the Peloponnesian War and perhaps a good deal later. One recent study argues it was completed around 414 B.C. Thus Thucydides may have known nothing about Herodotus' work when he set out to write his own history at the beginning of the war. Nor is it certain that he had read the work prior to his own exile in 424 or had access to it until his return to Athens in 404. It is quite possible, in other words, that Thucydides' own approach to history was already developed and parts of the *Histories* written when he first studied Herodotus' masterpiece.

His reactions to that work were, it would seem, highly ambivalent. His admiration for

Herodotus has often been conjectured from his careful avoidance of any significant overlap between the two works and from occasional echoes in language and technique. But Thucydides' criticisms are clear. Above all he was determined to focus on the war itself rather than on setting that conflict in a wider frame by incorporating ethnographic accounts and utilizing frequent digressions. Thucydides is Herodotus' rival, and on this point he adopts no pose of false modesty. Some historians disingenuously complain that the truly great subjects have already been taken by their predecessors. They then proceed to demonstrate their virtuosity and brilliance in the treatment of an ostensibly less promising theme. Thucydides will have none of that. He affirms in the first sentence of his work that he expected from the outset of the war that it would be a great one and the one most worth narrating of all those that had preceded it. The second sentence makes the claim even more forcefully: "For this was the greatest movement for the Hellenes, and for some portion of the barbarians and so to speak even among the widest circle of men" (1.1.1).

This assertion—so directly contradicting conventional views about the grandeur of the past and the greatness of both the Trojan and Persian wars—shapes Thucydides' "Archaeology," and gives his disquisition on the past and his demonstration of method a further level of significance. The "Archaeology" also functions as an attack on conventional views about the scale of these wars and on the significance of the subjects adopted by Homer and Herodotus. This is a bold challenge and not easy to sustain. The Trojan War is treated at some length in chapters 10 and 11, but the Persian War is not mentioned until late in the "Archaeology," when Thucydides writes: "Of earlier actions the greatest accomplished was the Persian war and this had a speedy resolution through a pair of naval battles and a pair of land battles" (1.23.1). The battles are not even specified, perhaps because to name Artemisium, Salamis, Thermopylae, and Plataea would too strongly evoke the immense fame of those engagements.

Instead Thucydides emphasizes the great length of the Peloponnesian War and the frequency and intensity of the suffering that attended it.

This is ultimately the criterion on which Thucydides bases his claim that the Peloponnesian War was the greatest—not in the number of participants or scale of the battles, but the intensity of suffering. His phrasing was carefully chosen. This war was the greatest *kinesis* (movement or disturbance). At first the phraseology seems purely descriptive, but later its emotional content becomes clear: "so many cities deserted . . . so many exiles, so much slaughter, some from the war itself and some from civil strife" (1.23.2).

Thucydides' concentration on the element of suffering *(pathos)* in his subject matter sets him apart from Herodotus and his other predecessors in historical writing, and is the basis of his implicit claim to have surpassed them. The ancient critics recognized and responded to the power and vividness of Thucydides' representation of suffering; they knew that his avoidance of explicit comments did not betoken a lack of concern but rather a technique for drawing the reader into the action and evoking the reader's reactions and responses. Modern critics, misconstruing his use of implicit techniques and his adoption of a detached viewpoint, have often found this feature of the work more difficult to appreciate. He has seemed cold and unconcerned, even an advocate of the harshest realpolitik, because he only rarely comments in his own voice about the cruelties and miseries of the war. Yet when one reads his account of the hairbreadth escape of the Mytileneans (3.49) or the atrocity at Mycalessus (7.29) it is clear that his techniques evoke an intense response.

Hence the frequent comparison between Thucydides and tragedy. Many of these comparisons, to be sure, are trivial or fail to specify precisely in what sense the comparison is intended. Almost all historical narratives are tragic in the sense that they concern suffering and loss. More significant are attempts to show that the *Histories* share techniques or a viewpoint with contemporary tragic drama. Yet the contemporaneity itself may account for some similarities. Greek art, literary and visual, during this period is rigorously selective, concentrates on the individual in ways that develop the relationship to ideal types, and works by careful contrasts and significant minimal variations on type scenes and formulae. All these features can be detected in both Attic tragedy and Thucydides, but need not imply an especially close relationship between the two. More significant still is the view shared by Thucydides and some of the tragic dramatists that the sufferings of the heroes arise in large part from the qualities and characteristics that cause their greatness. Oedipus is destroyed because of his concern, integrity, and determination; the Athenians are defeated, at least in part, because of the qualities that made them great and powerful—their restless energy and boldness.

For the tragic poets this connection between the qualities that provoke our admiration and the destruction that compels our pity and terror raises with considerable regularity the problem of divine justice. Destiny, fate, the gods are constantly under scrutiny, either through choral meditations or by the explicit comments of the major characters, or sometimes through the actual appearance of a divinity on stage. Nothing in Thucydides directly corresponds to this. Some critics, to be sure, have argued that some of the abstractions that figure prominently in his work, such as hope (*elpis*), sexual attraction (*eros*), and indeterminacy (*tyche*), function as superhuman and semidivine forces, as analogues to the divine powers in Greek tragedy. The abstractions have been personified, capitalized, and made into manifestations of a Thucydidean theology or theodicy. This interpretation, eloquently argued many years ago by F. M. Cornford, has constantly tempted Thucydidean scholars but never commanded general assent. It provides an explanation for the reader's feeling that this seemingly detached and totally prosaic text somehow attains an intensely poetic quality. But it fails to account for

the great difference between Greek tragedy's direct confrontation of the cosmic implications of suffering and Thucydides' reluctance to be drawn out. At the point where Greek tragedy would ask how the gods could allow such suffering, Thucydides returns to the role of Hippocratic observer, noting the details as precisely as possible and recording men's reactions to them. Of the gods or of cosmic justice there is no trace. As a good child of the Enlightenment, Thucydides knows that the causes of human history are to be found in human decisions and actions and in the nature that shapes them. And this is awesome enough, for there are within nature regularities no less inspiring of pity and fear than the will of the gods and the rule of destiny.

THE THUCYDIDEAN QUESTION

The more one studies Thucydides in the intellectual and literary setting of his time, the clearer it becomes what an immense task he set for himself. It is hard to say which challenge was the greater: the problems of historical research—the secrecy of the Spartans, the inadequacy of Greek recordkeeping, the complexity of the events, the partialities of the witnesses—or the difficulties of shaping this material into a literary form. That it was a long undertaking is clear from Thucydides' own statements that he began work on the project when the war broke out (1.1.1) and that he lived through the entire war (5.26.5). The work thus took at least twenty-seven years to bring to its present form (it stops at a semicolon in the middle of the events of 411 B.C., the twenty-first year of the war).

Over this period it is inevitable that Thucydides changed and modified his views; that notes were taken, assessed, and reassessed, drafts written and revised; and that new information and new events set old actions and interpretations in different lights. If one could determine the stages of Thucydides' thought, one would have a fascinating view into the nature of the work, the mind of the author, and perhaps into the intellectual climate of the age. Since the mid-nineteenth century, an immense effort has been made, especially by German scholars, to detect the inconsistencies and changes in style, technique, and attitude that would identify the successive stages in the composition of the work. Surely in a book as complex as this, developed over so many years, there must be signs of its evolution. Thus "separatism," the attempt to identify the stages in which the work was composed, has dominated Thucydidean studies and often represented itself as *the* Thucydidean question.

The treatment of the Sicilian expedition provides an instructive example. Thucydides first mentions the great, disastrous Athenian attempt to subjugate Sicily in book 2, during a digression on Pericles and his successors. He emphasizes the intense rivalries and the struggles for first place among the successors and then observes:

> From these came many other mistakes, as one would expect in a city large and imperial, and above all the expedition to Sicily. This was not so much a mistake in deciding whom to attack as it was the result of those who sent out the expedition failing to make the right further decisions concerning what was beneficial for those who had gone. Instead, by their slanders concerning the leadership of the citizen body they dulled the cutting edge of the expedition and they threw the affairs of the city into extraordinary confusion among them.
>
> (2.65.11)

This is a coherent, although highly compressed, interpretation of the failure of the Sicilian expedition. Ultimately it may even be consistent with the interpretation advanced in books 6 and 7, in which the course of the expedition is reported; but the emphasis is radically different. In the later narrative a great deal is made of the initial error of deciding to attack Sicily. In the earlier passage that mistake is subordinated to an ill-explained failure to support the expedition with "what was benefi-

cial" and to the civic disorder caused by competing politicians. There is little room for the factors that later appear so significant: the importance of cavalry, the arrival of Gylippus and his success in war and diplomacy, the delays of Nicias, and the perseverance, growing confidence, and skill of the Syracusans. There is thus a great tension between the earlier passage and the later, fuller account of the expedition. From this it has been concluded that the two passages cannot have been written at the same time. The excursus on Pericles' successors, in which the comments about Sicily occur, alludes to the end of the war and hence must have been written after 404 B.C. The Sicilian narrative then must have been written earlier. Or was it written even later? Or was it simply written in a different mood?

Such is the stuff of which separatism is made. Its immense expenditure of intellectual effort has not produced consensus. Each critic has a different view of the divisions within the work and their dates of composition, and each has a different sense of the evolution of the work and of Thucydides' thought. Such inconsistency does not discredit the attempt, for an improved method may yet produce more decisive results, but it has led other students of Thucydides to apply their energies in yet a different direction and to study those elements that unite and integrate the work. Critics of this persuasion, often called "unitarians," have achieved impressive results and have succeeded in bringing the fundamental consistency of the *Histories* more clearly into focus.

Since World War II, the conflict between unitarians and separatists has become less pronounced, and critics who disagree on the composition problem have sometimes found it possible to agree on other fundamental issues. The treatment of the cause of the Peloponnesian War is one example. Separatists had often believed that the first book of the *Histories* combined two inconsistent or at least chronologically distinct views of the cause of the war: an original view that emphasized the specific disagreements between Athens and the Peloponnesians over Corcyra and Potidaea, and a later view that ascribed to the growth of Athenian power the fear that pushed Sparta into war. Recently, especially since the book by Jacqueline de Romilly on Thucydides and Athenian imperialism, it has come to be widely agreed that the two views are closely integrated and form a coherent, perhaps even profound, etiology of the war.

Thus it is not surprising to find a moratorium, albeit incomplete, on separatist studies and a redirection of scholarship toward subjects on which agreement is more likely. The composition problem, surely, can no longer be considered *the* Thucydidean question. Instead, a large number of valuable studies have focused on Thucydides' treatment of various topics. There have been lively and significant debates about Thucydides' political views, his representation of realpolitik, his belief in the utility of history, and the degree of optimism and pessimism within the work. Agreement, however, has again proved elusive, despite the best efforts of excellent scholars.

One example of scholarly disagreement centers on Thucydides' treatment of realpolitik. Several speakers in the *Histories* urge that decisions be made on the basis of the self-interest of the more powerful party and not on moral principles or conventions. That attitude, as we have seen, is often expressed by using the rhetorical antithesis between the advantageous and the just and is sometimes grounded in the conflict between *physis* (nature) and *nomoi* (conventions). The implication is that nature drives men to act out of self-interest and, hence, appeals to convention will be irrelevant and ineffective. There is, in effect, a law of nature that the strong will rule and the weaker will obey (5.105.2 and 1.76.2–3). Herodotus, Plato, and many of the Sophists were also investigating this idea and its radical implications, but none expressed it as strongly and openly as Thucydides. Since he gives repeated expression to this view, and since there is no equally eloquent advocacy of traditional Greek ideas of justice and restraint, it has often been

inferred that Thucydides himself believed in this doctrine and intended his work in part to illustrate or expound it. He would then be, in some sense at least, an advocate of the right of the stronger and a critic of those who expect great powers to be bound by moral constraints. Hence he would be likely to agree with those speakers who argue that in acquiring and holding on to its empire Athens had done nothing unnatural or reprehensible. He would also regard as foolish those—for example, the Melians—who think that a great power can be deflected or stopped from pursuing its self-interest.

If this view of Thucydides is correct, the work emphasizes the superiority of what is natural over artificial restraints. It is an Enlightenment text, expressing and reinforcing views developed by the radical thinkers of the period, and a Great Power text, since it implicitly exculpates the self-aggrandizement of the powerful and tacitly urges the weaker to accommodate.

Views such as these have been strongly advocated and widely adopted in recent Thucydidean studies. But they run directly counter to other interpretations, usually based on analyses of literary technique, that suggest that Thucydides was in sympathy with the Melians, the Plataeans, and the other victims and near victims of the war's violence. In such interpretations Thucydides expresses—perhaps even exaggerates—the realpolitik of the belligerents, but does not himself accept it. His own preference is for restraint and the traditional moral standards of earlier Greece. Thucydides, in this view, is a traditionalist, a virtual dinosaur, the product of a pre-Enlightenment world, who has somehow survived to enter a totally alien environment. His text is not a brief for the powerful, but a Third World text illustrating the dangers of polarization.

In this case the conflict between two radically different views of Thucydides may be susceptible to some resolution. The *Histories* illustrate in various ways a process whereby the success and power of the stronger provokes fear and eventual unification among the weaker. As Socrates pointed out to Callicles in Plato's *Gorgias*, "stronger" is by no means an easy or simple concept. For example, what if the weaker combine to resist domination and thereby, though individually weaker, become collectively stronger? Hermocrates of Syracuse, urging the Sicilians to unite and prevent Athenian intervention in the affairs of their island, develops a similar argument in the *Histories*:

> For the Athenians to seek to aggrandize themselves and to plan ahead is completely excusable. I do not blame those who wish to dominate, but those who are inclined to yield. For the nature of mankind is to rule on every occasion anyone who gives way, but to ward off the aggressor.
>
> (4.61.5)

In this passage Thucydides implies that there is another side to the law of the stronger, no less deeply rooted in nature: the tendency of those who are threatened by a superior power to resist and to unite. He does not suggest that the necessary unity of action is easy to obtain or that resistance is always successful. The processes are slow and difficult and their outcomes uncertain. There is no swift rallying around the Melians to help them ward off Athenian enslavement. But awareness of past Athenian conduct encourages Sicilian resistance to their operations (6.33.4 and 6.88) and contributes to Athens' eventual defeat. The *Histories* illustrate the folly of thinking that a superior power is easily deflected from attaining its objectives, but the work is no mere restatement of the familiar law of the stronger. Instead, it leads to a new level of complexity as far removed from the conventional wisdom of realpolitik as from the archaic belief in a *kosmos* in which unrestrained growth (*hybris*) provokes a moral blindness (*atē*), and leads to destruction. The work, in other words, is not an attempt to regress to an earlier moral system, but an effort to go one step beyond the Enlightenment.

In the treatment of realpolitik the text itself contains, if our suggestion is correct, a resolution to some of the conflicts in interpretation. But it is by no means clear that this is always so. In other instances scholarly disagreements may reflect unresolved tensions within the work. Thucydides' attitudes toward various forms of government is one example. Here the interpreters have disagreed almost totally. Hobbes, who was not an insensitive reader of Thucydides, saw him as a critic of democracy and an advocate of monarchy:

> He says Democracy's a Foolish Thing;
> Than a Republic wiser is one King.
> ("The Life of Mr. Thomas Hobbes
> of Malmesbury Written by
> Himself . . . ," 1680)

Modern scholars have often agreed that he had no sympathy for democracy and assured us that he "ended his life as he had begun it, a confirmed oligarch who had never renounced the creed of his fathers" (M. McGregor, *Phoenix* 10:102 [1956]). Yet John Finley and others have called attention to the importance of democratic institutions in Thucydides' view of Athens' greatness. They wondered, if he is made into a critic of democracy, "what becomes of the attitude of apparent approval and even profound admiration of the Periclean democracy expressed in the Funeral Oration?" (G. M. Kirkwood, *American Journal of Philology* 93:94 [1972]). The effort to develop a consistent formulation of Thucydides' political views has led to some very strained interpretations of individual passages, some dubious critical procedures, and, again, unrelenting disagreement among the interpreters.

Behind such difficulties is a methodological problem. Much of the so-called "evidence" of Thucydides' views is so deeply embedded in specific contexts that any attempt to extract it and generalize from it is likely to fail. We recognize the problem in passages such as book 6, chapter 54, in which Thucydides points out that the Pisistratid tyranny in Athens was not oppressive and exacted only a five percent tax, while it beautified the city, waged war effectively, and made the proper sacrifices to the gods. It is clear that Thucydides is not advocating tyranny or even giving a comprehensive list of his criteria for good government. The comments are tied to the immediate context and constitute a typically Thucydidean corrective to the imprecise views of his contemporaries. They resist generalization.

Other passages present stronger temptations. Thucydides' explicit admiration for Pericles, for example, and the glowing tone of Pericles' Funeral Oration (2.35–46) have led many critics to conclude that Pericles embodies Thucydides' political ideal. Yet even here, closer reading reveals ambiguities and tensions, and any attempt to generalize confronts Thucydides' explicit praise of the limited democracy (or moderate oligarchy) that followed the regime of the Four Hundred in 411 B.C.:

> for the first time in my life time the Athenians appear to have governed themselves well. For a measured mixture between the few and the many came about and this first revived the city from the miserable circumstances which had beset it.
>
> (8.97.2)

This passage implies that Thucydides had some reservations about the government of Athens in Pericles' time. Yet it too is closely tied to its context and has an important literary function in marking a stage in Athens' surprising endurance in the war and in her recovery after the disaster in Sicily. It also contributes to an important theme in book 8—the connection between internal politics and external affairs. There is a danger of overburdening the comment if it is made into an indication of a systematic political philosophy. One can be quite sure that Thucydides knew and was attracted by some theory of a "mixed" constitution, one that included elements of both democracy and aristocracy. But that such a theory sums up his political views or is to be read into other passages is far from certain.

Many of Thucydides' comments about forms of government function in a similar way. They are closely tied to context, and often emphasize the importance of a specific episode. They mark significance rather than affirm a political philosophy, as can be seen from another example derived from the account of the year 411 B.C. When the oligarchy of the Four Hundred overthrows the democracy, Thucydides emphasizes the difficulty of the task:

> it was difficult to deprive the Athenian common people of their freedom now approximately one hundred years after the suppression of the [Pisistratid] tyranny—a people who had not only avoided submission but had for over half of that time been accustomed to rule others.
>
> (8.68.4)

Thucydides adopts the democrat's identification of "freedom" with democratic government, but it would be risky to try to generalize about his political views from such a statement. His remarks emphasize the significance of the moment and convey a good deal about the mood of the city, but they do not provide a basis for any systematic treatment of Thucydides' political views.

And, after all, why should they? What warrant do we have that such a work will contain an outline of its author's political views? It is a history, not a political science textbook or a treatise on political philosophy. The literary techniques employed in it suggest a deliberate avoidance of authorial judgments and skillful efforts to draw the reader into making his own assessments of events. It would be very surprising if, coexisting with these techniques, there were a series of propositions that would enable a systematic exposition of the author's political views.

Scholarly disagreement about his political philosophy, then, is not in the least surprising. The text was constructed to resist such explication. The proper question to put to it is not its author's views but how it affects the reader. How does it shape the reader's response; what reactions does it evoke?

THUCYDIDES AND HIS READER

We return then to the question that can never fully be answered but must constantly be asked: What is the relationship between Thucydides and his reader? The intended reader, we have seen, is not the typical man in the street—whether the street be ancient or modern. The text appeals to an elite, to readers who recognize the new methods of analysis it employs, to those who are willing to doubt conventional interpretations and dogmas, and to those prepared to struggle with thought as sustainedly complex as its style is involved and perplexing. This readership emerges directly out of the Greek Enlightenment and its new attitude toward the past. It is sophisticated, proud of its cleverness, eager to be free of the folly of conventional views and of the repression of traditional restraints.

Yet Thucydides' relationship to his reader is not a simple one. His text does not simply restate or reaffirm the consensus of the Greek Enlightenment, nor the position of one school within it. Rather, it constantly explores ambiguities and complexities and contemplates new possibilities. This may in large part explain the notoriously difficult style of the *Histories*. If one borrows the terminology of Tzvetan Todorov (in *Poetics of Prose* [1977]) and speaks of the "figuration" of the work, then one will surely emphasize the tendency toward unresolved antithesis at every level of the text. The traditional, highly polarized Greek sentence style is maintained, but there are constant shifts in the balance—an unexpected word or idea is interjected, a construction modified, a new complexity introduced. In the speeches the same figuration can be detected; they are presented in pairs, with sharply contrasting arguments and ideas. At a practical level a resolution follows; one speaker carries the day and wins the vote. But at an intellectual level, the issues persist and are rarely fully settled on any one occasion. In the Mytilene debate, for example, Diodotus carries the day by his clever exploi-

tation of the argument from advantage, but his exclusion of the consideration of justice raises new questions that cannot be resolved in the immediate context. These questions recur at important moments throughout the *Histories* and are still unresolved, even at the point where the narration breaks off. The same treatment applies to the fundamental antitheses out of which much of the work is constructed—the oppositions between reason (*gnome*) and passion (*orge*), or speech (*logos*) and deed (*ergon*), or nature (*physis*) and convention (*nomoi*). The conflicts are sharp, increasingly complex, and never fully resolved.

Most Thucydidean scholars have assumed that this is largely the result of the incomplete state of the *Histories*, and that if Thucydides had lived to complete and fully revise his work a clear resolution would have emerged. But is this assumption secure? It appears instead that the distrust of simple solutions characterizes the text at every level and reflects a fundamental strategy of the author. Indeed, considering the steady progression throughout the work toward greater complexity and more subtle analysis, one can hardly expect that the completed work would affirm unequivocally the claims of nature over convention, or advantage over justice, or reason over passion—or vice versa.

Modern readers, accustomed to more explicit modes of exposition, may find this puzzling, even while recognizing the affinity between Thucydides' approach and that of the Socratic questioning, the Platonic dialogues, and the dramatic techniques of Euripides. But the approach derives not from some intangible zeitgeist but from very practical considerations. The audience to which the work was directed was not likely to be reached by mere assertions. Nor was sustained argumentation likely to convince them—not, at least, until a long series of rejoinders and surrejoinders had been completed. Thucydides recognized that a different technique was required. His audience had to see things anew, to reexperience the war and rethink its implications. This is the explanation for the coexistence in the work of an austere generalizing narrative and a visual element that often takes readers by surprise. Suddenly Thucydides will turn to an episode that seems minor or trivial and accord to it a fullness of treatment disproportionate to its apparent significance. The narrative becomes more and more graphic; sometimes the account seems about to conclude and then resumes with a detail more horrible than anything that has preceded it. When, for example, Thucydides relates the Thracians' brutal attack on the little town of Mycalessus, he adds: "There was no little disturbance; every form of destruction took place. And falling upon a school for children, which was the largest one there and the children had just entered, they cut them all into bits" (7.29.5).

The ancient critics recognized in passages such as this a technique of writing that they called *enargeia* (vividness):

> The most effective historian is the one who makes his narrative like a painting by giving a visual quality to the sufferings and the characters. Thucydides certainly always strives after this vividness in his writing, eagerly trying to transform his reader into a spectator and to let the sufferings that were so dazzling and upsetting to those who beheld them have a similar effect on those who read about them.
>
> (Plutarch, *On the Fame of the Athenians,*
> ch. 3, in *Moralia* 347a)

The technique is especially suited to conveying emotions and representing suffering, that is, to narrating the *pathos* (suffering) that Thucydides considered so significant an aspect of the war and the true measure of its greatness.

Later Greek historians often imitated Thucydides' vividness and recognized in him something far different from the cold, detached, scientific historian described in modern handbooks. But they seem rarely to have perceived the full significance of Thucydides' treatment of *pathos*. For Thucydides, the suffering during the war was not only the mark of its greatness but also the factor omitted in much contemporary thinking about the war. It had no place in the calculations of realpolitik, nor in the analyses of advantage. Even Pericles, in his mighty prevision of the war and confidence in Athens' ability to win, seems not to have considered the full cost of the war, the intensity of suffering that would attend it, and the loss not only of human and material resources but of so many of the qualities that made Athens great.

The suffering also set the conflict between nature and convention in a new light. Nature, as many of the Enlightenment thinkers predicted, proved stronger. One convention after another was violated. Ambassadors were illegally detained and ultimately executed; bodies were denied proper burial; supplications, promises, oaths all lost their binding force. But the disintegration of convention did not bring the expected liberation. As the *Histories* follow the progress of the war, we see what a state of nature is like, and it turns out to be not the culmination of man's slow progress but a return to the most primitive violence and horror. The civil strife (*stasis*) that afflicted the city of Corcyra in 427 B.C. is described in detail in book 3, not only because it is typical of the problems that beset many cities as the war went on, but also because it shows what human nature is like when the cloaks and ameliorations of a more prosperous existence are removed:

> And many atrocities afflicted the cities that suffered civil strife, things that continue to happen and will keep happening in the future as long as the nature of men remains the same, though more intense or more tranquil, modified in form depending upon the attendant circumstances. For in peace and good times both cities and individuals form better plans since they do not experience pressures over which they have no control. But war, by taking away the prosperity of daily life, becomes Violence's teacher and assimilates the dispositions of ordinary men to their circumstances.
>
> (3.82.2)

As the discussion of the Corcyrean revolution proceeds, a new aspect of the conflict between nature and convention becomes apparent. The triumph of nature results not so much in the annihilation of conventions as in their enslavement. They do not disappear, but are reshaped in the service of self-aggrandizement. Language, recognized as a form of convention, changes under the pressures of the war and becomes an agent of violence. Thucydides emphasizes that the factions in the civil strife "modified at their whim the accustomed relationships of names to deeds. Thoughtless rashness was considered 'courage on behalf of the party'; a thoughtful delay was 'specious cowardice'; restraint was 'an excuse of the unmanly.' Intelligence in each detail was 'inactivity throughout'" (3.82.4). In this episode one detects one part of a much broader process wherein *logos* (speech) and *gnome* (reason), which among many Enlightenment thinkers were expected to resolve conflicts and lead to progress, perform the opposite function: that of abetting violence and the most destructive forms of self-aggrandizement.

Thucydides' history is always prepared to contemplate such complications. As we have seen, it resists simplified resolutions and the imposition of the views of an omniscient narrator. But it invites the reader to reexperience the war and to re-create the thoughts and suffering generated by this great "disturbance." If the work cannot be reduced to propositions and generalizations, it nonetheless holds out to the reader who perseveres a deepening understanding of the war and its implications, and justifies thereby its bold claim to be "something to keep forever."

Selected Bibliography

TEXTS

Historiae, edited by H. S. Jones. Revised by J. E. Powell. 2 vols. Oxford, 1942.

La guerre du Péloponnèse, edited and translated by Jacqueline de Romilly, L. Bodin, and R. Weil. 5 vols. Paris, 1953–

TRANSLATIONS

Crawley, R. *The History of the Peloponnesian War.* London, 1874. Reprinted with introduction by John Finley. New York, 1951.

Hobbes, Thomas. *Eight Bookes of the Peloponnesian Warre.* London, 1629. Reprinted with introduction by Richard Schlatter. New Brunswick, N. J., 1975.

Smith, C. F. *Thucydides.* 4 vols. London, 1919–1923.

Warner, R. *History of the Peloponnesian War.* Harmondsworth, England, and Baltimore, Md., 1954.

COMMENTARIES AND WORD INDEXES

Bétant, E.-A. *Lexicon Thucydideum.* Geneva, 1843. Reprinted Hildesheim, 1961.

Classen, J., ed. *Thukydides.* Revised by J. Steup. 8 vols. Third and subsequent editions. Berlin, 1892–1922.

Essen, M. H. N. von. *Index Thucydideus.* Berlin, 1887. Reprinted Darmstadt, 1964.

Gomme, A. W., A. Andrewes, and K. J. Dover. *A Historical Commentary on Thucydides.* 5 vols. Oxford, 1945–

Hude, C., ed. *Scholia in Thucydidem.* Leipzig, 1927. Reprinted New York, 1973.

CRITICAL STUDIES

Cornford, F. M. *Thucydides Mythistoricus.* London, 1907. Reprinted London, 1965.

Dover, K. J. *Thucydides.* Greece and Rome: New Surveys in the Classics, no. 7. Oxford, 1973.

Luschnat, Otto. *Thukydides der Historiker.* Stuttgart, 1971. Separate publication of the article in A. F. Pauly and G. Wissowa, ed., *Realencyclopädie.* Supplement 12, cols. 1085–1354. Stuttgart, 1970.

Pritchett, W. K. *Dionysius of Halicarnassus on Thucydides.* Berkeley, 1975.

Rawlings, Hunter R. *The Structure of Thucydides' History.* Princeton, 1981.

Romilly, Jacqueline de. *Histoire et raison chez Thucydide.* Paris, 1956.

———. *Thucydides and Athenian Imperialism.* Translated by P. Thody. Oxford, 1963.

Schwartz, Eduard. *Das Geschichtswerk des Thukydides.* 2nd ed. Bonn, 1929.

Stahl, H. P. *Die Stellung des Menschen im geschichtlichen Prozess.* Munich, 1966.

W. R. CONNOR

ARISTOPHANES

(*ca.* 445–385 B.C.)

I

ARISTOPHANES WAS BORN about 445 B.C., possibly on Aegina, the island that looks across toward Piraeus, the harbor of Athens. We know very little about his life. His first play, *Banqueters*, was produced in 427 at the Dionysia (the major annual dramatic festival) to some success (second prize out of three); the second, performed the following year, was *Babylonians*, in which the young playwright attacked the demagogue Kleon. Both plays are now lost, but their fragments suggest that they were, at least to some extent, a programmatic announcement of some of Aristophanes' leading themes: generational conflict and city versus country in *Banqueters* and political satire in *Babylonians*. For the latter Aristophanes won first prize and also provoked a law suit from the comedy's enraged target. He seems to have enjoyed the publicity, since Kleon's threats became, in 425, the subject for more dramatic needling in *Acharnians* (our first complete extant play) and then the catalyst for a full-scale satire in *Knights* (424 B.C.).

Aristophanes is a character in Plato's *Symposium*, with a dramatic date of 416. Although the dialogue's intent is plainly philosophical and ethical rather than biographical, it is worth noting that Aristophanes' speech, which occupies the central position in the seven praises of love, is the most charmingly mythic. Plato's *Apology*, possibly more factual, again makes reference to the lampoon of Socrates in Aris-

tophanes' *Clouds* (first produced in 423 B.C.). But the comedy's original version and the trial of the philosopher are separated in time by nearly a quarter of a century. It is recorded that Aristophanes in old age allowed his son Araros to produce at least two of his comedies (*Kokalos* and *Aiolosikon*). No tradition surrounds his death; it is commonly assumed that he died in 385, some three years after the performance of his last extant play, *Plutus*.

The playwright's life is thus even more sparsely documented than those of the fifth-century tragedians. Although Aristophanes is commonly thought to have been a contemporary of Euripides, one of his favorite targets, he was born some ten years after Euripides first competed at the festival (455 B.C.): their dramatic careers overlap (from 425 to 406), but Aristophanes was decidedly of a different generation.

Like the tragedians, he was uncommonly prolific: he composed some forty dramas, of which eleven survive. This is a higher proportion of extant plays than for any other Greek dramatist, but his total output is still less than half of that of Aeschylus, Sophocles, Euripides, or Menander. Perhaps connected with this fact are the distinctive demands of the genre in which Aristophanes wrote, Old Attic Comedy. Comic playwrights, as opposed to tragedians, were forced to invent new stories, rather than relying on the inherited narratives of myth and legend.

We do not know how comedy began. Aristotle (*Poetics*, ch. 5) mentions the "leaders of the phallic processions"; but the circumstances of the processions and the actions and words of the leaders remain obscure. Two words that may be involved in the etymology of *komoidia* are often cited to support the hypothesis that the genre developed from rural fertility festivals: *komos* meaning "festival" or "revel," and *kome* meaning "village." But this is only to speculate, since the etymology is uncertain. The enthusiasm with which Dikaiopolis and his family celebrate the Country Dionysia in *Acharnians* (237–279), with the accoutrements of a religious procession and a hymn to Phalles (the personified, divinized phallus), is notable. But the passage need not represent a literary recrudescence of comedy's primitive origins. Attempts to explain the development of the genre from literary sources (such as Megarian farce or the earlier fifth-century plays of Epicharmus of Syracuse) have been generally unconvincing.

Whatever comedy's origins, the first formal performances came to Athens relatively late. The evidence of the Parian marble testifies to a victory by the poet Chionides in 486 B.C. If this was the first comedy in Athens, Aristophanes (and his rivals Kratinos and Eupolis) wrote within the first several generations of the comic theater. Kratinos was born *ca.* 484, and would have watched some of the first comedies as a youth; the dates of Eupolis are uncertain, but we know that his career flourished approximately from 430 to 410. That the Romans regarded this trio as the leading exponents of fifth-century Athenian comedy is attested by the opening of Horace's *Satires*:

> *Eupolis, atque Cratinus, Aristophanesque poetae,*
> *atque alii quorum comoedia prisca virorum est....*
> (1.4)

The poets Eupolis, Cratinus, and Aristophanes, and the others who composed old comedy....

By Horace's time, it was conventional to designate fifth-century comedy as "Old Comedy" and the plays of Menander, Diphilos, and Phi-lemon, composed some 75 to 125 years later, as "New Comedy." (The inevitable scholarly temptation to fill in the missing link of "Middle Comedy" does not seem to have arisen before Apuleius, in the second century A.D.; see *Florida* 3.16.)

Old Comedy is highly topical and relentlessly lampoons the leading politicians of the age (Pericles, Kleon, Alcibiades, Hyperbolos). Along with these, a host of minor functionaries—poets, quacks, philosophers, and figures-about-town—are singled out by name for ridicule. In their freedom of speech (*parrhesia*, "saying everything") the plays of Aristophanes are unique in the history of Western literature; despite the internal strains caused in Athens by the Peloponnesian War, such liberty appears to have been abridged only twice in the late fifth century, for comparatively brief periods. The topical character of the comedies makes an edition or translation with good notes and a glossary of names essential for students of Aristophanes and his contemporaries. It may be of some consolation to note that the learned Aristotle, barely a century after the plays' production, would not have understood a large proportion of their references.

Parrhesia, which the Romans called *ius nocendi* ("the right to injure"), often takes the form of obscenity and scatology. Like the costuming of comic actors, who almost certainly were outfitted with exaggerated leather phalluses and padding in the rear, these features of Aristophanic diction are reflexes of the comic tendency to smash taboos; they are, in short, funny. But these aspects of Aristophanic style pose another considerable barrier for readers of Aristophanes in translation, since numerous bowdlerized versions often present something quite different from what Aristophanes wrote. The Victorian translations of B. B. Rogers tone down the piquancy of the original text, although they have the virtue of conveying Aristophanes' extraordinary metrical virtuosity. The American versions of William Arrowsmith and Douglass Parker, despite their liberties, are closer to Aristophanes' pungent spirit.

ARISTOPHANES

It is generally held that Old Comedy possessed a set of strict formal conventions. Thus critics have distinguished among the parts of the play: the *prologos* (prologue); the *agon* (dramatized debate); the parabasis (or "turning aside" of the chorus to address the audience directly); the episodic encounters of the hero with various *alazones* (imposters, phonies, buffoons); and the *exodos* (finale).

The parabasis itself is elaborately structured, with seven parts: *kommation* (short introduction), parabasis proper, *pnigos* (literally "choking song": a short lyric said all in one breath), ode, epirrhema, antode, and antepirrhema. The final four parts are often called collectively the "epirrhematic syzygy": the ode and antode are metrically identical, as are the epirrhema and the antepirrhema; lyric sections (ode and antode) alternate with rhetorical ones (epirrhema and antepirrhema). The evidence of the plays themselves confirms such structural elements. But the practice of Aristophanes also shows that their placement and combinations were far less conventional than is commonly assumed. For example, the parabasis may appear in full form (as in *Acharnians, Knights, Wasps,* and *Birds*), or as continuation of the agon and in considerably altered form (as in *Lysistrata*), or in a severely truncated state (as in *Thesmophoriazusae*). There may be a second parabasis (as in *Knights, Wasps, Peace,* and *Birds*), or the parabasis may be absent altogether (as in *Ecclesiazusae* and *Plutus*). The persona of the playwright may be adopted by the chorus in the parabasis, or the chorus may consistently maintain its dramatic character (as in *Birds*). The parabasis is usually placed toward the end of the drama's first half; but special considerations may force its postponement until the play is two-thirds over (as in *Wasps*).

Normally the episodic scenes in which *alazones* interrupt the hero and are unceremoniously ejected occur in the comedy's second half. But the most coherent interpretation of the very first scene of *Acharnians* is that Aristophanes has adapted this structural element for an opening tableau (compare also the feast of Polemos in *Peace*, the second scene of the play, where the hero is forced temporarily into the role of a subordinate *alazon*, in an inversion of the usual structural pattern). The *agon*, which often occurs before the parabasis, may be expanded to occupy the entire second half of the play (as in *Clouds* and *Frogs*).

A second commonplace of Aristophanic criticism is that the comedies typically possess a self-assertive hero, whose grandiose fantasy transforms him from decrepitude and frustration into a marvelously rejuvenated figure by the end of the play. This is certainly true in a number of the extant dramas. For example, Dikaiopolis in *Acharnians* achieves a private peace with the Spartans for himself and his family: the thirty-years' truce permits the hero to enjoy the fruits of prosperity, and he ends the play by winning a drinking contest, mocking the vainglorious general Lamachus, and anticipating a night of sexual revelry (not with his wife, but with two rather younger flute-girls). In *Knights*, Agorakritos, a common sausage seller, replaces Kleon as the leader of the people; in *Wasps*, the old juror Philokleon frustrates his son's desire to keep him on the straight-and-narrow, escapes from the house, and returns from a revel with a young girl on his arm, beating up those who accost him in the street; in *Peace*, Trygaios, an Attic farmer, assails the heavens to liberate the goddess Peace herself and returns to earth a triumphant hero. Perhaps this pattern, if such it be, is most resplendently illustrated in *Birds*, where Pisthetairos founds a new utopia in the sky, Cloud-cuckoo-land, and is crowned king of the universe, the new Zeus, at the end of the play.

Fantasy pervades nearly all of Aristophanes' comedies. But two qualifications of the thesis of comic heroism are necessary. First, there is no single hero-figure in a number of the comedies, for example, *Thesmophoriazusae* (where Euripides and the Kinsman split the heroic role) and *Clouds* (where Strepsiades, Socrates, and Pheidippides are all shown to be buffoons). In *Lysistrata, Frogs,* and *Ecclesiazusae* the heroic roles of Lysistrata, Dionysus, and Praxagora are all attenuated. Secondly, there are important differences even among the undisputed heroes. Dikaiopolis' private peace in *Acharnians* does not resemble Pisthetairos' ambiguous utopia in *Birds*, and the fulfillment of both these characters' fantasies is quite separate from the pan-Hellenic pastoral dream of Trygaios in *Peace*. As with structural elements, so with the analysis of comic heroism: we must be careful to take each Aristophanic comedy on its own terms.

A third standard judgment in the criticism of Aristophanes is that in contrast to the well-made plays of Menander and New Comedy, Old Comedy is episodic and loosely structured. Such an assessment ignores the fact that, to a considerable degree in Aristophanes, language tends to become plot; the coherent unities of comic poetry are to be sought in the unique realm of the fantasy itself. Aristophanes' verbal art, in metaphor and pun, coordinates and unifies his plays far more than does the action of his plots, in the Aristotelian sense of *mythos* (a logically organized plot). For example, the apparently irrelevant lyric of abuse at *Birds* 1470 ff., despite the stanzas' separation, is skillfully composed to refract and anticipate various elements of the scenes that surround it; the elaborate symmetry of the parabasis in *Lysistrata* mirrors the structured interrelationships of political and domestic life, of male and female, that are central to that play; and *Peace* can well be described as a series of variations on the theme of festivity. This is not to deny the well-known differences between Aristophanic comedy and the New Comedy of Menander. It is, rather, to advance at the outset the suggestion that Aristotelian canons of literary criticism may be as inadequate for appreciation of the playwright's poetic art as they are for the oral poetry of Homeric epic. Let us turn now to an analysis of the individual plays themselves.

II

The first of the extant comedies is *Acharnians* (425 B.C.). The prologue presents an old farmer named Dikaiopolis ("Mr. Just City"), sitting at dawn on the hill Pnyx, where public assemblies were held in Athens, lamenting his many sorrows. His introductory speech suggests an imaginative equation that often recurs in Aristophanic drama, the identification of good tragedy with good government (see especially *Frogs*); Dikaiopolis complains that he has seen all too little of either recently. Also prominent in the prologue is the theme of the country and the city, a major motif not only of *Acharnians*, but also of *Clouds*, *Peace*, and the New Comedy of Menander.

Dikaiopolis is a frustrated minority of one, favoring a peace with Sparta in the Peloponnesian War (begun in 431). He ironically comments on the greed and pomposity of various state officials, including the ambassadors to the Persian court, the Persian emissary Pseudartabas ("the Great King's Eye"), and the smooth but unpersuasive Theoros, who had been sent by the Athenians to procure an alliance with the Thracian king Sitalces. Thoroughly outraged at the assembly's failure even to consider a truce, Dikaiopolis commissions Amphitheos to negotiate a private peace for himself and his family. Amphitheos' name is both bombastic and ironic; we might suspect that a character who boasts of divine descent on both sides of the family will prove to be yet another *alazon*, but he is actually the instrument of Dikaiopolis' salvation. A nimble messenger, he returns from Sparta to Athens within fifty lines of dialogue: almost certainly, he is a parody of a Euripidean *deus ex machina* (only this time in a comedy, and in the first scene rather than the last); he is also, perhaps, a remote precursor of the Roman *servus currens* (running slave). For eight drachmas, he has bought for Dikaiopolis a selection of truces on approval. The hero selects—not the five-years' variety, which smells of shipyards (naval preparations), not the ten-years' peace, which smacks of diplomatic dickering—but the thirty-years' truce, which has the comforting bouquet of divine nectar. All the "truces" are, in fact, skins of wine; the verbal pun on *spondai* ("libations" and thus by extension peace treaties) is the first example in Aristophanes of a marvelous facility with language that converts symbolic abstractions into physical manifestations or props, richly exploiting various fields of meaning and linking indissolubly the concrete with the fantastic.

Thus Dikaiopolis achieves his principal objective very early in the play. By the second scene he is prepared to reenact the Country Dionysia with his family and is readying a great celebration. But now he must face more serious obstacles, since success—as in Pindar—breeds anger and envy. The chorus of the Acharnians, his old neighbors from the rural district of Acharnai, are outraged that he has dealt with the enemy; the pompous and belligerent general Lamachus (whose name puns on the Greek word for fighting, *machē*) adds his threats to the Acharnians' intimidation. What is Dikaiopolis to do?

To deal with the hostile chorus, Dikaiopolis decides to make an oration about the causes of the Peloponnesian War. To present himself as pathetically as possible, he needs an appropriate costume, and supplicates the playwright Euripides for his aid. (The scene at 395 ff., when Dikaiopolis approaches the house of Euripides and importunes him for assistance, becomes something of an Aristophanic trademark; see the variations at *Clouds* 221 ff., when Strepsiades calls on Socrates for aid, and *Thesmophoriazusae* 39 ff., the visit of Euripides and the Kinsman to the house of Agathon on a similar errand.) Euripides was well known in Athens for his iconoclasm in dressing mythical heroes in sackcloth (Oeneus, Phoenix, Philoctetes, Bellerophon, Thyestes, and Telephus: *Acharnians* 418 ff., a valuable inventory of Euripidean dramas pre-425, all of which are now lost). After some hesitation, Dikaiopolis settles on the costume of Telephus. Attired in this indecorous outfit, he addresses his defense to the Acharnians. Emboldened by its partial success—one half of the chorus agrees with him, while the other half obstinately reviles him—Dikaiopolis mockingly insults Lamachus. The general declares that he is off to fight the good fight; the farmer announces his intention to set up a personal trading post with the enemy.

The parabasis now intervenes (626–718). The first three sections (introduction, parabasis, and *pnigos*) are occupied with a choral defense of Aristophanes the playwright; the poet should be congratulated by the people as an able counselor on state affairs, who cleverly detects and thwarts the enemies of the public interest—that is, Kleon, to whom Dikaiopolis has already referred in 502–508, lines that have led some critics to the hasty conclusion that the playwright himself acted the hero's role in this play. In the latter four sections of the parabasis the chorus resumes the persona of the old Acharnian countrymen. After an invocation of the Acharnian Muse (a piece of charcoal), the oldsters lament their being pushed aside by young, fast-talking city-slickers. The passage marks the first appearance of one of Aristophanes' major themes, the conflict of the generations, which is the mainspring of *Clouds* and *Wasps*, important in *Frogs*, and possibly significant in the lost *Horai (Seasons)* and *Pelargoi (Storks)*. In the extant dramas, Aristophanes always seems to side with age against youth, not necessarily because he was conservative in politics (or anything else), but because the unexpected triumph of age promised more fun.

After the parabasis, Dikaiopolis is shown marking the boundaries of his *agora* (private marketplace), much as the herald had outlined the physical area of the assembly in the prologue (*Acharnians* 43–44). The hero trades with a wretched Megarian, from whom he buys two little girls (the starving man's daughters), and with a Boeotian, on whom he palms off an Athenian informer. These scenes are among the best of the episodic interruptions by *alazones* in Aristophanic comedy. Especially in the encounter with the Megarian (*Acharnians* 728–817), Aristophanes presents a skillful concatenation of motifs. He playfully mocks the man's dialect; Megara's distress in the Peloponnesian War in real life is ironically reflected in the starving trader's gratitude for salt and garlic in exchange for his daughters (or "piglets," in a double entendre of the word for female genitals); Dikaiopolis' sexual innuendo with the girls is capped by the Megarian's avarice, as he exits wishing that he could also part with his mother.

After several more interruptions the finale of *Acharnians* pits Dikaiopolis directly against Lamachus. Two messengers enter: one to order Lamachus to the front, the other to invite Dikaiopolis to a drinking contest, replete with culinary and nubile dainties. Both prepare to take their leave, Dikaiopolis mockingly and exuberantly summarizing each line of Lamachus' lament in pointed, stichomythic exchanges. Lamachus endures further misery. A messenger enters to announce in paratragic language an absurd and inglorious series of misfortunes: the general has impaled himself on a vine-pole while leaping over a ditch, turned his ankle, and bashed his head against a stone. Meanwhile our sense of time, and that of Dikaiopolis, is utterly dissolved. Although it was December and time for the Country Dionysia earlier in the play, it is now February, season of the Anthesteria (another festival in honor of Dionysus). The hero enters, flushed with insolence and wine from his victory at the drinking contest of the *Choes* (part of the Anthesteria celebrations) and sporting a young girl on each arm. The closing lines of the chorus (1232–1234) raise a song of praise to the hero and his wineskin, the prop that is by now a symbol of peace and festivity.

Acharnians contains an astonishing number of Aristophanes' leading motifs. The parallelism between good theater and good government is explicit in *Frogs*; the tension between the city and the country preoccupies Strepsiades in the prologue of *Clouds* and is an important motif in *Peace* and *Birds*; the generational conflict that dominates the parabasis of *Acharnians* is the leading theme of *Clouds* and *Wasps*; the war and its consequences furnish the background of *Peace* and *Lysistrata*; Euripides reappears as a character in *Thesmophoriazusae* and *Frogs*. Of the leading motifs in the extant plays, only the comic inversion of the real-life role of women (in *Lysistrata*, *Thesmophoriazusae*, and *Ecclesiazusae*) is absent in *Acharnians*.

Knights (424 B.C.) continues the attack on Kleon: it is one of Aristophanes' most openly political comedies. The plot, as in many other cases, is an extended *agon*: this time, between a Paphlagonian slave (who represents a thinly disguised, blustering Kleon: compare the Greek verb *paphlasdein*, to bluster) and an obscure and lowly sausage seller, Agorakritos ("chosen by the assembly"). These two struggle to capture the favor of an old man, Demos, who is the Athenian people personified. Two slaves open the play (as in *Wasps* and *Peace*), decrying the voracity and viciousness of their fellow servant, the Paphlagonian. A reference to the Athenian victory at Pylos, in which Kleon and the general Demosthenes had participated, has led some commentators to identify the servants as Demosthenes and Nicias (another prominent politician during the Peloponnesian War). The two steal some of the sleeping Paphlagonian's oracles, and learn that a sausage seller is fated to replace Kleon in Demos' affections. When such a tradesman presents himself, the servants immediately set about indoctrinating him, with the assurance that he will have the support of the aristocratic cavalrymen, the knights, in his battle against Kleon.

The sausage seller, timorous at first, gradually acquires confidence in a preliminary skirmish with the monstrous Paphlagonian. Much of *Knights* consists of a parody of political abuse and mud-slinging; when the two antagonists are not insulting each other, they compete in outrageous political promises, first to the council (offstage), and then to the old master himself. Demos admits that he has been lazy and lacking in vigilance, in that he has allowed the Paphlagonian to cheat him and to usurp his rightful powers. He awards the sausage seller the trusted seal-ring that is the symbol of chief stewardship of his affairs; the Paphlagonian discovers from his own stock of oracles the prediction of his defeat, and snarlingly yields to Agorakritos the eminence he had enjoyed and abused.

Knights carries forward a motif implicit in *Acharnians*: the parallelism between private ordering of the household and public governance of the state. But whereas Dikaiopolis had evaded the public preoccupation with war by concluding his own fantastic private peace, in *Knights* Aristophanes presents an allegory. Demos is characterized as an ostensibly confused, dithering old man, who may or may not know what his servants are really up to. The latter are the politicians of the day. Among them, the leading steward of the household has the power to drain Demos' resources or to rejuvenate him: the finale of *Knights* (probably incomplete in our text) seems to celebrate the old man's new lease on life with the exile of the Paphlagonian (who retires to the profession of none other than sausage selling) and the triumph of Agorakritos. It is part of the play's humor, however, that the latter is not nobler than his predecessor; indeed, the chorus explicitly hails him as more vicious (*Knights* 329). The allegory does not move in the direction of consistent political criticism. As in *Clouds*, *Lysistrata*, and (to some extent) *Frogs*, the Aristophanic *agon* does not possess an unequivocally moral theme but is rather bent on eliciting fun from the excesses and outrageousness of both sides of the argument. (Compare the portrait of Pisthetairos in *Birds*, who is permitted to triumph not because of his nobility, but because he is the greatest *alazon*, or fraud, of all.) The reaction of the audience seems to confirm the ambivalence of the play. Aristophanes was rewarded with first prize by the play's judges; Kleon was, within weeks, reelected as one of the ten *strategoi* (generals) of Athens for the following year.

Clouds (432 B.C.) does not now exist in its original form. After the play's failure (it received third prize), Aristophanes seems to have revised the parabasis, the *agon*, and the finale; it is doubtful that the revised version (generally dated 419–418) was ever presented on stage. In the prologue the old countryman Strepsiades laments the debts and aristocratic pretensions of his son, Pheidippides. He is determined to send Pheidippides to the school of Socrates and Chairephon, the *phrontisterion* ("thinkery"), where he hopes the young man may learn the elements of Sophistic rhetoric and so be able to confute the father's creditors in court. But Pheidippides refuses to be enrolled, protesting that he has no desire to exchange horse-racing for pasty-faced intellectualism. Consequently Strepsiades presents himself as a student, despite the fact that he is old and his memory is failing. After a preliminary interview he is introduced to Socrates himself, who appears suspended in the air in a basket (the better to probe the mysteries of meteorological phenomena). Socrates initiates the old buffoon in the mores of the school and in the worship of its patron deities, the clouds (here symbols of vacuous abstraction); but his patience is sorely tried by Strepsiades' forgetfulness and vulgarity. After the parabasis, Strepsiades reverts to his original plan, forcing his son to take his place at the thinkery. Pheidippides witnesses an extended *agon* between right and wrong logic (or "stronger argument" and "weaker argument"), a model display of rhetorical abuse and shifty argumentation. Armed with some pointers from his son, Strepsiades is able to bamboozle two of his creditors. But it is soon apparent that the son has absorbed the "new education" all too well, since he settles a dispute about poetry with his father by beating up the old man. Strepsiades' pain turns to horror when Pheidippides "rationally" justifies the assault by claiming that old age is second childhood and that he strikes Strepsiades for his own good. The son adds that he can also present arguments for striking his mother. At this point, Strepsiades' faith in the new education is destroyed, and he recants his heresy to the clouds, who reveal that they have been leading him on only to punish him. In a fury Strepsiades and his slaves attack the *phrontisterion* with torches, and as the thinkery burns, its dismayed inhabitants flee from a volley of stones and blows.

The failure of *Clouds* was a bitter disappointment to its author, as we can see both from the parabasis of the revised version (518–525) and from the parabasis of *Wasps* (1043–1050). Why did it fail? It was bested by Kratinos' *Wine Jug (Pytinē)* and Ameipsias' *Konnos*: the former was apparently a confessional allegory with the poet himself deserting his true wife, Poetry, for a mistress named Drunkenness, while the latter was a satire on Sophistic philosophy. The character of Ameipsias' play makes it improbable to suppose that *Clouds* failed because its subject matter was too esoteric for Athenian audiences. And the example of *Knights*—in which Aristophanes won first prize for an unflattering portrait of Kleon, who was then reelected by the people—tells against the theory that *Clouds* offended because of the portrait of Socrates. We know too little about contemporary taste and possess too little evidence for detailed comparison with the competing plays to formulate a convincing hypothesis.

Clouds is different from many of the surviving comedies in several respects: the about-face of the chorus toward the end, the lack of a triumphant finale, and the fragmentation (some would say the absence) of the heroic role. But it contains extraordinarily ingenious dialogue and displays the typical Aristophanic fusion of satire and fantasy. The portrait of Socrates is a comic tour de force: as with Kleon, Euripides, and Lamachus, the poet has combined real-life traits susceptible to caricature with totally imaginary ones. It is idle to protest that Socrates did not champion the doctrines with which he is associated in the play, or that he did not, like the Sophists, accept money for his services. These distinctions, although significant for the history of philosophy and ethics, are not terribly important for comedy or satire. Socrates' well-known idiosyncrasies (see *Birds* 1282, 1555; *Frogs* 1491; Ameipsias, frag. 9) made him a convenient target for a sally of jabs against the Sophists (*Clouds* contains echoes, many of them distorted, of the doctrines of Protagoras, Diogenes of Apollonia, Prodicus, Gorgias, Antiphon, and others).

In *Wasps* (422 B.C.) Aristophanes exploits to the fullest an important subtheme of *Acharni-*ans and *Clouds*: the battle between the generations. The contemporary Sophists had directed attention to the possibilities of strain between parents and children (see Antiphon, frag. 44a); and the split between young and old in politics is clear in Thucydides' description of the public debate on the eve of the Sicilian expedition of 415 (see Thucydides, *History* 6.13 ff.). In *Acharnians*, the portrait of oldsters being confounded by young Sophistic upstarts (676–718) is consistent with the scene in *Clouds* in which Pheidippides confounds his father with "Socratic" rhetoric (1321–1446). But in *Wasps* the tables are turned; it is now the old man, Philokleon, who is presented as a slippery rogue, whereas his son, Bdelykleon, is a model of propriety and restraint.

The significance of the characters' names is only tangential; Philokleon, the old father of the play, "loves Kleon" because, as his son claims, he is the dupe of demagogic politicians who manipulate his love of jury service in order to prosecute their enemies and line their own pockets. Bdelykleon is "repelled by Kleon" and sensibly tries to curb his father's excesses and alert him to the truth. But Kleon himself does not appear, as in *Knights*; and the real point of the play has little to do with politics. Rather, *Wasps* is a satire on Athenian litigiousness and a delightful fantasy of irrepressible *vis comica* in the old.

At the play's beginning, we hear from Philokleon's two slaves that the master suffers from a strange disease: an obsession with jury service in the law courts. His son has tried every expedient to confine him to the house (much as, in later comedy, the "blocking character"—an old father or guardian—attempts unsuccessfully to confine a young lover). But Philokleon, in a series of imaginative maneuvers, soon proves that his mania for judging is not to be cured easily. In efforts to join his old friends, the chorus of wasps (so named because they delight in "stinging" defendants in court with harsh penalties), Philokleon pretends that he is the smoke escaping from the chimney, hides himself under a donkey (as Odysseus had clung to the belly of a ram when escaping from Cyclops), and threatens to gnaw through a net covering the window. With difficulty his son persuades him and the chorus to listen to his exposé of official rapacity. Although Bdelykleon convinces the chorus, the father is reluctant to agree that his time-honored prerogatives are in reality only sops for the ignorant. To reawaken his interest in domestic life, his son arranges for a mock trial to be held at the house, and the case of a dog who has stolen some cheese is duly entered on Philokleon's docket. To his dismay, Philokleon is tricked into voting for the dog's acquittal.

After the parabasis, which is postponed until comparatively late in this play, Bdelykleon proceeds to press his advantage; he urges his father to lead a more social life and sends him off to a dinner party. But the anarchic energies that the old man had previously channeled into judging are now released in a different arena: he returns from the party riotously drunk, having stolen someone else's slave girl and beaten up the passersby in the street. He proclaims himself rejuvenated and sweeps aside the protests of his son. In the finale, he crowns his exuberance by leading a wild dance. The circular structure of the dance mirrors the dramatic structure of the comedy: Bdelykleon's efforts to repress his father's carousing instinct have led full circle, with the only change being that Philokleon has substituted the private sphere for the public one.

Peace (421 B.C.) was produced at the City Dionysia (where it won second prize) just weeks before the conclusion of a truce between Athens and Sparta after ten years of war (the so-called Peace of Nicias: see Thucydides, 5.20.1). It is thus the only play of Aristophanes that is topical in its entirety. A countryman, Trygaios (whose name is a pun on Greek *tryx*, "wine lees," and also suggests *trygoidia*, another word for comedy), determines to journey from Athens to Olympus to seek the goddess Peace. He accomplishes this on the back of a winged dung-beetle (parodying the mythical flight of Bellerophon on the winged horse

Pegasus); of course he is more successful than his tragic counterpart, to whom Euripides had devoted a play some years earlier (see *Acharnians* 427). Hermes, as gatekeeper, informs Trygaios that the gods, appalled at the violence of war among mortals, have abandoned their customary seats, yielding Olympus to Polemos, the personified god of war. Trygaios must undergo an interview with this fearsome deity, as Polemos prepares to grind up the Greek cities in a giant mortar and devour them in a ghastly banquet. But the hero persists: he bribes Hermes with a golden goblet, promising him that all the festivals in Greece will henceforth be celebrated in Hermes' honor, and he is able to rescue the goddess Peace from the deep cavern in which she is interred. Together with a chorus of farmers (who at various points in the play seem drawn from all over Greece and at others are referred to as Attic), Trygaios escorts Peace and her handmaidens Opora (Harvest) and Theoria (Festival) back to earth. In triumph he prepares for his own wedding with Opora, symbolic of the material blessings of peace; he surrenders Theoria to the Athenian council.

Assessments of this comedy often include the terms "static" and "symbolic"; it is not generally regarded as one of Aristophanes' better plays. The comparative lack of dramatic tension and the blurring of the chorus' precise identity are undeniable; the static plot, the symbolic features of the play's language and of some of the characters, and the insistence throughout on the motif of festivity all suggest something of an experiment on Aristophanes' part. Although *Peace* is normally classified as a political play, it represents a transition from the earlier comedies of the 420's to the more self-contained fantasies of *Birds* and *Lysistrata*. Its more curious, distinctive qualities have little to do with contemporary events and personalities; to the usual admixture of satire and fantasy, a substantially new, lyrical element has been added (or, rather, the lyrical elements of earlier comedies have been greatly expanded and varied). As in no other play, we are presented with the extensive celebration of simple country joys, the fertility of the fields, and release from care of every kind. Such a celebration is anticipated by the reenactment of the Country Dionysia at *Acharnians* 247 ff., but *Peace* presents a large-scale instance of this impulse.

The play begins and ends with mention of food: the disgusting cake of dung for the beetle and the luscious delicacies of Trygaios and the chorus. In between, the feast of Polemos (itself a perverted parody of the normal *komos* or revel of comedy) is succeeded by a vignette of the triumphant poet at a festival banquet (769–774), by a picture of Peace as hostess of a symposium (996–999), and by a lengthy, dramatized account of a rural celebration (see the second parabasis at 1127–1191, and note the name Komarchides, "leader of the revels," at 1142). The play thus moves from negative (repellent) feasting to positive (desirable) festivity, from Polemos and his ghastly mortar to Trygaios and his tasty wedding feast. It is even suggested that the hero will "eat" his bride Opora in a passage of double entendre at 925 ff.

Birds (414 B.C.) is the longest and perhaps the greatest of the extant plays. A decrepit oldster named Pisthetairos* ("companion persuader"), accompanied by his friend Euelpides ("high hopes"), sets out for the country of the birds, determined to escape debts and taxes in Athens. They encounter the hoopoe, who had originally existed as King Tereus. Pisthetairos conceives a brilliant idea: why not establish a new commonwealth in bird-land? In the *agon* he persuades the chorus of birds, initially hostile, that they are the primeval rulers of the universe, and offers himself as the leader who can restore the avine power and prestige that men have usurped. Fusing fantasy and realpolitik, Pisthetairos points out that the birds are strategically located between gods and men: if either group should balk at their sovereignty, they may attack humanity from above and intercept the smoke of sacrifices to the gods from below. De-

lighted, the chorus abandons its suspicions and urges Pisthetairos to swing into action.

After the parabasis, the action turns to the building and naming of the new fortress in the sky, Cloud-cuckoo-land. Two series of *alazones* interrupt Pisthetairos in his preparations for a great triumphal feast; they are supplemented by two messengers, the goddess Iris and the Titan Prometheus, and finally a delegation of gods (Poseidon, Herakles, and a barbarian deity called Triballos). These last are hoodwinked by the hero into agreeing that he be allowed to marry Basileia, the fabulously attractive personification of Zeus's sovereignty. As the comedy concludes, the dedication feast is transformed into a wedding banquet; ironically, many of the choicest delicacies are roast fowl.

Several passages in *Birds* remind us of the contemporary political climate of high hopes for the success of the Sicilian expedition. The name of Pisthetairos' sidekick, Euelpides, should be compared with Thucydides' description of the Athenian character (*Histories* 1.70.3) and with his comment on the city's optimism as the expedition set sail (6.24.3); *euelpides* occurs in both contexts. The latter passage is especially suggestive for its use of erotic metaphor, also a prominent strand of imagery in *Birds*. Pisthetairos, at the very moment of his inspiration to found a new city-state *(polis)* in the sky *(polos)*, suggests that the birds will destroy the gods with a Melian famine (*Birds* 186); the joke refers to the Athenian subjugation of the small Aegean island of Melos two years before, in 416. Later in the play, he threatens Iris with death, even as he recognizes that she is immortal. His rationale is expressed in terms that might come straight from Thucydides' account of the Melian incident (compare Thucydides, 5.87–116): "We will suffer a grievous fate indeed, it seems to me, if while we rule over others you are unchastened and will not recognize that you, in your turn, must obey those who are more powerful" (*Birds* 1225–1228). At 1596 ff., Pisthetairos' negotiations with the gods also take a Thucydidean turn when he urges

*The hero's name, more correctly, is Peisetairos; but the version given here will be more familiar to many readers.

their capitulation in a speech that sophistically claims nonaggression and recommends the "just course" (*dikaion*):

> We never started the war against you in the past, and now we are willing to make peace, if you should promptly make up your mind to do the just thing. And the just course is this: for Zeus to return the scepter [of sovereignty] to us birds. If we can frame a truce on these terms, I invite the ambassadors to lunch.
>
> (*Birds* 1596–1602)

In both passages, the echoes of the negotiations of the war are mingled with bathos and fantasy. We should beware of any critically reductive interpretation of the play that makes it either (a) a satire of Athenian imperialism or (b) an escapist, utopian fantasy. *Birds* is the clearest, most brilliant illustration of the Aristophanic synergy of the satirical and the fantastic.

Lysistrata (411 B.C.) is probably the best known and most frequently performed of the comedies. Its structure depends on an elaborate series of parallels between the political sphere (war between Athens and Sparta) and the domestic sphere (war between the sexes). The semichoruses of old men and old women, which do not unite until late in the play, constitute a visual emblem of strife, and they are balanced by the contingents of Athenian and Spartan negotiators in the final episodes. Political *eris* (strife) is plausibly blamed by Lysistrata for the destruction of domestic *eros* (desire); true to her name ("dissolver of armies"), she plans the sex strike to end the war, using domestic *eris* to restore political reconciliation.

The topical references in *Lysistrata* are comparatively infrequent, and this may have something to do with its stage popularity in modern times. The richest source of the play's energy is its invocation of domestic life, especially evident in such passages as Lysistrata's extended simile of wool-working (567–586), the parabasis (614–705), and the lyric extending the spurious invitations (1043–1071; 1189–1215). But just as we should not overemphasize the political resonances of *Birds*, we should not dismiss the po-

litical implications of *Lysistrata*, at least as they are transformed in comic myth: especially striking is the speech of the Athenian ambassador at 1228–1238, where the fruitless embassies and captious misinterpretations of diplomacy are comically recalled.

Interpretations of *Lysistrata* as an ancient model for present-day women's liberation are not uncommon. But the play itself does not lend unambiguous support to such readings, since (a) Lysistrata and the other women do not dispute but rather are made to illustrate the very charges that men commonly bring against them, and (b) Lysistrata herself retires from the action toward the end of the play, presumably content to return to obscurity once peace has been established. On the other hand, the position of women in Athens in the fifth century B.C. is concisely summarized by Kalonike at line 16 ("it is difficult for women to get out of the house"), and Lysistrata offers a pointed and poignant criticism of the prevailing double standard at 594–597, when she tells the *proboulos* (commissioner) that the war affects men and women very differently. One of the most striking images in the play concerns the role of women as mothers, as at 651, where the chorus of old women implicitly liken themselves to tribute-paying allies of Athens, "assessed" for young sons for the war effort. On the whole, however, *Lysistrata* and the other "women's plays," *Thesmophoriazusae* and *Ecclesiazusae*, exploit the notion of "women on top" for the same reason that Aristophanes champions the old over the young: the humorous reversal of expectation.

Despite some differences of opinion, it is likely that *Thesmophoriazusae* (*Women at the Thesmophoria*) was performed later in the same year as *Lysistrata*, at the Dionysia of 411. The two plays could not be more different. *Lysistrata* is a blending of political fantasy with domestic life, *Thesmophoriazusae* a dramatically more audacious combination of farce and literary parody. Unaccountably neglected by commentators and critics, *Thesmophoriazusae* is skillfully composed and unified. The principal motifs are set out in the prologue and then developed in two distinct segments: the *ekklesia* (assembly) of the women, with the prosecution and defense of Euripides, and the paratragic rescue of the Kinsman.

As the play opens, Euripides seeks the aid of his fellow tragedian Agathon. Since Euripides is to be put on trial at the Thesmophoria by the women of Athens as their defamer, he pleads with Agathon (presented here as an effeminate dandy) to infiltrate the exclusively women's festival and defend him. Agathon, who is in the middle of composing a new tragedy, declines; Euripides must turn to his Kinsman (sometimes identified as Mensilochos) for aid. The Kinsman duly undergoes a ritual of shaving and disguise, and defends the tragedian at the festival in a somewhat ambivalent fashion. His arguments only have the effect of increasing the women's ire; upon the information of the epicene Kleisthenes, the Kinsman is stripped and recognized indisputably as a man. He is bound and guarded, and must implore Euripides for a "means of salvation" *(mechane soterias)*, in an obvious parallel to the plots of numerous Euripidean tragedies. The rest of the play depicts Euripides' attempts to set the Kinsman free. After abortive efforts based on the rescue plots of his own plays, *Helen* and *Andromeda*, the playwright finally conquers his reluctance to disguise himself as a woman. He dresses up as an old bawd and employs a shapely young girl as a decoy to distract the Scythian policeman guarding his relative. The policeman, a remote precursor of Dogberry in Shakespeare's *Much Ado About Nothing*, cooperates; and the scoundrels finally escape.

The programmatic function of the prologue in *Thesmophoriazusae* is clear: rhetorical pyrotechnics, the motif of disguise (specifically transvestism), the notion of *mimesis* (imitation), and the setting at the festival constitute the play's givens. Ambiguities of language and of the theatrical process—which are both representations of reality and thus "mimetic"—emerge from the preliminary jests of Euripides and the Kinsman on seeing and hearing (*Thes-mophoriazusae* 5–11), and from Agathon's "imitation" of the parts of both the actor and the chorus in the rehearsal of his play. Agathon's physical appearance introduces a second major theme: ambiguities of gender and sex role. His theory of *mimesis*, which insists on a proper empathy between a playwright and his poetry, is a focal point, not of literary criticism but rather of a comedy that plays on the theory's consequences: the potential disjunctions between gender and sexual identity and between aesthetic "imitation" and its objects.

The Thesmophoria thus functions as a rich, symbolic setting for the play, since even in real life something of the disjunction between the sexes marked the festival's observance. It extended for three days in October, and marked a major focus for women on the calendar. They left their homes to pitch tents in an exclusive area (the Thesmophorion), where they slept in groups and cooked their food in the open air when they did not have to fast. The dedication of the whole observance to Demeter and Kore involved one day's abstinence from food and, probably for some women, abstinence from sex for a longer period before the festival began. The women chose their own officials for the ceremonies and were supported (at least in some cases) by financial contributions from their husbands. A requirement of secrecy (as in the Eleusinian mysteries) underscored the solemnity of the rite, whose purpose was probably connected with fertility.

Some aspects of the Thesmophoria (encamping in the open air, the autonomy of the women, the posting of guards, and the financial subsidies) suggest the structural framework, at least, of a military operation; the ritual contained an implicit *mimesis* of social roles that were, outside the sacred precinct of the Thesmophorion, typically confined to males. The *mimesis* of Aristophanes' poetic fantasy converts the festival to an *ekklesia*, where the women may function in even more atypical ways within the framework of an informal play-within-a-play. (It is interesting that archaeological evidence suggests that the Thesmophorion in Athens was located very near the Pnyx, where assemblies restricted to adult male citizens were held.) The central images of the parabasis (*Thesmophoriazusae* 819–829)—the *kanon* (weaving-rod/spear-shaft) and the *skiadeion* (parasol/shield)—are a verbal emblem of the sexual ambiguities that pervade the play. These ambiguities are exploited through parody after the parabasis, with the extensive comic versions of Euripides' *Helen* and *Andromeda* (produced in 412, the year before *Thesmophoriazusae*).

Euripides is a character, rather than a target, in *Thesmophoriazusae*; the comedy is not a satirical attack on him, any more than it is a polemic on the position of women: the antagonists, after all, are reconciled at the conclusion.

In *Frogs* (405 B.C.) Euripides again appears as a character. Dionysus, god of the theater, has been reading Euripides' *Andromeda* and a great yearning to see its recently deceased author has seized him (*Frogs* 52–66). He and his slave Xanthias set out for the underworld, with Dionysus somewhat imperfectly disguised as Herakles, one of the few heroes to undertake successfully a round trip to that destination. In the play's opening scenes, the two encounter Herakles himself, who after some irreverent jests points the way for them; a corpse who refuses to carry their luggage; and Charon, the fearsome ferryman guarding the lake that borders Hades. Xanthias goes around the lake on foot, while Dionysus is transported by Charon in his boat, to the mocking accompaniment of a chorus of frogs. Once on the other side, the two survive a series of terrors; the chorus of forgs gives way to a chorus of initiates in the Eleusinian mysteries. At the house of Hades, misunderstandings arise because of Dionysus' costume; a servant who thinks he is Herakles accuses him of stealing the dog Kerberos. After several panicky exchanges of costume with Xanthias, the god proclaims his identity (631); but he and Xanthias are forced to submit to a whipping in order to establish which one of them is really immortal.

The parabasis intervenes, an epirrhematic syzygy that presents a serious plea for political amnesty in Athens (675–737). The second half of the play is an extended *agon*, as in *Clouds*. Dionysus is installed as the most suitable judge for a literary dispute between Euripides, newly arrived in Hades, and Aeschylus. The prize in this contest will be the ultimate reward: the chance to reascend with Dionysus to the upper world. The two playwrights are first invited to defend their work in general terms. Euripides boasts of his innovative techniques, having introduced, as he says, *oikeia pragmata*, "everyday (literally household) things," on the tragic stage (*Frogs* 959). He attacks Aeschylus for the ponderous inflation of his style. Aeschylus defends himself by adducing the good moral example of his heroic themes and faults Euripides for his characters' depravity. The playwrights then proceed to a detailed analysis in three areas: prologues, lyrics, and the "weight" of individual verses on a scale; the last is determined literally, rather than figuratively. Dionysus, who has periodically interrupted the contenders with buffoonlike remarks, finally becomes serious. He is hard put to choose between them; one is so "clever," the other so "pleasing" (Euripides and Aeschylus, respectively). He finally tries to make a decision on political grounds rather than aesthetic criteria, on the premise that the true test of tragedy is whether it produces sound advice for the city. Even this test, however, produces no clear result, and Dionysus ends by choosing Aeschylus rather arbitrarily (1471). The play concludes with the victor joyously preparing to revisit the light and instructing Pluto to accord his chair of tragedy to Sophocles during his absence.

Frogs is valuable evidence for the continuation right through the fifth century of a largely oral culture in Athens. In a society where books were rare, it is remarkable that Aristophanes could anticipate the appreciation by a vast audience of detailed literary parody, with a minimum of farcical stage action in the second half of the play (contrast *Thesmophoriazusae* in this respect). *Frogs* succeeded admirably: it was accorded first prize and also the unique honor of a repeat performance—although the ancient evidence singles out the parabasis (rather than the literary contest) as the focus of contemporary praise. In the subsequent development of comedy, the role of the slave Xanthias is especially significant. He is a precursor of Karion in *Plutus* (discussed subsequently) and the forerunner of an army of mischievous and impertinent slaves in New Comedy: see especially his dialogue with Pluto's slave on the pleasures of gossip, eavesdropping, and prying into the master's business at *Frogs* 738–755.

In the two fourth-century comedies, *Ecclesiazusae* (392 B.C.) and *Plutus* (388 B.C.), the development of the genre is clear. Neither play possesses a parabasis, and the role of the chorus in *Plutus* is reduced to less than fifty lines. In *Ecclesiazusae (Assemblywomen)* the fantasy is a takeover of the assembly by women disguised in their husbands' clothes, under the direction of the heroine Praxagora. The women institute a new regime of communal property and communal sex; the consequences are exploited in two amusing scenes in the second half of the play. The first presents a cynic who refuses to hand in his property; the second exhibits three old hags, each one uglier than the last, who squabble over the right to have sex with a young man (the new laws give the old and the ugly first priority). A grand banquet of celebration ends the play; Praxagora's husband, Blepyros, hastens to the feast to the accompaniment of a choral praise of food, most notable for its seventy-eight-syllable word for soup (*Ecclesiazusae* 1169–1175), comparable to any *pnigos*. The relationship of the play's central idea to the description of communal property, wives, and children in Plato's *Republic*, book 5, has long been observed; but it is not necessary, as K. J. Dover has noted, to suppose that Aristophanes is specifically satirizing Plato, whose ideas may have been circulating for some time before the *Republic* was written.

Plutus (Wealth) also possesses general philosophical motifs: the ethical questions posed by wealth's uneven distribution among the just and the unjust. The old man Khremylos and his slave Karion have consulted the oracle at Delphi to determine if Khremylos' son should lead a virtuous life in order to be financially successful. Apollo has advised the father that he is to fasten on the first man he meets when he leaves the shrine: this proves to be an old blind man, who identifies himself under pressure from Karion as Wealth. Zeus has deprived Wealth of his sight so that he may not know the difference between good men and bad. Khremylos and Karion, overjoyed at their good luck in finding Wealth himself, lead him to the sanctuary of Asklepios, where they hope his sight may be restored. But they are interrupted by a menacing old woman named Poverty, who argues in an attenuated *agon* that if Wealth recovers his sight, men will no longer fear Poverty and thus become idle and dissipated. Her arguments do not convince Khremylos and his friend Blepsidemos, and she retires grumbling that men will soon need her services again.

Soon after the exit of Poverty, a choral song (now lost) interrupts the action (*Plutus* 626); the manuscripts of the play have the same, or similar, notations after lines 321, 770, 801, 958, and 1096. Karion announces that Wealth is cured. The house of Khremylos is now magically transformed into a palace, with gold and silver tableware and servants playing dice for stakes worthy of Monte Carlo. Word of the household's good fortune spreads swiftly, and a series of *alazones* is quick to appear. Significantly, however, the informer and the melancholy old hag are balanced by a just man, who joyfully announces his sudden new prosperity; and the dramatic situation, analogous in some respects to the second half of *Birds*, is manipulated to emphasize moral behavior (*Plutus* 1158), rather than the acquisition of unlimited power. When Hermes arrives to complain of the gods' starvation (sacrifices have ceased on earth), he is won over by Karion and magnanimously accorded a job in the kitchen (1099–1170), perhaps the most amusing scene in the play.

Ecclesiazusae and *Plutus* are hardly devoid of fantasy, and are linked to the fifth-century comedies in certain important motifs (see especially *Ecclesiazusae* with *Lysistrata*, and *Plutus* with *Peace* and *Birds*). But the tone and the diction of both comedies show, in their relative lack of extravagance, a shift from satire to comedy of manners (although pungent political allusions may still be found: such as on Agyrrhios at *Ecclesiazusae* 102, 184 and *Plutus* 176; on Neokleides at *Ecclesiazusae* 254, 398 and *Plutus* 655 ff.). The evidence of an ancient biographer of Aristophanes indicates that this shift was not confined to the plays that have been preserved through popularity, chance, or both. *Aiolosikon*, produced by Araros (Aristophanes' son) sometime after 388, also lacked a chorus; and *Kokalos* apparently focused on domestic affairs in a fashion familiar to us from New Comedy. If we possessed more of the plays of this period, Aristophanes might well be credited with the origins of New Comedy as well as with the imaginative perfection of Old.

The preceding survey has focused on the outstanding structural and thematic characteristics of the extant plays. Let us now turn to an analysis of what Aristophanes says about his own originality, and to an assessment of his place in the Western comic tradition.

III

Aristophanes was keenly aware of his place in the tradition of comic poets down to his own day: see his comments on his predecessors Magnes, Kratinos, and Krates at *Knights* 506–544. His status as poet was inextricable from his profession as dramatist; it is well to remind ourselves that neither the Greeks nor the Romans were aware of the possibility of writing drama in prose, and the modern separation of "dramaturgy" and "poetics" would have been meaningless to them. The numerous exploitations of dramatic conventions in the comedies (such as Trygaios' address to the crane operator at *Peace* 174–176) and the complex network of vaunting and lyrical images that Aristophanes

applies to his own poetry (the *pnigos* of the chorus at *Wasps* 1050–1059) are thus aspects of the same, self-conscious perception of the poet vis-à-vis his precursors and contemporaries.

Aristophanes' own appreciation of his originality typically combines elements of fantasy and elements of realism. It is generally couched in boasts of cleverness:

> But in the future, wondrous friends, love and cherish the poets who look for and invent something new to say, and store up their thoughts: throw them in your chests with the apples. If you do that, your clothes will smell all year—of cleverness!
>
> (*Wasps* 1051–1059)

Since Aristophanes, in this parabasis, has just made the chorus upbraid the audience for ignoring the virtues of his own play of the previous year (*Clouds*), it is clear which of the poets this passage has in mind. His plays, the poet claims, are veritable feasts, whose aroma is the scent of cleverness. They thrive on novelty (*kainon*:1053); *Clouds* surpassed the efforts of Aristophanes' rivals (in the author's own estimate, if not in actual fact) because it was fertile with "the most novel ideas" (1044).

Cleverness and novelty: they are conjoined also in the parabasis of *Clouds*:

> I'm not a poet who puts on airs, and I don't try to deceive you by bringing on the same acts two or three times; but I'm always inventing clever new routines for you, each one different and all of them ingenious.
>
> (545–548)

The assertion of novelty and cleverness is, at first sight, disingenuous. Shortly before this passage in *Clouds*, Aristophanes has disarmingly declared that his comedies avoid all of the following: obscene joking with the phallus, mockery of bald-heads, the *kordax* (a vulgar dance), witless old men with stale jokes, and wild commotions with torches and clamor (*Clouds* 537–544). But the fact is that we can document most, if not all, of these elements in Aristophanic comedy, and several of them are especially evident in the revised version of *Clouds* (line 543 is in fact a good description of the end of the play, where Strepsiades uses a torch to set the *phrontisterion* on fire). Comic rivalry and infighting, which are alluded to in the chorus' accusation (*Clouds* 553 ff.) that Eupolis plagiarized Aristophanes' famous eel simile at *Knights* 864–867, make the whole passage "suspect"—not in terms of its authenticity, but in the sense of its rhetorical quality as a smokescreen. The poet pretends not to employ the very techniques that in fact he favors; he boasts of his great originality and cleverness; and for good measure he attacks rivals who are charged with being far less original and clever. Ironically the frequency of such tactics and their typical concentration within the parabases suggest that the boasts of novelty and cleverness were well-known formulas of Old Comedy. The paradoxical fun for the audience was in the expectation of these formulas from the comic choruses, and in the uncertainty as to which poet would invent the most outrageously tongue-in-cheek routine. Jokes, to be successful, must build both on the familiar and the unfamiliar; and Aristophanes' appreciation of the dynamics of humor is crystallized in the exchange of Dionysus and Xanthias in the opening lines of *Frogs*, where—even as the god of the theater and his porter satirize the "old jokes"—they elicit the spectators' laughter (*Frogs* 1–18).

Aristophanes also belied his boast of novelty by often reusing material that had proved successful, a practice that may be systematically documented in most of the successful comic playwrights who lived after him, including Menander, Plautus, Shakespeare, and Molière. With Aristophanes, the evidence for this practice ranges from the simple level of personal attack to more complex repetitions of metaphor, theme, and parody. For example, it is striking that many of the minor scoundrels of Athenian real life are referred to not just once but twice or more within individual plays: to take only

one comedy, Exekestides and his citizenship at *Birds* 11, 764, and 1527; Chairephon, represented as a bat at *Birds* 1296 and 1564; Orestes the hooligan at *Birds* 712 and 1490; Opountios the one-eyed informer at *Birds* 153 and 1294; Teleas at *Birds* 168 and 1025; the cowardly Kleonymos at *Birds* 290 and 1475. Some of these multiple references may be explained by a principle of preparation; the poet familiarizes the audience with the target at first, then unleashes an even more witty assault later, to greater laughter.

When we look beyond the confines of a single play, we notice the same technique, such as the repeated jabs at the fat and cowardly Kleonymos over a period of more than a decade, including *Acharnians* 88, *Clouds* 353, *Wasps* 20, and *Birds* 290 and 1475; or the mockery of the effeminate Kleisthenes at *Acharnians* 118, *Knights* 1374, *Clouds* 355, *Birds* 831, *Lysistrata* 621, *Thesmophoriazusae* 574 ff., and *Frogs* 426. On a more imaginative level, the technique of the reuse of material is implemented in metaphor: compare the personification of war (Polemos) as a drunken guest at a symposium (*Acharnians* 979–987) with the presentation of a nefarious host named Polemos in a dramatic episode four years later (*Peace* 236 ff.). The self-reflectiveness of Aristophanic comedy is striking when we notice, in turn, that the scene early in *Peace* is a comic parody of the revel at the end of plays like *Acharnians*, *Birds*, and *Peace* itself, where the hero, engaged in preparing a banquet, is irregularly interrupted by *alazones*. At the beginning of *Peace*, Polemos' preparations for a grisly meal in which he will devour the cities of Greece function as a thematic and structural inversion of Trygaios' triumphant banquet at the end.

Peace also provides numerous examples of the imaginative reuse of motifs from earlier plays. Both Trygaios and Dikaiopolis extensively parody the situation of Euripidean tragic figures (Telephus and Bellerophon, respectively: *Acharnians* 280 ff. and *Peace* 58 ff.). In both *Peace* and *Acharnians* there are elaborate, humorous, and quite fantastic accounts of the origins of the Peloponnesian War (*Acharnians* 515 ff., *Peace* 605 ff.). Just as we learn in the prologue to *Wasps* that Philokleon is suffering from a new illness (*Wasps* 71), so the master in *Peace* is said by his slaves to be under the spell of a strange mania (54, 65); in the prologues to both plays, slaves jest with the interpretation of riddles (*Wasps* 20, *Peace* 47). Part of the parabasis of *Peace* is directly quoted from that of *Wasps* (compare *Peace* 752 ff. with *Wasps* 1030 ff.); we also have particularly emphatic abuse in both plays of the crablike Karkinos and his sons (compare *Wasps* 1501 ff. with *Peace* 781 and 864).

All this does not prove that *Peace* is a derivative play; much the same analysis could be adduced for all the fifth-century comedies. The same motifs, images, and jokes, once they have entered a comedian's repertory, are likely to be used again if they "play" well with audiences. The same rationale applies even to larger-scale repetitions and adaptations, such as the parodies of Euripides' lost play *Telephus* in *Acharnians* and *Thesmophoriazusae*. Aristophanes' penchant for presenting the same play in two versions (*Clouds, Peace, Thesmophoriazusae,* and *Plutus*) may also be linked with the urge to reuse material, even if it did not initially encounter audience approval (as in *Clouds*).

But even as we acknowledge the playwright's reuse of material (and are thus forced to take his claim of novelty with a grain of salt), Aristophanes' imaginative achievement remains intact. Very seldom are motifs and characters exactly duplicated; and the more fundamental meaning of novelty is certainly that Aristophanes and his contemporaries were charged with a task from which the tragedians were exempt: the task of dramatic myth-making. Antiphanes, a poet of Middle Comedy, is almost plaintive in his reminder that, whereas tragedians may retell the well-known stories of legend, comic dramatists must invent "new names, new business, and new plots" (frag. 191). And so Pisthetairos, the hero of *Birds*, is admired by the chorus as an old fellow who is "of novel judgment" and an "accomplisher of

novel deeds" (*Birds* 256–257). The birds themselves become the "new" gods (848, 862); and in a passage that might come from *Clouds* the distracted poet Kinesias tells Pisthetairos that he wants wings so that he may hang suspended in the air, plucking snow-clad preludes for his dithyrambs: thus, his poems will be "novel" (1384). Let us turn to the analysis of two examples of Aristophanic novelty in detail.

The parabasis of *Birds* affords an excellent illustration, not only of the comic myth-making process but of Aristophanic style. In some respects the poem is unusual: at 125 verses, it is the longest parabasis in the extant plays; the artistic claims of the poet are not advanced; and the chorus maintains its dramatic persona throughout. Furthermore a mute character, the nightingale (who has entered at 665 before the parabasis commences), seems to remain on stage during the choral address to the audience; she accompanies the poem on the flute (682–684). The introduction invokes the nightingale and her sweet song (676–681); the bird is then entreated to "begin the anapests," the usual meter for the parabasis proper (684). In the latter, the birds address men on earth, "shadowy, dream-like ghosts, creatures of a day" (685–686), and purport to instruct them on the origins of the universe and the majesty of birds, the original divinities. In a parody of Hesiod's *Theogony* (and probably of the Orphic hymns as well) the birds proclaim the beginnings of the cosmos in Chaos and darkness; black-winged Night then laid a wind-egg, from which Eros, gleaming with golden wings, was hatched (695–697). Eros, in turn, mingled with Chaos and begat all subsequent generations of birds.

The myth continues with a pastiche of Homeric language, Hesiodic structure, and a dash of the pre-Socratic philosophers here and there (notably Empedocles). Eros is said to have brought together all things in mingling (700–701); only then did the race of immortal gods begin. In a recapitulation of Pisthetairos' arguments in the *agon*, the birds then boast of their associations with beauty, youth, love, the seasons, the blessings of nature, and even the divine oracles (703–722: also 465 ff.). The parabasis proper concludes with a pun on the very word *ornis* (which may mean both "bird" and "omen"); the birds proclaim themselves a collective "Apollo" for mankind (722): Apollo was associated with prophecy and divination.

The third section of the great parabasis is the *pnigos*, or "choking lyric"—so called because it is said all in one breath. As with the mention of the anapests at 684, the chorus specifically identifies the *pnigos* at 726. The birds promise a cornucopia of goods to men, if only men will tender them their proper worship and substitute them for Zeus and the Olympian gods as the true divinities (723–736). With the conclusion of the *pnigos*, we reach the end of the first movement of the parabasis.

The four-part syzygy that follows constitutes the second major movement: the birds provide specific illustrations of the benefits that they can confer upon mankind. The syzygy consists of ode (O), epirrhema (E), antode (AO), and antepirrhema (AE). Lyric meter alternates with trochaic tetrameter. O (739–751) comprises another invocation of the nightingale, the "woodland Muse," whose sacred melodies suggest the honey-sweet tragic choruses of the tragedian Phrynichus. AO (769–784) corresponds with O both with respect to metrical structure and to theme; here the swans, sacred birds of Apollo (see Plato, *Phaedo* 84e), gather by a river praising the god with their songs and the noise of their wings. E and AE are most pungent and satirical in tone; but certain motifs, especially the notion of flying and the pun on *nomos* (which can mean both "melody" and "law"), connect these passages to O and AO. The birds hold out tantalizing prospects to men if they will join them in the new city. They may beat their fathers if they feel like it, like the cocks; branded slaves may run away to liberty, like speckled francolins; all, in short, that is prohibited by the laws and customs of society (755) is not only legal but admirable in bird-land. AE (785–800) expands this idea by linking wings to the smashing of a number of personal taboos: with wings, a man may escape from boring tragedies

at the theater, or fly away to answer nature's call, or even facilitate a secret adulterous affair. Finally, one of the central dreams of comedy, to exchange obscurity for power, is illustrated by the chorus with another ridiculous pun: "Captain Horse-Cock" Dieitrephes, a minor military official whose promotions in the service were, presumably, inversely proportional to his competence, but are here fancifully linked to the fortune he had made in manufacturing wicker "wings" (or handles) for wine-flasks (798–800).

The parabasis is a *kainos logos*—a novelty—in the fullest sense. With stunning virtuosity, Aristophanes' parody ranges over the whole of Greek literature and philosophy since Homer and Hesiod. His myth of the cosmic wind-egg is a fantasy invested with credibility through the numerous echoes of prior speculations on the beginning of the universe. If the best romance is grounded in reality, so too are the most evocative fantasies, since the fantastic operates through a precise reversal of reality, and hence the very process of fantasy contains a code for the world from which it proceeds. Within the parabasis itself, this polarity is crystallized in the birds' summation of life in bird-land: "All the things that are shameful here and forbidden by the law are beautiful (and legal) among us, the birds" (755–756). The contemporary debates of such Sophists as Protagoras, Antiphon, and Prodicus (for the last, see 692) on the relationship of *nomos* (law) and *physis* (nature) may lurk in the background here; but it would be a mistake to extract an Aristophanic "position" on them. It is simply more fantastic, and funnier, to imagine law and nature, fathers and sons, birds and gods, turned topsy-turvy.

The comic myth-making in the parabasis of *Birds* really proceeds on two levels, indicated by the division of the poem itself into two movements (676–722; 723–800). First is the fanciful evocation of a golden age in the past (the birds' hegemony); second is the construction of a utopia in the future (men growing wings to become birds). As if to underline this structure, the first half of the parabasis looks backward—not only to previous Greek literature, but also to the earlier arguments of Pisthetairos. The second half of the parabasis looks forward, especially in AE, where the vignette of the Muses, the Graces, and Apollo suggests a divine royal wedding and anticipates Pisthetairos' union with Basileia and his apotheosis (1718 ff.). The poem also suggests that the passage from a fantastic past to an idealized future is a circular one; the parabasis contains a clear example of ring-composition (the tawny nightingale at 676 and the tawny Dieitrephes at 800, the first and last verses of the parabasis), and the nightingale's presence, in both music and language, furnishes a unifying theme. The rhetorical structure of AE is also evidence of carefully planned composition: note the repeated expression "fly back again" at the verse end of 789, 792, and 796; and the symmetry of "winged" at 786 and 797. Two of the examples of wings' utility (786–792) seem specifically set at the theater; there is perhaps an oblique hint in the birds' suggestion that one can fly away from the tedium of tragedies that it is comedy (and, above all, Aristophanic comedy) that serves to fulfill man's most grandiose dreams.

Immediately after AE, when the flute music of the nightingale ceases, Pisthetairos enters with precisely the accoutrements the chorus has praised (785: "there is nothing better or more pleasurable than growing wings"). Looking at Euelpides perhaps, but more probably adopting the stance of a spectator of the parabasis itself, Pisthetairos comments, "So much for that part of the play. By God, I've never seen anywhere a funnier affair than this!" (801–802).

Besides the novelty of the avine cosmogony, the merging of past and future, and the fantasy of man's growing wings, the comic myth-making in *Birds* derives energy from reinterpretations of existing myth. Such is the impulse behind the passages dealing with Procne the nightingale (her name in some versions of the myth is Philomela, which means something like "sweet song"). The traditional myth of Tereus, Philomela, and Procne was a ghastly story of lust and revenge (Ovid, *Metamorphoses* 6). King Tereus raped Philomela, sister of his wife

Procne, and then cut out her tongue to prevent her from exposing the outrage. But Philomela, mute and imprisoned, managed to inform Procne of the crime by weaving the story on a tapestry and sending it to her sister. Procne enacted a hideous revenge on Tereus. She slaughtered their child Itys and served him up to Tereus at a banquet. When she told him of the atrocity, Tereus attacked her in rage; but the gods put an end to the savage misery of all three characters by intervening to transform them into birds: Procne became the nightingale, Philomela the swallow, and Tereus the hoopoe.

Aristophanes has radically altered the Tereus myth to suit the festive connotations of Pisthetairos' quest in *Birds*. In three passages, invocations to the nightingale provide much of the play's lyrical impulse (209–222, the hoopoe's song, and the very similar lines at 676–684 and 737–751 in the parabasis); they are connected to constitute a leitmotif. The sweetness of the nightingale's song is an emblem of the utopian land of heart's desire in the play. The flute that imitates her voice provokes elaborate praise from Euelpides at 223–224, and her actual appearance at the beginning of the parabasis instantly kindles the lust of both old men (667 ff.). She is metamorphosed into a joyous, rather than sorrowful, symbol of Eros. Even though she is said in the hoopoe's song to chant "laments" (211) and the boy Itys is "mourned with many tears" (212), Procne magically becomes a desirable figure of purity (215–216). Her songs enjoy the antiphonal response of Apollo himself (217–222). Her hymns are associated with the sounds of spring (683) and the sweet verses of Phrynichus (748–750). In short, the nightingale, far from evoking the destructive powers of Eros (as in Euripides' *Helen* 1107–1113, a passage probably influenced by *Birds*), is transformed into the central figure of a new myth: the comic fantasy of utopia.

The finale of *Lysistrata* also illustrates the power of Aristophanic myth-making. In this case the novelty proceeds not from a revision of myth but through a transformation of history. With the entrance of the principals at 1241, who come from a great symposium honoring the play's truce between Athenians and Spartans (and men and women), the stage is set for the concluding lyrics. Of these the majority are given to the Spartan semichorus, however we order the lines (they sing 1247–1272 and 1297–1320 in the Budé text). The two semichoruses of the finale obviously balance the earlier choruses of old men and old women, graphically underlining the play's central equation between political and domestic strife.

The Spartans start by recalling the battles of Artemisium and Thermopylae in the Persian Wars at the beginning of the fifth century. The Athenians are praised as "godlike" for their heroism at Artemisium; as for Leonidas and his followers at Thermopylae, they are accorded an elaborate Homeric simile (1254–1258: compare *Iliad* 20.168). In this passage the Persian Wars are recalled as an idealized example of the cooperation between Athens and Sparta, and ornamented with linguistic evocations of glorious, antique heroism; contrast Lysistrata's ambiguous allusion to the role of the Persians in real life, in the Peloponnesian War, at 1133. The language for Leonidas also recalls the Iliadic narrative of Greek unity in a war in the more remote past; even the Trojan conflict will be romantically transformed in the Spartans' second lyric at 1297 ff.

The Athenian semichorus intervenes to invoke a long series of divinities; special emphasis is laid on the Graces (1279), who head the list, and on Hesychia (Serenity) and Aphrodite (1289–1290), who conclude it. Dionysus and his maenads are mentioned (1284–1285): this reference is complemented by the Spartans in their concluding song (1312–1313). Cries of victory are raised (1291 ff.); but it is the victory of Hesychia, not of Ares, that the chorus celebrates.

The final lyric invokes the Spartan Muse to celebrate Apollo at Amyklai (1298) and the cult of Athena *Chalkioikos* (Athena of the Brazen House) (1300, 1320). The Spartans evoke a charming vignette of young maidens by the river Eurotas; their chorus is like that of Dio-

nysus' Bacchae. But the surprise is that the leader of this chorus is none other than Helen, daughter of Leda, who is now *hagna choregos euprepes*, the "pure and fair leader of the dance" (1315). Helen has been referred to once before in *Lysistrata* in quite a different context: when Lysistrata explains her plan of the sex-strike to the women, the Spartan Lampito recalls that Helen's seductive charms sufficed to make Menelaus forget his rage after the Trojan War and forgo vengeance upon her (155–156). The tradition that Menelaus "dropped his sword" when he was reunited with Helen was extensively exploited by Euripides in tragedy several years before *Lysistrata*: in the *Trojan Women* (415 B.C.), for example, Menelaus is set up as the judge of his own wife's guilt but is clearly shown to weaken; although the actual reconciliation of the couple is not presented, the chorus prays apprehensively that the pair not be allowed to return to Greece together on the same ship, thus allowing love to thwart justice (*Troades* 941–1114).

But in the context of comic myth-making the "dropping of the sword," or the triumph of love (*eros*) over strife (*eris*), is decidedly desirable. This explains the mention of Helen by Lampito and the chorus' reference to her in the concluding lyric. She becomes, not the catalyst of war, but pure and lovely, an emblem of war's exorcism and the leader of an imaginary chorus, sacred to Dionysus, that parallels the chorus on stage at the end of Aristophanes' comedy. As such, her beauty is beneficial, like that of the personified character Reconciliation, and she complements the mention in the previous song of Hesychia and Aphrodite.

The epithets for Helen are arguably *kaina onomata*, in Antiphanes' sense of new names; and the poetry of Aristophanes converts even her ambiguous charms to beneficence. In effect, the comic poet constructs a new myth about the Trojan War: the conflict is poetically refashioned and limned in the glow of heroic, pan-Hellenic unity. As Helen is exculpated, so the cult of Athena of the Brazen House, ostensibly a cause or claim in the Peloponnesian War, is similarly transformed. Thucydides reports that the Athenians claimed that, through the death of Pausanias, the Spartans had brought a curse upon themselves, since Pausanias had sought refuge in Athena's sanctuary (Thucydides, 1.128 ff.). Athens demanded reparation, in response to the Spartan demand for restitution after the curse of Kylon. These acrimonious preliminaries to the war are skillfully transformed into a graceful, unifying salutation in the final lyric of Aristophanes' play, however; Athena of the Brazen House telescopes the patron of the Acropolis (prominently identified with the entire action of *Lysistrata*) with Spartan cult, and the curses associated with the prewar embassies are implicitly expiated with the invocation of the goddess.

The finale of *Lysistrata*, then, shows comic myth-making as an exorcism of strife. Aristophanes recalls the Trojan War, the Persian War, and several prominent episodes of the Peloponnesian War—if only to recast them poetically. Helen is reenvisioned as pure; Thermopylae and Artemisium serve as examples of pan-Hellenic harmony; Athena *Chalkioikos* transmutes curses into blessings. The whole scene is an impressive reenactment of the past for the benefit of the future: compare the relationship of the golden age and utopia in the parabasis of *Birds*, discussed previously. Through the use of metaphor, rhetoric, and selective historical reference, Aristophanes creates a poetic myth of peace for an audience still at war in real life—a novelty, in the most profound sense of Antiphanes' term.

The originality of Aristophanes is thus to be measured, ultimately, through the mythopoeic qualities of his work. We do not possess enough comparative evidence to assess these specifically with reference to his contemporaries. Certain features of his plays that may appear to us as charmingly idiosyncratic (such as the animal choruses) were in fact employed by other poets of Old Comedy. His popularity in antiquity more probably derived from the energetic combinations of fantasy and satire that almost all the extant plays reveal. Because of the difficulty

of his language and the topical references of his plays, he was not often directly imitated in antiquity or afterward. But the continuities of theme between Old Comedy and New are undeniable (see "Menander" in this series); and it is probable that Aristophanes influenced the fourth-century comedians both in his own right and through his significant impact on Euripides, the tragedian whom he took such pleasure in mocking and who was revered by Menander, Diphilos, and Philemon. The similarities of Euripidean and Aristophanic style are implicit in the celebrated phrase of Kratinos (frag. 307), which refers to *euripidaristophanizein* ("to write like a 'Euripidaristophanizer'") in a context that seems to highlight the enigmatic, novel qualities of the plays of both dramatists. But we have more than this fragment as evidence. Both dramatists created novel works; both indulged in metrical innovations; and the practice of including a parabasis is attested in tragedy only for Euripides (see Pollux, 4.111, where the grammarian mentions the lost *Danae* and "many [other] dramas" as exceptions to the norm whereby parabases were restricted to comedy). In addition, one may compare *Birds* 209–219 with *Helen* 1107–1113, and *Thesmophoriazusae* 253–265 with *Bacchae* 830–836 and 925–944.

In more recent times, the comedies of Ben Jonson (1572–1637) have been compared in spirit to those of Aristophanes; but satire outweighs fantasy in *The Alchemist* and *Bartholomew Fair*. Racine adapted *Wasps* in his only comedy, *Les Plaideurs* (1668). The closest contemporary analogues to the spirit of Aristophanic comedy are in American films: Charles Chaplin's *City Lights*, which presents the triumph of the little man, and Stanley Kubrick's *Dr. Strangelove*, which combines mordant satire with surrealistic motifs. The tradition of the American political cartoon possesses Aristophanic elements; but few cartoonists would dare to portray their targets in a truly Aristophanic fashion. In tone, if not in themes, Aristophanic comedy is unique. With *Ecclesiazusae* and *Plutus*, the playwright himself initiated the shift that would lead to the more typical wellsprings of the modern comic tradition.

Selected Bibliography

TEXTS

Aristophane, edited by V. Coulon. 5 vols. Paris, 1923–1930. Budé edition. The standard text.

Aristophanes, edited by J. Van Leeuwen. 11 vols. Leiden, 1893–1906. With commentary in Latin.

Aristophanis Comoediae, edited by F. W. Hall and W. M. Geldart. 2 vols. 2nd ed. Oxford, 1906–1907. Reprinted Oxford, 1970.

The Comedies of Aristophanes, edited by B. B. Rogers. 11 vols. London, 1902–1916. With commentary.

TRANSLATIONS

Aristophanes: The Acharnians, The Clouds, Lysistrata. Translated by A. H. Sommerstein. London, 1973.

Aristophanes. Collected Works. Translated by B. B. Rogers. 3 vols. Cambridge, Mass., and London, 1960–1963. Loeb Classical Library.

Aristophanes, Four Comedies. Translated by W. Arrowsmith, D. Parker, and R. Lattimore. Ann Arbor, Mich., 1969.

Aristophanes; Four Comedies. Translated by D. Fitts. New York, 1962.

Aristophanes: The Knights, Peace, The Birds, The Assemblywomen, Wealth. Translated by D. Barrett and A. H. Sommerstein. Harmondsworth, 1978.

Aristophanes: Plays. Translated by P. Dickinson. 2 vols. New York and London, 1970.

Aristophanes, Three Comedies. Translated by W. Arrowsmith and D. Parker. Ann Arbor, Mich., 1969.

Aristophanes: The Wasps, The Poet and the Women, The Frogs. Translated by D. Barrett. London, 1964.

COMMENTARIES

Dover, K. J. *Clouds.* Oxford, 1968.
MacDowell, D. *Wasps.* Oxford, 1971.
Platnauer, M. *Peace.* Oxford, 1964.
Ussher, R. G. *Ecclesiazusae.* Oxford, 1973.

CRITICAL STUDIES

Arrowsmith, W. "Aristophanes' *Birds:* The Fantasy Politics of Eros." *Arion* n.s. 1,1:119–167 (1973).

Cornford, F. M. *The Origin of Attic Comedy.* 2nd ed. Cambridge, 1934.

Dearden, C. W. *The Stage of Aristophanes.* London, 1976.

Dover, K. J. *Aristophanic Comedy.* Berkeley, 1972.

Ehrenberg, V. *The People of Aristophanes,* 2nd ed. Cambridge, Mass., 1951.

Forrest, W. G. "Aristophanes' Acharnians." *Phoenix* 17:1–12 (1963).

Fraenkel, E. *Beobachtungen zu Aristophanes.* Rome, 1962.

Gelzer, T. *Aristophanes der Komiker.* Stuttgart, 1971.

Gomme, A. W. "Aristophanes and Politics." *Classical Review* 52:97–109 (1938).

Henderson, J. *The Maculate Muse.* New Haven, 1975.

———, ed. *Aristophanes: Essays in Interpretation.* Yale Classical Studies 26. New Haven, 1980.

Hofmann, Heinz. *Mythos und Komödie.* Hildesheim, 1976.

McLeish, K. *The Theatre of Aristophanes.* London, 1980.

Moulton, C. *Aristophanic Poetry.* Göttingen, 1981.

Murphy, C. T. "Aristophanes and the Art of Rhetoric." *Harvard Studies in Classical Philology* 49:69–113 (1938).

Murray, Gilbert. *Aristophanes.* Oxford, 1933. Reissued New York, 1964.

Newiger, H. J. *Metapher und Allegorie.* Munich, 1957.

———, ed. *Aristophanes und die Alte Komödie.* Wege der Forschung 265. Darmstadt, 1975.

Prato, C. *I canti di Aristofane.* Rome, 1962.

Rabkin, E. *The Fantastic in Literature.* Princeton, 1976.

Rau, P. *Paratragodia.* Munich, 1967.

Sommerstein, A. H. "Aristophanes and the Events of 411." *Journal of Hellenic Studies* 97:112–126 (1977).

Taillardat, J. *Les Images d'Aristophane.* 2nd ed. Paris, 1965.

Whitman, C. H. *Aristophanes and the Comic Hero.* Cambridge, Mass., 1964.

CARROLL MOULTON

ISOCRATES

(*ca.* 436–338 B.C.)

WHEN ISOCRATES WAS born, Athens was at the height of its imperial power and prosperity. By the time of his death ninety-eight years later, the battle of Chaeronea had been fought, the days of Athenian greatness were over, and the future of Greece depended on the Macedonians. For fifty years Isocrates published his views on what should be done, and for us his main importance is as an index of Athens' and Greece's slide to disaster. As long as we are interested in ancient Greece he will surely be attentively read. For antiquity, however, his importance was quite different. Inevitably, in a world so dependent on the spoken word, the art of public speaking was supremely valued, and it was for his place in the development of that art, both as writer of speeches and as teacher of rhetoric, that he was studied and esteemed. References to him are frequent in the rhetorical treatises of Cicero and Quintilian, in which Demosthenes was of course the unchallenged master but Isocrates was praised for the mellowness and gracefulness of his style. In Isocrates' ideas, however, later writers manifested no interest whatever. Plato, with whom Isocrates seems to have fought a running battle about how best the young were to be educated, profoundly affected the cultural inheritance of Cicero, but there is not a word in the whole of Cicero's writings to suggest that Isocrates had more to him than "empty elegance of speech" (*De oratore* 3.141). Only in modern times has he been taken seriously as a political thinker. Whether rightly, or in what sense, needs to be discussed.

LIFE

Our best source of information is, of course, Isocrates' own orations and letters, principally the fifteenth oration, *On the Exchange,* written when he was eighty-two (para. 9), in which he reviewed his whole career. The various lives deriving from the Roman period help, if used with caution. The great orators of the fourth century were of considerable interest to Hellenistic scholars, and by the first century B.C. there was a consistent enough tradition, which Dionysius of Halicarnassus epitomized at the start of his essay on Isocrates and which Cicero could draw on for his rhetorical treatises. The *Life* in Plutarch's *Moralia* (836e–839d), which most scholars agree was not actually written by Plutarch, retails a good deal: one wishes one could fully trust it. There is also an *Anonymous Life* of a later date that confirms and supplements this tradition, but in general one has to remain somewhat skeptical about this sort of ancient literature.

The main outline is clear enough. He was born in 436/435 B.C., son of a man rich enough to be appointed *choregus,* that is, responsible for providing the choruses for plays, a costly business that greatly depended on the generosity of the individual concerned. The man for whom Lysias wrote his twenty-first oration claimed to have spent as much as 2,000 and 3,000 drachmas on separate occasions. These were large sums. Isocrates' father, Theodorus, must have been, in Athenian terms, very rich, and it is no surprise that he was able to provide for his son an expensive education with Prodicus of Ceos, Tisias of Syracuse, and the most expensive of all, Gorgias of Leontini (15.155 ff.), whose fee was fabled to have been 100,000 drachmas a pupil (Suidas, "Gorgias," in *Lexicon*). The first two presumably taught in Athens, but for the latter Isocrates probably had to go to Thessaly (Cicero, *Orator* 176), where Isocrates himself placed Gorgias' school (15.155). All this argues Theodorus' wealth. There is another small corroborative detail: Not only was Isocrates an outstanding figure among the young Athenians receiving such expensive education (15.161), but also, if we may trust the story (*Moralia* 839c), as a boy he rode in a horserace, and a bronze figure of him on a horse was set up on the Acropolis. Only the rich could keep a horse or commission a statue.

Then, in the closing years of the Peloponnesian War, came disaster. Theodorus had derived his wealth from the use of slaves in the business of flute-making, just the sort of skilled craftsmen who deserted in large numbers during the Spartan occupation of Decelea (Thucydides, 7.27), and the family was impoverished (15.161). Forced to earn his own living, Isocrates turned his hand to the writing of speeches for others, a profitable if slightly contemptible business (see Plato, *Phaedrus* 257c) in a notoriously litigious city. Where Lysias, a few years his senior, had found fame, Isocrates could hope to succeed. It particularly suited his talents. As he tells us again and again, he lacked both the voice and the temperament for speaking in public and was therefore excluded from public life; speeches had to be learned and delivered in dramatic style. In the courts, however, only the parties to a suit or those who could claim a personal interest were allowed to speak. So there was ample and lucrative work for the speechwriter if he could artfully adapt himself to the needs of the artless. Some of these forensic speeches survive, and there is no need to question their authenticity. Aristotle asserted that booksellers had whole bundles of Isocrates' law court speeches for sale (Dionysius of Halicarnassus, *Isocrates* 18). Doubtless a great many of these were not authentic, but Dionysius accepted the statement of a pupil of Isocrates' that his master did write a number of forensic speeches. In the 350's, his adoptive son, Aphareus, seeking to save his father from the burden of paying for a year's upkeep of a trireme by arguing that he was not as rich as commonly believed, declared that Isocrates did not write for the law courts. He was correct about the 350's and probably about the three preceding decades, but the statement should not be taken as proof that Isocrates had never done so. After the collapse of the family fortunes, speechwriting was the inevitable opening.

Presumably he was successful, for he was shortly able to turn his rhetorical training to the more respectable profession of teaching others to speak. Whether, as some asserted (*Moralia* 837b), he opened a school in Chios or not, by the later 390's he had probably begun to teach in Athens. One of his most illustrious pupils was Timotheus (*Moralia* 837c), the son of Conon, with both of whom Isocrates was on familiar terms (epistle 8.8 ff.). Conon died in 392–391, by which time his son was probably active in public life, his education completed. Presumably the father had sent him to his friend in the mid-390's. The famous school of what Isocrates chose to call *philosophy* had begun and was to continue, as far as we know, for many decades.

Isocrates was a gifted teacher. He became celebrated throughout the Greek world, though not without the aid of some contrived publicity (15.87; 9.74). Athens was "the education of Greece" (15.295), and Isocrates its most illustrious teacher. His services were sought by a succession of gifted and influential pupils. In his oration *On the Exchange*, he had to face the claim that his wealth was derived from the instruction not only of private citizens but of "orators, generals, kings and tyrants," coming from "Sicily and Pontus and the other places" (15.30, 224). The names he chose to give were those of unexceptionable Athenians (para. 93). Other, less palatable names were available to his critics. Epistle 7 shows that they included the shameful Clearchus, tyrant of Heraclea in the Pontus, and his son Timotheus, of whom better things had been hoped. Other "kings and tyrants" can only be conjectured. The Cyprian Orations might suggest that Nicocles, ruler of Salamis in Cyprus, had been a pupil, although that is never stated; certainly Isocrates had visited the island before 374 B.C. (*Moralia* 838 – 839). His two most celebrated "overseas" pupils became, with his encouragement, the two great historians of the third quarter of the fourth century, Ephorus of Cyme and Theopompus of Chios, of whom the story is repeated again and again that Isocrates remarked, "I have two pupils, of whom one needs the whip, the other the bit." It is a remark by no means surprising to those familiar with the fragments of their histories. For the rest, the list of his pupils is indeed long if we believe all we read in the ancient lives and the *Lexicon* of Suidas. One name of special interest is that of the orator, Python of Byzantium, later found in the employ of Philip of Macedon (*Anonymous Life* 1.105; see also Demosthenes, 7.35, etc.). His Athenian pupils possibly included Lycurgus and Hyperides, even Isaeus (*Moralia* 837d, 841c, 848d; Dion. Hal., *Isaeus* 1). All in all, an illustrious list, reflecting the luster of the master.

Isocrates became rich. He claimed not to have taken money from Athenian pupils (15.164). He did not need to. His regular fee was 1,000 drachmas for a course (*Moralia* 838e; Demosthenes, 35.40 and 42), and in addition very large sums were allegedly paid him by Nicocles: 30 talents for the *Evagoras*, 20 for *To Nicocles* (*Moralia* 838a; hypothesis to oration 2). So he would seem to have been fabulously rich. But was he? The question is important. In the 350's he was challenged in a court of law by

Megaclides, either to "exchange" property or to undertake the support of a trireme, an expense already imposed on Megaclides. Did the great upholder of upright conduct, so frequently groaning about the burdens of the rich (see 8.128), actually seek to dodge his duty by concealing his wealth, as he claimed many others did (15.159–160)? Were all his pious pleas for a crusade against Persia a cover for shabby self-interest?

He was rich enough to be liable for the "liturgies" that Athens laid on her more prosperous citizens (15.145; 12.12), but not as rich as Megaclides would have the court believe. In 357 B.C. the system of financing the navy was changed, and by the law of Periander the functions of serving in person and of footing the bill were separated. Isocrates, who had long been past the age for service, was now in line for payment. But the city was so impoverished that it set up boards of as many as sixteen persons, the *symmories*, to provide the money needed for a single trireme; thus it would seem that the duty of trierarchy was no longer imposed on individuals. So Megaclides must have been challenging Isocrates to prove that he was less rich than a member of a *symmory*, for Isocrates lost the case and by the date of oration 15 had already three trierarchies to boast of (see para. 145). He may have concealed his wealth, but not to the extent that he could escape even membership of a *symmory*. It is likely that Megaclides exaggerated and that his statements— for example, those about the gifts of Nicocles (15.40)—were unsupported by evidence, although accepted by posterity; the speech in defense of Isocrates survived (Dion. Hal., *Dinarchus* 13), and the accuser's may have too. The truth was probably much more modest. Isocrates spoke in the oration *On the Exchange* of the wealth of Gorgias (15.155 ff.), with whom he claimed comparison. Gorgias, the most expensive teacher of rhetoric, left, according to Isocrates, a mere 1,000 "staters"; of what city and whether of gold or silver, he did not say, but no great amount seems to be implied; and he probably meant silver, hence a sum not in excess of a single talent. If this is right, Isocrates was, in Athenian terms, rich, but not prodigiously so. He lost his case but not his credit—not, at any rate, with posterity.

The verdict put him much out of countenance. Though he well knew that in Athens verdicts constantly reflected political sympathies, it rankled that he had not been believed. For three years he nursed his grievance and paid his share. Then in 354–353 B.C. his pupil and friend, Timotheus, was prosecuted for treachery and fined an impossible 100 talents (15.129; also Nepos, *Timotheus* 3), and shortly died in exile. This was too much for Isocrates, who saw the verdict as a savage injustice similar in kind to his own treatment. He published a long apologia for his whole career, oration 15, *On the Exchange*, in the form of an answer to another (wholly fictitious) demand for an "exchange" (paras. 6–8). This allowed him to speak of his theory of education, his wealth, and his pupils, including a long justification of Timotheus (paras. 101–139), and to attack the role of sycophants in public life, portraying them as troublemakers seeking whom they might devour for their own profit. He had been stung and wanted his revenge, even though he would not be able to forget (see epistles 2.22, of 345 B.C., and 12.15, of 342 B.C.).

The speech is tell-tale. He chose to imagine himself accused of corrupting the young, the charge leveled against his teacher Socrates more than forty years before, and he saw nothing comic in presenting himself as a similar victim of popular justice. As he rounded off his remarks on Timotheus, he wrote words that he probably felt applied as much to the master as to the pupil. He recounted how he had advised the great general—whose nature was as ill suited to licking boots as it was well suited to handling great affairs—to court the favor of the people's favorites, and how Timotheus had agreed but had been unable to change his nature. Isocrates concluded thus: "He was a true gentleman and worthy of his city and all Greece, but he could not get on with the sort of man who happens to resent his natural supe-

riors" (paras. 131–138). There speaks Isocrates of himself? Modesty was not one of his impediments.

From 353 B.C. to his death, he lived in Athens writing speeches that "counseled the city and the Greeks at large about their interests" (12.2; see also 15.46 and 79) and dispatching epistles to sundry rulers of the Greek world. Earlier he had absented himself from the city. There is the story of a visit to Cyprus (*Moralia* 838f), the alleged school on Chios (*Moralia* 837b), and the claim that with Timotheus he visited many cities (*Moralia* 837c), which one may doubt; but he certainly was abroad with Timotheus at some time when the latter was sending home dispatches denouncing the king of Macedon, for Speusippus was later to claim in his *Letter to Philip* that Isocrates had helped in the drafting (para. 13). From the 350's onward, he remained in Athens, too old for travel and fearful of offending the city by displaying connections that might be disapproved of (epistle 6.1–3), but his prestige was by then such that Greece visited him, or so he claimed (epistle 2.22). He did not, unlike his pupil Theopompus, have the disillusionment of visiting Macedon or ever seeing for himself what sort of man Philip was and what sort of power he was seeking to win over to his Hellenic designs.

In 338 B.C. came the defeat of free Greece at Chaeronea, and shortly afterward Isocrates, in despair, starved himself to death. How shortly is debated. Two views have been held on the strength of differing statements in the Plutarchean *Life*. One is that he did so as soon as he heard news of the battle (837e). The other is that he did so "at the time of the funerals of those who had fallen at Chaeronea" (838b), and if those public burials took place at the same time of year as was usual in the Peloponnesian War (Thucydides, 2.34), there may well have been quite an interval between the battle and the suicide. Which is correct? Again, the question is important. Did Isocrates dread any form of concord that was not achieved solely by common consent? Or had he accepted that the use of force was inevitable but resented the way in which Philip threatened to use his victory? The resolution depends on whether one accepts that epistle 3, professedly addressed to Philip after the battle, was written by Isocrates; if so, it was not the battle but something later that induced despair and suicide. Here, the epistle is presumed authentic. Its conclusion is optimistic:

> I can thank my old age for this, if nothing else, that it has extended my life to the point that what I had in mind and tried to put into words in the *Panegyric* oration and the letter I sent you [see oration 5] in part I now see being realized through your actions, in part I look forward to.

His optimism did not last. Greece was to be clapped into "fetters" (Polybius, 18.11.5), that is, garrisoned. He died in despair.

This much about the life of Isocrates would win wide, if not universal, assent, and, compared with our information about other eminent literary figures, it is a lot. But much is lacking. We hear nothing of military service, the experience or lack of which makes a great difference to men, nor of his part in the oligarchic revolutions of 411 and 404 B.C., nor of the personal experiences that formed his reactions to events and conditioned what he thought and wrote. But some observations may be hazarded.

His father's wealth is significant, for it places him in the class of knights, distrusted by demagogues and the democracy (see Xenophon, *Hellenica* 3.1.4). Isocrates is especially severe on the popular politicians who succeeded Pericles. Unlike Plato, who thought Pericles' influence was harmful, Isocrates speaks of him with approval (15.234 ff., 307; also 16.28), but he is scornful of his successors, "wicked radicals" *(poneroi)*, "full of rash ideas," whom he holds responsible for the oligarchic revolutions, the revolts of Athens' imperial subjects, and the final ruin of the city (15.316–319), a predictable enough view for a knight. It is, however, worth noting that by 418–417 B.C. Isocrates would have been old enough to attend the assembly, and the decisions of the declining years of the Peloponnesian War are likely to have made a great and lasting impression on him. One point is of particular interest. He names with disrespect the radical demagogues Hyperbolus and Cleophon (8.75) but avoids discussion of Alcibiades (save in oration 16, the forensic speech *On the Team of Horses*, written for Alcibiades' son). When he speaks of the folly of the Sicilian expedition, it is not the folly of 415, for which some would have found Alcibiades much to blame, but the folly of 413, when, after the recall of Alcibiades from Sicily and despite the Spartan occupation of Decelea, Athens chose to commit even further forces (8.84; see Thucydides, 7.19 ff.). This is very odd. One may guess that Isocrates was a supporter of Alcibiades (though the words on the excellence of his policies in oration 16.36 ff. may have been somewhat tongue-in-cheek). It would be consistent with this that he seems to have been a sympathizer, if not a pupil, of Theramenes. Both the Plutarchean and the anonymous lives tell a story of Isocrates standing up for Theramenes and seeking to defend him when he was being led off to execution in 404. Diodorus' account (14.5) confirms the event, if the name Socrates in paragraph 2 is amended to Isocrates, an almost inevitable emendation; since the revaluation of Diodorus following the discovery of the Oxyrhynchus historian, his account is no longer to be discarded, but the unamended text cannot be correct, for if Socrates had tried to save Theramenes we would have heard of it elsewhere. So we may tentatively place Isocrates among the moderates, a posture similar to, if not identical with, that of the young Xenophon, a rich young equestrian, no admirer of democracy and its follies, but detesting still more Critias and the "madness" of the Thirty Tyrants, who ruled Athens after the Peloponnesian War (see 7.62 ff.; 8.108). Like Xenophon, who was five years or so his junior, and Alcibiades, about fourteen years his senior, Isocrates had been in the Socratic circle (Plato, *Phaedrus* 279a), or at any rate on the fringes, though too early, or perhaps not aristocratic enough, to make an appearance in Xenophon's *Memorabilia*.

In the fourth century Isocrates' views and his affections are reflected in his writings, and his hopes and fears can be imagined where his words fail us. On the one hand, he saw that Athens was in a sad decline under its imperialist politicians, approaching bankruptcy, both financial and spiritual, in the Social War (357–355 B.C.). His great oration *On the Peace* (8), directed against General Chares and his ilk (Aristotle, *Rhetoric* 1418a32), was a plea for a change of heart, just as his *Areopagiticus* (7), shortly after, pleaded for a change of political life. On the other hand, he saw the domination of Greek politics for decades by the king of Persia. The *Panegyric* (4) was the most notable expression of Isocrates' reaction against Persia. But one wonders about its sincerity. After all, he professed friendship for Conon (epistle 8), who had been a Persian admiral (and Isocrates, as far as we know, never redeemed the promise to explain that he made in 9.57). The great evils of Persian rule over Greeks paled beside the evils inflicted by the Greeks on each other, and Isocrates' indignation seems to have lessened in the course of time. Perhaps his denunciation of Persia was rather a matter of fashion than of deeply felt injustice. But he set his hopes on the anti-Persian crusade as the cure for Greece's ills, and he looked to Macedon to save Greece from itself. In so doing, he assisted in its ruin, and his suicide was fit comment on fifty years' devotion to folly.

THE WRITINGS OF ISOCRATES

We have twenty-one speeches and nine letters. In the Roman period sixty orations were attributed to him, of which only twenty-five were genuine according to Dionysius of Halicarnassus, and only twenty-eight according to Dionysius' contemporary, Caecilius (*Moralia* 838d). Whether they included all those we have, we cannot tell. Such pruning of titles was common. Of the 425 speeches ascribed to Lysias, the same two critics pronounced genuine only 233, and the process continues; K. J. Dover has concluded that there is only one speech that "we can safely affirm to have been written in its entirety by Lysias and by him alone." How confident can we be that the works we have were actually written by Isocrates? In fact, although we may be mistaken, modern criticism has not succeeded in discrediting any of the speeches we have. The letters are more dubitable. The genre affords ample opportunity for literary exercise and forgery. Unlike the speeches, they were not cited or discussed in rhetorical treatises, nor is it easy to envisage how and why some of them would have been published. Yet Isocrates was not the man to deprive others of the enjoyment of reading anything he had written, and he may have published those we have in order to forestall any suggestion of shady communications. No single letter is discredited by discernible errors of fact. The onus of proof is on those who would deny authenticity. So far, such proof is lacking.

Aristotle (*Rhetoric* 1358b7) made a threefold classification of speeches: the kind delivered in the courts (forensic); the kind, whether delivered in public or in private, aimed at exhorting or dissuading (symbouleutic); and the kind aimed primarily at displaying the orator's powers (epideictic). This classification is not particularly helpful for Isocrates.

Although the forensic speeches (16–21) do stand apart, the others are less distinguishable in kind. For instance, the *Encomium of Helen* (10) might seem to be a pure example of the epideictic on a theme handled by his master Gorgias and treated by Isocrates with what he claimed was refreshing novelty (para. 15). In fact the introduction is a discussion of what is valuable in rhetorical training—the instruction of pupils in the practical affairs of the city (para. 5). The praise of Helen is merely offered as proof that he can do that sort of thing if required (para. 15). So in a sense the speech is rather a disparagement of the purely epideictic.

On the other hand, two of the so-called Cyprian orations might seem to be purely hortatory: *To Nicocles* (2), advising the ruler how to exercise his power, and *Nicocles* (3), advising the Salaminians how to submit to that power (para. 11). But in all probability such speeches were aimed in large measure at advertising Isocrates' school. For not only did he have to publish to get an audience at all, since he could not deliver the speeches himself, but he was also well aware of the value of advertisement (15.87; 9.74). In the very early days of his school he published a prospectus, explaining his methods and critizing others' (15.193), the oration *Against the Sophists* (13).

Some of his apparently symbouleutic speeches are really samples of his rhetorical skill on display. The *Archidamus* (6), for example, professedly written for the son of the Spartan king to deliver in the Spartan assembly, was most ill suited to Spartan political conditions; such fullness would have been much out of place (Thucydides keeps Spartan speeches comparatively short, even in the case of Brasidas, whom he pronounced "not ungifted as a public speaker" [4.84]), nor was policy really made in the Spartan assembly. Rather, the speech was a demonstration that Isocrates, and by implication a man trained by him, could turn his hand to any theme. The supreme example of his epideictic oratory, the *Panegyric* (4), is a serious statement of the right policy for the Greeks, in large measure symbouleutic. Aristotle's classification is of little use here.

A more satisfactory division of the nonforensic speeches may be made. The main speeches for the understanding of Isocrates' political ideas are the *Panegyric* (4: 380 B.C.), the *On the Peace* (8: 355 B.C.), the *Areopagiticus* (7: ca. 355 B.C.), the *Philippus*, sometimes called *The Letter to Philip* (5: 346 B.C.), and the *Panathenaic Oration* (12: 339 B.C.). Then there are the advertisements: *Against the Sophists* (13: later 390's) is straightforward; the *Encomium of Helen* (10) and the *Busiris* (11), both of early date, are disguised advertisements; *On the Exchange* (15: 353 B.C.), a defense of his system as well as of himself, is an advertisement of a sort. *To Nicocles* (2) and *Nicocles* (3), both of the later 370's, are in large measure samples to show that what anyone else could do he could do better. The *Evagoras* (9), of similar date, is purely epideictic, the encomium of a dead ruler. The *Demonicus* (1) defies classification and dating, a mere rag-bag of precepts. And what of the *Plataicus* (14: after 373 B.C.) and the *Archidamus* (6: after 366 B.C.)? It is not clear whether they express his views or merely advertise his talents.

We should not take Isocrates seriously in a sense he did not intend. He was aware that he could be, and perhaps had been, accused of saying anything that suited the moment (see 15.243: "too ready to shift his ground"), and the ancients as well as the moderns were apt to demand a consistent attitude. The speech *To Nicocles* had been interpreted as commendation of monarchy, and he felt the need to rebut the charge (15.70). Such demands were and are unfair. The puzzling pieces were no more than his speechwriting, once practiced for the courts, continued in other genres. To probe the *Archidamus* or the *Plataicus* in search of a consistent political stance is energy misapplied, just as treating the Cyprian orations as a sign that Isocrates hankered after monarchy is to miss their point. In all these he was the speechwriter, though one can understand why the description could be used in a mildly opprobrious way.

Isocrates did not work under pressure. Unlike politicians writing speeches for an imminent debate, he could take as long as he liked. The dramatic dates[1] of his speeches can be fixed, generally speaking, accurately enough. The dates of publication are more dubitable. Sometimes the situation demanded prompt completion, such as the *Letter to Philip* of 346. It was apparently written between the making of peace between Philip and Athens and Philip's swearing three months later to observe it. The letter must have been written and dispatched in that period since it was intended to influence Philip. But generally Isocrates was free to take as long as he liked. His *Panegyric*

---

[1]The date at which a writer affects to be writing, even though he may have been writing long afterward in fact.

is reputed to have been ten years in preparation (Dion. Hal., *De compositione*, p. 208, Radermacher, ed.). Longinus wittily remarked that "Alexander took less time to conquer the whole of Asia than Isocrates took to write the *Panegyric* proposing the war against the Persians" (*On the Sublime* 4.2). The three years or so he took over the *Panathenaic Oration* (12) were, he alleged (paras. 267–270), due to illness. But in general he took his time and polished and polished. As Cicero remarked (*Orator* 38), he wrote "not for a contest in the courts but to please the ear"; in Thucydides' phrase (1.22), "a possession forever."

Stylistically speaking, the great influence of his life was his teacher, Gorgias. Isocrates had been too young to be present in the assembly in 427 and share in the Athenians' amazement on first hearing the gorgeous contrivances of Gorgias' rhetoric.

> He was the first man to work out a theory of rhetoric . . . and he astounded the Athenians, naturally clever and fond of speeches as they were, with his exotic style of speech. . . . He was the first to employ somewhat extravagant and oddly contrived forms of expression, with antitheses, sentences of balancing structure and length, assonances, and so on. At that time they were taken up because of the novelty of contrivance, though nowadays they seem overdone and present a downright ridiculous appearance when used so often as to be a glut.
>
> (Diodorus, 12.53)

To this influence the young Isocrates was exposed, and every page he wrote, after he had ceased his forensic speechwriting, bears the mark of it. But his use is moderate. One is never tempted even to smile. The antitheses are there, sentence balances sentence and clause balances clause, sounds find their echo, and the prose, though not poetic, is rhythmical (see Cicero, *Brutus* 32). The clash of vowel and vowel (*hiatus*) is studiedly avoided; yet the style is never stilted. It is no wonder that, when he died, the statue of a siren was placed on his tomb, "a mark of the harmoniousness of the man's words" (*Anonymous Life* 181), the quality that Cicero (*De oratore* 3.28) termed "suavitas," Quintilian (*Institutio oratoria* 10.1.108), "iucunditas." Isocrates reads uncommonly easily and well, albeit a trifle soporific.

ISOCRATES' SYSTEM OF EDUCATION

"A great orator, a consummate teacher" was Cicero's judgment (*Brutus* 32). Pupils came, as already remarked, from all over the Greek world, not just men of great intellectual gifts or political influence but also "men of good sense and good taste in their conduct of life, but who were quite without natural aptitude for other employment or pursuits" (epistle 4.2). What did they come for? What did they get?

The opening pages of Plato's *Protagoras* (especially 314–320) provide a lively picture of higher education in classical Athens. If one wanted to learn about medicine, one attached oneself to a Hippocrates; if astronomy, to a Hippias; for a general education without "mathematics, astronomy, geometry, music," one went to a Protagoras. When Socrates and his young companion arrived at Callias' house, where Protagoras was staying, he found separate groups around their chosen specialists receiving instruction. Protagoras' group was partly Athenians, partly foreigners who were following the master from city to city; the scene is described by Plato in his delicate style of wit. Elsewhere (*Hippias Minor* 368) the wide range of instruction on offer from Hippias is described. Prodicus, one of Isocrates' teachers, would for fifty drachmas give a course on "names" (*Cratylus* 384b). One could have a tutorial or a seminar (*Protagoras* 316d). It was all very personal, far removed from the lecture hall of the modern university. Of course, there were also lectures. In the *Hippias Minor* (368b) we hear of Hippias lecturing "in the Agora beside the bankers." According to Aristotle (*Rhetoric* 1415b16), when Prodicus noticed his audience nodding drowsily, he would wake them up with a dash of his celebrated fifty-drachma course—a lecturer's, not a tutor's, trick.

Isocrates was no lecturer. The number of his pupils at any one time was not large. In the *Panathenaic Oration,* he speaks of reading the first draft of the speech to "three or four young men who regularly attended my school" (para. 200). He was said to have had "about a hundred" pupils (*Moralia* 837c), and they stayed for three or four years (15.87); since he taught for over fifty years, there cannot have been on average more than six at any one time, though he may have had more in early days than later. It was an exclusive school indeed. But he did not go in for lectures to a wider audience. He lacked the voice and the nerve for that. Not for him even the sort of wider discussion that develops in the *Protagoras* (317d). "Two is an audience, three a theaterful," someone remarked (*Moralia* 838e), not necessarily Isocrates himself. His instruction was entirely of small groups, tutorial.

But what did he teach them? Of course there was formal training in the making of speeches, though whether he wrote a handbook on the subject is disputed. According to the *Anonymous Life,* Aristotle mentioned a technical treatise that Isocrates had written on rhetoric, and Aristotle, one would think, must have known what he was talking about. Although later it was not universally agreed that Isocrates had so written (*Moralia* 838f), there are various passages from later writers that are best understood as citations from such a work, and one passage seems quite explicit. (The passages are cited in the Budé *Isocrate, Discours,* vol. 4, pp. 229–233.) So, despite difficulties, it may be affirmed that Isocrates did write such a treatise. In any case, it is certain that his pupils were trained in the making of speeches, and, as Aristotle's *Rhetoric* shows, by the later fourth century B.C. there was many a rule to master.

But on what subjects were they trained to speak? It is easier to say what he did not concern himself with. He would have nothing of

the business of the law courts, which must have been a fairly large field of study. Critics might accuse him of such a concern (15.2); doubtless not all his pupils subsequently abstained from that sort of activity, and one can understand why he was so accused (and why his adoptive son, Aphareus, saw fit to deny flatly, but not quite truthfully, that Isocrates had ever even written for the courts). But Isocrates emphatically denied that his school was in any way engaged in such study (15.40). Nor did he concern himself with "astrology, geometry, and the like," which at best, he held, did no harm but were of no use "either in personal matters or in public affairs"; pupils forget all about them "because they are irrelevant to life, constitute no aid to action, and have nothing to do with what they have to be concerned with" (15.261 ff.); they are really of lasting use only to those who choose to teach them, and nit-picking with astrology and geometry and other "hard" subjects can only prepare pupils for the study of "more serious and more worthwhile matters" (15.265). Nor would he have anything to do with the logic-chopping of dialectic, "the so-called eristic dialogues" (12.26). In the oration *Against the Sophists,* he denounces (para. 7 ff.) all such concern with paradoxes *(enantioseis)* as so much "idle talk and hair-splitting" *(adoleschia kai mikrologia).* Later he conceded that those who "hold sway in eristic discussions" (15.261) did no harm, but the real business of education was not there.

For Isocrates the true concern of higher education was "discussion of general and practical matters," of politics in an elevated sense (15.258 ff.). Again and again he insisted that educated men were the men trained for discussion and action in the sphere of the practical, who by reason "persuade each other and define aims" (15.254), who "carefully weigh their words and make fewer mistakes in their actions" (15.292) and prove "useful to the city" (15.305). What exactly such "policies," such "great affairs" (15.3) are, he does not specify, but it is to be understood that the sort of matters discussed in his own speeches provided the themes for his pupils' speeches (the Isocratean equivalent of the modern student's essay—monarchy, oligarchy, imperialism, unification of Greece, and so on).

In all this, Isocrates was strongly opposing the education offered by Plato and the Academy, in which it was presumed that certain knowledge rendered a man fit to rule. Only those trained in the Platonic sort of philosophy would have knowledge of the Good, which alone equipped men for the just exercise of power. In this system of education, mathematics and dialectic, which Isocrates regarded as useless, were central. Plato thought that one had to think certain things to think well. Isocrates in sharp contrast held that it was how, not what, one thought that mattered in education.

The antipathy was explicit enough for Athenians to have no doubt about whom exactly Isocrates was criticizing in the later part of the oration *On the Exchange*. Plato had already had his say in a famous passage of the *Phaedrus*, a dialogue much concerned with the nature of speeches and discourse. It was written long after Isocrates had begun his school and proclaimed his contempt for the utopian ideas that Plato's *Republic* expressed, but the dramatic date of the dialogue's action is in the period when Isocrates was a young man. Phaedrus asks Socrates about "the handsome Isocrates." He replies:

> Isocrates is still young, Phaedrus, but I am willing to say what I predict of him. . . . I wouldn't be surprised if, when he gets older, he's very much better at the sort of speeches he's now attempting [forensic speeches] than any boy who's ever put his hand to speeches and, if that doesn't satisfy him, some divine impulse will take him on to higher things. There's a natural love of wisdom of a sort in the fellow's mind.
>
> (279a)

These were biting words (though some have refused to see them as such) that must have hurt.

Time had shown Plato that Isocrates had nothing of real philosophical importance to say. Isocrates constantly referred to his educational system as providing training in philosophy. It was nothing of the sort to Plato, nor to his greatest pupil, Aristotle, who parodied a line of Euripides: "'Twere base to keep silence and let Isocrates have his say" (Quintilian, *Institutio oratoria* 3.1.14). To the Academy, Isocrates was a windbag who condemned true philosophy, for which he had no aptitude.

Isocrates' pupils thought otherwise. They kept coming, in greater numbers than to all the other teachers of philosophy, according to Isocrates (15.40), who also declared that when they left at the end of their three or four years, there were tears and passionate longings to remain (15.88). His most gifted pupils, in the judgment of Dionysius of Halicarnassus (*Isaeus* 19), sought to imitate the master's style. Consummate teacher indeed.

THE POLITICAL VIEWS OF ISOCRATES

What were the "proposals" of Isocrates that were "great, noble, humane, and concerned with affairs of general importance" (15.276)?

A starting point is provided by the *Areopagiticus* (7), in which he set out his views about the polity of Athens and how it formulated its policies. The dating of the speech is important. The Social War (357–355 B.C.), in which three major states of the Athenian Confederacy—Rhodes, Chios, and Byzantium—succeeded in breaking free, was over (para. 10); Athens had been near to "extreme disaster" (para. 17), a phrase that could only mean for Athenians the horrors of the close of the Peloponnesian War, when with Persian aid Sparta had cut off the Athenian grain route past Byzantium; the hostility of the king of Persia had been reawakened (paras. 8, 10) and hostile letters had been received from him (para. 81), a plain reference to the Persian ultimatum that ended the Social

War (Diodorus, 16.22). The long struggle to recover Amphipolis in Thrace continued, which was *the* war (para. 82), the war by sea as opposed to peace on land (para. 1); and despite the complacency of some (citizens,) it was time for radical discussion of the condition of the city. Men were denouncing the state of affairs and declaring that "policy had never been worse conducted while the city was a democracy" (para. 15). Clearly then, the speech belongs to the troubled times after the Social War, let us say to 354 B.C., when the city's income, which had regularly been, and needed to be if the routine administration was to continue, 460 talents, was down to 130 (Demosthenes, 10.37), and Xenophon, descrying from Corinth the city's plight, was moved to write his treatise *On Revenues*, with its mixture of bizarre and sensible proposals for the restoration of Athens' prosperity, some of which were shortly to be incorporated in the financial reforms of Eubulus. Things were indeed serious, and Isocrates was emboldened to speak out.

Isocrates' solution for Athens' troubles was to propose the restoration of the constitution that had obtained before the great reform of Ephialtes in 462 B.C., whereby the ancient council of the Areopagus, composed of all those who had held the chief magistracies in the city, was deprived of most of its functions.

> When the Areopagus was in charge, the city did not have its fill of law-suits and accusations, of war-taxes, poverty, and wars, but the Athenians lived in contentment with each other and at peace with all men. They made themselves trusted by the Greeks and feared by the barbarian [that is, the Persians]. For the former they had procured salvation; from the latter they had exacted justice of such a kind that he was content if there was an end to his sufferings. . . . The Areopagus freed the poor from hardship by work and by the charity of the rich, the younger men from excesses by moral conduct and by its supervision, the politicians from immoderate designs by its punishments and the impossibility of escaping justice, and the senior citizens from demoralization by the honors ac-

corded by the state and by the respect paid them by their juniors. How could there be a more worthwhile constitution than that, which managed all things so well?
>
> (*Areopagiticus*, paras. 51–55)

The reform of Ephialtes was indeed a watershed in Athenian history. It marked the end of the aristocratic state and the emergence of the democratic. Its essence was the abolition of the "guardianship of the *nomoi*" exercised by the aristocratic Areopagus. In aristocratic states what a man did was regulated by *nomos*, not just "law" but also "custom." For Isocrates to demand the restoration of the guardianship of the *nomoi* was to demand the restoration of a world in which men's actions were subject to the scrutiny and censorship of their betters.

> Our ancestors . . . set the Areopagus to look after orderly behavior and it was open only to the sort of man who was well-born and had given in his life ample proof of virtue and moderation . . . It was not that they had many in charge of them in boyhood and then when they became men they could do what they liked, but in this prime of life they got greater supervision than when they were boys. . . . For it is not by legal enactments but by morality that cities are well run.
>
> (*Areopagiticus*, paras. 37, 41)

This world of moral leadership and censorship, which Isocrates lauded, was contrasted with democratic Athens by Pericles in the Funeral Oration in Thucydides. He was particularly concerned with the contrast between the effortless superiority of the open society of Athens and the effortful inferiority of the closed society of Sparta, as he proudly proclaimed the democratic principles of free participation in public life and tolerance in private (Thucydides, 2.37.2). Sparta was the purest example of aristocracy—its customs and laws were indistinguishably ascribed to the lawgiver Lycurgus—but in modified form what Pericles said about aristocratic Sparta could be said of the world of the Areopagus, which, according to the Aristotelian *Constitution of the Athenians* (3.6), "like a master punished and fined all those who did not behave themselves," and according to the learned and (by us) highly esteemed third-century historian of Athens, Philochorus, "in olden times would summon before it and punish all those who were wastrels and lived beyond their means." The Areopagus and the radical democracy were "clean different." When the democracy was overthrown in 404 B.C., the laws of Ephialtes were rescinded (*Constitution of the Athenians* 35.2), and when in 321 B.C. the Macedonians suppressed the democracy, the supervision of morals seems to have begun again.

One might be tempted to think therefore that Isocrates was fundamentally opposed to democracy and favored aristocratic oligarchy. Indeed, having expounded his cure, he felt he had immediately to explain that he was not an opponent of the democracy nor sought "to throw the city into oligarchy" (para. 56 ff.). We should believe him. A careful reading of the speech shows that what he wanted was not oligarchy but a return to the world of the men who fought at Marathon, the world of Cleisthenes (para. 16), the man whom Herodotus (6.131) had pronounced "the founder of the democracy," under whose constitution the Areopagus had continued its guardianship of *nomoi* and the Athenians had founded the Delian League and fought against Persia.

> We could not find a constitution more democratic than that or more advantageous to the city. There is most powerful testimony; the men who had the benefit of it, after doing many noble deeds and gaining a goodly repute with all mankind [having broken the Persian invasion of 480/479 B.C.], received from the Greeks and with their compliance the role of leader [formed the Delian League].
>
> (*Areopagiticus*, para. 17)

It was to the period of the Delian League that he referred when in a passage already quoted (para. 51) he said that under the Areopagus "they made themselves trusted by the Greeks and feared by the barbarian." His constitutional proposal is no less and no more than the demand for a return to the great days of the two decades following the Persian Wars. There is no dark and sinister yearning for oligarchy, let moderns bay as they will. He simply wanted Athens in the state it was in when with such glorious success it led the Greeks against the Persians and before Athenian imperialism had brought evils on the city and on all Greece.

Here, as in all his speeches, Isocrates was the Panhellenist striving for the union of Greece in a crusade against Persia. The most famous, though not the first, statement of that doctrine is the *Panegyric Oration* (4). Panhellenism had a long history. After the withdrawal of the Persians from Greece in 479 B.C., Athenian policy had wavered between vigorously prosecuting the war of revenge and seeking a compact with Persia and power in Greece. Themistocles and Pericles represented this latter Panathenian policy, Cimon the former Panhellenism. Cimon's view was aptly expressed when the Spartans in the crisis of the Helot Revolt of 465 appealed to Athens for aid; he supported them, calling on the Athenians "not to see Greece lamed or Athens deprived of her yoke fellow" (Plutarch, *Cimon* 16), that is, Greece must be united under a shared hegemony of the war against Persia. Similarly, at Sparta there was a division between men like Lysander, who did not scruple to seek Persian aid to destroy Athens, and men like Callicratidas, whose disgust at trafficking with Persia is enshrined in a famous dictum, later echoed by Teleutias, stepbrother of the most notable Spartan Panhellenist of all, Agesilaus (Xenophon, *Hellenica* 1.6.7 and 5.1.17). Such political Panhellenism evoked its own literature. The most famous theorist of the fifth century was Isocrates' master, Gorgias, who in his Olympic oration "counseling the Greeks to seek concord, sought to turn them against the barbarians and to persuade them to make as prizes of their arms not each others' cities, but the barbarians' land" (Philostratus,

Lives of the Sophists 1.9). This was the same line as that taken by Aristophanes' Lysistrata when she sought to reconcile Sparta and Athens (*Lysistrata* 1130 ff.); no matter whether Aristophanes was himself a Panhellenist, her speech shows that the doctrine was current. No other clear literary traces survive from the fifth century. It may be noted, though, that twice in Herodotus' account of the 490's (5.50, 6.84) an anabasis, a march up-country barely conceivable before the defeat of the Persians, is proposed, probably reflecting fifth-century Panhellenist dreams. It is clear that Isocrates was heir to a well-established doctrine, as he himself indicates at the start of the *Panegyric* (para. 3): "I come to give counsel about the war against the barbarians and about concord amongst ourselves, not unaware that many of the self-professed Sophists set out on this theme." He was confident that he would do it better than his predecessors, but many predecessors there had been.

The essentials of the doctrine are all there: The problem is how to unite Greece; its divisions have led to the shameful state of affairs in which Persia controls Greek politics and deprives the Asiatic Greeks of liberty; so Greece must find unity by attacking Persia, which will be an easy task, so weak have the Persians shown themselves; the time is ripe, and by exploiting the wealth of Asia, Greece can provide for its multitude of impoverished people. This doctrine was the setting for the speech, but Isocrates' main purpose was to argue that for this crusade Athens was as well suited as Sparta to lead, his version of Cimon's plea about shared hegemony. (The date of the speech is 380 B.C. [see para. 126], just two years before the foundation of the Second Athenian Confederacy, formed to confront Sparta.) Some have seen the speech as a plea for such a league. This is unlikely. He took a whole decade to write it, and "a writer who polishes an essay for ten years does not write for the moment."

He never abandoned the doctrine, but there was an important later development. In the *Letter to Philip* (5) of 346 B.C. he sought to persuade Philip to unite the Greeks and lead a campaign against Persia; it would be easy and, if colonies were founded, those "roaming around Greece" could be settled in prosperity. What is different from the *Panegyric* is his attitude to hegemony. There he had thought of it as shared between Athens and Sparta; now he looked to Philip. But this development was not new in 346. A passage in Speusippus' *Letter to Philip* makes clear that Isocrates' appeal to Philip had been in much the same terms as his earlier appeals to Agesilaus of Sparta, Dionysius of Syracuse, and Alexander of Pherae in Thessaly. Those had been in vain, indeed absurd. Now he saw that Philip really was the man for the job, and from 346 his hopes centered on him. Almost with his dying breath Isocrates called on Philip to "compel the barbarians to be Helots to the Greeks" (epistle 2.5).

Two speeches seem to deviate. In the oration *On the Peace* (8) of 355 B.C. he demanded (at first glance astonishingly) a renewal of the King's Peace (para. 16) and seems to have forgotten all about a crusade against Persia; the plan for colonies was still there (para. 24), but in Thrace, not Asia. It is not really astonishing. Even Isocrates could see that with the king threatening to intervene with arms in Greece itself (Diodorus, 16.22) talk of intervention in Asia was absurd. Nor was the demand for renewal of the King's Peace so paradoxical. He probably referred not to the peace of 387–386 against which he had fulminated in the *Panegyric*, but to the peace of 375, which was the King's Peace renewed, but with the important modification that Athens should share with Sparta the defense of the peace. That would have offered him a basis for hope; Greece united under a shared hegemony could move forward, at a more apt time, to the great design. But the speech is a freak in Isocrates' writings, for it was written in uncommonly adverse times.

The other apparently deviant speech is the *Panathenaic Oration*, begun in 342 B.C. and completed in 339, which made no mention of Philip and, far from preaching the crusade, spoke of it as a vanished hope (para. 13). Again, the time was out of joint. He had set his hopes on Philip's persuading, not coercing, the Greeks; but the Greeks, chiefly the Athenians, had shown themselves unwilling to be persuaded. Philip had been rebuffed. The war party at Athens was increasing its hold. Isocrates had only to fear. In these circumstances, he retreated into simple laudation of Athens. His Panhellenist appeals had been disregarded; troublemakers were in power; the speech is a gesture of resignation. But after the disastrous defeat of Chaeronea, it was no longer necessary for Philip to persuade, and Isocrates' hopes rekindled, as the final epistle to Philip shows. He was at his end, as he had been for fifty years, a Panhellenist pure and simple.

THE INFLUENCE OF ISOCRATES

There was nothing original about his views, but originality of a sort has been claimed for Isocrates, namely, that he inspired Philip with the idea of a Panhellenic crusade against the Persian Empire. The thesis is absurd. So little is known of Philip's thoughts and intentions that the assertion could not be proved—even if there were not evidence to the contrary, which there is. In his letter to Philip of 338 B.C. Isocrates declared that, when asked whether Philip owed his plan to him, he could only reply that he did not know for sure but he supposed that Philip had thought of it for himself and his letter of 346 had been merely consonant with desires already formed (epistle 3.3). So Isocrates himself conceded that the credit was not his. Indeed, if Philip's demand for alliance with Athens all through the peace negotiations of 346 is rightly taken to mean that he needed the help of Athens' navy because he planned to attack Persia, the plan may have been formed as early as 348 (Aeschines, 2.15). In any case Philip

was too clear-sighted a statesman to need or even heed an Isocrates, except in a limited sense: Isocrates' writings gave Philip insight into Greek public opinion and perhaps helped Philip perceive the way to win support among the Greeks.

His influence elsewhere, however, was considerable. His pupils were often men of power and importance (15.30), and three or four years of Panhellenist proselytizing must have had their effect. Then too, publication had secured him a very wide audience. His rhetorical fame was such that his writings must have become familiar in every school of rhetoric in the Greek world (see 9.74, 5.84). People cribbed his arguments (5.11; epistle 6.7), a sign of the esteem in which he was held, but the real measure of his influence is provided by the epistles. He did not hesitate to write to Dionysius of Syracuse with no suspicion that his opinion would not be seriously received (epistle 1), or to the magistrates of Mytilene in an almost condescending tone, requesting a favorable reception for the teacher of his grandsons (epistle 8). The sons of Jason of Pherae invited him to take up residence at their court (epistle 6). Men approached him for letters of recommendation to his pupil Timotheus of Heraclea (epistle 7) and to Philip's right-hand man, Antipater (epistle 4). Isocrates did not hesitate to address the powerful and did not expect to be ignored. Men visited the city to hold discussions with him, arousing others' envy (epistle 2.22). All this suggests that he was a man of considerable influence.

The Panhellenist doctrine was widely held. Xenophon wrote no specifically Panhellenist tract, but his writings betray his sympathy for the cause and suggest widespread sympathy in his circle of aristocratic friends. If more of the literature of the fourth century had survived, we would doubtless find many others of the same ilk. Isocrates' distinction was to write, in Alexander Pope's phrase, "what oft was thought but ne'er so well expressed," and he was most seriously considered throughout the Greek world.

ISOCRATES

THE JUDGMENT OF ISOCRATES

Isocrates must be rated a singularly naive man, with no trace of Thucydidean hard-headedness. In the *Letter to Philip* of 346, he revealed that, before Philip and Athens made the peace in which Athens was obliged to surrender its claim to Amphipolis, he had been engaged in writing a speech about the war for Amphipolis, arguing that it was to Philip's advantage that Athens should hold the city; the friendship of Athens was worth more to Philip than the revenues thence derived (paras. 1–7). This is astonishing. Amphipolis, at the only crossing point on the lower Strymon River, was the key to Thrace, and if Athens had held it, Philip's whole eastward expansion would have been blocked. Isocrates had missed the point. Similarly, he had no notion of what Philip's position would be once he had successfully cut off the western provinces of the Persian Empire. Philip, he declared, did not need any more wealth or power, but the campaign would increase his glory (para. 133 ff.) by serving the cause of Greece; the Persian provincial governors would welcome Philip as the bringer of freedom (para. 104). He did not reflect on the serious consequences for Greek independence of the establishment of such an enormous power. Again, in the *Areopagiticus* he showed similar naiveté over the affairs of Athens. He saw no difficulty in a return to the simpler days of the Delian League and the Cleisthenic constitution. For him history could simply be undone. He had little understanding of why the Athenian Empire and the democracy had developed, nor did he recognize that the maintenance and extension of power was the true concern of politics.

He was indeed naive but probably not vicious. Some have regarded him as the visionary who perceived that the days of the free city-state were over and that Greece needed a ruler who would secure the unity that the Greeks had been unable to achieve for themselves—which would have been a most villainous betrayal of

liberty. But he apparently had no such thoughts. He supposed that Philip would produce concord by persuasion, that the Greeks would be beyond the reach of the royal power, for Philip was to exercise monarchic power over the Macedonians and imperial rule over as many barbarians as possible, but would merely "benefit" the Greeks—principally, one supposes, by founding comfortable colonies (5.16, 154, 140; and see Demosthenes, 7.35). He seems to have given no real thought to what the precise position of Philip would be vis à vis the Greeks, once he had "persuaded" them to unite. In his mind the relation of the Greeks with Philip would be comparable to that of the Spartans with their king or that of the Macedonian "Companions" with theirs (5.80), a very suggestive comparison. Spartan kings had no special political powers but were in essence hereditary generals, and the Companions were the core of the Macedonian army of which Philip was general. The truth is that Isocrates was naively looking for a military leader for his crusade, no more. Speusippus' *Letter to Philip* (para. 13) is most revealing. That Isocrates could send much the same letter to Agesilaus, Dionysius, and Alexander of Pherae shows how little he had in mind; he merely wanted a general, for it is inconceivable that he ever thought of any of those three gaining political mastery in Greece. With sublime naiveté he concentrated on the leadership of his crusade and thought not at all of what either the crusade or its success would mean to Greek liberty.

Panhellenism, which he espoused, was disastrous folly. Its premises were false. The moral and military weakness of Persia was a myth; Agesilaus in the 390's or Alexander in the 330's might easily enough defeat Persia's provincial forces; the royal Persian army was a different matter, and the destruction of Persian power on the battlefield of Gaugamela was "a damned close-run thing." Nor was the condition of the Greeks of Asia all that bad. Isocrates wildly exaggerated in the *Panegyric*; the tribute paid to Persia, no greater than that once paid to

Athens, was not heavy; some cities were garrisoned but for most of the fourth century many cities hardly ever saw a Persian soldier; military service for Asiatic Greeks was trifling compared to the constant demands on the Greeks of the mainland; above all, the cities had autonomy in large measure. Isocrates came later to realize the truth and kept off the subject of the Asiatic Greeks, as the real evils of Greece itself absorbed him more and more; but the cry for the liberation of the Asiatic Greeks went on. By preaching that Greece would find unity in attacking Persia, the Panhellenists helped blind the Greeks to the real menace to their liberty, "the bandit rising to power on their very doorsteps in the heart of Greece," as Demosthenes (10.34) called Philip. Panhellenism was indeed disastrous folly and held foolish men like Isocrates in thrall.

Ironically, Greece's disaster was also its salvation. In the fourth century B.C. Greece was falling into ever worse social and economic confusion. Revolution and bloodshed abounded, with great numbers of poor forced into mercenary military service and many exiles ready to lead them. Greece was, for whatever reason, growing poorer, and the cities founded by Alexander and his successors provided Greece with an outlet. Thus Isocrates' and the Panhellenists' demands for colonies were proved not to be idly conceived. Of course, the settlements founded by Alexander were not at all what Isocrates had envisaged. They were in remote areas of the East, in Cicero's phrase, "bulwarks of empire," Macedonian rather than Greek. Isocrates had thought of "exploiting Asia," with comfortable Greek cities in Asia Minor (4.133, 160; 5.120), the sort of colonies that, with the exception of Alexandria in Egypt, did not come until after Alexander's death. Nor did Isocrates have in mind more than a physical transportation of Greece's poor. He did not foresee that the economic salvation of Greece would be not so much the colonies themselves as the trade that developed between the Hellenistic foundations and Old Greece. Still, even though he "intended an ode that turned out a sonnet," he deserves credit for drawing attention to the social misery of the age and offering a practicable solution.

Selected Bibliography

TEXTS AND INDEX

Isocrates, edited by Benseler-Blass. 2 vols. Leipzig, 1879. The Teubner, with critical appendix.
Isocrates, edited by Englebert Drerup. Vol. 1. Leipzig, 1906.
Preuss, Siegmund. *Index Isocrateus*. Leipzig, 1904. Reprinted Hildesheim, 1963.

TRANSLATIONS

Isocrates. 3 vols. Translated by G. Norlin and L. van Hook. London, 1928–1945. Loeb Classical Library. Text and translation.
Isocrate Discours. 4 vols. Translated into French by Georges Mathieu and Emile Brémond. Paris, 1928–1966.

COMMENTARIES.

Forster, E. S. *Isocrates: Cyrian Orations*. Oxford, 1912.
Laistner, M. L. W. *Isocrates: De Pace and Philippus*. New York and London, 1927.
Sandys, J. E. *Isocrates: Ad Demonicum et Panegyricus*. Cambridge, 1868.
Treves, P., ed. *Isocrate: Il Panegyrico*. Turin, 1932.
——. *Isocrate: A Filippo*. Milan, 1933.

BIOGRAPHICAL AND CRITICAL STUDIES

Baynes, N. H. *Byzantine Studies and Other Essays*. London, 1955. Pp. 144–167.
Blass, F. W. *Die Attische Beredsamkeit*. 2nd ed. Leipzig, 1892. Pp. 1–331.
Bringmann, Klaus. *Studien zu den politischen Ideen des Isokrates*. Göttingen, 1965.
Buchner, Edmund. *Der Panegyrikos des Isokrates*. Wiesbaden, 1958.
Cloché, Paul. *Der panhellenische Gedanke im 4 Jahrhundert vor Christ und der "Philippus" des Isokrates*. Vienna, 1968.
Dobesch, G. *Isocrate et son temps*. Paris, 1963.
Fuks, Alexander. "Isokrates and the Social-eco-

nomic Situation in Greece." *Ancient Society* 3:17–44 (1972).

Jaeger, W. W. *Paideia*. Vol. 3. Berlin and Leipzig, 1936. Reprinted New York, 1945. English translation, pp. 46–155.

Jebb, R. C. *The Attic Orators*. Vol. 2. London, 1893. Reprinted New York, 1962.

Kennedy, G. A. *The Art of Persuasion in Greece*. Princeton, N.J., 1963. Pp. 174–203.

Levi, M. A. *Isocrate*. Milan, 1959.

Markle, M. M. "A Study of Isokrates' *Philippus* and Speusippus' *Letter to Philip*." *Journal of Hellenic Studies* 96: 80–99 (1976).

Marrou, H. I. *Histoire de L'Education dans L'Antiquité*. 6th ed. Paris, 1964. Pp. 131–147. English translation, London, 1956.

Mathieu, Georges. *Les idées politiques d'Isocrate*. 2nd ed. Paris, 1963.

Perlman, S. "Isocrates' *Philippus*—A Reinterpretation." *Historia* 6:306–317 (1957).

———. "Isocrates' Advice on Philip's Attitude Towards Barbarians." *Historia* 16: 338–343 (1967).

Seck, F., ed. *Isokrates*. Neue Wege der Forschung 351. Darmstadt, 1976.

Wilcken, U. "Philipp II von Makedonien und die panhellenische Idee." *Sitzungsberichte Berlin* (1929), pp. 291–318.

Zucker, F. "Isokrates' Panathenaikos." *Berichte über die Verhandlungen der Sächsischen Akademie, Philologische Historische Klasse* 101, no. 7 (1954).

G. L. CAWKWELL

XENOPHON

(ca. 428– ca. 355 B.C.)

THE WORKS

XENOPHON, HAILED IN antiquity as the one philosopher whose deeds were equal to his words (Eunapius, *Lives of the Sophists* 1.1) and set beside Plato as the "twin star of Socratic charm" (Aulus Gellius, *Noctes Atticae* 14.3), is now less highly valued. But his *Anabasis* remains one of the great adventure stories of all time; his Socratic writings inform us of the standards by which an Athenian gentleman of the old school measured his own conduct and that of the rest of the world; and his historical works, though they offer no adequate analysis and are not even a satisfactory chronicle, are imbued with the Athenian codes of honor and piety and frequently report vividly events that the author either witnessed himself or of which he was personally informed by participants.

In the modern canon of Xenophon's works, the *Hellenica* stands first, and it has been maintained that the first two books of this history of Greece represent his earliest writings. But the dates at which he composed his different works are so problematical that it seems better, in tracing Xenophon's personal development, to start with his Socratic recollections, the *Memorabilia* and *Symposium*, and the light that they throw on his education. His active career as a soldier may be considered next, especially as it is revealed in his *Anabasis*; then the historical writings, including those minor works in which he praises his friend and patron, the Spartan king Agesilaus, and examines more critically the nature of the Spartan constitution. (The *Constitution of the Athenians*, which has come down to us among Xenophon's works, is certainly not by him, and must have been written while he was still a child. However, it reflects the political prejudices with which he grew up.)

The *Oeconomicus*, though formally belonging with the Socratic writings, seems to reflect Xenophon's own life as a retired general and the owner of an estate, rather than whatever teaching he may actually have received from Socrates. Xenophon's own experience also underlies the short practical handbooks of instruction that are included among his minor works. Of these the *Art of Horsemanship* justly continues in high esteem. The *Cynegeticus*, on hunting, seems to be only partly from Xenophon's hand, and in any case describes techniques that have little to do with any modern form of the sport. Nor have the treatises on the Athenian revenues and on the duties of a cavalry commander more than antiquarian interest. The same is true of the practical advice offered throughout the *Cyropaedia*, Xenophon's great historical novel, whose hero is Cyrus, founder of the Persian Empire and namesake of the rebel prince with whom Xenophon marched from Sardis to Babylonia in 401 B.C. Written in the last years of Xenophon's life, the book sums up its author's views on everything from table manners to grand strategy, and for centuries was regarded as his masterpiece, though it is neglected nowadays.

XENOPHON

THE SOCRATIC WRITINGS

Xenophon was the son of Gryllus, an Athenian of the parish of Erchia. He was modest and of great physical beauty. They say that Socrates first met him in an alleyway and blocked his passage with his staff, while he asked him where different products were to be bought. Xenophon answered, and Socrates again questioned him and asked where men might become honorable and virtuous. Xenophon confessed his ignorance, and Socrates replied, "Then follow me and learn." From that time on Xenophon was the disciple of Socrates.

Perhaps this story, from a source (Diogenes Laertius, *Lives of the Philosophers* 2.48) centuries later than the time of Socrates and Xenophon, does not truly describe their first meeting. Indeed, it bears a suspicious resemblance to the complaint that Xenophon himself puts into the mouth of Socrates (*Memorabilia* 4.4.5), that teachers could be found in abundance for would-be shoemakers or carpenters, horsemen or coppersmiths, but none to instruct in justice. Yet there is no sufficient reason to doubt that Xenophon and Socrates did meet, or that the memory of Socrates and his teaching influenced Xenophon through the rest of his life, even though more of that life was spent in practical affairs than in philosophical inquiry.

Whatever the circumstances, the meeting must have taken place about the time that Xenophon came of age, during the later years of the Peloponnesian War. Xenophon seems, on his own evidence, to have been born about 430–425 B.C.; he was apparently younger than his friend Proxenus the Boeotian, whom he accompanied on Cyrus' expedition, and Proxenus was "about thirty" at the time of hsi death in 401 B.C. (*Anabasis* 2.6.20 and 3.1.14). So Xenophon can hardly have met Socrates earlier than about 413 B.C., and probably a few years later. The story that Socrates saved Xenophon's life in the battle of Delium in 424 (Diogenes Laertius, 2.22) must be a romantic invention. Their association definitely ended with Xenophon's departure for Asia in 401, two years before Socrates' death.

Xenophon's conduct during the retreat of Cyrus' Greek mercenaries proves that he was a seasoned soldier and a master of tactics, so it is likely that he saw considerable service during the Peloponnesian War itself and in the subsequent civil war that led to the overthrow of the Thirty Tyrants imposed on Athens by Sparta as part of the peace settlement. We can only guess at the details, but we can be fairly certain that he was a cavalryman; if so, most of his service would have been in Attica, trying to restrict the systematic devastation of the countryside by the Spartans and their allies, who had established a permanent base a few miles outside Athens. Perhaps he sailed with the Athenian fleet in 406 B.C., when, in the crisis before the battle of Arginusae, he tells (*Hellenica* 1.6.24), many of the cavalry embarked. It may even be true, though the story is only found in a late source (Philostratus, *Lives of the Sophists* 1.2), that he was taken prisoner by the Boeotians. If so, he was lucky, for the story adds that he was paroled and attended the lectures of the fashionable rhetorician Prodicus of Ceos, who was teaching in Thebes at the time. Perhaps Xenophon owed this favorable treatment to the "ancient ties of friendship" between himself and Proxenus.

At all events, it seems clear that Xenophon's discipleship with Socrates must have been intermittent and based on informal association rather than regular instruction. If the "thinking-shop" shown in Aristophanes' *Clouds* ever existed, Socrates must have abandoned it years earlier. Xenophon perhaps preserved some recollection of it and certainly is defending his master's memory against the sort of charge that Aristophanes brings, when he insists repeatedly (*Memorabilia* 1.1.10–17; 4.7.1–5) that Socrates, while urging his pupils to master such sciences as geometry and astronomy to the extent that they were of practical use to a man of affairs, cautioned against pursuing them too far or wasting time in abstract speculation on metaphysics and the supernatural, which could only lead to religious doubt, as the example of Anaxagoras proved. For Socrates the proper study of mankind was man, not speculations about the One and the Infinite, or whether all things were in flux or remained immutable.

> His own talk was always about humanity, investigating the nature of the pious, the impious, the honorable, the shameful, the just, the unjust, good sense, folly, courage, cowardice, the city and the good citizen, government of men and the man fit to govern, and other matters by knowledge of which, so he thought, men were honorable and good, and through ignorance of which they deserved to be called slavish.
>
> (*Memorabilia* 1.1.16)

The conversations that Xenophon records are set against the background of a lost war and postwar depression. Socrates' associates include members of the new poor, who have been ruined in defeat: Eutherus once possessed property overseas but had no inheritance in Athens and now had nothing to look forward to but a laborer's life and a pauper's old age; Charmides had come down in the world but still moved in society and could claim that his losses had freed him from slavery to the tax-collector and fear of burglars and informers—a ruined, dangerous man, ready to hit back (*Memorabilia* 2.8.1 ff.; *Symposium* 4.2.9 ff.). But ruined or not, they still regarded themselves as gentlemen—*kaloi kagathoi* (honorable and good).

Xenophon presents his view of morals and politics from the side of the propertied classes, not from that of the democrats. His guiding principle is not equality but power to those best qualified to serve the state—that is, those whose possessions enable them to fit themselves out with weapons, armor, and horses for military service on land; who equip the galleys on which the poor embark as rowers; who finance expensive theatrical productions; who make large donations in cash to the treasury. Certainly Socrates himself was a poor man (though his trade as a sculptor must have brought at least a lower middle-class income

earlier in his life when he served in the army as a foot soldier). Xenophon (*Memorabilia* 1.2.58–59) defends him against the charge—brought posthumously, rather than at his trial—that he despised the poor. It was true that Socrates used to quote approvingly Homer's description of the conduct of Odysseus in the assembly (*Iliad* 2.1.188, Pope ed.):

> But if a clamorous vile plebean rose,
>   Him with reproof he check'd, or tam'd with blows;
> "Be still, thou slave, and to thy betters yield,
> Unknown alike in council and in field!"

But of course, says Xenophon, Socrates, himself a poor man, did not mean that the poor should be struck and silenced. "He meant that those who are useless in word and deed; who can give no help when wanted, either to an army or to the city or to the people; above all, those who are impudent as well as useless, must be restrained by all means, even if they happen to be very rich" (*Memorabilia* 1.2.59). But the examples of impudence and uselessness in Xenophon's historical writing are mostly demagogues.

Aristocratic villains might be impudent, but they were not useless; they were dangerous because they had abilities that they used to bad ends. Socrates had associated with the two most notorious—Critias, "under the oligarchy the most ambitious and violent," and Alcibiades, "under the democracy the most incontinent and insolent." They were of the generation before Xenophon's and had both come to violent ends some years before Socrates was brought to trial for corrupting youth, but they must have been very much in the judges' minds. Xenophon is at pains to show (*Memorabilia* 1.2.12) that Critias and Alcibiades did not act upon Socratic principles. They associated with Socrates, in order to master what they needed of Socratic technique, and while they were doing so Socrates restrained them and influenced them for good despite themselves. Then they went their own way, to the ruin of the state.

XENOPHON

Xenophon illustrates the use to which Alcibiades put the "Socratic method":

They say that, before he was twenty years old, he held the following conversation with Pericles, his guardian and the leading statesman of Athens, on the subject of the Laws. "Tell me, Pericles, could you teach me what is Law?" "By all means," said Pericles. "Then teach me, for God's sake," said Alcibiades. "I hear some men praised as law-abiding citizens, and I think that one could not justly earn this praise without knowing what law is." "What you want to know is easily answered," said Pericles. "Laws are everything that the people in assembly have scrutinized and enacted, pronouncing what is authorized and what is prohibited." "Enjoining good actions or wicked ones?" "Good, for Heaven's sake, my dear boy, and by no means wicked!" "If it is not the people, but, as in the case of an oligarchy, a small number who meet to enact what is authorized, what is that?" "Everything that the authority in a city, after due deliberation, enacts as authorized, is called law." "Then if a tyrant is the authority in a city and enacts authorized conduct of the citizens, this is law too?" "Even what a tyrant in power enacts is also called law." "Well, Pericles, is not violence a form of lawlessness? For example, when the stronger compels the weaker to do as he wishes not by persuasion but by force?" "I suppose so," said Pericles. So Pericles admits that what the tyrant enacts by compulsion rather than persuasion is lawlessness, not law, and then is driven to the same admission about the oligarchy and, finally, the people. He concedes with a sour "When I was your age I was clever at this sort of argument," and is answered, "If only I had known you, Pericles, when you were at the height of your powers!"

(*Memorabilia* 1.2.40–46)

Xenophon's Socrates often uses question and answer less for the sake of disputation than to bring some acquaintance to agree to some particular course of action, which serves as a moral example, without the underlying principles being closely examined. For example:

I know that he debated somewhat as follows with Diodorus, who was his associate. "Tell me, Dio-dorus, if one of your household slaves runs away, do you take steps to recover him?" "Indeed yes," he replied, "and I call on others for help by publishing a reward for his recovery." "Well then," said Socrates, "if one of your slaves is ill, do you look after him and call in doctors to save his life?" "Certainly." "But if one of your acquaintance, who is more worthy than your slaves, is in danger of perishing through want, do you think it unworthy of you to take steps for his preservation? You know, of course, that Hermogenes is no stranger to you, and would be ashamed, if he were helped by you, not to give you some assistance in return. Yet to have a servant, willing and well-disposed and faithful and capable of obeying orders, and not merely capable of obedience, but able to make himself useful on his own initiative, with foresight and forethought, is, I think, worth many slaves. Good housekeepers, when they buy something of value at a small price, say that it is a buyer's market. And now the situation is such that good friends can be bought cheap."

(*Memorabilia* 2.10.1)

A small lesson in good manners follows; Diodorus must invite Hermogenes himself, not send Socrates to do it for him, and the story concludes with a note that the friendship fulfilled Socrates' expectations. In a few lines we have been told a good deal about accepted relations between master and servant, patron and dependent, friend and friend, and given a sound, practical lesson in worldly wisdom. But there is no search for underlying principles; contrast the manner in which Plato (*Republic* 1.332d ff.) explores just one of the topics that Xenophon touches on, the obligation to repay service with service, to "do good to one's friends and harm one's enemies"—and this too as a mere prelude to the examination of the whole concept of justice.

The Socratic dialogues of the *Memorabilia*, besides being short and limited in scope as compared to Plato's, are restricted to Socrates and the person whom he is interrogating. (The more elaborate *Symposium* is perhaps a deliberate attempt at the Platonic manner.) We may assume the presence of others, including Xenophon himself, who sometimes says that he "heard" the conversation, but Xenophon shows none of Plato's elaborate stagecraft in introducing the company and establishing the mood of the conversation that is to follow. We see glimpses of Socrates at dinner warning his young friends to enjoy the pleasures of the table only as far as they are needed to satisfy hunger and thirst (*Memorabilia* 1.3.5–8) and rebuking the glutton who neglects the bread that forms the substantial part of the meal and eats only the relishes that are meant to accompany it (*Memorabilia* 3.14.2). The gentleman whose education prepares him to rule others should not allow himself to fall slave to his own physical desires; idleness and incontinence are the object of even more Socratic rebukes than gluttony—including one addressed to Critias, who was told in the presence of a large company that "his passion was swinish; he rubbed himself against his beloved Euthydemus like a pig against a rock" (*Memorabilia* 1.2.30). And Socrates practiced what he preached:

> He was of all men most continent as regards sexual pleasures, and food and drink. He was most able to endure heat and cold and physical labor. He was so disciplined in the moderation of his needs that, though his possessions were very small, they easily sufficed. How could such a character have made others impious, law-breakers, luxurious, sexually incontinent or too soft to endure hardship?
>
> (*Memorabilia* 1.2.1)

There is no need to follow those modern scholars who claim that Xenophon's model is not Socrates, whom (they allege) he hardly knew, but Antisthenes the Cynic, who also appears in Xenophon's writings to preach the doctrine that true riches are not found in men's possessions but in their souls (*Symposium* 4.34). The Socratic dialogue certainly became established as a literary form during the first half of the fourth century B.C., and Xenophon did use it as a conventional way of expressing his own opinion. But he would not have needed to insist so emphatically that he was defending the memory of Socrates from "the accuser" if he had merely wished to present in conventional guise the doctrines that he had learned from other teachers. And in fact he expressly attributes to Prodicus (though he makes Socrates tell it) the story of how Heracles, when he passed from childhood to youth, dreamed that he stood at a crossroads where he was approached by two beautiful women—Virtue, adorned with simple modesty, and "Pleasure, or as those who hate me call me, Vice." Each invited him to choose her way, and Heracles chose the hard road which, by making him worthy to serve Hellas, led to honor in life and undying fame after death (*Memorabilia* 2.1.21–34).

Nor, if Xenophon had not known Socrates well and remembered his influence all his life, would there have been any reason for him to introduce an allusion to his condemnation into the *Cyropaedia*, written some forty years afterward (3.1.38–40). The story does not demand it; it seems that Xenophon himself felt his debt to Socrates was so great that he could not allow his major work on education to appear without a tribute to his master. So we should not be too skeptical about using the *Memorabilia* as evidence for what the historical Socrates was like, at least toward the end of his life. For example, Plato's Socrates, like Xenophon's, argues that the virtue of particular arts or instruments is to be judged by how well they function in relation to the objects to which they are directed. It seems consistent for Socrates to develop this further, as Xenophon makes him do (*Memorabilia* 1.4.2–19), and confute an atheist by arguing that the fitness of the parts of the human body, as well as of various natural beings, to function in relation to the object of human well-being argues the design of a supreme creator who is concerned with human happiness. We may also suppose that Socrates was bent on training future leaders of the state, even if he himself abstained from politics (*Memorabilia* 1.6.15); that to this end he encouraged his associates to learn arts like military tactics and blamed their teachers, not because they neglected underlying metaphysical principles, but because their instruction was limited to the parade ground and so of small practical value.

Plato makes Socrates question the value of instruction in rhetoric, for which all fashionable Athens was running to the sophist Protagoras, by asking which of the practical matters of statecraft, such as naval policy or the architecture of public buildings, the rhetorician will be qualified to direct by virtue of his rhetorician's art (Plato, *Protagoras* 319b–323a). Xenophon's Socrates (*Memorabilia* 3.6) restrains a young friend who, though not yet twenty years old, is setting himself up as a statesman, by leading him to confess his ignorance of practical affairs. How is he to advise on finance, when he does not even know the city's revenues and expenditure? "But, Socrates, one can enrich the state at its enemies' expense." But the young statesman is not qualified to advise on military matters either: he is ignorant not only of the total military resources of Athens, but of details such as the siting of the frontier forts. He "guesses" that they are badly placed and garrisoned and is told to stop guessing and ascertain the facts. The fact that Socrates is talking not with a professional teacher of rhetoric but with Plato's brother Glaucon might suggest that Xenophon is making an underhand attack on his rival; but in fact he acknowledges that Socrates' concern to stop Glaucon from making a fool of himself was prompted by his special regard for Plato.

He does not mention Plato elsewhere, and Plato never names him. We can fairly conclude that they did not know each other well when they were both young men, with very different interests, and not yet famous, rather than that Xenophon did not know Socrates. Nonetheless, his claim to have heard particular conversations is not to be taken at face value. He does not record the voice of Socrates as James Boswell recorded Samuel Johnson's; at best we have recollections of conversations set down perhaps a third of a century later. And it must be acknowledged that Xenophon did work his own opinions into his dialogues—though we may well imagine that he asked himself what Socrates would have advised in a certain situation. For example, Socrates discusses the military situation with General Pericles, son of the great statesman. This is quite in keeping with the historical Socrates, as far as we can reconstruct such a figure; compare the discussion that opens Plato's *Laches*. But the military situation at the period in which, for dramatic purposes, the reader is supposed to imagine the dialogue taking place—shortly before 406 B.C.—was quite different from that which the dialogue examines. Why is it, Socrates asks, that the Athenians, whose ancestors the Boeotians were afraid to face even in their own country without Peloponnesian support, now in their turn fear a Boeotian invasion? This was the situation during the 360's, after the Thebans had defeated the Spartans at Leuctra and the Athenians, allied to Sparta, feared a Theban invasion. Xenophon is manifestly giving his own opinions in the conventional form of the Socratic dialogue, and no doubt in the assurance that Socrates would have approved.

THE SOLDIER

Modern scholars have judged Xenophon in very different ways. That he is not a great abstract philosopher is generally, though not universally, admitted; that he is less than adequate as a historian is certain. Whether his virtues make up for his failings is the real point at issue. If he lacks historical judgment and breadth of vision, does he at least tell us the truth as far as he knows it? If he contributes little to the theory of moral philosophy, was he at least an honorable man who tried to live in accordance with the best standards of his own age? Evidence must be sought in the *Anabasis*, the only one of his works largely concerned with his own conduct.

Here certainly is a story of heroic adventure against impossible odds. "One of the very first works that antiquity has left us. Perfect in its kind," as the historian Thomas Macaulay considered it. But when we probe, we find reasons for disquiet. Xenophon, the associate of Socrates who had been preparing himself to be one of the leaders of the Athenian state, instead enters the service of a barbarian prince, the constant enemy of Athens in the last years of the Peloponnesian War. The Socratic lessons that a general must be an efficient administrator as well as a gallant leader in the field and that the commander needs the skills of the politician and orator as well as proficiency in arms (*Memorabilia* 3.3–4) are applied to the management of a band of mercenary adventurers. The seemingly honest narrator, who freely admits his own errors as well as reporting his successes, is accused by some of his critics of suppressing the achievements of his colleagues and stealing the credit for a great feat of arms in which his own part was nearly always subordinate. Worst of all, perhaps, the man who makes a great show of his piety, who respects portents and dreams sent from the gods, who consults soothsayers and the entrails of sacrifices before every important move, and who claims to rest all this on the precept and example of Socrates, begins his expedition by prevaricating with his master and with Apollo's Delphic oracle.

But Xenophon should be allowed to tell the story for himself. In the early books of the *Anabasis* we catch a glimpse of him reporting to Cyrus as the armies are about to join in battle on the field of Cunaxa; another of him strolling beyond the lines with his friend Proxenus one evening during the retreat (*Anabasis* 1.8.15–17; 2.4.15). It is not until the generals of the Greek army have been cut off by treachery and Xenophon is about to offer himself as a leader in place of his lost friend Proxenus that he tells us how he came to join the expedition:

> There was in the army a certain Xenophon of Athens, attached to it neither as a general nor as a captain nor yet as a private soldier. Proxenus had invited him from his home because they were linked by ancient ties of hospitality, and promised him, if he came, to gain him the friendship of Cyrus, whom he himself, so he said, valued above his native country. Xenophon read the letter and communicated the proposed expedition to Socrates the Athenian. And Socrates expressed doubts that by becoming a friend of Cyrus he might expose himself to political reprisals, because Cyrus seemed to have supported the Lacedaemonians eagerly in their war against Athens, and advised Xenophon to go to Delphi and consult the gods about the expedition. So Xenophon went and asked Apollo to which of the gods he should sacrifice and pray in order to make the journey that he had in mind best and most fairly, and come through successfully and safely. And Apollo told him the gods to whom he ought to sacrifice. When he came home, he told the oracle's answer to Socrates, who blamed him because he did not first ask whether it would be better for him to go or to stay, but decided for himself that he ought to go and then asked how he could accomplish his journey most fairly. But since he did not put the question this way, he should do, said Socrates, as the god commanded. So Xenophon sacrificed as Apollo had commanded and set sail, and overtook Proxenus and Cyrus at Sardis when they were just on the point of starting their march inland, and was presented to Cyrus. And since Proxenus urged him to remain with them, Cyrus joined in urging him, and promised to send him home immediately upon the conclusion of the expedition, which he said was directed against the Pisidians. So Xenophon joined the army deceived—but not by Proxenus.

> (*Anabasis* 3.1.4–10)

Whatever else we may make of this story, Xenophon must at least be credited with being honestly ready to take the blame for his own mistakes and to clear the memory of his friends. His reasons for making up his mind to go may be guessed. After the final surrender to Sparta in 404 B.C., the Athenian democracy had been abolished, and Xenophon, like others of his class, had probably initially supported the Thirty Tyrants led by Critias, who had held out the prospect of a state controlled by responsible property owners rather than the mob. By the time democracy was restored in 403, Xenophon had certainly realized his mistake. The noble speech that he puts into the mouth of Thrasybulus, the democratic leader, at the time of his triumphant entry into Athens (*Hellenica* 2.4.39–42), shows that he was well aware that the "best people" had proved themselves inferior by their own standards of justice and valor, and that the Spartans, on whose friendship they relied and whose institutions they admired, had handed them over to the people "like muzzled curs." Xenophon also acknowledges that the democrats had respected their oaths and not taken revenge on their opponents, and we know from other sources (notably Lysias, 16.8) that former supporters of the Thirty did subsequently rise to office and military command under the democracy. But in 401 B.C. Xenophon was probably ashamed of his own conduct at Athens and despairing of the career for which he had striven to qualify himself. Whatever Socrates might say, Xenophon was already compromised politically, and the chance to make his name and fortune abroad was too good to miss.

Xenophon's professed belief that Cyrus' great army had been collected for a local punitive expedition might seem to mark him either as a liar or a simpleton. Cyrus had gathered more than eleven thousand Greek heavy infantry, an army comparable to the largest that any combination of Greek cities had put into the field in the previous generation. His Asiatics, though of less military value, were several times more numerous. But the Greeks took it for granted that Asiatic princes numbered their armies by myriads. Of course Cyrus would have a huge army—however disproportionate the objective. And of course King Artaxerxes' own army would be much larger still (Xenophon actually estimates his forces in the field at Cunaxa at a million men) and his capital cities several months' march away, so that Xenophon may not have realized that Cyrus was marching against his brother simply because the whole

notion seemed fantastic. Most of the Greeks seem to have been equally duped—or perhaps they were only pretending to be taken in, so that at successive stages in the journey they could make a show of refusing to march to the next objective and extract promises of higher pay.

"Deceived—but not by Proxenus": yet Xenophon does not show any resentment against Cyrus, whom he represents as a prince valiant in battle and in the hunt, skilled in arms and horsemanship, superbly generous to his friends and to all who served him, ready to forgive personal injury but stern in the execution of public justice. In the description of Cyrus that follows the account of his death, Xenophon says:

> Nobody could say that he allowed criminals to laugh in his face. He was most unsparing in exacting punishment, and one could often see along the highways men whom he had deprived of their feet and hands and eyes. So that in Cyrus's province both Greek and barbarian, provided they did no wrong, could journey without fear whenever they wished, taking their property with them.
>
> (*Anabasis* 1.9.13)

"If Cyrus had only lived"—Xenophon even puts the wish into the mouth of Socrates (*Oeconomicus* 4.18–19), and it is sometimes echoed by modern historians, who imagine the hero-prince revitalizing the Persian Empire and even anticipating the supposed designs of Alexander the Great and achieving the fusion of Greek and oriental civilizations. It was his brother, the drunkard who could sit neither his throne nor his horse worthily (Plutarch, *Artaxerxes* 6.3), who stayed at home over his wine instead of leading his courtiers in the manly sports of their ancestors (*Cyropaedia* 8.8.12), who brought Persia to ruin.

Xenophon ignores the very real political achievements of Artaxerxes, who during a long reign not only saved his empire from the total disintegration that threatened it but forced the Greeks to submit to his authority as they had not done to any of his ancestors. Xenophon might claim and make Socrates repeat (*Anabasis* 1.9.29–31; *Oeconomicus* 4.18–19) that

> though Cyrus was a slave [the Greeks affected to regard all Persians as slaves of the great king], nobody deserted from him to the king, except that Orontas attempted it. And even he soon found that the man whom he thought trustworthy was a better friend to Cyrus than to himself. But from the king many deserted to Cyrus, when they became enemies to each other.

But by the "deserters" from the king Xenophon apparently means the miserable conscript rank and file of his army who threw down their arms and surrendered when the Greeks charged them. Orontas, who had been betrayed in an attempt to lead his cavalry regiment over to Artaxerxes, was a great Persian noble—and of the Persian nobility none joined the rebellion except those who had been subject to Cyrus in his original province. "Villain! unworthy of the name of Cyrus!" exclaimed the captain of the royal horseguards as he hurled his spear (Plutarch, *Artaxerxes* 9). Perhaps if Artaxerxes had been defeated, his brother would have destroyed the empire instead of saving it. The Persian nobility, rather than submit to a usurper supported by foreign mercenaries, might have rallied to other claimants or declared themselves independent.

But "if only Cyrus had lived" haunted Xenophon for the rest of his life. When he summed up for posterity the lessons of his long and distinguished career in a fictional biography of the ideal ruler, he did not make his hero a Greek or place him in the context of a city-state—the uncorrupted Sparta of Lycurgus the lawgiver, for instance. He chose as a pattern for rulers and generals the first Cyrus, founder of the state that to most Greeks was the ancient enemy, the opponent of all that either Sparta or Athens represented; against which Xenophon himself had borne arms not merely in the rebellion of the younger Cyrus but under the Spartan king

Agesilaus. It is true that Xenophon's Cyrus the Great, joking with his peers around the mess table or knocking an awkward squad of recruits into shape, obviously owes more than a hint to Agesilaus, and it is also true that the superhuman figure of the ideal ruler is better displayed against a background extending from the Nile to the Oxus than in a corner of the Peloponnesus. But the first inspiration of the *Cyropaedia* was Xenophon's memory of Cyrus the Younger.

In the *Cyropaedia* everything, of course, from the moment that the young hero recruits his Persian peasants and starts to turn them into soldiers to his return home after the conquest of Asia and Egypt, goes according to plan—something we must allow to the daydreaming of an old man whose own plans in life consistently went wrong, perhaps through no fault of his own. But the *Cyropaedia*—which the poet Edmund Spenser, nineteen centuries later, preferred to Plato's *Republic*, "so much more profitable and gratious is doctrine by ensample, than by rule"—was intended not as escapism, but as practical instruction by one who was, among other things, a master in the art of war. In it, Xenophon allots his hero one great setpiece battle, to which his army, with its perfectly organized supply train, advances under perfect control. The smoke of campfires, dust clouds, tracks of men and animals, and the sight of foraging parties supplement the efforts of the Persian secret service and reveal the presence of the enemy, Croesus of Lydia, with his huge army. Cyrus rests and feeds his troops before bringing them into action, consults the gods by sacrifice and examination of the victims, fights his battle according to the tactical scheme that he has drawn up in advance and discussed with his officers, and wins a glorious victory (*Cyropaedia* 6.3.1–7.1.49). Contrast all this with the younger Cyrus' march to Cunaxa (*Anabasis* 1.7.1–1.8.3). An order of battle had indeed been planned, and the troops had been marshaled and reviewed at the boundary of Babylonia. But Artaxerxes abandoned the defensive lines without a fight. Silanus, the Greek seer, correctly predicted that no battle would take place within ten days. The strong force of enemy cavalry whose tracks had been noted constantly melted away before the rebels as they advanced. Cyrus persuaded himself that, after all, he would win Babylon without a fight and continued his march

> seated in his chariot, with a few men in good order in front of him, but most of his army was marching in disorder, and many of the soldiers' weapons were being carried on the wagons and baggage-animals. And now it was about the hour when the market fills [late morning], and the station where it was intended to fall out was near, when Pategyas, a noble Persian of the household of Cyrus, appeared at full gallop with his horse in a lather, shouting out in Persian and in Greek to everyone he met that the king was approaching with a great army ready for battle.
>
> (*Anabasis* 1.7.20–1.8.1)

Though the Greeks at least managed to form their line of battle before the enemy was upon them, they went into action unfed and unrested; and though Cyrus leaped from his chariot, seized his javelins, mounted his horse, and led his bodyguard like a hero, he had clearly not done all that was required of a general, and Xenophon knew it, though he would not go so far as to criticize his prince directly.

The Greek generals he observed shrewdly, both on the long march from Sardis to Babylonia, when they were intriguing for first place in Cyrus' favor and for popularity with the troops, and after the battle, when the hopes of fortune had vanished and, in their desperate situation, Clearchus the Spartan "commanded, and the rest obeyed, not because they had elected him, but because they saw that he alone understood a commander's duties, while the others were without experience" (*Anabasis* 2.2.5). Clearchus, a fifty-year-old veteran who had risen to high command at the end of the Peloponnesian War but had been exiled from Sparta for plotting to seize Byzantium for himself, had even before the battle been recog-

nized by Cyrus as the leading Greek general, though he was not given the undivided supreme command. Xenophon describes him as a man passionately devoted to soldiering, who

> chose to make war when he could have lived in peace without shame or injury, and when he could have possessed wealth without danger chose to diminish his riches in warfare. His daring, his skill in stratagems, his forethought in provisioning his army, the force of his discipline, were universally recognized. He was well capable of impressing on all present that Clearchus was to be obeyed. He achieved this by severity. His appearance was repellent, his voice harsh. He punished rigorously, and sometimes in anger, so that even he occasionally repented of it. But he also punished deliberately. For he thought that, unless disciplined by punishment, an army was useless, and people said that he used to remark that the soldier must fear his officer more than the enemy if he is to stand guard or keep his hands off his friends or march against the enemy at a moment's notice.
>
> (*Anabasis* 2.5.6–15)

Xenophon's own friend Proxenus offers a complete contrast. Twenty years younger than Clearchus and liberally educated under the famous Gorgias, ambitious for fame, power, and wealth but restrained by a resolve to pursue his ambitions only as far as was consistent with honor and justice, he was

> able to command gentlemen. But he was incapable of instilling either respect or fear for himself into his soldiers. He actually reverenced his soldiers more than they did him. And he was obviously more afraid of making himself disliked by the soldiers than they were of disobeying him. He thought that, in order to be and appear to be a good officer, it was enough to praise good conduct and not to praise bad.
>
> (*Anabasis* 2.6.16–20)

Though without official responsibilities, Xenophon had evidently impressed his friend's subordinate officers as a capable and efficient soldier. So they were ready to accept him as their general when the Persian satrap Tissaphernes seized Clearchus, Proxenus, and the other principal commanders, including Plato's friend Menon the Thessalian, whom Xenophon hated and suspected of treachery. From this point (*Anabasis* 3.1.4) Xenophon takes over the chief part in his narrative, though he always refers to himself by name and in the third person, in accordance with the convention established by Thucydides. Throughout the extraordinary march across the snow-covered mountains of Kurdistan and Armenia to Trapezus at the eastern extremity of the Black Sea; thence along its shore to Byzantium; and finally in Thrace where the survivors of the army were hired by King Seuthes, Xenophon displayed (if we are to believe him) all the qualities of a model commander.

And there is in fact no real reason to doubt him. The Greeks, adventurers from twenty different states who had joined the standard of a rebel prince in the hope of making their fortunes, were under no sort of legal authority. They accepted discipline because without it there was no hope of safety, and as danger diminished so did their readiness to obey orders. As Xenophon himself put it (*Anabasis* 5.8.20-21), when the soldiers called the generals to account for their actions after the army had reached the sea and the furthest outposts of the Greek world, they were like sailors who, when the seas run high, jump to obey their officers' merest nod, but become slack in a calm. An unpopular or inefficient officer would have been removed at any time, with swords serving as ballots. Moreover, as an Athenian, Xenophon was to most of the army a foreigner and to some a former enemy. His own most trusted officers—Eurylochus of Lusii, Agasias of Stymphalus, Callimachus of Parrhasia—and most of the rank and file were from the Peloponnesus. For all this, Xenophon not merely kept his command of Proxenus' brigade but eventually was accepted as sole commander of the army during its last independent campaign, and retained his

position after the "Cyreans" as a body were absorbed into the army with which the Spartans, from 399 B.C. on, attempted to liberate the Greeks of Asia Minor from Persia.

Though Xenophon shows us his personal qualities, he does not brag about them. He was a gallant leader in action, but when he describes how he exposed himself in covering the withdrawal of the rear guard during the march through Kurdistan, he keeps his praise for Eurylochus, who covered Xenophon with his shield from the enemy's cloth yard arrows when the general's own shield bearer ran away (*Anabasis* 4.2.20-21). Xenophon was a skilled tactician, adept at handling men in formation and also in adapting formations to suit the ground and the enemy's dispositions (see especially *Anabasis* 4.8.9-19). But he acknowledges that he made mistakes, particularly during the early stages of the retreat through the flood plain of the Tigris, when he was at first unable to counter the attacks of the Persian cavalry and light infantry upon the heavy infantry of the rear guard, which he commanded (*Anabasis* 3.3.1-20). As a disciplinarian he was neither weak like Proxenus nor unduly harsh like Clearchus: he was evidently pleased to be recognized as "the soldiers' friend" (*Anabasis* 7.6.4)—even if the man who so described him did not intend it as a compliment. He resorted to corporal punishment, as he freely admitted when, with the other generals, he was called upon to give an account of his conduct, but only as a last resort, to keep the men moving when they would otherwise have lain down and died in the snow, or, once at least, when it was thoroughly deserved. The first to complain against him was a muleteer, who had resented being forced to unload his animal in order to carry a sick man.

"I sent you on," said Xenophon, "and caught up with you again when I brought up the rear guard. And I found you digging a pit to bury the man, and, when I learned what you were doing, I praised you. But as we stood beside him, the man bent his leg and the bystanders shouted that he was alive. And you said 'Let him live as much as he likes, but I shan't carry him!' Then I did strike you."

(*Anabasis* 5.8.8–10)

Needless to say, Xenophon's conduct was thoroughly approved. Xenophon certainly did not wish his soldiers to fear him. On the contrary, he thought it an important point of leadership to be directly accessible at all times, to the ordinary soldier as well as to his officers. "All men know that he could be approached both at breakfast and at dinner, and even if he were asleep he could be awakened to be told military information" (*Anabasis* 4.3.10).

Personal example, in facing the day-to-day hardships of campaigning even more than in action, is perhaps the aspect of leadership that Xenophon most emphasizes. Already he had noted how Clearchus, when the irrigation ditches in Babylonia had to be hurriedly bridged and the work was allotted to the younger men, had gone into the mud himself to bear a hand, making the older soldiers ashamed not to join in (*Anabasis* 2.3.11). So Xenophon on at least two occasions dismounted from his charger and led on foot—the first time because an infantryman of another brigade complained that it was all very well for the general, with a horse to ride and no heavy shield to carry, to tell the men that they must race the Persians for possession of a hill; the second a year later, when he needed no such prompting but, Seuthes of Thrace having called on the heavy infantry to make a forced march to support his cavalry and light-armed troops, Xenophon dismounted. The king in surprise asked why he did so when speed was essential and was told, "I know that you do not need me by myself. The heavy troops will run faster and more cheerfully if I, their leader, am on foot too" (*Anabasis* 3.9.37–49; 7.3.44–45). Again, one night in Armenia when the soldiers were covered by snow as they lay in their bivouacs and reluctant to stir from them, Xenophon set the

example by rising naked and starting to chop wood.

Soon another man got up and took the cleaver from him and began to chop. Then others got up and kindled a fire and rubbed themselves down. They found plenty of grease there, which they used instead of olive oil, lard, and oil of sesame, bitter almonds, and turpentine. Even myrrh was found from these same places.

(*Anabasis* 4.4.11–13)

But Xenophon's merits as an officer do not guarantee fairness as a reporter. Diodorus Siculus (14.18–31), who wrote, four centuries later, a general history, *Bibliotheca Historica*, that includes a short account of Cyrus' rebellion and its consequences, does not name Xenophon at all in his account of the retreat through Asia, but only later (D.S., 14.37) when he briefly mentions the Thracian campaign. It has been argued that Xenophon deliberately exaggerates his own part and misrepresents that of the other generals, especially Chirisophus the Lacedaemonian, who, says Diodorus, was given the chief command after the death of Clearchus. Xenophon has, in fact, plenty to say about Chirisophus, nearly all of it good, but represents him as his senior colleague rather than his commander. Besides, he usually comes into the story when Xenophon himself hurries up from the rear to discuss some tactical development, or brings some essential information—the position of an unguarded fort, or the report of an intelligent native guide. Obviously the vanguard, which Chirisophus commanded, must have done much more than Xenophon reports. If Chirisophus had lived to write his memoirs, instead of dying of a sickness apparently brought on by the strain of responsibility (*Anabasis* 6.4.11), we might see the retreat from a very different point of view. But this does not mean that Xenophon is misrepresenting him. It is from *his* point of view that he writes—memoirs of an eyewitness, not a balanced account drawn from many sources. If we demand of him what he does not pretend to give us, we are ourselves guilty of injustice.

THE HISTORIAN

Xenophon's *Hellenica* provides us with lively accounts, a few at first hand, many more taken in all probability directly from eyewitnesses, of some of the great events of an important period in Greek history. We have no other contemporary historical narrative of his times, though we know that others existed and were used, often clumsily, by much later writers. We have therefore every reason to be grateful that the *Hellenica* has survived, and there is a temptation to offer the same sort of defense for it that has just been given for the *Anabasis*: Xenophon does not tell us everything that we would like to know, but at least he sets down truthfully much interesting material. But leaving aside for the moment the question of his truthfulness, which has been challenged, this defense will not do. A historian should do more than transmit information; he should actively seek it out, and try to understand the causes of events as well as narrating their course. Here Xenophon fails, and his failure is the more disappointing because, by beginning his work at the point where that of Thucydides ends, he invites direct comparison.

Diogenes Laertius, in his biography of Xenophon (2.57), says that "the books of Thucydides were lying unpublished, and he brought them into esteem when he could have claimed the credit for himself." From this it has been deduced that Xenophon served as Thucydides' literary executor, inherited his notes, and even collaborated with him. But in that case Xenophon's *Hellenica* might have been expected to continue Thucydides' narrative smoothly; instead, Thucydides leaves us in mid-sentence, at Ephesus where the Persian satrap Tissaphernes, deep in intrigue with the Greek powers, has come to sacrifice to Artemis, and Xenophon, with no more than an abrupt "after this"

to serve as connection, takes us at a bound to the Hellespont. Even "after this" the two narratives do not dovetail neatly; the city of Cyzicus, which Thucydides left in Athenian hands, is held by Sparta when Xenophon first mentions it. It has even been argued that two important events in the early chapters of the *Hellenica*, an Athenian naval victory off Abydos and the arrival of the Spartan Clearchus at Byzantium (*Hellenica* 1.1.2–7; 1.1.35), are muddled repetitions of actions that had already been told by Thucydides. Without accepting this last suggestion, we can still find enough reason to suppose that Xenophon did not know what Thucydides had in mind when he broke off.

Nonetheless, the early part of the *Hellenica* does complete Thucydides' work by carrying the story of the Peloponnesian War from 411 B.C. to its end. It does attempt to adhere to the Thucydidean chronological scheme of recording events by summers and winters—that is, by campaigning seasons. And the war itself imposes a pattern and unity. Nor is this unity broken by the fact that the second book (*Hellenica* 2.3–4) ends with an account of postwar Athens down to the restoration of the democracy in 403 B.C. The defeat of the attempt to install in Athens a narrow oligarchy, like those in the other cities of the Spartan alliance, was in fact a continuation of the war, and it was the settlement between the Athenian political parties that finally established peace.

The last five books of the *Hellenica* have no such unity of theme and do not attempt a continuous narrative, season by season. Continuity is broken at the very beginning of book 3, where a gap of nearly four years between the reestablishment of the Athenian democracy and the outbreak of war between Sparta and Persia in Asia Minor is inadequately bridged by a paragraph referring to Cyrus' rebellion and the account of it that has already been published by "Themistogenes of Syracuse"—probably a pseudonym used by Xenophon himself. The gap may also indicate that books 1 and 2 were written many years earlier than books 3 through 8. Xenophon does not offer any account of affairs in European Greece at this point, and confines himself to the war in Asia, where he goes into considerable detail on the intrigues of satraps and the movements of Spartan generals. In these events he was himself playing a considerable part, though he mentions himself only once (*Hellenica* 3.2.7), and then not by name but as "the commander of the Cyreans," the survivors of Cyrus' mercenaries who had finally been brought over as a body into the Spartan service. In fact, Xenophon is not giving us Hellenic history so much as a memorial of his times.

In 396 B.C. the new king of Sparta, Agesilaus, arrived in Asia to take personal command of the war. Xenophon prepares us for his arrival by describing (*Hellenica* 3.2.21–3.3.11) the last campaigns of King Agis, his brother and predecessor, the intrigues that led to Agesilaus' succession, and a dangerous conspiracy among the underprivileged, who formed the great majority of the Spartan population. This narrative provides valuable evidence to the modern historian interested in the social order of ancient Sparta or the nature of the league through which the Spartans at this time controlled their allies. But Xenophon does not pause to examine these topics analytically; he merely sets down his story, as he might have heard it from the officers who had come out with Agesilaus, or from the king himself.

For with the entry of Agesilaus into the story, fresh considerations arise, affecting our estimate of Xenophon's honesty as a historian and honor as a person. We know that he continued in the Spartan service during the two years that the king remained in Asia, though he was superseded by a Spartan as commander of the Cyreans in 395 B.C., if not earlier (*Hellenica* 3.4.20). He became the king's personal friend and accompanied him in 394, when Agesilaus was recalled to Europe with his army to face the coalition of states that had been formed with Persian help to try to break the domination of Sparta.

Xenophon represents these states as traitors to the cause of Greek liberty, but he himself may seem to be the traitor. For in the coalition against Sparta, Athens took a leading part, and now Xenophon was fighting against his own city.

How he is to be judged depends in part on the date and circumstances of the decree of exile from Athens that we know was passed against him. One ancient version (Pausanias, 5.6.5) has it that he was banished for joining Cyrus, the deadly enemy of the Athenian democracy, and this has some support from Xenophon's own statement that Socrates warned him before the expedition that it might expose him to a political prosecution. His remark at the end of the *Anabasis* that he had "not yet" been banished also suggests that the decree followed soon afterward (*Anabasis* 3.1.5; 7.7.57).

But Diogenes Laertius says (2.51–52) that Xenophon, after joining Agesilaus in Asia, conveying to him the mercenary Cyreans and winning his friendship, was banished from Athens on a charge of supporting Sparta. While this is clearly incorrect, as Agesilaus was not yet in Asia, or even king, when Xenophon entered the Spartan service, it does leave us in doubt whether in 394 B.C., when he accompanied Agesilaus to Europe, he was an Athenian citizen in good standing who marched against his city for the sake of the king's friendship and the material rewards that went with it, or a stateless man bearing arms against the city that had banished him, put Socrates to death, and crippled the efforts of Sparta against the Persians, the common enemy of Greece.

With this question is bound up that of Xenophon's honesty as a historian. At some time after 394 B.C., he was settled by the Spartans on a large estate at Scillus near Olympia in territory liberated from Elis, and here he remained until he was expelled during the disturbance that followed the defeat of Sparta by the Thebans at Leuctra in 371 B.C. The account of this period in the *Hellenica*, written from the Spartan viewpoint, gives great prominence to the doings of Agesilaus and his relations and omits completely matters of great importance—the revival of the Athenian naval alliance; the victory of the Athenian fleet off Naxos; and the early careers of Epaminondas and Pelopidas, the Theban soldiers and statesmen who eventually broke the Spartan power. It has been maintained that these omissions are deliberate and dishonest, that Xenophon was attempting not history but propaganda.

This accusation can be met in part with excuses; in an age in which the transmission of news was so casual and accidental that Athenians first learned of the destruction of their great armament in Sicily from a chance visitor to a barber shop, how could Xenophon, managing his estate at Scillus, learn what was going on in the world? The appearance of an Athenian fleet off the west coast of the Peloponnesus (*Hellenica* 6.2.27–32) no doubt roused the country as far inland as Scillus, but for the most part he would have been collecting information from his friends—Spartans of Agesilaus' own circle or like-minded aristocrats from other Peloponnesian cities, perhaps when they visited Scillus on their way to the Olympic festival, perhaps when he himself traveled to Sparta, where his sons were being educated.

However, the omissions continue even after the battle of Leuctra, when Xenophon had escaped to Corinth (Diogenes Laertius, 2.53) and was certainly once more in close touch with Athens. (The decree of banishment against him was repealed; he sent his sons to serve in the Athenian army; his pamphlets *On Revenues* and *The Cavalry Commander* give advice on various aspects of Athenian financial and military policy at the time.) But the viewpoint of the *Hellenica* is still Spartan; Xenophon does discuss, not without admiration, Epaminondas' conduct of his last campaigns in the Peloponnesus (*Hellenica* 7.1.41–42; 7.5.4–27), but he does not revise his account of the battle of Leuctra in order to give Epaminondas the credit. Nor does he describe the Theban statesman's greatest achievements—the liberation of Messenia from Sparta and the foundation in the heart of Messenia and at Megalopolis in

southern Arcadia of great fortress-cities, designed to confine Spartan power permanently to Lacedaemon. Messenia and Megalopolis do appear as independent cities and allies to Thebes (*Hellenica* 7.5.5), but if we had no other source of information than Xenophon, we should be left guessing and reading between the lines. On the other hand, he describes in detail for us a nonevent—a battle that was never fought because Agesilaus extracted his army with great skill from a difficult position (*Hellenica* 6.5.15–21).

This affair is, no doubt, described not merely to illustrate the king's coolness and skill but as a practical example worthy of study by the would-be tactician. To provide examples was perhaps, in Xenophon's eyes, the main purpose of history, and of course moral examples mattered even more than practical ones. It is Xenophon's moral examples that prove he was not setting out to write an apology for Agesilaus and the Spartans.

Among the worst crimes of the Spartans during their period of power was the treacherous seizure, in time of peace, of the Cadmea, the citadel of Thebes. The officer responsible had disobeyed orders to march to Olynthus, and the home authorities had been about to discipline him, when Agesilaus directed them to act on the old law that justice required the punishment of conduct prejudicial to Spartan interests but initiative was permissible for the good of the state. Not only did the Spartans keep possession of the Cadmea and install a puppet government in Thebes; they put to death Ismenias, their chief opponent in the city (*Hellenica* 5.2.25–36).

Xenophon tells all this without comment. But when he comes to tell of the liberation of Thebes he begins his story with the observation that

One could show by many examples, from Greek history as well as from that of foreign nations, that the gods do not overlook impious or sacrilegious men. Now I shall tell the present instance. For the Lacedaemonians, after swearing to leave the other cities independent, seized the citadel of Thebes. And they were punished by none other than the men whom they had wronged, they who had never been conquered in past history by anyone at all. As for the Thebans who brought them into the citadel and had wanted to enslave their city to the Lacedaemonians so as to become tyrants themselves, to overthrow their government required no more than seven of the exiles.

(*Hellenica* 5.4.1)

The man who wrote this was no Spartan propagandist. As for the charge that Xenophon deliberately omits from the *Hellenica* things that might have distressed his Spartan friends, it is significant that he does include several important facts about the career of Agesilaus that he omits from his *Life*. For example, after the liberation of Thebes in 378 B.C., the Spartans continued to hold several neighboring towns, and Sphodrias, military commander at Thespiae, attempted to seize the Piraeus by a night march, though Athens was at peace with Sparta. His humiliating failure left him without even the defense that his treachery had benefited Sparta. But he was saved because his son Cleonymus was the beloved of Archidamus, the son of Agesilaus. Xenophon reports the affair at some length in the *Hellenica* (5.4.20–33) but leaves it out of the *Agesilaus*, in which he tries to present a wholly favorable picture of the king's character.

Further complicated questions about Xenophon's truthfulness in dealing with Agesilaus, his memory of events that happened long before he wrote his account of them, and the amount of information that he possessed in the first place were raised at the beginning of this century by the discovery of a considerable fragment of a historical work now known as the *Hellenica Oxyrhynchia*. It has proved impossible to determine the identity of the author, but he was in all probability Xenophon's contemporary and, like him, the author of a history of Greece that began where Thucydides left off. Even the fragment of his work that survives gives valuable information, previously quite

unknown, about the political organization of Boeotia, and it seems clear that the author was much better informed than Xenophon about what was happening in European Greece from 401 to 394 B.C., when Xenophon was campaigning with the Spartans in Asia Minor. But the fragment also contains the account of an event that Xenophon does record and that he ought to have understood very well—the victory of Agesilaus at Sardis in 395, which finally broke the power of Xenophon's old enemy Tissaphernes. Xenophon's account of the affair (*Hellenica* 3.4.20–24)—an encounter action in which the king's army, marching on Sardis from Ephesus, routed the Persian cavalry—was, until the new historian was discovered, generally accepted. Diodorus Siculus (14.80) tells a totally different story, containing geographical details that at first sight appear authentic but lead to contradictions when they are examined closely, and describing how Agesilaus trapped the whole Persian army between his main force and a detachment set in ambush. This was dismissed as an elaborate concoction, until the essentials of the same tale, shorn of some of its extravagances, were found in the *Hellenica Oxyrhynchia*. Since then, many scholars have felt that Xenophon was discredited. He was no longer in command of the Cyreans; therefore, it is argued, he was not present at the battle, learned nothing from the secretive Spartans about what really happened, and made up a story to magnify the reputation of his friend Agesilaus. But quite aside from the fact that it is the other version that magnifies the king's victory, it seems most implausible that Xenophon, who, whether he fought in the battle or not, was with the army both before and afterward, never learned what happened. His story may therefore be accepted and the other perhaps accounted for as the invention of a man who knew little more about the battle than that it had been won and invented a tale to illustrate his own theories on the proper tactics for Greeks against Persians.

To sum up, Xenophon as a historian seems essentially truthful, though sometimes forgetful or careless; biased not so much because he deliberately wrote Spartan propaganda, but because he did not seek out balanced sources of information; unable to discover any large pattern in the events that he records, but valuing history as a guide to conduct, both practical and moral. Yet the virtues that Xenophon admired, above all in Sparta, proved to be illusions. In 404 B.C. the Spartan fleet sailed into the Piraeus, and its fortifications were demolished to the music of flutes, while men thought that this day was the beginning of freedom for Greece (*Hellenica* 2.2.23). In 362 the great battle of Mantinea, contrary to all men's expectations, resolved nothing but left Greece in worse confusion than before (*Hellenica* 7.5.26–27). In between, the "best people" throughout Greece had lost both political standing and respect as men of honor, and Xenophon did not know how it had come about.

THE COUNTRY GENTLEMAN

In the *Anabasis* (5.3.6–13), Xenophon gives us a passing glimpse of life on the estate at Scillus near Olympia, where he was settled by the Spartans after his return from Asia with Agesilaus. He tells how he laid out the monies set aside from the plunder of the Cyreans as a dedication to the goddess Artemis, and he carefully describes her temple and statue, which reflected, as far as their petty scale and rustic materials allowed, the great temple of Ephesus and the annual festival in her honor. Here the whole neighorhood gathered to feast on the wheat and barley, wine and animal sacrifices that "the Goddess provided" by means of a tithe paid from the produce of land that Xenophon had purchased in her name. Here, too, the sons of Xenophon and his neighbors brought game, "some from the holy ground itself, and some from Pholoe, boar, and fallow-deer and red-deer."

This pleasant mixture of rustic sports and festivals may reflect also the way of life that Xenophon would have enjoyed on his family's estates outside Athens, had it not been for the Peloponnesian War. The life of the Athenian country gentleman, as it ought to have been, is described in the longest and in some ways the most interesting of Xenophon's Socratic dialogues, the *Oeconomicus*.

The abrupt beginning of the work suggests that it was originally conceived as no more than a continuation of the *Memorabilia*, a brief dialogue on household management between Socrates and his young friend Critobulus, who was to be shown how to keep his expenses within bounds and reminded at the same time of the Socratic lesson that no man is free who is the servant of his own desires. But as the subject developed, Xenophon perhaps found himself being carried away by his own love of country life, which hardened men's bodies for the service of their country while supplying them not merely with the necessities but the luxuries of life; which taught piety and justice; and whose amenities and rustic festivals offered the most delightful existence, not to the countryman alone but to all his family (*Oeconomicus* 5).

Here, if anywhere, Xenophon seems to be using Socrates as a mouthpiece for his own sentiments. (Plato tells us—*Phaedrus* 230—that the real Socrates was a lover of the town.) Indeed, by making Socrates, whom he never saw again after his departure for Asia, discuss the virtues of the younger Cyrus as manifested down to the day of Cyrus' death (*Oeconomicus* 4.18–19), Xenophon shows quite clearly that he did not hear this dialogue, as he claims in its opening words. But the notion of describing the ideal life of a large landed proprietor evidently pleased him and if Socrates was clearly the wrong man to do it, he could present Socrates interrogating a representative of the country gentry, as he had interrogated representatives of other classes and occupations.

But the Socrates of the *Oeconomicus* is not the Socrates of Plato's *Apology* (21e–22c). He does not expose the lack of universal wisdom that underlies skill in one particular craft. He does not seek to show that Ischomachus, whose name he has heard on all lips as that of the perfect gentleman (*Oeconomicus* 6.17), is pompous, self-satisfied, and not as clever as he thinks he is. On the contrary, he listens attentively and approvingly to all that Ischomachus tells him, answers instead of asking the questions in a short Socratic dialogue, and thereby discovers that he knew all along such important secrets of agriculture as the right season to plow and the proper depth at which to set fruit trees (*Oeconomicus* 16–19).

But we are not let very deeply into these secrets. The perfect gentleman is no field laborer. When Socrates meets him first (*Oeconomicus* 7.1–3) he is sitting in the stoa of Zeus Eleutherios at leisure, but only because some acquaintances have missed an appointment. Almost his first words make it clear that he is one of the richest class of citizens upon whom the heaviest burden of public service is laid, and though he spends his time out-of-doors, leaving the management of his house to his wife, and prides himself on hardening his body by activity in the open air, he takes his exercise by riding out from town to his estate, by practicing martial horsemanship once he gets there, and by jogging home again. The actual labor of the fields is performed by slaves, whose work he supervises and corrects—and even this duty, in view of the master's political activities, has to be entrusted largely to overseers chosen for honesty, knowledge of their business, and above all for power of command. For Ischomachus (and certainly his sentiments are those of Xenophon, the retired general officer) leadership is the most important aspect of "household management" (*Oeconomicus* 13.6–12). Men—even slaves, whose training would seem to be like that of animals—are not like horses or dogs who can be taught only by punishing them when they act against their master's will and rewarding them by some immediate gratification when they please him. Men can be persuaded with words or won by praise or by such rewards as the gift of better cloaks and shoes to those who do their duty properly. "Some natures hunger for praise no less than others do for food and drink," says Ischomachus. But, if he does not rule his estate with the harsh discipline of a Clearchus, neither does he fall into the error of Proxenus, but is quite ready to punish his overseers if they are won by favor or flattery to reward undeserving men.

Still more interesting than Ischomachus' account of his own activities is the description that precedes it (*Oeconomicus* 7.14–10.13) of how he received his wife from her parents when she was not yet fifteen years old, disciplined to control her bodily appetites but otherwise knowing no more than how to produce a cloak out of a given weight of wool. He tells how he has trained her to become the "queen bee"—mistress in fact as well as in name of his whole establishment, with its large staff of servants and quantities of different stores whose expenditure must be carefully regulated so that a year's supply is not consumed in a month. He shows her round the great house, built for comfort and convenience rather than ostentation, insisting on the importance of order and regularity: a place for everything and everything in its place, so that never again will she have to blush and bite her lips in mortification when her husband asks for something that she cannot find on the spot. The point is characteristically illustrated by comparisons between well- and ill-managed households and between armies in disorder and those that are properly marshaled.

Ischomachus insists that his wife and he himself are equal partners in their joint-stock enterprise, although the monetary value of the dowry that she has brought to him is obviously less than that of his estate. He makes it clear that "mother told me to be modest" does not sum up the whole duty of woman; she is to be his active partner. Once again, leadership in directing a large household of servants forms the most important part of her duties. She is to be helped, in her inexperience, by a carefully chosen housekeeper, but she is not simply to delegate authority to the senior servant. And she must see to the health and welfare of the slaves as well as to the performance of their duties; nursing the sick may be an unpleasant task, her husband suggests, but she replies that, if their gratitude helps to attach them to their masters, it will be pleasant indeed.

But if husband and wife are equal partners, their activities are still kept separate, as the gods and human law prescribe. Socrates may praise the wife's "masculine intelligence," as demonstrated by her wish to safeguard her husband's interests and property (*Oeconomicus* 10.1), but Ischomachus insists on the distinction between male and female. Their physical differences are designed for the perpetuation of the race and for the provision of supporters in the parents' old age; and since humans, unlike the beasts of the field, need shelter as well as provisions brought in from outdoors, woman is naturally fitted for the home and man for the open air.

Has Ischomachus nothing to say about "love" in any of the senses in which we use the word? The gratification of sexual passion was not one of the stated reasons for which "I took you, and your parents gave you to me" (*Oeconomicus* 7.10), and Ischomachus does not violate the rule that no man is free who is a slave to his own desires. He does allow that, as the gods have made the animals of each kind pleasant to each other, so mankind finds most pleasure in the pure human body, but this observation forms part of a severe rebuke to his wife after he has caught her using cosmetics—a cheat, he says, no less shameful than if he were to use false coins to deceive her. And though he goes on to recommend exercise to her as the way to true beauty, there is no suggestion that she should share in any of his recreations. She is to "stand up to the loom like a mistress," to bustle around the house seeing that all is in order, to shake out and fold the blankets. He offers her not "romance," but the hope that by showing herself better than her husband in her share of their partnership, she may eventually make him her servant, with the knowledge (*Oeconomicus* 7.37) that her honor, stemming not from her youthful charms but from her virtues, will increase with her advancing years.

If we compare all this with the liberated communal life of Plato's *Republic*, Xenophon appears a typically narrow-minded, selfish, insensitive male traditionalist. Yet Xenophon is not giving us his view of what woman's life should ideally be in some imaginary perfect state, but of the best possible marriage given the actual conditions of Athenian society. It is notable that he praises, in the *Constitution of the Lacedaemonians* (1.3 ff.), the free life of Spartan girls (from a eugenic, not a romantic, standpoint). Still more remarkable are two tales of married love woven into the *Cyropaedia*, which strengthen its position as the ancestor of the romantic novel, not merely an instructional handbook disguised as fiction. The love story of the virtuous Panthea ends tragically with her suicide over the body of her husband, who has fallen heroically in battle. The other romantic heroine, the wife of Tigranes, prince of Armenia, is not even named, but her husband declares his readiness to ransom her "with his own soul" when the Armenian royal family is captured by Cyrus; and, after Cyrus has magnanimously released the captives, she alone has nothing to say about his splendid figure, because she has seen nobody but "the man who said he would give his own soul to ransom me from slavery" (*Cyropaedia* 3.1.35–41).

Finally, one cannot take leave of Xenophon without a tribute to his *Art of Horsemanship*, which is still read by modern horsemen, not merely as a historical curiosity but as a work of genuine though limited practical value. The essential principle, that the horse is to be trained by immediate reward when he acts according to his rider's wishes and immediate punishment when he misbehaves, is still repeated by modern riding masters. Xenophon's insistence that horses and humans must be brought to understand, not compelled by force, and that one should never lose one's temper with animals or with children, has more value than much that has been written about education in the past 2,500 years.

What else has Xenophon to offer the modern world? Scrupulous piety toward long-discarded gods seems ridiculous, if it is not dismissed as a hypocritical sham. Self-control is scorned as inhibition, and we have seen too much of "the big wars that make ambition virtue" to regard the soldier as the perfection of manly virtue. Modern scholars too often dismiss Xenophon with contempt; or run to the other extreme and find hidden in his philosophical writings their own insights; or, because they themselves have seen through Ischomachus or Agesilaus, detect a subtle irony in Xenophon's treatment of these characters. It seems better to accept him at face value, not as a profound metaphysician or master of political theory, but as that obsolete but not ignoble character, "an officer and a gentleman."

Selected Bibliography

TEXTS AND TRANSLATIONS

Cyropaedia. Translated by W. Miller. New York and London, 1914.

Hellenica and *Anabasis*. Translated by C. L. Brownson. Cambridge, Mass., and London, 1947–1950.

Memorabilia and *Oeconomicus*. Translated by E. C. Marchant. London, 1933.

Scripta Minora. Translated by E. C. Marchant and G. W. Bowersock. London, 1925.

Symposium and *Apology*. Translated by O. J. Todd. London, 1922.

Xenophon. 7 vols. Cambridge, Mass., 1914–1968. Loeb Classical Library. Greek text with English translation; the standard.

Xenophontis opera omnia, edited by E. C. Marchant. 5 vols. Oxford, 1900–1920. The standard text.

GENERAL CRITICAL STUDIES

Anderson, J. K. *Xenophon*. London, 1974.

Breitenbach, H. R. "Xenophon." In A. F. Pauly and G. Wissowa, eds., *Realencyclopädie*. Vol. 9 A 2, cols. 1567–2052. Stuttgart, 1967.

———. *Xenophon von Athen*. Stuttgart, 1966. Reprint of the above.

Delebecque, E. *Essai sur la vie de Xénophon*. Paris, 1957.

Higgins, W. E. *Xenophon the Athenian: The Problem of the Individual and the Society of the Polis*. Albany, N.Y., 1977.

Nickel, R. *Xenophon*. Darmstadt, 1979.

CRITICAL STUDIES OF INDIVIDUAL WORKS

HELLENICA

Anderson, J. K. *Military Theory and Practice in the Age of Xenophon*. Berkeley and Los Angeles, 1969.

———. "The Battle of Sardis in 395 B.C." *California Studies in Classical Antiquity* 7:27–54 (1974).

Breitenbach, H. R. "Hellenica Oxyrhynchia." In A. F. Pauly and G. Wissowa, eds., *Realencyclopädie*. Supplement 12, cols. 393–395. Stuttgart, 1970.

Bringmann, K. "Xenophon's *Hellenika* and *Agesilaos*: zu ihrer Entstehungsweise und Datierung." *Gymnasium* 78 (1971).

Bruce, I. A. F. *An Historical Commentary on the Hellenica Oxyrhynchia*. Cambridge, 1967.

Henry, W. P. *Greek Historical Writing: A Historiographical Essay Based on Xenophon's Hellenika*. Chicago, 1967.

Krafft, P. "Vier Beispiele des Xenophontischen in Xenophons *Hellenica*." *Rheinisches Museum* 110:103–150 (1967).

Sordi, M. "I caratteri dell'opera storiografica di Senofonte nelle Elleniche." *Athenaeum* 28:3–53 (1950) and 29:273–348 (1951).

Warner, R. *Xenophon: History of My Times*. Harmondsworth, 1966.

Westlake, H. D. "Individuals in Xenophon's *Hellenica*." *Bulletin of the John Rylands Library* 49:246 ff. (1966).

MEMORABILIA

Fritz, K. von. "Das erste Kapitel des zweiten Buches von Xenophons Memorabilien und die Philosophie des Aristipp von Kyrene." *Hermes* 93:257–279 (1965).

Gigon, O. *Kommentar zum ersten Buch von Xenophons Memorabilien*. Basel, 1953.

———. *Kommentar zum zweiten Buch von Xenophons Memorabilien*. Basel, 1956.

Guthrie, W. K. C. *A History of Greek Philosophy*. Vol. 3. Cambridge, 1968. Especially pp. 333–348.

Luccioni, J. *Xénophon et la Socratisme*. Paris, 1953.

Strauss, L. *Xenophon's Socrates*. Ithaca, N.Y., 1972.

XENOPHON

OECONOMICUS

Erbse, H. "Sokrates und die Frauen." *Gymnasium* 73:201–220 (1966).

Gil, J. *Jenofonte: Economico.* Madrid, 1967.

Novo, S. T. *Economica ed Etica nell'Economico di Senofonte.* Torino, 1968.

Strauss, L. *Xenophon's Socratic Discourse: An Interpretation of the Oeconomicus.* Ithaca, N.Y., 1970.

ANABASIS

Barnett, R. D. "Xenophon and the Wall of Media." *Journal of Hellenic Studies* 83:1–26 (1963).

Erbse, H. "Xenophons Anabasis." *Gymnasium* 73:485–505 (1966).

Kromayer, J. *Antike Schlachtfelder.* Vol. 4. Berlin, 1924–1931. Pp. 223 ff.

Lendle, O. "Der Bericht Xenophons uber die Schlacht bei Kunaxa." *Gymnasium* 73:429–452 (1966).

Nussbaum, G. B. *The Ten Thousand: A Study in the Social Organization and Action in Xenophon's Anabasis.* Leiden, 1967.

Parke, H. W. *Greek Mercenary Soldiers from the Earliest Times to the Battle of Ipsus.* Oxford, 1933.

Rouse, W. H. D. *The March Up Country.* Ann Arbor, 1958. English translation.

CONSTITUTION OF THE LACEDAEMONIANS

Momigliano, A. "Per l'unita logica della *Lakedaimonion Politeia* di Senofonte." *Rivista di Filologia* e *d'Istruzione Classica* 14 fasc. 2:170–173 (1936). Reprinted in *Storia e Letteratura* 108: 341–345 (1966).

HIPPARCHICUS

Delebecque, E. *Xénophon: le commandant de la cavalerie.* Paris, 1973.

ART OF HORSEMANSHIP

Anderson, J. K. "Notes on Some Points in Xenophon's *Peri Hippikes.*" *Journal of Hellenic Studies* 80:1–9 (1960).

———. *Ancient Greek Horsemanship.* Berkeley and Los Angeles, 1961.

Delebecque, E. *Xénophon: de l'art equestre.* Paris, 1950.

———. *Xénophon: de l'art equestre.* Paris, 1978.

Morgan, M. H. *Xenophon: The Art of Horsemanship.* London, 1894. Reprinted London, 1962.

Widdra, K. *Xenophontis de re equestri.* Leipzig, 1964.

CYNEGETICUS

Delebecque, E. *Xénophon: l'art de la chasse.* Paris, 1970.

Hull, D. B. *Hounds and Hunting in Ancient Greece.* Chicago, 1964.

ON REVENUES

Gauthier, P. *Un commentaire historique des Poroi de Xénophon.* Geneva and Paris, 1976.

J. K. ANDERSON

PLATO

(428–348 B.C.)

INTRODUCTION

THE WRITINGS OF Plato are known mainly through medieval manuscripts, the oldest of which are dated to the ninth century. These contain (1) the *Defense of Socrates*, (2) thirty-four dialogues of varying length, (3) thirteen letters, and (4) seven smaller works written after the fashion of Plato but accepted by no one as his.

The titles of the dialogues are taken mostly from one of the major interlocutors or from the content (the *Statesman*, the *Laws*) and probably originated in Plato's time, though we cannot say if they are his. Five to ten of the dialogues are thought by many scholars to be spurious for reasons of style and content, and the weight of opinion holds that most, if not all, of the letters were not written by Plato, although there is genuine and precious biographical information in the seventh letter. What the manuscripts contain is all that Plato committed to writing. We know that he lectured in the Academy, the school he founded, but we know almost nothing about the relationship between his lecturing and his writing. Thus speculation on possible unwritten doctrines of Plato is fruitless. The text of Plato is unusually well preserved, and the preservation was assisted by the strong school-traditions of Platonism in Athens (the Academy lasted over 900 years), Alexandria, and Constantinople.

The unusual and universal form of citation used in referring to passages (such as *Republic* 464e1–5) is taken from the sixteenth-century printed edition of Henri d'Etienne (in Latin, Henricus Stephanus): the column in a Stephanus page was divided into five sections (a through e), with approximately the same number of lines in each section.

LIFE AND BACKGROUND

A native of Athens, Plato (428 –348 B.C.) was born into an aristocratic family and could trace his lineage back through Solon, the poet and lawgiver of the sixth century, to the much earlier period when Athens was ruled by kings. This aristocratic background colored, if it did not determine, his attitude toward social questions. Of most details of his life we are very poorly informed, and the dialogues could hardly be less autobiographical. After the death of Socrates in 399, Plato left Athens to travel. He made three trips to the court of the tyrant of Syracuse in Sicily. On one of these trips he apparently tried to practice some of his theories of education on the tyrant's son—with singular lack of success. He instituted his school in Athens, the Academy, apparently in the 380's, and spent the rest of his life teaching and writing.

Although aristocratic birth and connections were no longer a prerequisite for a political career, they were still an advantage. It is stated in the seventh letter that Plato once envisaged such a career with some eagerness. An opportunity came with the second oligarchic revolution in the last decade of the fifth century, when many of the oligarchs (some of whom are characters in the dialogues) were his friends and relatives. They invited him to join them, but he was repelled by their illegal excesses. Hardly more attractive were the political conditions when the democracy was restored, for it was this government that put to death Socrates, whom, Plato said, "I would hardly be ashamed to call the most just man of the time." One suspects that Plato would not have been very comfortable in political life. He was not impressed with the quality of contemporary politicians and was far too radical an intellectual critic of Greek—not only Athenian—society. His contributions to politics were his writings and the Academy: many of his students went on to political careers of varying success in Athens and other parts of the Greek world.

Plato's youth and young manhood coincided with the war that pitted Athens against Sparta and involved most of the Greek world from Sicily on one side to Asia Minor on the other. As described by the historian Thucydides, the effects of the war were convulsive. It left Athens without its empire (though it retained intellectual leadership of Greece), with a population reduced by battle and recurrent plague, and with an increasingly radical democracy, itself shaken by two short-lived oligarchic revolutions in 411 and 404 B.C. This period also saw the culmination of the long and brilliant development of tragedy and comedy by Sophocles, Euripides, and Aristophanes. Dramatic productions continued, but the quality declined severely. As an intellectual vehicle, poetry gave way to the relatively new medium of prose in the genres of historiography, public oratory, and philosophy.

Of prime importance was the revolution that took place in education. What corresponded to precollege education is well described in a passage from Plato's *Protagoras*:

As soon as a child understands what is said to him, his nurse, mother, tutor, and his father him-self strive to make him as good as possible, teaching him with every word and deed, and pointing out that this is just, this unjust, this is noble, this shameful, this is holy, this unholy, and "do these things," "don't do those things." If the child obeys willingly, fine; if not, they treat him like a bent and twisted piece of wood and straighten him out with threats and beatings. Afterward they send him to teachers who are instructed to pay much more attention to the children's good behavior than to teaching them letters or musical instruments. The teachers attend to this, and when the children learn letters and begin to understand the written word, as they already understand the spoken, they provide at their desks the works of good poets to read, and compel them to learn them by heart: these contain many admonitions, many complimentary descriptions and encomia of good men of old, so that the child in emulation may imitate and desire to become like them. The music teachers in turn do the same; their concern is controlled behavior and that the young don't do wrong. In addition, when they learn to play an instrument, they are taught the works of other good writers, lyric poets, which are set to music. The teachers compel the students to adapt and internalize the rhythms and the harmonies so that they become more gentle; by becoming more graceful and well adjusted, they will be more useful members of society in speaking and acting. A person needs these qualities throughout his life.

In addition to this, they send the children to the physical trainer, so that they can more skillfully follow the directions of the mind with their bodies in better physical shape and so that they won't be forced to slack off in battle or in other activities because of poor physical condition.

The people who enjoy this type of education are those who have the greatest opportunity to do so (that is, the wealthier) and their sons; these are the pupils who enter school at the earliest age and are the last to leave. After they finish their schooling, it is the turn of the state, and the state compels them to learn the laws and to live according to the model they impose.

(325c)

The passage reflects conditions that were slightly more advanced than those of the fifth century. Evidence for the earlier period is scanty, but the process then seems to have been even more clearly restricted to aristocratic families, more an informal method of association than formal instruction, intended to produce the "gentleman" skilled in battle and sport, especially in hunting and horse racing. Literacy became fairly widespread only in the fourth century. The schooling Plato describes was clearly one of transmitting the values of family and society. It was not analytical nor given to criticism of these values; it was not concerned with abstract thought; it was not, in a word, particularly intellectual.

The assumptions of this kind of education were shaken with the advent of a group of professional educators, the Sophists (a term that did not originally have the pejorative connotation it later gained). Most of these were non-Athenians who traveled from town to town in search of pupils whom they would instruct for a fee. They gave public lectures to advertise their skills, and their form of instruction also included lecturing to small groups in private homes or public buildings. Some taught particular skills that were not subjects of instruction in the kinds of schools Plato describes in his *Protagoras*, or that were the same subjects on a higher level: these included arithmetical calculation, geometry, astronomy, painting, and criticism of literature.

Those Sophists of greater ability made wider claims. According to Plato (*Protagoras* 318e), the Sophist Protagoras taught "intelligent planning of one's personal affairs, so that a man could manage his household most efficiently, and of public affairs, so that he could become most effective in speech and action in the political arena." This latter goal was based on an ability to speak and argue persuasively, a prerequisite for success under a democratic form of government.

But more was involved than the ability to persuade one's fellows on a practical level, and it is difficult to exaggerate the Athenians' fascination with the powers of speech (*logos*) and the problems of language at this period. When the Greeks came into contact with other societies through trade and travel, they noted the phenomenon of different customs in various parts of the world, customs in many cases very

different from their own. This observation inevitably raised the question of the relative superiority of individual customs and led to the intellectual antithesis of *nomos* (custom/law) and *physis* (nature). Most simply put, the problem raised in the antithesis is: Are things the way they are purely by conventional agreement or do they have a reality rooted in nature? The antithesis was relevant to different aspects of thought and action and produced various intellectual stands. In religion, for instance, what most Greeks knew about their gods they had learned from their poets, beginning with Homer. But Homer's portrayal of the gods had long been criticized. In the sixth century B.C. the Ionian Xenophanes had said that Homer and Hesiod ascribed to the gods actions—theft, adultery, deceit—that are held reprehensible among men. He also said that if oxen, horses, and lions had hands and could make portraits and statues as humans do, their representations of the gods would resemble oxen, horses, and lions. Further, he said, Ethiopians believe that their gods are snub-nosed and black-skinned, while people in northern Greece have gods with red hair and blue eyes. These statements suggest that there is a gap between the reality and the language used to describe that reality. They can further lead to the agnosticism of Protagoras, who said, "Of the gods I cannot know that they exist or that they do not exist, nor what appearance they have. There are many things that prevent this knowledge, including lack of clarity and the shortness of human life" (Diogenes Laertius, 9.51). The next state is atheism, where poetic functions of the gods (Zeus sends thunder and lightning) are given natural or scientific explanations.

This kind of skepticism can become almost pervasive. What is the relationship between language and the things language describes? If people can use various languages to speak of the same thing, which language, if any, best describes the thing? Is all language totally conventional? Do we simply agree to use certain terms, implicitly agreeing that the language we use tells us nothing objective about the thing it purports to describe?

The effects of this kind of skepticism on language in society are almost predictable. Let us consider democratic government. In theory, it was based on human equality and the freedom to live as one wished. In Greek practice, it was the rule of the majority (including the poorer segment of the population), exercised through a popular assembly. Yet equality did not include everybody, for slavery was an integral component of society. Nor are people equal by nature; some are born with more talent, wealth, and strength than others. Is it fair to treat such people the same way as the less talented? In a democratic society, statute law exists to protect the weaker against being the victims of force. Yet is not democratic government, based on the power of the majority, also implicitly based on (the threat of) force?

Some theorists tried to bridge the gap between *nomos* and *physis* by appealing to conditions of the animal world, in which the survival of the fittest is the rule. This criterion was applied to international relations, in which, so it was claimed, it is a law of nature that the strong hold sway over the weaker. Yet if the same criterion is applied internally to a society, it leads to a tyranny or an oligarchy, and in practice to *stasis*, civil war.

These were some of the perceived effects of the gap between language and the reality it purported to describe, and they were issues that Plato constantly returned to. The gap, he came at some point to realize, could not be bridged unless the whole question of the real was treated in a fashion less dependent on ordinary language than it had been. This radical step— the so-called theory of Ideas—he arrived at only after a "Socratic" period in which he used the central figure of Socrates to show that normal and accepted attempts to describe reality were defective.

SOCRATES

The Sophists made another wide claim, that *aretē*—a term usually translated as "virtue" or "excellence," and referring to that congeries of human qualities that leads to success in the world—was something that could be taught by formal instruction rather than something that was inborn, to be nourished and developed in an aristocratic environment. This claim can serve as a convenient introduction to the man who was most influential in shaping Plato's philosophical career.

According to a biographical passage in *Phaedo* (96), Socrates began his intellectual career within an older tradition of philosophizing: natural science. His particular slant was to search for the causes of natural phenomena and the explanation of how things came to be as they are. Contemporary theories, especially those involving mechanistic explanations, could give no satisfactory answer to this teleological question. How long this scientific interest lasted or how intense it was we cannot say. It is at least partially consistent with the portrayal of the character "Socrates" in Aristophanes' comedy *Clouds* (423 B.C.). There "Socrates" is the director of a think tank, investigating celestial phenomena and teaching rhetoric. In the *Apology* Socrates denied that his intellectual interests in any way coincided with Aristophanes' parody. The denial is certainly true of the Socrates portrayed by Plato and others of Socrates' associates whose interests were metaphysical and moral. Possibly the solution is that Socrates in the *Apology* is referring to the last twenty years of his life.

Those years were devoted to the fulfillment of what Socrates conceived to be his divine mission. At an unknown date and for unclear motives, a young friend of Socrates, Chairephon, inquired of the god Apollo at Delphi— the prophetic center of the Greek world—if there were anyone wiser than Socrates. The oracle said no. In disbelief, Socrates decided to refute the oracle by quizzing various of his fellow citizens who had reputations for wisdom or intelligence. He approached certain politicians, who he discovered, were not wise; certain poets who were less able to explain the meaning of their own works than some members of their audience and who must therefore have written by a kind of divine inspiration; and certain craftsmen who admittedly had knowledge of their own crafts and thought that this justified them in claiming to have knowledge in other and more important areas. Socrates concluded that the god meant that so-called human wisdom was almost worthless, and that he was wisest because he realized this.

He also seems to have interpreted the answer of the oracle in such a way that it led him to act as a gadfly to the people of Athens, to convince them that the assumptions on which they acted were wrong or, if not wrong, at least unexamined ("the unexamined life is not worth living") and that their usual goals in life were delusory. In the course of his trial he suggests the possibility that he might be acquitted if he stopped acting the way he had. He says:

> Gentlemen of Athens, I am extremely fond of you, but I will obey the god rather than you. And, so long as I am able and there is breath in me, I will not stop playing my part in the pursuit of wisdom, encouraging you and pointing out to each of you with whom I come in contact, saying the kinds of things I usually say: "My dear sir, you are an Athenian, living in a city that is very great and most renowned for its wisdom and strength. Are you not ashamed to be concerned only with getting as much money as possible and reputation and honor, and not to be concerned or even to care about things of the mind and truth and making your soul as good as possible?" If one of you disputes this and claims to be so concerned, I will not go off and let him be right away, but I will ask him questions and examine him and dispute him. If he does not seem to me to possess virtue (arete), but claims to, I will reproach him for putting a very low value on things that are worth the most and a higher value on things that are rather insignificant.
>
> (Apology 29d)

The reaction to Socrates was varied. To some, especially the young, it was electric. Plato puts these words in the mouth of the brilliant Alcibiades at a drinking party:

> Whenever anyone, man, woman or youth, listens to you, we are gripped and our minds are dazzled. If I weren't to seem absolutely blotto to you, gentlemen, I would have taken an oath about the kind of reaction to him I have had and continue to have. Whenever I hear him, my heart leaps up more than an ecstatic dancer's, and the tears pour forth at his words. I see many others with the same reaction. When I listened to Pericles and other good speakers, I used to think that they spoke very well, but I never used to experience anything like this, nor was my soul thrown into turmoil, nor was I irritated at being made to feel as helpless as a slave. But this was how I was made to feel by this Marsyas [a mythical satyr], here, and I didn't think I could keep on living the same kind of life.
>
> (Symposium 215d)

Other listeners did not have the same experience. The reaction of many of the people whom Socrates questioned, and their friends, was simply hatred, and it was this hatred that must in large part have led to his death.

THE APOLOGY OF SOCRATES

In 399 B.C., Socrates was brought to trial and condemned to death by a jury of 500 of his peers. The general charge was impiety; the hardly more specific details were that Socrates corrupted the young and did not believe in the gods sanctioned by the state, but instead introduced new divinities. Much remains mysterious about the whole affair and its antecedents. There is evidence that accusations of impiety were used in the prosecutions of a few intellectuals in the fifth century, but the evidence is generally late and uninformative on details. A point relevant to Socrates is that the charge seems to have been used against some associates of the influential statesman Pericles and was doubtless intended to damage him.

Many hold that the primary impetus to the charge was Socrates' association with men like Alcibiades and Critias, who turned out to be traitors to the democracy. There is sufficient material in Plato and Xenophon to show that Socrates thought that Athenian democracy was not a particularly intelligent or efficient form of government, with many offices filled through allotment rather than through election of those most qualified, and with important decisions taken in the Assembly, the members of which had little theoretical ability to grasp many of the issues and were frequently swayed by appeals to emotion. Most of his associates (the younger ones would be thought to be his pupils) were from the upper levels of Athenian society. Many of them would have had no theoretical commitment to Athenian democracy and many again were involved in the first of the oligarchic revolutions. Add to this the natural assumption that the deeds of a pupil are the result of indoctrination by his teacher and it becomes plausible that a certain guilt by association was an important factor in the whole business.

This conclusion is somewhat supported by remarks that Plato puts in Socrates' mouth. Unlike the ordinary citizen of Athens, Socrates did not take part in public life, for he would have felt constrained to oppose the Athenian assembly or any other city's assembly if it did not act in accordance with his standards of fairness and legality, and a person who consistently opposed the assembly could not expect a long life (31e). Again, he takes pains to deny that he was anyone's teacher or that he ever formally communicated any doctrine (*mathema*: the same word Protagoras used to describe his profession), and that those who say he did are lying and slandering him.

In using Socrates' words in this way, I am implicitly assuming that there is some historical truth to Plato's work, but to what *extent* it is true is still a matter of dispute. The question is complicated by the fact that there were two other contemporary *apologiai*. One of these, by Xenophon, is extant. It is reported at second hand, is one-quarter as long as Plato's version, and has several points of similarity with Plato's. My own opinion is that the content of the *Apology* is largely faithful to the facts, but that the expression is largely Plato's own. I think that this is especially true of a large part of the speech (28b–35d) that may properly be called Socrates' *apologia pro vita sua* and that shows a degree of literary elaboration unparalleled in the rest of the work.

Socrates believed that the factors that most influenced the jurors were the personal enmities he had caused by questioning people and the prejudice that had been aroused against him by his detractors. The prejudice was of long standing. Its most irritating aspect was that the detractors were all anonymous, with one exception, a comic poet (the reference is to Aristophanes). Socrates felt that he had to speak to the prejudice, which he calls the older accusation, as well as to the specific legal indictment, the new accusation. He treats both accusations as being of a piece by a clever use of the structural device of parallelism. In 19a8–24b4, he defends himself against the earlier accusation; in 24b6–28a4, against the later. He joins the two by beginning and ending each of these sections with the same language, 19a8–b4 corresponding to 24b6–c2, and 24b3–4 to 28a3–4. He treats the earlier accusation as if it were a legal charge by taking the language of different parts of Aristophanes' comedy and presenting that language as if it made up a formal legal charge: "Socrates acts illegally and excessively by investigating subterranean and celestial phenomena, by making the weaker argument appear the stronger, and by teaching these subjects to others" (19b4). This is formally and grammatically paralleled by the actual legal charge: "Socrates acts illegally by corrupting the young and by believing not in the gods whom the state sanctions but in different new divinities" (24b8).

The purpose of this double parallelism—of language and structure—is to persuade the jurors that the legal indictment has all the truth and validity of a comic plot, and is to be taken just that seriously. When Socrates speaks to the details of the indictment, it is quite easy for him to show how baseless they are. He does this by engaging his prosecutor, Meletus, in a mini-dialogue on quite a low intellectual level of argument. He claims that Meletus brought the charge relying on the efficacy of the old prejudice (19b1); applies language used by comic poets to Meletus' procedure (24c5, 27a2, 27c6); characterizes his mode of argumentation with the curt phrase, "this is the work of a joker"

(27a6); and, in his final reference to the indictment, coins a word (*epikomoidon*) to suggest that Meletus is producing a second comedy (31d1).

What follows in the *Apology* is much more seriously intended. I suggest that Plato, in reacting against Aristophanes' depiction of Socrates as a comic character, intended to make of him quite the opposite, an epic hero. A capsule definition of epic heroism is preserved in the words of Achilles' father to his tutor, Phoenix, that he teach Achilles to be a "speaker of words and a doer of deeds" (*Iliad* 9.443); in other words, that he become effective in deliberative assembly and on the battlefield. This dichotomy came to be articulated in fifth-century thought as the antithesis between *logos* and *ergon*, word and act. Attached to the first were implications of guile, appearance, pretense; to the second, clear-cut action, reality, truth. Traditionally in Greek literature, Odysseus typified the former and Achilles the latter. In the earliest literature there are already traces of this dichotomy. The *Odyssey* (8.75) contains a reference to a quarrel in the Greek camp about the correct strategy to be followed in taking Troy. Achilles recommended the direct path of courageous force, Odysseus more devious tactics, which an ancient commentator to the passage says involved the use of *logos*. Again, in the *Iliad* (18.105–6), in a context that we will examine later, Achilles claimed that he was preeminent on the battlefield, but admitted that others were superior in the Assembly.

If it was Plato's intention to portray Socrates as a second Achilles, he was faced with a large initial problem. Apart from the fact that the societies of the Homeric war and of fifth-century Athens were very different, Socrates was quintessentially a man of words. Plato overcame this difficulty by connecting both terms of the dichotomy to Socrates' divine mission. Socrates mentions his war record and participation in three battles (28d) and says that it would have been as disgraceful for him to have left the position assigned to him in battle as to neglect the civic duty assigned him by the god. In a passage noted before (31d), he says that it was again on the instructions of the god that he did not speak in deliberative assemblies, political *logos*. He continues in this line by pointing to the two occasions when he was involved in politics and, significantly, refers to these instances as matters not of *logos* but of *ergon*. The first was when he opposed an illegal motion in the assembly, although some of those present called for his arrest. The second instance was when he opposed an assignment by the oligarchs to participate in an illegal act. He claims that he would have been executed for this refusal, had not the oligarchic regime been thrown out of power shortly thereafter.

In further developing the connection between Socrates and Achilles, Plato relies on the literary devices of association, allusion, and quotation. After he has been condemned to death, Socrates' penultimate words are concerned with the possible advantages of life after death.

> In my opinion, I would have a marvelous time in Hades, where I could meet Palamedes and Telemon's son Ajax, and any other men of old who died because of an unjust decision, comparing my experiences with theirs. (I think that would not be unpleasant.) It would be particularly pleasant to spend my efforts examining and questioning people there as I did people on earth, as to who of them is wise and who thinks he is wise but is not. How much do you think it would be worth, gentlemen of the jury, to question the men who led the great expedition to Troy, or Odysseus, or Sisyphus, or many others I could mention, male and female? I would be immensely happy if I could associate with and examine people like these.
>
> (41b)

The names are from the world of epic poetry, a world so rich in characters that we are entitled to ask why Plato focuses on these. There are two groups. The first consists of victims of injustice. Traditionally, Palamedes had been responsible for the reluctant presence of Odysseus at Troy. He was later condemned to death by the Greek host on a charge of treason; the evidence for this was a letter forged by Odysseus. Ajax, the greatest Greek warrior after Achilles, competed for Achilles' armor after his death. Details of the competition are confused in various versions, but Ajax lost and committed suicide; Odysseus won. The second group is made up of people Socrates would like to examine to see if their reputation for and claim to wisdom is true: Agamemnon, whose seizure of Achilles' war captive, Briseis, precipitated the anger of Achilles and the plot of the *Iliad*; Sisyphus, a mythical trickster who tried to cheat death (unlike Socrates, who welcomed it) and was in some versions the father of Odysseus; and Odysseus himself, whose quarrel with Achilles has been mentioned. It is clear, then, that the criterion for inclusion in the two groups is the pro-Achilles or anti-Odysseus stance illustrated by the individual characters.

This denigration of the character of Odysseus is also pointed up by the technique of literary allusion. Several scholars have noted a series of verbal parallels between the *Apology* and another work of approximately the same period and have suggested that Plato used that work as a model. The work was a speech of defense written by the Sophist Gorgias: in it the defendant was Palamedes, the prosecutor Odysseus.

The clearest link between Socrates and Achilles is effected by quotation. At 28b, Socrates replies to a hypothetical question:

Perhaps someone might say, "Are you not *ashamed*, Socrates, to have engaged in the kind of activity that in all probability will lead to your *death*?" I would reply, with all justice: "You are mistaken if you think that [a] a man from whom even minimal utility is expected should [b] have only the slightest *consideration* of the *risk of death*, and should not consider this alone when he acts, [c] whether he is acting *justly* or unjustly and whether his acts are those of a good man or a bad man. Your question shows that you think little of the demi-gods who died at Troy and particularly of Thetis' son. Faced with submitting to something *shameful*, his contempt for danger was such that when his goddess-mother spoke to him—his mind being set on killing Hector—saying something like "My son, if you avenge the

slaying of your companion Patroclus, you will *die* yourself, for," she said, "your fate is at hand, directly after Hector's." When he heard this, [1] he thought little of *death* and *danger*, [2] having a far greater fear of living [c-1] the life of a bad man and [3] not avenging his friend. "Let me die," he said, "immediately after I inflict a *just* penalty on the wrongdoer, so that I won't remain here, an object of ridicule and a burden on the earth, beside the curved ships." Do you think that he cared about *death* and *danger*?

For this is the truth of the situation, men of Athens. Wherever a man stations himself because he thinks it is best or wherever he is stationed by a superior officer, there in my opinion he must remain, and *risk* his life, showing no *consideration* of *death* or of anything else over against what is *shameful*.

(28b; italics added)

Plato begins with a brief characterization of the person under consideration: one who will be a help to his society [a]. This person is defined by two criteria, negative [b] and positive [c]. These criteria are exemplified by Achilles and Socrates. The verbal echoes (the italicized words and phrases) make it clear that the two men are to be treated as parallels, partly in the sense that Achilles is a model for Socrates, and partly in the sense that both men are acting according to the same general criteria. So much is this true that it seems fair to say that what is stated explicitly of one is implied of the other. Not to act as a bad man (c-1) is part of the criterion specifically applied to Achilles, but it is also to be understood of Socrates. To avoid committing an act that brings shame upon oneself is exemplified by both characters and is thus implicit in the positive criterion.

On a more narrowly textual level, Plato's manipulation of Homer's text is evident. The "quotations" of Thetis and Achilles are partly in the language of Homer, partly in language added by Plato. When Thetis says, "My son, if you avenge . . . ," Plato introduces Achilles' response with three clauses (marked 1, 2, 3). Only the last of these is directly relevant to Thetis' statement; the other two are dictated by the criteria of activity that Plato has set up earlier.

Some of the language Plato puts in Achilles' mouth ("inflict a just penalty on the wrongdoer") is alien to the language of Homer but, reflecting the situation in which Socrates finds himself, is part of Athenian legal terminology.

Apart from adapting the text of Homer to his own thematic demands, Plato has also changed it in two places to achieve similar ends. First, in Achilles' final words, the original Homeric text has "useless burden": the epithet has been removed, and (to preserve the demands of the meter) has been replaced by the epithet "curved," which is frequently applied to ships in Homer. Second, a Homeric expression for "sitting" has been expanded into "remain here, an object of ridicule." Although both changes have been imputed to faulty memory, they are more likely deliberate. Since Plato is attempting to establish a connection between Socrates and Achilles in the context of being useful to one's society, an epithet to the contrary effect would have been out of place. The purpose of the second change becomes clear only when it is realized that Plato is once again using literary allusion, and that the change has Sophoclean overtones. More than Aeschylus or Euripides, it was Sophocles who transferred the Homeric hero to the tragic stage, and, in the *Apology*, Sophoclean influence is occasionally detectable in the language. Of immediate relevance, it is particularly characteristic of the Sophoclean hero that he refuses to be mocked, and it is perhaps not accidental that this trait is especially marked in the plays *Ajax* and *Philoctetes*, whose heroes were both traditional enemies of Odysseus. In his last work (*Laws* 817) Plato said that the most genuine form of tragic drama was the representation of the best and noblest life, and it seems clear that there is much in the *Apology* that satisfies this definition.

THE DIALOGUE

With the formal institution of higher education in Athens in the fourth century and the concomitant professionalization of philosophy, the essay or treatise became the most common medium of philosophical exposition, as it has continued to be in the Western tradition. The form became firmly established in the school of Plato's pupil Aristotle (the Lyceum) and his successors, although its origins may be traced to earlier sources: the lecture format adopted by the Sophists or the treatises on natural phenomena by Ionian thinkers. In his last works, Plato slightly tended toward this form to the extent that the chief interlocutor has far more to say than the others, but he never totally deserted the dialogue form, with which he began.

There were several reasons for the choice of this form. Traditionally, dialogue had been used in the different genres as the main vehicle for treating the issues and ambiguities of human and divine activity. This is the case with the earliest pieces of Greek literature, the *Iliad* and *Odyssey* of Homer, in which, so far as these themes are important, they are conveyed through the speeches of the characters rather than by the poet speaking in his own person. It became increasingly the case in the development of Athenian tragedy, with the lessening importance of the chorus and increasing focus on the actors, and this tendency culminated in the plays of Euripides, who was called the philosopher of the stage.

There is a credible tradition that Plato's first literary efforts were dramatic, although it is probably a pleasant fiction that he burned the manuscripts of his tragedies on first listening to Socrates. His tendencies toward dramatic poetry—which he criticized in the *Republic*, perhaps the more harshly because he so deeply felt its emotional power—found expression in the possibilities inherent in the dialogue, with its interplay of character and opinion in the drama of the mind.

Of greatest importance, it seems clear, was that the dialogue form was most true to the historical Socrates, and this is also why others of Socrates' disciples, like Aeschines of Sphettus, wrote dialogues featuring him. (These are preserved only in fragments.) When Socrates made the claim that he was not a teacher, this meant that he was not so committed to any positive set of doctrines that he could confidently give it some semipermanent validity by putting it in written form, and in fact he wrote nothing. This also made the lecture format of the Sophists—with its inherent exhibitionism—unsuitable for an accurate portrayal of Socrates. While it would be difficult to claim that any Platonic dialogue was intended to be a closely factual account of a historical occasion, the dialogues were intended to be true to Socrates' method of philosophic activity. It is clear also that they had an apologetic purpose. By showing Socrates in action, Plato is implying over and over that his activity is irrelevant to the charges brought against him and certainly incommensurate with the penalty he suffered.

Perhaps as an inheritance from the Socratic method of question and answer, Plato mistrusted the usefulness of books in education. In a famous passage at the end of *Phaedrus*, he compared the written word to the human figures in a realistic painting. They appear to be alive but are speechless when questions are directed at them. So the written word imposes a rigid finality on philosophical inquiry, a finality totally alien to the questing spirit that marked Plato's approach to intellectual problems.

The dialogues are usually divided into three groups loosely demarcated by various criteria (prominence of Socrates, analysis of style, philosophic theme), although absolute agreement about the relative dating of all the dialogues has not yet been reached. (A list of dialogues in the three groups is in the appendix.) The early dialogues contain the most accurate picture of the Socratic method. As later in the *Laches*, the interlocutors try to define moral terms: temperance *(sophrosyne)* in *Charmides*, friendship *(philia)* in *Lysis*, and piety *(hosiotes)* in *Euthyphro*.

It is the middle group about which most questions arise: particularly, what dialogues are to be included therein and to what extent Plato continues to depict the historical Socrates. The differences from the earlier dialogues are marked. These are longer—sometimes much longer—and thus less realistic as records of conversations. The interlocutors tend to be professionals, like Protagoras and Gorgias in the works so named, with the occasional admixture of the amateur Athenian. Socrates now has answers of positive content and is no longer merely the questioner and critic of others' opinions. These considerations suggest that Socrates is here serving as Plato's mouthpiece. But it is perfectly plausible that the historical Socrates actually discussed the issues with which these dialogues are concerned—justice, the proper functioning of society, the use of rhetoric in political discourse. This is most obvious in the last group. Many of the topics discussed in this group—logical division in the *Sophist*, the physics of the universe in the *Timaeus*—had their origin not in Socratic thought but in discussions in Plato's Academy. In Plato's last and longest work, the *Laws*, Socrates has disappeared, to be replaced by an Athenian Stranger, an alias for Plato himself.

LACHES

This dialogue allegedly recounts a conversation in Athens around 420 B.C., a decade after the outbreak of the Peloponnesian War. The initial participants are Lysimachus and Melesias, undistinguished sons of distinguished Athenian statesmen of the past, and Nicias and Laches, high-ranking military officers. The first pair has invited the second pair to view an exhibition of a man fighting in armor, their purpose being to ascertain whether this kind of training is a useful component in the upbringing of their own sons. Nicias is positive: it is good physical exercise, it is a useful introduction to the actual conditions of battle, and, with that kind of experience, the young men may well aspire to higher military positions and the knowledge of military matters that such positions require. Drawing from his own experience, Laches objects to these somewhat abstract and theoretical considerations: People who give such exhibitions never give them in Sparta (the prime example of the militaristic state; presumably they would not be appreciated there); Laches himself has met and bested some of them in battle; and technical innovations in weaponry can lead to disaster on the field (as was the case with the person who invented a newfangled combination spear and hook; the hook got caught in the rigging of an enemy whip and the weapon had to be let go, leaving the man undefended).

This impasse reached, they turn to Socrates as an impartial arbiter. That the conversation is going to take a different tack is signaled by comments of Nicias that serve as an intellectual introduction of Socrates to those of the group who are not familiar with his ways:

> You don't seem to know what happens to anyone who engages Socrates in close and serious conversation. It always turns out that, although he has begun to talk about some other topic, Socrates will drag him around in the conversation until he finds himself describing the kind of life he has led and is now living. And when he finds himself in this state, Socrates will not let him go until he has finished questioning him sharply and closely.
>
> (187e–188a)

Accordingly Socrates begins as if he will totally ignore the original problem. Actually, though implicitly, he subsumes it under a larger question. This kind of training is only one aspect of education viewed more widely. Education is intended to effect improvement toward a good: that combination of moral qualities that the Greeks called *aretē* (human excellence). To discuss all these qualities is too large a task, Socrates says, and we must here focus on the virtue that skill in fighting is expected to produce: courage. But just as an ophthalmologist cannot help a patient unless he knows about eyes and sight, so no teacher or trainer can expect to produce a moral quality unless he knows what the quality is. What, then, is courage?

The answer of Laches, as that of an experienced military man of the fifth century, is predictable: a man is courageous if he is willing to remain at his assigned post in battle and not flee from the enemy. This answer is quickly seen to be defective, because it applies to only one type of individual in one type of situation (infantry battle with contemporary tactics). Socrates broadens the inquiry: What about the courage of other types of soldiers (cavalry, for instance); of people in other situations, in danger at sea, in disease and poverty, in politics? What common quality that we call "courage" is shared by all of these, in the same way that the quality we call "quickness" is shared by activities of the body, of the tongue, and of the mind?

Laches suggests that its shared quality is a kind of endurance of the soul; a moral endurance, we would say, as distinct from a physical endurance. This definition is vague enough to fit the situations just described, but Socrates wants to make it more precise and takes the discussion in a slightly different direction. Courage is a noble quality, yet endurance may be intelligent or unintelligent. He gives two examples: a doctor may refuse to give medication to a patient who requests it, but his obduracy—a kind of endurance—may be simply irrational. Again, a soldier may be more ready to endure in battle if he knows that he has more men on his side or if he possesses certain skills that his opponent lacks. In such a case, we are likely to say that the opponent, lacking support or lacking skills and yet enduring, is in fact the braver man, and that a quality that is ignoble—foolish endurance—is at the same time courage. This contradicts the assumption with which this part of the discussion began, that courage is something noble. When Socrates playfully suggests that, despite the impasse they have reached, they should be courageous and endure in pursuing the argument, Laches begs off:

> I am ready to continue, but I'm not used to discussions like this. I would like to win the argument and I am really irritated that I cannot express what I mean. I think I know what courage is but somehow—I don't know how—it has just escaped me so that I can't put it in words and say what it is.
>
> (194a)

Socrates now asks the second general, Nicias, to come to the aid of his friends, a playful use of a military metaphor. Nicias suggests that they begin with a maxim he has often heard Socrates enunciate: A man is good at something he knows about, bad at that in which he is ignorant. The particular knowledge involved here is knowledge of what causes fear and confidence in battle and in other situations. Laches makes the obvious objection that a doctor knows what is dangerous in disease and a farmer what is dangerous about agriculture, but that we do not on that account call the doctor or the farmer courageous. Nicias counters with the rather odd statement that doctors know about diseases but do not know whether this sick person should be cured or should be allowed to die, or in general whether life is better than death; only the courageous man knows this. If this is so, says Laches, a soothsayer, who can predict the future, is courageous. No, says Nicias, a soothsayer can predict what will happen but does not know whether what will happen is better for the individual who will be affected. Laches can only conclude that unless Nicias means that no one is courageous except a god, he has put himself into a position from which he cannot extricate himself and refuses to admit that he is talking self-contradictory nonsense.

Socrates has remained silent during the increasingly rancorous byplay between Nicias and Laches, mainly because the discussion has lost its focus and is destined to get nowhere. He tries to give it a surer direction by going back to Nicias' original definition, that courage is the knowledge of things that inspire fear and confidence. By this definition, are we, using ordinary language, to say that certain animals (lions and panthers) are brave? If so, these animals know what many men (doctors and soothsayers) do not know. Somewhat impatiently, Nicias distinguishes between courage and what may be called boldness or rashness or fearlessness. This is the quality animals and children have, but their actions lack intelligence and therefore are not brave. When Laches complains that this is to misuse ordinary language—we do talk about brave lions—he is reminded by Socrates that Nicias is a friend of his son's teacher Damon, and that Damon is an associate of Prodicus, the Sophist most renowned for his skill in distinguishing the meanings of words.

The final state of the argument takes up a theme introduced near the beginning of the dialogue: that courage is *arete*, or virtue, but only a part of *arete*, which comprises also temperance, justice, and other qualities. Socrates appropriates Nicias' definition of courage and expands its application. Courage is knowledge of things that create fear and hope: the former are bad, the latter good. Fear and hope are both concerned with the future. Now, if courage is knowledge, it must have an object, something known. But knowledge is not only of things known in the future, but also of things past and present. The analogies here are the sciences of medicine, agriculture, and generalship. (For the latter, Socrates notes that this is why the law puts the future-predicting soothsayer under the general; it is the skilled and experienced general who is likely to know what will happen in battle.) Thus, the revised definition of courage, dealing as it does with future goods and evils, is concerned with the subject matter of one-third of courage. By the same token, if courage as a whole deals with all good and evil, past, present, and future, courage would comprise the whole of *arete*. This conclusion, like the contradiction in Laches' argument, contradicts the original premise that courage is only a part of virtue.

Socrates: Well, Nicias, we have not discovered what courage is.

Nicias: Apparently not.

Laches: I certainly thought that you would discover it, Nicias my friend, since you were contemptuous of my replies to Socrates' questions. I had quite high expectations that you would discover it with the wisdom you got from Damon.

Nicias: It's marvelous, Laches, that you still think it nothing that you were clearly shown to know nothing about courage.

But if I will be shown to be in the same difficulty, you fix on this, and it will still not matter, it seems, that you as well as I have no knowledge of things that a man who thinks he is something should know. What you are doing, it seems to me, is something quite human: looking at others but not at yourself. I think I have spoken moderately well about the topics we were discussing. But if some of these topics have not been treated adequately, I will rectify the situation later with the help of Damon—whom you think you are laughing at although you have never even set eyes on him— and others. And when I am sure of my arguments, I will instruct you, I won't begrudge it, for you seem to me to be very much in need of instruction.

(199e)

The dialogue closes with an ironic suggestion from Socrates that, despite their age, all three go back to school.

At the beginning of many of the earlier dialogues, we are told where the conversation took place—a wrestler's training area (*Charmides*), the house of Cephalus in the port of Athens (the *Republic*). This feature is lacking in the *Laches* (for no particular or discernible reason), but otherwise this small work has features common to other dialogues. These include (1) the introduction of the characters; (2) the posing of the topic, initially in general terms that are later refined and made more specific; (3) the educational purpose and value of the topic, especially as it involves and affects the young; (4) the practical relevance of the topic to the activities of human life and to the Greek ideal of *arete*; (5) the notion that a life well lived is a skill, and that ethical activity has analogues in the techniques and skills of the professions, especially medicine; (6) the central position of Socrates as the main interlocutor; and (7) the conclusion in the form of an *aporia*, a difficulty: various solutions to the problem, initially put forward with confidence by the interlocutors, are ultimately found to be unsatisfactory.

At least in literary terms, the Socrates of the dialogues is a creation of Plato, and it is an endlessly debated question how far he is a philosophic creation as well. In plainer language, to what extent is the Platonic picture of Socrates historically accurate? As we have seen, the question is complicated by interpretative versions of Socrates written by Aristophanes and some companions of Socrates. It is further complicated by the fact that the Socrates of the earlier dialogues differs from the picture of him in the later ones.

The question may be approached from two aspects—Socratic method and Socratic doctrine. About the first there is little disagreement. As exemplified in the *Laches*, Socrates was attempting to arrive at an objective definition of a moral quality (courage, temperance, justice). By his time, the need for such definitions had become self-evident. Thucydides reports one of the effects of the civil strife that befell many Greek states in the Peloponnesian War:

People claimed the right to change the meanings of words in relation to acts. Irrational boldness became courage in support of the group, hesitation based on foresight specious cowardice, moderation the cover of unmanliness, an intelligent approach to the whole situation inactivity in everything.

(*Histories* 3.82)

Precise definition is necessary for intellectual and moral reasons. If two people do not agree on the meaning of a term, they literally cannot communicate intelligently and intelligibly. Similarly if a word means what an individual or group wants it to mean, that meaning is only private and objective, and is the inevitable basis of moral relativity. Socrates' method is the *elenchus*, an attempt to arrive at such a definition by a process of question and answer. One of the interlocutors will be asked what he understands by such and such a moral term: his answer will invariably be too general or too specific.

Thus, when Nicias defines courage as a knowledge, Socrates must get him to be more specific (194e): it is not, Socrates says, knowledge of how to play the flute nor skill at playing a lyre, but, we finally learn, the knowledge of things that cause fear and confidence. The examples of musical skills adduced by Socrates are deliberately ridiculous and trivial, but their very triviality underscores the need for precision, for musical skills are forms of knowledge.

A more typical form of *elenchus* is Socrates' treatment of Laches. In this case, the initial formulation of the moral quality is not a definition; instead, a specific instance of the quality is used as an illustration. It is quickly discovered that the specific instance does not exhaust all the situations to which the quality may be relevant. Laches initially attempts a definition by illustration: the courageous man remains at his assigned post and fights the enemy. Socrates points out that this cannot literally be true. In general, it excludes cavalry soldiers who wheel, retreat, and advance; it does not apply to specific military actions, such as that of the Spartans at the battle of Plataea, who, having retreated until the ranks of the pursuing Persians became disorganized, then turned and routed them. Nor is Laches' illustration at all relevant to nonmilitary situations where the use of courage-terminology is appropriate.

There is also a personal purpose to the Socratic method. Each major interlocutor was a historical figure (some better known than others), and Plato occasionally alludes to the actual facts of their lives. For instance, the briefly discussed role of the soothsayer in this dialogue does not materially forward the argument, but it takes on historical significance when we know that Nicias, according to Thucydides, was in fact rather superstitious. His credulity played a part in a decision that ultimately led to the failure of the Athenian expedition against Sicily and his to own death.

It is probable that the character traits marking Laches as a blunt man of action, not comfortable with abstract thought and language, and Nicias as a foil to him—competitive, in love with wordplay and theory (although not very skillful at either), eager to embrace Sophistic method—are true to life. It is more important that they are typical characters, representative of many like themselves in ancient Athens. Such men are very much the products of their own experience, and it is part of the educational process to which Socrates exposes them to realize (and occasionally to admit) that their experience does not equip them to deal fully or intelligently with people whose perspective is different or with matters within a different frame of reference.

In another sense, the dialogues are unrealistic. The give-and-take of the argument is represented as something spontaneous, but it is of course always controlled by Plato. It is one aspect of his dramatic technique that the logic of the argument can be of lower or higher quality: lower, when the interlocutors are amateurish and are content to engage in *eristic*, a type of debate in which the opponents want to score points off each other; higher, when the interlocutors are engaged in genuine *dialectic*, in which one starts from firmly held opinions but is willing to change them if objective analysis so persuades him.

When we turn to the question of what is peculiarly Socratic in the content of the dialogues, problems abound. Socrates professed to teach no doctrine and claimed to be ignorant in terms of human wisdom. His method was largely destructive of others' opinions, and the dialogues end in *aporia* (a difficulty). Yet he was no nihilist, and the charismatic effect he had on people (as evidenced by Alcibiades' words in the *Symposium*) could hardly have been so great if his attitudes were entirely or mainly negative. In fact, evidence from various sources identifies him with a specific attitude and a general doctrine. The attitude was that the individual's main concern should be the proper development of his *psyche* (soul/spirit) rather than things external to the inner self, like the acquisition of wealth or reputation or even the demands of the body. The doctrine was that human excellence (*aretē*) consisted of knowledge, and the paradoxical corollary was best expressed in Socrates' words: "no human being does wrong voluntarily, but all who act this way act involuntarily" (*Protagoras* 345d).

The theory that moral activity has an intellectual basis is a Socratic insight that Plato never abandoned—indeed it pervades his writings. It is a valid psychological principle that few people choose an action unless they perceive that there is something good in it for them. While it is hardly possible to isolate in the dialogues the implications Socrates himself drew from these principles, it is fairly clear how they influenced Plato's philosophical development. In psychological terms, Socrates' insistence on the development of the soul assumes in theory a duality of soul and body. One implication of "no one does wrong voluntarily" is that to know the correct good is to do it: this, in turn, entails the same duality, for it assumes that the mind controls the body. Aristotle sharply criticized this bipartition, on the ground that it took no account of the irrational elements of the soul, the sources of the emotions. The criticism was anticipated by Plato, who constructed a tripartite psychology: the intellectual, the spirited (source of nobler passions and desires), and the appetitive (source of baser passions and desires). This construct, brilliantly described in the simile of the charioteer and his two horses in *Phaedrus* (253a), permeates the educational and social schemes of the *Republic*.

The equation of Good with the goal of moral activity led Plato along a slightly new and different avenue of approach: how to define Good, how to distinguish real from apparent Goods. This last topic led to the epistemological questions of appearance and reality and ultimately to the theory of Ideas.

THE REPUBLIC (POLITEIA)

Discussion of what is generally agreed to be Plato's greatest work may begin with two passages, one an analogy, the other a claim. The first is usually known as the allegory of the cave, though Plato himself called it an image of our natural condition with respect to education and lack of education. He describes a cave (514a1–515e6; perhaps modeled on a cave high on a hill in Vari, near the coastline of Attica), the inside of which slopes down from its entrance. At the far end, there is a group of people, chained since childhood in such a way that they can look only in a forward direction. At some distance behind the prisoners is a fire. Closer, but still behind them, is a low wall along which men are carrying artifacts, statues of people and animals. The only "reality" to which the prisoners are exposed consists of sights and sounds: the flickering shadows of the artifacts cast by the fire onto the opposite wall and echoes of the voices of the men carrying them.

Education begins when one of the prisoners is released and is compelled to make the painful journey back up to the daylight. At each stage of this journey, he is exposed to greater degrees of reality— the artifacts, the fire—but, conditioned by habituation and dazzled by the light, he continues to think that what he formerly saw is more real. Ultimately he leaves the cave and, adapting himself by stages, is able to progress from the vision of shadows and reflections in water to objects themselves, from the nighttime vision of sky, stars, and moon to the daytime vision of the sun and its light.

In context, the specific purpose of this image is graphically to illustrate Plato's new ontology—the theory of Ideas—with its distinction between true reality and reflections or images of reality, and to introduce the system of education by which one can learn to comprehend this reality, paralleling the journey of the released prisoner. But like a Homeric simile the image has a life of its own. Plato goes on to describe what happens to the prisoner when he returns to the cave of ordinary mankind. Reluctant to leave his newfound reality, he has no desire to engage himself in the activities of society, and finds it so difficult to adjust that he cuts a ridiculous figure.

The allegory of the cave points up what was

for Plato the fundamental defect in contemporary societies: a failure to comprehend true reality and an inability to distinguish the image or reflection from the real. The picture of the prisoner reentering the cave is intended to remind the reader of the second passage referred to above: Plato's proposed solution to this defect. His claim is as follows:

> Unless philosophers become kings in their states or unless those who now are kings and rulers genuinely engage in philosophy and attain a sufficient level of proficiency, unless political power and the love of knowledge are joined in the same person, and the many people who go in one or the other direction are absolutely prohibited from doing so, there is no cessation of trouble for our cities, nor, I think, for the human race, nor will the political society that we have just described enter the realm of possibility and see the light of day.
>
> (473d)

In a sense, these two passages provide the key to the purpose, content, and structure of the *Republic*. The work suggests such a radical reformation of society and contains so many innovative, controversial, and, to some, unattractive proposals that it is tempting to dismiss it as merely utopian and impossible of realization. But a fanciful utopia was not what Plato had in mind. He realized fully how controversial some of his proposals were and how difficult it would be to bring such a society into existence. Yet it is difficult to see why he would have bothered to compose the work if he thought the task impossible—at least at the time he wrote it. It is true that by the time he wrote his last work, the *Laws*, his goals were less lofty and he replaced the rule of the philosopher-king by the rule of law, but even there he praised the system of the *Republic* as the best. Nor is it in the Platonic spirit to treat the contents of the *Republic* as discrete parts, rejecting some (the censorship of literature, the abolition of the nuclear family) and keeping others as desirable elements of a social fabric. Plato's state was a whole, all its principles rooted in a particular ontological or metaphysical system and all necessitated by that system. Plato claims that if a state is to achieve and maintain certain goals—internal stability being a prime one—it is the special vision of the philosopher-king that will determine the means toward that goal.

It is also this ontological system that informs the structure of the *Republic*. It falls roughly into two halves, corresponding to the two worlds of becoming and being. The ontological dichotomy can also be characterized by the correlative sets of terms: appearance and truth, opinion and knowledge, imitation and reality. The treatment of the same general topics in each half is affected by this dichotomy. Thus, the system of education presented in the first half is intended to produce correct opinion, not knowledge. The potential literary component of this education is chosen to produce correct opinion; when pieces of literature or other kinds of artistic representation do not produce correct opinion, they are censored. The system of education presented in the second half is nonliterary, based on mathematics and abstract thought, and leads to knowledge of the ideas. The treatment of artistic representation in the second half of the work is the ontological justification for the censorship of art in the first half: literature and the plastic arts cannot produce knowledge because they are representations of objects and of actions that are themselves imitations of the real world.

The work begins in much the fashion of the early dialogues, and some hold that the first book was originally a dialogue and later integrated into a larger whole. The quality that is originally to be defined is justice or righteousness (*dikaiosune*). As usual, the first attempts at definition are unsuccessful—but in this case, unsuccessful for unusual reasons that set the *Republic* apart. As we saw in *Laches*, to possess a moral quality is assumed to be good in itself. This assumption is here challenged, and the argument works toward an *apologia pro justitia*: How does being just lead to personal happiness? Next, Plato introduces two new contexts of moral activity as they affect the individual.

The first context is internal or psychological. Although Socrates seems to have held no theory of the human personality more advanced than a primitive dualism of body and soul, Plato divided the soul into parts according to its three major activities: moral and intellectual activity was to be ascribed no longer to the individual as a whole but to these three internal divisions. The second new context is external. For Socrates, moral activity was political only when it was confined to and determined by a political end, such as bravery in defending one's country. In the *Republic,* responsibilities for some activities and restrictions on others devolve upon the individual not as an individual but as a member of a political class.

The amateur interlocutors—Cephalus, a wealthy alien resident at Athens, and his son Polemarchus—define justice from their own experience and the Greek traditional culture: it is to repay one's debts to god and man, to benefit friends, and to harm enemies. Shown to be defective in the usual manner, these definitions are almost irrelevant to the new contexts. It is not until the intervention of the Sophist Thrasymachus, who espouses one of the principles of the new power-politics—justice is action leading to the advantage of the stronger—that the focus of the question is extended beyond the level of the individual. For the sake of the definition, the model of just activity that Thrasymachus chooses is the faction-state. Justice so defined means, for example, that the oligarchic state makes laws to ensure that the members of the oligarchy keep power, and the laws produce that result if they are obeyed by the rest of society—the subjects. When Socrates attempts to use the analogy of the professions to show that people in authority (a doctor or ship's captain) use their power or skill to the advantage of those subject to them (health for the patient, a safe and successful voyage for the crew), Thrasymachus' reply is withering:

> On the question of the just and justice, the unjust and injustice, you are so far off the mark that you are unaware that justice and the just are in reality the good of another [person], the advantage to the stronger and the ruler, but bring personal harm to the subject and inferior. Injustice is quite the opposite, and it rules over men who are truly simple and just: subjects do what is to the advantage of the stronger, and by serving him they make him happy, themselves not at all. Socrates, most naive of men, you must realize that on every occasion the just man comes off worse than the unjust. First, whenever they set up a partnership with contracts, you would never find that the just man comes out with more when the partnership is dissolved, but always less. Second, take dealings with the state. Whenever taxes are imposed, the just man pays more, the other less, although they have the same capital. Whenever there are subsidies from the state, the one profits not at all, the other much. When each becomes an officeholder, the result is that, even if the just man suffers no other loss, his personal affairs are in poorer condition, because he has to neglect them, and he makes no profit from the public treasury, because of the fact that he is just. In addition to these losses, he is hated by his relatives and friends, because he is unwilling to do favors for them illegally. The situation is totally different in the case of the unjust man. As I was just saying, I mean by the unjust man the one who has a great ability to come out ahead. If you want to judge how much more personally advantageous it is to be unjust rather than just, your judgment will be easiest if you go to the ultimate limit of injustice: the condition that makes the wrongdoer most happy and those who are his victims, but who are themselves unwilling to commit wrong, most miserable. This condition is tyranny, which robs the possessions of others both secretly and with open force—property sacred and profane, private and public—not in gradual stages but all at once.
>
> (343c)

Thrasymachus goes on to distinguish between the petty criminal, branded as temple robber or kidnapper and penalized if caught, and the criminal on a large scale, the tyrant, who is envied by his fellow citizens even after he has enslaved them, and is deemed blessed and happy. Men condemn justice only because they fear to become its victims.

We know almost nothing about Thrasymachus as an historical person, nor can we say if this eloquent cynicism represents the view of a single individual. More probably it is a conflation of views known to be current at the end of the fifth century and selected by Plato to fit his own purposes. In mentioning interpersonal and intrastate forms of injustice, Plato seems to be excluding relations between states. This is partly because he has little to say about them in general, and partly because his approach to the problem of justice is based on an analogical relationship between the individual soul and the state. Thrasymachus' choice of the tyrant as the embodiment of ultimate, and profitable, injustice has a structural as well as thematic importance, for it foreshadows Plato's lengthy treatment of the psychology of the tyrant as the embodiment of political and individual weakness.

Thrasymachus' statements about how justice operates are conditioned by history and experience. To avoid this kind of conditioning, Plato seeks in book 2 of the *Republic* to investigate justice in the abstract and begins with a theory on the origin of society. People gather into primitive social units because each is unable to provide for himself certain basic needs—food, clothing, and shelter. These needs are most efficiently met if there is a specialization of function, with each person performing, for the common good, that task for which his natural ability best fits him—one man a farmer, another a shoemaker, and so on. The initial goal of society is economic self-sufficiency, and this is achieved on a minimal level with a minimal number of people.

As the population expands, new needs are felt, new expectations are aroused, and more and different economic functions and institutions are thought necessary—import and export, retailing, currency. Constant expansion beyond the satisfaction of basic needs leads from a kind of natural state to a luxurious state, with the creation of poets, musicians, chefs, beauticians, physicians. The final result of this expansion is that the original acreage occupied by the society is no longer sufficient to support

it, and neighboring land must be appropriated. Plato locates the origin of war in the transition from a society that provides for basic needs to one that is engaged in the limitless acquisition of wealth; and war, whether defensive or offensive, necessitates the creation of a warrior class.

In his initial statements about the specialization of labor, Plato has little to say about how various functions would be distributed apart from the assumption that natural dispositions or talents would produce the desired match between worker and work. His contempt for the luxury professions is such that he does not even consider the matter when treating them. This relative lack of interest is partly to be explained by the fact that, although the consuming segment of society is its largest, Plato is least interested in it. Another part of the explanation is that the large majority of the basic functions, however necessary they are, require no special talent. This is not true of men in the military class. They have to be born with innate physical and mental abilities, both of which are to be developed by training and education.

The traditional carrier of literary culture in Greece had been the works of the poets: the epic poetry of Homer and Hesiod, the choral lyrics of Pindar, and the plays put on at the annual dramatic festivals. For the future guardians of his state, Plato thinks that much of this literature is not only inadequate but harmful. Particularly repugnant to his own religious views are such literary statements as those stating that the gods are responsible for human evils, that they appear to men in various disguises, that they are untruthful. Unsuitable to moral training are depictions of characters of heroic stature acting less than heroically, like Achilles writhing on the ground in grief at the death of Patroclus or the many emotionally distraught figures of Greek tragedy. Passages like these are simply to be censored, and poets who write this kind of material are not to be admitted to this society.

Plato's treatment of literature has been much criticized, and to modern tastes it seems like an overreaction to the possibly harmful effects of performances of epic and tragedy. Plato's answer would be that at this level—prerational—education consists almost entirely of imitation of that to which the young are exposed, and he is consistent in applying the same strict criteria to music, to the plastic arts, and to architecture:

> We must try to find craftsmen who have the natural talent to search for and express the essence of the noble and the graceful.... The young man who is nurtured in this area will keenly perceive those works of craft or of nature that are defective; he will rightly be angered by these, but will take pleasure in and praise beautiful things. Accepting them into his *psyche,* he will be nourished by them and himself will become noble and good. Ugly things he will rightly hate and reject, even while he is still young, before he is capable of using reason. When reason comes, he will recognize it with joy, because of its likeness to himself. (401c)

After the class of guardians has been produced by the educational system—which it is its duty to preserve unchanged—its members will also be controlled by the principle of one man, one function. Lest they be distracted from performing this function efficiently by the need to acquire and maintain private property and possessions, they are forbidden to have them; they will receive the minimally necessary support from the state. Making further use of Spartan institutions, Plato has his soldiers live in a camp and eat at common messes.

When the objection is made that this life doesn't sound particularly attractive, Plato's reply seems somewhat feeble. He says that their purpose in fashioning a particular type of society is not to make any one group or class in it happy, but the society as a whole. This kind of happiness depends upon certain conditions: society must be stable, free from internal dissension and external aggression, and economically secure. These conditions depend upon the principle of one man, one function. If happiness for a farmer is defined as a continual round of parties, little farming will get done; if

others neglect their functions in the same way, ultimately the society will collapse. Once stability is secured, Plato says "we must allow nature (or the nature of the class) to provide each class with its proper share of happiness" (421c).

This last comment describes a transition from what may be called a natural state—a society created to satisfy natural needs like food, clothing, and shelter—to a society in which natural processes are refined and perfected by a system of eugenics, and in which a system of higher education is superimposed upon a type of education familiar in actual Greek life. Even at this stage of its development, Plato thinks it justified to say that the society is good, that is, both moral and efficient. To be good, it must have the traditional and almost canonical virtues of wisdom, courage, moderation, and justice. A wise society is one that conducts its internal and external affairs correctly; a courageous society has right opinion about what is and is not to be feared; and a moderate society recognizes who is to rule and who is to be ruled (a quality that entails the consent of the governed). Some aspects of these definitions require explanation. Only some of these virtues are shared by all the population. Wisdom, the rarest of these qualities, is found in the smallest group, the rulers; this group is represented by the best of the soldiers, those who have received advanced education. Courage is found in the next-largest group, the soldiers; and moderation is required of all. While wisdom is a specific kind of knowledge, courage and moderation are correct opinion, not achieved independently by the individual but implanted by educational indoctrination.

The question of moderation and justice is a bit more complicated and linked both to Plato's theory of human psychology and to the analogy in the *Republic* between the *psyche* and society. The three parts of the personality—the cognitive, appetitive, and desiring elements—parallel the ruling, military, and consumer classes, and have a similar hierarchic relationship. With the other virtues defined, justice turns out to be very like the principle on which the society was originally founded—one man, one function—but it is now invested with new content. In the state, moderation is the intellectual recognition of who is to rule and who is to be ruled; and, in the individual, it is the recognition that one part of the person, the mind, should direct the other parts. Justice, therefore, is the psychic disposition according to which each part of the individual or of society should play its own role. In society, then, injustice exists when one class or a member of that class attempts to appropriate a role for which it or he is not equipped by nature or by training.

Plato thinks to ensure the permanence of this social structure through two controversial proposals: a system of genetic inbreeding and the abolition of the nuclear family within the guardian class. The first flows from Plato's insight that women as a class are not essentially different from men in fulfilling the intellectual and political tasks of the guardians. The proposal includes carefully regulated sexual intercourse between the most talented members of both sexes as well as common sharing of mates: no permanent marriage of two individuals is to be permitted. Also, Plato thinks that the preservation of the family, with its bonds of individual affection, would dilute the loyalty that members of this class should feel toward the class as a whole. Since the claim has been made that Plato was the spiritual ancestor of modern theories of an ethnic "master race," it must be emphasized that these proposals, along with the common use of property, were intended only for the ruling class, not for the large majority of the population, for which they would have been unworkable and irrelevant.

Plato began his treatment of the philosopher in society with the challenging statement quoted near the opening of this section. Hitherto, the combination of philosophical intelligence and political power had not really been envisaged—for various reasons: the ignorance of those who thought that the ability to acquire power was a guarantee of its successful use; the frequency with which the young man of high talent was early corrupted by groups in society that perverted that talent to their own ends; and the bad name given to philosophy by its professed practitioners. To these phenomena Plato opposes a society in which the majority agrees to be ruled by the smaller group, to an educational system that isolates the young from sources of corruption, and to a new kind of philosopher dealing with a new vision of reality.

Central to this vision is the theory of Forms or Ideas. More will be said about this theory later, but it will be remembered that the world of forms stands to the world of becoming as the world of natural phenomena stands to the conditions of the cave. To illustrate the relationship, Plato uses an image: a line divided into four segments (AB, BC, CD, DE) of which AB is to BC as CD is to DE. The segments represent, respectively: AB—images and reflections of objects; BC—the objects themselves; CD—mathematical entities; and DE—the forms. Corresponding to each of them is a type or state of cognition: imagination, opinion, reasoning, and understanding. Higher education for the future rulers will comprise, in series, arithmetical calculation, geometry, astronomy, harmonics, and logic. The subject matter will be increasingly removed from sensible things, and at the end of the course a ruler will be capable of achieving knowledge of the form of the Good. As the sun is responsible for the existence of natural beings that are characterized by growth and nurture, and is the source of light by which things are seen accurately, so the idea of Good is the cause of everything that exists and is the source of true knowledge of things. Once he gains this vision, the philosopher will be compelled to reenter society (as the freed prisoner was compelled to reenter the cave) to apply his knowledge to its governance and to educate others to be his successors.

For many readers, the most valuable and interesting contribution of the *Republic* to political theory is not the construction of the ideal state but Plato's analysis of the psychological bases of actual societies. The ideal state is a human construct, and, like everything human, subject to corruption and decay. The process of degeneration results, successively, in a series of societies that replace higher values with lower. The analyses are coordinated to the themes of the whole work in three ways. Thrasymachus' original claim—that the life of the tyrant, the man of injustice par excellence, is the happiest—requires an answer, which is supplied by Plato's picture of what the life of the tyrant is really like. But tyranny comes at the end of the degenerative process, and this must be described first. Plato justifies his original claim that there is no salvation for society unless love of wisdom is wedded to political power by showing what different forms of society are like without this condition. The original analogy between man and state is here fundamental to the principle that the character of a society is determined by the collective psychological character of the segment of the population that has effective governing power.

The analyses are both dynamic and static: Plato describes how each political form comes into existence and what its permanent condition is; the psychology of the individual that corresponds to the political form receives the same treatment. The prime cause of the degenerative process is the denigration of that valuing of the intellect that characterizes the aristocracy of the ideal state. A compensatory inflation of the spirited element of the *psyche*—the love of honor and victory—gives its name to the next form, *timocracy*. Since the desiring element is the largest part of the soul, this gives rise to not one but three forms of government. Desire for honor is replaced by desire for wealth in the oligarchy. These focused desires may be replaced by indiscriminate desire: in a democracy there is so much freedom of choice that the fragmented *psyche* cannot be satisfied with any one desirable object. Finally, the tyranny: instead of being the happiest of mortals, as Thrasymachus had thought, the tyrant turns out to be the most miserable. Totally the victim of irrational desire, he is totally in the control of others whom he needs to satisfy those desires.

Much in the social thought of the *Republic* has proved offensive to modern thinkers of a liberal persuasion, and it is not to be denied that Plato's state is paternalistic and authoritarian. But it may be suggested that authoritarian measures would be used only where compulsion failed and that all classes, not only the ruling class, would be subject to such measures. It is also a society based on a mutual interdependence of the three classes; one in which Plato thought bonds of mutual affection could develop between the members of the classes.

THE THEORY OF FORMS OR IDEAS

The focus of Socrates' philosophical activity was the search for definitions of moral qualities or value terms. Taken together, the early dialogues give a composite picture of such a definition: it is comprehensive, including those acts that display the quality, and exclusive, omitting those acts that do not; it can be comprehended by human beings, but it is not only a human construct, for that would make its base subjective; and finally, since moral qualities are evinced only in action, it must serve as a criterion of action.

The failure of Socrates' method to achieve these definitions suggested to Plato that the fundamental cause of the failure was a confusion between states of mind and the objects the mind was dealing with. If one does not have knowledge of a thing, one may have an opinion about it, and the opinion may be totally wrong or more or less close to the truth. It also began to be clear that differences of opinion could partially be traced to the fact that objects of opinion appeared different to different people. While Socrates had concerned himself with the problem of knowledge in moral matters, Plato realized that the problem should not be restricted to moral matters only. If we define two terms, knowledge and opinion, corresponding to two states of mind or modes of apprehension, there must also be two corresponding objects of apprehension, and, if they are two, they must be different. Thus, the difference is not only one of epistemology—how we perceive or know—but also one of ontology—what we perceive or know.

The issue may adequately be illustrated by considering the maxim "beauty is in the eye of the beholder." Beauty is a very vague concept, since the predication "beautiful" can normally be applied to such different types of objects as people, artifacts, ideas, natural phenomena, and so on. If the term is not to be used so indiscriminately and subjectively that it totally loses meaning, Plato thought, there must be some objective reality that we could know and through this knowledge recognize beauty in particular, concrete things. This object he called the form or idea *(eidos)* of Beauty. The term he used underlined the visual aspect of knowledge (*eidos* is etymologically cognate with the most common word for knowledge, *oida*: compare Latin *video*, "I see"). This emphasized the first of the two terms of the correlation "knower/known"; to emphasize the second term, he exploited the potential of the Greek language. He could combine the definite article with the neuter gender of the adjective to produce a class name—the Beautiful; or he could point up innate quality by an abstract noun—Holiness; or he could suggest transcendent, independent existence by the use of an intensifying pronoun, the Beautiful Itself or Holiness Itself. Although these illustrations are drawn from the sphere of morals and aesthetics, it must be kept in mind that Plato originally thought this theory comprehensive of all of reality: there would be forms of natural phenomena, artifacts, mathematical objects (Circle, Square), and relations (Equality, Largeness, Smallness). The result was two ontological worlds: the one of the eternal, unchangeable, imperishable forms—the world of being; the other our sensible world, in which the forms are imperfectly realized in particular phenomena, changing, shifting, perishable—the world of becoming.

In attempting to bridge the gap between the knower and the known, Plato may seem initially to have complicated the problem by creating another gap, between the worlds of being and becoming, for this led to three further questions: (1) What is the ontological relationship between the two worlds? (2) How is one even to become aware of the existence of the world of forms? (3) Once aware of it, how is one to know it? The second question is not as innocent as it seems. According to the strict logic of the Socratic method, with human beings looking for answers from human experience, this kind of awareness is impossible. For an answer, Plato had recourse to an extraordinary strain of Greek religion that emphasized morality—sin, punishment, and reward. Its tenets included one called *metempsychosis*, the transmigration of souls, according to which each soul lived several lives in different bodies, animal and human. Plato adapted this to his own needs and claimed that each soul was exposed to the world of forms in its disembodied state. When it enters a body, the soul loses memory of this exposure; but in life, when the human being perceives concrete instances of specific phenomena, the soul is reminded, however dimly, of the forms of which phenomena are imitations. This adaptation is called the theory of recollection (*anamnesis*).

To achieve knowledge of the forms in human life means that the soul must come as close as possible to its original disembodied state, and for the *psyche* to be able to achieve this psychological condition is one of the purposes of the ascetic educational system of the *Republic*. Once achieved, this condition would allow the untrammeled use of the mind's powers to intuit the forms.

The problem that Plato was never able to explain satisfactorily was the precise relationship between the worlds of being and becoming, and particularly how the former was the cause of the latter. He seems first to have emphasized the language of immanence: somehow the forms were present to or in the concrete particulars, or the latter received or shared in the forms. Later, he used the language of transcendence: here the separateness of the forms is emphasized, and the particulars resembled or imitated them.

Plato never relinquished his personal faith in the validity of the theory. Characteristically (or Socratically), he was most reluctant to jettison forms of moral qualities. For the history of philosophy, however, the non-Socratic aspects of the theory have remained important: analysis by logical categories, the distinction between essence and accidental properties; those physical and mathematical laws of motion apprehensible only by the mind.

Of similar importance is Plato's influence in the history of religious thought. Although the only work of Plato known in the West throughout much of the Middle Ages was a Latin translation of the *Timaeus,* versions of Platonic thought were spread from the East to the West through representatives of the popular neo-Platonic school tradition that affected St. Augustine so deeply before his conversion to Christianity. Some neo-Platonic ideas were perversions of what Plato believed (that matter was evil, for example) and others were adaptations (that the ideas were thoughts in the mind of the creative God), but central to both earlier and later systems was the tenet of monotheism, the oneness of God.

Some interpreters have stressed what they conceive to be a deep strain of mysticism. Poetic inspiration is probably a more accurate explanation of Plato's frequent use of invented myth to convey what seemed to him essential religious truths not subject to intellectual, empirical control. Such truths include the question of human freedom and responsibility versus divine determinism, both in the myth of Er in the last book of the *Republic* and in the creation myth of the *Timaeus.* In the end, however, Plato was basically a rationalist who recognized that both poetic language and scientific discourse were necessary to communicate different aspects of reality. The relative importance he attached to each mode of language may be illustrated by his *Phaedo.* The dialogue ends with a brilliant and imaginative description of the abodes of the soul after death. Necessary to this myth is the conception of the immortality of the soul. Plato devotes over four times as much space to establishing this conception as he gives to the myth, and his mode of establishing it is logical argumentation.

Appendix

About the publication dates of Plato's writings there are two secure facts: the *Apology* was written after 399 B.C. and the *Laws* was his last work, edited after his death by a pupil. Traditionally, Plato's activity is divided into three periods: to *ca.* 385; *ca.* 385 to *ca.* 370; and after *ca.* 370. If this division is retained, the following placements are probably fairly accurate (alphabetic arrangement):

I	II	III
Apology	*Cratylus*	*Critias*
Charmides	*Euthydemus*	*Laws*
Crito	*Menexenus*	*Parmenides*
Euthyphro	*Phaedo*	*Phaedrus*
Gorgias	*Republic*	*Philebus*
Hippias Minor	*Symposium*	*Sophist*
Ion		*Statesman*
Laches		*Theaetetus*
Lysis		*Timaeus*
Meno		
Protagoras		

Selected Bibliography

TEXTS AND TRANSLATIONS

The Collected Dialogues of Plato, edited by E. Hamilton and H. Cairns. Princeton, N. J., 1969. A preferred and more varied translation.

The Dialogues of Plato, edited by B. Jowett. Oxford, 1953. Traditional but now somewhat archaic.

Plato. London and Cambridge, Mass., 1914–1952. Greek text with English translation. Loeb Classical Library.

Platon. Paris, 1930–1964. Budé series. Greek text with French translation.

Platonis Opera, edited by J. Burnet. Oxford, 1902–1906. Greek with French translation.

PLATO

GENERAL STUDIES

Crombie, I. M. *An Examination of Plato's Doctrines.* 2 vols. London, 1962, 1963.

Field, G. C. *The Philosophy of Plato.* 2nd ed. Oxford, 1969.

Friedlander, P. *Plato.* 3 vols. New York, 1958–1969.

Gosling, J. C. B. *Plato.* London, 1973.

Grube, G. M. A. *Plato's Thought.* London, 1935.

Guthrie, W. K. C. *A History of Greek Philosophy.* Vols. 3, 4. Cambridge, 1969, 1975.

Havelock, E. A. *A Preface to Plato.* New York, 1967.

Jaeger, W. W. *Paideia.* Vols. 2, 3. 2nd ed. Oxford, 1965.

Riginos, A. S. *Platonica: The Anecdotes Concerning the Life and Writings of Plato.* Leiden, 1976.

Ryle, G. *Plato's Progress.* Cambridge, 1966.

Shorey, P. *The Unity of Plato's Thought.* Chicago, 1904.

————. *What Plato Said.* Chicago, 1978.

Taylor, A. E. *Plato, the Man and His Work.* 6th ed. New York, 1949.

SPECIAL STUDIES

Barker, E. *Greek Political Theory: Plato and his Predecessors.* 5th ed. London, 1960.

Cherniss, H. *The Riddle of the Early Academy.* Berkeley, 1945.

Dover, K. J. "The Freedom of the Intellectual in Greek Society." *Talanta* 7: 24–54 (1976).

Field, G. C. *Plato and His Contemporaries.* 3rd ed. London, 1967.

Gould, J. *The Development of Plato's Ethics.* New York, 1972.

Gouldner, A. W. *Enter Plato: Classical Greece and the Origins of Social Theory.* New York, 1965.

Gulley, N. *Plato's Theory of Knowledge.* London, 1962.

————. *The Philosophy of Socrates.* New York, 1968.

Irwin, T. *Plato's Moral Theory.* Oxford, 1977.

Keuls, E. *Plato and Greek Painting.* Leiden, 1978.

Levinson, R. B. *In Defense of Plato.* Cambridge, Mass., 1953.

Lodge, R. C. *Plato's Theory of Art.* London, 1953.

O'Brien, M. *The Socratic Paradoxes and the Greek Mind.* Chapel Hill, N. C., 1967.

Popper, K. *The Open Society and Its Enemies.* 5th ed. Vol. 1. Princeton, 1966.

Robinson, R. *Plato's Earlier Dialectic.* 2nd ed. Oxford, 1953.

Ross, W. D. *Plato's Theory of Ideas.* Oxford, 1951.

Solmsen, F. *Plato's Theology.* Ithaca, N. Y., 1942.

Stewart, J. A. *The Myths of Plato.* London, 1905.

Taylor, A. E. *Platonism and Its Influence.* New York, 1927.

Vlastos, G., ed. *Plato: A Collection of Critical Essays.* 2 vols. New York, 1970, 1971.

————, ed. *The Philosophy of Socrates.* New York, 1971.

————. *Platonic Studies.* Princeton, N. J., 1973.

————. *Plato's Universe.* Seattle, Wash., 1975.

Voegelin, E. *Plato.* Baton Rouge, La., 1966.

White, N. *Plato on Knowledge and Reality.* Indianapolis, Ind., 1976.

BIBLIOGRAPHIES

Cherniss, H. "Plato 1950–1957." *Lustrum* 4, 5 (1959, 1960).

McKirahan, R. D. *Plato and Socrates: A Comprehensive Bibliography, 1958–1973.* New York, 1978.

JOHN J. KEANEY

ARISTOTLE

(384–322 B.C.)

Poi ch'innalzai un poco piu le ciglia,
 vidi 'l maestro di color che sanno
 seder tra filosofica famiglia.
Tutti lo miran, tutti onor li fanno.

And when I lifted my eyes a little higher,
 I saw the master of those who know
 Sitting in the midst of a philosophical family.
All look to him, all do him honor.
(Inferno 4.130–134)

S O DANTE, IN the luminous high space of a green meadow closed eternally from the sun, walking in the company of sober souls with slow-moving eyes, encountered his master Aristotle. This portrait, which tells us at one and the same time one deep truth about Aristotle and a great deal more that is perversely, though influentially, false, seems to be, for its very contradictions, a good place to begin our exploration of Aristotle's thought. The truth is that Aristotle is indeed great. The problem, however, is that if he were a philosopher such as Dante describes—a complacent and dogmatic figure concerned with being in the know, surrounded by docile and worshipful disciples—he would not be a great philosopher for us, and perhaps not a philosopher at all. We tend to feel that philosophers should be continually inquiring, willing to follow argument and intuition even when they lead to the overthrow of dogma, flex-ible seekers of truth rather than makers or followers of authority.

Fortunately, however, Dante's *maestro* is not the Aristotle of the extant texts. What we shall encounter here is thought that combines ambition for order with responsiveness to the complexity and variety of human life and language, a thinker who would be less likely to be discovered on a lofty throne than sitting on the seashore observing the movements of shellfish. In place of the "master" with his chillingly affectless sobriety, we discover a comprehensive lover of living beings (including human beings), who is capable of equal concern for the characteristics of a good joke, the nature of the heavenly bodies, the digestive structures of a bird. It was not Dante's Aristotle who said this to a group of students disgusted at the prospect of studying the "blood, flesh, bones, blood-vessels, and parts of this sort" of which both they themselves and other animals are made:

> We must not enter upon the study of the lesser animals with childish disgust. For in every natural thing there is something wonderful. There is a story which tells how some foreigners once wanted to meet Heraclitus. When they entered, they saw him warming himself in front of the stove. They hesitated; but he told them, "Come in; don't be afraid; there are gods here too." In the same way, we must proceed towards the study of each kind of animal, without making a sour face.

In every one of them there is something natural and beautiful.

(*Parts of Animals* 1.5.645a15–23)

As we pursue the complex structures of Aristotle's thought, we shall try to keep in view the features of his philosophical personality revealed in this passage: fascination with inquiry of every sort, love of the mutable and the material, responsiveness to the wonder of the imperfect.

LIFE

Aristotle was born in 384 B.C. in Stagira, a Greek-speaking town on the coast of the peninsula of Chalcidice. His father, Nicomachus, was a doctor, a member of the guild of the Asclepiadae, and court physician to Amyntas II, then king of Macedonia. Aristotle's interest in biology may well have developed early, as a result of his father's medical career, although there is no reason to think that he began any actual research at this time. Asclepiad doctors taught their sons dissection, but since both of his parents died when he was extremely young, Aristotle probably did not receive this training.

When he was seventeen, he traveled to Athens and entered Plato's Academy; here he remained as a student and associate until Plato's death in 348 B.C. The importance of Plato's philosophical influence is apparent in all of Aristotle's work. Even when he is critical—which, in the extant writings, is a great part of the time—he expresses a deep respect for Plato's genius. Some critics have supposed that the Academy was a place in which no dissent from the thought of the master was tolerated; they therefore conclude that all works in which Aristotle takes issue with a view of Plato's must have been written after Plato's death. This supposition is implausible. Plato's own work reveals an unusual capacity for searching self-criticism. What is even more interesting is that, more than once, the self-criticisms we find in

the later dialogues resemble Aristotelian criticisms of the earlier Platonic views. An attractive possibility is that it was his brilliant pupil's arguments that stimulated Plato to rethink some of his most deeply held positions. In the *Nicomachean Ethics*, just before his devastating criticism of the Platonic Form of the Good, Aristotle writes:

> This inquiry is difficult, since men who are dear to us have introduced the Forms. But it would seem to be better, in fact to be necessary, to uproot even what is one's own for the sake of preserving the truth—both as a general principle and because we are philosophers. For when both the people and the truth are dear to us, it is fitting to put the truth first.
>
> (1096a12–17)

It is in this spirit that we should think of Aristotle's days in the Academy.

At Plato's death, he left Athens. His Macedonian court connections may have made him politically unpopular; he may also have disapproved of the choice of Speusippus as Plato's successor, since Speusippus' work developed the strands in Platonism to which he was least sympathetic. He went to Assos in the Troad, at the invitation of Hermias, then tyrant of that region, but formerly a fellow student in the Academy. Here he spent some three years as a member of a small intellectual circle; he married Hermias' adopted daughter Pythias. While at Assos, and afterward at Mitylene on the island of Lesbos, he did the original biological research on which his later scientific writings are based. These works refer frequently to the place-names and the native species of the area. His observations, especially in marine biology, were unprecedented in their detail and accuracy. His work in these areas remained without rival until the time of William Harvey (1578–1657), and was still much admired by Charles Darwin (1809–1882).

Summoned by Philip of Macedon to the capital of Pella in 342 B.C., Aristotle became the tutor of Philip's son, Alexander, later the Great, then a boy of thirteen. Little is known about the content of Aristotle's instruction. It probably covered the standard literary texts; but it very likely ventured also into political theory and political history, areas in which Aristotle did so much later writing. Aristotle's opinion of his pupil's philosophical ability is unknown. But in later years the relationship does not appear to have been a warm one. In the *Politics* Aristotle writes that rule by a single absolute monarch would be justified only if a person appeared on earth who was as far superior to existing humans, in both intellect and moral character, as humans are to animals. He conspicuously fails to mention any case in which these conditions have been fulfilled.

After his tutorship ended, Aristotle returned to Stagira for several years and then came once again to live in Athens as a teacher of philosophy. Concerning this return, he is alleged to have composed the following epigram:

Returning to the famous land of Cecropia,
He reverently erected a monument of lofty
  friendship
for a man whom inferior men should not even
  praise.

The context makes it clear that he is referring to Plato—and, it is supposed, to his own great body of philosophical writing, most of which was produced in this period. He thus acknowledges his lifelong debt to Plato's teaching, also implying that critical pursuit of truth would be in this case an even higher tribute than praise.

As a resident alien, Aristotle was unable to own property in Athens; he therefore rented some buildings outside the city. Here, in what came to be called the Lyceum, he established his own school. (From the colonnade, or *peripatos*, attached to the main building, his followers were later called Peripatetics.) He delivered some popular lectures, but most of his time was spent in writing or in lecturing to a smaller group of serious students. Most of the surviving works are lectures written for this group, which

included a number of thinkers, like Theophrastus and Eudemus, who later achieved distinction. We find in the works a number of hints about Aristotle's classroom: notes as to where diagrams should be presented, references to objects that were presumably in the lecture room, even little jokes about his own physical appearance. (At the end of a *Metaphysics* 5 discussion of the senses of the word "mutilated," he remarks that one would not call a bald man mutilated.) There are frequent references back to previous lectures and ahead to material yet to be covered. Sometimes there are indications that Aristotle gave more than one course of lectures on a single topic, putting the same discussion in different contexts according to his plan for the series. Sometimes, too, he has obviously changed his view on a topic and introduced a substantially different discussion. In addition to the lecture courses, Aristotle encouraged his students to undertake research projects, especially in natural science and in political history (where he projected a complete collection of historical and comparative descriptions of different regimes, like the one preserved in the *Constitution of Athens*).

Aristotle's wife, Pythias, died early in this period; they had one daughter. For the rest of his life he lived with a slave woman named Herpyllis, with whom he had a son, Nicomachus, after whom the *Nicomachean Ethics* was named. Although in his will Aristotle praises Herpyllis' loyalty and kindness, he granted her freedom from legal slavery only upon his death. Aristotle, unlike Plato and very many educated Greek males of his time, appears to have been exclusively heterosexual. He does not seem to have accorded women much respect, or even careful attention. (Once he even states that they have fewer teeth than men, though some scholars have found this passage beyond belief and have moved to emend the text.) His opinion of women's intellectual and moral potential, as expressed in his political writings, was far lower than Plato's; his judgment concerning the advisability of giving them political rights, far more conservative. (He claims that women's emotions are naturally so violent and unruly that they can never, even with the best of education, become people of practical wisdom.) To his male colleagues and friends, however, Aristotle seems to have been generous and loyal; this can be seen especially in his will, which survives.

At Alexander's death in 323 B.C., Aristotle was forced by the revival of anti-Macedonian feeling in Athens to leave the city. Evidently he believed his life to be in danger, for, referring to Socrates' execution, he said that he would not allow the Athenians "to sin twice against philosophy." He retired to Chalcis, the home of his mother's relatives. A year later, he died there of illness.

WORKS

Aristotle left all his personal papers to Theophrastus, his successor as head of the Lyceum. Because of the uncertain political situation in the years following Theophrastus' death, his heirs are said to have had them removed to a cellar at Skepsis in Asia Minor. The same report goes on to say that the works remained completely hidden and unused until a rich collector, Apellicon, purchased them and brought them to Athens early in the first century B.C. This is seriously misleading. There is copious evidence that some of Aristotle's major works were used and consulted by his successors in the Lyceum, as well as by Epicurus and numerous Alexandrian intellectuals. At this stage, the works were not edited in anything like the form in which we know them, although their content, to judge from paraphrases and references, corresponds closely to that of the works we know. A list of Aristotle's works dating from the third century B.C. and prepared by a successor of his at the Lyceum (although the list has also been ascribed to an Alexandrian librarian) mentions most of the major extant works, under some identifiable description, as well as a number of works that now appear to be lost to us. (Although the biological works are not mentioned,

they were extensively consulted and cited in Alexandria during this same period.) In addition, it mentions a number of dialogues, more popular works probably published during Aristotle's lifetime. Although none of these works survive in their entirety, they were among the most popular for several centuries following Aristotle's death. We can perhaps judge from descriptions of Aristotle's style written in this period—for example, Cicero's remark that Aristotle's prose is like a "golden river"—that these works were written rather differently from the more technical treatises. In many cases, we can reconstruct portions of the dialogues and other lost works through citations in later authors.

When Sulla captured Athens (86 B.C.), the papers held by Apellicon were brought to Rome. Here they were edited, around 30 B.C., by the great scholar Andronicus of Rhodes, whose edition is the basis for all subsequent ones. He grouped books into works, arranged them in order, and also left copious notes about the authenticity and grouping of various works. (Two Arabic texts of the thirteenth century A.D. preserve the table of contents of Andronicus' edition.) Many works branded by Andronicus as minor or spurious have subsequently disappeared. We possess most of the works that he considered major and genuine in manuscripts produced between the ninth and sixteenth centuries. The transmission during the intervening period is represented by several papyrus fragments from the third century on. Some of these commentaries, especially those of Alexander of Aphrodisias (third century A.D.), prove valuable sources of information about the lost works; all pre-ninth-century commentaries are useful aids in establishing the text of the extant works.

We may group the extant treatises as follows:

1. Logic and Metaphysics
   Categories
   On Interpretation (De Interpretatione)
   Prior and Posterior Analytics
   Topics
   On Sophistical Refutations
   Metaphysics

2. Philosophy of Nature and Natural Science
   Physics
   On the Heavens (De Caelo)
   On Coming-to-Be and Passing-Away (De Generatione et Corruptione)
   Meteorologica
   Investigations about Animals (Historia Animalium)
   On the Parts of Animals (De Partibus Animalium)
   On the Movement of Animals (De Motu Animalium)
   On the Progression of Animals (De Incessu Animalium)
   On the Reproduction of Animals (De Generatione Animalium)
3. Philosophy of Mind
   On the Soul (De Anima)
   Parva Naturalia (a group of short treatises: *On the Senses, On Memory and Reminiscence, On Dreams, On Divination through Dreams, On Length and Shortness of Life, On Youth and Old Age, On Respiration*)
4. Ethical and Political Works
   Eudemian Ethics
   Nicomachean Ethics
   Magna Moralia (authenticity disputed)
   Politics
   Constitution of Athens (authenticity disputed)
5. Works about Art
   Rhetoric
   Poetics

Of the works surviving only in fragments, the most important are the dialogues *On Philosophy* and *On the Good*, the *Protrepticus*, and *On the Forms*, a valuable discussion of Plato's theories.

These groupings will immediately be seen to be ad hoc and insufficiently complex. Aristotle's metaphysics is very closely connected with his views about nature and natural beings; his work on the soul is a work about plants and animals as well as about human mental life; among the scientific works, some are concerned with the recording of detailed information, some with the discussion of general issues concerning explanation, or time, or the nature of motion; the *Rhetoric* is a work of moral psychology as well as a technical treatise. One of the most salient characteristics of Aristotle's thought is always its range and comprehensiveness: his ability to see the implications of arguments in one area for thought about a quite different subject and, at the same time, his ability to illuminate a single issue by approaching it from quite different points of view. This makes his thought both especially difficult and especially exciting to pursue.

There has been a great deal of speculation about the status of the "Aristotelian corpus." Scholars have not only raised questions of authenticity about particular works, but have also, in some cases, called into question the Aristotelian origin of the entire corpus. It is agreed by most that the general line of thought is to be attributed to Aristotle, but some have held that the exact choice of words, or even the detail of the arguments, is the work of students or imitators. These are difficult questions, requiring the most careful use of both external and internal evidence in each case. On balance, the most plausible story is that extant treatises (excepting the *Historia Animalium*, his biological data book) were written, but unpolished, lectures, never finally revised for publication by Aristotle himself. We can rely on the exact wording of most of the material, but not always on its final ordering. We cannot rely on the order of books within a treatise as Aristotelian, nor always even on the order of chapters within a book. All titles and many introductory and concluding sentences are likely to be the work of later editors. Cross-references to other works can be genuine, but they should be suspected if they are not well integrated into their context. Throughout, we are, in addition, faced by many textual problems, some of which require the transposition of substantial passages for their solution. Some chapters, on the other hand, may have been left poorly organized by Aristotle himself and are best regarded as assorted notes that were never worked into a finished discussion (for example, *De Anima* 3.6–7).

The most serious philosophical problems raised by the state of the corpus come from its duplications: (1) multiple discussions of a single problem, and (2) a single discussion repeated in more than one context. There are numerous cases of the first type. Sometimes the discussions are very similar, sometimes apparently incompatible. Sometimes the incompatible discussions appear in close proximity in what appears to be the same work. Doublets of the second type may be very brief, or they may be several books long; sometimes the repetition is verbatim, and sometimes there are changes and reorderings. *Metaphysics* 1 and 13 have many chapters in common, with small but significant changes. *Metaphysics* 11 compiles material from other books of the *Metaphysics* and from the *Physics*. The most perplexing problem is that books 5–7 of the *Nicomachean Ethics* also appear as books 4–6 of the *Eudemian Ethics*. It is unclear whether they were originally intended to stand with one or the other or with both (see below). In each case of duplication we must ask how likely it is that Aristotle would have put the repeated portion in both contexts himself; if on this hypothesis there appear to be problems in the argument of the work as a whole, we must ask whether these problems are only apparent, and, if they are not, whether it is clear that Aristotle himself would have been aware of the problem. Where we have two or more differing accounts of a single issue, the most important question will be whether these differences amount to incompatibility or merely to a shift of perspective or a difference of starting point. We must decide, furthermore, what sorts of discrepancies justify us in invoking a chronological hypothesis.

Medieval philosophy viewed Aristotle's thought as a closed, consistent system, totally without internal development. The "master of those who know" never changed his mind. Internal discrepancies were either explained away or not fully noticed. This view of the corpus was brilliantly overthrown early in this century by Werner Jaeger's important work, which forcefully presented evidence of philosophical development, especially with regard to Aristotle's view of Platonic metaphysics. Jae-ger recovered and stressed the flexibility and lack of dogmatism in Aristotle's philosophizing. Whether or not we finally agree with the particular story he tells, his work began a new era in Aristotle scholarship and made it possible to take Aristotle seriously once again as a genuine philosopher. Unfortunately, modern scholars have sometimes gone to the other extreme in reaction, making irresponsible use of developmental explanations, often assuming incompatibility before expending much effort to resolve the difficulty.

The general picture endorsed by Jaeger and by his more influential followers, such as W. D. Ross and F. Nuyens (though in some important respects their accounts differ from Jaeger's), is of an Aristotle initially subservient to Plato but gradually developing his own views. Given a discrepancy of doctrine, the assumption is that the more nearly Platonic view is the earlier of the two. Some critics even claim to be able to guess how many years have elapsed between two works by the extent of the divergence from Plato. We have already questioned the psychological plausibility of these assumptions, which also ignore the extent to which Plato's thought developed during Aristotle's years in the Academy. We are best off relying, where we can, on firmer evidence of chronology: historical and geographical references; cross-references to the arguments of other works, where these are well embedded in their context; discernible philosophical reliance upon or criticism of the exegesis and/or argument of other works. We know that the writing of the biological works must postdate Aristotle's period of research in Assos and Lesbos; this often proves helpful in dating other related texts. Evidence of stylistic development is difficult to use and to assess, since the status of these works as finished literary compositions is itself in question. More dangerous still is the assumption that a view which appears "better" or "more mature" to us is bound to be later. We are not always good judges of philosophic worth; and philosophers have been known to decline.

In general, it is important to recognize the

extent to which Aristotle's problems and interest in a particular work dictate the way he will present an issue; difference of perspective and emphasis too often is read as a change of view. (Aristotle himself often remarks that "the natural scientist" would say one thing about a certain problem, but another character, for example, the first philosopher, would say something different.) We can preserve Jaeger's important insight that Aristotle's thought is flexible and not dogmatic, centered around certain problems and questions rather than around the goal of establishing a closed system, without relying, as Jaeger did, on a chronological premise that assumes the very psychological principles that it ought to establish.

METHOD: APPEARANCES AND UNDERSTANDING

At the beginning of book 7 of the *Nicomachean Ethics*, Aristotle pauses to reflect about his philosophical method:

> Here, as in all other cases, we must set down the appearances *(phainomena)* and, first working through the puzzles, in this way go on to show, if possible, the truth of all the beliefs we hold *(endoxa)* about these experiences; and, if this is not possible, the truth of the greatest number and the most authoritative. For if the difficulties are resolved and the beliefs are left in place, we will have done enough showing.
>
> (1145b1 ff.)

Proper philosophical method is committed to, and limited by, the appearances, or *phainomena*, here interchangeable with *endoxa*, shared beliefs. (Later in the passage, *phainomena* is replaced by *legomena*, what we say.) The job of the philosopher, in each area, is to gather and work through our shared beliefs and conceptions on the subject, our human interpretations of the world—often as revealed in what we say. If the philosopher resolves the puzzles or contradictions, while at the same time preserving as true the deepest and the

greatest number of these beliefs, he has done his job sufficiently.

For a long time, Aristotle scholars did not take Aristotle at his word. They were willing to grant that this was his method only in a limited range of cases, if at all. First of all, they were reluctant to believe that a method that begins from our beliefs and interpretations could have anything to do with science. In the grip of a scientific inquiry modeled on that of Francis Bacon, interpreters believed that any good scientist must begin from hard data gathered by precise observation that remains uninfluenced by our beliefs and theories about the world. If, as seemed likely, Aristotle was a serious scientist, his method must have been something like this. Hence, even when the scientific works presented them with methodological remarks very similar to the one quoted, and using the word *phainomena*, interpreters translated *phainomena* as "observed facts" or "data of perception," thereby concealing its connection with belief and interpretation and making Aristotle look more reliably Baconian.

Contemporary philosophy of science has taken a more subtle view of the connection between theory and observation, a view much more like the one explored by the Aristotle of the undoctored texts. It does not shock us now to find a distinguished thinker suggesting that all observation is in some way theory-laden, a part of the complex structure of human beliefs and human discourse about the world. We are now able to see with interest that Aristotle's *Physics* is primarily taken up with inquiry into our human conceptions of place, time, and change, usually starting from observation of what we say; that his theoretical works of biology are deeply concerned with our conceptions of substance and matter; and that even his most specific empirical research in biology and cosmology presents itself as the recording of human appearances. Of course, there are important differences among types of observation that will be relevant in the different cases; but by using *phainomena* of all "data," and by indicating that there is, in general, a single method in all the cases, Aristotle stresses what all the cases share: a concern with investigating the structure of the world as perceived (therefore interpreted), demarcated, believed in by human beings.

There is, however, another serious difficulty to be faced: how we are to reconcile this account of Aristotle's method (which seems to conform rather well to his practice in the *Physics*, *Metaphysics*, and many other works) with his description of the structure of scientific understanding, or *epistēmē*, in the *Posterior Analytics*. There he argues that scientific understanding has the structure of a deductive system, internally consistent and hierarchically ordered, depending on first principles that are true and basic, and explanatory of the other conclusions of the science. The scientist has *epistēmē* (understanding) when he is able to show how the more basic principles of his subject explain the less basic—when, in general, he is able to give the appropriate explanation for what he knows.

Put this way, Aristotle's interest in *epistēmē* already coheres more closely with his interest in the *phainomena* than it does in some traditional accounts, where *epistēmē* is (misleadingly) rendered as "certain knowledge" and Aristotle's interest is taken for epistemological certainty. Aristotle's point is that when we understand a subject thoroughly we must be able to do more than cite a series of truths; we must be able to show how they are related to one another, how less basic ones follow from more basic ones. There is an important distinction between knowing (and using) a principle and *understanding* it. What understanding requires is a full and thorough survey of all the relevant *phainomena* and their ordering in a perspicuous system. This is not a research program or a heuristic device. One does not have to understand a geometrical principle in order to know and use it; nor does one have to understand, for example, the central role of substance-concepts in human practices of counting in order to do some counting and to claim to know that one's answer is correct. But if one wishes to claim that one *understands* a geometric principle, or

the human practice of counting, one must be prepared, Aristotle holds, to give explanations and accounts that would locate these principles appropriately within their larger context in the relevant body of human knowledge.

The first principles, however, remain a source of difficulty. Through the medieval tradition we have received the account that each Aristotelian science rests on principles that are not discovered through experience at all (are not *phainomena*), but are grasped instead by special acts of intellectual intuition. The story tells us that in addition to the method of gathering and adjusting *phainomena*, Aristotle invokes, at the most basic level, an entirely different intellectual process, an activity of the pure intellect a priori. This is supposed to be the only way we can provide an epistemically sound foundation for any kind of understanding.

This reading of the *Analytics* runs into trouble immediately when we look at the way Aristotle actually does go about defending his most basic principles. In *Metaphysics* 4.4, for example, he responds to an opponent who has assailed the validity of the Principle of Non-Contradiction (contradictory predicates cannot both be true of the same subject at the same time). This principle he calls "the most secure principle of all." If the medieval story were correct, we would expect that, in reply to the opponent's request that he demonstrate the truth of this principle, Aristotle would say that we do not need to demonstrate it, since we know it with certainty, a priori, by a special act of intellectual intuition. He says nothing like this. He says that, although we cannot demonstrate it, since it is the most basic of all and is presupposed by all our discourse, we can give the opponent what he calls an "elenctic demonstration": we can show him that all of his discourse, including his denial of the principle, actually relies on the principle. First, he says, you must find out whether the opponent will in fact say anything to you or not. If he will not say anything, then you can stop worrying about him. "It is comical to look for something to say to someone who won't say anything. A person like that, insofar as he is like that, is pretty well like a vegetable" (1006a13–15). But if he *does* say something, something definite, then you can go on to show him that in so doing he is presupposing and making use of the very principle he attacks. For in order to be saying something definite, he has to be ruling out something else as incompatible: at the very least, the contradictory of what he has asserted.

It is obvious that this reply has nothing in common with the story of certainty through intellectual intuition. It remains entirely inside human practices and human experience and aims at displaying perspicuously the ground-level basic role of this logical principle in all human discourse. It does not even claim any harder sort of certainty than that. In this view, understanding of a basic principle is not some special sort of grasp but a clearer view of the fundamental role played by that principle in a certain area of human experience. It is evident that this would be fully compatible with the method of appearance saving described in the *Ethics* passage.

It emerges, in fact, that this is also the best way to read the disputed text of the *Analytics*. What *nous*, or intellectual insight, does in *Posterior Analytics* 2.19 is not to move us away from experience to the sphere of the a priori but to give us insight into the explanatory role of principles that we got from experience and were using all along. To understand the Principle of Non-Contradiction is simply to see that we could not communicate without it. We achieve this kind of *nous* by practice in, and reflection on, our human world.

Aristotle does not hold inflexibly to the claim that in every area understanding will display a fully consistent hierarchical system, self-contained and autonomous from other areas of inquiry. First of all, there are some areas, in particular ethics and politics, where he denies from the start that the end is any sort of hierarchical deductive system. The indeterminancy and fluidity of what he calls "the matter of the practical" would make any such systematization an oversimplification. Furthermore, Aristotle probably believed that there could be a

conflict between two genuine obligations and that such a conflict would not always lead us to revise the system; inconsistency of this sort in ethics is not objectionable, as inconsistency in a system of mathematical or scientific beliefs would be. But even in science itself, as Aristotle began to think less about mathematics (the model science of the *Analytics*) and more about astronomy and biology, he seems to have become less interested in hierarchical systematization; and he probably dropped altogether his demand for autonomy. At any rate, his late treatise *On the Motion of Animals* shows an interdisciplinary approach to biology and cosmology that would not have been permitted by the strictures of the *Posterior Analytics*.

I have said nothing about one of Aristotle's major philosophical achievements, the development of formal logic. It is easy to underrate this contribution, since we take it for granted that a philosopher will have some acquaintance with logic and will, at any rate, subject his own arguments to rigorous scrutiny. In Aristotle's day, however, nobody had ever attempted to give a general account of validity in argument; although arguments were recognized and criticized as invalid, the absence of a general formal account made fallacy much harder to detect; it is clear that sophistical characters capitalized on this situation, hoodwinking the public and giving all of philosophy a bad name. To go into detail about syllogistic inference would be beyond the scope of this essay, but we can certainly say that Aristotle's *Prior Analytics* is a towering achievement. In an area where nothing had been done before, Aristotle created a formalization that was the dominant system of logic until early in this century.

METAPHYSICS: THE SEARCH FOR SUBSTANCE

The central question in Aristotle's metaphysical writings is the question "What is substance?" or "What are the substances?" Aristotle tells us that this is, in his view, the central and guiding question of his entire philosophical tradition:

> And indeed the question that was asked long ago, and is asked now and always, and is always a matter for perplexity, viz. the question what being *(to on)* is, this is the question what substance *(ousia)* is; for it is this that some assert to be one in number, some more than one, and some limited, others unlimited.
>
> (*Metaphysics* 1028b2–6)

The general question about the nature of "what is" reduces to, or is equivalent to, the question about a certain part or type of that which is, namely *ousia*, usually translated as "substance." (*Ousia* is simply a verbal noun formed from the participle of the verb "to be.") It is not intuitively evident just what this question means. In order to have any idea of what Aristotle's theory attempts and accomplishes we must first try to get a better purchase on his question: what is one searching for when one searches for substance or substances, and to what real problems that might grip or trouble us does such a search respond?

It is difficult to trace this problem to its pre-philosophical roots, since even the word *ousia* is primarily an Aristotelian word, with no very clear philosophical or extraphilosophical history in earlier texts, especially as distinct from *to on*, "that which is." Fortunately, in the following portions of *Metaphysics* 7, Aristotle gives us a number of examples of theories of *ousia*; he claims that various early Greek thinkers were all answering the question about *ousia* when they put forth their very different theories about the nature of the universe. Although none of these thinkers, with the exception of Plato, used the term *ousia* or described himself as searching for *ousia*, Aristotle clearly thinks that there is a way we can view their inquiries as motivated by a common question, one that he calls the question of *ousia*. To see what concerns these earlier theories share should, then, help us to understand Aristotle's search.

Aristotle's examples here appear very het-erogeneous: the material monism of Thales and Anaxagoras; the Pythagorean number-cosmogony; Plato's theory of forms. But if we examine Aristotle's use of them as precedents for his inquiries here and elsewhere, we pick out two large and closely connected questions around which their enterprises, and his, seem to converge: a question about change and continuity; a question about identity.

As early Greek philosophers observed process and change in the world around them—the cycle of the seasons, the birth, growth, and death of living creatures, the evaporation of water in time of heat, its replenishment from the upper air—they were moved to ask how we ought to talk about and explain such changes. Early mythology was content to invoke the capricious will of anthropomorphic beings constrained by no general laws of nature. Early scientists looked instead for explanations that were both naturalistic, introducing no nonempirical entities, and lawlike, bringing the confusing matter of nature into a perspicuous, graspable order. They had to confront, in the process, a number of distinct questions that they themselves did not always very clearly distinguish.

First, they had to ask themselves what sorts of entities in the world were the primary subjects, or substrates, of change. That is, to what sorts of persisting entities do growth and process happen? A coherent story of change seems to presuppose our ability to pick out from its surroundings and identify some underlying item that is the "substrate" or "underlying thing" (Aristotle's *hupokeimenon*) of that change, something that itself persists as one and the same throughout the change. Plato expressed this demand forcefully in the *Theaetetus* in his criticism of the "Heracliteans," who are said to hold that everything is always changing in all respects. Plato points out that this would make all coherent discourse about change—including their theory itself—impossible; unless you can single out something *to which* the change belongs, which itself remains unchanged, we will have no subject for our discourse about the change, and we will be able to say nothing at all—except perhaps, Plato adds, "not even so, said in an indefinite way" (*Theaetetus* 183b). The search for substance is, in part, a search for the most basic substrates: the persisting entities that form the basis for our discourse about change. This question, Aristotle believes, should be distinguished, at least initially, from several other questions that one might ask about change—questions asking for an account of how, physiologically, change takes place in natural substances; and questions about alternative models of explanation, such as whether an efficient-causal or a teleological explanation is preferable for the growth and movement of living creatures. These questions seem to demand a prior answer to the substrate question; for only when we know what it is that is undergoing the change do we have a hope of comparing different accounts of its development and investigating its concrete physical structures.

The second major question is more difficult to articulate; but it also forms a deep part of the Greeks', and our own, prephilosophical questioning about the world. This is what Aristotle calls the "What is it?" question. Suppose I am considering some particular item in my experience: let us say, Socrates. I have a sense that, in order to pursue my curiosity about this creature further, I must have some answer to the question "What is this?" I want to know what it is about this individual that makes him the individual he is: what enables me to single him out as a distinct particular and mark him off from his surroundings; what enables me to re-identify him at a later time as the same individual I encountered earlier. What I really seem to be asking for is a separation of the properties of the observed specimen into two groups: properties that are just incidental and have no bearing on whether or not this item is Socrates (for example, pale color, which might depart if Socrates gets a suntan, without making him cease to be the same entity); and properties whose departure would mean the end of this individual. I am asking what features Socrates must have

as long as he continues to exist as one and the same particular; this seems to amount to asking what Socrates really is—what, in the mixture that impresses itself on our sight, is the real Socrates. In the human case, the question takes on a special urgency, since it becomes connected with complicated ethical and political issues, such as the determination of death and the treatment of the severely handicapped. Any adequate detailed answer to the question would have to embody our most serious thinking about personal survival and human species membership.

These two questions (distinguished by Aristotle in several places) are obviously very closely intertwined. For an adequate theory of change must single out, as its substrates, items that are not only relatively enduring, but also definite and distinct; items that can be identified and characterized. Unless we can single it out, individuate it from its surroundings, and say something about what it is, we can hardly make it the cornerstone of our explanatory enterprise. On the other hand, when we ask the "What is it?" question about a particular—for example, Socrates—one of the things we are asking is, what changes can Socrates endure (as a substrate) and still persist as one and the same individual? What about him must remain constant, even though other properties may come and go? Thus answers that are inadequate to the one question are likely to fail to answer the other at the same time.

As Aristotle sees it, early natural scientists went wrong because they believed that the "What is it?" question, asked about natural entities, was equivalent to the question "What is it made of?" and that a list of material constituents was an adequate account of the identity or nature of any particular. Aristotle traces this belief to their overriding interest in explaining change, which they took to require substrates that were the most enduring or permanent items that could be found. Seeing that material stuffs persisted when substances like men and horses perished, seeing that the death of an individual like Socrates leaves around a heap of flesh, blood, and bones (or, in more elementary terms, earth, air, fire, and water), they concluded too quickly that matter must be the primary substrate of change and hence also the basic nature of things. A question about a thing's identity was construed as a request for a list of the persisting stuffs that preexisted it, compose it, and will survive it.

> Most of those who first did philosophy thought that the only principles of all things were material stuffs. For whatever things come from, and whatever they perish into in the end, while *its* being remains, though the affections change, this thing they took to be the element and principle of things. And this is why they thought that nothing ever comes to be or passes away, since this sort of nature was always preserved.
>
> (*Metaphysics* 983b6–17)

We can see to what paradoxical conclusions the materialist view of identity and explanation could lead. If substances *are* (are identical with) their constituents, then, in a very real sense, no substances ever perish, so long as the sum total of material stuffs remains constant. This account cannot, then, make the distinction that is fundamental in our discourse and practices, between property change (what Aristotle calls *alloiōsis*) and real coming-into-being and going-out-of-being, between the change that happens to Socrates when he gets a suntan and the change that takes place in the world when Socrates is born or dies. Aristotle will insist that any good theory of change must take this distinction as among its most basic starting points, "save" it, and show its importance.

The Platonist answers to our two questions are peculiar in a rather different way. The Theory of Forms has a tendency to treat a living being—for example, Socrates—as a sort of mixture of various form-instances, in which no one is more fundamental than any other in determining the particular's identity and in explaining what happens to it. Each thing that is or comes to be true of Socrates is explained with reference to his participation in a certain form

(or his coming-to-participate in that form). Socrates is a human being in virtue of his participation in the form of the human, just as he is white in virtue of his participation in the form of whiteness, and just in virtue of his participation in the form of justice. Where, in all this, is Socrates himself? We are never clearly told. One problem is the obscurity of the notion of "participation," never fully explained. But an equally serious difficulty is that no form is given any sort of privileged status in fixing the identity of the particular. This means that it becomes very hard to say what sorts of changes Socrates, the substrate, can undergo and still remain one and the same individual. Will he still be Socrates if he loses his white color? his justice? his humanness? To these legitimate questions, questions to which our ordinary practices of individuating and identifying offer answers that are there to be perspicuously recorded, Plato has little to say. In the *Phaedo* he offers only the somewhat uninformative answer that he remains alive as long as the form of life is instantiated in him, and no longer. What the connection between the form of life (or the livingness of a particular human) and whiteness, humanness, or justice might be, we are never told. Even in the *Theaetetus*, in the passage we have discussed, he insists only that for any case of change there must be *some* persisting item to which the change belongs; he does not go further and ask whether there are persisting entities that play this substrate role in a privileged way in our discourse and our practices.

Such was the situation with which Aristotle was confronted. Let us now follow in more detail his attempt to improve on it, developing theories of change and of the identity of particulars that will be more adequate than these to the complexities of human practices.

Both his Platonist and his materialist predecessors, as we have seen, blurred the distinction we ordinarily make between substances and their properties, substantial change and property change. Accordingly, Aristotle's first step in building an account of the identity of persisting things is to reintroduce and explore this distinction. The *Categories*, a compressed and probably early work, develops a complex system of classifications intended to enable us to see the central role played by certain concepts, which we might call species or substance concepts, in classifying and identifying the particulars of our experience. Aristotle first introduces a fourfold distinction of "the things that are." This distinction cuts across the later very famous distinction of the ten "categories," which we might see as answers to different sorts of questions that we might ask about a particular in our experience. (The ten are substance, quantity, quality, relation, place, time, position, having, doing, being affected.) The fourfold distinction functions to separate substance from all the other categories and to separate particular from general or universal in each category:

1. Things said of a subject, but not in a subject (Aristotelian name: "secondary substance"; examples: man, horse)
2. Things in a subject, but not said of a subject (particulars in nonsubstance categories; examples: this particular knowledge of grammar, this particular white)
3. Things both in and said of a subject (nonparticulars in nonsubstance categories; examples: knowledge, color)
4. Things neither in nor said of a subject (Aristotle's "primary substances"; examples: this man, this horse)

This is all, so far, somewhat obscure. The real motivation for this distinction becomes clear only later, when Aristotle explains the classifying role of general conceptions and the central importance of both "primary substance" and "secondary substance" in any good answer to our questions about change and identity. The point of the distinction between being "said of" and being "in" a subject seems to be as follows. Take two sentences: "Socrates is a human being," and "Socrates is pink." Platonist philosophy, as we saw, failed to make any salient distinction between these two; the situa-

tions they describe were analyzed in strictly symmetrical fashion in terms of participation in the forms of humanity and pinkness. Socrates, let us say, just has all these items *in* him: humanness, pinkness, etc. The problem, as we saw, is that we then seem to have no way of understanding how we individuate and identify Socrates himself. The theory conceives of him as a bare container of properties; but it is entirely unclear how we are to individuate a bare container and trace it through space and time. And yet these are things that we do in fact do; and a theory of substance should reflect and display this. The materialist theory is not much different, since it conceives of Socrates as a set of modifications of some underlying material stuffs, which it then seems to require us to individuate and trace through space and time.

Aristotle's basic insight is that we do not individuate either bare containers or bare, uncharacterized matter. Our discourse and our experience of the world relies very fundamentally on a certain sort of classification, a classification according to substance concepts, such as human being, dog, horse, tree. We pick Socrates out as a subject of discourse and a substrate of change (the Greek word *hupokeimenon* stands both for grammatical subject and for substrate of change) only when we pick him out *as* a human being. Only under such species concepts do we identify and reidentify particulars, count them, mark them off from their surroundings. Questions such as "How many?" and "Is it the same as . . . ?" must be asked relatively to some covering concept of this kind. The question "How many things are there in this room?" has no definite answer, until we substitute for it the concrete questions: "How many human beings?" "How many horses?" "How many desks?" Similarly, when we ask the "What is it?" question, pointing to an item in our experience, we have given a better answer when we say "a human being" than when we say "a white thing" or "a five-foot-tall thing"; for only the first answer will provide us with ways of reliably tracing Socrates through time and answering identity questions about him. This Aristotle conveys by saying that it is secondary substances such as "human being" and "horse" that "reveal the being" of the primary substance (*Categories* 2a30). Socrates' color and height may change, while he remains "numerically one and the same"; he cannot cease to be human and remain one and the same. Therefore it is humanness, rather than color, that tells us what Socrates really is.

Aristotle argues not only that secondary substance concepts play a basic role in our individuation and discourse about substantial particulars such as Socrates and this horse. He wants us to see, in addition, that it is substantial particulars, identified under a substance concept, that are, in our discourse, the most basic subjects of discourse and substrates of change. We cannot and do not pick out an individual piece of white and trace it through time and change. Universals in nonsubstance categories play a limited classifying role: we classify white as a color, and that gives us a way of answering a "What is it?" question about a particular bit of white. But this answer is not self-sufficient. White is, in our experience and discourse, always the property of some substance or other, and our ability to individuate it, and other nonsubstantial items, relies on our prior ability to individuate substances.

> It seems peculiar to substance that an item that is numerically one and the same is able to receive opposites. For example, a color that is numerically one and the same will not be light and dark.... But ... an individual human being, being one and the same, becomes now light and now dark, and warm and cold, and mediocre and praiseworthy.
> (*Categories* 4a10 ff)

Property change can have a coherent account only when we pin it to an underlying substance, identified by its appropriate substance concept.

In the *Categories*, Aristotle said nothing about the coming-to-be and passing-away of substances. He showed only how substances play a fundamental role in the explanation of other sorts of change. But without a discussion of what he calls "simple coming-to-be," his alternative to the materialist theories will remain seriously incomplete. For the early scientists, as we saw, claimed that matter was the basic substrate of change, on the ground that it was what remained when particular substances came to be and passed away. It is a great strength of Aristotle's writing about change that he explores this position fully and shows its strength, before going on to indicate what considerations should lead us to reject it. In *Physics* 1 and in *On Coming-to-Be and Passing-Away,* he articulates our intuitive distinction between "alteration" *(alloiōsis),* or property change, and "coming-to-be" *(genesis),* or substantial change. He does this (compare especially *Physics* 1.7) in characteristic fashion by pointing to features of our talk about change and then going on to show the importance of the distinctions embodied in our talk. Aristotle acknowledges (especially in *Physics* 1.7–8 and in *Metaphysics* 7.3) that if one thinks of the search for the basic substance as, primarily, a search for a persisting and continuous substrate, one might well be tempted to think that bare, undifferentiated material stuffs should be the primary substances. But he goes on to argue that this is a temptation that the natural philosopher should reject. "For being separable and a definite this are attributes that seem especially to belong to substance" (*Metaphysics* 1029b27–8). The idea is that a truly perspicuous explanation of change must attribute the change to something definite that can be picked out, marked off from its surroundings, identified, and reidentified. Material stuffs, even when sorted into "lumps" and "heaps," are not definite enough, lack sufficiently clear criteria of identity and persistence, to play this role. Suppose we think of identifying Socrates' "nature" with his constituent matter, rather than, say, with his functional or formal structure; suppose we think of explaining the various changes that happen to Socrates during his lifetime as modifications of these elemental stuffs. There will be two problems with this. First of all, matter does not even, with regard to a particular living substance, persist. Socrates is constantly changing his particular material constituents. Food comes in, wastes are excreted; and yet Socrates remains one and the same particular. Our theory of change must encompass this fact; but it cannot do so if it persists in attempting to identify the living creature with any particular set of its changing material constituents. Second, the material stuffs simply are not definite enough; matter, as such, has no principle of individuation. Of the elemental stuffs, Aristotle writes in *Metaphysics* 7.16, "None of these is a unity, but a kind of heap, until they are concocted and some one thing comes to be from them." The moral is that any theory hoping to account for the changes of natural substances must begin, not with material constituents and their interactions, but with some account of the persisting substance itself that does the changing.

> It is not enough to state simply the substances out of which they are made, as "out of fire," or "out of earth." If we were describing a bed or any other like article, we should endeavor to describe the form of it rather than the matter (bronze or wood)—or at any rate, the matter, if described, would be described as belonging to a concrete whole.
>
> (*Parts of Animals* 640b)

To be sure, the natural philosopher will have to deal with many cases of "absolute coming-to-be" in which no substance persists: the death of Socrates, or, at an even more fundamental level, the reciprocal transformations of the various elements. But Aristotle insists, first of all, that this is no reason for the philosopher to blur the important distinction between the two types of change. Second, in every case he should look for the most definite available substrate. It is only in the case of ultimate elemental change that Aristotle speaks of the theoretical entity, "prime matter," which was wrongly thought by his medieval interpreters to serve, in his view, as matter for every change. In *On Coming-to-Be* 2.4–5, he seems to concede that in order to explain the changes of earth, air, fire, and water

into one another, one does need to introduce a bare theoretical entity that is not capable of separate existence and has no properties in its own right. But he is not happy with this solution, and he clearly would rather explain as many natural changes as possible as changes belonging to some persisting definite substance. He even claims in several places that there is no continuous material substratum for, for example, the death of Socrates: since we cannot identify constituent matter except as constituent of a substance, playing a functional role in the life of that substance, we ought to deny that the stuff left around after Socrates' death is really "flesh" or "blood." It cannot be, he says, since it does not play the functional role in the life of that particular with respect to which we were able to identify it and speak of it in the first place.

If material stuffs neither serve as the basic substrates for the explanation of change nor provide us with perspicuous answers to identity questions, what does play this role? What *is* the "nature" or essence of Socrates, with which he is truly identical throughout his career? Most of *Metaphysics* 7 (see also *Physics* 2.1) is devoted to exploring this question and to defending a particular candidate, the *eidos*, or "form" of the concrete substance. Throughout the continuous life processes of a particular natural being, what does, what must, remain the same about it is not material composition, for that continually alters; nor is it properties such as color, size, shape, or position, for those too could alter without taking the individual out of existence. It is the structure or organization of the individual, the formal-functional structure that it shares with other members of its species. Socrates is, as long as he lives, identical with a certain example of characteristically human functional organization. When he ceases to be organized so as to think, move, and nourish himself in characteristically human ways, he exists no longer. Socrates is the same in *kind* as any other human being; there is, in other words, nothing that we can say about the essential properties of Socrates that would distinguish him from Callias. But he is a particular, definite example of the species type that traces a unique path through space and time, realized in gradually changing materials. The so-called "form" is not a *part* of the thing or a component element in the thing. It has the best claim to be identical with the thing; it is the thingness of the thing, what the thing is. At its breakdown that thing will no longer exist.

Aristotle's question about substance broaches many of the most complicated questions that are implicitly raised by human life and discourse. His inquiry (the depth and complexity of which have hardly been hinted at here) has the great virtue of grasping the complex interconnections among many different questions and problems, and of trying to keep these complexities in view in the theoretical solution. For these reasons his theory provides us with the basis for an account of the identity of persons, and their continuity through time, that is still enormously powerful against the dominant materialist and reductionist theories of our day, which are as vulnerable to Aristotle's criticisms as were the theories of his predecessors.

I have not, of course, even touched upon many other rich areas of Aristotle's metaphysical thought: his accounts of the basic logical principles in *Metaphysics* 4; his development of an anti-Platonist philosophy of mathematics in *Metaphysics* 10, 13, and 14; his development of a rational theology in *Metaphysics* 12. I have tried to follow one line of his thinking in some detail; but this should not imply that other areas are not equally worthy of serious philosophical attention.

NATURAL PHILOSOPHY: THE TYPES OF EXPLANATION

We can already see how closely intertwined metaphysics and philosophy of nature are in Aristotle's thought. The paradigmatic cases of unitary, persisting substances are, for him, living organic creatures, things that "have within themselves a principle of change and of staying unchanged" (*Physics* 192b13–14). Our criteria of identity and distinctness are even clearer for these things than they are for other substances, such as artifacts. (We are much more clear about what counts as the death of Socrates than about what sorts of repairs to my house will make it a numerically different house.) For this reason, Aristotle's search for substance, as he himself frequently says, is, first and foremost, an inquiry into the natures of living creatures. But in the *Physics* 2, Aristotle also goes on to develop a complex account of explanation, asking what the relative merits are of different competing explanatory structures. Some of this material overlaps with the *Metaphysics*, renewing and pressing further the attack against the various forms of materialism and reductionism in the philosophy of nature. But the account of the famous "four causes" in 2.3 and 2.7 contributes important new insights as well.

In enumerating the types of "causes" or *aitiai*, Aristotle is pointing to different ways in which we can answer "why" questions about objects or events in our experience. We observe a thing or a happening and ask "on account of what" *(dia ti)* did that happen, why is that the way it is? Aristotle is interested in stressing the variety of the types of answers we do in fact offer to these requests for explanation in our ordinary speech; on this basis he will go on to criticize the tradition of natural science for offering overly narrow and reductionistic models of scientific explanation. *Metaphysics* 1, in its detailed history of pre-Socratic science, shows us how slowly science and philosophy returned to the richness and complexity in explanation giving that Aristotle shows, in *Physics* 2, to be characteristic of our ordinary speech.

There has been a great deal of discussion about the proper translation of the words *aitia* and *aition*, Aristotle's central terms in these discussions. The traditional rendering in Aristotelian contexts is "cause"; hence, we hear of Aristotle's "theory of the four causes." The problem with this interpretation is that it pries Aristotle's usage away from the ordinary usage of the Greek term; it also misleads us into thinking Aristotle's interests narrower than in fact they are. The most common meaning for the adjective *aitios* in pre-Aristotelian Greek is something like "responsible for" or "explanatory of." A demand to know the *aition* of an event is indeed, just as Aristotle says, a "why," a request for an explanation; and the person, event, or thing that is found to be *aition* is so because, in one way or another, that entity figures in the answer to the "why" question. If *x* is, or happens, on account of *y*, then *y* can be called an *aition* of *x*. (Frequently these words occur, as we might expect, in contexts of the judicial ascription of responsibility.) The English word "cause," in its most common usage, suggests a particular way in which one thing can be explanatory of the occurrence of something else: the way that Aristotle will call the "moving" or "efficient" *aition*. When we use this translation for all four types of answer to "why" questions, we are tempted to try to assimilate all four patterns of Aristotelian explanation to efficient causality. In the case of teleological explanation, in particular, this has produced disastrous misreadings of Aristotle's thought, as we shall see. We should, then, bear in mind that Aristotle is beginning from the most general interest in explanation; he is interested in exploring the variety of ways in which we offer explanations, and asking what the value of each major explanatory type is to the student of nature. We may continue to use the translation "cause" if we realize that it is not quite right and avoid being led by it into misreading.

When Aristotle surveys the explanatory patterns present in our talk about things and events in the world, he discerns four main types. The first is what is generally known as the "material cause": "something is said to be explanatory *(aition)* of something else if the thing comes to be out of it and persists as a constituent, as the bronze is explanatory of the statue and the silver of the bowl" (*Physics* 194b23-5). Aristotle is thinking of a situation in which, when asked something like, "Why is this statue (man, horse) as it is?" he answers, "Because it is made of bronze (flesh and blood,

bones)." He repeatedly stresses that this sort of answer, a favorite of the early natural science tradition, as we saw, is no good on its own; an enumeration of the material constituents of Socrates is no better answer to questions about how Socrates comes to be as he is than it is to the question about his identity or essential nature. This brings us to the central importance of the second sort of explanation, usually known as the "formal cause," and called by Aristotle here "the formula of the essence," "the substance," and "the definition." Here, when asked why the horse or human being is as it is, he answers by saying whatever he can about the formal or functional character that is common to all members of that kind. Aristotle is at pains to insist that by "form" he means not surface shape or configuration, but the underlying structure in virtue of which a thing performs the functions characteristic of that sort of thing. This sort of explanation of a thing is prior to the enumeration of its constituents; it is only when he has picked out the statue as a formal or functional entity that he can go on to ask what *it* is made of. Constituents must be enumerated as parts *of* a complex whole.

The next type of explanation, "the origin of change," usually called "the efficient cause," corresponds rather closely to our notion of cause. Aristotle has in mind the situation in which, in order to explain why an event happened or a thing is as it is, he mentions some other event or agent that acted in such a way as to produce it. For living creatures he is thinking particularly of the way in which the parent, and the parent's nature, are explanatory of the nature and development of the child.

Finally, we reach the most difficult interpretive problem in this section: the teleological explanation, or "final cause," what Aristotle often calls "the end" or "that for the sake of which." Aristotle gives particular importance to this sort of explanation, in which we say that *x* is, or happens, for the sake of *y*. In several of his works on animals, he insists that we ought to give accounts of growth and development in this form, explaining the various life processes in the growing animal as tending toward the end of mature adult functioning, as specified in our account of what it is to be that sort of creature. (We see here the very close connection between formal-functional and teleological explanation, frequently stressed by Aristotle.)

> For coming-to-be is for the sake of being (ousia), not being for the sake of coming-to-be. . . . Hence we should, if possible, say that because this is what it is to be a human being, therefore this human being has these parts; for he cannot be without them. . . . And because he is a thing of this sort, his coming-to-be must happen the way it does. And that is why this part comes to be first, and then this.
>
> (*Parts of Animals* 640a18 ff.)

We can perhaps best approach this difficult issue by sketching a traditional understanding, which wrongly conflates Aristotelian teleology with later Stoic and Christian views, and then distinguishing Aristotle's view from it. According to the common story, Aristotle views all of nature as ordered in a harmonious teleological system, so that each event and each natural being can be seen to have its place in contributing to the ideal order. Everything happens for the sake of the good of the whole. This reading is contradicted by Aristotle's text in several ways. (1) He repeatedly insists that it is only living beings whose movements and parts should be explained as "for the sake of" something. Rocks, eclipses, even functionless systems of living beings (for example, the appendix) are not for the sake of anything. (2) The *Physics* 2.7 chapter strongly insists that teleological explanation should be given "not simply, but with reference to the being (ousian) of each sort of thing." In other words, we are not to explain anything about dogs as taking place for the sake of cows or humans. What we are supposed to do, as the cited passage shows, is to explain various processes and organs in the living being with reference to the overall functional nature

of the creature. The biological works give hundreds of examples of this. What we are doing, when we explain the heart, for example, as being there "for the sake of" some function that is essential to the characteristic life of a being of that kind, is integrating the diverse movements and parts of a complex creature into a systematic account of its functioning.

Aristotle's teleological explanations introduce no mysterious nonempirical entities. They certainly do not allege that goals exert a mysterious efficient-causal power from the future, pulling things into being. (This has sometimes been falsely inferred from the translation "final cause.") What they do accomplish is perspicuously to display the interworkings of the complex systems of "things that have within themselves a principle of change," showing the contribution made by different systems to overall mature functioning. They also display the self-maintaining nature of living organic systems, what Aristotle in the *De Anima* calls "the first and most common capacity of soul, the one in virtue of which life belongs to all that has life." A self-maintaining creature is a creature who, in a variety of situations, will act or grow so as to promote its own continued life and functioning. This is so (and can be invoked to explain behavior) whether or not the creature is conscious of so acting. Plants grow toward the sun for the sake of continued life and nourishment; and we can advance this as a general explanation for diverse movements of plants in a variety of different situations. For this reason, Aristotle believes, an explanation that first stated what the characteristic life and functioning of a plant was and then showed how its movements in different conditions contributed to the maintenance of this life would convey *understanding* and a general grasp of the activities of this plant in a way that a complex conjunction of efficient-causal accounts could not.

Aristotle's teleology, then, grows not from a religious cosmology, but from a biologist's understanding of the organic character of growth and the plastic character of living systems. It is a model of explanation intended to capture those features of the living being in a way that previous models had not. Modern biologists and philosophers of biology have recently begun to see the depth and value of Aristotle's insights, and to return to these texts as viable alternatives to behaviorism and other forms of reductionism.

Once again, I have been able to give an idea of only a very few of the concerns of Aristotle's philosophy of nature. The *Physics* contains valuable discussions of our conceptions of time and place, of various types of change and motions, and of Zeno's paradoxes of motion. It ends with a global discussion of the self-motion of living beings, which argues that an adequate account of movement and change in the universe as a whole requires us to postulate the existence of a being outside the physical world, a being that imparts movement without itself undergoing any sort of change. Thus Aristotle's god is introduced by detailed and rigorous physical argument. In *Metaphysics* 12, Aristotle argues that this divine being (a bodiless substance whose essential nature is the ceaseless activity of intellect) imparts motion to the heavenly spheres (which Aristotle believes to be living beings) as an object of love and longing.

The *De Caelo* contains Aristotle's cosmology, developed mostly from the work of Eudoxus rather than from original research. It also includes a theory of the "natural motions" of elemental bodies that is disappointing in its simplicity. *On Coming-to-Be and Passing-Away* contains a valuable discussion of the distinction between coming-to-be and qualitative change, and, as we have noted, asks penetrating questions about the explanation of low-level changes. The biological works form a portion of Aristotle's work far too little consulted. They are fascinating on many levels: as excellent science, as good writing on explanation and identity (especially *Parts of Animals* 1 and *On the Motion of Animals*), and, often, as shedding new light on other issues of philosophical importance.

SOUL AND MIND

Before we can begin discussing Aristotle's work *On the Soul*, we must say something about the ways in which "soul" is a potentially misleading translation from the Greek *psuchē*. We would assume that a philosopher who believes in the existence of souls and decides to write a work about the soul has a distinctive view of persons and their faculties: namely, that persons are composites of a body and an immaterial substance. The immaterial substance, in such views, is particularly associated with the "higher" functions of the person—with contemplation and deliberation, rather than with appetite, bodily movement, and nutrition. We would therefore expect that a work entitled *On the Soul* would concern itself primarily with these functions and with creatures capable of these functions. Finally, a belief in the soul is usually linked with some sort of belief in an afterlife; we might expect, then, that a work *On the Soul* would concern itself with religious beliefs.

The Greek word *psuchē* has no such implications. It is simply the general word for whatever it is in virtue of which living things are alive. The Greek word for "living thing" is *empsuchon*, or "thing with *psuchē* in it." All that one is believing, when one believes that there is such a thing as *psuchē*, is that there is a difference between the living and the lifeless. An inquiry into *psuchē* is any inquiry into the nature of that difference. Early Greek thinkers (many of whose views are discussed by Aristotle in *De Anima* 1) had a wide variety of theories about *psuchē*, most of which would not be theories of soul in our sense, since they recognize no nonmaterial entities. Some believed *psuchē* to be one of the material constituents of a person; some believed it to be a group of these, specially mixed; some thought it a state of harmony among all the bodily constituents. Finally, there were some, of whom Plato was the most important, who did believe *psuchē* to be a separable nonphysical substance, temporarily housed in the body. What in our terms would appear as a distinction between thinkers who believe in the soul and thinkers who do not appears in the Greek tradition as a debate about what is the best theory of *psuche*. Theorists agree on the explananda: motion, growth, perception, imagination, thought. They disagree about the best explanatory theory. Thus, the work *De Anima* not only has no dualist presuppositions, it also need have no special connection with the "higher faculties" to the exclusion of the lower. Aristotle feels entitled, at the opening of his work, to take his predecessors to task for focusing too exclusively on the human being and the higher faculties; he can make this criticism only because the theorist of *psuche* implicitly accepts the task of accounting for all the livingness of the living. Finally, a theory of *psuche* may or may not include an eschatology; this depends entirely on the nature of the theory, since Platonist dualism is compatible with individual survival in a way that materialism is not.

Aristotle's own theory of *psuche* is very closely connected, as we might expect, with the theory of the identity of particulars developed in his metaphysics (see above). There he had already used the word "*psuche*" interchangeably with the term "substantial form" for animate beings. In the *De Anima*, he argues first against theories that make *psuche* a property, or nonessential attribute; we should view *psuche* as the *ousia* of the living creature, that which makes the creature what it is. This, as the *Metaphysics* has already argued (see above), will not be the list of the creature's material components, but rather their characteristic functional organization. Aristotle's working definition of *psuche* in *De Anima* 2.1 is "the first entelechy of a natural organic body." He substitutes "first entelechy" for the word "form" *(eidos)*, which he used earlier in the chapter, in order to stress the fact that it is not actual functioning (for example, actual thinking or seeing) that is the *psuche*, but rather the organization-to-function. A person who goes to sleep and ceases to exercise his life capacities is not for

that reason dead. By "organic" he seems to mean "equipped with materials that are suitable for performing these functions." (Greek *organon* means "tool.") He is saying, then, that the essential livingness of Socrates, that without which Socrates would not live, is a certain sort of functional structure or organization that makes it possible for him to perform characteristic human activities.

This theory of *psuche* is an interesting alternative both to the materialism and to the Platonist dualism of Aristotle's day. It goes against materialism by stressing (as in the *Metaphysics*) that a list of constituents does not tell us what a thing is or how it lives its characteristic life. The only account that can do this is one that remains on the functional and structural level, since these functions can be realized in continuously changing particular materials. Aristotle would thus oppose any attempt to reduce psychological processes to physical processes, not on the ground that psychological processes involve nonmaterial substances, but on the ground that the reduction does not cite the features that are really relevant to the continuity and the etiology of these processes, which can, of course, be realized each time they occur in slightly different particular matter. The materialist does not give us *understanding*, because his account will necessarily lack comprehensiveness and integrative power. At the same time, Aristotle's theory opposes itself to Platonist views of soul as an immaterial substance. Here he seems to put the burden of proof on Plato, alleging that Plato has not made out any case for the nonphysical nature of most life activities of the person. His painstaking study of self-nutrition, imagination, perception, and movement in plants and animals generally (those that have these faculties) suggests that there is no good reason not to view all of these as activities of living organic systems, realized in each case in some sort of suitable matter. Most of *De Anima*'s books 2 and 3 are occupied with very interesting explorations of these particular life functions.

With the intellect, Aristotle arrives at a different conclusion. Here (*De Anima* 3.4–5) he concludes that there is some good reason to think that a nonphysical entity is at work. He is struck, above all, by two things about the intellect: (1) its apparently limitless flexibility, its ability to "become everything," and (2) its selectivity—the fact that, despite its flexibility, it does not simply receive every impression, but focuses, actively and apparently freely, now on this and now on that. This second aspect of intellect, the "active" intellect, or intellect that "makes" the thought, he believes to be nonphysical and separable from the body of the living creature. Perhaps this is because of the nature of his own particular theory of matter, which would make such complicated selectivity particularly difficult to explain. Perhaps, however, he is worried here by some sort of question of determinism and believes that any totally physical account of intellect would remove the free power of thought to choose its objects.

Unfortunately, we cannot really tell what was motivating Aristotle here. This famous chapter is among the briefest and least finished in the corpus. We can, however, say something to those who use it as evidence for a chronological development within Aristotle's psychological views, arguing that its closeness to Platonism is indicative of an early date. This "explanation" really does not take Aristotle seriously as a philosopher. When he says that there is no good case to be made for Platonist dualism with respect to faculties A, B, and C, but there is a good case to be made in the case of faculty D, because faculty D is different in relevant ways from faculties A, B, and C, he seems to be arguing philosophically in a perfectly coherent way. There is no reason why a good philosopher should either accept every detail of a position or totally damn it; nor is there reason to believe that the only reason he could see some merit in Plato's position here was that he was still a schoolboy under the master's influence. In fact, his care and open-mindedness could serve as an example for philosophers of mind in all periods; we have too often seen very general talk of "the mental"

rather than this careful attempt to distinguish the different explananda, asking whether the same account will do for all.

Among the other achievements of *De Anima* (and the related *Parva Naturalia* and *On the Motion of Animals*) might be mentioned a complex theory of perception and perceptual imagination, which seems to stress the active and selective aspects of these processes; a related theory of animal activity, which insists that we must explain the movements of animals with reference to the world as they experience and interpret it; accounts of memory and dreaming that are of considerable psychological and philosophical interest.

ETHICAL AND POLITICAL THOUGHT

Aristotle's ethical treatises are among the greatest works ever written about human choice and human values. Their special distinction is that they combine intellectual and theoretical power with a keen responsiveness to the complexity of lived practical choice, the hardness and messiness of living well in the world. Unfortunately, it now requires a considerable effort of interpretation, and even of decipherment, to recover the full force of these texts; the tradition of translation and exegesis has in several important ways obscured them. To say something about these misunderstandings will begin also to illuminate the distinctive features of Aristotle's position.

Modern ethical thought has been dominated by two theories: Kantianism and utilitarianism. These two views, which differ radically in their accounts of the ethical right and good, of the relation between the right and the good, and even of the underlying questions to which ethical theory offers an answer, have come to seem exhaustive alternatives. Any ethical theory must be, at bottom, either one or the other. For the utilitarian, the basic question of ethics is "How shall I (or, in a nonegoistic version, we) be happy?" The end or good is taken to be the maximization of a certain desirable psychological state (happiness, contentment, pleasure), and the right, in practical choice, is taken to be whatever effectively serves to maximize this good. For the Kantian, the first question to be asked is not a question about the good at all, but a question about right or duty. In choosing, I am to ask myself what my responsibility or duty is in these circumstances, without allowing myself to be swayed by considerations of pleasure or happiness. Now if one reads Aristotle's ethical works, especially in an English translation, it will seem obvious that they give priority to questions about happiness. Indeed, it is apparent that the central and organizing question of Aristotle's practical philosophy is a question about eudaimonia, which always gets translated as "happiness." This question is treated as equivalent to a question about the "human good." It has thus seemed natural to interpreters, especially Kantian interpreters, to assume that Aristotle's theory must be an anticipation of utilitarianism: he holds that the human end or good is happiness, where this is a psychological state of contentment or pleasure, and asks about the instrumental means to this state. Even though he claims to be asking the question "What is eudaimonia?" he cannot really be doing this, since it is obvious what happiness is; he must, then, really be asking, throughout, only about the means that are productive of the desired psychological state. This reading appeals for support to the numerous passages in books 3 and 6 of the Nicomachean Ethics in which Aristotle says (in the versions of all post-eighteenth-century translators): "We deliberate not about ends, but about means to ends." This reading has the consequence that all of the virtues of character so carefully explored by Aristotle for most of the work—courage, moderation, justice, and so on—and, in addition, friendship, to which two entire books of the Nicomachean Ethics are devoted, all have the status merely of useful instrumental means to the state of contentment. They have no intrinsic value in themselves; I am to choose them only because, and only when, they are productive of the desired psychological end.

It is plain, however, that this cannot be what Aristotle has in mind. He repeatedly insists that friendship and virtuous action are ends in themselves; in fact, he stipulates that an action is genuinely virtuous only if it is chosen for its own sake. Even early in book 1, he enumerates a number of goods that are chosen "both for their own sakes and for the sake of eudaimonia." Soon after, he concludes that "the human good is activity of the psuche according to excellence" (Nicomachean Ethics 1098a16–17). And it would appear to the unbiased reader that the rest of the work is aimed at producing a more concrete specification of "activity according to excellence," by asking, in the different spheres of human choice, what excellent activity would be like. Even the apparent support derived by a utilitarian reading of the word "happiness" collapses on further examination. For "happiness," insofar as it is associated with a psychological state of contentment or pleasure, is inappropriate as a translation for Greek eudaimonia, which Aristotle paraphrases with the words "living well and doing well." Eudaimonia is not a psychological state, but a complex way of living; it is the sort of human life that an admirable person would choose for himself, and, unless prevented by acute misfortune, would achieve. (One recent critic, John Cooper, has suggested the helpful translation "human flourishing," in order to convey the association of eudaimonia with being active.) Pleasure, Aristotle adds in book 10 of the Nicomachean Ethics, supervenes on and perfects this good activity; but it is not a uniform or single psychological state that one could separate from the activity and seek on its own.

Aristotle's ethical theory is organized, then, neither around the question "How shall I maximize the feeling of happiness?" nor around the question "What is my duty?" but around the very general question "How shall I live well?" This question need not lead to any form of egoism, since it can, and does, turn out that part of what it is for me to live well is to benefit friends "for their own sake" and to treat fellow citizens with fairness. The point, however, is that I am starting out only with the most vague and general idea that I want to have the sort of life that is a good life for a human being. And I go on to produce an ever more concrete specification of that good human life, asking both about *what it is*, what its components are, and about instrumental means to these. In book 1 of the *Ethics*, Aristotle sets down several formal marks of a good life on which he thinks most of us are already in agreement. It ought to be *active*: we do not think that a man who sleeps all his adult life lives well, even though he may have an excellent character. It ought to be "sufficient," or inclusive of all the goods that we believe, on reflection, such a life ought to have; and it ought to be "final"—that is, sought for its own sake, rather than for the sake of something further. In the succeeding books, Aristotle directs his attention, in turn, to many different areas in which human beings characteristically make choices; he attempts, in a provisional and open-ended way, to give a characterization of excellent human action in each of these areas that will harmonize with our practical intuitions. He relies, as he tells us, on the fact that his audience will be people of considerable maturity and experience. They will already have fairly well-developed practical intuitions and responses, and will be ready to work through and refine these rationally, in order to have a clearer view of their value and aims, the good life at which they are aiming. (Aristotle compares this procedure to an archer aiming at a target, and says that his ethical writing is designed to give the audience a clearer view of their target.) The procedure is, thus, Socratic in that its material will be the experienced perceptions of the interlocutor or the reader who, in each case, will test Aristotle's sketch against his own experience.

But if Aristotle's ethics is really aimed at working on the question "How shall I live?" that is, at providing us with specifications of *eudaimonia*, rather than with instrumental means to some predetermined psychological state, how are we to understand the repeated claim that we deliberate not about ends, but only

about means to ends? For this surely seems incompatible with the idea that rational deliberation can help us to specify the components of the end itself. The first thing to emphasize is that this is not, in fact, what the text, in these passages, says. Aristotle actually writes, "We deliberate not about ends, but about what is *toward* the end" or "what *pertains to* the end." There is nothing here to suggest that instrumental means alone are in question; in fact, Aristotle's examples in several places strongly indicate that he wishes us to think of enumerating or specifying the components of the end, as well as of finding means to these. (The correct, literal translation is to be found in Thomas Taylor's eighteenth-century version, but disappears with the advent of utilitarianism.) His point is only that for any given piece of deliberation, there must be something that it is *about*, which is itself not up for question in that particular piece of deliberation. But within that piece of deliberation, I can ask both for means to that end and for a further specification of the end. And another piece of deliberation can always call into question the end that was held firm for this one. For example, suppose that my question is "How shall I become a good scholar?" Aristotle's point is that, so long as I am pursuing this question, I cannot at the same time be asking *whether* I should become a scholar. But I can ask both about instrumental means to being a scholar (for example, about how to get into graduate school) and also about what, more specifically, a good scholar *is*, what qualities of skill, diligence, responsiveness, and moral character I ought to cultivate in myself if I wish to *be* a good scholar. These will be constitutive of, not merely means to, good scholarship. And, of course, in the context of some other deliberative question—for example, the question "How shall I promote political justice in my country?"—I might very well be led to ask *whether* being a scholar is at all compatible with the appropriate pursuit of that important value. Thus, Aristotle does not hold that any deliberative question is purely about means; one can always press for a further specification of the end. Nor does he hold that any deliberative end—with the exception of the ultimate end of "living well," and possibly the end of physical health—is an end about which no deliberation at all is possible.

What, then, is Aristotelian deliberation like? It does not, evidently, take the form of precise utilitarian calculation, reducing the apparent plurality of values to some common coin and seeking to maximize that. (In my example, it does not consist in making scholarship and political justice commensurable on some single scale, let us say, personal pleasure, and then choosing the course that maximizes that.) Nor does it take the form of a kind of deliberation often defended by Kantian and Christian philosophers, including so-called Christian Aristotelians, in which one subsumes the case at hand under some antecedently set and fixed rule that forms a part of a closed system of universal practical principles. Aristotle is always at pains to stress that rules are never prior to the good particular judgments of a perceptive judge. Rules, in his view, are useful for purposes of moral education; also, where there is no time to perform the entire deliberation, or where some strong bias might distort the objectivity of one's judgment. But he holds that rules, at best, are only summaries of the particular judgments of people of practical wisdom. If we follow them against our intuitions, we will become fixed and inflexible just where we should most of all be responsive and flexible. In the *Nicomachean Ethics* 5, Aristotle invokes an architectural analogy. A person who tried to make every decision according to a principle held firm and inflexible would, he says, be like an architect who tried to use a straight rule on the intricate curves of a fluted column. Instead, he observes, good architects use a device known as the "Lesbian Rule," a strip of metal that "bends to fit the shape of the stone and is not fixed" (1137b30). Thus, in my example, when I wish to decide what sort of pursuit of scholarship will be compatible with my attachment to social justice, I will not attempt to look to some antecedent system of fixed rules that predetermine the choice. Nor will I expect, as the systematic-rule view implies, that all my concerns will form a coherent system making consistent claims. I will realize the extent to which, in the act of choosing, I am myself deliberating about my own ends, what will, from that time on, count for me as living humanly well. And I will not expect that all the ends to which I have attached value can be fully satisfied in the contingent circumstances of the world. That is a part of what Aristotle means when he denies that practical wisdom is scientific understanding: the "matter of the practical" is such that scientific consistency may not be attainable, or even desirable.

The person of practical wisdom brings to the concrete situation of choice a disparate plurality of attachments and commitments, most of which have been nourished by early moral training, long before reflective adulthood. He also brings his prima facie reflections about what, for him, will count as a good life for the human being, reflections such as those exemplified in Aristotle's detailed discussions of the excellence of character. It is the virtue of these reflections to have made him well acquainted with his "target," his own desires, attachments, obligations. This means that in a new situation confronting him, he, unlike the child or the unreflective person, will be able to single out those features that bear on his conception of the good and to see how, in this case, they relate to one another. In the commonest case, he will be able to choose in such a way as to satisfy and perhaps to further develop his scheme of values; his finely tuned self-awareness and his responsiveness to the complexities of the case (what Aristotle calls "perception") will lead him, often without conscious or elaborate reflection, to choose in accordance with his developing conception. But sometimes, too, a new situation might call forth deliberation about his major ends themselves, and lead either to a new specification of some major end or, more fundamentally, to a new sketch of *eudaimonia* itself. In the present example, I might decide that the tension between my ends is so deep and divisive that I must devote myself exclusively either to one or to the other.

But Aristotle's emphasis on the human importance both of intellectual achievement and of social action warns us that such choices, though the world may at times require them, are frequently better viewed as involving the loss of an important good than as involving a change to another equally appropriate plan of the good. Very seldom, Aristotle believes, will we find reason, in our deliberation, to reject completely from our plan any of the major values to which we have become attached in early education. If we are prevented from pursuing the entirety of our inclusive conception in a harmonious way because of the way the world has arranged the constraints of time, place, and social position (as Aristotle was prevented from political action through his lack of citizen status in Athens), that is a way in which the world has diminished the goodness of our good living, and it is better to acknowledge this fact than to pretend that one lives equally well regardless of one's circumstances.

Thus, a major difference between Aristotle's ethical view and most modern theories is that he believes good living to be vulnerable: he believes that the world and its contingencies can affect not only my happiness but actually the quality of my life. It has been the persistent effort of modern ethical theory, as it was also that of Plato and of both Stoicism and Epicureanism, to describe an ideal life for the human being that is immune from luck and contingency. Supreme value, in such theories, is accorded to things about human life that appear to be completely in the human being's own control, and not subject to the vicissitudes of circumstance. Hence, the Epicurean's defense of the calm, contemplative life, removed from the hazardous political arena and from the risks of love; hence, too, the Stoic image of the sage on the rack, happy, despite both constraint and pain, because of his superior inner character. Hence, too, Kant's image of the "good will" that "shines forth like a jewel for its own sake" despite the ravages of "step-motherly nature."

Aristotle, by contrast, is determined to preserve in his ethical theory the insight that there are deep and important human values that are not self-sufficient, or immune to contingency, and that a human life is a poorer, meaner life if it seeks to avoid commitment to these values. For example, he devotes one-fifth of the *Nicomachean Ethics* to the subject of love and friendship, displaying the value contributed to our lives by different types of attachments, especially those based on mutal respect and shared aspirations. This idea needed emphasis: Plato and other contemporaries had been urging that the good agent should wean himself from exclusive attachments to particular contingent individuals who could die or go away, in order to cultivate an invulnerable contemplative purity. Aristotle shows, in his investigation of both love and political action, that one purchases invulnerability in this way only at a great cost in richness and value of life. He arargues that close enduring love between individuals, besides being good in itself, is an invaluable aid to the moral and intellectual development of the individual. We grow to understand our own aspirations better by seeing a good life lived by another person whom we love and respect; and we are sustained in our intellectual pursuits by the inspiration and support of another person who shares our aims.

In the area of political activity, Aristotle seems to argue that good living requires having some voice in the determination of one's political environment. Political thought must begin with a consideration of human needs; and the job of politics is to provide human beings with what they need for living well. One of our deepest needs, Aristotle believes, is the need for practical reasoning and choice. If a person does not actively choose his or her own values and activities, that person cannot be said to live well, no matter how worthy a life he or she leads. These considerations lead Aristotle to argue, in book 3 of the *Politics*, for a political system that distributes citizenship and its associated rights quite broadly. If one is not a citizen, "free" and "equal" alongside other adult citizens of one's regime, one has been deprived of an important human good. Aristotle seems to concede, however, that the economic requirements of society will continue to force some people naturally equipped for citizenship to perform a kind of degrading labor that will not give them the leisure to educate themselves for citizenship. He does not try to beautify this fact, or to represent the situation of these deprived individuals as anything but deprived. The discussion of "natural slavery" in book 1 makes it clear that Aristotle believes coercive treatment of adults to be justified only when we can be sure that the person in question naturally lacks the capacity for foresight and rational planning.

Aristotle's account of moral virtue, like the other parts of his views that we have so briefly discussed here, would seem surprising to a theorist determined to banish contingency from the moral scene. For a start, the very name "moral virtue" is obviously inappropriate as a generic translation of what Aristotle himself calls "excellences of character." The excellences described by Aristotle as important components of a good human life are enormously diverse, and Aristotle does not cordon off one group of them for special praise in the way that a modern theorist would separate "moral" excellences from other excellences of temperament and character. A sense of humor and a just estimation of one's talents find their place alongside justice and courage. Aristotle's method is simply to consider, in turn, the different areas of life in which human beings act and choose; he then asks, in each case, what sort of behavior and response a person of practical wisdom will deem appropriate. (Frequently the appropriate is discovered negatively, by consideration of what behavior would be either excessive or defective; this is why Aristotle speaks of excellence as the disposition to choose "the mean." It does not imply that we should always choose a safe middle course, or that it is never appropriate to act or feel in some very intense manner. It means only that we must consider what is *appropriate*, that is, neither excessive nor defective, for the particular situation in

which we find ourselves.) The result of this procedure is a complex discussion of a wide range of human excellences, in which absolute priority is accorded to none, and in which a large role is played by traits that may not be entirely under the control of the rational will. Aristotle emphasizes that training and habituation are the most important factors in developing all of these excellences; but he does not try to select for special praise a group of excellences over whose development luck and nature can have no influence.

Another aspect of Aristotle's theory of excellence that would trouble a Kantian is the role it accords to feeling and emotional response. Being a person of good character, for Aristotle, is not simply a matter of making the right choices—or even of being disposed to make the right choices. It is also a matter of appropriate passional response. A person who always ate and drank the appropriate amount, but did so only with constant effort and reluctance, would be, for Aristotle, less excellent in character than a person who had trained his desires to harmonize with his choices. Conflict between rational choice and passion is, in Aristotle's view, a sign of moral immaturity. *Enkrateia,* or effortful self-control, is less admirable than full excellence, which requires a harmony of passion and action. Worse still is *akrasia,* or choice of a worse course of action, despite knowledge of the better; this results, in Aristotle's view, from improper or incomplete training of the passions.

Aristotle, then, unlike Kant and the Plato of the middle dialogues, makes emotional and appetitive response a full part of excellence. We can discover several reasons for this difference. First, he clearly believes that emotions, and even appetites, can be trained to select appropriate objects and to manifest themselves appropriately. Emotions (as we discover in book 2 of the *Rhetoric* especially) are not simply blind surges of affect; they are complexes of belief and feeling; they are responsive to reason and, in a mature person, can often aid and guide reason itself. Second, as we have already said,

Aristotle is more willing than many modern theorists to allow that contingent and not entirely will-governed features of the person may be at least partially constitutive of that person's goodness. He is certainly concerned with something like our question of responsibility: he is concerned to ask under what conditions praise and blame are justified or rational. But he seems to believe that, if a person has been brought up in accordance with some communal conception of the good that has shaped his feelings as well as his choices, it will be rational to praise that person for his goodness of passion and action, even though they are the product, not of some isolated free choice of will, but of normal patterns of socialization and acculturation. Similarly, if a person with that normal upbringing failed to profit from it, and either developed a bad character or failed to develop any stable character, it would be rational to blame that person. The question of defective upbringing is not often broached; but in the section on "bestial vice" in *Nicomachean Ethics* 7, he indicates that certain sorts of defective upbringing may prevent a person from being a candidate for any sort of moral assessment.

Book 10 of the *Nicomachean Ethics* confronts the interpreter with an especially grave problem. Throughout books 1–10, Aristotle has indicated that the human good is an inclusive plurality of actions according to excellence, in which intellectual activity will be one component, side by side with other constituents of intrinsic worth, such as activity according to excellences of character and activity benefiting friends. Most of book 10 develops this view. But 10.7 abruptly shifts to the defense of a life single-mindedly devoted to theoretical contemplation, seeking to maximize this as the single intrinsic good. Interpreters have tried in various ways to minimize this problem but it remains. According to the view expressed in 10.7, friendship and excellence of character could not have intrinsic value; if we chose to pursue them, it would only be because, and insofar as, they seek to maximize contemplation. But their intrinsic worth is clearly defended in the other

books. Again, in the books on friendship, Aristotle claims that it is incoherent, when deliberating about the good, to think of the good of some other sort of being, for example, a god. But in 10.7 he says that we *ought* to "immortalize as much as possible," identifying ourselves not with our complex human nature, but only with its intellectual element.

It is extremely difficult to know what to make of this chapter, since *Magna Moralia* and *Eudemian Ethics* also, and even more clearly, defend the complex, inclusive view. Perhaps the best that one can say is that Aristotle, like anyone who has been seriously devoted to the scholarly or contemplative life, understood that, thoroughly and properly followed, its demands are such as to eclipse all other pursuits. Although he tried to articulate a conception of a life complexly devoted to politics, love, and reflection, he also felt (whether at different times or in different moods at the same time) that really fine reflection could not stand side by side with anything else. He would, then, be doing what the agent in my earlier example of deliberation did: revising his conception in accordance with a new perception of a conflict between the full demands of one cherished value and all other values. At any rate, this nonsolution to the dilemma, unlike artificial chronological hypotheses, has the merit of expressing a lived truth about human choice; and this seems to me to make it more worthy of Aristotle than others that have been put forward.

I have not entered into a comparative study of Aristotle's different ethical treatises, but I have, as is the convention, confined myself primarily to the *Nicomachean*. There are a number of grave problems here: the question of the authenticity of the *Magna Moralia*; the relative chronology of the *Eudemian* and *Nicomachean* works; the question of whether the three shared books belong to one or the other, or to both. There has been a great deal of writing on this topic recently. Its principal merit has been to remind us that the *Eudemian Ethics* is an interesting philosophical work in its own right that deserves much more serious scrutiny than it has received. The question of the shared books remains a difficult one; the alleged stylometric evidence for a *Eudemian* placement is not conclusive, because it cannot show that Aristotle, having written the books at the time of the *Eudemian* work (if even this much is established), did not himself transfer them, perhaps with philosophically significant alterations, to the *Nicomachean*. Anyone who has given a course of lectures over a period of time, making substantial changes in some sections, should be familiar with this possibility. The *Magna Moralia* certainly does not come from Aristotle's own hand; even its defenders concede that its style is very unlike that of Aristotle. But it seems likely that it is a more or less faithful report of some early lectures of Aristotle's on ethical subjects; it can give us interesting and authentic information about a number of topics.

POETICS *AND* RHETORIC

Plato, in the *Republic*, had rejected the traditional claim of dramatic poetry to be a source of moral education. He had two main arguments for this. First, he argued that poetic texts are unable to teach the real truth about anything, since they, and their makers, are unable to answer our demand for general accounts of the essences of the moral virtues. In the absence of these general definitions, poetic stories, however exemplary, are not sufficient for genuine ethical teaching. Second, all dramatic poetry, especially tragic poetry, depicts, and appeals to, powerful human emotions such as grief, fear, pity, and passionate love. In so doing, Plato held, it "feeds fat" these emotions, making them more troublesome and distracting to practical reason. True teaching would cultivate the perfection and separateness of the rational part, allowing it to function, as much as possible, "itself by itself," apprehending "clearly" or "purely" (*katharōs*), uncontaminated by the influence of the baser elements in the soul (compare especially *Phaedo* 66de, *Republic* 606 ff.).

It can readily be seen that these arguments against poetry depend on features of Plato's moral psychology that Aristotle has decisively rejected. For Aristotle, grasping ethical truth is, as we have seen, not a matter of apprehending general rules or definitions, but a matter of refining one's intuitive perception of the salient features of the complex situations with which life confronts us. "Among statements about conduct, those that are universal are more general, but the particular are more true, for action is concerned with particular cases, and statements must harmonize with these" (*Nicomachean Ethics* 1107a29–32). A detailed account of a complex particular case will be "more true" than a universal account. And we learn better by taking a competent judge as a model for emulation than we do by slavish adherence to rule. But this suggests that poets and other storytellers who depict the deliberations of rational agents, presenting them to us for assessment and response, can once again claim to be offering us genuine instruction. Aristotle's position on this issue is complicated. In chapter 9 of the *Poetics*, he ranks poetry above history in philosophical value on the ground that its stories are more representative and therefore more helpful to human beings seeking understanding. For moral learning, not just any true story will do, only stories "such as might happen." Human probability is more important than literal historical truth, which might be too idiosyncratic to teach a truth about human choice. But the fact remains that stories about particulars educate better than abstract formulae because they are closer to the complex and indefinite "matter" of our actual deliberations, which cannot be exhaustively summarized in a system of rules.

To Plato's second argument, Aristotle would reply that the emotions are not always sources of disturbance and conflict. They can often be positive sources of learning and guidance; often we recognize what to do, what action harmonizes with our character and principles, not by performing acts of pure reason, but simply by noticing how we feel. Furthermore, Aristotle has argued that appropriate emotional response is actually a part of good character itself, something without which the good and virtuous agent will be less good. Thus, a very important part of an Aristotelian program of moral education is the appropriate training of the emotions and feelings. This can best be accomplished, Aristotle feels, through proper exposure to musical and poetic works that represent human emotion or deliberation or both. (This position is also clear from the account of moral education in books 7–8 of the *Politics*.)

The text of the *Poetics* survives in an incomplete form. Most of the surviving portion is concerned with tragedy, but even here we lack important portions of Aristotle's discussion. The work begins with a general discussion of artistic *mimēsis*, or representation. Aristotle claims in chapter 4 that *mimēsis* is a natural tendency in human beings, connected with our love of learning and making distinctions. Unfortunately, the *Poetics* itself, as it stands, says little more about the connection between poetry and moral education. It is not difficult, however, to imagine an account of this that would harmonize with the ethical works. In general, the *Poetics* should never be read in isolation, but only in connection both with the ethical and political treatises and with the detailed discussion of various emotions in book 2 of the *Rhetoric*.

Aristotle defines tragedy as

> the representation of a serious and complete action having size, in pleasant style, this being done separately for each kind of style in the different parts, performed by actors and not told through report, accomplishing, through pity and fear, the *katharsis* of experiences of this kind.
>
> (*Poetics* 1449b24–28)

This famous definition, which was intended by Aristotle less to serve as a constraint on future poets than to provide the basis for an informed and self-conscious critical discussion, has probably generated more commentary than any other sentence in Aristotle's work. Most mysterious, and most vigorously debated, is the important remark about the function or effect of

tragedy, which probably was further discussed in material now lost to us. Renaissance criticism argued that *katharsis* is a kind of moral purification: our pity and fear at the excessive passions of the tragic characters curbs our own tendency to irrationality in real life.

The nineteenth century replaced this uplifting interpretation with a flat materialist account. Jacob Bernays and his successors, connecting this passage with contemporary medical texts and with remarks in the pseudo-Aristotelian *Problemata*, argued that *katharsis* was nothing more than physiological purgation. Through the emotions experienced in the theater, the spectator is purged of congested bodily humors that would have made him unbalanced in the absence of purgation. There is no evidence for this interpretation within the *Poetics* itself, nor does it derive support from anything in Aristotle's ethical theory. No authentic Aristotelian passage gives evidence of a belief in the theory of humors. Furthermore, the account is reductionistic in a way that seems very uncharacteristic of Aristotelian psychology. Aristotle probably believed that all experiences and activities of the person (with the possible exception of intellectual contemplation) are realized, each time they occur, in some matter. But this emphatically does *not* mean that a materialist account has adequately *explained* the process and made the psychological language otiose (see above). Material accounts, Aristotle insists, are never explanatory by themselves; "the material element must never, all by itself, be said to be the thing" (*Metaphysics* 1035a8–9). So even if *katharsis*, like most everything else about human beings, is physiological, this should not pose as an answer to our question about what sort of psychological process it is and how it affects the moral life of the agent who experiences it. The medical "answer" is not a real answer to our question, whether or not it is true. Finally, insofar as the purgation theory does incorporate an answer to our question about the function of art, it is an answer of disappointing simplicity. "Theoretically," writes D. W. Lucas, one of the view's leading exponents, "the *katharsis* might equally well be provoked by a dose of medicine, but Greek physicians seem to have lacked confidence in their power to control black bile." In other words, the only reason we have works of art in our lives is that our doctors do not trust their medicine. If Aristotle had really believed this, it seems highly unlikely that he would have devoted so much respect and attention to works of art, when he was as capable as any scientist of his time of getting on with the requisite medical research. It is hardly necessary to report that Aristotle nowhere speaks of a research project whose success would do away with the need for art. He probably would have criticized this view in much the same way that he criticizes other forms of pseudoscientific reductionism.

If we want an adequate understanding of the psychological and epistemological importance of *katharsis*, it seems promising to begin with Plato. In Plato's middle dialogues, this and related words occur frequently in connection with the "pure" or "clear" state of the rational soul when it is freed from the troubling influences of the senses and emotions. The intellect achieves "purification"—or "clarification," since the word obviously has a cognitive meaning—only when it goes off "itself by itself." To any Platonist, it would be profoundly shocking to read of clarification of the practical intellect produced through the influence of pity and fear, the very emotions to which the *Republic*'s discussions of poetry devote the most negative attention. Aristotle is fond of delivering such shocks. In his moral view, we do learn more about our "target," about the content of our character and principles, through our emotional response to a tragic situation. When we see Agamemnon, torn between disobedience to the command of a god and the equally horrible murder of his daughter, we pity his dreadful dilemma and feel fear for ourselves lest a similarly insoluble moral conflict should ever come our way. In so responding, and in attending to these responses, we are likely to learn more about the values we ourselves attach to piety and to the protection of children; we are also likely to achieve a clearer understanding of the nature of moral conflict and natural necessity. (The chorus of the *Agamemnon* strikingly exemplifies this sort of responsive deliberation.) We achieve "clarification," or "illumination."

Fortunately, we are able to defend this interpretation from the text of the *Poetics* itself. It has frequently been noticed that every element in Aristotle's definition of tragedy comes out of some part of the discussion in the first five chapters. Aristotle himself introduces the definition with the words "taking up the definition of its essence that has come into being from what we have said." The phrase about *katharsis*, if we adopt either the moral purification or the purgation reading, would have to be an exception to this. It is a strong prima facie advantage for a view of *katharsis* if it can show that *katharsis*, too, has in fact been discussed in some way in the earlier part of the work. As we have already mentioned, Aristotle argues in chapter 4 that our interest in *mimēsis* is based on a cognitive interest: "For this reason human beings take pleasure in seeing representations: because it happens that as they contemplate these they learn, and reason concerning what each thing is, e.g., that this is that." On the suggested interpretation of *katharsis* (slightly different versions of which have been defended by the scholars H. D. F. Kitto and Leon Golden), our response to tragic events engenders moral learning and refines our practical "perceptions" so that we will be better able to pick out the ethically relevant features of a complex situation in our own experience. When we watch Agamemnon's particular situation, we are led, through our emotional responses of pity and fear, to learn something about the nature of moral conflict which will make us more perceptive judges when confronted with such situations in our own experience. Since Aristotle clearly attributes a cognitive role to the emotions in his ethical works, there is no problem about seeing tragic learning as working *through* our emotional responses. (Golden, thinking that this is a problem, interprets "through pity and fear" to mean "through the representation of pitiable and fearful events"; this interpretation is unnecessarily baroque.)

The phrase which I have translated "of experiences of this kind" remains ambiguous. Earlier interpretations tended to take the "experiences" in question to be our emotional responses, which were purified or purged through themselves. Recent interpreters such as Gerald F. Else and Golden have pointed out that, in the immediate context, the Greek word is used to refer to the tragic events themselves and have understood Aristotle's point to be that there is a *katharsis* concerning the tragic events. (Else holds that the *katharsis* is not in the spectator at all, but in the working out of the plot, which purifies the hero's pollution in our eyes.) Either type of reading could accord with our general interpretation. When I learn from tragic events, I achieve clarification concerning "experiences similar in kind" to the tragic events. But certainly part of my learning will be about the emotions themselves and their role in the good life. We should probably prefer the first reading because it allows a more inclusive account of tragic learning and does not restrict it to learning about emotions.

Two other famous critical problems about the *Poetics* deserve briefer comment: the nature of tragic *hamartia,* and the relation of plot to character. In chapter 13, Aristotle tells us that the protagonist of a tragedy ought to be a person "who is not surpassing in excellence and justice, but who changes to ill fortune not through a defect and evil character, but through some *hamartia.*" This sentence gave rise to the famous theory of the "tragic flaw," according to which the hero has some defect in his moral character that brings about his downfall. It has more recently been recognized that this cannot be the correct reading, since *hamartia* is plainly here contrasted with a defect of character. Attempts have been made to return to a close look at contemporary use of the word, and at Aristotle's own informative discussions in the *Nicomachean Ethics* (5.8, 1137b11 ff.) and the *Rhetoric* (1.13, 1374b6 ff.). It is clear that *hamartia* is not a stable disposition of character,

but some sort of mistake in judgment or action, a "missing the mark." What remains controversial is whether Aristotle's use of *hamartia* here includes both blameworthy and excusable errors, or only one of these, and if only one, which. This becomes important because Aristotle's later discussion of recognition gives preference to plots like that of the *Oedipus,* where the agent did wrong in (apparently excusable) ignorance.

According to Aristotle's ethical views (in *Nicomachean Ethics* 3.1) there are a number of types of errors that neither proceed from a vicious character nor are excusable. Acts of *akrasia,* in which untrained passions overwhelm good judgment, would be of this sort; so would acts done in ignorance of some essential feature of the situation, where we judge that the agent ought to have known the feature in question, as, for example, where we judge that the ignorance arose through some fault, like drunkenness. Bad actions will be fully excusable when there was some sort of direct physical compulsion involved, or where the agent acted in ignorance that was not due to a fault of his own. Where there is indirect compulsion (for example, when the agent acts under threat, or in a situation of moral conflict) there will be mitigation of blame, but not full excuse. The *Nicomachean Ethics* discussion of the difference between *hamartēma* and other sorts of bad action makes it very clear that *hamartēma* is not the sort of error in action that proceeds from badness of character. The account of its difference from *atuchēma,* or mere (blameless) misfortune, is less clear. Aristotle says two things to distinguish the two: (1) *hamartēma* is not "contrary to expectation," though it is done in ignorance either of the person, or the means, or the consequences, etc.; *atuchēma* is done in ignorance *and* "contrary to expectation"; (2) the agent *hamartanei* "when the origin of the cause is in him," and the *atuchei* when it is "from without." The problem here is that these criteria fail to inform us clearly about the status of actions like those of Aristotle's salient example, Oedipus, who appears to have acted in fully excusable ignorance; the real nature of his acts was indeed "contrary to expectation," and not only to his own actual expectation but to all rational expectation in the circumstances. But (according to the apparent criteria of *Nicomachean Ethics* 3.1) the "origin" of his act was in him, not outside him, since no external compulsion was involved. Thus, his mistake would be an *atuchēma* on the first criterion, but a *hamartēma* on the second. Clearly the second criterion would allow us to include both blameworthy and fully excusable errors in the class of *hamartēmata*, whereas the first might seem to restrict this class to the blameworthy sort of error. One possible solution to the difficulty would be to understand "contrary to expectation" to mean not "contrary to the rational expectation of a good agent in those circumstances," but as "contrary to the expectation of someone with full knowledge of all relevant information." Oedipus' story is not a story of sheer chance misfortune; to somebody with full knowledge of all the persons and causal forces involved, the downfall of Oedipus can perfectly well be predicted. Part of the strength of the myth lies in its combination of inextricable causal logic with excusable ignorance. We in the audience can and do foresee what will happen, though, given the restrictions on Oedipus' knowledge, we excuse him for not foreseeing. Aristotle's point would then be that we do not want tragedies based on sheer coincidence, where the plot has no predictable causal logic at all, and what happens to the agent seems to happen from outside rather than from his own reasons and choices. (One example he gives in the *Ethics* is the case where the wind picks someone up and drops him in such a way that he does damage.) We want, in other words, tragedies whose action is "not contrary to expectation." But the hero can make mistakes that come from fully excusable ignorance, given his particular situation; he might equally well err from a blameworthy ignorance, so long as it does not come from a settled bad character (for example, a mistake made through erotic passion or fear). This inclusive understanding probably comes closest to doing justice to Aristotle's interest in *hamartia*.

As for the phrase "who is not surpassing in excellence and justice," we should not take this to imply that the hero must have defects of character; the context explicitly rules this out, at least as a source of his downfall. The emphasis should be on "surpassing," and we should compare this passage with Aristotle's discussion of "heroic" or "divine" excellence in book 7 of the *Nicomachean Ethics*. There he briefly dismisses this sort of excellence from consideration, since it is not of much use to human beings who are interested in getting an account of *human* excellence. If our tragedies had characters who resembled gods more than humans, we would not learn from them anything that would pertain to our own deliberations. The *Rhetoric* connects the tragic emotion of fear with a perception of *similarity* between ourselves and the person suffering misfortune. Furthermore, really surpassing excellence would probably imply omniscience, which would make most of the *hamartēmata* that are at the heart of tragic plots impossible.

It is not possible to speak at length about another problem that has vexed readers of the *Poetics*: Aristotle's apparent preference for plot above character. But it is important to realize that what Aristotle is ruling out in his remarks about the priority of plot is not a tragedy with full psychological development of character; it is an actionless character portrait. The genre familiar to us from the *Characters* written by Aristotle's primary pupil, Theophrastus, needed to be marked off from drama, which, as its name implies, has an indissoluble connection with acting and doing. Theophrastus' character portraits are not dramatic; drama must show its characters acting and choosing. Aristotle would probably say, in fact, that a character portrait that simply mentions general traits, without giving us a picture of the person's concrete choices, would not be the best way of showing character. He repeatedly insists that we judge people's characters by seeing the nature of their choices. Aristotle also insists that virtuous dispositions by themselves, without the possiblity of action, will be insufficient for good living. The sage on the rack does not live well because, however good his character is, he is unable to *act* well. This would be another area in which dramatic portrayal of character could teach us more than static portraiture of the Theophrastean kind: it could show us the interaction between character and circumstances and the relevance of both for living well. If we follow out these suggestions as we read the *Poetics*, we will see that Aristotle does not subordinate character to plot; he shows, instead, how the great tragic plots serve as superior vehicles for the study of human character and of its fortunes in the world.

Aristotle's great rhetorical treatise argues, against Platonic strictures, that rhetoric is a subject that can be treated systematically. Defining rhetoric as "the capability of recognizing in each case the possible means of persuasion," he argues for its autonomy as a *techne* (art or science) and goes on to offer a comprehensive discussion of persuasion through speech. Although some of this discussion is concerned with matters of structure, form, argumentation, and style, the larger portion deals with subjects that we might associate with ethics: the causes of human action, the nature of pleasure, the structure of various emotions, the types of human character. This material, which is of great interest to students of Aristotle's moral philosophy as well, gives the treatise a depth and richness rarely encountered in works on this topic. Aristotle's work on rhetoric has had enormous influence for centuries; it is even now returning to prominence in the work of contemporary literary critics.

Because of its difficulty and its precision, Aristotelian philosophy can seem, to the unfamiliar reader, to be a remote discipline with little connection to the world of ordinary life and discourse. Aristotle, however, was always at pains to stress its continuity with basic human desires and interests, showing his audience a motivation for overcoming this obstacle. The *Metaphysics* begins with the claim that "all human beings by nature reach out for understanding." And the discussion that follows these famous words traces the development of philosophy back to a natural inclination, on the part of all human beings, to sort out and interpret the world for themselves, making distinctions, clarifying, finding explanations for that which seems strange or wonderful. Other creatures live by the impressions and impulses of the moment; human beings seek to comprehend and grasp the world under some general principles that will reveal an order in its multiplicity. A major part of this human effort is the search for general and more simple explanations for the variety of phenomena: our natural desires will not be satisfied so long as something apparently arbitrary eludes our grasp. Philosophy grew up as the expression of this natural urge to comprehend, this hatred of being at a loss in the world.

> It is because of wonder that human beings undertake philosophy, both now and at its origins.... The person who is at a loss and in a state of wonder thinks he fails to grasp something; this is why the lover of stories is in a sense a philosopher, for stories are composed out of wonders.
> (*Metaphysics* 982b12–19)

Our encounter with the world is, he continues, rather like what happens when we watch a puppet show performed by mechanical marionettes, with no visible human control: we wonder, and we look for an explanation for the apparently wondrous motion. There is a natural continuum between wonder and storytelling, between storytelling and theorizing; continually, we seek to expand the comprehensiveness of our grasp.

But as we seek this order, reduction and oversimplification remain ever present dangers. For this reason, Aristotelian philosophy must also remain in touch with the stories and the discourse from which it grew, opposing (as we have seen here) the oversimplifications that it detects in other philosophies. This determination to return to "appearances" can cause difficulties for the reader in another way. Aristotle's work can seem mundane, clogged, less exciting than the lofty structures of Platonism. But properly understood, this return can be seen to be its greatest strength. Aristotle's philosophy seeks order and clarity while avoiding specious or misleading clarity. It helps us proceed toward understanding without effacing the complexities on which a properly human life is based. Like (and as a part of) our human nature, it exists in a continual oscillation between too much order and disorder, ambition and abandonment, excess and deficiency, the superhuman and the merely animal. The good philosopher would be the one who manages humanly, guarding against these dangers, to improvise the mean. In so doing he helps all human beings to fulfill their natural desires. To do that, as every work of Aristotle reminds us, is to do something "rare and praised and noble" (*Nicomachean Ethics* 1109a29–30).

Selected Bibliography

TEXTS

Bekker, Immanuel, ed. *Aristotelis Opera* 1 & 2. Berlin, 1831. The classic edition, on whose pages and columns modern reference numbers are based. In most cases, however, Bekker's text has been superseded by more recent editions, and editions of most of Aristotle's works may be found in several series: Oxford Classical Texts (OCT, Clarendon Press, London), Teubner (Leipzig), Budé (Paris), and Loeb (Cambridge, Mass., and London). In most cases, the Loeb does not present a new edition of the Greek text. The following is a list of recommendations in the order of works according to Bekker's numbers.

Minio-Paluello, L., ed. *Categories, De Interpretatione.* Oxford, 1949. OCT.

Ross, W. D., ed. *Prior and Posterior Analytics.* Oxford, 1964. OCT.

———. *Topics* and *Sophistici Elenchi.* Oxford, 1958. OCT.

Brunschwig, J., ed. *Topics* 1–4. Paris, 1967. Budé.

Ross, W. D., ed. *Physics.* Oxford, 1950. OCT.

Allan, D. J., ed. *De Caelo.* Oxford, 1936. OCT.

Moraux, P., ed. *De Caelo.* Paris, 1965. Budé.

Joachim, H. H., ed. *De Generatione et Corruptione.* Oxford, 1922. Reprinted Olms, 1970.

Fobes, F., ed. *Meteorologica.* Cambridge, Mass., 1919.

Ross, W. D., ed. *De Anima.* Oxford, 1956. OCT.

———. *Parva Naturalia.* Oxford, 1955. OCT.

Dittmeyer, L., ed. *Historia Animalium,* books 1–6. Leipzig, 1907. Teubner.

Peck, A. L., ed. *Historia Animalium,* books 1–6. Cambridge, Mass., and London, 1965; 1970. Loeb. Vol. 3 is in preparation.

———. *De Partibus Animalium.* Cambridge, Mass., and London, 1968. Loeb.

Nussbaum, M. C., ed. *De Motu Animalium.* Princeton, 1978.

Jaeger, W., ed. *De Incessu Animalium.* Leipzig, 1913. Teubner.

Drossaart Lulofs, H. J., ed. *De Generatione Animalium.* Oxford, 1965. OCT.

Hett, W. S., ed. *Mechanics.* Cambridge, Mass., and London, 1936. Loeb.

Ruelle, C. A., ed. *Problems.* Leipzig, 1922. Teubner.

Jaeger, W., ed. *Metaphysics.* Oxford, 1958. OCT.

Ross, W. D., ed. *Metaphysics.* Oxford, 1924.

Bywater, I., ed. *Nicomachean Ethics.* Oxford, 1894. OCT.

Susemihl, F., ed. *Magna Moralia.* Leipzig, 1883. Teubner.

———. *Eudemian Ethics.* Leipzig, 1884. Teubner.

Dreizehnter, Alois, ed. *Politik.* Munich, 1970.

Kassel, R., ed. *Rhetoric.* Berlin, 1976. Vastly superior to the Teubner and OCT editions.

———. *Poetics.* Oxford, 1965. OCT.

TRANSLATIONS

Smith, J. A., and W. D. Ross, eds. *The Works of Aristotle Translated into English.* Oxford, 1912–1952. The basic English translation of Aristotle's work, soon to be reissued, with some useful corrections and substitutions, by Princeton University Press, and edited by J. Barnes.

COMMENTARIES

Commentaria in Aristotelem Graeca. Berlin, 1882–1909; with *Supplementum Aristotelicum.* Berlin, 1882–1903. The ancient Greek commentaries on Aristotle, some of which are extremely valuable.

Aquinas, Thomas. *On De Interpretatione, Posterior Analytics, Physics, De Caelo, De Generatione et Corruptione, Meteorologica.* Rome, 1882–1886.

410

On De Anima, Metaphysics. Turin, 1924–1926. The commentary on *Posterior Analytics* has been translated into English by F. R. Larcher (New York, 1970). The following modern commentaries are listed in the order of works by Bekker's numbers:

Ackrill, J. L. *Aristotle's Categories and De Interpretatione.* Oxford, 1963. Clarendon Aristotle Series (CAS). The most serious defect of the Oxford translation is its rendering of the *Categories;* Ackrill's will replace the old Oxford version in the forthcoming Barnes ed.

Ross, W. D. *Aristotle: Prior and Posterior Analytics.* Oxford, 1949.

Brunschwig, J. *Aristotle: Topiques 1–4.* Paris, 1967. Budé.

Ross, W. D. *Aristotle: Physics.* Oxford, 1936.

Charlton, W. *Aristotle's Physics 1 & 2.* Oxford, 1970. Clarendon Aristotle Series.

Moraux, P. *Aristote: du Ciel.* Paris, 1965. Budé.

Elders, L. *Aristotle's Cosmology.* Assen, 1966.

Joachim, H. H. *Aristotle on Coming-to-Be and Passing-Away.* Oxford, 1922. Reprinted Olms, 1970.

Düring, I. *Aristotle's Chemical Treatise.* Göteborg, 1944.

Rodier, G. *Aristote: Traite de l'Ame.* Paris, 1900.

Hicks, R. D. *Aristotle: De Anima.* Cambridge, 1907.

Ross, W. D. *Aristotle's de Anima.* Oxford, 1956.

Hamlyn, D. W. *Aristotle's De Anima 2 & 3.* Oxford, 1968. Clarendon Aristotle Series.

Ross, W. D. *Aristotle: Parva Naturalia.* Oxford, 1955.

Sorabji, R. R. K. *Aristotle on Memory.* Providence, 1972.

Ross, G. R. T. *De Sensu et De Memoria.* Cambridge, 1906.

Peck, A. L. *Historia Animalium, 1–6.* Cambridge, Mass., 1965; 1970. Loeb.

———. *De Partibus Animalium.* Cambridge, Mass., 1937. Loeb.

McKeon, R., ed. *The Basic Works of Aristotle.* New York, 1941. Useful short version of the Oxford trans.

———. *An Introduction to Aristotle.* Chicago, 1973. An even more abridged version of the Oxford trans.

The following are recent translations, listed in the order of works according to Bekker's numbers, that may be used in place of the Oxford version.

Barnes, J., trans. *Aristotle's Posterior Analytics.* Oxford, 1975. CAS. In some respects a clear improvement over the Oxford.

Charlton, W., trans. *Aristotle's Physics 1 & 2.* Oxford, 1970. CAS.

Hamlyn, D. W., trans. *Aristotle's De Anima 2 & 3.* Oxford, 1968. CAS.

Sorabji, R. R. K., trans. *Aristotle on Memory.* Providence, 1972.

Peck, A. L., trans. *Historia Animalium 1–6.* Cambridge, Mass., 1965; 1970. Loeb.

Balme, D. M., trans. *Aristotle's De Partibus Animalium I and De Generatione Animalium I.* Oxford, 1972. CAS.

Nussbaum, M. C., trans. *Aristotle's De Motu Animalium.* Princeton, 1978.

Kirwan, C., trans. *Aristotle's Metaphysics* Γ, Δ, E. Oxford, 1971. CAS.

Annas, J., trans. *Aristotle's Metaphysics M & N.* Oxford, 1976. CAS.

Robinson, R., trans. *Aristotle's Politics 3 & 4.* Oxford, 1962. CAS.

Golden, L., trans. *Aristotle's Poetics.* Englewood Cliffs, N.J., 1968.

Butcher, S. H., trans. *Aristotle's Theory of Poetry and Fine Art.* New York, 1951.

von Fritz, K., and E. Kapp, trans. *Aristotle: Constitution of Athens.* New York, 1966.

Ross, W. D. *Aristotle: Metaphysics.* Oxford, 1924.

Burnyeat, M. F., et al. *Notes on Z.* Study Aids Monograph no. 1. Sub-Faculty of Philosophy, Oxford, 1979.

Gauthier, R. A., and J. Y. Jolif. *Aristote: l'Éthique à Nicomaque.* 2 vols. Louvain, 1970. Best commentary on the *Nicomachean Ethics.*

Grant, A. *The Ethics of Aristotle.* London, 1885.

Stewart, J. *Notes on the Nicomachean Ethics of Aristotle.* Oxford, 1892.

Burnet, J. *The Ethics of Aristotle.* London, 1900.

Joachim, H. H. *Aristotle: The Nicomachean Ethics.* Oxford, 1955.

Dirlmeier, F. *Aristoteles: Nikomachische Ethik.* Berlin, 1966.

Jackson, H. *Aristotle: the Fifth Book of the Nicomachean Ethics.* London, 1879.

Greenwood, L. H. G. *Aristotle: Nichomachean Ethics, Book 6.* Cambridge, 1908.

Rodier, G. *Aristote: Éthique à Nicomaque, livre 10.* Paris, 1897.

Dirlmeier, F. *Aristoteles: Magna Moralia.* Berlin, 1968.

———. *Aristoteles: Eudemische Ethik.* Berlin, 1962.

ARISTOTLE

Newman, W. L. *The Politics of Aristotle.* Oxford, 1887–1902.

Susemihl, F., and R. D. Hicks. *The Politics of Aristotle.* London, 1894.

Barker, E. *The Politics of Aristotle.* Oxford, 1966.

Cope, E. M. *The Rhetoric of Aristotle with a Commentary.* Cambridge, 1887.

Else, G. M. *Aristotle's Poetics: the Argument.* Cambridge, Mass., 1957.

Lucas, D. W. *Aristotle: Poetics.* Oxford, 1968.

INDEXES

Bonitz, H. *Index Aristotelicus.* Berlin, 1870.

Organ, T. W. *An Index to Aristotle in English Translation.* Princeton, 1949.

CRITICAL STUDIES

GENERAL WORKS

Allan, D. J. *The Philosophy of Aristotle.* Oxford, 1952.

Düring, I. *Aristoteles.* Heidelberg, 1966. In German, but the most complete and detailed work; a shortened version may be found in Düring, *Aristoteles.* Stuttgart, 1968.

Grene, M. *A Portrait of Aristotle.* Chicago, 1963.

Lloyd, G. E. R. *Aristotle.* Cambridge, 1968.

Randall, J. H. *Aristotle.* New York, 1960.

Ross, W. D. *Aristotle.* London, 1923. Still the best general book in English.

COLLECTIONS OF ARTICLES

ANTHOLOGIES

Barnes, J., M. Schofield, and R. R. K. Sorabji, eds. *Articles on Aristotle.* 4 vols. London, 1975–1979. Excellent collection of modern scholarship, with some new translations of French and German pieces; full bibliographies. (Hereafter referred to as Barnes, *Articles.*)

Moravcsik, J. M. E., ed. *Aristotle.* Garden City, N.Y., 1967. (Hereafter referred to as Moravcsik.)

Rorty, Amélie, ed. *Mind and the Good: Essays in Aristotle's Moral Psychology.* Berkeley, 1980. Mixture of new and reprinted pieces on ethical topics.

SYMPOSIA ARISTOTELICA

Proceedings of triennial international meetings; articles appear in the author's language of presentation.

Aubenque, P., ed. *Études sur la Metaphysique d'Aristote.* Paris, 1977.

Berti, E., and M. Mignucci, eds. *Aristotle on Science: The "Posterior Analytic."* Padua, 1981.

Düring, I., and G. E. L. Owen, eds. *Aristotle and Plato in the Mid-Fourth Century.* Göteborg, 1960.

Düring, I., ed. *Naturforschung bei Aristoteles und Theophrast.* Heidelberg, 1969.

Mansion, S., ed. *Aristote et les problèmes de méthode.* Louvain, 1961.

Moraux, P., ed. *Untersuchungen zur Eudemischen Ethik.* Berlin, 1970.

Owen, G. E. L., ed. *Aristotle on Dialectic.* Oxford, 1968.

Owen, G. E. L., and G. E. R. Lloyd, eds. *Aristotle on Mind and the Senses.* Cambridge, 1978.

There are also excellent German language collections in the Wege der Forschung series.

STUDIES OF PARTICULAR TOPICS

LIFE AND WORKS

The following works are in addition to those cited under "General Works" above.

Chroust, A. H. *Aristotle.* London, 1973.

Düring, I. *Aristotle in the Ancient Biographical Tradition.* Göteborg, 1957.

Moraux, P. *Les listes anciennes des ouvrages d'Aristote.* Louvain, 1951.

Moraux, P. *Der Aristotelismus bei den Griechen.* Peripatoi 5. Berlin, 1973.

DEVELOPMENT AND RELATIONSHIP TO PLATO

Block, I. "The Order of Aristotle's Psychological Writings." *American Journal of Philology* 82:50–77 (1961).

Cherniss, H. *Aristotle's Criticism of Plato and the Academy.* Baltimore, 1944.

Jaeger, W. *Aristotle.* Translated by R. Robinson. Oxford, 1948. First German ed. Berlin, 1923.

Nuyens, F. J. *L'Évolution de la psychologie d'Aristote.* Louvain, 1948. Originally published in Flemish in 1939.

Owen, G. E. L. "The Platonism of Aristotle." *Proceedings of the British Academy* 50:125–150 (1965). Reprinted in Strawson, P. F., ed., *Studies in the Philosophy of Thought and Action.* Oxford, 1968. Also in Barnes, *Articles,* 1.

———. "A Proof in the *Peri Ideōn.*" *Journal of Hellenic Studies* 77:103–111 (1957). Reprinted in

ARISTOTLE

R. E. Allen, ed., *Studies in Plato's Metaphysics.* London, 1965.

————. "Dialectic and Eristic in the Treatment of the Forms." In Owen, ed., *Aristotle on Dialectic* (see above).

Ross, W. D. "The Development of Aristotle's Thought." *Proceedings of the British Academy* 43:63-78 (1957). Reprinted in Düring and Owen, *Aristotle and Plato in the Mid-Fourth Century* (see under "Symposia Aristotelica" above) and in Barnes, *Articles,* 1.

LOGIC

Anscombe, G. E. M. "Aristotle and the Sea-Battle." *Mind* 65:1-15 (1956). Reprinted in Moravcsik.

Hintikka, J. *Time and Necessity: Studies in Aristotle's Theory of Modality.* Oxford, 1973.

Kneale, W. C., and M. Kneale, *The Development of Logic.* Oxford, 1962.

Lear, J. *Aristotle and Modern Logic.* Cambridge, 1980.

Lukasiewicz, J. *Aristotle's Syllogistic.* Oxford, 1957.

Patzig, G. *Aristotle's Theory of the Syllogism.* Translated by J. Barnes. Dordrecht, 1969.

METHOD

Barnes, J. "Aristotle's Theory of Demonstration." *Phronesis* 14:123-152 (1969). Reprinted in Barnes, *Articles,* 1.

Burnyeat, M. F. "Aristotle on Understanding Knowledge." In Berti and Mignucci (see above).

Evans, J. D. G. *Aristotle's Concept of Dialectic.* Cambridge, 1977.

Kosman, A. "Explanation and Understanding in Aristotle's *Posterior Analytics.*" In *Exegesis and Argument,* edited by E. N. Lee, A. P. D. Mourelatos, and R. Rorty. Assen, 1973.

Lesher, J. "The Role of *Nous* in Aristotle's *Posterior Analytics.*" *Phronesis* 18:44-68 (1973).

Nussbaum, M. C. "The *De Motu Animalium* and Aristotle's Scientific Method." Essay 2 in Nussbaum's *Aristotle's De Motu Animalium.* Princeton, 1978.

————. "Saving Aristotle's Appearance," In *Language and Logos,* edited by M. C. Nussbaum and M. Schofield. Cambridge, 1982.

Owen, G. E. L. "'*Tithenai ta Phainomena.*'" In *Aristote et les problèmes,* edited by S. Mansion (see above). Reprinted in Barnes, *Articles,* 1, and in Moravcsik.

METAPHYSICS

General

Anscombe, G. E. M. "Aristotle." In Anscombe amd Geach, *Three Philosophers.* Oxford, 1961.

Aubenque, P. *Le Problème de l'Être chez Aristote.* Paris, 1966.

Jaeger, W. *Studien zur Entstehungsgeschichte der Metaphysik des Aristoteles.* Berlin, 1912.

Leszl, W. *Aristotle's Conception of Ontology.* Padua, 1975.

Owens, J. *The Doctrine of Being in the Aristotelian Metaphysics.* 3rd ed. Toronto, 1978.

The Nature of First Philosophy

Irwin, T. M. "Aristotle's Discovery of Metaphysics." *Review of Metaphysics* 31:210-29 (1977).

Merlan, P. *From Platonism to Neoplatonism.* The Hague, 1960.

Owen, G. E. L. "Logic and Metaphysics in Some Earlier Works of Aristotle." In Düring and Owen, *Aristotle and Plato* and in Barnes, *Articles,* 3.

Substance, Essence, and Identity

Albritton, R. "Forms of Particular Substances in Aristotle's *Metaphysics.*" *Journal of Philosophy* 54:699-708 (1957).

Bolton, R. "Essentialism and Semantic Theory in Aristotle." *Philosophical Review* 85:514-545 (1976).

Cohen, S. M. "Essentialism in Aristotle." *Review of Metaphysics* 31:387-405 (1977-1978).

Dancy, R. M. "On Some of Aristotle's First Thoughts About Substance." *Philosophical Review* 84:338-373 (1974).

Hartman, E. *Substance, Body and Soul.* Princeton, 1977.

Lesher, J. H. "Aristotle on Form, Substance, and Universals." *Phronesis* 16:169-178 (1971).

Matthews, G., and S. M. Cohen. "The One and the Many." *Review of Metaphysics* 21:630-655 (1967-1968).

Miller, F. D. "Did Aristotle Have a Concept of Identity?" *Philosophical Review* 82:483-490 (1973).

Owen, G. E. L. "Inherence." *Phronesis* 10:97-105 (1965).

————. "Particular and General." *Proceedings of the Aristotelian Society* (1979-1980).

White, N. P. "Aristotle on Sameness and Oneness." *Philosophical Review* 80:177-197 (1971).

————. "Origins of Aristotle's Essentialism." *Review of Metaphysics* 26:57-85 (1972-1973).

ARISTOTLE

Wiggins, D. *Sameness and Substance*. Oxford and Cambridge, Mass., 1980.

Woods, M. J. "Problems in Metaphysics Z, Chapter 13." In Moravcsik.

Matter

Code, A. "The Persistence of Aristotelian Matter." *Philosophical Studies* 29:357–367 (1976).

Jones, B. "Aristotle's Introduction of Matter." *Philosophical Review* 83:474–500 (1974).

Lukasiewicz, J., G. E. M. Anscombe, and K. Popper. "The Principle of Individuation." *Proceedings of the Aristotelian Society Supplement* 27:69–120 (1953).

McMullin, E., ed. *The Concept of Matter in Greek and Mediaeval Philosophy*. Notre Dame, 1963.

Miller, F. D. "Aristotle's Use of Matter." *Paideia* (1978). Special Aristotle issue.

Robinson, H. M. "Prime Matter in Aristotle." *Phronesis* 19:168–188 (1974).

Contradiction

Barnes, J. "The Law of Contradiction." *Philosophical Quarterly* 19:302–309 (1969).

Dancy, R. M. *Sense and Contradiction*. Dordrecht, 1975.

Lukasiewicz, J. "On the Principle of Contradiction in Aristotle." *Review of Metaphysics* 95:485–509 (1971).

Potentiality, Actuality, and Necessity

Ackrill, J. L. "Aristotle's Distinction between *energia* and *kinesis*." *In New Essays on Plato and Aristotle*, edited by R. Bambrough. London, 1965. Pp. 121–141.

Hintikka, J. *Time and Necessity: Studies in Aristotle's Theory of Modality*. Oxford, 1973.

———. "Aristotle on Modality and Determinism." *Acta Philosophica Fennica* 29:1–124 (1977).

Penner, T. "Verbs of Identity and Actions." In *Ryle*, edited by G. Pitcher and O. Wood. New York, 1970. Pp. 393–453.

Sorabji, R. R. K. *Necessity, Cause and Blame*. Ithaca, N.Y., 1979.

PHYSICS, NATURE, AND EXPLANATION

General

Mansion, A. *Introduction à la physique aristotelienne*. Louvain, 1945.

Solmsen, F. *Aristotle's System of the Physical World*. Ithaca, N.Y., 1960.

Wieland, W. *Die aristotelische Physik*. Göttingen, 1970. Two long excerpts are translated in Barnes, *Articles*, 1.

Explanation

Balme, D. M. *Aristotle's Use of Teleological Explanation*. London, 1965.

Brody, B. A. "Towards an Aristotelian Theory of Scientific Explanation." *Philosophy of Science* 39:20–31 (1972).

Gotthelf, A. "Aristotle's Conception of Final Causality." *Review of Metaphysics* 30:226–254 (1976–1977).

Hocutt, M. "Aristotle's Four Becauses." *Philosophy* 49:385–399 (1974).

Moravcsik, J. M. E. "Aristotle on Adequate Explanations." *Synthèse* 28:3–17 (1974).

———. "*Aitia* as Generative Factor in Aristotle's Philosophy." *Dialogue* 14:622–638 (1975).

Nussbaum, M. C. "Aristotle's Use of Teleological Explanation." Essay 1 *in Aristotle's De Motu Animalium* (see "Commentaries").

Motion, Space, and Time

Annas, J. "Aristotle, Number and Time." *Philosophical Quarterly* 25:97–113 (1975).

Carteron, H. *La notion de force dans le systeme d'Aristote*. Paris, 1923. Partly translated in Barnes, *Articles*, 1.

Furley, D. J. *Two Studies of the Greek Atomists*. Princeton, 1967.

———. "Aristotle and the Atomists on Infinity." In Düring, *Naturforschung* (see above).

———. "Aristotle and the Atomists on Motion in a Void." In *Motion and Time, Space and Matter*, edited by P. K. Machamer and R. J. Turnbull. Columbus, Ohio, 1976.

Kosman, A. "Aristotle's Definition of Motion." *Phronesis* 14:40–62 (1969).

Miller, F. D. "Aristotle on the Reality of Time." *Archiv für Geschichte der Philosophie* 56:132–155 (1974).

Owen, G. E. L. "Aristotle on Time." In *Motion and Time, Space and Matter* (see above).

Aristotle's Reply to Zeno's Paradoxes

———. "Zeno and the Mathematicians." *Proceedings of the Aristotelian Society* 58:199–222 (1957–1958). Also appears in Salmon (see immediately below).

414

Salmon, W. C., ed. *Zeno's Paradoxes*. Indianapolis, 1969.

Vlastos, G. "Zeno." In *Encyclopedia of Philosophy*, edited by P. Edwards. London, 1967.

Soul and Mind

Ackrill, J. L. "Aristotle's Definitions of Psuchē." *Proceedings of the Aristotelian Society* 76:119–133 (1972–1973). Also in Barnes, *Articles*, 4.

Barnes, J. "Aristotle's Concept of Mind." *Proceedings of the Aristotelian Society* 75:101–114 (1971–1972). Also in Barnes, *Articles*, 4.

Hartman, E. *Substance, Body and Soul*. Princeton, 1977.

Kahn, C. "Sensation and Consciousness in Aristotle's Psychology." *Archiv für Geschichte der Philosophie* 48:43–81 (1966). Also in Barnes, *Articles*, 4.

Nussbaum, M. C. *Aristotle's De Motu Animalium* (see "Commentaries," above). Especially essays 3 and 5.

Schofield, M. "Aristotle on the Imagination." In Barnes, *Articles*, 4, pp. 103–32.

Sorabji, R. R. K. "Body and Soul in Aristotle." *Philosophy* 49:63–89 (1974). Also in Barnes, *Articles*, 4.

Wiggins, D. *Sameness and Substance*. Oxford and Cambridge, Mass., 1980.

ETHICS

General

Cooper, J. *Reason and Human Good in Aristotle*. Cambridge, Mass., 1975.

Gauthier, R. A. *La morale d'Aristote*. Paris, 1963.

Hardie, W. F. R. *Aristotle's Ethical Theory*. Oxford, 1968.

Rorty, A., ed. *Mind and the Good* (see under "Anthologies" above).

Comparative Study of the Three Ethical Works

Cooper, J. "The *Magna Moralia* and Aristotle's Moral Philosophy." *American Journal of Philology* 94:327–349 (1973).

———. Review of Kenny, *The Aristotelian Ethics*. *Nous* 13 (1979).

Kenny, A. *The Aristotelian Ethics*. Oxford, 1978.

Rowe, C. J. *The Eudemian and Nicomachean Ethics*. Cambridge, 1971.

Eudaimonia

Ackrill, J. L. "Aristotle on *Eudaimonia*." *Proceedings of the British Academy* 60:339–360 (1974). Also available as a separate pamphlet.

Austin, J. L. "*Agathon* and *eudaimonia* in the Ethics of Aristotle." In Moravcsik and in Austin, *Philosophical Papers*. Oxford, 1970. Pp. 1–31.

Kenny, A. "Happiness." *Proceedings of the Aristotelian Society* 66:93–102 (1965–1966). Also in Barnes, *Articles*, 2.

Nagel, T. "Aristotle on Eudaimonia." *Phronesis* 17:252–259 (1972). Also in Rorty (see above).

Prichard, H. A. "The Meaning of *agathon* in the Ethics of Aristotle." *Philosophy* 10:27–39 (1935). Also in Moravcsik.

Deliberation and Choice

Anscombe, G. E. M. "Thought and Action in Aristotle." In *New Essays on Plato and Aristotle*, edited by R. Bambrough. London, 1965. Also in Barnes, *Articles*, 3.

Irwin, T. H. "Aristotle on Reason, Desire and Virtue." *Journal of Philsophy* 72:567–578 (1975).

———. "Reason and Responsibility in Aristotle." In Rorty (see above).

Kenny, A. *Aristotle's Theory of the Will*. London, 1979.

Wiggins, D. "Deliberation and Practical Reason." *Proceedings of the Aristotelian Society* 76:29–51 (1975–1976). Also in Rorty (see above).

Virtue

Burnyeat, M. F. "Aristotle on Learning to Be Good." In Rorty (see above).

Hardie, W. F. R. "Aristotle's Doctrine that Virtue is a Mean." *Proceedings of the Aristotelian Society* 66:183–184 (1964–1965). Also in Barnes, *Articles*, 2.

Sorabji, R. R. K. "Aristotle on the Role of Intellect in Virtue." *Proceedings of the Aristotelian Society* 74:107–129 (1973–1974).

Urmson, J. O. "Aristotle's Doctrine of the Mean." *American Philosophical Quarterly* 10:223–230 (1973).

Justice and Friendship

Cooper, J. "Aristotle on Friendship." In Rorty (see above).

Williams, B. A. O. "Aristotle on Justice." In Rorty (see above).

Akrasia

Davidson, D. "How Is Weakness of Will Possible?" In *Moral Concepts*, edited by J. Feinberg. Oxford, 1969.

ARISTOTLE

Santas, G. "Aristotle on Practical Inference, the Explanation of Action, and Akrasia." *Phronesis* 14:162–189 (1969).

Walsh, J. *Aristotle's Conception of Moral Weakness.* New York, 1963.

Watson, G. "Skepticism About Weakness of Will." *Philosophical Review* 86:316–339 (1977).

Wiggins, D. "Weakness of Will, Commensurability, and the Objects of Deliberation and Desire." *Proceedings of the Aristotelian Society* 79:251–277 (1978–1979). Also in Rorty (see above).

Pleasure

Festugiere, A. J. *Aristote: le plaisir.* Paris, 1946.

Gosling, J. C. B. "More Aristotelian Pleasures." *Proceedings of the Aristotelian Society* 74:15–34 (1973–1974).

Kenny, A. *Action, Emotion and Will.* London, 1963. Chapter 6.

Lieberg, G. *Die Lehre von der Lust in den Ethiken des Aristoteles.* Munich, 1958.

Owen, G. E. L. "Aristotelian Pleasures." *Proceedings of the Aristotelian Society* 72:135–152 (1971–1972).

Ricken, F. *Der Lustbegriff in der Nikomachischen Ethik.* Göttingen, 1976.

Rorty, A. O. "The Place of Pleasure in Aristotle's Ethics." *Mind* 83:481–493 (1974).

POLITICS

Barker, E. *The Politics of Aristotle.* Oxford, 1966.

Mulgan, R. G. *Aristotle's Political Theory.* Oxford, 1977.

von Fritz, K., and E. Kapp. *Aristotle's Constitution of Athens and Related Texts.* New York, 1950.

RHETORIC

Cope, E. M. *Introduction to Aristotle's Rhetoric.* London, 1967.

Fortenbaugh, W. *Aristotle on Emotion.* London, 1975.

Grimaldi, W. M. A. *Studies in the Philosophy of Aristotle's Rhetoric.* Wiesbaden, 1972.

POETICS

General

Butcher, S. *Aristotle's Theory of Poetry and Fine Art.* London, 1932.

Bywater, I. *Aristotle on the Art of Poetry.* Oxford, 1909.

Cooper, L. *The Poetics of Aristotle, Its Meaning and Influence.* New York, 1927.

Else, G. *Aristotle's Poetics: the Argument.* Cambridge, Mass., 1957.

Gulley, N. *Aristotle on the Purposes of Literature.* Cardiff, 1971.

Jones, J. *Aristotle and Greek Tragedy.* London, 1962.

Lucas, D. W. *Aristotle: Poetics.* Oxford, 1968.

Katharsis

Bernays, J. *Grundzüge der verlorenen Abhandlung des Aristoteles über Wirkung der Tragödie.* Breslav, 1857. Reprinted Olms and Hildesheim, 1970.

Golden, L. "Catharsis." *Transactions of the American Philological Association* 93:51–60 (1962).

———. "Mimesis and Catharsis." *Classical Philology* 64:145–153 (1969).

Hamartia

Bremer, J. M. *Hamartia.* Amsterdam, 1969.

Dawe, R. D. "Some Reflections on Ate and Hamartia." *Harvard Studies in Classical Philology* 72:89–123 (1967).

Dodds, E. R. "On Misunderstanding the *Oedipus Rex.*" *Greece and Rome* 13:37–49 (1966).

Harsh, P. W. "*Hamartia* Again." *Transactions of the American Philogical Association* 76:47–58 (1945).

Stinton, T. C. W. "*Hamartia* in Aristotle and Greek Tragedy." *Classsical Quarterly* 25:221–254 (1975).

BIBLIOGRAPHIES

Barnes, J., M. Schofield, and R. Sorabji. *Aristotle: A Bibliography.* Study Aids, vol. 7. Sub-Faculty of Philosophy, Oxford, 1977.

Philippe, M. D. *Aristoteles.* Bibilgraphische Einführungen in das Studium der Philosophie, 8. Berne, 1948.

Schwab, M. *Bibliographie d'Aristote.* Paris, 1896

MARTHA CRAVEN NUSSBAUM

DEMOSTHENES

(ca. 384–322 B.C.)

NO CRITIC IN antiquity ever doubted that Demosthenes was the greatest of the Greek orators. When Plutarch wrote his *Parallel Lives of Greeks and Romans*, it was as inevitable to pair Cicero with Demosthenes as to match Caesar against Alexander. And just as the Roman republic died with Cicero, so the independent city-state of Athens came to an end with Demosthenes. Some of his critics, both ancient and modern, have questioned his wisdom in insisting that the Athenians must not give in to the aggressive King Philip of Macedon, and his reputation as a statesman has suffered because Athens lost the decisive battle and he was responsible for the policy that led to the defeat. But his gifts of persuasion are not diminished because the course that he urged Athens to adopt led to disaster. And it is Demosthenes the orator, not Demosthenes the statesman, whose work is under consideration here.

In Greek city-states every ambitious politician had to learn the exacting art of making himself intelligible and persuasive to large crowds in the open air. In the law courts also speakers often had to address a much larger audience than a modern jury, because the Athenians believed that the size of the jury should correspond with the importance of the question they had to settle: five hundred or a thousand for trials that might have serious political consequences. Pleaders in court, moreover, whether politicians accused of corruption or treason, with their political careers in danger, or private individuals in civil lawsuits, were expected to speak for themselves. Only if they could convince the jury that they were incapable of making a coherent speech were they permitted to ask a "friend" to explain their case.

Demosthenes prepared and presented his own first case in the courts when he was only eighteen. Some of the speeches that he delivered in this lawsuit have been preserved, and most of what we know about his young days comes from passages in these speeches. He was born in or about 384 B.C., and his father, also called Demosthenes, was a man of moderate wealth who operated two small factories or workshops producing furniture (couches) and cutlery (knives and daggers). The workers, fifty in number at one time, were slaves in his possession, and since there was no machinery, no expensive tools, and no valuable premises, they constituted his principal capital. He died when his son was seven years old, leaving a will that appointed three guardians to hold the property in trust until young Demosthenes came of age, ten years later. One of these men was to marry his widow or find a suitable husband for her (the will provided for a dowry); another was given similar responsibility for Demosthenes' sister when she grew up (she was only five at the time). Unfortunately, these guardians were either dishonest or incompetent, and when the time came for Demosthenes to enter on his inheritance, he found that most of it had "disappeared" (this is his own expression). Most of the slaves had been sold to raise cash (this too had vanished), no husbands had been found for his mother and sister, and there was no trace of the dowries. All that was left was the house and a few slaves, about a tenth of what the estate should have been worth, if the businesses had been kept running properly and the income from them had been used to maintain the children and their mother without drawing on the capital.

Such, at least, is the way Demosthenes argued when he prosecuted the guardians for breach of trust after he came of age. He was successful in his suit and was awarded the sum of ten talents that he asked for, but he had considerable difficulty in collecting the full sum. All this we learn from the speeches, the texts of which are preserved because his success in pleading his case led him to adopt the profession of a speech writer. And like other speech writers he published some of his speeches, in finished literary form, as an advertisement to attract clients.

There was no regular legal profession in Athens at this time, but people who needed help in litigation could consult a speech writer, who, in return for a fee, would decide how their case should be presented and provide them with a suitable speech, which they would have to deliver themselves. Lysias, in the previous generation, and Isaeus, in Demosthenes' youth, acquired distinction as speech writers, and a good many of the speeches that they published have been preserved.

Demosthenes quickly became a master of the speech writer's art. Litigants were not necessarily gifted or fluent speakers, and they needed speeches that were easy to deliver, without pretentious phraseology or long parentheses, which might cause them to stumble and lose the attention of their audience. A pleader had to tell a story, and tell it in such a way as to lead the jury to the right conclusion. And his time was limited, measured by a water clock; he could not afford to be slow or repetitious; but the clock was stopped while he presented evidence or any other kind of written document or statement. After the speakers had had their turn, each being allowed a short rebuttal, the jury did not retire at the end of the day to deliberate among themselves, but gave their vote

immediately by ballot. And the vote of the majority decided the issue.

Though the jurors took a solemn oath to observe and enforce the law, there was no learned judge presiding at the trial to explain to them how it applied to the case before them. Each speaker could explain the law in the way that suited his argument; he could paint the blackest possible picture of his opponent's private life; and the speeches abound in remarks that would draw an indignant protest from opposing counsel in a modern courtroom and a stern rebuke from the judge. In Athens it was the pleader's responsibility to decide how far he could use or abuse his right to free speech without losing the goodwill of the jury.

All these considerations must be borne in mind if we are to appreciate the quality of Demosthenes' forensic speeches. Out of the sixty orations in the manuscript collection—the Demosthenic corpus, as it is called—only sixteen are political speeches addressed to the Assembly. Two of these are certainly the work of others, and three more cannot have been delivered or intended for delivery in the form in which we have them. Of the remaining speeches in the collection, all that can be accepted as authentic are intended for the courts. Seven are classified as public orations, speeches for the prosecution or the defense in important criminal trials; and three of these were written for clients in Demosthenes' capacity as speech writer. There remain at least twenty genuine private orations, so called because the trials for which they were written were not criminal trials of great public interest, but civil actions in which a plaintiff sought satisfaction from the defendant for some private injury. Most of these were written for clients who sought his services, not for himself.

Thus, in what survives of Demosthenic oratory, more was written for others than was written for himself. And his work as a speech writer, which began ten years before he spoke himself in any important criminal trial or started his active career as a politician, should command our attention first. It is in these private orations that we can see how he discovered and developed his talent for presenting a case. Taken by themselves, they would not have earned him his reputation as the master orator of antiquity, but many of them are so well written and so perfectly adapted for their purpose that they can be considered little masterpieces of their kind. They are also of enormous interest for the light they shed on the manners and morals of contemporary Athens, showing how and why Athenians fought with one another and what drove them to litigation.

Handbooks of public speaking that circulated in the time of Demosthenes recommended that a speaker should begin by commending himself to his audience and winning its sympathy. Aristotle, in the *Rhetoric*, goes further and points out that one of a speaker's strongest arguments, stronger very often than any logical argument, is the argument from character, the character that his speech reveals to his audience. This opinion must have been reinforced, if not actually prompted, by reading Demosthenes' speeches. In almost all his forensic speeches the speaker makes a point of contrasting his character with that of his opponent, showing how he himself has always been devoted to his family, a good neighbor, and a public-spirited citizen, not the kind of person to do what he is accused of doing by his totally unscrupulous opponent, who is notorious for his constant litigation and his irregular personal life, the kind of man who is likely to continue in his evil ways if not checked now that the jury has the opportunity to check him. An opponent might complain that these remarks are not only untrue but irrelevant, because the case should be decided on the evidence and according to the law. But any speaker might hope that the jury would decide to vote in favor of "the better man," thinking the evidence inconclusive or falsified (accusations of false witness were frequent in Athens).

We cannot often be sure what the facts were or make up our mind how we should vote, even when we have the speeches on both sides of a case, as sometimes happens. We should be content, therefore, to enjoy the human comedy that these speeches present and admire the brilliance with which Demosthenes fights for himself and his clients in trials conducted under Athenian conditions.

In his prosecution of Aphobus, one of the three guardians, he introduces himself as a modest young man, simple and inexperienced, ready to make some compromise with Aphobus, if only he were willing to let friends of the family act as arbitrators and avoid an open breach. But he also declares himself courageous and confident in the justice of his cause, though at a disadvantage in having to contend against men like Aphobus and his associates, who are experienced, unyielding, crafty, and ready to use every trick in the book. He goes on to tell his story, which will illustrate the contrast and develop the characterization further: "My father, Demosthenes, left property worth about fourteen talents, and he left me, a boy of seven, and my sister aged five, as well as our mother, who had brought fifty minas into the family."

The point of mentioning these fifty minas (nearly a talent) is to show that their mother came of a respectable but not a wealthy family (since this is a good but not a large dowry), in case the jury might think that she was not a good enough wife for Aphobus or that her family could well afford to look after her without his help. Demosthenes' narrative is much more than a simple narrative of "the facts," as he pretends that it is. Every detail that can be introduced without appearing to be irrelevant is designed to make things more difficult for Aphobus, to make his excuses and explanations invalid: "My father put everything in the hands of these three men. Two of them were his nephews, the other was an old friend since boyhood."

So he had every reason to trust them, the jurors are expected to say to themselves. And in a second speech Demosthenes drives the point home further, describing the scene in which his father solemnly entrusted the two children and their mother to their care, "putting me on this man's knee," and explained to the men the income they would receive from part of the capital during the next ten years, to repay them for their trouble.

A conventional orator might let the jury see that he was using the conventional figure of *amplificatio*:

> Not only is he a thief, but he has robbed two helpless children and their mother, not only is he dishonest but he is without shame or pity, not only has he betrayed a sacred trust, but he has proved faithless to a man who had every reason to have faith in him.

Demosthenes does not spell out the argument in this way, but it has the greater effect if it is left to the jury to work it out for themselves.

The speakers in many of these speeches promise that they will tell the whole story, even though they often know only part of what happened, and sometimes it will suit their purpose to suppress part of it. They will certainly not want to introduce details that raise problems or doubts. Demosthenes is remarkably successful at making an incomplete story seem complete and coherent, with persons behaving as one might expect them to behave in view of their known character. Subtle characterization has no place in the speech of a plaintiff or defendant. Both the good men and the villains must be types familiar to the jury. They will recognize the kind of man Demosthenes means when, in *For Phormio*, he describes the behavior of Apollodorus, the extravagant young man who wears expensive clothes, maintains one hetaera (mistress) and finds a husband for another when he discards her (and he is a married man too). He walks about with three servants attending him, trying to play the part of an aristocratic Athenian and to disguise the fact that he is of foreign birth, the son of Pasion, a former slave who rose to be director of a banking business.

For Phormio is generally considered to be one of the very best of the private speeches, and it reveals an extremely interesting story.

Phormio had been a slave of the banker Pasion in Athens, who also owned a shield factory. Pasion, himself a former slave and hence without the prejudices of a free-born Athenian, promoted Phormio to be his chief assistant, gave him his freedom, and enabled him to become an Athenian citizen. When he died, he left a will instructing Phormio to marry his widow, to be one of the guardians of his younger son, Pasicles, and to remain in charge of the bank until Pasicles was old enough to take over. This was about 370 B.C. Phormio married the widow, who bore him two sons, and the bank prospered, weathering a financial crisis. But Pasion's elder son, Apollodorus, who was anxious to enter politics and had expensive tastes, was greatly disappointed because he was not allowed to take possession of the bank or the shield factory until his younger brother came of age.

If we try to reconstruct the whole story of what subsequently happened, we soon see how shrewdly Demosthenes in his speech has told the tale in such a way as to help Phormio without telling us all that we should like to know. The speech was written for a trial that took place about 350 B.C., by which time Demosthenes was well established as an experienced speech writer. It is twenty years since Pasion's death, his widow is no longer living, and it is ten years since Pasicles came of age. Apollodorus has made various demands for money over the years, and (so we are told in the speech) the family has made many concessions to him so as to avoid an open quarrel. But now that he comes with a suit claiming that Phormio has held back eleven talents that is due to him from Pasion's estate, it is time to seek professional help from a good speech writer. It is decided to block his suit with a *paragraphe*, a counter suit declaring that his action is not legally admissible because some years previously he signed a formal release that barred him from making further claims. One might think, therefore, that no long speech was needed, but Athenian juries could not be counted on to respect purely legal argument. Demosthenes' speech has to show that Phormio is an honest, conscientious man, who has been unjustly harassed for many years by Apollodorus.

The speaker begins by saying, "You can see for yourselves that Phormio is quite unable to make a speech," and we must imagine that the poor man has stammered out a sentence or two and then called upon his "friend" to present his case. The speech is written to be delivered with restraint and dignity. Documents are presented to show that Pasion withheld eleven talents of the bank's assets when he leased the bank to Phormio, that this money was invested in loans and Pasion wanted to deal with these transactions himself. Apollodorus apparently had hoped to persuade the jury, whose grasp of bookkeeping might be uncertain, that these eleven talents constituted a debit of the bank, not a credit, and hence that they were owed to the bank by Phormio. He also refused to accept his father's will as genuine, maintaining that Pasion was not the kind of man who would authorize Phormio to marry his widow. Thus it is particularly necessary to establish Phormio's good character, to show that he is in fact a better man than Apollodorus, who is an unworthy son of his father.

When a man is speaking for himself, it is hard for him to sing his own praises; but the speaker is able to pay a handsome tribute to Phormio, emphasizing the high esteem that he enjoys in banking circles, his gifts to the city, and his generosity to individuals in need.

The speech was completely successful, as we learn from a subsequent speech of Apollodorus, when he attempted to reverse the verdict of this trial by bringing an action for false witness against Stephanus, one of Phormio's witnesses: "The speech made such an impression on the jury that they would not listen to a single word from me." A number of speeches written to be delivered by Apollodorus, who was a persistent litigant, are preserved in the manuscripts of Demosthenes; and they reveal interesting stories and situations, but they are not well written and are certainly not from the pen of Demosthenes. This particular speech, however (*Against Stephanus* I), is well written and

presents a difficult case skillfully, and most critics are prepared to believe that it is a genuine work of Demosthenes and that he wrote it for Apollodorus as a political favor, because Apollodorus supported him in one of his political moves. We know hardly anything of the professional ethics that may have prevailed among speech writers, but a modern reader will think the worse of a man who wrote for both sides. The facts are very uncertain, however, and we have no reason to believe Aeschines when he accuses Demosthenes of showing his speech *For Phormio* to Apollodorus before the trial.

Readers must be left to find their own favorites among the private speeches, but two more may be mentioned briefly. One is *Against Boeotus*. In *For Phormio* the speaker takes for granted that the jurors will be respectable family men who will disapprove of Apollodorus' way of life, but here the sympathy of the jury is needed for a young man trying to defend the good name of his father, who may have been guilty of bigamy. The speaker, Mantitheus by name, maintains that his father, Mantias, was married only once, and that he is the legitimate eldest son. But his opponent also calls himself Mantitheus, and insists that he and his brother are also legitimate sons, that his mother, Plangon, was married to Mantias before he found a wife of better family.

In the speech it is neither denied nor admitted that Mantias lived with Plangon for several years and that she bore him two sons. But it has to be admitted that she forced him, shortly before his death, to acknowledge them publicly as his sons, so that they could be registered as citizens. The speaker says they were named Boeotus and Pamphilus, the grandfather's name, Mantitheus, being reserved for him as the eldest legitimate son. There was no register of marriages in Athens, and the only way to prove that a marriage took place twenty years earlier was to provide convincing witnesses. It is said in the speech that Boeotus associates with men who have a reputation for legal fraud, and the jury may be expected to disbelieve the evidence of the marriage that is offered.

But evidently the jury believed their evidence, because Mantitheus lost his case. He then made a second attempt with another speech writer, whose speech is preserved as *Against Boeotus* II. This is a much less dignified assault on Plangon and her two sons, and we are left wondering if these rougher tactics proved to be more successful.

The speech *Against Conon* also deserves mention, because here the jury must be persuaded to vote for "law and order," though they may sympathize with the defendants. A young man is complaining that he was brutally assaulted by a group of men in the Agora, the public square of Athens. But he cannot pretend that the attack was unmotivated, because when they were in camp on military service he and his comrades had complained to the commanding officer of the unruly and drunken conduct of these men. It is all too probable that the jury, remembering their own days in the service, will despise him for running to the authorities for help and will dismiss his case.

Demosthenes' solution is to make the speaker describe his sufferings (and how they drove his family to despair) in such a way that he will appear to be a simple, well-bred young man cruelly maltreated by a gang of ruffians whose reputation is well known. The speech was admired in antiquity as an example of the "simple" style of pleading, and it is exactly in this simplicity that its effectiveness lies. It is not recorded what the defendants had to say or what the verdict was.

For Phormio, written about 350 B.C., must be one of the latest of the private orations, because Demosthenes had been taking an active part in politics since 355, and when he wrote a speech for a client or appeared in court himself, it was generally because politics and politicians were involved. One of the ways in which a politician tried to eliminate a rival was by charging that he had made an illegal, unconstitutional proposal to the Assembly. If he was found guilty, the defendant's political career was at an end, because he could be condemned to pay such a heavy fine that he would prefer to evade it by going into exile, finding some means of saving part of his property from confiscation. But the state did not initiate criminal prosecutions, and individuals who undertook the responsibility did so at considerable risk to themselves. It was the prosecutor who had to propose the penalty, and if he obtained less than one-fifth of the jury's votes, he would himself have to pay one-sixth of the amount proposed as a fine, one obol for every drachma. The Athenians took a serious view of frivolous or malicious prosecutions.

If a prosecutor could maintain convincingly that the defendant's proposal was not only illegal, because it contravened some existing law, but was positively unwise or harmful, he could argue that this proved the defendant a dangerous man, who should not be allowed to take further part in public life. But if the proposal had in fact seemed reasonable at the time, and had perhaps actually been passed without serious opposition by the Assembly or the Council of Five Hundred (which would have to accept it first), other arguments would have to be found to show that the man was an undesirable character, with a record of corruption and incompetence, totally unfit to advise the people of Athens or influence their course of action. And if the defendant could not deny his technical guilt, he might still win the day by refuting these other accusations, arguing that his policy had been the right one, and that he was a better man than his adversary, who had just told a pack of lies.

This is indeed what actually happened in later years, after the battle with Philip had been fought and lost, when Aeschines, instead of attacking Demosthenes directly, prosecuted Ctesiphon, who had proposed that Demosthenes be rewarded with a gold crown for his services to Athens. Aeschines found a technical illegality in Ctesiphon's proposal, but his real object was to prove that Demosthenes was unworthy of the reward and was directly responsible for the defeat of Athens. And when Demosthenes replied in his oration *On the Crown* (330 B.C.), though he spoke nominally in defense of Ctesiphon, most of his time and effort went to vindicating his own political career and character. The jury decided to overlook the legal technicality, Ctesiphon was acquitted, Aeschines failed to obtain one-fifth of the votes and had to go into exile.

The first prosecution of this type in which Demosthenes was involved also concerns the offer of a crown. Androtion had proposed that the Council of Five Hundred be awarded a crown in appreciation of its work during the year, but his proposal was attacked as illegal, because the Council had not taken steps to provide the navy with new ships, as it was bound to do by law. The speech *Against Androtion* was written for one of the two prosecutors, and it is of great interest in showing the kind of character assassination that was practiced in these prosecutions and the degree of rhetorical virtuosity that could be employed. It sets out to establish that Androtion was a man of undemocratic character, that his disregard for the law was shown not only by his illegal proposal but also by the high-handed manner in which he had collected arrears of taxes, forcing his way into the houses of Athenians:

> What are you to think of it, men of Athens, when a poor man, or maybe a rich man who has had many expenses and for some perfectly good reason happens to be short of money, had to climb over the roof of his neighbor's house or creep under the bed so as to avoid being seized and dragged off to prison, or had to submit to other indignities that befit a slave rather than a free man, and in the sight of his wife whom he had married as a free citizen?

The speaker, Diodorus, was a politician, and presumably an experienced and capable orator, if he could handle this sort of indignant outburst without making himself ridiculous. An explosive passage of this kind must be carefully written, so that it can be delivered at speed and with intensity, not giving the listeners time to reflect that the tale is unsupported by any evidence. One must ask, of course, how closely any of the written versions of the speeches cor-

respond to what was actually said. But a published version is surely meant to invite a reader to try his hand at delivering it. Even a modern reader, who reads the Greek with some imagination, can discover for himself how carefully these occasional outbursts have been written, how well adapted for fast delivery.

There is evidence from other quarters that Androtion was an honest public servant with a good reputation. The jury in fact acquitted him. And we may want to complain that unsupported, irrelevant accusations are out of place in a legal trial. But we must recognize that they are part of the tradition in which Demosthenes worked, and that an orator would be blamed by no one, except his adversary, for using a weapon that would almost certainly be used against him.

Also, if we think we could not keep a straight face listening to this passage, we must remember that the Athenians did not think it at all funny that a man's dignity should be outraged. A man who showed no respect for the personal and civic dignity of his fellow man could be accused of that unforgivable offense, *hubris*. And that is precisely the charge that Demosthenes makes in *Against Meidias*, one of the speeches that ancient critics especially admired. He begins with absolute confidence: "As for the criminal arrogance, gentlemen of the jury, and the *hubris* which Meidias shows in his relations with everyone on every occasion, I imagine that no one of you and no single citizen of Athens is unfamiliar with it."

Then he explains what he himself has suffered at the hands of Meidias. He had volunteered to be a *choregus*, to pay for the training and performance of a chorus in the annual competition at the festival of Dionysus, and Meidias had done his best from the start to prevent him from putting on a good show. He had tried to ruin the costumes of the chorus, including the gold crowns they were to wear, he had bribed the chorus trainer to abandon his task (fortunately, the experienced flute player took over), and had attempted to influence the judges by bribes and threats. Such, at least, is

Demosthenes' story. And then, on the day of the competition, Meidias came out onto the floor of the theater and punched him in the face, in full view of everyone.

Demosthenes retaliated with an appeal to the Assembly, protesting that this was not simply a personal affront but an outrage to the sanctity of the festival. The Assembly duly censured Meidias, but the vote had no immediate effect except to authorize Demosthenes to prosecute. "So now," the text runs, "here I am to press the charge against Meidias, though I was offered a large sum of money if I would drop it." Despite this statement he probably did accept Meidias' offer of a settlement out of court. Aeschines says he did, and it would scarcely have been possible to say so publicly if the trial had actually taken place. This means that the speech cannot have been delivered, but that the written text represents what Demosthenes was prepared to say.

As in other speeches, he is not content to describe and "amplify" what he has suffered at the defendant's hands and demand punishment for such outrageous behavior. He wants to expose Meidias as a vicious bully who has terrorized many Athenians, and also as a coward who has made himself ridiculous trying to play the part of a dashing cavalryman in elaborate costume ("though he cannot even ride a horse in procession across the Agora") and carefully avoiding any dangerous action in the field. What emerges is more like a grotesque caricature than a credible portrait of a man. As a rhetorical tour de force the speech is magnificent and has always been greatly admired. But we must be warned against believing that Demosthenes always tells the truth.

By this time he had been active in politics for some years and was one of the regular speakers in the Assembly. The Assembly met in the open air, on the hill of the Pnyx, and it is no easy task to speak intelligibly and effectively to a large crowd on a windy hillside. In fact, his first attempt to address the Assembly was a disastrous failure. Plutarch tells us that he was not well received, that he lost his bearings and his language became confused, that his voice seemed not to be strong enough and he was troubled by shortness of breath.

Accordingly, taking the advice of an actor, who would know the problems of speech in the open air, he subjected himself to a rigorous course of training in an underground studio, where no one would hear him, shaving one side of his head so that he could not decently appear in public. The point of practicing with pebbles in his mouth, so Cicero tells us, was to force him to speak long sentences without taking breath, and the good results of this training can be seen in his later speeches, which contain many long sentences that must be delivered in one breath if they are to have their full effect.

For speakers who had not trained their voices and developed powers of breath control, the alternative was to speak slowly, pausing for breath after every five or six words. Demosthenes' first speeches to the Assembly, *On the Symmories* and *For the Megalopolitans*, and to a lesser extent *For the Freedom of the Rhodians*, are written in a style which recalls that of the speeches in Thucydides' history. Like them they cannot be understood readily unless they are taken very slowly, one phrase at a time, and they are evidently intended for delivery with pauses for breath at the end of every phrase. One must suppose that Demosthenes adopted this deliberate, even ponderous style of delivery because he had not yet taught himself to address an open-air audience with the fluency that he found effective in a courtroom. And it is likely that this was the way in which most people spoke when addressing the Assembly, as many speakers do today before large audiences, even when using microphones.

The mode of argument in these early political speeches is also reminiscent of Thucydides. The Thucydidean speeches are remarkable for their abstract quality, as though the speaker's purpose was to establish some general principle as well as recommend a particular course of action, and to support his recommendation by appealing to political or strategic principles instead of describing and interpreting the immediate situation. So also when Demosthenes in *On the Symmories* proposes that groups of taxpayers (known as *symmories*), which had been designed originally for collection of property tax, be reorganized in order to provide money for naval armament, he offers no convincing explanation of the foreign threat that makes it necessary to build new ships.

He apparently thinks it unnecessary to describe the situation and is content to complain that it has been misinterpreted by previous speakers. He says it is a great mistake for Athenians to be alarmed at what appear to be aggressive moves by the Persians and to threaten reprisals that may provoke a real quarrel; but he never tells his audience exactly what he thinks the Persians are doing and intend to do. And while he wants the Athenians to undertake a shipbuilding program in preparation for resistance to Philip of Macedon, he offers no real comparison of the Persian threat with the danger from Macedon. The speech has considerable interest as a rhetorical composition, but most modern readers will find it lacking in immediacy, and they are unlikely to find it very interesting unless they know something of the situation in 355 B.C., when it was delivered, and the developments in the following years that prompted him to deliver the *First Philippic* in 351, a speech that revealed a much more forceful Demosthenes to the Assembly.

In the 370's Athens was able to build up an extensive organization of allies, which was intended to check Spartan aggressiveness; but after the Spartans were defeated by the Theban army at Leuctra in 370, and the hegemony of the Thebans that resulted came to an end when they were defeated at Mantinea in 362, neither Sparta nor Thebes nor Athens was strong enough to pose a serious threat to the other two. And while Athens was anxious to retain the allegiance of her allies, many of them saw no reason why they should continue to increase Athenian power and influence by contributing money or ships. One after another they fell away, defying Athenian efforts to force them to stay in the organization. War had become more expensive than in former days, since the fighting now was done mostly by professional mercenary soldiers, instead of conscripts who received only minimal pay, and by 355 Athenians were ready to support any group of politicians that advocated peace and economy, preserving financial resources instead of wasting them on futile efforts to humble recalcitrant allies.

The whole situation was altered, however, when Philip, who became king of the Macedonians in 359, started to use his army of Macedonians, trained on the Greek model, to extend the borders of his kingdom. He pushed eastward into Thrace, where many Athenians had earned a living as mercenary soldiers in the service of Thracian princes, and was able to exploit a rich goldfield there. This made it possible for him to supplement his military efforts with another effective weapon—money. There were a number of Greek cities settled on or near the coast, bordering on Macedonia, some of them allies or former allies of Athens, and in all Greek cities there were politicians who were ready to let an external power dictate policy to them, if they were paid well enough, so that Philip made remarkable progress in bringing city after city under his control. Demosthenes comments in a later speech that Philip had a special advantage because Greece in his time had produced a rich crop of "traitors, receivers of bribes, and such men as the gods hate, a richer crop than anyone can remember occurring in the past."

What Athens and other cities of central Greece now had to decide was how far these developments in the north threatened their own security and independence, and what measures, if any, they were prepared to take in the face of them.

Our understanding of Greek politics in these years is less than perfect, because Xenophon's history does not go beyond 362, and the accounts of later events by contemporary historians, like Ephorus, Theopompus, and Callisthenes, have all been lost. The only firsthand accounts that we possess come from Demosthenes and other orators, who may always be bending the truth a little to suit their purpose. No one tells us how Demosthenes made his entry into public life. Since he does not propose military action in his earliest speeches, some scholars have argued that he must have joined the party of Eubulus, which wanted to keep military expense to a minimum, and that he broke away from it in 351, when he delivered the *First Philippic* and urged the Athenians to take the initiative against Philip. But there is no direct evidence of an early attachment to Eubulus and nothing to suggest that Demosthenes was under an obligation to any politician for opening a way into politics for him. In fact, we do not know how a newcomer was expected to introduce himself, or even if he needed someone to help him catch the eye of the presiding officer in the Assembly when he asked the formal question, "Who wishes to speak?"

Our knowledge of the exact procedure on these occasions is deficient, but it is worth noticing that in the earliest speeches, *On the Symmories* and *For the Megalopolitans*, Demosthenes has been preceded by several other speakers on the same topic. When he comes to deliver the *First Philippic* it looks as though he has gained some recognition, because he opens the meeting:

> If the subject proposed for discussion were a new one, men of Athens, I would have waited until some of the usual speakers had expressed their opinions. If I had been satisfied by some proposal of theirs, I would not have risen to speak. If I had not been satisfied, my turn to say what I thought would come after them. But since we are now discussing matters about which these men have often spoken in the past, I think I may be excused for being the first to come forward.

This speech is the first of a series that ancient critics called the *Philippics*, a series which includes not only the four orations that we call *Philippics*, but also the *Olynthiac Orations, On the Peace*, and *On the Men in the Chersonese*. *On Halonnesus*, the sixth oration in order, is not by Demosthenes at all, but by Hegesippus, and the *Reply to Philip's Letter* is probably a speech written by the historian Anaximenes for his history.

The subject for discussion in the *First Philippic* is Philip's progress, and Demosthenes has no need to describe the problem, because speakers in previous sessions of the Assembly have done so and failed to find any satisfactory solution to it. But instead of telling them how serious it is, he says they have every reason to be optimistic,

> ... because the crisis has arisen while you have been doing none of the things you should do, whereas (we must admit) if things were as they are after you had done all the right things, we could not even hope for any improvement. And here is something else to think about. You have heard from others, and some of you will remember from your own experience, how strong the Spartans were not so long ago, and how splendidly you did what was right, refusing to act in a way unworthy of the city, how you took up the cause of justice and went to war against them. And why am I saying this? So that you will understand, men of Athens, and see clearly that there is nothing you need fear so long as you stay on your guard—and nothing will turn out as you want it to if you are negligent. You must take as examples, first the strength of the Spartans in those days, which you overcame by keeping your mind on what had to be done, and the present outrageous behavior of this man, which is throwing you into confusion, because you are not thinking about the right things.

> Suppose now that one of you, men of Athens, reasons that Philip is a hard man to fight, noting the size of the army available to him and our loss of all these towns to him. His reasoning of course is perfectly correct, but here is what you must bear in mind, that there was a time when Pydna and Potidaea and Methone and all the country round them belonged to us, and when many of the population now under Philip's control were self-governing and free and more inclined to side with us than with him. Suppose that Philip at that time had taken the attitude that it was difficult to fight the Athenians, when they held all these strong places from which they could attack his country, while he had no allies. In that case he would have

done nothing of what he has done and would not have acquired all this power. But there is something, men of Athens, that he saw clearly. All these places were lying ready to be picked up as prizes of war, and it is the nature of things that when people are not there, their property is taken up by people who are there, and if they are negligent it falls into the hands of anyone who is willing to make an effort and take risks. . . . If then you, men of Athens, are willing to take this kind of attitude. . . .

As always with Greek literature translation is inadequate and has to be supplemented by explanations and an appeal to the reader's imagination. Critics of later antiquity, who had never heard Demosthenes or spoken with anyone who had heard him, insist nonetheless on his tremendous emotional impact—how, as they read him, they find themselves carried away by one emotion after another. If one imagines Demosthenes delivering this passage with intensity and at quite a fast pace, having mastered the art of holding the attention of a large crowd in the open air, never pausing between one sentence and the next, one can perhaps feel something of the effect he must have had. The object is to shame the Athenians into changing their attitude, as he will constantly say they must do. He does not tell them what actual steps they should take until he thinks he may have succeeded in changing their attitude. They must be "willing to be their own masters" and stop thinking that someone else will do their work for them.

This means that they must be willing to take the field themselves, instead of relying on mercenaries, who so often discover a more profitable mission than that which they are sent out to execute. Here again he appeals to examples from the past, telling them how regularly Athens has accomplished what it set out to do when citizen soldiers have been fighting side by side with mercenaries. Demosthenes is very skillful at making his point by appeals to examples (paradeigmata, as the rhetoricians call them), with specific instances from past history, using less well-known military and diplomatic suc-

cesses as well as the glorious examples of victories like Marathon and Salamis. Here he hopes to trap his audience into accepting his conclusion before they can think of reasons why the example may be misleading or irrelevant.

Demosthenes prepares the way carefully for his actual proposal. He calls for fifty triremes, which must be manned by citizens, and an infantry force of two thousand, of whom five hundred must be citizens. And this force should be based on one of the northern Aegean islands, ready for action at short notice, to prevent the kind of destructive sudden raids that Philip has been making, one of which actually brought him as far south as Attica, where he landed at Marathon and seized the ceremonial "sacred" trireme. Philip must not be allowed to keep the initiative. Athenians must anticipate events, not allow themselves to be led by them, but at present they are behaving like barbarians who don't know how to box, "letting their hands fly to where they are hit, instead of putting up a guard." Since Demosthenes is trying to shame the Athenians into action, he does not spare their pride as he tells them, "The strongest force that can drive any free man is the shame at what has happened."

In speeches before the Assembly it was not permissible to attack rival politicians by name, charging them with corruption or treasonable behavior, as was customary in the law courts. But neither custom nor law protected foreigners from unsupported accusations, and throughout the *Philippics* Demosthenes attacks the character of Philip unmercifully. Like a prosecutor trying to persuade the jury that the defendant is both dangerous and contemptible, he wants to convince the people that Philip threatens their security but can be resisted and must be resisted, because he is quite unworthy of any respect and in many ways not strong at all. He may be ruthless and unscrupulous, but he is after all a mere Macedonian, "coming from a land where you could not buy even a slave that was worth anything," and "he does not want men of real ability about him, but prefers men who will keep him company in his drunken orgies."

We may think this kind of scurrilous abuse offensive and unworthy of a statesman, but Demosthenes is fighting for his country's independence, and thinks himself entitled to use any weapon that is available to him. He can also use the more dignified weapon of the simile, as when he insists that Philip's power is built on an unsound basis: "Just as in a house and a ship and all such structures the foundation must be the strongest part, so in political activity the basis on which everything rests must be sound and honest." If Philip's power is built on deceit and bribery, it cannot last, and it cannot survive an attack, as explained in the famous simile of the "body politic":

It is the same as in the human body. A man may be unaware of any trouble so long as he is in good health, but the slightest indisposition can throw everything into disorder and reveal any latent weakness, a fracture or sprain or whatever it may be; likewise with cities and autocrats, so long as the fighting is outside their own territory, the population is unaware of the troubles, but as soon as war starts on their own borders everything is revealed.

The *First Philippic* failed to rouse the Athenians to take action, and in the three *Olynthiac Orations* (349 B.C.) he tried, without success, to persuade them that they should make some effort to save the city of Olynthus from falling into Philip's hands. The Athenians thought other measures were more important, and it may indeed be doubted if any intervention in the north could have succeeded. The difficulty was that no combined force of allies could be organized to oppose Philip, and the distrust and enmity that prevented Greek cities from working together soon gave him the opportunity to extend his influence farther south.

Athens and Sparta had given some support to the Phocians of central Greece in their ten-year war against their neighbor Thebes, which they had financed by looting the sacred treasures of Delphi, an openly sacrilegious act. The Thebans in this so-called Sacred War had the support of the Delphic Amphictyony, an ancient quasi-Panhellenic organization that was sworn to defend the integrity of Delphi. But without help from Athens or Sparta the northern cities that controlled votes in the Amphictyonic Council had little strength to offer, until Philip saw his opportunity to ingratiate himself with the forces of religion and good order by offering his help. The Athenians had hoped to restrain him from further movement by binding him with a peace treaty that would let him keep his northern acquisitions, but he moved too fast for them; and by the time that the peace was signed, the Phocians were totally defeated, Philip as his reward had been given the votes in the Amphictyonic Council that the Phocians had previously possessed, and he was now the sworn friend of Thebes, Athens' bitter enemy and close neighbor. There was nothing now that the Phocians could do to prevent him from coming to the borders of Athens if he chose. The few Phocians who remained farming the land were reduced to the condition of villagers, stripped of their political existence, because their cities were completely destroyed as punishment for their sacrilege. This was the status quo that the Athenians were obliged to observe by the terms of the peace—the peace of Philocrates—which they had devised themselves.

Philocrates, Aeschines, and Demosthenes had been the members of the embassy that went to Macedonia to present Philip with the terms of peace and obtain his sworn agreement to them. They had been outwitted, and someone would have to pay for this diplomatic disaster. Demosthenes, who had quarreled with his fellow ambassadors, accused Aeschines of betraying his trust as ambassador, saying he had taken bribes from Philip. Philocrates also came under fire and, rather than face the prosecution that Hyperides was preparing, withdrew into exile. But Aeschines was more sure of himself, faced trial, and answered Demosthenes' furious attack with an equally confident reply. He was acquitted by the majority vote of the jury.

As we compare the two speeches we can see

how bitterly the two men had come to dislike and distrust one another after they had been thrown together as companions on two frustrating journeys to Macedonia. There is no direct evidence of Aeschines' guilt, but Demosthenes seems so completely convinced of it that it is hard to think of him as entirely innocent. From the very start of the speech *On the Embassy* he invites the jury to take for granted that Aeschines is a despicable scoundrel, who was well paid by Philip to arrange the ruin of Phocis and wreck Athenian efforts to establish an acceptable peace ("It was just a job for him, like any other"). He describes the desolation of the Phocian countryside, as he saw it on a journey to Delphi: "houses pulled down, city-walls dismantled, no sign of any young men in the fields, just a few women and children and pitiful old men." And he describes how the news of the Phocian disaster reached the Athenians, when the Assembly was in session in Piraeus:

> You were of course deeply shocked to hear of the disaster, and you voted to bring in the women and children from the country, to prepare the defence posts and fortify the Piraeus, and to celebrate the country festival of the Heracleia inside the walls of the city. And in the midst of all this turmoil and confusion our wise and clever friend here, with the beautiful voice, without any authorization from the Council or the Assembly, set off on his mission to join the man who was responsible for all these disasters. He never thought how shocking it was that he had previously reported a price put on his head by the Thebans, and now, with the Thebans in control of Phocis as well as all Boeotia, he walks right into the middle of Thebes and the Theban camp. He was so completely beside himself, so totally taken up with the prospect of the pay he had earned, that he dismissed all other thoughts from his mind or chose to ignore them.

Aeschines will reply that he went to Thebes in a last desperate attempt to save the situation, but there is a fair chance that the jury will refuse to believe him. It is not the task of this essay to determine how many of the charges against Aeschines are pure fabrications. No one could hope to win a case in an Athenian court by sticking to the truth and the evidence, and since Demosthenes is determined, rightly or wrongly, that Aeschines must be barred from public life, he is not going to be scrupulous in the tactics that he uses.

He is convinced that Philip is as dangerous as ever and will soon start brushing aside the terms of the peace treaty. In the *Second Philippic* (344), delivered before the Assembly a few months before the case against Aeschines was heard, he insists that Philip's "whole policy is directed against Athens," that he wants to establish an empire "and realizes that you are the only people who can stop him." "But he cannot buy the Athenians" as he bought the Thebans, "who were willing to let him do whatever he wanted in return for what he gave them." And in the *Third Philippic* in 341 Demosthenes does his best to frighten the Athenians into decisive action by telling them not only how far Philip has progressed toward establishing an empire, but how he has done it: by choosing carefully the men who will serve his interests best if he pays them well enough, and by flouting the established conventions of warfare. He still insists on Philip's *hubris*, his autocratic methods that will always defeat the slower methods of democracies, his advantage over governments that will not take military action until some formal declaration of war is made, and his skill in exploiting any signs of political disunity:

> It is not because he has a hoplite phalanx that we hear of Philip going wherever he wants, but because he has light-armed troops, cavalry, bowmen, mercenaries and so on. And when he attacks a city that is unhealthy within itself, when no one comes out to defend his own city, through lack of trust, that is when he is able to bring up his machinery and start besieging the place. I need not point out that he makes no distinction between winter and summer.

Open war with Philip began in 340. He laid siege to Byzantium, and attacked and captured the Athenian merchant ships from the Black Sea that were assembled awaiting naval convoy across the Aegean to Piraeus. Just as in 346, there was nothing to stop him from advancing into central Greece, and in the autumn of 339 he was at Elatea in Phocis. But this time Thebes was ready to join Athens in resisting him, and next summer they fought and lost the battle of Chaeronea. Demosthenes played a leading part in arranging the alliance with Thebes and in the military preparations. Despite the disastrous defeat his services were recognized by the Athenians, and in traditional style it was proposed by Ctesiphon that he be honored with the gift of a golden crown, as was discussed earlier.

Aeschines, however, blocked the proposal in the Assembly by objecting that Demosthenes was still holding public office and could not legally be honored until he had submitted his accounts to audit. He also argued that the motion should have been made at a meeting of the Assembly, not in the Theater of Dionysus—and, above all, that it was illegal to propose to honor a man who was guilty of bringing ruin on Athens.

The alarming events that followed—Philip's murder and Alexander's descent on Thebes and his destruction of that city, which shocked the Hellenic world—prevented Aeschines from proceeding with his action against Ctesiphon, and it was not until 330 that he thought feeling in Athens was sufficiently favorable for him to revive the issue and bring Ctesiphon to trial. Here at last was his opportunity to take revenge on Demosthenes for prosecuting him in 343. He hoped to ruin him by proving that he was more like a traitor than a patriot. His speech as prosecutor, which survives, bears the title *Against Ctesiphon*, and Demosthenes' reply, the magnificent speech *On the Crown*, is nominally in defense of Ctesiphon; but in reality each of them is defending his whole political career and knows that if he loses his case he will have to withdraw from public life. And they are just as merciless in attacking one another as in their speeches *On the Embassy*.

Demosthenes cannot maintain that his anti-Macedonian policy was a success. He is nevertheless prepared to argue that, even though every step that Athens took was a step toward disaster, Athens was right to do as she did, because the alternative of making a pact with Philip and surviving as a minor partner in Macedonian imperialism would have been dishonorable and degrading, a betrayal of all Athenian principles and ideals, if she had been willing to let the rest of Greece be subjected so that she could enjoy comfort as a third-class power. He has to convince the audience that this would have been no better than agreeing to help Xerxes conquer Greece. Thebes had made a pact with Xerxes, as it did with Philip, and now that Thebes is in ruins, can anyone say that such treachery was even true self-interest? The jurors must be made to understand that if they vote for Aeschines, they have failed to see where true self-interest lies and have betrayed the honor of their country. It is this tremendous challenge to his powers of persuasion that gives the speech *On the Crown* its very special character. The jury gave less than one-fifth of their votes for Aeschines, Ctesiphon was acquitted triumphantly, and Aeschines had no alternative except to disappear into exile.

In contrast with the patriotic fervor of the speech in its finest passages is its venom in attacking Aeschines. Demosthenes dares not risk giving offense by spending too much time in description and justification of what he has done or attempted to do. He prefers to establish his integrity and intelligence by pointing to corruption and stupidity in others, especially in Aeschines, and he gives what he considers to be notorious examples of Aeschines' failings, always preferring specific detail, however distorted or even fictitious, to generalities and innuendo. He cannot refute the technical charges against Ctesiphon. But he can, and does, complain that they are charges such as only a pedant would make, a man with no sense of true values like Aeschines, who had worked at dismal clerical jobs, but quoted long passages of poetry in court, hoping to make a good impression: "You heard him crying out 'O earth and sun and true worth,' like an actor on the stage, and appealing to 'Intelligence and culture, which teach us to distinguish right from wrong.'" Readers have sometimes thought, mistakenly, that Demosthenes is revealing himself as a snob, looking down on Aeschines as a man of humble origins and little education. That would have been a fatal mistake for anyone pleading in an Athenian court. Rather, he is jeering at Aeschines for his absurd attempt to play the part of a cultured gentleman, as he had tried to do without success during his career as an actor. He wants the jury to conclude that Aeschines is a man without any standards of his own and without any real integrity.

Pretending that he is reluctant to reveal sordid details, but is compelled to do so because Aeschines has told such scandalous lies about him, Demosthenes says that Aeschines' father obtained Athenian citizenship illegally, that he had been the slave of a schoolmaster, that the only education Aeschines received was cleaning up the schoolroom, and that his mother was a notorious prostitute who worked for a disreputable religious sect and let her little boy roll on the floor among the drunkards. The jury ought not to believe a word of this fantastic tale, but they must have listened avidly, not forgetting a word that he said—the damage was done. Some of the jury would say to themselves that a boy brought up by such parents would naturally grow up to accept the worst practices of corrupt politics, and that this helped to explain his guilt (whereas Demosthenes came of a respectable family and went to a good school). Even those who shook their heads at such gross slander might not think any the worse of Demosthenes for employing it.

It is almost impossible to offer a brief summary of *On the Crown* because its structure is quite unorthodox. After a careful introduction Demosthenes starts what seems to be a narrative of events since 355: "When the Phocian War broke out, not through any fault of mine, because I was not yet active in politics. . . ." He gives an admirable account of the general political situation at that time, noting how completely disunited and distrustful of one another the various cities were, and how Philip took the opportunity to recruit traitors ("agents," as we should call them) in many places. But, unlike Aeschines, who generally follows chronological order and presents a consecutive account, which historians welcome, Demosthenes allows himself to be interrupted by thoughts that occur to him and take him into later or earlier years, as though he were departing from a prepared plan. It is most unlikely that he is in fact speaking extempore, but he may want to give the impression that he is doing so.

The result is that he never remains long enough on any single topic to exhaust his arguments or weary his hearers, and can return to it later with new arguments. He raises the central issue quite early in the speech, insisting that Athens was bound to resist Philip: "Was it to abandon its pride and worth, to put itself on a level with Thessalians and Dolopians and destroy all that its ancestors thought right and valuable?" This appeal to Athenian tradition will be repeated several times, whenever he can prepare the way for it.

Demosthenes offers no systematic account of his various Philippic orations, being content to say such things as "I never stopped warning the people and telling them that they must not give up." He does not want to draw attention to his failure to influence events, though he constantly ridicules Aeschines for recalling with pride speeches that he made, but which accomplished nothing. It is only when he finds occasion, about halfway through the speech, to recall the events of 339, that he can speak with satisfaction of the occasion when he dominated the Assembly. This is a celebrated passage, much admired by ancient critics:

> It was evening when a messenger came to the *prytaneis* [the executive committee of the Council] with the news that Elatea was in Philip's hands. At once they got up in the middle of their dinner, cleared the people out of the shacks in the Agora and set fire to the wicker screens, while others were busy sending for the generals and calling for the trumpeter. The whole city was full of confusion. Next morning, at break of day, the *prytaneis* called a meeting of the Council in the

Chamber, while you were on your way to the Assembly; the whole citizen body was seated on the hill before the Council finished its business and prepared its draft proposal.

Then, when the Council had come into the Assembly, and the *prytaneis* reported the news they had received, after the messenger had been brought forward and made his announcement, the herald put his question: "Who wishes to speak?" And no one came forward.

He lists the various people who could or should have come forward but did not:

Now I was the man who came forward on that day, and told you something to which I shall ask you to pay special attention, for two reasons. I want you to know that I was the only speaker, the only politician who did not desert his post in the hour of danger, but was ready to present himself, to speak and make the necessary proposals on your behalf. The other reason for asking you to listen is so that, with the expense of only a little time, you will have a better understanding of national affairs hereafter.

It is our misfortune that no text of this speech has been preserved. Demosthenes' advice was taken, a delegation was sent to Thebes to arrange an alliance and make plans for military action. By taking charge of the situation, he says, he "caused the danger that threatened the city to pass like a cloud." As for Aeschines, he showed that he knew better how to act heroic parts on the stage at village dramatic festivals than to face a real crisis.

Demosthenes does not describe the battle of Chaeronea, how Athens was defeated, or the consequences of the defeat. His responsibility ended before the battle; and after the defeat, he says with inevitable malice, it was friends of Philip, like Aeschines, who were found useful. But since Aeschines never offered any alternative policy to resistance, what right had he now to complain of the defeat? And how could Athens have refused to fight? How could she face the world now, if others had fought and lost and Athenians had remained idle?

It cannot be that you were wrong, men of Athens, in taking up the struggle in defense of the safety and freedom of all. No, I call to witness the men who first faced the enemy at Marathon, who stood in the ranks at Plataea and served in the ships at Salamis and Artemisium, and all of those who lie buried in public graves, brave men all of them, all honored alike by the city, Aeschines, not only those who won a victory, and rightly so honored, because all of them did their duty as brave men, and the destiny that they met was that which the gods allotted to them.

The speech is only two-thirds finished. There is much more that Demosthenes has to say, and it is no small part of his art that he can relax the tension after this climactic point and still keep people listening. This is something that no summary account can explain, and readers must go to the actual text to see how it is done.

No speeches from later years have been preserved, but Demosthenes' final effort to recover Athenian independence must be described briefly. Harpalus, who had been Alexander's treasurer in Babylon, arrived at Piraeus, early in 324 probably, with an enormous sum of money in gold that he had stolen from the treasury, offering to finance a new Greek movement against Macedonia. Some politicians were in favor of accepting his offer; but when Alexander's order to surrender Harpalus arrived, it was decided, on the proposal of Demosthenes, to arrest Harpalus (who later escaped from Athens and was killed in Crete) and keep the money on the Acropolis, in the Parthenon treasury, until Alexander sent a representative to claim it. Then, when further demands came from Alexander, asking to be recognized as a god by the Greeks and ordering all Greek cities to recall their exiles, anti-Macedonian feeling grew stronger, and Demosthenes found himself at the head of an embassy that was sent to protest these orders—they went not to Macedonia, but to Olympia, where the orders were to be proclaimed.

Before long, however, it was discovered that nearly half of the gold that was supposed to be on the Acropolis was not there, and Athenian politicians accused one another of stealing some or all of what was missing. Demosthenes, among others, was put on trial and, rightly or wrongly, was found guilty. He went into exile to escape imprisonment or death, but was recalled and welcomed back when the movement against Macedonia, after Alexander's death, made a good start with support from various quarters in Greece. But the Macedonian forces under Craterus and Antipater were too strong; and after the battle of Crannon, in the autumn of 322, Athens had to accept Antipater's hard terms. Demosthenes was declared an outlaw, was hunted down where he had taken refuge in Poseidon's sanctuary at Calaureia, and took poison.

An essay on Demosthenes is traditionally permitted to finish with an anecdote told of Aeschines. After he went into exile he is said to have opened a school of oratory in Rhodes, and one day, as an exhibition of his powers, he read to his pupils his speech *Against Ctesiphon,* and on the next day he read Demosthenes' *On the Crown.* And when everyone applauded, he said: "But just imagine if you had heard the brute himself speaking."

Selected Bibliography

TEXTS AND TRANSLATIONS

Private and Other Orations, translated by Charles Rann Kennedy. Volume IV of the Bohn's Classical Library edition of *The Orations of Demosthenes.* London, 1882.

On the Crown, edited by William W. Goodwin. London, 1901. Reprinted New York, 1979. Greek text with notes.

Demosthenis Orationes, edited by Samuel H. Butcher and William Rennie. 3 vols. Oxford Classical Texts. Oxford, 1903–1931. Greek text.

Public Orations, translated by Arthur W. Pickard-Cambridge. Oxford, 1912.

Harangues, edited by Maurice Croiset. 2 vols. Collection Budé. Paris, 1924–1925. Greek with French translation.

Demosthenes, edited and translated by James H. Vince, Augustus T. Murray, et al. 7 vols. Cambridge, Mass., and London, 1926–1949. Greek with English translation.

Plaidoyers politiques, edited by Octave Navarre, Pierre Orsini, Jean Humbert, Louis Gernet, and Georges Mathieu. 4 vols. Collection Budé. Paris, 1947–1959. Greek with French translation.

Plaidoyers civils, edited and translated by Louis Gernet. 4 vols. Collection Budé. Paris, 1954–1960. Greek with French translation.

Greek Political Oratory, translated by Arnold N. W. Saunders. Harmondsworth, 1970.

Six Private Speeches, edited by Lionel Pearson. Norman, Okla., 1972. Greek text with notes.

Demosthenes and Aeschines, translated by Arnold N. W. Saunders. Harmondsworth, 1975.

SECONDARY STUDIES

Blass, Friedrich W. *Die attische Beredsamkeit.* 2nd ed. 3 vols. Leipzig, 1887–1898. Reprinted Hildesheim, 1962.

Cawkwell, George. *Philip of Macedon.* London, 1978.

Cloché, Paul. *Démosthènes et la fin de la démocratie athénienne.* Paris, 1937.

Jaeger, Werner W. *Demosthenes: The Origin and Growth of His Policy.* Berkeley, 1938. Reprinted New York, 1963.

Kennedy, George. *The Art of Persuasion in Greece.* Princeton, 1963.

Pearson, Lionel. *The Art of Demosthenes.* Meisenheim, 1976. Reprinted Chico, Calif., 1981.

Pickard-Cambridge, Arthur W. *Demosthenes and the Last Days of Greek Freedom, 384–322* B.C. New York and London, 1914. Reprinted New York, 1978; 1979.

LIONEL PEARSON

MENANDER

(ca. 342–ca. 291 B.C.)

AN ESSAY COMPARING Aristophanes and Menander is attributed to the ancient biographer Plutarch. Much of the content, contrasting the two playwrights' style, plot construction, and characterization, is unexceptional. What may strike us as surprising, however, is the consistent bias of this early critique in favor of Menander; at almost every point of comparison, the later playwright is judged the more accomplished. If the author had been concerned solely with deprecating the vulgarity of Aristophanes' diction and the immorality of his characters (points that are vigorously noted), his preference for Menander might impress us as less emphatic, an encomium faute de mieux. But such is not the case. Rather, Menander is the subject of lively and perceptive appreciation; near the conclusion the author asks rhetorically: "For what other reason, truly, would an educated man go to the theater, except to see a play by Menander?"

Ever since this early essay it has become customary to compare Menander, the only poet of Greek New Comedy from whom complete plays and substantial fragments are preserved, with Aristophanes, whose eleven extant plays are the sole representatives of Old Comedy in Athens a century earlier. In modern criticism such comparison could begin to assume specific form only with the discovery and publication of substantial fragments of Menander, found on papyrus in archaeological excavations in Egypt, in the twentieth century. Large portions of three plays (*The Arbitration, She Who Was Shorn,* and *The Woman of Samos*) were first

published in 1907; since the mid-1950's nearly all of the *Dyskolos* ("Grouch"), most of the remaining portions of *Samia* (*The Woman of Samos*), and lengthy fragments of several other plays have come to light. This second phase of discovery, which has enabled us to examine two virtually complete comedies for the first time, has occasioned a spate of critical writing, much of it preoccupied with the necessary scholarly tasks of establishing the Greek text, supplying commentary on difficult points, and adjusting previous reconstructions of lost scenes in the light of our new knowledge of Menander's dramaturgy.

The broader framework of dramatic criticism, however, has remained unchanged. In literary history Menander must still be reckoned the fountainhead of the premier tradition of romantic comedy, which extends through the Roman adaptations of Plautus and Terence to William Shakespeare and Molière, the comedy of manners, and modern situation comedy. Even before the modern discoveries, the testimony of the ancients and the short fragments of Menander's plays that survived in quotations by other authors had permitted George Meredith to couple Menander with Molière ("An Essay on Comedy," 1877): "[They] stand alone specially as comic poets of the feelings and the idea. . . . Menander and Molière have given the principal types to comedy hitherto." Aristophanes, for all his fertility of invention, stands sui generis. Meredith did not consider that he was likely to be revived, and quoted Jonathan Swift's jaunty couplet:

MENANDER

But as to comic Aristophanes,
The rogue too vicious and too profane is.

In the words of one modern scholar, Aristophanes died "intestate." Various explanations have been offered to relieve the apparent paradox of Menander's dominance of the comic tradition: the unique political freedom of democracy at the time of Aristophanic comedy in fifth-century-B.C. Athens, the difficulty of Aristophanes' Greek for the Romans, and the indulgence of Old Comedy in obscene and scatological language. These three examples, however legitimate as partial assessments, are ultimately unsatisfactory, even in the aggregate, for a student of the theater. They do not begin to tell us about Menander and what may have motivated people to return to the theater to see his plays.

Menander was born in Athens, of distinguished parentage, about 342 B.C. Little is known of his life. His first production, at the age of twenty (*Orgē*, or "Anger"), probably won him the prize at the Lenaean festival, one of the two principal occasions for the presentation of comedy in Athens. Alexander the Great had died the previous year (323 B.C.); the politics of his successors were to dominate the mature years of the playwright and his contemporaries, whose public experience was that of the garrison town under a sequence of dictatorships. In 317–316 the *Dyskolos* was staged at the Lenaea; some months before, Demetrius of Phaleron, who with Menander had been a pupil of Theophrastus, Aristotle's most celebrated student, had been installed by Cassander as governor at Athens. *The Woman of Samos*, as well, may belong to this early period, although the lack of precise topical references in the plays makes the dating of all but a very few of them highly conjectural. Menander's professional career embraced three decades, and his total output is placed at 108 plays by ancient testimony. We can identify ninety-six titles; it seems possible that some plays may have been first produced in theaters outside Athens (Corinth, Sikyon, and Rhodes are likely candidates). Papyrus fragments, ancient quotations and summaries, and the indications of various art objects, including the mosaics of the "House of Menander" discovered at Mytilene, offer firm evidence on the plot and characters of about sixty plays; but full-scale dramatic analysis must be restricted to the half-dozen or so that exist in substantial fragments of several hundred lines or more. Menander is said to have learned his craft from Alexis, one of the great poets of Middle Comedy, who may have been his uncle. Unfortunately, the fragments of the latter's plays are too scanty to permit reliable conclusions of value on the relationship of the two dramatists. Ancient tradition records that Menander was drowned while swimming off Piraeus.

The audiences of New Comedy who attended the plays of Menander and those of his principal competitors, Diphilos and Philemon, may well have been familiar with older plays, both comic and tragic, through revivals. In the main, however, the set of conventions for comedy was quite different from that of the late fifth century. Most obviously, the extensive use of the chorus in Old Comedy, often in extravagantly fanciful personae, had given way to the convention of detached choral interludes between the episodes, or acts, of the play; in the *Poetics* Aristotle records this as an innovation in tragedy introduced by Agathon, Euripides' contemporary, in the closing years of the fifth century B.C. The sharply reduced role of the chorus in Aristophanes' last two extant plays, the *Ecclesiazusae* and the *Plutus*, shows the older comic playwright adapting to the new trend. Although the language of Menander and some of his contemporaries reveals occasional mild scurrility, it is clear that diction in New Comedy generally avoided the extraordinary range of Aristophanes, and that verse approximated the rhythms of correct, conversational speech. Setting, costume, and masks were functionally appropriate to the middle-class milieu of New Comedy plots, which revolved around the triumph of love over the obstacles of family and society, and conventionally culminated in the wedding of young lovers or the recognition and reunion of those already married. Every plot of Menander, so far as we know, conforms to this basic pattern of elements. The logic and decorum of the playwright's dramaturgy are epitomized in the famous story told about him by Plutarch (*Moralia* 347e). As the time of the festival approached, a friend is reported to have asked Menander about his progress. "I've completed the comedy," he replied, "the theme is sketched out: all I have to do is fill in the words."

The basic plot of romantic comedy is capable of a broad range of variations, as is the relatively small number of character types on which New Comedy conventionally relies: the miser, the braggart soldier, the innocent young lovers, the courtesan, the cooks, parasites, and slaves. The exploitation of this range of plot complications and character traits posed the challenge to the ingenuity of New Comedy.

Menander and his colleagues inherited some prototypes from Old and Middle Comedy. For example, we know that the self-important cook was well established on the comic stage by Menander's day, and one may even venture to suggest that the cook's typical, buffoonish impostoring *(alazoneia)* evolved from aspects of the heroes of Old Comedy, for whom the personal preparation of a feast was often an elaborate concern (compare Dikaiopolis in *Acharnians* and Pisthetairos in *Birds*).

The braggart soldier furnishes a case for which we have more developed evidence: the prototype of Lamachos in *Acharnians* was susceptible to very different elaborations in Menander, ranging from Thrasonides in *The Hated Man*, Bias in *The Flatterer* (the original of Terence's Thraso in the *Eunuch*), and Stratophanes, hero of *The Sikyonian*, to Polemon in *She Who Was Shorn*. Like Lamachos, these soldiers have "speaking names," which are common in all periods of Greek comedy; unlike him, several of them are made the heroes of their plays, and at least one, Polemon, furnishes an unusual portrait of sympathetic regretfulness.

Such examples could be multiplied. The joy of the clever slave, for instance, in doing verbal battle with his master, eavesdropping on others' conversations, and intervening (or meddling) in their affairs is clearly anticipated by Xanthias in Aristophanes' *Frogs*; but these general traits are ramified to an almost infinite degree in the slaves of New Comedy, and the personalities behind the stock masks and names (such as Geta and Daos) are subtly individualized.

However we balance the continuities and differences between the plays of the late fifth century and Menander's comedies, an audience at the latter had undergone two fundamental shifts in expectation. Instead of the fantastic flights of fancy of Old Comedy, spectators anticipated the realism of everyday life: characters no longer traveled to the skies or to the underworld, but remained solidly planted on earth, generally in their own neighborhood. And the domestic circle of the private family unit, rather than serving as an incidental background for the more public focus of Aristophanic satire and fantasy, had become for New Comedy the principal, indeed the sole, dramatic interest.

The *Dyskolos*, first published in 1959, well illustrates the new form. Set in Phyle, a country district of Attica, the play is our earliest surviving dramatization of romantic love at first sight. The god Pan, who speaks the prologue, informs us that Sostratos, a rich young man from the city, had one day ventured on a hunting expedition outside Athens. He had glimpsed the beautiful daughter of Knemon, a crusty old farmer, and immediately fallen in love with her. In the first scene he returns to the neighborhood, hoping to introduce himself, and has a sudden opportunity: the girl is in distress, since her old nurse, Simiche, has carelessly let their bucket drop down the well. The young hero gallantly offers to fetch water; but just as he reenters, their conversation is overheard by a servant of Gorgias, the girl's half brother, who lives nearby. Gorgias, suspicious and proud, demands to know Sostratos' intentions; already the division in temperament between the city characters and the rustics is developed as a major theme. Gorgias is reassured, but advises Sostratos that the young man will never get permission from the girl's father to marry her: Knemon is a misanthrope, and talks to nobody. The only possibility of approaching him is to join the work party out in the fields. Sostratos agrees enthusiastically, and with the help of Gorgias and his rather cynical slave dresses up as a workman, determined to prove by physical labor that he is a worthy suitor.

Coincidentally, Sostratos' mother, the night before, has had a frightening dream of her son in chains, condemned to labor in the fields. She has decided to sacrifice to the god Pan in order to avert the evil omen, and takes her daughter and a retinue of servants, complete with Sikon, a professional cook, to the shrine of Pan and the cave of the nymphs, which are located in the same area of Phyle as Knemon's house. The servants amusingly irritate the old grouch, who is about to set out for the fields and is in no mood to see strangers from the city near his front door. When they ask to borrow various cooking utensils for the sacrifice, he threatens and abuses them, and resolves to stay home so he can keep watch. Sostratos, back from work in the fields, where he awaited Knemon in vain while nearly breaking his back, complicates matters by inviting Gorgias to his mother's feast after the sacrifice. Meanwhile, Simiche tries to retrieve the bucket from the well with a hoe; she only succeeds in dropping the hoe to the bottom. Enraged, Knemon climbs down to fetch the hoe and bucket himself; slipping, he too falls down the well, and is severely injured. Sikon the cook, who had been cursed by Knemon, cynically allows that poetic justice has been served. Sostratos, seizing his opportunity to earn the old father's gratitude, rushes to aid Gorgias in rescuing him.

Laid out on a litter and full of self-pity, Knemon admits that he was wrong to try to live his life divorced from society; the day has come when he needs others around him. He vows to change his ways. But when he is introduced to Sostratos, who has helped save him, he at first turns away, proving that new resolutions are hard to keep. He reluctantly consents to the betrothal of his daughter to the youth when Gorgias tells him that Sostratos is a good farmer. The latter is overjoyed by this somewhat premature assessment, and gratefully undertakes to arrange a match between Gorgias and his sister. But the consent of Kallippides, Sostratos' rich father, must be secured, and he proves a bit of a stumbling block. Just as the poor are suspicious of the rich, so the rich are wary of the poor when it comes to family alliances. Kallippides at length yields to his son's philosophical pleas, and is persuaded that money is less important than good character. A double wedding ends the play, with the servants forcing the cantankerous old Knemon to join the sacrificial feast.

The themes of this early comedy, produced when Menander was twenty-five, recur in much of his work that survives. In particular the conflicts between rich and poor, which are worked out in the *Dyskolos* largely within the framework of a contrast between the city and the country, are an important leitmotiv in Menander's drama. One may compare the tensions between the two old men, Demeas and Nikeratos, in *The Woman of Samos*, or the situation at the beginning of *Georgos* ("The Farmer"), where the young man wonders how to extricate himself from an arranged marriage so that he may wed a poor widow's daughter, with whom he has had an affair.

The integrity of family ties, to which all the characters in the *Dyskolos* are sensitive in varying degrees, is perhaps most dramatically treated in *She Who Was Shorn*, where Glykera, rather than reveal what she believes to be her own low birth and that of her brother Moschion, risks both the youth's amorous attentions and her husband's abuse; appropriately, the goddess Agnoia (Ignorance) speaks the prologue of that play.

The emphasis on chance and good fortune, which initiate Sostratos' love affair and bring it to a successful conclusion so speedily that even he is surprised (see *Dyskolos* 39 ff., 860 ff.), is virtually a convention of New Comedy. Indeed, in *Aspis* ("The Shield") the goddess Tychē, Lady Luck personified, plays a role similar to that of Agnoia, and sacrifices considerable dramatic surprise by outlining the events of the play in a delayed prologue; somewhat coyly postponing her own identification, she ends the speech by pronouncing herself "empowered to govern and direct all these events" (*Aspis* 146–148). Finally, the individuality of slave characters, adumbrated in the *Dyskolos* in the quite different treatments of the misogynistic Geta and the sardonic Daos, is fully developed in other plays, most notably *Epitrepontes* (*The Arbitration*), where Onesimos assumes a principal role in the plot, and is endowed with speeches of soliloquy and philosophical reflection (see especially 557 ff. and 1087 ff.).

To this selection of typical themes and techniques we may add the more general point that female characters become important for the first time in comedy—that is, if we regard Aristophanes' Lysistrata and Praxagora as departures from the norm of Old Comedy. In the *Dyskolos* Knemon's daughter (whether or not she is named Myrrhine), Sostratos' mother, and the old servant Simiche all possess roles of some importance. Habrotonon, the courtesan in *The Arbitration*, Glykera in *She Who Was Shorn*, and Chrysis in *The Woman of Samos* are principal characters in their respective plays. For this innovation, like other features of his dramatic technique, Menander is probably most indebted to the tragic playwright Euripides, for whom the poets of New Comedy reserved special admiration.

Besides the prominence of female characters, Euripides' plays had been marked by considerable psychological realism, which the playwrights of New Comedy developed substantially. Roughly a century after Menander's death, the scholarly Aristophanes of Byzantium rhapsodized: "Oh, Menander! Oh, life! Which of you imitated the other?" In the first century of the Christian era, Quintilian's tribute to Menander praises the same quality of realism; the first professor of literary criticism in Rome concludes that the careful study of Menander alone would suffice to make one a good orator, so perceptive is the dramatist's insight into human nature. The external features of New Comedy—well-motivated entrances and exits in ingeniously ordered plots, scenes and characters from everyday life, and emphasis on the family—help to define only one dimension of this realism: the praise of the ancients is most cogently validated when we examine Menander's subtlety in character portrayal.

Take for example, Knemon, the title character in the *Dyskolos*. This stock *agelast*, or blocking character, is carefully individualized in the later scenes of the play. In Pan's prologue Knemon is introduced as a man who has exiled himself from humanity: *apanthropos . . . anthropos* (6). He appears briefly in Act 1 and Act 3, alternating between fits of rage and outbursts of self-pity; much of Act 2 revolves around a description of his many quirks. He is a hard worker, yet wastes the fruits of his farm by throwing them at intruders (121). He watches his daughter carefully, and has decided that the only suitable husband for her will be a man exactly like himself (335 ff.). He rejects the concern and attention of everybody, and his bad temper has managed to alienate the affections of most people. Despite all these faults, which are developed almost to the point of caricature in the first half of the play, Menander does not mean us to dismiss Knemon as a crank. Early in the play his love for his daughter is a hint that he will eventually have a claim on the audience's sympathy, as are the indications that his character is as much a torment to himself as an annoyance to others. In the crisis of Act 4, when misfortune suddenly makes him dependent on goodwill that he scarcely deserves, his monologue reveals him as a thoroughly believable, and somewhat sympathetic, human being.

Rescued from the well, Knemon delivers his great speech probably from a rolling litter, or pallet. Catching sight of Sostratos, who had helped save him, the old man irritably asks him what he is doing there. We are unprepared for the "conversion" of his ways that he announces:

> . . . Not one of you could make me change my mind. You'll have to let me have my way. I think I've made just one mistake. That was to feel that I alone was self-sufficient and would need no one. Now that I see how death can be so swift and sudden, I know that I was wrong in this. A man needs someone standing by to help him out. I hadn't admitted that before, because I thought that every man around cared only for his own profit. By God, I thought there wasn't one of them who was concerned for other men. That was what blinded me. One man has just now proved the opposite: Gorgias, who's done a deed that's worthy of the finest gentleman. I never let him near my door, or gave him help in anything, or greeted or conversed with him, and still he saved me. Another man might well have said: "You don't allow me in—well, I won't come. You've never helped us out—I won't help you."
> *(Catches sight of GORGIAS, who has now returned, and looks embarrassed)*
> What's the matter, boy? If I should die—I think that's likely, seeing as how I feel—or whether I live, I'm making you my legal son, and heir to what I own. It's yours. And take the girl: she's in your care. Find her a man. For even if I live, I won't be able to. Not a single one will ever please me. If I survive, though, let me live the way I want. Do all else as you wish. Thank God, you're sensible. You're just the man to be your sister's guardian. Give half of my estate as dowry for her; the rest can feed me and your mother.
> *(To MYRRHINE)*
> Help me lie down, my girl. I think it's not a man's job to say more than he has to. *(He sits up again)*
> But child, I want to add a bit about myself and how I lived. If everyone lived so, there'd be no courts, men wouldn't drag each other off to prison, war would vanish—all would be content with modest lives.
> *(To the audience)*
> But your ways suit you better, doubtless. So, live on.

(Almost to himself, with some self-pity)
The difficult old *dyskolos* won't hinder you.
(*Dyskolos* 711 ff.)

The speech is a complex outburst, marked by an unusual meter (trochaic tetrameter) as the turning point of the play. Knemon reasserts his cussed single-mindedness at the outset, and even his admission of error is mingled with self-justification as it begins ("just one mistake"). He gives Gorgias his due; but the young man's embarrassment triggers a self-indulgent impulse, the parenthetical remark on his own poor condition, and then further generosity. Knemon clearly recognizes that his own crankiness stands in the way of a future marriage for his daughter, but is determined, if he should live, to follow his own course. Relieved at the practical disposition of his estate, he sinks back to rest, self-consciously reflecting that men worth their salt limit their words strictly to what has to be said. The impulse of moral conviction, however, is too strong for him to let it go at that; like the jack-in-the-box, he springs back up, with the extraordinary claim that his life has been a paradigm for the improvement of humanity.

In the apologia Knemon exhibits all the cantankerousness that we have come to expect of him. But he adds a credo that ironically bears out the romantic speculations on nobility uttered earlier by Sostratos (see 388–390). The youth imagines that his beloved has been "nurtured nobly in the country by her father, who's a man that loathes life's evil ways." Knemon does indeed loathe life's evil ways, and has in his odd fashion been motivated by something close to utopianism. Of course, this utopianism is combined with hypochondria, melancholy self-righteousness, and the marvelously disingenuous self-pity that closes the speech ("The difficult old *dyskolos* won't hinder you": 747). Yet there is no reason why we should not take his admission of error and his generous, sensible dispositions for the future at face value.

But Menander is too much the realist to let matters rest here. Immediately after the great speech, Knemon reverts to his old habits, in his sharp refusal to be introduced to Sostratos and in his crusty appraisal of the young man's character through the observation that he is sunburned, as a farmer should be (751 ff.). In Act 5 we see Knemon once again as his old self, the grouch who blocks festivity, and we are likely to remember as more significant, and ultimately true to nature, his plea in the apologia to "let me live the way I want" (735–736). Did he only go through the motions of a recantation so that he could ensure being left alone? We may now suspect his motives, which Menander probably intends us to do. But the outcome renders such skepticism irrelevant; at the end Knemon is brought willy-nilly to join the party.

The alternation between self-pity and irascibility, established early in the play, forms the underpinning of Knemon's speech in Act 4; his admission of error is set in the context of the habits of a lifetime. The speech and its aftermath display a psychological realism that, for its depth and range of detail, is substantially new in Attic drama. It also goes far beyond the realism of the *Characters* of Theophrastus, the contemporary collection of short sketches that was certainly part of the background for the stock characters of New Comedy. There is no passage of Aristophanes that resembles Knemon's apologia in this respect; once again Menander's closest analogue is Euripides.

Menander's individualized treatment of stock characters becomes even clearer when we lay the portraits of Demeas and Nikeratos, the old fathers in *The Woman of Samos*, beside that of Knemon. Unlike Knemon, Demeas is rich and urbane; but his sophistication does not prevent a gross error (*hamartia*; compare *Dyskolos* 713, *Samia* 707): the misapprehension that his adopted son, Moschion, has cuckolded him with Chrysis, the free-born woman of Samos who lives with him as a common-law wife. In two remarkable soliloquies in Act 3 (*Samia* 206 ff., 324 ff.), Demeas reveals how he overheard Moschion's old nurse sentimentally chattering about a baby's paternity; what he does not know is that the baby's mother is not Chrysis,

but Plangon, daughter of Nikeratos, whom Moschion had raped at the festival of the Adonia some months before, while his father was away.

But Demeas concludes that Moschion and Chrysis have betrayed him in his absence; Moschion's status as an adopted son and Chrysis' position as a mistress rule out any question of incest, but pose a tormenting dilemma to Demeas of what he believes to be rank ingratitude on both sides. Demeas resolves to expel Chrysis, since he infers, unjustly and more than a bit ironically, that she must have been the seducer: after all, before he kept her in style, she was a poor courtesan. Actually, as we know from Moschion's prologue, it was he, raised in luxury, who must bear the responsibility for Plangon's pregnancy. Once again the theme of rich and poor is exploited in the exposition of Demeas' complex motivations; the monologues combine dramatic irony with psychological subtlety.

Demeas' cruel expulsion of Chrysis is followed by a confrontation with his son. Moschion's desire to conceal the real reason he must marry Plangon results in an ironic dialogue of mounting tension, since Demeas believes Moschion is prevaricating for an entirely different reason. When the truth comes out, Demeas is quick to apologize for his misgivings, with sensible straightforwardness. But Nikeratos is now irate, and Moschion plans his own revenge against his father: a charade of going off to military service and abandoning his family and prospective bride.

Despite these complications the wedding, which had been amiably agreed upon by the two fathers at the end of Act 1, is in progress at the end of the play.

If we compare Demeas, possibly the most complex characterization in our extant fragments of Menander, with Nikeratos, it is again clear that Menander is at elaborate pains to individualize character. Both old men threaten to disrupt the wedding at different points in *The Woman of Samos*, but how different are their personalities and motivations! From the moment of their first entrance, back from a business trip to Byzantium, their speech is differentiated: Nikeratos, the poorer, is given short, staccato phrases (*Samia* 98 ff.), while Demeas is afforded longer, more elegant reflections in which the rhyming devices frequently serve to heighten emotion (for instance, 153 ff., 266 ff., 472 ff.).

Aside from well-marked distinctions in diction, the two men are most effectively juxtaposed at the end of Act 3, when, after Demeas' tormented second monologue and his excited scene with Chrysis, Nikeratos comically ambles on stage with his contribution to the prospective wedding feast, a sheep so thin and scrawny that after the sacrificial obligations are satisfied, the only thing left to pass around to the banquet guests will be the skin (399 ff.).

Demeas deals with his assumed betrayal through philosophical reflection, self-questioning, and verbal accusation; Nikeratos, when he finds out that his daughter has been violated, comes to blows with his old friend toward the end of Act 4. Demeas is capable of tenderness and sensitivity, but also of considerable cruelty, as his sarcastic taunting of Chrysis shows (see 390 ff.). Nikeratos' blunt practicality is enlivened by outlandish, melodramatic abuse when he becomes enraged; his pomposity is delightfully deflated in Act 4, as first he accuses Moschion of outdoing all the famous criminals of tragedy in villainy (495 ff.), but then is reluctantly calmed by Demeas' sophistic analogy of Plangon's pregnancy with that of the tragic heroine Danaë, who lost her virginity to Zeus when he appeared in the form of a shower of gold (589 ff.). Demeas slyly asks his friend if perhaps he has a leak in the roof at his house; the tension abates when the comparatively poor Nikeratos admits that his roof is in terrible disrepair (593). Demeas' tactfully playful use of mythology manages to revive the two families' projected alliance.

Demeas and Nikeratos may be compared, in turn, with yet another *senex*, the miserly and scheming Smikrines in *Aspis*. From the somber opening scene, in which the slave Daos announces (mistakenly) the death in battle of his young master Kleostratos, it is clear that Smikrines, the soldier's greedy uncle, has his eye on the rich booty that the young man's party has brought home from Lykia. By Athenian law this treasure, together with Kleostratos' other property, passed to his sister on the soldier's death; Smikrines, standing on his rights as the eldest male of the family, proposes to cancel his niece's engagement to young Chaireas, and marry her himself.

The first half of the play is preserved relatively intact; we are thus able to appreciate the comic artistry with which Menander presents the miser, whose distracted questioning of Daos precisely betrays his lack of concern for the young soldier's fate and his consuming preoccupation with the extent of the booty. From the prologue we learn that Kleostratos is not really dead, and we can be certain that the scheme of the old rogue will somehow be aborted. Almost buffoonish in his haste, Smikrines sweeps aside the sensible objections of his rich younger brother Chairestratos (260: "Am I the only older man to get married?"). Fittingly he is duped by an appeal to avarice: Chairestratos, on the advice of Daos, pretends to die, and Smikrines accordingly drops his plan, lured by the more tantalizing prospect of marrying Chairestratos' daughter, a niece who stands to bring him an even greater fortune. Smikrines is informed of his brother's "demise" by a foreign "doctor," played by one of Chaireas' friends.

The second half of the play (of which we have only sketchy fragments) must have contained an amusing series of scenes in which first Kleostratos and then Chairestratos "returns from the dead" to upset the miser's plans. The two pairs of young people celebrate a double wedding in the fifth act; possibly, as W. G. Arnott suggests, the play concluded with a scene in which Smikrines is tormented by Daos and a cook (see the corresponding situation at the end of the *Dyskolos*). Certainly, Smikrines is presented as totally unsympathetic: tightfisted, childless, and greedy, he would be a caricature were it not for the real and formidable power he acquires from Athenian law and his precise knowledge of it (*Aspis* 153 ff., 182 ff., 269 ff.). But as we find in Molière, the old man's avarice makes him vulnerable.

The comedy of Smikrines' ambitions and their frustration is played out against two tragedies, a plot device that is accented by the diction of the play (*Aspis* 1–18, 329 ff., 399–432) and that helps to make the miser's depiction even more vivid. The first tragedy, Kleostratos' death, is assumed by the characters but quickly dispelled by the prologue speech of Tychē (Chance). Daos' solemn narration is juxtaposed with Smikrines' cautious questioning, as the latter tries to make sure that Kleostratos is really dead, yet betrays himself with a remark complimenting Daos on his escape from the surprise attack (62), and lingers on the details of the booty (82 ff.); polite but pointed touches in Daos' diction (85, 89) show that the slave is quite aware of the old man's greed.

The second tragedy, Chairestratos' pretended death, is devised by the characters and is linked effectively with the first through Chairestratos' genuine grief (305 ff.). Daos embellishes this play within a play through a series of tragic quotations when he announces Chairestratos' "death"; the astonished Smikrines can only grumble that the slave is "wearing him down" (425). In this and the succeeding scene with the "doctor," Smikrines is for the first time not in control. Just as the second tragedy is closely connected with the first, so the duping of the miser plays on the same fault in his character that had kindled his ambition in the first scene. Throughout, Smikrines' nervous questioning and exaggerated defensiveness constitute a comic foil to the ostensibly serious actions of the plot.

Such comparisons could be extended; the art of Menander's subtle manipulation of diction for purposes of individualized character portrayal continues to be recognized, after the seminal studies of F. H. Sandbach. In the *Dyskolos*, for example, Sostratos and Gorgias, the two young men, are differentiated through several idiosyncratic stylistic features, including the form of oaths, the presence or absence of qualifying phrases, and the frequency of gnomic reflections. On the other hand, Menander avoids the temptation to infuse the speech of individual characters with distinctive mannerisms; distinctive stylistic touches are employed deftly and sparingly, with some attention to dramatic pacing and the particular needs of the dramatic situation in individual scenes. Geta, Daos, and Sikon, as well as the parasite Chaireas, are individual personalities in the *Dyskolos*; Sikon the cook, in particular, is endowed with uniquely colorful language, which renders his egotistic authoritarianism more comic: Sikon uses more metaphors, swears by more gods, and is more lyrically effusive than any other character in the play (see his description of the party to Knemon at 931 ff.).

It is clear that, despite the absence of fantasy in Menander's comedy and of the broad verbal range that regularly accompanies the fantastic, the artistic success of the plays is bound up with a refined, subtle attentiveness to individual traits of character and expression. This discovery (or rediscovery, if we may suppose that this feature of Menander's style animated his popularity with ancient audiences) of variety beneath the surface homogeneity of Menander's language is probably the most significant result of research on Menander since the recently discovered fragments of his plays have been published.

Other subjects of inquiry, scarcely less fertile, are the dramatic and philosophical backgrounds to New Comedy. With our fragmentary picture of comedy after the end of the fifth century B.C., each new papyrus discovery has enlivened discussion of the development of comedy after the death of Aristophanes, and has expanded our notions of the relationship between the poets of New Comedy and Attic tragedy, especially Euripides. It seems clear that the rhetorical wish of Philemon, who professed he would be content were he able to meet and converse with the shade of Euripides in the underworld, is scarcely exaggerated as an emblem for the age of New Comedy: in dramaturgy (recognition scenes, mistaken identity, the treatment of family relationships, prologue and messenger speeches) Menander at least may be shown to have borrowed numerous techniques from tragic melodrama.

Occasionally characters in Menander refer explicitly to Euripidean plays—for example, Onesimos, who quotes the *Auge* in *The Arbitration*. More often the influence of the tragedians is indirect, or obliquely indicated, as with Menander's frequent practice of introducing the stricter form of iambic trimeter, peculiar to tragedy, on certain occasions in the comedies to convey sober reflection or serious emotion: examples include Moschion's account of the rape in *The Woman of Samos* (45 ff.) and Daos' narration of the tragedy in Lykia in *The Shield* (1–18). The latter play furnishes especially intricate illustrations of Menander's use of tragedy, since Daos adopts a contrived, tragic "plot" (the death of Chairestratos) in order to trick Smikrines. Thus, a "tragic" play within a play both parallels and contrasts with the solemn opening narration, in which young Kleostratos' death is reported (erroneously, as it turns out). As S. M. Goldberg observes, Menander's technique in such references to tragedy is best described as a "mixture of modes," a technique in which the playwright is, again, most closely anticipated by Euripides.

As for the comic background, we have already touched upon some of the continuities in theme and characterization that link Aristophanes and Menander. In scene construction it is illuminating to compare the end of the *Wasps* with the finale of the *Dyskolos*. Aristophanes' hero, old Philokleon, illustrates the folly of obsessive preoccupation with the law courts; like some of Menander's old men, Knemon especially, Philokleon is a *senex* with a tic. The litigiousness of Athenian life was never far from the comic stage; Smikrines' machinations in *The Shield* display a keen legal mind, while Syriskos in *The Arbitration* observes that merely to survive in Athens a man must put everything aside and devote himself to study of the laws and the prosecution of suits (417–418).

At the end of the *Wasps*, Philokleon returns drunk from a party, having stolen someone else's girl and enlivened his progress home by beating up people in the street. Eagerly anticipating a sexual orgy, he turns aside the protests of his son and crowns his physical exuberance at the finale with a wild dance; Aristophanes draws attention to the novelty of such a conclusion for a comedy in the final verses (see *Wasps* 1536–1537). A very different party is in progress at the end of the *Dyskolos*: a decorous, middle-class wedding feast. But vestiges of earlier comedy may be discerned in Sikon's description of events (*Dyskolos* 949 ff.):

> The drinking went on, and on, and on. You're listening? A tipsy girl, a maid, who veiled her youthful face, stepped out to dance. The flower blushed as she began the rhythm. She trembled, shyly—but another joined her hand in hers and waltzed!
>
> (*Dyskolos* 949 ff.)

This account—in fact, the whole concluding scene with Geta, Sikon, and Knemon (*Dyskolos* 880–969)—is performed to the intermittent accompaniment of flute music from the party. This is also an unusual ending, or at least one for which there is no parallel in extant Menander. In addition, most of the scene is played in a relatively unusual meter, iambic tetrameter. As E. W. Handley notes, the end of the *Dyskolos* shows signs of being a descendant of the *exodos* (the concluding scenes of a play) of Old Comedy. In the final scene the hints of physical aggression by Geta and Sikon are only hints: Knemon is tamed verbally and psychologically. In Menander the Aristophanic inversion of generational stereotypes is abandoned. The *Wasps* presents a mischievous, carousing father who chafes under the restraint of his sober son and is eager for *kōmos* (revelry) and *gamos* (sex). In the *Dyskolos* it is the young who properly look forward to *gamos* (here a legitimized marriage) and the old who are reproached for hardening of the arteries. Knemon, of course, is persuaded to go the party at the end of the play. Although this may represent the process of social reintegration that is often described as one function of comedy in general, the last scene nevertheless leaves us with the impression that the success of Geta and Sikon with the old man has been strictly limited. After all, we never see Knemon dance.

If the sketch above testifies to some of the differences between the fifth- and fourth-century Athenian comic stage, it should also signal some important structural similarities. In fact, the two finales we have been considering are very similar, and it is possible that psychological criticism would regard the second as merely a "sublimated" version of the first. On stage the scene from Menander, if less outrageous, is potentially just as comic: New Comedy is more energetic theatrically than is commonly supposed. Clearly, though, this energy differs from that of Aristophanes. It has, in the main, been elevated from satire and farce to the realm of romantic comedy and the comedy of manners.

The varying influences of Euripidean tragedy and Aristophanic Old Comedy may thus be discerned in Menandrean comedy, with no detriment to the playwright's originality. Similarly, Menander appears to have been capable of fusing many of the themes of contemporary philosophy with drama, without running the risk of too programmatic an approach. Certainly the scrutiny of character and virtue in his plays, the tests of what constitutes justice (dikē), and the tolerant love of mankind (philanthrōpia) for which he was famous may serve to link Menander's plays with some of the doctrines of Aristotle and Theophrastus; even the variations of plot in some of the comedies suggest an application of the Poetics. But Menander seldom presses a specific idea to the extent that we can link a particular character's speech with philosophical theory in a precise relationship; the exemplar of Aristophanes' Ecclesiazusae and Plato's Republic is instructive, since it illustrates the difficulty of pinning philosopher and playwright in a post hoc, ergo propter hoc dependence.

However much some of the plays, or isolated quotations, may recall the Ethics or the Rheto-

ric, or anticipate some of the doctrines of the Stoic and Epicurean schools that were formed during Menander's dramatic career, it is plain that his relationship with contemporary philosophy was not that of the pamphleteer. One may recall the parallel intellectual exchange a century earlier, in the drama of Euripides and the doctrines of the Sophists. Menander's gift of pithy expression simplified many philosophical reflections to epigrammatic form; he is one of the most quotable authors of antiquity.

Julius Caesar, a devoted admirer of Terence, nevertheless admitted that his favorite Roman playwright was a dimidiatus Menander, a Menander "cut down by half." His remark points to the subsequent influence of the Greek playwright in Rome: four of Terence's six plays are known to have been based on Menandrean originals (Andria, Heautontimorumenos, Eunuchus, and Adelphoe). Plautus also based four of his twenty surviving plays on Menander (Aulularia, Bacchides, Cistellaria, and Stichus). The discovery of a papyrus fragment makes possible the comparison of a scene from the Bacchides with its original, the Dis Exapatōn ("The Double Deception"). The analysis of E. W. Handley, in Menander and Plautus: A Study in Comparison, is a suggestive indication of the ways in which Plautus altered his Greek model in the direction of "stronger colours . . . more obvious staging . . . and more comic comedy." Handley's final assessment, while conceding Plautus' heightened theatricality, points to the "paradox . . . that, with our present almost documentary standards of realism in this kind of drama, Menander seems so much more modern."

The varying treatments of Menandrean originals by Plautus and Terence constitute the principal link in antiquity in the transmission of Greek New Comedy to the modern stage and to the romantic comedy of twentieth-century films and television drama. Shakespeare's formulation in A Midsummer-Night's Dream, "Jack shall have Jill/Naught shall go ill," is a suitable epigraph for thousands of subsequent variations of the typical New Comedy plot; and it is not inapposite in any appraisal of Menander's originality to reckon the readiness and the range with which he and his Roman adapters were imitated.

Menander stands behind the stylized farce of Pierre de Marivaux in *Le Jeu de l'amour et du hasard,* even as his plots provide the essentials of Oscar Wilde's *The Importance of Being Earnest* and the fantasies of late-twentieth-century situation comedy. Plautus adapted him to raucous musical comedy; Terence, to the sober drama of smiling *humanitas.* The ancient panegyrics that laud Menander's realism, in this perspective, are reminiscent of Samuel Johnson's praise of Shakespeare as preeminently the poet of "general nature." Fortuitously, since Shakespeare could not, as far as we know, have read Menander's Greek, the motifs of his late romantic comedies are often strikingly similar to Menander's plays in their combinations of tragic possibilities with comic recognition and restoration (compare, for example, Polemon in *She Who Was Shorn* with Leontes in *The Winter's Tale*). If the genius of Aristophanes stands alone, Menander's originality was to give birth to a remarkably vital tradition in the theater that, after more than two thousand years of variation, is still capable of self-renewal.

Selected Bibliography

TEXTS

Koerte, A., and A. Thierfelder, eds. *Menandri quae supersunt.* 2 vols. Leipzig, 1957–1959. Teubner text.
Lloyd-Jones, H., ed. *Menandri Dyscolus.* Oxford, 1960.
Jacques, J.-M., ed. and trans. *Ménandre, Le Dyscolos.* Paris, 1963.
———, ed. *Ménandre, La Samienne.* Paris, 1971.
Sandbach, F. H., ed. *Menandri reliquiae selectae.* Oxford, 1972.

TRANSLATIONS

Allinson, F. G. *Menander, the Principal Fragments.* Cambridge, Mass., 1921. Revised ed., 1951.

Arnott, W. G. *Menander.* Vol. 1. Cambridge, Mass., and London, 1979. Loeb Classical Library. First of three projected volumes to replace Allinson's translation.
Casson, L. *The Plays of Menander.* New York, 1971.
Moulton, C. *Menander, The Dyskolos.* New York, 1977.
Turner, E. G. *The Girl from Samos or The In-laws.* London, 1972. The title that is more commonly used is *The Woman of Samos.*
Vellacott, P. *Menander, Plays and Fragments.* 2nd ed. Harmondsworth, 1973. Together with Theophrastus' *The Characters.*

COMMENTARIES

Gomme, A. W., and F. H. Sandbach. *Menander, A Commentary.* Oxford, 1973.
Handley, E. W. *The Dyskolos of Menander.* Cambridge, Mass., 1965.

CRITICAL STUDIES

Arnott, W. G. *Menander, Plautus, Terence.* Greece and Rome, New Surveys in the Classics 9. Oxford, 1975).
Charitonidis, S., L. Kahil, and R. Ginouvès. *Les Mosaïques de la maison du Ménandre à Mytilène.* Antike Kunst, Beiheft 6. Berne, 1970.
Fantham, E. "Sex, Status and Survival in Hellenistic Athens: A Study of Women in New Comedy." *Phoenix* 29: 44–74 (1975).
Feneron, J. S. "Some Elements of Menander's Style." *Bulletin of the Institute of Classical Studies* (London), 21: 81–95 (1974).
Goldberg, S. M. *The Making of Menander's Comedy.* London, 1980.
Gomme, A. W. "Menander." *Essays in Greek History and Literature.* Oxford, 1937. Pp. 249–295.
Handley, E. W. *Menander and Plautus: A Study in Comparison.* London, 1968.
———. "The Conventions of the Comic Stage and Their Exploitation by Menander." *Ménandre.* Entretiens Fondation Hardt 16 (Geneva, 1970). Pp. 3–26.
Holzberg, N. *Menander, Untersuchungen zur dramatischen Technik.* Nuremberg, 1974.
Knox, B. M. W. "Euripidean Comedy." *Word and Action: Essays on the Ancient Theater.* Baltimore, 1979. Pp. 250–274.
Lloyd-Jones, H. "Menander's *Samia* in the Light of the New Evidence." *Yale Classical Studies* 22: 119–144 (1972).

MENANDER

Meredith, G. "An Essay on Comedy." *Comedy*, edited by W. Sypher. Garden City, N.Y., 1956.

Moulton, C. "Introduction." *Menander, The Dyskolos*. New York, 1977.

Sandbach, F. H. "Menander's Manipulation of Language for Dramatic Purposes." *Ménandre*. Entretiens Fondation Hardt 16. Geneva, 1970. Pp. 111–136.

Segal, E. "The *Physis* of Comedy." *Harvard Studies in Comparative Philology* 77: 129–136 (1973).

Webster, T. B. L. *Studies in Menander*. 2nd ed. Manchester, 1960.

———. *Monuments Illustrating New Comedy*. 2nd ed. *Bulletin of the Institute of Classical Studies* (London), Supp. 24 (1969).

———. *Studies in Later Greek Comedy*. 2nd ed. Manchester, 1970.

———. *An Introduction to Menander*. Manchester, 1974.

BIBLIOGRAPHICAL SURVEY

Mette, H.-J. "Der heutige Menander." *Lustrum* 10:5–211 (1965); 11:139–143 (1966); 13:535–568 (1968); 16:5–80 (1971–1972).

CARROLL MOULTON

HELLENISTIC POETRY AT ALEXANDRIA:
The Epigrammatists, Callimachus, and Apollonius of Rhodes

IN THE THIRD century B.C., in Egyptian Alexandria, a small group of gifted poets revolutionized Greek poetry. So successfully did they alter its outlook and idiom to suit a changed world that Roman poets, centuries later, learned their philosophy from Athens but their literary aesthetics from Alexandria.

FOURTH-CENTURY ROOTS

Plato and Antimachus

The Alexandrian literary revolution did not materialize out of air but had aesthetic, philosophical, and political roots in the previous era. The literary glories of the fourth century were philosophy, history, and rhetoric, all prose media. Greek poetry—epic, lyric, tragic, and comic—went into virtual eclipse. Aristophanes associates the ruination of tragedy with the influence of Socrates (*Frogs* 1491–1495). Although changes in the political and social order of Athens certainly played the major part, there is some truth in Aristophanes' jibe. Socrates took a perverse pleasure in challenging hapless poets to give a rational account of their work

(*Apology* 22b–c), and his pupil Plato banned poets and poetry altogether from his ideal state (*Republic* 10.595a–608b).

Despite his theoretical objections to poetry, Plato had a favorite poet. Cicero reports (*Brutus* 191) that when Antimachus of Colophon gave a public recital of his huge epic *Thebaid* (frags. 1–55) the audience deserted in droves—all, that is, but Plato. Antimachus was not displeased. "I will read on," he said, "for to me Plato alone is equal to a hundred thousand." Plato himself believed that the judgment of the wise few was preferable to the approbation of the mob, and this attitude was later to appear among the Alexandrian poets, who wrote for a select audience of cognoscenti.

Although the *Thebaid* once spanned twenty-four books (Porphyro in Horace, *Ars Poetica* 146), less than fifty lines remain, so it is impossible to judge its contents. The fragments are enough, however, to show that Antimachus was a revolutionary poet in his own right. He had edited both the *Iliad* and the *Odyssey* and produced his epic *Thebaid* by a remarkable new technique, a self-conscious reworking of Homeric verse based on a direct and intimate knowledge of the texts of early hexameter poetry. Homeric formulas appear in the *Thebaid* intact, but in new contexts or broken apart and restitched in combinations that had never occurred to Homer. Antimachus especially liked to use glosses, rare words whose meanings were obscure even in antiquity.

A proper appreciation of Antimachus' technique requires a knowledge of the ancient texts equal to the poet's, for he did not merely mine the texts for diction but expanded, contracted, conflated, and otherwise renovated specific lines of Homer and Hesiod to suggest new meanings from the old. The opening line of the *Thebaid*, for example, conflates the first line of the *Odyssey*, "Sing, Muse," with a line from Hesiod's *Theogony* (76) describing "nine Muses, daughters of great Zeus," yielding "Sing, daughters of great Zeus, son of Kronos." By combining the two verses, Antimachus invokes the ghost of Homer as a literary antecedent while correcting Homer's mythology on the authority of Hesiod. This is an entirely new form of literary expression, in which the artist uses the literary tradition itself as a creative medium.

In addition to the epic *Thebaid*, Antimachus wrote the elegiac *Lyde* (frags. 56–73). Only a few fragments remain, but we have a sense of its contents from Plutarch (*Consolatio ad Apollonium* 9), who says that Antimachus wrote the poem to console himself on the death of his beloved wife, Lyde, enumerating heroic suffering to lessen his own grief. It may have been influenced by the lost "Nanno" of the sixth-century-B.C. elegist Mimnermus. The *Lyde* was much admired by some Alexandrians and was probably an important forerunner of the kind of narrative elegy popular in the third century B.C.

After Antimachus' death, Plato sent his pupil Heraclides Ponticus to Colophon to collect all that remained of the poet's work (*Timaeus* 1.216). In spite of these efforts, Antimachus' poetry attracted no known imitators in the fourth century. His achievement would not be recognized nor his techniques perfected until the third century B.C. and Alexandria.

Aristotle and Alexander

Antimachus' approach to literary composition presupposes a specialist's knowledge of the poetic tradition that can be acquired only by making literary texts the object of detached study. The fourth century B.C. witnessed a great surge of scientific investigation, but most of it was directed at nonliterary objects. The moving force behind the collection and organization of general knowledge at this time was Plato's pupil Aristotle.

On the death of Plato in 347 B.C., Aristotle left Athens, but he returned in 335 B.C. to organize an association dedicated to the Muses, the famous Peripatos in the grove of Apollo Lyceius. There he founded his library, the largest to date in the ancient world, and assembled a group of scholars dedicated to compiling and organizing facts of scientific, philosophical, and historical interest. Although philological studies were not among his chief interests, Aristotle did produce a work entitled *Homeric Problems* (frags. 142–179, Rose ed.), which may owe something to his association with Heraclides Ponticus, who also wrote on this subject (frags. 171–175, Wehrli ed.). The tradition that Aristotle made a special edition of the *Iliad* is of dubious value, but his broader, theoretical treatments of rhetorical prose and poetry, the *Rhetoric* and the *Poetics*, were immensely influential.

As Greek tyrants had supported literary and artistic enterprises in the sixth and fifth centuries, Aristotle's library and research interests were underwritten by Alexander the Great, who had been his pupil in 343–340 B.C. Aristotle inspired Alexander's interest in natural science, and throughout his eastern campaigns until his death in 323 B.C., Alexander surrounded himself with philosophers and scientists who collected material and facts for Aristotle's delectation. Alexander's relationship with Aristotle's school was the model for interaction between the monarchy and the scholarly community in third-century Alexandria.

In the spring of 334 B.C., Alexander crossed

the Dardanelles and began his Asian conquests. After conquering Syria and capturing Tyre by siege (332 B.C.), he entered Egypt to free it from Persian hegemony and to consult the oracle of Zeus Ammon. In 331 B.C., at the western end of the Nile delta, between Lake Mareotis and the sea, he founded Alexandria, the first and most important of the many cities bearing his name. According to Arrian (3.1.1. ff.), Alexander himself laid out the plans for the city: the extent and direction of the wall, the location of the marketplace, and the sites of the temples of the gods, Greek and Egyptian.

The city prospered from the first, drawing a large, cosmopolitan population of Macedonians, Greeks, Egyptians, and Jews. It was already playing a major role in the economics of the Aegean in 323 B.C., when Alexandria with the rest of Egypt came under the control of Alexander's general and biographer Ptolemy, later known as Ptolemy Soter and Ptolemy I.

THE ALEXANDRIAN BACKGROUND

Ptolemy Soter, the Museum, and the Library

As an associate of Alexander and a man of considerable intellectual capabilities, Ptolemy Soter could not escape the influence of Aristotle and the Peripatetic school. Soter invited eminent scholars from all over the Greek world, including Aristotle's successor Theophrastus (Diogenes Laertius, 5.37), to take up residence in his city. Although Theophrastus refused the invitation, his own successor, Straton of Lampsacus, was tutor for a while to Soter's son Ptolemy Philadelphus (Diogenes Laertius, 5.58).

Another eminent Peripatetic and pupil of Theophrastus, Demetrius of Phalerum, fled to Alexandria when his tyranny was overthrown in Athens (307 B.C.). Demetrius was a prolific writer on moral, philosophical, and occasionally literary themes (Diogenes Laertius, 5.80–81). A fully extant treatise, *On Style*, has come

down from antiquity bearing his name, and although the ascription and date are controversial, it may be taken as an example of Peripatetic literary theory after Aristotle. It begins with a preliminary section on the Greek period marked by frequent citations of Aristotle and Theophrastus (1–35). Then follow the definitions of four kinds of style (36–37): slight, elevated, elegant, and forcible. Suitable subject matter, diction, and principles of arrangement are detailed for each. While the theoretical framework seems to have been designed for rhetorical criticism—the forcible style, for instance, is tailor-made for Demosthenes—illustrative examples are frequently taken from poetry.

The four-style scheme is an elaboration of a simpler and earlier notion of two kinds of style: slight and grand. Demetrius himself admits (*On Style* 36) that other critics accept only these two because they alone are mutually exclusive. The influence of theoretical schemes such as these on the critical theory of the Alexandrian poets will be readily apparent when we examine their work.

Demetrius advised Ptolemy Soter on lawmaking (Aelian, *Varia Historia* 3.17) and probably on the organization and foundation of the famous Museum and Library. Following Alexander's example, Soter endowed a research foundation and library organized on the Peripatetic model (Plutarch, *Non posse suaviter vivi secundum epicurum* 13). The research foundation was known as the Museum because it took the form of a religious association dedicated to the Muses. Strabo (793–794) tells us that it was situated within a part of the city known as "the palaces," that it had a covered walk or *peripatos*, a gathering place or *exedra*, and a large building that housed a dining room. It possessed corporate funds and was headed by a priest appointed by the king. It is not known whether the member-scholars lived on the premises or whether they held formal classes there.

The buildings of the Museum appear on a

list of the city's tourist attractions made by the poet Herodas (*Mimiambi* 1.26–31). The Library is not mentioned, probably because it was part of the Museum complex. The Library's collection grew to be very large, 490,000 papyrus rolls by Tzetzes' estimation (Kaibel, *Com. Graec. Frag.* p. 19, Pb. 20), thanks to the Ptolemies' rather heavy-handed methods of acquisition. Galen (*Commentary on Euripides' Hippolytus* 3.17a.606–607) describes how Ptolemy Soter's grandson, Ptolemy Euergetes, gave orders that all books found on ships unloaded at Alexandria should be confiscated for the Library and only copies returned to the owners. Euergetes also "borrowed" the official Athenian copies of the works of Aeschylus, Sophocles, and Euripides on deposit of fifteen talents that he cheerfully forfeited.

The Ptolemies' bibliomania was motivated in part by self-aggrandizement but also by a respect bordering on awe for the Greek literary tradition and a fear that much of it was in danger of perishing. Since books were transcribed by hand, there were never many copies in circulation. Many important books did not survive long enough to find their way to the Library at all, and when the Library was accidentally burned by Julius Caesar in 48 B.C. a precious heritage was lost forever.

Philitas, Zenodotus, and Ptolemy Philadelphus

Among the most brilliant of the intellectual immigrants of this period was Philitas of Cos. Philitas was a poet and scholar (Strabo, 14.657) in the tradition of Antimachus. Although he was not a text editor, he made a collection of *Miscellaneous Glosses* (frags. 29–59, Kuchenmüller ed.) so well known in the third century that the comic poet Strato portrayed a cook who used rare Homeric words for everyday objects and drove his poor master to the "books of Philitas" (Athenaeus, *Deipnosophistai* 9.382c).

We have only the smallest fragments of Philitas' poetry: the elegiac *Demeter* (frags. 5–8,

Kuchenmüller ed.), the *Hermes* (frags. 1–4, Kuchenmüller ed.), the *Paignia* (frags. 10–11, Kuchenmüller ed.), and the *Epigrams* (frags. 12–13, Kuchenmüller ed.). According to Ovid (*Tristia* 1.6.1–2), he wrote of a beloved named Bittis, but we know nothing more of the poem.

Athenaeus (12.552b) tells us Philitas was so slender that he had to put balls of lead around his feet so he would not be swept away by the wind. The story is a reflection not on Philitas' physique but on his poetry, which was written in a slight as opposed to a grand style. In contrast, Antimachus' *Lyde* was "fat" (Callimachus, frag. 398, Pfeiffer ed.).

Philitas was a mentor of poets and a teacher of kings and scholars. The king was Ptolemy Philadelphus, the son of Ptolemy Soter, who was born on Philitas' native Cos in 308 B.C. He succeeded his father in 283 B.C. in spite of the opposition of Demetrius of Phalerum, whose death followed shortly (Diogenes Laertius, 5.78–79). Like his father, Ptolemy Philadelphus was a great patron of scholarship and the arts. We learn from Tzetzes that Philadelphus himself provided the impetus for the first editing of literary texts.

When books are copied by hand, as they were until the invention of the printing press in the fifteenth century, errors are bound to creep into the text on account of the carelessness or ignorance of scribes. Lines or even whole passages can be truncated or lost. Marginal comments can migrate into the text, words can be misspelled or blotted, and rodents or insects can feed on the pages. It was apparent in the third century that many literary texts that had been in circulation for a long time were badly in need of correction. The Library was an ideal site for the job.

Ptolemy set Lycophron to edit the comedies, Alexander the Aitolian to edit the tragedies and satyr plays, and Zenodotus to edit Homer and the other poets. They were all poets as well as scholars: Lycophron and Alexander were both noted tragedians; Zenodotus, another pupil of Philitas, was an epic poet. No trace of Zenodotus' poetry has survived, but the impress of his editorial work can still be found in modern texts of the *Iliad* and *Odyssey*.

Zenodotus' greatest contributions were his use of critical signs to indicate verses he wished to eliminate because they seemed superfluous or inappropriate, and his division of the *Iliad* and *Odyssey* into twenty-four books, an arrangement that others after him maintained and refined. His editions were well known to contemporary poets, and many of his textual criticisms have come down to us in the Homeric scholia. He was the first to have the official title "librarian," and he held the position while tutoring Philadelphus' son Euergetes.

While Zenodotus was librarian, a catalog was begun of the Library's holdings. The cataloging was the work of Callimachus of Cyrene, the greatest poet of his age (whose life and poetry are discussed subsequently). His catalogs were called the *Pinakes* or *Tables of All Those Who Were Eminent in Any Kind of Literature and of Their Writings in 120 Books* (frags. 429–453, Pfeiffer ed.).

In order to make the *Pinakes*, it was necessary to devise suitable principles of organizing literary works. Callimachus' broadest categories were genres, some of which had traditional names and definitions, but Callimachus must have improvised others. Within genres, authors were arranged alphabetically. A brief biography was appended to each name, and the author's works were listed by title and opening words (frag. 436, Pfeiffer ed.). The works of individual authors could also be grouped according to various principles. Simonides' victory odes, for example, were arranged by type of athletic contest (frag. 441, Pfeiffer ed.); Pindar's, by location of the contest (frag. 450, Pfeiffer ed.). Writers who did not fit into any of the main categories were put into *miscellanea* (frags. 434–435, Pfeiffer ed.).

Later scholars sometimes protested the choices Callimachus made. Aristarchus complained that he misplaced a *dithyramb* among the *paeans* of Bacchylides (*P. Oxy.* 2368), and

Apollonius the Eidographer maintained that Callimachus wrongly placed the poem we call Pindar's "Second Pythian Ode" among the "Nemeans" (frag. 450, Pfeiffer ed.). Although many corrections and supplements were subsequently devised, it is clear that Callimachus' work was widely consulted and had a decisive influence on the way literature and literary history were understood in Alexandria and afterward.

In addition to the general *Pinakes*, we know of two special *Pinakes*: *The Table and Register of Dramatic Poets, Chronologically from the Earliest Times* (frags. 454–456, Pfeiffer ed.), and *The Table of Glosses and Compositions of Democritus* (*Suda*; see Callimachus). There were also numerous prose compendia, including two patterned directly after works of Aristotle: *Non-Greek Customs* (frag. 405, Pfeiffer ed.) and *On the Games* (frag. 403, Pfeiffer ed.). *A Collection of Marvels in All the Earth According to Localities* (frags. 407–411), *On the Rivers of the World* (*Suda*; see Callimachus), and *The Foundations of Islands and Cities and Changes of Name* (*Suda*; see Callimachus) were others. The titles *On Fishes* (frag. 406, Pfeiffer ed.), *On Winds* (frag. 404, Pfeiffer ed.), *On Birds* (frag. 414–425, Pfeiffer ed.), and *The Names of the Months by Tribes and Cities* (*Suda*; see Callimachus) may be chapters of a work called *Local Nomenclature* (frag. 406, Pfeiffer ed.).

The Peripatetic spirit shines clearly through Callimachus' prose work. Although he himself was never called a Peripatetic, two of his pupils, Hermippus and Satyrus, were given that title, and the adjective was ultimately applied to Alexandrian scholars in general.

THE REBIRTH OF POETRY

The Ptolemies were altogether successful in translating Peripatetic aims, methods, and institutions to a new setting. Unlike the original Peripatos, however, the Museum and Library were strongly oriented in the direction of literary scholarship. This must have been due to the predispositions of the early Ptolemies and their intellectual advisers, Demetrius of Phalerum and Philitas of Cos. The emphasis they placed on preserving and studying the Greek literary tradition, their eagerness to attract literary men from abroad, and their willingness to support them economically encouraged not only scholarship but the creation of new poetry.

Poetry had died in the fourth century, paralyzed by its own spendid success and demoralized by the recent destruction of the political institutions and religious beliefs that had been its lifeblood. The monumental intellectual and artistic difficulties faced by poets in the postclassical era are described most poignantly by Choerilus of Samos, who despaired of following in Homer's footsteps:

Blessed was he who was skilled in song,
a servant of the Muses, when the meadow was yet undefiled.
Now, when everything has been searched out and arts have limits,
we, the hindermost, are left behind, off the road; nor is there a place
where someone, searching all about, might bring near a new-yoked chariot.

(frag. 1, Kinkel ed.)

Choerilus is asking a question: How can a serious poet presume to write an epic poem after Homer? Or a lyric poem after Sappho? Or anything at all in the face of the glorious Greek literary tradition?

Choerilus' own answer was to find new subject matter for epic poetry in recent history. Antimachus revitalized diction; and Philitas, style. In an age when most poets did nothing more than grind out slavish imitations of the old masters, these three seriously addressed the problem of poetic renewal and showed the way to a true renaissance of Greek poetry in the third century.

When it came, it was a revolution as well as a rebirth. The new poetry grew out of the Greek poetic tradition, but everything about it was different. The old literary genres still provided rules governing the general shapes of poetic compositions, but they were expanded, contorted, and conflated in ways that would not have been possible before Callimachus' *Pinakes*. Traditional myths still provided the content of most poetry, but they often appeared in unusual versions discovered in library research. Poetic diction was also given new life. Koine, the common Greek dialect of the third century that had developed to suit the needs of commerce and politics, was not intrinsically poetic, so it was leavened with semantic and syntactic exotica to please the intellect and the ear. Antimachus' poetry of literary reference reappeared in elegant and sophisticated forms, transforming the entire Greek literary tradition into a gold mine of poetical language and vastly increasing the possibilities of multiple meanings for a learned audience.

These changes in diction, content, and form were fueled by the poets' scholarly work, but they were subordinated by the best poets to entirely artistic aims. These aims are defined, to the extent that artistic aims are ever capable of definition, by literary theory of the sort put forth in Demetrius' *On Style*. In Alexandrian poetry, for the first time in the western tradition, it is possible to observe the interplay of literary theory and literary practice.

The true nature of the Alexandrian literary revolution is best revealed in the individual works of the best poets. It is to these that we now turn.

THE EPIGRAMMATISTS: ASCLEPIADES AND POSIDIPPUS

The Epigram

The earliest extant examples of Greek writing, dating from the eighth century B.C., are metrical inscriptions. One, on a vase, promises it as a prize for the best dancer. The other, in mixed iambic and hexameter lines, on a bowl from Ischia, says,

> Away with Nestor's fine cup.
> Whoever drinks from this cup will be seized at once
> with a longing for lovely-crowned Aphrodite.
> (*Rendiconti Lincei* [1955], 215 ff.)

These are epigrams. Similar verses—anonymous, brief, and to the point—were inscribed on tombstones and votive offerings throughout Greek history. In the sixth and fifth centuries, owing to Ionic influence, the elegiac couplet became their usual metrical form, and their style became more polished; but their purpose and content were essentially unchanged.

The beginning of a trend to expand the limits of the genre can be detected in the fourth century in the epigrams ascribed to Plato, which include fictitious epitaphs on famous poets such as Pindar (*Anthologia Palatina* 7.35) and Aristophanes (*Life of Aristophanes*). Once the notion took root that an epigram could be entirely a work of the imagination and could be copied on papyrus rather than incised on stone or painted on pottery, the way was clear for rapid development of the genre.

Asclepiades

The earliest Alexandrian epigrammatist whose work is extant is Asclepiades of Samos. Two of his poems give some indication of when he lived. The first (*Anthologia Palatina* 1014 ff., Gow–Page ed.) refers to a Queen Cleopatra, most likely the sister of Alexander the Great who was murdered in 309 B.C. The other (*Anthologia Planudea* 995a ff., Gow–Page ed.) describes a portrait of Berenice, probably Berenice I, the wife of Ptolemy Soter. From these we gather that Asclepiades was a contemporary of Philitas, with whom he is coupled by the poet Theocritus (*Idylls* 7.39–41), and was active in the last part of the fourth and first part of the third centuries.

Like Plato, Asclepiades acknowledges the original uses of the epigram by inventing fictitious sepulchral and votive inscriptions. In *Anthologia Palatina* 832 ff. (Gow–Page ed.) a prostitute dedicates a golden spur to Aphrodite; in *Anthologia Palatina* 939 ff. (Gow–Page ed.) a comic mask announces that it was presented to the Muses by a schoolboy in honor of a prize for good penmanship. Tombstones declare their occupants missing at sea (*Anthologia Palatina* 950 ff., Gow–Page ed.) or lost at too early an age (*Anthologia Palatina* 962 ff., Gow–Page ed.). There is some experimenting with iambic meter in the last, but on the whole these are Asclepiades' most traditional efforts.

In other poems he expands the epigram by incorporating into it the forms and contents of other genres. *Anthologia Palatina* 920 (Gow–Page ed.), for example, is a miniature mime. When a prospective host orders his slave to buy rose wreaths for a dinner party, he discovers that his budget has been overspent. The slave is then dispatched for expensive perfume to be procured by blackmailing the shopgirl.

The genre most successfully incorporated into the epigram was the drinking song (*skolion*), which often had erotic themes. The model for this innovation is the inscription on the bowl from Ischia. Here is one of the best:

> Wine is the test of love. Many toasts
> convicted Nicagoras who denied to us that he was in love.
> He wept, and hung his head, and looked somewhat downcast.
> His wreath was askew.
> (*Anthologia Palatina* 894 ff., Gow–Page ed.)

The theme of "truth in wine" is an old one in Archaic drinking songs, and Asclepiades' immediate source was probably the seventh-century lyric poet Alcaeus (frag. 243, Lobel–Page ed.). The literary reference neither diminishes the poignancy nor destroys the economy of Asclepiades' verse.

In this epigram the lover remains disconsolate at the party, but another favorite motif is the *paraclausithyron*, where the lover pursues his beloved to his or her very door only to find himself excluded. In the usual situation, the disappointed lover makes his recriminations and departs (*Anthologia Palatina* 860, Gow–Page ed.) but endless elaborations are possible. In *Anthologia Palatina* 854 ff. (Gow–Page ed.) the lover defies the elements to deter him from his passionate expedition. In *Anthologia Palatina* 866 (Gow–Page ed.) his beloved has given him an explicit invitation, but still denies him admittance.

Erotic themes are also given other forms. *Anthologia Palatina* 624 ff. (Gow–Page ed.) puts erotica in the form of an *ekphrasis*, a description of a work of art that has been a feature of Greek poetry since Homer:

> Once I played with persuasive Hermione, O
> Paphian Queen.
> She wore a gaily colored girdle
> with golden letters. It was written, "Always love
> me,
> and do not grieve if another has me."

Anthologia Palatina 1002 ff. (Gow–Page ed.) combines erotica with the epitaph. The tomb speaks:

> I hold Archeanessa, the prostitute from Colophon,
> on whose very wrinkles sweet Eros sat.
> You lovers who plucked the first flowers of her
> youth,
> through what a furnace you came.

In finding new directions for the epitaph, Asclepiades went one step further than Plato, who wrote epitaphs for famous poets. Asclepiades wrote epitaphs for famous poems. They speak their name, race, and fame as if from the grave:

> I am Lydian by race and Lyde by name.
> On account of Antimachus I am grander than all
> the descendants of Codrus.

For who has not sung of me? Who has not read the
> Lyde?
> The joint writing of the Muses and Antimachus?
> (*Anthologia Palatina* 958 ff., Gow–Page ed.)

> This is the sweet work of Erinna, not much,
> but enough for a nineteen-year-old girl, and
> more powerful than many others. If Hades
> had not quickly come to me, who would have such
> fame?
> (*Anthologia Palatina* 942 ff., Gow–Page ed.)

These epitaphs are not far from being prefaces to the works they memorialize. Asclepiades' choice of Antimachus and Erinna no doubt reflects his own literary taste.

Posidippus

Asclepiades' success in expanding the possibilities of the epigram is most evident in the work of his younger contemporaries, who not only use his themes, motifs, and conceits as literary stocks-in-trade, but sometimes refer directly to his verses in theirs. One of the most important of these was Posidippus of Pella, whose poems on the Pharos lighthouse (3100 ff., Gow–Page ed.) and the temple of Arsinoe-Aphrodite (3110 ff., 3120 ff., Gow–Page ed.) combined with epigraphical evidence place him in the first half of the third century.

Posidippus wrote the obligatory epitaphs on children dying young (*Anthologia Palatina* 3174 ff., Gow–Page ed.) and shipwrecked sailors (*Anthologia Palatina* 3130 ff., Gow–Page ed.), as well as votive epigrams (*Anthologia Planudea* 3155 ff., Gow–Page ed.) and drinking songs. His convivial and erotic epigrams feature literary men. In *Anthologia Palatina* 3074 ff. (Gow–Page ed.) he pits reason against Eros, and in *Anthologia Palatina* 3074 ff. (Gow–Page ed.) he declares that love cannot torture the Muses' cicada, the poet, who has been tried before in his books. In *Anthologia Palatina* 3086 ff. (Gow–

Page ed.) he cites literary precedents for poets in love:

> For Nanno and Lyde pour two, and one for the
>   lover
> Mimnermus, and one for wise Antimachus,
> and mix the fifth for me, Heliodorus, and at the
>   sixth
> say "For anyone whoever happened to love."

As Posidippus' poems are often peopled with literary characters, so his poetry is self-consciously literary. In *Anthologia Palatina* 3070 ff. (Gow–Page ed.) the poet challenges the Erotes (the Loves) to shoot him down, if they have the power. It begins, "Yes, yes, shoot, Loves!"—a line he has taken directly from Asclepiades (*Anthologia Palatina* 892, Gow–Page ed.). By using Asclepiades' verse, Posidippus is deliberately contrasting his own confidence with the despondency of Asclepiades, who begs the Erotes to leave him alone or kill him outright because he can no longer stand the pain of love.

Other poems also show Posidippus reacting to Asclepiades, but the problem of establishing literary influence is complicated by difficulties in ascribing the poems to their rightful authors. In many cases the epigrams are labeled with two possible authors, but even when there is only one name, we cannot be certain that it is the correct one. The uncertainties about authorship accrued over the years as the epigrams were copied from one anthology to another. Two anthologies are now extant, the *Palatine* (*ca.* A.D. 980) and the anthology of Maximus Planudes (A.D. 1301). These were both based on the anthology of Constantinos Cephalos (*ca.* A.D. 900), who used as his sources three earlier anthologies, including the *Garland* of Meleager, which was compiled about 100 B.C. and contained the early Alexandrian material. Meleager himself may have gathered the poems from yet earlier anthologies (*P. Harris* 56, *P. Teb.* 3).

In the age when books in the form of papyrus rolls were being gathered, sorted, and copied in the Library, it is not surprising that small poems such as epigrams would be collected together. Since the scholars themselves were often literary men, it seems reasonable that they might think of collecting their own work and publishing it as a corpus. Posidippus apparently did just this. A scholium on the *Iliad* 11.101 indicates that Aristarchus, the third librarian at Alexandria, possessed two collections of Posidippus' epigrams. The first, entitled the *Soros*, or *Heap of Winnowed Grain*, contained an epigram with the name "Berisos" that was altered or omitted from a second collection in response to Zenodotus' criticism of the reading of that name in the *Iliad* 11.101. This information shows how Posidippus incorporated into his poetry the most up-to-date findings of literary scholarship and how he published not only first but second editions of his work. A third-century papyrus (*P. Lond.* 60) with the title *Assorted Epigrams of Posidippus* confirms the existence of a collection made and published in the author's lifetime.

An author making a collection of his own short poems would doubtless exercise his artistry in arranging the works and might fit out the collection with special poems at the beginning and possibly the end. Ultimately each individual poem would be written with the entire collection in mind. We cannot show that Posidippus took this final step, since most of his poems have disappeared and their original order is gone, but we do have a badly preserved elegiac poem of his that seems very much like a signature poem that might serve as an introduction (see H. Lloyd-Jones). It was found in very poor condition on a pair of wooden tablets of the first century A.D. now in Berlin.

Fellow-citizen Muses,
if ever you have heard something beautiful,
with keen ears, either from Apollo of the golden
  lyre
on the dells of snowy Parnassus, or from Olympus,
leading off the trietic altars for Bacchus,

support now the grievous old age of Posidippus,
writing on the golden columns of tablets.
Leave the peaks, O Heliconians, and come into the
walls of Piplian Thebes . . .
And you who once loved Posidippus, Cynthian,
Son of Leto, Farworker [Apollo]. . . .

The text is very corrupt. In subsequent verses the poet mentions an oracle in connection with the seventh-century poet Archilochus, seeks the acknowledgment of all the Macedonians, including his own hometown of Pella, envisions a statue of himself in the agora, and concludes with a wish to come to his death in an honored old age. The elaborate invocation in so brief a poem, the concluding prayer, and the poet's reference to himself twice by name, and to his place of birth, suggest the signature passages that professional singers sometimes attached to hymns (e.g., *Homeric Hymn to Apollo* 166–178).

Similar introductions can be found in other contemporary poems. The most elaborate of these is the prologue to Callimachus' *Aitia*, in which the poet also speaks of his old age (frag. 1.33–36, Pfeiffer ed.), the love the Muses had for him in his youth (frag. 1.37–38, Pfeiffer ed.), the tablets on which his poetry is written (frag. 1.21–22, Pfeiffer ed.), and his literary predecessors (frag. 1.10–11, Pfeiffer ed.). The poem is discussed subsequently.

So many motifs in common raise the question of deliberate adaptation. Uncertainties about chronology render this question ultimately insoluble, although the complexity, integrity, and imagistic brilliance of the *Aitia* prologue, together with Posidippus' predisposition to borrow from other poets, strongly suggest which one is the original. Setting aside the question of originality, the *Aitia* prologue is clearly a prologue, and so, we can assume, is the elegy of Posidippus. It may introduce a work that is entirely lost, but it could equally well introduce the *Soros*, or more likely the second edition of Posidippus' *Epigrams* mentioned by Aristarchus.

Alexandrian Epigrams

We have seen how the third-century epigrammatists of Alexandria expanded a minor literary form that once served only to mark tombstones and votive offerings into a full-fledged genre by incorporating into it the contents and forms of other genres. Asclepiades in the first generation seems to have pioneered this technique and underscores it by referring in his poems to literary predecessors who were not epigrammatists. Posidippus, in the second generation, does not hesitate to cite Asclepiades himself, making Asclepiades' redefinition of the genre into a new canon.

Like earlier epigrams, Alexandrian epigrams are constrained by their brevity to be logically and stylistically simple; but unlike their predecessors, they are written in the context of literary history and, at least in the case of Posidippus, published in the context of a poetry book. The definitions of the genres and the idea of a poetry book can be traced directly to the scholarly work at the Library. Callimachus, the man responsible for much of that work, also happens to be an epigrammatist.

CALLIMACHUS

In antiquity, Callimachus' scholarly achievement was recognized, but it was his poetry that brought him fame. No other Greek poet is mentioned so often and with such admiration by the best Roman poets. No other poet except Homer is quoted so frequently by grammarians, metricians, and lexicographers. No other poet but Homer and Euripides appears so frequently in the papyrus remains.

Life

In spite of his fame, we know little about Callimachus' life. The *Suda*, which is late (tenth century A.D.) and often unreliable, provides our only account. It begins with the names of his parents, Mesatma and Battus of

Cyrene. The Battiads were the founding family of Cyrene, and a direct connection with them would make Callimachus a descendant of royalty. The source of the *Suda*'s information is doubtless an epigram Callimachus wrote as a mock epitaph for himself:

> You are passing the tomb of Battus' son,
> well-versed in song and in laughing, moderately,
>   over his wine.
>
>   (35, Pfeiffer ed.)

The Romans frequently call him Battiades, but neither the epigram nor the Romans guarantee his aristocratic lineage. There was a fashion among Greek poets to be called by patronymic pseudonymns, as Theocritus calls himself Simichidas, and Asclepiades Sikelides (*Idylls* 7.21, 40). Callimachus Battiades may mean nothing more than Callimachus of Cyrene.

The *Suda* also says that Callimachus was a pupil of Hermocrates the grammarian, an authority on Greek accents, that he was married to the daughter of Euphrates of Syracuse, and that he taught grammar at Eleusis, a suburb of Alexandria, before he was introduced to the king. A stint as schoolmaster early in life does not seem illogical, although this "fact" may be only inferred from his fifth iamb, which is addressed to a lascivious schoolmaster.

The *Suda* says that the king in question is Philadelphus (285–247 B.C.) and that Callimachus survived to the time of Euergetes (247–221 B.C.). Three of his poems that refer to public events place him in the same period. His epic celebrating the marriage of Philadelphus and Arsinoe (frag. 392, Pfeiffer ed.) was written between 278 and 273 B.C. His lyric poem the "Apotheosis of Arsinoe" (frag. 228, Pfeiffer ed.) must have been composed shortly after her death in July 270 B.C., and the famous elegy the "Lock of Berenice" was written to honor her marriage with Euergetes in 246 B.C. Callimachus, then, was a contemporary of Posidippus.

There is no doubt that Callimachus was a prolific writer. The *Suda* credits him with more than 800 titles and lists 24 without mentioning

some of his most famous extant poems. We discussed his scholarly writing previously, and it remains to characterize his poetry.

Epigrams

When Martial wished to compliment a fellow Roman epigrammatist in the first century A.D., he could think of no better way than to compare him to Callimachus (Martial, 4.23). Of Callimachus' epigrams, sixty-four are extant, preserved mainly in the *Anthologia Palatina* (*The Greek Anthology*). For artistry, wit, and sheer emotional force, none can match them.

On the whole, Callimachus does not stray far from the limits of the genre as Asclepiades redefined them, and he often has his predecessor in mind as he writes.

> Our guest had a wound, but kept it hidden.
> Did you see how painfully he heaved up his breath
>   from his chest,
> when he drank the third cup? And all the roses
>   from the man's wreaths,
> were on the ground shedding petals.
> He was burned terribly, by the gods. My guess is
>   not
> out of line. Set a thief to catch a thief.
>
>   (43, Pfeiffer ed.)

This poem should be compared with one by Asclepiades (*Anthologia Palatina* 894 ff., Gow–Page ed.) translated previously.

Callimachus' debt to his predecessor is clear, yet his poem is utterly different. Callimachus defines the situation and the action more precisely and dramatically. The lover's weeping and hanging his head is now a painful, heaving sigh: the verb "to heave," *anegageto*, has also been used to describe a man dying of consumption (Plutarch, *Cleomenes* 30). Asclepiades' misplaced wreath is now a shower of rose petals resembling a ritual leaf-pelting. The vague "many toasts" have become one, the third of three ritual toasts, to Zeus the Savior.

There are also differences in narrative technique. Unlike Asclepiades' simple narrative aimed at a faceless reader, Callimachus uses direct address ("Did you see?" line 2), coupled with a mild oath ("by the gods," line 5) to imply a speaker and listener who witness the lover's behavior and are on friendly terms with one another. Both poets summarize their point in a proverb. Asclepiades states his straight out in the first line, "Wine is the test of love," and uses his narrative to illustrate the theme. Callimachus reserves his proverb, more dramatically, for the end, where it calls attention to the narrator, as much as the lover, and binds the two inextricably.

Asclepiades leads the way to literary epigrams by writing epitaphs for his favorite poems. Callimachus uses a similar technique to make a scholarly argument and a literary judgment:

> I am the work of the Samian, who once at home
>   received the divine singer.
> I celebrate Eurytus and the things he suffered
> and yellow-haired Ioleia. I am called "Homeric,"
> For Creophylus, dear Zeus, a great [*mega*] thing.
> (6, Pfeiffer ed.)

Here Callimachus seems to be arguing a question of authorship, but it is only to disparage the work as a Homeric imitation in the grand style. Callimachus' distaste for the cycle of epic poems that grew up over the years around the *Iliad* and *Odyssey* is thought to be attested in epigram 28 (Pfeiffer ed.), which combines literary and erotic themes.

> I hate the cyclic epic, nor do I enjoy the road that
>   carries many here and there.
> I also detest the roving lover, and I do not drink
>   from the public well. I despise all common
>   things.
> Lysanias, you are beautiful, yes, beautiful, but
>   before Echo says this clearly someone says,
>   "He's another's."
> (28, Pfeiffer ed.)

At the outset the poem seems to be a literary manifesto, a denouncement of derivative epic poetry, which is grouped with crowded roads, roving lovers, and public wells, to be avoided because it is overused and polluted. In the last two lines, however, the poet retreats wittily from his position, at least as far as the roving lover is concerned. The point of the last lines is lost in translation. The words "yes, beautiful" (*naichi kalos*) were pronounced in Greek so that they rhymed in reverse with the words *allos echei*, "another has him," hence the echo. The plain meaning is that Callimachus continues to admire one particular boy in spite of the boy's promiscuity. The implication is that the same indulgence might be given to a particularly beautiful poem, even in an overworked genre.

When Asclepiades introduced convivial and erotic themes into the epigram, he opened the way to using an essentially public genre for the expression of personal feelings. Callimachus extends that license beyond the symposium to include one of the most moving expressions of personal grief ever written, best known to English-speaking people through Cory's translation:

> They told me, Heraclitus, they told me you were
>   dead,
> they brought me bitter news to hear and bitter
>   tears to shed.
> I wept as I remembered how often you and I
> had tired the sun with talking, and sent him down
>   the sky.
>
> And now that thou art lying, my dear old Carian
>   guest,
> a handful of grey ashes, long long ago at rest,
> and still are they pleasant voices, thy nightingales,
>   awake,
> for death, he taketh all away, but them he cannot
>   take.
> (2, Pfeiffer ed.)

The historic use of epigrams for funerary inscriptions made the development of a lamentory epigram entirely natural.

In other funerary epigrams Callimachus'

mood is lighter. An epitaph for a twelve-year-old boy reads:

His twelve-year-old son, his father Phillip laid to
  rest
here, his great hope, Nicoteles.

(19, Pfeiffer ed.)

There is no obvious artifice here, but the simplicity of the poem is deceptive. The father's name, Phillip, means "horse-lover." *Ten pollen elpida* is "the favorite," and *apetheke* ("laid to rest") can have the sense of "sent to pasture." The puns build on one another and end with the pathetic irony of the boy's name, Nicoteles, "Victor." Ferguson, in his article "The Epigrams of Callimachus," first suggested this interpretation. He translates the poem this way:

Mr. Ryder senior retired
his twelve-year-old son
here, the favorite,
Victor.

The epitaph for Nicoteles is a purely literary effort with punning effects that create almost a parody of the genre. Other epigrams are more obvious parodies: the dedication to the Cabiri of a salt box by Eudemos, who saved himself from storms of debt by eating cheap salt and from the salt found salvation (47, Pfeiffer ed.), depends for its point both on puns (salt and sea) and on the thousands of dedications made by sailors for rescue at sea. Epitaphs that address bystanders from the tomb are parodied in 13 (Pfeiffer ed.), where a passerby conducts an interview with the ghost of Charidas, who responds to the inquiries by revealing that Hades is very dark, return is impossible, and Pluto is a myth—but the good news is that you can buy a large ox for a penny.

The writing of parodies requires a sense of humor and a clear understanding of the rules and limits of the genre. Callimachus' wit was his own natural gift, but his feeling for genre must, to a large extent, be the product of his la-

bors on the *Pinakes*. We will see touches of parody in many of his other poems.

Hymns

Of Callimachus' 800 works, only the hymns have survived complete. For this we may thank the scribe who copied them onto a manuscript with the hymns of Homer, Orpheus, and Proclus. There are six altogether.

Hymns are songs addressed to a deity to win divine favor on behalf of the singer or his city. The singer addresses the god directly or through the Muses in simple prologues and epilogues; he may refer as well to himself, the difficulty of his task, and his hope of pleasing the god. The major part consists of a narrative from one or more of the traditional myths associated with the subject of the hymn, generally containing both descriptive material and direct address. It may be embellished with genealogies, lists of honors, prerogatives, and other information enhancing the prestige of the god.

Thirty-three extant hymns have been attributed to Homer, although his authorship was questioned even in antiquity. The hymns are written in Homer's dactylic hexameter, using many traditional Homeric formulas. Thucydides calls one of them, the "Hymn to Apollo," a *prooemion*, that is, a prelude. A number of the hymns contain sign-offs at the end referring to songs that follow (*Homeric Hymn* 6, 10, 31, 32). Four of the hymns (*Homeric Hymn* 2, 3, 4, 5) are far too long to be preludes to anything. These are literary developments of the original form, and Callimachus took them as models for his own hymns.

The Hellenistic period saw a rebirth of interest in the composition of hymns. Some of these poems were quite bizarre. We know of a "Hymn to Demeter" in choriambic hexameters by Philicus of Corcyra that begins "Grammarians, I bring you gifts, the strangely-written composition of Philicus" (Hephaestion, *Enchiridion* 21, Consbruch ed., p. 30).

Callimachus' hymns do not require such an

introduction. The first, his "Hymn to Zeus," follows the Homeric models quite closely. After a rhetorical question introducing his theme, the poet considers which of two birth stories he should tell.

> How shall we sing of him, as Dicteaean or
>   Lycaean?
> My heart is divided, since his birth is disputed.
> Zeus, some say you were born on the hills of Ida,
> Zeus, others say in Arcadia. Which of these are
>   lying?
> "Cretans always lie."
>
> (hymn 1.4–8)

The rhetorical review of suitable topics before the selection of one is called a *priamel* and is a traditional feature of the hymn (e.g., Homer, *Hymn to Apollo* 207–215). The listing of alternatives enhances both the dignity of the god, whose attributes are shown to be many, and the particular theme the singer selects, which is always the last and by implication the best. Callimachus makes his choice on the basis of the famous opinion of Epimenides of Crete on the veracity of his fellow countrymen (frag. 5, Kinkel ed.). Callimachus was undoubtedly aware of the implications of the fact that Epimenides himself was a Cretan but proceeds in any case to describe Zeus' birth in Arcadia (hymn 1.10 ff.).

No sooner does Rhea, mother of Zeus, end her labor than she finds herself in need of water (hymn 1.15–16). Callimachus describes waterless Arcadia by listing six local rivers that had not yet started to flow (hymn 1.18–27). This passage seems like a bit of Alexandrian pedantry by a scholar who wrote a treatise *On Rivers* (frag. 457, Pfeiffer ed.), but the use of geographical lists has direct parallels in the Homeric hymns (e.g., *Hymn to Apollo* 30–46).

Rhea makes the waters flow and gives the baby to the nymph Neda to carry to Knossos in Crete. On the way, his navel falls away in a place called Omphalion, the Plain of the Navel (hymn 1.43–45). An explanation such as this, of how some thing or some place received its name or how a civic or religious institution began, is called an *aition* (plural: *aitia*). *Aitia* can be found in earlier Greek literature—Euripides was especially given to them—but their ubiquity in Hellenistic poetry is due to the influence of antiquarian scholarship and Callimachus.

Baby Zeus is nurtured on honey and serenaded by the Curetes, and quickly grows to manhood when Callimachus says to him,

> Your relatives, though older,
> did not object to your having heaven as your
>   allotted home.
> The ancient poets were not altogether truthful.
> They said that the lot apportioned homes in three
>   ways among the sons of Cronus.
> Who would draw lots for Olympus or Hades?
> Who but a fool?
>
> (hymn 1.57–63)

The ancient poets who describe the allotments are Homer (*Iliad* 15.187 ff.) and Pindar (*Olympian* 1.7.54 ff.). In contrast, Hesiod tells how the other gods requested Zeus to rule them (*Theogony* 881 ff.). In ostentatiously embracing Hesiod's version, Callimachus is making a literary judgment while moving his narrative in a particular direction.

This passage has also been interpreted politically, as a reference either to Ptolemy Soter's acquisition of Egypt with the consent of Alexander's other generals or, more commonly, to Soter's choice of Philadelphus as his successor with the consent of Soter's older brothers. Neither of these interpretations exactly fits the historical facts, and Callimachus' intent here will always be in doubt. It is clear, however, from the conclusion of the narrative, where Callimachus postulates a special relationship between Zeus and "our ruler" (hymn 1.79–88), that the hymn is meant to link Ptolemy to Zeus and to glorify them both.

The hymn ends with a brief epilogue in

which the poet greets the god and remarks on the impossibility of doing justice to his theme.

> Who could sing your works?
> There is no one, nor will there be, who will sing
>   the works of Zeus.
>
> (hymn 1.92-93)

In form, then, the first hymn is very traditional. The introductory priamel, the mythic narrative, and the concluding epilogue all have analogies in the Homeric hymns. Callimachus' second hymn, to Apollo, is more inventive. It begins dramatically with an epiphany of the god.

> How the laurel branch of Apollo has been shaken;
> how, the whole shrine. Away, away the sinner.
> Phoebus knocks at the door with his lovely foot.
> Do you not see?
>
> (hymn 2.1-4)

We have no earlier examples of mimetic representations of epiphany rituals, but it may only be that Callimachus' models have been lost (see Alcaeus, frag. 307, Page ed., for a possible example).

The poet strikes up an accompaniment of lyres (2.12-16), requests reverential silence (2.17-24), and begins the choral paean.

> Shout hie hie. It is evil to contend with the blessed
>   gods.
> Whoever fights with the blessed ones would fight
>   with my king.
> Whoever fights with my king would fight with
>   Apollo.
> Apollo will honor the chorus that sings according to
>   his heart.
> He is able for he sits at the right hand of Zeus.
>
> (2.25-29)

The scholiast identifies "my king" as Ptolemy Euergetes. He may only be guessing, and many scholars prefer to see Philadelphus here. These lines in no way suggest a date for the hymn nor anything about the circumstances of its composition, as some have alleged. As in hymn 1, Callimachus shies from equating the king directly with the god but only indicates that they have a close community of interests.

The song covers a wide range of topics: Apollo's ritual objects (2.32-35), his appearance (2.36-41), his skills (2.42-46), his patronage of flocks (2.47-54), and his founding of cities (2.55-64). The poet expands this last topic into a description of Apollo's role in the founding of his own Cyrene (2.65-96). The ritual cry, "*Hie, hie Paieon,*" is heard again at line 97, where it is explained etymologically: when Apollo drew his bow at Pytho, the crowd shouted, "Shoot, shoot, Son, the arrow."

The hymn concludes with the famous epilogue:

> Envy spoke secretly in the ear of Apollo,
> "I do not admire the poet who does not sing as
>   much as the sea."
> Apollo drove away Envy with his foot, and said
>   this,
> "The stream of the Assyrian river is great [*megas*],
>   but it
> carries much filth of earth and much rubbish in its
>   water.
> The Melissai carry water to Demeter, not from
>   every source,
> but that which comes pure and undefiled,
> from the holy fountain, a small [*olige*] spring, the
>   ultimate flower.
> Hail Lord. And Blame, let him go where Envy is.
>
> (2.105-113)

The scholiast says of line 106, "In these words he rebukes those who scoffed at him for not being able to write a big poem, which taunt drove him to write the *Hecale.*" The scholiast sees Envy as a literary critic who accuses Callimachus of not writing a large-scale epic. Scholars, beginning with Voss in 1684, have understood the "sea" to refer specifically to the epic *Argonautica* of Apollonius of Rhodes. They have interpreted this epilogue as a polemical statement in a hypothetical quarrel between Apollonius and the champions of the "big book" against Callimachus, the poet of "slender" verse. Other evidence relating to this alleged quarrel will be examined later. It is important to note here that this critical passage is not an intrusion into the hymn but is essentially hymnal in form and function. It is a *sphragis*, a conventional epilogue, discontinuous with the body of the hymn, devoted to prayers or apologies to the god, to stating the singer's inability to treat adequately such difficult themes and his hope to please the god with his song. The singer's fear of disapproval is personified as Envy and Blame. Envy tries to persuade Apollo that the singer has not covered the material sufficiently—that is, he has not hymned Apollo as much as the sea. This would correspond with the brief epilogue at the conclusion of hymn 1, where the poet says, "Who could sing your works? There is no one . . . ," a rhetorical question to which there is no reply. In hymn 2, the god actually answers the singer's self-doubts by approving his work and kicking out Envy.

The hymnal function of the epilogue does not exhaust its meaning. How do we explain the water metaphors—the polluted Assyrian river and the pure drops from the holy fountain? Both of these are developed from Envy's equation of size and the sea, and they refer to different kinds of literary style. The qualities separating them are purity and magnitude. The words "great" (*megas*), describing the river, and "small" (*olige*), describing the spring, indicate physical size, that is, the length of a poem. They are also technical terms describing the grand and slight styles defined by Demetrius that include judgments about diction, subject matter, and composition as well as length (see the subsequent discussion). Demeter, who receives water from a small spring, is Philitas' elegiac "Demeter," a perfect example of poetry in the slight style. A pure style would be slight or grand in respect to all of its features. Demetrius expresses this idea of stylistic consistency in section 120 of his treatise *On Style* (122), where he illustrates it with two examples. In the first, Xenophon describes a small but beautiful river

in a concise, elegant construction that embodies the very idea it expresses. In the second, an anonymous writer describes a similar river as if he were writing about the cataracts of the Nile. The relationship between Callimachus' views of literary style and Demetrius' treatise *On Style* will be discussed in more detail subsequently.

In his second hymn, then, Callimachus replaces the conventional prologue with an epiphany and the epilogue with an elaborate parable setting forth his views on literary style. The parable is hymnal rather than polemical. It is designed to highlight Callimachus' own views by presenting them dramatically and contrasting them with their opposites. There is no need to see in Envy a flesh and blood enemy.

Other hymns have other interesting features. Hymn 3 to Artemis is written in the spirit of the Homeric hymn to Hermes. It presents the goddess as a baby, sitting on father Zeus's knee and plucking hairs from the Cyclops' chest. Hymn 4 is addressed not to a god but to Delos, the island on which Apollo was born, and features Leto's search over many geographical sites for a birthing place and Apollo's prophesying from her womb the birth of Ptolemy Philadelphus, the extent of his kingdom, and his victories over some rebellious Celtic mercenaries. Hymns 5 and 6 both begin with divine epiphanies, of Pallas Athena in the fifth and of Demeter in the sixth. Unlike the first four hymns, 5 and 6 are written in a literary Doric dialect. The fifth is composed in elegiac meter, while the sixth is in dactylic hexameters like the other hymns. The narrative portions of 5 and 6 are both cautionary tales, warning the reader against failure to respect the goddesses. The fifth hymn tells the story of Teiresias, who accidentally saw Athena as she was bathing. The goddess took his sight but gave him prophetic powers in return. In the sixth hymn, Erysichthon ignores fair warning and deliberately levels a grove belonging to Demeter. He is punished with insatiable hunger and literally eats his family out of house and home.

As the meter, dialect, content, and form of Callimachus' hymns reflect his Homeric models, so too does the diction. The Homeric hymns are composed of Homeric formulas amplified with new formulas made according to traditional principles. In the fourth century, we observed, Antimachus broke apart and restitched the old formulas to form an entirely new literary language with a much wider range of expression. Callimachus goes several steps further. He expands epic vocabulary by fitting out new words in epic shapes, by using diction from nonepic (especially tragic and lyric) sources, often within the context of Homeric-like formulas, and by artfully employing Homeric glosses, those rare words Philitas had collected.

The use of glosses is not merely decorative. Since the meaning of individual glosses was often in dispute, a poet's use of a rare word was tantamount to a scholarly opinion on the subject. For example, Callimachus uses the word *dieros* to describe the weeping rock that had once been Niobe (hymn 2.22–23). The meaning was disputed in antiquity. In Hesiod's *Works and Days* (460), it apparently means "wet," but this will not do for its two Homeric appearances (*Odyssey* 6.201, 9.43), where it modifies the words "foot" and "mortal." Aristarchus suggested the translation "living." By using *dieros* to describe the weeping rock into which Niobe was transformed while still living, Callimachus sets his seal of approval on both meanings.

The story of Niobe was told in book 24 of the *Iliad,* and the authenticity of the passage describing her metamorphosis (*Iliad* 24.614–617) was disputed. Philitas signaled his approval of the passage by referring to it in his "Demeter" (frag. 6, Kinkel ed.), while the scholars Aristophanes and Aristarchus thought it should be eliminated. Callimachus' reference to Niobe's transformation here in hymn 2 is tacit support for Philitas' opinion (details in Callimachus, *Hymn to Apollo,* Williams ed., pp. 32–34).

Thus, in two not inelegant lines, Callimachus delivers two scholarly opinions on complex textual questions. He presumes, of course, that his readers will recognize his scholarly allusions here and elsewhere, but it is possible to enjoy his poetry without catching every nuance. The scholarly substructure does not make Callimachus' poetry even remotely ponderous, for his elegance and wit never fail.

Callimachus' sense of artistry extends beyond the individual hymns to the group of six as a whole. Taken together they give a distinct impression of organized diversity. The first hymn, linking Zeus and Ptolemy in an otherwise traditional format, using the epic Ionic dialect and the dactylic hexameter of the Homeric hymns, seems a perfect introduction to the group. It is linked to the hymns that follow by dialect, meter, and general format, and to hymn 2, specifically, by its joining of human and divine patrons. Hymn 2 introduces the divine epiphany that recurs in 5 and 6, binding them to the group, although 5 differs from it in meter and both 5 and 6 in dialect. The lengths of the poems vary also, increasing from 1 (95 lines) to 4 (326 lines), then dropping back in 5 (142 lines) and 6 (138 lines).

We cannot be absolutely certain that the order in which we have the hymns is the order in which Callimachus published them, but the arrangement is at least as old as the second century A.D. and probably much older. The notion that the hymns were published together in an organized format like Roman poetry books, which exhibit the same organized diversity, seems preferable to the view held by some that the hymns were written for and performed at actual religious festivals. This idea is based on the success of the poet's epiphany passages, the festival settings of three of the hymns, and Callimachus' skillful use of traditional religious lore. That scholars have allowed themselves to be duped by Callimachus' realism is a testament to the power of his poetry.

Aitia

Many of Callimachus' 800 works are only names, most not even names. Only sixty-four epigrams and the six hymns have come down to us intact. A few others are preserved in fragments either found on pieces of papyri or preserved as quotations in the works of lexicographers, grammarians, or metricians. Callimachus' most celebrated poem, the *Aitia (Origins)*, is known to us only through fragments, most of them small. It was an elegiac poem composed in four books and preceded by a very elaborate prologue preserved almost intact on *P. Oxy.* 2079. It begins this way:

> The Telchines mutter at my song, ignorant and
>   no friends of the Muses,
> because I did not finish one continuous poem
> in many thousands [of verses]
> about kings or . . . heroes,
> but I spin a small tale
> like a child, although the decades of my years are
>   not few.
>
> (frag. 1.1–6, Pfeiffer ed.)

The Telchines are proverbial sorcerers, described by Hesychius as *phthoneroi*, "enviers." They are analogous to Envy in hymn 2, who tells Apollo that he cannot abide poets who do not sing as much as the sea (hymn 2.105–113). The Telchines have a similar complaint here about the length of Callimachus' poetry, its contents, and its lack of continuity.

A scholiast (Pfeiffer ed., p. 3) identifies the Telchines as Asclepiades and Posidippus, whose epigrams we discussed earlier, and Praxiphanes of Mitylene, a Peripatetic grammarian. These identifications have been taken very seriously by many scholars since the publication of the scholia in 1933, but it is hardly possible that they are correct. How could Asclepiades and Posidippus have complained about short poems with unheroic content while they were writing epigrams, rarely more than four lines long, about drinking parties and love? Why should the Peripatetic Praxiphanes have been so critical of the most Peripatetic of scholars? An elaborate case has been made by K. O. Brink to justify the identification of Praxiph-

anes by showing how Callimachus violates Aristotle's canons of literary unity set out in the *Poetics*, but a careful study of the structure of Callimachus' poems, especially his use of the technique of ring-composition, shows that Callimachus was particularly sensitive to this requirement. In any case, there is no reason to assume that Praxiphanes would have ascribed to every article in the *Poetics*.

The fact that the scholiast feels the need to identify the Telchines himself suggests that Callimachus did not. The scholiast's conjectures, made centuries after Callimachus' lifetime, are based not on special knowledge of Alexandrian gossip but on literary evidence that is partly available to us. The scholiast's choice of Asclepiades and Posidippus as the first two Telchines is based on the fact that both of them mention Antimachus' *Lyde* approvingly in their epigrams, whereas Callimachus calls it "thick writing and unclear" (frag. 398, Pfeiffer ed.). These adjectives refer to literary style and link the *Lyde* with the kind of poetry symbolized by the large and polluted Assyrian river in hymn 2. We do not know the specific context of this line, but it comes from one of Callimachus' epigrams, and it may have been written with the epigram of Asclepiades in mind. Nevertheless, an aesthetic disagreement over *Lyde* is hardly proof that Asclepiades and Posidippus castigated Callimachus for failing to write Homeric-style epics. The *Lyde* was an elegy, and its subject was love.

The scholiast's identification of Praxiphanes as the third Telchin is based on the fact that Callimachus wrote a treatise called the *Pros Praxiphanen*, often translated as *Against Praxiphanes*. Our only notice of this work comes from the scholiast on the *Phaenomena* of Aratus, who notes that Callimachus praises Aratus there as "much-learned and the best poet" (frag. 460, Pfeiffer ed.). This does not give us reason to believe, however, that the *Pros Praxiphanen* was essentially a work of literary criticism. Other prose works with similar titles are glossological or grammatical in nature: Aristarchus' *Pros Philitan* was written in reference to Philitas' *Miscellaneous Glosses*, not his poetry. It seems most likely that Callimachus added a friendly adjective or two to Aratus' name while citing one of his verses to illustrate a scholarly point in a scholarly tract. There is no reason to suppose that Praxiphanes cared about the length or content of Callimachus' poetry.

The scholiast on the *Aitia* prologue assumed that the Telchines were real enemies of Callimachus, then sifted through his poetry in search of possible candidates. Since none of his guesses is convincing, there is nothing to prevent us from rejecting his initial assumption and assuming instead that the Telchines, like Envy and Blame in hymn 2, are personifications of criticism introduced as a foil for the poet's own theory of literature. The remaining parts of the prologue elaborate this theory further:

> I [say] this to the Telchines, "Race
> [   ] knowing how to melt down a heart,
> [   ] few lines, but the bountiful
> Demeter draws down the great [   ]
> and of the two, the *Catalepton* taught that
> Mimnermus was sweet,
> [   ] not the big woman."
> > (frag. 1.7–12, Pfeiffer ed.)

The empty brackets indicate gaps in the text that greatly complicate interpretation. The scholia say that the "bountiful Demeter" is Philitas' poem of that name and that the poet is comparing the "Demeter" and Mimnermus' "Catalepton" with two other poems described as *makren* (big) and *megale* (grand). It is not at all clear whether the big poems are other poems by Philitas and Mimnermus or poems of different authors.

The key terms of the comparison are *leptos* in the title of Mimnermus' poem (a known attribute of Philitas' style), which corresponds to the slight style of Demetrius, and *megas*, which corresponds to his grand style. Here, the slender poems are said to triumph over the big ones, and Callimachus uses the remainder of the prologue to announce his intention of writing in the slight style.

According to Demetrius, each of the styles has its own suitable subject matter (75, 120), diction (77, 143–145), and length (204). Callimachus addresses the issue of length in line 4, where he says that he has not written poems in many thousands of lines. This hardly seems credible, since the length of the *Aitia* itself has been estimated at 4,000–6,000 lines. Callimachus reconciles long length and the slight style by organizing his material episodically rather than continuously (frag. 1.3, Pfeiffer ed.). In doing so, he precisely contradicts the advice given by Demetrius for creating a grand effect (Demetrius, 47).

In the opening lines, Callimachus rejects kings and heroes as unsuitable subject matter for the slight style (frag. 1.3–.5, Pfeiffer ed.), and again in lines 13–16:

> Let it fly from Egypt to Thrace,
> that crane who loves the blood of pygmies.
> And let the Massagetai shoot far at the Medes.
> > (frag. 1.13–16, Pfeiffer ed.)

Grand diction is also unacceptable:

> Judge by art
> not by the Persian mile.
> Do not seek after a great [*mega*], noisy song to be born
> from me. It is not for me to thunder, but for Zeus.
> > (frag. 1.17–20, Pfeiffer ed.)

Demetrius uses the word "thunder" as an example of the bulky sound that characterizes diction in the grand style (Demetrius, 177).

Apollo annunciates Callimachus' literary theory in hymn 2, and here also Callimachus' point of view is attributed to the god:

> When first I put a tablet on my knees,
> Lycian Apollo said to me,
> [   ] Poet, make a sacrificial animal as
> fat as possible, keep the Muse slender.

Also I tell you, walk paths that wagons do not
   frequent,
and do not drive your chariot along the common
   road,
nor the wide way, but on paths
unworn, even if narrower.
                   (frag. 1.21–28, Pfeiffer ed.)

Apollo introduces a new image into the great/ slender comparison, the choice of paths, which is adapted from Hesiod (*Works and Days* 287 ff.) via Choerilus. Grand poetry is a wide path that many frequent. Few tread the narrow. The notion expressed here is that slender poetry is exclusive and original.

Our text of the prologue concludes with the poet rhapsodizing on the cicada, whose clear voice and lightness embody the concept of the slight style (frag. 1.29–38). Posidippus also called himself the Muses' cicada (3086 ff., Gow-Page ed.), perhaps with the same idea in mind.

The prologue is one of the best-preserved pieces of the *Aitia*. The rest can be only partially reconstructed from more than 190 fragments and scholia. Following the prologue is the "Dream" (frag. 2, Pfeiffer ed.), in which the poet recalls Hesiod's meeting with the Muses on Mt. Helicon (Hesiod, *Theogony* 22 ff.). We learn from the scholia (Pfeiffer ed., p. 11) and an anonymous epigram (*Anthologia Palatina* 7.42) that Callimachus described a dream in which he was conveyed from Libya, that is, Cyrene, to Helicon, where he met the Muses, who taught him the *aitia*, or origins, of the heroes and gods.

In recalling and repeating Hesiod's poetic initiation, Callimachus is putting Hesiod forth as his poetical model for the *Aitia*. We know from hymn 1 and the epigram at 1297 ff. (Gow-Page ed.) that Callimachus generally admired Hesiod's content and manner. Hesiod's style was considered the plainest of the epic poets' (Dionysius of Halicarnassus, *De compositione verborum* 23). Callimachus' citing Hesiod indicates more than admiration, however, for in the *Aitia* Callimachus has essentially taken content

suitable for dactylic didactic poetry like Hesiod's and recast it in elegiacs. We know of no earlier elegiac poems that are remotely like it.

In the first two books of the *Aitia* that follow the "Dream," the poet organizes his material around the conversation with the Muses begun on Helicon:

Why, O Goddesses, does an Anaphian man
sacrifice to Phoebus with shameful words,
and Lindus worship Heracles with curses?
                (frag. 7.19–21, Pfeiffer ed.)

The result is a variety of themes in short segments within an organized whole. In book 1 Callimachus' topics include the Parians' sacrifice to the Graces (frag. 3.7–14), the return of the Argonauts and the rite at Anaphe (frag. 7.19–21, Pfeiffer ed.), the sacrifice at Lindus (frags. 22–23, Pfeiffer ed.), Thiodamas the Dryropian (frags. 24–25, Pfeiffer ed.), Linus and Coroebus (frags. 26–28, Pfeiffer ed.), and Diana of Leucas (frag. 31, Pfeiffer ed.).

One of the most celebrated episodes of the *Aitia* is the charming story of Acontius and Cydippe (frags. 67–75, Pfeiffer ed.). Acontius saw Cydippe at a Delian festival and fell in love with her. He followed her to the temple of Artemis, where he rolled at her feet an apple inscribed with the words, "I swear by Artemis to marry Acontius." Cydippe read the inscription aloud, binding herself to the oath. Her father arranged three marriages for her, but each had to be canceled when the bride became mysteriously ill. Finally he sent to Apollo at Delphi, who revealed the cause of her distress. The marriage of Acontius and Cydippe followed soon after.

Near the conclusion of the narrative Callimachus addresses Acontius.

We heard of your charming love
from ancient Xenomedes, who once
described the whole island in a mythological
   memoir.
                (frag. 75.53–55, Pfeiffer ed.)

The presence of scholarly citations in the text is without precedent in classical poetry, but not unsuitable for Callimachus, who once boasted, "I sing nothing unattested" (frag. 612, Pfeiffer ed.). The versification of prose genres had a vogue in Alexandria in this period. The most successful was the *Phaenomena* of Aratus, an elegant hexameter version of an astronomical treatise of the same name by Eudoxus of Cnidus. Callimachus' admiration of Aratus' feat is evident in the fragment of the *Pros Praxiphanen* and in epigram 27 (Pfeiffer ed.), where he links Aratus with Hesiod, his own mentor for the *Aitia*. With its store of mythological information from prose sources, the *Aitia* is certainly Callimachus' interpretation of a didactic poem in the slight style.

The Acontius and Cydippe episode also offers proof that Callimachus was up to date on the latest editorial work at the Library. Callimachus describes (frag. 67.13, Pfeiffer ed.) Cydippe taking part in "the dance of sleeping Ariede." At *Iliad* 18.592, Zenodotus read "Ariede" where the other editions all had "Ariadne." Like Posidippus, Callimachus incorporated into his own text the fruits of Zenodotus' labor.

The *Aitia* concluded with the renowned "Lock of Berenice" (frag. 110, Pfeiffer ed.), best known from Catullus' Latin translation. Berenice II, the wife of Euergetes, dedicated a lock of her hair at the temple of Arsinoe-Aphrodite at Zephyrium in honor of her husband's safe return from the Third Syrian War (247–246 B.C.). When the lock mysteriously disappeared, the astronomer Conon identified it in a constellation known thenceforth as the Lock of Berenice. The poem, then, is an *aition* on a contemporary subject designed to flatter the royal house. It is narrated in the first person by the lock itself in the style of a dedicatory epigram.

A newly discovered fragment of the *Aitia*, a poem celebrating Berenice's victory at Nemea, has been identified by P. J. Parsons as the first *aition* of book 3. The two Berenice poems form a frame for the *aitia* of books 3 and 4 that do not have any organizing device like the conversation with the Muses in books 1 and 2.

Following the "Lock" is a brief epilogue that recalls Hesiod's talk with the Muses on Helicon (frag. 112.5–7, Pfeiffer ed.) and concludes,

Hail Zeus, you great one, preserve the whole house
  of the kings,
but I pass on to the foot pastures of the Muses.
                    (frag. 112.8–9, Pfeiffer ed.)

These lines are precisely like the conclusions of hymns in which the singer signs off one song and introduces the next. Callimachus' next song, the "foot-pastures of the Muses," must be the *Iambi*, for Horace calls his own iambic poems his "pedestrian Muse" (*Satires* 2.6.17; *Epistles* 2.250). The *Iambi* follows the *Aitia* directly, both in the principal papyrus (*P. Oxy.* 1011, fourth century A.D.), and in the *Diegeseis* (second century A.D.), which are brief prose summaries of some of Callimachus' poems.

The interpretation of these lines as an introduction to the *Iambi* lead Pfeiffer (*Callimachus*, vol. 2, pp. xxxvi–vii) to conjecture that Callimachus published the *Aitia* originally in his youth, then reissued it in old age with a new prologue (the "Address to the Telchines") and a new epilogue (the "Lock of Berenice") in an edition of his collected works where it was followed by the *Iambi*. This theory accounts for the fact that the poet describes himself as an old man in the "Address to the Telchines," but a youth in the "Dream," and for the fact that the "Lock" has been found in papyrological contexts separated from the *Aitia*. If the editor of the new papyrus of "Berenice's Victory" is correct in placing it at the beginning of book 3, the "Lock" appears as a more integral part of the poem, linking the end of book 4 with the beginning of book 3. It becomes necessary, then, to assume that in his youth Callimachus published only books 1 and 2, which were introduced by the "Dream" and organized around the conversation with the Muses, and in old age added the prologue to the Telchines and books 3 and 4, beginning and concluding with the Berenice poems.

Since we know that Callimachus' contemporary Posidippus republished his own work, Callimachus certainly could have done the same. A prologue that Posidippus wrote for his collection was described previously as having many motifs in common with the *Aitia* prologue, including an emphasis on the poet's old age and the love the Muses had for him in his youth. One poet may have borrowed these motifs from the other to emphasize the fact that their poems were written in similar circumstances, but it is also possible that the borrowing was a purely literary act. In this case the poets' reference to themselves in youth and old age would have no biographical significance whatever and Callimachus' collected works would be only a fiction of modern scholarship.

Iambi

The origin of iambic poetry is obscure, but it seems to have had ritual associations and an abusive, sometimes obscene nature. The first extant iambs, the work of Archilochus of Paros in the seventh century B.C., are not overtly religious, however, and encompass many different kinds of themes in a variety of meters. There are convivial (frag. 120, West ed.) and erotic (Merkelbach–West ed.) iambs, personal (frag. 128, West ed.) and public iambs (frag. 3, West ed.), iambs that insult his enemy Lycambes, directly (frag. 172, West ed.) and through animal fables (frags. 185–187, West ed.).

The next great iambic poet was Hipponax of Ephesus, who lived in the sixth century B.C. He used a modification of the iambic trimeter, the choliamb or limping iamb, and wrote more obscene poetry set in the Ionian demimonde. His literary archenemy was Boupalus. Both Archilochus and Hipponax were said to have driven their enemies to suicide by the venom of their verses, although both victims seem to have been literary rather than real-life characters.

Like the *Aitia*, Callimachus' *Iambi* is extant only in fragments. He begins the first by raising the ghost of Hipponax from the dead, speaking in Hipponax's own choliambic meter and Ionian dialect:

> Listen to Hipponax. For I have come
> from the place where an ox costs a penny.
> (frag. 191.1–2, Pfeiffer ed.)

Hipponax is in Alexandria, outside the great temple of Serapis, haranguing the scholars of Ptolemy's Museum. Serapis gives dream visions to the sick who come to him in search of a cure, and Hipponax's ghost is the answer to their prayers.

Hipponax begins by castigating "men who are now" (frag. 191.6, Pfeiffer ed.). The text is full of holes, but his subject appears to be literature (frag. 191.7–23, Pfeiffer ed.). When continuous text resumes, he is comparing the scholars to swarming flies and wasps, in Homeric similes. One member of the crowd, a bald man in danger of losing his cloak, is singled out for abuse (frag. 191.29–30, Pfeiffer ed.). The garment suggests that he is a Cynic philosopher, and the vignette is ironic because Hipponax himself is taking the role of a Cynic diatribist who complains publicly about the sins of the present and embellishes his speech with moralizing fables.

Hipponax's fable, the story of Bathycles' cup, begins at fragment 191.31 (Pfeiffer ed.). On his deathbed, the Arcadian Bathycles instructs his middle son, Amphalces, to give a golden cup to the best of seven wise men. Amphalces presents it to Thales, whom he finds scratching a geometrical figure in the ground (frag. 191.56–58, Pfeiffer ed.). The figure was devised not by him, we are told, but by Phrygian Euphorbus, whom Pythagoras, the sixth-century mysticmathematician, claimed was an earlier incarnation of himself (Diodorus Siculus, 10.6.1). A joke on Pythagorean vegetarianism follows (frag. 191.61–63, Pfeiffer ed.). Our text fails, but we can glean that Thales passed the cup to Bias, another of the seven wise men, who passed it on in turn. After each of the seven had rejected it, it was returned to Thales, who dedicated it to Apollo. At the conclusion there is a moral: men who are truly wise do not fight for preeminence among themselves. Our prose summary, the *Diegeseis*, applies this thought to the dramatic circumstances of the poem, saying that Hipponax tells the scholars not to be jealous of one another (*Diegeseis* 6.5–6). The surly Hipponax hardly seems the one to stop them.

The remainder of the poem is fragmentary and obscure. At the end, literature, very likely iambic poetry with its inelegant and poverty-stricken Muses (frag. 191.92–93, Pfeiffer ed.), is the topic, and in line 97 Hipponax announces that it is time for him to sail back.

Iamb 2 is a brief animal fable of a typical sort, or so it seems at first, set in an earlier age when animals could talk (frag. 192.1–3, Pfeiffer ed.). When the animals complain to the gods about old age and the rule of Zeus, he transfers their voices into men (*Diegeseis* 6.27–29). Thus,

Eudemos has the voice of a dog;
Philton of an ass;
[   ] of a parrot;
And the tragedians have the voice of those living
    in the sea.
(frag. 192.10–14, Pfeiffer ed.)

The appearance of the tragedians leaves no doubt that Callimachus is here indulging in a bit of literary polemic. Eudemos and Philton may be stock comic characters rather than contemporary writers, and his aim nonspecific. The point is summarized in lines 13–14: "All men are verbose and over-wordy."

Iamb 3 also contrasts the corrupt present with a golden past but it takes the form of a typical moralizing poem of the day, such as Phoenix of Colophon might have written, decrying the practice of putting wealth before morality (*Diegeseis* 6.34–35) and railing at sexual abuses (frag. 193.13–14, Pfeiffer ed.). It is not long, however, before the motive for this grandiloquent outburst becomes clear: the narrator has been rejected by the boy Euthydemos, whose

mother has introduced him to a rich man. He wishes that he had never become involved with the boy at all. He would have been better off as a eunuch devotee of Cybele or Adonis (frag. 193.34–38, Pfeiffer ed.), rather than mad (*margos*) because he is a poet (frag. 193.38–39, Pfeiffer ed.). The remains of the final line are unclear, but it seems to be a proverb: "I have kneaded my bread and now I must eat it." If *margos* is given its usual meaning of "gluttonous," the proverb is especially appropriate.

In iamb 3, then, the poet uses the form of contemporary moralizing poetry to express anguish at a failed love affair. Unlike iambs 1 and 2, the narrative of iamb 3 is presented in the first person, giving the impression that the poet is talking about his own experiences and feelings. This intimate tone, nearest in feeling to the Latin love elegy, is all the more admirable since Euthydemos is likely to have been not an actual acquaintance of the poet's but an archetype for a youthful lover on the Socratic model (Plato, *Symposium* 222b; Xenophon, *Memorabilia* 1.2.29; 4.2.1–6).

Iamb 4, the best preserved of the iambs, returns to the fable form. The *Diegeseis* supplies the setting for the poem: a certain Simos, or "snub-nose," interrupts a quarrel between the poet and an unnamed rival, asserting that he is the equal of both (*Diegeseis* 7.2–5). The poet roundly abuses the interloper (*Diegeseis* 7.5–6) and instructs him with the fable of a proverbial quarrel on Mt. Tmolus between an olive and a laurel tree that is interrupted by a thorny bramble bush.

As the text begins, the trees' debate is already in progress. The olive and laurel present cases for their own superiority in high rhetorical style. Both give careful consideration to organization, marshaling their phrases with a view to symmetry and variety while burnishing their lines with alliteration and assonance. In spite of the formality of their arguments, the trees have lively personalities. The olive is sophisticated and ironic, while the laurel has the feisty temper of an iambicist. She lashes out at the presumptuous bramble bush with lines worthy of Hipponax himself:

> Oh pernicious outrage!
> One of us? You? May Zeus forbid.
> When you are near you suffocate me.
> (frag. 194.102–105, Pfeiffer ed.)

Line 103 recalls the first line of the poem, indicating that the bramble is to be equated with Simos, the son of Charitades, who interrupted the poet and his rival at the start. Scholars have been tempted to see in the laurel and olive reflections of Callimachus and his own literary rivals, but none of these allegorical interpretations is very convincing.

Callimachus' point here is rather to exaggerate the essentially rhetorical nature of the fable by presenting two trees holding an elaborate debate, constructed in the fashion of professional rhetoricians. In this way Callimachus both acknowledges the true nature of the genre and comically burlesques it. The verbal finesse of the arboreal rhetoricians also parodies certain contemporary literary types and attitudes, including several that Callimachus himself assumes from time to time.

The remaining iambs are very diverse. Iamb 5 is another attack on moral corruption, this one aimed at a schoolteacher accused of abusing his pupils. Callimachus patterns the opening on a poem of Hipponax (frag. 195.1–3, Pfeiffer ed.; frag. 118.1–6, West ed.), but delivers the bulk of his "friendly advice" in obscure riddles, the very opposite of Hipponax's typically direct approach. Iamb 6 has neither fable nor abuse, but a technical description of the length, height, and width of the base, throne, and footstool of the statue of Zeus at Olympia for a friend who is sailing off to see it. It combines elements of two subgenres, the *propempticon*, or farewell poem, and the *ecphrasis*, a description of a work of art, but it must be said that nothing else like this poem is known to us from antiquity.

Iambs 7, 9, and 11 have the form of extended epigrams in which a statue or tomb narrates its story. Iambs 7 and 11 are also *aitia*, as are iambs

8 and 10; 8 has the form of an *epinicion*, or victory poem, and 12 is a birthday song for the child of the poet's friend.

Meter and dialect are as varied as the contents, but all the variations are resolved in iamb 13, which is choliambic and Ionic like iamb 1. Here the poet addresses his cantankerous contemporaries whom Hipponax tried to mollify in iamb 1. The poem begins with an invocation and libation for the Muses and Apollo but quickly proceeds to an attack on Callimachus by his critics:

> Neither having mingled with Ionians
> nor gone to Ephesus, which is . . .
> Ephesus, where those who are about
> to give birth to choliambs are set afire,
> if they are clever.
>
> . . .
>
> This is interwoven and babbling . . .
> Ionian and Dorian and the mixed dialect.
> (frag. 203.11–14; 17–18, Pfeiffer ed.)

Here Callimachus is charged with not showing proper regard for his model, the choliambs of Hipponax of Ephesus, and of mixing up dialects. These charges presumably apply to the twelve preceding iambs. The fragments do not make clear who is speaking, but it is very likely Callimachus himself who is quoting his critics to set up a target he will subsequently attack.

The text of Callimachus' defense speech is in very bad shape, but even so we can see many close verbal connections with Hipponax's speech in iamb 1. According to the *Diegeseis* (9.34–36), Callimachus defends himself here against charges of *polyeideia*, writing in many different genres, a criticism that may be directed at his work as a whole or only at the iambs in which he incorporated the forms of many different genres. Although we have lost the content of Callimachus' defense, it is clear that in iamb 13 we have an iambic version of the *Aitia* prologue and the epilogue of hymn 2, in which Callimachus sets forth his own poetic program. Scholars who assume that Callimachus circulated some of the iambs before writing this poem, and that they had met with criticism that he is here answering, are taking literally a dramatic device designed to give a lively character to literary theorizing.

This is not to say that there was no literary rivalry in Alexandria. The last part of the poem describes what fierce rivalry has done to the literary community. One poet brands another as a slave (frag. 203.54–56, Pfeiffer ed.). The Muses leave town, fearing for their reputation (frag. 203.58–59, Pfeiffer ed.). This recalls Hipponax's plea to the quarreling scholars in iamb 1. It is well to note that in both cases Callimachus identifies himself with the peacemaker, not the combatants.

In meter, dialect, dramatic setting, and attitude, iamb 13 comes full circle back to iamb 1. These points of comparison and Callimachus' use of the poem to delineate his literary principles show that iamb 13 was the original endpoint of Callimachus' iambs. Four other poems, labeled "Mele" ("Lyrics") by Pfeiffer (frags. 226–229), follow them in the *Diegeseis* and in *P. Oxy.* 1011, but these were not part of the original group (Clayman, *Callimachus' Iambi*, pp. 52–54). The variations of form, meter, and dialect within the iambs conform to the principle of organized diversity that characterizes Roman poetry books and are evident in the hymns. The formal introduction in iamb 1 and conclusion in iamb 13 that echo one another closely guarantee that the iambs were composed and published as a unit.

Hecale

By the admission of all, both ancient and modern, the greatest poet in the Greek tradition was Homer. The greatest challenge for a poet, therefore, was to write an epic poem that might rival the master's. For centuries after the *Iliad* and *Odyssey* were in circulation, poets composed sequels to them on a variety of related mythological themes. These were the cyclic epics. Only a minuscule number of fragments remain, but to judge from the comments of Ar-

istotle and Callimachus himself, their quality was not high.

A new approach to the writing of epic poetry was begun by Antimachus in the fourth century (discussed earlier). He found a way to employ Homeric diction in a scholarly and creative way that had a profound influence on poetry in all genres throughout the postclassical period. Callimachus' unfortunate comment on Antimachus' *Lyde* (frag. 398) suggests that Callimachus was less than satisfied with the aesthetic quality of Antimachus' work.

Callimachus' ultimate answer to the cyclic poets and to Antimachus could best be made not through sniping remarks but by writing an epic poem of his own. The scholiast at the conclusion of hymn 2 who said that Callimachus wrote the *Hecale* to prove to his critics that he could write a big book may have overinterpreted the passage, but there is no doubt that the *Hecale,* a treatment of an authentic Greek hero in dactylic hexameters, is a Callimachean epic.

Our knowledge of the plot comes mainly from Plutarch's *Life of Theseus* (which seems to be drawn from the same prose source Callimachus used) and the *Diegeseis* (10.18–11.7). They tell us that Theseus was being carefully guarded by his father after Medea had tried to kill him. He wished, however, to set out against a monstrous bull who was ravaging the country around Marathon, so he secretly escaped from his father's house at night. When an unexpected rainstorm came up, he sought shelter in a small hut belonging to an old woman called Hecale, who entertained him as well as her poverty allowed. At dawn he set out for Marathon and promptly dispatched the bull, but when he returned to Hecale with the good news, he found her dead. To repay her hospitality he set up a deme named in her honor and a sanctuary to Zeus Hecaleios.

The brevity of the *Diegeseis* suggests that the poem itself was quite short as epics go: 1,000 lines is the usual estimate of its length. It is also clear that, far from making a grand epic sweep, it concentrated on just one incident in the life of just one hero. In reducing the size and unifying the contents, Callimachus exactly followed the guidelines laid down by Aristotle for translating to the epic some of the virtues of tragedy (*Poetics* 1459b). Callimachus apparently interpreted Aristotle's cryptic statement—that ideally, the length of an epic poem should equal the length of the tragedies presented at a single entertainment (*Poetics* 24.5)—to mean that an epic should be the length of one tragedy.

Although there are 147 fragments of the *Hecale* extant, most of them are tiny and impossible to place, so we know little about the way Callimachus handled the details. It appears that he greatly emphasized Theseus' visit to Hecale's hut, which he invited the reader to compare to Odysseus' visit to the hut of the swineherd Eumaeus by many literary references to the *Odyssey* (frags. 243, 313, Pfeiffer ed.). He described in detail her modest lifestyle and recorded at length their shared reminiscences, which gave him the opportunity to narrate a number of obscure Attic legends. The killing of the bull seems to have occupied relatively little space.

The *aitia* that conclude the poem are very much in character for Callimachus. Their placement at the conclusion suggests the influence of Euripides, who wrote about Theseus in two of his tragedies. Callimachus' frequent use of tragic diction, along with usual and unusual Homeric forms, is consistent with his merging other elements of the two genres.

Conclusion

Callimachus was a major force in the renewal of Greek poetry that took place in third-century Alexandria. He gave the old genres new life by wedding them to others previously quite distinct. He discovered new content for his poems in prose sources and remedied the banality of Koine Greek with new diction created by fusing diverse elements of older poetic language. At every turn his poetry reveals a vast knowledge of the Greek literary tradition acquired through years of work on the *Pinakes*.

His penchant for writing poetry books as well as individual, occasional poems can also be traced to a scholar's experience.

How many of these innovations originated with Callimachus is difficult to say, since his most eminent contemporaries—Apollonius, Aratus, and Posidippus, among others—were all moving in similar directions and constantly influencing each other. There are several ways, however, in which Callimachus appears to be unique. One is his extraordinary versatility. Some of his contemporaries tried their hand at more than one poetic genre, and others wrote scholarly prose as well as poetry, but none came close to approaching the range of Callimachus' literary output and its consistently high quality. A second unusual aspect of Callimachus' work is his abiding interest in the theory of literary criticism. He defines his own literary style in practice, as all writers do, but also in abstract discussion within the poems themselves.

Finally, there is the marvelous grace and humor of his verse. In spite of the scholarship and literary theory in them, his poems are never unreadable and are often, when we have enough consecutive lines to follow the argument, a delight. It is certainly no accident that the best Roman poets cite Callimachus more than all the other Greeks as their artistic inspiration.

APOLLONIUS OF RHODES

Callimachus' contribution to the renewal of epic poetry in the *Hecale* is for the most part lost to us. To see in detail what an Alexandrian poet might do with the epic genre we must look instead at the *Argonautica* of Callimachus' student, Apollonius of Rhodes.

Life

The biography of Apollonius is better documented than that of Callimachus, but the sources are confusing and contradictory. We are told (*P. Oxy.* 1241) that Apollonius was the librarian at Alexandria before Eratosthenes, most likely second after Zenodotus, and that he was tutor to Ptolemy Euergetes, as Zenodotus had tutored Philadelphus. Euergetes was born about 282 B.C. Since he would not have needed a tutor until 272 or later and could have dispensed with one by 260 or so, Apollonius must have begun his librarian-tutorial post sometime between those dates. He retired from it in 246–245, when Euergetes came to the throne, and gave the position to Eratosthenes. Apollonius is said to have fled to Rhodes, but the reason for his resignation is unclear. Euergetes may have had a personal dislike for his old teacher, or Apollonius may have had enough of the job. Tradition assigns two other causes: a disastrous public recital of the *Argonautica* from which Apollonius fled in shame, and a raging feud with Callimachus. The two reasons are usually connected: the recital failed because Callimachus did not like it.

The story of Apollonius' recital is detailed in two accounts of his life appended to a tenth-century manuscript of the *Argonautica*. The first reads:

Apollonius, the poet of the *Argonautica*, was an Alexandrian by birth of the tribe of Ptolemais. . . . He lived in the time of the third Ptolemy; student of Callimachus. At first he was with Callimachus, his own master. . . . Later he turned to making poetry. It is said that while he was yet a young man he gave a public presentation of the *Argonautica* and was condemned. Being ashamed before the citizens, and not abiding the rebuke and slander of the other poets, he left his fatherland and went to Rhodes. There he polished his poems and corrected them and gave a successful performance. Therefore he calls himself the Rhodian in his poems. He taught brilliantly there and was deemed worthy of citizenship and honor.

There is a contradiction in this account. Apollonius could not have begun writing poetry "later" and also have given a public performance in his youth. The contradiction is not re-solved by the second Life, which adds to the story of his flight to Rhodes the following:

Some say that he returned to Alexandria and again giving a public performance there, was well received, so that he was deemed worthy of the libraries and the Museum, and was buried with Callimachus himself.

There is no room in the chronology of librarians for Apollonius to have held the office twice, so the story of his return to Alexandria must be apocryphal. It may have been inspired by a confusion between our Apollonius and the fifth librarian, Apollonius the Eidographer. The author of the Life who introduced the story of the return with "some say" was less than certain of its truth.

There is a clue to the origin of the story of Apollonius' failed recital in the scholia to the *Argonautica*, which refer in six places to variant readings from a *proekdosis*, an earlier edition (Wendel, *Scholia* 1.285; 1.516; 1.543; 1.726; 1.788; 1.801). The authors of the Lives, who may have known even more of these readings, obviously assumed that the *proekdosis* was a preliminary edition made by Apollonius himself that he revised in the face of criticism. This interpretation was then embellished with the story of the recital for the purpose of explaining Apollonius' departure for Rhodes.

If the *proekdosis* really was the poet's preliminary edition, it is best to view it in the context of Posidippus' and Callimachus' reissuing of their poetry—not as an extraordinary act requiring special explanation but as the ordinary result of an Alexandrian scholar-poet's casting a critical eye on his own work. Alternatively the *proekdosis* may be not the author's autograph at all but an early edition made by a scholar and so designated to distinguish it from a later one. The *proekdosis* of the *Iliad* mentioned in the Homeric scholia was made by Aristarchus, not by Homer (Fraenkel, *Apollonii Rhodii Argonautica* 5–6).

We must also ask why it was necessary for Apollonius' biographers to devise a motive for

Apollonius to leave Alexandria and go to Rhodes. The contradiction they were trying to solve is this: Apollonius was a citizen of Alexandria, but he called himself Apollonius of Rhodes. Their solution, that Apollonius went from his native Alexandria to Rhodes, where he was given citizenship, is very odd since virtually all of the renowned scholars and poets who were active in Ptolemaic circles in the third century came from elsewhere to Alexandria, many at the express invitation of Ptolemy. It is conceivable, therefore, that the author of the first Life, or his source, devised an explanation precisely opposite to the truth and that Apollonius was, in fact, a native Rhodian who, like all of his colleagues, emigrated to, not from, Alexandria. There he was given Alexandrian citizenship, which was easily acquired in the city's youth (Fraser, *Ptolemaic Alexandria*, pp. 38–92). The author of the second Life, who knew the first, was also aware that Apollonius was buried with Callimachus in Alexandria, so he added the story of the return trip in order to accommodate the joint burial. In this way the story of Apollonius' life became more and more complicated and less and less factual.

If the trips to Rhodes and back are eliminated, the chronological contradictions disappear, and a new picture emerges of a young Apollonius who came from Rhodes to Alexandria to study with the great Callimachus. He spent his youth in scholarship and was rewarded with the librarianship and Alexandrian citizenship. He retired from the Library at the ascension of Euergetes and took up poetry. He was immensely successful and at his death was buried with his beloved master.

There is no room in this account for a feud with Callimachus. Evidence for such a falling out is dubious at best and is all of a late date. First there is the *Suda*'s description of Callimachus' lost poem "Ibis": "A poem created for obscurity and abuse against a certain Ibis who was Callimachus' enemy. This was Apollonius who wrote the *Argonautica*." A sixth-century-A.D. epigram that also identifies Apollonius as Ibis may have been the *Suda*'s source (Testimonia 23, Pfeiffer ed.). Since Callimachus fails to identify his critics by name in the *Aitia*, *Hymns*, and *Iambi*, it is unlikely that he did so here in a poem that was notably obscure. The "Ibis" was an example of the genre of *arai*, or curse poems, and was probably directed at no one in particular. Ovid describes the poem in his own "Ibis" as *exiguus libellus*, "a thin little book" ("Ibis" 449).

Apollonius' name is also mentioned by the *Diegeseis* (second century A.D.) as one of two possible identifications of the lascivious schoolmaster lampooned in Callimachus' fifth iamb (7.20–21). If Apollonius' name had been mentioned in the poem itself, the *Diegeseis* would not have given us two choices.

From Apollonius' camp there is a single epigram of very doubtful attribution, translated by John Ferguson:

> Callimachus: Muck
>   Trifle
>   Blockhead
> Original: Callimachus, for writing *Origins*.
>   (*Anthologia Palatina* 11.275)

In Planudes and Eustathius the epigram is labeled anonymous. It may have been assigned to Apollonius after the story of their feud became current in late antiquity (Wilamowitz, pp. 96–97).

What prompted scholars in late antiquity to postulate the feud and what has sustained the notion all these years is undoubtedly the way Callimachus presents his own poetic program in the *Aitia* prologue, the conclusion of hymn 2, and the thirteenth iamb. In our earlier discussion of these passages, we showed how Callimachus gives dramatic definition to his poetic ideals by contrasting them with their opposites. In the *Aitia* prologue, for example, he tells us what he will not write: a poem of great length, a continuous narration on exotic military subjects in loud thundering diction, just like everybody else. Although Callimachus does not say that he despises all such poems and appeals to us to judge only by art and not by external criteria like length, it is easy to see why readers might begin to look about for works that fit Callimachus' definition of the poem he will not write. Everyone's first candidate is the *Argonautica*, the most influential epic poem written at Alexandria in the third century. It remains to show, then, that the *Argonautica*, which is fully extant, could not be the poem Callimachus shuns in the *Aitia* prologue.

Argonautica

The *Argonautica* describes the journey of Jason and the Argonauts to Colchis to win the golden fleece. Books 1 and 2 describe the outward journey. The third book details how Jason procured the fleece from the unwilling King Aeetes with the help of his daughter Medea, and the fourth tells how the Argonauts fled the pursuing Colchians, eluded dangers at sea, and returned triumphantly home.

The first criterion in Callimachus' literary analysis is length. The *Argonautica*, totaling 5,835 lines, may be longer than the *Hecale*, but it is short by the standards of Homer and Antimachus. Apollonius' choice of this length, like Callimachus' choice of approximately 1,000 lines for the *Hecale*, seems to be based on that ambiguous sentence in the *Poetics* where Aristotle recommends that the length of an epic poem be the length of the tragedies presented at a single entertainment. One possible interpretation is the length of three tragedies and a satyr play, or just about the length of the *Argonautica*.

Not only does the *Argonautica* fail the test of length, it also fails the test of continuity. True, it tells a single story, in a way that the *Aitia* does not, but then, so does the *Hecale*. Epic poetry demands an epic story. Within the story frame, Apollonius' narrative proceeds episodically. The episodes vary considerably in length and content in observance of the principles of organized diversity that characterize Callimachus' poetry books. Many of them take on a life of their own, which seems to some observers to detract rather than add to the power of the poem.

Callimachus' third criterion is subject matter. Apollonius does not, it is true, entirely avoid the kind of subject matter that Callimachus characterizes as "cranes who love the blood of pygmies and arrow-shooting Massagetai." The *Argonautica* includes a fight with giants (1.989–1011), an airborne pursuit of the Harpies (2.262–290), the yoking of fire-breathing bulls (4.1278–1314), and a number of other violent episodes. By choosing to tell the legend of the Argonauts, Apollonius committed himself to including a number of these incidents, which were integral parts of the tradition. Callimachus could exclude violent exotica altogether from the *Aitia*, but it had a legitimate place in Greek epic. Even Theseus had to kill the Marathonian bull. The test is not the presence or absence of such incidents, but how the poet handles them. Apollonius acts with great restraint, rationing them out in small quantity, always with clear dramatic purpose. Jason's entire encounter with the fiery bulls and the sown men, his heroic *aristeia,* is given only 129 lines (3.1278–1407), yet it serves excellently as the dramatic climax of book 3, in which Jason's other efforts have been diplomatic.

On the matter of diction, Apollonius is squarely in Callimachus' camp. He draws rare and interesting words from Homer and renovates ordinary Homeric diction by putting old words in modern dress and new words in old formations. To these he adds vocabulary from other genres and authors, including Callimachus himself. One phrase (1.1309) is taken whole from Callimachus (frag. 12.6, Pfeiffer ed.), and the borrowing is remarked by the scholiast. Other apparent borrowings are single words or pairs, so that it is difficult to judge who took them from whom. Apollonius shares other rare diction with Aratus and Lycophron. It may be that all the poets were dipping into a single pool rather than borrowing directly from one another.

Apollonius' occasional use of a rare word from Antimachus (Wyss, *Antimachi Colophonii Reliquiae* 48 ff.) has sometimes supplied a motive for adding him to the list of Antimachus-loving Telchines, but we know that Apollonius directly contradicted Antimachus on at least two points, the reason why Heracles left the expedition (1.1207–1272) and the genealogy of Phineus (2.237–239). We also know of a prose work in which Apollonius quotes Antimachus for the rare word *pipo*, "woodpecker." To Apollonius, Antimachus was just another source of interesting words.

Based on the four criteria of length, narrative unity, subject matter, and diction, the *Argonautica* would easily pass Callimachus' scrutiny. In addition to these, there are other aspects of the poem essentially Callimachean. We recall that Callimachus wrote about Theseus' visit to Hecale's hut in a way calculated to remind us of Odysseus' visit to the hut of the swineherd Eumaeus in the *Odyssey*. Apollonius also draws on Homer to give his episodes recognizable literary antecedents. For example, Medea's first meeting with Jason recalls many details of Odysseus' meeting with Nausicaa in book 6 of the *Odyssey*. Medea driving with her attendants to the temple of Hecate where she will meet Jason (3.869–875) reminds us of Nausicaa driving with her maidens to wash her clothes in the river where they will meet Odysseus (*Odyssey* 6.81–84). Jason is radiantly beautiful as he approaches Medea (*Argonautica* 3.919–926), as is Odysseus when he appears before Nausicaa after his bath (*Odyssey* 6.229–237). Both Jason (*Argonautica* 3.210–212) and Odysseus (*Odyssey* 7.14–17) are concealed in mist while they make their way to the palaces of their potentially hostile hosts.

By deliberately recalling passages in the *Odyssey*, Apollonius is able to imply many things about his characters without saying them directly. Jason is in some ways like Odysseus, a hero caught in a situation where he must rely on a young female to help him. Both depend on their charm and good looks to seduce the girl, and both are aided in their efforts by divine patrons. Medea is in some ways like Nausicaa, a young virgin in a mysterious land who falls in love with a handsome stranger. There are also important differences in the characters, and it is the author's intention that the reader notice the differences as well as the similarities. Medea is a naive young lady, but she is also a witch. When she rides through town with her maidens, the people look away in fear of her evil eye (*Argonautica* 3.885–886). Nausicaa offers Odysseus only food, clothing, and advice, at little cost and little gain to herself, for Odysseus soon departs. Medea provides Jason with magical powers to help him yoke the bulls and win the fleece. She is repaid with marriage to Jason, but the price for helping Jason is a direct betrayal of her father, and it ultimately leads to her complicity in the murder of her brother. When Nausicaa goes to the washing her mind is clear. She is acting innocently, with no idea of her motive. Medea goes to Hecate's temple after a night of intense psychological torment. She has weighed the risks involved and is acting in full knowledge of the possible consequences.

In this way Apollonius counts on his reader's knowledge of Homer to convey many of his ideas about the characters and their circumstances. This technique was apparently pioneered by Callimachus in the *Hecale*.

Like Callimachus' writing in general, the *Argonautica* is replete with miscellaneous knowledge from prose sources, among them geographies and medical tracts. The itinerary of the *Argo*'s return is based on the work of Timagetus. The description of the pain of Medea's love, "about the fine nerves and right up to the lowest part of the brain" (3.762), alludes to a recent discovery that the nerves originate in the brain. Most Callimachean of all are Apollonius' many *aitia*. There are more than thirty throughout the *Argonautica*, most of them etymological. Of these, we know that four were also treated by Callimachus. Their accounts of two, the ritual jokes at Anaphe and the origin of the Etesian winds, are especially close.

In drawing on Homer for diction and plot, and using geographical, medical, and especially aitiological material, Apollonius is thoroughly Callimachean. The fragmentary state of the text of the *Hecale* prevents us from ever knowing the true extent of Apollonius' dependency, but it is not likely to be complete. Two very important aspects of Apollonius' poem do not have demonstrable precedents in the *Hecale*. The first is Apollonius' use and development of Homeric similes to describe one thing in terms of another:

> Just as plowing oxen labor, working
> the damp field and endless sweat streams
> around from their flanks and neck; their eyes
> are turned askance under the yoke; the hot
> breath comes from their mouth in gasps; all day
> they labor, putting their hooves in the earth.
> Like them the heroes were dragging their oars
> through the sea.
>
> (*Argonautica* 2.662–668)

Similes make the unfamiliar familiar. They create pauses to help the poet manage the ebb and flow of the narrative, and they evoke emotions in the reader that enhance his response to the poem. Similes are a special feature of the Homeric epic that Apollonius adapts with extraordinary skill to the needs of his own poem.

In many cases Apollonius uses similes from Homer: Jason is compared to a war horse (3.1259–1261) like Paris in the *Iliad* (6.506–511). Sometimes the shared simile is given a new application, so that its evocative power is increased. As Achilles approaches Troy he appears like the beautiful death-star Seirios (22.26–31). Apollonius uses the same simile to describe Jason as he approaches Medea (3.957–959), suggesting that her encounter with Jason will be no less devastating than Achilles' with Hector.

For another occasion the simile may be completely transformed. As Jason approaches Hypsipyle's city and the love-starved Lemnian women, he is compared to another kind of star:

> He went to the city like a shining star,
> which maidens shut up in newly built rooms
> gaze at; rising above their homes,
> and through the dark air, it charms their eyes,
> a beautiful red; and the girl rejoices
> wanting the youth who is away among foreigners,
> whom her parents have arranged for her to marry.
>
> (1.774–781)

Note the pictorial description of foreground and background and the isolated figure of the girl contrasted with the youth who is being entertained in company. In Apollonius' similes no detail is superfluous.

The second aspect of Apollonius' poem that cannot be directly linked to Callimachus is his characterization of Jason and Medea. No typical hero, Jason is irresolute, easily discouraged, dispirited, and inept. Even at the embarkation, as he hears the seer Idmon prophesying the success of his mission, Jason falls into despair:

> Here the son of Aeson, helpless, thought over
> each thing in his mind, as if depressed.
>
> (1.460–461)

He is chided by Ides, a more typical hero, who relies on his spear more than on Zeus (1.463–471).

The adjective *amechanos*, "helpless," characterizes Jason more often than any other in the poem. When the *Argo* sets sail at Mysia, leaving behind the great Heracles searching for his beloved Hylas, the crew breaks out into a quarrel over their abandonment and,

> The son of Aeson, bewildered by their
> helplessness,
> said not a word, good or bad, but he sat, eating
> out
> his heart from the bottom with heavy grief.
>
> (1.1286–1289)

Here it is the hero Telamon who rails at Jason's inaction, and well he might, for Jason set sail without knowing that the men had been left behind.

The mighty Heracles, symbol of the vitality of the old heroic order, is everywhere a foil for Jason's new and peculiar kind of heroism. It is Heracles who extricates Jason and the crew from the embraces of the Lemnian women, but he is also an anachronism whose aggressive attitudes and brute strength are not adequate to the supernatural forces that await Jason in Colchis. It is no accident that Heracles is lost before Jason attempts his central task, the winning of the fleece. Jason may be difficult to admire and impossible to love, but it is he who wins the fleece and the girl, too. His virtues, such as they are—his good looks, his smooth tongue, his tendency to hang back rather than to act or speak rashly—finally become assets in a highly unusual situation in which he finds himself pitted against the forces of black magic.

The story of the Argonauts is a traditional one—it is mentioned in the *Odyssey* (12.70)—and although Apollonius had some leeway to choose among incidents to include or disregard, he was tied to the basic plot and its manner of resolution. He has characterized Jason as if he had asked himself what kind of a man could have done the necessary deeds: got through the first interview with Aeetes, electrified Medea, faced the bulls, murdered Medea's brother, and ultimately, outside the epic, deserted her for another woman. His Jason is a psychologically realistic portrait of just such a person cast into the role of an epic hero.

Apollonius' model for this kind of psychological realism is Euripides. From Euripides also comes the compelling portrait of Medea's passion. From the time Eros shoots her with his arrow all else is forgotten but the fire in her heart. Her cheeks turn from red to white and white to red. She hears the king challenge Jason and is beset all night with violent dreams of Jason, marriage, and bulls. When her sister suggests that she could be of use to him, she joyfully enlists herself in his cause, but her decision is followed by a long night of anxiety, self-reproach, and thoughts of suicide. She pulls herself together in the morning and drives with her maidens to the rendezvous like, but not quite like, Nausicaa going to the washing. At her first sight of him her heart stands still, a mist descends on her eyes, and her cheeks flush. Her feet are rooted to the ground.

After Jason successfully vanquishes the bulls and sown men, Medea panics in fear of what her father will do when he learns of her part. Her eyes burn. There is a roaring in her ears. She groans, clutches her throat, and tears her hair. She runs to the *Argo* and begs Jason at his knees to rescue her. It is panic that motivates her rages in book 4 and her complicity in the murder of her brother. Their wedding is a grim affair. Happiness for either is impossible.

The *Argonautica* is formally an epic, but in many ways it is a tragedy, and its principal characters are drawn from the drama of Euripides. In this Apollonius goes further than Callimachus in interpreting Aristotle's suggestions for the further development of the epic. The extra length of the *Argonautica* and the nature of the story allow Apollonius more latitude in characterization. Apart from this extra length, the *Argonautica* is in no fundamental way different from what we know of the *Hecale*. We must conclude that there are no grounds for believing the story of a feud between Callimachus and Apollonius. It was no accident that Apollonius chose as the theme of his epic a story best known through Pindar's fourth *Pythian Ode*, presented to honor the victory of Arcesilaus IV, king of Cyrene and ancestor of Callimachus.

ALEXANDRIANISM

When Choerilus of Samos thought of writing an epic poem in the fourth century B.C. he despaired of following in Homer's footsteps and sought new areas for his creative impulses by writing epics on historical subjects. Antimachus tried to solve the same artistic dilemma by renewing Homeric diction; Philitas, by aiming at a slight style. Their purpose was serious: to make Greek poetry again an important creative medium. It was the genius of the Alexandrians to combine their insights and solve their problem.

They were aided immeasurably by the Ptolemies and the intellectual adventurism of the age. The Museum and the Library gave them the leisure and the means to bring to their poetry the fruits of their literary and scientific research. The work of Zenodotus and his successors on the texts of the classical poets gave them a broad knowledge of poetic diction. The work of Callimachus on the *Pinakes* provided a clear formulation of the concept of genre. The labor of scientists, geographers, antiquarians, and mythographers provided new raw material for content. Demetrius and other literary theorists supplied concepts of stylistic consistency.

The best poets could control all the elements at their disposal, producing new and exciting work, able to reach readers at many levels. Intellectualism never overwhelmed them. They used it for their own ends. Aitiology is the occasion for Callimachus' wit. Medical terminology is the medium through which Apollonius fashions Medea's passions.

The ability of these poets can be judged by their less successful peers. "Alexandrianism" often has a pejorative sense, implying esoteric learning, want of emotional force, and admirable technique squandered on trivial subject matter. The excesses of certain Alexandrian poets do, indeed, conform to this description. Lycophron's *Alexandra* is obscure to the point of incomprehensibility. Nicander wastes his formidable technical skills versifying handbooks on the treatment of snakebites and food poisoning. These poems are technical tours de force in which a single aspect of Alexandrian poetic practice is exaggerated and other elements of good poetry are neglected altogether. Needless to say, it is unfair to characterize an age by its worst poets.

The success of Callimachus and Apollonius can also be measured by the influence they had on the Romans. Propertius begins the first poem of his third book this way:

> Shades of Callimachus and sacred rites of Coan
>   Philitas,
> Allow me, I beg, to come into your sacred grove.
> (3.1.1–2)

Vergil's melancholy Aeneas and tragically lovelorn Dido depend more than a little on Jason and Medea. Prominent among the works of Catullus is a translation of the "Lock of Berenice." Catullus also wrote epigrams, Propertius *aitia*, and Horace iambs that owe something to Cal-

limachus. His influence was less on subject matter and form than on style. When Horace defends the content and style of his odes he says:

> Phoebus Apollo struck his lyre
> when I wished to speak of wars and conquered
>   cities,
> lest I spread small sails
> on the Tyrrhenian sea.
> (4.15.1–4)

Vergil reports a similar experience in his *Eclogues*:

> When I would sing of kings and battles
> Apollo plucked my ear and warned, "Tityrus,
> a shepherd ought to raise fat sheep,
> but sing a slender song."
> (6.3–6)

The voice they heard was not Apollo's but Callimachus'.

The Alexandrians found a way to make poetry live again in an age that was all too conscious of its own inadequacies. The Romans, coming afterward, were at a double disadvantage. The story of how they adapted Alexandrian ideas and ideals to their own needs, as the Alexandrians had taken what they needed from classical poetry, is told in other chapters.

Selected Bibliography

TEXTS, TRANSLATIONS, AND
COMMENTARIES

GENERAL
Collectanea Alexandrina, edited by John U. Powell. Oxford, 1968.

ANTIMACHUS
Antimachi Colophonii Reliquiae, edited by Bernhard Wyss. Berlin, 1936. Text and commentary.

PHILITAS
Philetae Coi Reliquiae, edited by G. Kuchenmüller. Baden, 1928. Text and commentary.

THE EPIGRAMMATISTS

Anthologia Palatina [*The Greek Anthology*], edited by Andrew S. F. Gow and D. Page. 2 vols. Cambridge, 1965. Text and commentary.

Anthologia Palatina [*The Greek Anthology*], edited by William R. Paton. 5 vols. Cambridge, Mass., 1916–1918. Loeb Classical Library. Text and English translation.

CALLIMACHUS

Callimachus, edited by Rudolf Pfeiffer. 2 vols. Oxford, 1949–1953. Text and commentary.

Callimachus: Aetia, Iambi, Hecale, Fragments, edited by Constantine A. Trypanis. Cambridge, Mass., 1958. Reprinted New York, 1975. Loeb Classical Library. Text and English translation.

Callimachus: Hymns and Epigrams, edited by Alexander W. Mair. Revised ed. Cambridge, Mass., 1960. Loeb Classical Library. Text and English translation.

Callimachus: Hymn to Apollo, edited by Frederick J. Williams. Oxford and New York, 1978. Text and commentary.

Callimachus: Hymn to Zeus, edited by G. R. McLennan. Rome, 1977. Text and commentary.

Hymnus in Dianam, edited by F. Bornmann. Florence, 1968. Text and commentary.

APOLLONIUS

Apollonii Rhodii Argonautica, edited by Hermann F. Fränkel. Oxford, 1961.

Apollonius Rhodius: Argonautica, edited by Robert C. Seaton. Cambridge, Mass., 1912. Loeb Classical Library. Text and English translation.

Fränkel, Hermann F. *Noten zu den Argonautika des Apollonios*. Munich, 1968. Commentary.

Scholia in Apollonium Rhodium Vetera, edited by Carl Wendel. 2nd ed. Berlin, 1958. Text of scholia.

OTHER AUTHORS

Cory, W. J. *Ionica*. London, 1891.

Epica Graeca Fragmenta, edited by G. Kinkel. Leipzig, 1877.

Hephaestion. *Encheiridion*, edited by M. Consbruch. Leipzig, 1906.

Iambi et Elegi Graeci, edited by M. L. West. Oxford, 1971.

Kaibel, G. *Comicorum Graecorum Fragmenta*. Berlin, 1899.

Poetarum Lesbiorum Fragmenta, edited by E. Lobel and D. Page. Oxford, 1955.

Rose, V. *Aristotelis qui ferebantur librorum fragmenta*. Leipzig, 1886.

Wehrli, F. *Die Schule des Aristoteles 7. Heraclides Pontikos*. Basel, 1953.

PAPYRI

P. Harris = The Rendel Harris Papyri of Woodbrook College, Birmingham, edited by E. J. Powell. Cambridge, 1936.

P. Lond. = Greek Papyri in the British Museum, edited by F. Renyon and H. Bell. 5 vols. London, 1893–1917.

P. Oxy. = The Oxyrhynchus Papyri, edited by B. P. Grenfell, A. S. Hunt et al. London, 1898–

P. Teb. = The Tebtunis Papyri, edited by B. P. Grenfell et al. 3 vols. London, 1902–1938.

CRITICAL STUDIES

Brink, K. O. "Callimachus and Aristotle." *Classical Quarterly* 40:11–26 (1946).

Clayman, D. L. *Callimachus' Iambi*. Leiden, 1980. Interpretation.

Ferguson, J. "The Epigrams of Callimachus." *Greece and Rome* 17:64–80 (1920).

Lloyd-Jones, H. "The Seal of Posidippus." *Journal of Hellenic Studies* 83:75–99 (1963).

R. Merkelbach and M. L. West. "Ein Archilochus-Papyrus." *Zeitschrift für Papyrologie und Epigraphik* 14:97–113 (1974).

Parsons, P. J. "Callimachus, Victoria Berenices." *Zeitschrift für Papyrologie und Epigraphik* 26:1–50 (1977).

Wilamowitz-Moellendorff, U. von. *Hellenistische Dichtung in der Zeit des Kallimachen*. Berlin, 1924. Reprinted Berlin, 1962. Interpretation.

HISTORICAL STUDIES

Fraser, Peter M. *Ptolemaic Alexandria*. 3 vols. Oxford, 1972. History and interpretation.

Pfeiffer, Rudolf. *History of Classical Scholarship*. Oxford, 1968. History and interpretation.

DEE LESSER CLAYMAN

THEOCRITUS

(End of Fourth Century to Middle of Third Century B.C.)

INTRODUCTION

WILLIAM EMPSON, IN his book *Some Versions of Pastoral* (1935), remarks: "They seem able to bring off something like a pastoral feeling in Spain and Russia, but in an English artist, whatever his personal sincerity, it seems dogged by humbug." It may be that pastoral has been dogged by humbug for centuries, even outside of England, but the humbug was not there at the beginning in the hands of Theocritus. Perhaps the pastoral has never fulfilled its potential, perhaps the pastoralists of following ages succeeded in transmuting gold into lead. Certainly, Theocritus and his art bear looking at closely with regard to the nature of his writings and particularly with regard to the ingredients and structure of his pastoral. Consequently, our main concern will be with these visible constituent elements in the observed poetical structures. But we must not forget that below the visible lies the mostly invisible, and largely undefinable, generative complex of intricate interconnections between the artist's life, personality, and experiences, the age and its culture, and the relation of the age to earlier periods.

A great deal is known about one part of the complex: the Hellenistic age and its art, and its connection with the preceding Hellenic period. One must hasten to admit that, in seeking a concise characterization of the significant differences between the two periods, one runs the risk of oversimplification, of overstatement, of glossy generalities, of high-flown bromides, and even of common nonsense.

It is a view widely accepted that in the fourth century B.C., after the conquests of Alexander, a cycle of the historic process ended and another opened up. Radical changes occurred in man's view of himself, of his society, of his environment. Political freedom was greatly diminished. The system of a large number of independent, small city-states, loosely joined by common bonds of religion and language, sometimes temporarily and opportunistically federated in response to outside pressures—for example, Persia—disappeared for the most part. It was replaced in Greece itself by leagues and elsewhere by monarchic regimes that extended over huge territories, great complex organisms, managed by new royalties: the Seleucids, the Attalids, the Antigonids, the Ptolemies. The life of the *polis* was no longer everything for the Greeks. The horizons of their minds had been enlarged and embraced a world. People, or at any rate the leaders and intellectuals, began to view themselves as cosmopolitan; the *agora* (marketplace) was not the center of their existence.

The Hellenistic artist and his art reflected the altered orientations of this new world. Social and religious contingencies and necessities were no longer rigidly compelling determinants; the vicissitudes of practical life no longer imparted the occasionality and particularity so characteristic of Hellenic expression, no longer favored the heroic sense of life and the capacity for feeling with tragic passion. The new art found its sanctions in attitudes that were anti-heroic, rationalistic, naturalistic. In fifth-century-B.C. Athens, Aristophanes, in comedies with fantastically contrived situations, with ribaldry and lyricism, dealt with actual problems of city life that were under current debate: war and peace, Socrates and the Sophists, the new communism and feminism. His plays reflected the everyday talk and particular problems of that city at that moment, and the people whom he ridiculed on the stage were often the very same ones, with their exact names, who sat in the audience and were recognized and pointed out by their fellow spectators. During the fourth and third centuries B.C. in Athens, Menander wrote plays that presented not real contemporary Athenian citizens, but human types that lived as though outside of space and time. Each represented a vice or virtue: the stern or indulgent father, the prudent or dissolute son, the miser, the spendthrift, the clever or stupid slave, and the like. These universalized characters paraded through these comedies of manner in cleverly designed, intricate plots whose resolution depended upon fortuitous recognitions and lucky chances. The poet sought the likely, or at all events the possible, and avoided the improbable and fantastic; he aimed for the typical and the reasonable and avoided the personal and historic.

Hellenistic literature has been summed up over and over again, tritely perhaps, but aptly, by such adjectives and descriptive phrases as these: richly psychological, introspective, soft, intimate, gracefully polished, rigorously delicate, ironic, plaintive, erudite to the point of obscurantism, miniaturizing, sentimental, idyllic.

LIFE

About the other part of the artist-milieu complex, Theocritus himself, little is known. Exter-

nal evidence is sparse and late, inaccurate and contradictory, trivial and confused. The citation of two examples of such evidence will suffice:

1. Prolegomena. A. *Genos Theokritou* (C. T. E. Wendel, *Scholia in Theocritum Vetera* [Stuttgart, 1967], p. 1): "(a) Theocritus, the composer of bucolics, was a Syracusan in origin, his father being Simichus, as he himself says (7.21): 'Simichidas, now where are you footing it in the noontide?' But some say 'Simichidas' was a nickname—for it seems that he (i.e., Theocritus) was snub-nosed *(simos)* in appearance—and that his father was Praxagoras and his mother Philina. He became a pupil of Philetas and Asclepiades, of whom he makes mention (7.40). His *floruit* was about the time of Ptolemy Philadelphus, the son of Ptolemy the son of Lagus. Since he was naturally gifted [literarily] he acquired a large reputation in the composition of bucolics. According to some, he was named Theocritus though calling himself Moschus."

"(b.) Be it known that Theocritus was a contemporary of Aratus and Callimachus and Nicander. He lived in the time of Ptolemy Philadelphus (283–246 B.C.)."

2. Suidas (the lexicon called "the stronghold") under the entry *Theokritos:* " . . . And there is another man [called] Theocritus, son of Praxagoras and Philinna, but others say son of Simmichus, a Syracusan, whereas others say he was a Coan and was an alien resident in Syracuse. He wrote verse called "bucolic" in the Doric dialect. Some assign to him also these works: *The Daughters of Proetus, Hopes*, hymns, *Heroines*, dirges, lyrics, elegies and iambs, epigrams. Be it known that there were three composers of bucolics, namely Theocritus as aforementioned, Moschus from Sicily, and Bion from Smyrna from a little place called Phlōssa."

These passages contain little information that is not in the idylls[1] or that cannot be de-

[1]The Theocritean corpus of idylls consists of:
1. Authentic poems
   (a) bucolic: nos. 1, 3, 4, 5, 6, 7, 10, 11 (761 lines total)
   (b) nonbucolic: nos. 2, 12, 13, 14, 15, 16, 17, 18, 22, 24, 26, 28, 29, 30 (1299 lines total)
2. Poems of uncertain authorship
   (a) bucolic: nos. 8, 9, 20, 27 (247 lines total)
   (b) nonbucolic: nos. 19, 21, 23, 25 (419 lines total)

duced from them. Theocritus lived during the very last years of the fourth century B.C. and the first half or so of the third. He was probably born in or near Syracuse in Sicily, as evidenced by 11.7, where he speaks of the Cyclops Polyphemus as his countryman; by 28.16 ff., where he alludes to the distaff that he is sending as a gift to his friend's (Nicias') wife as coming from his country (Sicily) and from the town (Syracuse) that Archias of Ephyra founded; and by the variably styled 16, which is a self-advertising begging plea to Hiero II of Syracuse for future patronage, wherein occur these lines of a Pindar-imitative prayerful eulogy of a Sicily to be restored:

> O Zeus, Athena, Persephone: may harsh necessity send the enemy [the Carthaginians] from our isle over the Sardinian waves with news of the fate of loved ones to their children and wives, so few surviving from so great a host. May the towns be peopled again with the citizens who lived there before, all those towns that the hands of the foe pillaged utterly. May they work the luxuriant fields. May unnumbered thousands of sheep, fattened by rich pasturage, bleat across the plain. May herds of cattle on their way to their stalls speed the traveler at twilight. May the fallow lands be tilled for sowing while the cicada overhead, watching the shepherds in the noonday sun, sings in the branches of the trees. May the spiders spin their gossamer webs over the armor and may the name of war exist no more.
>
> (85-97)

At an unknown date for unknown reasons Theocritus left Sicily. We do not know what his immediate destination was. At some time he must have traveled in some parts of Magna Graecia, as shown by the southern Italian color of idylls 4 and 5. Certainly he lived for a period of time on the island of Cos, in the eastern Mediterranean right off the southwestern coast of Asia Minor. Here he possibly belonged to a literary coterie headed by the scholar-poet Philetas, who had a considerable reputation as an elegist. Here too he may have met and become

the friend of the doctor-poet Nicias of Miletus, who may have frequented the famous medical school on Cos. Idylls 11 and 13 are addressed to Nicias. The evidence for Theocritus' residence on the island is idyll 7, one of the bucolic poems, which is a remembrance of a day passed on Cos. Whether the day was an actual one spent as described or represents the distillation and idealization of numerous experiences is not to be determined. One suspects the latter because the poet (ironically?) takes such pains, especially by means of a plethora of place names and personal names, to anchor the scene in a very specific place on a particular, noteworthy occasion:

Idyll 7: Thalysia ("Harvest Festival")

It was a time when Eucritus and I were strolling out of the city toward the Haleis River and Amyntas along with us made a third. The reason was that Phrasidamus and Antigenes were holding a harvest thanksgiving in honor of Demeter—they, the two sons of Lycopeus, who was the noblest of well-born men, of the lineage of Clytia and Chalcon himself who by dint of his foot made the fountain Burina by thrusting his knee hard against the rock. And there by the fountain poplars and elms wove a well-shaded grove, overarching with their green leaves, wearing their foliage aloft. And we had not yet journeyed halfway nor had we even glimpsed the tomb of Brasilas when we came upon a wayfarer by the grace of the Muses, a goodly man from Cydonia, named Lycidas. He was a goatherd and no one, looking at him, would have mistaken him for anything else. He was very much of a goatherd. He had the yellowish hide of a shaggy rough-haired he-goat on his shoulders, one smelling of fresh rennet, and round about his chest an old cloak was tightly bound with a broad belt and in his right hand he held a crooked staff of wild olive. Quietly, with a grin, he spoke to me with an amused glance and laughter played on his lips: "Simichidas, where are you striding along at noonday when even a lizard is asleep in the rough stone wall and crested larks are not a-wing? Are you in a hurry to reach a feast, an uninvited guest, or are you making a beeline for the wine bin of some one of the townsmen? Every stone that strikes against your walking shoes as you travel along makes such a ringing sound!" And I answered him: "Friend Lycidas, all men say that you among the herdsmen and the reapers are by far the best player of the pipes. This gladdens my heart very much! And yet, as I think about it, I have hopes of holding my own against you. I'm on my way to the harvest festival. Some friends are holding a feast in honor of fair-robed Demeter and are offering the first fruits of their riches. In full measure the goddess has filled their threshing floor to overflowing with wealth of barley. Come along now. The road belongs to both of us and the day too. Let us sing the bucolic. Perhaps one of us will delight the other. I am the clear voice of the Muses and all call me best of bards. But, by Heaven, I don't believe it. As I see it, I am not yet the master in singing of the noble Sicelidas [Asclepiades] nor Philetas, but like a frog against locusts I contend with them." Thus I spoke with a purpose. The goatherd said with a pleasant laugh: "I make you a present of this staff because you are a sprout [*ernos*, metaphorically "scion"] fashioned by Zeus wholly in the pattern of truth. How I detest the builder [poet] who tries to construct [compose] a house [poem] the size of a Mount Oromedon, how I detest the cocks of the Muses [lesser poets] who toil in vain against the Chian bard [Homer] with their crowing! Come, let us straightway begin the bucolic song, Simichidas. And I—well, look, friend, see whether this pleases you, the ditty that I worked out the other day on the hillside."

(1–51)

Lycidas sings for his loved one, Ageanax, an elaborately ornate *propempticon* (bon voyage poem) in which are embedded resumés of two songs by Tityrus, one about Daphnis, who pined for Xenea, one about the goatherd Comatas, who was imprisoned in a chest for a year and was fed on honeycomb by bees (52–89). Simichidas (Theocritus) now caps Lycidas' song with one just as preciously elaborate that concerns the love affair of his friend Aratus (96–127). Both songs are highly sophisticated, elegant products possessed of much erudition. The lines that follow the songs present the most famous *locus amoenus* (a locale of great charm and natural beauty, with Edenlike qualities) in the Theocritean corpus.

Those were my words and he, laughing pleasantly as before, gave me the staff to be a farewell gift from the Muses. Veering off to the left he went along the road to Pyxa while Eucritus and I and handsome Amyntas turned toward the house of Phrasidamus and reclined joyously on deep beds of sweet rush and on newly cut vine leaves. High above our heads many a poplar and elm swayed. Nearby a holy stream trickled from out the grotto of the Nymphs and gurgled on its course. On the shady branches the burnt-colored cicadas kept busy with their chatter. From far off the nightingale trilled its notes in the thick thornbushes. The larks and linnets were singing, the turtledove was cooing, and the humming bees kept flying about the springs on every side. Everything was highly fragrant of the richness of harvest time, fragrant of fruit time. The wild pears kept rolling by our feet, apples kept rolling by our sides, in profusion. Young branches laden with sloe-plums hung down to the ground. The four-year-old pitch seal was loosened from the neck of the wine jar. O Nymphs of Castalia who haunt Mount Parnassus, did old Chiron ever set a bowl like this before Heracles in the rocky cave of Pholus? That shepherd who dwelt by the Anapus, mighty Polyphemus, who used to throw mountains at ships, was he ever set to dancing among his folds by such a nectar as that which you Nymphs mixed for us to drink that day by the altar of Demeter of the threshing-floor? Once again may I plant the great winnowing fan on her grain heap the while she [a statue of her] smiles benignly with sheaves and poppies in either hand.

(128–157)

Either before the time spent on Cos or, more probably, afterward, Theocritus was "called," so to speak, to Alexandria in Egypt, where he became a poet in good standing at the court of the Ptolemies and presumably frequented the Museum Library, that ancient Institute for Advanced Study, where he must have met and associated with the great scholars and scientists and philosophers and literary figures of the day. Idyll 15, which is an urban mime, shows a detailed knowledge of Alexandrian people and life. It concerns two housewives of Syracusan origin who set forth to attend the festival of Adonis that is being celebrated lavishly by Queen Arsinoe at the palace:

Gorgo: Is Praxinoa in?

Praxinoa: Gorgo dear, what an age since I've seen you! I'm home all right. It's a wonder you got here even now. Eunoa, see about getting a stool for her. Throw on a pillow too.

Gorgo: That's fine, no need for a pillow.

Praxinoa: Do sit down.

. . .

Gorgo: I barely got here alive, Praxinoa. What a huge mob! What a lot of four-horse chariots! Everywhere men with heavy boots! Men with Macedonian cloaks! And the road's endless! You live further away every time you move!

Praxinoa: That's the doing of my crazy husband. He went to the end of the earth and took a hovel, not a house, so that we couldn't be neighbors, out of spite, the brute! He's always the same.

(1–10)

. . .

Gorgo: Come on, get your long dress on and your wrap. Let's be off to the palace of the king, rich Ptolemy, to see the *Adonis.* I hear the queen is getting up something fine.

(21–24)

. . .

Praxinoa: Eunoa, get a move on. Bring some water. . . . Why are you watering my slip, you dolt? Stop! . . . Where's the key to the big chest? Bring it here.

Gorgo: Praxinoa, this full-bodied dress is awfully becoming. Tell me, what did it cost you straight off the loom?

Praxinoa: Don't remind me, Gorgo. More than two *minae* hard cash. And I put my very heart's blood into the work on it.

Gorgo: Well, it's turned out just as you wanted it. This you can say.

Praxinoa: Bring me my wrap and sun-hat, Eunoa. Fix them properly. I'm not going to take you, child. Boo! Bad horse bite little boy! Cry as much as you like. I don't want you lame for life. Let's be off! Phrygia, take the little fellow and amuse him; call in the dog; lock the door.—Ye

gods, what a crowd! How and when's a person to get through this plagued mob? . . . Gorgo dearest, what's to become of us? Here come the king's warhorses.—My good man, don't walk on me. The bay horse has reared bolt upright. Look how wild he is! Eunoa, you reckless thing, get out of the way. He'll kill the man that's leading him. I'm awfully glad my baby's indoors.

(27–55)

. . .

Gorgo: Praxinoa, come over here. Look at these embroideries. How delicate and charming! They are truly "robes of the gods."

Praxinoa: Lady Athena! What spinners made these! And what artists drew these precise designs! How true to life they stand and how true to life they move around on them! They're alive, not woven patterns. Man's a clever creature! And Himself—Adonis I mean—how wondrous to see he reclines on his silver chair, . . . thrice loved Adonis, who is beloved even in Hades.

(78–86)

. . .

Gorgo: Be still, Praxinoa. The daughter of the Argive woman is just about to sing the "Adonis" song, that clever singer, the one who was the best in dirge-singing last year. She'll give out with something beautiful, I know for sure. She's already clearing her throat.

(96–99)

Then follows the highly embellished Adonis song (100–144), which invokes and celebrates Aphrodite and her beloved Adonis and also, implicitly, celebrates the divinity-aspiring Philadelphus and Arsinoe.

Two other idylls attest the Egyptian connection. In 14, another urban mime, which concerns Aeschinas' erotic difficulties with Cynisca, Thyonichus advises Aeschinas to solve his problem by leaving the country and taking service as a mercenary under Ptolemy, whom he then eulogizes when asked by Aeschinas what kind of a man Ptolemy is:

The very best! Fair-minded, a lover of the Muses, a devotee of Eros, exceptionally agreeable, one who knows a friend, still more one who knows the man who isn't a friend, generous to many, one who doesn't refuse when asked for something, the sort of person a king should be. But you must not ask for something on *every* occasion. Aeschinas. So, if it please your fancy to wear military garb and if, standing firm on both feet, you have the courage to abide the onslaught of the bold shield-bearer, be off with you to Egypt with all speed.

(60–67)

Idyll 17, on the pattern of a Homeric hymn and also having resemblances to Callimachus' *Hymn to Zeus* and *Hymn to Delos,* is a fulsome encomium, not so much of Ptolemy Philadelphus as, in order to supply him a suitable mythic background as god-king, of his lineage—Sōter and Berenice, the *theoi sōtēres* (savior deities), and *their* lineage—his vast domain, his riches, and Arsinoe, his sister and wife who with him formed the duality *theoi adelphoi* (brother and sister deities). The idyll appears to be payment for patronage conferred.

This essentially is the sparse Theocritean part of the "poet and his age" combination.

RANGE OF POETRY

It should be noted that Theocritus was a versatile composer with competence in numerous genres other than pastoral; he wrote epic pieces, hymns, lyrics, and mimes.

Epic

His treatment of the epic material is typically Alexandrine in that it avoids the better-known parts of the legends and seeks to focus on the lesser-known, or at any rate less-written-about, areas. Idyll 24 is an example. Following, in general, Pindar's *Nemean* 1 but expanding greatly and transposing events from a heroic to a middle-class environment, it tells the story of the infant Heracles' throttling of the two huge snakes sent by Hera to kill him; recounts Alcmena's consultation with Teiresias and his prophecy of the future greatness and divinity of Heracles; and describes the early schooling of

the young hero by a formidable number of famous tutors eruditely catalogued by the poet. The poem's mythological time precedes that of the twelve labors and the mature Heracles. Be it noted that both Alexander the Great and Ptolemy I (and therefore succeeding Ptolemies) claimed Heracles as ancestor and through him Zeus. Therefore, as with idyll 17, the poet is supplying an appropriate mythic setting that could make the god-king and goddess-queen feel comfortable in their developing divine aspect.

Idyll 13, an epistle addressed to Nicias, is also concerned with Heracles, a humanized and deheroized Heracles, and a vain search by him for his beloved Hylas, a theme treated by Theocritus' contemporary, Apollonius of Rhodes, at greater length toward the end of book 1 of his *Argonautica.* Theocritus' poem is tighter, more compact, well-rounded, more of a whole. Some think it is an illustrative comment upon Apollonius' diffuse, more loosely organized treatment of the story:

> Not for us alone, Nicias, did he beget Love, as we used to think, whoever the god was that once had this child. We are not the first to see beauty as beautiful, we who are mortals and shall not look upon the morrow. Amphitryon's son, whose heart had the strength of bronze, who stood against the wild lion, he loved a boy too, the lovely Hylas . . . and he taught him all, as a father teaches his son, all he had learned himself and so had gained virtue and renown.

(1–9)

When Jason sailed to seek the Golden Fleece, among the Argonauts were Heracles and Hylas. The *Argo* sped over the waves and came to the Hellespont, and the crew anchored it within Propontis just where the Ciani lived. The men disembarked and made ready the evening meal.

> And golden-haired Hylas with bronze pitcher in hand went off to bring water for the meal. . . . And soon he marked a spring in a low-lying place where rushes grew profuse and dark celandine and pale-green maiden hair and blooming pars-

ley and creeping marsh-grass. In the waters, midst Nymphs were performing their dance, the sleepless Nymphs, dread goddesses in the minds of country folk, Eunice and Malis and Nycheia with springtime in her eyes. The lad held out the wide-mouthed jar to the water, eager to dip. But they all clung to his hand. Love for the Argive boy made the hearts of them flutter. Into the dark water he fell headlong as when a fiery star plunges from the sky into the sea. . . . The Nymphs held the weeping boy on their laps and comforted him with soothing words. But Amphitryon's son was alarmed about the boy and went off . . . three times he called "Hylas" as loud as his deep throat could. And three times the lad answered but his voice came faintly out of the water and, though very near, he seemed far away. . . . And Heracles in his longing ranged frantically about in the trackless brambles.

(36–65)

Immediately following the Hylas incident in the *Argonautica,* there comes at the beginning of the second book an account of the pugilistic duel between Amycus, king of the Bebryces, and the Argonaut champion Polydeuces, one of the Dioscuri. Theocritus also handles this duel in idyll 22 more elegantly, making it a well-integrated part of a larger whole that has important literary significances. It may indeed be that this is another instance of a Theocritean rewriting of Apollonius. The idyll is an interesting piece. It has a hymnic frame reminiscent of Homeric hymn 33, consisting of a prologue (1–26) and an epilogue (212–213). Within the frame is a diptych panel that shows two insets containing epic material, the Polydeuces–Amycus contest *(agōn)* just mentioned, and the Castor–Lynceus contest. Castor was the twin of Polydeuces and Lynceus the twin of Idas. The latter contest is a nonurbane potpourri of Homerisms that seems to be set as a deliberate balancing contrast to the first contest and to serve as an example both in terms of style and moral content of how not to handle epic material. In addition to its hymnic and epic features, the idyll contains features of the bucolic, of the encomium, and of the mime. In a sense the poem is a kind of exemplary literary essay illustrating an Alexandrian predilection for the mixed genre.

Hymn

Idyll 18 also deals with epic material in the form of another type of hymn, an epithalamium, a lyric expression that celebrates the virgin maid Helen, child of Tyndareus but also daughter of Zeus, at the moment of her marriage to Menelaus, younger son of Atreus and by this marriage now son-in-law of Zeus. The poet is indebted to Sappho generally and specifically to a lost poem about Helen by the sixth-century-B.C. Stesichorus of Sicily. In many phrasings, conceits, motifs the poem has similarities to idyll 17, which suggest a pairing of Menelaus–Helen with Philadelphus–Arsinoe. Perhaps one should use the phrase "quasi-epic material" since Helen as pure virginal girl, as bride-to-be, does not appear in any extant epic or drama. The emphasis upon youth is similar to the presentation of Heracles in idyll 24. Of course the mature Helen in all her guises, as well as the mature Heracles, is always in the mind of the poet and his audience:

Once in Sparta at yellow-haired Menelaus' house, maidens with hyacinth blossoms in their hair set up a dance in front of the new-painted bride-chamber, twelve in all, the elite of the city, a sizable bevy of Spartan girls, at the hour when the younger of Atreus' sons, he who had wooed Helen, locked the bridal door behind this beloved child of Tyndareus. All in unison they sang, dancing with interlacing steps to a single tune, and the house rang with the bridal hymn.

(1–8)

Rising Dawn reveals her lovely face, O Mistress Night, as bright Spring reveals hers at winter's end. So too did Helen shine among us. As a tall cypress shoots up to adorn the fertile field or garden, or as the Thessalian steed is an adornment to the chariot, so too is rose-complexioned Helen an ornament to Lacedaemon.

(26–31)

Farewell, O bride, farewell, o bridegroom, son of a great father.

(49)

Sleep, and breathe love and desire into each other's breast, but do not forget to wake at dawn. We will return before light . . . Hymen, O Hymenaeus, take joy in this marriage.

(54–58)

Here, perhaps, mention should be made of the puzzling idyll 26, which has a close that some regard as characteristic of a hymn that may have been composed for some local festival. With extreme brevity in twenty-six lines the poem tells the story of King Pentheus of Thebes being torn to bloody pieces at the hands of the Dionysus-possessed maenads; Pentheus' mother, Agave; and her sisters, Ino and Autonoe. Except for a few differences (but maybe they are critical) the story is that treated by Euripides in the *Bacchae*. There may be no need to view the piece as hymnic. Lines 1–26 can be considered a miniaturized messenger-speech, and the "I" that expresses the moral conclusion (27–32) and utters the farewell (33–38) to Dionysus and his mother, Semele, sister of Agave, and the others can be regarded as the chorus making its typical comments. However, it cannot be denied that the poet is concerned not merely with the story of Pentheus but with presenting a just, deorientalized Dionysus, a justified Agave plus sisters, and an implicit apotheosis for them and Semele. Nor can it be denied that Dionysus as an ancestor figure is one of the most important gods in Ptolemaic cult and myth. Therefore, it is possible that Theocritus is giving Philadelphus and Arsinoe a redefined deity to include in their exclusive pantheon.

Lyric

Set apart by meter and dialect from the rest of the authentic Theocritean poems are the three lyric pieces, 28, 29, and 30, which are modeled on the works of the sixth-century-B.C. Lesbian poets, Alcaeus and Sappho. The dialect is Aeolic; the meter of idylls 28 and 30 has the sixteen-syllable scheme $xx|-uu-|-uu-|-uu-|ux$; that of 29 has the fourteen-syllable scheme $xx|-uu|-uu|-uu|-ux$. The other authentic poems—except for the epigrams, of which 1–16 and 23 are in the elegiac couplet and 17–22 and 24 are in other meters—are written in the dactylic hexameter line, namely $-uu$ or $--|-uu$ or $--|-uu$ or $--|-uu$ or $--|-uu$ or $--|-x$, and the dialect is a mixture of epic, Syracusan Doric, choral lyric Doric, and other Doric dialects, such as Coan and Rhodian. As mentioned previously, idyll 28 is a poem that accompanied the gift of a distaff from Theocritus to Theugenis, Nicias' wife. Along with idyll 12, which is in Ionic and composed in hexameters, idylls 29 and 30 are pederastic songs that express the usual conventional conceits associated with this type of erotic poetry in all periods of Greek literature: You do not love me enough. Why do you hurt me? You treat a new lover well, the old lover badly. Remember that youth has wings. You won't always be young. One day you will change from beloved to lover. Love is an unlucky disease. Love is a wound. Love eats away the inmost marrow. Wily Love cannot be conquered. Eros trips up even Zeus and Aphrodite. Man is his plaything.

Mime

As we have seen, Theocritus wrote mimes. Originally the mime was popular theater, subliterary, rendered in prose, largely improvised, emphasizing delineation of character, not plot, relating to everyday life and to the lower levels of society. It must have been very much like some of the vaudeville skits that flourished in the early 1900's and even later and also like some features of this century's burlesque shows. The mime came into literature only exceptionally. One case was in the fifth century B.C., in the hands of Sophron of Syracuse. It seems certain that Theocritus was indebted to him, but to what extent cannot be determined because all that survives of him is fragmentary.

He wrote in Doric prose and his subjects were realistic. Another writer of mimes was Herodas, who lived sometime in the third century B.C., but we cannot be sure whether he was older or younger than Theocritus and whether either influenced the other. In his eight extant mimes, Herodas imitated the choliambic meter and the language of the sixth-century-B.C. Hipponax of Ephesus.

Idylls 14 and 15, from which parts have been presented previously, are urban mimes in dialogue form. Idylls 4 and 5, as well as being bucolics, are rustic mimes with dialogue structure. We will look at 5 later. Idyll 10 may also be termed a rustic mime-bucolic; that is, a dramatic dialogue whose setting is agricultural, not pastoral. The mime structure is the poem's outer frame and presents the give and take between two reapers, the lover Bucaeus and Milon, the antilove figure:

> Milon: Farmer Bucaeus, what's the matter with you these days, poor fellow? You can't cut a straight swathe the way you used to, and you don't keep up with the reaper next to you. You're left behind like a ewe with a cactus-spine in her foot. What sort of worker are you going to be toward evening or even in the afternoon if you can't get going on your row at the very start?
>
> Bucaeus: Milon, you late-in-the-day mower, you flinthead, hasn't it ever happened that you yearned for somebody who's absent?
>
> Milon: Never! What's a farmer got to do with yearning for things that have nothing to do with his work?
>
> Bucaeus: Haven't you ever passed sleepless nights because of love?
>
> (1-10)

There is further banter. Then come two songs set within the frame. Milon invites Bucaeus to sing a song about Bombyca, the flute girl, and his love for her. He does so (24-37). Then Milon responds with a Hesiodic work song (42-55). The mime frame ends the poem with an insult to Bucaeus by Milon (57-58).

Idyll 2, with the title *Pharmaceutria* ("Sorceress"), is also a mime, an urban mime in the form of a dramatic monologue performed by the young, lower-middle-class girl Simaetha, who tries to regain by magic spell and incantation the love of the young, higher-class Delphis, who has grown tired of her. She is helped in the magic rites by her slave Thestylis, who does not have a speaking part. The spells are addressed to infernal Hecate, whose celestial aspect is Selene, the Moon, and whose terrestrial aspect is Artemis, at whose festival Simaetha met Delphis. The rites are executed in the moonlight that shines in her room, and when she has despatched Thestylis to Delphis' house to carry out some specific magic, she turns and pours out to the Moon the whole story of her love with an intensity that we find approached only in Sappho. Simaetha is a true sister to the Medea of the third book of the *Argonautica;* the intimate, insightful analysis of their passions forms a most important part of the Alexandrian legacy to European poetry. Idyll 2 ranks as one of the greatest short poems in Greek literature. It cannot be savored in excerpts but must be read in its entirety, if not in the original then in poetical translation. A few years ago Roger Sessions composed a magnificent musical interpretation of the poem entitled *An Idyll of Theocritus,* which was recorded by the Louisville Symphony (Columbia Records).

Pastoral

This is the final part of the Theocritean poetic spectrum that remains to be scrutinized. We must try to determine the distinctive common denominators of the genre as established and handled by its inventor, and the pattern or patterns in which the constituent elements allow themselves to be arranged; we must identify the structure-points and the structure. There are certain assumptions implicit in such a statement that have to be mentioned. First, genres do exist, in the sense that literary works can be grouped on the basis of outer and inner form. Matters of outer form, such as the nature of the hexameter line, the makeup of the "salon" Doric, grammatical idiosyncrasies, kinds of Homeric echoes and echoes of other writers, high style versus colloquial, diverse types and functions of word-repetition including the refrain, and so forth, belong to the domain of the specialist. Secondly, the genre cannot have purity, cannot be unmixed, in the sense that it cannot be an amalgam of unique, novel ingredients, but rather represents a totality of devices, motifs, materials that are on hand, available to the artist, and already familiar in some degree to his audience. Thirdly, a genre is what one finds it to be at a given moment in time in the hands of a given artist. Furthermore, however slowly, it undergoes historical change. Fourthly, in the analysis to follow, the goal is description not prescription. Any resultant summarizing statement about Theocritean pastoral that emerges has no normative or regulative value.

There is more than one way of looking at the bucolic. On the level of form there is, for example, the *frame*, which is composed of narrative or dramatic machinery: the prologues, the epilogues, the introductory and intercalary dialogues, sometimes monologues. Within the frame is the *nucleus*, which is generally made up of the nonrustic song or songs performed by rustic actors. The song tends to be the essential element; it is a given of the bucolic piece (it may also occur in idylls that are not bucolic), and one of its main roots is in the popular song, both the semiliterary and folk types, about which we know a little from several fragments that have turned up in the papyri. The Theocritean song is not a real song but a literary facsimile. Previous allusion was made to songs in connection with idylls 7 (those of Lycidas and Simichidas), 10 (those of Bucaeus and Milon), 15 (the Adonis song), and 18 (the epithalamium). In idyll 1, as we shall see, there is the song of Thyrsis on the passion and death of Daphnis; in idyll 3 is the goatherd's serenade to Amaryllis, a *paraclausithyron* (lament of the urban lover shut outside his beloved's door) amusingly delivered in front of a door that is not there since Amaryllis lives in a cave; in 6 there are competing songs, as in 7 and 10, of Daphnis and Damoitas on the Polyphemus–Galatea theme; in 11 the same theme is treated and there is one song, the love song of Polyphemus himself.

There is another way of viewing the bucolic. It involves the level of scene and content. Here there is an enveloping element, the pastoral world, which is firmly rooted in the reality of a countryside and rustic society that the poet personally knows—specifically, the rural regions of southern Italy, Sicily, and Cos. But there is no attempt at a total realistic portrayal of that countryside or society. It is a simplified, selected world. The human actors are few, mostly cowherds, shepherds, and goatherds hierarchically arranged in that order. Except for idylls 4, 5, and 10, there is hardly an attempt at differentiation of character. There is little action in this world, and what there is is of a sameness. The natural setting, realistically presented, is always there, in the background, but despite the poet's lively appreciation of nature's beauties, there is no nature for nature's sake, no soft, romantic, sentimental glorification of the countryside. In contrast with this enveloping world in which simplicity and order and symmetry prevail, there is an embedded element that consists of the ordinary, everyday, urban world. This is unsimple, and imperfect and chaotically intricate. It also is largely rooted in reality, the reality of a complex Hellenistic civilization and sophisticated society that the poet personally knows: specifically, at a minimum, Syracuse, Cos, the eastern Mediterranean area, and Alexandria and the Ptolemaic court. This world is the one in which the poet and his audience live from day to day. But again there is no attempt in the bucolic idylls at a total realistic portrayal of it. In fact, it never appears on the surface but exists in a symbol like the intricately carved ivywood bowl in idyll 1 or the tone and structure of a sophisticated song like that of Lycidas or Simichidas in 7 or in the urban *kōmos-paraclausithyrastic*[2] situation in 3 or 6 or 11.

In addition to these components, namely the

---

[2]Pertaining to carousing (*kōmos*) in the very early hours of the morning and serenading one's beloved.

two worlds or scenes, there are other elements in the genre as established and used by Theocritus. There is the prelude music, the music, mainly of the pipes, the single-reed pipe *(aulos monokalamos)*, or the polyreed Pan-pipe, the syrinx. Actually, of course, no such music was ever played in conjunction with a Theocritean bucolic. The poem was designed for a listening or reading audience and, if it ever was read aloud to members of a literary circle on Cos or to the sophisticates of Ptolemy's court in Alexandria, it is hardly likely that there was any playing of the herdsman's pipe. Yet, in most of the pastorals the music had to be there as a constituent element, there in the consciousness of the poet and in the consciousness of those who read or listened, evoked in the memory by the context and poetical pattern and scene, sometimes called immediately to the mind by direct statement. So, the first idyll opens with these words: "Honey-sweet the whispering song of the pine, goatherd, there, by the springs. Sweet too your sibilant pipes" (1–3). The flavor of the "sibilant pipes" has a unique quality that is lost to most moderns. It can be recaptured by listening to certain recordings of modern Greek folk music that involve the single-reed shepherd's pipe or clarinet and *laouto* (lute). Pastoral music produced by pipe or by clarinet plus *laouto* in this modern folk music often culminates in a song. It can be conjectured that some such folk form as this was one of the roots of Theocritean pastoral.

Another component, typical of so much Hellenistic poetry, is the erotic. The whole body of Theocritean verse is permeated with love, and almost all the songs in the pastoral idylls have erotic themes. The poetic treatment is a rather uncomplex one and somewhat conventional: tragic or heroic love never, but simply pathetic love, love as suffering, love as a malady or wound for which the only remedy or easement is the poetry of song that comes from the Muses. This is the view of the poet's address to his doctor friend Nicias at the opening of 11: "There is no other *pharmakon* [magic medicine] for Love, my Nicias, nothing except the Pierides [Muses]

and their song. Its effect upon men is gentle and sweet, but it is not easy to find" (1–4). As the poem continues it shows us Polyphemus, the Cyclops, as a case in point. He sits land-bound upon some high crag and, looking out over the sea, forlornly sings a song to his milk-white Galatea, the lovely sea-nymph. He has found the magic medicine. In this piece and others the tone is whimsical, the hand of the poet is light; his mildly comic, sometimes ironic touch alleviates a pathos that might have been cloying. Even more noteworthy than the semihumorously handled pathos is the restricted nature of the erotic attitude and action. Throughout the bucolics (and in the nonbucolics such as 2, 13, 14, 29, and 30) the main emphasis is upon the striving to attain, the beseeching, besieging aspect of the action. Courtship is the keynote, incomplete and unsuccessful courtship containing a quality of suspension that images an eternal prolonging of the state of unfulfillment. This competitive erotic process is a dominant action in the pastoral's structure of movement; it analogizes the most important and distinctive component of the genre, namely the contest, the match.

The basic situation in Theocritean bucolic is one of contest. In some sense all the actors, including the poet himself, are contestants. The contest assumes numerous forms and appears on various levels. The most common form is that of a singing match where the performance is one of two sorts: either a recitation of set pieces, songs previously composed and presented from memory, or improvised amoebean versifying with couplets or tercets or short stanzas on a given theme or themes dictated by an arbiter or by one of the contestants. There exist tape recordings of singing matches of the improvising sort between villagers on Cyprus involving the village champion and a challenger from outside the village. These recordings date from a post–World War II period. There cannot be much doubt that Theocritus here, as with the instrumental music, built on a folk pattern.

Idyll 5 is the example par excellence of the improvised singing match and, in fact, exemplifies numerous features of the rustic contest. The contestants are Comatas, a goatherd, and Lacon, a shepherd. The poem begins immediately with a rapid-fire contest in amoebean invective and vituperation that is not part of the singing match proper:

Comatas: Goats, steer clear of that shepherd fellow over there, that Sybarite, that Lacon. He pinched my fleece jacket yesterday.

Lacon: Hey, lambs, get away from that spring. Don't you see Comatas, the fellow who stole my Pan-pipe the other day?

(1–4)

And so it goes on: vilification, bragging, scoffing, and gross erotic allusions all adding up to the slanging contest, the competition in insult (*loidoria*), which as anthropologists and folklorists know is to be found everywhere in the most diverse cultures. The inverse form of such a match is a contest in courtesy, and vestiges are to be found in other idylls, such as 6 and 7. Sandwiched among the insults in 5 are other formal features: the issuance of the challenge, its acceptance, and the setting of the prizes. Every game or contest has its stake, which can be of material or symbolic value or both:

Lacon: If you want to stake a kid, although that's nothing much, I'll sing you a match until you surrender.

Comatas: . . . Look, there's the kid, my stake. Come on now, you put up a fatted lamb.

Lacon: And how will that be fair, you fox? . . .

Comatas: . . . Since the kid isn't enough of a stake for you, look, here's the he-goat. Start the contest.

(21–30)

Next comes the stakeout of the contest area and then the choice of the referee:

Lacon: Come on, stroll over here, and you'll sing the pastoral for the last time.

Comatas: I'll not come. There are oak trees here, and galingale too. Here the bees buzz prettily by their hives. There are two springs of cold water and the birds warble in the treetops and the shade isn't like that over there by you. . . .

Lacon: If you come over here, you'll have sheepskins to walk on and fleeces softer than sleep. Those goatskins there beside you smell worse than you smell. . . .

Comatas: If you'll come here, you'll walk on soft feather fern and blooming pennyroyal, and there'll be a carpet of skins of young kids four times softer than those lambskins. . . .

Lacon: All right, start the contest from there, sing the pastoral from there. Walk on your own ground and keep your old oaks.—Who will be our judge? . . .

Comatas: We'll call that fellow if you want, that woodcutter, the one who is chopping away at those heather bushes over there. It's Morson.

(44–65)

This concern about the choice of the terrain for the singing match, the desire of each contestant to secure the territory favorable to his performance, is a literary reflex, an inheritance from folk material, of the ritualistic, ceremonial marking off of the game ground and the players' territories, and is an analogue of the circle within which the marbles are set, or the chessboard and its squares on which the pieces are moved, or the net and the court and subcourts where the ball is put in play.

After the umpire is selected, the singing match soon begins. It consists of thirty-three alternately rendered competing couplets on diverse rustic subjects: goats, sheep, cheese, love of boys, love of girls, roses, wild apples, the ringdove, fleece, the wild olive tree, the oak tree, mixing bowl, shepherd dog, locusts, cicadas, foxes, beetles, buggery. Then the judge selects the winner. The winner delivers the closing speech of the poem. That in barest outline is idyll 5. Elements of this form appear in varying proportions in the other bucolic poems.

The contest component of pastoral thus illustrated by idyll 5 needs further comment. Certainly contest is an integral element of everyday existence in business, politics, war, commerce, and so forth. But there is a special kind of contest that resides elsewhere—in the realm of play.[3] This type of contest is highly organized conflict-play. Play has primeval roots; it is precultural, in fact prehuman. Various modes of animate life indulge in it as training exercise to prepare for the grim realities of existence. Also, play is temporary activity occurring within clearly marked limits of space and time whose dimensions are relatively small. It is extremely formal in that it has rules, freely accepted by the players, that are strictly binding for the duration. Play can be described as constructed on order and symmetry, on pattern or patterns, and repetition of them, and so, for the time it lasts, it brings limited perfection into an imperfect world and into the confusion of life. It lies outside the constraints of necessity and logic and practicality and material utility and duty; it has its aim in itself, and the participants for a while have the feeling that it is different from ordinary life. The mood of play is one of joyful and at the same time serious enthusiasm and enthrallment. Exaltation and tension accompany the action; joy and relaxation follow. In other words, play momentarily transports the spectators and the players into a sphere of delight and tranquillity. It takes many forms. It is a factor operative throughout the cultural process, functioning as a social impulse that produces many of the fundamental forms of social life. It can be martial and physical, religious and philosophical, legal and political, and, of course, artistic and linguistic.

All poetry is play or at least partly play. But in much poetry the linguistic forms and their referents lift the poem in varying degrees out of pure play into the domain of ideation and judgment, whereas Theocritean pastoral tries not to leave the play sphere, the contest sphere. In a sophisticated manner Theocritus isolates the play elements, keeps them as pure as he can, and forms a structure that is patently a play structure. The framing pastoral world is the playground where the special rules obtain and the games are played. There is an interesting inversion here. In life the various playgrounds, such as the stage and screen and baseball diamond and football field, are temporary worlds within the ordinary world. In Theocritus, so often the ordinary world is inside the temporary world, but the temporary world has been literarily fixed into permanence and so there is reversal of the norm. In this structure the great contest is between the worlds, and the desired and felt result is the ordering of the disordered, the refinement and refreshment of the world of life that has become too complex and variegated, whose civilization has grown too serious and lost touch with play. Or to put it in Theocritus' own terms, as song is the magic medicine for Polyphemus' lovesickness, so perhaps the poet's pastoral song is the magic medicine for his audience's uncertainties and disorders and perplexities.

It should prove profitable for understanding and appreciating Theocritean pastoral to subject a complete bucolic idyll to careful scrutiny with regard to the formative features revealed by our analysis. The programmatic idyll 1, one of the poet's finest, will serve admirably for the purpose.

Thyrsis, the shepherd, begins, sets the pastoral scene, initiates a contest of courtesy, and suggests gift-prizes:

Honey-sweet the whispering song of the pine, goatherd, there by the springs. Sweet too your sibilant pipes; and after Pan yours the prize. He-goat his, then she-goat yours. If he takes her as prize, you shall have the kid. The flesh of a kid is tasty until she comes to an age to milk.

(1-6)

The goatherd takes up the implicit challenge and vies in courtesy, replying: "Sweeter, shepherd, flows your song than flows the echoing stream over there from the rock above. If the Muses take the suckling ewe-lamb as their gift, your prize shall be the stall-fed lamb. But if *this*

[3]See Johan Huizinga, *Homo Ludens: A Study of the Play Element in Culture.* Translated by R. F. C. Hull (London, 1949). This paragraph and part of the next one are a recapitulation of some of the ideas expressed in chapter 1, "Nature and Significance of Play as a Cultural Phenomenon."

lamb be their pleasure, then yours be the ewe herself" (7–11).

Thyrsis invites the goatherd to perform: "Will you, in the name of the Nymphs, will you, goatherd, sit and play your pipe here by this sloping knoll and these tamarisks? I will tend your goats for you in this very spot" (12–14).

The goatherd pretends to decline:

It is not right, shepherd, it is not right for me to play the pipe at high noon. I fear Pan. He is tired of the hunt and rests at this hour. He's sharp-tempered; pungent anger always sits by his nostril. But, Thyrsis, since you are wont to sing the *Passion of Daphnis* and have become skilled in the pastoral muse, come, let us sit beneath the elm, facing Priapus' image and the springs, right there where the shepherd's seat is, where the oak trees are. [This is a reflex of the marking off of the contest-grounds.] If you will sing as you once sang in your match with Chromis from Libya, I will let you have three milkings of a goat that is the mother of twins, one whose milk fills two pails even after she has suckled the kids.

(15–26)

Here ends the first episode, which is a kind of prologue, characterized as far as the action is concerned by the playful, amoebean striving (that is, verbal give and take) of the two herdsmen to entice each other into beginning the singing contest. The poet has carefully established the pastoral world, the seemingly simple, uncomplex world of flocks and herds and their keepers, of whispering pines and shady elms and grassy slopes and trickling streams, the world of nature at high noon—warm, drowsy, alive, remote. This is a real pastoral scene. However idealized and conventionalized it may be, it still belongs in the world of sights and sounds. Real country scenes and country life lie back of it.

As one moves on into the idyll, the enticement of Thyrsis' Muse continues and the listing of the contest gift-prizes goes on, but there is a shift of world. The goatherd is still speaking:

And I will give you a deep ivywood bowl [*kissubion*], coated with sweet beeswax, two-han-

dled, newly made, with a fresh wood smell. Ivy twines on top along its edges, ivy dotted with goldflower, and along it the tendril twists a meandering way rejoicing in its yellow berry. Within there is fashioned a woman, an intricate work of art such as the gods might make; she is decked out in flowing robe and headband. And close to her, on either side, two lovers with beautiful long hair alternate strife of words. But their words do not touch her heart. Now she glances at one with a laugh, now again she flings the other a thought. Their eyes are heavy with love's long sleeplessness and their efforts are useless. Next to them are fashioned an ancient fisherman and a rock, a crag, on which the old man with eager strength gathers up a great net for his cast like a man working his hardest. You would say that he is fishing with all the might of his limbs, so swollen are the sinews all over his neck and throat and shoulders even though he is gray-haired; yet his strength is that of a young man. A little way off from the sea-worn old man there is a vineyard beautifully laden with clusters of purpling grapes, and a small boy sits idly on a stone wall and watches the vineyard. There are two vixens, one on either side. One is running up and down the vine rows plundering the ripe fruit while the other plans every sort of trick to get his knapsack and says she will not let the lad be until she lands his lunch. But he is weaving a pretty locust cage out of asphodel stems, fitting it with rush, and he cares not so much for the knapsack or the vines as he takes pleasure in his weaving. All about the bowl spreads pliant acanthus. It is a sight for a goatherd to wonder at. The marvel of it would amaze you. [End of section that is a surrogate for a song by the goatherd.] To pay for it I gave the ferryman of Calydna a goat and a large cheese of white milk. The lip of the bowl has never touched mine. The bowl is still pure. I'll give you it with great pleasure if you'll be my friend and sing that lovely hymn. I mean what I say. Come, man, you shan't keep your song for Hades, which brings oblivion.

(27–63)

Except for the material of composition, wood, this intricately wrought ivywood bowl does not belong to the pastoral world. It's the product of a tediously learned craft and of a highly self-conscious art that delights in variety and minuteness of detail. The bowl symbolizes the world of an intricate, complex society. By means of its three vignettes it pictorializes and freezes somewhat preciously different segments of life's pattern.

The first scene (the adult world of erotic passion) presents a contest between the coquette and the two swains, and also a contest between each of them as they alternate strife of words to win her over. But she remains unaffected and unwon, all the while showing attention now to one, now to the other. Their eyes are swollen from lack of sleep, and their toil is heavy; but it is in vain, and so their goal is unachieved.

The next scene (old age and hard work) shows the initial stage of a contest between the old, gray-haired fisherman on the high rock and the sea. Like a man working his hardest he gathers up the great net for the cast. He is using all his strength, and over his neck and throat and shoulders his sinews swell and writhe. The poet chooses to leave the outcome of the contest unfinished; the cast is not made; the fish are not caught.

The third scene (the world of innocent childhood) is similar to the first. The boy, the vineyard's guardian, imperturbable like the coquette, takes pleasure in weaving his toy and does not care about the vixens. The vixens, like the long-haired dandies, are engaged in a contest. The boy is the focus. One pillages the ripe grapes and subverts the boy's guardianship, the other plans every sort of trick to win his knapsack away from him. One vixen achieves her goal, but, so far as the poet allows us to see, the other does not.

In each case there is described or implied an action of striving to attain, of besieging, of wooing, of attempt at ensnarement: the two lovers of their lady, the fisherman of the sea, the vixens of the boy. These scenes suggest the unconcluded struggle, the unachieved aim, life unfinished. The *kissubion* then is the second episode in this drama, and the scene it symbolizes is that of the present, near-at-hand, complicated society of the artist where the strands of existence twine and twist and are interwoven like the ivy tendrils about the edge of the bowl. In a manner of speaking the bowl is

the scene and the whole idyll is a drama expressed in terms of scene or spectacle, not in terms of plot or character or thought. The different scenes or worlds make up the plot and character and thought. There are actors: Thyrsis, the goatherd, the coquette, the fisherman, the boy, and in the section next to be presented, Priapus, Aphrodite, Hermes, Daphnis, and there is conflict between them, and there is dialogue and movement; yet the total effect is that of posed tableaux fused. The idyll is a series of scenic slides that somehow stand out from one another and at the same time mingle and merge. As the performance takes place, the spectator is only partially aware of the operator's insertion of the next slide. The relation and interaction of the slides constitute the poem.

The next slide, contrasting with the ivywood bowl of life, is the drama within the drama, the *Passion and Death of Daphnis*. This, like the bowl, has its own series of slides, marked off by the refrain lines, many of them verbal slides, not patently pictorial, but possessing the same static quality:

Begin, dear Muses, begin the pastoral song. This is Thyrsis from Aetna and Thyrsis' voice. Where were you then when Daphnis pined, where were you, Nymphs? Peneius' lovely valley? Or Pindus'? Not by Anapus' mighty course, nor Aetna's peak, nor Acis' holy stream. Begin, dear Muses, begin the pastoral song. For him the jackals howled, for him the wolves howled; the lion from out the oakwood mourned him as he died. Begin, dear Muses, begin the pastoral song. Around his feet many cows, many bulls too, many heifers and calves moaned for him. Begin, dear Muses, begin the pastoral song. First Hermes came down the hill and said: "Daphnis, who tortures you? Whom do you love so deeply, friend?" Begin, dear Muses, begin the pastoral song. The cowherds came; the shepherds, the goatherds came, all asking of his ills. Priapus came and said: "Poor fool, Daphnis, why do you pine? The maid runs past all the springs and through all the groves—Begin, dear Muses, begin the pastoral song—looking for you. Ah! you're too gauche a lover and impotent too. You were called the oxherd, but you're like a goatherd now. When the goatherd sees how the bleating she-goats are covered, he weeps his eyes out that he wasn't born a he-goat—Begin, dear Muses, begin the pastoral song—and when you see how the girls laugh, you weep because you don't share their dance." [Priapus' speech is a reflex of the insult contest.] The herdsman gave them no answer but bore his bitter love and bore his fate to the end. Begin, O Muses, begin again the pastoral song. Finally Cypris [Aphrodite] came too, the sweetly laughing goddess, but displaying a heavy displeasure, and said: "Ah, you boasted, Daphnis, that you would give Love a fall. Cruel Love gave you the fall, didn't he?" Begin, O Muses, begin again the pastoral song. Then, in turn, Daphnis answered her: "Pitiless Cypris, dread Cypris, Cypris hated by men, I suppose you think that all my suns have already set? Even in Hades Daphnis will be a bitter pain to Love. Begin, O Muses, begin again the pastoral song. They say, do they not, that Cypris and the herdsman?—Well, you know. Off with you to Mount Ida, off to Anchises! There there are oaks and galingale, there the bees hum prettily by their hives [ready to sting adulterers]. Begin, O Muses, begin again the pastoral song. Adonis too is ripe [for plucking]; he also [like Anchises a rustic] tends flocks and kills hares and hunts all the beasts of the wood. Begin, Muses, begin again the pastoral song. Daphnis tells Aphrodite to go stand by Diomed and say: 'I am the conqueror of the oxherd Daphnis. Come, fight with me!' [This Aphrodite–Daphnis exchange is also a vestige of the insult contest.] Begin, O Muses, begin again the pastoral song. Wolves, jackals, bears in your mountain dens, farewell! No more am I your herdsman Daphnis in the woodland, no more in the thickets, no more in the groves. Farewell Arethusa and rivers that pour fair water down Thybris. Begin, O Muses, begin again the pastoral song. I am that Daphnis who here tended the cattle, that Daphnis who here watered the bulls and calves. Begin, O Muses, begin again the pastoral song. Oh, Pan, Pan, whether you be on the high hills of Lycaeus or roam mighty Maenalus, come here to Sicily and leave Helice's peak and that lofty tomb of Lycaon's son that is admired even by the blessed gods. Cease, Muses, come cease the pastoral song. Come, lord, and take this waxen pipe that breathes out honey, this beautiful pipe whose lip is spirally bound. For now I am drawn down to Hades by Love! Cease, Muses, come

cease the pastoral song. May brambles, may thorns bloom with violets. May the lovely narcissus wear its flowers on the juniper! May all with all be confounded! May the pine tree bear wild pears! Daphnis is dying! May the stag drag down the hounds, and from the hills may the owls sing against the nightingales." Cease, Muses, come cease the pastoral song. And with these words he ended his say. And Aphrodite wished to restore him. But all the threads of Fate were spun and Daphnis went to the stream. And the spiraling waters washed over the man, beloved of the Muses, not unloved of the nymphs. Cease, Muses, come cease the pastoral song [end of Thyrsis' song].

(64–142)

This is a third world, not that of everyday living, the *kissubion* world, and not the simple, reality-rooted pastoral world. It has a bucolic setting, its trappings are pastoral, there are cowherds and shepherds and goatherds, beasts of the field and beasts of the woodland on the scene. Still, it is a rarefied pastoral with no roots in reality, no smell of the earth. Literally it is a no-man's-land. The leading players are supernatural creatures or powers: Hermes, Priapus, Aphrodite, and Daphnis the idealized bucolic hero. They move like statues and talk like symbols. This is the "Strange Other World of Daphnis' Passion and Death." In its obvious contrast with the *kissubion* of life it is the world of death, but its suggestive potency goes beyond that. Such is clear from listing merely the significances of Daphnis: the virgin youth, the hunter, the opponent of Aphrodite, a Hippolytean figure; the steadfast rebel, resistant to the last, a Promethean figure; Daphnis half-man, half-"natural," mediator between man and god, between man and nature; Daphnis the simple man in touch with nature, perhaps symbolizing the aspirations of a society that wants itself to be in touch with nature; Daphnis, the dying god, the Adonis-figure; Daphnis the sacrificial tragic hero, the scapegoat figure that has a magical importance to all men.

The action of this third world seems to bear a relation to that of the scenes on the *kissubion*. It is a kind of besieging action of increasing intensity. Daphnis is the focal point. First Hermes, sincerely concerned; so too the cowherds, shepherds, and goatherds; then the mocking, scoffing Priapus with gross innuendos; finally the dread Aphrodite, making the ironic onslaught that breaks through Daphnis' silence. In this conflict with whatever Eros and Aphrodite represent, he is overcome by their superior might, but in place of the erotic-seeking action they have wished to force him into, he makes the tragic, heroic choice of death; here is the struggle concluded, the aim achieved, life finished. It is the finale of the world of Daphnis' passion and death but not the poem's. There is one more slide.

The poet returns us briefly to the simple, pastoral world. Thyrsis says: "Now give me the goat and the bowl that I may milk her and pour a libation to the Muses. Farewell, Muses, many farewells! I will sing you a sweeter song another day" (143–145). The goatherd speaks the closing speech:

> "Thyrsis, may your fair mouth be full of honey, and full of honeycomb, and may you nibble on the sweet fig of Aegilus, for you sing better than the cicada. See, here is your bowl [award of the gift-prize]. Look, friend, how pleasantly fragrant it is. You will think that it has been washed in the springs of the Seasons.—Come here, Cissaetha! Thyrsis, you milk her. And you young she-goats, stop frisking about, else the he-goat will mount you."
>
> (146–152)

Before leaving idyll 1 and Theocritean bucolic, we should look once again at the *kissubion*, that product of a meticulous workmanship that delights in exact, delicate tracery of complex detail. It provides us with a key image that permeates the poem in numerous forms. It consists of a series of, not identical, but similar and related patterns of interweaving, crisscrossing, zigzagging lines and movements. The key word is *helix*, meaning "tendril," but also "spiral, whirl, convolution." On top of the bowl the ivy twines *(maruetai)* about the edges, interlaced with *helichryse*; the tendril *(helix)* twists its

meandering way *(heileitai)*. The coquette is an intricate piece of workmanship *(daidalma)*. The great net *(mega diktuon)* suggests a maze of crisscrosses. The bulging sinews *(ines)* of the old fisherman's neck and throat and shoulders form a network of curves and spirals. The grape clusters in the vineyard are masses of circles. The one fox runs up and down the vine rows. The boy is weaving *(plekei)* a locust cage, and he delights in his weaving *(plegmati)*. The pliant acanthus is spread out *(peripeptatai)* all over the bowl.

When groups of images persistently recur, it is a reasonable conjecture that one is dealing with symbol. The symbol occurs or is implied elsewhere in the idyll, although it is not necessarily always of a visual kind.

This *helix* figure is encountered everywhere in numerous word and phrase matchings; in the numerous balancings and interweavings of conceits; in the heavy use of the refrain line, which creates a spirallike effect; in the circling and recircling presentation in various guises of the "besieging" theme. At the last in the finale of the world of Daphnis' passion and death, it occurs twice within two lines in its visual form: first indirectly in *ta ge man lina panta / ek Moiran* ("The last spiral of life's thread had been unwound from the Fates' distaff": 139–140) and secondly, quite directly, in *Daphnis eba rhoon. Ekluse dina / ton Moisais philon andra, ton ou Numphais apechthe* ("Daphnis went down to the stream. / A spiraling, whirling eddy washed over the man beloved of the Muses, not unloved of the Nymphs": 140–141).

The symbol seems to wind and twist its way like the tendril of the vine throughout the poem on various levels, giving it unity, coiling around the different worlds, the real pastoral world, the world of the *kissubion*, the world of Daphnis' passion and death, binding them together. The spiral and its associated patterns make the poem a daedal thing. The poem's significance is to be reckoned partially in terms of the evocations that this nexus of patterns, in its visual and auditory and conceptual forms, effects for the poem's audience.

This is Theocritean pastoral: *daidalma,* "an intricate work," and *pharmakon,* "the magic remedy" of poetic song that brings easement.

Selected Bibliography

TEXTS

Bucolici Graeci, edited by A. S. F. Gow. Oxford, 1966. Greek text; the standard.

Theocritus: Select Poems, edited by K. J. Dover. London, 1971. Greek text with introduction and commentary.

TRANSLATIONS AND COMMENTARIES

Beckby, Hermann. *Die griechischen Bukoliker.* Meisenheim am Glan, 1975. German translation with commentary.

Gow, A. S. F. *Theocritus.* 2 vols. Cambridge, 1952. Vol. 1: introduction, text, and English translation; vol. 2: commentary, appendix, indexes, and plates. The standard.

Holden, A. *Greek Pastoral Poetry. Theocritus, Bion, and Moschus. The Pattern Poems.* Baltimore, 1974. English verse translation with introduction and notes.

Legrand, Ph.-E. *Bucoliques Grecs: Tome 1, Théocrite.* Paris, 1960. Greek text and French translation.

Rist, A. *The Poems of Theocritus.* Chapel Hill, N. C., 1978. General introduction; English verse translation with introductions to individual poems.

Staiger, E. *Theokrit: Die echten Gedichte.* Zurich and Stuttgart, 1970. German verse translation.

HISTORICAL BACKGROUND

Fraser, P. M. *Ptolemaic Alexandria.* 3 vols. Oxford, 1972. Vol. 1: text; vol. 2: notes; vol. 3: indexes.

CRITICAL STUDIES

Bignone, E. *Teocrito.* Bari, 1934.

Cameron, A. "The Form of the *Thalysia.*" In *Miscellanea di studi alessandrini in memoria di Augusto Rostagni,* pp. 291–307. Turin, 1963.

Edquist, H. "Aspects of Theocritean Otium." *Ramus* 4:101–113 (1975).

Effe, B. "Die Destruktion der Tradition: Theokrits mythologische Gedichte." *Rheinisches Museum für Philologie* 121:48–77 (1978).

Elliger, W. "Theokrit." In *Die Darstellung der Landschaft in der griechischen Dichtung,* pp. 318–364. Berlin and New York, 1975.

Giangrande, G. "Polisemia del linguaggio nella poesia alessandrina." *Quaderni urbinati di cultura classica* 24:97–106 (1977).

———. "Théocrite, Simichidas et les Thalysies." *L'Antiquité classique* 37:491–533 (1968).

Griffiths, F. T. *Theocritus at Court.* Leiden, 1979.

Horstmann, A. *Ironie und Humor bei Theokrit.* Meisenheim am Glan, 1976.

Lawall, G. *Theocritus' Coan Pastorals.* Washington, D. C., 1967.

———. "The Green Cabinet and the Pastoral Design." *Ramus* 4:87–100 (1975).

Legrand, Ph.-E. *Étude sur Théocrite.* Paris, 1898.

Merkelbach, R. "Boukoliastai (Der Wettgesang der Hirten)." *Rheinisches Museum für Philologie* 99:97–133 (1956).

Ott, U. *Die Kunst des Gegensatzes in Theokrits Hirtengedichten.* Spudasmata 22. Hildesheim, 1969.

Rosenmeyer, T. G. *The Green Cabinet: Theocritus and the European Pastoral Lyric.* Berkeley, Calif., 1969.

Schmidt, E. A. "Der göttliche Ziegenhirt: Analyse des fünften Idylls als Beitrag zu Theokrits bukolischer Technik." *Hermes* 102:207–243 (1974).

Segal, C. "Landscape into Myth: Theocritus' Bucolic Poetry." *Ramus* 4:115–139 (1975).

———. "Thematic Coherences and Levels of Style in Theocritus' Bucolic Idylls." *Wiener Studien* n.s. 11:35–68 (1977).

Serrao, G. *Problemi di poesia alessandrina.* Rome, 1971.

———. "L'Idillio 5 di Teocrito: campestre e stilizzazione letteraria." *Quaderni urbinati di cultura classica* 19:73–109 (1975).

White, H. *Studies in Theocritus and Other Hellenistic Poets.* Amsterdam and Uithoorn, 1979.

Wojaczek, Günter. *Daphnis: Untersuchungen zur griechischen Bukolik.* Meisenheim am Glan, 1969.

SAMUEL D. ATKINS

PLAUTUS
(254–184 B.C.)

TITUS MACCIUS PLAUTUS, Rome's first surviving author and her greatest playwright, flourished in the late third and early second centuries B.C. The dates of his birth and death are traditionally given as 254 and 184. He is said to have been born in the town of Sarsina, to the north of Rome, in Umbria. Sarsina still exists—a quiet country village, consisting of a handful of buildings clustered around a piazza that now bears Plautus' name, nestled in beautiful, rolling hills. It is just the sort of town from which a young man interested in the theater would want to escape as soon as possible.

But Plautus had more to do than simply shake the hayseed from his hair and set out for the metropolis. At his time the people of Umbria, including, presumably, Plautus himself, did not speak Latin. Though Umbrian is commonly called an Italic dialect, surviving inscriptions make it clear that it was different enough from Latin to warrant being called a separate language. If the tradition about Plautus' origin is correct, therefore, he, like so many other early Roman poets and playwrights, was not only a stranger to Rome but initially a stranger to Rome's own language. His absolute mastery of Latin thus becomes all the more impressive.

His name, as well as his birth, raises some questions—and, as with so many other Plautine problems, the answer lies in a joke, and a joke lies in the answer. Umbrians do not seem to have employed the standard triple nomencla-ture of the Romans, familiar to us from such resounding titles as Gaius Julius Caesar or Marcus Porcius Cato—names that almost beg to be engraved at the foot of a statue. At home our would-be playwright would probably have been known as plain Titus. Apparently he created a mock Roman name for himself, using names of traditional theatrical characters, the equivalents of Punch or Harlequin. From Maccus, a clown figure, he made Maccius, using the added "i" to produce a counterfeit Roman gentile, or clan, name; Plautus ("flat-foot") he used as a cognomen. Hence his full professional name meant something like "Titus, the clown and mime"—but its Latin form carried an irreverent solemnity that is lost in translation.

Tradition tells us that he earned money in the theater working as an actor or stagehand, lost the money in a business enterprise, and was forced to earn his living working in a mill, during which time he started to write plays. Now, ancient biographical tradition is suspect at best. Even when dealing with well-known figures, biographers tended to start with an ideal image of their subject's achievements and character, and arrange, juggle, or invent the facts to suit this image. In the case of a popular entertainer this problem would be compounded by contemporary scholarly indifference to the lives of everyone other than highborn political and military leaders. Plautus' biography, therefore, may well be muddled or even completely fictitious, but from our knowl-

501

edge of his milieu and from the intrinsic quality of his surviving work, we can draw two conclusions about him with some confidence: first, he was a professional who earned his living with his pen (and this makes him practically unique among ancient writers); and second, he was intimately involved with the theater from the very beginning of his career.

The theater itself was hardly a new phenomenon in the Rome of Plautus' day. Romans had been enjoying professional and amateur presentations of song-and-dance acts and improvised satirical revues for generations. And, since 240 B.C. at least, fully staged adaptations of Greek comedy and tragedy had been a regular feature of holiday entertainment. The attitude of the state toward this activity was ambiguous. On the one hand, the theater was suspect in the puritanical minds of Rome's leaders. They associated drama of any sort with what they saw as Greek licentiousness and degeneracy, and it was for this reason that the erection of any permanent theater in the city was forbidden in Plautus' day, and indeed for more than a century thereafter. The magistrates also distrusted the theater as a possible instrument of sedition, and it appears (though here again the record is cloudy) that they were not above throwing in prison playwrights who were responsible for the production of unacceptable political pronouncements, even of the most mild sort. Furthermore, acting itself, as in other cultures and eras, was looked upon as a debased calling, so much so that anyone appearing as a professional actor immediately lost his citizenship.

On the other hand, theatrical performances were sponsored by the state: the *aediles* (high-ranking officials who were responsible for public works of all sorts) would buy scripts from playwrights and hire the producers whose companies would perform them. The scripts would eventually be deposited in the public archives (the only reason for their survival today). And the performances were not simply matters of state but matters of state religion. They were performed on religious holidays, and as an integral part of religious ritual they were taken very seriously, however frivolous their apparent content: mistakes or interruptions in their enactment were matters of grave concern. A story is told, apocryphal in its details but enlightening as a general picture of the time, of an old man who was dancing a mime before a Roman audience when the alarm went forth that Hannibal was at the gates of the city. The audience—citizen-soldiers all, of course—sprang to arms and rushed off to defeat the enemy. When they returned to the stage, they were delighted to find that the old man had continued his dance in their absence, thus keeping the ritual intact, and from this a lovely proverb arose: *salva res est: saltat senex* ("We are saved: the old man is dancing").

Under this curious combination of official support and opposition the Roman theater flourished throughout the second century B.C., eventually providing more opportunities for public dramatic performances than were available in Athens during the age of Pericles. The acting companies were all-male, professional, made up of a combination of slaves and freemen; the troupes presumably supplemented their income by touring in other Italian towns. One of Plautus' actors, Marcus Publilius Pellio, was well enough known to provide the butt of a friendly insult (spoken, perhaps, by himself) in a Plautine play, but it was not until a century or so later that we find an actor like Roscius (famous, by the way, for his Plautine revivals), who could earn a fortune in the theater and move freely in the most exalted circles. There is no direct evidence that Plautus was a member of an acting company, though it is hard to imagine otherwise.

Roman producers were never limited to using three or any other number of actors, but structural oddities in certain plays make it clear that there was considerable doubling of roles. Masks would seem the most obvious tool to facilitate such doubling (they would also make plays about twins much easier to produce), but one source says they were a post-Plautine importation; perhaps the actors had to make do with wigs and makeup. Male characters all wore a Greek cloak called the *pallium*, whence the Roman term for Plautus' sort of comedy, the *comoedia palliata*. Performers were accompanied by a musician playing a flutelike instrument called the *tibia*. This musician stood on the stage throughout the performance; by convention he was invisible, though in one or two raucous scenes his presence is recognized, and he is invited to join in the fun. The name of one such musician, Marcipor, the slave of Oppius, survives; since he shared top billing with Pellio, it is logical to assume that he was responsible for the composition as well as the performance of his music.

Plays were enacted on a broad, shallow, wooden stage, erected for the occasion in the Forum or some other likely spot. (One would like to suppose that the *Pseudolus*, specially commissioned for the formal opening of the temple of the Magna Mater in 191 B.C., was performed on the still-extant steps of that edifice.) This stage generally represented an urban street; it was furnished with an outdoor altar that sometimes figures in the action, and a backdrop with two or three sets of doors representing houses. The arrangements, if any, made for the audience are a moot point among modern scholars. Some evidence would suggest that no seating whatever was provided, but if this were true, the jokes and references to a seated audience in the scripts themselves would lose their point. Perhaps a few rows of benches were provided for dignitaries while the rest of the audience stood. Standing throughout a two-hour comedy may seem rather a penitential form of amusement to us, but the Romans were more accustomed to remaining on their feet for long periods of time than we are, and in fact they took pride in their ability to do so as evidence of their toughness.

The Romans had more than strong legs to take pride in during the time of Plautus. As victors in the Second Punic War (218–201 B.C.), they had survived the devastating invasion of Italy by Hannibal of Carthage; they retained the loyalty of their Italian allies through this challenge, and emerged as masters of the western Mediterranean. It was as if the English had destroyed the Armada and defeated Napoleon in a single war. Ancient historians were unanimous in regarding this as the moral, if not the material, high point in the history of republican Rome. Veterans of the Carthaginian campaigns were doubtless to be found in Plautus' audiences, but in a real sense all Romans, male and female, rich and poor, young and old, slave and free, were veterans of this war. Understandably, they were feeling pretty good about themselves, and understandably too, Plautus (whose plays, as we know from references in the scripts, were open to all Romans, regardless of status) made a point of saluting them in his prologues as the best of warriors—and of chafing them, now and again, as "porridge-eating barbarians," a lighthearted insult that they obviously loved.

These "barbarians," then, could laugh at themselves from time to time. But a full-scale theatrical satire of Roman life would have been a little harder to take—and at any rate, as we have seen, it would have been unacceptable to the authorities. Plautus and his predecessors and contemporaries solved this problem by setting their plays in Greece. This was an imaginary Greece, a Greece where people spoke Latin, referred casually (sometimes unconsciously) to Roman customs and values, and mentioned "nearby" Roman landmarks. But when things threatened to get a little wild, the characters could always fall back for defense on their Greek setting, saying, implicitly and in one case perfectly explicitly: "Remember, folks, we're in Greece. We Greeks can get away with this sort of thing."

But the cloak and the mise-en-scène were not all that was Greek about the *comoedia palliata*. The plots as well, sometimes titles and all, were taken over by Plautus and his fellow playwrights from the Greeks, from the vast body of post-Aristophanic drama known by the Aristotelian term New Comedy, which flourished in Athens and was performed throughout the

Greek world about a century before Plautus' time. Exactly what was involved in this take-over has been the central issue of Plautine scholarship for almost a century and a half. Was it straight translation? Free adaptation? Or was it simply no more than the sort of opportunistic behavior, typical throughout most of the history of the Western theater, of almost all playwrights (and librettists), who as a class have been notoriously unwilling to invent an "argument" when they could find promising material to borrow or steal? Plautus' own term for the process was *vortere barbare*, "to turn into a barbarian language"—an amusing example of his self-deprecating irony, but not very enlightening when it comes to answering this question.

Until fairly recently this problem was made more difficult, and more intriguing, by the fact that none of the New Comedy (to say nothing of the particular New Comedies Plautus used) survived, except in fragmentary quotations. The New Comedy, especially the plays of the Athenian Menander (*ca.* 342–291 B.C.), enjoyed a very high reputation in antiquity, so the solution of the problem seemed to offer scholars the possibility of reconstructing lost masterpieces, as well as exposing the secrets of Plautus' workshop. But how was one to separate the Roman from the Greek material in a given Latin comedy? The question attracted the attention of some of the greatest of modern classicists, and the methods they have used to attack it are ingenious. As a starting point, direct Roman allusions ("I guess I'll have to take a job as a porter at the Porta Trigemina") were an obvious sign of Plautus' hand. But one could go much further than that. Untranslatable puns provided some evidence; for example, "The Olympic games are nothing compared to the games we'll play on this old fool" is Plautus' line, despite the reference to the Olympics, since "games" cannot be used in this double sense in Greek. Finally, one could isolate a number of marked stylistic features scattered throughout the Plautine canon but not found in any surviving Greek work; the hyperbolic comparison involved in the line about the Olympics

is generally accepted as an example of one such stylistic touchstone.

The discovery in the twentieth century of papyruses containing the texts of several Menandrian plays, one of them in its entirety, as well as a tantalizing scrap of a play that Plautus adapted, has led to a redoubling of such scholarly probing. How successful it has been is another story. It would be grossly unfair to say that it has been a waste of time; even the most ardent advocate of Plautine originality can learn a great deal from it. On the other hand, it can hardly be said to have produced a scholarly consensus with regard to Plautus' methods. No doubt almost all scholars would agree that he painted with broader strokes than his Greek predecessors, that he was more interested in fun for its own sake, that his wide (and very effective) use of music and song made his plays more extravagant and festive than the Greeks'. And few would deny that he was responsible for strengthening the role of the *servus callidus* (clever slave), especially since such characters constitute some of his most memorable heroes. But when analysts use alleged plot inconsistencies or loose ends to demonstrate the existence of Plautine cutting and pasting, or point to various interchanges and scenes as irrelevant and therefore Plautine, they part company with many of their fellow scholars. It is not surprising that in the last decade or so, many critics, particularly in the United States, have taken simply to examining the individual plays as they stand, ignoring or skirting the question of Plautus' responsibility for them.

A primary *desideratum* for the critical consideration of a prolific author would clearly be the establishment of a sound chronology for his work. In the case of this Plautine question, too, ingenuity, coupled with much sound scholarship, has not been wanting. But once again it has not produced a consensus. A modern Shakespearean critic would hardly feel it necessary to argue that *The Tempest* is a late play (though it stands first in the early collections), or that *A Comedy of Errors* is early. Such enviable unanimity cannot be claimed for Plautine studies. Two plays are specifically dated in the manuscripts; there seems to be a general agreement that several others are early or late. But this is as far as it goes.

Twenty-one comedies (one of them very fragmentary) survive under Plautus' name. "Under Plautus' name" is not simply a circumlocution. The question of the authenticity of the Plautine canon was much debated in antiquity. Plautus was a very popular playwright in his day, but several centuries elapsed before scholars got around to establishing, or trying to establish, an authoritative text (a typical sequence of events for a popular entertainer). This combination of circumstances led to enormous difficulties. Plautus' popularity meant that his name had been attached to any number of plays by unscrupulous producers, while the passage of so much time meant that hard external evidence for sorting the genuine works from the spurious was totally lacking. Stylistic arguments were all the ancient scholars had to fall back upon, and our list of twenty-one plays is the result of their consensus. It is a little disconcerting to discover that a play called the *Commorientes*, specifically ascribed to Plautus in the prologue of a play by Terence produced less than a generation after Plautus' heyday, failed to make the list, and it is equally disconcerting to learn from the fragmentary remains of the works of Plautus' contemporaries that their style is very similar, if not identical, to his own. But despite this, or perhaps faute de mieux, the canon has met with a general acceptance among modern scholars.

Perhaps the safest generalization one can make about these twenty-one plays regards their language. Every word of them is in verse, in a bewildering variety of meters that is enough to challenge even the most accomplished of modern metrical specialists. And while the effect of these lines of verse is extraordinarily natural—they are in fact a treasure-house of information on spoken Latin, and this is one of the reasons they have received so much scholarly attention—at the same time they are unlike any language ever spoken by

mortal Roman. From beginning to end they exhibit every verbal trick imaginable: puns, one-liners, alliteration, anaphora, assonance—the list could be extended through the whole alphabet, though it would take a Plautus to do it. The result is utterly untranslatable. If one could imagine a Gilbert and Sullivan patter song, extended for 1,000 lines, not falling back on repeated refrains, aurally entrancing while still totally comprehensible, carrying with it dialogue, characterization, and plot, one might have some idea of the effect of Plautus' language.

This incredibly artful language is a major cause of a second important general characteristic of Plautine comedy, an attitude of ironic detachment that is evident throughout the canon, even at the most solemn moments. Both playwright and audience clearly share what might (perhaps a little unkindly) be called a sense of superiority toward the plot and characters being portrayed. There are enough obiter dicta and obvious bits of plot manipulation in the plays to convince anyone that this feeling of detachment, which some modern theatrical critics seem to believe was invented by Bertolt Brecht, was deliberately and consciously sought after by Plautus. And, on reflection, one wonders how it could be otherwise. In the Greek New Comedy, Plautus and his audience were faced with an image of a society that in their eyes was effete, oversensitive, and refined to the point of vacuousness. How were they, having been through what they had, to take seriously stories of supposititious infants, love-besotted youths, gullible dotards, shrewish matrons, and kindhearted prostitutes? But Plautus' attitude is never unpleasantly contemptuous. He approaches the whole enterprise with a spirit of joy; as he makes one of his young men say, "It's no fun being in love unless you're foolish."

This is a sophisticated stance, and the Roman audience, contrary to the statements in some handbooks, was fully capable of appreciating it. They were good soldiers and good engineers, their society was hardheaded and authoritarian, but they were not anti-intellectual, or to be more precise (since it is true that they distrusted what they saw as the pointless quibbling of philosophers), they were not antiverbal. They were keen connoisseurs of the spoken word in forum and law court as well as theater. Though the Romans came to written literature late in comparison to the Greeks and were in fact impelled into it by the Greek example, once they actually started writing they were never primitives. All their surviving prose and poetry, at whatever level of intent or achievement, exhibits an extraordinarily self-conscious sophistication. To a Roman the written word was a product of art. This is the Roman mainstream, and Plautus stands at the head of it.

The variety of Plautine comedy is so great that further generalization about its contents would be misleading. Taking a cue from the most recent Plautine critics, let us examine the canon play by play. "There is wit and fun in this comedy," as Plautus says in a prologue, "and it's worth your while to attend."

The *Amphitryon* (*Amphitruo* in Latin), appropriately enough for the point I have just made, is unique in Greco-Roman New Comedy. It is set in the heroic age, concluding with the birth of Hercules, an "event" that occurred before the Trojan War. The plot concerns the deception of Alcumena, depicted as a highly respectable Theban matron, by Jupiter, who disguises himself as her husband Amphitruo in order to sleep with her. Such participation by the gods (Mercury also appears, acting as Jupiter's Leporello) in the action of a play is unparalleled in Plautus' work, and he insists in the prologue (spoken by Mercury) that the result should be called a tragicomedy. At first glance this discussion of nomenclature appears to be nothing more than a concern, perhaps a hypersensitive concern, with generic propriety. But there is more to the matter than this. When deception is carried out by a character who is ordinarily subservient and helpless, such as a slave, it is not very difficult to make the situation funny. But deception of a human being by

an all-powerful god is usually the stuff of tragedy; "as flies to wanton boys are we to the gods" is not a comic line. Plautus might have loaded the dice by making Alcumena flighty and Amphitruo pompous, but he does not. Alcumena is treated with perfect dignity throughout the play, and is given a memorable (and very Roman) set piece on matronly virtue. Amphitruo is confused and bewildered throughout most of the action, but basically his dignity is unimpaired, and his essential worthiness is established by another set piece (again very Roman in style and content), a song describing in heroic detail his triumph over his enemies, which is sung before he arrives on the scene. Even Amphitruo's slave, Sosia, who is mocked by his temporary twin, Mercury, in the play's most farcical scene, concludes this very scene with some deeply disquieting remarks about how his identity has been stolen from him.

The play has been deprived of what may have been its most comic episode, the face-to-face confrontation of Amphitruo and the disguised Jupiter, by an accident of text transmission: apparently a couple of hundred lines have been lost. This scene may well have contained the answer to the question of how Plautus extricated himself from the perilously tragic situation he created. The few surviving fragmentary quotations show that the scene was full of farcical slapstick, but as our intact text resumes, Jupiter has just departed and we are left with an Amphitruo who has been almost literally driven mad with fury and frustration. In the earlier portions of the play Plautus humanizes the gods by permitting them to address the audience directly: Mercury in a long and chatty prologue, and both gods in a continual series of extended, prologuelike asides. Ostensibly these speeches explain the plot to the audience (an explanation that is totally unnecessary, since once the simple premise is grasped the plot explains itself); their real purpose is to make the spectators identify with the gods rather than their victims. At the play's conclusion Jupiter appears *ex machina* (sound of thunder offstage), admits what he has done, and prophesies the future glory of the newborn Hercules, the product of his union with Alcumena. Amphitruo accepts the explanation without any difficulty or hesitation, but we may find it a little harder. The *Amphitryon* is a memorable and at times hilarious play, but in the end it remains more than a little disquieting.

Lupus est homo homini ("Man is a wolf to man") is a line from *The Comedy of Asses* (*Asinaria*) quoted by Sigmund Freud in his classic essay "Civilization and Its Discontents" (1929). And it is hard to imagine how anyone could be contented with the civilization depicted in this particular play (contemporary Athens is the scene, but it could be any Greek city). Without exception, the characters are as unsympathetic as their actions are unedifying. A young man needs a large sum of money to buy the exclusive favors of his mistress for a year. His aged father, purely out of spite, agrees to help him swindle his mother out of the money (the purchase price of a team of asses is involved; hence the play's title). The execution of the trick is left to a pair of slaves, who succeed, though they spend most of their time insulting each other and bragging of the savage punishments they have endured in the past and no doubt will endure in the future. They hand the money over to the lovers only after teasing them interminably. The father demands an evening with the girl as his reward, a request that the son supinely grants. The ensuing interlude is enacted for us, as far as theatrical limitations and ordinary decency will permit, with the son moaning out his self-pity, the old man salivating, and the girl, who had earlier shown at least a bit of spunk in resisting her greedy mother's arguments against yielding to sentiment, going along with the game in a truly whorish fashion. A henchman of a rival of the young man betrays them all to his aged and shrewish mother, who bursts in on the "party" and, after an appropriate interval of verbal torment, hauls her cringing husband home by the ear as the play ends.

It used to be the fashion to condemn plays of this sort out of hand, purely on moral grounds.

Most critics today would agree that it is perfectly feasible to make a good play out of bad characters. But Plautus does not seem to have done this with *The Comedy of Asses.* The focus of the plot is poor, so much so that it has been suggested that two Greek originals have been conflated here. If there is any unifying theme to the play, that theme is sadism, with one character after another alternately playing the role of torturer and victim. In fact, if we accept this analysis, we could say that the play is quite tautly and neatly organized thematically. The trouble is that sadism, like pornography, is ultimately boring, at least as the subject of mimetic art. We will meet characters of this sort again—lecherous dotards, whores with hearts of lead, and the rest—in other Plautine comedies, and we will see that Plautus could be considerably more successful in dealing with them.

The Pot of Gold (*Aulularia*) illustrates a theme that has been a favorite of comic playwrights from the time of Plautus' Greek precursors down to our own day: an old man, living in angry isolation, is redeemed, or at least restored to society, through the medium of the exuberance and innocent loves of the younger generation. Having said this, we have not said very much, since such a process is common enough in real life, and it forms the theme of plays ranging in quality from a masterpiece like *The Tempest* to a prentice effort like Menander's *Dyskolos. Le bon dieu se trouve dans les détails* ("But God is in the details"), and *The Pot of Gold*, thanks to the skill with which it is worked out, is generally recognized as one of the more successful examples of the theme.

The central character is Euclio, a poverty-stricken old miser who has found a pot of gold buried under the floor of his house. We are told in the prologue, which is spoken by the Lar, or tutelary god of Euclio's household, that this discovery was a reward for virtue—not Euclio's virtue, but his daughter's. She has always paid due honor to the Lar, and furthermore has had the misfortune to be raped (and impregnated) by a rich young neighbor. The pot of gold, says the Lar, will provide the dowry to make marriage to this young man possible. In addition, the Lar has arranged that the young man's uncle will ask Euclio for the girl's hand, simply to speed things up a bit.

The girl never appears on the stage. It would be unthinkable for a respectable young Greek woman to appear in public, or even to be seen by a young man in her own house. Therefore a rape of this sort—they occur in many comedies, always during nocturnal festivals—is almost the only way a dramatist can initiate a romantic attachment between young people. It is an unavoidable dramatic convention, and one can only hope that it was less common in real life than it was on the stage.

Euclio's poverty has obviously isolated him badly enough throughout his life. His discovery of the gold, which he is determined to keep a secret, isolates him even more. He suspects everyone, from his aged serving woman to strangers on the street. He is terrified to leave his house, and when he must go, he tells his servant to open the door to no one, not even Good Fortune herself. When (just as the Lar predicted) his wealthy neighbor asks to marry his daughter, he at once concludes that his secret is out—mistakenly, of course, as is emphasized by an earlier scene in which the neighbor expounds his motives for seeking out a penniless bride. The cooks sent by the neighbor to prepare the wedding feast drive Euclio into a paranoiac frenzy.

Thanks to his isolation, Euclio continually talks to himself, and this habit (always dangerous in Plautine comedy, where asides can be overheard at the playwright's will) is his undoing. An eavesdropping slave of the young lover finds Euclio's gold and steals it, a theft that leads to two great scenes: a splendid monody in which Euclio bemoans his loss and vainly begs the audience for help, and a hilarious dialogue in which the young man tries to confess to Euclio, who thinks the boy means the ducats when he speaks of the daughter. This is finally straightened out, and the young man is con-

fronting his slave about the gold when—our manuscripts break off. Common sense, as well as the prologue and the ancient plot summaries, tells us that the play ended with the appropriate marriage. The extent of Euclio's conversion, or at least his return to normality, can be judged by a single line of his that happens to survive from the play's denouement: "I never had a bit of rest day or night watching it: now I shall sleep."

The title of *The Two Bacchises* (*Bacchides*) refers to a pair of twin courtesans, who, by an improbable but common comic convention, are both known by the same name, Bacchis. The same textual accident that caused the loss of the end of *The Pot of Gold* has lost us the beginning of this play. This makes for a bit of difficulty for the reader at first, but in fact the plot is quite straightforward. Two young Athenians are infatuated with the twins, much to their fathers' dismay. One of them needs money to pursue his infatuation, and, after some ups and downs, this money is acquired through trickery. Even though one of the fathers is the victim of this trickery, the opposition of both of them to the whole arrangement melts away, thanks to the warmth of the working girls, as the play concludes.

The rich profusion of comic characters in *The Two Bacchises* makes orderly analysis difficult for a critic, though an audience would no doubt simply revel in them. These characters contain enough possibilities to provide the focal point for whole plays (as indeed they do, elsewhere in the Plautine canon). A braggart warrior, for example, is allowed to make a brief appearance and is then dismissed. The confusion resulting from the existence of identical twins is exploited very effectively for a scene or two; then the matter is dropped. And for the first time (in the canon, that is, not chronologically as far as we know) we meet an example of Plautus' greatest comic creation, the *servus callidus*, or clever slave.

This is Chrysalus, whose name, as he reminds the audience, comes from the Greek word for gold. He is the slave of one of the father-and-son pairs, though it might more accurately be said that they belong to him. The son depends on him utterly to trick his father out of the money needed to keep his girl, and when, thanks to the son's stupidity, this trick is exposed and goes for naught, Chrysalus is splendidly undaunted. He specifically warns the old man to be on his guard, and predicts to the son that in no time at all his father will be down on his knees begging Chrysalus to take the money—a prediction that is fulfilled to the letter. In a memorable monody he compares his exploits to the sack of Troy, and himself to its captors, who took the city more by brains than brawn. The comparison is totally justified.

The recent discovery of a small scrap of Menander's *Dis Exapaton* (*The Double Deceiver*), the Greek original of Plautus' *Two Bacchises*, adds a special scholarly interest to the play. We can now, for example, directly compare a short monologue spoken by Chrysalus' young master with its source. Menander's monologue is serious, realistic, psychologically convincing. Plautus' is stylized and comic, full of deliberately illogical twistings and self-interruptions—thus strengthening the feeling of ironic detachment mentioned earlier as a general characteristic of his work. We also know that Plautus has added a formal, almost ritualistic exchange of greetings between the two young men (one of whom has just returned from abroad), an exchange that ends with an unexpected comic twist—as similar exchanges do throughout the canon. And, perhaps most important, we know that Menander's name for the character Plautus called Chrysalus was Syrus. With this fact in mind, it takes no great detective to interpret the claim Plautus is making for his art when he has *his* slave sing triumphantly, as he pats his chest:

> Here is a man who is worth his weight in gold: here is a man who ought to have a gold statue set up for him. Why, I've done a double deed today,

been graced with double spoils.... I haven't any use for those Parmenos, those Syruses that do their masters out of two or three gold pieces. There's nothing more worthless than a slave without brains....

> (4.4.640–650)

Since the time of the eighteenth-century playwright and theorist Gotthold Lessing, *The Captives* (*Captivi*) has been specially valued among the plays of Plautus for its high moral qualities. Plautus himself, if we can take his prologue and epilogue at face value, regarded *The Captives* as unique in this regard, as indeed it is in many ways. The noble slave Tyndarus, by exchanging identities with his young master, enables him to escape from his captor, or rather his temporary jailer, an old man who has been buying up prisoners of war in the hope of finding someone he can exchange for his son, who has been captured by the enemy. Meanwhile, the audience can savor the delicious and edifying irony of the fact that this same Tyndarus, though no one realizes it, is the old man's second son, who had been stolen from him many years before. How natural that Tyndarus should show such loyalty to his young master (his equal, in reality), and address his unknown father with such noble pride when his trick is discovered. Tyndarus is led away to the quarries, but virtue is rewarded as the play concludes with the return of the first son and the recognition of Tyndarus as the second, amid general rejoicing.

But an unalloyed picture of virtue rewarded, Plautus seems to have realized, could hardly make for a successful comedy. Hence the inclusion of a representative of one of his favorite types of comic character, logically unnecessary to the plot but wonderfully useful to the play, Ergasilus the parasite. Parasites were penniless men who "earned their living" by cadging free meals from the rich in exchange for their witty dinnertime patter and their willingness to put up with insults. Such people were surely not to be found in the real-life Rome of Plautus' day, and it is difficult to imagine that they were all that common even in Greece, but to a comic author they offered irresistible possibilities, and so they appear in play after play. The "unnecessary" Ergasilus comes close to dominating *The Captives*, from the opening scene, in which he bemoans at length, in comically lugubrious language, the agonies his belly is enduring as a result of the loss of his generous patron (the captured son), to the climax, as he rushes in from the port with the news of the son's safe return, to the tune of a magnificent song of impending gastronomic triumph.

In Plautus' eyes, furthermore, since Tyndarus is (temporarily, at any rate) a slave, the trick he plays, however altruistic its motives, makes him a *servus callidus*, and his victim, though in "reality" an upstanding gentleman and a kindly master, can only be the sort of *senex iratus* who is the clever slave's favorite gull. And their language, as the trick is plotted, played, and ultimately discovered, reflects these comic expectations. "Now the old geezer's in the barber's chair," says Tyndarus in an aside; "yep, now we've got the clippers on him." The joy of the play's conclusion, moreover, is tempered by the appearance of the slave (conveniently discovered by the returning young men) who stole the young Tyndarus away from his father in the first place; Iago-like in his unrepentant wickedness, he concludes the play with a sour wisecrack as he holds out his wrists for the handcuffs. There is morality enough for anyone in *The Captives*, but it is a morality colored by the usual fascinating combination of Plautine exuberance and irony.

It would be difficult to argue any deep moral purpose to the *Casina* (a girl's name, accented on the first syllable). This is Plautus' bawdiest and most raucous comedy. The proportion in it of lyric to spoken lines is greater than in any other play in the canon: the product, some scholars argue, of a progressive evolution in Plautus' career. If they are right, the *Casina*, which might be called a sort of farcical opera,

represents the culmination of his work as a playwright, and it is a sign of the direction that he hoped (vainly, as it turned out) that Roman comedy might take in the future.

The theme of the *Casina* is frustrated lust. An old man is smitten with a slave girl in his household (Casina herself, who never appears on the stage); to facilitate his "suit" he enlists the aid of his steward, who is to marry the girl and make her available to his master whenever he wishes. The old man's wife counters this by proposing that Casina marry a rival slave. They draw lots to see who gets the girl, and the old man's side wins. His wife, apparently acquiescing in defeat, goes inside to prepare for the wedding.

But she and Plautus have a surprise for us, one not predicted or hinted at until the play is three-quarters over. The wife's slave, Casina's disappointed suitor, is clothed and veiled as a bride, and it is this "Casinus" who is presented to the steward bridegroom and his slavering master. The farcical slapstick and splendidly unedifying dialogue that result from this substitution, as we see the "bride" led from her house and hear, a little later, of the "honeymoon" activities offstage, can easily be imagined, and unfortunately some of it must be, since a number of key lines at this point have been lost in transmission, thanks either to an accident or to a censorious copyist. The lecherous old man is thoroughly and publicly disgraced, and his wife, "that," in her words, "we may not make this long play longer," agrees to forgive him as the *Casina* ends.

What is left out of the play is in many ways just as interesting as what is included in it. There is a romantic framework to this unseemly conflict: the old man's son is also in love with the girl, and his mother is acting on his behalf (a psychoanalyst could have a field day with this); ultimately the girl is discovered to be the freeborn daughter of a neighbor, thus paving the way for the young lovers' marriage. But the framework remains just that: a framework. It is dealt with entirely in the prologue, in which we are specifically told that the son will not appear in the play ("Plautus would not have it so—he broke down a bridge that lay on the youth's route"), and the epilogue, in which the marriage is foretold. The arrangement practically amounts to a programmatic statement on Plautus' part as to what was really important in his sort of comedy, and if modern scholars, who generally agree that Plautus suppressed a scene of return and recognition that capped his Greek original, are right, this antiromantic shift in focus was conscious and deliberate.

The *Casina* is also unique in that its surviving prologue, in large part at any rate, was written for a revival of the play that occurred a generation or so after Plautus' death. The words of the prologue suggest that this wild farce had been a favorite among the older generation of Roman theatergoers; it is easy to see why.

If the *Casina* is one of the most cynically antiromantic of Plautus' plays, *The Casket Comedy* (*Cistellaria*) is the closest thing to its opposite one could ask for. Here the young lovers, far from being invisible, are very much in the forefront. As the play opens, the girl is tearfully bemoaning her threatened separation from her beloved and reminiscing tenderly on how they first met; her warm sentiments are set in strong relief by the hardheaded comments and unfeeling advice of her interlocutors. And soon we see her anxious young man invoking the gods and calling for a sword in the very ecstasy of love (reminding us that after all these are *comic* lovers).

Despite the prologue, spoken by the god Succor (*Auxilium*), it is difficult to follow the plot of *The Casket Comedy*, not because of any sloppiness on Plautus' part, but because vast portions of the play have been lost or mutilated during the vagaries of manuscript transmission. The scattered material that is left is certainly unstageable and very nearly unreadable. We do know, however, that the girl is a foundling, the offspring of one of those distressingly common comic rapes. She was exposed as an infant along with a little casket of birth tokens that gives the play its name. Like the rapes, such exposures are ubiquitous in New Comedy, and for the same reason: they make a love interest possible, since the exposed child can be recognized as freeborn and hence marriageable. Infant exposure was not unknown in real life, but historians now argue that it was less common than was once believed; if we allow ourselves to take comedy as a guide in this matter, we are putting ourselves in the position of foreigners who come to America expecting to find nothing but cowboys and gangsters.

The course of true love is diverted by threats of an arranged marriage for the young man (the fragmentary text allows us a glimpse of the conclusion of an engaging lovers' quarrel), but the casket is discovered in the nick of time, the meaning of its contents is deciphered by the appropriate characters, and (offstage) the lovers are reunited. So enough survives of *The Casket Comedy* to give us an attractive, if tantalizing, suggestion of Plautus' infinite variety.

There is a pair of young lovers in the *Curculio*, but the world of this play could hardly be called romantic. The title is the central character's name; its literal meaning is "weevil," which, of course, provides an excuse for a joke or two. The name is Latin rather than Greek, and this would suggest a special investment of Plautine attention in the development of this character, as with Chrysalus in the *Bacchides*.

The *Curculio* is the shortest of Plautus' surviving plays; even if, as has been suggested, a prologue predicting the recognition scene with which it ends has been lost, the play would still be very brief. As befits a short play, it is remarkable for the economy with which Plautus exploits certain established comic situations and expectations. There is a warrior; therefore, we "know" he is a braggart, and jokes can be made about this even before he sets foot on the stage. There is a lover; therefore, he is a fool, and stamped as such before he even opens his mouth. There is a parasite; therefore, he is hungry—more grist for comedy, even though hunger has little to do with his actions or motivations.

This economy of expectation can go even further. For example, the heroine is in the clutches of a *leno* ("pimp" is the usual translation, but a *leno*'s work was lawful, if not very reputable). Therefore, he is hateful: that goes without saying. And therefore, he must be tricked out of the girl. Why tricked? Usually because a young man in comedy has no money. The young man in the *Curculio*, however, appears to have plenty of money. No matter: his girl is held by a *leno*, so the *leno* must be tricked; this is comedy.

And Curculio is the man for the job. Just when things look darkest, he bursts on the scene with enormous energy, spouting a splendidly irrelevant tirade against anything and anyone that might be met up with on a Graeco-Roman street. He cooks up his plot in seconds and pulls it off with aplomb, catching the *leno* and an equally villainous moneylender in his toils. The girl is found to be the long-lost sister of the warrior, and everyone lives happily ever after.

Though the plot of the *Curculio* is hardly unique, the comic strength of the central character is enough to make it a success, and a number of important minor details make it unusually interesting. Alone among the plays, it is set in Epidaurus, a center of healing in antiquity; the stage features a shrine of Aesculapius, in which the *leno* has been passing his nights in the hope that a divinely inspired dream will help him cure a painful (and hilariously described) stomach ailment. An early scene with the young lover contains the first example of a *paraclausithyron*, or lover's serenade to a closed door, to be found in Latin literature, a more songlike (in our sense) composition than anything Plautus wrote elsewhere. And halfway through the play there is a unique interruption in which the stage manager suddenly appears on the scene and, after worrying out loud about whether or not the tricky Curculio is going to return his props, proceeds to give the audience a set lecture on the Roman Forum, listing, monument by monument, the places where disreputable characters generally hang out: a treasure-house for Roman topographers.

"Now take the *Epidicus*: it's a comedy I love as well as my own self, but there's not a one I so object to seeing, if Pellio's playing in it." This little wisecrack, uttered by Chrysalus in *The Two Bacchises* (a character perhaps played by Pellio himself), serves a double function: it enables Plautus to get in a sly dig at the man who was no doubt his favorite actor, and it enables him to offer a bit of harmless advertisement for what was no doubt one of his favorite plays.

It is not hard to see why: the title role of the *Epidicus* is played by another example of that quintessentially Plautine creation, the clever slave. Epidicus faces the usual challenge: he must use his wits to free his young master's beloved. But the situation is made more difficult than usual by the young man's fickleness. Epidicus, as we learn from the exposition scene, has already succeeded in arranging for the purchase of one girlfriend (and in doing so has accomplished the extraordinary feat of making the boy's father believe he is freeing his own long-lost daughter); now the young man has returned from the wars with a new girlfriend in tow. Once again money is needed, and Epidicus, the sole and only indispensable man, must do the job. Through a combination of ingenuity, nerve, and luck he succeeds, in a juggling act that is sometimes as tricky for the spectator to follow as it is for Epidicus to manage: three different girls appear on the stage at one time or another, and the identity of each of them is the subject of confusion. Epidicus, meanwhile, punctuates his nefarious activities with comic monologues that sometimes read like lighthearted inversions of the soliloquies in *Hamlet* ("Now you are alone. . . . Epidicus, your hour has come").

The two masters, father and son, as well as their slave, have their contributions to make to the play's interest. The young lover is less attractive than his confreres in other comedies, and not simply because of his errant heart. Perhaps he has seen too many Plautine comedies; at any rate, he is unpleasantly brusque in the way in which he takes Epidicus' help and talents for granted. His erotic dreams are dashed when he learns that his newly found beloved is actually his long-lost sister (a *real* sister, this time), but, given his character, this is hardly upsetting to us. The old man, on the other hand, is rather more attractive than usual. In one scene he has a touching reunion with an old flame of his own; in another he resists Epidicus' impudent invitations to exercise "masterly" sadism; and when, as the play concludes, he wryly echoes Epidicus' earlier insults as he releases the unrepentant trickster at once from physical bondage and servile status, we strongly suspect that Epidicus, as a new freedman, has acquired a thoroughly worthwhile patron.

Recently, it has been very plausibly argued that the peculiar varieties of minor confusions with which the plot of the *Epidicus* is riddled (even to list them would require microscopic analysis of a sort impossible here) make it very possible that this particular Plautine play had no Greek original at all. Thus far, this is no more than a strong suggestion—but even such a suggestion would have been rank heresy among scholars not too long ago. What in large part makes it possible now, ironically enough, is our new knowledge (through unearthed papyruses) of the Greek New Comedy itself, and with it a new appreciation of the great difference between Plautus and the genre he took for his model.

The Two Menaechmuses (*Menaechmi*) is in every sense the classic comedy of mistaken identity. It is classic in its role as a model for later imitation, in its deliberate rejection of the romantic, and in its beautifully taut, well-balanced construction. For anyone willing to suspend disbelief in its absurd but necessary premise, namely, that a man who is searching the world for his lost twin brother would never imagine that he has found him when he arrives at a strange town and meets a series of strangers who claim to recognize him, the *Menaechmi* will emerge as a masterpiece of farce.

It would almost take a mathematical model of some sort to demonstrate the play's total economy: no comic situation in it is repeated. The out-of-town Menaechmus arrives and is mistaken for his brother. The local brother is then faced with certain difficulties as a result of this mistake, and finally the out-of-towner confronts the problems that arise because of his brother's actions. It looks as if this could go on forever, but in fact it does not: the play stops there, having taken just enough twists and turns and no more.

To later playwrights one obvious use of the mistaken-identity situation is the creation of romantic problems. Plautus was not unaware of the comic possibilities that lay in this direction, as the *Amphitryon* and *The Two Bacchises* make clear, but in this play they are not exploited. The local Menaechmus has a wife and a mistress, but the former is a shrew and the latter a grasping harlot, and his brother's encounters with them are anything but romantic. The reunited twins go off hand in hand at the end of the play, but the local Menaechmus' family and dependents are not invited to join in the reunion. Neither brother is sentimental by nature—quite the contrary—and the play in which they star is unsentimental as well.

The *Menaechmi* is set in the seaport of Epidamnus; the name of the town offers opportunities for Latin puns (*damnum* is "loss" of any sort) that are not ignored. To the newly arrived Menaechmus, Epidamnus is a fantasy world (he calls his experiences a "dream" at one point), and Plautus' use of music and meter reinforces the events of the plot in establishing this theme. The first scene, for example, which features the local Menaechmus, is a song set in various lyric meters. The newcomer, on the other hand, always speaks in unaccompanied iambic lines (the nearest thing to prose in Plautus), except twice when he is drawn into the musical world of Epidamnus: once as he enters the house of his brother's mistress, and a second time when he feigns madness to escape the attacks of his brother's wife and father-in-law (a very funny scene, with an equally funny sequel, marked by the arrival of a magnificently pompous physician). The scene of recognition and reunion that ends the play is, of course, set to music too.

It has been argued that Plautus was more faithful to his Greek original in composing *The Merchant* (*Mercator*) than he was in any of his other plays. If so, this may go a long way toward explaining why the resulting product is, relatively speaking, so uninteresting. The characters are flat, and there is no real conflict in the play; the only problem that arises turns out not to be a problem at all.

A young man (the merchant of the title) returns home from a trading voyage with a new slave mistress, whom he pretends he has bought as a maid for his mother. The father is immediately smitten with the girl and plots to make her his own. But as soon as he learns the truth about his son's relationship with her, he gives up these attempts. Senile lust, in Plautus, is usually made of sterner stuff. And the son has no more backbone than his father. His only reaction to this temporary misunderstanding is a threat to run away from home, and in fact a great proportion of this disappointing play is given over to his maudlin monologues of self-pity.

The comic character after whom *The Braggart Warrior* (*Miles Gloriosus*) is named has proven to be a perennial and surefire favorite throughout the history of the theater. Plautus was not the inventor of the type; the technical term critics often use for it, *alazon*, is Greek, and in fact Plautus tells us in his prologue that *Alazon* was the name of the Greek original of his play. But for the later theater the character of the braggart warrior in all his comic glory, marked by bombastic language, bottomless conceit, puerile gullibility, and a mistaken certainty of his unlimited attractiveness to women, was established for all time by the *Miles Gloriosus*.

It is natural to assume that the military operations in which Rome was so continually involved during Plautus' lifetime had something to do with the popularity of this figure (who appears in several other plays besides this one) on the Roman stage. But when Plautus, in his prologues makes direct reference to Rome's wars, he is always in deadly earnest, and his tone is thoroughly respectful. His braggarts are not Roman soldiers, but Greek mercenaries, with long, tongue-twisting Greek names of a sort the Romans seem to have found hilarious (Pyrgopolynices plays the title role in this comedy, and in the opening scene he mentions an adversary with the even more splendidly ludicrous name of Bumbomachides Clutomistaridarchides). It may well be that the Romans regarded themselves as strong, silent types, and thus found it all the easier to laugh at a phenomenon they saw as essentially foreign.

Pyrgopolynices has a girl in thrall who must be restored to her young lover; the rest of the characters in the play band together to accomplish this. They bamboozle him twice, and the two tricks are so disconnected that scholars have argued, as they have in other cases, that Plautus has here combined two Greek plays to make one Latin comedy. It may seem a little farfetched to postulate such an apparently unnatural process (known to modern critics as *contaminatio*), but in fact Terence, Plautus' successor, states in the prologue to one play that he has inserted in it a scene taken from a second Greek original, and remarks that he is not the first Roman playwright to do this. So it is conceivable that something of the sort happened here.

The first trick (in which an imaginary twin is created for the girl) is relatively harmless, but the second, in which the warrior is convinced that a respectable matron has conceived an adulterous passion for him, leads to his utter defeat: he is beaten mercilessly and even threatened for a time with castration. Scenes of this sort, though popular enough with playwrights in the past, tend to leave a bad taste in the mouth of a modern audience; the prolonged punishment of Shakespeare's Malvolio, for example, strikes us as rather sadistic, and our feeling as he leaves the scene (growling "I'll be revenged on the whole pack of you") is one of extreme discomfort. Plautus avoids this danger by giving Pyrgopolynices the last word in his play; he addresses the audience directly, admitting that he has been a fool and assuring the spectators that his punishment has been richly deserved.

The first trick in *The Braggart Warrior* (the fictitious twin) is amusingly gratuitous, since there is no way in which it can lead to a permanent solution of the lovers' problems. The plot of *The Haunted House* (*Mostellaria*) consists of nothing but a series of such ultimately pointless tricks. If seeing the *Oedipus Rex* can be compared (as one critic has said) to watching a blindfolded man groping his way to the edge of a cliff, in *The Haunted House* we see a fully sighted hero consciously making his way in the same direction.

The slave Tranio and his young master have been "acting like Greeks" (as Plautus, and the Romans, put it) during the absence of the young man's father; they have wasted the family fortune and incurred an enormous debt. Once this precarious situation is established in the exposition, Tranio comes rushing from the harbor and, in a classic example of the *servus currens* (running slave) speech, announces (with appropriately hyperbolic verbosity) the disastrous news that the old man's ship has just pulled in. Of course, the moment the father returns, the jig is up in reality, but Tranio is not one to let reality bother him. Blithely ignorant of strategy, he is a master of tactics. The old man is on his way, so the son and his disreputable companions must be hidden. Where? In the nearest available spot, of course: Tranio shoves them into the family house and locks the door. Now how to get rid of the old man, who is hardly going to stand for being locked out of his own house? Simple enough: make him believe that the house is haunted. Unlike the hapless heroes of modern horror films, the old man is ready enough to believe this; he runs off in terror, but Tranio's respite is brief. His master soon re-

turns, and sees a moneylender dunning Tranio. What now? Tell the old man the debt in question was incurred to buy a replacement house. What house? the master demands. Again, Tranio picks the nearest one available: the next-door neighbor's. But now, naturally enough, the old man wants to inspect this new property. How on earth is this to be arranged? And so on, and so on.

It is all a house of cards, of course, and sooner or later it must come tumbling down. A house of cards: and a recent critical study has shown how the idea of a house is central to the theme as well as the action of this play. Tranio's young master introduces himself with a long monody in which he compares the successful, or unsuccessful, rearing of the young to the construction and proper maintenance of a house. And the image is continued through the language of the remainder of the play: for example, during the amusing tour conducted by Tranio, temporarily cast in the role of a real-estate agent, through the neighbor's house, simultaneously convincing the neighbor that the old man is simply looking for remodeling ideas and the old man that the neighbor has denied selling the house simply because he regrets the bad bargain he has made.

When the inevitable collapse occurs, the solution is deliberately and comically simple. A companion of the son's, acting as *deus ex machina*, offers to pay off the debt. This satisfies the old man, who is doubly satisfied when Tranio reminds him that he will no doubt be committing some new outrage sooner or later that will enable his master to take a double vengeance. And, under one guise or another, no doubt he will.

The Persian (*Persa*) is a puzzling play for the modern reader and critic. The difficulty does not lie in the plot, which is simple enough: a pimp is tricked into buying a freeborn girl who is offered to him for sale as a foreign captive by a "visiting Persian" (the product of a disguise provided, as the plotters admit with amusing frankness, by the stage manager). His money is lost when the girl's father, by prearrangement, comes to "rescue" her. The prime mover and beneficiary of all this is a clever slave (nothing new in that), but the slave is also a lover, and this is unparalleled in Plautine comedy.

The main difficulty lies in the character of the girl, the fictitious captive, who serves as the unwilling agent of this plot. Her services are offered to the scheming hero by her father, a parasite, in return for the promise of the usual parasite's reward. In other Plautine plays women enter into such plots with as good a will as any of the other characters, and accompany their participation with cheerful remarks to the effect that no one need give *them* lessons in wickedness. But the unnamed girl in *The Persian* is very different. She at first resists her father's suggestion as shameful and yields to it only at length, and under compulsion. As she enters in disguise, she punctuates her conversation with high-minded (and apparently sincere) statements about civic virtue. And when she finally carries off the deception, she manages to do it without actually telling a lie; in fact she makes a number of very true (though necessarily ambiguous) statements about the embarrassing situation in which she has been placed. There is a certain wry irony in all this, but it is hard to see how it could be very funny, though critics have argued that humor does arise from the enormous contrast between the girl's social position and her lofty sentiments. Skillfully playing the character as a total prig may possibly have produced successful comedy.

Modern readers may also be puzzled by the appearance of long scenes of irrelevant, almost ritualistic insults exchanged by pairs of characters at several points in the play. These appear to be relics of the *versus Fescennini*, or Fescennine verses, a form of improvised lampoon mentioned by Livy, Horace, and others as a feature of Italian popular entertainment. A possible modern parallel would be the "Arkansas Traveler" sketch that is still occasionally staged in the southern United States.

The Persian concludes with the beating and humiliation of the pimp, in a scene reminiscent of the finale of *The Braggart Warrior*. But this example is rather less successful to modern taste. The putative wickedness and folly of the pimp, unlike that of the warrior, have not been fully established dramatically, and his parting statement to the audience is much briefer and less reassuring.

During the time of Plautus, as we noted earlier, Rome and Carthage were engaged in a fight to the finish, the ancient equivalent of the two world wars. In general, the Romans' behavior during war was reasonably civilized by the standards of the day; the popular picture of them as a sort of ancient Gestapo is grossly unhistorical. But the hatreds of the Punic Wars ran very deep indeed, and in the Third Punic War, fought a generation after Plautus' death, the Romans destroyed Carthage forever, leveling the city and sowing its fields with salt. Hence, it is doubly surprising that Hanno of Carthage, an elderly wanderer who plays a vital role in *The Little Carthaginian* (*Poenulus*) is, with the special exception of Alcumena in the *Amphitryon*, the only fully sympathetic character in the whole of Plautus.

Hanno, whose reunion with his long-lost daughters caps the play, is handled with extraordinary dignity. His prayer to Jupiter as he finally sees the girls is one of the few moments in Plautus that can be called genuinely moving. As one of the other characters remarks, simply by virtue of his devotion to truth he seems to be accomplishing what usually in comedy is brought about by roguishness and deceit. And Hanno is not simply a cosmopolitan New Comedy father who happens to come from Carthage. On the contrary, in his appearance, his dress, and even his language, his Punic origin is continually stressed.

The Punic language provides some of the play's most memorable moments. Hanno's first appearance is marked by a long speech in Punic (immediately repeated in Latin), in which he announces his quest and prays to the gods for help. In the scene that follows, a roguish slave who claims to know Punic conducts a hilariously fractured conversation with the new arrival. The slave's linguistic boorishness—he seems to believe that bluff, bluster, and a vocabulary of half-a-dozen words are all one needs to deal with foreigners—is very reminiscent of the attitude of the English soldiers in Kipling's poems and tales of India. And like those soldiers, it is the slave and other characters in the play who suffer by comparison with the dignified Hanno, even (or especially) when they are mocking him with what one imagines were standard anti-Carthaginian insults. And all this, we must remember, was performed before an audience that must have consisted largely of veterans of the wars with Hannibal.

But there is much more to *The Little Carthaginian* than the scenes with Hanno. The prologue, for instance, contains the most vivid picture we possess of the Roman audience (though its references to that audience's unruliness have been taken too literally by some commentators). There is love interest, with a moonstruck adolescent (he, not Hanno, is the little Carthaginian of the title). There is a scheme featuring the aid of a group of *advocati* (hired counselors), self-consciously respectable freedmen who speak in unison and who, one imagines, march solemnly across the stage in step with one another. There are a remarkable number of amusing violations of dramatic illusion: a joke admitting that a sack of gold is really stage money, for instance, or a reminder to one character to get on with his scene, since the audience is thirsty. The unnecessary elaborations of trickery in the plot have led critics to condemn *The Little Carthaginian*, but in many ways it is one of Plautus' richest and most interesting plays.

As for the *Pseudolus* (a slave's name, accented on the first syllable), however, there is little argument: critics ancient and modern have acclaimed this play as Plautus' masterpiece. But the modern reader who expects from this judgment to find something strikingly new or different in the play will be disappointed or at least mystified. Pseudolus, as usual, is a clever slave; as usual, his master is in love; as usual, he must use his wits to free the master's girl from a pimp. Nothing new or different here. But Plautus was working in a traditional art, and a traditional artist is not judged by how far he departs from his tradition, but by how well he works within it. And in the *Pseudolus*, Plautus is working within the Roman tradition very well indeed.

The characters are raised to unprecedented heights of hilarity. Calidorus is the quintessence of the comic young man in love, wallowing deliciously in ludicrous self-pity, reveling in mock-tragic orations, doltishly infatuated with his silly girl, and above all enjoying the whole business immensely (he is the author of the great statement that it is no fun being in love unless you are foolish). Ballio the pimp is his enemy, Plautus' greatest comic villain. If in other plays Plautus can be accused of failing to give an adequate dramatic demonstration of a pimp's villainy, he certainly cannot be accused of this in the *Pseudolus*. Ballio's first appearance, in the company of the full retinue of his disreputable establishment, is one of the most remarkable achievements in the canon: an enormous, leering, snarling, growling, whipcracking monody. And Ballio's conscious, gleeful malevolence mounts in an ever-rising crescendo throughout the play, right up to the very moment of his defeat. A splendid role: it is no wonder that Roscius was famous for his enactment of it in revivals of the *Pseudolus* more than a century after Plautus' death.

Ballio meets his match in Pseudolus, the ultimate Plautine clever slave. The trick Pseudolus plays is not unusually complex or brilliant, but complex and brilliant tricks are not the true mark of a clever slave. It is a question of words rather than deeds, of attitude rather than accomplishment. Pseudolus is great because he *says* he is, and says it surpassingly well. He can run rings around the other characters with words. He can manipulate *us* as well, stopping the whole play in the midst of a monologue (for a musical interlude) simply at his whim. For the vulgar details of real action he uses others, directing, coaching, and even costuming them. As he closes the play with a comic dance and an invitation to tomorrow's performance, it is hard to resist the conclusion that this play is Plautus' statement about his own craft, and that Pseudolus is to be identified with Plautus himself.

If the *Pseudolus* is Plautus' ultimate play about the machinations of men, *The Rope* (*Rudens*) is his most attractive demonstration of the machinations of the gods—not, as with the *Amphitryon*, in the foreground and for their own dubious motives, but behind the scenes, where one feels more comfortable with them, and for altruistic purposes of justice and decency. The setting, on a lonely seacoast, the old man who inhabits it, and the storm that buffets it as the play opens, inevitably suggest a parallel to *The Tempest*, but in fact the parallel ends there. Old Daemones is hardly an all-powerful Prospero, and his Miranda, far from sharing his exile, has been lost to him for many years. Righteousness and true love are served in Plautus' play as well as Shakespeare's, but not, for the most part, through conscious human action.

The prologue is spoken by the minor divinity Arcturus (wearing a star on his forehead to assist in his identification), who assures us of the gods' close interest in human behavior, and informs us that, thanks to a storm he has stirred up, Daemones' long-lost daughter and another slave girl are being blown ashore in a lifeboat, while the rascally pimp who was sailing off to sell them in Sicily has been shipwrecked. The ensuing action is simple enough: the girls take refuge from the pursuing pimp in a nearby shrine of Venus, the gruff but kindly Daemones offering a strong secular arm to this sanctuary when needed, and finally a slave of Daemones' finds the shipwrecked pimp's treasure chest, which contains the tokens necessary to unite father and daughter, and daughter with the lover who has come in search of her. (A little incongruously, the rope with which the chest is dragged onto the stage gives the play its name.)

Despite the simplicity of its action, *The Rope* is one of Plautus' longest plays, enabling us to savor at leisure not only the ironies of the basic situation but also a number of memorable vignettes: a grouchy slave's detailed complaints about the damage done by the storm, a lively eyewitness description of the girls' final dash to shore, a choral song by a group of fishermen on the subject of their hard life (included for atmosphere only; it serves no purpose in the plot), the hilariously lugubrious entrance of the pimp and his henchman, soaking wet, teeth chattering, each blaming the other for the disaster, and a splendid, elaborate aria by the slave who has discovered the chest, who builds verbal castles in the air (including a city named after himself) as he imagines—vainly, as it happens—all the wonders this untold wealth will bring him. And through all this, in conscious and unconscious words and actions, we are constantly and artfully being reminded that the Venus whose shrine shares the stage with the house of Daemones knows how to take care of her own, so that it is easy to agree with a recent study in which it is suggested that *The Rope* is a kind of reenactment in high comedy of the goddess' mythic birth from the foam. As old Daemones says at one point while recounting a dream, "The gods produce plays for us humans in wondrous ways."

The *Stichus* (a slave name) is perhaps the most puzzling piece of work in the whole Plautine canon. While a number of other plays are constructed loosely enough, this one seems to make a deliberate mockery of the whole idea of construction. It falls into three almost absolutely distinct parts; the conflicts established in each are left unresolved. The play has a beginning, but not much of a middle, and certainly nothing that Aristotle would have called an end. The firmly established fact that the author of the Greek model was the workmanlike Menander only deepens the mystery.

In the first part of the *Stichus* a father threatens to make new marriages for his two daughters, since their husbands have been absent and unheard from for three years. In the second part the husbands return, but the conflict with their father-in-law is almost totally ignored; instead, most of this segment is devoted to the discomfiture and rejection of a parasite who had hoped to get a free meal out of the family reunion. The third part consists entirely of a party celebrated by the two slaves of the returning brothers and their mutual girlfriend.

Ironically, we have a greater amount of reliable external information about the *Stichus* than about any other Plautine play, but even this information raises as many questions as it answers. For instance, we know that the famous Pellio acted in this play—but in what role? Was he the unhappy parasite, with his Chaplinesque pathos? Or did he play the carousing, singing, and dancing slave Stichus? If the latter, this odd play may have been specially created as a vehicle for Pellio's musical talents; if the former, we might conclude that Pellio was particularly adept at the parasite role, and that a good actor could do things with this stock character that are not immediately apparent to us from the bare script (which, in fact, makes it a little hard to understand why the character was so attractive to the Romans). We know that Marcipor, the slave of Oppius, played and presumably composed the flute music with which the *Stichus* was accompanied (and indeed, his presence is acknowledged in the play, when the celebrating slaves break what little dramatic illusion is left at that point by inviting him to take a drink). Was the availability of a first-rate musician a rare enough event to encourage a playwright to turn a comic drama into a musical revue? We know that the *Stichus* was quoted by a scholar of late antiquity under the title *Nervolaria* (the meaning of which is unexplained). Is this (a modern scholar has asked) evidence of a revision? And was the *Stichus* the revised version, or was the revision made from the *Stichus*? And by whom? Finally, we know that the *Stichus* was produced in 200 B.C. It is a tantalizing bit of knowledge, for if the date were somewhat earlier or somewhat later, we could at least make a guess at the direction Plautus' dramatic career was headed in: either toward the sort of loosely organized musical

comedy we have here, or away from it. Unfortunately, the date 200 B.C. is close enough to the dead center of Plautus' career (as far as we know) to tell us nothing whatsoever. All in all, it is hard not to emerge from the *Stichus* as frustrated as the parasite who manages to dominate, in a negative fashion, one section at least of this confusing play.

The *Three-Penny Day* (*Trinummus*, so named by a professional swindler who is paid three *nummi* to carry out an impersonation in the play) reads like a deliberate, high-minded inversion of almost all the rest of Plautine comedy, the *Mostellaria* in particular. It is as if Plautus, after so many celebrations of roguery, deceit, and barefaced impudence, has decided to give old-time morality, courtesy, generational decorum, and responsible altruism their chance at last.

Consider a few details: a young man (who, to be sure, has been a wastrel before the play opens; without this necessary precondition we would have had no plot at all) spends the whole play competing with a friend of his in lofty unselfishness. As if this were not enough, despite his earlier misdeeds he is actually longing for the return of his absent father—a sentiment shared by his slave. Meanwhile his friend and rival in nobility is treated to an endless lecture on proper behavior by his father—a lecture that he accepts without the least sign of impatience or demurral. Money is needed, not to buy a prostitute but to provide a dowry for a respectable young girl. A deception is arranged—by an *old* man, with a *young* man as intended victim. A rogue is hired for an impersonation, is decked out in the usual traveler's costume, and fails utterly—unmasked by another old man. This clever, witty, and intelligent old man is the long-absent father; after out-talking and outwitting the professional swindler, he approaches his house. A running slave appears—delivering a serious sermon on public morality. He tells the old man that the house has been sold—and it really has been. But never fear: the sale has saved the old man's fortune rather than destroying it. The joyful cast assembles; the old man's return has solved every problem. Girl gets dowry; boy gets girl; all is forgiven; and everyone lives happily ever after.

Even for the stage, it all sounds more than a little too good to be true, especially given the sort of universe Plautus has depicted in most of the rest of his work. The inversions of normal expectation are so numerous and so pat that one would like to believe the *Trinummus* is a deliberate tongue-in-cheek exercise, aimed at a sophisticated and experienced audience. It must be admitted, however, that so far the critics have taken the play at face value. Perhaps the Romans did as well.

Modern analysts seem unanimous in calling the *Truculentus* (the title comes from the name of a rustic slave who figures briefly in the action) a satiric comedy. The play certainly shares a number of the generic characteristics of Roman satire, especially its misogyny, its preoccupation with sex, and its general assumption that civilization is going to pot. It is a bleak but interesting play. Cicero's statement that the aged Plautus rejoiced in the *Truculentus* is usually taken to mean that the play can be dated toward the end of his career.

The action centers around a prostitute named Phronesium. She manages to convince her soldier-lover that a baby she has borrowed is their son, thus multiplying the soldier's already prodigal generosity toward her. It is discovered that the father is really another of Phronesium's lovers; the mother is a respectable girl; the baby is the product of yet another rape. A shotgun marriage is arranged for the more-or-less repentant young man, who, however, lets Phronesium keep the baby for a day or two while she strings the soldier along.

Such a plot summary, while true enough, gives a mistaken impression of the real effect of the *Truculentus*. The focus is not on the irony of the young father's situation, as he helps Phronesium with her scheme, unwittingly before the baby's recognition and wittingly afterward. Rather, we get an episodic and cumulative picture of an endless stream of besotted lovers—besides the young father and the soldier there is a young man from the country and his surly slave, Truculentus—being drawn again and again into the morass of Phronesium's establishment, yielding with ever-increasing generosity to her ceaseless demands for "gifts." The process is almost hypnotic, and the truth about the baby's parentage is only incidental to it. Therefore, recent scholars are agreed in rejecting an earlier suggestion that the facts about the baby were expounded in a lost portion of the play's prologue, on the ground that this information would weaken the focus of the play as we have it.

It may take rather a strong stomach to appreciate Phronesium, but she is clearly meant to be appreciated; in her own way she stands in the line of such great comic villains as Ballio of the *Pseudolus*. She shares some of the characteristics of Plautus' clever slaves as well. Like them, she must live by her wits; she has nothing to fall back upon (except a bed, of course). Like them, she takes a dramatist's delight in directing her plot; she shares her schemes with the audience; she employs the usual metaphors (military and the like) of the *servus callidus*, and at one point she even calls her trade a *quaestum callidum*. Her victims, like those of the slaves, are the rich and supposedly powerful. Her most redeeming feature, dramatically at any rate, is her infinite capacity to enjoy her own wickedness.

The twenty-first and last play in the Plautine canon is *The Tale of a Traveling Bag* (*Vidularia*). Unfortunately, because of its position at the end of the manuscripts, it has been almost completely lost—a fate with which those whose names begin with alphabetically late letters will sympathize. We seem to have lost an interesting play, something akin to *The Rope*, with a rural coastline setting rather than the usual city street. The mutilated text allows us a tantalizing glimpse of a young man-about-town who has obviously never done a stroke of honest work in his life asking a gruff farmer to take him on as a day-laborer. The farmer is lecturing him sternly on the rigors of country life as the manuscript fragments, like an ill-kept fresco, crumble away into ruins.

It will be clear from our examination that there is no such thing as a typical Plautine comedy. The twenty-one plays show great variety in plot, in purpose, and (it should be admitted) in quality. Yet different as they are, they are interdependent in a way that gives them a definite unity as a group and can lead to misunderstandings on the part of readers who confine themselves to studying one or two of them. This interdependence is the result of Plautus' conscious manipulation and suggests an attentive and sophisticated audience. For instance, we must know the characters of clever slaves like Pseudolus if we are to appreciate what Mercury is doing to poor Sosia in the *Amphitryon*, what sort of role each is playing. Knowledge of parasites is needed to explain the apparent oddities in the behavior of Curculio, and the pathos of the *Stichus*. The full originality of the *Casina* and the nihilistic cynicism of the *Truculentus* become evident only if we are aware of the norm established by such plays as *The Rope* in the matter of love and marriage. And the whole meaning of the *Trinummus* may well depend on a thorough knowledge of Plautus' methods in the rest of his work.

Plautus continually sides with the underdog—as a comic playwright almost inevitably must; we have seen in the *Amphitryon* how difficult it is to make comedy out of the operations of the powerful. And the more Plautus sides with the underdog, the greater his comic achievement; he reaches his highest peaks with his clever slaves, who weave their marvelous webs of words and wit in a genuinely heroic fashion. But none of this is really social commentary in any programmatic sense, though some scholars have tried to show that it is. The greatest moral, social, and economic weakness of ancient society was its reliance on slave labor, and Plautus is fully aware of the dangers slavery carries for the master, as well as the pain it causes the slave. But he cannot really imagine an end to the system—a weakness he shares with all his predecessors and contemporaries, including the greatest social philosophers. Nor is he really arguing for any other moral reforms. The tirades against pimps and prostitutes that pepper his plays have the air of set pieces, and probably refer more to the imaginary universe of the *comoedia palliata* than to any real conditions in Plautine Rome. And with other issues as well, such as war, male chauvinism, and the conflicts between generations and social classes, Plautus is basically inclined to take the world as it is, all the while having as much fun with it as he possibly can.

It is this lack of any programmatic message in Plautus that has led to the relatively low esteem in which he is held by modern dramatic historians, who tend to feel uncomfortable with a comic playwright who concentrates on being funny, rather than on expounding Fabian socialism or preaching an end to the Peloponnesian War. Theatergoers and readers of antiquity, including the most discriminating, had no such problem. The plays of Plautus were revived continually for many years after his death, and later, as material for reading, they were regarded almost unanimously as literary classics of the first rank, and went on being so regarded until the fall of the Roman Empire. Ancient connoisseurs of Plautus included such diverse figures as Cicero, the antiquarian Aulus Gellius, and St. Jerome. No doubt they enjoyed Plautus' characters and comic situations, but if there is one common denominator to their appreciation of him it is the almost voluptuous delight they take in his language.

With the European Renaissance there was a rebirth of interest in Plautus, as there was with so many other Latin authors. His plays were printed and produced in the original language and in translation, and soon inspired a host of imitations. These provide a veritable gold mine for modern students of comparative literature, who can match *The Two Menaechmuses* with *The Comedy of Errors*, *The Pot of Gold* with *L'Avare*, and the *Amphitryon* with the host of dramas (there are far more than thirty-eight of them) that lie between that play and Jean Giraudoux's *Amphitryon 38*, and still only scratch the surface of this subject. But concentrating exclusively on such direct comparisons is apt to be misleading, for two reasons. First, it can obscure the fact that Plautus' vitality and his ultimate value to us lie not in his influence on such amusing froth as *The Boys from Syracuse* and the novels of P. G. Wodehouse, though such influence exists and is worth studying, but in his work itself, if only we can acquire the knowledge, imagination, and good will needed to approach it in the proper spirit. Second, one-on-one comparisons with modern plays are simply not enough to do Plautus justice. There is an enormous difference between medieval drama on the one hand and Renaissance and all later European drama on the other. The first, while beautiful, impressive, and often of very high quality, is almost insurmountably foreign to us, while the second, to put the matter plainly, speaks our own language from the very beginning. A major reason for this great difference is the rediscovery and use of the Roman dramatists, and Plautus in particular. As Yeats reminds us, it was Plautus, in productions staged by the duke of Urbino, who set the pace for Italian comedy—and the same thing happened all over Europe. Or, as an anonymous modern tag has it (and our playwright would have appreciated its form as well as its sentiment),

> Plautus
> Taught us

If we let him, he can continue to do so.

Selected Bibliography

TEXTS

Plauti Comoediae, edited by F. Leo. 2 vols. Berlin, 1895–1896.
Plauto, le commedie, edited by G. Augello. 3 vols. Turin, 1968–1972.
T. Macci Plauti Comoediae, edited by W. M. Lind-say. 2 vols. 2nd ed. Oxford, 1910. Oxford Classical Text; generally regarded as the standard.

TRANSLATIONS

Bovie, P., ed. *Five Roman Comedies*. New York, 1970. Includes *Amphitruo*, *Mostellaria*, and *Poenulus*.
Casson, L. *Six Plays of Plautus*. Garden City, N.Y., 1963. Includes *Amphitruo*, *Aulularia*, *Casina*, *Menaechmi*, *Pseudolus*, and *Rudens*.
Copley, F. O., and Moses Hadas, trs. *Roman Drama*. Indianapolis, 1965. Includes *Menaechmi*, *Mostellaria*, and *Rudens*.
Duckworth, G. E., ed. *The Complete Roman Drama*. 2 vols. New York, 1942. Includes the complete works in vol.1 and in vol.2, pp.1–135.
Nixon, P., tr. *Plautus*. 5 vols. Cambridge, Mass., and London, 1916–1938. Includes the complete works, with Leo's Latin text printed on facing pages. Most of the quotations used in the essay are taken from this edition, which is the nearest thing to a standard English text in existence.
Roche, P., tr. *Three Plays by Plautus: Amphitryon, Major Bullshot-Gorgeous, The Prisoners*. New York, 1968.
Segal, E., tr. *Plautus; Three Comedies*. New York, 1969. Includes *Menaechmi*, *Miles Gloriosus*, and *Mostellaria*.
Watling, E. F., tr. *The Rope and Other Plays*. Baltimore, 1964. Includes *Amphitryon*, *Mostellaria*, *Rudens*, and *Trinummus*.
———.*The Pot of Gold and Other Plays*. Baltimore, 1965. Includes *Aulularia*, *Captivi*, *Menaechmi*, *Miles Gloriosus*, and *Pseudolus*.

GENERAL BACKGROUND STUDIES

Beare, W. *The Roman Stage*. 3rd rev. ed. London, 1963.
Dorey, T. A., and D. R. Dudley, eds. *Roman Drama*. London, 1965.
Duckworth, G. E. *The Nature of Roman Comedy: A Study in Popular Entertainment*. Princeton, 1952. Reprinted often.
Fraenkel, Eduard. *Plautinisches im Plautus*. Not available in English. The Italian translation by Franco Munari, *Elementi plautini in Plauto* (Florence, 1960), is now the standard edition.
Segal, Erich. *Roman Laughter: The Comedy of Plautus*. Cambridge, Mass., 1968.

Wright, John. *Dancing in Chains: The Stylistic Unity of the Comoedia Palliata.* Rome, 1974.

CRITICAL STUDIES

AMPHITRUO

Fantham, E. "Towards a Dramatic Reconstruction of the Fourth Act of Plautus' *Amphitruo.*" *Philologus* 117: 197–214 (1973).

Forehand, W. E. "Irony in Plautus' *Amphitruo.*" *American Journal of Philology* 92: 633–651 (1971).

Galinsky, C. K. "Scipionic Themes in Plautus' *Amphitruo.*" *Transactions of the American Philological Association* 97: 203–235 (1966).

ASINARIA

Konstan, D. "Plot and Theme in Plautus' *Asinaria.*" *Classical Journal* 73: 215–221 (1978).

AULULARIA

Konstan, D. "The Social Themes in Plautus' *Aulularia.*" *Arethusa* 10: 307–320 (1977).

BACCHIDES

Clark, J. R. "Structure and Symmetry in the *Bacchides* of Plautus." *Transactions of the American Philological Association* 106: 85–96 (1976).

CAPTIVI

Konstan, D. "Plautus' *Captivi* and the Ideology of the Ancient City-State." *Ramus* 5: 76–91 (1976).

Leach, E. W. "Ergasilus and the Ironies of the *Captivi.*" *Classica et Mediavalia* 30: 145–168 (1969).

CASINA

Forehand, W. E. "Plautus' *Casina*: An Explication." *Arethusa* 6: 233–256 (1973).

MacCary, W. T. "Patterns of Myth, Ritual, and Comedy in Plautus' *Casina.*" *Texas Studies in Language and Literature* 15: 881–889 (1974).

EPIDICUS

Goldberg, S. M. "Plautus' *Epidicus* and the Case of the Missing Original." *Transactions of the American Philological Association* 108: 81–91 (1978).

MENAECHMI

Leach, E. W. "Meam quom formam noscito: Language and Characterization in the *Menaechmi.*" *Arethusa* 2: 30–45 (1969).

Segal, Erich. "The *Menaechmi*: Roman Comedy of Errors." *Yale Classical Studies* 21: 75–93 (1969).

MILES GLORIOSUS

Cleary, V. J. "Se sectari simiam: Monkey Business in the *Miles Gloriosus.*" *Classical Journal* 67: 299–305 (1972).

MOSTELLARIA

Leach, E. W. "De exemplo meo ipse aedificato: An Organizing Idea in the *Mostellaria.*" *Hermes* 97: 318–332 (1969).

PSEUDOLUS

Wright, John. "The Transformation of Pseudolus." *Transactions of the American Philological Association* 105: 402–416 (1975).

RUDENS

Leach, E. W. "Plautus' *Rudens*: Venus Born from a Shell." *Texas Studies in Language and Literature* 15: 915–931 (1974).

STICHUS

Arnott, W. G. "Targets, Techniques, and Tradition in Plautus' *Stichus.*" *Bulletin of the Institute of Classical Studies* 19: 54–79 (1972).

TRINUMMUS

Segal, Erich. "The Purpose of the *Trinummus.*" *American Journal of Philology* 95: 252–264 (1974).

Stein, J. P. "Morality in Plautus' *Trinummus.*" *Classical Bulletin* 47: 7–13 (1970).

TRUCULENTUS

Dessen, C. S. "Plautus' Satiric Comedy, the *Truculentus.*" *Philological Quarterly* 56: 145–168 (1977).

BIBLIOGRAPHIES

Arnott, W. B. *Menander, Plautus, and Terence.* Greece and Rome, New Surveys in the Classics 9. Oxford, 1975.

Hanson, J. A. "Scholarship on Plautus since 1950." *Classical World* 59: 103–107, 126–129 (1965); 141–148 (1966).

Hughes, J. D. *A Bibliography of Scholarship on Plautus.* Amsterdam, 1975.

Segal, Erich. "Scholarship on Plautus 1965–1976." *Classical World* 74: 353–433 (1981).

JOHN WRIGHT

POLYBIUS

(205?–125? B.C.)

POLYBIUS BEGINS WITH the assumption that there can be no one of any worth who would not wish to know "how, and by a state with what sort of constitution, almost the whole of the known world was conquered and fell under the single rule of the Romans in a space of not quite fifty-three years" (*Histories* 1.1.5). The time in question runs from the 140th Olympiad (220–219 B.C.) to the Roman settlement of Greece in 167 B.C. that abolished the kingdom of Macedonia. This last event marked for him the final point in the expansion of Roman rule. What he saw in the years following led him to extend his work, both in time and in depth. Conquest (or defeat) was not the end pure and simple. There were lessons to be learned from the behavior of conquerors and conquered (or, rulers and ruled, as they were then) alike. Hence, the decision to continue past 167 B.C. and to give an account of

> the subsequent policy of the conquerors and their method of universal rule, as well as of the various opinions and appreciations of the rulers entertained by others. And I must also describe what were the prevailing and dominant tendencies and ambitions of the various peoples in their public and private life.
>
> (3.4.6)

The ultimate reason for this decision:

> For it is evident that contemporaries will be able to see from these things whether the dominion of the Romans is an evil or, on the contrary, a good, and future generations whether their rule should be considered to be worthy of praise and emulation or rather of censure.
>
> (3.4.7)

In this Polybius sees "the usefulness" of his *Histories* (3.4.8), and he is surely right. The approach is new and important. Judgment about empire is to be based upon evidence about its effect upon rulers and ruled. It is for the historian to provide this evidence. The material will come from the years down to the time of "troubled confusion and movement" (3.4.12), which began in the 150's B.C. and continued to the destruction of Carthage and Corinth in 146 B.C. and the immediate aftermath. This he treats as a separate period: "About the time of trouble, owing to the importance of the actions and the unexpected character of the events, and chiefly because I not only witnessed most of them but even directed some, I was induced to write, making as it were a new beginning" (3.4.13). The reasons he gives for these enlargements of his work and his theme should be taken at face value. When did he take the decisions to add these two dimensions, and how far had he written when he did so? The events of 146 B.C. clearly prompted the final extension. How long before this (if at all) he decided to treat the period of Roman rule per se is bound to remain a matter of debate, but it is most likely a separate question. By 146 B.C., at any rate, he had probably written the first fifteen books, down to the end of the Hannibalic war.

Birth and subsequent fortune placed Polybius exceptionally well for his task. His father, Lycortas of Megalopolis, was a leading figure in the Achaean League, especially in the 180's B.C., and, along with Philopoemen, one of the architects of the doomed Achaean attempt to treat with Rome on a basis of equality during those years. Polybius himself was to have gone on an Achaean embassy to Alexandria in 181–180. (The mission did not happen owing to the death of Ptolemy V just then.) Polybius was in his twenties at the time. In 170–169, during the Roman war against Perseus, he held the second-highest magistracy of the Achaean League, the hipparchy. In 167, he was one of the thousand Achaeans deported to Italy after the Roman victory over Perseus at Pydna in the previous year. The following sixteen years he spent mostly in Rome and in the company of L. Paullus' grandsons, Q. Fabius Maximus Aemilianus and P. Cornelius Scipio Aemilianus. His friendship with the latter was particularly close. After his captivity ended in 151 he traveled extensively but the connection with Scipio and, more important, that with Rome, endured. He was with Scipio when Carthage was burned and razed, and perhaps with him later at Numantia; and he helped in no small way to usher in the Roman settlement imposed upon Greece after the Achaean war. He is said to have died after falling from a horse at the age of eighty-two. It is not impossible.

As finally conceived and written by Polybius, the *Histories* ran to forty books. The narrative proper begins in book 3 with the start of the 140th Olympiad (220–219 B.C.) and the outbreak of the Hannibalic war, and extends to a total of thirty-four books. Books 1 and 2 look back from the starting point and provide what Polybius saw as a necessary background:

> As neither the former power nor the early history of Rome and Carthage is familiar to most Greeks, I thought it necessary to prefix this book and the next to the actual History, in order that no one after becoming engrossed in the narrative proper may find himself at a loss, and ask by what counsel and trusting to what power and resources the Romans embarked on that enterprise which has made them rulers over land and sea in our part of the world; but that from these books and the preliminary sketch in them it may be clear to readers that they had quite adequate grounds for conceiving the aim of universal rule and dominion and adequate means for achieving their purpose.
>
> (1.3.8–10)

Book 3 itself follows the Hannibalic war down to the battle of Cannae (216 B.C.). Books 4 and 5 treat separately of the contemporary history of Greece and Asia to just beyond the Peace of Naupactus (217 B.C.), which at once brought an end to the Social War in Greece and marked the entwining of the theretofore separate histories of west and east (see below). There follows at this point book 6, Polybius' account of the Roman constitution (including Roman military arrangements), so instrumental in facilitating Rome's recovery from disaster and in enabling the Romans to form and to carry out their project of universal domination. Books 7–11 contain the decade after Cannae (216–215 B.C. to 207–206 B.C.), the period of Philip V of Macedon's involvement in Rome's war with Carthage. Book 12 comprises Polybius' treatment of the Sicilian historian Timaeus of Tauromenium, an extended series of more or less violent attacks upon Timaeus and corresponding statements by Polybius about who ought to write history and how he ought to go about doing it. Continuous narrative of the next fifty-four years (206–205 B.C. to 153–152 B.C.) occupies twenty-one more books. This is the period of the Roman conquest and of Roman rule in a more or less stable world. Book 34 is devoted to geography and provides a break before the account of the time of trouble (152–151 B.C. to 146–145 B.C., books 35 to 39). Book 40 seems to have contained a kind of chronological summary and index of the whole work.

By no means all of it is extant. Books 1–5 remain intact. After that it is a matter of excerpts and quotations by other writers. The "Excerpta Antiqua" are a continuous abridgment of books 1–18 and provide the majority of what remains of books 6 to 18. With book 7 the slightly later "Constantinian excerpts" (a collection of excerpts, under various headings and from many Greek historians along with Polybius, made for the emperor Constantine VII Porphyrogenitus in the tenth century A.D.) begin to be important. Some Polybius is preserved under the titles (themselves not completely preserved) "de virtutibus et vitiis" (124 excerpts from books 2–39, about 130 pages); "de sententiis" (166 excerpts from books 1–39, some 120 pages); "de legationibus gentium ad Romanos" (119 excerpts from books 18–36, about 135 pages); "de legationibus Romanorum ad gentes" (35 excerpts from books 1–38, about 45 pages); "de insidiis" (one three-page excerpt from book 15). By contrast with the "Excerpta Antiqua," these excerpts (which are of widely varying length) do not constitute any sort of abridgment but are kept as quite separate passages, and the excerptor's hand can often be detected in awkward, and sometimes quite misleading, attempts to provide summary contexts at the beginning of an excerpt. Within each set, the passages have been copied out in the order in which the excerptor found them in the text before him, but the arrangement of the lot into one continuous set (there are some overlaps but not many)—representing part of the text of books 7 to 18 and virtually the whole of it after that—is a different matter. The task may now be said to be about complete. The arrangement put forward by F. W. Walbank (*Historical Commentary*, vol. 3, pp. 1–62) makes almost all the adjustments that need to be made to T. Buettner-Wobst's text for the Teubner edition, which itself was a great improvement in this respect upon the earlier text of F. Hultsch. In all of this it must be remembered that each of the excerptors was looking for, and copying out, only certain kinds of passages, and it must be added that they certainly did not register all the passages relevant to their themes. From five books there are no excerpts at all (17, 19, 26, 37, 40), and these must be assumed to

have been lost before the excerpts were made. A few quotations from 19, 26, and 37 are found in other authors; 17 and 40 have perished without trace. The geographical book 34 was most referred to, especially by the ancient geographer Strabo, and some twenty-five pages of citation or paraphrase from it have been assembled.

What has made it possible not only to reconstruct the skeleton of the *Histories* but also to replace accurately what of the flesh has survived is precisely the careful and consistent arrangement of the work that Polybius reckoned would enable readers of the whole to come to terms with it. Previous writers had arranged disparate material by subject matter or had adopted a chronological framework based upon the Olympiad. Polybius, having to fashion into a single story events spread over three-quarters of a century and the whole of the Mediterranean world, combined the two in an original and perfectly fitting way. Vertically, the arrangement is by Olympiads, each Olympiad containing four years that could be numbered (compare, for example, 23.1.1, beginning the account of the 149th Olympiad: "In the 149th Olympiad . . ." and 23.9.1, beginning the account of the next year: "In the second year . . ."). Polybius' Olympiad years are not meant to be rigid or formally correct, running from midsummer to midsummer, but are cut to fit the course of events. They generally begin and end in the autumn, with the close of the campaigning season, but this rough limit could be, and was, stopped short of or run over if the events being narrated required. Within the year he offers more precision by reference to the various stages of spring, summer, and winter, which are to be taken as based quite precisely upon astronomical phenomena. Thus, for Polybius, the beginning of spring is closely associated with the vernal equinox, that of summer with the heliacal rising of the Pleiades (about 20 May then), that of winter with their cosmical setting (about 7 November). The most common arrangement was for a single book to contain half an Olympiad, two years. This is the way with fourteen books: 7–11 (Olympiad 141.1–143.2); 13 (Olympiad 143.3–4); 16–18 (Olympiad 144.3–145.4); 23 (Olympiad 149.1–2); 24 (Olympiad 149.3–4); 27 (Olympiad 152.1–2); 35 (Olympiad 157.1–2); 36 (Olympiad 157.3–4). But this arrangement also was varied to suit the importance of the events and the amount of material available. Thus, eight books contain the events of a single year: 14 (Olympiad 144.1); 15 (Olympiad 144.2); 20 (Olympiad 147.1); 28 (Olympiad 152.3); 29 (Olympiad 152.4); 37–39 (Olympiad 158.1,2,3). Apart from the special case of books 3–5, eight contain the events of an entire Olympiad: 19 (Olympiad 146); 22 (Olympiad 148); 25 (Olympiad 150); 26 (Olympiad 151); 30–33 (Olympiad 153, 154, 155, 156). Only book 21 contains the events of three years (Olympiad 147.2–4), and no book begins other than at the beginning of an Olympiad year.

Horizontally, the guide is provided by Polybius' adoption of a geographical framework. Within each year, there is a fixed progression from west to east: first, the events in Italy (with Sicily, Spain, and Africa), then Greece and Macedonia, then Asia, then Egypt. Demands of subject matter could occasion departure from this schedule; such departure required announcement and explanation (15.24a and 25.19; 32.11.2), and so at least once did its maintenance (38.5). The framework could give rise to oddities, such as reporting the arrival of an embassy at Rome before its dispatch from Rhodes, as happens in book 28, and upon which Polybius himself comments:

> I have already reported in the section dealing with Italian affairs their speech to the Senate and the answer they received from it; and how after the kindest possible reception they returned. As regards this matter it serves some purpose to remind my readers frequently, as indeed I attempt to do, that I am often compelled to report the interviews and proceedings of embassies before announcing the circumstances of their appointment and dispatch. For as, in narrating in their proper order the events of each year, I attempt to comprise under a separate heading the events that

happened among each people in that year, it is evident that this must sometimes occur in my work.

> (28.16.9–11)

To judge from his remark here, this problem must have arisen often, and, given the fragmentary state of the later books, it is a point to bear in mind. But such occasional oddities are, as Polybius recognized, a small price to pay for keeping the parallel status of events spread over a wide area in constant focus. It is not a history of Rome that he was writing, but an account, first, of the process whereby the Mediterranean world came to be conquered by Rome and, then, how its several peoples (including the Romans) fared during the time of Roman rule. The Italian section of each year necessarily precedes the others, but, equally necessarily, it does not stand alone.

In this respect, the arrangement of the narrative reflects Polybius' conception of the essential unity of his subject. This unity, the interconnection of events east and west, had a fixed beginning, the peace conference at Naupactus in the late summer of 217 B.C.

> It was this time and this conference that first connected the affairs of Greece, of Italy, and of Africa with one another. From this point both Philip and the leading statesmen in Greece ceased to make wars, truces and treaties with one another in the light of events in Greece alone, but fixed their attention upon the issues in Italy. And very soon the same thing happened with the islanders and the inhabitants of Asia Minor. Those who were displeased with Philip, and some of the opponents of King Attalus of Pergamum no longer turned towards the south and east, to Antiochus and Ptolemy, but henceforward looked to the west, some sending embassies to Carthage and some to Rome. Likewise the Romans sent embassies to the Greeks, since they were disturbed by the audacious nature of Philip's policy and wished to guard themselves against an attack by him now that they were in difficulties.

> (5.105.4–8)

Polybius thus reckons to have shown "how and why Greek affairs became involved with those of Italy and Africa" (5.105.9) and in the remainder of book 5 takes his narrative of Greek history down to Hannibal's victory at Cannae. Prior to this unification a different approach had been required:

> But in order that my narrative may be easy to follow and lucid, I think it most essential as regards this Olympiad (the 140th) not to interweave the events with one another, but to keep them as separate and distinct as possible until upon reaching the next and following Olympiads I can begin to narrate the events year by year and in parallel.
>
> (5.31.4–5)

The events of Greece and the east are accordingly narrated quite separately in books 4 and 5, but all are located within their Olympiad year and are, moreover, kept within sight of one another by the occasional synchronizing of important points in the history of Greece, Asia, and the west (compare 5.31.3). It is a question whether the turning point was as complete or as radical as Polybius portrays it, whether Agelaus' "clouds from the west" speech (5.104) so altered men's thinking in the course of a day, whether the news of the Roman defeat at Lake Trasimene and what Demetrius of Pharos whispered about Italy in Philip's ear (5.101) so changed the direction of that king's policy. The last is hardly defensible even on chronological grounds, and the embassies to Rome and Carthage of which Polybius speaks are met only much later, if at all. But Philip did begin to treat with Hannibal on the morrow of Cannae, and the Romans did respond. This linked the affairs of Rome and the west with the already intertwined ones of Greece, Asia, and Egypt. One might wish to see an inextricable connection between Italian and Greek events going back to the first Illyrian war (or indeed a good deal further). Polybius might in turn have argued that only in 217–216 B.C. did the royal house of Macedon become directly involved with Roman affairs. There is, at least, no question that from 216–215 B.C. and the beginning of book 7 the story is a single one and Polybius' synoptic approach is admirably suited to its telling.

In the course of Polybius' enumeration of Timaeus' defects as a historian we learn something of what he thought a historian ought to be and do. Plato said that human affairs would go well when philosophers became kings or kings took up the study of philosophy. So, for Polybius, history will be well written either when "men of affairs" write history (in a serious and concentrated way) or when those who would write it regard training in actual affairs as an indispensable basis from which to proceed (12.28.1–4). Such background is necessary, but by no means sufficient. "Pragmatic" history (the account of these "actual affairs" that maintains, as will be seen, its focus upon the need for explanation) has three parts (12.25e.1). The first involves "the diligent study of memoirs and documents and the collation of the material in them"; the second, "the survey of cities, locales, rivers, harbors, and in general all the special features of land and sea and the distances from one place to another"; the third concerns "political actions." It is clear that what Polybius has in mind is contemporary, or what might better be called "accessible" history. This he reckons to be the only kind that can be written with confidence, and it is certainly what he sees himself doing in his narrative proper. He considers his chosen starting point appropriate both because it was about then that the memoirs of the Achaean statesman Aratus finished and

> because the period following upon this and included in my History coincides with my own and the preceding generation, so that I have been present at some of the events and have the evidence of eyewitnesses for others. It seemed to me indeed that if I comprised events of an earlier date, repeating mere hearsay evidence, I should be safe neither in my judgments nor in my assertions.
>
> (4.2.2–3)

Thus books 1 and 2 are background, preparatory material attached "before the History" (1.3.8), and not part of the history itself. Thus also the third part of pragmatic history becomes its distinguishing and most essential element.

Inquiries from books require only leisure and access to a library or a city rich in documents. "Personal inquiry [the critical examination of witnesses], on the contrary, requires great hardship and expense, but it is of great importance and is the greatest part of history" (12.27.6). Polybius knew the value of homework; he had read extensively both inside and outside his own period (as the range of the discussion in book 12 and stray references throughout the history show), and he was no stranger to the use of documents (see especially 3.22–26 on the early treaties between Rome and Carthage). But for him, only direct personal acquaintance or painstaking questioning of those who have it can provide the historian with the requisite knowledge of the actual affairs, the events or actions that are the basis of his account. These include not only what the characters did but also what they said; speeches are reckoned as much political actions as deeds. In 12.25b the immediate emphasis is upon speeches, but he is evidently talking about facts of both kinds:

> The peculiar function of history is to discover, in the first place, the words actually spoken, whatever they were, and next to ascertain the reason why what was done or spoken led to failure or success. For the mere statement of a fact may interest us; but when the reason is added, the study of history becomes fruitful. For it is the mental transference of similar circumstances to our own times that gives us the means of forming presentiments about what is going to happen, and enables us at certain times to take precautions and at others by reproducing former conditions to face with more confidence the difficulties that menace us. But a writer who passes over in silence the speeches made and the reason for what actually happened and in their place introduces false rhetorical exercises and discursive speeches destroys the peculiar characteristic of history.

Here, of course, as indeed in so much else, he is with Thucydides in seeing the need to make what was said the subject of the same kind of rigorous inquiry as what was done. Yet he also goes beyond Thucydides in his insistence that it

is the element of explanation that gives historical work its value. Accuracy and clarity are necessary, but not sufficient. To these must be added the reason for what happened.

The importance Polybius attaches to this element is explicit here but could have been guessed from the care and emphasis with which he explains his view of historical causation early in book 3. After taking to task those who fail to distinguish between the beginning of something and the reason for it, he states his own position:

> I maintain that the beginnings of anything are the first attempts and actions of those who have already taken decisions, but that the reasons are what lead up to the decisions and judgments; I refer here to ideas and states of mind and reckonings about these and the things through which we come to take decisions and form projects.
>
> (3.6.7)

A more precise statement on the subject will not be found among ancient writers, but the principle behind it is not novel. For Polybius, as for Thucydides and Herodotus alike, to explain why something happened is to explain why someone did something. To explain the outbreak of a war is to explain why someone made the first move in it. Such explanations are inevitably always personal at base, and founded upon judgment as to essentially individual motives. So for Croesus deciding to invade Cappadocia, so for Darius and then Xerxes deciding to launch campaigns against Greece. So, more subtly, for the Spartans initiating the Peloponnesian War. The basically individual motive, fear, is there, but the fear is occasioned by Athenian growth. Polybius maintains the Thucydidean subtlety—the focus on the effect of someone's action upon someone else—and includes in the causal nexus all that leads to decisions to act. It is worth stressing that it is exactly this subtlety that makes it clear that neither writer can be seen as attempting to assign responsibility for, say, the start of a war, at least not when (as seems always to be the case) actions of each side are involved in the chain of explanation.

Polybius' account of the outbreak of the Hannibalic war illustrates his principles. For some, Hannibal's attack on Saguntum and his crossing of the Ebro River were the reasons for the war. Polybius reckons these events, correctly, as its beginnings (3.6.1–3). The reasons are further to seek. First (in chronological order), the wrath of Hamilcar Barca, arising from the fact that, undefeated, he had had to yield to circumstances; second and most important, the seizure by the Romans of Sardinia and concurrent increase of the indemnity at a time when the Carthaginians were powerless to resist; third, the success of the Carthaginians in Spain and the confidence it inspired in them (3.9.6–10.6). All of these factors operated upon the Carthaginians in general, and upon Hannibal in particular. The first act in the war (the beginning) was on their side, but, for Polybius, there is no value in knowing that, without the addition of the explanation of why they acted as they did.

> So, if one posits the destruction as the reason for the war, it must be granted that the Carthaginians began the war unjustly, both in view of the treaty of Lutatius, according to which the allies of each were to have security from attack by the other, and also in view of the agreement with Hasdrubal, according to which the Carthaginians were not to cross the Ebro River for purpose of war. But if [one posits as the reason for the war] the seizure of Sardinia and the accompanying money, it must certainly be agreed that the Carthaginians fought the Hannibalic war with good reason: for, after yielding to circumstances, they defended themselves when they could against those who harmed them.
>
> (3.30.3–4)

It is only for the Hannibalic war that Polybius' explanation of the reasons survives, but from it one can see how the system worked. It was a great war of conquest for the Romans, but they did not start it. That said, Roman actions must, on Polybius' account, be seen as instrumental in bringing it about. In those cases where Polybius' explanation is not preserved, the same approach should be used. The chief reason for the war between the Romans and Antiochus III is the anger of the Aetolians (3.7.1–2; compare 3.3.4). But this arises from their feeling of having been slighted by the Romans in many respects having to do with the end of the war against Philip (3.7.2), and it is (or will have been) this process that is important in the explanation. Similarly, Philip V is seen as having planned the war against Rome that Perseus undertook as his executor (22.18.10). What matters is how and why he came to this decision, and there is enough left of book 22 to show that the process was essentially a reaction against Roman behavior toward him (see 22.13–14 and 18, with 22.1.5), in much the same way as the Carthaginians are reckoned by Polybius as having reacted to Roman behavior toward them. Something will be said below about the Dalmatian war of 156 B.C., but there is a point to be made here about the "second" Macedonian war. There is, notoriously, no trace of a discussion of the reasons for this war. Indeed, had there been such a discussion, it would have been referred to at 3.3.2, but there Polybius looks forward to relating "the naval battles of Attalus and the Rhodians against Philip, also the war of the Romans and Philip: how it was fought, who were the persons engaged, and what its end was." There was no separate treatment of its reasons. There was no need for one, for the war against Philip "took its origins from the war against Hannibal" (3.32.7). Evidently, there was for Polybius only one war with Philip. Rome's conflict with him was seen as a single affair beginning with Philip's intervention in the Hannibalic war.

The reasons and the explanations are, then, of paramount importance throughout. Like Herodotus before him, Polybius was alive to coincidences and capable of being struck by them. And like Herodotus he was not unwilling, in connection with them, to see something suprahuman at work in the universe; for Polybius it takes the form of Fortune, *Tyche* (compare, for example, 1.4, 29.19, 38.18). But Polybius was even more reluctant to attribute any kind of agency to the supernatural, and expressly so. He devotes a chapter (17) of book 36 to the question of what sort of events do not admit of rational explanation. Very few are like this. And with the exception of the Macedonian support for the pretender Andriscus in 149–148 B.C., inspired by "a kind of heaven-sent madness" (36.17.15; compare 28.9.4 for the notion), none of the events with which Polybius concerns himself falls into this category.

At the beginning of the history Polybius' question was "how, and by a state with what sort of constitution, almost the whole of the known world was conquered and fell under the single rule of the Romans." A good part of the answer to the question "How?" lay in Polybius' treatments of the outbreaks of the wars of conquest, the Hannibalic war, and the wars with Philip, Antiochus, and Perseus. Another factor informs most of the period, namely what Polybius saw as Rome's desire for world rule, Rome's "universal aim" (see 1.3.6 and 3.2.6 for this expression). It was not there from the beginning, but developed. In quite the same way that success led to a widening of Roman aims in the first war with Carthage (1.20.1–3) and in the struggles against the Gauls in the 220's B.C. (2.31.8), success against Carthage in the Hannibalic war led to an ultimate widening. "Thus and then [with the victory over Carthage] for the first time were the Romans emboldened to reach out their hands for the rest and to cross with forces into Greece and the regions of Asia" (1.3.6). What this "universal aim" led to was "universal rule and dominion" (1.3.10). This was what the Romans sought, and it receives definition in Polybius' account in terms of its practical content. A summary statement in the introduction to book 3 provides the key:

The fifty-three-year period came to an end with these events [that is, in 168–167 B.C.], and the increase and extension of the Romans' dominion was completed. And it seemed to be agreed universally as a matter of strict necessity that what remained was to harken to the Romans and to obey their orders.

(3.4.2–3)

Orders on the one side and on the other obedience. Rome's universal dominion meant that everyone must in practice obey Roman orders. The "universal aim" of Romans is accordingly their intention to bring this state of affairs about. This is the story told by their actions. In 200 B.C., Philip V is required to obey Roman orders or face war with them (16.27.2–3; 16.34.4). Orders are given to Antiochus at Lysimachia in 196 (18.47.1, and so on), and the list goes on and on, taking in the great—Philip again, and Perseus—and the less great—for example, the Boeotian and Achaean Leagues—alike. The Dalmatian war of 156 is indicative. On the outbreak of that war Polybius, in Rome when it was declared, offers the following comment:

Therefore they planned, by initiating a war against the aforementioned people [the Dalmatians] both to renew, as it were, the drive and zeal of their own masses, and, by terrifying the Illyrians, to compel them to obey their orders. These, then, were the reasons on account of which the Romans made war on the Dalmatians; to the outside world they proclaimed that they had decided to go to war on account of the insult to the ambassadors.

(32.13.8–9)

Polybius' remarks here also point us in the direction of another aspect of his answer to the question "How?" particularly as that appears in 3.3.9. There, after a summary of the main events of the Roman conquest of the east, he states that "all the above events will enable us to perceive how the Romans managed individual affairs in making the whole world subject to themselves." The Dalmatian war occurs after the completion of the extension of Roman rule, but the idea of putting about a special version of things for the consumption of the "outside world" is of wider applicability and can be generalized. And it is what Polybius says of the decision to make war on Carthage for the last time that requires one thus to generalize:

> This decision had long ago been ratified in their individual minds, but they were looking for a suitable occasion and a pretext that would seem respectable to the outside world. The Romans were wont to pay much attention to this matter. And in doing so they displayed very good sense, for, as Demetrius [of Phalerum] says, if the inception of a war seems just, it renders victories greater and ill successes less dangerous, but if it seems to be dishonorable or base, it has the opposite effect. So on this occasion too they differed with one another about the opinion of the outside world and almost abandoned the war.
>
> (36.2)

The Carthaginians, of course, behaved conveniently in the end. Number 99 among the fragments of Polybius is of uncertain attribution. If the words are his, they join the above passages in offering a nice comment on the practical side of the "just" (or "defensive") war:

> For the Romans took no ordinary forethought not to appear to be the initiators of unjust actions and not to appear to be attacking those around them when they took on wars, but always to seem to be acting in self-defense and to enter upon wars out of necessity.

All this bears upon one aspect of Roman management of individual affairs. Another one, by no means unrelated, is illuminated by Polybius' comment on Rome's handling of the Egyptian question in the 160's B.C. The aim: to keep the place weak; the method: to keep the contending parties at odds with one another; the device: to assent to whichever of the opposing claims suited themselves in their aim. Polybius again generalizes in his comment:

> Measures of this kind are frequent among the Romans. Using the ignorance of those around them they extend and solidify their own rule in a practical way, at the same time doing a favor and ap-

pearing to confer a benefit upon those who are in the wrong.

> (31.10.7)

The reference in this to the "extension" of Roman rule, a process complete by 167 B.C., guarantees its applicability to the period of conquest. Even if we detect a wry smile as he thought of how the Romans over the years gratified Spartan or Messenian claims against the Achaean League, no criticism is evident here. The emphasis is upon the "practical"—"pragmatic" is the word. Throughout, Roman actions are carefully fitted to the general aim. This is how they handled individual affairs, and this is how they made the whole world subject to themselves, subject, that is, to Roman orders. At least it is as much as remains in what is left of the text of Polybius about how they did it.

Along with the question "How?" went another: "With what sort of constitution?" For Polybius this was not a separate question. The constitution is intimately bound up not only with recovery after Cannae, but with the conquest itself, as his announcement that he will devote an entire book to it indicates:

> Halting the narrative at this point [namely, at the end of book 5] we shall draw up our account of the Roman constitution, as a direct sequel to which we shall point out that the singular nature of the constitution contributed not only very greatly to their reacquisition of mastery over the Italians and Sicilians, and to their attainment of rule over the Spaniards and Gauls, but also, finally, to their forming the conception of their universal aim when they defeated the Carthaginians in the war.
>
> (3.2.6)

There is both a political and a military (6.19–42) dimension to the constitution and its contribution. The focus here will be upon the former. Book 6 combines the theoretical and the practical. Polybius begins with a general account of how constitutions develop and change that contains two elements. The first is the theory of an-

acyclosis—the cycle of constitutions, as it were—that provides the overall pattern. Along with this theory goes the biological principle of the orderly process of birth, acme, and decay, which applies to the individual stages within the pattern. Polybius recognizes three basic forms of constitution: kingship, aristocracy, and democracy, each of which is reckoned as having a perverted form: tyranny, oligarchy, and ochlocracy, or mob rule. To these three "good" and three "bad" types a seventh is added, neither good nor bad, a kind of primitive monarchy, or rule by one man, that is seen as the first form of what can be called political organization in any nascent human society. Thus, in the beginning there is chaos until "the man who excels in bodily strength and courage" comes necessarily to rule over the rest (6.5.7). As notions of what is base and what is noble, and of justice, grow up, and as the ruler is seen to throw the weight of his authority on the side of what is noble and therefore advantageous, the people

> yield obedience to him no longer because they fear his force but rather because their judgment approves him; and they join in maintaining his rule even if he is quite enfeebled by age, and they join in defending him with unanimous spirit and battling against those who conspire to overthrow his rule. Thus by insensible degrees the monarch becomes king, ferocity and force having yielded supremacy to reason.
>
> (6.6.11–12)

Kingship is the first "constitution" proper. It has arisen because the people have consented to be ruled, in this case by one man. This element of consent, of the people granting the authority to someone to rule over them (or withdrawing this consent), is basic to all that follows. Eventually the successors of the king, bred to power, come to cherish it for its own sake and for what it permits them. This is tyranny. Hatred, resentment, and conspiracies spring up among the people. The leaders are the "best men," and the people join with them

in overthrowing the tyrant and then entrust the rule to these best men. This is aristocracy. But the descendants of these best men, knowing only power and nothing of the misfortunes that brought it to them, go the way of the king's descendants, and aristocracy becomes the collective tyranny known as oligarchy. The people respond by killing or banishing the oligarchs, but there is now nowhere else for them to turn. "The only hope still surviving unimpaired is in themselves, and to this they resort, making the state a democracy instead of an oligarchy and taking to themselves the responsibility for the conduct of affairs" (6.9.3). But power without knowledge of how or why it came to be held corrupts no less in this case.

> When a new generation arises and the democracy falls into the hands of the grandchildren of its founders, they have become so accustomed to freedom and equality that they no longer value them, and begin to aim at preeminence; and it is chiefly those of great wealth who fall into this error.
>
> (6.9.5)

Their lust for power and reputation is pursued by bribing the people and thereby creating among them "an appetite for gifts and the habit of receiving them" (6.9.7). Democracy gives way to force and the rule of violence. Slaughter, banishments, and redistributions of land ensue, until the people "descend back into a state of savagery and find once more a master and monarch" (6.9.9). This is the *anacyclosis*, the cycle according to which constitutional changes happen. Each of the individual forms of government is born, has its acme, and decays according to the biological principle. The progress from one kind of constitution to the next is always in the same order or pattern, and it is to this process, a cyclical one in the end, that the name *anacyclosis* is given. The *anacyclosis* itself has no birth, acme, or decay; these notions are appropriate only to the individual stages of the process. The ideas of three (or six) types of constitution and of the biological principle are, of course, not new. Not so the combination of these (and the primitive monarchy) with the apparently novel *anacyclosis* into a single and coherent theory of constitutional development. This is Polybius' own.

Knowledge of the process is important in two respects. It will enable one to judge where a state is in its development and to predict how (if not when) it will change. It also makes one realize that the best constitution will not be simple and uniform but will have united in it

> all the good and distinctive features of the [three] best governments, so that none of the individual elements should grow unduly and be perverted into its allied evil, but that, the force of each being neutralized by that of the others, none of them should prevail and outbalance another but that the constitution should remain for long in a state of equilibrium like a well-trimmed boat.
>
> (6.10.6–7)

This is the kind of constitution that Lycurgus in his knowledge and prescience gave to Sparta. The Romans arrived at the same result "not by any process of reasoning, but by the discipline of many struggles and troubles, and always choosing the best in the light of the experience gained from misfortunes" (6.10.14). Polybius saw Rome as having reached the ideal in a thoroughly natural way (6.9.13: natural, too, the inevitable decline), a constitution in which the three elements existed side by side, in a state of balance, exercising checks upon one another (compare 6.18.7). The ideal is achieved by tension and balance, not mixture, and indeed Polybius never speaks of the Roman constitution (or any other) as "mixed."

How the Roman constitution, with its checks and balances, looked in practice is the subject of chapters 11–18 of book 6. The description is tied to the time of Cannae but must be seen as reflecting rather the time when Polybius was in Rome half a century later. It is always worth remembering that he is here describing, and speaking in terms of, Rome's constitutional machinery. To the purpose thus limited, magistra-

cies and assemblies are relevant, things such as *clientela* or *nobilitas* are not. Kingship is found in the consuls, aristocracy in the Senate, democracy in the popular assemblies and the tribunate. He describes the competencies of the respective elements and the ways in which they could check one another in fairly brief compass and in a manner that tends somewhat toward overschematization. At issue here is a desire to portray these elements of the state in terms of specific functions and powers *(exousiai)*. The requirements of writing for a Greek audience may be seen to lie behind this method. It works well enough for some things, such as the power of the consuls in the field or the role of the assembly in elections and trials, less well for others. Thus, in 6.17 the *demos* seems to consist of public contractors and those involved in their works; they were important, and their constitutional place was in the democratic element, the assembly, but they do not add up to the *demos*. There are problems of this kind in the descriptive section, and it is not (nor was it intended to be; see 6.11.3–8) a complete account. The problems do not vitiate the picture, and there is enough in the text to make Polybius' point about the presence of, and relations among, the three basic constitutional components in the Roman state as it then was. How it came to be that way is another question.

The development was natural, Polybius says. The section he devoted to the account and explanation of this development is now lost. One can only guess at what it contained. In the beginning there were kings. After a time, a tyrant naturally arose (Tarquinius Superbus). He was put down by a conspiracy led by nobles, and aristocracy took hold (domination by patricians and the Senate). But the element of kingship was not rooted out altogether; it was kept on in a collegiate form (compare Sparta) in the consulship. Eventually, aristocracy degenerated, as it must, into oligarchy (perhaps with the decemvirate), and the people took power back to themselves. But not all the elements of aristocracy were abolished; they kept on the Senate, now effectively under the control of the people

535

through electoral and judicial assemblies. The result of this or some such process would be a constitution that was essentially a democracy but that incorporated in its institutions independent elements of kingship and aristocracy.

However the "archaeology" in book 6 ran, it must have come to such a conclusion, for Polybius did see the Roman constitution as essentially a democracy. His statements about its inevitable decline in 6.57 require this interpretation. First, the description of that decline is almost identical to his earlier account of the transition from democracy to ochlocracy (6.9.4 ff., and see above); second, it is precisely into ochlocracy that Polybius says the Roman constitution will decline. Rome had then come to have not a mixed constitution but a democracy held in check by the institutionalization of the lessons of its past, all developing naturally and in accordance with the *anacyclosis*.

The prediction of the eventual decline and the course it would follow is in its detail remarkable. Of more direct concern here is the fact that he saw its first signs appearing before his eyes:

> When a state has weathered many great perils and subsequently attains to supremacy and undisputed mastery, it is evident that under the influence of long-established prosperity life will become more extravagant and men more fierce in their rivalry for office and other objects than they ought to be. As these defects go on increasing, the beginning of the change for the worse will be due to the love of office and the disgrace entailed by obscurity, as well as to extravagance and purse-proud display.
>
> (6.57.5)

And later, in 161–160 B.C.:

> It was just at this period that this present kind of behavior [extravagance and love of luxury] shone forth, as it were, first of all because they thought that now after the fall of the Macedonian kingdom their universal dominion was undisputed, and next because after the riches of Macedonia

had been transported to Rome there was a great display of wealth both in public and private.

> (31.25.6)

The similarity is more than striking, and the two passages were clearly written at much the same time. The context of the second is Polybius' praise of his young friend and protégé, Scipio Aemilianus, for, among much else, his temperance in the face of rampant luxury and his lack of concern for "the disgrace entailed by obscurity." It was, as Polybius knew, not with the mechanics of the constitution that the real trouble would come, but when the people behind it, and their "customs and laws," changed for the worse. This view is implicit even in the account of the *anacyclosis*. It is explicit in 6.47 (especially paragraph 4). With the Romans this kind of change began in some degree when they started to embark upon overseas wars (18.35), but it is after the acquisition of universal rule that the "change for the worse" sets in seriously.

Polybius had promised "to describe what were the prevailing and dominant tendencies and ambitions of the various peoples in their public and private life" (3.4.6) after the final establishment of Roman rule down to the time of trouble and disorder. We have, in the above, at least some part of that promise fulfilled as far as it concerns the Romans. This fulfillment came in the part of the work that extends from the middle of book 30 to book 33. Here would also have come the account, promised at the same time, of "the subsequent policy of the conquerors and their method of universal rule." The two, of course, go together. Most of what he wrote on this subject is lost, but some fragments survive.

In the Peloponnesus the atmosphere was one of "unconcealed anger and hatred" against Callicrates and those like him (30.29.1), who wished to persuade the Romans to support those who put Rome's wishes and orders above all else. The Senate proceeded with the object of "shutting people's mouths and making them obedient to the party of Callicrates in Achaea, and to those in the other states who were thought to be the friends of Rome" (30.32.8). The policy of Callicrates had borne bitter enough fruit since it won the day at Rome in 180 B.C. (see 24.8–10). Even stronger support from Rome now evoked even more brutal manifestations of it by its practitioners in Greece. The doings of Charops in Epirus are only the best known (32.5–6). The death within a short period of a number of these men was marked by Polybius as "a sort of purification of Greece" (32.5.3; compare 30.13.4 for their prominence in the aftermath of Pydna). The long-standing Roman desire that nothing should be done without Rome's knowledge and approval (see especially 23.17) was securely catered to in these years by Callicrates and the others (compare 33.16.7). Kings could behave in an analogous fashion. After Pydna, Prusias of Bithynia, who had previously appeared before Roman envoys in a freedman suit, groveled unsurpassedly before the Senate; and "showing himself to be utterly contemptible, he received a kind answer for this very reason" (32.18). Callicrates, Charops, Prusias, and the rest are a response to, and a reflection of, Roman policy. Some aspects of "the policy of the conquerors" after 168–167 B.C. were noted earlier in another context. In addition to these and the indications just mentioned, one or two others may be cited. In 167–166 B.C. the Thracian king Cotys sought to explain his agreement with Perseus and to obtain the release of his son, who had fallen into Roman hands. "The Romans, thinking that they had achieved their aim, the war against Perseus having gone as they planned, and that their difference with Cotys no longer had any point, allowed him to take back his son" (30.17.2). Similar is the Roman response, in 160–159 B.C., to an embassy from Demetrius, who had established himself on the Seleucid throne after his escape from Rome. He sent to Rome the self-confessed murderer (and his accomplice) of the Roman envoy, Cnaeus Octavius. The gesture was not welcomed.

For the Senate, as it seems to me, supposing that it would seem to the people that the murder had been avenged if they took over and punished the guilty ones, scarcely received them, but kept the charge open, in order to have the power to make use of the accusations when they wished.

(32.3.11–12)

The account offers an explanation, but no judgment. So it is in all the cases cited here and above, except insofar as Roman behavior was reckoned "pragmatic." These do not add up to all the surviving illustrations of Roman policy and of the state of affairs in the various places during the period of Roman rule, but there are not a great many more, and none of them is of very different tenor. True to his promise, Polybius gave us the evidence, and the excerptors have preserved enough of the text for us to see what the evidence looked like. Judge he did not. Judgment in its different forms was for those on the spot and for future generations, including our own.

The account in the last four books (35–39) is insulated from what goes before by the geographical excursus in book 34, a work made possible by Polybius' own travels and observations. It marks the end of the long and continuous narrative of the Roman conquest and the description of Roman rule (books 13 to 33 in an unbroken run); what follows is the time of trouble par excellence, including especially the culmination (but not the beginning, which belongs in book 33) of the chaotic Celtiberian war, the last war with Carthage, and the Achaean war. Polybius saw the history of these years as a new and different undertaking. And during this time some Greeks saw a new and different policy adopted by the Romans. Roman treatment of Carthage prompted a variety of comments on Roman policy that are reported by Polybius in 36.9 (some of "the various opinions and appreciations of the rulers entertained by others": 3.4.6). Some felt that lust for power was overtaking the Romans as it had overtaken Athens and Sparta before, and that instead of making war against people until they were compelled to obedience, they now set about exterminating them altogether; others defended or attacked them in other ways. It is extremely tempting to treat some of the opinions expressed in 36.9 as Polybius' own, but it would be equally hazardous to do so. Certainly, the ascription of any of them to him is not susceptible of proof. The Spanish and Carthaginian narrative, though by no means complete, is apparently straightforward. The Achaean narrative is also quite incomplete, but what there is does raise a problem that cannot be left unmentioned.

To all appearances, Rome's decision to deal harshly with the Achaeans was taken in 149 B.C. and communicated only in 147 B.C. by the embassy of L. Aurelius Orestes, after the war against the pretender in Macedonia was won. Orestes' embassy required the Achaeans to detach certain cities from their league. The envoys received a violent response. The order was repeated, with blandishments, by Sextus Julius Caesar later that year. The Achaeans, led by Critolaus, temporized. Shortly after, in the beginning of 146 B.C., the Romans declared war on the Achaeans, alleging the violence offered to Orestes and his fellow ambassadors as the reason. Polybius must have known all this. Yet his account of the Achaean assembly at Corinth in the spring of 146 B.C. (38.12) seems at first sight to tell a different story. There the Achaeans, under the influence of Diaeus and Critolaus (whom, along with their adherents, Polybius characterizes throughout as madmen and as finally responsible for the disastrous war), are portrayed as bringing the war upon themselves, in complete ignorance of the Roman declaration. Something is amiss. Possibly Polybius, in a passage now lost, explained how Critolaus and company concealed the Roman declaration of war from their people. But the account in 38.12 does not make it sound as if he did. The other possibility is that all the Achaeans were genuinely unaware that war

had been declared against them and of the staggeringly duplicitous conduct on the part of Rome that this would entail. If so, then it must emerge that Polybius has concealed this fact and this conduct from his readers. He did not hesitate to notice when Roman policy took this kind of turn elsewhere (see above on the Dalmatian war [32.13] and the last war with Carthage [36.2]), but he chose not to do so here. Why? By portraying the Greeks as entirely responsible for their own disaster (and compare 38.1 and 3, not least 3.8) and the state of affairs that preceded and led up to it in an irredeemably negative light, he shows, by implication at least, the Roman settlement that followed (in which he was involved and of which he was, in part, an architect) to have been pure blessing. Responsible they were, but misguided. The real blame lies with Critolaus, Diaeus, and the few other statesmen who led the Achaeans and other Greeks into the abyss and were the true authors of their folly. If the blame can be thus fixed upon these few, the many may be forgiven. And Polybius' concern was for his fellow Greeks at large: "In times of danger it is true that those who are Greek should help the Greeks in every way—by active support, by cloaking faults, and by trying to appease the anger of the rulers—as I myself actually did at the time of the events" (38.4.7). Did he in fact go further than this in his account of the events? If it was indeed such as to fix the blame upon these few and did not speak of Roman conduct, there will have arisen from it no cause for the forgiven many to censure the Romans or their settlement, or indeed to do anything but welcome it. "Had we not perished so soon we would never have been saved" (38.18.12). The object is not to exculpate the Romans. Polybius wished to tell his countrymen what he thought it best for them to know. Perhaps this is how "he succeeded after a certain time in making men welcome the constitution that was given them" (39.5). "But," the statement in 38.4 continues, "the record of the events meant for posterity is to be kept free from any taint of falsehood." The problem remains, but, in the light of this statement, it may after all require a different solution.

The sympathetic author of 39.5 reported that, in response to Polybius' role in the Roman settlement that followed the Achaean war, "each city took every means to confer the highest honors on him during his life and after his death." We know from inscriptions that he spoke the truth. This would have delighted Polybius at least as much as would the knowledge that among the writers of Greece and Rome his achievement as a historian is unparalleled.

Selected Bibliography

TEXTS

Polybe. Histoires. Texte établi et traduit par Paul Pédech et al. Paris 1969– . Collection Budé. A new text, in progress and appearing one book at a time, with a long way to go.

Polybii Historiae. Recensuit apparatu critico instruxit Fridericus Hultsch. 2nd ed. of vols. 1 and 2. Berlin, 1870–1892.

Polybii Historiae. Editionem a Ludovico Dindorfio curatam retractavit Theodorus Buettner-Wobst. 2nd ed. of vol. 1. Leipzig, 1889–1905; and since reprinted. Bibliotheca Teubneriana. This is the standard text.

Polybii Megalopolitani quidquid superest recensuit, digessit, emendatiore interpretatione, varietate lectionis, adnotationibus, indicibus illustravit Iohannes Schweighaeuser. Leipzig, 1789–1795.

Polybius. The Histories. London, 1922–1927; and since reprinted. Loeb Classical Library. With an English translation by W. R. Paton. The text is based upon the Teubner edition of Buettner-Wobst.

TRANSLATIONS

See also above. The best translation is easily Schweighaeuser's Latin version. There are two com-plete English translations, those of Paton in the Loeb Classical Library (above) and Shuckburgh. Of the two Shuckburgh's is, on balance, the more accurate, but it is based upon the text of Hultsch, whose arrangement of the excerpts is often wrong. A new English version, complete, accurate, and based upon a sound and correctly ordered text, is needed.

The Histories of Polybius. Translated by Evelyn S. Shuckburgh. London, 1889; since reprinted (for example: Bloomington, Ind., 1962, with a new introduction by F. W. Walbank).

Polybius. The Histories. Newly translated by Mortimer Chambers, edited and abridged with an introduction by E. Badian. The Great Histories. New York, 1966.

Polybius. The Rise of the Roman Empire. Translated by Ian Scott-Kilvert, selected with an introduction by F. W. Walbank. Penguin Classics. Harmondsworth, 1979.

Polybius on Roman Imperialism. The *Histories* of Polybius translated from the text of F. Hultsch by Evelyn S. Shuckburgh, M.A. Abridged with an introduction by Alvin H. Bernstein. South Bend, Ind., 1980.

COMMENTARY

Walbank, F. W., *A Historical Commentary on Polybius.* 3 volumes. Oxford, 1957, 1967, 1979. Not only are they essential for the study of Polybius, these volumes constitute a masterpiece.

GENERAL WORKS AND SPECIAL STUDIES

Derow, P.S. "Polybius, Rome and the East." *Journal of Roman Studies* 69:1–15 (1979).

Mauersberger, Arno. *Polybios-Lexikon.* Berlin 1956– . In progress.

Moore, J. M. *The Manuscript Tradition of Polybius.* Cambridge, 1965.

Walbank, F. W. *Polybius.* Berkeley, Calif., 1972. Sather Classical Lectures, vol. 42. This book and the *Commentary* are the starting point, after the text itself, for the study of Polybius. Both contain extensive bibliographies and references to books and articles.

P. S. DEROW

TERENCE

(*d.* 159 B.C.)

PUBLIUS TERENTIUS AFER, whose name has been anglicized as Terence, was the author of six comedies produced between 166 and 160 B.C. They survive, and antiquity knew no others. His work became a classic, studied by schoolboys, commented on by scholars, and seen upon the stage perhaps even as late as the fourth century A.D. During the Middle Ages monasteries, which were the centers of learning, had many monks who allowed their admiration for his literary gifts to overcome their disapproval of his subject matter; we still possess more than 100 manuscripts written before the fourteenth century. With the revival of learning and the invention of printing, his popularity increased by leaps and bounds. There were at least 446 complete editions before 1600. In England and on the continent of Europe, he was made an instrument for teaching boys Latin; and boys acted his plays in their schools. In Italy, Niccolò Machiavelli translated his *Andria* for the stage (1517), and similarly Lodovico Ariosto composed a version, now lost, of *Phormio* (performed 17 February 1509); in France he was a favorite of Michel Eyquem de Montaigne (1533–1592). More importantly for the history of drama he was, along with Plautus, an inspiration to the authors of comedy in the vernacular, who learned from him the importance of plot and characterization.

The concern of this essay, however, must be not with theatrical history, but with the nature and merits of Terence's plays and with the very little that is known of his biography. Suetonius, writing in the second century A.D., believed that Terence had been brought to Rome as a slave from Carthage and had been educated by his master, one Terentius Lucanus, whose name he took when he was set free. If this story is not an invention based on his name Afer (literally "African," but borne by some Romans)—ignorance did not deter ancient literary biographers from writing the lives of their subjects—it makes more remarkable and more creditable the purity of his Latin, for which he was praised by Julius Caesar, himself a man with a genuine care for correctness of vocabulary and syntax. Soon after 160 B.C. he is said to have sailed for Greece, and the varied, inconsistent accounts of his death suggest that he was not heard of again.

He was accused of receiving constant help and collaboration in the composition of his plays from members of the aristocracy; in the prologue to his last play, *Adelphoe (The Brothers)*, he neither admits nor rejects the charge but replies that he takes it as a compliment. In later times no one knew for certain who were meant, but it was a by-no-means impossible tradition that they were the younger Scipio and his friends, junior to Terence; we may see them as interested in drama, but prevented by their social status from writing plays for public performance. At any rate it is clear that Terence enjoyed the support and patronage of some prominent men; this was a necessary condition for his work and explains its nature.

Terence's plays demand an intelligent, quick-witted audience who could follow a complicated plot, understand rapid dialogue, and appreciate character drawing. But they were produced on public holidays in wooden theaters erected for the occasion and open free to all comers; they were paid for by politicians who hoped that such generosity would win them votes. It is, therefore, remarkable that he wrote for an elite and made no significant attempt, as Plautus had done, to hold the attention of the more simpleminded. *Hecyra* failed twice: on the first occasion because of counter-attractions and chattering among the audience; on the second because the theater was invaded by a crowd who had heard that there was to be a gladiatorial show. But there must have been a core of educated persons to whom serious drama would appeal and whose approval was valued by his sponsors. That is not to say that the sponsors were actuated merely by selfish motives; they may at the same time have had a genuine wish to encourage the development of dramatic art in the Latin language.

Some critics have written about Terence as if he were an independent author, a pardonable method, perhaps, since his plays cannot be directly compared with the lost Greek originals from which they were adapted: *Andria (A Woman from Andros)*, *Heautontimorumenos (One Who Punished Himself)*, *Eunuchus (The Eunuch)*, and *Adelphoe (The Brothers)* from Menander (342–292 B.C.), who was acknowledged to be the greatest writer of New Comedy; and *Hecyra (A Mother-in-law)* and *Phormio* from Apollodorus of Carystus, who belonged to the generation after Menander. Yet if the modern reader wishes to assess Terence's stature as a dramatist, he must neither ascribe to him merits due to a Greek nor shirk the attempt to discover what he contributed that was new. The task is not hopeless but cannot be crowned with more than partial success. Only changes that all or most scholars accept have been admitted to this chapter. More far-reaching modifications, supported by some, may occasionally

have hit on the truth, but they are for the most part marked more by ingenuity than by plausibility. In the end, the reader may be content to enjoy the plays in themselves and disregard the problems of dividing the credit between two dramatists.

Terence's first play, *A Woman from Andros*, was performed in April 166 B.C. The prologue takes a form of which we posess no earlier example, but which was destined to have many successors. Among the Greeks the prologue to a comedy, so far as is known, had been used to acquaint the audience with the situation with which the play opens; it might be spoken by one of the characters, whom convention allowed to confide in the public, or, if no character was in possession of all the facts, an omniscient divine figure would perform the office. Terence's prologues were spoken by an actor, not in the part of a character but as the mouthpiece of the poet or as the representative of the company; they named the play but said nothing of the plot; instead they engaged in controversy with a rival author or in appeals to a difficult public. Only in his last play, *The Brothers*, did he follow this controversial prologue with a monologue spoken by a character and addressed, in the Greek manner, to the audience.

The Greek spectator, if informed by a divinity, a method to which Menander frequently adhered, could watch the action from a position of quasi-divine superiority; he could see how the ignorance of the characters involved them in unnecessary agitation or unsuspected danger, yet be confident that the emergence of the unknown facts that had been confided to him would bring a happy ending. The dramatist gained this advantage at the price of limiting the possibilities of surprising his audiences; he could not introduce unexpected persons or previously unknown circumstances halfway through the play. Whoever first abandoned this sort of prologue changed the rules, so to speak: at the end of the fourth act of *A Woman from Andros* a man turns up who has never been mentioned before and who recognizes the heroine as an Athenian, the long-lost daughter of one of the characters, thus enabling her to be given in marriage to the hero. This is contrary to all that we know of Menander's practice, and there can be little doubt that Terence suppressed a divine prologue.

But a divine prologue cannot be simply suppressed without more ado. It reveals facts that the audience must be told. If it disappears, the facts must be conveyed in some other way, introduced into an actor's speeches. Terence became quite clever at this, but in this play, his first, he failed to disguise matter from the prologue that he put into the mouth of the slave Davos, who, after reflecting on the dangerous dilemma in which he stands, irrelevantly adds:

> But that's not all that's wrong; this Andrian, wife
> Or mistress, is with child by Pamphilus.
> Their daring impudence deserves your hearing,
> An enterprise of madmen, not of lovers:
> They've planned to raise whatever child is born,
> And now they're cooking between them some
>   pretense
> The woman's an Athenian citizen.
> "There was an old man once, a merchant-trader,
> Shipwrecked on Andros Island, where he died.
> The little orphan castaway was then
> Given a home by Chrysis' father." Stuff!
>
> (215–224)

To return to Terence's prologue, in reply to a malevolently critical older rival, who can be identified as one Luscius from Lanuvium, he explains that Menander wrote *A Woman from Andros* and *A Woman from Perinthos* with not dissimilar plots but "dissimilar language and style"; he admits that he has taken from the latter play what was suitable for the former. His critics say that plays should not be "adulterated"; he replies that he follows the precedent of Naevius, Plautus, and Ennius, whose "carelessness" he hopes to imitate rather than his enemies' "obscure carefulness." In other words, he rejects the ideal of close adherence to the Greek model or to a single model. The same position is taken in other prologues; those to *The Eunuch* and *The Brothers* confess the addition of material from another play.

The commentary that goes under the name of the fourth-century-A.D. scholar Aelius Donatus reports that, apart from the opening scene, only two other passages (not specified) of twenty and eleven lines, respectively, were taken from *A Woman from Perinthos*. The fact is that Terence's prologues are very clever rhetorical exercises in half-truth, evasion, and illusion. His reference to *A Woman from Perinthos* distracts attention from other more important changes that he made.

The opening scene in Terence's *A Woman from Andros* contains the exposition. Simo, one of two fathers who are among the leading characters, explains how he has discovered that his son, Pamphilus, who had been promised in marriage to the daughter of his neighbor, Chremes, is actually in love with the sister of a woman from Andros, a professional courtesan who has recently died. Learning of this, Chremes has called off the marriage. Simo now proposes to pretend that it is about to take place, in the hope that his son will not refuse to go through with it and Chremes will then relent. In Menander's *A Woman from Andros*, Simo communicated all of this to the audience in a monologue, while in *A Woman from Perinthos* he conversed with his wife. Terence uses the dialogue form of the latter play, but makes Simo talk not to his wife, but to a freedman, Sosia. The probable reason for the change is that the wife must already have known much of the background, which in Menander's play was supplied in the divine prologue.

It follows that the twenty excellent lines of conversation that open the play, depicting both Simo's trust in his freedman and Sosia's loyalty and gratitude to the man who had once been his master, are entirely the work of Terence. Less perfect is the end of the scene. Terence had to find a reason why Simo should send for the freedman and tell him the story:

> Your part is to keep up this pretense of marriage,
> To terrify Davos, and to keep an eye
> On what my son does and plans the pair may
>   make.
>
> (168–170)

This command is unconvincing and becomes more so when the freedman plays no part whatsoever in the rest of the play.

But Terence made an even greater change; he introduced two characters who, according to Donatus, were not in Menander: Charinus, a young friend of Pamphilus, and Byrrhia, his slave. Charinus is in love with Chremes' daughter Antiphila. Davos, rightly inferring that Simo's declaration that his son must marry Antiphila is a mere blind, persuades Pamphilus to raise no objection. His scheme goes wrong because Chremes, impressed by Pamphilus' apparent willingness to give up the other girl, abandons his opposition and is once again ready to give his daughter in marriage to him. Opportunity is thus afforded for two scenes between Pamphilus and a jealous Charinus, who has been informed by Byrrhia of what is afoot. In the first, Pamphilus can clear himself of any intention of marrying Antiphila; in the second, he appears to be trapped. Charinus appears again at the end of the play, where he is encouraged to hope for his beloved. Whether Terence invented these scenes or adapted them from another Greek play, he is revealed as more than a translator and as less than candid in his prologue.

When the second play, *A Mother-in-law*, was first staged in 165 B.C., it did not capture the attention of the noisy audience, who had hoped to see boxers and a tightrope walker. It was revived in 160 as an entertainment at the funeral of L. Aemilius Paulus, the younger Scipio's father, but was once again interrupted. Later the same year it was presented by the same actor-manager, L. Ambivius Turpio, who in the prologue recounted his successes in establishing the plays of Caecilius, Terence's great predecessor, who had himself experienced initial failure. He appealed to the audience, perhaps more select through having paid for admission, to help him to encourage the playwright: "You have the power to make theatrical entertainment glorious; do not allow dramatic art to become the preserve of a handful." As the prologue of the almost contemporary play *The Brothers* makes clear, Terence was still subject to rancorous attacks from critics and rivals.

The story is that a young man, Pamphilus, in obedience to his father, gave up his mistress and married his neighbor's daughter, Philumena. The marriage was not consummated, although he slowly came to love her, moved by her patience in humiliation. On his return from a trip abroad to collect a legacy for his father, he finds that his wife has gone to live with her mother, refuses to see her mother-in-law, and says that she is ill. Thinking that his mother and his wife have proved incompatible, Pamphilus decides that he must give up his wife. Entering the neighbor's house he finds Philumena in labor. Her mother explains that she had been raped by some unknown man before her marriage; and by an emotional appeal she persuades him to say nothing of the child. He agrees, expecting it to be quietly made away with (Athenian morality did not require one to rear an unwanted infant) and intending to divorce his wife, which Athenian law allowed him to do at will. But things go wrong for Pamphilus. His mother, who believes that Philumena's withdrawal must be due to dislike of her, insists on retiring to the country, to remove the only obstacle to the young couple's reunion. Moreover, his father-in-law, upon discovering the child, assumes that he will acknowledge it and keep it, even if he divorces Philumena. Pamphilus' difficulties are resolved when his father, guessing that his daughter-in-law had been removed by her mother on suspicion that Pamphilus had continued to consort with his former mistress (whom he had in fact visited for a time), summons the mistress to deny the charge. She is found to be wearing a ring that Philumena had been wearing when she was raped; Pamphilus had given it to his mistress, confessing that he had just taken it from some unknown girl who had been his victim. So all is well.

More than any other play by Terence, *A Mother-in-law* makes no concessions to the audience. There is little light relief, only that offered by Pamphilus' slave, Parmeno, whom he sends off on a fool's errand, and who is bewildered at the end when he is made the uncomprehending bearer of good news. There is a surfeit of admirable characters: everybody's motives are of the best. That is not accidental, but it makes for monotony. The play is also slow to get under way: there is a long opening scene of exposition in which Parmeno accidentally meets a courtesan of his acquaintance just back from two years in Corinth, who is talking to another about Pamphilus' marriage; he explains the situation to them, and they never appear again. The modern reader must in addition find Pamphilus unattractive. He prefers his mother to the wife he professes to love, and he determines to divorce his wife on discovering her misfortune. This may be understandable in the light of ancient attitudes, but even so he cuts a poor figure in contrast with Charisios of Menander's *Epitrepontes*.

The two plays have often been compared, somewhat unprofitably. The similarities are superficial and concern elements of plot rather than treatment. In atmosphere the plays are quite different. Much of *Epitrepontes* is lighthearted, and there is a great range of characters, connected in some way with the central problem, but contributing to its solution unwittingly and by the pursuit of their own ends. The characters of *A Mother-in-law* all deliberately and altruistically concentrate their efforts on the attempt to save Pamphilus' marriage. But the greatest difference is that *A Mother-in-law* is permeated by anxiety and distress; this emotional impact is the heavier because of the absence of a divine prologue, which would have informed the spectators that Pamphilus, although he did not know it, was the father of his wife's child, and perhaps would have promised them a happy outcome. Whether it was Apollodorus who so constructed the play or, more probably, Terence, the result is novel and effective. The audience, knowing no more than the characters, can be fully involved in their painful emotions; they can equally misunderstand the wife's withdrawal and be equally surprised by its explanation. The denouement must also come as a surprise, even to an experienced playgoer who has noticed the preparatory hint (574).

The first scene of *One Who Punished Himself* is as good as any opening in Terence. With some difficulty Chremes gets out of Menedemus, his new well-to-do neighbor, whom he finds still plying a heavy mattock as the evening draws on, the story of why he punishes himself. Chremes is excellently characterized as inquisitive, opinionated, self-satisfied, and insensitive, yet genuinely moved by the other man's situation and ready to extend his unwanted help. Menedemus' story of how his opposition to his son Clinia's love affair had driven the boy to go to the wars is vividly told; equally lifelike is the sequel of his repentance, which had caused him to adopt a manner of life as hard as that to which his son was bound. But he is less fully characterized than Chremes, which is justified because, although the play is named after him, he is not at the center of the plot, as Chremes is. Chremes is immensely pleased with himself; he knows all the answers. When the son unexpectedly returns, he gives Menedemus bad advice on how to behave; yet he is ignorant of his own son's affair with an expensive courtesan. He is constantly mistaken about what is going on under his own nose and is manipulated by his own slave, Syrus, in spite of distrusting him. But, although ridiculous, he is not contemptible: he is well-meaning and genuinely wants to be helpful and live up to the standards that will win him approval. Syrus tricks him by appealing to his belief that he will be expected to act generously (790–799), and his wife knows how to handle him:

Your mind's by nature steadier, more forgiving;
May my folly in your justice find protection.
(645–646)

The plot is ingenious and complicated, partly because unforeseen recognition of Clinia's loved one as Chremes' long-lost daughter upsets Syrus' original plan, and partly because there are two young lovers whose interests are to be furthered. Terence had introduced a second young man in love to his *Woman from Andros*; for his last four plays he chose originals with a double love interest, finding this a scheme that appealed, whether to himself or to his audience. It allows the dramatist to illuminate characters by contrast. Here Menedemus' son is hesitant, afraid of his father, and swings from anxiety and despair to ecstasy; Chremes' son, Clinia's friend Clitipho, a shallower man, speaks with confidence, criticizes and upbraids Syrus, but is completely under his thumb.

Other merits of the plot are the way in which expectations are cheated again and again, expectations that the audience has been made to share with the characters, and the paradox by which Syrus achieves his ends by telling the truth, knowing that his master will disbelieve it.

In the last act Chremes, furious at being deceived, declares that he will give the whole of his property to his daughter as her dowry and so deprive his son of any chance of squandering it. Syrus advises Clitipho to ask his parents whether he really is their son, that he can be treated so. The suggestion upsets his mother but not his father, who confirms his parenthood but remains stern, until with Menedemus' aid she prevails upon him to relent, on condition that Clitipho make a respectable marriage.

There are many details in this conclusion that may disturb an alert reader and lead him to infer that Terence made some innovations. The motif of suspected illegitimacy introduces a complication that leads nowhere; it has no effect upon Chremes. Terence liked to add "thickening" to his plays, and he may have also added a fourth character to the last scene, since Menander never, so far as is known, used more than three actors. Unfortunately, Donatus' commentary for *One Who Punished Himself* is missing, and with it the chance of external evidence for change.

Many scholars have seen another alteration. The play is unusual among New Comedies in that the action is not confined to a single day; a night intervenes between lines 409 and 410. They have thought that this was an alteration made by Terence, who supposedly converted Chremes' hospitality (162, 170, 211, 455) from a lunch to a dinner. His motive would have been that Romans would find strange such an early start to the enjoyment of food and wine. The absence of a chorus from the Roman theater would facilitate such a change. If the theory is right, Terence went to a good deal of trouble to emphasize the new time scheme (248, 410, 422, 461, 491, 498 ff.). For my part, I find it improbable that Menander would have made his glutton for work break off for lunch and spend one and a half acts and two entr'actes over his meal.

There is a much-discussed, puzzling incident at line 170. Chremes leaves the stage, saying that he must remind his neighbor Phania to come to dinner, and returns immediately, having learned that his guest is already in his house. It is probable that in Menander, Chremes' absence provided the opportunity for a "delayed" prologue by some divinity. Such a prologue was not absolutely necessary, but it would be in accord with Menander's methods, so far as they are known, to explain the parentage of Clinia's love. A prologue might also have explained how this girl had come to be associated with Clitipho's courtesan and to pass as one of her household, a thing that Terence's play leaves to guesswork.

But why should Terence retain an incident that had lost its structural reason? Perhaps he thought that the fruitless errand would provide some movement between two static scenes and a little amusement to the spectators. He may also have seen that it is symptomatic of Chremes' blindness to what is going on in his own house.

The Eunuch is the liveliest and most varied of Terence's plays. The basic story is that a young man, Phaedria, passionately in love with the courtesan Thais, is jealous of a soldier whom she is for the moment encouraging because he has bought a girl who had passed as her sister. Thais hopes to receive the girl from him as a gift. The importance of this is that she believes the girl was born an Athenian citizen and was kidnapped as a child. Thais intends to restore her to her family, whom she is on the point of identifying, and so secure for herself friends and protectors.

Phaedria, not to be outdone in generosity, is giving Thais two slaves, one a eunuch. Phaedria's younger brother, Chaerea, catches sight of the girl as she is being taken to Thais, is set alight by her beauty, exchanges clothes with the eunuch and so gains admission to the house, and is left in charge of the girl during her mistress's absence at dinner with the soldier. He takes advantage of the opportunity to rape her. Thais, on learning what has happened, shames him by her dignity; and he is eager to repair his crime by marrying the girl, whose citizen birth and consequent eligibility have meanwhile been established.

Suppression of a divine prologue, which many find all but certain, caused a difficulty. It was essential for the audience to know that Chaerea's victim was not the slave he imagined her to be. Otherwise, they would not have attached any importance to his design. The problem was solved in the opening scene by making Thais give Phaedria the girl's history with what the reflective reader will recognize as unnecessary detail for its context. What makes the solution unsatisfactory is the attentive presence in this scene of the slave Parmeno, who will later suggest to Chaerea his disguise as the eunuch. When the frivolous suggestion is—to his horror—taken seriously, he does not say that the girl is probably not a slave but an Athenian, the one argument that might have deterred the young man. If Terence noticed the improbability of this, he may have hoped that it would pass unobserved on the stage, as the audience's attention was held by the rapid, gripping exchanges.

The major alteration, however, is announced in the prologue. Two characters were introduced from Menander's *Kolax (The Toady)*, Thraso,[1] a mercenary soldier, boastful and cow-

ardly, and his malicious hanger-on, the toady, whose irony Thraso is too stupid to detect. Being essential to the plot, they must replace two less colorful characters in Menander's *Eunuchus*: a soldier or merchant, who was Phaedria's rival, and perhaps one of his slaves. With them they bring some matter that is most entertaining, although irrelevant to the plot of *The Eunuch*: the introductory monologue by the toady (232–264) and the conversation between him and the soldier (391–433). Later the two of them and their slaves mount an attack on Thais's home to recover the girl, whose brother's resistance makes the cowardly soldier abandon the effort. This amusing scene (771–804) must be adapted from *The Toady*.

If Donatus' commentary is to be believed, as I think it should be, Terence improved a monologue in which Menander's young man had informed the audience of his doings in Thais's house by providing a friend to whom Chaerea could tell the story. He is so plausibly introduced, and his remarks are so apt, that Terence must be applauded for an advantage gained at the expense of adding a dozen lines (562–573) to inform the friend of what the audience already knew. His motive for the change may have been a desire for greater realism, but he was less averse to monologues addressed to the audience than is sometimes supposed; there are several in his plays that cannot be excused as being soliloquies. Perhaps he thought that Chaerea might more properly confide in a friend than boast of his crime to the world at large. In any case the scene gains both in liveliness and in humor.

But it seems certain to many that he spoiled the end of the play by making Phaedria and the soldier agree to share Thais's favors, with the soldier paying for both, and the toady transferring his allegiance to Phaedria. This may be taken from *The Toady*, where the soldier's rival was an impecunious youngster and the girl was a slave whose inclinations were of no account. Terence's finale is comic, but at odds with the preceding play, in which Phaedria has been wildly jealous of the soldier, and Thais is a wealthy free woman who could not possibly be

---

[1] In Menander he was called Bias. The names of Terence's characters are sometimes known to differ from those in the Greek originals. Maybe they usually differed, since he even more than Menander made use of the practice of employing the same name in play after play. Thus he had three women all called Sostrata and three men called Chremes. Perhaps the changes were a symbol of his originality.

so disposed of behind her back. Nor would Phaedria have any use for the toady.

Phormio, an original and interesting play, with more appeal to the intellect than the emotions, was from the Greek of Apollodorus, who had entitled it *Epidikazomenos*, a word that would have meant nothing to the Roman public, since it was a technical term of Athenian law. (If a citizen died, leaving only an unendowed daughter for whose marriage he had not provided, her next of kin was obliged to marry her himself or to equip her with a dowry.) The opening scene of the play is exposition. Two brothers, Demipho and Chremes, live side by side; Geta, the former's slave, explains the situation to an interested friend. Both brothers had gone abroad, and he had been left in charge of their sons, youths named Antipho and Phaedria. Phaedria had fallen in love with a girl belonging to a slave dealer, but being without money he could do no more than accompany her to her music lessons. Antipho had gone with him, and while waiting in a barber's shop—a common place to pass the time in Greece—heard of a friendless beautiful girl in the neighborhood whose mother had just died. He visited her; it was love at first sight. Next day he had approached the old woman who was the only other person in the house; she had told Antipho firmly that the girl was a citizen of good birth, and he could have her only by marrying her. Of that he saw no prospect; his father would never allow him to marry an unknown girl with no dowry. A somewhat disreputable acquaintance, Phormio, had suggested that he should represent himself as the girl's family friend and bring an action against Antipho, alleging him to be her next of kin. If Antipho did not contest the case, he would be obliged to marry her. The scheme had been successfully carried through and the marriage had taken place.

The ingenious and excellently constructed plot centers on the conflict between the hot-tempered and insensitive Demipho, who on his return wishes to annul the marriage, and the cool, clever Phormio, who is always master of the situation and succeeds in causing Demipho

unwittingly to provide the money necessary to buy the girl whom Phaedria loves. Antipho's wife turns out to be Chremes' daughter by a bigamous marriage in Lemnos; this delights both brothers. At the end Phormio, threatened by Demipho with a legal action, tells Chremes' wife of her husband's bigamy, which puts Chremes in her power and secures her protection for Phormio.

Radical changes by Terence in Apollodorus' play seem unlikely, except that those critics may be right who think he was responsible for Antipho's presence in Act III. If they are, this is more evidence of Terence's desire to increase the pathos and of his ability to write first-rate original dialogue to promote an inherited plot. But some changes, parallel to those more certain in his other works, may be suspected. They cannot be asserted, because nothing is known of Apollodorus' technique. Menander would almost certainly have informed his audience by a divine prologue that Antipho's love was his uncle's daughter, the fruit of an affair that he had carried on under the assumed name of Stilpo. But Apollodorus may have anticipated Terence by reserving the matter to create a surprise. If, on the other hand, he followed the Menandrean model, the god presumably set out much of the matter recounted by Geta to a character whose sole function is to provide a listener, like Sosia in *A Woman from Andros* or Philotis in *A Mother-in-law*.

The prologue describes Phormio as a *parasitus*, but in the action he does not display any of the normal characteristics of that type. He makes no attempt to gain any advantage for himself by his efforts on behalf of his young friends, and his own house is to be the venue for drinks (837). It is to be suspected that the passage 325–345, quite unnecessary to the plot, is Terence's addition, intended to paint Phormio in familiar colors as a comic thug and boastful sponger. Another departure from Apollodorus' conception has been seen at the end of the play, where some critics have alleged that Phormio should accept Chremes' offer (947), which gives him all he needs. If he were a calculating machine, perhaps he would;

but Phormio is enjoying playing a part and teasing the old men. This is no adequate reason for assigning all that follows to Terence. But the adaptor's hand may be seen in the presence of four speakers in the last scene, something probably unusual, perhaps unknown, in Greek New Comedy, but found in three other of Terence's endings. The simplest solution would be to eliminate Demipho, who has very little to say in this last scene apart from 1014–1020, which is hard to reconcile with 1012; in the Greek, the actor playing that character may have entered his house at 984 and emerged at 990 as Chremes' wife Nausistrata, followed by a *persona muta* wearing Demipho's mask. Yet this may not be enough, for it leaves an awkwardness that some find easier to ascribe to Terence than to Apollodorus: Demipho enters his house to fetch slaves to seize Phormio, a flatly illegal assault, and then abandons his purpose without a word.

Clearly Terentian, however, is the way in which Demipho brings three witnesses to his second interview with Phormio (making six speakers); in an amusing passage, two give opposite advice, while the third solemnly declares that the matter needs further thought (445–459).

The Brothers is the most fascinating of the plays, because it is concerned not merely with personal problems but with a subject of perennial interest—the right way for a father to treat and educate his son. Is it that of the permissive, generous, and humane Micio, who knew the value of leisure, or that of his brother Demea, strict, parsimonious, and self-centered, for whom work on the farm left no time for pleasure? The question had been adumbrated in a less clear-cut fashion in *One Who Punished Himself*, where it was not so prominent. For most of the play, Micio appears to be the indisputable winner; when he discovers that Aeschinus, his adopted son (Demea's child by birth), has concealed the fact of having got a poor citizen girl with child, his understanding treatment causes the youth to protest that he could not have a better father. Micio is open with his disapproval, but more for refusal to face facts than for the original act of passion;

and he has no doubt that the girl must be married, although she is not the bride he would have wished for his son.

The end of the play brings a surprising change. Demea, who has always been cast in an unfavorable light, announces that if generosity is the road to popularity, he will outdo his brother. He starts by speaking with forced geniality to two slaves; then he causes Micio's garden wall to be broken down and Micio to agree to marry the girl's mother, and, to promise a whole series of other generous acts. Micio attempts some feeble resistance, but allows Aeschinus to overrule him. Demea then declares that he has done all this to show that the right way of life is not Micio's, one of indulgence and generosity, and offers himself as a guide to the young, an offer that Aeschinus accepts.

This scene has long been a puzzle. Literary men such as Denis Diderot, Gotthold Ephraim Lessing, and Johann Wolfgang von Goethe have been offended by it; some scholars have defended it; others, more plausibly, see in it another example of Terence's willingness to sacrifice character for a lively comic ending. The rehabilitation of Demea and the humiliation of Micio may have seemed right to an audience with more belief in parental authority than in the Greek virtue of humanity.

Some claim the moral of the play is that correct education would be a middle course between Micio's permissiveness and the severity of Demea. This view, for which the text offers no support, may be connected with a belief that a young man should not be assisted to sow wild oats. This overlooks the vast differences between the prospects and possibilities for a rich young man in Western societies and those available in Athens at the end of the fourth century B.C. Micio may not be perfect—a saint would not provoke his elder brother (746–752)—but Menander drew him as one whose actions were essentially correct and successful, not one who would collapse weakly without the courage of his convictions.

Terence's own testimony confesses, or rather boasts of, the change he made at the beginning. Aeschinus had broken into a slave-dealer's house and abducted the girl whom his brother, Ctesipho (also Demea's son), passionately desired, to prevent her being taken abroad. In Menander this was recounted. Plautus, in his adaptation of a play by Diphilus, omitted a scene in which such a theft was enacted outside a slave-dealer's house. In his prologue, Terence says that he had transferred it "word for word" to his own play. Since Terence's slave-dealer did not have a house on the stage, some alteration was inevitable; the original act of kidnapping had to be replaced by Aeschinus and the girl's arrival at Micio's house, with the dealer in hot pursuit. The scene is lively; blows are struck, and no doubt the audience was entertained. But there was a price to pay: on the one hand, the dealer arrives on the stage before he is wanted for the progress of the play, and must stand about as the idle witness of a scene between the two brothers; on the other hand, he comes too late, since in the preceding scene the kidnapping has already become the talk of the town. Moreover the climax of Diphilus' scene is a declaration that the girl was freeborn (and therefore not his property). Nothing more is heard of this; the girl is indubitably a slave in Terence's play; no doubt he was unwilling to sacrifice the *coup de foudre* and left anyone who wished to invent an explanation for the false claim free to do so.

It has appeared that Terence's identifiable changes in the plots of his originals often resulted in some damage to their structure and their characterization. This was offset by an undoubted gain in liveliness and variety. It is clear too that he showed much skill in the introduction of additional material; whether it was invented or adapted, original writing was required to fit it to the context. One may ask whether even in the scenes where he followed his main model he did so in his own way.

A translator of verse into verse is bound to reshape his original, even if he wishes to be faithful to it. Fidelity is not a virtue for Terence; he wanted to improve his Greek models, or at least make them more suitable for the Roman theater. Accordingly, one may suspect that there were more changes than can be detected.

Some novelties, however, are made certain by comparison with Menander's practice.

Terence could employ more than three speaking actors, and thus could give a few words to slaves, who in a Greek comedy would have been played by supers and have obeyed orders silently. He could keep characters on the stage for scenes in which they were in no way essential but might contribute an occasional comment. Once, it is highly probable, he enriched his play be dividing a part; in *The Eunuch* the slave-girl Dorias seems to be a double of the other slave Pythias, whose place she temporarily takes and with whom she later remains on scene. He makes far more use than either Menander or Plautus of interjections, which mark the close attention and emotional reaction of the man who utters them. His actors were probably masked, like those of Greek comedies, and so unable to use facial expression for these purposes. He develops what already occurred in his predecessors, the breaking up of dialogue into brief phrases, often incomplete. For example, five lines in *The Brothers* (323–327) contain fifteen changes of speaker; and four times Geta does not get beyond the first word of a sentence. All this is realistic, and also dramatically effective.

Terence was no committed champion of realism; he made an increased use of some conventions—eavesdropping by an unseen person and, more particularly, "asides." Addressed to the audience, asides are a device to inform them of what is passing in someone's mind; realistically they would be heard by the man near whom he is talking, and whose failure to respond allows them to be imagined as their speaker's silent thoughts. These conventions were to have a long and useful life on the European stage.

Of the few lines that survive from the Greek originals of Terence's plays a number have no parallel in his Latin. When new material was introduced, compensatory excision of the old must have been necessary. He seems to have been willing to forego many of the generalizing statements to which Greek dramatists were attached; once he can be detected in converting

550

a generalization into an explicit reference to the situation. In *One Who Punished Himself* (384),

> Your talk showed me what character is yours

in Menander had been,

> One's character becomes known from one's talk.

Such comparisons are rarely possible, and it is dangerous to assume that they are typical. But when Menander's "one maid ... in a filthy state" becomes "one little maid ... dressed in rags, neglected, filthy, and unwashed" (*One Who Punished Himself* 293–295), that is characteristically Terentian in its desire to engage the emotions, to rouse feelings of pity.

It is characteristic also that Terence minimizes the Greek coloring; and when he very occasionally introduces an element from Roman society, the engagement ring (*The Brothers* 347) or allowing the hair to grow in mourning (*Phormio* 106), it is not aggressively Roman. His plays are intended to be about universal human beings rather than about members of a particular culture. In accord with this is a tendency to avoid the specific. Menander's midwife, giving instructions on the feeding of her patient, says,

> And after that, my dear,
> The yolk of four eggs,

while Terence's midwife issues a reminder without content,

> Then afterwards ...
> To drink give what and how much I have told you.
> (*A Woman from Andros* 483)

No doubt he thought the elimination of inessential detail was an improvement. Unfortunately, it is detail that individualizes a character and makes him lifelike. Terence did not match Menander in creating an illusion of real men and women.

However much or however little Terence adapted his Greek originals, his language was his own. It has long been highly praised. It is correct Latin in the sense that it eliminates loan words from Greek, comic formations such as enlivened Plautus' work, indecencies, and vulgar expressions. Its positive merits include concision, elegant ease, variety of construction, and a vocabulary adequate to reveal thoughts and emotions. Essentially homogeneous, perhaps rooted in the speech of educated Romans, this style can allow delicate differences between different characters. The occasional archaisms occur mainly in the speech of the elderly, who are fond of using dimunitives as they refer to the young and to women. A happily drunken slave invents the words *prodeambulare* (expromenade) and *parasitaster* (piddling parasite) in *The Brothers* 766 and 779. *Mi* (my dear) with a vocative is a favorite blandishment for Thais in *The Eunuch*.

An air of naturalness is given by the way in which characters, above all in quick exchanges, will break off in midsentence, or by the omitting of verbs, thereby shortening a phrase to its essential elements. It is a technique that sometimes approaches the limits of intelligibility. In longer speeches there are no wasted words; joining of nearly synonymous expressions is uncommon and deliberately used for emphasis. Emphasis is also secured by alliteration, that frequent ornament of Latin verse. It may at times be accidental: for example, *The Brothers* (333), *in sui gremio positurum puerum patris*; but often it is clearly intended to lend force or weight to the words: for example, *The Brothers* (322), *oppido opportune te obtulisti obuiam*, or *One Who Punished Himself* (209), *necessest, Clitipho, consilia consequi consimilia*. It is sometimes an element in the effectiveness of lines whose lapidary form has given them immortality:

> *amantium irae amoris integratiost*
> Lovers' quarrels renewal are of love
> (*A Woman from Andros* 555)

> *fortis fortuna adiuuat*
> Fortune favors the brave.
> (*Phormio* 203)

But it is absent from the most famous of all:

> quot homines, tot sententiae
> As many opinions as there are persons.
> (*Phormio* 454)

Like all authors of ancient comedy, Terence wrote in verse. His technical skill cannot be illustrated here. But there is one feature that needs attention. Menander had used the iambic trimeter predominantly, with some scenes in trochaic tetrameters; other meters were exceptional. Terence employed a much greater variety and never went as far without a change; *senarii* (six-foot iambics), the Latin equivalent of Greek trimeters, and the measure he uses most, never much exceed 150 lines in succession. Did he think this an improvement? Or did he bow to the expectations of his audience? Plautus had used "meters without number," including lyric measures delivered in a singing voice. Such passages in Terence are short and infrequent, but nearly half his lines are long verses, iambic or trochaic, which contrast with the shorter *senarii*. The contrast was greater in the theater because these long lines were recited to an accompaniment by a piper; the importance of the music is evidenced by the official records, which preserved both the name of the composer, who was a slave, and also the performer and the type of instrument he played (always some form of double pipe with a reed). Terence often used more than one kind of long verse in a sequence; one may guess that the music emphasized the changes, which we are in danger of overlooking.

The play always opens with a long passage in *senarii* and ends with a shorter one in seven-foot trochaics; in-between meters seem to be chosen with an eye to variety, subject to the condition that there should be at least one extended passage of *senarii*. It cannot be said that a change of meter is always connected with some particular way of feeling or type of subject matter. A new meter may do no more than mark a section in a scene, caused for example by the departure of some character or the appearance of one not previously there. But it is hard to be sure that the dramatist did not intend to mirror some change of emotional or dramatic color. Sometimes the intention is clear. For example, at *The Brothers* 676, the change to seven-foot trochaics marks the point at which Aeschinus' pretense breaks down and Micio becomes serious; at 706, Aeschinus, left alone, uses long iambic lines to reflect upon his father's goodness, and then goes off (712) with an even longer iambic line, as he thinks of his own affairs.

On the Roman stage a play was performed without intermissions. The Greek originals had been divided into five acts, separated by irrelevant songs by the chorus. Terence had no chorus, and if he were not to impose a strain on his spectators, he was bound to provide them with variety in some other way. Following the lead of his predecessors at Rome, he retained the musical element by integrating it with his play. He does not seem to have been embarrassed by the absence of a chorus, whose performance had been used by the Greeks to mark the passage of time. An audience can easily accept the substitute of a momentarily empty stage. Ancient critics, who believed that a play ought to have five acts, attempted to find them in Terence; and those marked in modern texts, sometimes convenient for reference, are the descendants of that misguided endeavor.

Terence's choice of plays to adapt shows that he was attracted by Menander's skillful construction, lifelike characters, and interest in psychology rather than action. He seems to have welcomed dramas in which the stock figures of comedy had lost or modified their traditional characteristics: there is no out-and-out miser and the courtesans are not entirely self-seeking. Bacchis in *A Mother-in-law* insists again and again on her good nature, unique (she says) among women of her profession; her namesake in *One Who Punished Himself* is kindness itself to Antiphila; and Thais in *The Eunuch* confesses her affection to Phaedria. Even if some of this is due to Terence, his conception of what personages should be portrayed stands revealed. Really unpleasant creatures have no part on his stage. The slave-dealer of *The Brothers* is not, outside the scene translated from Diphilus, an impudent, conscienceless bully, but an anxious, ill-treated trader. There are no lecherous old men. Intriguing slaves are never protagonists, nor outstandingly successful in their intrigues; they are Menandrean, not Plautine. No cook is even mentioned, but it is unlikely that this standard comic figure was absent from all six Greek plays; probably Terence suppressed him as specifically belonging to Greek society.

But it must not be supposed that Terence was single-minded in his desire to avoid traditional elements, violence on the stage, and improbable but dramatically effective actions. He wanted to write successful plays and was prepared to do what was necessary. He tricked Phormio out in the colors of the conventional parasite and introduced in Thraso a conventional soldier, boastful, stupid, and cowardly. He enlivened *The Brothers* with a bit of knockabout and *The Eunuch* with the siege scene. He enjoyed drawing character and vied with Menander in making a man's words hint at thoughts and emotions underlying their superficial meaning; but he was willing to sacrifice consistency in order to provide an audience with a finale to arouse their mirth.

What must win unqualified admiration is his ability to write in a fashion that grips the attention and illuminates the speaker. The basis may have been in the Greek, but he had to find the Latin words to transmute the effect. Nothing could be better than the scene in *The Eunuch* (292–351) where young Chaerea enters, enraptured by the beauty of the girl he had seen in the street and entertainingly contemptuous of the everyday beauties whose mothers inflict on them the current fashion for drooping shoulders and no bosom. The mastery of language shown there, and consistently in all of Terence's plays, is a virtue unfortunately inaccessible to those who are forced to read him in translations, but inescapable by those who have even a little Latin.

Selected Bibliography

TEXTS

P. Terenti Afri Comoediae, edited by R. Kauer and W. M. Lindsay. Oxford, 1926. Addenda by O. Skutsch (Oxford, 1958). Oxford Classical Texts.

TRANSLATIONS

Borie, P., C. Carrier, and D. Parker, trans. *Complete Comedies of Terence.* New Brunswick, N.J., 1974.

Marouzeau, J., ed. and trans. *Terence.* 3 vols. Paris, 1942–1949. French translation in the Budé series.

Radice, B., trans. *Terence, the Comedies.* Harmondsworth, 1976. Penguin Classics.

Sargeaunt, J., ed. and trans. *Terence.* 2 vols. Cambridge, Mass., and London, 1912. Loeb Classical Library. English translation.

BIOGRAPHICAL AND CRITICAL STUDIES

Arnott, W. G. *Menander, Plautus, Terence.* Oxford, 1975. Report of work in this century.

Beare, W. *The Roman Stage.* London, 1950. Revised and enlarged 2nd ed. London, 1955; 3rd ed. London, 1964.

———. "The Secret of Terence." *Hermathena* 56:21–39 (1940).

Bruder, H. W. *Bedeutung und Funktion des Verswechsels bei Terenz.* Zurich, 1970.

Büchner, K. *Das Theater des Terenz.* Heidelberg, 1974.

Duckworth, G. E. *The Nature of Roman Comedy.* Princeton, N.J., 1952. Contains a chapter on later influence and a large bibliography.

Earl, D. C. "Terence and Roman Politics." *Historia* 11:469–485 (1962).

Flickinger, R. C. "A Study of Terence's Prologues." *Philological Quarterly* 6:235–269 (1927).

Focardi, G. "Linguaggio forense nei prologhi terenziani." *Studi italiani di filologia classica* 44:55–88 (1972).

———. "Lo stilo oratorio nei prologhi terenziani." *Studi italiani di filologia classica* 50:70–89 (1978).

Gaiser, K. "Zur Eigenart römischer Komödie." *Aufstieg und Niedergang der römischen Welt* 1, no. 2:1027–1113 (1972).

Gomme, A. W. *Essays in Greek History and Literature.* Oxford, 1937. Pp. 254–297.

Haffter, H. "Terenz und seine kunstleriche Eigenart." *Museum Helveticum* 10:1–20, 73–102 (1953).

TERENCE

Henry, G. K. G. "The Characters of Terence." *Studies in Philology* 12:57–98 (1915).

Jachmann, G. "Terentius." In A. Pauly and G. Wissowa, *Realencyclopädie der Altertumswissenschaft* 5a:598–650 (1934).

Jenkins, E. B. *Index Verborum Terentianus.* Chapel Hill, N.C., 1932. Reprinted Hildesheim, 1962.

Lefèvre, E. *Die Expositionstechnik des Terenz.* Darmstadt, 1969.

Ludwig, W. "The Originality of Terence and His Greek Models." *Greek, Roman and Byzantine Studies* 9:169–182 (1968).

McGlynn, P. *Lexicon Terentianum.* 2 vols. London and Glasgow, 1963–1968. Vol. 1: A–O; vol. 2: P–V.

Marti, H. *Untersuchungen zur dramatischen Technik bei Plautus und Terenz.* Zurich, 1959.

Mattingly, H. B. "The Terentian didascaliae." *Athenaeum* n.s. 37:148–173 (1959).

Norwood, G. *The Art of Terence.* Oxford, 1923.

————. *Plautus and Terence.* New York and London, 1931.

Perelli, L. *Il teatro rivoluzionario di Terenzio.* Florence, 1973.

STUDIES AND EDITIONS OF INDIVIDUAL PLAYS

THE BROTHERS (ADELPHOE)

Dziatzko, K., and R. Kauer, eds. *P. Terenti Afri Adelphoe.* Leipzig, 1903.

Fantham, E. "*Heautontimorumenos* and *Adelphoe:* A Study of Fatherhood in Terence and Menander." *Latomus* 30:970–998 (1971).

————. "Terence, Diphilus and Menander." *Philologus* 112:196–221 (1968).

Grant, J. N. "The Ending of Terence's *Adelphoe* and the Menandrian Original." *American Journal of Philology* 96:42–60 (1975).

Martin, R. H., ed. *Terence, Adelphoe.* Cambridge, 1976.

Rieth, O. *Die Kunst Menanders in den Adelphen des Terenz.* Hildesheim, 1964. Postscript by K. Gaiser.

Tränkle, H. "Micio and Demea in den terenzischen Adelphen." *Museum Helveticum* 29:242–255 (1972).

A WOMAN FROM ANDROS (ANDRIA)

Oppermann, H. "Zur Andria des Terenz." *Hermes* 69:265–285 (1934).

Shipp, G. P., ed. *Terence, Andria.* Oxford, 1938.

Steidle, W. "Menander bei Terenz." *Rheinisches Museum* 116:303–325 (1973).

Thierfelder, A., ed. *P. Terentius Afer, Andria.* Heidelberg, 1951; 2nd ed. 1961.

THE EUNUCH (EUNUCHUS)

Brothers, A. J. "Terence *Eunuchus* 189–216." *Classical Quarterly* n.s. 19:314–319 (1969).

Ludwig, W. "Von Terenz zu Menander." *Philologus* 103:1–38 (1959).

Rand, E. K. "The Art of Terence's *Eunuchus.*" *Transactions of the American Philological Association* 63:54–72 (1932).

Steidle, W. "Menander bei Terenz." *Rheinisches Museum* n.s. 116:326–347 (1973).

ONE WHO PUNISHED HIMSELF (HEAUTONTIMORUMENOS)

Lefèvre, E. "Der 'Heautontimorumenos' des Terenz." In *Die römische Komödie: Plautus und Terenz,* edited by E. Lefèvre. Darmstadt, 1973.

Steidle, W. "Menander bei Terenz." *Rheinisches Museum* n.s. 117:247–276 (1974).

A MOTHER-IN-LAW (HECYRA)

Carney, T. F., ed. "P. Terenti Afri Hecyra." *Proceedings of the African Classical Association.* Suppl. 2 (1963).

Posani, M. R. "Originalità artistica dell Hecyra di Terenzio." *Atene e Roma* 3, no. 8:225–246 (1940). See also 3, no. 10:141–152 (1942).

Schadewaldt, W. "Bemerkungen zur 'Hecyra' des Terenz." *Hermes* 66:1–29 (1931).

Sewart, D. "Exposition in the *Hecyra* of Apollodorus." *Hermes* 102:247 (1974).

PHORMIO

Arnott, W. G. "Phormio Parasitus." *Greece and Rome* 17:32–57 (1970).

Dziatzko, K., and E. Hauler, eds. *P. Terenti Afri Phormio.* Leipzig, 1913.

Lefèvre, E. "Der Phormio des Terenz und der Epidikazomenos des Apollodor von Karystos." *Zetemata* 74. Munich, 1978.

Martin, R. H., ed. *Terence, Phormio.* London, 1959.

BIBLIOGRAPHIES

Kauer, R. *Bursians Jahresbericht* 143:176–270 (1909). Covers the years 1898–1908.

Marti, H. *Lustrum* 6:114–238 (1961) and 8:5–101 (1963). Covers the years 1909–1959.

F. H. SANDBACH

CICERO

(106–43 B.C.)

INTRODUCTION

THE ROMAN CRITIC Quintilian said that Cicero was the name "not of a man, but of eloquence itself." Insofar as the general public still knows of Cicero, it is perhaps as the author of speeches that may seem too verbose and artificial to appeal to modern taste, and perhaps also as a vain and tiresome man. But a closer acquaintance reveals him as impressively many-sided; he also wrote treatises on the art of speaking, on political questions, and on philosophy—being to all intents and purposes the first to write seriously in Latin on this last subject—and by immense good fortune we have surviving a large part of his collected correspondence, ranging from formal epistles to casual and elliptical notes written to his great friend Atticus (a few letters from other figures of his period, ranging from Julius Caesar to Caesar's murderers, Brutus and Cassius, are included). He was also in his youth well regarded as a poet. He nearly wrote a history of Rome; he certainly took an interest in historiography and antiquarianism, as in linguistic and grammatical subjects. Above all, he was a politician who has been described in modern times as "more than half a statesman," and it should be remembered that for him both oratory and philosophy were the necessary preparation and weapons of the public man, rather than ends in themselves.

Many of Cicero's writings, including some of those most celebrated in antiquity, are lost, but what remains is greater in bulk than what we have of almost any other ancient writer. It enables us to know the man as we know no one else in antiquity, and also to know, through him, his fascinating period; a period in which Rome was reaching, under Greek influence to a great extent, a new intellectual and artistic maturity, even while the political structure of the Roman republic was collapsing in chaos and civil war. Cicero was not a profoundly original genius. But he combined and summed up, with unique sensitivity and breadth of knowledge, the Roman tradition, which was largely political and moral, and the Greek one, whose triumphs were intellectual and artistic. And he thus contributed largely to the coming of age of Roman cultural life in his time. His great adversary in politics, Julius Caesar, paid him the most magnificent of compliments in saying that he had extended the boundaries of the Roman spirit—implying perhaps that his own achievement in extending the boundaries of the empire to Gaul was a lesser one. And Quintilian, writing primarily of Cicero's style, said that a student may judge of his own proficiency by the satisfaction that he receives from Cicero. There is some truth in this in a wider sense as well; the intelligence and literary subtlety of Cicero grow on one, the more one knows of him and of his background.

CICERO

LIFE AND POLITICAL CAREER

Marcus Tullius Cicero was born on 3 January 106 B.C. at the attractive country town of Arpinum, some eighty miles southeast of Rome, into one of the leading families of the place, active in local politics and in touch with certain great aristocratic figures in Rome itself. His father, a student of literature who suffered from poor health, seems to have taken his son, who probably already showed great promise, to Rome for his education. This education would have been based at first on literature, primarily poetry, in both Latin and Greek, and later on rhetoric, which he seems to have studied perhaps exclusively with Greek masters, though he avidly read such Latin speeches as were available and, slightly later, at least practiced speaking in both languages. He was subsequently also entrusted to a distinguished legal consultant and public figure, in order to improve his knowledge of law, and began to study Greek philosophy with leading Greek scholars visiting Rome.

In 91 B.C. there broke out a savage war against such parts of the peninsula as had not yet received Roman citizenship but were demanding it, and in this conflict young Cicero served. The war passed almost insensibly into a period of civil strife and disturbance, during which Cicero, whose family was clearly unsympathetic to the regime in control at Rome for most of this time, continued his education rather than trying to enter public life. He later thought that he owed much to this unusually extended period of preparation. When, by the late 80's, Sulla had restored the conservative rule of the Senate at Rome, Cicero began to make his name, in the usual way for aspirants to public office, by pleading in the law courts. Political issues were often involved in trials, and the advocate could make his political position clear. Shaky health and a consequent desire to change his overstrenuous manner of speaking caused him to interrupt this life for a further period of study of philosophy and rhetoric, with the best masters in Athens and the

Greek cities of Asia Minor, especially Rhodes, which had a proud tradition in rhetoric.

Soon after his return, Cicero was elected to the junior financial magistracy that gave entry to the Senate. One of his background counted as a "new man," since none of his forefathers had held office in Rome. It would not be difficult for one of his talent and connections to rise to a certain level, but the Roman aristocracy was loathe to see such a new man hold the supreme magistracy, the consulship. But Cicero, whose maxim from a boy was the line of Homer "Always to be the best and far to excel all others," probably soon had his eye on this prize. He worked immensely hard in the courts, usually representing the defense, in order to collect the wide range of personal supporters that the great nobles inherited (since advocates were not paid, their clients were under a deep obligation to them, to be worked off by assistance of varying kinds). But it was by a prosecution, that of the unscrupulous governor of Sicily, Gaius Verres, that Cicero's name was finally made, in 70 B.C. The case was entwined with a program of political reform, aiming to return the power that Sulla had removed from them to the popular magistrates known as tribunes of the people, and to see that more control was exercised over individual senators at home and abroad.

This program was somewhat *popularis*; that is to say, though not fully democratic, it asserted the latent sovereignty of the Roman people. Cicero's background and convictions were conservative; he had particularly close ties with the *equites*, or "knights," the class of wealthy men outside the Senate, sometimes engaged in financial or commercial affairs, and though he believed that the Senate should rule, he advocated close cooperation between these two orders. However, he deprecated recent senatorial scandals, and he always thought it essential to conciliate the people as far as possible. In the next years he also had to do this for electoral purposes, especially as he attached himself to the star of Pompey the Great, who was not only immensely popular but at this time somewhat *popularis* too. Cicero's first speech to the people, given when he was praetor in 66 B.C., was in favor of a great command for Pompey; but he did his best not to offend the nobility, and in 64 B.C. he was rewarded for all his efforts. Partly because Catiline and another candidate for the consulship were talking wildly about measures for the abolition of debt, almost the whole aristocracy came round to Cicero as a fundamentally safe prospect, and he, a new man, was elected top of the poll and at the earliest possible age, to the consulship. It was an unparalleled achievement.

During Cicero's year of office, Catiline turned to outright conspiracy and rebellion, and it was in the course of putting the trouble down that Cicero delivered the famous "Catilinarian orations." For a while he was triumphant, lauded even by most of the nobility, but his position created jealousies, which his own desire to hear as much praise of himself as possible did nothing to abate (to do him justice, he could laugh at himself over this). And he failed, on Pompey's victorious return from the East, to persuade the conservative nobility to embrace the great general, who was now willing enough to be embraced. In the end, in order to get his arrangements in the East ratified and his veterans settled on allotments of land, Pompey was forced into the arms of Caesar, whom Cicero distrusted, and of Marcus Crassus, whom he loathed. This alliance was the so-called First Triumvirate. Cicero refused, on his conservative principles, to make a fourth in it, though invited to do so. As a result, the dynasts proved unwilling to save him from his enemy, the aristocratic demagogue Publius Clodius, who in 58 B.C. passed a bill exiling Cicero on the ground that he had put a number of the self-confessed conspirators to death without public trial in 63 B.C. Cicero could answer that the Senate had voted for this action, and that an emergency decree deployed by it had deprived the men concerned of their status as citizens, which alone entitled them to trial. But the great nobles, too, did not or could not help him, and he left Italy in despair.

When he was recalled, with Pompey's aid, Cicero tried once more to split his old friend from his present allies, but he was called smartly to heel by the three, and spent several unhappy years in which he had to defend adherents of theirs in the courts, though many of them were obnoxious to him. It was in this period that he began to write treatises on oratory and politics, which were well received, though fashion was beginning to turn against his oratorical style. In 51 B.C. Cicero was dispatched, protesting, to govern a province in Asia Minor—for him Rome was the center of the world, though he also loved the Italian countryside, where he had several villas—but he found he took some pleasure in ruling honestly and beneficently; he hoped, having done some minor campaigning, to reenter Rome with all the pomp of a triumph. But he returned to Italy late in 50 B.C. only to be faced with the outbreak of civil war between Pompey and Caesar (Crassus was dead in the East), in which at first he hoped to mediate. After long agonizing—though he resolutely rejected Caesar's attempt to gain his active support—he joined Pompey in Greece, mainly owing to a feeling of personal obligation, for he now thought Pompey almost as likely as Caesar to institute a tyranny if he won. He found himself very unhappy with the policies of Pompey and his followers, and after the disastrous battle of Pharsalus he hurried home to Italy.

But he hated Caesar's autocratic regime, in which he could speak freely in neither courts nor Senate, and turned back to his books, writing again on oratory and beginning to treat of philosophy, in which, especially after the death of his beloved daughter, Tullia, he found some consolation and felt he was doing Rome some service. He was not privy to, but rejoiced in, the assassination of Caesar in 44 B.C., and after some months of uncertainty he flung himself into the struggle against Mark Antony, who seemed to be trying to step into Caesar's shoes. A very senior ex-consul, and the embodiment of those republican principles on which he had written so much, he was for some months the real ruler of Rome, especially after the consuls of 43 had left the city to fight Antony in northern Italy; the *Philippics*, speeches named after those in which the great Greek orator Demosthenes had tried to stir up the Athenians to resist Philip of Macedon, document his course. But it proved impossible to hold together a motley alliance that included Caesar's adopted son, the nineteen-year-old Octavian (later the emperor Augustus) on the one hand, and Caesar's killers, the so-called Liberators, on the other, and Octavian and Antony finally joined forces. They proscribed numerous opponents, including Cicero. He was caught fleeing, not very decisively, from Italy, but died bravely, on 7 December 43 B.C.

This rapid sketch should serve at least to remind us of Cicero's deep involvement in the major events of his time (it is a great mistake to undervalue his importance just because he sometimes overvalued it) and the wide experience that he could bring to bear in his later years on problems of ethics and politics as well as oratory.

CICERO THE POET

Cicero's poetry is the aspect of his written work that we can deal with most rapidly. Most of it was the product of his youth, and it was probably largely because this was a time very thin in poets that he gained his reputation. He wrote easily—too easily—and probably from not a real poetic impulse but a desire to practice, and show off, his versatility and virtuosity with words. His remark that the Greek lyric poets were not worth reading shows the limitations of his poetic taste, which tended to the didactic or political. He once said that he honestly thought his brother a better poet than himself; but he remained proud of his version of the Greek astronomical poet Aratus, quoted it often, and perhaps had even revised it in maturity. It is the only one of his poems of which part has come down to us in an independent manuscript. We have too little contemporary

material to be certain, but it looks as if both Lucretius and Vergil may have imitated certain passages, and it is possible that Cicero infused a certain amount of feeling into the clarity and objectivity of the Greek, thus pointing the way to a characteristic of much later Roman poetry. Technically, his use of the hexameter was probably advanced for his time; a certain suppleness and elegance place him closer to Vergil than to the poets of the second century B.C. (whom nevertheless he loved) or even to his contemporary the archaizing Lucretius, though he still uses some of the heavy compound adjectives that early Latin had coined on the Greek model, but that do not really suit the language. And there is a prosaic explicitness in much of the work that prevents its taking a really high place among the remains of Latin poetry that we possess (there are also mistakes in the astronomy that suggest that, not untypically for his culture, he had never really looked at the heavens).

Later in life Cicero attempted to glorify his own political achievements and vicissitudes in heroic verse, with all the traditional epic machinery of councils of the gods and so on. These poems were a mistake; certain vainglorious lines became notorious, and Cicero the poet became something of a laughingstock. The historian Tacitus was to comment, "Caesar and Brutus also wrote poetry, not better than Cicero, but with better luck, for fewer know that they did so."

THE SPEECHES OF CICERO

It was otherwise with his speeches. Cicero was fortunate, of course, in living when he did, when the power of eloquence in courts, Senate, and popular assemblies was still enormous (under the more repressive and authoritarian government of the emperors, the practitioners of the art had far fewer real opportunities, and this, as Tacitus knew all too well, proved damaging), and when Greek training and influence had just brought some Latin speakers, such as Cicero's early mentors Lucius Crassus and

Marcus Antonius, to considerable heights. As the later historian Velleius Paterculus said, "oratory and forensic skill and the perfected glory of eloquence in prose so burst into flower in all their forms in the time of Cicero, their chief exponent, that there are few before him whom one can enjoy, and none whom one can admire save those who had either seen him or been seen by him" (1.17.3). But none of this entirely explains Cicero's greatness.

The Greeks had codified the rules of rhetoric in detail, and in Cicero's youth their teaching was being transferred into Latin, as his own early treatise *De inventione* shows ("invention" in rhetoric is the finding of arguments and other material); so does the more complete treatment, once ascribed to but certainly not by him, known as the *Rhetorica ad Herennium*. Like their Greek models, these works are organized as *artes*, in which the subject matter is carefully defined and subdivided, an arrangement ultimately derived from the Greek philosophers. It is impossible here to outline the teachings of the rhetoricians (which anyway diverge in detail), but one might note that they divided speeches into three types: judicial or forensic, delivered in the law courts, most typically for the defense; deliberative, concerned with public policy and delivered to some form of council or assembly; and demonstrative (in Greek, *epideictic*), which usually took the form of eulogy or invective, in Greece often delivered as a showpiece at a festival, but in Rome mainly employed either at funerals of great men or as an element in other forms of oration.

The orator has to excel in five fields—"invention," *dispositio* or organization, diction or style, memory, and delivery. A judicial speech (and with minor differences a deliberative speech) also has five parts—an introduction or *prooemium*; a narrative of the facts concerned; a *divisio* distinguishing the matters to be dealt with; a *confirmatio*, the arguments supporting one's case, which could be subdivided in various ways; and then, perhaps by way of a *digressio* or digression, which gave variety and relief, on to the often indignant or pathetic *per-*

oratio or peroration. The rhetoricians sometimes also spoke of the three styles of oratory: the low or plain, the grand or sublime, and the middle style, rather unsatisfactorily defined, but sometimes seen as formal and elegant, though not passionate. "Figures of speech" and "figures of thought" were also listed. Formal and artificial as all this may appear to us, it did encourage the giving of a clear if often rather standardized shape to a speech, something that the more primitive Romans had probably needed to learn, and provided a vocabulary for discussion and criticism. There was much choice, too, built into the rules; if fifteen different topics for arousing pity were cataloged, one was, of course, only expected to choose those most suitable to the case in hand, and room was left for natural talent as well as art. Cicero came to find traditional rhetoric jejune and inadequate, but he never tried to throw overboard its basic categories.

The stress on delivery and memory as two of the chief departments of the orator must also remind us that the most eloquent written speech from antiquity is only a shell, and that it was originally given life by a great variety of vocal tones (sometimes even by mimicry) and a great variety of gestures. Cicero may not have employed the positive language of gesture that Quintilian describes in his eleventh book (and he taught his own pupils to avoid beating time to their own rhythms or making faces), but he certainly thought one might stride up and down, stamp the foot, and strike the thigh or the forehead in moments of emphasis or emotion. The orator's art was considered to be allied to that of the actor, though Cicero was to think that it should be somewhat more restrained; but he was in his early years a friend and admirer of the great Roman actor Quintus Roscius, a proud and conscious artist from whom he probably learned much. Even a published speech would be judged by the ear rather than the eye, for one would either read it aloud oneself (for one thing, inadequate punctuation made this easier than silent reading) or, very commonly, would have a slave read it out to one.

CICERO

The conditions of the Roman courts also need to be understood; among other reasons, because they made it difficult to follow the rules of rhetoric precisely. In criminal cases the advocate was addressing a large jury of fifty or, later, seventy-five men (chosen among senators and later *equites* as well, not from the men in the street). He spoke in the open air—Quintilian was to say that the advocate must be ready to speak in sun or wind, wet or heat—though it has been supposed that the courts moved indoors in the winter. This fact, like the large audience, which also included a circle of bystanders, must have affected the style of speaking required. Though we know little of the acoustics of the Forum, it is clear that there was a certain amount of playing to the gallery, although in the first instance it was a fairly well-educated gallery; but Cicero certainly cared for the applause of the *corona*, the circle of bystanders, as well as the jury. Oratory, he thought, was not like poetry, which need only appeal to the cognoscenti. In some civil cases a single judge might be involved, in others a large panel of a hundred or more.

The main speech was usually delivered at the start of a case, before the witnesses were heard, and a briefer intervention was made afterward. Often, especially in important criminal cases and in Cicero's later years, several advocates shared a single brief, and since Cicero himself usually spoke last, in the place of honor, and was expected to cope with any general, perhaps political, aspects of the case and, often, to provide the pathetic peroration at which he was so skilled, such mundane matters as the narration of the facts and the refutation of some or all of the actual charges had already been dealt with. But parts at least of the rhetorical framework are usually visible in his speeches, though often, as we shall see, in surprising and unexpected forms.

Cicero came into court, we are told by Quintilian again, with his *prooemium* fully written out, and for the rest mere notes (his freedman Tiro later published these, and we may wish that they had survived). The published versions of the orations, which might combine parts of both the speeches actually made in court and sometimes part of the cross-questioning as well, were written up afterward (on feast days and holidays, says their author, when the rest of the world was at leisure), and how close they were to what was actually delivered it is very hard to say. Sometimes the speech was published quite soon after its delivery, to catch the interest that the trial had aroused or as political propaganda; but though in this case some readers might be able to compare the spoken and written versions in their minds, we do not know how much change they expected to find. Minor stylistic or factual changes Cicero certainly did make, as we see from the letters to Atticus, who in the 40's was responsible for making and disseminating at least some elegant and accurate copies of Cicero's new works, though perhaps not on the scale really to deserve the term publisher. (One often borrowed a book one wanted, whether from the author or another, and copied or had one's slaves copy it out.) But it was not till three years after his consulship that Cicero put out a collection of the speeches of that period, primarily for political reasons, and it has been suspected that political considerations may have prompted various insertions and changes. For one of these speeches, the famous *First Catilinarian Oration*, there can hardly have been even any notes to go on, for it must have been entirely improvised, since apparently no one had expected Catiline, to whom it is largely addressed, to come into the Senate that day; while the version that we have is so concise and brilliant that it must surely have been carefully worked on. Nevertheless, Cicero did tell Atticus that the written speeches would show him "what I said and what I did"— and both men were in fact conscientious historians.

A contemporary writer assures us that he had heard a famous speech, now lost, the *pro Cornelio*, delivered in court by Cicero, and that the peroration was almost identical with the published version. But Cicero may have prepared his perorations with some care, even if he did not write them out fully, though he tells us that he was so overcome by emotion himself on these occasions that he gave the impression, at least, of hardly knowing what he did or said. He was famous for his appeals to the jury for mercy. Scenes theatrical in the extreme might be staged; by Roman tradition the accused man's aged parents, or even better his small children, might appear dressed in mourning and weeping, and the advocate would exploit the possibilities to the hilt. Cicero tells us that he once delivered a peroration with a baby in his arms (one would like to have seen that), and another orator once tore the tunic from a defendant's shoulders, to show the honorable scars that he bore. Cicero certainly often wept real tears—the prosecution in the case of Cn. Plancius, trying to prevent yet another dramatic finale, jeered at the *lacrimula*, the little tear, that he had shed on a recent occasion. "Say rather whole floods," retorted Cicero unrepentantly in the *pro Plancio*, and he refused to be balked of his great scene, which seems to have had its usual effect—at any rate his client got off. This one concentrates on Plancius' devotion to Cicero himself and the succor he gave Cicero in his exile, and on Cicero's desperate anxiety to save him in return, and tears all round are at least imputed. Cicero was, in fact, an intensely emotional man (this was one of his problems as a politician, if one of his strengths as an artist), though at times his emotions were roused somewhat too easily and had no great depth—this is far from being always true, however. He was a nervous man, too, and claimed toward the end of his life that he had always felt uneasy before a big case.

It is difficult for us to set Cicero's speeches in their proper literary context; for though we have much interesting discussion and evaluation of earlier Roman speakers in his history of oratory at Rome (the *Brutus*), we have only the most miserable fragments of his immediate predecessors, such as his admired L. Crassus, or of his coevals. We must particularly regret the loss of the speeches of Quintus Hortensius, the elder contemporary whom Cicero at first attempted to rival and in time surpassed—though we are told that Hortensius, whose most remarkable gifts were in voice, movement, and an astounding memory, was better heard than read, which helps to explain why nothing of his has survived; his style was floridly "Asianic," as Cicero ultimately came to call it. Even more do we miss the younger orators who criticized Cicero in the 50's and 40's as verbose, flaccid, and overconcerned with the rhythms in which his phrases and periods ended. (Ciceronian rhythm is a complex and disputed subject; but whole periods, and many shorter sections within them, tend to end in one of a certain number of rhythms. Cicero's opponents claimed in particular that he was overfond of the phrase, and rhythm, *ĕssĕ vĭdĕātŭr*. The rhythms of recognized verse forms he carefully avoided.)

And perhaps worst of all is the loss of all recent and contemporary formal prose in Greek, in other words, that of the Hellenistic period. It was swept away in the rage for a purity of language and style based on the dialect and manner of Athenian writers of the fifth and fourth centuries B.C. that overcame the Greeks soon after Cicero's death. In this grievous dearth we have to fall back on scraps such as the self-laudatory inscription of an oriental king from the fringe of the Greek-speaking world, whose *clausulae* or metrical phrase endings appear to be very close to Cicero's, and suggest that he was modeling himself to some degree on Hellenistic precedent. In general, Cicero seems, especially in the works of his earlier maturity, to be attempting with considerable success to naturalize in Rome the ample periodic style of Greek that the fourth-century author of political pamphlets Isocrates had been one of the first to develop (though Cicero's sentence structure is by no means identical with that of Isocrates, his clauses being rarely so exactly balanced and parallel but tending to greater variety and unexpectedness). There are those who admire a more concise and forceful style as more truly Latin and more suited to the genius of the language. But Cicero could be on occasion concise and forceful too. There can be no doubt that he greatly expanded the capacities of his native tongue and paved the way for his admirer Livy's mastery of the period, though Livy's periods are typically narrative rather than argumentative, and his rhythms are different and less marked.

One ought, however, to speak not of Cicero's style but his styles—which depend on context and occasion. When speaking in a property suit before a single judge it was necessary to use a simpler and quieter manner than when addressing a large body of jurors in a great criminal case with political overtones. In the *pro Roscio comoedo*, however, in which he represented his friend the actor in one of the civil cases that he later gave up, Cicero experiments with a condensed and pointed style unlike his usual, more amply flowing one, which some have thought to be, perhaps, one of Hortensius' manners. Another speech for a property case, the *pro Caecina*, he later described as being entirely in the plain style, which aims at convincing the intellect. In the same passage (*Orator* 102) he says that his speech to the people on behalf of the law of Manilius, which gave Pompey his great command in the East, was in the middle style, and that one of his speeches as a consul, that for Rabirius, a case of (possibly) unlawful killing of crucial political importance, in which Cicero felt that the whole authority of the Senate and welfare of the state were involved, was in the grand style throughout. These three speeches survive, the last incompletely. It is worth noting that the *pro lege Manilia* is largely taken up with praise of Pompey, bringing it close to the epideictic genre of oratory.

Cicero goes on to say that his *pro Cluentio* has passages in all three styles. And this in fact would seem to be more usual. The *prooemium* would be a careful piece of work, but usually quiet; the narration should be brief and clear, as Cicero's generally are (unless, as in the *pro Cluentio*, he positively wishes to confuse us); the *dispositio* and the *confirmatio*, normally fairly down-to-earth; a digression might be a showpiece, on a subject suitable for *amplifica-tio*, worked up with rhythms, figures, and so on; and the peroration, as we saw, emotional in the extreme. Cicero admitted that the grand style was ludicrous and disgusting in the wrong place, and he deplored the tasteless Asian rhetoricians who chanted or howled their unremittingly rhythmical compositions, giving an impression of insincerity. But he remained convinced that oratory should be capable of moving as well as persuading, and be able to rise to the level of grandeur, as Demosthenes could do. He wrote to Atticus about the speech Brutus had made to the people after Caesar's murder and was now publishing:

> he has achieved in this speech with perfect taste the manner he prefers and the style he thinks best for oratory. I, rightly or wrongly, have aimed at something else. . . . if you recall the thunders of Demosthenes you will see that it is possible to be both Attic and impressive.
>
> (*Ad Atticum* 15.1 and 2)

But he was immensely proud of his varied abilities. In the *Brutus* (322 ff.) he indicates that there was no one to equal him (he is speaking of the earlier part of his career) in calling up witnesses from the past out of his abundant knowledge of history, or who could by brief and witty mockery of his adversary relax the jury and incline it to mercy rather than severity, or who could move the discussion from the particular circumstances onto a more general plane. The first and third of these abilities were due to his unusually wide early education and continued reading; for the second he was famous, though he also got a reputation for maliciousness and a certain lack of the proper Roman quality of *gravitas*, a certain weighty seriousness. "What a comic consul we have," said Cato pointedly in 63 B.C., as a speech that mocked devotion to Stoic philosophy was arousing gales of laughter. In fact, collections of Cicero's jokes were made in his time, and individual examples have come down to us (as well as those in surviving writings); unfortunately, for the most part they do not survive

CICERO

translation (he was fond of puns) or isolation from their circumstances.

Linked with Cicero's humor was his skill in character drawing, what the Greek rhetoricians called *ethos*, and thought very important in judicial oratory; standards of relevance were lax and the whole lives of defendant, prosecutor, or witnesses were brought up for discussion; it was vital to give these people convincing characters, praiseworthy or otherwise, that would explain their actions in a way that suited the speaker. Cicero, with his wit and theatrical sense, was particularly good at this, and there are numerous memorable character sketches in his works, whether of persons actually involved in the trial or those who, by the figure of speech known as *prosopopoeia*, or "personification," were summoned up in imagination to make their contribution to the argument. There is an unforgettable paired *prosopopoeia* in the *pro Caelio*, where first the grave and antique statesman Appius Claudius the Blind is called up to reproach his unworthy descendant Clodia, and is followed by her degenerate young brother, Cicero's enemy P. Clodius.

Invective, too, suited Cicero all too well. Strictly a form of demonstrative or epideictic oratory, it could find a place in judicial or deliberative speeches—especially in the Senate, where, since the politicians almost all knew each other, clever hits could be really savored. Cicero's enemies L. Calpurnius Piso Caesoninus and Aulus Gabinius, whom he regarded as partly responsible for his exile, the one with a misleadingly severe appearance and bushy eyebrows but also a hidden taste for the Epicurean life of pleasure, the other a curly-haired dandy with a talent for dancing—not a respectable quality in a Roman consul—are pictured as brilliantly, and unfairly, as is the crapulous Antony of the *Second Philippic*. Strict truth was not demanded in this form, which had its own conventional topics; invective might offend, but often did not seriously damage, its victims. Vatinius forgave Cicero for the *In Vatinium*, and Piso's reputation seems to have survived the *In Pisonem*.

SELECTED SPEECHES

How cleverly Cicero makes use of, but avoids slavishly following, the pronouncements of the teachers of rhetoric we may see by a couple of brief illustrations. The *prooemium*, we saw, is expected to be calm. But the *First Catilinarian* opens with a tremendous effect of headlong urgency.

> *Quo usque tandem, abutere, Catilina, patientia nostra? quam diu etiam furor iste tuus nos eludet? quem ad finem sese effrenata iactabit audacia? nihilne te nocturnum praesidium Palati, nihil urbis vigiliae, nihil timor populi, nihil concursus bonorum omnium, nihil hic munitissimus habendi senatus locus, nihil horum ora voltusque moverunt? patere tua consilia non sentis, constrictam iam horum omnium scientia teneri coniurationem tuam non vides? Quid proxima, quid superiore nocte egeris, ubi fueris, quos convocaveris, quid consili ceperis quem nostrum ignorare arbitraris? o tempora, o mores! Senatus haec intelligit, consul videt; hic tamen vivit.*

How far, then, Catiline, will you go on abusing our patience? How long, you madman, will you mock at our vengeance? Will there be no end to your unbridled audacity? Is it nothing to you that there is a nightly guard on the Palatine, that there are patrols throughout the city, that the populace is in terror, that all honest men are rallying together, that the Senate meets in this stronghold, that the senators look on you with expressions of horror? Do you not see that all your plans are discovered? Do you not realize that you conspirators are bound hand and foot by the knowledge that every man here has of you? Which of us do you think is not aware of what you did last night, or the night before, where you were, whom you summoned, what plans you made? What times we live in, what scandals we permit! The Senate knows these things, the consul sees them; yet this man lives.

This is rapid and condensed (as the far wordier English translation makes evident); the individual sentences are not elaborately periodic; their constituent phrases and clauses are not linked by coordinating or subordinating words. Emphasis is given by the repetition of the same word in the same place in the phrase (*nihil* in the opening position six times)—this is the figure known as anaphora—and vividness by the address to Catiline and the use of the question, which was itself counted as a figure. Favorite rhythms appear in *iāctābĭt aūdācĭă* and *vŏl-tūsquĕ mōvērūnt*; and *ora voltusque* is one of Cicero's typical doublets, in which the second word, though nearly synonymous with the first, either adds a shade of meaning or improves the weight and rhythm of the passage. (It is not quite true that Cicero always uses two words where one could do.) The superlative *munitis-simus*, "most heavily defended," is also typical of Cicero's style on formal occasions.

After the passage quoted, the questions continue, and so does the use of figures; for example, hendiadys, *furorem ac tela*, "his fury and weapons" for "the fury of his weapons"; also metaphor, of which Latin is sparing, but which is always vivid when it does occur: "we are allowing the edge of the Senate's decree to grow blunt"; it is "as though hidden in its scabbard." There are *exempla* too, references to events of past history, brought forward in illustration of a point or as precedents and examples to follow or avoid; Aristotle had already thought this figure especially suitable for political speeches, but the Romans, with their reverence for the authority of the past, were particularly devoted to it—here we find the justifiable killing of Tiberius Gracchus and other more ancient plotters of tyranny in Rome. In paragraph 5, calming down a little, Cicero explains why Catiline is nonetheless allowed to live. It is because not everyone would yet think Cicero justified in putting him to death (he was an aristocrat with many influential friends); but he can do no harm, for Cicero knows all his plans. The consul's course is thus shown to be *prudent* and *not harmful*, recognized topics of deliberative oratory; but all this is done indirectly, through the address to Catiline, still full of rhetorical questions. And so, very boldly, is even the narrative of Catiline's recent activities and all that Cicero has discovered of his plots: do you not realize

that we know you were at Laeca's house, that you did such-and-such, and so on? The questions are interrupted only briefly in paragraph 9, by an address to the Fathers, the *patres conscripti*; there were clearly no rules about always addressing the house in general. In paragraph 10 Cicero bids Catiline leave Rome:

> Therefore, Catiline, continue on the path you have chosen: leave the city at last: the gates are open: go!

One notes how the brief paratactic (unsubordinated) clauses get progressively shorter and quicker, not, as so often, longer (the tricolon, three parallel clauses or phrases of increasing length, is elsewhere one of Cicero's favorite organizing devices).

The next section might loosely be described as proof, or at least argument, directed at making Catiline actually leave. In paragraph 13 there is some invective about his past life, still in rhetorical questions. As in most invective, what is said about his private affairs is probably not true (he is accused of incest and murder, among other things), whereas what is said in paragraph 15 about a supposed earlier conspiracy is almost certainly false. The tone changes in paragraph 16 from indignation to ironical pity for Catiline's isolated position in the Senate. In paragraph 17 the Fatherland, the *patria* who hates and fears him, is personified (another figure); in paragraph 18 the country actually speaks, in a dramatic prosopopoeia (the figure mentioned above in reference to the *pro Caelio*).

Catiline seems to have interrupted to say that if the Senate voted that he should go into exile he would obey. But the Senate was not a court of law and could not have voted such a thing. Cicero turns the interruption to splendid effect by pointing out the silence in which the Fathers heard the proposal; if it was suggested that anyone else from among them should go into exile—and he names various distinguished names—there would be uproar. After a further passage, about Catiline's future acts when he has left Rome, which some have thought may have been added with hindsight later, there is a second prosopopoeia, in which the *patria* now addresses Cicero in the archaic form used in the Senate: *Marce Tulli, quid agis?* What are you doing, Marcus Tullius? Why are you sending Catiline to head a hostile army? In paragraph 29 he answers, he says, her voice and the thoughts of those who feel as she does: it is because there are some who do not believe, or claim that they do not believe, in the conspiracy. Cicero's style is now becoming more periodic, but it is still brief and rapid; metaphors are still prominent, and so are pairs of words or doublets: *exstirpetur atque delebitur*, "will be rooted out and destroyed," or *stirps ac semen malorum*, "the root and seed of our ills."

And Cicero ends by turning, first back to Catiline, to urge him again to leave, and then to Jupiter Stator, in whose temple the Senate was meeting, asserting that he is indeed the stayer, or stay, of the city and the empire—such plays on words were felt to be perfectly serious. This, the final sentence, is a longer, but not a long, period, organized internally with two *tricola*, and marked by a solemn reference to Romulus, the founder of the city of Rome and of this temple, and by the lofty archaic word *mactare*, to punish, which ends the speech not only with a powerful metrical cadence but with a strong alliteration (the repeated *m* in *mōrtŭōsquĕ māctābīs*), something that was traditional in Latin, and so perhaps again archaic in its overtones, though not much favored in Greek or by Greek rhetoricians. But when the very preservation of Rome and its ancient traditions was in question, such an evocation of the past was highly appropriate.

> *Tu, Iuppiter, qui isdem quibus haec urbs auspiciis a Romulo es constitutus, quem Statorem huius urbis atque imperi vere nominamus, hunc et huius socios a tuis ceterisque templis, a tectis urbis ac moenibus, a vita fortunisque civium omnium arcebis et homines bonorum inimicos, hostis patriae, latrones Italiae scelerum foedere inter se ac nefaria societate coniunctos aeternis suppliciis vivos mortuosque mactabis.*

Thou, O Jupiter, who wert set here by Romulus with the same religious ceremony with which he founded the city, thou whom we truly call the Stay of this city and its Empire, ward off this man and his confederates from thy temples and those of the other gods, from the houses and fortifications of the city, from the lives and property of its citizens, and punish men who are enemies to all respectable people, traitors to their country, and brigands to Italy, with eternal torment both in life and beyond the grave.

The speech is perhaps almost entirely in the grand style, in spite of its speed and compression; the critic Demetrius had a fourth category, "forceful" writing, which might fit much of it well. It treats the rules with notable freedom; but it would not impress us so much as daring and unexpected if we did not know the rules and were unable to judge it in part by them.

This speech is unusually excited for one that was delivered to the Senate; formal oratory might have its place here, as in the speech described by Cicero in a letter to Atticus in 61 B.C. (a couple of years after his consulship and shortly after Pompey's return to Rome).

> As for me, good gods, how I showed myself off before my new hearer, Pompey: if ever periods or cadences or arguments of various kinds [he uses the Greek technical terms] came to my aid, they did then. In short, there were cheers. This was the theme, the dignity of the Senate, concord with the *equites*, the unity of Italy, the dying remnants of the conspiracy, the price of grain, peace at home. You know how I can thunder on those subjects. I think you must have heard me out there in Epirus [where Atticus was staying on his estate] so I won't dwell on the subject.
>
> (*Ad Atticum* 1.14.4)

The speech is lost but need not be regretted; Cicero thundered elsewhere on these subjects. Often, however, too formal a speech might seem artificial, and some of the most influential statesmen in Rome had spoken quite simply and naturally. Cicero may often have concentrated on the matter in hand in a similar way, though in such circumstances he would obviously not have troubled to publish his speech.

Speeches to the people were often rather generalized and appealed more to emotion (or prejudice) or even superstition than to reason. They had to be fairly short, as the men in the public meeting or *contio* stood rather than sat, and recurrent disorder also meant that it was essential to capture the attention. Again, Roman tradition meant that it was not always possible to stick precisely to the rules. For example, in a *suasio* or a *dissuasio*, aimed at persuading the people to pass or reject a particular bill, it might be useful to go through the clauses of the bill one by one, quoting and commenting on them, in a necessarily down-to-earth style. This is what Cicero does in the second speech *De lege agraria*, concerning a bill proposed at the start of his consulship, which proposed to acquire land in order to give allotments to the urban poor and to Pompey's veterans. And sometimes the main object of a *contio* (the word is also used of the speech itself) is simply to give information to the people. There were no newspapers; there was no official publication of senatorial proceedings, at least till Caesar in 59 B.C. introduced some sort of published summary of debates or decisions. The people therefore depended on a magistrate telling them in a *contio* what was going on; and Cicero makes a merit at times of doing so.

The *Third Catilinarian Oration*, especially, consists very largely of narrative: it is a prompt report on recent events, a clear, simple, and rapid account of the intrigue by the conspirators left in Rome after Catiline's departure with some envoys from a tribe in Gaul; of the latter's arrest outside Rome on their way home, arranged by Cicero, which meant the seizure of the letters that proved the conspirators' guilt at last; and of the subsequent scene in the Senate, with the confessions by a praetor and other conspirators of senatorial rank; and the decree with which the sitting ended. This *narratio* is sandwiched between an excited *prooemium* and a peroration on what the gods, and Cicero

himself—who is, it is hinted, almost to be regarded as a god himself—have done to save Rome.

Utterly different from any of these is the *pro Caelio*, a judicial speech in which Cicero was defending a talented but wild young friend and protégé, himself a very talented speaker but, as Cicero said in an unwonted boxing metaphor, the possessor of a better right than left, and thus in need of assistance in his defense. There were various charges, including an attempt to poison his mistress Clodia (possibly Catullus' Lesbia, though one of her sisters may be a better candidate for the post). The court had been convened, as for an emergency, on a holiday.

Now one of the most usual forms of *prooemium* stressed the importance of the subject on hand (which sometimes led to ridiculous exaggerations). Here, however, Cicero turns the tradition upside down; this is the most frivolous trial ever, in which an honorable young man is being persecuted by a woman who is no better than a *meretrix*, a prostitute, and so totally undeserving of credit. And on a holiday too! So Cicero sets himself to make up to the jurors for the theatrical shows that they are missing; the speech is full of situations that are treated as if they occurred in Roman comedy or farce—notably the bungled rendezvous at the baths at which a friend of Caelius was supposed to have handed over the poison to Clodia's slaves. There is also mythological burlesque, a common theatrical form; Clodia is not only a *meretrix*, a stock figure of comedy, but the Medea of the Palatine, the fashionable hill in Rome on which she lived. There are quotations from Terence and another playwright—the interpolation of verse was a recognized, if not very usual, figure of speech. Members of Clodia's family are vividly set before us. Much of the language is natural, even colloquial, though a famous character sketch of Catiline, with whom Caelius had unfortunately been friendly, evokes his contradictory vices and virtues in a memorably antithetic style, and a dramatic digression describes the deathbed of Clodia's husband, Metellus, poisoned by his wife—the tragic scene is perhaps not meant to be taken quite seriously. There is good-humored moralization on the theme "boys will be boys," a recognized *locus communis* or commonplace, suitable for various contexts. And there is a brief pathetic peroration—brief, because too long and serious a plea might be out of place in this speech, and with so bold a defendant (it concentrates therefore on his aged father), and because, as a Greek rhetorician quoted elsewhere by Cicero says, "nothing dries more quickly than a tear."

Even the *pro Caelio* has some rather repetitive and tedious passages; and there are certainly other speeches, notably some of those dating from the period after Cicero's return from exile, that make sad reading. They grind relentlessly, again and again, through the events leading up to his banishment, in a verbose and mechanical manner that betrays his embarrassment and wretchedness. Some were at one time even suspected of not being genuine because of their inferior quality. But even where the best speeches, with all their variety and brilliancy, are concerned, it is possible to feel dissatisfaction. Too often Cicero is pleading a bad case, whether in the courts, where many of his clients were patently guilty—such as Milo, who killed P. Clodius, though the speech composed (not in fact delivered) in his defense, the *pro Milone*, was revered as a model in antiquity; or in the Senate, where his somewhat narrow political views and his lack of real sympathy with the poor are visible, and where at several periods in his life he could not express his real views; or before the people, where he performs miracles of disingenuousness in order to persuade them that he is really a *popularis* at heart.

To a considerable extent these criticisms do not apply to the *Philippics*. In his late years, partly because a restrained style was considered suitable for an elderly man, partly because Cicero had had to defend himself against the criticisms of the so-called "Atticisers" at Rome,

led by Catullus' friend Calvus, who found models for their simpler style in the orators of classical Athens, he wrote what to modern eyes at least is some of his finest prose, more condensed than much of his earlier work, though not lacking in richness. In 43 B.C., indeed, there was no time to write long speeches—the struggle against Antony was too urgent. And Cicero was fighting for a cause in which he believed; indeed, he felt at last that he was holding the position in the state that his achievements warranted, and he was trying to play worthily the role of *rector reipublicae*, the statesman who led and guided his country, whose duties and qualifications he had detailed in his political treatise, the *De Republica*. These speeches above all cannot be measured by the rulebook, though Greek influence combines with Roman tradition. For example, in the last surviving speech of all, the *Fourteenth Philippic*, in proposing unusual honors to the soldiers killed in the battles by which, for a moment, it looked as if Cicero's cause had triumphed, he evoked in his hearers in the Senate the memory of the Athenian public funeral orations, spoken for those who had died in the service of the state by so many of Athens' greatest orators, and most memorably by Pericles, in the version given by the historian Thucydides. But he ended, as so many speeches in the Senate were bound to end, whatever the rhetoricians might say about perorations, with the formal proposal of the decree that was to authorize these honors. Thus it was legal Roman language, formulaic and old-fashioned, that was ringing in the Senate as Cicero came to the end of his speech.

But even with the *Philippics*, doubts may intrude. Nothing could be more sublime and moving than the plea to Antony at the end of the *Second Philippic*:

Respice, quaeso, aliquando rem publicam, M. Antoni, quibus ortus sis, non quibuscum vivas considera: mecum, ut voles: redi cum re publica in gratiam. sed de te tu videris; ego de me ipse profitebor. defendi rem publicam adulescens, non de-

seram senex: contempsi Catilinae gladios, non pertimescam tuos. quin etiam corpus libenter obtulerim, si repraesentari morte mea libertas civitatis potest, ut aliquando dolor populi Romani pariat quod iam diu parturit! etenim si abhinc annos prope viginti hoc ipso in templo negavi posse mortem immaturam esse consulari, quanto verius nunc negabo seni? mihi vero, patres conscripti, iam etiam optanda mors est, perfuncto rebus eis quas adeptus sum quasque gessi. duo modo haec opto, unum ut moriens populum Romanum liberum relinquam—hoc mihi maius ab dis immortalibus dari nihil potest—alterum ut ita cuique eveniat ut de re publica quisque mereatur.

(2.118)

Remember for once, I beg you, Mark Antony, the State; think of your ancestors, not your associates; treat me as you please, but make your peace with the State. But that is your affair; I shall speak for myself. I fought for the Republic when young, I shall not abandon her in my old age. I scorned the daggers of Catiline; I shall not tremble before yours. Rather I would willingly expose my body to them, if by my death the liberty of the nation could be recovered and the agony of the Roman people could at last bring to birth that with which it has been so long in labor. All but twenty years ago in this very temple I said that death could not be premature for one who had attained the rank of consul; how much more truly must I say it now that I am an old man. For me indeed, Fathers of the Senate, death is even desirable, after all that I have attained and accomplished. I have only two wishes, one that at my death I may leave the Roman People free—the immortal gods can grant me no greater boon than that; and secondly that each citizen may prosper according to his deserts toward the Republic.

One would not accuse Cicero of insincerity; doubtless he passionately believed every word as he penned it. But when, staying on the seacoast, he heard that Antony, whom he had already offended irreparably, was marching up Italy toward Rome with a strong force, though he made up his mind to go to the capital, he fell on the way into a panic lest Antony catch up with him and bolted to his remote birthplace at Arpinum, to return to Rome only when Antony had left it.

THE EARLIER DIALOGUES

The true Ciceronian is often happier with the treatises and the letters, where the author is usually saying what he really thinks, and where, on the whole, the vanity of which he is so often accused is not in evidence. This supposed vanity rested partly on the recurrent need to assert his political position, and for the rest on a sense of insecurity, which leads him often to self-criticism, when he does not need to present a confident face to the public. In these works, largely remote from the conventions of personal invective and eulogy, his judgments even of his opponents are often balanced and generous.

The dialogue was a form favored by the Greeks, partly because it sweetened the pill of serious discussion for the general reader, partly, in some cases at least, because it reflected the art of philosophic argument or dialectic, on which the philosophers laid so much stress. It seems that there had already been a few imitations of the form in Latin. Cicero was to be particularly influenced by the dialogues— in which such a great part is played by Socrates— of Plato, who was as great an artist and stylist as he was a philosopher, and of Aristotle, which are now lost to us. But on the whole he abjures the cut and thrust of debate—his characters put forward their differing views at length; and the framework of his discussions is more formal than that of Plato's dialogues, where often casual encounters in Athens lead insensibly to argument on serious matters. Cicero tends to bring together great Roman public figures, in a city mansion or a country villa, on some holiday that gives them leisure to talk; they are often accompanied by younger relatives or admirers. They decide deliberately to discuss some important problem, which they do with great courtesy. But there is considerable charm in, for example, the introduction to the

De Legibus, where Cicero, his brother, and Atticus are walking in his grounds at Arpinum, or in book 3 of the *De Finibus*, where we find Cato in the library of a country house outside Rome "wallowing" in books on Stoicism, or in book 5, set in Athens in its author's student days. Only at the end of his life does he seem to have become bored with the form; in the *Tusculan Disputations* it is vestigial, and in the *De Officiis* he does without it altogether.

Plato at least had cared little for anachronisms in his dialogues; Cicero is uncommonly scrupulous in trying to avoid these, and though, especially when he set his works back in the later second or early first century, his speakers had to be made more sophisticated and more conversant with Greek learning than really they had been, he did try to give a fair picture of them and their background, and factual statements are rarely erroneous. The letters show him, with Atticus' aid, going to considerable trouble to get details right. In fact, Cicero had strong historical interests, and was tempted by Atticus' urgings that he should write a history. They both, and doubtless others too, were aware that Rome had not yet produced a great historian to rival those of Greece, and Cicero, with his political experience and his literary genius (the ancients usually thought of historiography as a branch of oratory, that is, of literary prose) seemed the ideal writer to fill the gap. Cicero promised to devote himself to the subject in old age and in the last year of his life thought seriously of beginning, with the help of Atticus, who was himself something of a historian; but events moved too fast for him. However, he discussed the genre interestingly in the *De Oratore*, insisting that while it must not suppress or invent facts, it must reflect its author's views clearly so that the reader can learn from his experience, and in the third book, in which the introduction includes a longish account of the great orator L. Crassus' last political speech, his illness and death in 91 B.C., he perhaps gave a sample of what he could do in this line. The account is notably clear and precise, indicating its sources, although it reaches heights of eloquence at the end, in its meditation on the death of L. Crassus, by which he avoided the horrors of the ensuing civil wars.

L. Crassus, adviser and model to Cicero in his youth, is the leading figure in this first dialogue, written in 55 B.C. It is clear from its remoteness from the ordinary rhetorical handbooks how inadequate Cicero now found these. It is concerned largely with the broad education, partly on the Greek model, that Cicero thinks the true orator requires—in law and history, and above all in philosophy, which means primarily ethical and political theory. For a long time Greek rhetors and philosophers had quarreled over the education of the young, the rhetors holding that philosophy was abstruse and useless, the philosophers often arguing, in the wake of Plato, that rhetoric was frivolous and amoral. There were others, however, who held that rhetoric could be given serious intellectual and ethical content; Isocrates had even declared, in the fourth century B.C., that his high-minded political pamphlets constituted real philosophy. It is in their steps that Cicero treads. He disclaims far-reaching originality, declaring in a later letter that he had gone back to Isocrates and also to Aristotle, who had tried to justify rhetorical methods of argument as well as philosophical ones. Cicero, in fact, always gave eloquence an immensely high place, claiming that, as well as uniting intellectual and aesthetic excellence, it was even responsible for the creation of all civilized society.

The *De Oratore* also discusses some rather more technical subjects, such as the role of humor in oratory, which Cicero declares has never been treated fully. The organization of this section, as well, indeed, as much of the rest of the work, shows that though he did not suffer from the convert's mania for organization on the pattern of an *ars* that seems to have afflicted so many of his contemporaries—such as the great scholar Marcus Terentius Varro or, slightly later, the architectural writer Vitruvius—he did feel that some use of this framework was necessary for a large work on a serious subject. Indeed, part of his claim for the role of philosophy rests on the power of organization of this very kind, as well as on the capacity for logical argument that dialectic on the Aristotelian or Stoic model bestows on the orator. But Cicero was capable, as perhaps no one else in his time in Rome was, of treating the method with freedom and maturity. The work as a whole, too, in spite of some dull and over-lengthy passages, has a maturity never reached in Rome before.

In its identification of the true orator with the true statesman—L. Crassus came close to being both—the *De Oratore* was in a sense a political work. The *De Republica*, which followed on its heels, was explicitly political, and perhaps the first discussion of political theory in Latin; though the breakdown of the republican constitution in these years may have inspired historians and antiquarians to ask what had gone wrong, and in particular what changes in Roman customs and manners had had so disastrous an effect. Cicero sets this dialogue back in the second century, just when (as he saw it) the brothers Gracchus were alienating the People from the Senate, but statesmen of the Golden Age of the republic were still alive. Scipio Aemilianus, the great general and statesman, is asked to say what he thinks is the best form of government. He argues, as many Greeks had done, that a mixture of the three basic forms, monarchy, oligarchy, and democracy, is best and stablest, and that Rome is the best of several examples of this mixed constitution. Cicero writes him a brief and rather schematized history of Rome to show this, and there are also passages of interesting antiquarian argument about early customs in Rome, in which, if Cicero appears less learned than his contemporary Varro, who discovered many early documents, he probably shows much better critical judgment.

Most of the *De Republica* was lost until 1820, and much of the work is still fragmentary. There was a discussion of the role of justice and natural law in the state, based on a famous Greek debate; there seems to have been a consideration of education, which Cicero, against many Greeks but in accordance with Roman tradition, preferred to see centered in the home rather than controlled by the state. And there was a long account of the ideal citizen, who is also the ideal statesman. It used to be thought that he was advocating a quasi-monarchic protector of the constitution, but it is now generally agreed that there could be more than one such *rector* or *gubernator* guiding or steering the state, and that he was to rely solely on example, knowledge of the laws, and influence on public opinion. Cicero probably had himself in mind—rather than, as used to be thought, the military and inadequately educated Pompey—for the post. In a crisis, however, he thought that a dictator (for the Romans, a magistrate with overriding powers but a limited term of office), was acceptable. It is remarkable that in this work Cicero shows himself very aware of the power of oratory to mislead; his *rector*, unlike the ideal statesman of the *De Oratore*, will speak simply and briefly.

Scipio and his friends open the work by discussing astronomy and the claims of the life devoted to politics rather than private study—the old quarrel of the practical and the theoretical life, as the Greeks called it. It ends by returning to these themes, showing how carefully Cicero, who spent a great deal of effort on it, has constructed it. Plato sometimes, as in his own work on the ideal state, also known as the *Republic*, ended his dialogues with a myth, and Cicero here imitates him, as he does in certain other respects. In the famous "Dream of Scipio," his protagonist is transported to the heavens, where he is told by his grandfather Scipio Africanus, the conqueror of Hannibal, that true statesmen are rewarded by the gods with immortality; from his present position Aemilianus can see that the earth is an insignificant ball and realize that fame on earth, though it is the proper reward for a statesman, is evanescent—and so he will not be influenced by popular repute. The ancients, and Cicero himself as he is generally painted, were obsessed with glory; but here again, he shows himself more capable of detachment than is usually supposed, even if he is following in the footsteps of certain philosophers. He is arguing in effect that political activity should be altruistic; for about a future life and its rewards, Cicero was never dogmatic. The "Dream" was famous—and misunderstood—in late antiquity and the Middle Ages (it was the one part of the *De Republica* that was not lost); it has not the extraordinary imaginative qualities of Plato's myths, but it is a noble and eloquent piece of writing, though, as is so often the case with Cicero, rather too long to lend itself easily to quotation.

The *De Legibus* was meant as a supplement to the *De Republica* (the title again echoes Plato, who wrote a dialogue called the *Laws*). It was probably written shortly after it, though it may never have been finished and was perhaps not published in Cicero's lifetime. It is a less attractive piece of writing, in spite of its pleasant framework and some touches of humor directed at the conventions of the dialogue form ("you are aware, my dear brother, that in dialogues of this kind it is customary to say 'certainly' or 'quite true,' so that a new subject can be introduced"; "As a matter of fact I do not agree at all, but please go on to the next subject all the same"). Here, after another introductory discussion of natural law, on which to him all particular laws should rest, Cicero enunciates in archaizing legal language a religious and political code based on though not quite identical with the practices, themselves not fully codified, of the Rome he knows; the provisions are then discussed. The work as we have it is fragmentary and often obscure, something that is rare with this author; but it is typical of Cicero and of his breadth of mind that he tends to find support for his (often somewhat reactionary) changes in Roman practice in three sources, and sometimes in all three at once: Greek political thinkers; the practice of the *maiores*, the Roman ancestors; and his own experience. Scipio Aemilianus too had claimed to keep a balance between authority and experience in the *De Republica*. For the historian the *De Legibus*, difficult as it is, is a work of great importance, for it is here that one discovers what

changes Cicero, who was never much of a reformer in practice, would ideally have liked to see in Rome.

THE LATER RHETORICAL AND PHILOSOPHIC WORKS

After the Civil War, and when finally back in Rome, Cicero could take no active part in politics and turned to his books. As he wrote in a letter to Varro:

> Let this be agreed between us, that we will live together in our studies, from which we formerly sought only pleasure, but now our very being. We shall not be found wanting, supposing that anyone desires to make use of us in rebuilding the state, even if as workmen rather than architects, nay we shall hasten to offer ourselves. But if no one uses our assistance still we will read and write on political subjects; and if we cannot do so in the Senate House and the Forum, yet in writing and literature, like the wisest men of old, we will serve the state and inquire into manners and laws.
>
> (*Ad familiares* 9.2.5)

Perhaps he was thinking of finishing the *De Legibus*. But his first work was to be the *Brutus*, the history of oratory at Rome that we have already mentioned. In it, his interest in the political tradition of Rome and the great men who embodied it combines with a probably wider knowledge of surviving speeches from an earlier period than any contemporary could boast, to create an extremely interesting piece of cultural history. It is too tactful to deal with contemporaries, though there is high and probably deserved praise of Caesar's style, in his (lost) speeches as well as his commentaries. And Cicero rightly thinks that an account of his own education and development will be of interest; such a passage of intellectual autobiography may have had few precedents. We only regret that he did not, doubtless from a desire for brevity and stylistic uniformity, quote from the speeches he discusses, and that, since he is trying to show that Rome has, like Greece, a strong tradition of oratory, even if it does not go so far back and is only now reaching maturity, he does not tell us a great deal about Greek teachers of rhetoric in Rome and their influence. The dialogue form allows for legitimate differences of opinion, especially for some agreeably tart interventions by Atticus, who complains, for example, that Cicero, the main speaker, is too generous in his estimate of second-century orators. As this passage in fact shows, the work was also something of a contribution to the debate with his "Atticizing" critics, and a lament for the days of republican freedom, in which alone oratory could flourish. The praise of Caesar also introduces a hint that he should now restore the institutions of the republic; Cicero was perhaps also trying to suggest that associated with him in this hope was Brutus, a political (and indeed an intellectual) figure of growing importance.

Brutus never became quite as close to Cicero as the latter hoped, but he did ask Cicero to write a laudation of his uncle, Cato, now the martyr of the republic, who had committed suicide in Africa rather than ask Caesar for clemency; it was presumably to be a substitute for the laudatory funeral oration normally given over a great man's dead body in the Forum at Rome.[1] Cicero found the job difficult, for to be completely frank in praising Cato's political outlook was hardly possible; but he was finally quite pleased with the result, and Caesar, though he wrote an *Anti-Cato* himself, at least had generous words for Cicero's eloquence in it; it is a pity that it does not survive. (Cicero found completely impossible the writing of a letter of open political advice to Caesar, which he tried to write at Atticus' suggestion and on the model of certain Greek works, such as Aristotle's *Letter to Alexander*; Caesar's friends in Rome vetoed a first draft, and Cicero thankfully gave up.)

---

[1]Cicero occasionally wrote such funeral orations for friends to deliver, though he does not seem to have thought much of this traditional genre. None of his attempts at it survive.

Cicero's last major work on oratory, the *Orator*, has fewer political overtones, though it has in part an ad hoc purpose, the fuller refutation of the Atticisers, and also shows his revived interest in philosophy, for example, in the preface in which he modifies Plato's famous theory of Ideas in order to show what he means by an ideal orator. But he wrote to a friend, "I do believe I have put into that book any judgment I may have on the art of public speaking. If it is what you say you think it, then I too am worth something" (*Ad familiares* 6.18.4). This is not an exorbitant claim.

Much of the book is given immediacy by reflecting Cicero's new role as a teacher, which he had taken up on the request of several friends who now practiced "declamation" with him—though this was a new departure for a great public figure. But sometimes his precepts do not seem to coincide with his own practice, for example, in a long and not very clear discussion of rhythm, based on Greek sources. As in the case of the allied subject of sentence structure, the trouble is probably due to his wanting to argue that he is more truly Attic than his opponents, when, in fact, he drew partly from other and later Greek sources. There is some consideration of alternative forms of words, a subject very much alive at a time when grammarians and practicing writers were attempting to refine and fix the still fluid language, which was subject to the influence not only of Latin speakers from different parts of Italy, but also to that of the many foreigners in Rome. Cicero usually chooses between alternatives on the grounds of euphony, not attempting to be consistent, as those who represented the theory of "analogy" (as opposed to "anomaly") in language insisted on being. Caesar, who dedicated his book *De Analogia* to Cicero himself, was a rigorous proponent of logic and highly autocratic in his choice of forms.

A couple of very minor works on oratory also date from this period of Cicero's life. More importantly, before writing the *Orator*, Cicero had already produced a little work, the *Paradoxa Stoicorum*, that shows him moving toward philosophy. Again dedicated to Brutus, it declares that it will try to recommend by every resource of style some of the Stoic ethical paradoxes, such as that virtue is enough to make a man happy, that all good deeds are equally meritorious, and that the wise man can never really be poor, or an exile, or even a slave. "Nothing is so hard to believe that oratory cannot make it acceptable." Cicero presents the work as basically a set of exercises. He was never really a Stoic (nor was Brutus), but he had a hankering after the heroism of the Stoic ethical system. There is nothing in the least technical about the work; it recalls to some extent the moralizing treatises in Greek sometimes known as "diatribes" and often addressed to a fairly popular audience; it illustrates its arguments with figures and events of recent years in Rome—for example, its rich man is clearly based upon Marcus Crassus.

But, perhaps in the autumn of 46 B.C., Cicero seems to have formed a plan of giving Rome a real philosophic literature. He did not think the objection that anyone interested in philosophy could read it in Greek was a valid one. Not that he was aiming at a wide public; he was only concerned with an intellectual elite, preferably of the young, though he seems to have found in practice that it was mainly older men who appreciated his work, which was not au fait with the latest developments at Athens or Alexandria and in which weight is given to his often undramatic, and undogmatic, conclusions by his own experience of life. He argued that Roman poetry and oratory were worth reading, even though they were based on Greek models; why not philosophy in Latin too? His aims were partly political; he still thought philosophy a necessary part of the education of a true statesman. He also thought that it was to Rome's glory to have a philosophic literature, and the challenge of putting the subject into Latin attracted him. He was a pioneer, for apart from a few popular treatises on Epicureanism, and probably a dialogue on ethics by Brutus (also Lucretius' Epicurean poem and some other didactic verse), there was nothing in Latin on the sub-

ject, though some members of the upper class had studied it with Greek teachers—not always to a very advanced level, for Cicero had some difficulty in finding suitable interlocutors for his dialogues.

In both the letters and the treatises themselves he lets us see him at work, finding equivalents for Greek technical terms; Atticus, who was nominally an Epicurean but not a serious student of philosophy, did take an interest in this side of the program. It appears that such words as *qualitas, essentia,* and *moralis* were first coined by Cicero on the model of Greek philosophical terms, and later taken up by other writers; we are not usually aware of this when we employ "quality," "essence," or "moral." But the real problem lies in the syntax, which Cicero discusses less than the vocabulary. Even the fact that Latin has no definite article, as Greek has, provides a problem—it is easier to talk unambiguously about "the good" in Greek or English than it is in Latin. And Cicero was too sensitive to the nature of Latin to force it into unnatural patterns; as a result he sometimes translates the same Greek word or phrase differently in different contexts, or uses a paraphrase, thus obscuring the clarity of his train of thought. Nonetheless, his achievement is considerable. But the style of his philosophical dialogues still needs more study.

He began with a general work encouraging his readers to turn to philosophy, partly based on Aristotle's *Protrepticus* and similar works. The *Hortensius* was a dialogue set in his own youth, in which Hortensius praised oratory and Cicero himself philosophy. It is strange that the work is lost, save for a few quotations by later authors, for it was highly regarded in antiquity and in particular had a dramatic effect upon St. Augustine in youth:

> I came in the usual course of study to a work of one Cicero, whose style is admired by almost all, though not so his message. This book however contains his exhortation to philosophy; it is called the *Hortensius*. This book indeed changed my whole way of feeling. It changed my prayers to

thee, O Lord, it gave me different plans and desires. Suddenly all vain aspirations lost their value; and I was left with an unbelievable fire in my heart, desiring the deathless qualities of wisdom.

It seems to have urged with great eloquence the necessity for detachment from ambition and pleasure, the joy to be found in the search for truth—for Cicero does not promise that it can be attained—and the possibility that the purification of the soul by developing its intellectual part in this life will make it easier for it to return to its home in the heavens.

Cicero then got down to real work with his *Academica*, or *Academic Treatises*. He regarded himself as a follower of Plato's Academy at Athens, as it had become by the time of his own youth, when a thoroughgoing Skepticism, which Plato at least in his later years would not have approved of, was being modified, to the extent of allowing that probable views could be formed even if they could not be proved to be true; soon after, under Stoic influence, the reaction in the Academy went further. The Skeptical Academic was also expected to expound rival views fairly and discuss them politely, and Cicero tried hard to do this.

In the *Academica* Cicero introduces the various schools and their beliefs on epistemology: what, if anything, can we know? This discussion is often pretty technical. Cicero was proud of the work, which cost him some trouble: "my very clever books," he calls them; and he is probably somewhat misleading when he writes to Atticus, clearly of some of his philosophic works, that "they are transcriptions, requiring little work; I only contribute the words, of which I have plenty." Attempts to prove Cicero dependent for any lengthy section of a work on a single Greek predecessor have proved unsuccessful. It is clear from other passages that he read fairly widely (though sometimes in epitomes made for him by Greek scholars in Rome), and he showed some independence in organizing and selecting his materials and in passing his own judgment on them, as well as in giving a Roman color to the whole. His characters are all educated Romans, and they illustrate their words with examples of various kinds drawn from Roman life and literature.

Immediately on finishing the *Academica*, or perhaps even before, he turned to the *De Finibus Boni et Mali*, on ethics, which to him, as to most Romans—and some Greek philosophers of the period too—was "the most essential part of philosophy," as he had called it in the earlier work. Here he begins by refuting the Epicurean view that pleasure (though for them real pleasure involves virtue as well as simplicity of life) is the naturally desirable good; he despised Epicureanism on intellectual as well as moral grounds, though he treats it with reasonable fairness and insists that Epicurus and his followers (who included many of Cicero's friends) are personally admirable men. He next throws doubt on the Stoic belief that virtue is what man naturally desires and is enough by itself to make him happy. The idea of a recent Academic philosopher, that we instinctively desire also knowledge and action, is argued at length, though Cicero in his own person strikes a more strictly Skeptical note.

The *Tusculan Disputations*, set in Cicero's villa at Tusculum, outside Rome, are rather different in character and much less technical. There is a good deal of information as to what various philosophers have said, and an unusual amount of rapid argument between Cicero and an anonymous friend. But here Cicero is again using all his rhetorical armory, in order to help his readers—and, it cannot be doubted, himself—to despise death, to endure pain, and even to believe, with the Stoics, that virtue is sufficient for happiness. This is the kind of "declamation," or practice speaking, he says, that he now makes use of with his friends and pupils. Vivid anecdotes from Cicero's own career and quotations from the poets (often the Greek poets, in Cicero's own not very inspired translations) make the work approachable. We know that Atticus read at least the first book twice, and that he pressed the work on a business acquaintance with no philosophical training. There are passages that reach a poetic intensity, like perhaps this from the first book, on the fear of death:

Vetat enim dominans ille in nobis deus iniussu hinc nos suo demigrare; cum vero causam iustam deus ipse dederit, ut tunc Socrati, nunc Catoni, saepe multis, ne ille medius fidius vir sapiens laetus ex his tenebris in lucem illam excesserit, nec tamen illa vincla carceris ruperit (leges enim vetant), sed tamquam a magistratu aut ab aliqua potestate legitima, sic a deo evocatus atque emissus exierit. tota enim philosphorum vita, ut ait idem, commentatio mortis est. nam quid aliud agimus, cum a voluptate, id est a corpore, cum a re familiari, quae est ministra et famula corporis, cum a re publica, cum a negotio omni sevocamus animam, quid, inquam, tum agimus, nisi animum ad se ipsum advocamus, secum esse cogimus maximeque a corpore abducimus? secernere autem a corpore animum ecquidnam aliud est nisi mori discere? quare hoc commentemur, mihi crede, disiungamusque nos a corporibus, id est consuescamus mori. Hoc, et dum erimus in terris, erit illi caelesti vitae simile, et cum illuc ex his vinclis emissi feremur, minus tardabitur cursus animorum. nam qui in compedibus corporis semper fuerunt, etiam cum soluti sunt. tardius ingrediuntur, ut ii, qui ferro vincti multos annos fuerunt. quo cum venerimus, tum denique vivemus. nam haec quidem vita mors est, quam lamentari possem, si liberet.

(1.30.74)

For the god who is our master forbids us to leave our home here for another one without his command, but when the god himself has given a fair reason to do so, as he did then to Socrates, and recently to Cato, and has often done to many, then on my life the wise man of whom we have been speaking will pass rejoicing from the shadows here to the light beyond, and yet he will not break the bonds of his prison (for the laws forbid it) but will go forth, summoned and set free by the god, as though by some magistrate or some legitimate authority. For the whole life of philosophers, as the same man [Socrates] says, is a study of death. For what else do we do, when we call our soul away from pleasure, that is, from the body, and from our possessions, which are the ministers and servants of the body, from public life, from every sort of business, what, I ask, do we do, except summon our spirit to itself, force it to be independent and divorce it as far as possible from the body? But to separate the spirit from the body, what is it but to learn to die? And so, believe me, let us make this our study, and let us sever ourselves from our bodies, that is, let us accustom ourselves to dying. This, while we are still on earth, will resemble that heavenly life, and when we are freed from these chains and borne thither, the passage of our souls will not be delayed. For those who have always lived in the shackles of the body will even when they are freed move slowly, like those who have been in irons for many years. When we have come thither, at last we shall live. For this life is a death, and I could lament it if you so willed.

With the *De Natura Deorum*, Cicero turns to theology, which was regarded as closely allied to astronomy and cosmology; all were branches of philosophy, like the natural sciences in general. The Epicurean spokesman begins, outlining the gods of his system, who live in the remotest parts of the sky and take no care for men, but who are still strictly anthropomorphic. The Skeptic Cotta has little difficulty in pouring ridicule on this, and showing that it is not true that all mankind worships gods in their own image—what about the Egyptians' animal gods? (Cicero is never very interested in any traditions that are neither Greek nor Roman, but like the rest of his generation he knows something of a wide range of peoples; Roman horizons had been expanding rapidly.) The Stoic speaker then argues that the universe itself is divine and sentient, pervaded by the fire that is the principle of all life, and dilates on the beauty and order of the world, which proves that a superior intelligence lies behind it. Here Cicero writes with great splendor about this beauty and order—first that of the earth, then of the heavenly bodies, and here he rises from prose to poetry, quoting extensively from his own version of Aratus' astronomical poem. He then comes down to earth again to describe the amazing characteristics of the various animals, rising to another climax in his account of man, which foreshadows Hamlet's outburst, "What a piece of work is a man!" Cicero, like most Romans, was not much of a scientist, but if he is closely following a Greek source or sources here, he still transforms it into splendid language. At times he almost bursts the conventions of Latin prose style, pressing to its limits, for example, a curious use of abstract nouns to convey the amazing qualities of the things or creatures he describes:

> *Totam licet animis tamquam oculis lustrare terram mariaque omnia: cernes iam spatia frugifera atque inmensa camporum vestitusque densissimos montium, pecudum pastus, tum incredibili cursus maritimos celeritate.*
>
> (2.64.161)

> Let the mind as though it were the eye survey the whole earth and all the seas: you will behold now the fruitful and measureless expanses of the plains, the very thick clothing of the hills, the pasturage of the flocks, now passages over the seas of incredible swiftness.

The whole section is somewhat too long—one has some sympathy with the French sixteenth-century essayist Montaigne, who said that one could fall asleep for a quarter of an hour as one of Cicero's treatises was being read and wake up without having lost the thread—and occasionally goes into slightly ludicrous detail, but it forms one of the finest expressions in his work of demonstrative or epideictic eloquence.

Finally, Cotta again opposes the Stoic arguments, if rather tentatively. Much of his speech, which seems to have stressed the disorder and evil also to be found in the world, is lost—omitted, perhaps, by a pious copyist in Christian times. But Cicero indicates that he finds the Stoic point of view convincing. Even in its truncated form the *De Natura Deorum* had immense influence, first on Christian writers attacking pagan religion, who drew much from Cotta's first speech, and then in the seventeenth

and eighteenth centuries on philosophers anxious to establish some form of natural religion distinct from revelation, who turned to the Stoic arguments; and ultimately on the truly skeptical Hume himself, whose famous *Dialogues of Natural Religion* are distinctly Ciceronian in style and treatment.

The works *De Divinatione* and *De Fato* were in a sense supplements to the *De Natura Deorum*. The *De Fato* is only partly preserved; the *De Divinatione* is made attractive by Cicero's desire to serve his country by eradicating superstition—not the same thing, he insists, as the destruction of religion—and from the humor with which he lambasts the various methods of foretelling the future, whether from the flight of birds, the organs of sacrificial animals, dreams and trances, or astrology, which was making its way into Italy from the East at this period, and which he regarded as utter madness, rather than mere foolishness. In no sort of divination did he believe, though only a few philosophers (apart from the Epicureans, whom he despised) had been so bold. And Cicero's spirited fight was to have little immediate effect, as his world turned more and more, often led by those who claimed the title of philosopher, to the comforts of the supernatural. Indeed, Cicero's general openness of mind and lack of dogmatism, even joined as they were to occasional logical lapses and sometimes to frank contradictions, were to be a sad loss to Rome.

For another dialogue, either lost or never written, Cicero translated a long passage from Plato's *Timaeus*, which allows us, as a few briefer passages elsewhere do, to examine his translation procedures in detail. This work was to consist of argument against the mystico-scientific views of a friend and contemporary, Nigidius Figulus, a man of great erudition, who found magical correspondences everywhere in nature. Cicero's clear sight and sense of ridicule would no doubt have been brought into play again, while he broke his usual rule and gave a part to Cratippus, a professional Greek philosopher of the school of Aristotle, partly perhaps as a compliment to the man, who was teaching Cicero's son in Athens, but partly perhaps because no suitable Roman skilled in the rational biological learning of the Peripatetics was to be found.

The *De Gloria* is also almost entirely lost; one may wonder if it echoed a surviving speech, the *pro Marcello*, which is addressed to Caesar as Dictator and argues that the true glory is that of a statesman, not a soldier (this needed arguing, in a society as militaristic as the Roman and in an epoch in which Alexander the Great was widely regarded—though not by the philosophers—as the most famous man who ever lived); or whether it followed the "Dream of Scipio" in stressing that sub specie aeternitatis glory is a brief and petty thing. Hellenistic philosophers in general tended to be reserved toward it. There is no doubt that in his later years Cicero was trying, by means of his own philosophical studies, to argue himself into detachment both from popular success and acclaim, which under Caesar he could not have, and from the extreme emotions to which he had always been prone, and to satisfy himself with the approval of his own conscience. Even if he did not always quite live up to his aspirations, we may respect him for them.

Near the end of his life he dedicated two agreeable short dialogues to his friend Atticus, *Cato on Old Age* (not his contemporary, but a famous ancestor in the second century) and *Laelius on Friendship* (named for the faithful friend of Scipio Aemilianus); both are set in the period to which he looked back nostalgically, and deal with subjects of which both he and Atticus now had experience. He also wrote a much longer work, *De Officiis* or *On Duties*, for his son, who was then, as we saw, a student at Athens. It is based on a moderate Stoic source, but in its last book, where his source failed him, Cicero argued on his own account that duty and expediency can never really conflict. It is a markedly idealistic work. Though much admired in the Renaissance, when it was known in England as "Tully's *Offices*," it may interest us today largely for its comments on figures of the time, and young Marcus, who was not an

intellectual, was probably relieved that it was not followed by the series of other works that his father promised him. At some point, however, Cicero had also added to his ethical works a study of the four cardinal virtues, *De Virtutibus*, now lost.

Cicero is by no means an original philosopher, or even a strictly first-rate interpreter of other men's philosophies. But his achievement was nonetheless, in his circumstances, considerable, and it had great historic importance—first in the early Christian period, then in the Middle Ages, and later in the Renaissance, which turned to some extent away from logic and theology to the considerations of man and his place in this world. The climax of Cicero's reputation came perhaps in the late seventeenth and eighteenth centuries, in the time of the *philosophes*, who admired his easy style, his open approach and lack of credulity, and his opposition to political despotism. In the nineteenth century, a period of great original philosophical systems, in Germany at least, and of the exaltation of everything Greek as opposed to Roman, Cicero's standing fell disastrously, and only recently have we been coming round to a juster assessment of both his intellectual achievements and his political career.

He was the author of a number of other somewhat miscellaneous works, now lost, mention of which may serve at least to show us at how many points Cicero touched the intellectual life of his time. Famous in antiquity was the *Consolation* that he wrote for himself on the death of his daughter, Tullia; the genre was a well-recognized one, but Cicero says that nobody else had ever written one to himself. It lamented the woes of this life, from which Tullia had escaped, and promised to dedicate a shrine to her, to show the transcendence of her admirable qualities (this plan, after exercising Cicero for some time, ultimately fell through). A bitter memoir or "Secret History," based on the style of Theopompus, the Greek historian notorious for his frank and biting pen, attacked Cicero's political enemies; it was not published till near, or after, his death. There was a treatise urging the organization of the Roman civil law on the pattern of an *ars*, thereby making it easier to study (a preoccupation visible in some passages of extant dialogues). There was a work on augury, the ancient Roman tradition of divination by the flight and behavior of birds; Cicero had been made an augur in 53 B.C., and he valued this high position intensely, in spite of his disbelief in augury; the book must have been largely antiquarian. There was nearly a treatise on geography, but Cicero found this hard going (the mathematical side was perhaps beyond him) and his Greek sources contradictory, and so he gave it up.

THE CORRESPONDENCE

As for the letters, they can hardly be discussed; they must be read. A few are fairly formal, and were probably meant to be circulated; the epistle that opens the collection of letters to Cicero's brother Quintus is an essay on the duties of a provincial governor (*Ad Quintum fratrem* 1.1); there is a long apologia for Cicero's political career written in 54 B.C. to an important friend (*Ad familiares* 1.9); there is a careful description of the grand games given by Pompey in 55 B.C. sent to an invalid friend (*Ad familiares* 7.1); and a plea to a historian to write a favorable account of his consulship that its author described to Atticus as *valde bella*, very pretty, telling him to get a copy of it (*Ad familiares* 5.12). There are letters full of jokes, which are sometimes a little self-conscious, suggesting that their writer was well aware that joking letters were a recognized subdivision of the epistolary genre. There is a mass of brief but carefully composed letters of recommendation. Some of the above might have appeared in the collection of suitably revised letters that Cicero at one point in his last years was thinking of publishing; but the plan came to nothing, and what we have is far more valuable, a part of all the correspondence that survived his death, uncensored (or almost) and unrevised. The exchanges with several important figures, such as

Caesar and Octavian, which were known in antiquity, have been lost, as also that with an elderly lady called Caerellia, which is said to have been rather undignified, though Caerellia was apparently interested in philosophy, at least Cicero's philosophy, as well as gossip; we have only a part of the letters to and from Brutus (with one of his to Atticus, though this—and another—may not be genuine). What we do possess is the great collection addressed to Atticus, though without any answering letters from him; the smaller group addressed to Cicero's brother; and the miscellaneous collection known as *Ad familiares*, to (and sometimes from) a large number of figures less important in his life. This includes letters to members of his household, including his wife (but, unfortunately, not his daughter, Tullia) and his trusted freedman and secretary, Tiro, who is addressed in terms of real kindness and consideration. There is, unfortunately, nothing from Cicero's early years, and very little from the period before his consulship; the great mass comes from the last epoch of his life—barring the final six months, letters from which may have been suppressed because of their criticism of the future emperor Augustus or because his treatment of Cicero in this period appeared deceptive and discreditable.

Even though Cicero's judgment of events and people was often either overenthusiastic or overpessimistic, the collection throws an enormous amount of light on the political life of the time; shortly after Cicero's death a scholar commented that the letters to Atticus (which he probably knew before their final publication, which may have been delayed till the later first century A.D.) were almost a substitute for the history that Cicero did not in fact write. But there are also entirely private notes, especially to Atticus, dealing with family or financial affairs, and written in haste—we know that Cicero had a rapid scrawl, though sometimes he was so busy that he had to dictate to a secretary (Tiro at least knew shorthand)—and elliptically, certainly without a thought of other eyes viewing them. Yet in spite of all signs of pres-

CICERO

sure Cicero remains a master of language, as a close comparison with the style of letters from others that have been preserved with his own will show. Of course, highly elaborate periods, "amplification" in general, and the use of obtrusive rhythms would normally have been completely out of place; but Cicero is rarely awkward; he is colloquial but not vulgar or slangy. There are frequent happy and apposite quotations from the poets—often the Greek poets, for in informal prose there was no feeling against quoting in a foreign language, and indeed Cicero spatters his Latin with colloquial Greek phrases wherever they seem to convey his meaning better than Latin would do, rather as an educated letter writer in England a hundred years ago might have spattered his pages with French.

We get incomparably vivid glimpses of famous figures of the time. Here is Cato: "with all his good intentions and complete integrity he sometimes damages the public welfare; for he gives his opinion in the Senate as if he were living in the *Republic* of Plato, not on Romulus' dung-heap." And Pompey, who was regrettably disingenuous: "he spoke much of politics with me, regretting his own position—so he said, for one must always add that, in his case." And Caesar, who as dictator once came to dine with Cicero in one of his seaside villas; it went off well, "but my guest was not the sort to whom one says 'do please come again when you are back.' Once is enough. We did not talk of serious matters, but a great deal about literature." We get references to the books, often Greek classics of history and political theory, sometimes productions of the day, that Cicero has been reading; we get descriptions of Cicero's beloved country houses, "the jewels of Italy," for example, that at lonely Astura, where he delighted in "everything about the villa, the shore and the view of the sea," and where the house stood on a promontory "almost in the water"; also of the dinner parties he went to, especially under the Caesarian regime, like that at which he found himself in the company of a notorious actress and courtesan (mistress of Antony and

later the poet Cornelius Gallus): "even as a young man I was never attracted by anything of this kind, much less now that I am old. What I enjoy is the company. I talk about whatever comes up, and change my sighs into loud laughter." His devotion to Tullia is touchingly expressed: "such an incomparable daughter . . . so noble a creature," like that, later on, to Atticus' little daughter, a merry child but often ill with fever. So is his capacity for deep friendship: "on my life, my dear Atticus, I don't think—I won't say Tusculum, for the rest I am happy enough there—but even the Islands of the Blest would be worth being without you all day long." He turns continually to Atticus for advice, political as well as personal, financial, and literary; for example, before the outbreak of the Civil War: "after all, when the consul says 'Speak, Marcus Tullius,' am I to say 'Please just wait till I have seen Atticus'?"

The letters also document Cicero's frequent self-centeredness and lack of decision; the rediscovery of the collection of those addressed to Atticus proved a severe shock to Petrarch at the dawn of the Renaissance. The detached contemplative philosopher that Cicero had seemed to be to the Middle Ages was not to be found here. Indeed, the French historian Carcopino has used them in an attempt to prove that Cicero was guilty of every possible pettiness. But a more candid reader may feel that he finds in these pages, as in the treatises, a basically honest and certainly a very civilized man, from a period and a milieu in which not so many could claim these qualities. All in all, as Livy said, after noting his defects, he was "a great and memorable man, whose qualities it would require a Cicero to praise."

Selected Bibliography

TEXTS

Cicero. 28 vols. Cambridge, Mass., and London, 1913–1958. The Loeb Classical Library. Various volumes have been revised or reprinted.

Grilli, A., ed. *Hortensius.* Milan, 1962.

CICERO

TRANSLATIONS

Bailey, D. R. Shackleton. *Letters to Atticus.* Harmondsworth, 1979. The Penguin Classics.

————. *Letters to His Friends I and II.* Harmondsworth, 1978. The Penguin Classics.

Copley, F. O. *"On Old Age" and "On Friendship."* Ann Arbor, Mich., 1967.

Grant, M. *Murder Trials: In Defence of Sex. Roscius of America, In Defence of Aulus Cluentius Habitus, In Defence of Gaius Rabirius, In Defence of King Deiotarus.* Harmondsworth, 1978.

————. *On the Good Life; Tusculan Disputations, De Officiis, De Amicitia, De Senectute, Somnium Scipiomis.* Harmondsworth, 1979.

————. *Against L. Sergius Catilina, In Defence of the Poet Aulus Licimius Archias, In Defence of Marcus Caelius Rufus, In Defence of Titus Annius Milo, In Support of Marcus Claudius Marcellus, First Philippic.* Harmondsworth, 1979.

————. *Selected Works: Against Verres I, 23 Letters, Second Philippic, On Duties III, On Old Age.* Harmondsworth, 1960.

Higginbotham, J. *Cicero on Moral Obligation (de Officiis).* Berkeley and London, 1967.

Hubbell, H. M. *"Brutus" and "Orator."* Cambridge, Mass., 1971.

Poteat, H. *Selected Letters.* Boston, 1931.

————. *Brutus, On the Nature of the Gods, On Divination, On Duties.* Chicago, 1950.

Sabine, G. H., and S. B. Smith. *On the Commonwealth.* Columbus, Ohio, 1929.

Wilkinson, L. P. *Cicero's Letters, A Selection in Translation.* London, 1966.

COMMENTARIES

Asconius. *Orationum Ciceronis Quinque Enarratio,* edited by A. C. Clark. Oxford, 1907.

Austin, R. G., ed. *Pro Caelio.* Oxford, 1966.

Donelly, F. P., ed. *Pro Milone.* New York, 1935.

Douglas, A. E., ed. *Brutus.* Oxford, 1966.

Gigon, O., ed. *Tusculanae Disputationes.* Munich, 1970.

Kinsey, T. E., ed. *Pro Quinctio.* Sydney, 1971.

Nisbet, R. G., ed. *De domo sua.* Oxford, 1939.

————. *In Pisonem.* Oxford, 1961.

Pease, A. S., ed. *De Divinatione.* Urbana, Ill., 1920–1923. Reprinted Darmstadt, 1973.

————. *De Natura Deorum.* Cambridge, Mass., 1955. Reprinted Darmstadt, 1968.

Reid, J. S., ed. *Academica.* London, 1885.

————. *De Finibus.* Cambridge, 1925.

Ruch, M., ed. *Pro Marcello.* Paris, 1965.

Sandys, J. E., ed. *Orator.* Cambridge, 1885.

Shackleton Bailey, D. R., ed. *Cicero's Letters to Atticus.* Cambridge, 1965–1970.

————. *Cicero Epistulae ad Familiares.* Cambridge, 1977.

————. *Cicero Epistulae ad Quintum Fratrem et M. Brutum.* Cambridge, 1980.

Stangl, T. *Ciceronis Orationum Scholiastae.* Vienna, 1912. Reprinted Hildesheim, 1964. Collection of ancient commentaries to certain speeches by Asconius and others; primarily historical in nature. No translation available.

Traglia, A., ed. *Ciceronis Poetica Fragmenta.* Rome. 1963.

Tyrrell, R. Y., and L. C. Purser, eds. *The Correspondence of Cicero.* Dublin and London, 1904–1933.

Wilkins, A. S., ed. *De Oratore.* Oxford, 1892. Reprinted Amsterdam, 1962.

CONCORDANCES

Merguet, H. *Lexicon zu den Reden des Cicero.* Jena, 1877–1884.

————. *Lexicon zu den Schriften Ciceros, Teil 2, Philosophische Schriften.* Jena, 1897.

————. *Handlexicon zu Cicero.* Leipzig, 1905.

Oldfather, W. A.; W. V. Canter; and K. M. Abbott, eds. *Index Verborum Ciceronis Epistularum.* Urbana, Ill., 1938.

————. *Index Verborum in Ciceronis Rhetorica.* Urbana, Ill., 1964.

BIOGRAPHICAL AND CRITICAL STUDIES

Barwick, K. *Das rednerische Bildungsideal Ciceros.* Berlin, 1963.

Becker, E. *Technik und Szenerie des Ciceronischen Dialogs.* Osnabrück, 1938.

Boyancé, P. *Études sur l'humanisme cicéronien.* Brussels, 1970.

Broadhead, H. D. *Latin Prose Rhythm.* Cambridge, 1922.

Büchner, K. *Cicero: Bestand und Wandel seiner geistigen Welt.* Heidelberg, 1964.

————. *Somnium Scipionis: Quellen, Gestalt, Sinne.* Wiesbaden, 1976.

Dorey, T. A., ed. *Cicero (Studies in Latin Literature and Its Influence).* London, 1965.

CICERO

Douglas, A. E. "The Intellectual Background of Cicero's Rhetorica." In *Aufstieg und Niedergang der römischen Welt.* Berlin, 1973.

Fraenkel, E. *Leseproben aus Reden Ciceros und Catos.* Rome, 1968.

Gärtner, H. A. *Cicero und Panaitios: Beobachtungen zu Ciceros "De Officiis."* Heidelberg, 1974.

Geffcken, K. A. *Comedy in the "pro Caelio."* Leiden, 1973.

Gelzer, M. *Cicero: Ein biographischer Versuch.* Wiesbaden, 1969.

————, W. Kroll, et al. "M. Tullius Cicero." In A. F. Pauly and G. Wissowa, eds., *Realencyclopädie.* Stuttgart, 1970.

Gotoff, H. C. *Cicero's Elegant Style: An Analysis of the "pro Archia."* Urbana, Ill., 1979.

Haskell, H. J. *This Was Cicero.* New York, 1942.

Humbert, J. *Les Plaidoyers Écrits et les plaidoiries réelles de Cicéron.* Paris, 1925. Reprinted New York and Hildesheim, 1972.

Hunt, H. A. K. *The Humanism of Cicero.* Melbourne, 1954.

Johnson, W. R. *Luxuriance and Economy: Cicero and the Alien Style.* Berkeley, 1971.

Kennedy, G. A. *The Art of Rhetoric in the Roman World.* Princeton, 1972.

Klingner, F. *Ciceros Rede für den Schauspieler Roscius: eine Episode in der Entwicklung seiner Kunstprosa.* Munich, 1953.

Laughton, E. *The Participle in Cicero.* Oxford, 1964.

Laurand, L. *Études sur le style des discours de Cicéron.* Paris, 1907. 4th ed. Paris, 1938–1940.

Lebreton, J. *Études sur la langue et la grammaire de Cicéron.* Paris, 1901.

Lepore, E. *Il princeps ciceroniano.* Naples, 1954.

Michel, A. *Rhétorique et philosophie chez Cicéron.* Paris, 1960.

Mitchell, T. N. *Cicero: The Ascending Years.* New Haven and London, 1979.

Neumeister, C. *Grundsätze der forensischen Rhetorik gezeigt an Gerichtsreden Ciceros.* Munich, 1964.

Petersson, T. *Cicero, A Biography.* Berkeley, 1920.

Pöschl, V. *Römischer Staat und Griechisches Staatsdenken bei Cicero.* Berlin, 1936.

Pohlenz, M. *Antikes Führertum: Cicero "de officiis" und das Lebensideal des Panaetios.* Leipzig, 1934.

Poncelet, P. *Cicéron traducteur de Platon.* Paris, 1957.

Primmer, A. *Cicero Numerosus.* Vienna, 1968.

Rambaud, M. *Cicéron et l'histoire romaine.* Paris, 1953.

Rawson, E. *Cicero, A Portrait.* London, 1974.

Ruch, M. *Le préambule dans les oeuvres philosophiques de Cicéron.* Paris, 1958.

Schmid, W. *Über die klassische Theorie und Praxis des Prosarhythmus.* Wiesbaden, 1959.

Schulte, H. K. *Orator: Untersuchungenüber das ciceronianische Bildungsideal.* Frankfurt, 1935.

Shackleton Bailey, D. R. *Cicero.* London, 1971.

Stockton, D. *Cicero, A Political Biography.* Oxford, 1971.

Süss, W. *Cicero: Eine Einführung in seine philosophische Schriften.* Wiesbaden, 1966.

Traglia, A. *La lingua de Cicerone poeta.* Bari, 1950.

Weische, A. *Ciceros Nachahmung der attischen Redner.* Heidelberg, 1972.

Wilkinson, L. P. *Golden Latin Artistry.* Cambridge, 1963.

Zielinski, T. *Das Clauselgesetz in Ciceros Reden.* Leipzig, 1904.

————. *Cicero im Wandel der Jahrhunderte.* Berlin, 1912.

ELIZABETH RAWSON

CAESAR

(100–44 B.C.)

IT IS A curious paradox that two books written as personal records of spectacular achievement should have been reduced to the status of textbooks for elementary Latin students. Gaius Julius Caesar's accounts of the *Gallic War*, and to a lesser extent of the *Civil War*, have been generally read not as works of literature or of political and military history but for drill in the intricacies of Latin grammar. They have been known less for substance than for syntax, and too often not as the students' favorites. This anomalous fate has almost completely obscured for thousands of young readers the artistry and skill of the author, the sophistication of his selectivity and presentation, the revelation of his ambitions and attitudes, and the incredible accomplishments of a man who truly changed his world and helped to mold ours.

The work of any author consciously or unconsciously reflects himself and his times, but for Caesar the interrelation of his driving ambition and historical exploits with his written record demands that the text cannot be fully appreciated if it is separated from his political career and the events of the world around him.

Born at the turn of the first century B.C., which he was to dominate politically and militarily, Caesar came from an aristocratic noble family who traced its origins back before the founding of Rome through the Trojan Aeneas to the goddess Venus, whom he always regarded as his special patron. His early political career followed the *cursus honorum*, the customary passage through successively more responsible offices, and he attached himself to Marcus Licinius Crassus, an experienced politician and the wealthiest man in Rome, who helped to defray the expenses of the political rise of a young man whom he deemed useful.

In 60 B.C. the considerable political support of Crassus and of Gnaeus Pompey, the greatest general of the age, was thrown behind Caesar as a candidate for the consulship, the highest Roman magistracy. This alliance, the so-called First Triumvirate, was a private political coalition that was formed to secure for each of its members what he desired. Caesar as consul should contrive to settle certain financial problems involving Crassus' investments, to bring about ratification of Pompey's settlement of affairs in the East, and to provide a bonus of land grants for his veterans, which hitherto had been blocked by the reigning clique of the powerful senatorial oligarchy. Caesar and Pompey cemented their friendship by Pompey's marriage to Caesar's daughter, Julia. Despite yearlong in-fighting with his consular colleague Marcus Calpurnius Bibulus, Caesar fulfilled his preelection commitments. Because of imminent danger in Celtic Gaul, he also secured for himself the extraordinary proconsular command of the provinces of Cisalpine Gaul (the Po country of north Italy), Illyricum (Yugoslavia and Albania), and Transalpine Gaul (southern France, Provence), the first two by vote of the people and the third by senatorial action. His command was operative from 1 March 59 B.C. for a five-year term.

Caesar's next nine years were spent in hard campaigning in Gaul, Germany, and Britain, while in Rome his political rivals sought to recall him and put an end to his career. So ominous had the situation become in early 56 B.C. that the triumvirate met at Luca, the southernmost town of western Cisalpine Gaul, to take stock and plan for the future. Pompey and Crassus were elected consuls for 55, in which year they provided Caesar with an additional five-year term in his proconsular command and themselves with extraordinary commands of five years as well—Pompey in Spain, and Crassus in Syria, where he died ignominiously in 53. At Rome the situation steadily deteriorated into violence in the streets and at public functions; the government, continually mired in acrimonious political debates, was powerless to maintain control. By 52 matters had reached such a point that, in February, Pompey, who had never left Rome for his province, was named sole consul and so governed until the final months of the year when he coopted as his colleague his current father-in-law, Metellus Scipio.

In that year was passed a fateful law vital to Caesar's future, the Law of the Ten Tribunes, by which he was granted the special privilege of standing for the consulship in absentia, that is, of being a candidate without appearing in Rome. Such a law served to protect Caesar in the interval between the laying down of his command (as of 1 March), the time of the consular elections (July), and his entrance into office (1 January). It was Caesar's insistence upon exercising this option and his opponents' insistence upon preventing him that animated the arguments of subsequent years and finally resulted in the armed conflict of the Civil War.

Although there is no agreement among modern scholars upon the legalities of either Caesar's or his opponents' positions, an analysis of all the ancient evidence seems to lead to the conclusion that Caesar's command comprised a full ten years, due to expire as of 28 February 49 B.C.; that the Law of the Ten Tribunes provided for his standing for the consulship in July 49 while still in Gaul, thus implicitly prolonging that command; and that he would thereby hold his second consulship in 48, the year in which his iteration of office was legal. Whether his invasion of Italy can be condoned on the grounds of the threat to his future political life and of the moral bankruptcy of a government presided over by selfish, ambitious incompetents was and still is a personal and individual judgment.

With the dynamic leadership that had characterized his decisions in Gaul, in 49 B.C. Caesar led a legion across the Rubicon River, the boundary between his province of Cisalpine Gaul and Italy. This incursion of armed forces into Italy constituted high treason in formal law, and he thereby offered a military challenge to his opponents, who had declared him a public enemy and were now in arms under Pompey as their commander. Caesar and his officers and legions fought them all around the Mediterranean—in Italy, Spain, Marseilles, Africa, Illyricum, Greece, Alexandria, and again in Africa and Spain, where at Munda in early 45 he finally broke the will of Pompey's forces. In the few months left to him before his assassination he set in motion a variety of programs, including reforms of such disparate items as the calendar, the jury system, and the terms of provincial commands; the urban renewal projects of his forum and of the Basilica Julia; social legislation to reduce the recipients of public welfare, to offer prizes for having large families, and to limit private expenditures on luxurious living. He pardoned many of his former opponents, and his clemency became the hallmark of his regime. As the legal basis for his rule he held, often concurrently, the consulship and the dictatorship, which was voted to him for life in the winter of 44.

Fearing that he planned to set up a monarchy, a group of conspirators led by Brutus and Cassius murdered Caesar, ironically at the base of Pompey's statue, on the Ides of March 44 B.C., shortly before he was to set off to the East on a punitive expedition against the Parthians. The conspirators claimed to be acting in the name of liberty, that is, liberty for their clique to run the government in their own pre–Civil War way. Even if they acted from motives of highest purity, the result was civil war and chaos for years to come.

Like many Roman statesmen, Caesar tried his hand at various kinds of writing, technical and creative alike. Although only his war commentaries are extant from his prose works, his skill in oratory was said to rival that of Cicero, and he was the author of a technical treatise on grammar, *De Analogia*; an astronomical investigation, *De Astris*; a collection of witticisms, *Apothegmata*; and two books entitled *Anticatones*, which as the title suggests are a polemic against Cato. He also dabbled in poetry of genres as diverse as love songs and a tragedy, *Oedipus*. From these there remains only a six-line poem of literary criticism on the comic poet Terence (Suetonius, *Caesar* 56).

For us Caesar's literary reputation rests on the memoirs of his military campaigns, which were much admired by his contemporaries. Thus Cicero describes them (*Brutus* 262): "Bare, straight, beautiful, free from all ornamentation, like figures stripped of any garment." In his lean, precise style there is no room for affectation, emotional passages, or obvious rhetorical devices. The vocabulary is simple and repetitive; the narrative moves rapidly, the language dominated by verbs, especially that main verb which, like the commander-in-chief himself, firmly controls the action. Always in evidence is the "consummate elegance of his writing and his sure ability to explain his own policies," qualities that win the admiration and praise of Aulus Hirtius, who completed Caesar's history of the war in Gaul after Caesar's death (8. *Preface* 7).

The artistry is seen in the surface clarity, objectivity, and selectivity that often conceal what was best left unstated. Passionless, cool, and restrained in style, the narrative recounts a series of military engagements. Yet there are incidents that, read even in isolation as excerpts, arouse the imagination with the thrilling dramatic excitement of a good story: in Gaul the battle with the Nervii where Caesar himself rushes to the front line (2.15–29), the difficult invasions of Britain (4.20–36 and 5.1–25), the attacks on his officers' winter quarters in the north (5.26–52), and the winner-take-all siege of Alesia (7.68–89). The narrative brings to life the struggle with the Pompeians: the taking of Corfinium (1.14–23), the difficulties faced in Spain (1.38–55), Curio's disaster in Africa (2.23–44), and Caesar's defeat at Dyrrachium (3.55,57–74). Observations on the customs of Gauls, Britons, and Germans relieve the narrative of battles, and through his pages pass the figures of exotic Gauls; friends like the elder statesman of the Aedui, Diviciacus, his anti-Roman brother, Dumnorix, and Commius the Atrebatian, trusted comrade who in the end turned against Caesar; enemies like the wily Ambiorix of the Eburones, against whom Caesar seems to have waged almost a personal vendetta, and the Arvernian Vercingetorix, a foe worthy of Caesar, who alone was able to arouse and command the loyalty of almost all Gaul against the Roman invaders.

Probably the most striking first impression for the modern reader of the Latin text is the author's reference to himself in the third person. It is Caesar who moves and acts in these pages, not the egotistical *I*. The advantages of such a style are patent. Obviously the constant appearance of the name Caesar never allows the reader to forget what general is winning these victories. Equally compelling is the aura of impartiality created by the impersonal third person, since the reader tends to believe in the objectivity and veracity of the record to an extent he would not accord to an autobiographical account. It is easy to forget that narrator and commander are one and the same, for Caesar deliberately sets up a dual personality. Frequently he resorts to the first person, singular or plural, in a parenthetical clause, "as I have said above." Occasionally, he carries this separation of personae to an even greater extreme by differentiating the writer from the actor within the

585

same sentence: "Caesar, for the reasons which I have mentioned above, decided to cross the Rhine" (4.17.1). The general seems to have become the creation of the author.

This division is less obvious in the *Civil War*, more a convention than a device for objectivity. Since Caesar's role there was so personally important for his life and career, and the events were so well known to many of his readers through their own participation, any pseudoanonymity would have been incongruous. The use of the third person may, on the other hand, represent the conventional style of Roman memoirs. The fact that none of Caesar's contemporaries comment at all on this feature suggests that they found nothing unusual in it. Nevertheless it gives a unique effect that is destroyed by the regrettable decision of recent translators who settle for the first person and thus present us inevitably with a boastful, self-seeking Caesar.

To Hirtius (8.*Preface* 2) and to Cicero these memoirs were known as *commentarii*, by which they meant dossiers or notebooks of raw, factual information to provide material for the writers of history. Both agree that Caesar had written such a finished piece of work that there was no need or room for improvement. In Cicero's words:

> But although Caesar wanted others who wished to write history to have source material at hand which they might use, he has perhaps brought pleasure only to the inept who may wish to add elegant flourishes to his facts. He has, in truth, deterred men from writing, for there is nothing in history more pleasing than the pure and clear brevity of his work.
>
> (*Brutus* 262)

Apparently then, whether or not they represent a separate and distinct genre, in their straightforward, unadorned presentation, *commentarii* resembled the work of the annalists who recorded events year by year, in contrast to the writers of history, who under the aegis of the Muse Clio embellished their accounts with stylistic adornments, direct speeches created by the author, elaborate descriptive passages, and acknowledged prejudicial interpretations. Although we hear of other *commentarii*, such as those written by Sulla and Cicero, the only examples extant are those of Caesar. Hence any definition must rest on his writings alone and be formulated in accordance with individual scholars' opinions about the date and purpose of composition and their trust in Caesar's veracity.

Many scholars believe that Caesar wrote the entire account of the *Gallic War* at one time in the winter of 52–51 B.C. at his Gallic headquarters in Bibracte (Autun). This assumption is usually connected with a second assumption, that the book was political propaganda to justify his questionable imperialistic war of conquest to his peers in the Roman Senate. To use an assumed purpose to prove an assumed date and, conversely, to use an assumed date to prove an assumed purpose is ill-advised. It is true that Caesar in 52–51 faced serious problems regarding his tenure in command and regarding his political future, but these crises had been part of his life since the end of 57, when he had announced, prematurely, that "all Gaul had been pacified" (2.35.1; 3.71). Caesar's troubles arose from attempts on the part of his political enemies to replace him in the Gallic command by one of their own faction and to bring him home before the expiration of his extraordinary term. They might then bring him to trial on any number of the conventional charges faced by provincial governors on their return, and, thereby, block his iteration of the consulship or his assumption of any other public duty while under indictment.

Far from condemning his campaign, in 57 B.C. the Senate had voted him a public thanksgiving of fifteen days in honor of his victories, a length of celebration accorded to no one before him (2.35.4; Cicero, *De provinciis consularibus* 25); in 55 and again in 52 he was honored with public thanksgivings lasting twenty days (4.38.1; 7.90.8). The first of these tributes was voted by the Senate on the motion of Cicero

(*Pro Balbo* 61), who in his arguments presented to the Senate in the spring of 56 applauded Caesar's imperialistic ambitions and looked forward to the conquest of all Gaul (*De provinciis consularibus* 32,33). Cicero predicted, erroneously as it turned out, that "one or two summers' campaigns through fear or hope or punishment or rewards or arms would bind all Gaul in eternal chains" (34). Whatever were Caesar's plans and ambitions, the Senate voted in favor of Cicero's motion to retain him in his command, provided additional funds for his army, and ratified his special privilege of appointing his officer corps and increasing their number (*Pro Balbo* 61).

If anyone disapproved of the war or its extension, we hear nothing of it with the single exception of Cato's reaction to the massacre of the German Usipetes and Tenecteri (4.1–15), an incident recorded by the second-century gossipy writers, Suetonius (*Caesar* 24) and Plutarch (*Caesar* 22). Cato, leader of the most conservative group in the Senate, was affiliated by marriage to two of Caesar's bitter enemies: Lucius Domitius Ahenobarbus, husband of Cato's sister, whose canvass for the consulship of 55 included a threat to recall Caesar; and Calpurnius Bibulus, husband of Cato's daughter, Caesar's unfortunate and overshadowed colleague in the stormy consulship of 59. Cato's objection probably rested more on political than moral grounds. In any case, the Senate voted a public thanksgiving of twenty days for that year's campaigns (4.38.1).

It seems more reasonable that Caesar wrote the account of each year's campaign in the following winter. Whether these books were distributed annually or in groups or were published as a unit later, or whether there were first and second editions with interpolations by Caesar or someone else, can be argued indefinitely. Passages in the text can be used to support conflicting theories. Hirtius' statement that Caesar wrote his commentaries so "easily and quickly" (8.Preface 6) proves nothing about when or how they were composed; more cogent is his apology for including the events of the

years 51 and 50 in one book despite the fact that "Caesar completed a separate commentary for each year" (8.48.10).

The individual books vary considerably in length, style, emphasis, interest, details, and point of view; all of which suggests composition year by year rather than simultaneously. This unevenness forces itself to the attention of anyone who reads the volume straight through. A brief analysis of several books will demonstrate this variety and indicate the relationship of Caesar's political position to his work's form and content.

Any quick description of the first book is paradoxical. The book is both anecdotal and leisurely in its pace, generous with explanation and justification, and replete with records of negotiations, speeches, and conversations; on the other hand, it is clipped and almost brusque in the presentation of military operations, which in fact account for less than half its length. Caesar introduces his reader to the geography—"Gaul as a whole consists of three separate parts"—and to the situation that has created the emergency in Gaul. He does not appear on the scene himself until the seventh chapter. The content of Caesar's negotiations with Helvetian emissaries, his conversations with Aeduan leaders, and his interchanges with the German Ariovistus occupy about a third of the book, all reported by paraphrase in indirect discourse.

Two incidents in his camp are recorded in detail, as is the important council of the Gauls (30–33) held after the defeat of the Helvetians; there he was asked to deal with the German Ariovistus, who had migrated with his followers to Gaul. The first vignette in the Roman camp reveals the friendship of Caesar with the Aeduan senior statesman, Diviciacus, and the existence of a potentially dangerous anti-Roman faction among the Aedui (16–20), which was currently delaying a promised supply of grain. The second episode is unique in that it reveals Roman cowardice and a near mutiny, but not unique in showing Caesar's masterful handling of his men.

CAESAR

Twice in the first seasons' campaign Caesar had carried out operations the legality of which might have been questioned by the Roman Senate, and certainly have been by many modern scholars. He had left his province to pursue the Helvetians in Celtic Gaul and had attacked Ariovistus, "a friend and ally of the Roman people," a recognition achieved in some measure through Caesar's own recommendation (43.4). Furthermore, he quartered his legions for the winter in Gaul among the Sequani, not in his own province (54.2). Caesar does not conceal or apologize for his actions, but he does explain his reasons for taking them. These reasons take into consideration not only the jeopardy to Rome's interests in the current mass migrations of fierce fighting peoples but also the series of defeats suffered by Roman armies at the end of the second century at the hands of the Germanic Cimbri and Teutons, whose victories the contemporary generation of Helvetian and Germanic leaders had by no means forgotten (12.5; 13.3–7; 33.4; 40.5). No evidence of dissatisfaction in Rome is extant, but he received no official recognition of his victories, speedily accomplished though they were (54.2).

The second book is a distinct contrast in style and attitude. Shorter by sixteen chapters, it deals exclusively with military operations, except for the introductory chapter that explains the crisis arising among the Belgae, which necessitated an invasion of peoples neither included in Caesar's province nor subject to Rome.

This second book offers an opportunity to test Caesar's veracity by examining his handling of a specific episode. There is no way to verify his account of the war in Gaul through contemporary sources, nor are there any independent criteria by which to measure the reliability of those later ancient writers—Appian, Plutarch, Suetonius, Dio Cassius—whose versions differ in any marked degree. Asinius Pollio, one of Caesar's friends and supporters and himself a writer of tragedy and history, is reported to have offered this critique:

Caesar's commentaries were composed with too little care and with too little regard for the truth. Caesar trusted too readily in the accounts others gave of their deeds and he published some inaccuracies either purposely or because of a lapse of memory. Caesar, however, intended to revise and correct his material.

(Suetonius, *Caesar* 56.4)

Since Suetonius does not specify which of the commentaries are being evaluated; since it is unclear whether Pollio intends "inaccuracies" to mean small mistakes, like dates and locations, or major misrepresentations; and since the whole critique is one man's opinion repeated through at least one intermediary, it cannot be used as a serious indictment of Caesar's work as a whole.

Although some modern scholars have charged Caesar with deliberate falsehood, and others have tended to accept him at face value, a middle position seems more equitable: that Caesar's facts are true enough, but by rearrangement, omission, emphasis, style, and addition or deletion of cause and effect he manipulated those facts so that the total impression does not produce a completely true picture. The reality of any event, as has often been demonstrated, is seen differently by the different people involved in it, and, as time passes and the results of a given situation make themselves known, the factual details remembered are colored by hindsight. Reality becomes the subject matter with which the artist works. He must be selective about what he reports, and with that selectivity inevitably comes curtailment, censorship, and dramatic focus, no matter how objective he aims to be. Of course, Caesar wished to show himself in a good light, and no doubt the process of rationalization based on subsequent events enabled him to portray himself in some episodes as more far-seeing, more competent, and more successful than he might have been at the actual moment.

A close analysis of one engagement, the battle of the Sambre in 57 B.C., may give a clue to how Caesar could report an incident for his own greatest good. For almost half of the second book no decisive encounter has occurred, except for the abortive engagement at the River Aisne, which ended quickly in the withdrawal of the participating tribes to their own territories to await developments. Finally the Nervii, along with their allies the Atrebates and Viromandui, massed in force across the river Sabis (Sambre), awaiting the arrival of reinforcements from the Aduatuci. Caesar sent ahead a party to find a place suitable for camp and followed at the head of his marching column. As he learned later, some Gauls with his forces observed the Roman order of march and slipped away by night. They informed the Nervii that, since each legion was followed by its long transport train, it would be easy to fall upon the first legion when it arrived in camp, widely separated from the others, and by inflicting a major defeat discourage the rest of the Romans from making a stand. Caesar, however, changed the marching order, as was customary when nearing the enemy, so that he led six combat-ready legions, followed by the baggage train for the entire army; two legions, composed of recent recruits, protected the rear.

The campsite was on a gentle slope rising from the river, and across the water was a similar slope, the upper part of which was covered with trees in which the enemy was lurking. Only a small force of enemy cavalry was to be seen on the open field, and Caesar's cavalry were engaging them. The camp had already been laid out, and the six legions were beginning to throw up the standard protecting wall. As soon as the enemy in the forest saw the baggage train come into view, the agreed signal for attack, they launched their assault with incredible speed with all their forces.

In Caesar's words:

Everything had to be done by Caesar at the same time: the signal flag for battle had to be displayed, the alarm sounded by the trumpet, the soldiers recalled from the work of entrenchment and those who had moved out further to get material for the fortification summoned back, the battle line drawn up, the soldiers addressed and encouraged.

(20.1)

In the melee there were two mitigating factors, the knowledge and experience of his soldiers and his precaution of ordering the officers to remain with their legions during the construction work. Everyone knew what had to be done without having to be told. Caesar rushed to the nearest unit, the Tenth Legion, spoke briefly to them, and gave the signal to commit battle. The need for combat came so fast that many soldiers were not able to find their proper place in the battle line nor to put on helmets and take up their shields. The Ninth and Tenth Legions on the left, however, routed the attacking Atrebates and pursued them across the river, where they occupied the enemy camp. The Eleventh and Eighth in the center pushed back the Viromandui and engaged them at the river bank.

On the right the Twelfth and Seventh Legions were fiercely attacked on their now exposed left flank by the Nervii who divided their forces, one to hit that vulnerable side and the other to pillage the camp (23). The cavalry and noncombatants in the camp were in full flight, as were those in charge of the baggage train just arriving. The detachment of cavalry sent by the Treveri to aid the Romans saw the disarray, interpreted the scene as a debacle, and fled home to announce that the Romans had been routed and conquered and that the enemy had taken possession of their camp and baggage.

Caesar had moved from the Tenth Legion on the left to the right, where he found the Twelfth and Seventh Legions in difficulties caused by too close-packed a formation, the loss of centurions and standard bearer, the tendency of some recruits to hang back, and a general demoralization. Equal to the situation, Caesar

snatched a shield from one of the recruits, because he himself had come without one, advanced to the front of the line, called out to the centurions by name, encouraged the rest of the soldiers, and gave orders for the standards to advance and the ranks to be loosened up to facilitate the use of their swords. At his appearance the soldiers were instilled with new hope and restored courage, and the enemy attack was slowed a little, because each man desired to show himself to best advantage even at great risk in the sight of the commander-in-chief.

(25.2–3)

Then the soldiers of the two legions (Thirteenth and Fourteenth) who had followed the baggage train were seen by the enemy, and Labienus, now in possession of the enemy camp, sent the Tenth Legion back across the river to help. Even the Roman cavalry, which were routed in their first engagement, returned to fight. The Nervii fled in panic, and this day, as so many others before and after, belonged to the Romans.

Since Napoleon, military historians have criticized Caesar's handling of the operation, because he had not taken due precautions against a surprise attack, even though he knew the enemy was massed across the river, because he had no troops in line prepared for fighting, and because he risked his own life needlessly. Nevertheless, if we examine the details without being seduced by the drama, we see that Caesar had prepared carefully both his line of march and the building work, with both officers and soldiers ready for action, and that, although there was some scurrying around at the moment of attack, the four legions on the left and center were obviously battle ready, so much so that they overpowered the attack in their areas and advanced so quickly that they left both the right of the line and the camp exposed. Nor is there any indication that Caesar—in the front line with borrowed shield—was in any personal danger. There is, however, a good deal of colorful description designed to convey the impression that disaster was imminent; most of the havoc, however, was created among groups of little or no tactical import: cav-

alry, noncombatants in the camp with the baggage train, and the Treveri with their false assumptions. The nine chapters that narrate the engagement contain a disproportionate amount of detail emphasizing the pandemonium at the time of the attack, the hectic confusion on the battlefield, and the rout or stalemate of groups on the Roman side of the river. This imbroglio completely overshadows the successes on the right and center, the reactivation of the left, the supportive return of the Tenth Legion, the commitment of the two legions with the baggage train, and the recovery of the cavalry.

The immediate and lasting impression of Caesar versus the Nervii is that a near catastrophe was averted by Caesar's heroic posture and his coolness under fire. So, in fact, do two ancient authors see it. Valerius Maximus in his chapter on courage (*Factorum et dictorum memorabilium libri novem* 3.2.19) cites the Divine Julius as the "surest effigy of true courage," who by this act "restored the ebbing fortune of war." The second-century epitomizer Florus (*Epitomae de Tito Livio* 1.45.4) describes the whole battle only in terms of Caesar's valiant action.

Caesar had indeed achieved exactly what he wanted. In a season of campaign offering little opportunity to display military prowess, he managed to make the only real battle of the year memorable and himself exalted. In point of fact the most important and lasting result of the campaign was the immediate offer of friendship and surrender by the Remi, who had not joined in the Belgian conspiracy (3); they were to remain loyal to Rome and were one of the few tribes that did not join in the massive uprising of 52 B.C. Although Caesar claimed that the Nervii had been practically wiped out (28.1), both they and the Aduatuci, whom he besieged and defeated after the great battle of the Sambre (29–33), aligned themselves with Ambiorix and the Eburones and were back in arms to resist the Romans again in the hard campaigns of 54 and 53. The Nervii still had enough manpower to furnish a contingent for Vercingetorix in 52.

But if Caesar wrote the second book in the

winter of 57–56 B.C., he had no inkling of these future developments. He did, however, know the political situation at Rome, that Pompey was drawing close to the dominant oligarchs who were Caesar's enemies and had been Pompey's, that Cicero was proposing the rescinding of some provisions in the agrarian legislation passed in Caesar's consulship, and that efforts to recall him before the expiration of his term were being discussed. The news of his victories in official dispatches, strengthened and augmented by his dazzling performance in the field, had the desired effect of official reward. The campaign of 58 received the senatorial blessing "for the pacification of all Gaul" (35.1) and an extraordinary thanksgiving of fifteen days (35.4), and the literary publicity served to project the commander-in-chief as a true leader of men to his contemporaries, to later Romans, and even through the centuries to Miles Standish in the New World:

"Truly a wonderful man was Caius Julius
    Caesar! . . .
Now, do you know what he did on a certain
    occasion in Flanders,
When the rear-guard of his army retreated, the
    front giving way too,
And the immortal Twelfth Legion was crowded so
    closely together
There was no room for their swords? Why, he
    siezed a shield from a soldier,
Put himself straight at the head of his troops, and
    commanded the captains,
Calling on each by his name, to order forward the
    ensigns;
Then to widen the ranks, and give more room for
    their weapons;
So he won the day, the battle of something-or-
    other."
(Henry Wadsworth Longfellow, *The Courtship
of Miles Standish* 2.13.20–27)

The third book pales by comparison with the first two, and if anything Caesar wrote could be termed dull, this is it, probably because Caesar's presence is scarcely felt. To be sure he supervised the procuring and building of ships for the campaign against the Veneti and other maritime tribes, but much of the summer was wasted in futile attacks on towns admirably protected by their location on coastal promontories. The final decisive naval battle was commanded by Decimus Brutus and, although watched closely by the troops on shore and boldly carried out by innovative tactics in Caesar's sight, it is somewhat summarily described.

The book is the shortest of the seven, only twenty-nine chapters in contrast to the fifty-four of the first and ninety of the seventh. Caesar himself appears in less than half of the book: the ten chapters dealing with the maritime campaign and the concluding two describing the speedy expedition against the Menapii and Morini, undertaken "although the summer was already almost over" (3.28.1). The first six chapters finish the activities of the previous year when Galba in the late fall of 57 was sent against the tribes controlling the road to the Great St. Bernard pass; the inclusion of this foray in the third book rather than in the second supports the idea of serial composition, since presumably the second had been completed before a full report had been received from Galba. Three chapters (17–19) describe Titurius Sabinus' problems with northern maritime tribes and eight (20–27) the brilliant Aquitanian expedition of Publius Crassus, younger son of Caesar's political ally.

Thus, we hardly see Caesar at all and don't really know where he is and what he is doing. He says that after discovering that the Roman ships could not compete successfully with those of the Veneti, he was forced to wait for the construction of a fleet built according to different specifications (14.1). The picture of the dynamic and energetic Caesar sitting idly around in camp does not ring true. Probably his attention was focused on events in Rome rather than on this dragging maritime campaign. He may well have spent considerable time in Cisalpine Gaul where he could keep in closer contact with his supporters and agents in the city. It was, after all, the year 56, and we know that sometime before April or May he was at Ravenna where he conferred with Crassus and at Luca where both of them conferred with Pompey to renew and strengthen their political alliance. It was imperative to their interests that their political enemy, Domitius Ahenobarbus, candidate for the consulship of 55, be defeated and that Pompey and Crassus win that election. Cicero was prevailed upon to come firmly to the support of the triumvirate and persuaded the Senate not to supersede Caesar in his proconsulship. It is no wonder that military operations took second place and that the writing that winter was more perfunctory. Without detracting in any way from the excellence of young Crassus' military acumen, we may note that his exploits occupy a major share of the book written to record the events of that year crucial for the triumvirate and their manipulation of Roman politics.

The remaining four books are equally diverse. The fourth shows Caesar at the height of his form in audacity, speed, and showmanship. In 55 B.C., after dealing firmly with the Usipetes and Tencteri, who had migrated into Gaul near the mouth of the Rhine, he built his famous bridge, described in proud detail (17), crossed the Rhine, and remained only eighteen days to terrorize the Germans. That exploit, splendid as it was, did not fill out the campaign season, so, despite the lateness of the year, "when only a small part of the summer remained" (4.20.1), and despite his lack of knowledge about the ports of Britain, he decided to set out for the island that had continually furnished aid and comfort to his Gallic enemies. Although that invasion was hardly a military success, and his return was dangerous because of the proximity of the autumnal equinox, he could count the year's activities useful. He had carried Rome's standard across the mighty Rhine into the land of notoriously ferocious warriors and across the Ocean stream to a distant, fabulous, and mysterious island. The publicity attendant upon these exploits must have more than met his expectations. The affect on official Rome is shown by the Senate's decree of a public thanksgiving lasting twenty days (38.5).

Both the unfinished business in Britain and the Senate's signal accolade prompted his return the next year (54 B.C.) for a more thorough campaign mounted early in the season. This year he had time for a description of the geography of the island and of the customs of the Britains (5.12–14). On his return he had to deal with attacks on two of his winter quarters in Belgium, some of the most exciting narrative in the entire work (5.26–52). The impact of these wondrous expeditions to Britain can be seen in the eager plans of the brothers Cicero to write an epic poem on the invasion; Quintus was with Caesar in Britain, and Marcus urged his brother to send him information about the island that he could use for his work (*Ad Quintum fratrem* 2.15a.2; 16.4). In the same period the unhappy poet Catullus, breaking off his liaison with Clodia-Lesbia, asked two friends to carry a cruel final message to his faithless mistress. He pictures them as having declared themselves willing to accompany him anywhere in the world; whether he wishes to go to India or to Egypt, or

Whether Catullus intends to climb across the lofty Alps
To examine the records of great Caesar,
The Gallic Rhine, a frightening river, and
The Britains at the ends of the earth.

(11.9–12)

The sixth book describes the scorched earth policy carried out against the stubborn tribes of northeastern Belgium near the Rhine, the Eburones under Ambiorix with his allies, the Menapii and Treveri, and another brief sortie across the Rhine to discourage the Germans from continued meddling in Gallic affairs. The campaign had almost no pitched battles, except against the Treveri, since the Menapii and Eburones retired into the forest and swamps and waged guerrilla warfare against small Roman search parties. By pillaging and burning Caesar drove the Menapii into surrender but had little success with the Eburones (6.29.1–5), and Ambiorix lived on to plague the Romans again

(8.24.5). None of these campaigns was the stuff of which glorious accounts could be written, and furthermore, operations against these peoples had been reported before (3.28–29; 4.16–19, 38.3; 5.2–4, 24–41). Perhaps for that reason Caesar chose to devote more than a third of the book to a digression on the political, social, religious, and military habits of the Gauls and the Germans (11–28). Without this digression, presumably designed to appeal to Caesar's peers, and of utmost interest to modern critics, the book would be the shortest of them all.

The last and longest book records the momentous struggle of all Gaul united under the leadership of the Arvernian Vercingetorix. Only the Remi and the Lingones, who remained loyal to Caesar, and the Treveri, who were too far away and too involved with the Germans, did not join the Gallic alliance (63.7). Even the Aedui, long-standing friends of Rome, deserted Caesar and sent a contingent to Alesia to relieve the besieged Vercingetorix.

This is a book of hard fighting, as each side knew what was at stake—for the Gauls freedom, for Caesar triumph or ignominy to climax the work of the previous six years. Caesar's strategy, his resourcefulness in meeting the problems of the ever-spreading revolt, the difficulties of feeding his troops in hostile territory, the bravery and devotion of his soldiers, and the harrowing details of desperate warfare all make a vivid story. The bloody sack of Avaricum (Bourges) and the disappointing siege of Gergovia lead up to the final decision at Alesia in 52 B.C. In this town located on the summit of a steep hill, Vercingetorix was encamped with 80,000 men plus cavalry (71.1–3). Caesar besieged him there, constructing an elaborate circumvallation, trenches, and hidden traps of various kinds, still of interest to archaeologists. In danger of starvation Vercingetorix asked for a relief force, and an army of 250,000 infantry and 8,000 cavalry (76.3) came and threatened Caesar's camp. In contrast, the Roman forces were limited. Caesar had by now ten legions available in Gaul, a total force on paper of 60,000, but, owing to illness, deaths, leaves, retirements, and the slowness of replacements, the strength of a legion has been estimated anywhere from 3,600 to 4,500, rather than the theoretical 6,000. Vercingetorix, like Caesar, was clever and imaginative in his plans and commanded the wholehearted devotion of his men. The outcome was by no means certain, but in the end the Gauls were defeated, and Vercingetorix was handed over to Caesar.

The book is distinct from its predecessors. The detailed attention to military operations, almost suggestive of a daily journal or log, is a style that was later to characterize the *Civil War*. When he sat down at Bibracte to write the account of the year 52, he did so with well-earned confidence in his military prowess and with enthusiasm for military science.

Whenever and however Caesar wrote the *Gallic War*, he certainly wished to immortalize his name and his deeds for future generations. He also sought publicity and acclaim from his contemporaries. It was a glorious adventure for him personally and an immensely profitable one for Rome. So thorough a job did he do not only in conquering the Gauls but also in winning their friendship for and trust in Rome that in the coming years of civil war, when Romans were busy killing Romans, there was no unrest in Gaul. Caesar has left us a remarkable history of a monumental campaign, and he lives forever in its pages, moving among his troops, conspicuous in his red battle cloak (7.88.1).

Turning from the *Gallic War* to the *Civil War*, even the most casual reader is struck by the latter's explicit partisan propaganda, the minute detail of military operations, personal enmity for the foe, the greater presence of Caesar as general and politician, and the marked interaction between commander and soldiers. The *Civil War* is a less carefully composed work, perhaps a hastily sketched first draft, and may have been written in late 48 or early 47 B.C. in Alexandria, some two years before Caesar's final triumph over Pompey's party. It was published posthumously by Hirtius.

The three books cover the events of only two years, from Caesar's political struggle of 1 January 49 through 17 November 48, the opening skirmish of the Alexandrian War.* The third book is longer than any of those in the *Gallic War*, and the first is only three chapters shorter than the longest of that campaign (7). The annalistic composition of the *Gallic War* is discarded: all of the first two books and a small part of the third include the events of 49. Despite the expected pedestrian narrative of daily movements, skirmishes, and problems, the *Civil War* is an exhilarating piece of work. The reader is brought into the camp, onto the battlefield, and, what is more stirring, into the very mind of Caesar himself. In the first two books we are constantly at Caesar's side and, although we know full well the ultimate victorious result, the day-to-day operations create an aura of suspense in the midst of perilous difficulties and of awe at his unfailing dexterity and originality against trained Roman troops. Most of the second book, although enlivened by the exotic nature of its African setting, by the pungent personality of Caesar's general Curio, and by the vivid immediacy of direct speech, is the least successful, because Caesar himself was not in Africa at that time. His material had to come from copious dispatches from Curio and from information from survivors of that defeat.

Here there is no argument about the purpose in writing. Caesar must justify his role in a civil war, the legality of his position, and the rightness of his cause in contrast to the base, stubborn, and criminal motives of his enemies, even as they would have had to do had they been the victors. To take the offensive against Gauls, Germans, and Britains and to reduce many of them to Roman dominion was appropriate to the traditional concept of service to the state in fulfilling its predestined right to rule; but to kill Roman citizens in a civil war required an explicit presentation of a firm consti-

*The *Corpus Caesarianum*, the history of the subsequent campaigns in Alexandria, Africa, and Spain, was continued by anonymous authors, probably Caesar's officers.

tutional position and as much direct, as well as subliminal, propaganda as possible. Measured against other sources for the period, Caesar's account reveals a few false impressions, largely created by skillful arrangement, emphasis, and omissions; the most notorious omission is the abortive mutiny of the Ninth Legion in Cisalpine Gaul after the Spanish campaign. It is his side of the story he tells his readers; his opponents would have had a different version. He steadfastly maintains the justice of his position, the injustice of his enemies' plots both against him personally and against the laws of the state, and his constant efforts to settle matters peacefully in the face of the intransigence of Pompey's party. His tone is defensive, unlike anything in the *Gallic War*, and he is clearly the aggrieved party. Still there must have been at least a modicum of truth to his legal stance, since his contemporary readers were in a position to know first-hand the grievances out of which the dispute arose.

On one plane the Civil War was a struggle for *dignitas*, that almost concrete conception of paramount importance to a Roman noble, encompassing family, rank, prestige, honor of office, and personal honor. Caesar's *dignitas* had been impugned by his opponents' illegal attempts to prevent him from finishing his proconsular command and from exercising the right of canvassing for office in absentia, which had been duly conferred (1.9, 1.32, 1.85). He exhorted his troops to defend his reputation and *dignitas* from his enemies (1.7.7), claimed that part of his objective in the war was to restore his *dignitas* (1.22.5), and pledged that in the interests of arriving at a peaceful compromise he had been willing "to sacrifice his personal *dignitas* and position of command" (1.32.4). Pompey is accused of being unwilling to recognize anyone as equal to himself in *dignitas* (1.4.4). The later Roman historian Velleius Paterculus (*Historia Romana* 2.33.3) and the epitomizer Florus (*Epitomae* 2.13.14) saw the cause of the war in this way, as did the Neronian poet Lucan: "Caesar could no longer endure a superior, nor Pompey an equal" (*Pharsalia* 1.125–126).

Caesar continually represents himself as defending the constitution. It is his opponents who prevented the tribunes friendly to Caesar from exercising their most fundamental right, the veto, and drove them to seek refuge with Caesar (1.5.1–2). He used the same argument to gain the backing of his troops in January of 49 (1.7); he repeated this same charge of his opponents' perversion of the laws at Corfinium (1.22.5) and shortly thereafter in an address to the Senate (1.32.6). Moving from this specific instance to their general criminality, he claims as a principle for which he is fighting "the assertion of liberty for himself and the Roman people who had been oppressed by a small clique" (1.22.5).

By the time of the conclusive battle of Pharsalus (49 B.C.), Caesar's position and the people's liberty have become the battle cry. A veteran centurion of the Tenth Legion, Crastinus, shouted to his fellow legionaries when the signal to advance was given: "This one battle remains to be fought to restore his *dignitas* to our general and liberty to ourselves" (3.91.3).

The ready support of his cause by the townspeople of Italy and the frequent desertions from Pompey's forces to his own help Caesar to sustain the picture of himself as the true patriot, who despite the injuries done him "is prepared to suffer everything for the sake of the state" (1.9.5). Driven to war against his will, as he asserts at Pharsalus, "he never wished to shed the blood of his soldiers and deprive the state of either one of its armies" (3.90.2).

Nowhere does Caesar propose any change in the traditional government or suggest that he was thinking in terms of absolutism in rule. His ultimate aim, if that be what it was, is expressed in a letter to Metellus Scipio, Pompey's father-in-law, in Macedonia, again asking for a negotiated peace that would bring "harmony to Italy, peace to the provinces, and safety to the empire" (3.57.4). Caesar's claim that he was driven to war against his will is borne out by his

lament when he gazed upon the dead in Pompey's camp at Pharsalus: "They would have it thus; they drove me to it" (Plutarch, *Caesar* 46.1).

In the *Gallic War* the Gauls are presented as excitable and refractory, but Caesar respects their courage and recognizes their natural determination to fight for their freedom. Here, however, he constantly reminds his reader of the petty, cowardly, contemptible, and corrupt characters of Pompey's adherents, who have undermined the laws, refused to negotiate, and pursued war for personal and political power. The base motives of some individuals are highlighted: Cato's vengeance, Lentulus' avarice, and Sulla's ambition (1.4.1–2). After Caesar's setback at Dyrrachium (49 B.C.), they were already in dispute over who should replace Caesar as pontifex maximus, Lentulus claiming priority because of age, Domitius because of his influence and prestige, and Scipio because he was Pompey's father-in-law (3.83.1). "In short," he charges, "all were either arguing about rewards of honors or of money or about vengeance upon their enemies and were not planning how they might conquer but rather how they would enjoy their victory" (3.83.4).

Domitius, an old political enemy who was scheduled to replace him in Transalpine Gaul, had already been given a most unattractive portrait in his defense of Corfinium in the opening months of the war. A craven leader who had had to offer large bribes of land to his soldiers to ensure their loyalty, he planned to desert his troops and to escape with a few of his friends; his own soldiers arrested him and surrendered him and the town to Caesar (1.16–23).

The stalwart Labienus, who had performed bravely and efficiently in Gaul as Caesar's unofficial second-in-command, the only officer to desert to Pompey, comes in for expected censure. His brutality is illustrated by his address to a group considering negotiation: "Stop talking about a settlement. Surely we can have no peace until Caesar's head is brought in!" (3.19.8). Later this traitor taunted captured soldiers of Caesar and summarily executed them, according to Caesar, in order that he might prove his loyalty to his new affiliation (3.71.4). As the armies prepared for battle at Pharsalus, Labienus addressed the troops, denigrating the caliber of Caesar's soldiers, who, he claimed, "are not the veterans who conquered Gaul and Germany, most of whom have perished, but are rather recruits from north Italy and the best of those fell at Dyrrachium" (3.87.4).

Caesar's criticism of Pompey is more muted out of genuine respect for his ability, remembered friendship, former connection by marriage, recognition of his universal popularity, and almost legendary reputation. Pompey's natural ego is understood to have been played upon by Caesar's enemies (1.4.7). Later Caesar scores Pompey's duplicity to the Senate in undertaking an unnecessary war and in assuring his compatriots that he was prepared for a campaign when he was not (1.30.5). Caesar sympathized with the handicap Pompey suffered in the divisiveness among his senatorial supporters, who had their own ideas about how the campaign should be waged. Confident of easy victory at Pharsalus and a speedy return to Italy, they criticized the allegedly deliberate slowness of his plans for what should only be one day's work and complained "that he took undue pleasure in his high command and treated men of consular and praetorian rank like slaves" (3.82.2). However, they were certain of victory on the eve of battle, rejoicing in the assurances of "so skilled a general" (3.87.7).

Caesar's kindness and clemency to his enemies support his claims of wanting to arrange a settlement from the start and indicate his basic belief in negotiation rather than bloodshed. Mentioned fleetingly as *clementia* (mercy), *mansuetudo* (forebearance), and *consuetudo* (customary gentleness) in the *Gallic War*, these qualities are said to have been familiar to the Belgae from his earlier dealings with the Gauls (*Gallic War* 2.14.4, 31.3, 32.1); but although he treated the Gauls for the most part with restraint and leniency, he does not continue to use the same terminology. Because

clementia connotes the prerogative of a superior to his inferiors and carries a suggestion of a position above the laws, Caesar is chary of using it in relation to his humanity toward Romans; instead he speaks of his generosity and compassion in sparing his fellow citizens. He readily pardoned and freed the senators at Corfinium, the first real military engagement, and accepted the soldiers' oath of loyalty to himself (1.23). After his victory in Spain he even restored to the defeated soldiers any of their goods plundered by his troops and saw to their back pay (1.87.1–4). Soldiers of both armies, who had friends in each camp, were pleased when they realized that he would exact no penalty from the defeated, and "in the judgment of everyone Caesar reaped a great reward from his traditional mildness; his policy was approved by all" (1.74.7).

This sparing of the conquered, shown also to the soldiers at Pharsalus (3.98), is not merely a partisan ornament of the commentary but a conscious policy. In early March of 49 Caesar wrote to his agents Balbus and Oppius: "Let us try to see if we can win the hearts of all and gain a lasting victory. . . . This is a new way of conquering, to build strength by compassion and generosity" (Caesar, quoted in Cicero, *Epistola ad Atticum* 9.7c).

His desire to avoid armed confrontation is extended to his concern for his soldier's welfare in individual engagements since "it is no less the mark of a general to conquer by prudent planning than by the sword" (1.72.2). Such sympathy did not necessarily awaken a similar response among his men, who are always represented as eager for battle and sometimes vocally indignant that the enemy may escape. In one instance "they went to their centurions and junior officers to beg them to tell Caesar that he should spare neither their toil nor their danger. They were ready, able, and brave enough to cross the river" to engage the enemy (1.64.2).

The legions had been willing to follow Caesar in January of 49 in his invasion of Italy, partly out of loyalty to their great commander and his cause but also for their own hope of personal enrichment and advancement. Once the choice had been made, of course, there was little chance of survival in case of a change of heart. Caesar had a great advantage in that his was a trained army, molded by one commander-in-chief through the years. It had the kind of confidence, morale, and spirit engendered by the mutual experience of remembered victories. The blockade of Pompey's troops at Dyrrachium was maintained with difficulty by Caesar's smaller and less well-provisioned army. Nevertheless, the soldiers held out cheerfully, "for they remembered they had endured the same hardships last year in Spain and had won an important war. They recalled that they had survived deprivation at Alesia and even much more at Avaricum and had departed victorious over vast numbers of mighty peoples" (3.47.5).

His admiration for their bravery in the field and for their patient endurance of hardships in camp is matched by their eagerness for battle and their unswerving devotion to him. When they realized that they had failed him at Dyrrachium, for example:

> the whole army felt such remorse for the defeat and such a desire to repair their dishonor that, not waiting for the orders of their officers, each imposed on himself heavier labors for the sake of punishment and at the same time all hotly yearned for another encounter
>
> (3.74.2)

Caesar's army had become almost an extension of himself. This symbiosis between commander and the rank and file produced a reverent devotion that would outlast his death by many years and transfer itself to his successor and heir, the future Augustus.

There have been those who have looked upon Caesar's assassination as a noble, necessary, and glorious crime committed to rid the world of a despotic tyrant. On the other hand, Dante places Brutus and Cassius in the lowest part of Hell along with Judas Iscariot (*Inferno* 34). Such a man as Caesar in his own time and throughout history has excited strong emotions and fervent partisanship.

The demonstrations in the forum following Antony's funeral oration pointed in the direction of a kind of popular canonization, and the comet that appeared at the games in Caesar's honor in July of 44 was believed to be Caesar's soul en route to Olympus to join the gods. The official consecration of Caesar was decreed in January 42. The deification of Roman emperors, which became customary as an act of political fidelity, allegiance, and propaganda, should not obscure the fact that the deification of a real person was completely atypical for the Romans of the republic. Prior to Caesar's apotheosis only Aeneas, a Trojan from Homer's *Iliad* who migrated to Italy, and Romulus, son of Mars and founder of Rome, had achieved divine status. No doubt it is easier to add a deity to a polytheistic pantheon than to coopt one into a monotheistic system, but the fact that Caesar's divinity could even have been suggested—let alone adopted as official policy, complete with temple and priesthood—rather than laughed to scorn at the outset, is proof of the impact Caesar had on his contemporaries.

Shakespeare was wrong. It is not Brutus but Caesar "who was the noblest Roman of them all" (*Julius Caesar* 5.5.68).

Selected Bibliography

TEXTS

C. Iuli Caesaris commentariorum libri iii de bello civili cum libris incertorum auctorum de bello Alexandrino Africo Hispaniensi, edited by Renatus Du Pontet. Oxford, 1900. Reprinted 1958. Oxford Classical Texts; the standard.

C. Iulii Caesaris commentarii rerum gestarum, bellum Gallicum, edited by Otto Seel. Leipzig, 1961. Teubner text.

C. Iuli Caesaris commentariorum libri vii de bello Gallico cum A. Hirti supplemento, edited by Renatus Du Pontet. Oxford, 1900. Reprinted 1962. Oxford Classical Texts; the standard.

CAESAR

TRANSLATIONS

Caesar's War Commentaries, edited and translated by John Warrington. London, 1953; New York, 1958.

Caesar: The Civil Wars. Translated by A. G. Peskett. London and Cambridge, Mass., 1914. Loeb Classical Library; the standard.

Caesar: The Gallic Wars. Translated by H. J. Edwards. London and Cambridge, Mass., 1917.

War Commentaries of Caesar. Translated by Rex Warner. New York, 1960.

Julius Caesar. The Battle for Gaul. Translated by Anne and Peter Wiseman. Boston, 1980.

BIOGRAPHICAL AND CRITICAL STUDIES

Adcock, F. E. *Caesar as Man of Letters*. Cambridge, 1956.

Balsdon, J. P. V. D. "Caesar's Gallic Command." *Journal of Roman Studies* 29:57-73, 167-183 (1939).

———. "The Veracity of Caesar." *Greece and Rome* 2d ser. 4:19-28 (1957).

Chênerie, M. "L'architecture du *Bellum Civile* de César." *Pallas* 21:13-31 (1974).

Collins, John H. "Propaganda, Ethics and Psychological Assumptions in Caesar's Writings." Ph.D. dissertation, Goethe University, Frankfurt, 1952.

———. "On the Date and Interpretation of the *Bellum Civile*." *American Journal of Philology* 70:125-130 (1959).

———. "Caesar as Political Propagandist." *Aufstieg und Niedergang der Römischen Welt* 1.1:922-966. Berlin, 1972.

Conley, Duane F. "'Tendenz' in Caesar's 'Bellum Gallicum.'" Ph.D. dissertation, Yale University, 1975.

Cuff, P. J. "The Terminal Date of Caesar's Gallic Command." *Historia* 7:445-472 (1958).

Duval, P. M. "Une perspective nouvelle sur la guerre des Gaules et sur les Gaulois." *Journal des Savants*:19-31, 71-84 (1954).

Elton, G. R. "The Terminal Date of Caesar's Gallic Proconsulate." *Journal of Roman Studies* 36:18-42 (1946).

Gelzer, M. *Caesar, Politician and Statesman*. 6th ed. Weisbaden, 1966. Translated by P. Needham. Cambridge, Mass., 1968.

Gruen, Erich S. *The Last Generation of the Roman Republic*. Berkeley, 1974.

Hagendahl, Harald, "The Mutiny of Vesontio. A Problem of Tendency and Credibility in Caesar's *Gallic War*." *Classica et Mediaevalia* 6:1-40 (1944).

Harmand, J. "Des Gaulois autour de César." *Rivista storica dell'Antichità* 2:131-167 (1972).

Hastrup, Th. "On the Date of Caesar's *Commentaries of the Gallic War*." *Classica et Mediaevalia* 18:59-74 (1957).

Holmes, T. R. *Caesar's Conquest of Gaul*. London, 1899.

Kohns-Andernoch, H. P. "Der Verlauf der Nervierschlact. Zu Caesar, *Bellum Gallicum* II, 15-27."*Gymnasium* 76:1-17 (1969).

La Penna, A. "Tendenze e arte del *Bellum Civile* di Cesare." *Maia* 5:191-233 (1952).

Montgomery, H. "Caesar und die Grenzen. Information und Propaganda in den *Commentarii de Bello Gallico*." *Symbolae Osloenses* 49:57-92 (1973).

Radin, Max. "The Date of Composition of Caesar's *Gallic War*." *Classical Philology* 13:283-300 (1918).

Radista, L. "Julius Caesar and His Writings." *Aufstieg und Niedergang der Römischen Welt* 1.3:417-456. Berlin, 1973.

Rambaud, Michel. *L'art de la déformation historique*. Collection des Annales de l'Université de Lyon, 1952. 2nd rev. ed. Paris, 1966.

———. "Esquisse d'une stratégie de César d'après les livres 5, 6 et 7 du *de bello Gallico*." *L'information littéraire* 9:54-63, 111-114 (1957).

———. "Réflexions sur la veracité de César dans le *Bellum Gallicum*." *Giornale Italiano di Filologia* 21:313-324 (1966).

———. "César à travers les *Commentaires*." Conférences Société des Études Latines de Bruxelles, 1965-1966. *Collection Latomus* 92. Brussels, 1968.

———. "Pourquoi César a conquis la Gaule." *Humanités chrétiennes* 18:315-330 (1975).

———. "'Formation' et 'déformation' historique." *Revue des Études Latines* 55:54-60 (1977).

———. "A propos de la publication du *Bellum Gallicum*." *Hommage à la mémoire de Jerôme Carcopino* 245-251. Collection des études anciennes. Paris, 1977.

Ruch, M. "La veracité du récit de César dans les six premiers chapitres du *de bello civile*." *Revue des Études Latines* 27:118-137 (1949).

Sealey, R. "Habe Meam Rationem." *Classica et Mediaevalia* 18:75-101 (1957).

Stevens, C. E. "The Terminal Date of Caesar's Command." *American Journal of Philology* 59:169–208 (1938).

——. "The *Bellum Gallicum* as a Work of Propaganda." *Latomus* 11:3–18, 165–179 (1952).

Syme, Sir Ronald. *The Roman Revolution.* Oxford, 1939. Corrected reprint Oxford, 1952.

BIBLIOGRAPHIES

Collins, John H. "A Selective Survey of Caesar Scholarship Since 1935." *Classical World* 57:45–51, 81–88 (1963–1964).

Kroyman, Jürgen. "Caesar und das *Corpus Caesarianum* in der neueren Forschung: Gesamtbibliographie 1945–1970." *Aufstieg und Niedergang der Römischen Welt* 1.3:457–487. Berlin, 1972.

BETTY NYE QUINN